SharePoint 2010 as a Development Platform

Jörg Krause, Christian Langhirt, Alexander Sterff, Bernd Pehlke, and Martin Döring

Apress®

SharePoint 2010 as a Development Platform

ISBN-13 (pbk): 978-1-4302-2706-9

ISBN-13 (electronic): 978-1-4302-2707-6

President and Publisher: Paul Manning
Lead Editor: Jonathan Hassell
Technical Reviewer: Frank Binöder
Editorial Board: Steve Anglin, Mark Beckner, Ewan Buckingham, Gary Cornell, Jonathan Gennick, Jonathan Hassell, Michelle Lowman, Matthew Moodie, Jeff Olson, Jeffrey Pepper, Frank Pohlmann, Douglas Pundick, Ben Renow-Clarke, Dominic Shakeshaft, Matt Wade, Tom Welsh
Coordinating Editor: Anne Collett
Copy Editor: Damon Larson
Production Support: Patrick Cunningham
Indexer: Toma Mulligan
Artist: April Milne
Cover Designer: Anna Ishchenko

Distributed to the book trade worldwide by Springer Science+Business Media, LLC., 233 Spring Street, 6th Floor, New York, NY 10013. Phone 1-800-SPRINGER, fax (201) 348-4505, e-mail `orders-ny@springer-sbm.com`, or visit `www.springeronline.com`.

For information on translations, please e-mail `rights@apress.com`, or visit `www.apress.com`.

Apress and friends of ED books may be purchased in bulk for academic, corporate, or promotional use. eBook versions and licenses are also available for most titles. For more information, reference our Special Bulk Sales–eBook Licensing web page at `www.apress.com/info/bulksales`.

The source code for this book is available to readers at `www.apress.com`. You will need to answer questions pertaining to this book in order to successfully download the code.

Contents at a Glance

Contents

About the Authors

Jörg Krause has been working with software and software technology since the early '80s, starting with a ZX 81 using BASIC and assembler language. He studied information technology at Humboldt University Berlin but left to start his own operation in the '90s. He has worked with Internet technology and software development since the early days of CompuServe and Fidonet. He has been working with Microsoft technologies and software since the time of Windows 95. In 1998 he worked with one of the first commercial e-commerce solutions, and during this time he also wrote his first book in Germany, *E-Commerce and Online Marketing*, published by Carl Hanser Verlag, Munich. Due to the amazing success, he decided to work as freelance consultant and author to share his experience and knowledge of technologies with others. Since then he has written for Apress, Pearson, Hanser, and other major publishers, on a total of more than 40 titles. Additionally, he has written articles for various magazines and spoken at many conferences in Germany, including BASTA, VSOne, and Prio Conference. Currently he's working as a senior consultant for Microsoft technologies at Computacenter AG & Co. oHG in Berlin. He's a Microsoft Certified Technology Specialist (MCTS) for SharePoint and a Microsoft Certified Professional Developer (MCPD) for ASP.NET 3.5.

In his rare spare time, Jörg enjoys reading thrillers and science fiction books, and playing badminton in the winter and golf in the summer.

Christian Langhirt has been working with information technology since the early '90s. He began running his own software development business in 1998 during school. In addition to starting his own company, he studied information technology at the University for Applied Sciences Ravensburg-Weingarten. After that he received a master of science degree at Technische Universität München. Over the years, Christian has worked with a broad range of different technologies and is very familiar both with Java and .NET technologies. In the past years, he worked more and more with SharePoint, and he has used it as a development platform for modern intranet applications. Christian also speaks at conferences such as the German SharePoint conference. He currently works as a senior consultant at Computacenter AG and leads a highly skilled consulting team for Microsoft technologies. Christian cares deeply about his young son and his wife, and in his rare spare time he plays football passionately.

Alexander Sterff works as a consultant for Microsoft technologies at Computacenter AG. After many years of experience in object-oriented software development with Java and open source technologies, he started working with Microsoft products. Since then, he has participated in many different software projects, using his wide experience to guarantee their success. In the past years he has become an expert in building solutions that leverage the full potential of Office SharePoint Server, BizTalk, and InfoPath. Alexander received a bachelor's degree in informatics and a master's degree in information science, both at Technische Universität München.

Bernd Pehlke studied computer science at the University of Potsdam, Germany. He works as a software architect and technology consultant, focusing on Microsoft web technologies (ASP.NET and SharePoint). His main domain is enterprise business applications based on Windows SharePoint Services and SharePoint Server, especially conception and implementation of business process and integration scenarios.

He has spoken about business processes and integration using SharePoint and Microsoft Office technologies at several road shows and training courses.

Bernd is a Microsoft Certified Professional Developer (MCPD) for ASP.NET Developer 3.5 and Windows Developer 3.5, and a Microsoft Certified Technology Specialist (MCTS) for WSS 3.0/SharePoint 2007 configuration and application development.

Martin Döringbegan working with computers as a hobby in the mid-'90s, starting with writing code for MS-DOS in QBASIC and Turbo Pascal. Some years later he studied business computing and received a degree at the University of Applied Sciences Wildau (next to Berlin). After many experiences in software development with Java and open source technologies, his focus has moved to the .NET Framework—particularly web technologies and mobile devices.

Currently, Martin is working as a technology specialist for Microsoft technologies at Computacenter AG & Co. oHG in Berlin, applying his know-how in many different software projects across Germany.

When he is not in front of his notebook, Martin enjoys listening music at a concert or at home, or watching a movie at the cinema.

About the Technical Reviewer

Frank Binöder, MCTS, started his own film and IT business in 2001 while studying media informatics at the University of Applied Sciences in Dresden. He currently works as a SharePoint and Project Server consultant for Computacenter AG, and has over five years of experience engineering business solutions using Microsoft technologies. Frank has been dealing with the SharePoint and Project Server platform since the 2003 release. His passion is combining the functional requirements of customers with the creativity of developers. Frank also founded some of the local SharePoint user groups in Dresden and Hamburg.

Frank lives in Radebeul, near Dresden, Germany. When not working, Frank can be found riding mountain bikes with his son in the forests of Saxony.

Acknowledgments

We'd like to mention the people who helped us create this book and make it what it is. First, we'd like to thank David White for his amazing work smoothing out our style and cajoling it into readable English. We know you had a challenging task. We can't forget the support from Jonathan Hassell for our way into the Apress world, as well as the continuing help from Anne Collett. Thanks to our technical reviewer, Frank, who had a hard task getting our samples running within such a complex environment. His work greatly improved the quality of this book.

Last but not least, we'd like to thank our families and friends for understanding when we had to go back to the computer again and again to continue writing or installing SharePoint, from the first beta to the final release candidate.

Introduction

This With SharePoint 2010, Microsoft has shifted the developer experience toward a new paradigm—the paradigm of high-level development. This allows developers to extend Microsoft's software and adapt the parts to behave exactly as you would have designed them. However, things are not that clear on a closer look. SharePoint is multifaceted—it's an application, a platform, a server, a framework, and a database.

What Does This Book Cover?

This book is for experienced .NET and ASP.NET developers. It examines the SharePoint technology in greater depth than you'll find elsewhere, and it's full of practical tips and tricks from an experienced developer crew. You'll learn not only how things work, but also why. By adopting this knowledge, you will succeed in extending and adapting highly useful functionality in your own projects.

Imagine that your next customer wishes to run a couple of intranet tools, connect to line-of-business (LOB) applications, or customize beyond the limitations of the regular web UI and SharePoint Designer. SharePoint can handle this, but its out-of-the-box features won't be adequate. This book covers situations such as these in detail and shows you what to do when the SharePoint UI reaches its limits. You'll learn how to extend, customize, and enhance this platform to get what you want. "No more compromise" is our motto. That includes looking at SharePoint not just as a tool with some customization capabilities, but as a development platform and framework in and of itself.

Hence, programmability is covered in great depth. This book is for coders and real developers; it goes far beyond tinkering with XML and clicking aimlessly through an overcrowded UI.

Conventions Used in This Book

We understand that you're eager to start reading and learning, but it is worth taking a few seconds to look over this section—it will help you to get the most out of this book. Several icons and font conventions are used throughout the book:

- Screen messages, code listings, and command samples appear in `monospace` type.
- The same `monospace` font is used for HTML, ASP.NET controls (declarative listings), and XML snippets.
- Important parts of a listing are highlighted in **`bold monospace`**.
- All code-related terms in the body text of the book, including method names, class names, namespaces, and members, as well as URLs and path names, are set are set in `monospace` font as well.

Several icons highlight important definitions, cautions, and conclusions:

Tip This is a tip.

Note This is a note that explains a topic further, but is not required for understanding the main topic.

Caution This is a warning to keep you from common pitfalls.

Who Is This Book For?

This book is intended for advanced web developers interested in learning about how to use SharePoint as a development platform. We assume that you already have some experience writing web applications, you have created some web projects, and you have a basic understanding about ASP.NET, the .NET Framework, and related technologies.

We also assume that you already have some basic knowledge of skills and technologies often required as a web developer:

- HTML, CSS, and JavaScript
- Visual Studio basics, such as creating, running, and debugging a project
- Fluency with C#, as we use this language throughout the book exclusively
- ASP.NET basics, such as putting a control onto a page, customizing a control, and creating a user or custom control
- How to obtain database access, as well as how to use LINQ to query a database and write data back
- How to use XML as either a data source or storage

Prerequisites

This book is based on SharePoint 2010. As a basic platform, we use Visual Studio 2010 Ultimate running on 64-bit Windows Server 2008 R2 with IIS 7.5. When a client is involved, and when we run SharePoint in a client environment for development purposes, we use 64-bit Windows 7 Ultimate. (64-bit Windows is a requirement; you cannot even run the installer on 32-bit Windows anymore).

A similar platform is required for getting all the samples running. Nevertheless, we encourage you to look to the future and work with the most current tools and platforms you can obtain.

If you travel a lot and need to take your development environment with you, we suggest using a laptop with at least 4GB memory (8GB will be best if you can afford it) and Windows Server 2008 R2 x64 with Hyper-V installed. You can run several different development environments in virtual machines on such a computer. If you need external hard disk space, it's strongly recommended to use eSATA instead of USB. Connect to this machine using your regular laptop via remote desktop.

How This Book Is Organized

There are many ways of structuring a book. From our long-term experience in writing and publishing books, we know that different people read books very differently. Some read from beginning to end, just like a novel, while others start where they find an interesting topic. There is no book that can cover all reading styles; however, this book follows the same successful strategy we've used many times before.

We start with the basics: low-level concepts and background information necessary to *really* understand a topic. Then we proceed systematically through all the topics. This allows you to read from beginning to end, or to dip into an interesting chapter and skip the others. The many references in the book, pointing to chapters or sections where related parts are described in more detail, will help you get the information you need.

This book is full of code and examples, which are all available for download from the Apress web site (`www.apress.com`). Included with the package are subfolders named after each chapter (`chapter01`, `chapter02`, etc.). These folders contain several sample solutions or web sites in separate folders. Almost all examples are fully functional. Smaller code snippets that can't run on their own aren't included, to avoid confusion.

Support

We know that such a complex subject requires continuous support. We help the community by sharing our knowledge and expertise through our web sites. Feel free to visit our sites:

- `www.sharepointdeveloper.de`: The companion web site (in English; don't get confused by the de top-level domain)
- `http://blog.sharepointdeveloper.de`: The team blog, in English and German
- `www.aspnetextensiblity.com`: Jörg's ASP.NET site, in English

Several more sites driven by team members, colleagues, and partners are linked from there to give you access to more information. And if you want to have a look at Microsoft's official SharePoint 2010 site, visit `http://sharepoint2010.microsoft.com`.

Welcome to SharePoint Development

In this book we treat and express SharePoint as a development platform. This includes the fact that the applications developed on top of SharePoint must run in some kind of runtime environment. Having this in mind this lets you recognize SharePoint as an application server platform, too. It is, however, not an isolated piece of software. It is built on top of a broad range of interconnected technologies. One of these technologies is ASP.NET, a platform for creating web applications, and another is the .NET Framework, the underlying application platform, which consists of both developer capabilities and a runtime environment. SharePoint adds a bunch of functionality to these basic platforms. Applications designed for SharePoint are always built using the .NET Framework and quite often ASP.NET. They also make use of several services provided exclusively by SharePoint.

For developers, a deep knowledge of ASP.NET is essential. If you already have this, you'll have a head start into learning SharePoint development. Unless your organization is forcing you to use SharePoint, you might be struggling with the question of whether to use SharePoint as an application platform or stay with the ASP.NET platform. While ASP.NET is versatile and allows you to create powerful applications, there are some reasons that make SharePoint a viable alternative.

SharePoint is a technology that lets users create their own web applications without having to understand classic web site development. With SharePoint, rather than having to seek out a developer, users can now just talk to the database and server administrators, and start creating and deploying sites themselves. SharePoint provides various templates and features for modifying and customizing almost everything, from simple layout to the data structure held in lists. For the user, SharePoint acts like an application. Several tools accompany it, including Central Administration, SharePoint Designer, and the default site settings dialogs.

Developers can do even more with the SharePoint platform. SharePoint is extensible in many ways, and this extensibility gives developers access to almost all the internal modules. You can extend

SharePoint whenever a user cannot achieve a specific task with the embedded functions. Whether you need to make a slight modification or a large-scale one, such as adding an application page, you can extend the platform endlessly.

So, SharePoint is powerful both as an application platform and a developer platform. You can understand it in greater depth by looking at its main parts:

- *SharePoint Foundation*: Along with the other foundations, including Windows Communication Foundation (WCF), Windows Presentation Foundation (WPF), and Windows Identity Foundation (WIF), SharePoint bundles a collection of class libraries, runtime environments, tools, and support applications. The various tools address different roles, such as power users being supported by SharePoint Designer.
- *SharePoint Server 2010*: This is a product built on top of SharePoint Foundation that delivers a basic stack of features required to create an intranet- or Internet-aware application with little to no coding effort. It's a classic 20:80 ratio between effort and effect. Using SharePoint Server, you can create 80 percent of what an average site requires with 20 percent of the usual cost.

Using SharePoint as a development platform primarily involves SharePoint Foundation. However, you can develop on SharePoint Server as well. SharePoint became such a success worldwide because it allows you to reduce the risk of software project drastically by using it. SharePoint products provide what you need either out of the box or by extending the platform by coding.

SharePoint Applications

Ordinary users will be able to do lot of things with SharePoint by themselves (e.g., creating web sites, modifying the look and feel, adding certain features, and entering data), and developers equipped with at least basic SharePoint knowledge will be able to customize SharePoint further. This includes things such as adding a new menu item in site menus, creating Web Parts, adding code that invokes custom actions, and creating workflows beyond the built-in three-state limit.

Imagine that you're supposed to write a web-based application using ASP.NET, IIS, and SQL Server (as you may have done many times). Instead, you can use SharePoint Foundation to create your application, and you'll still have ASP.NET, IIS, and SQL Server at your disposal. Considering SharePoint as a development platform can only strengthen your development portfolio.

Figure 1 illustrates a general overview of SharePoint and its related technologies.

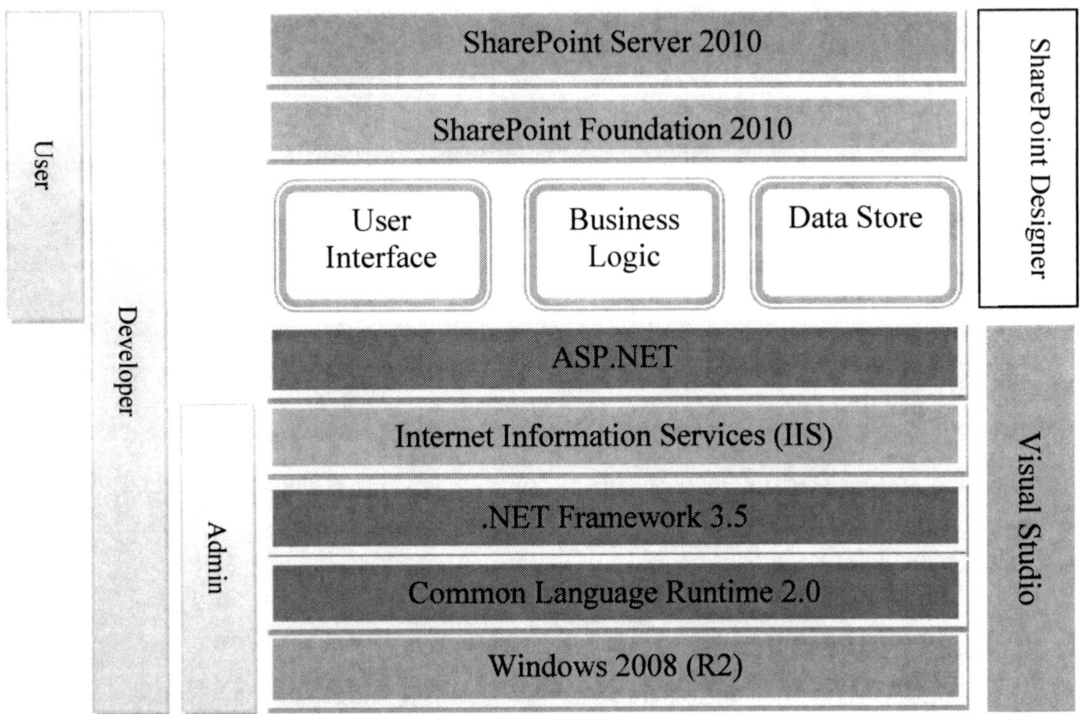

Figure 1. *A typical SharePoint application within the Windows Server stack*

The figure shows what a SharePoint application typically includes and how it relates to the Windows Server components. Users interact with some UI, the behavior is controlled by some business logic, and data is stored somewhere. Some development tools are used to empower both developers and power users. Additionally, SharePoint allows you to define three different roles: users, administrators, and developers. As you can see, the developer role spans all parts and is indeed the most demanding.

SharePoint is a platform that supports all of the following:

- The ability for administrators to maintain any installation, from a single server to a hierarchical farm
- A built-in way to work with data, including schemas created by end users
- The ability to create and execute business logic, including workflows
- A basic, easy-to-use UI, along with sophisticated customization features
- Visual Studio 2010 and a set of development tools that support everything from simple customization to huge team-based projects

While the developer support is not SharePoint specific, the other features are enhancements of the existing infrastructure. This is an important factor in considering SharePoint as a development platform.

The SharePoint Community

However, keep in mind that SharePoint is not just a huge piece of software. It is also part of an ecosystem of communities, information sources, consultant companies, third-party developers, forums, and books that provide support, help, training, and ideas. You can find people to communicate with, and meet to exchange ideas or discuss issues. There is a developer community, conferences exclusively devoted to SharePoint, MVPs, and authors you can hire. There are patterns and best practices available from Microsoft. While SharePoint may have a steep learning curve, it will be much easier if you don't walk alone.

Windows SharePoint Foundation for Developers

Before you start coding, you should understand what the pieces of the puzzle are. From one perspective, you can consider SharePoint to be built with tiers (although it's not really a multitier architecture behind the scenes, and the levels aren't as loosely coupled as you might like). But treating such a complex system as a collection of parts provides a well-structured way for you to understand it. From a developer perspective, we can identify six layers:

- The execution environment
- The data layer
- The business logic layer
- The UI layer
- The security layer
- The developer toolbox

Each of these layers is described in the following sections.

The Execution Environment

Executing a SharePoint application means using both the Common Language Runtime (CLR) and the ASP.NET engine. SharePoint itself comes with a bunch of services, along with tight integration with IIS using ASP.NET. In real-life applications, the complete scenario might appear more complicated. For example, in a farm with multiple servers, the execution environment will span several machines. While its logical structure still goes from farm to sites grouped into site collections, its physical appearance might be different. From a developer's perspective, the logical structure determines the objects you work with.

SharePoint provides a *site collection* as a container for sites. A site collection must have at least one site, the root site, which in turn can have child sites that run the applications. A site collection forms a multilevel hierarchy of instances that hold their own pages, lists, libraries, and individual users. SharePoint provides an inheritance mechanism that simplifies management of the sites. You can understand each site as a container of data, pages, and users working with that data. Each site can have its own administrator responsible for it and all its deriving sites.

The Data Layer

The sites that function as logical containers for data store that data in lists and libraries. Libraries are lists that have the ability to store documents or files. Libraries are the basic instances that make SharePoint act as a document management system.

Lists function similarly to relational database tables, but are much more versatile. While a table is a strongly typed container for rows of data, a list can be used more flexibly. Lists are, however, not containers for storing any sort of object regardless of its structure. Using content types to describe a lists schema, you can define the structure of the objects stored in that list. A list can be bound to many content types and therefore store different kinds of structured objects, the so-called list items. In real-life projects, this results in an object schema that imitates the real-world counterparts of the objects. For instance, when you need to handle offers, invoices, and packing slips for customers, a list called Customer Documents could keep all three document types together in one place. The variations in metadata between the individual document types would be too unwieldy to store in a relational database table. A database developer would suggest using four tables—three for the different types and one that joins them together. A SharePoint developer, on the other hand, would use just one list, extended with three content types. The relation is implicitly defined by this with no additional effort.

Additionally, lists are available through a UI that's powerful for both developers and end users. As a list's schema supports a data model that's closer in nature to an object than a relational database, it's easy for nondevelopers to use lists to create sophisticated structured data stores. Even working with list data is quite easy, because the UI for viewing, sorting, filtering, and manipulating data is available out of the box. Relationships between lists can be quickly and simply defined with a lookup feature, which forms a many-to-many connection. Complex fields can hold predefined sets of data contained in drop-down controls in forms. And the access control mechanism is available at the list and item stages, with no code required.

Internally, list querying is based on CAML (Collaborative Application Markup Language). The generated LINQ to SharePoint layer internally translates queries into CAML. Using CAML, both developers and users can create powerful selections of complex data.

The data layer is not limited to internal lists. You can even connect to external data from SQL server databases, web services, XML, or similar sources. Internally, that data appears in a similar format to lists. The external data is bound using Business Connectivity Services (BCS). However, this service is not a component of SharePoint Foundation; it's available in SharePoint Server only.

Exposing data to the outer world is another subject that's well addressed in SharePoint. SharePoint 2010 supports WCF Data Services for common REST-based access to any data stored internally.

The Business Logic Layer

If you use SharePoint as an application development platform, it's likely that you'll work on some sort of application logic as part of a development project. Such logic is usually encapsulated in modules that form a business logic layer. Technically, the logic makes use of the various built-in features, such as ASPX pages, web services, workflows, event receivers, and timers. Along with the .NET Framework, a huge toolkit is available to form the logic.

In simple projects it might be acceptable to spread the logic through the instances SharePoint provides—Web Parts, application pages, workflows, and event receivers. Such projects generally have only one or two of these instances and remain easy to maintain. However, from the perspective of professional software development and application life cycle management, a different strategy is needed. It makes sense to create a unique business layer that handles all relevant logic in one or more assemblies. The instances where the logic gets triggered should have interfaces only. That means you have to take care of your project's structure and the ways the data flows between the instances.

SharePoint itself does not come with a part that is dedicated to the logic. Moreover, the internal logic is spread over several parts, and cannot be found in one place. You should be aware of this, and instead create a dedicated business logic layer for your SharePoint application.

The User Interface Layer

The most sophisticated business logic is unusable if the user cannot exploit it easily. The UI layer is responsible for providing a modern and accessible way to interact with your application. SharePoint includes a browser-based engine and a web-based application. This has some nice implications, such as zero deployment and a broad range of clients, but it has some disadvantages compared with Windows applications as well (mostly concerning the limitations of HTML and browser environments). SharePoint defines basic UI elements and conventions for how to use these elements.

While you may be tempted to customize SharePoint's default design, we recommend against departing from it. Consider that the preferred way to extend SharePoint is through Web Parts. Web Parts can only appear in certain zones within a Web Part page, and users can arrange, close, or resize them. The available options don't change the UI—and neither should you while creating it. Treat regular application pages as part of an existing system.

Microsoft also recommends against creating new master pages, and instead recommends that you only change the basic layout and/or replace the company logo. This is something of a paradigm shift, since ASP.NET developers are used to having total freedom when designing their application's UI. But why should you accept these restrictions?

Primarily, many users have experience with the standard UI, and changing it could be potentially confusing for them. Likewise, you should anticipate new employees to arrive from other companies with SharePoint experience. If your intranet looks radically different from the standard, their prior experience won't be of use in your organization.

Silverlight Integration

The power of the SharePoint UI comes through its amazing collection of controls. You can use these to create similar pages with little effort. However, keep in mind that even the most sophisticated controls render as HTML and JavaScript, which have some limitations and pitfalls. In order to mitigate these, Microsoft introduced another paradigm shift with Silverlight—a new, small, autonomous framework that is mostly compatible with (but not identical to) the .NET Framework, and is available as a browser plug-in. Developers can create a GUI with animations and vector objects, based on the well-known XAML language that drives WPF (Windows Presentation Foundation) already. Using Silverlight, you can create ambitious applications that match users' needs without bending the existing UI. Silverlight's tight integration with SharePoint via the client object model makes it a serious alternative to HTML.

The Security Layer

Any security layer consists of two basic actions: authentication and authorization. Authentication identifies users by some combination of name and password, a token, or a smart card with a PIN (personal identification number). SharePoint has a comprehensive security model, and there is no need to reinvent the wheel. SharePoint makes use of IIS for authentication purposes, which in turn uses common data stores such as Active Directory. The authorization module itself is based on ASP.NET membership providers that can be replaced, customized, or enhanced using common techniques.

Once the user is authenticated, the security layer is responsible for informing other modules what the user is authorized to do or what data he or she is allowed to access. SharePoint comes with three predefined groups to handle users in categories. These groups can be extended by assigning common roles for data access. The security settings inherit from one level to another, such as from a site collection to its child sites. However, you can break the inheritance and choose another security model on any level; none of this configuration requires writing code. The security model works down from the farm level to the individual list items. For coders, the security model is available through particular classes. Specific base classes for application pages are available for use with the built-in security model or for allowing anonymous access explicitly.

Whatever you need to implement, you can extend and customize the ASP.NET security model that SharePoint is built on.

The Developer Toolbox

The toolbox is filled with everything you need to customize, extend, and adopt almost any part of SharePoint Foundation. This includes dedicated and exclusive tools such as SharePoint Designer, as well as common tools such as Visual Studio 2010, which comes with a couple of preinstalled project and item templates. There are several tools, notably `stsadm` and the PowerShell cmdlets, which support scripted administration and deployment processes. Also included is the SDK (software development kit), which consists of manuals, guides, step-by-step-instructions, samples, and references.

Because of SharePoint's two-pronged appearance, it's not a pure developer environment. While some other platforms may put all the power into the developer's hands, SharePoint also caters to end users and administrators with its tools. Consequently, for certain tasks, developers will need to use SharePoint Designer, the web UI, or Central Administration, as there may be no developer-specific alternative. In this way, your toolbox is not limited to Visual Studio and its relatives—it encompasses everything that comes with the standard installation. We strongly recommend that you treat SharePoint not just as couple of classes and controls, but also as your favorite platform for accomplishing daily tasks. SharePoint is used by Microsoft as a platform for Team Foundation Server administration, as the interface used by Project Server, and as the heart of the Office platform. This indicates that you're already in two roles—developer and user.

Microsoft SharePoint Server for Developers

SharePoint Server 2010 is everything SharePoint Foundation is. You can see SharePoint Foundation as a functional subset of SharePoint Server. Additionally, many high-level features have been added to SharePoint Server. The following list shows the areas that SharePoint server deals with exclusively:

- Content (document related)
- Search (mostly document related)
- Dashboards (data related)
- Forms and workflows (mostly data related)
- Community (people related)
- Content publishing (mostly people related)

We explain these subjects in the next few sections in more detail.

Content

Enterprise content management (ECM) is in the 21st century what file shares were in the past. The overwhelming quantity of documents and the various workflows that manage the ways people create, approve, edit, and update these documents create challenges for ECM systems. Content management systems consist of various built-in services, storage capabilities, and features to help developers focus on business logic and workflow creation, leaving infrastructure tasks to be completed by SharePoint.

Records management is another advanced subject in the field of ECM; it addresses the need for a reliable and auditable document store. Using ECM records management, it's possible to create custom solutions on top of the basic modules SharePoint Server provides.

Search

Document and enterprise management systems have been used to organize content in various ways, including taxonomies, category trees, and tagged documents. Since Google's success, we know that full-text search is a very user-friendly organization strategy. With the increasing number of documents found on file shares in companies around the world, search capabilities have become standard.

SharePoint's search capabilities are on par with this standard, offering you highly customizable and extensible ways to create sophisticated full-text search functionality.

Dashboards

The ability to access timely, pertinent data from many sources has become a necessity for company leaders. Knowing what's really going on in an enterprise is essential for managing a company well. To address this, SharePoint provides Web Parts that display key performance indicators, chart controls that express complex data simply, and business connectivity services that gain access to LOB systems quickly. SharePoint now acts as business dashboard.

Particularly impressive in this regard is the Excel services feature—available as a browser application—which extends the Web Part–based view into a full-blown spreadsheet environment. Spreadsheets are stored in document libraries, making them available under central rights management to the targeted audience.

Forms and Workflows

Forms management is part of almost every enterprise's intranet. From simple employee self-service to absence management, travel expense reimbursement, and internal orders for equipment, there are many applications that benefit from easy-to-create, flexible forms. Combined with workflows, forms management allows you to express internal processing through the SharePoint technology and automate daily tasks. Both forms and workflows in SharePoint are highly customizable, programmable, and well supported by additional tools.

Community

Blogs and wikis are available in SharePoint Foundation already. For most applications, these are the entry points into community support within an enterprise. SharePoint server adds some features that address a broader audience. They make social computing available to teams as well as entire enterprises. One core community-based feature is MySites, which allows employees to introduce themselves and express their thoughts in a managed and centralized way.

Content Publishing

Blogging allows users to express their ideas quickly in a relatively unstructured way. It complements the full-text search engine paradigm described previously. Adding and updating articles on a wiki is more structured, and complements the link paradigm that the whole Web is built on. Giving the ordinary user the power to create pages without knowing anything about HTML empowers common people to take part in creating content in a more powerful, less structured way. SharePoint's ability to allows users to create sites, blogs, and wikis has in part pushed it to its current level of popularity. While SharePoint Foundation offered these capabilities already, SharePoint Server's Publishing feature takes them even further. The larger an enterprise's sites and the greater its activity, the more it will benefit from content-publishing modules.

Applications Make the World Go Round

SharePoint has been recognized and widely accepted for its support for certain applications, including

- Business collaboration applications
- Portals for LOB applications
- Web Parts solutions

Collaboration features are an essential part of SharePoint—it only takes a few clicks to add collaboration capabilities to your application. Workflows and forms bring things together with little effort, and business applications with some specific SharePoint features added (what we call *business collaboration applications*) are commonly used.

Creating a portal for a LOB application is just like creating other types of applications. The use of built-in features such as the Dashboard Web Part, Business Connectivity Services, and integrated web services are common in such types of applications. Your application can add the requisite data collection services, filtering and sorting capabilities, and smart data displays using chart controls, and can employ rights management.

SharePoint also supports the creation of Web Part solutions, in which you create various Web Parts that you deploy to an existing SharePoint environment and let people use your modules to extend their pages. Web Parts can be complex, and the data connections between them can empower you to build a universe of solutions.

SharePoint brings developers to a new level of programming with a high-level foundation, an overflowing toolkit, and a base application that's already there before you start coding. Some people see SharePoint as the first platform of the future of coding. While it's not the only one out there, it's one that fits well into the existing development landscape.

PART 1

■■■

Basic Tasks

CHAPTER 1

Developer Basics

In this chapter you'll learn everything you need to start developing on the new SharePoint 2010 platform. In particular this chapter will explore in detail the primary development tool: Visual Studio 2010. You'll learn the strengths and weaknesses of SharePoint Designer 2010 and how it compares with Visual Studio.

The topics covered in this chapter are

- SharePoint developer support
- Debugging your code
- Installation scenarios and how to set up your development environment
- Visual Studio 2010 and the SharePoint tools
- Developing on 64-bit computers

Not all developer tasks can be accomplished using visual tools. The SharePoint SDK (software development kit—for SharePoint it's a collection of help files, manuals, and examples) is a great collection of tools, code examples, and documentation. This chapter will introduce the SDK and highlight the most useful tools.

SharePoint projects tend to become large. Visual Studio Team System and the Team Foundation Server are good bases for team development. We recommend, for optimal output from multiple developers, that you establish a shared environment based on a SharePoint farm. You'll learn how to set up and use such an environment and how to incorporate desirable software development practices such as continuous integration and rapid deployment.

Before You Start

This book assumes that you're already familiar with SharePoint—at least SharePoint 2007—and its underlying technologies and platform. However, it begins by clarifying some matters that might be unclear even for an experienced developer.

First and foremost, SharePoint is an *application platform*. An application platform is a software development foundation that consists of an operating system, one or more frameworks, and interfaces that applications use to accomplish tasks. Primarily, an application platform has the user in mind. Microsoft SharePoint is an example of a very good application platform.

The platform is a reliable, reusable, and well-documented set of products, technologies, and tools. While some of these modules are highly usable out of the box, others may be replaced, customized, or modified according to specific needs. The platform components are dedicated to specific services they provide and that other components can consume.

An application provides business capabilities to its users via its components. A platform is classified as having a service-oriented architecture (SOA) if the components provide a standard way to communicate via services. The services use providers that act as a transparent layer between the underlying data source and the service. SOA has evolved predominantly by using XML-based web services. However, these services are not limited to XML, and modern platforms may support many other data transmission standards. An application platform provides many ways to access the services, and this is true for SharePoint. As a developer you not only consume such services, but also create services, customize existing ones, and install providers appropriate to the business cases.

The production environment for the SharePoint application platform consists of the following:

- Windows Server as the common server platform. For SharePoint 2010, Windows Server 2008 (64 bit) is the minimum requirement. As parts of the operating system, you have to have access to the following:
    - Microsoft Management Console (MMC) as the common server interface.
    - The .NET Framework and the underlying Common Language Runtime (CLR), as well as the additional libraries such as Windows Workflow Foundation (WF).
- SQL Server 2005, SQL Server 2008/2008 R2, or a corresponding version of SQL Server Express edition. SQL Server must be a 64-bit platform regardless of the actual version.

SharePoint and SQL Server

It's worth thinking about the usage of SQL Server in your SharePoint installation. SharePoint makes use of any SQL Server database server found while installing. If there is none present, it uses a SQL Server embedded database or SQL Server Express. If you install a standalone version and there is no database preset, setup chooses the embedded version. If you choose a farm installation—which is always recommended—setup will choose the SQL Server Express version. For any other serious production installation, you should have a SQL server somewhere else up and running.

Setting Up a Development Environment for SharePoint

There are several ways to set up a development environment. It depends on whether you're on a team or you're a single developer, and whether you work for an enterprise or a small shop. First, consider your own development machine. The whole process of coding, packaging, installing, and running a SharePoint component takes time.

Working Outside a Server

When developing for SharePoint, the first impression is often that a new 64-bit development machine is required to run the server and the development environment together. We'll examine this scenario and its advantages and disadvantages in the next sections. The simplest option is to keep your client machine and work against a remote server running SharePoint. It makes you independent of local configuration requirements and reduces your cost outlay, particularly for your first, simpler projects. In Chapter 2, we explain what types of development are possible with SharePoint. As a preview, the different outputs are

- Web Parts
- Application pages
- Custom fields
- Controls

A legitimate concern as a developer on a disconnected machine is, "Won't my SharePoint projects require dependencies from SharePoint assemblies?" The most common development targets, Web Parts, have no such dependency. You simply derive your control from the ASP.NET `WebPart` class and use the SharePoint web services to access data. While this is not the most powerful tool set, it's easy to set up and maintain.

For a more professional and versatile environment, consider using a remote development configuration.

Considering Remote Development

Whatever configuration you choose, you should try to develop on your own server machine. That's the only way to get the Visual Studio 2010 *F5 deployment* feature. It makes your development cycles shorter and increases productivity.

For a team-working arrangement there are several extra prerequisites. SharePoint 2010 is a 64-bit–only product. That means your whole environment must run on 64 bits. If this is overkill, there are alternatives. We strongly recommend setting up a virtual server on a physical machine, such as Hyper-V or VMware on Windows Server 2008. Create your virtual development machines there and access them remotely. A cheap Windows 7 machine will suffice as such a client computer. SharePoint projects occasionally crash the server during heavy development. Re-creating a virtual machine is much easier than losing your whole personal computer.

Installation Scenarios

The following installation scenarios list the options you currently have to install SharePoint as a core component of a development environment. The 64-bit prerequisite limits the choice of operating system to the following:

- Windows Server 2008 x64
- Windows Server 2008 R2 x64
- Windows Vista x64
- Windows 7 x64

These descriptions are two-pronged, including instructions for the clients and the SharePoint server.

Developer Workstation on Windows Server 2008

The following list is the minimum needed for a working SharePoint development system. Depending on your specific needs, you may need to install additional components. The order is obligatory—meaning that SharePoint must be installed before Visual Studio. The help files are, of course, optional.

1. Install Windows Server 2008 x64.
2. Configure, at a minimum, the Web Server role.

3. Install SharePoint.
4. Install Visual Studio 2010.
5. Install help files and sample code if desired.

The server is now ready to act as a powerful development machine.

Developer Workstation on Windows Vista or Windows 7

The following section details the more complicated process to install SharePoint on Windows Vista or Windows 7. These instructions are intended for professional developer workstations and follow Microsoft's recommendations for such a development environment running Visual Studio 2010 and SharePoint Server 2010 on the same machine.

There are two limitations with this development environment: you cannot create a SharePoint 2010 farm, and SharePoint 2010 must not run in production on Windows Vista or Windows 7.

■ **Note** This installation can be disabled through Active Directory group policy if your organization wishes to prohibit SharePoint 2010 installations on Windows Vista or Windows 7 machines.

Be sure to run all the installation steps as a local machine administrator.

The recommended machine configuration is

- x64-compatible CPU (64 bit)
- Windows 7 x64 or Windows Vista SP1 (or SP2) x64
- 2GB of RAM minimum (4GB recommended)

Start with the `SharePoint.exe` file for SharePoint Foundation or SharePoint Server 2010. Extract the files from `SharePoint.exe` with the following command line. A user account control (UAC) prompt might appear at this point.

```
SharePoint.exe /extract:c:\SharePointFiles
```

This extracts all of the installation files to your hard drive. Use a folder you can recognize easily later, such as `c:\SharePointFiles`. This allows you to repeat the installation steps without extracting the package again and enables access to the configuration file that needs tweaking, to permit installation on Windows Vista or Windows 7:

```
c:\SharePointFiles\Files\Setup\config.xml
```

Add the following line to the end of the `config.xml` file:

```
<Setting Id="AllowWindowsClientInstall" Value="True"/>
```

The complete file should now look like this:

```
<Configuration>
  <Package Id="sts">
    <Setting Id="SETUPTYPE" Value="CLEAN_INSTALL" />
  </Package>
  <DATADIR Value="%CommonProgramFiles%\Microsoft Shared\Web Server
```

```
                    Extensions\14\Data" />
  <Logging Type="verbose" Path="%temp%" Template="Microsoft Windows
                                        SharePoint Services 4.0 Setup *.log" />
  <Setting Id="UsingUIInstallMode" Value="1" />
  <Setting Id="SETUP_REBOOT" Value="Never" />
  <Setting Id="AllowWindowsClientInstall" Value="True"/>
</Configuration>
```

If you miss this step, you will see an error dialog, as shown in Figure 1–1, when you run the installation.

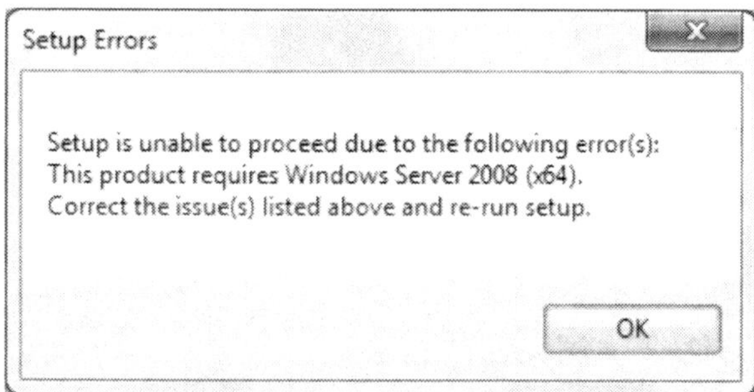

Figure 1–1. *Error if the package is not altered to run with Windows 7*

Before running the SharePoint setup, install the prerequisites described in the "Installing Required Windows Features" section of this chapter.

Steps for Vista SP1 Only

These three components are not required on Windows 7, because they are included with the operating system. For Vista with no service pack or SP1 only, they are required.

First, install the .NET Framework 3.5 SP1 from `http://download.microsoft.com/download/2/0/e/20e90413-712f-438c-988e-fdaa79a8ac3d/dotnetfx35.exe`.

Second, install PowerShell x64 from `www.microsoft.com/downloads/details.aspx?FamilyID=af37d87d-5de6-4af1-80f4-740f625cd084`.

Third, install the Windows Installer 4.5 redistributable from `www.microsoft.com/downloads/details.aspx?FamilyID=5a58b56f-60b6-4412-95b9-54d056d6f9f4`.

Installing Required Windows Features

The SharePoint 2010 prerequisite installer does not run on Windows Vista or Windows 7. You must manually configure the necessary Windows features and install the requisite software. The requirements include enabling almost all the IIS (Internet Information Services) features. Instead of checking almost all the boxes in the IIS section in Windows Features, you can enable them programmatically. At a command prompt, paste in the following command (for clarity the options are shown line by line, though you're supposed to enter them as a single line):

```
start /w pkgmgr /iu:IIS-WebServerRole;          IIS-WebServer;
IIS-CommonHttpFeatures;                         IIS-StaticContent;
IIS-DefaultDocument;                            IIS-DirectoryBrowsing;
IIS-HttpErrors;                                 IIS-ApplicationDevelopment;
```

```
IIS-ASPNET;
IIS-ISAPIExtensions;
IIS-HealthAndDiagnostics;
IIS-LoggingLibraries;
IIS-HttpTracing;
IIS-Security;
IIS-WindowsAuthentication;
IIS-RequestFiltering;
IIS-HttpCompressionStatic;
IIS-WebServerManagementTools;
IIS-IIS6ManagementCompatibility;
IIS-WMICompatibility;
WAS-ProcessModel;
WAS-ConfigurationAPI;
IIS-NetFxExtensibility;
IIS-ISAPIFilter;
IIS-HttpLogging;
IIS-RequestMonitor;
IIS-CustomLogging;
IIS-BasicAuthentication;
IIS-DigestAuthentication;
IIS-Performance;
IIS-HttpCompressionDynamic;
IIS-ManagementConsole;
IIS-Metabase;
WAS-WindowsActivationService;
WAS-NetFxEnvironment;
```

This may take some time. When it is finished, your Windows Features dialog settings should look like Figure 1–2.

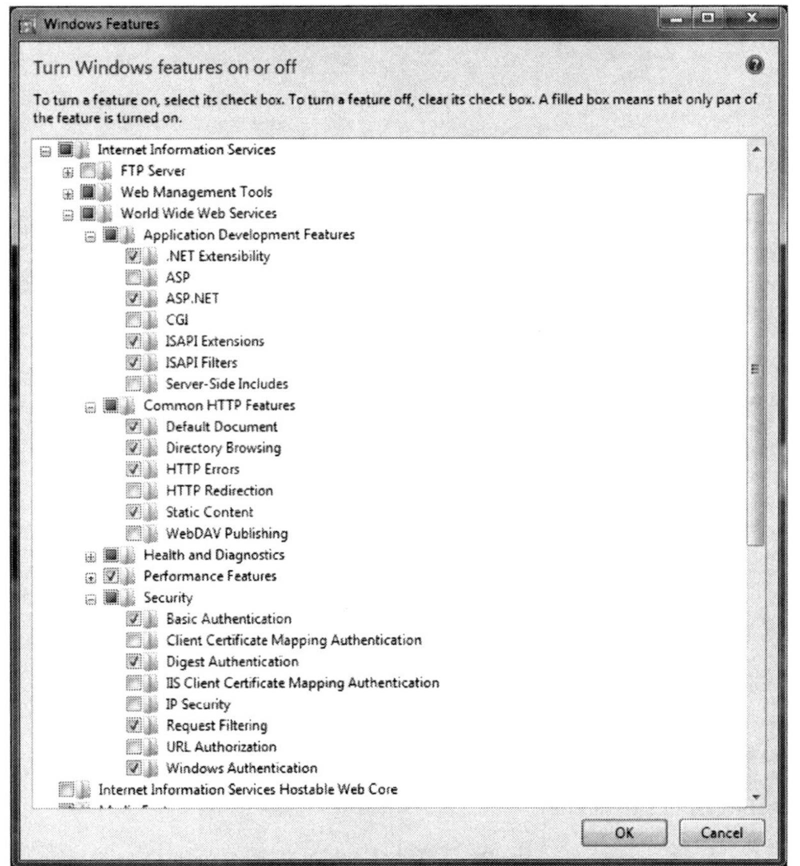

***Figure 1–2.** Check the prerequisites required for SharePoint 2010*

A reboot is required after the Windows Features update. Next, install FilterPack by running the command:

```
c:\SharePointFiles\PrerequisiteInstallerFiles\FilterPack\FilterPack.msi
```

This command runs a Windows installer application. There are no configuration steps—it simply installs its contents.

Install Windows Identity Foundation (WIF). This framework was formerly known by the code name Geneva. This is an update package and it's described in Knowledge Base article KB974405. It also has no configuration settings. The SharePoint Foundation needs the `Microsoft.IdentityModel` assembly with version 1.0.0.0.

Installing and Configuring SharePoint

Now you're ready to install SharePoint 2010 using `setup.exe`. After the start screen, you must accept the license terms. In the next step, choose Standalone as the server type, as shown in Figure 1–3.

■ **Note** A *Complete* installation allows you to add more servers. However, this requires access to Active Directory. If you install on a client operating system, this is probably not available. Using a *Standalone* installation is preferred on a client operating system intended for development purposes.

Click Install Now to start the installation.

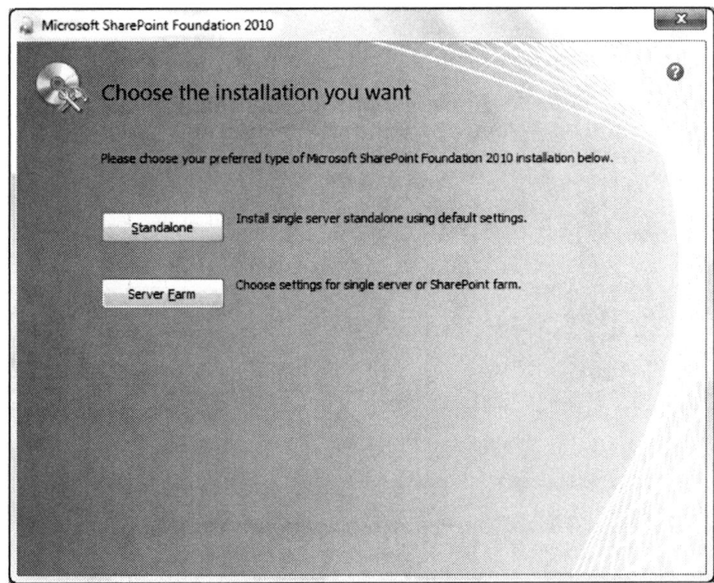

Figure 1–3. *Choose a Standalone installation.*

When the installer ends, you will be prompted to optionally start the SharePoint Products and Technologies Configuration wizard. With the check box checked, click Close to run it, as shown in Figure 1–4.

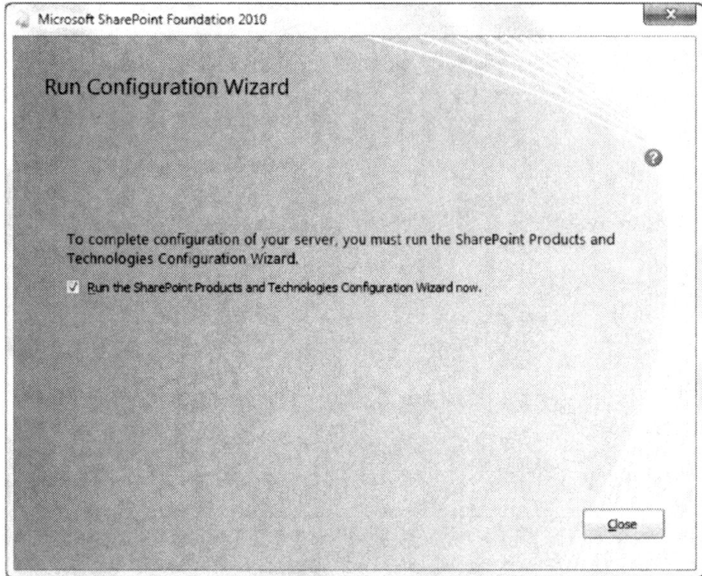

Figure 1–4. *Run the configuration wizard.*

The wizard leads you through several steps:

1. A splash screen outlines the information you might have to provide. Clicking Next displays a warning that installation on a client operating system does not support a production SharePoint environment (see Figure 1–5).

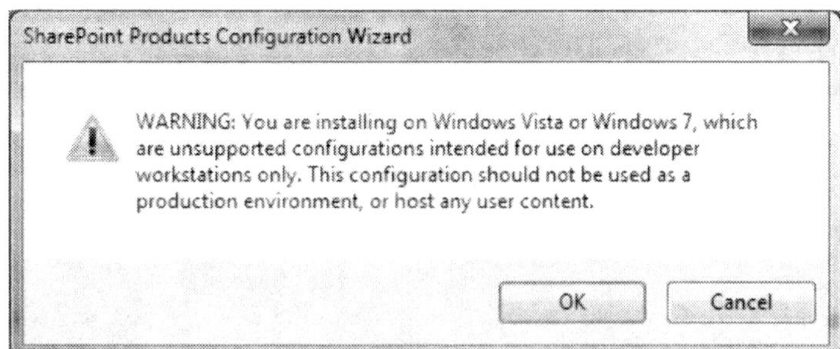

Figure 1–5. *Developers only: Installing on Windows 7 is not for production environments*

2. After this a second warning appears—explaining that several services might be restarted—confirm by clicking Yes.
3. Next, choose "Create a new server farm."

4. A standalone version runs on the internal embedded SQL server, requiring no further information. Otherwise, SQL Server 2008 Express is used, and you will need to enter the database server name, username, and password.
5. Let the wizard complete the remaining steps. No additional information is required. After this, Central Administration loads.

If the configuration is successful, you should install SQL Server 2008 SP1. If you install Visual Studio 2010 in the next step, this is not required, as the current release comes with the required service packs for SQL Server 2008 Express.

When it finishes, create a new SharePoint site using SharePoint 4.0 Central Administration under Administrative Tools.

■ **Tip** To avoid user authentication prompts, add your new local SharePoint site to the trusted sites list in the Internet Explorer options.

Installing Visual Studio 2010

Now install Visual Studio 2010 and the SharePoint development tools. The tools add several useful templates for creating SharePoint objects. The installation is straightforward, though you'll need to restart the computer once in the middle of the installation cycle.

■ **Tip** We recommend using Visual Studio 2010 Ultimate for this book (and in general).

Team Development

For team development, each team member needs access to the same code. Setting up a Team Foundation Server with its source code management feature is part of the solution. Each person should add his or her development machine as a farm computer to the SharePoint installation.

There should be one database server. It can run Central Administration, too. In large teams, we recommend restricting access to Central Administration to one or two people, not necessarily developers. You must ensure that the developers only use tools, plug-ins, features, and even Web Parts that are approved by the administrator to run on the production machine. The benefit is a much smoother deployment process later.

Optimizing Your Development Experience

Even on a fast machine, the development experience could be better. SharePoint is optimized for servers, and it runs a lot of background services that are not needed during development, so you could turn them off. There are a few exceptions—for example, when testing a deployment scenario, the SPTimer service might be needed in a farm environment. In the most common installations, such an optimization provides noticeable advantages.

To have the services available when they're needed, we recommend you create a suitable batch file. You can easily start up the server, stop the services, and restart later. Rather than stopping services manually in the Services snap-in and setting them to Manual, run a console command:

```
c:>net stop <Service>
```

The following services are not normally required on a development machine (the names are in the form that you'd use them from the command line):

- WebAnalyticsService
- OSearch14
- SPUserCodeV4
- SPSearch4
- SPTimerV4
- SPTraceV4
- FontCache3.0.0.0
- MSSQL$RTC
- ReportServer
- mqsvc
- MSASCui
- ntfrs
- OSPPSVC
- PresentationFontCache
- sqlwriter
- SYNCPROC
- ExcelServerWebService

Some services might not be installed or may already be stopped, depending on your machine's configuration. You can safely ignore such services.

■ **Note** When creating the batch file, be aware of the inconsistent naming of SharePoint 2010 services using the suffixes "4," "14," and "V4" (in no particular order).

Preparing to Use .NET 3.5

By default, SharePoint compiles using the C# 2.0 compiler. If you create an assembly using the 3.5 settings, you have all features of the C# 3.5 language available. However, if you have pages with embedded code, such as generic handler or web services, the ASP.NET compiler uses .NET 2.0. Features such as the var keyword will not work. To overcome this limitation, you must extend the settings in the web.config file. It's recommended to set this on a per–site collection basis to avoid side effects. The corresponding web.config can be found in the appropriate VirtualDirectory folder of IIS.

First, add the following section anywhere beneath the <configuration> node:

```
<system.codedom>
  <compilers>
    <compiler language="c#;cs;csharp" extension=".cs" warningLevel="4"
              type="Microsoft.CSharp.CSharpCodeProvider, System, Version=2.0.0.0,
                    Culture=neutral, PublicKeyToken=b77a5c561934e089">
      <providerOption name="CompilerVersion" value="v3.5" />
      <providerOption name="WarnAsError" value="false" />
    </compiler>
  </compilers>
</system.codedom>
```

This sets the required compiler version to 3.5.

Second, look for the <assemblies> node and compare carefully the list of assemblies, as shown here:

```
<compilation batch="false" debug="false">
  <assemblies>
    <add assembly="System.Core, Version=3.5.0.0,
                   Culture=neutral, PublicKeyToken=B77A5C561934E089" />
    <add assembly="System.Data.DataSetExtensions, Version=3.5.0.0,
                   Culture=neutral, PublicKeyToken=B77A5C561934E089" />
    <add assembly="System.Web.Extensions, Version=3.5.0.0,
                   Culture=neutral, PublicKeyToken=31BF3856AD364E35" />
    <add assembly="System.Xml.Linq, Version=3.5.0.0,
                   Culture=neutral, PublicKeyToken=B77A5C561934E089" />
    <add assembly="Microsoft.SharePoint, Version=14.0.0.0,
                   Culture=neutral, PublicKeyToken=71e9bce111e9429c" />
    <add assembly="System.Web.Extensions, Version=3.5.0.0,
                   Culture=neutral, PublicKeyToken=31bf3856ad364e35" />
    <add assembly="Microsoft.Web.CommandUI, Version=14.0.0.0,
                   Culture=neutral, PublicKeyToken=71e9bce111e9429c" />
    <add assembly="Microsoft.SharePoint.Search, Version=14.0.0.0,
                   Culture=neutral, PublicKeyToken=71e9bce111e9429c" />
    <add assembly="Microsoft.Office.Access.Server.UI, Version=14.0.0.0,
                   Culture=neutral, PublicKeyToken=71e9bce111e9429c" />
    <add assembly="Microsoft.SharePoint.Publishing, Version=14.0.0.0,
                   Culture=neutral, PublicKeyToken=71e9bce111e9429c" />
</assemblies>
```

The list might look slightly different on your system. You can extend the list if you need other parts of .NET 3.5 in your project. The changes take immediate effect and do not require a restart or an iisreset call.

SharePoint's Developer Support at a Glance

SharePoint 2010 opens a new era in developer support. It's moving from being just a powerful platform for collaboration, search, and content presentation, to becoming a developer framework. To increase developer productivity, it comes with tight integration within Visual Studio 2010. The Developer Dashboard gives an in-depth look into the state of the current request and the processing within SharePoint. A rich set of platform services are available for comprehensive data access. LINQ for SharePoint is a fast and reliable data access layer for type-safe access to lists, files, and folders. The business connectivity services allow smooth integration with line-of-business (LOB) systems. The deployment of applications within such a complex environment is just another challenge addressed by the improvements in SharePoint 2010. Team Foundation Server now supports the whole application life cycle. A standardized packaging solution allows easy deployment of your creations.

Bridging the Gap

SharePoint is a very large platform, especially from a developer perspective. It's not just an API (application programming interface) that you can hook into and start coding. Rather, it's a conglomeration of interrelated tools, administration sites, data, database schemas, and more. SharePoint sits on top of ASP.NET, which is another huge framework and another challenge to developers. ASP.NET in turn is built on the .NET Framework—yet another vast empire.

In the application development environment, there is another set of tools, too. Visual Studio is just one of the instruments in a powerful, reliable, and team-friendly development orchestra.

Connecting Your Systems

The first question that usually arises when starting development with SharePoint concerns how all these disparate parts fit together. What procedure do you have to follow to get the code running, the debugger watching, and the final application displayed in the browser?

It's helpful to start from the perspective of a web developer. In essence, SharePoint is a web application—a large one, but nevertheless just a web application. Each instance of SharePoint can have one or more web applications, and any number of SharePoint instances may reside in your farm. We'll explain later what roles these parts have. For now, consider a single SharePoint instance and a single web application in it. For this case, the architecture is as shown in Figure 1–6.

If you plan to work with Web Parts, code-behind with ASP.NET application pages, or web controls, you should hook up with the SharePoint object model. (Chapter 2 gives an overview and Chapter 3 contains a detailed explanation of the SharePoint object model.) The object model is used widely throughout the whole book. It is a rich set of classes that perform almost all required actions quickly and reliably. As shown in Figure 1–6, the web application occupies a central position. It builds the context in which your code runs. That means that the object model should primarily work within one web application. It's not intended to span multiple applications, even if this might be technically feasible.

To work on a higher level—against another web application or SharePoint instance, or somewhere beyond the boundaries of a SharePoint farm—use web services or REST-based data access. Web services provide another integration level and an even more reliable way to access your application. Due to the nature of web services, they might appear to perform poorly. It's a question of configuration, hardware, and usage scenarios as to whether the performance matters. As a best practice, we advise using web services and confirming that the required performance is supplied by a particular configuration. Using web services is easy, and the support to integrate them using Visual Studio is excellent. For several SharePoint-based applications, such as Project Server, web services provide extensibility without in-depth knowledge of another API.

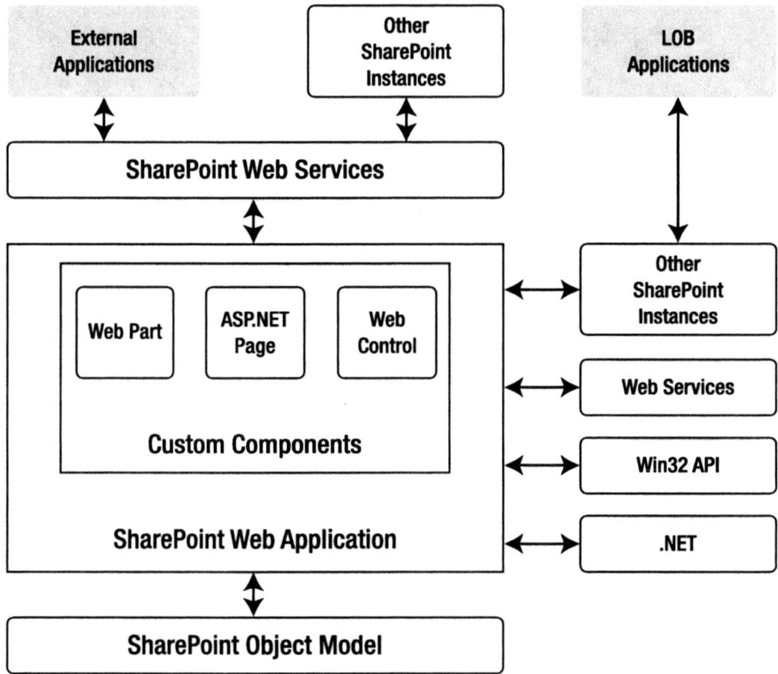

Figure 1–6. *SharePoint web application architecture at a glance*

When maximum performance is imperative, direct access is recommended if an API is explicitly exposed. That means, for example, when you program against Active Directory's LDAP protocol, the API is a better choice than using LDAP queries. The same applies for the Project Server Interface (PSI), for example. If the data source is supplied by a LOB system that provides either web services or direct database access, Business Connectivity Services (BCS; formerly known as Business Data Catalog) is a good choice. Even here you have an API to program against if the basic features provided out of the box lack power.

■ **Note** Never program against SharePoint's internal configuration or content databases. Even if it seems easy or the objects are publicly accessible, it's bad practice. Microsoft could change the data model, data structure, or internal behavior without warning. In that situation your application will eventually fail and you will have to rewrite it. However, sometimes under special circumstances you might need high-speed read access to the data. Then it's possible to code against the database as long as you strictly use read-only access and monitor schema changes.

Advantages of SharePoint Functions

When you first explore the SharePoint object model, you might feel lost. It's a vast desert of classes, classes, and more classes. Occasionally, you'll find an interface. As a result, developers tend to ignore the SharePoint object model for small projects and create their solution completely with standalone code. Even for big projects, some software developer teams follow this approach. They start creating wire frameworks, UML diagrams, and class models, and taking other preparatory steps. These methods are appropriate if the underlying framework is just a free programming platform, such as the .NET Framework. SharePoint is different. While it limits the freedom developers usually have, it empowers them by providing a rich infrastructure—an amazing number of functions all ready to use.

Instead of designing a project including the entire basic infrastructure, use the functionality that already exists in SharePoint. Handling the lists within your web application's administration, using the object model, and employing LINQ to SharePoint are much easier than writing it all yourself. You'll find out sooner or later that the object model empowers you and that it's worth learning at least the basic structure, the object hierarchy, and how the objects relate to each other.

SharePoint, like any other platform, has its strength and weaknesses. This book contains a collection of best practices and approved methods of coding, and a few warnings concerning some flaws. Because of the sheer volume of features, no book can describe all parts of SharePoint completely. So in case you get lost or can't find the right information, remember this advice: *never leave the object model.*

Do not start developing your own infrastructure. Do not start creating features that are supposedly part of SharePoint. Take the time to search and research. Sometimes you won't find the necessary information, either in the book or on MSDN. SharePoint 2010 is new and the documentation is patchy. With the previous versions of SharePoint, some information did not appear at all during the entire life cycle. Worse still, the deeper you dig into the internals and the more you use the features provided by the API, the less information you find. Sooner or later, even the blogosphere will fail and return nothing but garbage. You have to have techniques to help yourself and quickly devise a solution. (We understand the scenario where you're under pressure and your customer is yelling for results.)

Understanding the API

This book will explain the API as deeply and broadly as space allows. However, even that will not be enough. We'll even point to the entry points within the official documentation on MSDN. That's not enough either. If you need to know how something works internally to understand how to use it (instead of reinventing the wheel), use a tool like Reflector—it is priceless. Reflector is a free download from Red Gate—originally written by Lutz Roeder—and is able to decompile .NET code and reformat it into a few common languages, such as C#. Figure 1–7 shows Reflector in action.

■ **Tip** You can get your free copy of Reflector at `www.red-gate.com/products/reflector`.

There are some exceptions, but almost all major parts of SharePoint 2010 are written in .NET, and you can peek into the code and learn the Microsoft internals.

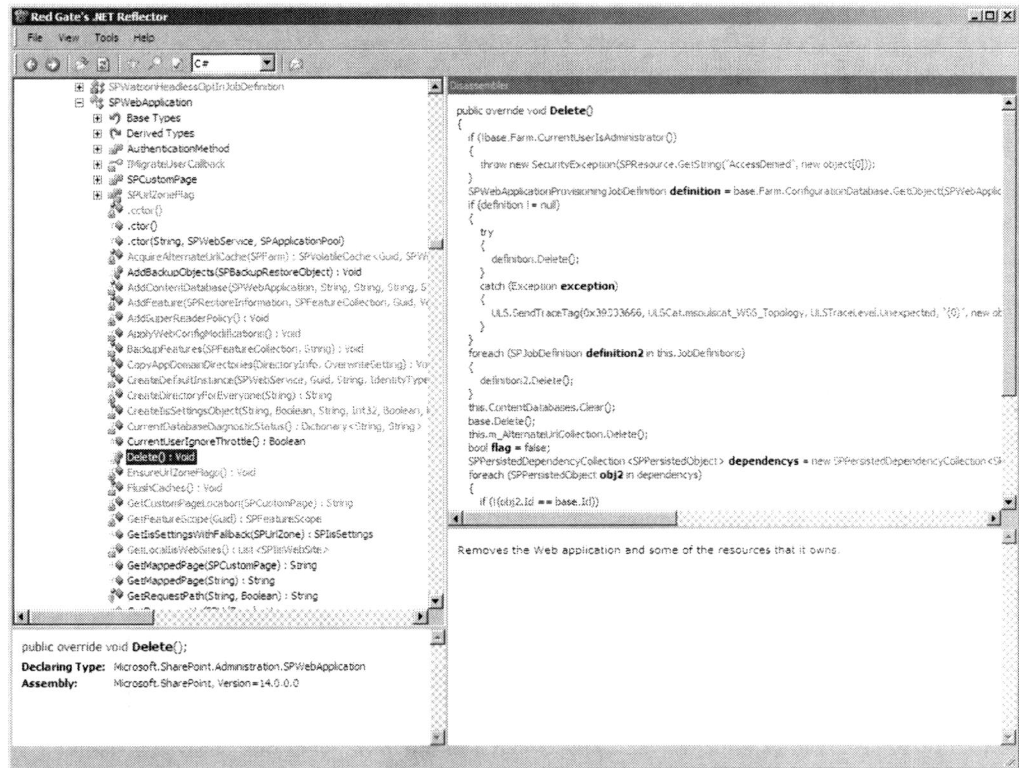

Figure 1–7. Red Gate's Reflector in action

Whatever your intention and whatever sort of code you're about to write, the API is your partner. Using the SharePoint controls and methods is the recommended approach. You can extend, customize, reformat, configure, preset, and generally do whatever you want with the existing components. But never reinvent something and write your own as long as you can find something comparable inside SharePoint. These components fit very well into the platform and they have many useful features. Adopting and changing is almost always better than writing your own from scratch.

Only if you can't find anything usable within SharePoint should you consider backing up a step and trying an ASP.NET component. Imagine a table you wish to use to present some data. First, try the `SPGridView` control. It's feature rich, and end users know it because it's the standard control used to present lists. It has such features as sorting and grouping. It's almost public, so you can easily hook into the interfaces and events and customize it. It's there for you. Only after you've experimented with customizing the `SPGridView` control and found it inadequate for your purposes should you try its base class, `GridView`, from ASP.NET. It might be simpler, but you can add your own features more easily. If even this fails, use the .NET Framework and write your own grid.

Once you have adopted, customized, and modified a component, think about team productivity. Repackage your component as another custom component, add configuration features, and make it installable. Redistribute it in your team and encourage others to make use of it. That way you ensure that your colleagues struggling with the API do not stray from the recommended approach.

Critical Tasks

SharePoint developers face many challenging tasks. With the appearance of Visual Studio 2010 and SharePoint 2010, some things are easier. The integration is improved and the support for server- and client-side programming is much better than it was in previous editions. With the new possibilities, however, a new level of application programming arises, and things become more challenging again. These challenges include

- How to distribute the results—creating and installing packages
- How to debug client-side code, especially Ajax behavior
- How to handle code issues on the server
- How to deal with issues that only arise on the production system (where there is no debugger)

If you develop on a team—and we assume that you do—things are even more complicated. You have to synchronize your work with others, take over their code, or provide yours to others. You must deal with configuration settings, farm maintenance, and the data stored in the shared database.

Debugging the Server

Having Visual Studio 2010 properly installed might look like the perfect environment to debug the code. We assume that you're already familiar with your IDE. In the section "Introducing Visual Studio 2010's SharePoint Support" is a brief introduction to the basic features concerning SharePoint.

A web application consists of several parts. IIS plays a significant role—each request and response passes through IIS. Debugging the server includes a way to debug IIS to see what data is transmitted from the browser to the server and back. Despite debugging, performance issues often arise. To test your SharePoint application under load, a stress test tool is essential.

If your SharePoint server does not respond as expected and the debugger does not reveal useful results—probably because an internal module beyond your access scope fails—you need more tools. SharePoint hides error message and replaces stack traces, exception messages, and logs with almost useless information. It's primarily designed for end users, and they might get frightened when a `NullReferenceException` is displayed (e.g., "Did I lose all my data now?"). In your development environment, you can turn on developer-friendly (and therefore user-unfriendly) error messages by setting the appropriate parameters in the `web.config` file:

```
<configuration>
  <SharePoint>
    <SafeMode CallStack="true" ... />
  ...
  </SharePoint>
  <system.web>
   <customErrors mode="off" />
  ...
  </system.web>
</configuration>
```

However, not all errors throw exceptions, and not all such messages are helpful. You need a plan for how to find the source of the trouble:

1. Look into the event log for SharePoint.
2. Look into the SharePoint logs.

3. Attach a debugger to the working process and watch for exceptions.
4. Look into the IIS logs.
5. Add tracing to your code and watch the traces.
6. Consider remote debugging if the target machine has no debugger installed.

Let's consider each of these alternatives in more detail.

Looking into the Event Log for SharePoint

The event log (see Figure 1–8) contains a special section for SharePoint, and the application event log can also contain some relevant information. It is even worth looking for events sent here from IIS. If the SharePoint application causes the worker process to die ungracefully, it can help to know when and why.

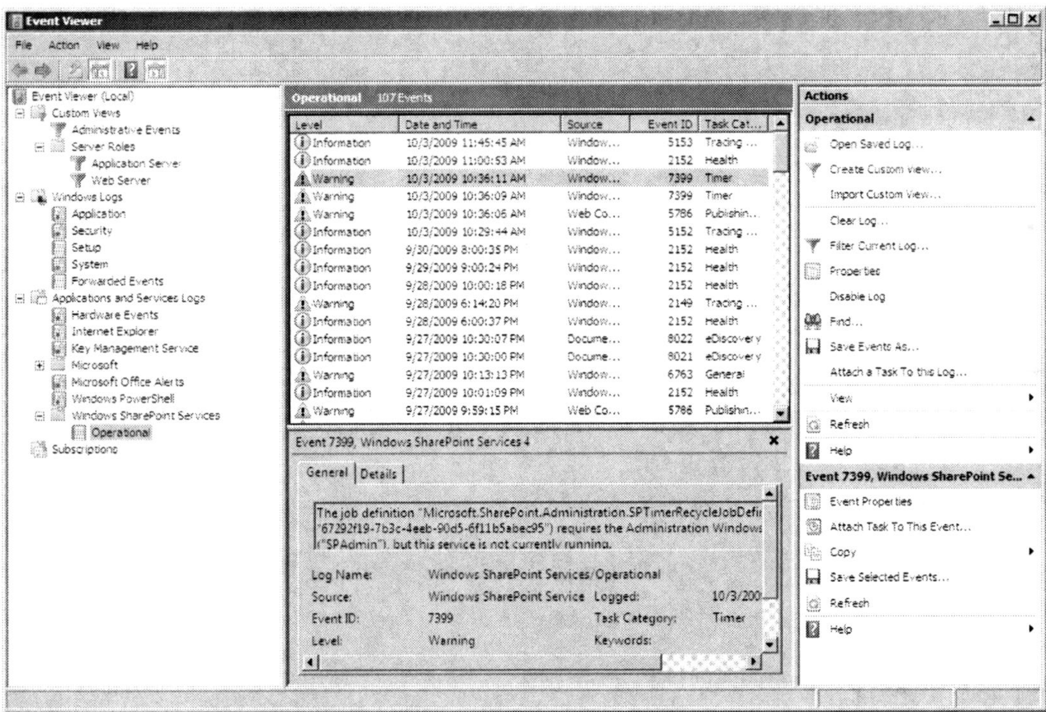

Figure 1–8. The SharePoint event log is now part of the Windows Event Viewer.

Looking into the SharePoint and IIS Logs

SharePoint itself writes a lot of data into the logs if it is enabled in Central Administration. During the development and test cycle, we strongly recommend activating the logs. You can find the logging files in

```
<%CommonProgramFiles%>\Microsoft Shared\Web Server Extensions\14\LOGS
```

The IIS logs are found here:

```
<%SystemRoot%>\System32\LogFiles
```

The IIS logs contain information about each request and the response. If you match certain reactions of SharePoint with the event of a specific request, there is a good chance of finding the reason for some unexpected behavior.
If you suspect that your code is causing the misbehavior and the debugger disturbs the data flow, a private trace is a good option. Just write useful information from your code to a trace provider. You can turn tracing on and off by setting the appropriate options in the application's `web.config` file:

```
<configuration>
 <system.web>
  <trace enabled="true" requestLimit="40" localOnly="false"/>
 </system.web>
</configuration>
```

The tracing framework is highly extensible and you can write the data to text files, the event log, or databases, or as XML. A full explanation is beyond the scope of this book. You can start here to learn more about tracing using the .NET Framework:

```
http://msdn.microsoft.com/de-de/library/1y89ed7z(en-us,VS.85).aspx
```

Using Common Debugging Techniques

In addition to these specific techniques, you should consider using advanced .NET debugging methods such as the following:

- Attaching a debugger to the working process and watching for exceptions
- Considering remote debugging if the target machine has no debugger installed
- Adding tracing to your code and watching the traces

These methods are not SharePoint-specific, but are nonetheless quite helpful.

The Developer Dashboard

Several tools are quite powerful, though not always appropriate on a production machine. The Developer Dashboard built into SharePoint 2010 provides at least basic information about internal processes.

Activating the Developer Dashboard Using stsadm

By default the Developer Dashboard is switched off. To activate it on your machine, you can run a `stsadm` command:

```
stsadm -o setproperty -pn developer-dashboard -pv ondemand
```

The command switch `-pv` accepts the following settings:

- `on`: Activate the Developer Dashboard (always appears at the end of a page)
- `off`: Deactivate
- `ondemand`: Activate on Demand

The ondemand option is usually the best choice, as it allows you to show or hide the information using the dashboard icon in the upper-right corner, as shown in Figure 1–9.

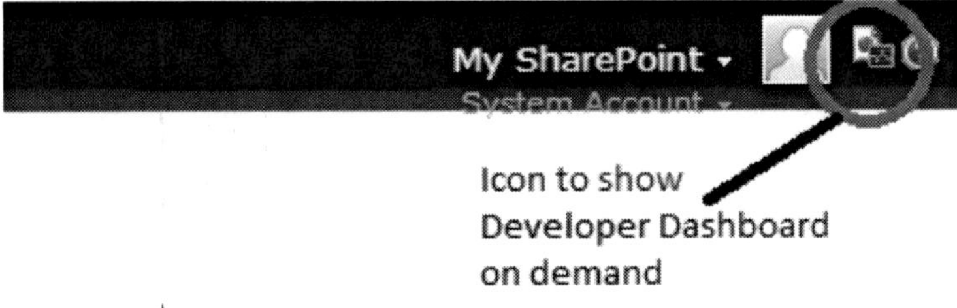

Figure 1–9. *The icon to show the dashboard on demand*

■ **Note** Launching this command takes some time even on a fast machine.

The on option is helpful if the layout of a page is destroyed or you can't reach the Dashboard icon for some reason.

Activating the Developer Dashboard Using PowerShell

To activate the Developer Dashboard via PowerShell, use a script such as this:

```
$level="Off"
[void][System.Reflection.Assembly]::LoadWithPartialName("Microsoft.SharePoint")
[void][System.Reflection.Assembly]::LoadWithPartialName
                                        ("Microsoft.SharePoint.Administration")
$contentSvc=[Microsoft.SharePoint.Administration.SPWebService]::ContentService
$contentSvc.DeveloperDashboardSettings.DisplayLevel=
                ([Enum]::Parse(
                [Microsoft.SharePoint.Administration.SPDeveloperDashboardLevel],
                $level))
$contentSvc.DeveloperDashboardSettings.Update()
Write-Host("Current Level: " + $contentSvc.DeveloperDashboardSettings.DisplayLevel)
```

The supported properties for the `$level` variable are the same as those for `stsadm`:

- `"On"`: Activate the Developer Dashboard (always appears at the end of a page)
- `"Off"`: Deactivate
- `"OnDemand"`: Activate on Demand

This code is good for running in a batch file using a parameter. To copy a command-line parameter to the variable, use something like this:

```
param($level)
```

There is neither error handling nor user help in this batch file. Consider adding such lines to turn this sample batch file into production-quality code.

Activating the Developer Dashboard Using Code

You're probably going to write some clever tools for SharePoint. Using code to activate the dashboard may help others to investigate what they are doing. A simple piece of code does the trick:

```
SPWebService svc = SPWebService.ContentService;
svc.DeveloperDashboardSettings.DisplayLevel = SPDeveloperDashboardLevel.OnDemand;
svc.DeveloperDashboardSettings.Update();
```

Note that the usage of the `SPFarm` object, which is shown in several blogs regarding earlier versions of SharePoint 2010, is no longer supported in the final SharePoint product.

Working with the Developer Dashboard

This tool will give you the following:

- A breakdown of the request/response cycle with timings for each operation
- A breakdown of the response times for each database query that the rendering process triggers
- A breakdown of the load times for each Web Part on the page

Use this information to narrow down the source of any error (see Figure 1–10).

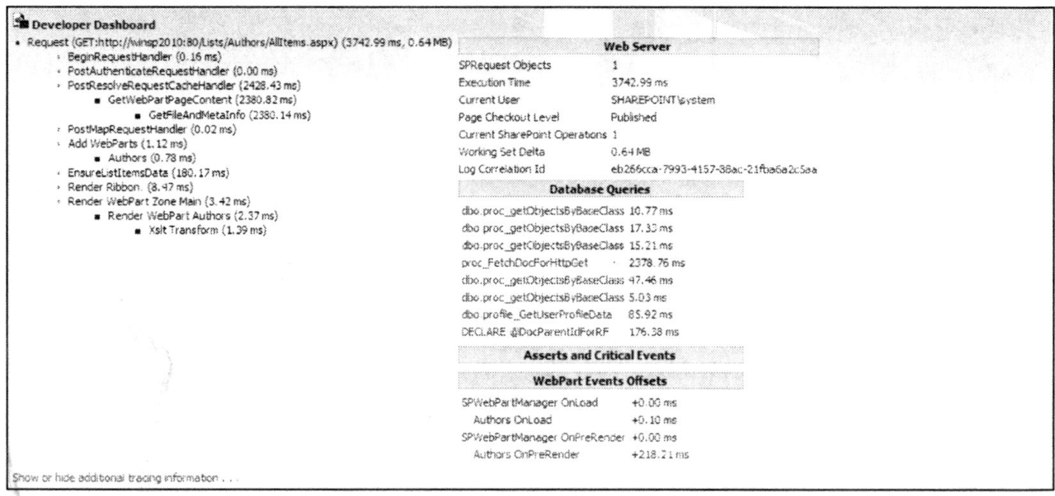

***Figure 1–10.** The Developer Dashboard reveals internal information.*

To access the dashboard, click the icon in upper-right corner to the left of the help button question mark. The dashboard analyses the current page only. The underlying ASP.NET engine has a lot more information beyond what the dashboard shows. It is written to the file `Trace.axd`, and can be displayed by clicking the small link at the end of the dashboard screen showing "Show or hide additional tracing information..." (see Figure 1–11).

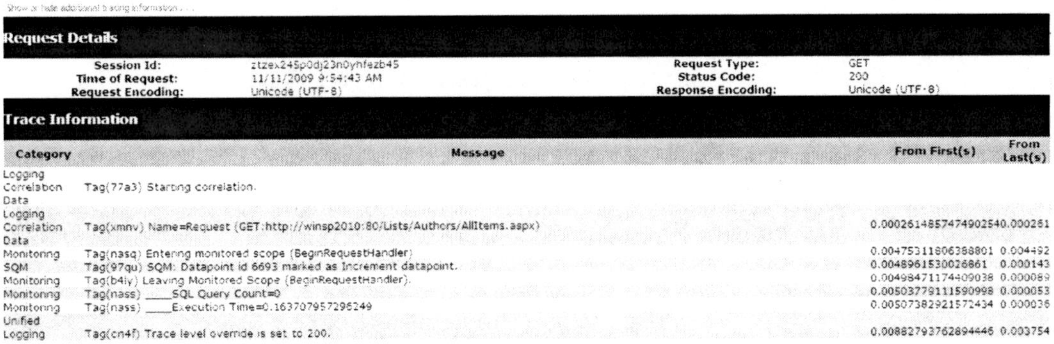

Show or hide additional tracing information . . .

Request Details

Session Id:	ztzex245p0dj23n0yhfezb45	**Request Type:**	GET
Time of Request:	11/11/2009 9:54:43 AM	**Status Code:**	200
Request Encoding:	Unicode (UTF-8)	**Response Encoding:**	Unicode (UTF-8)

Trace Information

Category	Message	From First(s)	From Last(s)
Logging Correlation Data	Tag(77a3) Starting correlation.		
Logging Correlation Data	Tag(xmnv) Name=Request (GET:http://winsp2010:80/Lists/Authors/AllItems.aspx)	0.00026148574749025	40.000261
Monitoring	Tag(nasq) Entering monitored scope (BeginRequestHandler)	0.00475311806388801	0.004492
SQM	Tag(97qu) SQM: Datapoint id 6693 marked as Increment datapoint.	0.0048961530026861	0.000143
Monitoring	Tag(b4iy) Leaving Monitored Scope (BeginRequestHandler).	0.00498471174409038	0.000089
Monitoring	Tag(nass) ____SQL Query Count=0	0.00503779111590998	0.000053
Monitoring	Tag(nass) ____Execution Time=0.163707957296249	0.00507382921572434	0.000036
Unified Logging	Tag(cn4f) Trace level override is set to 200.	0.00882793762894446	0.003754

***Figure 1–11.** The Developer Dashboard's trace information screen*

The ASP.NET trace shows virtually everything available from the current request/response cycle, such as headers, cookies, and form data. This includes internal traces, stack traces, and names of stored procedures and the time that they appeared. That makes the dashboard not only a perfect tool to find errors, but even more helpful to find performance flaws. The complete control tree is exposed and makes it possible to find the reason an element is not where you expect it or why it is missing altogether.

Making Your Code Dashboard-Aware

The dashboard displays any useful information that's available from the runtime environment. However, the reason for a malfunction, bad performance, or unexpected behavior could be in your code. It's good practice, in addition to using debugging tools, to add diagnostic output to your code that generates content to the dashboard.

You can use the `SPMonitoredScope` class to create a section that is logged and explicitly exposed to the dashboard's output.

■ **Note** The logging output generated by the `SPMonitoredScope` class is not available in sandboxed solutions.

Let's assume you create a visual Web Part and you want to know what happens inside the `Load` event, when is it called, and how much time a specific operation consumes. The following code explains how to use the `SPMonitoredScope` class:

```
using System;
using System.Web.UI;
using System.Web.UI.WebControls;
using System.Web.UI.WebControls.WebParts;
using Microsoft.SharePoint;
using Microsoft.SharePoint.Utilities;

namespace VisualWebPartDashboard.VisualWebPart1
```

```
{
    public partial class VisualWebPart1UserControl : UserControl
    {
        protected void Page_Load(object sender, EventArgs e)
        {
            using (SPMonitoredScope scope =
                   new SPMonitoredScope(this.GetType().Name))
            {
                Button b = new Button();
                b.Text = "Click me!";
                Controls.Add(b);
                using (SPMonitoredScope scopeInner =
                       new SPMonitoredScope("Inner Scope"))
                {
                    System.Threading.Thread.Sleep(500); // lengthy operation
                }
            }
        }
    }
}
```

In this code, the SPMonitoredScope class exposes two lines to the dashboard output. The first uses the current internal name of the control, while the second uses a constant string. The inner operation is delayed to show the effect of the timer.

The advantage of this method is that the output appears within the context of the execution tree, and you see not only your information, but also when your code is executed. You can also see in Figure 1–12 how the artificial 500-millisecond delay in the code affects the whole page.

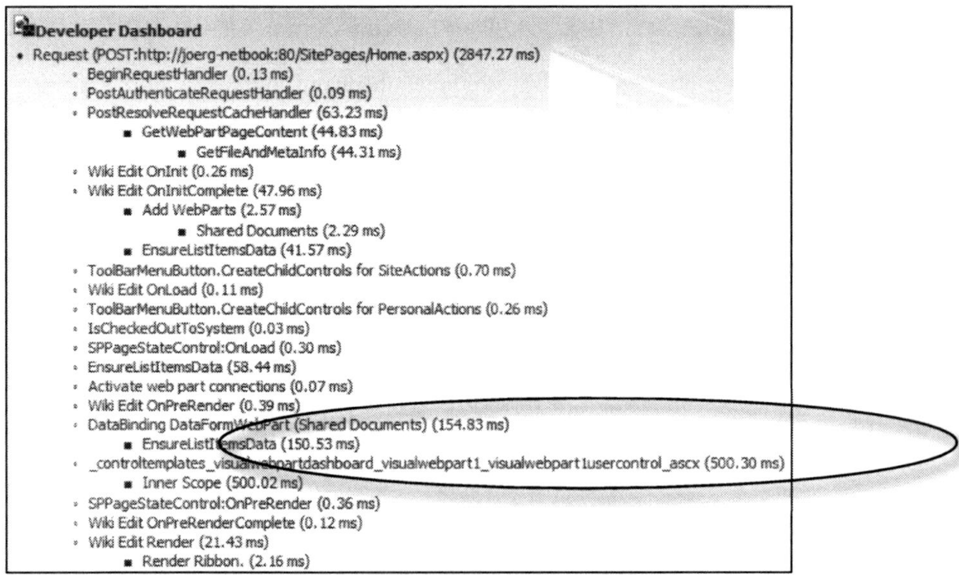

Figure 1–12. Private information shown in the Developer Dashboard

---

■ **Tip** To get more information about programming Visual Web Parts, refer to Chapter 6.

Debugging the Client

On the client, the same effort has to be made to ensure that it's working correctly. The situation here is more complicated because several different browsers need to be supported. The developers of SharePoint 2010 did well to support all common browsers, such as Internet Explorer 7 and newer versions of Safari, Opera, and Firefox.

■ **Caution** Note that Internet Explorer 6 is explicitly not supported by SharePoint 2010.

The application pages or Web Parts you create will programmatically send HTML, styles, and other content straight to the browser. You have to ensure that it runs without errors in the designated environment. Because SharePoint relies heavily on Ajax (asynchronous JavaScript and XML) and your customers invariably demand it, you may decide to use Ajax, too. Asynchronous calls from the browser to the server, while the page is visible, complicate things even further.

Using Fiddler to Understand What's Going on the Wire

Sniffing the protocol activity on the connection with SharePoint requires a tool like Fiddler (see Figure 1–13). It shows the data flow, headers, cookies, and raw data sent down to the server and back to the browser. Fiddler is a web-debugging proxy that sits between the browser and the network socket. It logs all incoming HTTP (and HTTPS) traffic. You can inspect the headers received and sent, investigate the raw data, and edit data to test your server. Fiddler itself is independent of a specific browser and works well with Internet Explorer, Firefox, Opera, and others. For advanced scenarios, Fiddler can be extended using .NET-based plug-ins to automate traffic analysis. There are several add-ons available.

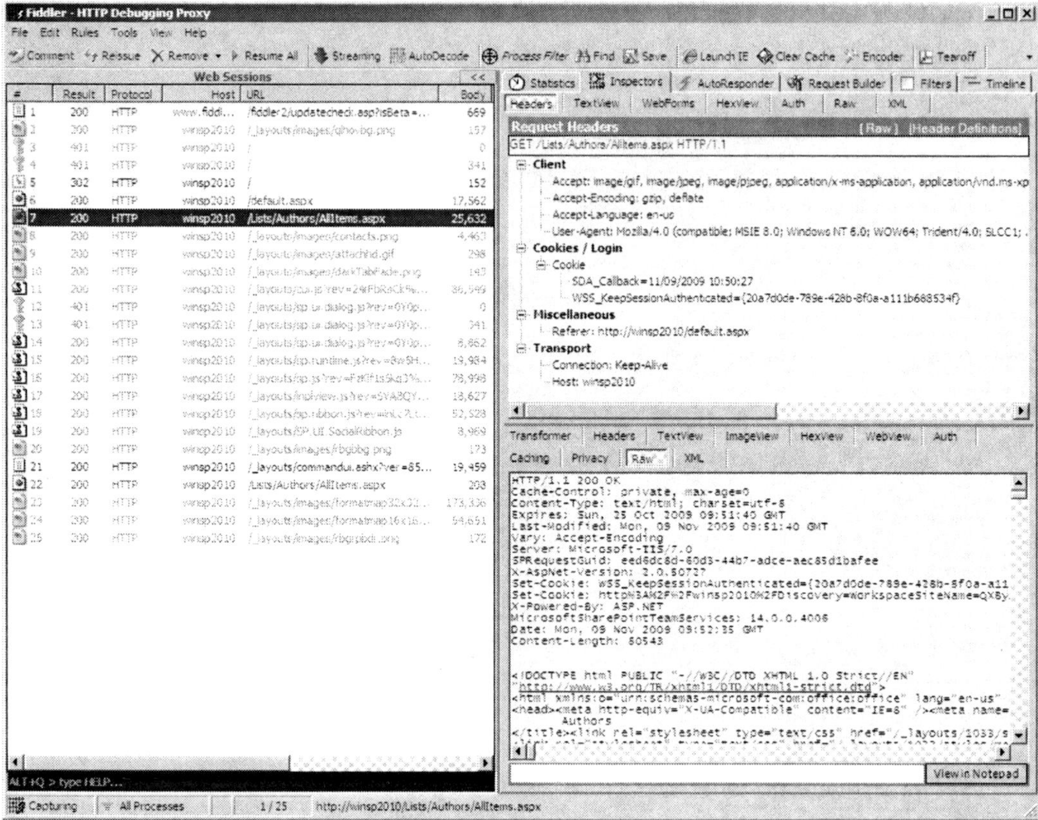

Figure 1–13. Fiddler snagging traffic

SharePoint makes heavy use of Ajax. Such calls to the server (called *postbacks*) run in the background. Fiddler is able to sniff this traffic and show what—if anything—happens.

To start Fiddler, you can use the icon that appears in the toolbar of Internet Explorer ( ). It runs as a separate application, so you can start it from the Start menu and use it with any other browser. After you start Fiddler, the program registers itself as a proxy for Internet Services (WinInet), the HTTP layer built into Windows. The proxy settings of the WinInet configuration dialog should express this, as shown in Figure 1–14.

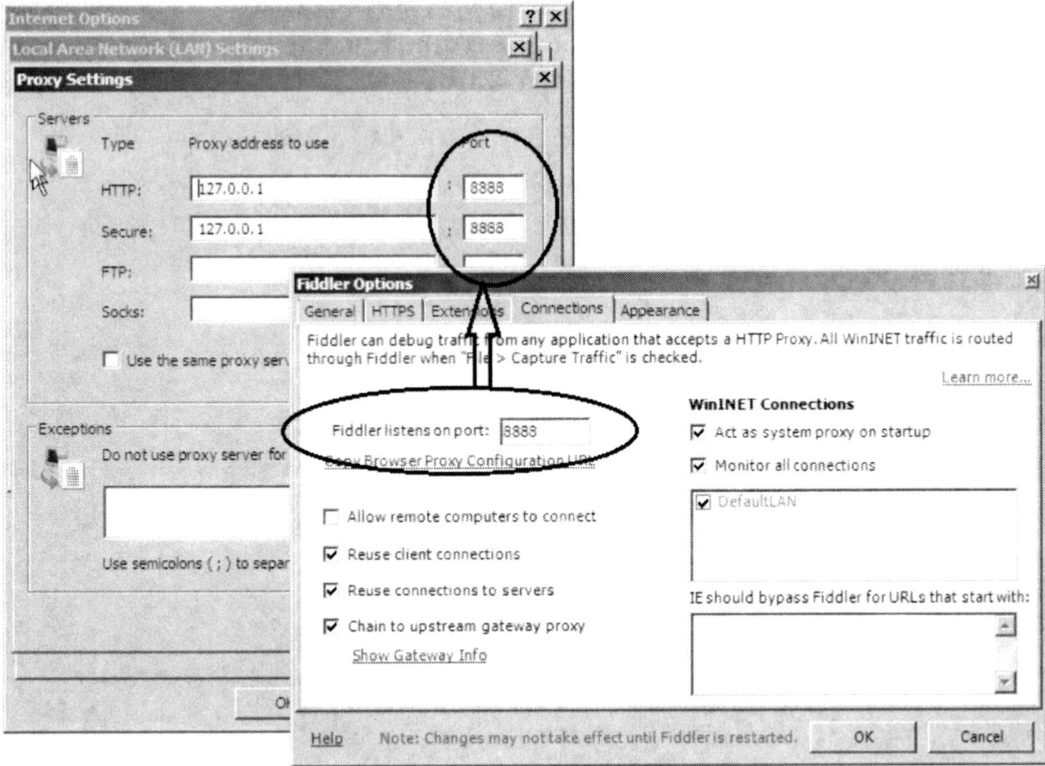

***Figure 1–14.** Proxy settings for Fiddler to get incoming and outgoing traffic*

When you close Fiddler, it unregisters itself automatically and restores previous settings.

Fiddler supports breakpoints. Because there is now code, breakpoints are based on conditions. If an incoming response or outgoing request matches your criteria, Fiddler will pause, allowing you to investigate the data further.

Fiddler has one serious limitation when sniffing local traffic—a common situation when debugging SharePoint. IE and the .NET Framework are hard-coded to not send requests for localhost through any proxies, and as a proxy, Fiddler will not receive such traffic. The workaround is to use your machine name as the hostname instead of localhost or 127.0.0.1. So, for instance, rather than navigating to `http://localhost/Default.aspx`, instead visit `http://machinename/Default.aspx`.

The latest version of Fiddler also supports some other monikers such as `http://ipv4.fiddler` to reach localhost on the IPv4 adapter, or `http://ipv6.fiddler` to access localhost on the IPv6 adapter. This works especially well with the Visual Studio 2010 internal web server, which is internally using the IPv4 loopback adapter.

Using Developer Tools to Investigate What's Running in the Browser

Eventually the page is rendered in the browser. If the rendered page does not display correctly, you will need to check the HTML, styles, and resources. The Internet Explorer Developer Toolbar will unlock

those and more. You can download a free copy from
`www.microsoft.com/downloads/details.aspx?familyid=E59C3964-672D-4511-BB3E-2D5E1DB91038&displaylang=en`.

Using this add-on you can

- Explore and modify the Document Object Model (DOM) of a web page.
- Locate and select specific elements on a web page through a variety of techniques.
- Selectively disable Internet Explorer settings.
- View HTML object class names, IDs, and details such as link paths, tab index values, and access keys.
- Outline tables, table cells, images, and selected tags.
- Validate HTML, CSS, WAI, and RSS web feed links.
- Display image dimensions, file sizes, path information, and alternate (`alt`) text.
- Immediately resize the browser window to a new resolution.
- Selectively clear the browser cache and saved cookies. You can choose from all objects or those associated with a given domain.
- Display a fully featured design ruler to help accurately align and measure objects on your pages.
- Find the style rules used to set specific style values on an element.
- View the formatted and syntax-colored source of HTML and CSS.

To get started with this tool, press F12 when working within Internet Explorer. You will see several tabs that give access to parts of the loaded data (e.g., HTML, CSS, and scripts).

■ **Tip** For the Firefox browser, a similar tool exists, called Firebug. You can get more information at `http://getfirebug.com`.

Introducing Visual Studio 2010's SharePoint Support

In this section you'll get a brief overview about SharePoint-related features included in Visual Studio 2010 and its SharePoint Extension.

Visual Studio 2010

In this section I'll introduce the support especially for SharePoint 2010 developers. If you already have experience with SharePoint 2007 and Visual Studio 2008, this may seem like a long list of obvious extensions. In essence, they will make third-party tools obsolete.

Preparing Visual Studio

If you use the SharePoint templates and create solutions or features for deploying, everything works well. However, if you start creating regular ASP.NET web applications that simply reference SharePoint and run standalone, the internal debugger and web server will fail. There are some requirements that you can easily fulfill using IIS. For details, refer to the "Handling 64-Bit Quirks" section later in this chapter. For Visual Studio 2010 it turns out that it's not trivial. One solution is to replace the internal web server with IIS, even for debugging purposes. To accomplish this, you have to set a few settings in your project. First, a web site is required. To create one, use IIS Manager. Follow the steps described in the "Configuring IIS to Run with the Right Account" section to set the correct application pool settings. Then configure your project as follows:

1. Open the Properties page of your web application project.
2. Change to the Web tab.
3. Select "Use Local IIS Web server" and enter the URL of the root web site—**Localhost:81**, for instance (see Figure 1–15). Use any port number that is not in use on your system. It must be configured in IIS as well.
4. You can now create a new virtual directory if several projects run under the same web. Enter the name of your project. If the root web points to the path above the project, the current project's leaf folder is converted into a virtual directory.

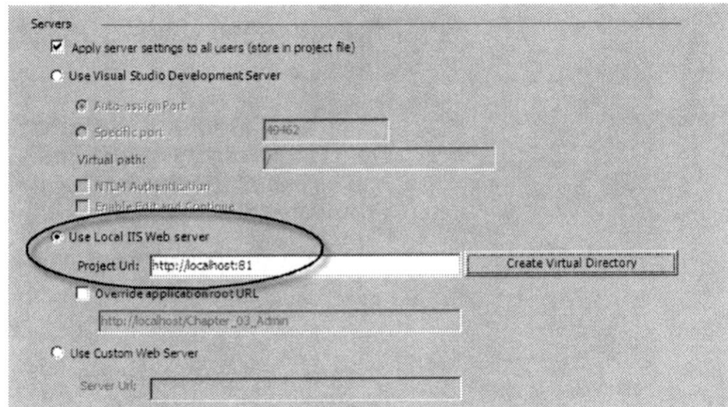

Figure 1–15. *Use IIS instead of the internal web server for debugging.*

You can now start debugging against IIS without worrying about the limitations of the internal web server.

The SharePoint Development Templates

Visual Studio 2010 comes with a set of templates ready to create SharePoint features. Table 1–1 gives an overview and short description of each template. Visual Studio supports SharePoint 2010 completely and SharePoint 2007 for workflow projects only. When you create a new project, you can find the appropriate path under the language selection. SharePoint templates are available for both VB .NET and C#. You can also choose to program against any of the supported .NET Frameworks: 2.0, 3.0, 3.5, or 4.0. This book uses C# as the preferred language, and you must use Framework 3.5.

Table 1–1. *SharePoint Project Templates for C# Developers*

Name	Icon	Description
Import SharePoint Solution Package		Creates a new solution based on an existing WSP (Windows SharePoint Solution Package)
Sequential Workflow		Creates a new sequential workflow
State Machine Workflow		Creates a new state machine workflow
Event Receiver		Creates an event receiver that handles events fired by SharePoint
Empty Project		An empty project to which you can add any item
Module		Creates a SharePoint module that can contain files
Business Data Connectivity Model		Creates a SharePoint Business Data Connectivity model that makes use of the Business Data Connectivity services.
Content Type		Creates a custom content type
List Definition		Creates a list definition for programmatically built lists
Import Reusable Workflow		Imports an existing declarative workflow from a WSP file created with SharePoint Designer
Site Definition		A template for defining a site programmatically
Visual Web Part		Creates a new web part using a visual designer

Each of these projects allows the addition of several items. Some of the templates are just an empty solution with at least one item predefined.

After choosing the most suitable template, a wizard appears. You can now choose against which site the project is to be deployed for debugging purposes (see Figure 1–16). Visual Studio takes care to deploy the required files and register the assembly in the Global Assembly Cache (GAC).

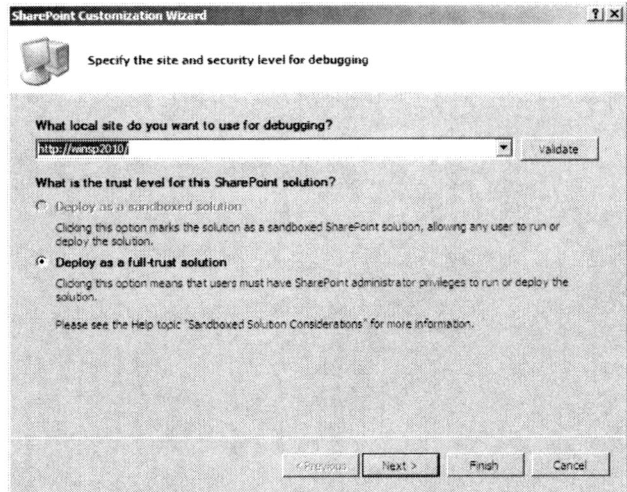

Figure 1–16. Choose the site the debugger uses for your solution.

The remaining tasks of the wizard depend on the item selected. Clicking Finish will create the project skeleton. As an example let's investigate a new list definition and its various settings. First, check the settings of the project by pressing F4 to open the properties pane (see Figure 1–17).

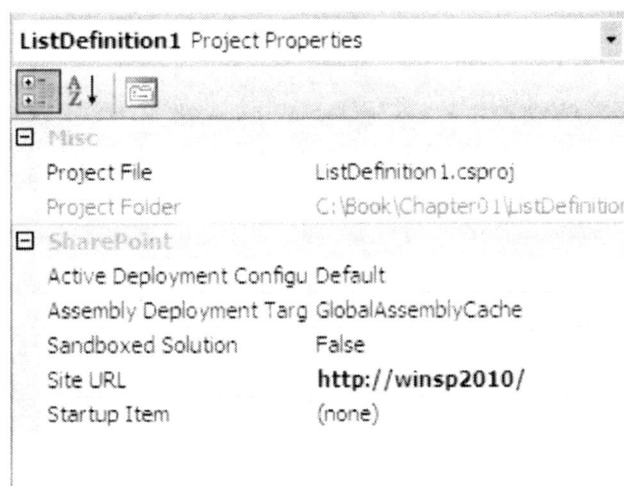

Figure 1–17. Check the settings for your project.

You can change the site and the assembly deployment target. If the project consists of only ASPX files or resources, you may deploy directly against the web application. If it is an assembly, it must be deployed into the GAC.

Adding Items to a Project

If you have a project created by some of the templates shown previously, you can add items from item templates. Apart from those available for any project type, such as `Class`, you can add SharePoint-specific items, as shown in Table 1–2.

Table 1–2. *SharePoint Item Templates for C# Developers*

Name	Icon	Description
Visual Web Part	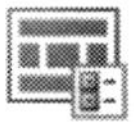	Web Part with an ASCX user control to create the visual part
Web Part		A regular Web Part with no designer support
Sequential Workflow		Creates a new sequential workflow
State Machine Workflow		Creates a new state machine workflow
Event Receiver		Creates an event receiver that handles events fired by SharePoint
Business Data Connectivity Model		Creates a SharePoint Business Data Connectivity model that makes use of the Business Data Connectivity services
Application Page	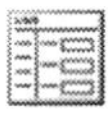	Adds an application page for highly customized applications
Module		Creates a SharePoint module
Content Type		Creates a custom content type
List Definition		Creates a list definition for programmatically built lists

Name	Icon	Description
List Definition from Content Type		Creates a list definition for programmatically built lists based on an existing content type
List Instance		Creates an actual list within a deployable project (the list can contain predefined data)
Empty Element		An empty element you can add code or configuration files to
User Control		An ASP.NET user control for further usage in Web Parts or application pages

Apart from these SharePoint-specific templates, you can add most of the item templates in the Web section to your project, such as JScript files, HTML, and other common resources.

Investigating a Package

The package contains several folders, even if it is something like a simple list definition. This structure represents a part of SharePoint's *14* hive—the SharePoint root. An item defined in the project is usually not able to act standalone. To deploy, it must be part of a feature or solution package. Hence, the project must meet specific requirements, and the templates take care of this. At least two items are required:

- Features
- Package

Under the Features folder, you'll find a feature definition as a configuration file. Each feature has a specific name. Just select the predefined name (Feature1) and rename it to whatever you choose. The files under the folder are then automatically renamed. A feature consists of at least an XML file. You could immediately start typing XML to create the feature. However, in a world of designers and graphical user interfaces (GUIs), you can also launch the Feature Designer.

The Feature Designer

The Feature Designer (see Figure 1–18) is primarily a collection of files comprising the solution. You can decide which files are parts of the feature.

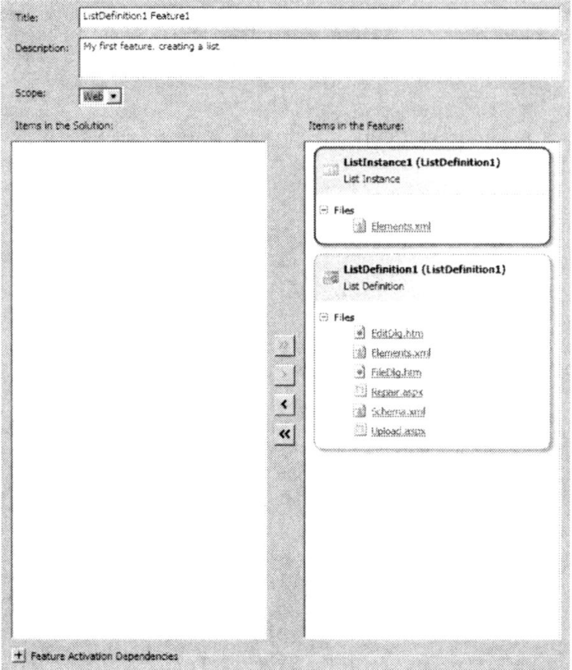

Figure 1–18. *The Feature Designer view*

The list definition template contains the support files for a list template and a list instance.

Working with SharePoint Designer Workflows

There is an import wizard to import workflows created and designed with SharePoint Designer 2010. Power users can now create workflows with SharePoint Designer and export them to a developer. The developer can import them and add further code or include them in a deployment package for further processing.

Importing Packages

The common package format `*.wsp` can now be imported and further used as the basis for a professional development package.

Creating a Package

Once the feature and its contents are defined, a package is required to transport the feature to another SharePoint server. You don't need a package to debug your solution; rather, you need one to make the results available to anyone else. A package creates a WSP file that merely consists of the resources, a manifest file, and assemblies. We'll dig deeper into the internals of the package definition in the Chapter 9.

Building and Deploying

There are several options for building a package and deploying it to the connected server. Deploying directly to the server allows a fast check of your work and provides immediate debugging capabilities.

The build step performs two tasks:

1. Building the solution and creating the assembly
2. Packing and creating the WSP package

The deploy step includes the build step and performs several more tasks:

1. Checking the WSP package
2. Recycling the application pool
3. Retracting a previously installed version
4. Deploying the current solution as a new version
5. Activating the features in the package

There is also a retract option to remove the current solution from SharePoint. Furthermore, the package option isolates the packaging step from the build step to refine the process in case you're hunting a difficult bug.

SharePoint Designer 2010 vs. Visual Studio 2010

While Visual Studio gives you low-level access to all programmable parts of SharePoint, SharePoint Designer provides a top-down approach (see Figure 1–19). Basically, SharePoint Designer starts by opening or creating a site. Once the connection to the existing or new site has been established, the user can apply various customization steps. That means the user can create a list, as it is possible with Visual Studio, but cannot easily export the list as an isolated installable instance. This means that SharePoint Designer is an end-user tool, empowering people working with an existing SharePoint server.

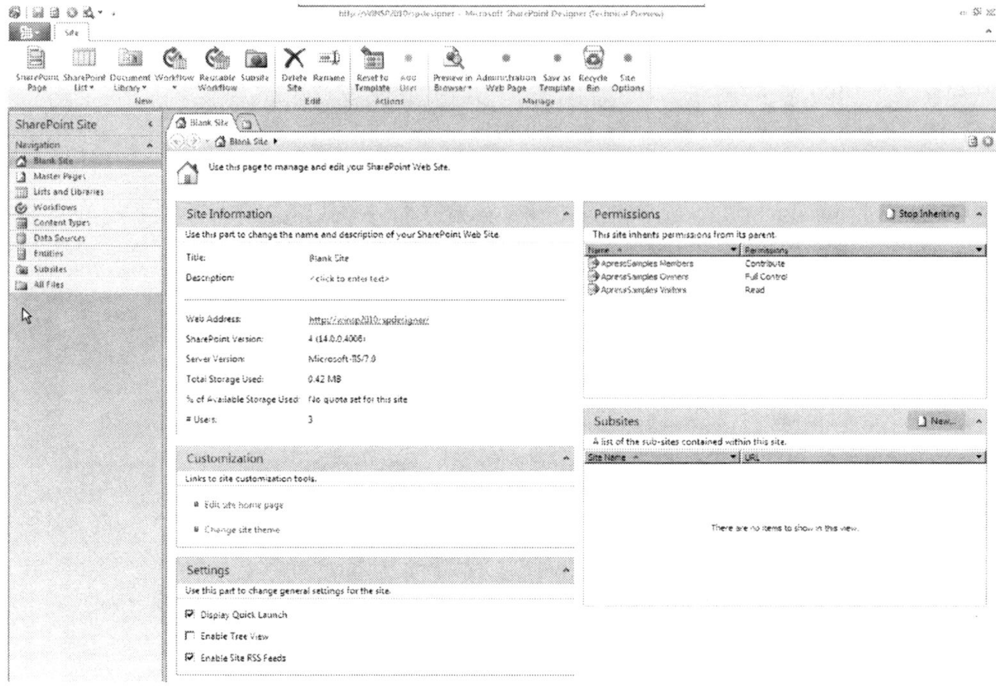

Figure 1–19. Initial information for a blank site in SharePoint Designer 2010

However, the biggest difference between the two products is the programming approach in Visual Studio. While you need direct access to a SharePoint system and the assemblies to program against, SharePoint Designer is limited to communicate via web services. The advantage is that you can use a 32-bit machine to run the appropriate version (an x64 version exists, too). A non-server operating system like Windows 7 is perfectly adequate for SharePoint Designer 2010 development.

SharePoint Designer 2010 for Professional Developers

When reading about SharePoint Designer in previous versions, professional developers used to regard it as a "forbidden" tool. SharePoint Designer 2007 operates against the database (read: production database) and has a number of powerful yet nontransparent functions. These aspects discourage developers from using SharePoint Designer, instead encouraging them to prefer Visual Studio.

With SharePoint 2010, the SharePoint Designer behavior is improved and some features seem to be sufficiently good to complement Visual Studio 2010. This section presents the more developer-oriented features.

Primarily, SharePoint Designer is positioned as a tool for power users. You can accomplish many common tasks, and it's quite helpful in smaller installations where the extensive effort required to create reinstallable components is unwarranted. For development and experimental installations, SharePoint Designer greatly complements the Visual Studio development approach. Hence, we recommend that all SharePoint developers attain an understanding of the basic features of SharePoint Designer 2010.

Among the many SharePoint Designer features, the most important ones are

- *SharePoint Designer rights*: Administrators can decide per site collection what exactly a power user operating SharePoint Designer is permitted to do.
- *New dashboard interface*: The new ribbon-based Office 2010 environment is now context sensitive.
- *Simplified object creation*: It's easy to create pages, lists, and workflows.
- *Easy usage of content types*: It's easy to create content types and use them immediately for a list or library.
- *Resource management*: You can use assets to store and deploy resources such as graphics, stylesheets, and support files.
- *XSLT views*: You can get the list views as XSLT and modify the views by editing the underlying XSLT.
- *Access data sources*: You can get access to external data sources such as web services, databases, XML files, and scripts.
- *Manage BCS*: The new BCS data sources can be created, modified, and connected easily.
- *Manage workflows*: You can create and modify list workflows, site workflows, and reusable workflows.

Installation Hints

The installation itself is straightforward. The only noteworthy aspect is deciding whether to install the 32-bit or 64-bit version. While your SharePoint development machine must run 64 bit, you can still use SharePoint Designer from this or another machine running either 32 bit or 64 bit. The SharePoint Designer version must match the version of an Office installation on the same machine. That means that if you run 32-bit Office 2010 on your development system, you must install 32-bit SharePoint Designer. If you already have 64-bit Office, the SharePoint Designer version must follow suit.

Features at a Glance

In this section you'll find some information about features that can simplify your life as a developer. Primarily, these options extend the capabilities of the browser-based user interface (UI).

SharePoint Designer Rights

Administrators can decide per site collection what exactly a power user operating SharePoint Designer is permitted to do. This gives the administrator the opportunity to manage the power users directly and without the need to check their systems for "forbidden" instances of SharePoint Designer.

You can change the required permissions via the "Site permissions" selection on the Site Actions menu. Choose Permission Levels on the ribbon's Permission Tools tab. Click Design to view the permissions associated with this level (see Figure 1–20).

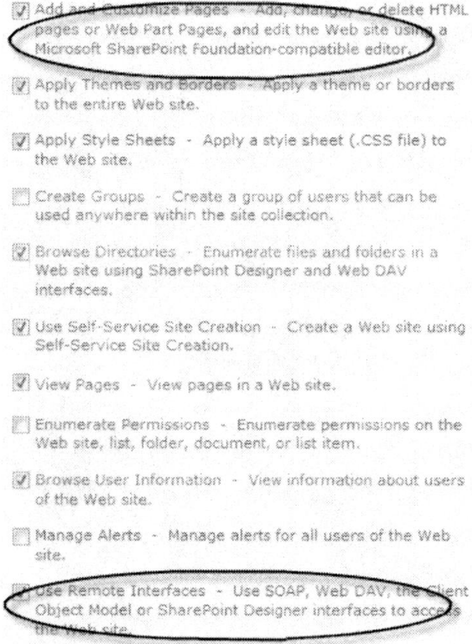

Figure 1–20. *By default, the design permissions include usage of SharePoint Designer.*

SharePoint Designer communicates remotely using web services; hence, the Use Remote Interfaces permission must be activated.

New Dashboard Interface

The new ribbon-based Office 2010 environment is now context sensitive (see Figure 1–21).

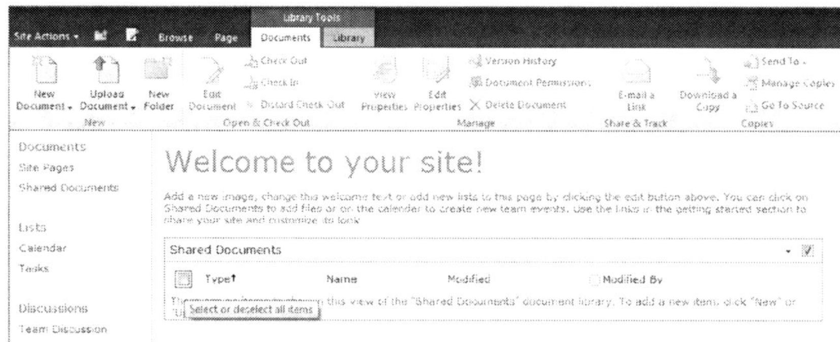

Figure 1–21. *The ribbon shows colored tabs for context-sensitive commands.*

Commands available only for specific elements appear on colorized tabs at the end of the ribbon bar. These tabs may be grouped, and several such tabs may appear. For example, if you edit an image within a Web Part, both the tabs for Web Part and Image Editing become visible.

Simplified Object Creation

It's easy to create pages, lists, and workflows (see Figure 1–22). The main screen allows you to browse any items of the currently opened site. For each element type, you can use the ribbon's first group, New, to create one.

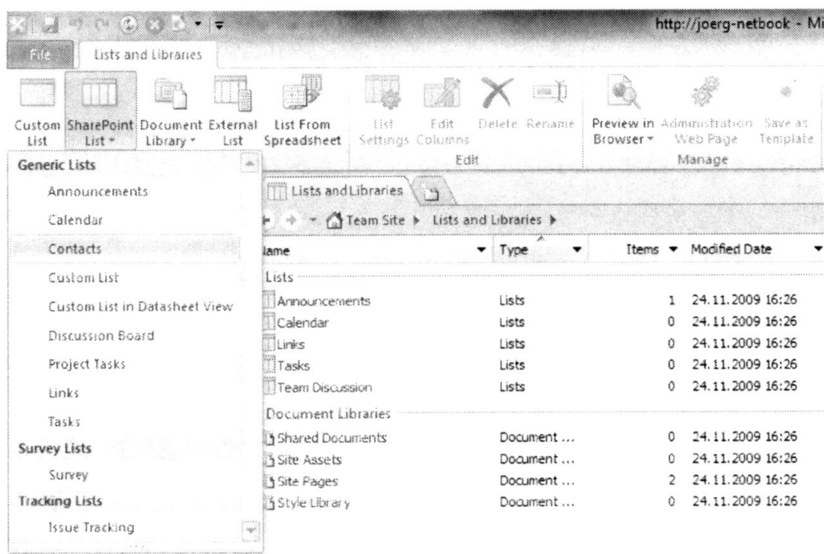

Figure 1–22. It's easy to create new lists, libraries, and workflows.

Once created, you can edit all settings of the list, such as the content types, columns, views, and edit forms.

Easy Use of Content Types

It's easy to create content types and use them immediately for a list or library. You can also associate workflows and set the appropriate forms for editing, viewing, and creating new elements based on this content type (see Figure 1–23).

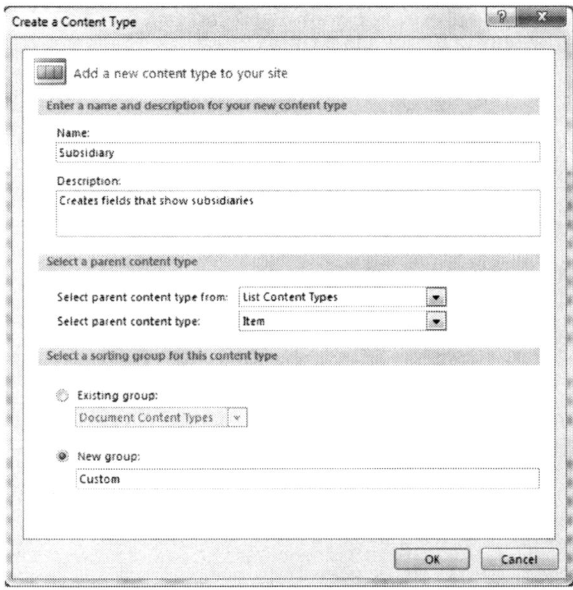

Figure 1–23. Creating a new content type using SharePoint Designer

Once the content type exists, you can add new columns from the list of site columns.

Resource Management

You can use assets to store and deploy resources such as graphics, stylesheets, and support files. An asset such as a CSS or JavaScript file can be edited directly using the integrated code editor (see Figure 1–24).

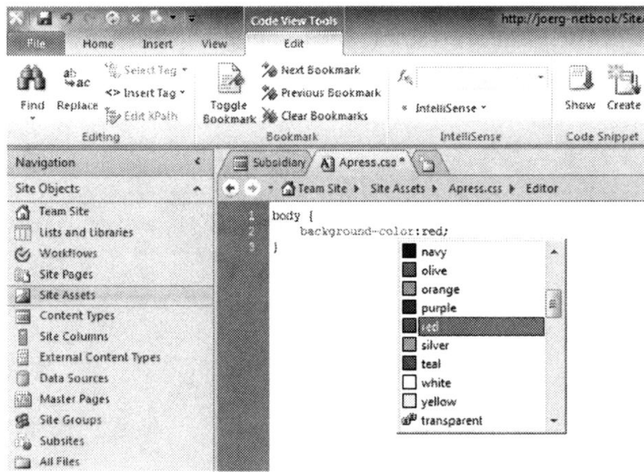

Figure 1–24. You can add and edit assets in one step.

By assigning Visual Studio as the default editor, you can also edit files in Visual Studio directly from SharePoint Designer.

XSLT Views

You can get the list views as XSLT and modify them by editing the underlying XSLT (see Figure 1–25).

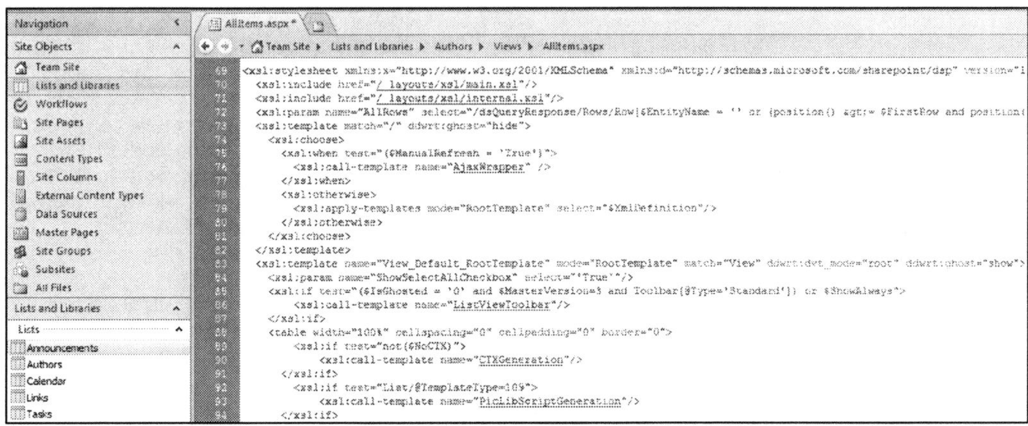

Figure 1–25. *Editing a list view reveals the underlying XSLT.*

XSLT allows dynamic changes to existing view forms. It's especially helpful when the generated HTML needs adjusting.

Accessing Data Sources

You can access external data sources such as web services, databases, XML files, and scripts via the Data Sources option. Any SharePoint list can be used as a data source too. Both SOAP and REST web services are supported.

Managing Business Data Connectivity Services

The new Business Data Connectivity data sources can be easily created, modified, and used. In SharePoint Designer, this option is called External Content Types (that's what it is internally, by the way).

Managing Workflows

You can create and modify list workflows, site workflows, and reusable workflows. Workflows can be bound to lists or content types.

Master and Site Pages

Two more sections contain all the master pages and sites stored in the database. You can edit any page available in the galleries. However, the editor does not allow any code editing of code-behind files.

SharePoint as a Development Toolkit and Framework

This book presents and teaches SharePoint as a toolkit and framework. It assumes that you're a web developer working with ASP.NET to create sophisticated web sites for intranet and Internet applications. Those applications are usually database intensive, with connectivity to LOB applications; they often implement an Enterprise Service Bus (ESB) and run inside a managed environment.

The .NET Framework, Visual Studio, and the Windows SDKs provide everything you need to get and build what you want. However, there are a lot repetitive tasks for every application. You need a UI for administrative purposes, pages to log users on and off, the ability to handle identities, and so on. With SharePoint, you get many of these features, providing more than 80 percent of a typical web application out of the box. That includes but is not limited to the administration functions, a set of powerful components, logging and maintenance capabilities, reporting and connectivity, and workflow and search engine support.

Even if you only need a few parts, the built-in functionality saves considerable time because you gain more than features. You get ready-to-use components that don't need any further testing or documentation.

Command-Line Tools

SharePoint comes with several command-line tools to support administration and automation tasks. Some of the tools particularly aid developers.

psconfig.exe

This tool configures a fresh SharePoint installation or repairs a damaged one. It's the same as the graphical SharePoint Products and Technologies Configuration Wizard, but the console mode allows it to be executed in batch files for automation purposes.

stsadm.exe

The most important tool is `stsadm.exe`. Almost all administrative tasks can be performed using this command-line program. Developers can extend it by adding private commands. It gives your administrators more power without introducing more tools. `stsadm` was the only automation tool for SharePoint 2007. With SharePoint 2010, Microsoft made a major shift to supporting PowerShell. PowerShell uses so-called *cmdlets* (pronounced *commandlets*).

It's important to note that `stsadm` supports several operations that have no equivalent in the Central Administration or Site Administration UI. That means that unless you program against the API, there is no alternative way to perform certain tasks without using `stsadm` (or its successors, PowerShell's SharePoint cmdlets). However, using PowerShell is the preferred way, because Microsoft is going to move all administration tools to cmdlets. Sooner or later, Microsoft is going to drop the antiquated batch support, whether you like it or not.

SPMetal.exe

Using `SPMetal` you can create a proxy class from existing lists and libraries to enable access using LINQ to SharePoint. The tool runs at the command line and can be invoked as a prebuild command within Visual Studio to create base classes for a type-safe data access layer.

Graphical Tools

Some graphical tools accompany the installation and support administrators and developers installing and configuring SharePoint properly.

psconfigui.exe

This is the common SharePoint Products and Technologies Configuration Wizard that is available after installation and from the Start menu. It supports basic configuration of a fresh installation or repair of an installation that doesn't work.

Handling 64-Bit Quirks

SharePoint 2010 runs on 64-bit hardware only. For you as a developer, this means that you have to create and build against the 64-bit version of the .NET Framework running on x64 processor architecture. Even with Visual Studio 2010 installed on the same machine, some settings need to be changed to support the right architecture.

For projects running inside the context of SharePoint, the templates ensure correct functionality. However, if you plan to develop administrative support tools, such as console applications or even a web site running in IIS and dedicated to helping administrators running advanced tasks, things are rather different.

Programming SharePoint Using a Console Application

For a console application, you merely set the processor architecture to 64 bit. Proceed with the steps shown in the following exercise.

Making a Console Application 64-Bit Ready

1. Create a new application using the Console Application project template.
2. Select .NET Framework 3.5 as the target framework.
3. Open the Properties pane from the project's context menu.
4. Click the Build tab.
5. Click the "Platform target" drop-down and select x64 (see Figure 1–26). If this entry isn't available, you must create the target:

a. Open the Configuration Manager via the Build ➤ Configuration Manager menu entry.

b. For your project, select <New...> in the Platform column.

c. In the next dialog, select x64 for "New platform" and x86 in the "Copy settings from" drop-down.

d. Click OK.

6. Build your project.

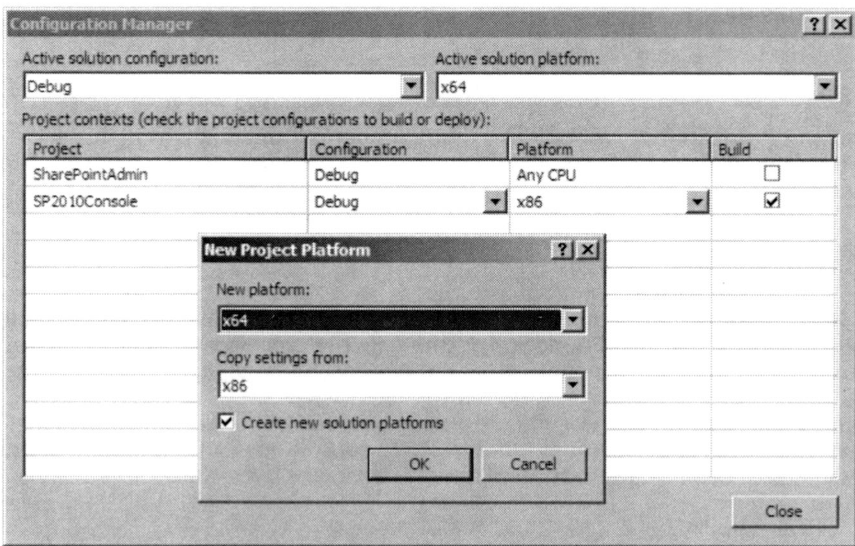

Figure 1–26. Adding a new platform target to your solution

The project is now able to run against the SharePoint assemblies.

■ **Note** The target framework is version 3.5, even if 4.0 is available on the target machine. The SharePoint assemblies are built against 3.5 and therefore can't interoperate with version 4.0. That means in turn that the features available are limited to what .NET 3.5 provides. In addition, it means that the ASP.NET runtime is still using 2.0, because .NET Frameworks 3.0 and 3.5 did not change the runtime. The next runtime version for ASP.NET is 4.0, and this is not available to program against SharePoint 2010.

Programming SharePoint Using ASP.NET

To create web applications, you don't have to run inside SharePoint. For administrative tasks in particular, it's recommended to use separate applications. While console programs are fine for scripting automated tasks, a web application provides an advanced UI, including help and support information.

Administrators lacking skills on the platform and users who help manage the servers may struggle with command-line tools. Therefore, creating administration web applications is common.

However, for ASP.NET, the same restrictions apply as for console applications. They must be configured to run on 64 bit. In addition, the application must run under the same account you would use to administer your SharePoint central administrations.

Preparing ASP.NET for the x64 Platform

To prepare ASP.NET for the x64 platform, you need to configure the application pool of your web site. The following exercise shows you how to set the appropriate property, `enable32BitAppOnWin64`, to `false`.

Configuring ASP.NET Applications to Run 64-Bit Code

1. Open IIS Manager.
2. Ensure that your ASP.NET application has a dedicated application pool. If not, create one and assign it to your web site.
3. Select the application pool from the Application Pools view and click Advanced Settings... on the Actions pane.
4. Search for the Enable 32-Bit Applications entry.
5. Select False from the drop-down as shown in Figure 1–27.
6. Close by clicking OK.

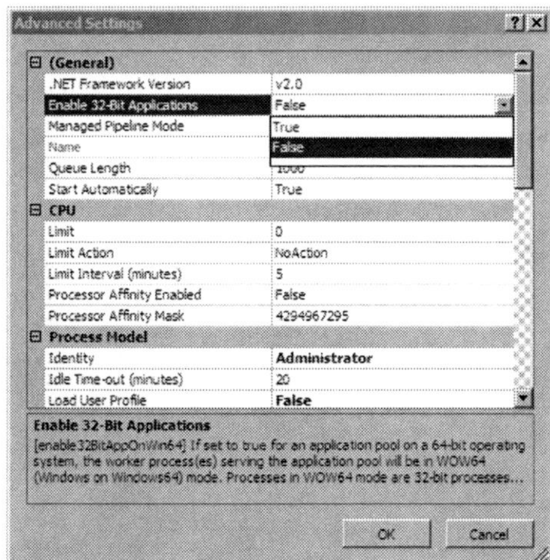

Figure 1–27. *Forcing ASP.NET to run 64 bit*

USE IIS Console or Scripting?

There are several blogs and a Knowledge Base entry regarding this issue that recommend using a script provided by IIS to change the settings via this command:

```
Cscript C:\inetpub\AdminScripts\adsutil.vbs set w3svc/AppPools/Enable32BitAppOnWin64 0
```

This script results in exactly the same setting change described previously, and simply changes an entry in the IIS settings. We recommend using the IIS management console method.

Configuring IIS to Run with the Right Account

For an ASP.NET application, two settings are required. First, you must set the application pool to run under the administrative account. The following exercise shows you how to configure it.

Running the Application Pool in the Appropriate Account

1. Open IIS Manager.
2. Ensure that your ASP.NET application has a dedicated application pool. If not, create one and assign it to your web site.
3. Select the application pool from the Application Pools view and click Advanced Settings... in the Actions pane.
4. Search for Identity in the Process Model group entry and click the ellipses (the default account is NetworkService).
5. In the next dialog, select "Custom account" and click Set...
6. In the next dialog, enter the account you want to use, such as "Administrator," and enter the password twice, as shown in Figure 1–28.

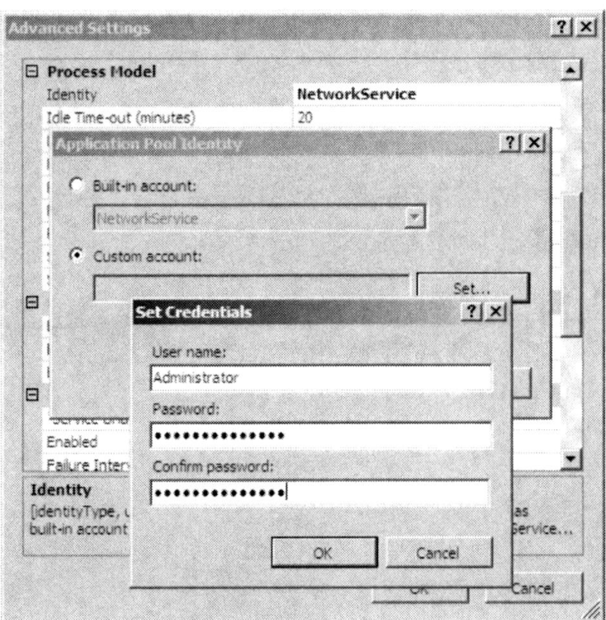

Figure 1–28. Forcing the application pool to use the SharePoint administrator account

---

Next you must ensure that the user you use is able to log onto your web site. You can either edit your `web.config` file or use the IIS Manager management console. In the `web.config` file, the following settings apply:

```
<configuration>
  <system.web>
    <authentication mode="Windows" />
    <authorization>
       <deny users="?" />
    </authorization>
  </system.web>
</configuration>
```

This code sets ASP.NET to authenticate using Windows authentication. The `<authorization>` tag prevents anonymous users from accessing the pages. Setting Windows authentication mode via the IIS management console requires the steps shown in the following exercise.

Forcing Authentication for an ASP.NET Application

1. Open the web site's Features view.

2. Click the Authentication icon.

3. From the list of available authentication modes, select Windows Authentication.

4. Click Enable in the Actions pane.

The settings apply immediately.

For the authorization part, a similar set of settings are required.

Setting Authorization for an ASP.NET Application

1. Open the web site's Features view.

2. Click the Authorization icon.

3. Click the Add Deny Rule... action.

4. In the next dialog, select "Specified users" and enter a question mark (?) here.

5. Close by clicking OK.

The settings change the corresponding `web.config` setting and take effect immediately.

■ **Caution** While the settings in IIS change the `web.config` file immediately, it seems that some settings changed in the `web.config` file do not automatically create similar entries in the IIS management console. If you use both approaches, watch carefully what finally appears in the `web.config` file (which is the master settings store). We recommend using `web.config` only, and using the IIS management console solely for tasks that set properties elsewhere.

Once everything is done, you can deploy and run your application.

Summary

This chapter first gave a short overview of why and how SharePoint is used as a development platform, how it is related to IIS, and what's so special about debugging custom code.

In this chapter you learned how to prepare your development environment for SharePoint 2010 and get the right tools for developing, debugging, and monitoring your work—tools such as the Internet Explorer Developer Toolbar, the web proxy Fiddler, and the Developer Dashboard. You also learned how to use command-line and graphical tools supplied by SharePoint. Some are intended to automate tasks or run as a prebuild event in Visual Studio.

Using Visual Studio 2010, you learned how to prepare ASP.NET and console applications to run code against SharePoint and the steps needed to run in a 64-bit environment.

Using SharePoint Designer 2010 enables power users to create sites, lists, libraries, workflows, and content types. The site administrator can control access through the SharePoint Designer tool. Developers can import projects created with SharePoint Designer and use them as the basis for professional development projects. The complete chain of tools is SharePoint UI for office workers, SharePoint Designer for power users, and Visual Studio for developers.

CHAPTER 2

Architecture

SharePoint 2010 is built on a comprehensive object model, supplying powerful features to access and manipulate internal data. This chapter introduces the SharePoint object model. The remaining chapters contain many useful scenarios and examples of what can be achieved via the object model—principally by extending, or customizing, the default behavior to suit your needs.

There are several quite diverse approaches to programming SharePoint, depending on your project's requirements, which we will explore.

Visual Studio 2010 with SharePoint 2010 has greatly improved the support for testing and debugging. We introduce the new features and show how to handle basic and more advanced everyday tasks.

At a glance, this chapter contains

- An architectural overview
- An introduction to the object model and its hierarchical view
- The technical integration with ASP.NET
- The building blocks, their design, and integration with the SharePoint platform
- The administrative model

The Architectural View

SharePoint consists of an amazing number of tools, functions, and modules (see Figure 2–1).

Because SharePoint is a set of products and technologies, we call it a platform. Its main function is the creation, organization, and rapid retrieval of information in the form of data and documents. Its presentation mode of web sites and pages is commonly used to build intranet and extranet portals. With particular support for team sites and public-facing Internet sites (plus many more predefined sets of web pages), it's a great platform for web-based applications. The close integration with the Microsoft Office System expands the handling of everyday tasks.

With SharePoint 2010 we see a stable, mature, scalable, well-supported product that is easy to integrate with other systems. For example, it integrates well with Outlook and all the other Office products, and with instant messaging via Office Communications Server. The refurbished data access layer can easily connect to line-of-business (LOB) applications, provided from companies such as SAP (www.sap.com).

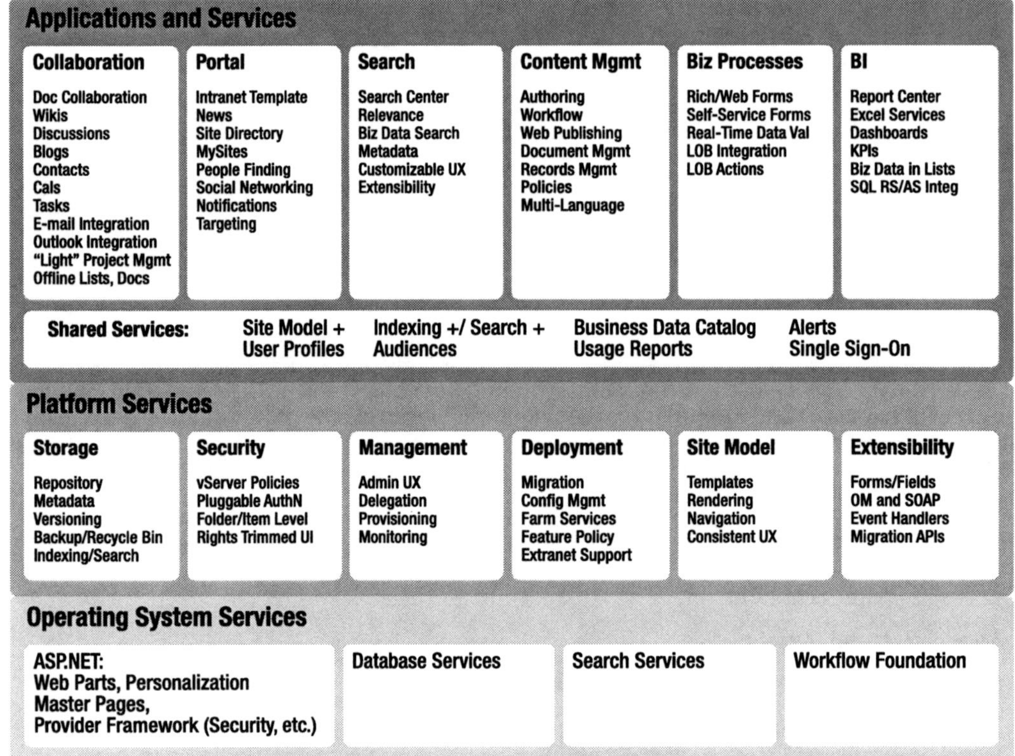

Figure 2–1. *Architectural components of SharePoint*

SharePoint 2010 Foundation

With a few exceptions, this book focuses on SharePoint Foundation—the platform on which all SharePoint products and SharePoint-enabled products are built. The foundation, formerly called Windows SharePoint Services, extends Windows Server System with a set of features for team collaboration and knowledge distribution. The foundation is built on ASP.NET 3.5 and is the basis for both a powerful application programming interface (API) and a highly scalable and reliable platform.

■ **Note** In this book we use the simple term *SharePoint*. By this we mean both SharePoint Foundation and SharePoint Server (see the following discussion). If we describe a feature available exclusively in SharePoint Server, we express this explicitly. Because SharePoint Foundation is a subset of SharePoint Server, we usually do not explicitly talk about SharePoint Foundation.

We treat SharePoint as a platform and framework. As you know, you can do many things just by configuring the server and activating whatever you need. A big feature of SharePoint is enabling ordinary people to build and maintain a complex web site without programming knowledge. However, this limitation is eventually reached. Each SharePoint site typically includes libraries, lists, calendars, tasks, announcements, and the like. Each of these is simply a highly customized instance of a basic list. Each list has its own distinct set of columns and views to create the UI. Events are used to launch actions when a specified condition is met. Organizing data is based on the concept of *content types*, which allows you to store different kinds of documents in the same library while keeping some structure. It is a bridge and partially a compromise between the typically unstructured world and highly structured storage, such as a relational database.

SharePoint Server

SharePoint Server comes in two flavors: Standard and Enterprise. The Enterprise edition includes extra features for enterprises, such as web content management functions (including publishing), single sign-on (SSO) to integrate with other portals, and record management—supporting storage of sensitive documents with an emphasis on security and audit trails.

Rendering InfoPath forms as HTML extends the forms environment to the Web. Accessing LOB applications integrates external data into the portal. Many new site templates have been added, enabling administrators to create common sites for their companies with ease.

Why Develop with the SharePoint Platform?

With all this power, it seems unlikely that you would ever need to extend the platform to add more features. However, our experience says you will. While SharePoint has so many features, the result is that people accomplish far more than they had ever expected with the product. The confidence this instills results in more people trying more things with the platform, some of which are not natively supported. This is the nature of all software systems created to be a platform or framework. They handle the common functionality (with a little configuration), but do not do everything. The advantage is that you get 80 percent of the solution done with minimal effort, and the remaining 20 percent can be built to suit the customer's requirements.

In this book we focus on the "20 percent" and demonstrate how to work with the API and its counterparts to achieve it. The amazing thing is that the platform extensibility is endless. Even books with thousands of pages will not be able to describe SharePoint completely. (We have tried, and yet this is still scratching the surface!) We describe many real-world examples from our experience, demonstrating specific strengths of SharePoint. Our aims are to broaden your expectations of SharePoint's capabilities and empower you to do more with less.

The Technical Integration

Before learning to customize SharePoint, first you need a basic understanding of its internals. SharePoint is built on top of ASP.NET and Internet Information Services (IIS). It makes heavy use of the ASP.NET extensibility model to customize the default behavior. It not only reveals the power of ASP.NET, but it also adds a new level of web programming to ASP.NET.

IIS also plays a key role. The performance, reliability, and security of each SharePoint page are the responsibility of IIS.

IIS and ASP.NET

When you see IIS mentioned in this book, we're referring to IIS 7 running on Windows Server 2008 or later. IIS 7 provides tight integration with ASP.NET to maximize performance. To explore this further, let's start with ASP.NET.

What Is ASP.NET?

In general terms, ASP.NET is a request-processing engine. It takes an incoming request and passes it through its internal pipeline to an endpoint, where you as a developer can attach code to process that request. This engine is completely separate from the HTTP runtime and the web server. In fact, the HTTP runtime is a component that you can host in your own applications outside of IIS or any other server-side application. The integrated development server within Visual Studio is a good example of an implementation that is independent of and unrelated to IIS. (SharePoint, on the other hand, runs on top of both IIS and ASP.NET.)

The HTTP runtime is responsible for routing requests through the ASP.NET pipeline. The pipeline includes several interrelated objects that can be customized via subclassing or through interfaces, making ASP.NET highly adaptable. Most of the extensibility points are exploited by SharePoint—demonstrating that there are very few limits when using ASP.NET.

Through the extensibility mechanism, it's possible to hook into such low-level interfaces as authentication, authorization, and caching.

The Internet Services API (ISAPI) is a common API. The ASP.NET engine interfaces with IIS through an ISAPI extension. On x64 Windows it is 64 bit, but it can run in mixed mode using the WoW64 (Windows-32–on-Windows-64) technique. Regarding SharePoint, you don't need to worry about the bits—it is 64 bit–only either way.

The ISAPI extension hosts .NET through the ASP.NET runtime. The ASP.NET engine is written entirely in managed code, and all of the extensibility functionality is provided via *managed code extensions*. The impressive part of ASP.NET is that it is very powerful but simple to work with. Despite its breadth and complexity, accomplishing your desired outcomes is easy. ASP.NET enables you to perform tasks that were previously the domain of ISAPI extensions and filters on IIS. ISAPI is a low-level API that has a very spartan interface. Typical .NET developers would find it difficult to develop anything on top of this interface. Writing ISAPI filters in C++ is not included in most current application-level development. However, since ISAPI is low level, it is fast. Thus, for some time ISAPI development has been largely relegated to providing bridge interfaces to other applications or platforms. But ISAPI did not become obsolete with the appearance of ASP.NET.

ISAPI provides the core interface from the web server, and ASP.NET uses the unmanaged ISAPI code to retrieve input and send output back to the client. The content that ISAPI provides is passed using common objects, such as `HttpRequest` and `HttpResponse`, that expose the unmanaged data as managed objects. Back in the .NET world, it is very easy to use these objects in your own code. Regarding SharePoint, you should know that it already extends ASP.NET in several ways. Changing the behavior or adding more extensibility code can work, but quite possibly it will disturb the internal behavior and make things worse. Here is where the SharePoint object model comes into focus, as it will protect you from doing foolish things with the flow of data.

From ISAPI to ASP.NET

The purpose of ISAPI is to access a web server such as IIS at a very low level. The interface is optimized for performance, but it's also very straightforward. ISAPI is the layer on which the ASP.NET engine is built. Understanding the relationship between ISAPI and ASP.NET aids in getting the most out of ASP.NET and subsequently your SharePoint applications. For ASP.NET the ISAPI level is just acting as a routing layer. The heavy lifting, such as processing and request management, occurs inside the ASP.NET engine and is mostly performed in managed code. Hence, SharePoint has a strong influence on how things proceed up and down the pipeline.

You can think of ISAPI as a type of protocol. This protocol supports two flavors: ISAPI extensions and ISAPI filters. Extensions act as a transaction interface; they handle the flow of data into and out of the web server. Each request coming down the pipeline passes through the extensions, and the code decides how the request is treated. As you might imagine, ASP.NET is one such extension. ASP.NET has several ways to give you as much control as possible to hook into this extension and modify the default behavior. The low-level ISAPI interfaces are now available as high-level .NET interfaces, named `IHttpHandler` and `IHttpModule`. This is very powerful while still providing good performance, because it's a well-written balance between lean access to the lower level and an easy-to-use high-level API.

As with any other ISAPI extension, the code is provided as a DLL and is hooked into the IIS management. You can find this DLL at `<.NET FrameworkDir>\aspnet_isapi.dll`.

SharePoint 2010 is not built on ASP.NET 4.0. Rather, the DLLs are built against the .NET Framework 3.5. It is important to note that the ASP.NET version number does not necessarily match the development cycle of the .NET Framework. While ASP.NET 3.0 and 3.5 were released with the corresponding framework, the DLLs and modules they consist of remained at version 2, at least regarding ASP.NET. ASP.NET 3.*x* was only a 2.0 revival with many new features supplied as add-ons. SharePoint 2010 now uses the Ajax features provided by the .NET Framework 3.5. The new assemblies providing Ajax features have internal version numbering schema beginning with 3.5. This sounds confusing, and it actually is a mess, but it is as it is.

The IIS 7 Integrated Pipeline

The IIS 7 integrated pipeline is a unified request-processing pipeline. Each incoming request is handled by this pipeline and routed through the internals of IIS. The pipeline supports both managed and native code modules. You may already know about creating managed modules based on the `IHttpModule` interface. Once implemented and hooked into the pipeline, such a module receives all events used to interact with the request passing through the pipe.

But what does the term *unified request-processing pipeline* mean? IIS 6 provided two different pipelines: one for native code, and on top of it, one for managed code. This was for historical reasons, because the managed code world arrived after IIS was first designed. In IIS 7, both pipelines are combined to become the unified request-processing pipeline.

For ASP.NET developers, this has several benefits:

- The integrated pipeline raises all exposed events, enabling existing ASP.NET modules to work in the integrated mode.
- Both native and managed code modules can be configured at the web server, web site, or web application level.
- Managed code modules can be invoked at certain stages in the pipeline.
- Modules are registered and enabled or disabled through an application's `web.config` file.

The configuration of modules includes the built-in ASP.NET managed code modules for session state, forms authentication, profiles, and role management. Furthermore, managed code modules can be enabled or disabled for all requests, regardless of whether the request is for an ASP.NET resource such as an ASPX file or a static file like an image.

Invoking modules at any stage means that this may happen before any server processing occurs for the request, after all server processing has occurred, or anytime in between.

IIS Sites, Applications, and Virtual Directories

IIS 7 and its architecture are crucial for SharePoint. A thorough understanding of the basic functions provided by IIS is a requirement for serious developers. One of these basic concepts is the relationship between sites and virtual directories.

Sites

IIS 7 has a formal concept of sites, applications, and virtual directories. Applications and virtual directories are separate objects, and they exist in a hierarchical relationship. It's a simple top-down approach. A site contains one or more applications, and each application contains one or more virtual directories. An application can be something running in IIS or something that extends IIS. Managed code applications form an -application domain that spans all virtual directories in it.

An IIS (web) site is an entry point into the server. The site is an endpoint that consists of an address, a protocol, and a handler that handles the request. The handler can be recognized as a path to an application. The protocol used by the endpoint is HTTP. The address is the configured IP address in conjunction with a defined port. For a web server, the standard port is 80. A site is bound to some sort of protocol. In IIS 7, bindings can apply to any protocol. The Windows Process Activation Service (WAS) is the service that makes it possible to use additional protocols. WAS removes the dependency on HTTP from the activation architecture. This is useful for technologies that provide application-to-application communication in web services over standard protocols. The Windows Communication Foundation (WCF) programming model is one such technology that can enable communication over the standard protocols of Transmission Control Protocol (TCP), Microsoft Message Queuing (MSMQ), and Named Pipes. This lets applications that use communication protocols take advantage of IIS features, such as process recycling, rapid fail protection, and configurations that were previously only available to HTTP-based applications.

Behind the scenes, the DNS (Domain Name System) protocol acts as a resolver to convert a human-readable address (such as `www.apress.com`) into a machine-level IP address (such as 66.211.109.45).

■ **Note** We strongly recommend investigating how DNS works for simple requests made from a browser to a server. However, this is beyond the scope of this book. Wikipedia has a very good explanation.

The DNS is able to forward the human-readable address to the endpoint. IIS can use the human-friendly hostname to resolve the address directly to the application. This technique is referred to as using a *host header*. To explain this with an example, consider two web sites, such as `intranet.apress.com` and `extranet.apress.com`. If the same server is configured to handle both sites and only one IP address is available on the network card, the DNS can't completely resolve incoming requests for both web sites. In that situation you can configure IIS to handle those addresses as host headers. The request containing the address as a header is forwarded and used to reach the right target. SharePoint uses this to provide multiple webs. Ports map in SharePoint to applications while host headers resolve this to the outside world. Host headers inform IIS what full server name is used (e.g., `http://app1.mydomain.com` or `http://app2.mydomain.com`). Both domains running on the same IIS server share the same IP address and port. The host header (`app1` or `app2`) is forwarded to the IIS server, which resolves this by routing the request to different applications.

Applications

An application is a group of files that delivers content or provides services over protocols, such as HTTP. When you create an application in IIS, the application's physical path becomes part of the site's URL. In

IIS 7, each site must have at least a root application. However, a site can have more than one application. In addition to belonging to a site, an application belongs to an application pool, which isolates the application from applications in other application pools on the server. In the case of managed code applications, each application pool is running the .NET Framework version that your application requires.

No matter whether a port number, an IP address, a combination of both, or a host header is used, at the end of the day the request is forwarded to a URL space. This is like a pool for all incoming requests of a specific type. A complete URL consists of the protocol moniker, the address portion, and the path to a resource (e.g., `http://intranet.apress.com:12683/Default.aspx`). To access resources, each such entry point maps to a physical folder on the file system of the server. In the most basic scenario—which applies if SharePoint is not yet involved—IIS simply reads the resource file from disk and delivers it to the client. If this fails, the common HTTP error 404 is returned. Delivering a resource means that the content is loaded into memory and streamed to the client.

IIS is responsible for authentication, too. The options are anonymous access, Basic authentication, and Windows authentication based on NTLM (NT Lan Manager) or Kerberos. Each web site can be configured differently. This is done by a stack of modules that handle incoming requests.

In addition to the direct mapping of an endpoint's address to a physical path to a file, IIS has the concept of virtual directories.

Virtual Directories

A virtual directory is a directory name (a sequence of which is better known as *path*) that you specify in IIS and map to a physical directory on a server. The directory name then becomes part of the application's URL. Users can request the URL from a browser to access content in the physical directory, such as your SharePoint application. If you specify a different name for the virtual directory than the physical directory, it is more difficult for users to discover the actual physical file structure. Moreover, SharePoint creates a complete virtual structure of paths that don't exist physically anymore.

In IIS 7, each application must have a virtual directory, which is called the root virtual directory, and which maps the application to the physical directory that contains the application's content. Regarding SharePoint, this is the directory you find in the `C:\inetpub\wwwroot\wss\VirtualDirectories` folder. However, an application can have more than one virtual directory. By default, IIS uses configuration from `web.config` files in the physical directory to which the virtual directory is mapped, as well as in any child directories within.

That means a virtual directory is always a child instance of an already defined URL space. It extends the root address, such as in `http://intranet.apress.com:12683/mysites/Default.aspx`.

In this address, the `/mysites` portion could be a virtual directory. Each virtual directory can be configured to point to a different physical path from the one defined for the root web site. In doing this, you hide the physical structure behind the undisclosed mapping between URL addresses and actual file locations. Since ASP.NET is tightly integrated with IIS, there are several options to extend this behavior. One approach is the *Virtual Path Provider* (see the "Virtual Path Provider" section later in the chapter). This provider is an abstract layer between physical storage of files and the virtual path to the resources. Using this feature, SharePoint stores the resources in a database while IIS behaves as if the files are still in the file system.

The Request Pipeline

When a request arrives, IIS checks for the file extension mapping and routes the request to the associated extension. In the case of ASP.NET, we assume that the request is something like `default.aspx`, so it's routed to `aspnet_isapi.dll` (see Figure 2–2).

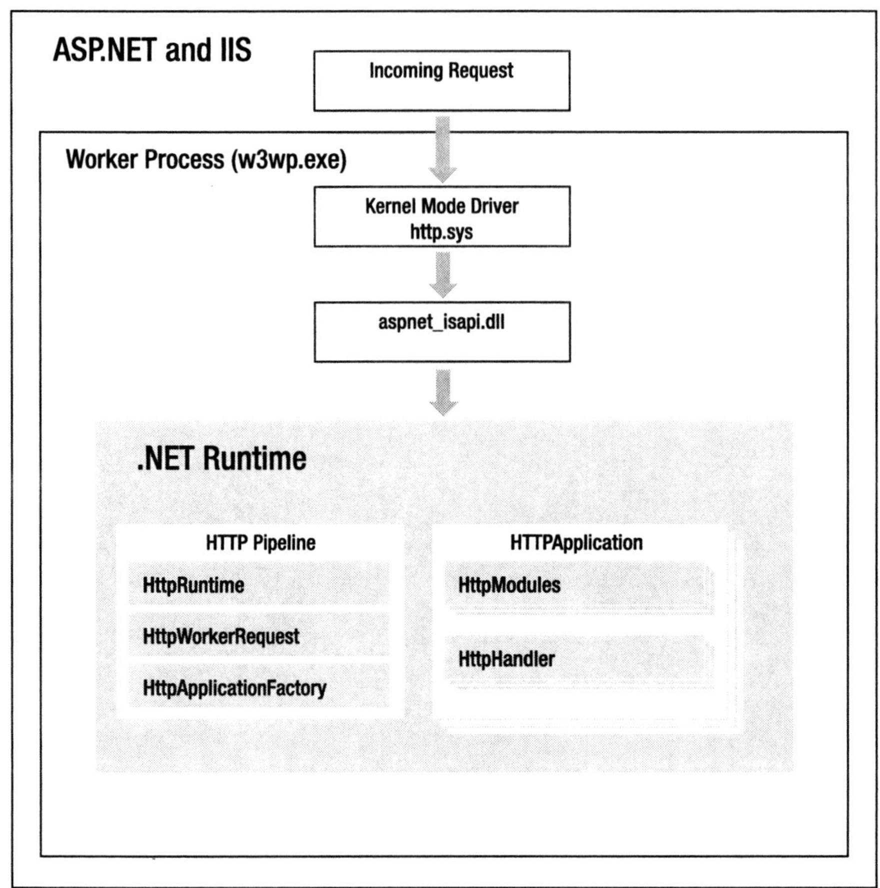

Figure 2–2. *Request flow through IIS to the ASP.NET runtime*

We assume that you have already worked with and configured the application pool. The application pool was introduced with IIS 6 to allow the complete isolation of applications from each other. This means that IIS is able to completely separate things happening in one application from those in another. Keeping applications together in one pool can still make sense, because another pool creates its own worker process, and (as shown in **Figure 2–2**) will use more resources.

Separate applications make the web server more reliable. If one application hangs, consumes too much CPU time, or behaves unpredictably, it affects its entire pool. Other application pools (and the applications within them) will continue to run. In addition, the application pools are highly configurable. You've already learned that the .NET Framework version can be different for each pool, which is very useful for migration scenarios. You can configure the security environment by choosing the impersonation level and customizing the rights given to a web application. Application pools are executables that run just like any other program. This makes them easy to monitor and configure. Although this does not sound very low level, application pools are highly optimized to talk directly to the kernel mode driver, `http.sys`. Incoming requests are directly routed to the pool attached to the application. At this point you may wonder where InetInfo is gone. It is still there, but it is basically just an administration and configuration service. The flow of data through IIS is as direct as possible, straight from `http.sys` to the application pools. `http.sys` is the basic driver that represents the TCP/IP protocol stack. This is one reason why IIS 7 is much faster and more reliable than any preceding version.

An IIS 7 application pool also has intrinsic knowledge of ASP.NET, and in turn ASP.NET can communicate with the new low-level APIs that allow direct access to the HTTP cache APIs. This can offload caching from the ASP.NET level directly into the web server's cache, which also dramatically improves performance.

In IIS 7, ISAPI extensions run in the application pool's worker process. The .NET runtime also runs in this same process, and thus communication between the ISAPI extension and the .NET runtime runs *in-process*, which is inherently more efficient.

ASP.NET Extensibility

ASP.NET's extensibility is the means by which SharePoint adds its own features. Extensibility is handled at several levels. This section provides a brief introduction.

■ **Tip** To read more about the extensibility model, we recommend the book *ASP.NET Extensibility*, by Jörg Krause (Apress, 2009).

Modules, Handlers, and IIS

IIS 7 web server features fit into one of two categories:

- Modules
- Handlers

Similar to the ISAPI filter in previous IIS versions, a module participates in the processing of each request. Its role is to change or add content to the request. Examples of some out-of-the-box modules in IIS 7 include authentication modules, compression modules, and logging modules.

A module is a .NET class that implements the `System.Web.IHttpModule` interface and uses APIs in the `System.Web` namespace to participate in one or more of ASP.NET's request-processing stages. We explained the stages of this pipeline in Chapter 1.

By contrast, a handler, similar to the ISAPI extension in previous IIS versions, is responsible for handling requests and creating responses for specific content types. The main difference between modules and handlers is that handlers are typically mapped to a particular request path or extension, whereas modules treat every incoming request. They also support the processing of a specific resource to which that path or extension corresponds. Handlers provided with IIS 7 include ASP.NET's `PageHandlerFactory`, which processes ASPX pages, among others. This kind of handler is a .NET class that implements the ASP.NET `System.Web.IHttpHandler` or `System.Web.IHttpAsyncHandler` interface. It uses APIs in the `System.Web` namespace to produce an HTTP response for the specific content it creates.

Modules

ASP.NET is tightly integrated with IIS 7. Even though it's possible to run ASP.NET with any host, thanks to its modular architecture, you should keep in mind that IIS is the best platform by design. Extending and customizing ASP.NET is only possible with a good understanding of IIS and its parts.

Microsoft changed large parts of the architecture of IIS 7 compared to previous versions. One of the major changes was the greatly enhanced extensibility. Instead of a powerful but monolithic web server, with IIS 7 there is now a web server engine to which you can add or remove components. These components are called modules.

Modules build the features offered by the web server. All modules have one primary task—processing a request. This can become complicated, however, as a request isn't just a call for a static resource. Rather, it can also include authentication of client credentials, compression and decompression, and cache management.

IIS comes with two module types:

- Native modules
- Managed modules

Native Modules

Native modules perform all the basic tasks of a web server. However, not all modules manage common requests. It depends on your installation and configuration as to whether a module is available and running. Inside IIS 7 are

- HTTP modules
- Security modules
- Content modules
- Compression modules
- Caching modules
- Logging and diagnosing modules
- Integration of managed modules

Managed Modules

Several managed modules are available in IIS if ASP.NET is installed. They include modules for authorization, authentication, and mapping, and service modules that support the data services.

Handlers

While modules are low level and run against every inbound request to the ASP.NET application, HTTP handlers focus more on a specific request mapping. This is usually a mapping of a file extension.

HTTP handler implementations are very simple in concept, but having access to the `HttpContext` object enables enormous versatility. Handlers are implemented through the `IHttpHandler` interface, or its asynchronous counterpart, `IHttpAsyncHandler`. The interface consists of a single method, `ProcessRequest`, and a single property, `IsReusable`. The asynchronous version has a pair of methods (`BeginProcessRequest` and `EndProcessRequest`) and the same `IsReusable` property. The vital ingredient is `ProcessRequest`, which receives an instance of the `HttpContext` object. This single method is responsible for handling a web request from start to finish.

However, simple does not imply simplistic. As you may know, the regular page-processing code and the web service–processing code are implemented as handlers. Both are anything but simple. Their power originates from the `HttpContext` object, which has access to both the request information and the response data. This means that, like a web server, a handler can control the whole process on its own. Whatever you want to implement on the level of specific mapping is achievable using handlers.

The Provider Model

Providers are software modules built on top of interfaces or abstract classes that define the façade for the application. The interfaces constitute *seams* in the architecture, which allow you to replace providers without affecting other modules. For instance, the data access provider enables access to any kind of data storage, including databases from different vendors. Hence, the provider model encapsulates the functionality and isolates it from the rest of the application.

Because almost all the major parts of ASP.NET are built using providers, there are multiple ways of modifying the internal behavior. Providers are responsible for the extensibility of ASP.NET. Creating your own providers gives you the ability to construct a sophisticated architecture that others might use—and to alter its behavior without disturbing internal processing. Consider an application such as SharePoint 2010, which is an ASP.NET application and a framework that others use as a foundation for their applications. A similar extensibility concept is supplied on this level. Providers build the core technology on which all of this is based.

When you work with providers for the first time, you may find that writing or extending a provider can be a complicated task. Due to the constraints of compatibility and transparency toward other modules, there is often no other option but to extend an internal interface. You may still need to decide whether or not to write your own provider model. This section gives you the information you need for making that decision.

Recall what the provider model was designed for:

- It makes ASP.NET both flexible and extensible.
- It's robust and well documented.
- It provides a common and modern architecture for your application.
- It's part of a multitier architecture.

The provider model does not consist only of simple provider modules. At the top level of the model are services. *Services*, in ASP.NET, is a generic term for separate modules, such as Membership, Site Maps, and Profiles. Almost all of them are replaced in SharePoint to achieve the specific functions. These are all high-level components, which make your life as a developer easier. Almost all of these services need some kind of data storage or at least a communication channel. From the perspective of a multitier application, the service should be independent of the particulars of data persistence.

The provider sits between the service layer and the data store layer (Figure 2–3). Modifying the provider allows the service to use a different data store or communication channel without changing the service functionality. From the perspective of the user, this architecture is transparent.

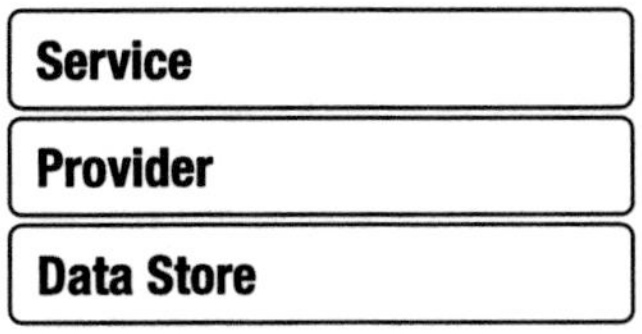

Service
Provider
Data Store

Figure 2–3. *The provider as part of a multitier architecture*

In addition, the provider is a readily configurable module. You can usually change the provider by editing the `web.config` file or by setting properties in base classes.

The Configuration Model

The extensibility of parts of the web.config file is not limited to configuring providers. Using the base classes within the System.Configuration namespace, you can create custom sections and handle them directly. If the settings defined in <AppSettings> are too limited for your application's needs, you can extend them.

The first step is to add a reference to the System.Configuration.dll assembly and the System.Configuration namespace. Creating a new project of the class library type for the new configuration definition is not required, but is recommended. This makes the code reusable and easier to test and deploy. Before you create a section like this, it's worth examining the anatomy of a configuration section.

The configuration section is based on the implementation of two abstract classes, ConfigurationSection and ConfigurationElement. ConfigurationSection is a parent of ConfigurationElement that makes it easy to create hierarchies of sections that contain elements on each level. The concrete ConfigurationSection is defined at the top of the web.config file:

```
<configSections>
  <sectionGroup name="system.web.extensions" type="...">
    <sectionGroup name="scripting" type="...">
      <section name="scriptResourceHandler" type="..."
               requirePermission="false" allowDefinition="MachineToApplication"/>
      <sectionGroup name="webServices" type="...">
        <section name="jsonSerialization" type="..." requirePermission="false"
                 allowDefinition="Everywhere" />
        <section name="profileService" type="..." requirePermission="false"
                 allowDefinition="MachineToApplication" />
        <section name="..." requirePermission="false"
                 allowDefinition="MachineToApplication" />
        <section name="roleService" type="..." requirePermission="false"
                 allowDefinition="MachineToApplication" />
      </sectionGroup>
    </sectionGroup>
  </sectionGroup>
</configSections>
```

The type attributes are empty for the sake of clarity. They contain the fully qualified assembly names of the type that holds the configuration definition. The top-level element, <sectionGroup>, defines in which group the new element appears:

```
<sectionGroup name="system.web.extensions">
```

The section <system.web.extensions> is thus defined as the location for all subsequent groups or elements, or any combinations of groups and elements. You can define exactly what appears there simply by implementing the base classes mentioned previously.

Virtual Path Provider

Complex sites with hundreds of pages are difficult to maintain. For some sections, a file structure with static data seems to be more productive, whereas other sections are composed dynamically from databases. This difference should be indiscernible to regular users and search engines alike. Search engines follow each link on a page and find the navigation paths through a site, indexing the content of each page on the way. Users bookmark pages and return directly to them later. However, neither of these behaviors are what developers are expecting when creating pages.

The Virtual Path Provider is designed to separate the internal and external structures. Like any other provider, it works transparently, using a pluggable approach. The difference is that the Virtual Path Provider does not access a database by default, and internally it's different from all the providers described so far. However, to implement a Virtual Path Provider, you'll have to inherit and implement an abstract base class—`VirtualPathProvider`.

A custom implementation usually uses the provider model. In this case it's rather different. There is no default provider, which means that each page is handled at its physical location. Implementing a Virtual Path Provider is all about changing the default behavior of the path resolution for a web site. SharePoint makes heavy use of this technique, because the pages that are at least partially stored in the database require a distinct way to pull them out at the right time.

The Virtual Path Provider is responsible for answering a request for a resource that ASP.NET assumes to be somewhere in the file system. Usually it is. However, the response consists not of a physical path, but of a stream of bytes (that make up the requested content). ASP.NET does not care about the source of the bytes. All files handled through the page's life cycle, including master pages and user controls, are loaded through a Virtual Path Provider.

SharePoint Integration with ASP.NET

After the introduction of ASP.NET as the basic layer, which SharePoint is based on, you'll find that there are a lot of extensions and customization. Quite often you'll find that SharePoint and its API provide neat solutions for common tasks. To program against the API, it's important to know when and why SharePoint has implemented its own features.

SharePoint integrates with ASP.NET at the level of an IIS web site. What SharePoint calls a web application is actually an IIS web site. Within Central Administration you'll find several ways to create, extend, or delete a web application. The connection between an IIS web site and a SharePoint web application is very close. It's not only for naming purposes, of course. SharePoint needs to route all incoming requests to its own runtime to handle them. However, that's not all it's about. SharePoint is a highly scalable and manageable platform. Creating a SharePoint web application means it can spread over several servers that constitute a web farm. That involves several instances of IIS running on these servers, and all of them need to be managed from one single point. Changing the settings using Central Administration mirrors the configuration and settings of all the IIS instances running across the farm. This step requires sufficient rights to perform the desired action—though the need to do so may be infrequent. Once at least one web application is created, several other levels to organize applications are provided, such as the creation of subsites.

The basic structure of a SharePoint application might include site collections and sites, and consequently a hierarchy of them. Adding custom code to sites or site collections or extending sites and site collections by application pages does not require you to touch either the web site within IIS or the web application within Central Administration. You may be struggling with the term *application*, as it appears at several levels in the hierarchy with different meanings. In this book we focus on the programmer or software developer. For these, a SharePoint application is a couple of ASP.NET pages, called *application pages*, that manifest as a part of a SharePoint site. That includes at least one SharePoint web application and in turn at least one IIS site that must exist. But it does not require you to program against these.

Understanding the Web Application

To create a web application, use Central Administration or the `stsadm` command-line tool or the corresponding PowerShell cmdlets.

■ **Note** Both PowerShell and `stsadm.exe` are part of the distribution and are used for automation. See Chapter 5 for more details.

You can create a web application either by converting an existing IIS web site or by building a new one from scratch. If it is a new one, SharePoint takes care of creating the required parts with IIS and spreading the settings across the farm. This is necessary since incoming requests have to be routed initially to the ASP.NET runtime. However, the default configuration does not know about all the file extensions used by SharePoint. As even SharePoint does not know about these yet, the routing forwards all requests. Instead of requests just being mapped to file extensions such as `.aspx` and `.ashx`, virtually all requests are routed to the ASP.NET runtime. This means that SharePoint can handle `.docx` and similar extensions.

The integration of ASP.NET with SharePoint starts with the use of the custom `HttpApplication` object, `SPHttpApplication`. This class is deployed in the `Microsoft.SharePoint.dll` assembly. The declarative expression of an application in ASP.NET is the `global.asax` file. Its code usually derives from `HttpApplication`. SharePoint changes the web application's `global.asax` to the following:

```
<@Application Inherits="">
```

As shown previously, several modules and handlers are responsible for handling incoming requests. SharePoint takes the same approach, but with a dramatic twist. It firstly eliminates all the default ASP.NET handlers and modules and replaces them with its own. The following snippet is taken from a site's `web.config` file. It shows that SharePoint replaces several modules to handle incoming requests.

```
<modules runAllManagedModulesForAllRequests="true">
 <remove name="AnonymousIdentification" />
 <remove name="FileAuthorization" />
 <remove name="Profile" />
 <remove name="WebDAVModule" />
 <add name="SPRequestModule" preCondition="integratedMode"
      type="Microsoft.SharePoint.ApplicationRuntime.SPRequestModule,
            Microsoft.SharePoint, ..." />
 <add name="ScriptModule" preCondition="integratedMode"
      type="System.Web.Handlers.ScriptModule, System.Web.Extensions, ..." />
 <add name="SharePoint14Module" preCondition="integratedMode" />
 <add name="StateServiceModule"
      type="Microsoft.Office.Server.Administration.StateModule,
            Microsoft.Office.Server, ..." />
 <add name="PublishingHttpModule"
      type="Microsoft.SharePoint.Publishing.PublishingHttpModule,
            Microsoft.SharePoint.Publishing, ..." />
</modules>
```

For the sake of clarity, some parts of the fully qualified assembly names have been removed.

`SPHttpHandler` and `SPRequestModule` are the classes used to handle incoming requests. First of all, both are required to initialize the SharePoint runtime. However, digging deeper you'll find that SharePoint still uses the default ASP.NET modules. Web configuration files build a hierarchy. Subsequent `web.config` files might add additional modules. That's exactly what happens with SharePoint sites. The central `web.config` file is augmented with the private modules and handlers that are positioned at the top of the pipeline. Each incoming request is handled there first. SharePoint adds some of the default handlers back into the pipeline. That means that the basic behavior of ASP.NET is still present. The initialization ensures that the API is accessible and the SharePoint object model is ready to operate.

It's helpful to get a basic idea of which modules and handlers are available with SharePoint and which have been replaced by custom variations. The global (machine-wide) web.config file contains the following section:

```
<configuration>
  <system.webServer>
    <handlers>
      <clear />
      <add name="PageHandlerFactory-Integrated" path="*.aspx"
           verb="GET,HEAD,POST,DEBUG" type="System.Web.UI.PageHandlerFactory"
           preCondition="integratedMode" />
      <add name="ScriptHandlerFactory" verb="*" path="*.asmx"
           preCondition="integratedMode"
           type="System.Web.Script.Services.ScriptHandlerFactory,
                 System.Web.Extensions, ..." />
      <add name="SimpleHandlerFactory-Integrated" path="*.ashx"
           verb="GET,HEAD,POST,DEBUG" type="System.Web.UI.SimpleHandlerFactory"
           preCondition="integratedMode" />
      <add name="StaticFile" path="*" verb="*" modules="StaticFileModule"
           resourceType="Either" requireAccess="Read" />
    </handlers>
  </system.webServer>
</configuration>
```

The handlers are sufficient for application pages and web services used by the client features. As you can see from the namespaces, none of these handlers are specific to SharePoint. A step further into a specific application it looks quite different. The web.config file that is responsible for a specific site has another set of handler assignments:

```
<handlers>
    <remove name="StaticFile" />
    <remove name="OPTIONSVerbHandler" />
    <remove name="WebServiceHandlerFactory-Integrated" />
    <remove name="svc-Integrated" />
    <add name="svc-Integrated" path="*.svc" verb="*"
         type="System.ServiceModel.Activation.HttpHandler, System.ServiceModel, ..."
         preCondition="integratedMode" />
    <add name="OwssvrHandler" scriptProcessor="C:\Program Files\Common
            Files\Microsoft Shared\Web Server Extensions\14\isapi\owssvr.dll"
         path="/_vti_bin/owssvr.dll" verb="*"
         modules="IsapiModule" preCondition="integratedMode" />
    <add name="ScriptHandlerFactory" verb="*" path="*.asmx"
         preCondition="integratedMode"
         type="System.Web.Script.Services.ScriptHandlerFactory,
               System.Web.Extensions ..." />
    <add name="ScriptHandlerFactoryAppServices" verb="*" path="*_AppService.axd"
         preCondition="integratedMode"
         type="System.Web.Script.Services.ScriptHandlerFactory, ..." />
    <add name="ScriptResource" preCondition="integratedMode" verb="GET,HEAD"
         path="ScriptResource.axd"
         type="System.Web.Handlers.ScriptResourceHandler,
               System.Web.Extensions,.../>
    <add name="JSONHandlerFactory" path="*.json" verb="*"
```

```
        type="System.Web.Script.Services.ScriptHandlerFactory,
              System.Web.Extensions, ..."
        resourceType="Unspecified" preCondition="integratedMode" />
    <add name="ReportViewerWebPart" verb="*" path="Reserved.ReportViewerWebPart.axd"
       type="Microsoft.ReportingServices.SharePoint.UI.WebParts.WebPartHttpHandler,
             Microsoft.ReportingServices.SharePoint.UI.WebParts, ..." />
    <add name="ReportServerProxy" verb="*" path="_vti_bin/ReportServer"
        type="Microsoft.ReportingServices.SharePoint.Soap.RSProxyHttpHandler,
              RSSharePointSoapProxy, ..." />
    <add name="ReportBuilderProxy" verb="*" path="_vti_bin/ReportBuilder"
        type="Microsoft.ReportingServices.SharePoint.Soap.ReportBuilderHttpHandler,
              RSSharePointSoapProxy, ..." />
    <add name="ReportViewerWebControl" verb="*"
        path="Reserved.ReportViewerWebControl.axd"
        type="Microsoft.Reporting.WebForms.HttpHandler,
              Microsoft.ReportViewer.WebForms, ..." />
</handlers>
```

For the sake of clarity and readability, some of the fully qualified assembly names are shortened (as noted by `...`). The crucial information here is what kind of handlers are being removed from the stack and which are added to handle the respective requests. Ignoring the various handlers responsible for reporting features (see Chapter 18 for more information), you can see that the handlers do not add anything specific here for common requests.

Understanding the Configuration

Whereas the basic configuration is on top of ASP.NET, SharePoint goes a step further and adds its own section to the `web.config` file. The extensibility model of ASP.NET allows such private configuration sections while still using the `web.config` file as the single point of configuration. If you plan to add your own custom pages, modules, handlers, Web Parts, and so on, it's strongly recommended to adopt the same tactic and extend the configuration model for tight integration within the infrastructure. In the section "The Configuration Model" earlier in the chapter, we explained the basics. SharePoint is doing exactly this. The `web.config` file's basic structure contains two SharePoint-specific sections (apart from various others that pertain to ASP.NET). First is the client section that is responsible for the heavily used JavaScript-based client components:

```
<microsoft.sharepoint.client>
  <serverRuntime>
    <hostTypes>
      <add type="Microsoft.SharePoint.Client.SPClientServiceHost,
                 Microsoft.SharePoint, Version=14.0.0.0, Culture=neutral,
                 PublicKeyToken=71e9bce111e9429c" />
    </hostTypes>
  </serverRuntime>
</microsoft.sharepoint.client>
```

Second are the server-side configuration sections:

```
<SharePoint>
  <SafeMode />
  <WebPartLimits />
  <WebPartCache />
  <WebPartControls />
  <SafeControls />
```

```
  <PeoplePickerWildcards />
  <WorkflowServices />
  <MergedActions />
  <BlobCache />
  <ObjectCache />
  <RuntimeFilter />
</SharePoint>
```

The sections WorkflowServices and ObjectCache are new in SharePoint 2010. The runtime reads the values provided within the attributes and subelements of the sections. Some of them, such as SafeMode, support developers and have an impact on the applications running within SharePoint. We'll look into this several times in this book—whenever it's necessary to configure code.

Using the Virtual Path Provider

Accessing the local file system has some limitations; in particular, it's hard to combine parts of files into one dynamically. Using a database, at least one like SQL Server, can overcome many of the drawbacks. However, storing pages in the database requires a different way to retrieve them at the right time. In the "Virtual Path Provider" section we explained the basics and the advantages of a custom path provider. The customized version in SharePoint is named SPVirtualPathProvider. It's initialized during the pipeline request using the SPRequestModule's Init method. The Virtual Path Provider is responsible for resolving predefined path tags, such as ~MASTERURL, ~SITE, ~CONTROLTEMPLATES, ~LAYOUTS, and ~SITECOLLECTION, as well as the file tags DEFAULT.MASTER and CUSTOM.MASTER.

In addition, the page parser ASP.NET uses to parse and eventually compile pages is inherited by another SharePoint-specific class, SPPageParserFilter. This class passes compilation instructions to the regular page parser. You can add settings to the web.config file to change the behavior.

The SPVirtualPathProvider, along with its siblings, handles one of the basic concepts of SharePoint: ghosting. Ghosting is an optimization feature that is used to improve the performance when scaling out pages across a farm. Understanding how ghosting works is necessary if you want a broad understanding of SharePoint.

GHOSTING AND UNGHOSTING

In SharePoint, most of the site pages derive from templates. The custom pages only store the difference between the custom page and the associated template. The template is loaded in memory and applied to the custom pages on the fly. Holding the template in the memory is like having it in a cache. This adds performance and flexibility. The flexibility is achieved when you change the template page—all the associated custom pages are updated with the new appearance. Custom pages are loaded from the file system. Such pages are called *ghosted* pages.

When page data is loaded from the content database, it's called an *unghosted* page. That's normally the default way you treat custom pages. Internally, the unghosted pages are supported by two tables. The page requires an entry in the document table because pages are elements within a document library. The content table contains the actual source code of the ASPX page required to execute the page.

When a page is requested, SharePoint first checks in the document table and then goes to the content table to load the page. If it does not find data for the page, it goes to the file directory to load the page. This entire page-loading process is performed by the ASP.NET runtime using the SPVirtualPathProvider mentioned earlier. This ensures flexible access as well as full control over the loading procedure.

SharePoint and Ajax

Ajax is a base technology used everywhere in SharePoint. You can use it in your own projects as well. This section introduces Ajax and some basic information to enable you to understand several examples in this book that use this technology.

What Is Ajax?

Ajax (Asynchronous JavaScript and XML) is a technology to retrieve data from a server directly from a web page without sending a form. The underlying techniques are old and well known. But they were dormant for some time before they were recognized as a powerful additional method to program web pages. Several frameworks were created to simplify adoption of Ajax by developers. (One such framework is Microsoft ASP.NET AJAX, formerly known under the code name Atlas.) With .NET 3.5, the framework on which SharePoint 2010 is built, the library is part of the main distribution, and there are no additional steps required to use the related controls.

The term *Ajax* is one you may hear in relation to the Web 2.0 phenomena, such as RSS feeds, blogs, and social web sites. Ajax is used by almost all of those web sites to makes them easier to use and encourage the users to stay longer. This is especially important if one is working with such a site every day or several times a day. If the site is slow and hard to use, such social behavior would be not possible—at least for the masses. Ajax exposes a simple idea to everybody. However, Ajax itself does not turn an ordinary site into a social web site. By default, Ajax does nothing but make the programming model a bit more complicated. So if there is absolutely no reason for you to use Ajax, you are not forced to do so. Now you have that in writing!

Despite that, improving the user experience of a web site is generally a good idea. JavaScript is well supported and widely accepted. Visual Studio 2010 has sophisticated support for JavaScript, including IntelliSense and debugging capabilities. Both Internet Explorer and Firefox have developer dashboards to aid in viewing, understanding, and debugging JavaScript and the several libraries involved when dealing with Ajax. But what is Ajax exactly?

Firstly, it's a combination of known technologies. As the name implies, it is a way to get data asynchronously. The browser's JavaScript engine is single threaded. Firing a web service call synchronously would block the UI until the response is received. Programming asynchronously is the only feasible way to get a good user experience. Second, the *j* in *Ajax* stands for *JavaScript*. This is widely accepted and supported; however, theoretically, any client language will do. Skipping the second *a* in *Ajax*, which is there just to create a catchy acronym, is the final technology, XML. This was the preferred way to transfer complex data. I say "was" because in recent years, JSON (JavaScript Object Notation) has proved to be a superior data format for Ajax. JSON defines a way to describe a serializable object using JavaScript instead of XML. This is both faster to evaluate and more compact in size. Size matters, by the way, because the bandwidth is still a bottleneck between the server and client. (So you could say "Ajax" or "Ajaj"; however, *Ajaj* is unknown perhaps because nobody can pronounce it easily.)

If you program using Ajax, you need a few more technologies, such as the DOM (Document Object Model) to access elements within a page; XML and XSLT to transform incoming data if it's not yet serialized using JSON; CSS (Cascading Style Sheets) and HTML to understand how to create and format objects dynamically; and at least a basic understand of HTTP, because it is still the protocol spoken between client and server. And last but not least, you must be fluent with JavaScript.

Security Model

Empowering users can harm any platform. As soon as a user is given the ability to do more, it increases the potential for malicious or damaging actions on your system. SharePoint is no exception, and the various ways that extend the platform make security considerations crucial. For development of controls this is particularly important, because this is frequently the way one codes for SharePoint.

Safe Mode

The <SafeMode> element in web.config controls the code execution behavior. Its basic structure looks like this:

```
<SafeMode MaxControls="200" CallStack="false" DirectFileDependencies="10"
          TotalFileDependencies="50" AllowPageLevelTrace="false">
  <PageParserPath AllowServerSideScript="false" />
</SafeMode>
```

Any customized page that can contain code is executed using so-called *safe-mode processing*. This adds some security, as no inline script is executed. That prevents intruders from infiltrating code through end user–enabled functions. To overwrite this behavior, set the AllowServerSideScript attribute to true, as follows:

```
<PageParserPath AllowServerSideScript="true" />
```

The MaxControls element prevents the server from rendering extensive pages with more than 200 controls by default. The attributes DirectFileDependencies and TotalFileDependencies address performance checks as well. Setting CallStack to true would expose the call stack if the page can show exception details.

Safe Controls

SharePoint is a highly customizable platform. That's true not only for administrators and developers, but for end users as well. While this is one of the key advantages the platform offers, it's also a risk for those operating the servers. Not only can users change content and create lists, but they can also upload Web Parts and add them to their sites. While one could simply prevent users from doing so, this would limit the attractiveness of a site. To give users a limited, policed power, SharePoint has *safe controls*.

That means that the administrator must explicitly allow the controls used on pages before anybody—regardless of his or her specific rights—is able to add and activate them. As a result, you no longer check and regulate "untrusted" users and their activities. Instead, you check the controls spread throughout your installation and give approval for them to be installed. Such approved controls can then be used by anybody who is allowed to import controls.

In the application's root web.config file is a <SafeControls> section that contains several elements to define which controls are allowed.

```
<SafeControl Assembly="MyWebPartLibrary, Version=1.0.0.0, Culture=neutral,
             PublicKeyToken=null" Namespace="MyWebPartLibrary" TypeName="*"
             Safe="True" AllowRemoteDesigner="True"/>
```

Use the Assembly attribute to define the fully qualified name of the assembly containing the type. Use NameSpace and TypeName to restrict which controls are permitted. For TypeName, the asterisk signifies "all controls." To make the control safe, set the Safe attribute to true. You might wonder why this is necessary, since just removing the entry would declare the control unsafe anyway. However, remember that web.config files form a hierarchy, and the final application folder can inherit settings from upper levels. Thus, an administrator can explicitly disallow a particular Web Part control anywhere deeper in the hierarchy to prevent users from using it. If this effect is desired, just repeat the definition and set Safe to false.

Manipulating web.config to Add Safe Controls Programmatically

Directly editing the web.config file is not recommended. Doing so could result in an invalid file, and the application could stop working. Even worse, it could become insecure in some way without you noticing. To avoid this, the process of Web Part deployment and registering the assembly or its parts as safe should be closely followed, as shown in the next code snippet.

```
public override void FeatureActivated(SPFeatureReceiverProperties properties)
{
    // A reference to the features site collection
    SPSite site = null;
    // Get a reference to the site collection of the feature
    if (properties.Feature.Parent is SPWeb)
    {
       site = ((SPWeb)properties.Feature.Parent).Site;
    }
    else if (properties.Feature.Parent is SPSite)
    {
       site = properties.Feature.Parent as SPSite;
    }
    if (site != null)
    {
         SPWebApplication webApp = site.WebApplication;
         // Create a modification
         SPWebConfigModification mod = new SPWebConfigModification(
              @"SafeControl[@Assembly="MyAssembly"][@Namespace="My.Namespace"]"
            + @"[@TypeName="*"][@Safe="True"][@AllowRemoteDesigner="True"]"
             , "/configuration/SharePoint/SafeControls"
    );
    // Add the modification to the collection of modifications
    webApp.WebConfigModifications.Add(mod);
    // Apply the modification
    webApp.Farm.Services.GetValue().ApplyWebConfigModifications();
   }
}
```

This code shows how to modify `web.config` using the appropriate classes called from a feature event receiver. If the Web Part is part of a feature and the feature is activated, the event is fired and the code executed. The code first checks the parent object the receiver refers to (i.e., the context object it's installed in). From that object, the `SPWebApplication` object is pulled to get the `web.config` file that contains the site's configuration. An XPath expression that contains the complete token and the path where it has to be added is used to get the configuration. A farm service is used finally to apply the modifications.

The feature event receiver is very flexible and powerful. However, adding an event receiver to merely modify the configuration is probably more work than it's worth. See Chapter 3 to learn more about event receivers and how to program them.

Making a Web Part Safe by Default

If you have a Web Part and want to make it safe anyway, you can add this information to the solution package, as shown in the following code. For more information about solution deployment, refer to Chapter 9.

```
<Solution SolutionId="{2E9DDE85-8822-42EC-3a92-E85537810BAA}"
          xmlns="http://schemas.microsoft.com/sharepoint/">
<FeatureManifests  />
<ApplicationResourceFiles />
<CodeAccessSecurity />
```

```
<DwpFiles />
<Resources />
<RootFiles />
<SiteDefinitionManifests />
<TemplateFiles />

<Assemblies>
  <Assembly DeploymentTarget="WebApplication" Location="Apress.WebParts.dll">
    <SafeControls>
      <SafeControl Assembly="Apress.WebPart, Version=1.0.0.0, Culture=neutral,
                             PublicKeyToken=a05eff78260564"
                   Namespace="Apress" TypeName="*" Safe="True"/>
    </SafeControls>
  </Assembly>
</Assemblies>
</Solution>
```

This technique is limited to your own Web Parts, where you have control over the packaging process. But it's the safest way to add controls to `web.config`. (You can review how to modify `web.config` using the SharePoint API in Chapter 3.)

The Foundation's Object Model

The SharePoint building blocks have a unique structure, object model, and behavior. In this book we show you how to work with and program against these blocks. This section contains a short introduction to each one, with links to other chapters where we elaborate on the building blocks in more detail. The list looks like this:

- Data-related building blocks:
  - Lists and document libraries
  - Files and documents
  - Columns and field types
  - Content types
  - Queries and views
- Deployment- and maintenance-related building blocks:
  - Features
  - Solutions
  - Web sites and site collections
- Building blocks to create the UI:
  - Mobile pages, controls, and adapters
  - Ribbon
  - Pages and UI
  - Web Parts

- Control flow, action, and events:
  - Event handling
  - Alerts
  - Workflows

For each part, we'll give a brief introduction and an overview of the entry points and the object model.

Data-Related Building Blocks

This section contains all the parts of SharePoint that deal with data. In particular, this includes lists and libraries, files and documents, and the parts they consist of, such as field types, column definitions (and templates for them), and content types. Furthermore, we explain how to query against such data containers using queries and views.

The data access techniques are explained in greater depth in Chapter 4.

Lists and Document Libraries

Lists are the basic data containers and document libraries are lists that contain documents. Lists have columns—internally called fields—to structure the data. Depending on the kind of customization you need, SharePoint offers several APIs regarding lists and libraries. There are three realms of APIs you can use:

- Server side, for working on the server (`Microsoft.SharePoint` namespace)
- Client side, for working on a client using JavaScript or Silverlight (`Microsoft.SharePoint.Client` namespace)
- Migrating content between site collections (`Microsoft.SharePoint.Deployment` namespace)

In addition to what the API provides, the list web services allow remote access.

SharePoint comes with many predefined lists and libraries that you can use as templates for your own creations. It's possible to export a list as a template and reuse it in custom code by adding a few more columns or modifying a field type. To manage list templates, the `SPListTemplate` class contains the relevant methods.

Lists form a hierarchy of list types, based on a primary type defined by the `SPBaseType` enumeration. The base types are

- `GenericList`: A generic list type for most custom lists
- `DocumentLibrary`: A document library for any kind of document
- `DiscussionBoard`: A discussion board list that's able to create discussion threads
- `Survey`: A survey list that handles surveys
- `Issue`: An issue list to store and track issues
- `UnspecifiedBaseType`: An unspecified base type for any other kind of list

The `SPListTemplateType` enumeration is used for default list template types in SharePoint. There is a relationship between the template and the base types. That means each list template has a specific base type. Each `enum` value also has an internal value used in XML configuration files. Table 2–1 shows this relationship for common types.

Table 2–1. List Template Types

Type	Value	Description
GenericList	100	Type used for a custom list
DocumentLibrary	101	Type that defines a document library
Survey	102	Type that defines a survey
Links	103	Type that defines a list that can store hyperlinks
Announcements	104	Type that defines announcements (news)
Contacts	105	Type that defines contacts with fields that store addresses, phone numbers, and so on
Events	106	Type that defines a calendar that supports events
Tasks	107	Type that defines tasks assigned to users
DiscussionBoard	108	Type that defines a discussion board list
PictureLibrary	109	Type that defines a library that has special views to show pictures
DataSources	110	Type that collects all data sources for a site
WebTemplateCatalog	111	Type that defines a site template gallery
UserInformation	112	Type that defines some user information
WebPartCatalog	113	Type that defines a Web Part gallery
ListTemplateCatalog	114	Type that defines a list template gallery
XMLForm	115	Type that defines an XML form library that stores InfoPath forms
MasterPageCatalog	116	Type that defines a gallery list that stores master pages
NoCodeWorkflows	117	Type that contains simple no-code workflows
WorkflowProcess	118	Type that defines custom workflows
WebPageLibrary	119	Type that defines a Wiki page library

Type	Value	Description
CustomGrid	120	Type that defines a custom grid for a list to present data
DataConnectionLibrary	130	Type that defines a data connection library for sharing information about external data connections
WorkflowHistory	140	Type that defines a workflow history
GanttTasks	150	Type that defines project tasks that can create Gantt charts
Meetings	200	Type that defines a meeting series
Agenda	201	Type that defines an agenda for a meeting
MeetingUser	202	Type that defines attendees of a meeting
Decision	203	Type that defines decisions of a meeting
MeetingObjective	207	Type that defines objectives of a meeting
TextBox	210	Type that defines the text box container for a meeting
ThingsToBring	211	Type that defines things to bring for a meeting
HomePageLibrary	212	Type that defines workspace pages for a meeting
Posts	301	Type that defines posts of a blog
Comments	302	Type that defines comments of a blog
Categories	303	Type that defines categories of a blog
IssueTracking	1100	Type that defines issue-tracking items
AdminTasks	1200	Type that defines administrator tasks used in Central Administration

The base of a list is the `SPList` class, which provides access to list properties common to all lists. If the list is a library, the more specific `SPDocumentLibrary` class can be used. You can retrieve an `SPList` object using the `List` property of the `SPWeb` object. In the client model, the type is `SP.List`. If the list uses external data, you'll need the `SPListDataSource` class or the corresponding `SP.ListDataSource` class.

Lists can fire events, especially when users add, modify, or remove elements. The `SPListEventProperties` class provides properties for list events, and the `SPListEventReceiver` class contains methods to trap events that occur for lists.

If you already have a list, the `SPListItem` class represents an item or row in it. An efficient way to return a list item or an `SPListItemCollection` is through the `GetItem` method of `SPList`. In the client object model, the type is `SP.ListItem`.

Also, lists support versioning. Using the `SPListItemVersion` class, you can access a version of a list item.

The Object Model at a Glance

Figure 2–4 shows the classes closely related to the `SPList` base class.

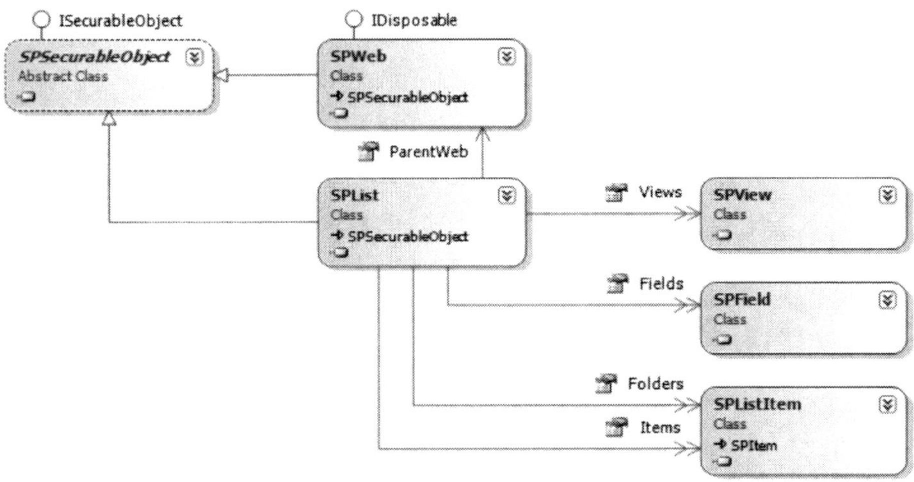

Figure 2–4. *Significant classes related to the SPList type*

Configuring Lists and Libraries

Using the API you can define lists; add, modify, and remove items; and use lists as powerful and highly flexible data containers. If you merely want to define lists for deployment purposes, it's easier to create XML files. The `schema.xml` file contains list definitions. See Chapter 7 for more details concerning XML-based list definitions. Views that show the data for a list in a specific way are constructed with XSLT.

Files and Documents

The previous section was about lists and libraries. Recall that libraries are lists that can contain documents. Documents usually start off as files on a local disk. However, in SharePoint, a file is everything that *could* be stored separately. This includes ASPX files, for instance. These files may reside on disk or in a database. Using the API you can read and write files with `Stream` objects.

A file is represented by an `SPFile` object. While the `Files` property of an `SPList` object returns all files, the same property of an `SPWeb` object returns the ASPX files associated with the web. In the client object model, the corresponding types are `SP.File` and `SP.Folder`.

As well as files attached to library items, a library supports folders. The SPFolder class provides the necessary properties and methods. A folder is a special item within a library. If you count items on an abstract level, the folders appear as items with a special property, namely FileSystemObjectType.

As files appear in collections, the type SPFileCollection is used to support adding, copying, and removing items. You can use SPFileCollectionAddParameters to add a file to a file collection. The SaveBinary method takes an SPFileStream and an SPFileSaveBinaryParameters object to save files to a stream. The target can be stored locally, written to disk, held in memory, or sent via HTTP. In the client object model, the method is called FileSaveBinaryInformation.

Like list items, even files can have versions. An SPFileVersion object represents a version of a file. In the client object model, SP.FileVersion is the equivalent.

The Object Model at a Glance

Figure 2–5 shows the classes closely related to the SPFile base class.

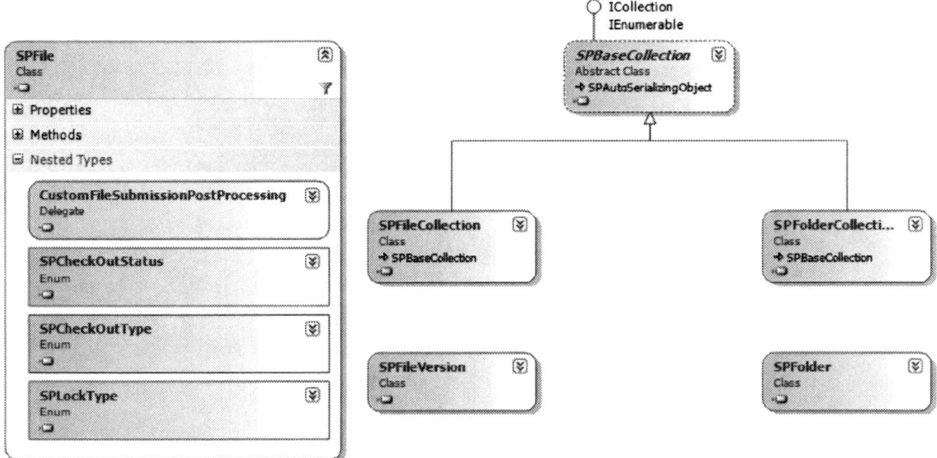

Figure 2–5. Significant classes related to the SPFile type

Configuring Files and Documents

In the XML definition, especially for deployment purposes, the <Module> element represents a file, as shown in the following code:

```
<?xml version="1.0" encoding="utf-8"?>
<Elements xmlns="http://schemas.microsoft.com/sharepoint/">
  <Module Name="Module1">
    <File Path="Module1\Sample.txt" Url="Module1/Sample.txt" />
  </Module>
</Elements>
```

The module encapsulates a collection of files that is part of the deployment package. In Chapter 7 we explain such files in more depth.

Columns and Field Types

Lists and libraries structure data via columns. In SharePoint, the term *field* is used to distinguish relational database tables from their columns. You may translate columns into field types, rows into items, and cells of a row into fields. In the object model, a collection of field definitions is called `Fields`. A single field containing data of one column is represented by an `SPField` object.

In SharePoint, fields not only contain data of a particular type, but they are themselves a kind of type because the same field type can be used on multiple lists with different data. That means all such definitions are created once and reused throughout the site. A field type can persist in the site column gallery. A site column from such a gallery can be added to any list in the site, either programmatically or through the UI.

Some of the site columns that are built into SharePoint include Address, Birthday, StartDate, and EndDate. Each column belongs to one of a small set of basic field types, called *scalar types*. These are, for example, multiple lines of text (`Note` in the `SPFieldType` enumeration), date and time (`DateTime`), single line of text (`Text`), and hyperlink (`URL`). The complete list of field types is specified in the `SPFieldType` enumeration. Table 2–2 shows the most important values.

***Table 2–2.** Basic (Scalar) Types That All Field Types Inherit From*

Type	Description
`Boolean`	A field that accepts only `true` or `false` as values.
`Calculated`	A field whose value is calculated at runtime from a mathematical formula.
`Choice`	A field that can have only one value, and the value must be from a finite list of values. There is also a `Multichoice` field type, which allows for more than one value from a list.
`Computed`	A field whose value depends on the value of another field in the same list item. It is usually the value of a logical operation performed on one or more other fields.
`Lookup`	A field that is similar to a `Choice` field, but the list of possible values comes from a column on some other list.
`Text`	A field that accepts a single line of text. There is also a field type for multiple lines of text called `Note`.

Chapter 4 contains a more detailed list, with examples. There is a rich object model to create and handle columns and field types. Use the `SPListItem` type to access a list item's data. The `SPListItem` object represents the list item, and you can use one of its indexers to reference a particular field. There is an indexer that accepts an `Int32` object as an ID, one that accepts a `String` object as the field name, and a third that takes a `Guid` object. `SPField` and its derivatives represent field types. For example, `SPFieldBoolean` represents `Boolean` fields and `SPFieldChoice` represents `Choice` fields. Any specified column in a web site's site column gallery is an object instantiated from one of these classes. The properties of the class differentiate the various columns of a specified field type. The Birthday column and the StartDate column are both objects of the `SPFieldDateTime` class, for instance, but they differ in the value of the `Title`. An important member of the `SPField` class is the `Update` method. It must be called to save changes made to the column. Otherwise, changing values has no effect.

Storing data in fields is only the half of the process. Presenting the data to the user is the other half. One core feature of the SharePoint API is tight integration between the data layer and the UI layer. Even if Microsoft publicizes that SharePoint has a multitier architecture, this is not strictly correct. For developers, though, it is an advantage. Having a field and defining its UI and behavior in one place simplifies both distribution and usage. The rendering behavior of a field in a particular list item is usually managed by an object derived from the `BaseFieldControl` class. For example, the `BooleanField` renders a Boolean value, as in `SPFieldBoolean`. `BooleanField` derives from `BaseFieldControl`, which derives from `System.Web.UI.Control`. The rendering control holds a reference to the field object exposed by the `Field` property. This relationship is established in both directions—the field has a reference to the control through the `FieldRenderControl` property. Both objects form a couple—one for the data and one for the user interaction. The transfer of the value is done using the `UpdateFieldValueInItem` method and the `Value` property.

As a developer, when you create a custom field, you can inherit from `BaseFieldControl` or from any of the derived classes.

Closely related to field controls is the concept of rendering templates for controls. A rendering template is an element in one of the ASCX controls stored in this folder:

```
%ProgramFiles%\Common Files\Microsoft Shared\web server extensions\14\
TEMPLATE\CONTROLTEMPLATES
```

You don't have to use templates, though it is recommended practice to do so by defining templates for public use. See Chapter 7 for more about this subject.

If your field holds more complex data than you will be able to present using a render template, you may consider using custom field types, too. There are a few built-in complex types, such as `SPFieldLookupValue`, which is used by the `SPFieldLookup` field type.

The Object Model at a Glance

Figure 2–6 shows the classes closely related to the `SPField` base class.

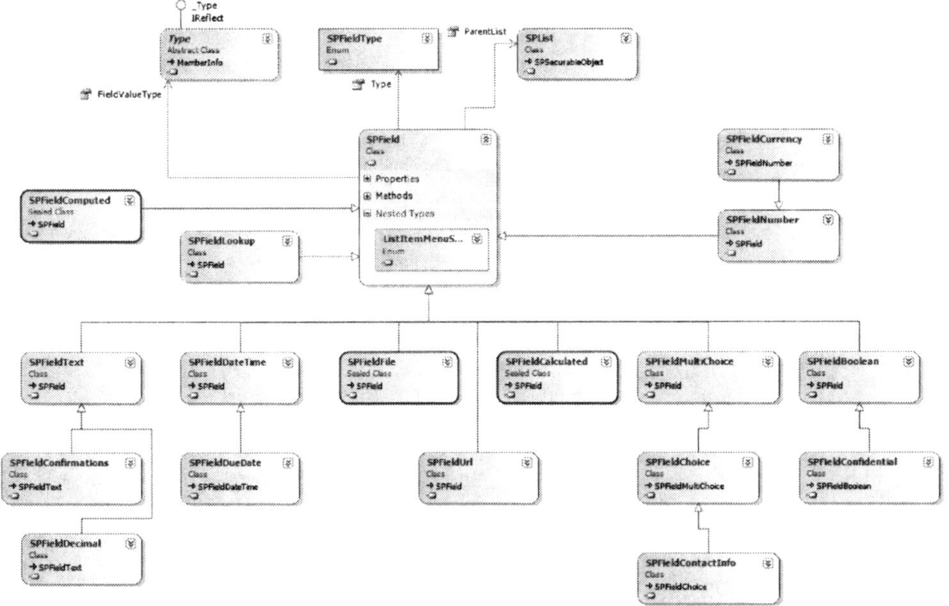

Figure 2–6. Significant classes related to the SPField type

Configuring Columns and Field Types

For the purpose of site, feature, or Web Part definitions and deployment, you use various XML files. XML is used for columns and field types, too. It is needed to register custom field types using `fldtypes*.xml` files located in this folder:

```
%ProgramFiles%\Common Files\Microsoft Shared\web server extensions\14\TEMPLATE\XML
```

To declare custom fields, you use XML definition files. They also allow you to define the render pattern used to display a field's data under specific circumstances. For instance, one of the patterns determines the appearance of data when the field is a column header. Moreover, the XML defines the variable properties. For example, the `Text` field type not only contains text, but it also supports constraints such as the text's maximum length. The property schema is where you enter a value for the variable property, such as `MaximumLength`. Sometimes you need more than a text box to enter variable data of custom properties. In these situations you can use an external editor. This is another ASCX user control, invoked by clicking an ellipses button. See Chapter 7 for more details about such definitions.

The object model provides access—albeit read-only access—to the field type and column definitions via the `SPFieldTypeDefinition` class.

SharePoint defines all field types available out of the box in a file `FLDTYPES.XML` in the same location.

The following example shows both—the field definition as well as a small portion of code that renders a view partially using dynamic expressions:

```
<FieldTypes>
    <FieldType>
        <Field Name="TypeName">Counter</Field>
        <Field Name="TypeDisplayName">$Resources:core,fldtype_counter;</Field>
        <Field Name="InternalType">Counter</Field>
        <Field Name="SQLType">int</Field>
        <Field Name="ParentType"></Field>
        <Field Name="UserCreatable">FALSE</Field>
        <Field Name="Sortable">TRUE</Field>
        <Field Name="Filterable">TRUE</Field>
        <RenderPattern Name="HeaderPattern">
          <Switch>
             <Expr><Property Select='Filterable'/></Expr>
             <Case Value="FALSE"></Case>
             <Default>
                <Switch>
                     <Expr><GetVar Name='Filter'/></Expr>
                     <Case Value='1'>
                         <HTML><![CDATA[<SELECT id="diidFilter]]></HTML>
                         <Property Select='Name'/>
                              <HTML><![CDATA["TITLE=]]></HTML>
                              <HTML>"$Resources:core,501;</HTML>
                         <Property Select='DisplayName' HTMLEncode='TRUE'/>
                              <HTML><![CDATA[" OnChange='FilterField("]]></HTML>
                              <GetVar Name="View"/>
                              <HTML><![CDATA[",]]></HTML>
                              <ScriptQuote>
                                <Property Select='Name' URLEncode="TRUE"/>
                              </ScriptQuote>
                               <HTML>
                                 <![CDATA[,this.options[this.selectedIndex].value,
                                          this.selectedIndex);' dir="]]></HTML>
                               <Property Select="Direction" HTMLEncode="TRUE"/>
```

```
                                        <HTML><![CDATA[">]]></HTML>
                                        <FieldFilterOptions
                                           BooleanTrue="$Resources:core,fld_yes;"
                                           BooleanFalse="$Resources:core,fld_no;"
                                           NullString="$Resources:core,fld_empty;"
                                           AllItems="$Resources:core,fld_all;">
                                        </FieldFilterOptions>
                                        <HTML><![CDATA[</SELECT><br>]]></HTML>
                                    </Case>
                                 </Switch>
                             </Default>
                        </Switch>
                 </RenderPattern>
         </FieldType>
</FieldTypes>
```

Content Types

Content types are designed to organize SharePoint content in a more meaningful way. A content type is a reusable collection of settings, features, and metadata that you can apply to a certain category of content. They manage metadata and extend the concept of lists and libraries with another level of abstraction.

Their main benefit is that content types enable you to add different types of items to the same library and still be able to handle the data in a structured way. This aids with organizing data in some kind of a matrix rather than flat tables. A mathematician would say that it adds another dimension to the organization structure. A content type includes different columns for metadata and can have different workflows assigned to it. Chapter 4 includes an overview of defining and using content types.

The Object Model at a Glance

Figure 2–7 shows the classes closely related to the `SPContentType` base class.

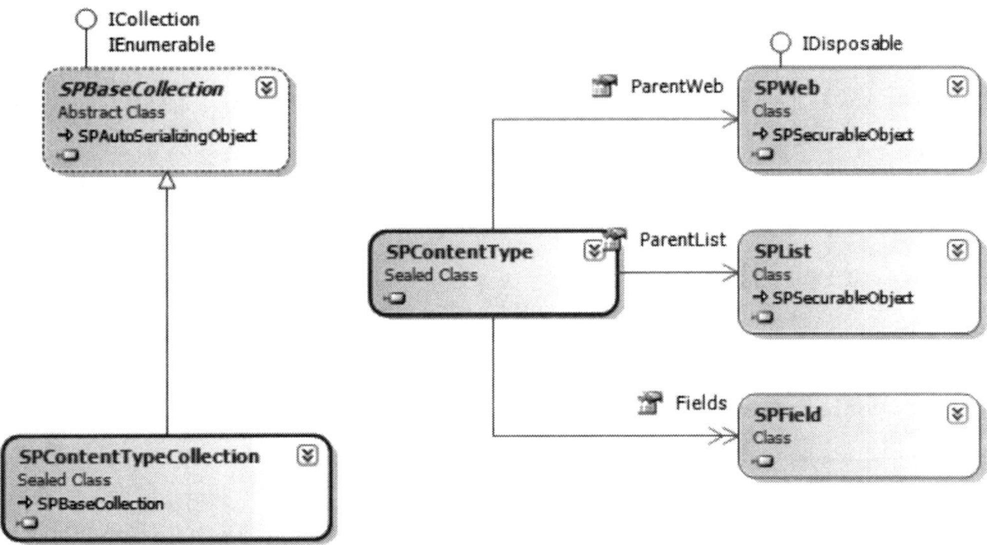

Figure 2–7. Significant classes related to the SPContentType type

Configuring Content Types

Custom content types can be part of any feature you deploy. Their basic configuration is via XML. Usually this is included with definitions of list templates and lists using this content type. However, it's possible to define the content type on its own, to allow for reuse.

A typical schema example looks like this:

```
<?xml version="1.0" encoding="utf-8" ?>
<Elements xmlns="http://schemas.microsoft.com/sharepoint/">
    <ContentType ID="0x0100E26A05B64C8B4e96A9B0461156806FFA"
        Name="Vehicle Data"
        Group="$Resources:List_Content_Types"
        Description="Store vehicle information of all kind."
        Version="0">
        <FieldRefs>
            <FieldRef ID="{CC5A31EF-CCD5-4ed4-A691-1C26DD405864}" Name="Brand" />
            <FieldRef ID="{B1105775-D16E-42ea-ABA1-1C26DD405864}" Name="Year" />
            <FieldRef ID="{6CC4C31C-AA19-43de-2009-1C26DD405864}" Name="Model" />
        </FieldRefs>
    </ContentType>
</Elements>
```

As you can see, the content type can't define columns directly. Instead, the `<FieldRef>` elements reference to some site columns, defined elsewhere. In custom list definitions, this can look like this:

```
<?xml version="1.0" encoding="utf-8" ?>
<Elements xmlns="http://schemas.microsoft.com/sharepoint/">
<Field ID="{CC5A31EF-CCD5-4ed4-A691-1C26DD405864}"
```

```
        Name="Brand"
        SourceID="http://schemas.microsoft.com/sharepoint/v3"
        StaticName="Brand"
        Group="Vehicle Information"
        Type="Text"
        DisplayName="Brand" />
<Field ID="{B1105775-D16E-42ea-ABA1-1C26DD405864}"
        Name="Year"
        SourceID="http://schemas.microsoft.com/sharepoint/v3"
        StaticName="Year"
        Group="Vehicle Information"
        Type="Text"
        DisplayName="Year" />
<Field ID="{6CC4C31C-AA19-43de-2009-1C26DD405864}"
        Name="Model"
        SourceID="http://schemas.microsoft.com/sharepoint/v3"
        StaticName="Model"
        Group="Vehicle Information"
        Type="Text"
        DisplayName="Model" />
</Elements>
```

In Chapter 7 you will find more information about the definition schema for site columns and content types.

Queries and Views

Defining the structure and storing data puts the items into the database. Queries and views are used to retrieve it. A query is a straightforward way to execute a data retrieval clause. It is very similar to an SQL statement. In fact, internally, with some steps removed from your code, an SQL statement is sent to the database.

In SharePoint you can use LINQ to SharePoint to execute queries. They are compiled into Collaborative Application Markup Language (CAML) queries and translated internally into SQL. You can also write and execute CAML directly. This is faster but more complicated and error prone than using LINQ.

Chapter 4 contains a comparison of all the data retrieval techniques.

A view defines a combination of UI (render) instructions and a query. A view always contains a query, while a query does not necessarily need a view. Figure 2–8 shows the interface users use to select the current view.

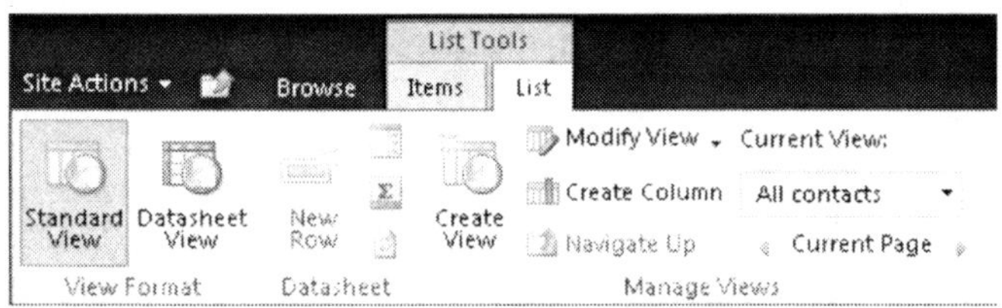

Figure 2–8. *The interface that users use to create, modify, and select views*

On the server side, the Microsoft.SharePoint.SPQuery class represents a query. Its Query property contains a CAML string that defines the query. You can pass the query object to the GetItems method of a list to get a collection of items that satisfy the query conditions.

From the client side, a similar CamlQuery type exists in Microsoft.SharePoint.Client and for JavaScript in the SP namespace, respectively.

For views, SPView represents a view of list data. A view contains a query. The Views property of SPList provides access to the list's SPViewCollection. This assumes that a list can have as many views as you need. In the client object model, the type SP.View exists. The SPViewFieldCollection type represents the collection of fields that are returned in a view. Furthermore, the SPViewStyle type contains a view style. The ViewStyles property of SPWeb provides access to the SPViewStyleCollection for a web site. View styles are defined globally in this XML file:

```
%Program Files%\Common Files\Microsoft Shared\Web Server
Extensions\14\TEMPLATE\GLOBAL\XML\VWSTYLES.XML
```

View styles determine the default formatting of a view. Lists are usually shown as tables, while contacts can appear in a boxed format like cards. View styles define such formats.

You can define views associated to a list in XML. The view can contain XSLT code to define how the data will be rendered. This is usually used to deploy complex lists.

Instead of using CAML and invoking queries directly, the LINQ to SharePoint provider simplifies working with large data structures. The provider is an object-relational mapping (ORM) between the content database and the SharePoint application. The SPMetal.exe tool creates a proxy from existing lists that contain a typed object model. This model is based on the DataContext class. The class contains code for querying and updating the content databases. It also supports sophisticated object change management. The EntityList<T> object represents a list that can be queried, and SubmitChanges writes changes to the content database.

Lookup relationships can exist between lists. These relationships can be one-to-one, one-to-many, and even many-to-many. EntityRef<T> is a reference on the "one" side, while EntitySet<T> is on the "many" side. Lookups in SharePoint can contain multiple values. Use the LookupList<T> class to represents the values of such a lookup field.

The Object Model at a Glance

Figure 2–9 shows the classes closely related to the `SPQuery` and `SPView` base classes.

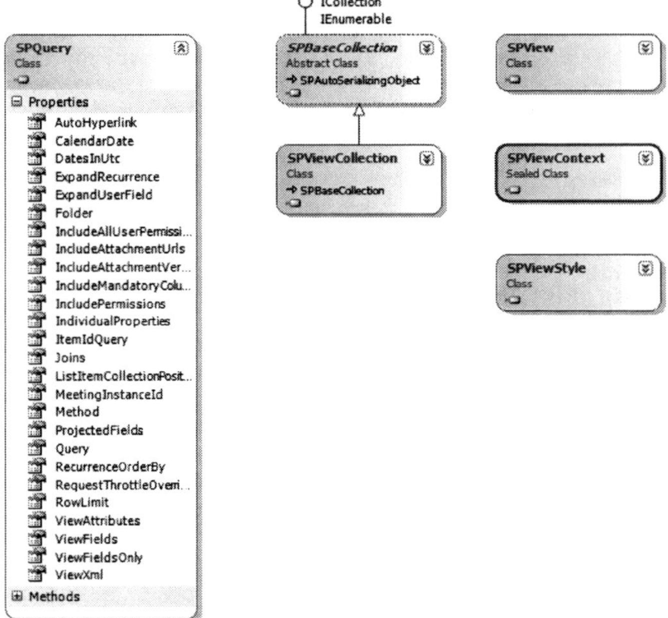

***Figure 2–9.** Significant classes related to the SPQuery and SPView types*

Configuring Queries

Queries use CAML. The corresponding schema is called a *query schema*; for views, there is a *view schema*. Both schemas are explained in Chapter 4.

A CAML query can look like this:

```
<Query>
  <Where>
    <Geq>
      <FieldRef Name="Expires"/>
      <Value Type="DateTime">
        <Today/>
      </Value>
    </Geq>
  </Where>
  <OrderBy>
    <FieldRef Name="Modified"/>
  </OrderBy>
</Query>
```

The view schema is more verbose. It supports control elements for conditional rendering and supports specific parts of the page explicitly. These include render instructions for the header, footer, groups, empty sections, and so forth.

The view definition code can contain HTML within CDATA (character data) elements to create the page's output.

```
<View Type="HTML" Name="Summary">
  <ViewBody ExpandXML="TRUE">
    <![CDATA[ <p><SPAN class=DocTitle><ows:Field Name="Title"/></SPAN>
      (<ows:Field Name="Author"/>, <ows:Field Name="Modified"/>)
      <ows:Limit><Field Name="Body"/></ows:Limit>
      </p>  ]]>
  </ViewBody>
  <Query>
    <Where>
      <Geq>
        <FieldRef Name="Expires"/>
        <Value Type="DateTime">
          <Today/>
        </Value>
      </Geq>
    </Where>
    <OrderBy>
      <FieldRef Name="Modified"/>
    </OrderBy>
  </Query>
  <ViewFields>
    <FieldRef Name="Summary"/>
    <FieldRef Name="Author"/>
    <FieldRef Name="Modified"/>
    <FieldRef Name="Body"/>
  </ViewFields>
</View>
```

As shown in the sample, the code can contain a query that filters the data further before it is displayed. Chapters 4 and 7 explain what to do with such a configuration and how to create it.

Deployment- and Maintenance-Related Building Blocks

Some parts of SharePoint are responsible for deployment of new functionality, called features. Features can be deployed using solutions, which have to provide everything an application might need. The structure they run in or build (define) consists of what SharePoint applications are—web sites and site collections.

Features

SharePoint is a highly extensible platform. To make extensions portable, the concept of features has been introduced. Features contain an XML file (`Feature.xml`) and one or more element files. These files describe the feature definition. Features contain all files required to get the extension running, such as templates and pages. They also come with assemblies that contain code for event handlers, workflows, and custom ribbons. Even support files such as images, CSS files, and JavaScript files are included in a feature.

Features appear in a specific scope, like a site or site collection. Features may depend on each other. For example, a feature for a site may require another feature on the site collection level. Other feature scopes are web and farm. From top to bottom, the scope levels are

- *Server farm*: The feature will be available in the server farm. This scope corresponds to the `SPFeatureScope.Farm` enumeration.
- *Web application*: The feature will be available in the web application. This scope corresponds to `SPFeatureScope.WebApplication` enumeration.
- *Site collection*: The feature will be available in a site collection. This scope corresponds to `SPFeatureScope.Site` enumeration.
- *Site*: The feature will be available in a single site. This scope corresponds to `SPFeatureScope.Web` enumeration.

■ **Caution** Note the discrepancies between the enumeration values and the scope names.

Features are typically activated by an administrator of the associated scope. During their activation or deactivation, a feature receiver can invoke code. For any change of the feature's state, such as activating, deactivating, uninstalling, or upgrading, the feature receiver's event handler can launch custom code.

Even features can be manipulated using the object model. This includes finding information, retrieving a list of installed features, and determining dependencies. The `Microsoft.SharePoint` namespace contains the `SPFeature` class. One `SPFeature` object represents one feature. A collection of features is stored in an `SPFeatureCollection` object. The `SPFeatureCollection` can be reached via the `Features` property on the `SPWebService`, `SPWebApplication`, `SPSite`, and `SPWeb` objects, depending on the scope of the feature. If a feature appears in the collection, it has been activated for the specified scope. That means that there is no activation method—adding the feature to the scope's container activates it. The `SPFeatureProperty` object represents a single property of an `SPFeature` object. Because there are multiple properties, they are stored in an `SPFeaturePropertyCollection` object and returned through the `Properties` property of the `SPFeature` object. If a feature depends upon another feature, an `SPFeatureDependency` object contains the associated information. Such dependencies can handle multiple types of data, which is why an `SPFeatureDependencyCollection` stores a collection of objects. You can use the `ActivationDependencies` property of the `SPFeatureDefinition` object to define that a feature depends on another one. For example, a feature on the site level may install particular Web Parts, while a feature on web level may install pages that use those Web Parts. The `Microsoft.SharePoint.Administration` namespace contains the `SPFeatureDefinition` class, which represents the base definition of a feature, including its name, scope, ID, and version. A collection of feature definitions is stored in an `SPFeatureDefinitionCollection` object. It can be accessed via the `FeatureDefinitions` property of the `SPFarm` or `SPSite` objects.

The `SPElementDefinition` class represents an abstract element that is provisioned when a feature is activated or used. The collection of elements is stored in an `SPElementDefinitionCollection` object and can be accessed using the `GetElementDefinitions` method of the `SPFeatureDefinition` class. Elements can be some types of objects, such as files.

The Object Model at a Glance

Figure 2–10 shows the classes closely related to the SPFeature base class.

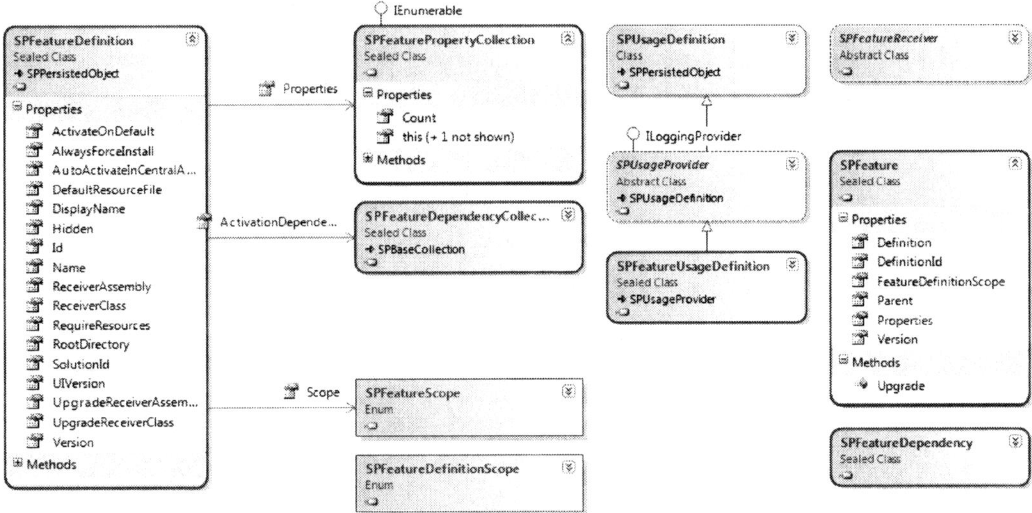

Figure 2–10. Significant classes related to the SPFeature type

Configuring Features

Features are defined by XML files to aid in deployment. You need at least two files: `feature.xml` and an element manifest file, which can have any name. These files define scope, dependencies, and related files. The `feature.xml` file specifies the location of assemblies, files, dependencies, and properties that the feature supports. A basic `feature.xml` file has the following form:

```
<Feature Title="Feature Title"
         Scope="FeatureScope"
         Id="GUID"
         xmlns="http://schemas.microsoft.com/sharepoint/">
  <ElementManifests>
    <ElementManifest Location="ElementManifestFile.xml" />
  </ElementManifests>
</Feature>
```

See Chapters 7 and 9 for more information about creating and using feature definition files.

Solutions

A feature extends an existing SharePoint installation. Site definitions are another distributable item, as are Web Parts. A complete installation may be provided as a solution and packed into a solution package (`.wsp`) file. Such a package contains a data definition file (DDF) and is compressed using the CAB file format. The API, enhanced with several tools, provides support for creating, deploying, and upgrading existing solutions to the servers of a farm.

In SharePoint 2010 there are two types of solutions: *sandboxed* and *full trust*. A SharePoint installation contains a gallery to store solutions for further installation and activation. Sandboxed solutions run with lower trust for hosted environments and secured production servers, and when testing foreign solutions.

■ **Tip** We recommend always creating sandboxed solutions. Always run production code as a sandbox whether it is self-hosted (on-premise) or uploaded to an online facility. Avoid Visual Web Parts and other project types that don't support sandboxed solutions.

A sandboxed solution uses a subset of features of the object model. When uploading a sandboxed solution, a *validator* can check the validity of the package. The farm's administrator can restrict allowed solutions to sandboxed solutions to protect the servers from malicious code. In contrast, full-trust solutions have access to the complete object model, and yet are deployed directly to the farm's servers.

Solutions can be administered using the object model. This includes deploying, upgrading, and removing solutions. You can also define solution validators and set usage limits for sandboxed solutions through the object model.

All solutions share some common objects. The `SPSolution` class represents a solution on a server farm. If all the solutions of a farm are retrieved, an `SPSolutionCollection` object is returned. Solutions can be localized. The language pack for a solution is held in an `SPSolutionLanguagePack` object, and if you support multiple languages, an `SPSolutionLanguagePackCollection` object is employed.

Sandboxed solutions use another part of the object model. The `SPUserSolution` class represents a sandboxed solution and `SPUserSolutionCollection` a collection of such objects. If the solution is blocked for some reason, it is copied to an `SPBlockedSolution` object. As well as exposing built-in validators, the `SPSolutionValidator` base class provides support for custom validators.

The Object Model at a Glance

Figure 2–11 shows the classes tightly related with the `SPSolution` base class. The sandboxed solutions have some additional types related to the `SPUserSolution` base classes.

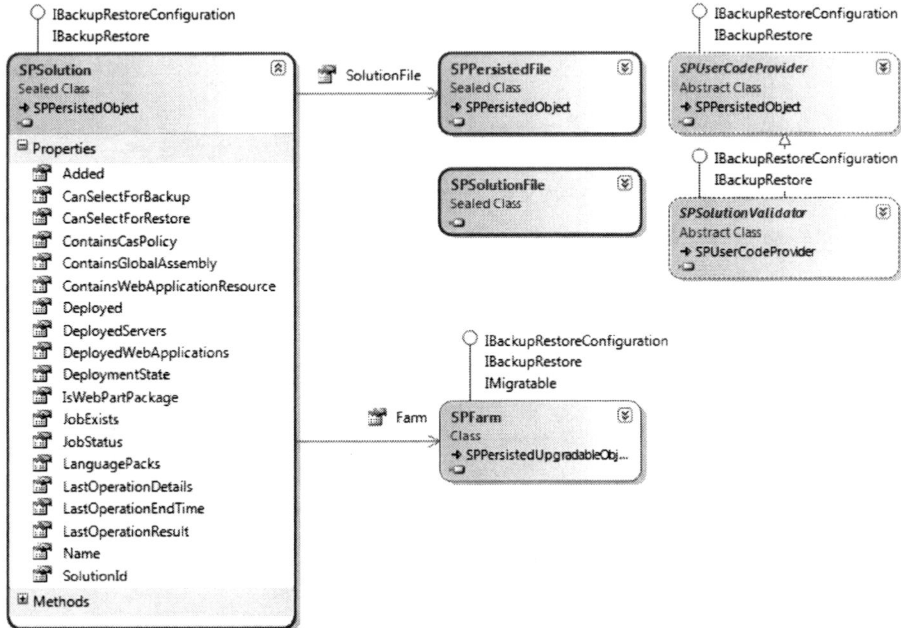

Figure 2–11. Significant classes related to the SPSolution type

Configuring Solutions

As in the previous sections, several XML files play a role in defining solutions. A solution is configured by a manifest file named `manifest.xml`. The solution manifest is stored at the root of the solution package and referenced from `feature.xml`. This file defines the features, site definitions, resources, and assemblies within the package.

```
<Solution SolutionId="SolutionGuid"
          xmlns="http://schemas.microsoft.com/sharepoint/">
  <FeatureManifests>
    <FeatureManifest Location="FeatureLibrary\feature.xml"/>
  </FeatureManifests>
  <TemplateFiles>
    <TemplateFile Location="ControlTemplates\Template.ascx"/>
  </TemplateFiles>
  <RootFiles>
    <RootFile Location="ISAPI\MyWebService.asmx">
  </RootFiles>
  <Assemblies>
    <Assembly DeploymentTarget="GlobalAssemblyCache"
```

```
              Location="ms.samples.sharepoint.myFeature.dll"/>
  </Assemblies>
</Solution>
```

Additionally, the DDF is required to create a complete package. It looks like this:

```
.OPTION EXPLICIT
.Set CabinetNameTemplate=MySolutionFile.wsp
.set DiskDirectoryTemplate=Setup
.Set CompressionType=MSZIP
.Set UniqueFiles="ON"
.Set Cabinet=on
.Set DiskDirectory1=Package
build\manifest.xml manifest.xml
build\MySolutionFile\feature.xml MySolutionFile\feature.xml
```

Again, Chapter 9 goes beyond these simple examples and explains how to distribute your code as a solution.

Web Sites and Site Collections

For end users organizing their applications, the top-level elements are site collections and sites. A site collection consists of a root web site and any number of child sites, which in turn can have child sites. Web sites contain lists, libraries, and elements used to support them, such as content types, custom fields, workflow instances, and more. Web sites can also contain application pages and Web Parts. The search engine can also search within the scope of a web site.

Web sites are containers for child web sites; hence, they build a hierarchy. The site collection is the root and is virtually a web site too. Elements available on a higher level or the root can be used deeper in the hierarchy. The site collection is typically used to store elements that all subsequent web sites share. Think of elements as Web Parts, list templates, themes, workflows, and features.

The security model is directly related to the site collection. Each site collection has its own administrator. Users can be assigned to a site collection as the highest available scope.

For developers, all parts of a web site are accessible through the API at runtime. The definition of a web site uses templates that contain several different types of XML files. A huge object model is available to deal with all the elements of a site collection and its child elements.

Firstly, the SPWeb class is the core type for web sites and site collections. It allows you to manipulate the look and feel of the web site and access a site's users and these users' permissions and alerts. Using an SPWeb object you can also open and modify galleries of list templates and Web Parts. Many of the child elements in the site, such as its child sites, lists, list templates, and content types, are collections that can be reached via properties of the SPWeb class. For objects that allow modification, the Update method writes changes back to the database.

One crucial thing is to get a reference to an SPWeb instance, because this type provides a bunch of basic properties that gain access to related objects, such as lists. Typically, you use the SPSite class to instantiate the root site collection address and open an SPWeb instance using OpenWeb. Site collections are represented by objects of the SPSite class. It has members that you can use to manage child objects, including features, subsites, solutions, and event receivers. As with the SPWeb type, there are multiple ways of getting a reference to an SPSite object.

Getting a reference to any of those objects is different from other classes, because these objects are primary ones that don't have parents. If you are running inside a SharePoint application, a Web Part, or an event receiver, you can use the current context to retrieve the site:

```
SPSite site = SPContext.Current.Site;
```

If your code runs in an application page (ASPX) and you only have the regular ASP.NET context (HttpContext), you can use the SPControl class instead:

```
SPSite site = SPControl.GetContextWeb(this.Context);
```

This code assumes that you're inside the System.Web.UI.Page class instance, and this.Context references the current page's context. If you inherit your application page from either UnsecuredLayoutPageBase or LayoutsPageBase, you can get an SPWeb instance from the Web property:

```
SPWeb web = this.Web;
```

■ **Caution** All of these methods use internal code to return SPSite and SPWeb instances. You're not supposed to dispose of or close any of these objects because the source instance takes care of this. Doing so results in unpredictable behavior.

The root web can be obtained using this code:

```
SPWeb root = SPContext.Current.Site.RootWeb;
```

Sometimes you need to go back from the current web to a higher level, such as the site or farm. The SPSite object gives direct access via the context's Site property:

```
SPFarm farm = SPContext.Current.Site.WebApplication.Farm;
```

The SPContext type does not exist in any application that runs outside SharePoint, such as a console application. In the case of a console application, you must access the site by calling the server:

```
SPSite site = new SPSite("http://myserver/site");
```

Here it's your responsibility to dispose of the site object, as there is no parent instance that can control this:

```
using (SPSite site = new SPSite("http://myserver/site"))
{
  // your code here
}
```

To get any web in the site collection, you can use the OpenWeb method like this:

```
using (SPWeb web = site.OpenWeb("webname"))
{
  // your code here
}
```

The using statement assures an implicit call to SPWeb's Dispose method. Chapter 3 discusses this and dives deeper into the various object creation and disposal methods.

The Object Model at a Glance

Figure 2–12 shows the classes closely related to the SPWeb and SPSite base classes.

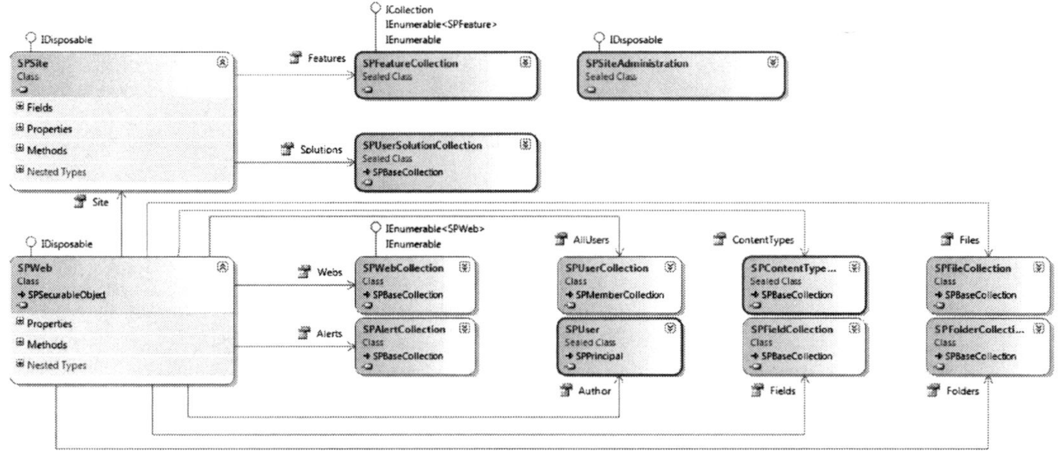

Figure 2–12. *Significant classes related to the SPSite and SPWeb types*

Configuring Sites and Site Collections

As for other elements, CAML is used to specify site definitions. Two types of files are required for site templates: WebTemp*.xml and Onet.xml.
The WebTemp*.xml file resides in the following directory:

```
%ProgramFiles%\Common Files\Microsoft Shared\web server extensions\14\
                TEMPLATE\<LCID>\XML\
```

The placeholder <LCID> is the numerical ID of the culture. Table 2–3 shows some common LCIDs.

Table 2–3. *Common LCID Values*

Language/Culture	LCID
English	1033
German	1031
Italian	1040
Spanish	3082
French	1036
Chinese (traditional)	2052
Chinese (simplified)	1028
Japanese	1041
Korean	1042

The markup contains templates and options from which the user creating a site from this template can choose.

As mentioned, you also need another essential file called `ONET.xml`. It resides in the following directory:

```
%ProgramFiles%\Common Files\Microsoft Shared\web server extensions\14\
               TEMPLATE\SiteTemplates\<SiteType>\XML\
```

The `<SiteType>` placeholder is the name of a site definition, such as internal ones like `STS` or `BLOG`. The markup provides metadata about the site type. It also itemizes and defines the lists, modules, and features that comprise the site type.

Site definitions are not the only way to define and distribute sites. Site definitions are intended to create an element chosen from administration and used to create several new sites from the same definition for subsequent customization.

Alternatively, there are site templates. Those templates are exported and stored as solution files (`.wsp`), and can be used to transfer templates from one server to another. The storage of solution templates as `.wsp` is new in SharePoint 2010—the former `.stp` format is still supported but deprecated.

Building Blocks to Create the UI

The UI is not just a collection of controls. Many parts of SharePoint offer extensible interfaces, a wide range of predefined elements, and comprehensive support for many devices.

■ **Note** Among the various building blocks, there is one especially for mobile controls. This book doesn't cover mobile controls and devices, and therefore we skip the definition. If you need information about this topic, please refer to `http://msdn.microsoft.com/en-us/library/ee536690(office.14).aspx`.

Pages and UI Support Elements

SharePoint is a web application, and such an application consists of pages. There are content pages that present lists and libraries, support pages that contain common functions (e.g., file upload), application pages that contain custom code, and master pages that define a common UI around all other types of pages.

Among the supported elements, you'll find everything you need to define a unique UI, including themes and CSS.

Content Pages

Content pages are any pages already used in a SharePoint application as part of the site definition. Users can change content pages using SharePoint Designer or Visual Studio, and even edit them using the embedded editors, such as the Web Part editor. Several common files (e.g., `AllItems.aspx`) are content pages. Unmodified content pages are stored in the file system and called *unghosted* or *uncustomized*. Customizing such pages transfers them into the database, and they become *ghosted*.

Caution Customizing server files to change them server-wide is not recommended. Instead, a better approach is to change master pages or add customized master pages to change the look and feel in your farm's applications.

Using Code in Pages

Content pages are ASPX pages, and are therefore intended to contain custom code. However, because end users can distribute such pages, and active code can potentially harm a server's reliability, there are several security restrictions. As a general rule, inline code is not supported within a custom content page. You are supposed to use code-behind classes to provide code to content pages to overcome this restriction. A special configuration section, `<SafeControls>`, defines the controls permitted on content pages.

To prevent users from uploading Web Parts containing harmful custom code, the code portion must be explicitly registered in the `<SafeControls>` section. Otherwise, SharePoint will not execute it. As a general rule you should avoid custom code in content pages. However, internal pages can execute code at any time. If you create a new site definition using modified content pages with custom code, they will execute just fine. If a user later modifies those pages, making them ghosted, the code will no longer execute. To avoid this confusing behavior you should not use custom code in common content pages.

However, as with most other extensible parts on ASP.NET, the administrator of a farm can override this behavior by configuring the Virtual Path Provider. This provider is responsible for retrieving the page from wherever it is stored (file system or database) and handing it over for execution. The following definition in `web.config` enables the execution of server-side code:

```
<SharePoint>
   <SafeMode ...>
    <PageParserPaths>
      <PageParserPath VirtualPath="/_mpg/*"

                      CompilationMode="Always"
                      AllowServerSideScript="true"

                      IncludeSubFolders="true"/>
   </PageParserPaths>
```

If you plan to create complete applications using code, using application pages is much more powerful and less confusing.

Application Pages

Application pages are regular ASPX pages that behave similarly to any other ASP.NET page. However, they run inside the context of SharePoint and have full access to the object model. The only restriction is that unlike content pages,[1] application pages cannot host SharePoint Web Parts zones. Application pages usually reside in a subfolder under the following base path:

```
%ProgramFiles%\Common Files\Microsoft Shared\web server extensions\14\
               TEMPLATE\LAYOUTS
```

---

1. Content pages are pages within SharePoint that usually reside in the database.

Chapter 3 contains a more detailed introduction to the world of application pages. For SharePoint developers, it's one of the most powerful ways to create sophisticated applications.

Master Pages

Master pages define a common layout for all other pages. You can change the look and feel and customize the UI just by changing the master page. A master page contains *placeholders*, which will be filled with controls by content and application pages. When a page is executed, the server first combines the master and the page into a final page. A master page can contain other master pages to form a hierarchy to accommodate complex scenarios. This includes a master that defines a global navigation, and another master that defines a subnavigation within this frame.

The default global master is named `v4.master`; `.master` is the common file extension for all ASP.NET master pages. You can find the global master page in

```
%ProgramFiles%\Common Files\Microsoft Shared\web server extensions\14\
             TEMPLATE\GLOBAL
```

In a SharePoint installation you can handle many master pages in custom galleries. This allows centralized administration and easy reuse in multiple sites.

■ **Note** Using master pages is a core concept for code reuse, consistent look and feel, easy maintenance, and centralized customization. As a general rule you should always use master pages, even for a single application page.

You can find more about master pages in Chapter 10.

Ribbon

The ribbon extends the UI and unifies the look and feel between SharePoint and Office products. A ribbon consists of tabs, and each tab contains groups of related UI elements called controls. The ribbon is stabler than a traditional menu or toolbar and makes it easier for a user to find a specific control. Several controls, such as drop-down lists, check boxes, and buttons, avoid the need for pop-up dialogs—meaning fewer clicks to accomplish an action. Context-sensitive controls are displayed in a tab with a highlight color at the end of the ribbon's tab row for rapid identification.

Ribbons reside in the rendered page only. While they can be configured and created on the server, you can use JavaScript on the client side to interact with ribbons via a large object model.

Use the `IRibbonMenu` interface to implement a new ribbon on the server. Within the ribbon you deal with menus, defined by `SPRibbonMenu`, and menu items, defined by `SPRibbonMenuItem`. Each control within a menu can issue a command, based on an `SPRibbonCommand` object.

On the client side, the `SP.Ribbon.PageManager` class is the entry point. To handle commands, the `CUI.Page.CommandDispatcher` and `CUI.Page.PageCommand` classes are used.

As a developer you can customize the ribbons of common pages. You can also create completely new ribbons for your application pages. We cover this in depth in Chapter 7.

The Object Model at a Glance

Figure 2–13 shows the classes closely related to the SPRibbon base class.

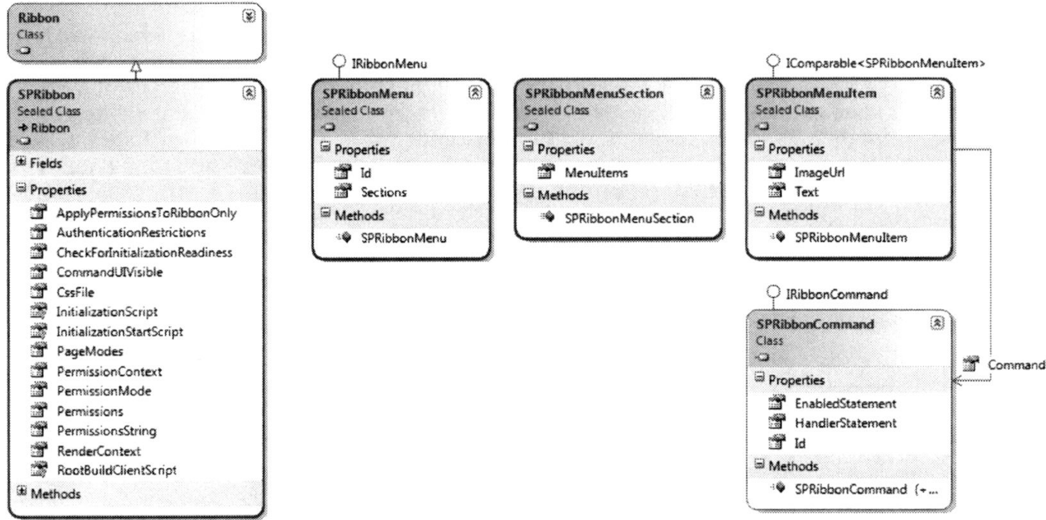

Figure 2–13. Significant classes related to the SPRibbon type

Configuring a Ribbon

Like most of the building blocks, a ribbon is also defined via XML. The following example shows such a definition:

```
<?xml version="1.0" encoding="utf-8"?>
<Elements xmlns="http://schemas.microsoft.com/sharepoint/">
  <CustomAction
    Id="Ribbon.WikiPageTab.CustomGroupAndControls"
    Location="CommandUI.Ribbon"
    RegistrationId="100"
    RegistrationType="List">
    <CommandUIExtension>
      <CommandUIDefinitions>
        <CommandUIDefinition
          Location="Ribbon.WikiPageTab.Groups._children">
          <Group Id="Ribbon.WikiPageTab.CustomGroup"
                 Sequence="55"
                 Description="Apress Group"
                 Title="Apress Group"
                 Command="EnableApressGroup"
                 Template="Ribbon.Templates.Flexible2">
            <Controls Id="Ribbon.WikiPageTab.CustomGroup.Controls">
              <Button
                Id="Ribbon.WikiPageTab.CustomGroup.Controls.CustomButton1"
```

```
                Command="CustomButtonShowAlert"
                Image16by16="/_layouts/images/FILMSTRP.GIF"
                Image32by32="/_layouts/images/PPEOPLE.GIF"
                LabelText=""
                TemplateAlias="o2"
                Sequence="15" />
            </Controls>
          </Group>
        </CommandUIDefinition>
       </CommandUIDefinitions>
      <CommandUIHandlers>
        <CommandUIHandler Command="EnableApressGroup" />
        <CommandUIHandler Command="CustomButtonShowAlert"
                          CommandAction="javascript:alert('Hello Apress!');" />
      </CommandUIHandlers>
    </CommandUIExtension>
  </CustomAction>
</Elements>
```

As you can see, it's neither trivial nor easy, but it's flexible enough to drive even an ambitious project.

Web Parts

Web Parts are probably SharePoint's most well-known component. SharePoint Web Parts are built on top of ASP.NET Web Parts, and share the same behavior and interfaces. Several built-in Web Parts plus an enormous list of third-party offers constitute a rich pool of powerful controls. A Web Part is simply a control you can place on a page. Web Parts can contain code, and can do everything from displaying a simple image to managing complex nested lists. Web Parts can interact through data connection interfaces. However, the most important feature is that end users can add, remove, and customize Web Parts without any coding, and without asking permission of an administrator or developer.

The object model mostly uses ASP.NET code, and is slightly extended to integrate well with SharePoint. The `WebPartManager` tracks the current state of the Web Parts on a page. This class provides the required JavaScript libraries, because Web Parts are managed on the client side. Within a page, one or more zones can be defined where the user can place Web Parts. The `WebPartZone` object creates such zones.

The Object Model at a Glance

Web Parts are one of the main types of controls that developers produce. Please refer to Chapter 3 for a comprehensive introduction, along with object class models and examples. When searching for more information, remember that Web Parts are plain ASP.NET controls, and the whole infrastructure resides in the `System.Web.UI.WebControls.WebParts` namespace, not `Microsoft.Sharepoint`.

Configuring Web Parts

Web Parts are defined with XML. The XML contains the information required to render it on the page and create the executable code. A sample XML file looks like this:

```
<?xml version="1.0" encoding="utf-8" ?>
<webParts>
  <webPart xmlns="http://schemas.microsoft.com/WebPart/v3">
    <metaData>
      <type name="TypeName, Version=VersionNumber, Culture=neutral,
```

```
                  PublicKeyToken=PublicKeyToken" />
      <importErrorMessage>Cannot import this Web Part.</importErrorMessage>
    </metaData>
    <data>
      <properties>
       <property name="Title" type="string">WebPart's Title</property>
       <property name="Description" type="string">WebPart's Description</properties>
    </data>
  </webPart>
</webParts>
```

This XML contains the fully qualified name of the assembly that holds the Web Part's code. Web Parts can be exported and imported into another site by the user. If a Web Part import fails due to missing dependencies, the `importErrorMessage` tag is displayed. The `<properties>` section is a bag that can contain any property supported by the basic `WebPart` object.

In Chapter 3 you'll find a complete description of Web Parts.

Web Parts and Security

The advantages of Web Parts—being accessible to and manageable by end users—are at the same time their biggest disadvantages. Importing a Web Part containing executable code opens a barn door–wide security hole in SharePoint. Therefore, you must register any Web Part in the central `web.config` file, which an end user can't access. The following `<SafeControl>` element shows such an entry:

```
<SafeControl Assembly="AssemblyNameWithoutDLLExtension,
   Version=AssemblyVersionNumber, Culture=neutral, PublicKeyToken=PublicKeyToken"
   Namespace="NamespaceOfYourProject" TypeName="*" Safe="True" />
```

Even the assembly registered here can face further security restrictions that follow the common code security model provided by the .NET Framework. SharePoint is built on top of this model. For example, the administrator can restrict the ability of assemblies to access the server's hard disks. The keyword here is *Code Access Security (CAS)*. We'll cover this in Chapter 3 in more detail.

Control Flow, Action, and Events

These blocks provide dynamic action to your application. Whenever an event occurs, your code is called. You can, for example, achieve a higher level of customization by doing something with the data before or after internal operations. Using alerts, users can interact closely with the system. Alerts extend the event model to the outside world, primarily by sending fragments of information by e-mail or text message (Short Message Service [SMS]). Workflows provide a higher level of control over the behavior of a whole application, using conditions and loops to define sequences of actions.

Event Handling

Creating interactive applications requires code that executes if a specific event occurs. In SharePoint, event receivers are used to create event handlers. It is a loosely coupled model. Lists or features can fire an event, and as a result, code executes somewhere. That's because SharePoint objects are often created using the UI, and there is nowhere suitable for attaching an event handler. Receivers are event handlers that can be attached by configuration through internal mechanisms.

For the `SPWeb` class you can define event receivers using the `SPWebEventReceiver` type, while the `SPList` object has an `SPListEventReceiver` type. To implement an event receiver, you inherit from one of these base classes or from their common base class, `SPEventReceiverBase`. The custom class has to be registered with the event source and a specific scope.

Event handlers are part of their designated source. All objects that support events have a corresponding event receiver, following the naming scheme *<Object>*`EventReceiver`, where *<Object>* is something like `SPList`, `SPWeb`, or `SPWorkflow`. However, there are some nasty exceptions to this rule. For example, the event receiver for features is named `SPFeatureReceiver`, not "SPFeatureEventReceiver" as you might expect.

Event receiver types are associated with property bags providing access to various properties. Event property bags follow a similar naming scheme to the events itself, using the suffix `EventProperties`. This reads as `SPWebEventProperties`, `SPListEventProperties`, and so forth.

The Object Model at a Glance

Figure 2–14 shows the classes closely related to the `SPEventReceiverBase` classes.

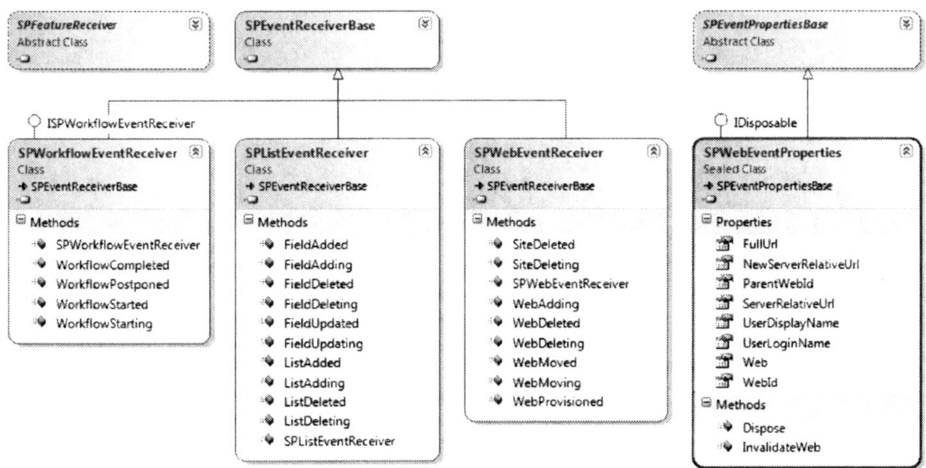

***Figure 2–14.** Significant classes related to the SPEventReceiverBase type*

The `SPWorkflowEventReceiver` class is defined in the `Microsoft.Sharepoint.Workflows` namespace, while all others are in the default `Microsoft.Sharepoint` namespace.

Registering an Event

Even events can be registered using XML files. Event receiver definitions are part of a feature, and therefore they are defined using the Feature Schemas XML. Typically, this looks like this:

```
<Elements xmlns="http://schemas.microsoft.com/sharepoint/">
  <Receivers
    ListTemplateOwner="ADDABAAA-1111-2222-3333-111111111111"
    ListTemplateId="104">
    <Receiver>
      <Name>SimpleUpdateEvent</Name>
      <Type>ItemUpdating</Type>
      <SequenceNumber>10000</SequenceNumber>
      <Assembly>SimpleUpdateEventHandler, Version=1.0.0.0, Culture=neutral,
              PublicKeyToken=10b23036c9b36d6d</Assembly>
```

```
      <Class>Apress.Samples.SimpleItemUpdateHandler</Class>
      <Data></Data>
    </Receiver>
  </Receivers>
</Elements>
```

This code defines a receiver that's associated with a list and coded in the specified assembly. Each receiver has several distinct methods, such as `Adding` (before item is added), `Added` (after item is added), `Deleting` (before item is deleted), `Deleted` (after item is deleted), and so forth. You can simply override the particular method of the base class, and SharePoint will call this method if the event occurs.

Alerts

Events within a web site are restricted in their reach. If you want to inform users about an event that occurs, writing something on a web site can only inform those users currently on the site. To overcome this limitation, SharePoint can reach the outside world through e-mail or SMS, or via other Office servers. Alerts define such transmissions. They operate at the item or list level.

The object model has several types to support alerts. The `SPAlert` class represents an alert, and includes such information as whether it is an e-mail or another message type, the template used, the alert frequency, and which user created the alert. To support reusability, the `SPAlertTemplate` class can define the content and format of an alert in a template format, such as the styles and rendering for e-mail alerts. The `SPAlertEventData` class is a container for information about an alert event. To define alerts in a more customizable way, use the base interface `IAlertNotifyHandler` for handling alert-sending events and `IAlertUpdateHandler` for handling changes that are made to an alert's definition.

The Object Model at a Glance

Figure 2–15 shows the types closely related to the `SPAlert` class. Note that the `SPAlert` class is sealed and can be used as is.

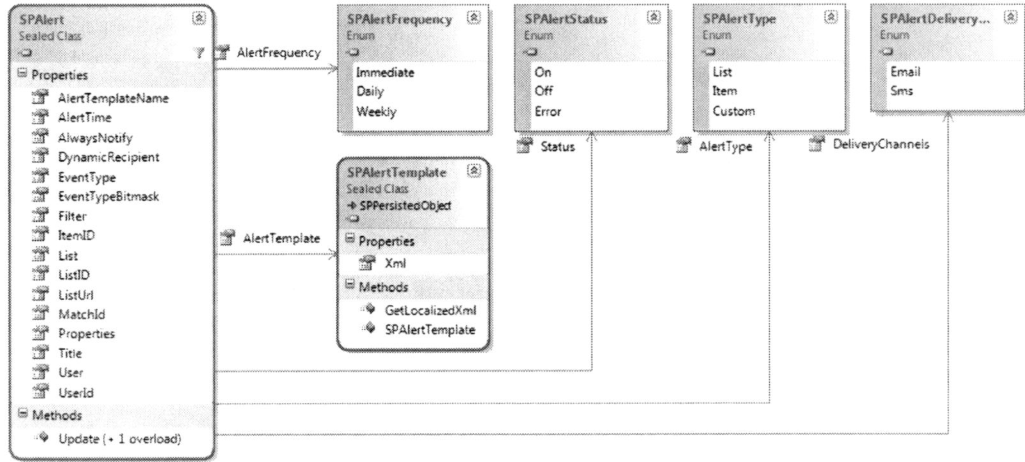

Figure 2–15. *Significant classes and enums related to the SPAlert type*

Registering an Alert

Because alerts communicate with the outside world, you need to specify a template. The templates define the layout of e-mails, along with placeholders and rules, to format the messages appropriately. Two template files, `AlertTemplates.xml` and `AlertTemplates_SMS.xml`, are located in the following folder:

```
%ProgramFiles%\Common Files\Microsoft Shared\web server extensions\14\Template\XML
```

You cannot change these files, but you can override any template with a template of your own. A `stsadm` command or corresponding `PowerShell` call overwrites the default template with your customized version, and that file is then stored in the configuration database.

Workflows

If a SharePoint application provides support for business processes, a workflow can control the flow of data. SharePoint uses the Windows Workflow Foundation (WF) engine. A workflow has a trigger point where it starts and an execution engine that tracks the state. The workflow consists of activities that execute predefined or custom code. In a graphical designer, such activities are often called *shapes*, as they represent specific steps in the flow. Shapes clarify the workflow's behavior and meaning for businesspeople.

Workflows gather information from users and data stores while running. The UI can be any list or library, an application page, or even an InfoPath form. Forms associated with a workflow expose their data to the flow for further processing.

As with any other component, you can use the object model to work with workflows. While the underlying engine uses WF, SharePoint extends it in several namespaces:

- `Microsoft.SharePoint.Workflow`: Contains the base classes and main entry points for developing custom workflows
- `Microsoft.SharePoint.Workflow.Application`: Contains three-stage workflow classes that are built into SharePoint
- `Microsoft.SharePoint.WorkflowActions`: Contains the workflow actions or activities that are included with SharePoint
- `Microsoft.SharePoint.WorkflowActions.WithKey`: Contains mirror classes that access workflows by using a string identifier

You can use the workflow designer in Visual Studio to build complex and highly customized workflows by dragging shapes onto the design surface to represent a business process. After that, they can be configured and programmed to execute specified code.

Please refer to Chapter 16 for an in-depth description.

The Object Model at a Glance

Figure 2–16 shows the classes closely related to the SPWorkflow base classes.

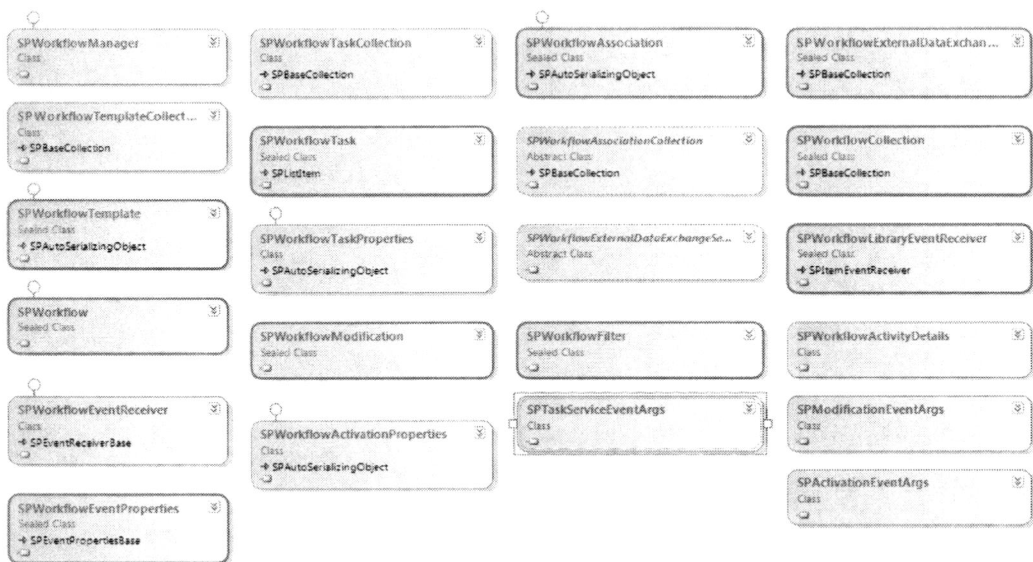

Figure 2–16. Significant classes related to the SPWorkflow type

Configuring Workflows

Workflows are associated with a list or library that provides an action to launch the workflow. The following code defines such an association.

```
<Elements xmlns="http://schemas.microsoft.com/sharepoint/">
   <Workflow Name="Moderation" Description="A standard WSS Moderation Workflow"
             TemplateBaseId="681127D0-0919-416a-945B-05F1643C07E2"
             WorkflowClass="Microsoft.SharePoint.Workflow.SPModerationWorkflow"
             WorkflowAssembly="Microsoft.SharePoint, Version=12.0.0.0,
                               Culture=neutral, PublicKeyToken=94de0004b6e3fcc5"
             CodeBesideClass="Unused"
             CodeBesideAssembly="Unused"
             HostServiceClass=
                      "Microsoft.SharePoint.Workflow.SPModerationHostServices"
             HostServiceAssembly="Microsoft.SharePoint, Version=12.0.0.0,
                                 Culture=neutral, PublicKeyToken=94de0004b6e3fcc5"
             EngineClass="Microsoft.SharePoint.Workflow.SPModerationEngine"
             EngineAssembly="Microsoft.SharePoint, Version=12.0.0.0,
                            Culture=neutral, PublicKeyToken=94de0004b6e3fcc5" >
      <Metadata>
       <Instantiation_FormURN>test.urn</Instantiation_FormURN>
      </Metadata>
```

```
  </Workflow>
</Elements>
```

A workflow is coded in an internal or custom assembly, which must reside in the GAC. You can find an in-depth description in Chapter 16.

The Administrative Object Model

SharePoint has APIs for more than just applications. Even administrative tasks, such as those in Central Administration or in tools like stsadm, rely on an API.

In this section you'll find the basic programming methods used for administrative functions. These include an introduction to the object model and its structure. This is accompanied by several links to the official documentation on MSDN. The types and classes discussed here are used for maintenance purposes, such as adding servers to a farm, creating sites programmatically, or checking the state of the content database.

Overview of Namespaces

The SharePoint object model consists of approximately 50 public namespaces (several more used internally) in a dozen assemblies that are used in SharePoint sites on the server that is running SharePoint Services. A complete list can be found here: http://msdn.microsoft.com/en-us/library/ms453225(office.14).aspx.

Namespaces and classes that support access to the whole farm, its servers, the webs, and the sites defined there are part of the administrative view. Administration utilities usually complement users by building sites and applications and maintaining them, and help administrators manage huge installations. Such tools are built using the administrative API. End user–driven applications are not likely to use such classes much. This section gives an overview of the administrative object model. In Chapter 17, we're going to show some typical administrative tasks with code examples.

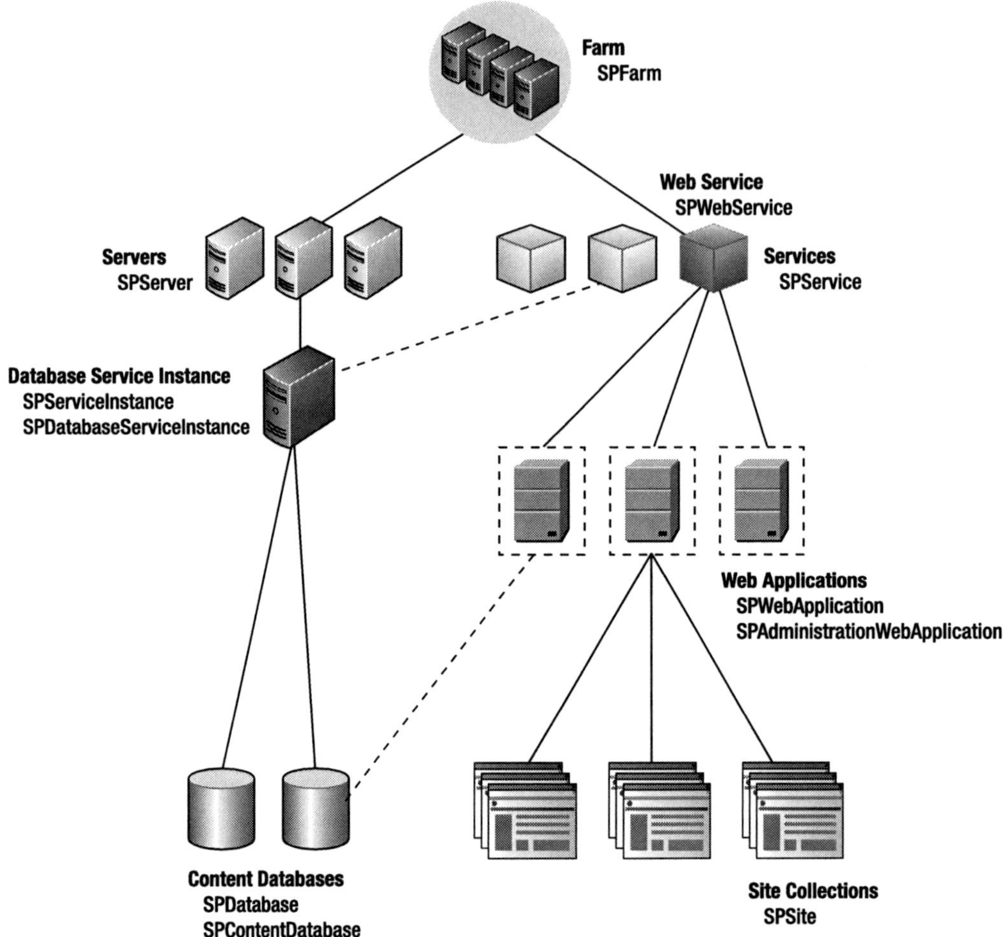

Figure 2–17. *The objects of the Administration namespace and their relationships*

An Administrative View

SharePoint offers a highly structured server-side object model that makes it easy to access objects that represent the various aspects of a SharePoint web site. You can drill down through the object hierarchy from higher to lower levels to obtain the object that contains the members you need to use in your code.

In this section we discuss the administrative aspects. These are the objects used to create the Central Application and several administration tools. You can use these classes to create your own tools, automate tasks, and extend the behavior of your distributed packages.

The Database Architecture

SharePoint has a two-pronged database architecture. There is one central configuration database and one or more content databases (see Figure 2–18). The configuration database contains references to such objects as

- Sites
- Content databases
- Servers
- Web applications

All objects that require persistence in the database inherit from the `SPPersistedObject` base class. They are stored with others in the Objects table.

Each content database exists once per web application. Sites can use multiple content databases to increase scalability. The databases store content and the following types of objects:

- Service details
- The structure of a site collection
- User content
- Files
- Security information

Session state information of additional services of the Enterprise version, such as Excel services and InfoPath forms services, are also stored in a service database.

The search database is separate to improve scalability and ease of management. You set search databases through configuration. They typically contain the following:

- Search data
- History log
- Search log
- Crawl statistics data
- Link tables and statistical tables

Index databases are stored in the file system and bound to the configuration database. If the configuration is part of a backup, this relationship ensures that the index files are saved too.

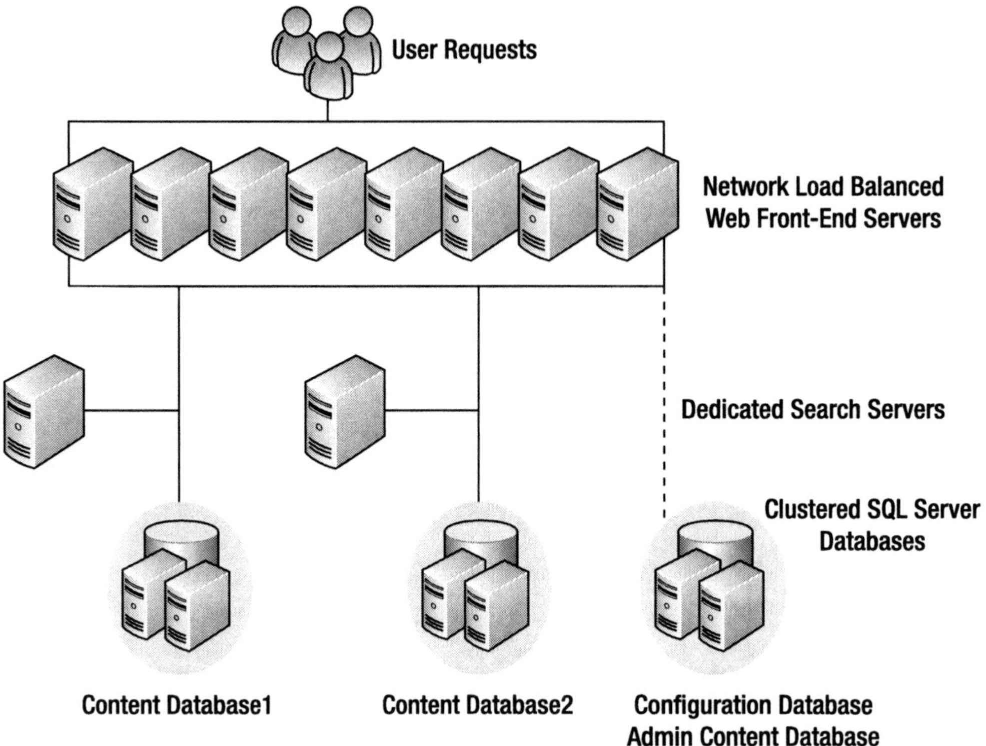

Figure 2–18. *Databases in a SharePoint farm*

Any part of SharePoint that runs custom code has access to the database server. Therefore, several applications use their own databases to store private data. These databases can be registered in the configuration and become part of the infrastructure tasks, such as backup and restoration.

The Server Architecture

Figure 2–19 shows the SharePoint server architecture for the collections and objects of the `Microsoft.SharePoint.Administration` namespace.

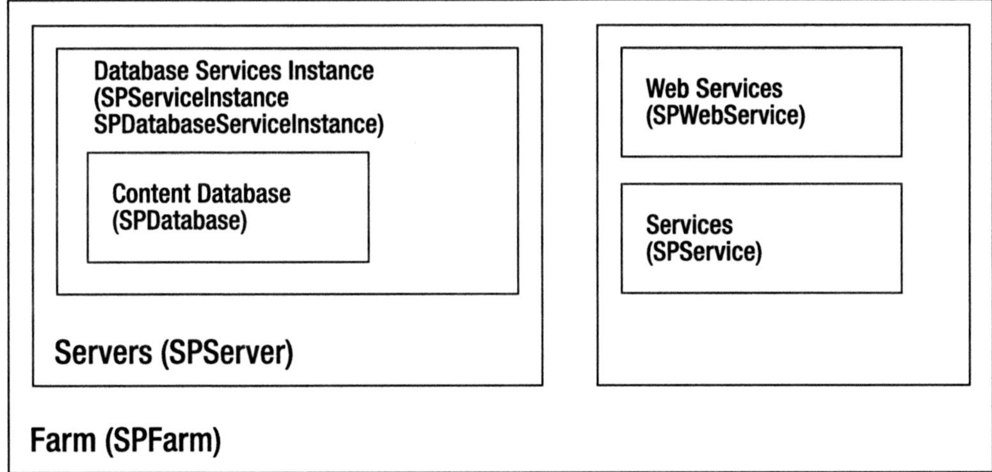

***Figure 2–19.** Top-level objects for administration functions*

The `SPFarm` object is the root object within the SharePoint object model hierarchy. Its `Servers` property contains a collection representing all the servers in the environment, and similarly the `Services` property has a collection representing all the services. Each physical server computer is represented by an `SPServer` type. The `ServiceInstances` property provides access to the set of individual service instances that run on the individual computers, each as an `SPService` type.

Each `SPService` object represents a logical service or application installed in the server farm. A service object provides access to farm-wide settings of the load-balanced service that a respective service instance implements. Derived types of the `SPService` class include, for example, objects for Windows services, such as the timer service, search, Microsoft SQL Server, the database service, and objects for web services.

An `SPWebService` object provides access to configuration settings for a specific logical service or application. Its `WebApplications` property gets the collection of web applications that run the service.

An `SPDatabaseServiceInstance` object represents a single instance of a database service running on the server computer. The `SPDatabaseServiceInstance` class derives from the `SPServiceInstance` class and thus inherits the `Service` property, which provides access to the service or application that the instance implements. The `Databases` property gets the collection of content databases used in the service. The web application forms another hierarchy that parallels the physical elements (see Figure 2–20).

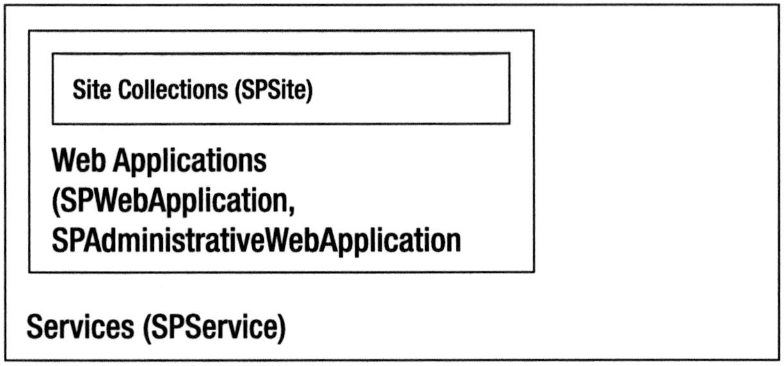

Site Collections (SPSite)

Web Applications (SPWebApplication, SPAdministrativeWebApplication

Services (SPService)

Figure 2–20. Administration objects, from web applications down to sites

Each SPWebApplication object represents a load-balanced web application based on IIS. The SPWebApplication object provides access to credentials and other server farm–wide application settings. The Sites property contains the collection of sites or site collections within the web application, and the ContentDatabases property is a collection of content databases used in the web application. The SPWebApplication class replaces the obsolete SPVirtualServer class, but it can still be helpful to think of an SPWebApplication object as a virtual server—that is, a set of one or more physical servers that appear as a single server to users.

An SPContentDatabase object inherits from the SPDatabase class and represents a database that contains user data for a SharePoint web application. The Sites property gets the collection of sites or site collections for which the content database stores data, and the WebApplication property gets the parent web application.

An SPSite object represents the collection of site collections within the web application. The Item property or indexer gets a specified site collection from the collection, and the Add method creates a site collection within the collection.

Working with Top-Level Objects

You can get the current top-level server farm object as follows:

```
SPFarm myFarm = SPContext.Current.Site.WebApplication.Farm;
```

If your application does not run inside the context of a SharePoint site, you have to retrieve the Site object based on its URL:

```
SPSite mySiteCollection = new SPSite("AbsoluteURL");
```

To return the top-level web site of the current site collection, use the RootWeb property:

```
SPWeb topSite = SPContext.Current.Site.RootWeb;
```

The SPContext class does not limit you to getting the current object of any given type. You can use the Microsoft.SharePoint.SPSite.AllWebs property to obtain a reference to any other web site than the current one. The following code returns the context of a specified site by using an indexer with the AllWebs property:

```
SPWeb webSite = SPContext.Current.Site.AllWebs["myOtherSite"];
```

■ **Caution** You should explicitly dispose of references to objects obtained through the AllWebs property. There are a number of nuances to best practices with regard to when objects should and should not be disposed of. In Chapter 3 you'll find a thorough explanation about the disposal issue.

Finally, to get a reference to either the server farm or the current physical server, you can use the static properties Microsoft.SharePoint.Administration.SPFarm.Local or Microsoft.SharePoint.Administration.SPServer.Local.

```
SPFarm myFarm = SPFarm.Local;
```

To use either of the Local properties, you must add a using directive for the Microsoft.SharePoint.Administration namespace.

Site Architecture

The following diagram shows the SharePoint site architecture in relation to the collections and objects of the Microsoft.SharePoint namespace.

Each SPSite object, despite its singular name, represents a set of logically related SPWeb objects. Such a set is commonly called a site collection, but SPSite is not a typical collection class, like SPWebCollection. Instead, it has members that can be used to manage the site collection. The AllWebs property provides access to the SPWebCollection object that represents the collection of all web sites within the site collection, including the top-level site. The Microsoft.SharePoint.SPSite.OpenWeb method of the SPSite class returns a specific web site. You'll learn later that there are numerous ways to open and access a web application.

Each site collection includes any number of SPWeb objects, and each object has members that can be used to manage a site, including its template and theme, as well as to access files and folders on the site. The Webs property returns an SPWebCollection object that represents all the subsites of a specified site, and the Lists property returns an SPListCollection object that represents all the lists in the site (see Figure 2–21).

Each SPList object has members that are used to manage the list or access items in the list. The GetItems method can be used to perform queries and retrieve items from the list. The Fields property of an SPList returns an SPFieldCollection object that represents all the fields, or columns, in the list, and the Items property returns an SPListItemCollection object that represents all the items, or rows, in the list.

Each SPField object has members that contain settings for the field. Each SPListItem object represents a single row in the list.

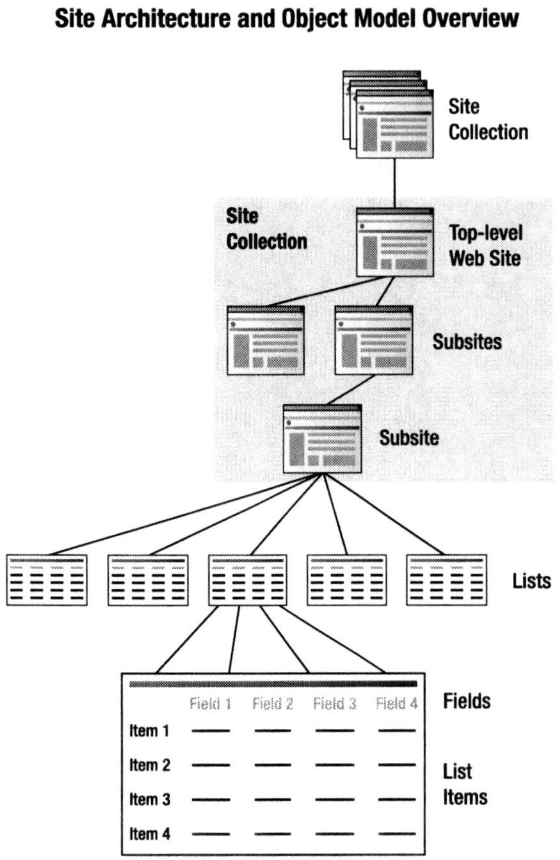

Site Architecture and Object Model Overview

Figure 2–21. *Object hierarchy from site collection down to list*

The Administrative Server Object Model Organization

After the administration object overview, what follows is a more structured view. When working with the objects described earlier, you will see several relationships and dependencies between the objects. To understand the various hierarchies, three different conceptual views are possible:

- Physical hierarchy
- Content hierarchy
- Services hierarchy

These views provide entry points into the object model. Some classes overlap the hierarchies and appear multiple times. Of course, they exist only once in the assemblies and namespaces. The hierarchies presented here are used only to explain the relationships between the objects.

Physical Hierarchy

The physical hierarchy (see Figure 2–22) contains objects that exist physically (e.g., the farm itself and the servers within the farm, as well as the folders and files containing the actual data). The *farm* term is always relevant, even if you have just one single server. In this case, this single server represents the farm.

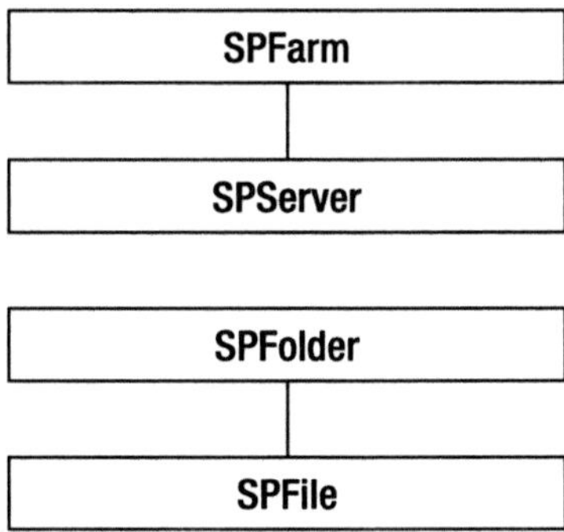

Figure 2–22. *Hierarchy of physical objects*

The term *physical object* does not necessarily mean that the objects exist separately on disk. SharePoint stores all objects in the content database. You may consider a physical object as something that might exist (such as a server machine) or that can be stored elsewhere (such as a file).

The `SPFarm` object is the top-level object in the hierarchy. You'll quite often start here to get access to various subobjects. Running an application on one of the servers, the `Local` property returns the farm object:

```
SPFarm myfarm = SPFarm.Local;
```

The `SPFarm` class has three child classes: `SPServer`, which represents a single server within the farm; `SPService`, which gives access to the farm's services; and `SPSolution`, which is used to deploy something to the farm. `SPFarm` is closely related to the configuration database. For instance, the `DisplayName` property of the `SPFarm` object returns the name of the configuration database. Like many other objects, `SPFarm` inherits from `SPPersistedObject`, which means the object's data is persisted in the configuration database. That's the reason so many objects have static properties returning useful information without any visible connection to other objects. They simply pull the data from the configuration database. (See the section "The Database Architecture" for more information about the configuration database.)

The `SPServer` class represents a physical server or machine.

■ **Note** Virtualization doesn't matter for the object model. A physical machine is everything running its own operating system, whether it's a box or just an instance of Hyper-V.

Typical properties of an `SPServer` object are the IP address (`Address` property) and the `Role` property. `Role` returns an enumeration of type `SPServerRole`:

- `Application`: The server runs a web application.
- `Invalid`: The server has not yet registered any role in the configuration database.

- SingleServer: The server is the only server in the farm (also called single-server installation).
- WebFrontEnd: The server is a regular front-end server in the farm.

As for SPFarm, the SPServer object has a static property, Local, that represents the local machine:

```
SPServer myserver = SPServer.Local;
```

Using the constructor with a server's address, you can instantiate any server's object from

```
SPServer myserver = new SPServer("myfarm-dev64");
```

SPServer's ServicesInstances property returns all its services. This includes SharePoint's Windows and web services.

Content Hierarchy

The content hierarchy (see Figure 2–23) contains classes that deal with the content the user stores in a SharePoint application. Most of the objects are containers that store other objects. The top level starts with the SPWebApplication class and steps all the way down to the SPField object, which contains data entered in a single field by an end user.

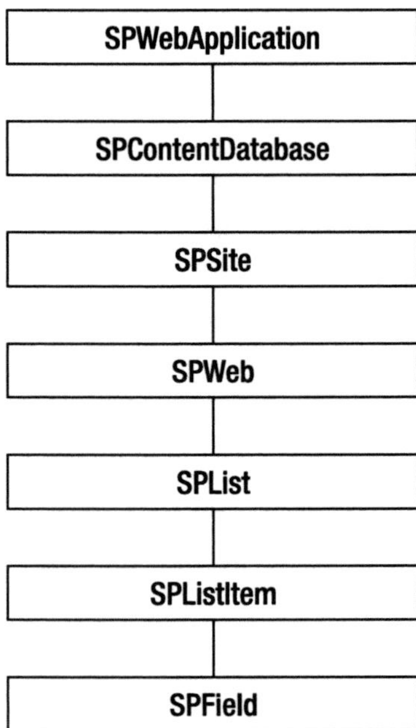

Figure 2–23. *Hierarchy of content objects*

The top-level object, SPWebApplication, represents a whole application. Usually this object is directly related to at least one content database. (See the section "The Database Architecture" for more information.) SPWebApplication inherits from SPWebService, because an application is treated internally like a service. The ContentDatabases property returns a collection of content database represented by

SPContentDatabase objects. Each web application is hosted in IIS; hence, the IisSettings property gives convenient access to the settings without needing a connection to IIS. Similarly, the ApplicationPool property gives access to the application pool. SPWebApplication is another object that inherits from SPPersistedObject, meaning that the object's data is persisted in the configuration database.

You can get an SPWebApplication object by different methods. Within a SharePoint application, you can use the current context:

```
SPWebApplication web = SPContext.Current.Site.WebApplication;
```

From anywhere else, such as a console application, use the following:

```
SPWebApplication web = new SPSite("http://myserver/site").WebApplication;
```

You've already learned that any request is handled by an ASP.NET application and represented by an HttpApplication object. SharePoint has its own implementation, SPHttpApplication, which is tightly coupled to SPWebApplication. Each web application runs its own SPHttpApplication object.

The content stored with the features provided by a web application is held within one or more content databases. Each database object has, along with the web application object, references to one or more SPSite objects. There is no physical difference between a site and a site collection. A site collection just contains other sites. It's still exposed as an SPSite object. A collection of sites can be represented by an SPSiteCollection object. Hence, sites form a hierarchy, whose top object is called the *root*. To indicate the root, the RootWeb property returns true for that site. The corresponding AllWebs property returns a collection of all subsites. Besides the confusing usage of the terms *web* and *site*, the model is quite helpful for administrative tasks. The root web object has its own type, SPWeb. Even webs can form a hierarchy; therefore, an SPWeb object can contain other SPWeb objects. It can also be the child of an SPSite object.

CONFUSING NAME RESOLVER

The naming of sites, site collections, and webs, together with the ability to make hierarchies out of them, causes some confusion. Moreover, the names used in Central Administration do not necessarily match those used for classes. A brief review of history may help to clarify this. In the first version of SharePoint Team Services, a site collection was simply called a site. This is usually an abbreviation for *web site*, and this is what confuses us. In SharePoint, a site (read: collection) is meanwhile a container of webs. Since the time of SharePoint Team Services, the corresponding class has been called SPSite. The webs in this class are represented by the class SPWeb.

You can read SPSite as "site collection," or "a *site* that has a *collection* of webs." Vice versa, you can read SPWeb as "a collection of pages" or "web site."

If IIS is introduced, things become even more bewildering. An SPWebApplication object in SharePoint is the containing instance for sites. In IIS it's what is named "web site." Hence, if you create a "web application" in SharePoint, a new "web site" is created in IIS that contains a hierarchy of site collections that contain webs. Hopefully, this clarifies the issue.

Because site collections are just containers, they must have at least one web. This is the root web that is shown at the top of a page in the breadcrumb navigation. This tight relationship between a site collection and its root is another snag. However, at the end of the day you come down to pages. If you think in terms of pages, the SPWeb object is the final container for them. Pages are ASPX files stored in the application's content database. Pages form the representational layer on which UI objects are exposed. Pages contain Web Parts, such as grid views that show list content, and simple published content. If you drill further down from the SPWeb level, the content is not stored as pages. It's stored in lists (SPList) containing items (SPListItem) or files (SPFile), and is organized using field definitions (SPField). Items in a list that's defined as a document library can be published as pages, but that's another subject.

Services Hierarchy

All services have the SPService base class. The most confusing thing here is that both Windows services and web services inherit from same base class. Moreover, the SharePoint-specific services, such as incoming e-mail, are in the same class hierarchy. This is another class that inherits from SPPersistedObject, ensuring persistence in the configuration database. The class provides members that return the assigned and currently running jobs. Most services process jobs in a queue. A service can have multiple instances. The Instances property returns them, and the SPServiceInstance class defines the objects representing an instance. An instance can be started or stopped.

WHERE HAS THE SHARED SERVICES PROVIDER GONE?

The Shared Services Provider (SSP) is finally gone. It has been replaced with a new concept called the *Services Architecture*. The services discussed in this section cover this as well. Your SharePoint installation will not have a separate SSP site, as previous versions did. You can now manage all of your familiar services, such as Search, BCS, and Excel Services, directly through Central Administration on the new Manage Service Application page.

Unfortunately, the term *service* is highly overused. In this case it does not refer to a WCF, web, or Windows service—it refers to the actual program that provides functionality used by other parts of the installation. A *service application* consists of the executable and the appropriate configuration on the farm. The provider of the service supplies you with a *service application proxy* to program against. This is an assembly that interacts with the service via WCF. If the service application is installed on multiple servers in the farm, a built-in load-balancing scheme will distribute requests among the servers.

Effectively, the Services Architecture is a new pluggable architecture that makes it possible for third parties to create their own services. You can now publish specific services and consume specific services from remote farms, giving a bit more flexibility. To access services in code, use the ServiceContext object.

Several web services support features provided by the API as well. The major difference is that web services can be used remotely. The API access is only possible if the code is executed on the target machine. The internal services that SharePoint provides can be configured in several ways. These services are

- Web Application service
- Administration service
- Timer service
- Diagnostics service
- Central Administration service
- Search service
- Outgoing E-mail service

- Incoming E-mail service
- User Code service
- Database service

Front-end servers usually run services such as the Web Application service. Application servers with a dedicated function run the Search service, for instance. Depending on the entire farm configuration, the services spread across the farm. The criteria to let one or another service run on a specific machine depend on the expected performance and physical capabilities of the hardware. If you know that the Search service takes 80 percent of the CPU power, then it would be unwise to locate it on the same machine as the front-end server.

From the class model perspective, the services structure has five specific variants:

- Windows services (`SPWindowsService`)
- Web services (`SPWebService`)
- Diagnostic services (`SPDiagnosticService`)
- Outgoing E-mail services (`SPOutboundEmailService`)
- Incoming E-mail services (`SPIncomingEmailService`)

All these classes inherit from `SPService`.

To investigate the current configuration of all services within the farm, the following code snippet is helpful. It consists of a small console application:

```
SPServiceCollection services = SPFarm.Local.Services;
foreach (SPService service in services)
{
   SPRunningJobCollection runningJobs = service.RunningJobs;
}
```

Services provide specific functions. The execution can be scheduled by a job. A job can be launched by a timer—either regularly (e.g., every 12 hours) or at a specific time (e.g., Monday at 7:00 p.m.)—or triggered by an event. They execute either on one server or on several servers on the farm, depending on the purpose of the service.

Summary

This chapter provided you with the basic technologies used behind the scenes of SharePoint Foundation. Based on ASP.NET plus its Ajax implementation, SharePoint is built on top of a highly extensible platform.

The description of the building blocks lead you through the major pieces making up SharePoint. This included an overview of the various namespaces and classes for programmatic access. The subsequent chapters describe many of these classes, with examples.

An administrative overview showed the parts of SharePoint that help administrators and power users maintain the server landscape and manage settings and applications. The object model builds the foundation to create tools or extend existing ones.

CHAPTER 3

Accessing the API

In this chapter we explain the basic techniques for programming SharePoint. This includes

- Programming the SharePoint Server API—finding the entry points
- Where to find helper classes and utility methods
- Working with internal objects—object disposal and security
- The security model, the user and group objects, and how to use them
- Writing isolated applications that access the server API

Accessing the API is not like implementing an interface or calling a method. SharePoint is both a platform that provides a programming environment and a framework that supplies features to aid in building high-level applications.

Developers new to SharePoint often struggle to find the entry points to the API. Even advanced developers occasionally get lost in the hundreds of classes. For historical reasons, the framework is not as clear and well designed as the .NET Framework. However, it contains almost everything you need to perform infrastructure work with a few lines of code—if you can find the right class. In this chapter we introduce the indispensable helper and utility classes.

A framework with the complexity of SharePoint has several guidelines and conditions. In particular, the internal objects based on COM (Component Object Model) layers require careful disposal. Most applications have security implications. User management, roles, and groups are part of any distributed application. Learning how to manipulate such data as objects is essential for SharePoint developers. Using the API is not limited to web pages and Web Parts. You can actually program against SharePoint using any kind of application, including console applications, Windows Forms, Windows Presentation Foundation (WPF), and anything else .NET supports. We call this the *isolated programming style* to indicate that it's a program running outside the context of SharePoint. You will discover the special ways to access and properly use the API from such isolated applications.

Finding the Entry Points

Depending on the type of custom solution you are creating, you use different entry points into the object model to obtain the appropriate objects. If you are building a Web Part, a custom web service, or a web application to work with site collections, individual sites, or lists, you can use members of the `Microsoft.SharePoint.SPContext` class to obtain the current site collection, web site, or list. When you create a web application in the `/_layouts` virtual directory, its functionality becomes available to all sites on the web server. Outside of an HTTP context, such as in a console application or a Windows application, use a constructor of the `SPSite` class to obtain a specific site collection and to reach objects within the collection.

To work with SharePoint data, your code must first obtain a reference to the objects with which it will be working, including web sites, site collections, and web applications. The methods depend on the sort of application you create. As we focus in this book on extending SharePoint using web applications, we run most of our samples in the context of SharePoint as physical application pages. For information on how to run code outside this context, refer to the section "The Isolated Programming Style" later in this chapter.

Establishing the Site Context

To work with SharePoint from a browser-hosted application, your code must first establish the site context or site collection context for requests sent to the server.
In your code you need to obtain the HTTP context of the request. Microsoft recommends that you do this via the `Microsoft.SharePoint.SPContext` class and its members. To return the current site collection, you can use the `SPContext.Current.Site` property. The `Microsoft.SharePoint` namespace must be imported to use the required classes.

```
SPSite site = SPContext.Current.Site;
```

To return the web site of the current request, you can use `SPContext.Current.Web`:

```
SPWeb web = SPContext.Current.Web;
```

Alternatively, when your code is contained in an ASPX file, you can use methods of the `SPControl` object with the `System.Web.UI.Page.Context` property as the parameter. For example, use the `GetContextWeb` method to get a reference to the current web site.

```
SPWeb web = SPControl.GetContextWeb(Context);
```

Finally, if your ASPX page inherits from `UnsecuredLayoutsPageBase` or `LayoutsPageBase`, instead of `Page`, you can use the `Site` or `Web` properties of the former classes to obtain references to the current site collection or web site, respectively. Or you can use the `System.Web.UI.Page.Context` property as the parameter to the `GetContextWeb` and `GetContextSite` methods. `LayoutsPageBase` gives you some extra SharePoint-oriented functionality beyond what is available with `Page`—mainly in connection with managing user rights to the page. (We'll look into this in more detail in Chapter 8—in particular in the section "Application Pages.")
For example, the following code, when used in an ASPX page that inherits from `LayoutsPageBase` (or in the code-behind page), gets a reference to the current web site:

```
SPWeb web = this.Web;
```

The `Microsoft.SharePoint.WebControls` namespace is required to run this code.

■ **Caution** You may know that the `SPWeb` object, among several others, needs to be disposed of explicitly. That's true for the context-driven access methods. However, you should not dispose of any `SPSite` or `SPWeb` object obtained by any of the methods provided by `LayoutsPageBase` or `UnsecuredLayoutsPageBase`. Calling the `Dispose` or `Close` method of these objects will result in unpredictable behavior. The SharePoint runtime will dispose of them after page completion. (See the "Object Disposal Issues" section of this chapter for more details.)

Utilities, Helper Classes, and Support Classes

Programming the API is not limited to accessing the object model or manipulating data. SharePoint is a vast infrastructure framework and comes with a number of classes that provide basic utilities—helper classes to achieve common tasks or to support coders with predefined constant values. Several types inherit from or make use of corresponding classes from the ASP.NET namespaces. The intention is to deliver similar behavior within the context of the SharePoint environment. Developers new to SharePoint tend to overlook these classes and reinvent functionality they think is missing. The SharePoint framework actually provides such functions—the trick is to find them. In this section we give an overview and some pointers to the official documentation.

Examining the Namespaces

If you search within the `Microsoft.SharePoint` namespace for a letter sequence such as *Util*, you'll find these among all the others:

- `Microsoft.SharePoint.JsonUtilities`: Helper classes for encoding and decoding JSON. This assists when writing client-side code using the client object model.
- `Microsoft.SharePoint.Utilities`: Several classes that support many parts of SharePoint. The most common methods are explained following.

SPUtility Class Examples

Next, we'll give some examples that demonstrate the use of various helper functions. (There are more, but they can often be found in code snippets and throughout other chapters of this book.) The examples assume that the code runs within an application page that derives from `LayoutsPageBase` and exposes the current `SPWeb` object through the `Web` property.

Formatting a Date Using SPUtility.FormatDate

This method allows you to format a given date to any of the `SPDateFormat` types:

```
DateTime curDate = DateTime.UtcNow;
DateTime regionDate = Web.RegionalSettings.TimeZone.UTCToLocalTime(curDate);
string result = SPUtility.FormatDate(web, regionDate, SPDateFormat.ISO8601);
```

This code returns the same date value in the `regionDate` and `result` variables, even if the type is different. Both are converted from UTC to local time according to the regional settings for the specified web. `FormatDate` always expects to convert from UTC. The code snippet assumes this. If you instead provided `curDate` as the input, it would return the wrong value. ISO8601 formats the output to look like `2010-01-19T16:55:04Z`. You might consider putting this method into an extension method to convert date fields in lists:

```
public static class MySPExtensions
{
  public static DateTime GetDateAsIso(this SPListItem listItem,
                                      string fieldName,
                                      DateTime defaultVal)
  {
     SPWeb web = listItem.Web;
     try
```

```
        {
          if (String.IsNullOrEmpty(fieldName))
          {
             return defaultVal;
          }
          if (listItem[fieldName] == null)
          {
             return defaultVal;
          }
          DateTime curDate = Convert.ToDateTime(listItem[fieldName]);
          DateTime regionDate = web.RegionalSettings.TimeZone.UTCToLocalTime(
             web.ParentWeb.RegionalSettings.TimeZone.LocalTimeToUTC(curDate));
          return Convert.ToDateTime(SPUtility.FormatDate(web, regionDate,
                                    SPDateFormat.ISO8601));
        }
        catch (Exception exception)
        {
           Debug.Write(exception.Message);
        }
        return defaultVal;
    }
}
```

This code assumes that the list resides in a web, rather than a site collection (because of the call to `ParentWeb`). That is, however, easy to change. The intention is just to give you an idea of how to extend common classes with fragments pulled from utility classes.

Getting the 14 Hive File System Path

The following code returns the file system path for the 14 hive (SharePoint root), or any of the folders beneath it. This is typically—though not always—located at

```
C:\Program Files\Common Files\Microsoft Shared\web server extensions\14
```

The argument is any relative path beneath the root—for example:

```
string featurePath = SPUtility.GetGenericSetupPath("template\\features");
```

An empty string returns the root path itself:

```
string featurePath = SPUtility.GetGenericSetupPath("");
```

Getting the Full (Absolute) URL

Some objects expose relative paths. To convert a relative path to the full URL, you add the current server, site paths, and so forth. Rather than performing path manipulation, use the `GetFullUrl` method instead:

```
SPList list = Web.Lists["Authors"];
string listUrl = SPUtility.GetFullUrl(site, list.DefaultDisplayFormUrl);
```

The variable `listUrl` now contains something like this:

```
http://myserver/site/Lists/Authors/DispFormASPX
```

Redirecting to Another Page

Sending an HTTP redirect to the client's browser is a common task, and Response.Redirect is the standard method for doing so in ASP.NET applications. However, within the SharePoint environment, extra internal processing is required. Instead, use SPUtility.Redirect:

```
string url = "http://myportal/Test/Pages/results.aspx";
string queryString = "author=Joerg";
SPUtility.Redirect(url, SPRedirectFlags.Default, Context, queryString);
```

There is an overload that omits the queryString parameter. The SPRedirectFlags enumeration has these possible values:

- CheckUrl
- Default
- DoNotEncodeUrl
- DoNotEndResponse
- RelativeToLayoutsPage
- RelativeToLocalizedLayoutsPage
- Static
- Trusted
- UseSource

As the name implies, the enumeration is flagged and the values can be combined. However, not all possible combinations make sense. The next few working examples indicate how this works.

Handling the Source URL with UseSource

If UseSource is part of the flags parameter of the Redirect method, the URL to which the user is redirected will be read from the query string of the original request (from the context parameter). The new URL will be the value of one of these query string parameters:

- Source
- NextUsing
- NextPage

If one of these parameters has a value, the new URL will be validated. Validation is performed by the IsUrlSafeForRedirect method of the Request property of the current SPWeb object. The URL in the query string of the original request needs to be relative. If this URL is not valid, or the UseSource parameter resulted in an empty string, the Url parameter that was originally passed will be used.

Working with a Static URL

If Static is part of the flags parameter, the URL is considered relative. Depending on the presence of RelativeToLayoutsPage in the flags parameter, the URL is relative to the _layouts directory. This is where your application pages reside. If so, SharePoint checks the flags parameter for the presence of RelativeToLocalizedLayoutsPage. If this is also present, a new absolute URL to the localized _layouts folder is assembled. If not, the URL is assembled for the root of the _layouts folder. The localized _layouts folder is merely the folder followed by the current web's language. If required, the value of SPGlobal.ServerCulture.LCID is added to the URL. This is 1033 for English, for instance.

Creating an Absolute URL

If Static is not part of the flags parameter, the user will be redirected to the value of the Url parameter, after it is validated. If Trusted is part of the flags parameter, then the URL is always valid, and the validation is skipped. If Trusted is not specified, the outcome of the IsUrlSafeForRedirect method of the Request property of the current SPWeb determines whether or not the URL is recognized as valid.

URL-Encoding Operations

URLs may need encoding. If DoNotEncodeUrl is not present, the URL is first encoded using SPHttpUtility.UrlPathEncode. (For more information about SPHttpUtility, see the section "The SPHttpUtility Class.")

Redirection Examples

Redirecting from one page to another is a common task. The redirect is a special HTTP header (302 redirect) that is sent to the browser. This forces the browser to issue another request retrieving a new page—the one defined within the header. In SharePoint you have to handle internal disposal and cleanup routines. A "hard" redirect might produce unpredictable behavior. Therefore, the SPUtility.Redirect method is available to invoke a safe redirect.

Following are several examples. Each is a one-line call to SPUtility.Redirect.

```
SPUtility.Redirect("http://mysite", SPRedirectFlags.Default, HttpContext.Current);
```

If this line is called from a page with the address http://mynet/site/Pages/default.aspx, there is no redirect, because the second parameter indicates that the server address should be the same. Even a query string parameter, such as &Source=data, does not influence the outcome.

```
SPUtility.Redirect("/news", SPRedirectFlags.Default, HttpContext.Current);
```

If this line is called from a page with the address http://mynet/site/Pages/default.aspx, redirection to http://mynet/news will occur. The query string parameter has no influence at all.

```
SPUtility.Redirect("http://newsite", SPRedirectFlags.Static, HttpContext.Current);
```

Without a query string parameter, this code redirects. If the query string parameter contains a URL, such as http://newsite, it does not redirect because it expects a relative URL.

```
SPUtility.Redirect("http://newsite", SPRedirectFlags.UseSource,
                   HttpContext.Current);
```

This code redirects only if a query string parameter such as Source is present and it's relative. That means http://news/news does not redirect, while /news does. If the current site is http://mysite, it redirects to http://mysite/news and ignores the http://newsite instruction. This is obviously confusing and should be used in advanced scenarios only. If you want to redirect anyway, use this combination of flags:

```
SPUtility.Redirect("http://newsite",
                  SPRedirectFlags.UseSource | SPRedirectFlags.Trusted,
                  HttpContext.Current);
```

A URL such as this redirects to the site http://newsite:

```
http://mysite/site/Pages/default.aspx?Source=http://newsite
```

The same code redirects to http://intranet/news, if the current URL is

```
http://mysite/site/Pages/default.aspx?Source=/news http://intranet/news
```

Using the Trusted flag alone redirects to whatever is supplied in the first argument:

```
SPUtility.Redirect("http://newsite", SPRedirectFlags.Trusted, HttpContext.Current);
```

Working with application pages is common to many SharePoint applications. This code redirects to http://mysite/site/_layouts/demo.aspx:

```
SPUtility.Redirect("demo.aspx",
                   SPRedirectFlags.Static | SPRedirectFlags.RelativeToLayoutsPage,
                   HttpContext.Current);
```

Redirecting to SharePoint Success or Error Pages

These methods allow you to transfer the browser to the built-in error and success pages.

```
Exception ex = new Exception("Some error message");
SPUtility.TransferToErrorPage(ex.Message);
```

The TransferToErrorPage method has a second overload, in which you can specify the URL and text for a link that leads to a troubleshooting page (illustrated in Figure 3–1).

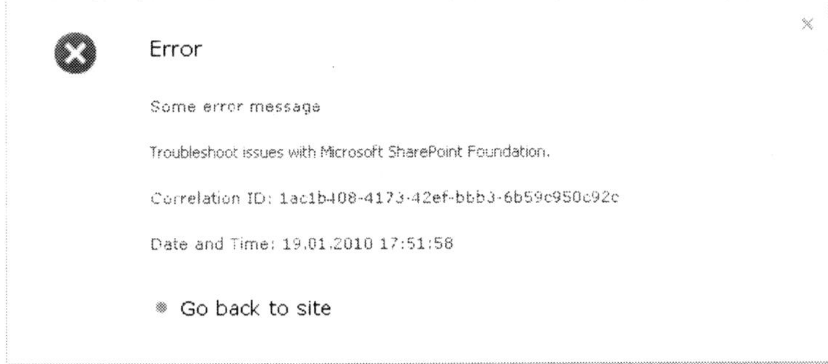

***Figure 3–1.** The built-in error page with a custom message*

You can also transfer to a success page (see Figure 3–2), and specify the URL to move to after OK is clicked by the user:

```
SPUtility.TransferToSuccessPage("Operation was completed", @"default.aspx", "", "");
```

The last two parameters seem to not have any effect.

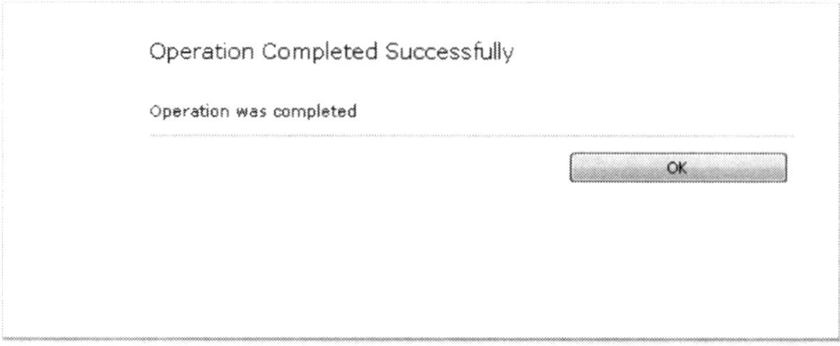

***Figure 3–2.** The built-in success page with a custom message*

The success page is not very impressive, but can save you some construction time.

Formatting Scalar Data

The SPUtility class comes with a few methods for formatting data. See **Table 3–1** for selected examples.

***Table 3–1.** Formatting Scalar Data Samples*

Method	Input	Output	Description
FormatSize	100000	976.6KB	Formats disk size information (1KB equals 1024 bytes)
ConcatUrls	http://mysite, pages	http://mysite/pages	Concatenates URLs with slashes
FormStringWithListType	http://mysite/*0*	http://mysite/list	Replaces the *0* placeholder with the type of an SPList object, such as list.
GetProviderName	provider:Joerg	provider	Extracts the provider from a string
GetAccountName	provider:Joerg	Joerg	Extracts the name from a string containing “provider”
HexStringToLong	AABBCC	11189196	Converts a hexadecimal value into decimal value within the “long” range
ParseDate	12/31/2009		Returns the appropriate DateTime object
StringToUInt64	0x1234	4660	Recognizes the optional 0x prefix and calls HexStringToLong if it’s present, and Convert.ToUInt64 otherwise
TimeDeltaAsString		3 months ago	Compares two DateTime objects and creates a useful string

We use the SPUtility class in many circumstances in this book. You will encounter more methods in their appropriate contexts in later chapters.

Common Utility Classes

Within the Microsoft.SharePoint.Utility namespace you can find many classes. Only a few of them seem to be useful for development projects. Some are dedicated to support specific site types, such as wiki pages.

The DateOptions Class

This class contains methods that extend what's already available in the DateTime class. Many of the methods are particularly useful in conjunction with the calendar. Instead of the more complex DateTime class, the DateOptions class works with the SimpleDate structure. This structure does not support time values. For internationalization, you might consider using the IntlDate class.

The SPUrlUtility Class

SharePoint is a web application, and most objects have a URL. Handling URLs is a very common task. The SPUrlUtility class has some methods and a property to make this easier. IsUrlFull and IsUrlRelative are particularly useful.

The SPHttpUtility Class

This class provides methods to encode and decode a string for usage in an URL, escape a string for JavaScript (ECMAScript), and add URL-safe quotation marks.

The SPDiffUtility Class

This class has a method Diff to compare two strings and return a merged version with HTML indicators of inserted, deleted, or changed text.

Object Disposal Issues

When using the API, you will frequently retrieve objects that implement the IDisposable interface. Such objects need manual cleanup after usage. The objects often consume large chunks of memory. The garbage collector might clean up the memory, but if underlying unmanaged objects keep holding references or if the server is under permanent pressure, the memory-tidying routine is going to leave affected objects in memory. This causes the server's memory consumption to ratchet upward and not completely return to normal. The problem is a lack of understanding regarding why and when SharePoint objects require explicit disposal.

Best Practice Advice

The general principles described previously do not answer all questions that arise regarding object disposal. One typical question is whether it's safe to dispose of an object or not. When in doubt, let

SharePoint decide. Not disposing costs memory, but it will not destabilize your system. Dereferencing an object that's still in use could cause unpredictable behavior.

What's more confusing is the internal disposal within the object hierarchy. If you dispose of an SPSite object, all SPWeb objects taken from there will be disposed of as well. Attempting to access any orphaned object will throw an exception. To avoid such issues, it's good practice to keep object creation and disposal as close together as possible. Creating an object that derives from SPPersistedObject extracts its definition from the database and instantiates it. Usually, this is straightforward and takes a short time. Hence, creating an object and disposing of it several times is better than risking orphaned objects. The easiest way is via the common using statement. Enclosing code in a using block ensures that the Dispose method is called implicitly at the end of the block.

First, here's an example that's typical, but not recommended practice:

```
SPList GetList(string webUrl, string listName)
{
   SPSite site = new SPSite(webUrl);
   SPWeb web = site.OpenWeb();
   return web.Lists[listName];
}
void AddItemToList(string webUrl, string listName, object item)
{
   SPList list = GetList(webUrl, listName);
   // Code for adding stripped for sake of clarity
   list.ParentWeb.Site.Dispose();
}
```

The disposable objects are SPWeb and SPSite. The creator of the GetList method can't ensure that the object is disposed of correctly because the call to Dispose is in a separate method from the list creation. If the AddItemToList method fails for some reason and the application is able to continue, the object is never disposed of. With a using statement, the code would look like this:

```
void GetList(string webUrl, string listName)
{
   using(SPSite site = new SPSite(webUrl)
   {
     using(SPWeb web = site.OpenWeb())
     {
        try
        {
           GetListHelper(web, listName);
        }
        catch { }
     }
   }
}
void GetListHelper(SPWeb web, string listName)
{
   SPList list = web.Lists[listName];
   // Do something with list
}
```

Both using statements ensure the disposal of the respective objects at the right time. It's easy to read, because the object flow is made visible through the braces. The helper method that's used do something useful has no influence, and the implementer can ignore the disposable objects.

Retrieving objects and disposing of them is only appropriate if you are the developer responsible for their creation.

■ **Caution** Only dispose of objects owned by the developer's code!

To clarify when this rule applies, here are some different examples of common sources of SPSite and SPWeb objects that may be your responsibility to call Dispose on.

Objects are owned by the developer if the SPSite constructor is called directly:

```
using(SPSite site = new SPSite(url))
{
   // Do stuff here
}
```

The same situation applies if a new site is created in code:

```
using(SPSite site = new SPSite(url))
{
   using(SPSite siteSelfServ = site.SelfServiceCreateSite(...))
   {
     // Process new Site
   }
}
```

As with sites, webs also need to be disposed of:

```
using(SPWeb web = site.OpenWeb())
{
   // Do stuff
}
```

The SPLimitedWebPartManager object returned by the GetLimitedWebPartManager method holds a reference to an internal SPWeb that it will not dispose of. The developer needs to call Dispose explicitly, as follows:

```
SPFile page = web.GetFile("default.aspx");
using (SPLimitedWebPartManager webPartManager =
        page.GetLimitedWebPartManager(PersonalizationScope.Shared))
{
   try
   {
      // Do stuff
   }
   finally
   {
      webPartManager.Web.Dispose();
   }
}
```

Handling Objects Used in a Publishing Web

The *Publishing feature* is available in SharePoint Server only. It supports the SharePoint content management system (CMS). As the publishing objects are based on regular objects and SharePoint Foundation, similar rules apply.

Microsoft.SharePoint.Publishing.PublishingWebCollection objects retrieved by indexing into or enumerating over this collection will hold a reference to an internal SPWeb that will not be disposed of by Close. Instead, the developer needs to call Dispose on the publishing web's web.

```
using(SPWeb web = site.OpenWeb())
{
   PublishingWeb parentWeb = PublishingWeb.GetPublishingWeb(web);
   PublishingWebCollection pubWebs = parentWeb.GetPublishingWebs());
   foreach(PublishingWeb pubWeb in pubWebs)
   {
      try
      {
         // Do stuff
      }
      finally
      {
         pubWeb.Web.Dispose();
      }
   }
}
```

For the Microsoft.SharePoint.Publishing.PublishingWebCollection.Add method, the developer needs to call Close on the returned PublishingWeb object, as follows:

```
using(SPWeb web = site.OpenWeb())
{
   PublishingWeb newPubWeb = null;
   try
   {
      PublishingWeb pubWeb = PublishingWeb.GetPublishingWeb(web);
      PublishingWebCollection pubWebs = pubWeb.GetPublishingWebs();
      newPubWeb = pubWebs.Add("NewPubWeb");
   }
   finally
   {
      if(null != newPubWeb)
      {
         newPubWeb.Close();
      }
   }
}
```

The Microsoft.SharePoint.Publishing.PublishingWeb.GetVariation method returns a PublishingWeb object that needs a call to Close too:

```
using(SPWeb web = site.OpenWeb())
{
   PublishingWeb varPubWeb = null;
   try
   {
      PublishingWeb pubWeb = PublishingWeb.GetPublishingWeb(web);
      VariationLabel label = Variations.Current[0];
      varPublWeb = pubWeb.GetVariation(label);
      // Do stuff
   }
```

```
   finally
   {
      if(varPublWeb != null)
      {
         varPublWeb.Close();
      }
   }
}
```

All the publishing examples need disposal, because internally they call the OpenWeb method on an SPWeb object.

The Microsoft.Office.Server.UserProfiles.UserProfile.PersonalSite property creates an SPSite object that needs to be disposed of:

```
using (SPSite site = new SPSite("http://sharepointdevelope"))
{
    SPServiceContext context = SPServiceContext.GetContext(site);
    UserProfile profile = ProfileLoader.GetProfileLoader(context).GetUserProfile();
    using (SPSite personalSite = profile.PersonalSite)
    {
        // Do stuff
    }
}
```

Disposing of Objects and Collections

SharePoint is all about collections. Sites contain collections of webs, webs contain collections of lists, and this goes on down to the field and item level. When iterating through SPSite or SPWeb collections, you need to handle the disposal carefully.

Assume you have a simple loop to iterate over SPWeb objects:

```
foreach (SPWeb subweb in rootweb.Webs)
{
   // Do stuff
}
```

There is obviously no Dispose call, and therefore the SPWeb objects remain in memory. Looking into the internal code reveals that the OpenWeb method is called implicitly for each item when looping through the collection. Consider using the following code instead, to obtain and dispose of each object correctly:

```
for (int i = 0; i <= rootweb.Webs.Count; i++)
{
   using (SPWeb subweb = rootweb.Webs[i])
   {
      // Do stuff
   }
}
```

When using LINQ, things are not as straightforward. You can replace foreach with for statements, but the internal way LINQ processes collections can't be changed. However, we still encourage you to use this sophisticated technology to query SharePoint. To fool the object creation and disposal procedure, the following extension method is safe to use:

```
public static IEnumerable<SPWeb> SafeEnumerable(this SPWebCollection webs)
{
```

```
  foreach (SPWeb web in webs)
  {
    try
    {
       yield return web;
    }
    finally
    {
       web.Dispose();
    }
  }
}
```

This method extends the SPWebCollection class. The yield statement returns an item for each loop. The try...finally block ensures that the object is disposed of under all circumstances after usage. To use it, call the extension method, as shown next:

```
var lists = from w in site.AllWebs.SafeEnumerable()
            from SPList l in w.Lists
            where !l.Hidden && !w.IsRootWeb
            select new
            {
                WebTitle = w.Title,
                ListTitle = l.Title
            };
```

The extension method can be defined in a central place and should be part of any project. SPWebCollection and SPSiteCollection objects are used at many places in SharePoint, such as

- Microsoft.SharePoint.Administration.SPContentDatabase.Sites
- Microsoft.SharePoint.Administration.SPVirtualServer.Sites
- Microsoft.SharePoint.Administration.SPWebApplication.Sites
- Microsoft.SharePoint.SPSite.AllWebs
- Microsoft.SharePoint.SPWeb.Webs
- Microsoft.SharePoint.SPWeb.GetSubwebsForCurrentUser()
- Microsoft.SharePoint.Meetings.SPMeeting.GetWorkspacesToLinkTo()

Objects retrieved by adding to, indexing into, or enumerating over these collections always need to be disposed of. Here is one way to do this:

```
using(SPSite site = webApp.Sites[0])
{
   using(SPWeb newWeb = site.AllWebs.Add("MyNewWeb"))
   {
      // Do stuff
   }
   foreach(SPWeb web in site.RootWeb.GetSubwebsForCurrentUser())
   {
      try
      {
         // Do stuff
      }
```

```
        finally
        {
           web.Dispose();
        }
    }
}
```

Objects Owned by SharePoint

Some objects are owned by SharePoint and must not be disposed of in custom code. The SPWeb object returned by SPSite.RootWeb is such an example.

This property returns a shared SPWeb instance and is used internally in several methods and properties. It should never be disposed of explicitly. The following sample code does not dispose of anything:

```
SPSite site = SPContext.Current.Site;
SPWeb rootWeb = site.RootWeb;
SPWeb web = SPContext.Web;
SPWeb web = SPContext.Current.Web;
SPSite site = SPContext.Site;
SPSite site = SPContext.Current.Site;
```

Objects Used in a Feature Receiver

The object returned by the SPFeatureReceiverProperties.Feature.Parent property for a site- or web-scoped feature receiver should not be disposed of:

```
public override void FeatureActivated(SPFeatureReceiverProperties properties)
{
    SPWeb web = properties.Feature.Parent as SPWeb;
    // Do stuff
}
```

The following event receiver objects do not require disposal either:

```
SPWebEventProperties.Web
SPListEventProperties.Web
SPListEventProperties.List.Web
SPItemEventProperties.ListItem.Web
```

SPItemEventProperties implements IDisposable to clean up the SPSite object it creates; the others do not. It is not yet clear if the framework actually handles these correctly, so it may be safer to avoid these properties in favor of creating a new developer-owned SPSite object.

```
public override void ItemAdded(SPItemEventProperties properties)
{
   using (SPSite site = new SPSite(properties.WebUrl))
   {
      using(SPWeb web = site.OpenWeb())
      {
         SPList list = web.Lists[properties.ListId];
         SPListItem item = list.GetItemById(properties.ListItemId);
         // Do stuff
      }
   }
```

```
    base.ItemAdded(properties);
}
```

Objects Used with Personal Pages

The Microsoft.SharePoint.Portal.WebControls.IPersonalPage interface has two properties that return SPSite and SPWeb objects, respectively: IPersonalPage.PersonalSite and IPersonalPage.PersonalWeb. My Site pages, which implement IPersonalPage, implement these properties as shared instances that should not be disposed of by controls that use them.

```
IPersonalPage currentMySitePage = this.Page as IPersonalPage;
if (currentMySitePage != null && !currentMySitePage.IsProfileError)
{
   SPSite personalSite = currentMySitePage.PersonalSite;
   // Do stuff
}
```

Some other functions used internally return the same objects:

- UnsecuredLayoutsPage.Web
- LayoutsPageBase.Web
- SPControl.GetContextWeb()
- SPControl.GetContextSite()
- SPWebProvisioningProperties.Web

There is one special property that might be owned by the developer or SharePoint: SPWeb.ParentWeb. This property will allocate an SPWeb object the first time it is called. The caveat is that once it is disposed of, any reference to the property will return the disposed-of object. If an SPWeb object is not owned by the developer, its ParentWeb object should be considered not owned as well. For example, there could be a problem if two components both depend on SPContext.Current.Web.ParentWeb, and one calls Dispose before the other is finished. Official Microsoft guidance is to never explicitly call Dispose on ParentWeb.

Example of Incorrect Disposal

In their eager fight against undisposed-of objects, developers sometimes overreact. The following code shows such an example. The intention is presumably an implicit disposal after usage.

```
public static SPWeb GetSPWeb(string url)
{
  using (var site = new SPSite(url))
  {
    using (SPWeb web = site.OpenWeb())
    {
      return web;
    }
  }
}
```

The using statements force the compiler to include the Dispose calls within the block. That means the web is disposed of before it is returned.

Finding Incorrectly Disposed-Of Objects

To monitor memory consumption, Windows provides several techniques and tools. Because monitoring is not a solution, administrators often set a threshold based on a memory limit. Each time the limit is reached, the application pool gets recycled, and you can simply monitor the event log to check for memory leaks. It is good practice to set the threshold at the right level and let the pool be recycled. However, finding the right limit value takes some time. For instance, with at least 2GB of RAM you can set the value between 800 and 1500MB. If the value is well set, the application pool recycling should appear occasionally—less than once per day, for instance. If the pool is recycled frequently under a higher load—say, more than once per hour—you probably have incorrectly disposed-of objects.

You can determine whether the cause is a memory leak due to incorrectly disposed-of objects by checking the SharePoint log files. Look for the files in this path:

```
C:\Program Files\Common Files\microsoft shared\Web Server Extensions\14\LOGS
```

Each instance of `SPSite` and `SPWeb` contains a reference to an `SPRequest` object, which in turn contains a reference to an unmanaged COM object that handles communications with the database server. SharePoint monitors the number of `SPRequest` objects that exist in all threads, and adds entries to the logs under some circumstances. For such objects, a threshold is configured—eight by default. If the threshold is exceeded, a warning is added to the log. The threshold settings are stored in a registry key:

```
HKLM\SOFTWARE\Microsoft\Shared Tools\Web Server Extensions\HeapSettings
```

There are two values that aid in finding the problem:

- `LocalSPRequestWarnCount`: By default set to 8, this is the number of objects required to log a warning.
- `SPRequestStackTrace`: Set this to `1` to add the complete stack trace to the log when the warning appears. You can use this to drill down to your code.

SharePoint Security: Users and Roles

This section provides a basic introduction to the security model that SharePoint provides and some parts of the API you can use to access users, roles, and related objects.

Security Primer

SharePoint's security model is closely related to Windows, IIS, and ASP.NET. There are a few additions required to handle internal objects, such as Web Parts.

Authentication

In order for someone to use a SharePoint application, the application must validate the user's identity. This process is known as authentication. SharePoint is not a directory service, and the actual authentication process is handled by IIS. However, SharePoint is responsible for authorization to its sites and content after a user successfully authenticates. The user points his or her browser at a SharePoint site, and IIS performs the user validation using the authentication method that is configured. If this procedure is successful, SharePoint renders the pages based on the access level of the user. If authentication fails, the user is denied access to the site.

Authentication methods determine which type of identity directory is to be used and how users are authenticated by IIS. SharePoint supports these methods of authentication:

- Windows Authentication
- ASP.NET Forms Authentication
- Claims-based security
- Web Single Sign-On

Windows Authentication

Windows Authentication is the most common authentication type used in intranet deployments. It uses Active Directory to validate users. When Windows Authentication is selected, IIS uses the Windows Authentication protocol that is configured in IIS. The options are NTLM, Kerberos, certificates, Basic, and Digest protocols. The security policies that are applied to the user accounts are configured within Active Directory. For example, account expiration policies, password complexity policies, and password history policies are all defined in Active Directory, not in SharePoint. When a user attempts to authenticate to a SharePoint web using Windows Authentication, IIS validates the user against NTFS and Active Directory; once the validation occurs, the user is authenticated and the access levels of that user are applied by SharePoint (see Figure 3–3). The `SPUser` object that represents the user internally reflects the method and actual credentials.

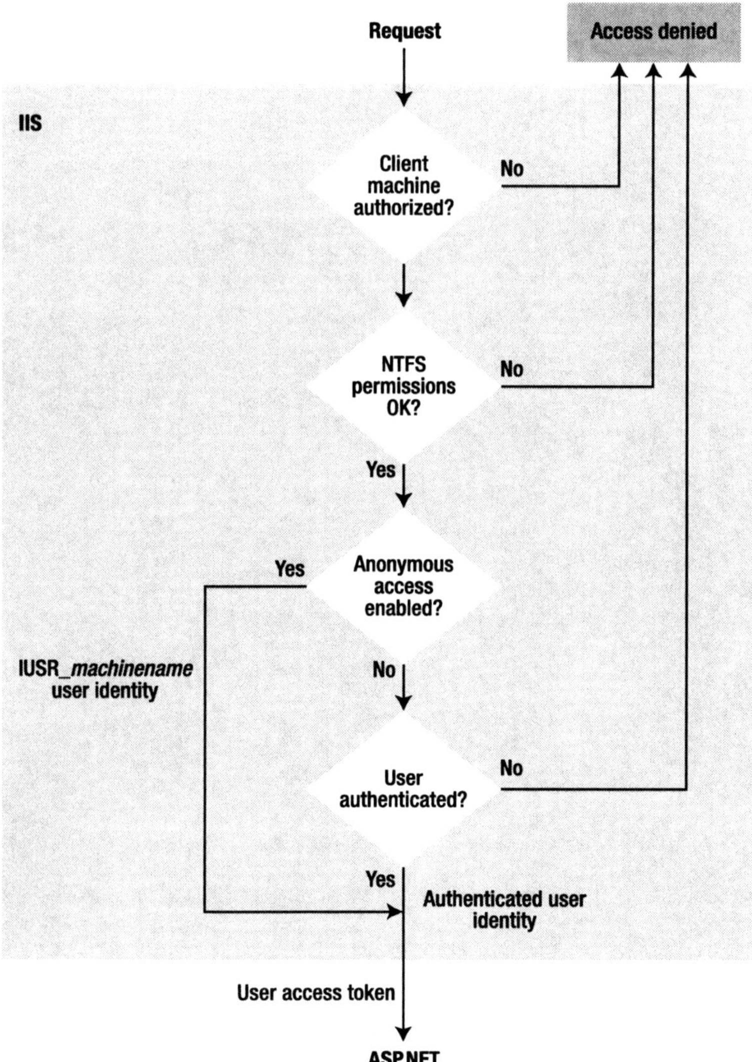

Figure 3–3. The SharePoint authentication process

Anonymous Access

Anonymous access is considered to be a Windows Authentication method because it associates unknown users with an anonymous user account (`IUSR_machinename`). It is commonly used in Internet sites. However, this configuration is disabled by default. The default configuration assumes that the SharePoint server runs in an intranet. In order to configure anonymous access to a SharePoint application, anonymous access must be enabled in IIS and the SharePoint application, and the anonymous user account must be provisioned. Users using anonymous access still face several limitations compared to authenticated users. By default, anonymous users are only allowed to read, and they are unable to edit, update, or delete content. Additionally, anonymous users are not able to utilize personalization features such as Microsoft Office integration, check-in/checkout, alerts, and page personalization.

Forms-Based Authentication

The ASP.NET Forms Authentication method is commonly used in situations where a custom authentication provider is required. Imagine using a custom LDAP directory, SQL Server, or another type of identity repository to store user account information. This is common in extranet environments, such as partner collaboration sites, where either it is not practical to create Active Directory user accounts for users, or a different type of directory is required.

Claims-Based Security

Claims-based identity is a security model for authentication and authorization based on the Windows Identity Foundation (WIF, formerly called Geneva), and was first introduced with SharePoint 2010. Claims-based identity provides a common way for applications to acquire identity information from users inside their organizations, in other organizations, and on the Internet. Identity information is contained in a *security token*, often simply called a token. A token contains one or more claims about the user. Think of it as metadata about the user that stays with them throughout their session.

Primarily, the WIF-enabled security model decouples SharePoint from an authentication provider. It supports multiple authentication providers per URL. Identity tokens can be passed without Kerberos to enable federation between organizations. When talking about claims-based security, the term *claim* plays an important role. First, it means an attribute of an identity. While the identity is a user's account, his or her claim may consist of things like a login name, an Active Directory group, and so on. Second, the term is related to an *issuer*. An issuer is a trusted party that issues claims. Third, a security token is a set of claims serialized and digitally signed (e.g., in Security Assertion Markup Language [SAML]). The security token is another crucial component of the security model. Security tokens are built, signed, and issued by a *security token service (STS)*. A relying party may make decisions about the authorization of an identity based on a security token. This relying party is often called an *authority*. Technically, you can regard this as a web service.

SharePoint 2010 supports two scenarios: incoming claims and outgoing claims. Incoming claims require an external STS that creates identity tokens. The incoming identity is mapped to the `SPUser` object used internally. This means that it is transparent for API access because it's the very same object as any other authentication method creates. SharePoint is decoupled from the identity provider. The connection between the external STS and SharePoint is handled by STS. Because the identity can be any kind of token used for security reasons, the object might contain not just a user, but even a role, group, or something similar. Consequently, an `SPUser` object might be more than just a user—every claim is seen as an `SPUser` object. Outgoing claims are related to service applications. Whenever a SharePoint application calls services, external line-of-business (LOB) systems, or external SharePoint farms, it transfers the token via a WCF (Windows Communication Foundation) service to the client applications. WIF is able to convert the token to a Windows identity object or whatever the client requires, evaluating what claims the caller requests and what authorization it permits.

Web Single Sign-On

The Web Single Sign-On authentication method is used in environments configured for federated identity systems. An independent identity management system integrates user identities across heterogeneous directories and provides the user validation for IIS. This includes Microsoft Identity Information Server with Active Directory Federation Services, Oracle Identity Management with Single Sign-On and Web Access Control, and Sun Microsystems Java System Identity Manager. Large enterprises often implement federated identity models to ease the administration of user provisioning for systems that span across subsidiaries and companies. Single sign-on systems are used to consolidate user accounts across heterogeneous systems, allowing the end user to authenticate to systems with one set of credentials, rather than having to use a different set of credentials for each unique system.

Combined Access

In SharePoint it is possible to configure a combination of authentication methods. For instance, employees and external partners can use different methods, such as Active Directory for internal people and a SharePoint list via Forms Authentication for others. This is achieved by defining two zones and associating authentication methods with the zones. The intranet zone would be configured with Windows Authentication and an extranet zone would be configured with ASP.NET Forms authentication.

Access

A SharePoint application includes sites, content pages, and web parts. SharePoint has several management controls in place for provisioning access to and within a web application. Users, groups, permissions, and permission levels are used to configure access within a SharePoint application.

SharePoint provides management and configuration functionality for such objects. Users are added from a directory service such as Active Directory. Once users are provisioned to a site collection, they are added to groups and assigned permissions on sites, lists, and items. SharePoint groups are used to maintain memberships internally. Additionally, Active Directory security groups may also be used directly. Active Directory group memberships are managed in Active Directory.

■ **Note** In this book we cover the SharePoint features only. Depending on your project's requirements, you might need access to the Active Directory Services API and .NET security namespaces as well. If you're not familiar with these, we strongly recommend reading about basic security techniques.

Permissions

Users and groups gain access or are restricted access to sites and Web Parts based upon permission levels. Permissions are individual rights that may be performed by a user in a site, list, or list item. These types of permissions are referred to as *site permissions, list permissions,* and *item permissions,* respectively. SharePoint comes with a number of predefined permissions. You can even create your own permissions.

Permissions are applied to users and groups using *permission levels.* Permission levels allow roles to be defined, consisting of unique combinations of individual permissions, or a set of permissions. SharePoint provides some default permission levels, such as Contribute and Full Control. In addition, you can extend the default permission levels to add custom permission levels in cases where a more appropriate name is desired or a unique combination of permissions is more appropriate.

The relationship between sites, lists, and items is hierarchical in nature. The same applies to permissions—they are inherited by child objects from the parent objects. In cases where business requirements require an object to have different permissions from the parent, the permission inheritance chain may be broken manually (see Figure 3–4). This is done by using the access control list of the child object.

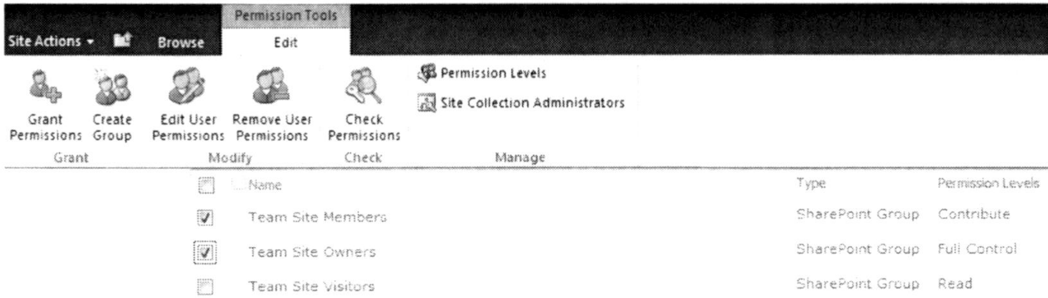

Figure 3–4. *Site permission settings*

The access control lists for sites, lists, and items are very similar. In addition, document libraries can contain folders, and it is possible to set permissions on these folders.

Audiences

Only those Web Parts that contain items such as lists and document libraries have access control lists to manage permissions. However, all Web Parts support audiences. Audiences are used to target content to users. SharePoint groups, Active Directory groups, Active Directory users, and global audiences may be used to define the audience of a particular Web Part. Audiences are used to restrict and filter certain content that exists on a content page to users who would otherwise have some level of access to the page. For example, an organization may have a portal that serves employees and external partners. If there is an employee announcement on the home page exposed by some Web Part, it might not be appropriate for external people to read. It is possible to target the Announcements Web Part to a specific audience, such as a security group assigned to employees only.

Search

In SharePoint, users are able to search for content across many different content sources, such as portals, web sites, file shares, data stored in LOB systems, and people profiles stored within Active Directory. The security model is fully integrated with the search feature, and therefore all of the content access concepts that apply to sites, Web Parts, and items also apply to search results. There are several management controls available that allow for custom tailoring of how content is crawled, what content can be searched, and how the search results appear to users.

Users, Groups, and Roles

In this section we give an overview of the security model. This includes ways to access the currently authenticated user using the `SPUser` object and its related classes. This section complements the programming tasks introduced in Chapter 8, where you can find more about how to work with groups, roles, and users. Here we focus more on how to get the current user object and identify the various properties and conditions to make security decisions.

Retrieving Users

There are several ways to retrieve user collections. Users of a SharePoint site can be divided into sections at the site level:

- All users of a site
- All users of a site collection
- All authenticated users

Some objects, such as alerts, can expose user collections, too. If you work with the specific rights concerning users along with the SPGroup object, collections of assigned users can be retrieved from there as well. (See the "Working with Groups" section, which follows, for more details about security considerations.)

To retrieve all users, you should start from the current SPWeb object using the AllUsers or SiteUsers method. SPUserCollection is the type returned. While SiteUsers returns the users that belong to the site, the AllUsers property returns these and others that browse the site as members of a domain group. This assumes that the SharePoint farm runs within an Active Directory environment. The example in Listing 3–1 retrieves all users and shows them unfiltered using a GridView control placed on an application page.

Listing 3–1. *Retrieving All Users and Binding to a GridView Control*

```
using System;
using Microsoft.SharePoint;
using Microsoft.SharePoint.WebControls;

namespace Apress.SP2010.UserManagement.Layouts.UserManagement
{
    public partial class RetrieveUsers : LayoutsPageBase
    {
        protected void Page_Load(object sender, EventArgs e)
        {
            if (!IsPostBack)
            {
                gvUsers.DataSource = Web.AllUsers;
                gvUsers.DataBind();

            }
        }
    }
}
```

The SPWeb object is retrieved from the Web property exposed by the LayoutsPageBase base class. If this code runs in a different context, you can use SPContext.Current.Web instead. The collection contains SPUser objects, which provide several useful properties, as shown in **Table 3–2**. The type derives from SPPrincipal, which in turn inherits SPMember.

Table 3–2. Useful Properties of the SPUser Type

Properties	Description
Email	The e-mail address
Groups	The collection of groups (SPGroup) to which the user belongs
ID, Sid	The internal ID and the security ID (SID) of the network account
LoginName	The login name
Name	The display name
UserToken	Access to the SPUserToken object
Notes	Some additional notes for this user
Xml	The XML used internally to store all the information
RegionalSettings	Property that returns an SPRegionalSettings object that exposes access to regional settings
IsSiteAdmin	A Boolean value that indicates whether the user is a site administrator
IsSiteAuthor	A Boolean value that indicates whether the user is a site author
IsDomainGroup	A Boolean value that indicates whether the user is a member of a domain group

You can set some basic properties such as Name, Email, and Notes, and save the changes by calling the Update method. To get access to the groups to which the user belongs, you use the Groups property.

■ **Note** The SPRole type is now obsolete and exists for backward compatibility only. Instead, you can use the SPRoleAssigment class to deal with groups and users that belong to them.

Retrieving the Current User

To get the current user, the SPWeb object is again the best choice. Call the CurrentUser property:

```
SPUser user = SPContext.Current.Web.CurrentUser;
```

If you change the current user when creating an SPSite object, this property returns the creating user:

```
SPUser userAlex = Web.Users[@"sharepointdevelope\alex"];
```

```
SPSite site = new SPSite("http://sharepointdevelope", userAlex.UserToken);
using (SPWeb web = site.OpenWeb())
{
   lblCurrent.Text = web.CurrentUser.LoginName;
}
```

In this example, the Label control lblCurrent is defined in the markup. After this code is executed, the label shows sharepointdevelope\alex. This is the preferred way to elevate permissions, because the administrator can define and control the account used to access the site.

■ **Caution** If the user executing the page has fewer rights, the code will still execute (same with RunWithElevatedPrivileges) and the user will gain higher rights. It is remarkable that a password is not required using this procedure. This is a security risk, and you should use this method with caution.

Getting a Specific SPUser Object

To get a particular user of type SPUser from the root web site in the root site collection of the current web application, you can retrieve it like this:

```
SPUser user = SPContext.Current.Site.WebApplication.Sites["/"].RootWeb.Users[name];
```

The EnsureUser method will return the SPUser object for the specified user login. The user will be added to the site if the user does not already exist. This will ensure an SPUser object is always returned.

```
SPContext.Current.Web.EnsureUser(@"domain\user");
```

Working with Groups

Assigning permissions directly to users is not a scalable and maintainable solution. Simplifying the management effort is one argument, scalability is another in large enterprises. If the database grows, the permission checks can impact performance. Using groups make such security checks faster. SharePoint creates three predefined groups to which you can assign your users. Each group has a typical set of permissions. The groups are

- *Owners*: Members of this group get full control.
- *Members*: Members of this group can contribute content.
- *Visitors*: This group provides its members read-only access to the site.

You can define any number of groups at the site collection level and assign specific permission sets, such as Full Control, to your groups.

The next example assumes you have several ASP.NET controls on an application page:

```
<asp:TextBox runat="server" ID="txtGroup" />
<asp:Button runat="server" ID="btnAddGroup" Text="Add Group" OnClick="btnAddGroups_Click" />
<br />
Existing Groups:
<asp:DropDownList runat="server" ID="ddlGroups" />
```

The code-behind is used to create a new group with the name given in the TextBox control. The DropDownList shows the current list of groups for the site collection in which the page runs. The code in Listing 3–2 assumes that the executing user has the appropriate permissions.

***Listing 3–2.** Code to Retrieve Groups, Add a New Group, and Assign Users*

```
using System;
using Microsoft.SharePoint;
using Microsoft.SharePoint.WebControls;

namespace Apress.SP2010.UserManagement.Layouts.UserManagement
{
    public partial class AddGroup : LayoutsPageBase
    {
        protected void Page_Load(object sender, EventArgs e)
        {
            if (!IsPostBack)
            {
                GetGroups();
            }
        }

        private void GetGroups()
        {
            ddlGroups.DataSource = Web.Groups;
            ddlGroups.DataTextField = "Name";
            ddlGroups.DataValueField = "ID";
            ddlGroups.DataBind();
        }

        protected void btnAddGroups_Click(object sender, EventArgs e)
        {
            // Retrieve root collection
            SPSite site = new SPSite("http://joerg-netbook");
            using (SPWeb web = site.OpenWeb())
            {
                string newGroup = txtGroup.Text;
                // Create
                web.SiteGroups.Add(newGroup, web.CurrentUser, web.CurrentUser,
                                   "A group created by code");
                // Assign to site
                SPGroup group = web.SiteGroups[newGroup];
                SPRoleAssignment roles = new SPRoleAssignment(group);
                SPRoleDefinition perms = web.RoleDefinitions["Full Control"];
                roles.RoleDefinitionBindings.Add(perms);
                web.RoleAssignments.Add(roles);
                // Add users to this group
                SPUser user1 = web.AllUsers[@"joerg-netbook\bernd"];
                SPUser user2 = web.AllUsers[@"joerg-netbook\martin"];
                group.AddUser(user1);
                group.AddUser(user2);
            }
            GetGroups();
```

```
            }
        }
}
```

The code that creates the group is in Button's click event. The current user becomes the default member and the group's owner. Adding the required permissions is not that straightforward. You first have to create an SPRoleAssignment object for the new group. Then you retrieve a permission as an SPRoleDefinition object from the current site collection. In this example, the Full Control permission is used. As you can see, the properties expose indexers. You can easily search in the collection or run a foreach loop to check or show the existing values. Once you have the right permission, you add it to the RoleDefinitionBindings collection. Finally, the object is assigned to RoleAssignments.

The reason for this procedure is the structure of collections. A site collection can have any number of groups, which can have any number of users and any number or roles, which in turn represent a collection of specific permissions.

When the group is ready, you can start adding users. In the example, this is hard-coded, and the users must exist. Remember to add error-checking code in a real-life solution. The settings for users, roles, groups, and so on do not require any call of an Update method. Calling the appropriate Add method creates the object immediately.

Security Issues in Custom Code

The application pool identity plays a significant role in SharePoint applications. This account is used to run the application itself. This means that internally, all connections to the content and configuration databases rely on the same account. In a single-server environment, this can be a local network service account. In a domain environment with several servers running in your farm, consider using a domain account. By using domain accounts, you can distinguish between the account used for Central Administration and those used for all other applications. In this section we show how to raise the current execution privileges to the application pool account. Running the whole farm with one account means that users can accidentally get access to features only available to the administrator. We strongly recommend decoupling the application pool account of Central Administration before deploying any code that raises the user's privileges.

Internally, SharePoint maps domain accounts or external accounts to internal ones. The same happens with the application pool account, which is mapped to the SHAREPOINT\system account. If you retrieve all users, as shown in the previous examples, the system account appears in the list too. However, you cannot do much with it, and it will cause most operations that apply to SPUser to fail. It doesn't matter whether the actual account is NetworkService or a domain account. It will always map to the same internal account, which is named statically. When you run code by using the SHAREPOINT\system identity, you're using the mapped Windows account—the one used by the application pool. Changing the settings is shown in Figure 3–5.

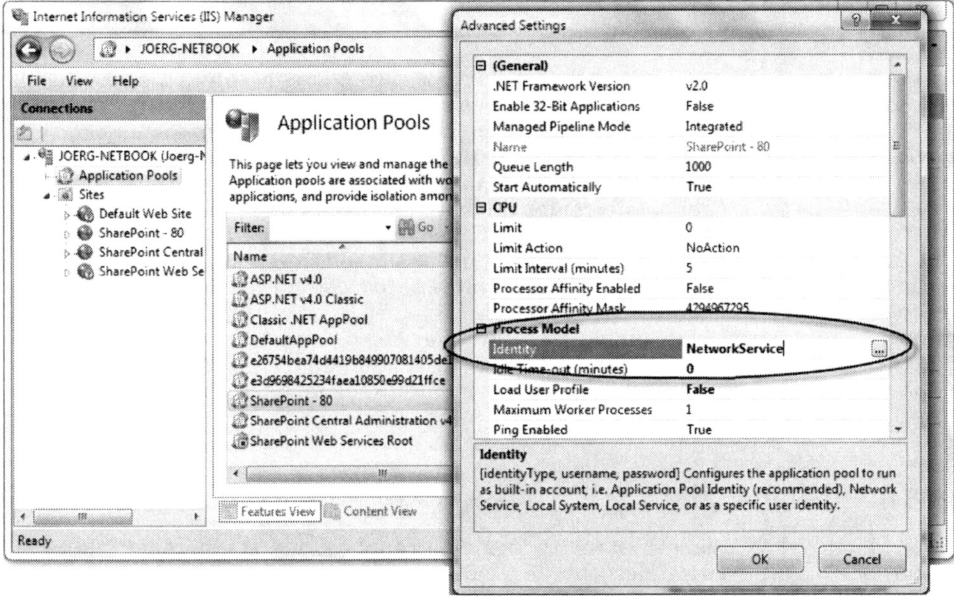

***Figure 3–5.** Getting and setting the application pool identity*

Running with Elevated Privileges

The SPSecurity class exposes a method called RunWithElevatedPrivileges, which gives you an option to elevate the privilege to the application pool identity under which your code is executing. In SharePoint it's common practice to run code with elevated privileges in order to avoid using additional accounts. The basic code example uses a delegate to encapsulate the code:

```
SPSecurity.RunWithElevatedPrivileges(
   delegate()
   {
      // Privileged code is running here
   }
);
```

If you like lambda expressions or just want to feel better, you might prefer this syntax:

```
SPSecurity.RunWithElevatedPrivileges(() =>
   {
      /* Some privileged expressions */
   }
);
```

For example, retrieving the current Windows account user would look like this:

```
string name;
SPSecurity. RunWithElevatedPrivileges(
            () => name = WindowsIdentity.GetCurrent().Name);
```

However, impersonation is not that simple. In order to get this method call to properly impersonate your application pool identity, you need to do further work. SPSite and SPWeb objects created outside the delegate or lambda expression do not have full control, even when referenced inside the delegate (anonymous method), so you need to find out their GUIDs before impersonation is performed, and re-create the context again. Finally, never forget to dispose of your objects. (See the "Object Disposal Issues" section earlier in the chapter for more details.)

You essentially need to create a parent SPWeb object again via creation of a new SPSite object, SPWeb object, and so on within the RunWithElevatedPrivileges block:

```
SPWeb webInUserContext = SPContext.Current.Web;
SPSite SiteInUserContext = SPContext.Current.Site;
Guid webGuid = webInUserContext.ID;
Guid siteGuid = SiteInUserContext.ID;
SPSecurity.RunWithElevatedPrivileges(delegate()
{
   // Get the site in the impersonated context
   using (SPSite site = new SPSite(siteGuid))
   {
      // Get the web in the impersonated context
      using (SPWeb web = site.OpenWeb(webGuid))
      {
         web.AllowUnsafeUpdates = true;
         // Do your work here
      }
   }
});
```

While the RunWithElevatedPrivileges method seems to be easy to use and solves several problems, using this approach isn't recommend for general purposes. Elevated privilege can be used to bypass or work with security, and can be performed either through SPSecurity or impersonation techniques involving the SPUserToken and SPSite classes. It's one of the most misunderstood aspects of the SharePoint API, but in general you should always prefer impersonation using the SPSite class and SPUserToken objects.

To impersonate the system, use the SystemAccount.UserToken property of the current SPSite context—for example:

```
var site = new SPSite(SPContext.Current.Site.ID,
                      SPContext.Current.Site.SystemAccount.UserToken);
```

If you need a specific user, use a similar approach (replace the *<username>* placeholder with a SharePoint user's name):

```
try
{
    SPWeb web = SPContext.Current.Web;
    SPUserToken token = web.AllUsers["<username>"].UserToken;
    SPSite site = new SPSite(SiteId/SiteUrl, token);
    // Do stuff
}
catch
{
}
```

The SPSite object returned is now running with explicit rights, and you have more control over when and how you dispose of it.

It can, however, be useful to run code under the context of the application pool for code that accesses network or file resources, or for SharePoint code that does not support impersonation through the SPSite object. Without further introduction, here's a list of best practices for elevated-privilege code in SharePoint that will help you create more reliable applications for the enterprise:

- Avoid using SPSecurity.RunWithElevatedPrivileges to access the SharePoint object model. Instead, use SPUserToken to impersonate SPSite with a specific account, as shown previously.
- If you do use SPSecurity.RunWithElevatedPrivileges, dispose of all objects in the delegate. Do not pass SharePoint objects out of the RunWithElevatedPrivileges method.
- Only use SPSecurity.RunWithElevatedPrivileges to make network calls under the application pool identity. Don't use it for elevation of privilege of SharePoint objects.

Avoid passing SharePoint objects between different security contexts (SPSite instances), with the exception of SPUserToken used in the SPSite constructor. An SPUser object created from one SPSite object cannot be passed reliably to another SPSite object. This can be the source of obscure bugs in production that are difficult to reproduce in development.

■ **Tip** Never use elevated privilege to bypass security—always use it to work with the security model your site needs.

To add to the previous explanation regarding the usage of the SPUser object and related types, the next section describes working with users.

Common Challenges with RunWithElevatedPrivileges

If you run code with elevated privileges and you create new objects, such as list items within a list, the user automatically assigned as author or editor is SHAREPOINT\system. If you use another user's token, it's of course the user you currently use. However, this might not be your intention. A user might expect to be the owner of an item with his or her current credentials. To handle this, you must first retrieve the real credentials, and then elevate the privileges. The example in Listing 3–3 shows how to deal with this issue of two identities.

Listing 3–3. *Save Method That Handles Elevated Privileges*

```
private void Save(SPList fictitiousList, bool ifAnonymous)
{
   SPUser user = ((LayoutsPageBase)Page).Web.CurrentUser;
   Guid siteID = fictitiousList.ParentWeb.Site.ID;
   Guid webID = fictitiousList.ParentWeb.ID;
   Guid listID = fictitiousList.ID;
   SPSecurity.RunWithElevatedPrivileges(() =>
   {
      using (SPSite site = new SPSite(siteID))
      {
         using (SPWeb web = site.OpenWeb(webID))
```

```
            {
               web.AllowUnsafeUpdates = true;
               SPList elevatedList = web.Lists[listID];
               SPListItem item = elevatedList.Items.Add();
               SPUser systemUser = web.AllUsers[@"SHAREPOINT\system"];
               SPFieldUserValue currentUser = new SPFieldUserValue(
                      item.ParentList.ParentWeb, user.ID, user.Name);
               if (!question.Anonymous)
               {
                  item["Author"] = currentUser;
                  item["Editor"] = currentUser;
               } else {
                  item["Author"] = systemUser;
                  item["Editor"] = systemUser;
               }
               item.Update();
            }
         }
      }
      );
   }
}
```

The code can access a fictitious list (FictitiousList) that the current user cannot normally access (even the usual read permission has been removed). This prevents users from accessing the list by entering the URL directly. From the current list, the IDs are retrieved to reinstantiate the SPList, SPWeb, and SPSite objects with elevated privileges. Within the delegate, a new list item is created. The Anonymous parameter determines whether the standard Author and Editor fields take the system account or the current user. However, the SPUser object exposed by SPWeb.CurrentUser is SHAREPOINT\system within the privileged block. That's why the user object is retrieved first from the current SPWeb object. The code assumes you run a Web Part or user control that resides on an application page that derives from LayoutsPageBase, as recommended in Chapter 2. The Web property contains the user credentials of the user currently logged on.

This code has several advantages:

- The user can access the list data through your code, but any other access is blocked, including directly entering the AllItems URL.
- You can decide in your code to set the user's data or leave the item in an anonymous state.
- You can manipulate the Author and Editor field values to suit.

Securing Objects

Identifying users serves two operations: authentication and authorization. While the common login procedure authenticates a user and creates the assigned token for further identification, the authorization process gains access to particular objects using the current credentials. In SharePoint, this association is resolved via securable objects. An object is securable if it inherits the abstract Microsoft.SharePoint.SPSecurableObject class. It is shown in **Listing 3–4**.

Listing 3–4. SPSecurableObject Class

```
public abstract class SPSecurableObject : ISecurableObject
{
   protected SPSecurableObject();
   public virtual SPRoleDefinitionBindingCollection AllRolesForCurrentUser { get; }
   public abstract SPBasePermissions EffectiveBasePermissions { get; }
   [Obsolete("Use FirstUniqueAncestorSecurableObject instead")]
   public ISecurableObject FirstUniqueAncestor { get; }
   public abstract SPSecurableObject FirstUniqueAncestorSecurableObject { get; }
   public virtual bool HasUniqueRoleAssignments { get; }
   public abstract SPReusableAcl ReusableAcl { get; }
   public virtual SPRoleAssignmentCollection RoleAssignments { get; }

   public virtual void BreakRoleInheritance(bool copyRoleAssignments);
   public virtual void BreakRoleInheritance(bool copyRoleAssignments,
                                            bool clearSubscopes);
   public virtual void CheckPermissions(SPBasePermissions permissionMask);
   public virtual bool DoesUserHavePermissions(SPBasePermissions permissionMask);
   public abstract SPPermissionInfo GetUserEffectivePermissionInfo(string userName);
   public abstract SPBasePermissions GetUserEffectivePermissions(string userName);
   public virtual void ResetRoleInheritance();
}
```

The SPWeb, SPList, and SPListItem classes implement this base class. That's why you can assign access permissions down to the item level. The base class provides methods to check permissions (DoesUserHavePermissions) interactively or force an exception (CheckPermissions) immediately.

Specific permissions are defined in the SPBasePermission enumeration. This is a flagged enum with the values described in Table 3–3.

***Table 3–3.** SPBasePermission enum (Source: MSDN Documentation)*

Name	Value	Description
EmptyMask	0	No permissions on the web site. This option is not available through the user interface.
ViewListItems	1	View items in lists, documents in document libraries, and web discussions.
AddListItems	2	Add items to lists, documents to document libraries, and web discussion comments.
EditListItems	4	Edit items in lists, edit documents in document libraries, edit web discussion comments in documents, and customize Web Part pages in document libraries.
DeleteListItems	8	Delete items from lists, documents from document libraries, and web discussion comments from documents.
ApproveItems	16	Approve a minor version of a list item or document.
OpenItems	32	View the source of documents with server-side file handlers.

Name	Value	Description
ViewVersions	64	View past versions of a list item or document.
DeleteVersions	128	Delete past versions of a list item or document.
CancelCheckout	256	Discard or check-in a document that is checked out to another user.
ManagePersonalViews	512	Create, change, and delete personal views of lists.
ManageLists	2048	Create and delete lists, add or remove columns in lists, and add or remove public views of lists.
ViewFormPages	4096	View forms, views, and application pages, and enumerate lists.
Open	65536	Open a web site, list, or folder to access items inside that container.
ViewPages	131072	View pages in a web site.
AddAndCustomizePages	262144	Add, change, or delete HTML pages or Web Part pages, and edit the web site using a Windows SharePoint Services–compatible editor.
ApplyThemeAndBorder	524288	Apply a theme or borders to the entire web site.
ApplyStyleSheets	1048576	Apply a stylesheet (CSS file) to the web site.
ViewUsageData	2^{21}	View reports on web site usage.
CreateSSCSite	2^{22}	Create a web site using self-service site creation.
ManageSubwebs	2^{23}	Create subsites such as team sites, Meeting Workspace sites, and Document Workspace sites.
CreateGroups	2^{24}	Create a group of users that can be used anywhere within the site collection.
ManagePermissions	2^{25}	Create and change permission levels on the web site and assign permissions to users and groups.
BrowseDirectories	2^{26}	Enumerate files and folders in a web site using the Microsoft Office SharePoint Designer 2007 and WebDAV interfaces.
BrowseUserInfo	2^{27}	View information about users of the web site.
AddDelPrivateWebParts	2^{28}	Add or remove personal Web Parts on a Web Part page.
UpdatePersonalWebParts	2^{29}	Update Web Parts to display personalized information.
ManageWeb	2^{30}	Grant the ability to perform all administration tasks for the web site.
UseClientIntegration	2^{31}	Use features that launch client applications; otherwise, users must work on documents locally and upload changes.

Name	Value	Description
`UseRemoteAPIs`	2^{32}	Use SOAP, WebDAV, or Microsoft Office SharePoint Designer interfaces to access the web site.
`ManageAlerts`	2^{33}	Manage others' e-mail alerts.
`CreateAlerts`	2^{34}	Create e-mail alerts.
`EditMyUserInfo`	2^{35}	Allow a user to change his or her user information, such as adding a picture.
`EnumeratePermissions`	2^{36}	Enumerate permissions on the web site, list, folder, document, or list item.

There is an additional value called `FullMask` (hex: `7FFFFFFFFFFFFFFF`) that includes all the permission flags shown in the table.

The permissions are grouped into several roles to simplify their usage. The `SPRoleDefinition` object holds those roles. **Table 3–4** shows the predefined sets.

Table 3–4. *Default Role Sets*

Role	Permissions (from SPBasePermissions; See Table 3–3)
Full Control	`FullMask`
Design	`ViewListItems`, `AddListItems`, `EditListItems`, `DeleteListItems`, `ApproveItems`, `OpenItems`, `ViewVersions`, `DeleteVersions`, `CancelCheckout`, `ManagePersonalViews`, `ManageLists`, `ViewFormPages`, `Open`, `ViewPages`, `AddAndCustomizePages`, `ApplyThemeAndBorder`, `ApplyStyleSheets`, `CreateSSCSite`, `BrowseDirectories`, `BrowseUserInfo`, `AddDelPrivateWebParts`, `UpdatePersonalWebParts`, `UseClientIntegration`, `UseRemoteAPIs`, `CreateAlerts`, `EditMyUserInfo`
Contribute	`ViewListItems`, `AddListItems`, `EditListItems`, `DeleteListItems`, `OpenItems`, `ViewVersions`, `DeleteVersions`, `ManagePersonalViews`, `ViewFormPages`, `Open`, `ViewPages`, `CreateSSCSite`, `BrowseDirectories`, `BrowseUserInfo`, `AddDelPrivateWebParts`, `UpdatePersonalWebParts`, `UseClientIntegration`, `UseRemoteAPIs`, `CreateAlerts`, `EditMyUserInfo`
Read	`ViewListItems`, `OpenItems`, `ViewVersions`, `ViewFormPages`, `Open`, `ViewPages`, `CreateSSCSite`, `BrowseUserInfo`, `UseClientIntegration`, `UseRemoteAPIs`, `CreateAlerts`
Limited Access	`Open`, `BrowseUserInfo`, `UseClientIntegration`

Now you can use the enumeration values to retrieve the current permissions in custom code. Using the `EffectiveBasePermissions` property of `SPWeb` class, this can look like the following:

```
if ((Web.EffectiveBasePermissions & SPBasePermissions.ViewListItems)
                                   == SPBasePermissions.ViewListItems)
{
}
```

The binary operator is used to mask the bit flags of the enum type. However, it's more efficient to use the methods defined in SPSecurableObject to check the permissions before a security exception is thrown.

Handling Authorization Failures

Working with the security model actively delegates the responsibility of handling authorization tasks to your code. This includes two actions. First, you must check the required permissions for the user using his or her credentials. Second, you have to let your code execute properly.

There are many ways to show an authorization failure. Some internal features simplify this, as shown in Listing 3–5, which demonstrates an application page that requires administrative permissions.

Listing 3–5. *Manually Securing an Application Page*

```
using System;
using Microsoft.SharePoint;
using Microsoft.SharePoint.WebControls;
using Microsoft.SharePoint.Utilities;

namespace Apress.SP2010.SecurityModel.Layouts.SecurityModel
{
    public partial class SecurePage : LayoutsPageBase
    {
        protected void Page_Load(object sender, EventArgs e)
        {
            // This page requires Admin permissions
           if (Web.CurrentUser.IsSiteAdmin)
            {
                lblName.Text = Web.CurrentUser.Name;
            }
            else
            {
                SPUtility.Redirect(SPUtility.AccessDeniedPage,
                                   SPRedirectFlags.RelativeToLayoutsPage,
                                   Context);
            }
        }
    }
}
```

This code simply checks the IsSiteAdmin property exposed by the SPUser object. If the current user is not an administrator, the page is redirected to the built-in Access Denied page (see Figure 3–6). With just one line of code, you get the default error message.

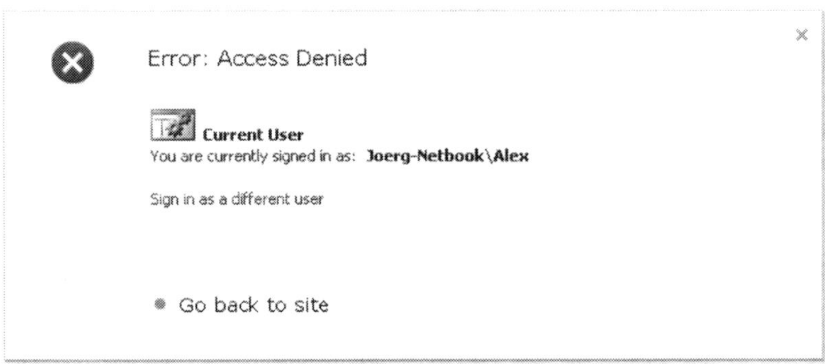

Figure 3–6. *Built-in "access denied" message*

You can achieve the same effect with the following code:

```
SecurityException ex = new SecurityException();
SPUtility.HandleAccessDenied(ex);
```

This method takes an object of type `System.Security.SecurityException`, which you can use further for logging purpose. The `HandleAccessDenied` method redirects to the same page as used in **Listing 3–5**.

This is good if your users are comfortable with the default SharePoint environment. External users, for instance, might be better served with standard HTTP messages. The HTTP return code for a security failure is 401 (Access Denied). Sending this as shown in Listing 3–6 lets the browser decide how to present the issue.

Listing 3–6. *Creating a 401 HTTP Message*

```
using System;
using Microsoft.SharePoint;
using Microsoft.SharePoint.WebControls;
using Microsoft.SharePoint.Utilities;
using System.Security;

namespace Apress.SP2010.SecurityModel.Layouts.SecurityModel
{
    public partial class Http401Page : LayoutsPageBase
    {
        protected void Page_Load(object sender, EventArgs e)
        {
            // This page requires Admin permissions
            if (Web.CurrentUser.IsSiteAdmin)
            {
                lblName.Text = Web.CurrentUser.Name;
            }
            else
            {
               SecurityException ex = new SecurityException();
               SPUtility.SendAccessDeniedHeader(ex);
            }
```

```
            }
        }
    }
```

The browser is now forced to present the common logon dialog to request the appropriate credentials. If the user fails to enter the expected logon data, the message "401 UNAUTHORIZED" is shown. Different browsers might show this message in distinct ways in response to the Access Denied header.

Using Helper Classes

In addition to SPUser, which is mostly used in the context of lists, you can use SPPrincipal to work with user information. The example in Listing 3–7 shows how to search principals and display available information.

Listing 3–7. *Searching Principals and Binding to a GridView*

```
using System;
using Microsoft.SharePoint;
using Microsoft.SharePoint.WebControls;
using Microsoft.SharePoint.Utilities;
using System.Collections.Generic;

namespace Apress.SP2010.UtilityExperiment.Layouts.UtilityExperiment
{
    public partial class SecurityUtils : LayoutsPageBase
    {
        protected void Page_Load(object sender, EventArgs e)
        {
            bool maxCount;
            IList<SPPrincipalInfo> users = SPUtility.SearchPrincipals(Web,
                txtInput.Text,
                SPPrincipalType.All,
                SPPrincipalSource.All,
                null,
                100,
                out maxCount);
            grdPrincipals.DataSource = users;
            grdPrincipals.DataBind();
        }
    }
}
```

This code searches principals for a word taken from a TextBox control's Text property. The results grid shows the properties that the SPPrincipalInfo class exposes (see Figure 3–7).

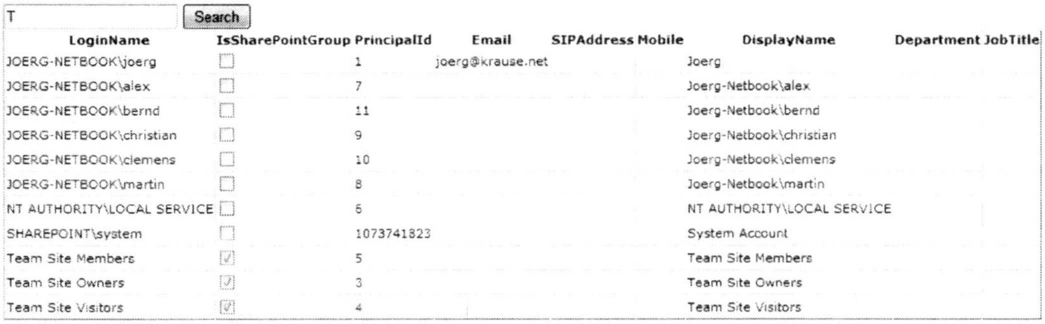

T [Search]

LoginName	IsSharePointGroup	PrincipalId	Email	SIPAddress	Mobile	DisplayName	Department	JobTitle
JOERG-NETBOOK\joerg	☐	1	joerg@krause.net			Joerg		
JOERG-NETBOOK\alex	☐	7				Joerg-Netbook\alex		
JOERG-NETBOOK\bernd	☐	11				Joerg-Netbook\bernd		
JOERG-NETBOOK\christian	☐	9				Joerg-Netbook\christian		
JOERG-NETBOOK\clemens	☐	10				Joerg-Netbook\clemens		
JOERG-NETBOOK\martin	☐	8				Joerg-Netbook\martin		
NT AUTHORITY\LOCAL SERVICE	☐	6				NT AUTHORITY\LOCAL SERVICE		
SHAREPOINT\system	☐	1073741823				System Account		
Team Site Members	☑	5				Team Site Members		
Team Site Owners	☑	3				Team Site Owners		
Team Site Visitors	☑	4				Team Site Visitors		

Figure 3–7. *Principal objects of type SPPrincipalInfo*

To retrieve a single item instead of a list, see the following example:

```
SPPrincipalInfo userInfo = SPUtility.ResolvePrincipal(web,
                                                      "Test User",
                                                      SPPrincipalType.All,
                                                      SPPrincipalSource.All,
                                                      null,
                                                      false);
```

The `ResolvePrincipal` method returns `null` if the user can't be found.

The Isolated Programming Style

The methods shown thus far in this chapter have used the API and have been tightly integrated with the SharePoint environment. This dictates a particular coding style that has both advantages and limitations. The advantages are that the deep interdependence between the API, the base files in the SharePoint root, and the settings in Visual Studio make for a great development experience. The disadvantage is that you're limited to only what this environment allows. In particular, it requires you to program either Web Parts or application pages that run within the context of SharePoint and IIS.

Breaking this barrier allows you to program against the API from any sort of application, including console, Windows Forms, and WPF applications.

▒ **Note** Running an isolated application that makes use of the complete API requires executing the application on the server. To run an application from a remote location, where the DLLs are not available, you must use the client object model. The client object model uses web services to work with webs, lists, and list items. It has limited capabilities and cannot be used to create administration applications, such as code that operates at the farm or server level. The client object model is described in depth in Chapter 12.

Console-Based Applications

Programming SharePoint is not limited to the boundaries of SharePoint itself. Imagine you want to write a new command-line tool to automate common tasks in your environment. In that situation, you have to work with the SharePoint object model, but with your code running in an isolated fashion. The SharePoint object model supports this, and lets you instantiate the access to any part, whether administrative or data-driven, in a similar way. Console-based applications are excellent for automation tasks. Administrators can easily integrate them into batch files and scheduled tasks, or run them on demand with no interaction.

■ **Note** One rule for console applications is that they should not require any user action. It's possible to make them work interactively; however, this would force somebody to sit in front of a computer, which is what console-based applications are trying to avoid.

Creating a Console Application

Creating a console application (see Figure 3–8) with Visual Studio 2010 requires only a few steps. After creating the project, you must add the required references to `Microsoft.SharePoint.dll`. Remember that applications running the SharePoint object model must be compiled for "x64" types (or "AnyCPU") and use the .NET Framework 3.5.

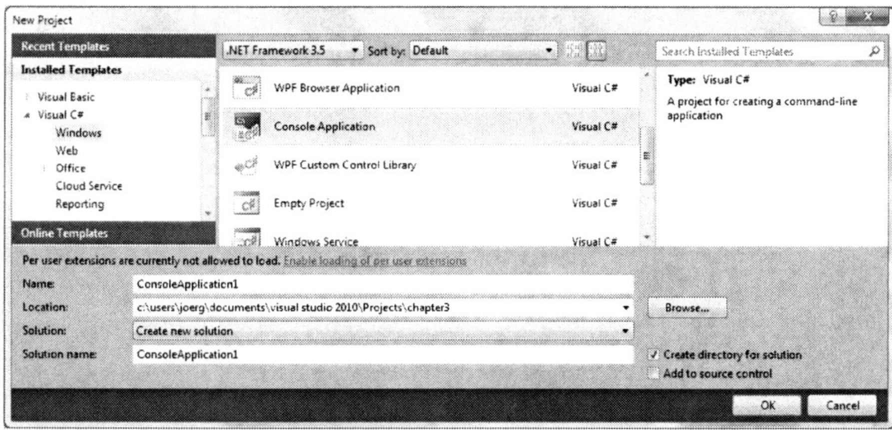

Figure 3–8. Project template for console applications in the Windows section

---

■ **Tip** Follow the instructions in Chapter 1 for details on how to set up a project for SharePoint 2010.

Set the x64 option in the Configuration Manager as shown in Figure 3–9 by selecting x64 from the "Active solution platform" drop-down.

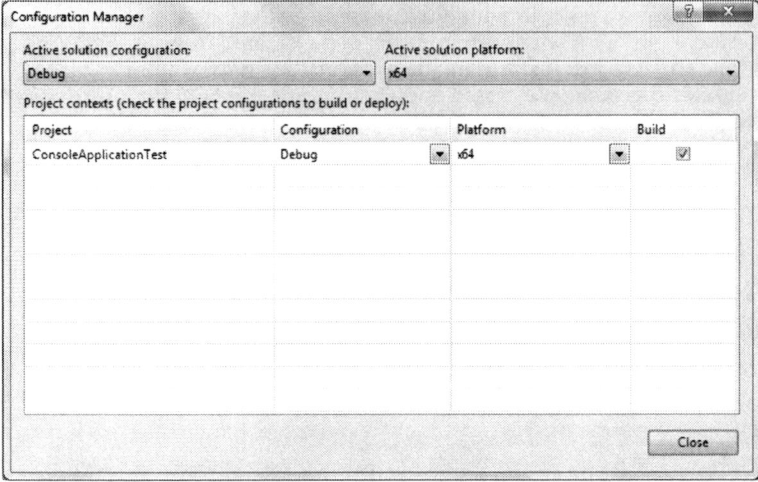

Figure 3–9. Select x64 from the "Active solution platform" drop-down.

This setting is required because SharePoint runs in 64-bit mode only. To program against the SharePoint API, you must add a reference to the SharePoint assembly (at a minimum), as shown in Figure 3–10.

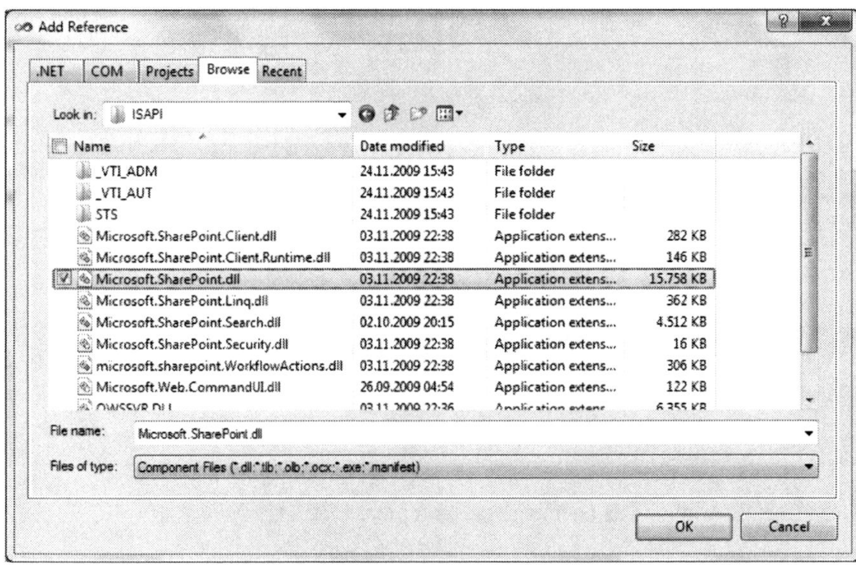

Figure 3–10. The SharePoint assembly must be added to the project references.

For specific namespaces, you might need to add more SharePoint assemblies. Most can be found in the ISAPI folder under the SharePoint root (also known as the 14 hive).

DO I NEED TO WORRY ABOUT THE CS1607 WARNING?

When you compile your projects, Visual Studio complains that referenced assemblies such as mscorlib target a different platform. That's because the project template includes the 32-bit version. Replacing them manually does not change the message either. Despite the warning, however, the project should compile and run without errors. So should you simply ignore the warning?

The assembly-loading procedure is part of the runtime. This means that the runtime takes care of what to load—and in the case of SharePoint 2010, this is the x64 version. Therefore, the right answer is to ignore this warning.

Controlling a Console Application Using Parameters

Using command-line parameters, you can control the behavior of console applications. This is well known, and you might consider copying the schema from one of the other SDK tools. It makes it easier for administrators to work with your new tool. The following code snippet shows how to extract multiple parameters from the command-line arguments.

Administrators love to organize their commands in files. It helps to hold things together. Consider that in a large enterprise, an administrator has to handle hundreds if not thousands of scripts. Your console application should be able to retrieve the parameters or switches from an external file. To do so, an XDocument object is used to read the data, extract it, and hand it over to the parameter parser (shown next).

This example (see Listing 3–8) does not contain any SharePoint-specific code. It's merely a skeleton used to create console applications with a powerful parameter parser. However, for the sake of clarity, the error checks and exception-handling parts are limited to some very basic checks. Before releasing this to a production environment, consider adding error checks and unit tests.

Listing 3–8. *Empty Console Application with Parameter Parser*

```
using System;
using System.Collections.Generic;
using System.Linq;
using System.Text;
using System.Xml.Linq;
using System.IO;

namespace Apress.SP2010.ConsoleApplicationTest
{
    class Program
    {
        static void Main(string[] args)
        {
            Properties p;
            if (args.Length > 0 && !args[0].StartsWith("xml"))
            {
                p = Properties.ReadArguments<Properties>(args);
```

```
            }
            else
            {
                string[] param = args[0].Split(new char[] {':'}, 2);
                if (param.Length == 2 && param[0].Equals("xml"))
                {
                    if (File.Exists(param[1]))
                    {

                        XDocument doc = XDocument.Load(param[1]);
                        p = Properties.Deserialize<Properties>(doc);
                    }
                    else
                    {
                        throw new FileNotFoundException();
                    }
                }
                else
                {
                    throw new ArgumentException("parameter 'xml' expected");
                }
            }
        }
    }
}
```

This simple parameter parser accepts either a list of values in any order that matches the structure of the serializable parameter class Properties, or an XML file that also contains a serialized object. The call to the console could look like this:

```
C:\>ConsoleApp.exe ShowAll:false WebUrl:"http://myserver" Filter:*
```

For the XML file, it would look like this:

```
C:\>ConsoleApp.exe xml:pathtofile\params.xml
```

An abstract base class (see Listing 3–9) that contains the serializers and deserializers delivers the appropriate functionality.

Listing 3–9. *Serialize, Deserialize, and Read Any Parameter*

```
public abstract class PropertyReader
{

    public static XDocument Serialize<T>(T source) where T : PropertyReader
    {
        XDocument target = new XDocument();
        XmlSerializer s = new XmlSerializer(typeof(T));
        XmlWriter writer = target.CreateWriter();
        s.Serialize(writer, source);
        writer.Close();
        return target;
    }

    public static T Deserialize<T>(XDocument doc) where T : PropertyReader
```

```
    {
        XmlSerializer s = new XmlSerializer(typeof(T));
        XmlReader r = doc.CreateReader();
        T props = s.Deserialize(r) as T;
        return props;
    }

    public static T ReadArguments<T>(string[] args) where T : PropertyReader, new()
    {
        T props = new T();
        foreach (string arg in args)
        {
          // Assume the parameter looks like param:value
          string[] param = arg.Split(new char[] {':'}, 2);
          if (param.Length != 2) throw new ArgumentOutOfRangeException("args");
          PropertyInfo pi = props.GetType().GetProperty(param[0]);
          if (pi == null) throw new ArgumentOutOfRangeException("args");
          object anyTypeValue = Convert.ChangeType(param[1], pi.PropertyType);
          pi.SetValue(props, anyTypeValue, null);
        }
        return props;
    }
}
```

This code assumes that the parameters are formatted as *param:value*. The Serialize and Deserialize methods are ready to use. The ReadArguments method uses Reflection to access the generic type properties and set the appropriate values. The foreach loop looks for corresponding properties and does not depend on any order. The class that is used to store the properties could look like this:

```
[XmlRoot(ElementName="Properties")]
public class Properties : PropertyReader
{

   [XmlElement(ElementName = "ShowAll")]
   public bool ShowAll { get; set; }

   [XmlElement(ElementName = "Filter")]
   public string Filter { get; set; }

   [XmlElement(ElementName = "WebUrl")]
   public string WebUrl { get; set; }

}
```

This class would produce the following XML:

```
<?xml version="1.0" encoding="utf-8"?>
<Properties xmlns:xsi="http://www.w3.org/2001/XMLSchema-instance"
            xmlns:xsd="http://www.w3.org/2001/XMLSchema">
  <ShowAll>true</ShowAll>
  <Filter>Tasks*</Filter>
  <WebUrl>http://joerg-netbook/</WebUrl>
</Properties>
```

You can use any serializable type here to store values in the XML file. To define a different schema, you simply change the `Properties` class. The serializer follows the `XmlRoot` and `XmlElement` attributes to create and read the file.

Handling Output of a Console Application

When your console application is running, it may need to output information. For example, the task may be going wrong, or a simple success message should be sent. Consider the following ways to return status information:

- Write to the console's output.
- Write to the Windows event log.
- Write to a file.
- Return a status code.

The most important thing is that the application must run even if the output is not handled by a human. So never use pop-up windows or wait at the console for input. You may consider writing it in a dual-function fashion: interactively and noninteractively. For testing purposes, it's often better to have a direct way to change parameters, instead of having to edit a file. However, command-line tools are not for daily use—they are primarily designed to support automation tasks.

The following example shows a tool that examines the farm's structure by reading information about the registered servers. If an error occurs, it writes a message to the event log.

Using Object Constructors

When working with console applications, there is no context equivalent to the `SPContext` class. Instead, you must use the `SPSite` constructor to instantiate an object that represents the site collection:

```
SPSite site = new SPSite("http://localhost");
  ...
site.Dispose();
```

■ **Note** Your code should dispose of any `SPSite` or `SPWeb` object obtained by using a constructor. The SharePoint runtime cannot take care of the object disposal, and to avoid a memory leak, explicit disposal after use is necessary. (See the earlier section "Object Disposal Issues" for more details.)

For a simpler programming style, take advantage of a `using` block to ensure that the object is disposed of:

```
using (SPSite site = new SPSite("http://localhost"))
{
  ...
}
```

The `localhost` name used in the example is an alias for the computer on which the code is executed. For console applications, you should always use `localhost`, because a console application can only operate on the local computer anyway. If you hard-code a server name, then your console application cannot be ported to another computer, and will break if the server's name is ever changed.

After you have a reference to a collection, you can use the AllWebs collection to obtain a reference to a particular web site in the collection:

```
using (SPWeb web = mySiteCollection.AllWebs["mySite"])
{
   ...
}
```

Alternatively, you can use the OpenWeb method, as shown in the following line:

```
using (SPWeb web = mySiteCollection.OpenWeb("mySite"))
{
   ...
}
```

Console Example

The next example loops through all objects of a farm and writes the GUIDs out to the console. It may not make much practical sense, but it looks like a grid and demonstrates how to access the object's tree.

The ReadFarm method (see Listing 3–10) is called from the entry point of the console application shown in the previous example.

Listing 3–10. The SharePoint Grid Code

```
private static void ReadFarm(Properties p)
{
    Console.ForegroundColor = ConsoleColor.Green;
    Console.BufferHeight = 1024;
    SPFarm farm = SPFarm.Local;
    Console.WriteLine(farm.Id.ToString("N"));
    var srvs = from s in farm.Services where s is SPWebService select s;
    Action<object> a = v =>
        {
            PropertyInfo pi = v.GetType().GetProperty("ID");
            if (pi == null || !pi.PropertyType.Equals(typeof(Guid))) return;
            Guid id = (Guid)pi.GetValue(v, null);
            Console.WriteLine(id.ToString("N").ToUpper());
        };
    foreach (SPWebService srv in srvs)
    {
        a(srv);
        foreach (SPWebApplication webapp in srv.WebApplications)
        {
            a(webapp);
            foreach (SPSite site in webapp.Sites)
            {
                a(site);
                foreach (SPWeb web in site.AllWebs)
                {
                    a(web);
                    foreach (SPList list in web.Lists)
                    {
```

```
                        a(list);
                        foreach (SPField field in list.Fields)
                        {
                            a(field);
                        }
                    }
                    web.Dispose();
                }
                site.Dispose();
            }
        }
    }
    Console.ReadLine();
}
```

The `Action` clause, defined first, reads any object and tries to get its `ID` property. If it is present, it writes the value out as a `Guid` without the hyphens. That's just a demonstration that makes the following `foreach` loops more compact and readable. Don't forget to dispose of objects as necessary to save memory. The output is shown in Figure 3–11.

Figure 3–11. The SharePoint grid

The general approach of getting objects out of a tree and doing something useful with them—except writing the ID to the console in green—is a basic pattern for most automation examples. Refer to Chapter 17 for more information about how to manipulate farm-level objects.

Windows Forms and WPF Applications

Windows Forms and WPF applications follow rules similar to console applications. However, because these applications have a powerful UI, the use of parameters is needless. Instead, users will probably manipulate the program's features by setting parameters interactively. Windows Forms and WPF are beyond the scope of this book. If you plan to write such applications to manage SharePoint, remember the following advice:

- Operations can take time. You should program asynchronously using background threads to keep the UI responsive.
- Add tracing to get information about the user actions to aid in investigating errors.
- Constrain the user's input as much as possible, and don't trust any textual input.
- Employ progress bars or hourglasses to inform the user that a lengthy operation is in progress.
- Check for appropriate user rights before starting the application.

Keep these in mind when adopting code samples from application programming.

Summary

In this chapter you got an overview about the basic SharePoint programming characteristics. We covered the entry points—the ways to access the object model from custom code to reach internal and custom data and properties. Whatever type of code you write, several utilities and helper classes support you by providing common tasks out of the box. The `Microsoft.SharePoint.Utilities` namespace, in particular, is a cornucopia of classes that save a lot of time.

SharePoint is mostly written in managed code. However, some critical parts responsible for performance and availability are based on COM components. This means that you have to carefully manage object disposal and keep your memory clean. Several best practices and examples show how and when to explicitly dispose of objects.

Each application developer needs to be concerned about security. SharePoint has a comprehensive built-in security model with integrated management of roles, groups, and users. The basic steps to access the collections of roles, groups, and users, and work with the retrieved objects, were explained in this chapter. Furthermore, you learned how to elevate privileges and work with a system account dynamically.

Programming SharePoint is not limited to Web Parts and web pages. Especially for tools and administrative tasks, it's possible to create Windows Forms, WPF, and console applications. Using the isolated programming style that decouples your development environment further from the SharePoint server, you can create standalone applications. We explained how to get access to the object model even in those circumstances.

CHAPTER 4

Data Access

Everything from the site level (`SPSite`) down to a list item (`SPListItem`) can be read, modified, and saved back to the database using the API. However, before using the object model, you need a basic understanding of lists and the content type model. Different data access techniques are necessary when dealing with large sets of data. They include querying with the Collaborative Application Markup Language (CAML) and the API based on its `SPQuery` object. SharePoint 2010 provides extensive support for accessing lists and libraries using Language Integrated Query (LINQ). Using `spmetal.exe`, you can create a type-safe object layer over any existing list or library. This layer uses LINQ to access and retrieve, write, or delete data. This method has some advantages, as you will see.

Learn more about data access in this chapter:

- How lists and libraries work internally and how to access data through the object model
- The event model that handles list and list item–related events
- CAML to query lists, and the `SPQuery` class
- LINQ to query data with type-safe objects

Organizing Data in Lists

Every application needs a flexible data model as a foundation. The user needs somewhere to store, deal with, and retrieve data. The data represents the natural and virtual objects managed in the application. SharePoint organizes data in lists and their derivatives, the libraries. Several objects assist with defining the list's structure, such as field types and content types.

Lists and Their Elements

Metadata is a semantically enhanced description of the data to express the meaning of data. For example, adding additional information (such as author, date, and keywords) to a document stored in a document library enhances the ability of a search engine to find it and order the results. SharePoint's list model is amazingly flexible. Moreover, it empowers ordinary users to create and manage their own data store—normally a function "for experts only." After years of computer technology advancement, the administration of a data model is no longer rocket science. However, this does not mean that you—as a developer—cannot programmatically interact with the data model. The whole power of the list model and its associated parts is available through the object model. Whatever the end user may do (and most of what they can't do) through the UI, you can accomplish with the object model.

Lists and Content Types

Early on in your contact with SharePoint lists, you should have encountered the term *content type*. Though they are ignored by many, they are, as a matter of fact, a core concept. The Microsoft definition on MSDN crystallizes their essential quality:

CONTENT TYPE DEFINITION

A content type is a reusable collection of settings you want to apply to a certain category of content. Content types enable you to manage the metadata and behaviors of a document or item type in a centralized, reusable way.

When designing a smart data model for your application, your first inclination will most likely be toward a similar structure as you would create for a relational database. You probably know that a lookup field can be used to define a many-to-many relationship without a helper table in between. It seems that this database-centric approach will result in a great data model.

But stop, this is not true! SharePoint is not just another UI layer on top of SQL Server. If you look into the SQL model, you will see that all list data is stored in the same table. It doesn't make sense to create a classic relational model within another generic one. Apart from the flawed performance, you will miss out on the advantages.

SharePoint has more subtle and powerful ways to structure data. That's necessary, because human-readable data is not well structured at all. Consider a taxonomy for storing documents in your company. You might keep the offers, invoices, and project documents in different libraries. Alternatively, you could store the documents by customer—collecting all the customer-specific data in one place, regardless of the type of document. In a relational model, things get complicated. You have a customer table, an invoice table, an offer table, and so on. They have relationships, of course, and retrieving data necessitates creating several joins over some or all the tables. However, not everyone needs everything. There are different consumers for the data. A co-worker will retrieve the offers, while another needs a summary of the projects in progress. A report for the board of directors includes a report on the overdue invoices. A developer modeling the data diagram needs access to everything.

With SharePoint, the data model is arranged very differently. The documents are stored in essentially an unstructured way. All documents are kept in one large library. Searching, filtering, reporting, and performing similar tasks are more efficient and easy to construct. On the other hand, to get access to particular data, more information about the documents is required. "More" is often expressed as "meta" in information technology. Instead of creating a complex and error-prone data model—which is still a compromise—each document has a distinct set of semantic data to describe itself. Each search instance can use all or some of the metadata to find the desired documents. If you think that additional columns in a relational data model table would offer equivalent functionality, that's not entirely true. If several different types of document share the same table—because they are "similar enough"—the number of columns would eventually exceed the capabilities of the database. Adding metadata means that you have the right amount of additional data restricted to the actual document type.

Such a predefined set of metadata fields is called a *content type*. Like a database table, lists in SharePoint have columns. Metadata expressed as content types are sets of columns. The clever feature is that each document in a list can be associated with its own content type. The content type has a private set of columns that describe the document (or data item) further without breaking the model. In other words, content types encapsulate the data schema on a very high level. The physical location of the data is no longer part of the schema. Having two schemas in one data container resolves the oldest conflict of a relational database—the target it's written for can be either one or another, but not both. In contrast to relational tables, it's like you have a superset of columns while each item (row) refers to a subset of columns. Each content type defines such a schema and several content types can be bound to the same list.

THE METADATA PARADIGM

In SharePoint, you can create multiple data schemas, in the form of multiple content types, and make them available on the same list or document library.

Content Type Elements

A content type includes a collection of information, such as the following:

- The columns that define the metadata
- Custom forms to edit the data, especially for New, Edit, and Display operations
- Associated workflows including the event or condition that invokes the workflow
- For documents, the template used to create a new document
- Associated custom code that's required to deploy and run custom content types

Creating and using content types is possible using the UI and the object model. In the section "Content Types" later in this chapter we explore the object model and learn how to program against lists and content types.

Working with Lists

Content types are a breakthrough in handling loosely structured data. They do, however, reside in lists. Before enhancing a list using content types, you need at least a basic list. It's good practice to check what internal lists are already available before creating your own.

■ **Note** In this section we refer often to *lists*. If not explicitly stated, this means both lists and libraries. Document libraries are a hybrid. They are lists, and they can store documents. Document libraries and their specific features are further explained in the "Document Libraries and Document Sets" section.

The Built-in Lists

SharePoint comes with several built-in lists (see Table 4–1). For simple projects, you probably don't need to create anything to store your user's data.

Table 4–1. Some Lists Built into SharePoint

List	Type	ID	Base Type	Description
Generic	List	100	0	Custom list's base type
Document	Library	101	1	Default document library supporting versioning, check-in and check-out, and workflows
Survey	List	102	4	Stores surveys and results
Links	List	103	0	Manages hyperlinks
Announcements	List	104	0	Timely news with expiration support
Contacts	List	105	0	Tracking people and contact information with Microsoft Outlook support
Events	List	106	0	Stores events in a calendar
Tasks	List	107	0	Activity-based items with workflow support
Discussions	List	108	3	Supports threaded discussions
Picture	Library	109	1	Stores slide shows, pictures, and thumbnails, and allows editing using the Microsoft Office Picture Manager
Data Sources	Library	110	1	Stores data connection files
Site templates	Library	111	1	Site template files
User Information	List	112	0	Information about users
Web part gallery	Library	113	1	Web parts
List templates	Library	114	1	List template definitions
Form	Library	115	1	Stores XML forms created with InfoPath
Master pages	Library	116	1	Master page gallery
No-Code Workflows	Library	117	1	Workflow library

List	Type	ID	Base Type	Description
Custom Workflows	Library	118	1	Workflows with code
Wiki Page	Library	119	1	Stores wiki pages
Custom Grid	Library	120	1	A customizable grid view
Data Connection	Library	130	1	Stores information about external data connections
Workflow History	List	140	0	The task history a workflow produces
Project Tasks	List	150	0	Tasks with Gantt chart rendering support
Issue tracking	List	1100	5	Stores issues with resolution information and prioritization support

The base type is defined in an SPBaseType enumeration that is defined like this:

```
public enum SPBaseType
{
    UnspecifiedBaseType = -1,
    GenericList = 0,
    DocumentLibrary = 1,
    Unused = 2,
    DiscussionBoard = 3,
    Survey = 4,
    Issue = 5,
}
```

Additional lists are available for specific purposes. The meeting workspace defines several lists in the number range from 200, and the blog site defines lists with an ID starting at 300.

An empty list definition called "Generic" is available to create your own set of columns. The base type shown in the table allows SharePoint to internally track the right columns for the specific item.

Creating a List Programmatically

You can easily create a new list using the Add method of the SPListCollection type. Listing 4–1 demonstrates this in a console application.

Listing 4–1. *Create a List in Code*

```
using (SPSite site = new SPSite("http://sharepointserve"))
{
  using (SPWeb web = site.OpenWeb())
  {
    SPList list = null;
    string listName = "Books";
```

```
      // Check whether the list already exists
      try
      {
        list = web.Lists[listName];
      }
      catch (ArgumentException)
      {
      }
      if (list == null)
      {
        Guid listId = web.Lists.Add(listName, "All our books",
                        SPListTemplateType.GenericList);
        list = web.Lists[listId];
        list.OnQuickLaunch = true;
        list.Update();
      }
      Console.WriteLine("Created list {0} with id {1}", list.Title, list.ID);
    }
  }
```

This code runs in a console application and creates a new generic (custom) list without any additional columns. Before creating a new list, you should check whether it already exists. You can either loop through all lists or try to access the new list and catch the exception thrown if it doesn't yet exist. An alternative approach is to use a LINQ query:

```
bool exists = (from l in web.Lists.OfType<SPList>()
               where l.Title.Equals(listName)
               select l).Count() > 0;
```

The list itself is not queryable and must be copied into a `List<T>` element using the `OfType` operator. That means the list is copied completely and uses a significant amount of memory if you have many lists. However, from the perspective of clean code, the pattern seems smarter than a `try...catch` block.

Once the new list is created, you can start changing properties and adding columns. In the example, only one property has been set—`OnQuickLaunch`. This enables instant access to the new list from the quick menu, as shown in Figure 4–1.

***Figure 4–1.** The new list has one default column—Title.*

Adding Fields to the List

Once the list exists, you can add fields. Fields represent the columns. Internally, a field is a type derived from `SPField`. SharePoint includes a number of predefined fields for specific types. The following example demonstrates adding several fields for scalar types:

```
list.Fields.Add("ISBN", SPFieldType.Text, true);
list.Fields.Add("LeadAuthor", SPFieldType.Text, true);
list.Fields.Add("Price", SPFieldType.Currency, false);
list.Update();
```

The `SPFieldType` enumeration contains all possible types. You can also define custom types and extend the list of field types. A field type is not only a scalar or complex value; it can also have a relationship to a custom field editor. (For more information, see the "Custom Field Types" section later in this chapter.)

The `Add` method has three overloads. These are the five possible parameters:

- Field name (`string`)
- Field type (`SPFieldType`)
- Flag to specify whether the field is mandatory (`boolean`)
- Flag indicating that the name is to be compacted to eight characters (optional) (`boolean`)
- An optional collection of values for choice fields (`System.Collection.Specialized.StringCollection`)

After all the fields have been added, you need to call the `Update` method, which changes the model in the database. Figure 4–2 shows the edit window of the modified list.

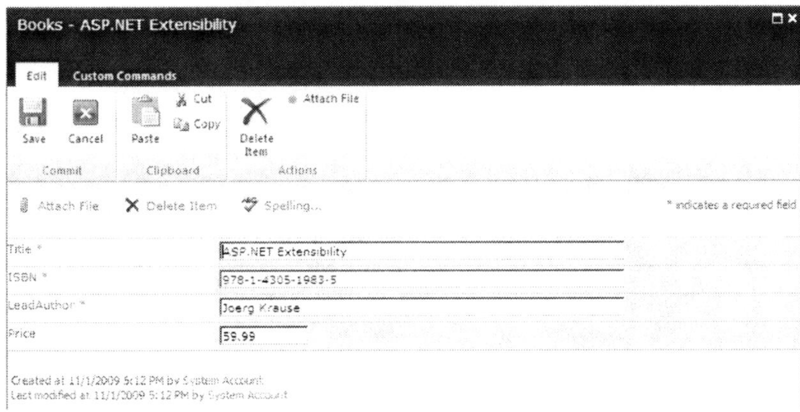

Figure 4–2. *Editing programmatically added fields*

Adding a lookup requires more information. A lookup creates a relationship between two lists. Instead of using the `Add` method, call `AddLookup`. This method requires three or four parameters:

- Field name (`string`)
- The `Guid` of the lookup list

- An optional Guid of another web where the lookup list resides
- Flag to make the field mandatory (boolean)

Adding a lookup field follows a similar process to adding any other field type:

```
using (SPWeb web = site.OpenWeb())
{
   SPList authorList = web.Lists["Authors"];
   SPList bookList = web.Lists["Books"];
   Guid listId = authorList.ID;
   bookList.Fields.AddLookup("Authors", listId, false);
   bookList.Update();
}
```

This code adds a lookup from books to the authors list (see Figure 4–3).

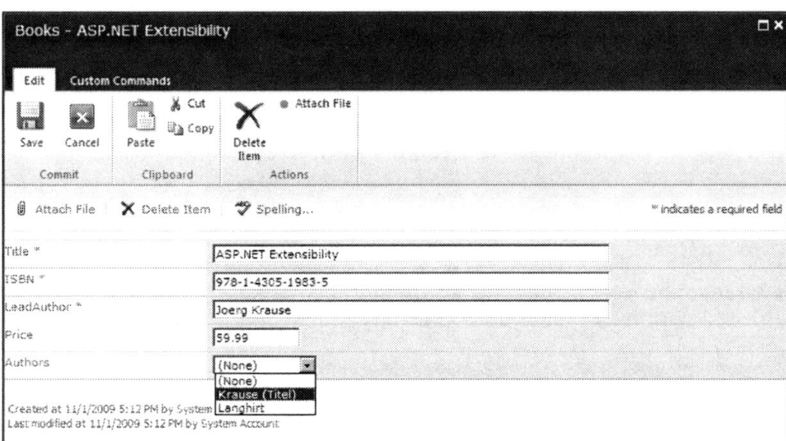

Figure 4–3. A programmatically added lookup field in the edit form

Again, the Update method commits the changes to the database model.

Changing Field Properties

Certain properties are not available through the UI. Even SharePoint Designer, with its advanced capabilities, eventually reaches its limits. The example in Listing 4–2 shows how to enable an invisible field to appear in the dialogs again and remove the read-only flag.

Listing 4–2. Change Field Properties Programmatically

```
using (SPSite site = new SPSite("http://sharepointserve"))
{
  using (SPWeb web = site.OpenWeb())
  {
    SPList questions = web.Lists["Questions"];
    SPField field = questions.Fields["Voters"];
    field.Hidden = false;
```

```
      field.ReadOnlyField = false;
      field.Update();
   }
}
```

The change affects only the SPField object—not the list. The code snippet assumes you have a Questions list with a Voters field that is hidden and read-only. The changes are assigned to the underlying content type if the column is defined there. There is no need to change the particular content type directly.

Enumerating the Fields Collection

Once the fields have been added—either programmatically or by using the UI—you can iterate through them and change properties. The foreach approach very simply iterates through all the fields:

```
SPList bookList = web.Lists["Books"];
foreach (SPField field in bookList.Fields)
{
   Console.WriteLine("{0}, Hidden:{1}, ReadOnly:{2}",
                     field.Title,
                     field.Hidden,
                     field.ReadOnlyField);
}
```

LINQ is an effective tool to filter the list:

```
foreach (SPField field in
         bookList.Fields.OfType<SPField>().Where(f => !f.ReadOnlyField) )
{
    Console.WriteLine("{0}, Type:{1}", field.Title, field.Type);
}
```

The OfType operator reads the complete list and converts it into List<SPField> type. Even if the result shows only a few fields, this operation reads all the fields and filters them in memory.

In the output, as shown in Figure 4–4, all the read-only fields are omitted. You can filter by any property the SPField type exposes.

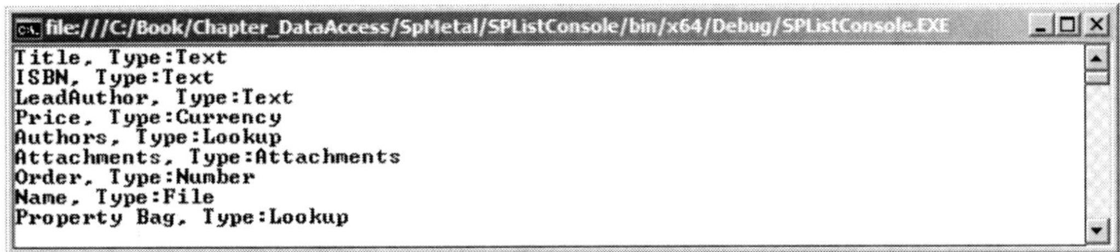
file:///C:/Book/Chapter_DataAccess/SpMetal/SPListConsole/bin/x64/Debug/SPListConsole.EXE
Title, Type:Text
ISBN, Type:Text
LeadAuthor, Type:Text
Price, Type:Currency
Authors, Type:Lookup
Attachments, Type:Attachments
Order, Type:Number
Name, Type:File
Property Bag, Type:Lookup

Figure 4–4. *A filtered list of fields*

Adding Items to the List

Adding items is as straightforward as adding fields. However, the procedure is not yet type-safe because the column's ID must be provided as a string or Guid. The field name you need to use here is the internal Name, not the DisplayName.

Using a string that clearly describes the field is recommended:

```
SPListItem item = list.Items.Add();
item["Title"] = "ASP.NET Extensibility";
item["ISBN"] = "978-1-4305-1983-5";
item["LeadAuthor"] = "Joerg Krause";
item["Price"] = 59.99;
item.Update();
```

An `ArgumentException` is thrown if a field name does not exist. Alternatively, you can use the field's zero-based index or its `Guid` to identify the field. This is recommended if the index or `Guid` is returned from any previous operation, to avoid errors due to mistyping.

Working with Collections

Some properties the `SPList` class exposes have specific types. Imagine that you have a Voters column, which can contain multiple users. The following code fetches the item with ID 1 from the Questions list. If there is no voter already attached, the current user executing the code is added. If there is already a user present, all users of the current web are added.

```
SPListItem item0 = questions.GetItemById(1);
if (item0.Fields["Voters"].Type == SPFieldType.User)
{
    if (item0["Voters"] == null)
    {
        SPFieldUserValue uv = new SPFieldUserValue(web, web.CurrentUser.ID,
                                                        web.CurrentUser.Name);
        SPFieldUserValueCollection coll = new SPFieldUserValueCollection();
        coll.Add(uv);
        item0["Voters"] = coll;
    }
    else
    {
        // add all users
        var users = from u in web.AllUsers.Cast<SPUser>()
                    where
                        !u.Name.Contains(web.CurrentUser.Name)
                        && !u.Name.StartsWith("NT AUTHORITY")
                        && !u.Name.StartsWith("SHAREPOINT")
                        && !u.Name.EndsWith("SYSTEM")
                    select new SPFieldUserValue(web, u.ID, u.Name);
        SPFieldUserValueCollection coll =
                                 (SPFieldUserValueCollection)item0["Voters"];
        foreach (SPFieldUserValue user in users)
        {
            coll.Add(user);
        }
        item0["Voters"] = coll;
    }
    item0.Update();
}
```

An interesting observation is that access to a field containing a collection is pernickety. If there is no user in the list, the `item0["Voters"]` call returns `null`. To add a new user, an object of type

SPFieldUserValueCollection must be assigned. Note that when you merely want to add another user to an already existing collection, you must assign the whole collection too. You can call Add for the SPFieldUserValueCollection object, but not directly to the property. This code will not work as expected:

```
((SPFieldUserValueCollection)item0["Voters"]).Add()
```

Unfortunately, it will not throw an exception but simply does nothing.

Working with Attachments

Each item in a SharePoint list has an associated SPAttachmentCollection array. The collection contains strings, which may seem odd, as you would expect SPFile objects instead. What you see is a direct representation of the underlying storage model. Attachments are part of the containing web. This means that all lists share all their attachments in one library. The names collection must be combined with the web's URL to give the complete address to the file in the repository.

Basic Techniques

Fortunately, the SPAttachmentCollection has several useful direct methods, such as Add, Delete, and Recycle.

```
SPList list = web.Lists["MyList"];
foreach (string fileName in item.Attachments)
{
    SPFile file = item.ParentList.ParentWeb.GetFile(
                  item.Attachments.UrlPrefix + fileName);
    // Work with SPFile
}
```

Listing 4–3 shows access to a specific item of a list.

Listing 4–3. *Read an Attachment for a Specific Item*

```
using (SPSite site = new SPSite("http://sharepointserve"))
{
    using (SPWeb web = site.OpenWeb())
    {
        SPList list = web.Lists["WordDocuments"];
        SPListItem item = list.Items[id];
        if (item.Attachments.Count > 0)
        {
            SPFile attachment = item.ParentList.ParentWeb.GetFile(
                                item.Attachments.UrlPrefix + item.Attachments[0]);
            Stream content = attachment.OpenBinaryStream();
            using (Package p = Package.Open(content))
            {
                // handle as a package (just a suggestion)
            }
        }
    }
}
```

This code assumes that you have a list, called WordDocuments. The current item is selected by using the variable id. The code checks whether one or more attachments are present, and if so, it reads the first attachment (index zero). The attachment is loaded into an SPFile object and read as a binary stream. We suggest you use the Package class to access files in the package format (such as XPS, DOCX, XSLX, and so forth). The Package class is defined in the namespace System.IO.Packaging—the containing assembly is WindowsBase.dll. (You can find more about working with Office packages in the section "Working with Office Documents.")

The example in Listing 4–4 retrieves the very same attachment, using the folder structure instead of the full URL.

Listing 4–4. *Read an Attachment via the Folder Hierarchy*

```
SPList list = web.Lists["WordDocuments"];
SPListItem item = list.Items[id];
SPFolder folder = web.Folders["Lists"]
                     .SubFolders[list.RootFolder.Name]
                     .SubFolders["Attachments"]
                     .SubFolders[item.ID.ToString()];
if (folder.Files.Count > 0)
{
    SPFile attachment = folder.Files[0];
    Stream content = attachment.OpenBinaryStream();
    using (Package p = Package.Open(content))
    {
        // handle as a package (just a suggestion)
    }
}
```

The twist is the direct access to the Attachments folder of the web, where the files are organized. As before, the variable id must contain a valid ID for the specified list.

Example: Adding an Attachment to an Item

In the same way that you can read an attachment, you can add an attachment to a list item. This is the preferred way to overcome the limitations of the common upload dialog and implement something more sophisticated (see Listing 4–5).

Listing 4–5. *Add an Attachment to an Item*

```
using (SPSite site = new SPSite("http://sharepointserve"))
{
    using (SPWeb web = site.OpenWeb())
    {
      SPList list = web.Lists["WordDocuments"];
      SPListItem newItem = list.GetItemById(id);
      byte[] contents = null;

      if (fileUpload.PostedFile != null && fileUpload.HasFile)
      {
         using (Stream fileStream = fileUpload.PostedFile.InputStream)
         {
           contents = new byte[fileStream.Length];
           fileStream.Read(contents, 0, (int) fileStream.Length);
           fileStream.Close();
         }

         SPAttachmentCollection attachments = newItem.Attachments;
```

```
            string fileName = Path.GetFileName(fileUpload.PostedFile.FileName);
            attachments.Add(fileName, contents);

            newItem ["AttachmentName"] = fileName;
            newItem.Update();
        }
    }
}
```

This code assumes you have an `.aspx` page with a `FileUpload` control named `fileUpload`. The user can use this to upload a file, where it's attached directly to the item. It is further assumed that your WordDocuments list has an AttachmentName column that takes the attachment's name for further reference. This column is of type `text`.

Example: Deleting an Attachment from SPList

As with reading and adding, you can delete an attachment (see Listing 4–6). The item is again selected by using the variable `id`.

Listing 4–6. *Delete an Existing Attachment*

```
using (SPSite site = new SPSite("http://sharepointserve"))
{
    using (SPWeb web = site.OpenWeb())
    {
      SPList list = web.Lists["WordDocuments"];
      SPListItem delItem = list.GetItemById(id);
      SPAttachmentCollection atCol = delItem.Attachments;
      if (delItem["AttachmentName"] != null)
      {
         string strFileName = delItem["AttachmentName"].ToString();
         delItem["AttachmentName"] = string.Empty;
         atCol.Delete(strFileName);
         delItem.Update();
      }
    }
}
```

In this example, the WordDocuments list contains an additional column, AttachmentName, that holds the URL of the attachment. As you can see, this avoids the URL operations to get the real URL of the attachment.

■ **Tip** If you work programmatically with attachments, it's helpful to store the complete URL in a hidden field of the containing list to have instant access to the file.

Example: Downloading an Attachment

To download an attachment, you must first find the download link and then redirect to another page. The ending of the response from current page does not affect the functionalities on the second one. The code shown in Listing 4–7 assumes you have a WordDocuments list and the AttachmentName column, as shown in the previous examples.

Listing 4–7. *Download an Attachment*

```
using (SPSite site = new SPSite("http://sharepointserve"))
{
    using (SPWeb web = site.OpenWeb())
    {
      string AttachmentURL = string.Empty;
      SPList list = web.Lists["WordDocuments"];
      SPListItem attItem = myList.GetItemById(NodeID);
      if (attItem["AttachmentName"] != null)
      {
          AttachmentURL = "/Lists/ WordDocuments/Attachments/" +
                          NodeID.ToString() + "/" +
                          attItem["AttachmentName"].ToString();

          System.Web.HttpContext.Current.Session["FileName"] =
                                     attItem["AttachmentName"].ToString();
          System.Web.HttpContext.Current.Session["Attachment"] =
                                     AttachmentURL.Trim();
       }
       else
       {
          lblReport.Text = "No File name found";
       }
       if (AttachmentURL != string.Empty)
       {
           Reponse.Redirect("download.aspx");
       }
    }
}
```

On the `download.aspx` page, you need to the code shown in Listing 4–8 to force the browser to download the file.

Listing 4–8. *Download a File (Code-Behind of an Otherwise Empty ASPX Page)*

```
if (System.Web.HttpContext.Current.Session["Attachment"] != null)
{
  string strName = System.Web.HttpContext.Current.Session["FileName"].ToString();
  string sbURL = System.Web.HttpContext.Current.Session["Attachment"].ToString();
  System.Web.HttpResponse response;
  response = System.Web.HttpContext.Current.Response;
  System.Web.HttpContext.Current.Response.ContentEncoding =
                                                  System.Text.Encoding.Default;
  response.AppendHeader("Content-disposition", "attachment; filename=" + strName);
  response.AppendHeader("Pragma", "cache");
  response.AppendHeader("Cache-control", "private");
  response.Redirect(sbURL);
  response.End();
}
```

The download page is standard fare used to set the appropriate headers that cause the browser to display an attractive download dialog with some values preloaded.

Example: Copying an Attachment from One Item to Another Using SPList

Copying an attachment is simply a combination of the previous techniques (see Listing 4–9). There is no direct copy method—only reading an attachment into a stream and writing it back into the new attachment.

Listing 4–9. *Copy an Attachment*

```
private void CopyAttachment(int fromID, int toID, string attachedFile)
{
  byte[] contents = null;
  SPList list = w.ParentWeb.Lists["Item List"];
  SPListItem toItem = list.GetItemById(toID);
  SPListItem fromItem = list.GetItemById(fromID);

  SPAttachmentCollection attColl = fromItem.Attachments;

  SPFile attFile = fromItem.ParentList.ParentWeb.GetFile(
                   fromItem.Attachments.UrlPrefix + attachedFile);
  string fileRead = fromItem.Attachments.UrlPrefix.ToString() + attachedFile;

  StreamReader fsReader = new StreamReader(attFile.OpenBinaryStream());
  using (Stream fStream = fsReader.BaseStream)
  {
    contents = new byte[fStream.Length];
    fStream.Read(contents, 0, (int)fStream.Length);
    fStream.Close();
  }

  toItem.Attachments.Add(attachedFile, contents);
  toItem.Update();
}
```

If you plan to copy very large files, such as 1 MB or more, we recommend you copy it in chunks. This reduces the amount of memory you need, because the byte array (`contents`) will hold a copy of the whole file into memory while the opened stream is doing the same already. A loop that reads chunks of 2,048 bytes, for example, is appropriate for most projects.

Handle Huge Lists

If a list becomes huge—Microsoft allows theoretically up to 50 million items—the direct handling using `SPList` and LINQ to Objects will fail. Instead, a CAML query, as described in the section "Query Data Using CAML and LINQ," can dramatically reduce the result set. However, if you want to modify all items in the list or need to page through a still substantial result set, this will not help. In a query, you can specify the current result set position using the `SPListItemCollectionPosition` class. The query is based on the `SPQuery` class, but the position does not require adding a specific condition—an empty query will also work. (See the section "Efficient Access to Huge Lists" in Chapter 5.)

Define and Use Views

The previous examples work well in code. However, when a user tries to access the list using the AllItems.aspx page, only the title is visible. The actual appearance depends on the base type from which the list inherits. In the example, the custom (generic) list is used. This type has the obligatory Title field only. To display more columns in the standard grid, you must change the default view or add a custom view. As with any other feature, it's also possible to customize the view in code.

Each list has a default view you can reach through the DefaultView property:

```
SPList mylist = SPWeb.Lists["MyList"];
SPView view = mylist.DefaultView;
// modify View
view.Update();
```

You can access the view object and save updates by calling the Update method. It is not possible to use the property directly, as in this snippet:

```
mylist.DefaultView.ViewFields.Add("NewField1");
mylist.DefaultView.ViewFields.Add("NewField2");
mylist.DefaultView.Update(); // saves the "NewField2" only!
```

The reason is that the property returns a new SPView instance with every call. To handle a single instance, you need to retrieve the object and modify it directly.

The next example retrieves all the lists and lets the user select any of the views of the chosen list. Within a GridView control, all the properties are displayed. First, the .aspx page shows how to deal with the values. The page uses the standard Master page's main placeholder, as shown in Listing 4–10.

Listing 4–10. *Application Page with a Ajax-Driven GridView*

```
<asp:Content ID="Main" ContentPlaceHolderID="PlaceHolderMain" runat="server">
    <div style="margin: 20px">
        <asp:UpdatePanel ID="up1" runat="server" ChildrenAsTriggers="true"
                         UpdateMode="Conditional">
            <ContentTemplate>
                <h2>
                    Available Lists in this Web</h2>
                <ul>
                    <li>Web:
                        <asp:Label ID="lblWeb" runat="server"
                                   Text="Label"></asp:Label></li>
                    <li>Lists:
                        <asp:Label ID="lblLists" runat="server"
                                   Text="Label"></asp:Label>
                        Lists<br />
                        <asp:DropDownList ID="ddlLists" runat="server"
                             AppendDataBoundItems="true" AutoPostBack="true"
                             OnSelectedIndexChanged="ddlLists_SelectedIndexChanged">
                            <asp:ListItem Text="Select a List" />
                        </asp:DropDownList>
                    </li>
                </ul>
                <h2>
                    Views in selected list</h2>
                Views:
                <asp:DropDownList ID="ddlViews" runat="server"
```

```
                    AppendDataBoundItems="true" AutoPostBack="true"
                    OnSelectedIndexChanged="ddlViews_SelectedIndexChanged">
                <asp:ListItem Text="Select a View" />
                </asp:DropDownList><br /><br />
                <asp:GridView ID="gvProperties" runat="server"
                              AutoGenerateColumns="false">
                    <Columns>
                        <asp:BoundField DataField="PropertyName"
                                        HeaderText="Name" />
                        <asp:BoundField DataField="PropertyValue"
                                        HtmlEncode="true" HeaderText="Value" />
                        <asp:BoundField DataField="PropertyType"
                                        HeaderText="Type" />
                    </Columns>
                </asp:GridView>
            </ContentTemplate>
        </asp:UpdatePanel>
    </div>
</asp:Content>
```

This markup defines a DropDownList control for the lists, another for the views of the selected list, and a GridView that displays all the public properties of the selected view. All the code to create and assign the data sources is in the code behind (see Listing 4–11).

Listing 4–11. *Code of the Application Page*

```
using System;
using System.Linq;
using Microsoft.SharePoint;
using Microsoft.SharePoint.WebControls;
using System.Reflection;

namespace Apress.SP2010.Layouts.CreateViews
{
    public partial class ViewsManager : LayoutsPageBase
    {
        private SPWeb web;

        protected void Page_Load(object sender, EventArgs e)
        {
            web = SPContext.Current.Web;
            if (!IsPostBack)
            {
                lblWeb.Text = web.Title;
                lblLists.Text = web.Lists.Count.ToString();
                ddlLists.DataSource = web.Lists;
                ddlLists.DataValueField = "ID";
                ddlLists.DataTextField = "Title";
                ddlLists.DataBind();
            }
        }

        protected void ddlLists_SelectedIndexChanged(object sender, EventArgs e)
        {
```

```
            Guid id = new Guid(ddlLists.SelectedValue);
            SPList list = web.Lists[id];
            ddlViews.DataSource = list.Views;
            ddlViews.DataTextField = "Title";
            ddlViews.DataValueField = "ID";
            ddlViews.DataBind();
        }

        protected void ddlViews_SelectedIndexChanged(object sender, EventArgs e)
        {
            Guid lid = new Guid(ddlLists.SelectedValue);
            SPList list = web.Lists[lid];
            Guid vid = new Guid(ddlViews.SelectedValue);
            SPView view = list.Views[vid];

            var props = from pi in view.GetType().GetProperties(
                                   BindingFlags.Public | BindingFlags.Instance)
                        orderby pi.Name ascending
                        select new
                        {
                            PropertyName = pi.Name,
                            PropertyValue = pi.GetValue(view, null),
                            PropertyType = pi.PropertyType.Name
                        };
            gvProperties.DataSource = props;
            gvProperties.DataBind();
        }

    }
}
```

In the final event handler attached to the ddlViews control that shows the views, the SPView object is retrieved. A LINQ query gathers all the public properties that are instance members. For each property, the type and value is read. Several properties contain XML. In the markup of the GridView, the value column has the HtmlEncode attribute set to make the XML visible (see Figure 4–5).

Figure 4–5. Retrieving all details of a view with few controls

The property that accepts XML can be filled with different CAML schemas. It depends on the property and usage what subset of CAML is appropriate. The most important is the `Query` property, which determines what the view returns. (CAML is described in more detail in the section "Understanding CAML" later in this chapter.)

Modifying an Existing View

Defining a view is very straightforward. You can see from the Change View dialog (select a list and then select List Tools ➤ List) in that it has many sophisticated options—as does the object model. Custom code can simplify the list creation task for a specific application. Adding the appropriate view should support at least adding the custom fields to the default view. For the Books list used previously, it looks like this:

```
SPList books = web.Lists["Books"];
SPView view = books.Views["All Items"];
view.ViewFields.Add("ISBN");
view.ViewFields.Add("LeadAuthor");
view.ViewFields.Add("Price");
view.Update();
```

The `AllItems.aspx` page now displays these fields, along with Title. As explained earlier, the internal properties sometimes return new objects with each call. Regarding `ViewFields`, it still works as shown, because the collections are synchronized internally. However, the recommended coding style is as follows:

```
SPList books = web.Lists["Books"];
SPView view = books.Views["All Items"];
SPViewFieldCollection svfc = view.ViewFields;
svfc.Add("ISBN");
svfc.Add("LeadAuthor");
svfc.Add("Price");
view.Update();
```

Creating a New View Programmatically

If a view does not yet exist, you can create one programmatically. This can be part of a feature—usually in the feature receiver—or any tool a user can use to change the current list.

The code in Listing 4–12 assumes you have a Books list with some entries. It has at least two fields: Publisher, which is a selection field, and Author, containing text.

Listing 4–12. *Creating a New View Programmatically*

```
using System.Collections.Specialized;
using System.Xml.Linq;
using Microsoft.SharePoint;

namespace Apress.SP2010.CreateNewView
{
    class Program
    {
        static void Main(string[] args)
        {
            using (SPSite site = new SPSite("http://sharepointserve"))
            {
                using (SPWeb web = site.OpenWeb())
                {
                    SPList books = web.Lists["Books"];
                    StringCollection fields = new StringCollection();
                    fields.Add("Title");
                    fields.Add("Publisher");
                    fields.Add("Author");
                    var query = new XElement("Where",
                                    new XElement("Eq",
                                        new XElement("FieldRef",
                                          new XAttribute("Name", "Publisher")),
                                        new XElement("Value",
                                          new XAttribute("Type", "CHOICE"),
                                          "Apress")
                                        )
                                    ).ToString(SaveOptions.DisableFormatting);
                    SPView view = books.Views.Add("ApressBooks",
                        fields,
                        query,
                        100,
                        false,
                        false,
                        Microsoft.SharePoint.SPViewCollection.SPViewType.Html,
                        false
                        );
                }
            }

        }

    }
}
```

You can add a new view to the SPViewCollection exposed by the Views property. You need to provide the fields as a StringCollection object. If the view should filter the data, a query can be applied using CAML. The XElement and XAttribute types aid in creating valid XML on the first attempt. The query is then assigned as a string. The Add method has some overloads. Table 4–2 explains the parameters this method supports.

Table 4–2. *Parameters of the Add Method Required to Create a View*

Parameter	Type	Description
viewName	string	The name for the view
fieldColl	StringCollection	The collection of field names
query	string	CAML query that filters the data
rowLimit	int	Maximum number of rows per page
paged	bool	Flag to indicate whether to show rows with paging
makeDefault	bool	Flag to indicate whether this view is the default view
type	SPViewType	The type of view—valid values are Html (default view), Grid (datasheet view), Calendar, Recurrence (recurring calendar items), Chart, and Gantt
isPersonal	bool	Flag to indicate whether the view is public (false) or personal to the current user (true)

There is no Update method—after adding a view, users can use it immediately.

Custom Field Types

A custom field type extends a field's behavior. A field is not only a simple storage location for data; it has additional functions:

- Constraints that limit the data value to a range or specific conditions
- Validation formula that checks data entered by user
- A field editor for the common edit forms

If you create a custom field type, you can modify all of these aspects. These features are independent of each other. If you want to display a drop-down to enter a selection of integer values, you will use a standard number field and simply change the editor, while a validation doesn't make sense (because the user can't manipulate the selection.)

A custom field type is usually accompanied with a custom editor, which appears in the default EditForm for the list. Building the editor is similar to building a user control or Web Part. It's therefore covered in Chapter 11 in more detail.

Content Types

As explained in the introduction, the content type has a significant role. Instead of modeling a list with a fixed set of fields, the content type can be bound to a list. A list may have different content types and accept different types. Content types are defined outside the scope of any list. This enhances reusability. Having defined content types to describe a specific set of items, you can use these definitions in as many lists or libraries as you want. As a developer, you can treat content types as a form of polymorphism. Content types are supported on several levels. Consequently, you can, for instance, search your site for all items of a specific content type, regardless of which list contains the item.

Content types support the concept of inheritance. This means that you do not usually create a new content type from scratch. Instead, you inherit from a similar one and add the fields and definitions you actually need. SharePoint includes several built-in content types for this purpose—making the process of creating a new one fast and simple.

Difference between Lists and Libraries

In this chapter, provided we're not referring to documents explicitly, we don't distinguish between lists and libraries. Content types have two base types, one for lists and one for libraries. As a result, if you want to create a new content type for a document library, it must inherit from the appropriate base type. A content type designed for a library will not work with a standard list.

Parts of a Content Type

The previous sections described fields. Content types define not only fields to create columns. They also define events or associated workflows—the item's behavior. For example, you can create a content type that is bound to a list, and when an item is created with that type, an associated event receiver uses the item to perform some calculations or check validity. Because of this power, creating and using content types is complicated. However, it's worth examining closer, for any real life project.

Like the content type itself, the fields it contains are not explicitly defined there. Instead, you create global fields (in the scope of the web or site) and assign a reference to such a field. SharePoint comes with many predefined global field definitions that can be used to create content types with standard field types. These appear as *site columns* in the SharePoint UI.

▒ **Note** While the global fields internally use the term *field*, the UI uses the term *column*. In this chapter, we use the term *field*, and you can regard this as equivalent to *column*. The authors prefer the term *field* because it expresses the nature of the data model with lists and items, while a *column* is closer to the relational model based on tables and records.

Internally, a content type is of type `SPContentType`. This type contains two collections, `Fields` (of type `SPFieldCollection`) and `FieldLinks` (of type `SPFieldLink`). If you want to add a field to the content type, you need to use an `SPFieldLink` object. The `Fields` collection is the corresponding list that gives access to the final definition of each column including a column's attributes. The resulting `SPField` object is a merged view of the part defined in the references field and the one inherited from.

■ **Note** Even if the object model appears to support addition or deletion of fields using the `Fields` collection, an exception is thrown if you try to do so.

Before you start creating your own fields, examine the list of predefined ones. It is likely that you will find one appropriate for your new content type, and it will save you time and effort. Figure 4–6 shows how site columns appear in the UI.

Create   Show Group: All Groups

Site Column	Type	Source
Base Columns		
Append-Only Comments	Multiple lines of text	ApressSamples
Categories	Single line of text	ApressSamples
End Date	Date and Time	ApressSamples
Language	Choice	ApressSamples
Start Date	Date and Time	ApressSamples
URL	Hyperlink or Picture	ApressSamples
Workflow Name	Single line of text	ApressSamples
Core Contact and Calendar Columns		
Address	Multiple lines of text	ApressSamples
Anniversary	Date and Time	ApressSamples
Assistant's Name	Single line of text	ApressSamples
Assistant's Phone	Single line of text	ApressSamples
Birthday	Date and Time	ApressSamples
Business Phone	Single line of text	ApressSamples
Business Phone 2	Single line of text	ApressSamples
Callback Number	Single line of text	ApressSamples

Figure 4–6. *Some predefined site columns available for creating content types*

You can find the complete list on MSDN—there are about 410 field definitions available. Hence, instead of creating one, take your time to find the right one. The following example shows both techniques, using an existing field type (site column) and a new one previously added to the field collection:

```
SPContentTypeCollection cts = web.ContentTypes;
SPContentType newctpy = new SPContentType(
   cts[SPBuiltInContentTypeId.Contact],
   cts,
   "Certificates");
// Add content type to the site
cts.Add(newctpy);
// Create site fields and link to the content type
SPFieldCollection siteFields = web.Fields;
siteFields.Add("Certificate", SPFieldType.Text, true);
siteFields.Add("Score", SPFieldType.Integer, true);
web.Update();
```

```
// Add fields to the new content type
newctpy.FieldLinks.Add(new SPFieldLink(siteFields["Certificate"]));
newctpy.FieldLinks.Add(new SPFieldLink(siteFields["Score"]));
newctpy.FieldLinks.Add(new SPFieldLink(web.Fields["Start Date"]));
newctpy.Update();
// Add content type to the list
SPList authors = web.Lists["Authors"];
authors.ContentTypesEnabled = true;
if (authors.IsContentTypeAllowed(newctpy))
{
   SPContentType certCT = authors.ContentTypes.Add(newctpy);
   authors.Update();
}
```

The content type is used to add certificates an author has earned to the Authors list used in the previous examples. The code starts with a reference to the web's `ContentTypes` collection. The new content type Certificates is added. Then two fields are added to the web's field collection: Certificate and Score. These and an existing field, Start Date, are added to the `FieldLinks` collection of the new content type. If no errors occurred, the list is enabled to support content types, and the content type is added to the list. The result can immediately be checked by comparing the content types in the site administration with those in the list.

In Figure 4–7 you can see that the custom site column is available.

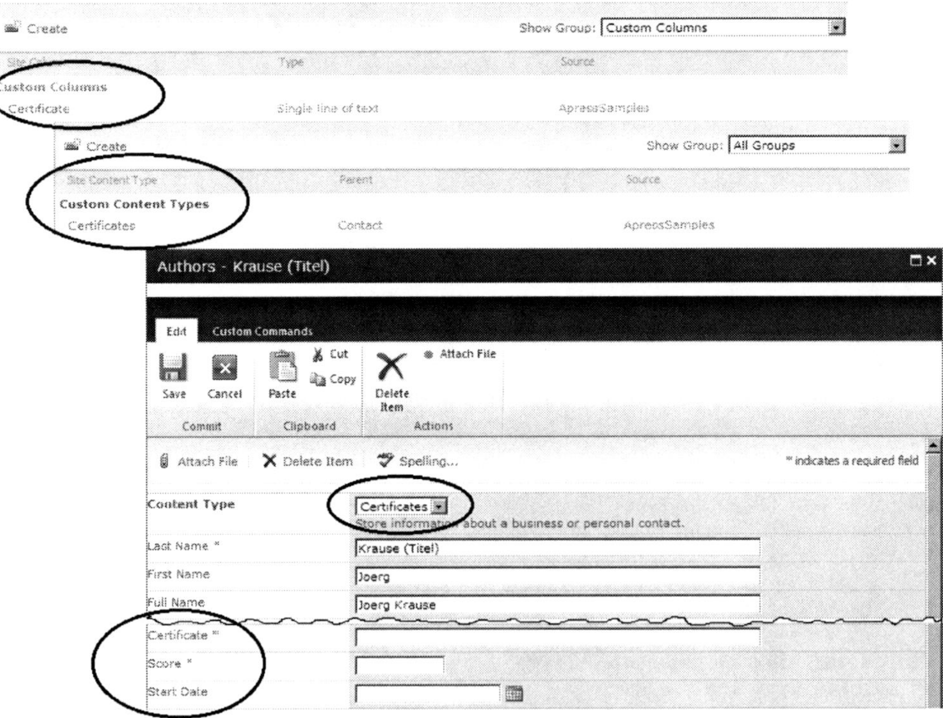

Figure 4–7. Custom content type with the custom column definition, the content type, and the editor

Also available are the custom content type using these columns and the built-in columns. When you start editing the items of the list, you can select your content type. This is because the existing list already implements the Contact content type. The new Certificates content type inherits from Contact and hence has the same fields plus the new ones. You can delete the existing content type if no existing items are using it:

```
list.ContentTypes["Name"].Delete();
```

When to Use Content Types Programmatically

In code that runs every day in your application, you will probably not use content types. Programmatic access to a site's content type is usually an administrative operation. Typically you deploy a new feature, and the users can create custom lists within your application. To minimize their effort, a custom content type is ideal. Consequently, the feature must be able to create the content type on activation. That's exactly when you invoke code similar to that shown previously.

There is some interaction between the UI and the settings made by custom code. First, when adding a content type to a list, the fields in the content type are copied to the list. That's why the edit form shows the fields immediately. If a user with appropriate rights now changes the field's definition, they change the copied definition. That means such modified fields remain local to that list and do not change the content type. Second, when changing the content type using the web's Site Settings dialog, the user has the choice to push changes to existing copies (see Figure 4–8).

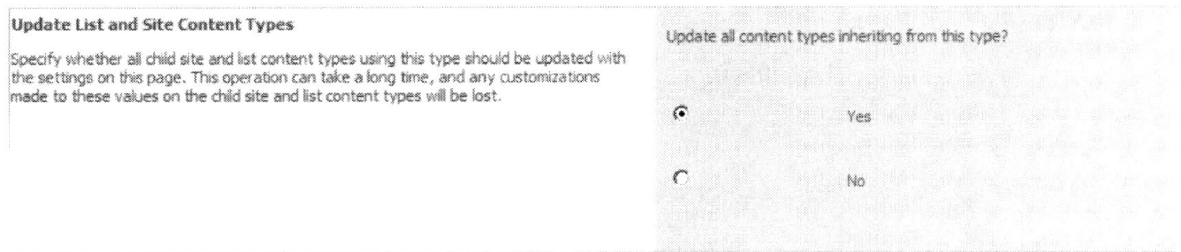

Figure 4–8. *The user has the option to push changes to existing content type copies.*

Item- and List-Level Event Receivers

To interact with lists and items, you can attach event receivers. With these your code is called when a specified condition is met in the attached list. The implementation uses the `SPListItemEventReceiver` base class—you simply override the methods you want to activate.

Synchronous vs. Asynchronous Events

SharePoint is rich with the events it exposes. We can categorize SharePoint events in two ways: by the "level" that fires the event (site, list, item) and by the type of the event (synchronous or asynchronous).

WHAT SYNCHRONOUS/ASYNCHRONOUS MEANS FOR EVENTS?

Synchronous events happen "before" the actual event. You have the `HttpContext`; you can display an error message in the browser, and if needed, you can cancel the event before it occurs.

Asynchronous events happen "after" the actual event. There is no `HttpContext`; you cannot directly show an error message, and you cannot cancel the event. On the other hand, you can handle what happens after the event is fired, including manipulating the object.

As examples of synchronous and asynchronous events, consider item-level events such as `ItemAdding` and `ItemAdded`. With `ItemAdding`, you can inspect the item, and, if necessary, cancel the addition and display an error message in the SharePoint page to the user. Inside the `ItemAdded` event, however, you know that the item is already in the SharePoint list, but you can start some post-add actions concerning that item.

List Item Events

Table 4–3 shows the full list of synchronous events you can handle with your receivers.

Table 4–3. *Synchronous Item-Level Events*

Event	Description
`ItemAdding`	Occurs when a new item is added to its containing object
`ItemAttachmentAdding`	Occurs when a user adds an attachment to an item
`ItemAttachmentDeleting`	Occurs when a user removes an attachment from an item
`ItemCheckingIn`	Occurs as a file is being checked in
`ItemCheckingOut`	Occurs before an item is checked out
`ItemDeleting`	Occurs before an existing item is completely deleted
`ItemFileMoving`	Occurs when a file is being moved
`ItemUncheckedOut`	Occurs before an item is being unchecked out
`ItemUpdating`	Occurs when an existing item is changed, for example, when the user changes data in one or more fields

Synchronous events are also called "before" events. They appear before the internal operation occurs. The event handler is also blocking the current flow. For this reason, we recommend you avoid time-consuming operations here.

Asynchronous events (see Table 4–4) are classified as "after" events. They are called asynchronously. Lengthy operations do not block the current thread. Because the internal operation is completed, you can safely manipulate the freshly added or changed data.

Table 4–4. *Asynchronous Item-Level Events*

Event	Description
`ItemAdded`	Occurs after a new item has been added to its containing object
`ItemAttachmentAdded`	Occurs after a user adds an attachment to an item
`ItemAttachmentDeleted`	Occurs after a user removes an attachment from an item
`ItemCheckedIn`	Occurs after an item is checked in
`ItemCheckedOut`	Occurs after an item is checked out
`ItemDeleted`	Occurs after an existing item is completely deleted
`ItemFileConverted`	Occurs after a file has been converted
`ItemFileMoved`	Occurs after a file is moved
`ItemUncheckingOut`	Occurs after an item is unchecked out
`ItemUpdated`	Occurs after an existing item is changed, for example, when the user changes data in one or more fields

List Events

List events (see Tables 4–5 and 4–6) occur for list operations that affect the whole list, such as schema changes. As for the list item events, you can choose synchronous and asynchronous events. The implementation uses the `SPListEventReceiver` base class—you simply override the appropriate methods.

Table 4–5. *Synchronous List-Level Events*

Event	Description
`FieldAdding`	Occurs when a field link is being added to a content type
`FieldDeleting`	Occurs when a field is being removed from the list
`FieldUpdating`	Occurs when a field link is being updated

Table 4–6. Asynchronous List-Level Events

Event	Description
`FieldAdded`	Occurs after a field link is added
`FieldDeleted`	Occurs after a field has been removed from the list
`FieldUpdated`	Occurs after a field link has been updated

■ **Note** Apart from list and list item events, several other objects in SharePoint support events, too. For site- and web-level events, refer to Chapter 3.

Developing and Deploying an Event Receiver

This section contains a step-by-step guide to developing event receivers and attaching them to the appropriate objects. In this example, we will create a simple receiver, which will handle two asynchronous events (`ItemAdded` and `ItemUpdated`) in all Document and Picture libraries at a SharePoint web site, and deploy it as a feature at the site level. The templates Visual Studio 2010 provides for this (see Figure 4–9) add the required configuration files. The template comes with a wizard that asks for the particular event you want to create. Therefore, there is just one template for all possible events.

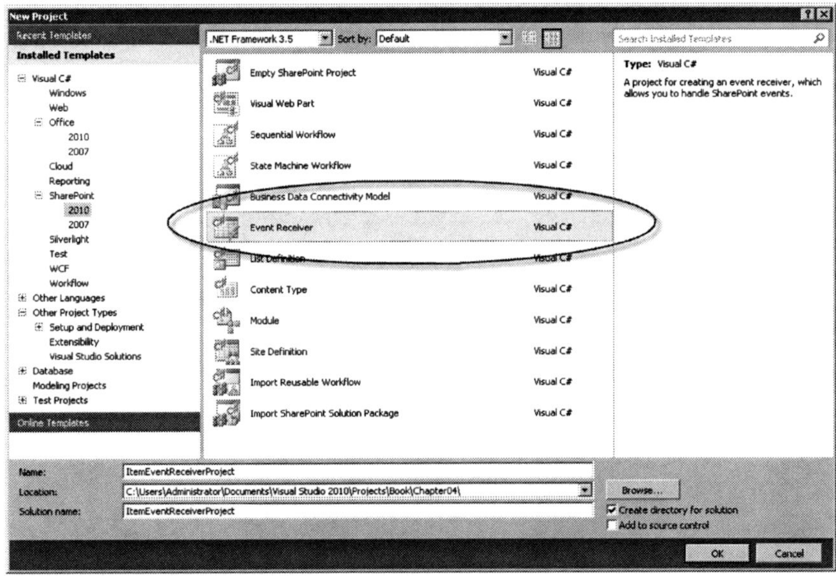

Figure 4–9. Create an event receiver project.

The wizard asks for the SharePoint site and whether the solution is a sandboxed or farm solution. Next (see Figure 4–10), you can select the type of event (List, List Item, and so on) and what specific event handler the wizard should create.

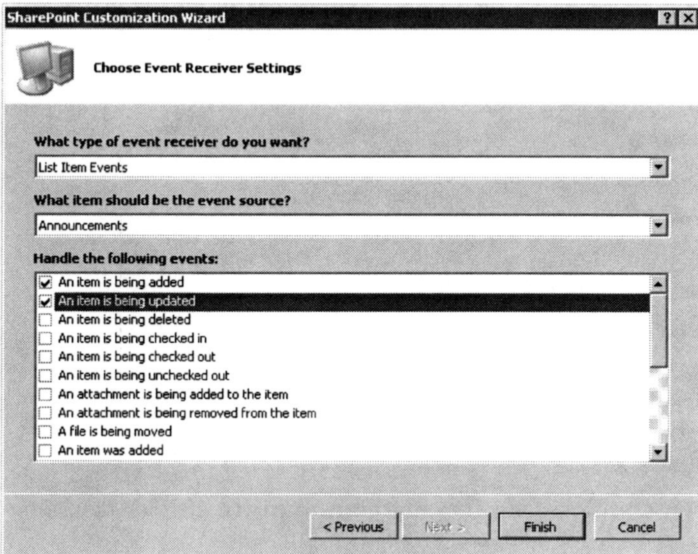

Figure 4–10. *Select the event type and particular handlers.*

The wizard creates the package (solution), the feature that activates and deactivates the event handlers, and the event handler definition. An event handler definition consists of an `Element.xml` file that defines events, where they attach and the entry point of the assembly that contains the code (see Listing 4–13).

Listing 4–13. *Elements.xml of an Event Receiver*

```
<?xml version="1.0" encoding="utf-8"?>
<Elements xmlns="http://schemas.microsoft.com/sharepoint/">
  <Receivers ListTemplateId="104">
      <Receiver>
        <Name>EventReceiver1ItemAdded</Name>
        <Type>ItemAdded</Type>
        <Assembly>$SharePoint.Project.AssemblyFullName$</Assembly>
        <Class>ItemEventReceiverProject.EventReceiver1.EventReceiver1</Class>
        <SequenceNumber>10000</SequenceNumber>
      </Receiver>
      <Receiver>
        <Name>EventReceiver1ItemUpdated</Name>
        <Type>ItemUpdated</Type>
        <Assembly>$SharePoint.Project.AssemblyFullName$</Assembly>
        <Class>ItemEventReceiverProject.EventReceiver1.EventReceiver1</Class>
        <SequenceNumber>10000</SequenceNumber>
      </Receiver>
```

```
  </Receivers>
</Elements>
```

This file defines two events, ItemAdded and ItemUpdated. Both are defined in the same class. The ListItemTemplateId attribute of 104 defines that the receiver is attached to one of the default lists—in this case, the Announcement list. See Table 4–1 earlier in this chapter for a list of built-in lists and their respective internal IDs.

The Elements.xml

Each Receivers node has following child nodes:

- Name: A unique name for the receiver—you can set it as you want for future reference.
- Type: This is actually the event name from the events table.
- SequenceNumber: An integer that determines in which order the event receivers will be fired.
- Assembly: The assembly that contains your event handler. The assembly will be deployed in the GAC.
- Class: The class in the assembly containing the handler methods.

The crucial parts here are the Assembly and Class tags. They must exactly match the class definition when they are deployed.

The Event Handler Code

The code snippet created by the wizard (see Listing 4–14) attaches the two events to their event handlers. This is shown "as is." No changes were made to fix namespaces or anything else.

Listing 4–14. *The Event Receivers Handler Methods*

```
using System;
using System.Security.Permissions;
using Microsoft.SharePoint;
using Microsoft.SharePoint.Security;
using Microsoft.SharePoint.Utilities;
using Microsoft.SharePoint.Workflow;

namespace Apress.SP2010.EventReceiver1
{
    /// <summary>
    /// List Item Events
    /// </summary>
    public class EventReceiver1 : SPItemEventReceiver
    {
       /// <summary>
       /// An item is being added.
       /// </summary>
       public override void ItemAdded(SPItemEventProperties properties)
       {
```

```
            base.ItemAdded(properties);
        }

        /// <summary>
        /// An item is being updated.
        /// </summary>
        public override void ItemUpdated(SPItemEventProperties properties)
        {
            base.ItemUpdated(properties);
        }

    }
}
```

The receiver class must inherit from SPItemEventReceiver. To attach other events, you can override the corresponding methods in this class and extend the Elements.xml to connect the handler with the event source. A closer look into the SPItemEventProperties reveals some options. Listing 4–15 shows an example.

Listing 4–15. *Using an Event Receiver to Change Permissions*

```
using System;
using System.Security.Permissions;
using Microsoft.SharePoint;
using Microsoft.SharePoint.Security;
using Microsoft.SharePoint.Utilities;
using Microsoft.SharePoint.Workflow;

namespace Apress.SP2010.EventReceiver2
{

    public class EventReceiver2 : SPItemEventReceiver
    {
        public override void ItemAdded(SPItemEventProperties properties)
        {
            updateItemPermissions(properties);
        }

        public override void ItemUpdated(SPItemEventProperties properties)
        {
            updateItemPermissions(properties);
        }

        private void updateItemPermissions(SPItemEventProperties properties)
        {
            try
            {
                this.EventFiringEnabled = false;
                SPListItem item = properties.ListItem;
                SPSecurity.RunWithElevatedPrivileges(delegate()
                {
                    SPList parentList = item.ParentList;
                    SPSite elevatedSite = new SPSite(parentList.ParentWeb.Site.ID);
                    SPWeb elevatedWeb =
```

```
                          elevatedSite.OpenWeb(parentList.ParentWeb.ID);
                    SPList elevatedList = elevatedWeb.Lists[parentList.ID];
                    SPListItem elevatedItem =
                          elevatedList.Items.GetItemById(properties.ListItem.ID);
                    if (!item.HasUniqueRoleAssignments)
                        item.BreakRoleInheritance(false);

                    SPUser editor = elevatedWeb.EnsureUser(
                           (new SPFieldLookupValue(item["Editor"].ToString()))
                                .LookupValue);
                    SPUser author = elevatedWeb.EnsureUser(
                           (new SPFieldLookupValue(item["Author"].ToString()))
                                .LookupValue);
                    SPRoleDefinition RoleDefReader =
                          elevatedWeb.RoleDefinitions.GetByType(
                                                     SPRoleType.Reader);
                    SPRoleDefinition RoleDefWriter =
                          elevatedWeb.RoleDefinitions.GetByType(
                                                SPRoleType.Contributor);
                    SPRoleAssignment RoleAssReader = new
                                     SPRoleAssignment((SPPrincipal)editor);
                    SPRoleAssignment RoleAssWriter = new
                                     SPRoleAssignment((SPPrincipal)author);
                    RoleAssReader.RoleDefinitionBindings.Add(RoleDefReader);
                    RoleAssWriter.RoleDefinitionBindings.Add(RoleDefWriter);
                    item.RoleAssignments.Add(RoleAssReader);
                    item.RoleAssignments.Add(RoleAssWriter);
                    item.Update();

                });

                this.EventFiringEnabled = true;
            }
            catch (Exception ex)
            {
            }
        }
    }
}
```

The receiver is attached to a list that has at least two fields—called Author and Editor—both of `User` type containing a user available in the current site. Usually the creator of the item becomes the owner. The event receiver overwrites the inherited permissions by setting the users added in the Author field with write permissions and in the Editor field with read permissions.

In addition, the code shows some basic principles. To change the permissions, you need sufficient rights. You can achieve this by elevating the privileges or by assigning a specific user's token to the `OpenWeb` method. In this example, the `RunWithElevatedPrivileges` method is used. The code checks whether the item already has specific permissions using the `HasUniqueRoleAssignments` property. This avoids rewriting the values again. If the permissions are at the default level, the inheritance hierarchy is broken by calling `BreakRoleInheritance`. Now you can assign user's roles. `EnsureUser` checks that the site's user is available in the list's web. The specific permissions are retrieved from the web's `RoleDefinitions` property and set to standard permissions (`SPRoleType.Reader` and `SPRoleType.Contributor`).

Because the changes will update the item and an event receiver connects to ItemUpdating event, you need to suppress events temporarily. This is done by setting the EventFiringEnabled property.

Document Libraries and Document Sets

Document libraries are lists that handle documents. Other than the attachments, which are stored in the containing web's central attachment library, a document library stores its files directly. The programmatic access to libraries is similar to lists. In addition to list-related functions, you use streams, such as a MemoryStream, when saving or loading files.

Libraries, Folders, and Documents

Several classes are dedicated to working with libraries, folders, and the files in them. In essence, a library is a list with a special content type. As a result, you can access any document library as a list and cast it to the SPList type. Each library contains at least one folder—the root folder—which provides access to any files in it. Because files are stored using an address relative to the site, even the SPSite object is a possible source. Precisely how to determine the correct storage location depends on what kind of library you use. The following examples in this section should give you ideas.

Example: Reading a File from the Shared Documents Library

Each site contains a library called Shared Documents. Listing 4–16 shows how to retrieve a file as an SPFile object.

Listing 4–16. *Read a File from a Folder Using SPFolder*

```
using (SPSite site = new SPSite("http://sharepointserve"))
{
   using (SPWeb web = site.OpenWeb())
   {
      if (web.GetFolder("Shared Documents").Exists)
      {
         SPFolder folder = web.GetFolder("Shared Documents");
         SPFile file = folder.Files["WordTemplate.docx"];
      }
   }
}
```

There is a more direct way to access a specific file using the SPDocumentLibrary (Listing 4–17).

Listing 4–17. *Read a File from a Folder Using SPDocumentLibrary*

```
using (SPSite site = new SPSite("http://sharepointserve"))
{
   using (SPWeb web = site.OpenWeb())
   {
      string url = SPUrlUtility.CombineUrl(web.Url, "/Shared Documents");
      SPDocumentLibrary lib = (SPDocumentLibrary) web.GetList(url);
      SPFile file = lib.RootFolder.Files["WordTemplate.docx"];
   }
}
```

Both examples fetch the same file. However, both will fail with an ArgumentException if the file does not exist. To check this, you cannot test the return value for null. Even an if statement such as the one shown next will not help:

```
if (lib.RootFolder.Files[["WordTemplate.docx"] != null)
```

Instead, use the GetFile method provided by SPWeb:

```
if (web.GetFile(fileName).Exists)
```

The interesting thing is that this method always returns an object. If the file does not exist, the method returns an SPFile object whose Exists property is set to false. There are still circumstances in which GetFile could return null. Hence, a helper method as in Listing 4–18 is desirable if you have many such file operations.

Listing 4–18. *Helper Method to Check for File (Retrieved from Internal Code)*

```
static SPFile GetExistingFile(SPWeb web, string serverRelativeUrl)
{
    SPFile file = null;
    bool exists = false;
    try
    {
        file = web.GetFile(serverRelativeUrl);
        if (file != null)
        {
            exists = file.Exists;
        }
    }
    catch (ArgumentException)
    {
        exists = false;
    }
    if (!exists)
    {
        return null;
    }
    return file;
}
```

Once you have the SPFile, you can do many things with it. The SPFile object gives access to some powerful properties and methods.

■ **Note** You can find the complete list of members for SPFile at http://msdn.microsoft.com/en-us/library/microsoft.sharepoint.spfile_members(office.14).aspx.

The main functions are the OpenBinaryStream method, which opens the file as a stream, and OpenBinary, which returns a byte array. Apart from these, you can do everything programmatically that users with appropriate rights can do from the UI.

Example: Adding a Folder to a Library

If you work with folders, your users might not be satisfied with the UI support. For greater capability, you can create a function (see Listing 4–19) that adds folders programmatically.

Listing 4–19. *Adding a Folder Using SPFolder*

```
using (SPSite site = new SPSite("http://sharepointserve"))
{
   using (SPWeb web = site.OpenWeb())
   {
      SPList lib = web.Lists["Shared Documents"];
      SPFolder parent = lib.RootFolder;
      SPFolder child = parent.SubFolders.Add("SubFolderName");
      parent.Update();
   }
}
```

This code adds a SubFolderName folder to the library's root. Exactly the same functionality is possible (see Listing 4–20) if you prefer to work with SPList.

Listing 4–20. *Add a Folder Using SPList*

```
using (SPSite site = new SPSite("http://sharepointserve"))
{
   using (SPWeb spweb = site.OpenWeb())
   {
       spweb.AllowUnsafeUpdates = true;

       SPList lib = spweb.Lists["Shared Documents"];
       SPListItem child =lib.Items.Add(lib.RootFolder.ServerRelativeUrl,
                                       SPFileSystemObjectType.Folder,
                                       "SubFolderName");
       child.Update();
   }
}
```

The previous example reveals that a folder is simply a special kind of item. That's indeed true and is the reason why some collections return all elements, regardless of the folder to which they are currently assigned.

Example: Saving Data to Libraries

To upload a file to a library, you use a similar approach (see Listing 4–21). The file must be available as a Stream or a byte array.

Listing 4–21. *Read a File from Disk and Save It to a Document Library*

```
using (SPSite site = new SPSite("http://sharepointserve"))
{
   using (SPWeb web = site.OpenWeb())
   {
       spweb.AllowUnsafeUpdates = true;
```

```
            SPFolder folder = web.Folders[site.URL + "/Shared Documents/"];
            byte[] content = null;
            using (FileStream filestream = new FileStream(@"C:\Sample.docx",
                                                          System.IO.FileMode.Open))
            {
               content = new byte[(int) filestream.Length];
               filestream.Read(content, 0, (int) filestream.Length);
               filestream.Close();
            }

            SPFile file = folder.Files.Add("Sample.docx", content, true);
            // do something usefil with file
        }
}
```

You can add the file to a specific folder:

```
SPFile file = folder.SubFolders["SubFolder"].Files.Add("Sample.docx",
                                                        content,
                                                        true);
```

The content variable is the same as shown previously in Listing 4–21.

Example: Deleting a File

Deleting a file is elementary. Listing 4–22 shows how to delete a file directly.

***Listing 4–22.** Deleting a File*

```
using (SPSite site = new SPSite("http://sharepointserve"))
{
   using (SPWeb web = site.OpenWeb())
   {
       web.AllowUnsafeUpdates = true;
       SPFolder folder = web.Folders[web.Url + "/Shared Documents/"];
       folder.Files["Sample.docx"].Delete();
       folder.Update();
   }
}
```

Recycling a file (Listing 4–23) uses a variation on the same approach. Recycling recycles the item into the Recycle Bin folder SharePoint provides.

***Listing 4–23.** Recycle a File from Parent Folder*

```
using (SPSite site = new SPSite("http://sharepointserve"))
{
   using (SPWeb web = site.OpenWeb())
   {
       web.AllowUnsafeUpdates = true;
       SPFolder folder = web.Folders[web.Url + "/Shared Documents/"];
       folder.Files["Sample.docx"].Recycle();
       folder.Update();
```

```
    }
}
```

Deleting a file from a subfolder follows the same rules (see Listing 4–24).

***Listing 4–24.** Deleting a File from a Subfolder*

```
using (SPSite site = new SPSite("http://sharepointserve"))
{
   using (SPWeb web = site.OpenWeb())
   {
       web.AllowUnsafeUpdates = true;
       SPFolder folder = web.Folders[site.Url + "/Shared Documents/"];
       folder.SubFolders["SubFolder"].Files["Sample.docx"].Delete();
       folder.Update();
    }
}
```

Working with Office Documents

Storing Microsoft Office documents in SharePoint is a common usage scenario. Creating such documents and filling them with data from SharePoint lists is more challenging. All Office products have an API that is available to .NET developers. However, the hierarchy of sections and paragraphs in Word, the structure of cells in Excel, or the slides in PowerPoint require several steps through the object model to write a single line of text. In addition, the products must be installed on the server. For complex document creation tasks, it's an impasse. Microsoft introduced a new document format with Office 2007—the `.docx`, `.xslx`, and `.pptx` file formats, respectively. Internally these formats are zipped packages that contain the main data file as XML (see Figure 4–11), all related resources, and a manifest.

The package itself is based on the packaging standard Open Packaging Convention (OPC), an ECMA International standards organization–approved format. To start working with it, you can take a `.docx` file, rename the file extension to `.zip`, and open the package. For the example in this section, we focus on Word and use `.docx`. Other Office formats follow a similar convention. However, the key to the solution isn't the package itself. The XML-based format is the clue. To generate a document, you need a template first. The template must be unpacked, modified, packed, and stored elsewhere as the final document.

```
- <w:tr w:rsidR="00E24DA0" w:rsidTr="00E24DA0">
  - <w:sdt>
    - <w:sdtPr>
        <w:alias w:val="Name" />
        <w:tag w:val="Name" />
        <w:id w:val="144975895" />
      - <w:placeholder>
          <w:docPart w:val="DefaultPlaceholder_22675703" />
        </w:placeholder>
        <w:showingPlcHdr />
        <w:text />
      </w:sdtPr>
    - <w:sdtContent>
      - <w:tc>
        - <w:tcPr>
            <w:tcW w:w="1842" w:type="dxa" />
          </w:tcPr>
        - <w:p w:rsidR="00E24DA0" w:rsidRDefault="00E24DA0" w:rsidP="00E24DA0">
          - <w:r>
              <w:t>Name</w:t>
            </w:r>
          - <w:r w:rsidRPr="00BD657F">
            - <w:rPr>
                <w:rStyle w:val="Placeholdertext" />
              </w:rPr>
              <w:t>.</w:t>
            </w:r>
          </w:p>
        </w:tc>
      </w:sdtContent>
    </w:sdt>
```

Figure 4–11. *A snap-shot from a .docx file*

Enriching a Word Document with Placeholders

The best way to add placeholders is via controls. To add placeholders, you first need to activate the developer toolbar (see Figure 4–12).

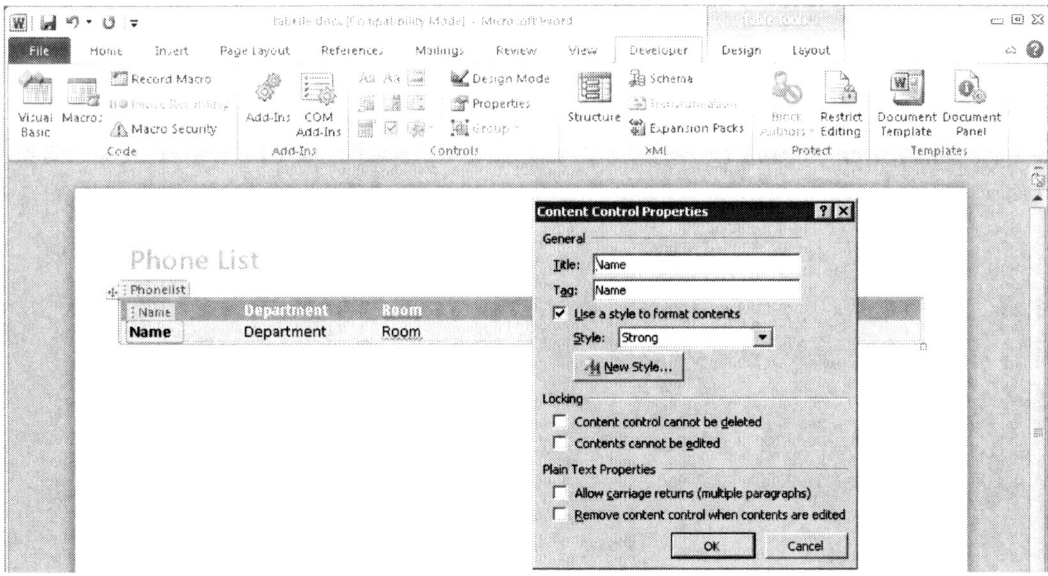

***Figure 4–12.** Adding controls from the Developer tab in Word 2010*

Before you can fetch a document from a library, you must have one. As shown in **Figure 4–11**, through the XML you have access to any part of the document. To build a template, you need to create a regular Word document and add placeholders at the appropriate positions. To construct a report, insert a table. Add one data row as a template and repeat this row for each line of data. Building the document can be accomplished with a few clicks, and an end user with some Word experience should be able to master this. They will, however, add an unpredictable amount of formatting styles to such a document. Therefore, you must be able to recognize the placeholders reliably.

ACTIVATE THE DEVELOPER MAIN TAB

To activate the developer main tab, follow these steps:

1. Open the Options dialog through the File pane (Office Button in Word 2007).
2. Click Options (Word Options in Word 2007).
3. Click Customize Ribbon (Popular in Word 2007).
4. Activate the check box near the Developer entry (Show Developer tab entry in the Main Tabs pane in Word 2007).

Figure 4–12 shows the activated tab with some controls already present.

On the activated Developer tab, click Design Mode, and you can add controls to your layout. For this exercise, use Text controls. In the Properties options, as shown in Figure 4–12, you can set the Title of the control (as it appears in design view) and the Tag name (as it appears in the XML).

Once the placeholders are inserted, you can save the document and upload it to the appropriate document library.

■ **Note** The techniques demonstrated here work with any combination of Office 2007 or Office 2010 product with SharePoint Foundation or SharePoint Server.

Creating Documents from Templates

The complex system based on SharePoint, Word, and package formats is now as easy as reading and writing XML. Using LINQ to XML makes this even more straightforward. However, you need the XML first. Begin by fetching the document into an `SPDocumentLibrary` object:

```
SPDocumentLibrary templateLib = web.Lists.Cast<SPList>().FirstOrDefault(
                                list => list.RootFolder.Name == "WordTemplates")
                                as SPDocumentLibrary;
```

The lambda expression is used to reference the list using the `RootFolder.Name` property. If you can use the `Title`, the `Lists` property's indexer will work, too. Call the `OpenBinaryStream` method to retrieve the file as a stream:

```
string documentUrl = SPUrlUtility.CombineUrl(
                     web.Site.MakeFullUrl(templateLib.RootFolder.Url),
                     templateName);
SPFile template = templateLib.RootFolder.Files[documentUrl];
Stream templateStream = template.OpenBinaryStream();
```

Working with Open Packaging Convention Packages

To work with OPC packages, you need classes from the `System.IO.Packaging` namespace. The assembly containing the classes is called `WindowBase.dll`.

CONFUSING NAME RESOLVER

The reason for the strange assembly name is that the first usage of OPC in .NET was in WPF where XML Paper Specification (XPS) is one of the supported formats. XPS is a device-independent document format. The techniques described here work for XPS as well. However, because of the editing capabilities you have with Microsoft Word, we prefer `.docx` and Word Markup Language (WordML).

You have to first unpack the document. SharePoint libraries return files as a stream, as shown previously. To open a file as a package, you can use code like this:

```
Package package = Package.Open(templateStream,
                               FileMode.Open,
                               FileAccess.ReadWrite);
```

The variable `templateStream` is of type `Stream`. From the `Package` object, you can now read the actual file:

```
Uri uri = new Uri("/word/document.xml", UriKind.Relative);
PackagePart part = package.GetPart(uri);
```

The PackagePart provides access to the document, as a stream that can be loaded into an XDocument:

```
Stream partStream = part.GetStream(FileMode.OpenOrCreate, FileAccess.ReadWrite);
XmlReader xmlReader = XmlReader.Create(partStream);
XDocument doc = XDocument.Load(xmlReader);
```

Creating the Report

Once the XML is in the right type, any further manipulation is simple using LINQ to XML. With minimal instructions you can locate the <w:sdt> element that creates a table:

```
XElement tablePlaceHolder = doc.Descendants(W.sdt).FirstOrDefault(
        x => x.Element(W.sdtContent).Descendants(W.sdt).FirstOrDefault() != null);
```

The content is found within <w:stdContent>, which this statement returns. From here you extract the table's row to use as a prototype for the rows being generated:

```
XElement prototype = tablePlaceHolder.Element(W.sdtContent).Descendants(W.tr)
.Where(x => x.Descendants(W.sdt).FirstOrDefault() != null).FirstOrDefault();
```

Before proceeding, you need to read the data from a SharePoint list. For the phone list, read from a list called Contacts:

```
SPList dataList = web.Lists.Cast<SPList>().FirstOrDefault(
                                        list => list.RootFolder.Name == "Contacts");
IEnumerable<SPListItem> allItems = dataList.GetItems(
                                        new SPQuery()).Cast<SPListItem>();
```

The items in allItems contain the data to display in the report rows. Listing 4–25 shows the complete code. The inner foreach statement reads the placeholders and replaces their contents with the data read from SharePoint. ContainsField is used to avoid exceptions if a user named the placeholder field accidentally with a name the list does not provide. li[celltag] fetches the data as input for a format instruction. Imagine additional operations here following either fixed rules or instructions added to the document. The prototype row is replaced with a number of rows—one for each line in the data list. The file is written back into the package, and the package is sent to another document library in SharePoint as the final report. You can find the complete solution in Listing 4–25.

Listing 4–25. *The Complete Solution: Generate Template-Based Reports in WordML*

```
using System;
using System.Collections.Generic;
using System.Linq;
using System.Text;
using Microsoft.SharePoint;
using Microsoft.SharePoint.Utilities;
using System.IO;
using System.IO.Packaging;
using System.Xml;
using System.Xml.Linq;

namespace Apress.SP2010.DocxDemo
{
    class Program
```

```
{
    static void Main(string[] args)
    {
        using (SPSite site = new SPSite("http://sharepointserve"))
        using (SPWeb web = site.OpenWeb())
        {
            SPDocumentLibrary templateLib =
               web.Lists.Cast<SPList>().FirstOrDefault(
               list => list.RootFolder.Name == "WordTemplates")
               as SPDocumentLibrary;
            SPDocumentLibrary reportLib =
               web.Lists.Cast<SPList>().FirstOrDefault(
               list => list.RootFolder.Name == "WordReports")
               as SPDocumentLibrary;
            SPList dataList = web.Lists.Cast<SPList>().FirstOrDefault(
               list => list.RootFolder.Name == "Finances");
            string templateName = "ReportTemplate.docx";
            string reportName = String.Format("DailyReport{0}.docx",
                                DateTime.Now.ToShortDateString());

            string documentUrl = SPUrlUtility.CombineUrl(
                   web.Site.MakeFullUrl(templateLib.RootFolder.Url),
                   templateName);
            SPFile template = templateLib.RootFolder.Files[documentUrl];
            Stream templateStream = template.OpenBinaryStream();
            Stream documentStream = new MemoryStream();
            BinaryReader templateReader = new BinaryReader(templateStream);
            BinaryWriter documentWriter = new BinaryWriter(documentStream);
            documentWriter.Write(
                templateReader.ReadBytes((int)templateStream.Length));
            documentWriter.Flush();
            templateReader.Close();
            templateStream.Dispose();

            Package package = Package.Open(documentStream,
                                           FileMode.Open,
                                           FileAccess.ReadWrite);

            Uri uri = new Uri("/word/document.xml", UriKind.Relative);
            PackagePart part = package.GetPart(uri);


            Stream partStream = part.GetStream(
                   FileMode.OpenOrCreate, FileAccess.ReadWrite);
            XmlReader xmlReader = XmlReader.Create(partStream);
            XDocument doc = XDocument.Load(xmlReader);
            xmlReader.Close();

            XElement tablePlaceHolder = doc.Descendants(W.sdt)
                     .FirstOrDefault(x =>
                     x.Element(W.sdtContent)
                     .Descendants(W.sdt)
                     .FirstOrDefault() != null);
```

```
XElement prototype = tablePlaceHolder.Element(W.sdtContent)
                      .Descendants(W.tr)
                      .Where(x => x.Descendants(W.sdt)
                      .FirstOrDefault() != null)
                      .FirstOrDefault();

IEnumerable<SPListItem> allItems = dataList.GetItems(
       new SPQuery()).Cast<SPListItem>();

prototype.Parent.Add(allItems.Select(
  li =>
  {
    var result = new XElement(prototype);
    foreach (var placeholder in result.Descendants(W.sdt))
    {
       string celltag = placeholder.Element(W.sdtPr)
                          .Element(W.tag)
                          .Attribute(W.val)
                          .Value;

       if (li.Fields.ContainsField(celltag))
       {
           placeholder.Element(W.sdtContent)
                      .Descendants(W.t)
                      .Single()
                      .Value = String.Format("{0}", li[celltag]);
       }
       else
       {
           placeholder.Element(W.sdtContent)
                      .Descendants(W.t)
                      .Single()
                      .Value = String.Empty;
       }
    }
  return result;
}));

prototype.Remove();

partStream.SetLength(0);

XmlWriter writer = XmlWriter.Create(partStream);
doc.WriteTo(writer);
writer.Close();
package.Flush();

string reportUrl = SPUrlUtility.CombineUrl(
   web.Site.MakeFullUrl(reportLib.RootFolder.Url),
   templateName);
SPFile report = reportLib.RootFolder.Files.Add(
   reportUrl, documentStream, true);
SPListItem reportItem = report.Item;
reportItem["Title"] = reportName; // Set Metadata
```

```
                reportItem.Update();
            }
        }
    }
}
```

Because you need access to WordML elements, it makes sense to create a helper class with predefined XName objects (in Listing 4–26).

Listing 4–26. Helper Class with WordML Elements

```
public static class W
{
  public static XNamespace w = "http://schemas.openxmlformats.org/
                              wordprocessingml/2006/main";
  public static XName body = w + "body";
  public static XName sdt = w + "sdt";
  public static XName sdtPr = w + "sdtPr";
  public static XName tag = w + "tag";
  public static XName val = w + "val";
  public static XName sdtContent = w + "sdtContent";
  public static XName tbl = w + "tbl";
  public static XName tr = w + "tr";
  public static XName tc = w + "tc";
  public static XName p = w + "p";
  public static XName r = w + "r";
  public static XName t = w + "t";
  public static XName rPr = w + "rPr";
  public static XName highlight = w + "highlight";
  public static XName pPr = w + "pPr";
  public static XName color = w + "color";
  public static XName sz = w + "sz";
  public static XName szCs = w + "szCs";
}
```

This is the small subset of WordML tags used in the previous example. For other projects, it may be necessary to extend this list.

Document Sets

Documents sets are new in SharePoint Server 2010. Technically, these sets are another content type, with particular functionality. A document set is related to a document library and is similar to a folder. Like a folder, you can add multiple documents to one document set. While a folder can be opened, a document set is much more. Each document set can have a different set of content types. Creating a new document set means creating a set of different documents. Imagine you want to produce offers for customers. The offer can contain various Office documents, such as the quote, terms and conditions, a calculation sheet, a presentation with some company information, and more. All these can be assembled by a user with a single click.

■ **Note** Document sets are a document management feature of SharePoint Server 2010. They are not available in SharePoint Foundation. The assemblies necessary to access the features programmatically are not part of a SharePoint Foundation installation.

The types used to work with document sets are defined in the `Microsoft.Office.DocumentManagement.dll` assembly.

Advantages of Document Sets

Document sets have several advantages:

- Each set has its own version history. It's not necessary to track changes at the document level.
- You can assign access rights on a per-set level.
- You can assign and start workflows related to a set.
- Users can download the whole document set as a ZIP file.
- The home page related to a document set is a wiki page that can be edited easily.
- Documents that are part of a document set can share their metadata.

Before you can access and use document sets programmatically, some preparatory steps are required.

Prepare Document Sets

The document sets feature is available at the site collection level. To activate it, open the site settings and click "Site collection features." On the next page, click the Activate button near the Document Sets feature entry (see Figure 4–13).

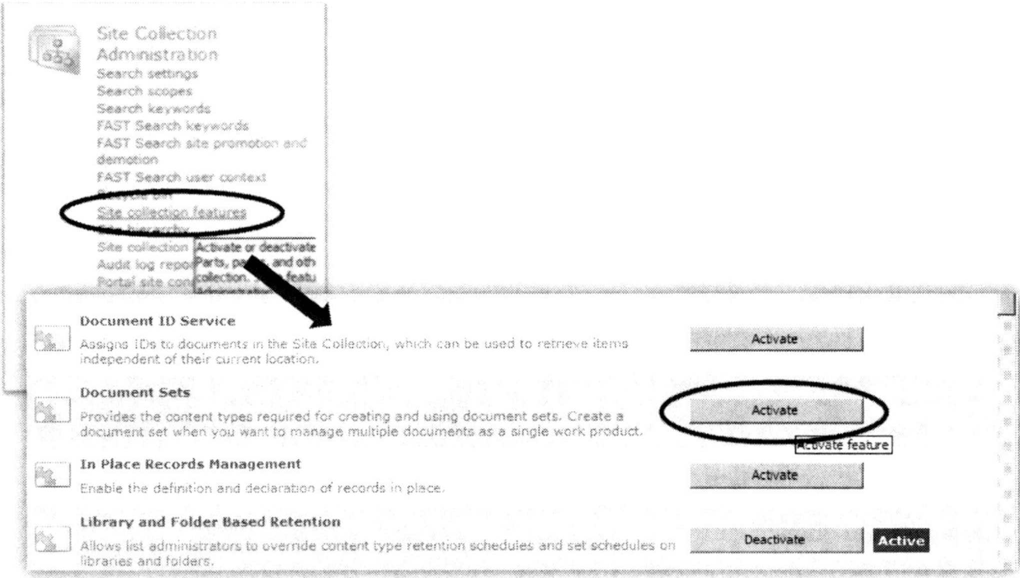

Figure 4–13. Activating document sets

A document set can now be created by adding a new content type, which inherits from the built-in content type Document Set. As with any other content type, you can add any number of metadata to modify the behavior appropriately. Additionally, you can configure multiple templates to support the documents the set can contain. The Document Set Settings function is available to modify the templates (see Figure 4–14).

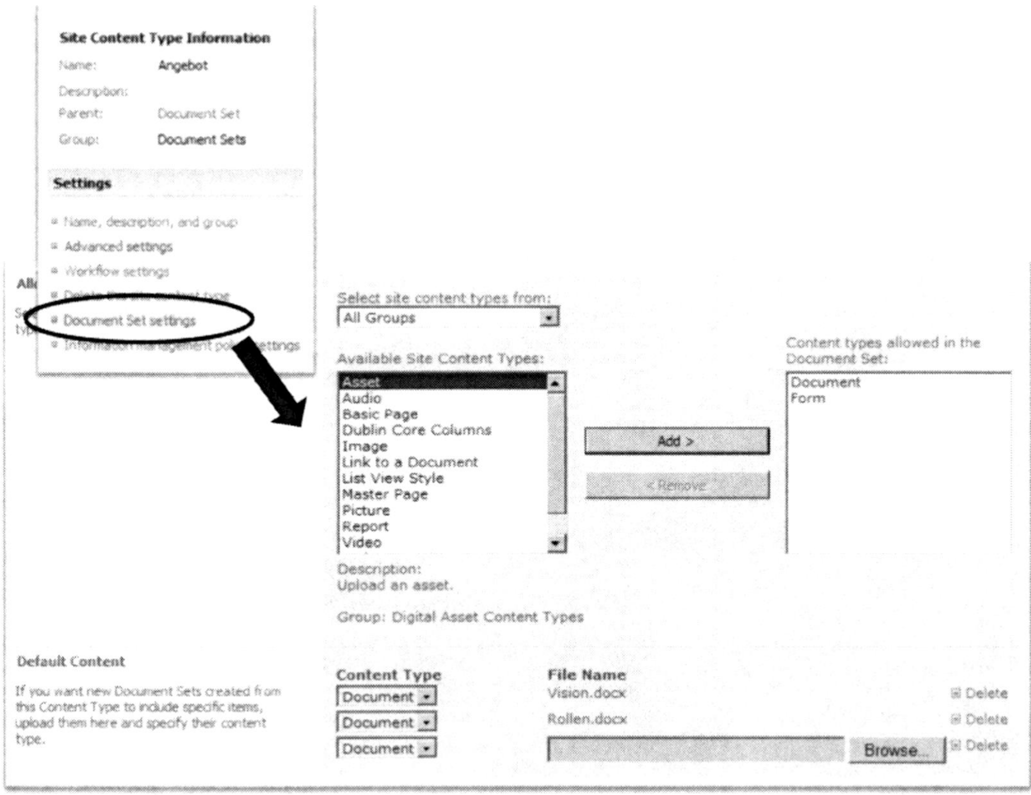

***Figure 4–14.** Edit the document set settings*

The various settings of the new content type are as follows:

- *Assigned content types*: These are the content types of the documents within the set.
- *Default content*: You can upload documents which automatically become part of a new set. These are usually static documents, such as “Terms and Conditions.”
- *Shared columns*: The columns defined here are shared between all documents of the document set.
- *Home page columns*: These columns are displayed on the document set’s home page—the standard wiki page.

After setting the appropriate properties, you can assign the new content type to any document library. Henceforth, this library supports document sets. The document library must generally support content types.

Access a Document Set Programmatically

All types required to access document set functions are defined in the namespace `Microsoft.Office.DocumentManagement.DocumentSets`. The namespace contains the classes shown in Table 4–7.

***Table 4–7.** Classes and Structures Related to Document Sets*

Type	Description
`AllowedContentTypeCollection`	A class that stores a list of the content types that can be included in an associated `DocumentSet` object
`DefaultDocument`	A class that represents a document that will be provisioned automatically for every `DocumentManagementDocumentSet` object based on the associated content type
`DefaultDocumentCollection`	A collection of `DefaultDocument` objects
`DocSetTooBigForExportException`	An exception thrown if an object exceeds 50 MB
`DocumentSet`	A document set item
`DocumentSetTemplate`	The template on which `DocumentSet` objects are based
`DocumentSetVersion`	Metadata that is associated with a major or minor version of the `DocumentSet` object and its files
`DocumentSetVersionCollection`	A collection of `DocumentSetVersion` snapshots
`SharedFieldCollection`	The list of metadata fields for the `SPContentType` object that is associated with the current `DocumentSet` object
`WelcomePageFieldCollection`	The list of metadata fields for the content type that is associated with this `DocumentSet` object
`DocumentSetVersionField`	A `struct` that represents display information for a `DocumentSetVersion` metadata field
`DocumentSetVersionItem`	A `struct` that contains metadata that is associated with a specific major or minor version of the current `DocumentSet` object and the files contained in the set

The most valuable class is `DocumentSet`. This class has three static methods you need frequently:

- `Create`: Creates a new instance
- `GetDocumentSet`: Creates an existing instance from an `SPFolder` object
- `Import`: Imports a document from a stream or byte array into a folder

Some methods are provided by a class instance:

- `Export`: Exports the document set to a stream or a byte array
- `Provision`: Places the default documents in the document set
- `SendToOfficialFile`: Submits a document set to the records management
- Moreover, all the current settings are exposed through properties:
- `ContentType`: Returns the content type for the document set
- `ContentTypeTemplate`: Returns the content type template associated with the `DocumentSet` object
- `Folder`: Returns the `SPFolder` object that contains this `DocumentSet` object
- `Item`: Returns the `SPListItem` object that is associated with this `DocumentSets` object
- `ParentFolder`: Returns the parent folder of the `DocumentSet` object
- `ParentList`: Returns the parent list of the `DocumentSet` object
- `VersionCollection`: Returns the version collection of the `DocumentSet` object
- `WelcomePageUrl`: Returns the URL of the Welcome page for the `DocumentSet` object

The relationship between a folder and a document set reveals the underlying approach. A document set is—from a developer's perspective—a folder that is associated with a specific content type. The examples shown in the next few sections express this in various ways.

Reading the Properties

A document set is specific folder based on a custom content type that inherits from a built-in content type. The new API necessary to deal with document sets is added to the existing model without changing basic classes such as `SPList` or `SPFolder`. To achieve this several new classes have been added, which provide some static methods (see Listing 4–27).

Listing 4–27. *Accessing a Document Set Programmatically*

```
SPListItem item = SPContext.Current.ListItem;
DocumentSet set = DocumentSet.GetDocumentSet(item.Folder);
Console.WriteLine("ContentType: {0}", item.ContentType.Name);
Console.WriteLine("Title: {0}", item.Title);
Console.WriteLine("WelcomePageUrl: {0}", set.WelcomePageUrl);
Console.WriteLine("ItemCount: {0}", set.Folder.ItemCount);
Console.WriteLine("Welcomepage Fields:");
DocumentSetTemplate template = set.ContentTypeTemplate;
WelcomePageFieldCollection fields = template.WelcomePageFields;
foreach (SPField field in fields)
{
     Console.WriteLine("{0}", field.Title);
}
```

The `DocumentSet` class encapsulates a document set. The `GetDocumentSet` method is used to convert the technical base (`SPFolder`) into a more appropriate object type. The home page for each document set is defined using the `WelcomePageFields` property. The `ContentTypeTemplate` property returns the template information as a `DocumentSetTemplate` type.

Example: Checking Whether an Item Is in a Set

You often need to know whether an item is already in a set. The method in Listing 4–28 checks this.

Listing 4–28. *A Method That Checks Whether an Item Is in a DocumentSet*

```
public bool IsDocumentSetItem(SPListItem itemToCheck)
{
   bool documentSetItem = false;
   if (itemToCheck.File != null)
   {
      DocumentSet documentSet;
      documentSet = DocumentSet.GetDocumentSet(itemToCheck.File.ParentFolder);
      if (null != documentSet)
      {
          documentSetItem = true;
      }
   }
   return documentSetItem;
}
```

The code asks the current item to return the containing set. If there is no set, then the item is not part of any document set.

Query Data Using CAML and LINQ

Storing data in lists and handling events are only part of the equation. More often you need to retrieve specific data and query a list for a particular result set. In previous versions of SharePoint, querying data has been tightly coupled with but not the sole domain Collaborative Application Markup Language (CAML). With SharePoint 2010, a new LINQ layer offers alternative data access options.

CAML vs. LINQ

This section explains both API data access methods: CAML and LINQ. It's a common misconception to regard LINQ as the successor to CAML. Although CAML was the only data access method for SharePoint 2007 and LINQ is new to SharePoint 2010, both methods are fully supported in SharePoint 2010.

The truth is that CAML is still the one and only data access method. There is a small performance penalty when using LINQ to SharePoint, because it translates queries into CAML before executing. However, the layer is thin and fast. Hence, it is worth knowing the advantages of LINQ and benefiting from them. First, LINQ uses built-in keywords, enabling the compilers (both C# and VB.NET) to check the syntax, types, and structure of a query. This eliminates invalid query statements, reduces unexpected responses, and improves the quality of your software. Second, strongly typed objects allow you to program against a real object model, rather than against generic types, such as `SPListItem`. This makes your code more readable, makes it less generic, and further improves code quality. Bear in mind that hardware is relatively cheap, and by adding another module of RAM, the LINQ to SharePoint method will win.

In the light of all this, we provide an insight into both methods. You have to decide for each project which to use. If overall performance is the uppermost criteria, CAML is superior. In all other cases, we encourage you to use LINQ.

Obsolete Methods in SharePoint 2010

While CAML is still the tool of choice for querying the data store, two other technologies are officially deprecated. SharePoint 2010 still supports them—though for backward compatibility only.

Avoid Using SharePoint Data Providing Web Services

SharePoint provides a set of web services to enable client interaction with the data model. Some of these are specifically designed for data retrieval or to support at least a subset of related functions. These services are still supported for backward compatibility and interoperability with web service clients. For reasons of both performance and ease, Microsoft recommends that you use either the object model API or the ADO.NET Data Services Framework. (Both methods are described in full in Chapter 5.)

Avoid Direct Calls to owssvr.dll

Access to SharePoint deployments using RPC calls into the `owssvr.dll` is still supported. However, Microsoft says that this is only to provide troubleshooting assistance to existing client applications. For maximum application compatibility, Microsoft does not recommend using this method of client access. We do not recommend it either and exclude it from further consideration.

Query Data Using CAML

CAML plays a significant role in SharePoint, not limited to querying data.

Understanding CAML

You can use CAML to do the following:

- Modify parameters to transport complex data
- Define the body of SOAP messages to transport data using web services
- Configure SharePoint for usage or deployment
- Add specific behavior to features

SharePoint utilizes many XML files to define behavior and content. Most of these files use CAML as the dialect to express SharePoint-specific settings. In this section, we examine more closely the usage of CAML to query the data store.

CAML is defined in several schemas. When you first attempt to understand CAML, it looks like an amalgam of many different dialects. However, it's simply a collection of schemas that make CAML powerful enough for both data schema definition and data retrieval. These schemas are as follows:

- Query schema
- View schema
- List schema
- Site schema
- Site Deletion Confirmation schema
- Regional Settings schema

- Document Icons schema
- General schema

For data access, the query schema provides a set of elements to build queries.

Using CAML to Retrieve Data

The Query schema is well documented, and numerous examples are available. However, the first time you try it, you'll discover it's not self-explanatory. All queries must be executed against a list. You need a reference to either an `SPList` or `SPView` object, which accepts a CAML query and can run it. The following examples demonstrate the bare bones of the technique.

The basic way to query data from SharePoint lists is to use queries constructed with CAML. Listing 4–29 shows a simple CAML query to fetch all items from a SharePoint list called Books whose Publisher is Apress.

Listing 4–29. *A Simple CAML Query*

```
public IEnumerable<SPListItem> GetBooksFromAPress()
{
    SPList list = SPContext.Current.Web.Lists["Books"];
    SPQuery query = new SPQuery();
    query.Query = @"<Where>
                      <Eq>
                        <FieldRef Name='Publisher' />
                          <Value Type='Text'>Apress</Value>
                      </Eq>
                    </Where>";
    IEnumerable<SPListItem> books = list.GetItems(query).OfType<SPListItem>();
    return books;
}
```

In this example, the list is obtained from the current `SPWeb` instance. A new `SPQuery` object is instantiated to contain the query. The query is written as an XML string fragment.

With CAML, you can easily build your own custom queries, including conditions (`Where`) and logical operators (AND, OR) in XML format. Internally, SharePoint translates the CAML query into a SQL query to retrieve the data from the SharePoint content database. You can consider CAML as a necessary abstraction layer to the database—necessary because it is responsible for security trimming and caching. A SQL query to the content database returns all queried items, even though the user who made the request may not be permitted to view the items. "Security trimming" means filtering out the items the user lacks permission to see. This is done internally by SharePoint's data access layer. There are also some caching mechanisms implemented that ensure that if the same CAML query is executed in quick succession, no direct database access has to be made after the first call.

■ **Tip** CAML allows single quotes (') for attributes. Using this style, you can write complete queries without escaping double quotes within the data, resulting in highly readable XML snippets within the C# code.

One big disadvantage of manually constructed CAML queries, such as the one shown in Listing 4–30, is a high error rate. If you make one small mistake, such as encapsulating your CAML query within

<Query></Query> tags, the query will execute without errors, but it will return all items instead of only those items whose Publisher is APress. This result can be very dangerous and subtle, and it can be time-consuming to find the error. There are alternative ways to construct a CAML query.

How to Create a CAML Query

You can use LINQ to XML and the XElement type to create a query:

```
SPQuery queryl = new SPQuery();
queryl.Query = new XElement("Where",
                 new XElement("Eq",
                   new XElement("FieldRef", new XAttribute("Name", "Company")),
                   new XElement("Value", new XAttribute("Type", "Text"))))
               .ToString();
```

While this approach takes care of closing tags correctly and will always create valid XML, it does not seem easier. The CAML keywords are strings, and hence they can suffer from typing errors. You might consider using constants to predefine such keywords:

```
const string WHERE = "Where";
const string EQ = "Eq";
const string FIELDREF = "FieldRef";
const string VALUE = "Value";
const string NAME = "Name";
const string TYPE = "Type";
SPQuery queryc = new SPQuery();
queryc.Query = new XElement(WHERE,
                 new XElement(EQ,
                   new XElement(FIELDREF, new XAttribute(NAME, "Company")),
                   new XElement(VALUE, new XAttribute(TYPE, "Text"))))
               .ToString();
```

That's indeed safe and compact, but it's still a manually built query. To overcome the manual construction of CAML queries, there are some useful implementations of CAML query builders that support creating a CAML query in a safe manner. To demonstrate this, check out an example using CAML.NET from John Holliday, which is a free project hosted on CodePlex (www.codeplex.com/camldotnet). Listing 4–30 shows how to use it.

Listing 4–30. *Simple CAML Query Using CAML.NET Query Builder*

```
public IEnumerable<SPListItem> GetBooksFromAPress2()
{
    SPList list = SPContext.Current.Web.Lists["Books"];
    SPQuery query = new SPQuery();
    query.Query = CAML.Where(
                    CAML.Eq(
                      CAML.FieldRef("Publisher"),
                      CAML.Value("APress")
                    )
                  );
    IEnumerable<SPListItem> books = list.GetItems(query).OfType<SPListItem>();
    return books;
}
```

If you need to use many manually constructed CAML queries, we strongly recommend using a CAML query builder such as CAML.NET. This is the least error-prone and most efficient method.

The Query Schema

The primary schema starts with a <Query> element that resembles the structure of a SQL query:

```
<Query>
  <Where>
    ...
  </Where>
  <GroupBy>
    ...
  </GroupBy>
  <OrderBy>
    ...
  </OrderBy>
</Query>
```

The <GroupBy> and <OrderBy> elements are optional. Within the elements a field reference is required. For the <Where> part, a more complex clause can be constructed that contains static values.

Referencing Fields and Values

To reference a field, use the <FieldRef> element. The Name attribute is compulsory. The element is also used in other CAML dialects, but several of its attributes are not supported in data queries. Table 4–8 shows the subset that are used for data retrieval. Boolean types are expressed by either TRUE or FALSE strings.

Table 4–8. *FieldRef Attributes for Data Queries*

Attribute	Type	Description
Name	Text	The field's name
ID	Guid	The field's internal ID (optional)
LookupId	Boolean	Determines that the value is a reference to a lookup list by its ID, if set to TRUE
LookupValue	Boolean	Determines that the value is a reference to a lookup list by its value, if set to TRUE

The <Value> element is used to reference static values against which the field's content is compared. In a query, this would look like the following for a simple field:

```
<Query>
   <Where>
      <Or>
         <IsNull>
            <FieldRef Name="Expires" />
         </IsNull>
         <Geq>
```

```
            <FieldRef Name="Expires" />
            <Value Type="DateTime">
               <Today />
            </Value>
         </Geq>
      </Or>
   </Where>
   <OrderBy>
      <FieldRef Name="Modified" Ascending="FALSE" />
   </OrderBy>
</Query>
```

Using lookups is more complex—the value's type must be set to Lookup. If the lookup uses the lookup table's ID field, set the LookupId="TRUE" attribute of the <FieldRef> element:

```
<Query>
  <Where>
    <Eq>
      <FieldRef Name="CatalogItem" LookupId="TRUE" />
      <Value Type="Lookup">1</Value>
    </Eq>
  </Where>
</Query>
```

Using Comparison Operators

To use comparison operators, you first need to join them. Logical joins are accomplished by the <Or> and <And> elements. Both elements accept two child elements. If you need to create more branches, you can use another logical join. For a three-part <Or> clause, this would look like the following:

```
<Or>
   <Or>
    <Eq>
     <FieldRef />
     <Value />
    </Eq>
    <Eq>
     <FieldRef />
     <Value />
  </Eq>
  </Or>
   <Eq>
     <FieldRef />
     <Value />
  </Eq>
</Or>
```

The equality operator <Eq> is used merely to express the syntax. Table 4–9 lists all such operators.

Table 4–9. Operators for CAML Queries

Element	Description
`<BeginsWith>`	Checks whether a string (Text) begins with another string
`<Contains>`	Checks whether a string (Text) contains another string
`<DateRangesOverlap>`	Checks that a date overlaps another date range
`<Eq>`	Equal to
`<Geq>`	Greater than or equal to
`<Gt>`	Greater than
`<IsNotNull>`	Is true if the field's value is not null
`<IsNull>`	Is true if the field's value is null
`<Leq>`	Less than or equal to
`<Lt>`	Less than
`<Membership>`	Checks the membership of a user
`<Neq>`	Not equal to

Working with Lists, Joins, and Projections

Joins between tables are well known in relational databases. The complexity and power of SharePoint lists overcome the need for frequent usage of joins. However, when working with views, you will find that it's occasionally desirable to add the odd field from another list. Lookups are a good way to do this, but they require navigating from the parent list to the related list in order to view fields. If you want to create a view that spans several lists and show the results in just one list, you need to use joins. Direct joins are a new feature in SharePoint 2010. Projections define the fields that become part of the result set's field list. This is comparable with the mapping of fields in the SELECT clause in SQL.

■ **Note** Though this may look like a replacement for lookups, it does not eliminate the need for them. A join uses a field reference previously defined by a lookup. Thus, you have to create a lookup field first.

Regular lookups can be multilookups—meaning that you can form a many-to-many relationship. Using joins, this is not possible; you must use a single-value lookup.

Joins and projections have a direct representation in views and queries. This includes the corresponding properties—Joins and ProjectedField—of the SPQuery and SPView objects. While both objects use CAML, the XML snippets do not become part of a regular query, and they are not child elements of the <Query> element. Instead, the root elements are <Joins> and <ProjectedField>, respectively. The XML is assigned to the properties of the SPQuery and SPView objects without their respective root elements.

■ **Caution** If you use joins and projections in list definitions, the root elements <Joins>, <ProjectedFields>, and <ViewFields> are required. If you assign the same XML to the respective properties of an SPView or SPQuery object, you must omit the root elements.

Joins

From SQL you may know that there are different kinds of joins. In CAML you can define two kinds of joins, INNER and LEFT, using the Type attribute:

```
<Joins>
  <Join Type="INNER" ListAlias="Authors">
   <Eq>
    <FieldRef Name="FullName" RefType="Id" />
    <FieldRef List="Authors" RefType="Id" />
   </Eq>
  </Join>
</Joins>
```

An inner join links two lists using an existing lookup. The result is a combination of both result sets. A left join (known in SQL as a LEFT OUTER JOIN) will return the same combination but includes the result of the parent list even if the related list does not have a matching entry. The common right join available in SQL is not supported by CAML. However, you can create an opposite lookup and reverse the parent and child lists before applying a left join.

As with SQL, in CAML you can combine several joins together. A chain of joins works like a JOIN statement in SQL but without the additional parentheses. A join B join C means that B acts as a parent for C, and A acts as a parent for the result from B and C. The default limitation for a chain of joins is eight. You can override this by setting the MaxQueryLookupFields property of the SPWebApplication object. However, keep in mind that the result set can become very large when using joined lists, and the more joins you have, the more data must be retrieved. Having more than a few (three or four) joins probably indicates an architectural mistake in your data model.

The meaning and usage of the ListAlias attribute (see the Join element in the previous sample) is worthy of a closer look. As described on MSDN, the second FieldRef, which references the actual list, must have the same name as the ListAlias attribute. That's irritating, as the term *alias* suggests that you can replace the internal name with something more descriptive. This is not so for the first join of chained joins or for the only join when there is just one. The name of the list must be defined using this List attribute, and the alias must correctly echo this name. If you have a second (subsequent) join to the same list that joins through to another, a conflict in the reference attribute occurs. The alias is used to resolve the conflict. However, the second join still needs a reference to an actual list. Therefore, the first FieldRef element gets yet another element List that tells the parser to which list it refers.

Projected Fields in Views

The ProjectedFields element enables fields from the foreign lists to be viewed in the list view. The fields must also be identified in the ViewFields child element of the View element. The foreign lists are identified by their aliases, as defined in the Joins element. Again, if there is only one join, then there is no alias that is different from the list's internal name. In this case, the reference in ViewFields uses the actual list name.

The ShowField attribute identifies which field from the foreign list is used in the view. This must be the internal name. The Type attribute always has the value Lookup—it does not indicate the data type of the field. The source type of a projected field is limited to a number of simple types:

- Calculated (converted into plain text)
- ContentTypeId
- Counter
- Currency
- DateTime
- Guid
- Integer
- Note (first line of multiline text only)
- Number
- Text

The ViewFields elements refer to the name of a field as defined in the ProjectedFields' Field element.

Example: Using Joins and Projected Fields

The following example shows how to use joins and projections. It is a console application that uses two lists: Books and Authors. The Books list relates to Authors through a field called LeadAuthor. The Authors list derives from Contacts and has an additional field called FullName.

The application (Listing 4–31) retrieves data from these two lists.

***Listing 4–31.** A Console Application That Joins Two Lists*

```
using System;
using System.Collections.Generic;
using System.Linq;
using System.Text;
using Microsoft.SharePoint;
using System.Xml;

namespace Apress.SP2010.CAMLJoins
{
    class Program
    {
        static void Main(string[] args)
        {
            using (SPSite site = new SPSite("http://sharepointserve"))
            {
```

```
                using (SPWeb web = site.OpenWeb())
                {
                    SPList bookList = web.Lists["Books"];
                    SPList authList = web.Lists["Authors"];
                    SPField la = bookList.Fields["LeadAuthor"];
                    SPField fa = authList.Fields["Full Name"];
                    string join = @"<Join Type='LEFT' ListAlias='Authors'>
                                         <Eq>
                                           <FieldRef Name='" + la.InternalName
                                                     + @"' RefType='ID' />
                                           <FieldRef List='Authors' Name='ID' />
                                         </Eq>
                                       </Join>";
                    string projField = @"<Field Name='Fullname' Type='Lookup'
                                           List='Authors'
                                           ShowField='" + fa.InternalName + "' />";
                    SPQuery query = new SPQuery();
                    query.Query = "";
                    query.Joins = join;
                    query.ProjectedFields = projField;
                    query.ViewFields = @"<FieldRef Name='Fullname' />
                                         <FieldRef Name='Title' />";
                    SPListItemCollection items = bookList.GetItems(query);
                    foreach (SPListItem item in items)
                    {
                        Console.WriteLine("{0} has these lead authors: ",
                                          item.Title);
                        if (item["Fullname"] == null)
                        {
                            Console.WriteLine("  no authors assigned");
                            continue;
                        }
                        SPFieldLookupValue sc =
                           new SPFieldLookupValue(item["Fullname"].ToString());
                        Console.WriteLine("  - {0}", sc.LookupValue);
                    }
                }
            }
            Console.ReadLine();
        }
    }
}
```

The join is from the parent list Books to the child list Authors. This is defined by `List='Authors'` in the join's second `FieldRef` element. The `ListAlias` attribute must echo this, as it is the only join. The first `FieldRef` refers to the parent list's lookup field, using the internal name. It's read from the `SPField` object that has a property `InternalName`.

The variable `pfld` stores the projected fields. The declaration contains one field, FullName, from the Authors list. `ShowField` is also defined using the internal name. The name defined in the `Name` attribute is used in the `ViewField` definition. The `Title` field is also added to the result set. The XML snippets are assigned to the appropriate properties of `SPQuery`.

The `GetItems` method executes the query. Because `item["Fullname"]` returns a lookup, the value it returns is in the form of "#1;Joerg Krause." To process it, we create an `SPFieldLookupValue` object, passing the data as a string into the constructor to re-create the lookup value. From this object the LookupValue returns the full name. Figure 4–15 shows the output.

```
ASP.NET: Tips, Tutorial, and Code has these lead authors:
  - Scott Mitchell
SharePoint Server 2007 has these lead authors:
  - Bill English
SharePoint 2007 Development has these lead authors:
  - Steve Fox
Pro InfoPath 2007 has these lead authors:
  - Philo Janus
Real World SharePoint 2007 has these lead authors:
  - Scott Hillier
Programming Microsoft Office Business Applications has these lead authors:
  - Steve Fox
Pro ASP.NET 3.5 in C# 2008 has these lead authors:
  - Matthew MacDonald
ASP.NET Extensibility has these lead authors:
  - Joerg Krause
SharePoint 2010 as a Development Platform has these lead authors:
  - Joerg Krause
ASP.NET 3.5 has these lead authors:
  - Joerg Krause
.NET WCF has these lead authors:
  - Joerg Krause
```

Figure 4–15. *The console output of a joined result set*

Using List Joins and Projections in Site Templates

If you create joins and projections in a site template or in the schema.xml of a list definition, you can use the same syntax, as shown earlier. Because the XML is now placed somewhere in between all the other schema elements, the root elements <Joins>, <ProjectedFields>, and <ViewFields> must be added appropriately.

You can find a thorough explanation of templates in Chapter 7.

Understanding LINQ

LINQ is a technology that integrates data queries directly into the programming language. Consequently, queries are type-safe and checked by the compiler. Before LINQ, you had to use string queries, either T-SQL against a SQL Server or CAML, to query SharePoint. Using strings, the compiler has no way to validate the queries or the returned objects.

Examining the LINQ Basics

In this section we'll give a brief overview about LINQ and how it works. You can skip this section if you're already familiar with it. The following "Queryable SharePoint Objects" section examines in detail the specific ways to query SharePoint data in a type-safe manner.

LINQ fills a gap between the worlds of data and code. Database queries written in the programming language improves both the programmer's productivity and the compiler's ability to help. LINQ itself is largely independent of the underlying data source. A data source specific API transforms LINQ queries into the format required by the data source. LINQ consists of an extension framework within the compiler. This means that there are no additions to the Common Language Runtime (CLR). The .NET 2.0 CLR is sufficient to run LINQ-based programs, and thus SharePoint is able to use it, too. However, the C# compiler must be at least version 3.0 to support the various extensions.

A few base technologies are used, and at points in the book we'll refer to them:

- Type inference
- Anonymous types
- Object initializer
- Extension methods
- Lambda expressions
- Expression trees
- Relaxed delegates
- Nullables

Architecture of LINQ

It is essential that you know at least the fundamental architecture of LINQ. Each data source has its own library containing methods to connect, retrieve, and update data. Figure 4–16 shows this.

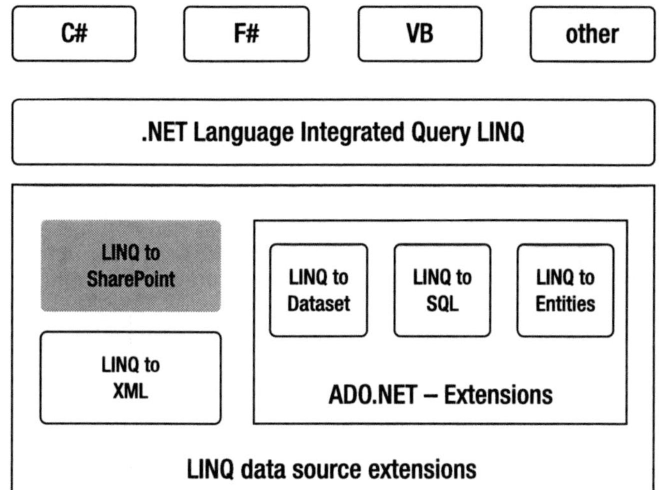

Figure 4–16. *LINQ architecture*

LINQ includes a well-defined set of keywords that is known to the API and the language compiler. This provides an abstraction level that allows you to write LINQ queries without needing to know the internals of SharePoint data object retrieval. However, once the objects have been fetched successfully, you need to work with them. From this point, LINQ drops out of the picture, and you're back into the world of CAML and SharePoint objects.

Keywords

LINQ uses keywords that are independent of the data source. The C# compiler supports this directly with new language keywords. The next example shows a simple array definition and a LINQ query to retrieve a filtered set from the array elements:

```
var data = new [] {0,1,2,3,4,5,6,7,8,9,10};
var res = from e in data
          where e < 5
          orderby e
          select e;
```

This query fetches all the numbers less than 5 from the array and stores them in the variable *res*. The keyword `var` is a variable type. Do not confuse this with `object`. A `var` type is set to a specific type at compile time by the compiler implicitly and is strongly typed then. That makes it somewhat type-safe, but you need not worry about the type before you get the data back. That's indeed crucial for working with SharePoint. Imagine you read data from a list. The list's columns might change depending on the query. The receiving variable must be robust enough to handle this. On the other hand, it's obviously a good idea to get the data from named properties instead of just string names.

The particular meaning of this small example doesn't matter here—rather, the internal structure is significant:

- `from e` defines the element's name (or in database terms, the name of a row).
- `in data` chooses the query data.
- `where e<5` defines the condition.
- `orderby e` adds sorting as a optional operation.
- `select e` selects the element to be returned.

This syntax is geared toward human readability. `from` and `in` are mandatory and must appear in that order. The compiler converts this into the corresponding lambda expressions. These are anonymous functions that represent queries internally. If you prefer, you could write such expressions directly:

```
IEnumerable<int> res = data.where(e => e < 5).orderby(e => e).select(e => e);
```

From this format with anonymous methods, the compiler can then compile the expression into IL code.

Enumerations

Each extension method returns at least an object that implements the `IEnumerable<T>` interface. Some queries also return the `IQueryable<T>` interface that provides additional features. This means that every query returns enumerable objects—like a collection. Even if the collection has only one element, it's still a collection. To access a single element, you can either use an iterator keyword, such as `for` or `foreach`, or use extension methods to get the first, last, or any other element that matches particular conditions.

Operators

The operators are similar to SQL operators. Table 4–10 summarizes them.

Table 4–10. LINQ Operators and Their Corresponding C# Syntax

Operator	C# LINQ Expression	
GroupBy	group … by …	group … by … into …
GroupJoin	join … in … on … equals … into …	
Join	join … in … on … equals …	
OrderBy	orderby …	
OrderByDescending	orderby … descending	
Select	select	
SelectMany	from … in … from … in …	
ThenBy	orderby … , …	
ThenByDescending	orderby … , … descending	
Where	where …	

Simple Queries

Before you start querying SharePoint, you should have a basic understanding of LINQ. Let's examine some examples. The use of where to add a condition to a query is the most common scenario:

```
int[] numbers = { 5, 4, 1, 3, 9, 8, 6, 7, 2, 0 };
var res =
  from n in numbers
  where n > 5
  select n;
```

To sort the results, add the orderby keyword:

```
var res =
    from n in numbers
    where n > 5
    orderby n
    select n;
```

Because each keyword is translated into its extension method counterpart, you could write the previous example as follows:

```
var res =
  (from n in numbers
   where n > 5
   select n).OrderBy(x => x);
```

Grouping follows a similar format, using the GroupBy operator.

```
var res =
  from n in numbers
  orderby n
  group n by n > 5 into g
  select new { GreaterFive = g.Key, Numbers = g};
```

In this example, the numbers are grouped into two groups. One group matches the condition `n > 5`, and the other group contains the leftovers. There are numerous ways to return the data. Here the `select` clause creates an anonymous type with two properties: `GreaterFive` and `Numbers`. `GreaterFive` contains the group's key to identify it later, while the property `Numbers` contains the retrieved data itself. Remember that the whole statement returns an enumerable object. In this case, the grouping would return two elements. Let's examine a more sophisticated example that deals with remainders:

```
var res =
  from n in numbers
  group n by n % 3 into g
  select new { Class = g.Key, Numbers = g};
```

Here the numbers are grouped together in classes dependent on the remainder after they are divided by three.

Anonymous types do not imply they are "untyped." The type is not explicitly defined in code, unlike a class. As soon as the data is assigned in the statement, the type is "safe." You cannot change it later. Hence, creating new enumerable constant data is easy:

```
var people = new [] {
   new {Name = "Langhirt", GivenName = "Christian", Author=true},
   new {Name = "Krause", GivenName = "Jörg", Author=true},
   new {Name = "Meurisch", GivenName = "Jörg", Author=false}
 };

var authors = from person in people
              where person.Author
              select new { Name=person.GivenName, person.Name };
```

The anonymous type is created with the `new` statement. The variable `people` is an array containing three objects. The object has three public properties. The types are inferred by the compiler and set to `string`, `string`, and `bool`, respectively.

If you want a specific person from the list, a suitable function is used. The first element could be retrieved like this:

```
string FirstAuthor = people.First().GivenName;
```

The more complex your questions, the more such operators are needed. Fortunately, LINQ comes with many of them. To get a selection of combined data, the `SelectMany` operator is helpful:

```
var books = new[] {
  new {Title = "ASP.NET Professional", Authors = Ã
    new[] {new {Name = "Fischer"}, new {Name = "Krause"}}},
  new {Title = "Windows Communication Foundation (WCF)", Authors = Ã
    new[] {new {Name = "Fischer"}, new {Name = "Krause"}}},
  new {Title = ".NET 3.5", Authors = Ã
    new[] {new {Name = "Fischer"}, new {Name = "Krause"}}},
  };
```

```
var publications =
  from book in books
  where book.Authors.Count() > 0
  from author in book.Authors
  select new { book.Title, author.Name };
```

If you have two lists and desire a cross-joined table, LINQ is even able to handle this:

```
int[] i = { 0, 1, 2, 3, 4, 5, 6, 7, 8, 9, 10 };
int[] k = { 0, 1, 2, 3, 4, 5, 6, 7, 8, 9, 10 };

  var cross = from x in k
              where x > 2
              from y in i
              where y > 3
              select new {x, y, product = x*y};
```

Remember that cross joins return the multiplied number of elements from both tables. In the example, you have 8 times 7 numbers, causing 56 elements being returned. More likely, you will deal with regular joins that follow a defined condition.

```
var names = new[]
{
  new {Name = "Fischer", id = 1},
  new {Name = "Krause", id = 2}
};

var givennames = new[]
{
  new {GivenName = "Jörg", id = 2},
  new {GivenName = "Matthias", id = 1}
};

var persons =
    from name in names
    join givenname in givennames
    on name.id equals givenname.id
    select new {givenname.GivenName, name.Name};
```

Aggregators

Aggregators are functions that reduce enumerable types. The most common is `Count`.

```
int[] i = { 0, 1, 2, 3, 4, 5, 6, 7, 8, 9, 10 };
int count = i.Count();
```

The LINQ library provides some other aggregate operators, such as `Sum<T>()`, `Min<T>()`, `Max<T>()`, and `Average<T>()`. The basic methods can handle scalar types only. To deal with complex types, you can use overloads that accept lambda expressions. The expressions resolve the data to be transformed in a way the aggregator can handle it, for example:

```
var objects = new [] {
  new {number = 0},
  new {number = 1},
  new {number = 2},
  new {number = 3},
```

```
    new {number = 4}
};

int sum = objects.Sum(x => x.number);
```

Selectors

You will often find that a query returns only one element. Even so, the query is built using either `IQuerable` or `IEnumable`. Both are enumerable and appear as collections. To extract the one and only element from the collection, the `First` selector is the best approach. This can fail, though, if the collection is empty. Using `FirstOrDefault` calls the `default(T)` method if there are no elements. You will usually get a new, empty element back.

```
int[] a = { 5, 4, 1, 3, 9, 8, 6, 7, 2, 0 }.First();
```

This example returns the number 5.

```
int[] a = { 5, 4, 1, 3, 9, 8, 6, 7, 2, 0 };
int res = (from n
                in a
                where (n > 3 && (n & 1) == 1)
                orderby n select n).FirstOrDefault();
```

To use a lambda expression, the same selectors are used:

```
int res = (a.OrderBy(n => n)).FirstOrDefault(n => (n > 3 && (n & 1) == 1));
```

You can retrieve the last element with `Last<T>()` and `LastOrDefault<T>()`, respectively. However, when processing large amounts of data, more functions are required. The extension methods `Take<T>(int n)` and `Skip<T>(int n)` either aid in selecting the first specified element or skip a number of elements and begin looping through the rest after this position. Using lambda expressions, this is all possible in a conditional manner using `SkipWhile<T>(Func<T,T,bool>)` and `TakeWhile<T>(Func<T,T,bool>)`.

```
int[] i = { 0, 1, 2, 3, 4, 5, 6, 7, 8, 9, 10 };
var r1 = i.Skip(5); // Skip 5 elements
var r2 = i.Take(6); // Take 6 elements
var r3 = i.SkipWhile(x => x < 6); // Skip all with x less than 6
var r4 = i.TakeWhile(x => x > 6); // Take all x greater than 6
```

LINQ to SharePoint

The SharePoint API gives you direct and powerful access to the data stored in lists and libraries. While this conventional access looks good, the flexibility and elegance of LINQ is particularly appealing.

LINQ is, as previously explained, a complete data abstraction layer. It's a provider between the data source (SharePoint) and the API. Its ability to extend the programming language and the tight integration is a big advantage while programming against SharePoint. You can regard LINQ as an object-relational mapper (OR mapper), defining entities to express your business object model. The LINQ to SharePoint provider uses entity classes to make the relational list model available in the object-oriented world of C#. This includes such features as object change tracking and deferred (or "lazy") loading. The primary feature is the abstraction between the SharePoint API and the object model. First, the object model can be closer to your business logic and a better expression of what you want to see as a developer. Second, the object model is robust against future changes of the API.

Understanding the LINQ to SharePoint Provider

The LINQ to SharePoint provider is defined in the `Microsoft.SharePoint.Linq` namespace. It translates LINQ queries into CAML queries, which means that you do not need to know how to write CAML queries or learn a different query language for each type of data source. In addition, LINQ queries can be executed against both the server and client operating models.

The gateway class for the LINQ to SharePoint provider is `Microsoft.SharePoint.Linq.DataContext`. It is equivalent to the `System.Data.Linq.DataContext` class in the LINQ to SQL provider. Just as the latter class has a `GetTable` method, which returns a `Table<T>` object that implements the `IQueryable<T>` interface, `DataContext` class has a `GetList` method. It returns an `EntityList<T>` type, which in turn implements the `IQueryable<T>` interface.

The following is an example of how to use LINQ to query a SharePoint list:

```
// Get DataContext from page context
DataContext data = new DataContext(SPContext.GetContext(this.Context).Web.Url);
// Get the SharePoint list
EntityList<Customer> Customers = data.GetList<Customer>("Lists/Customers");
// Query for customers from London
var londonCustomers = from customer in Customers
                      where customer.City == "London"
                      select customer;
```

You can now bind these data to some sort of control.

Query Joined Lists

One important aspect of the LINQ to SharePoint provider is that queries can be inefficient even if they appear to be well written and they produce valid results. An inefficient query is defined as one that requires more queries to the server than there are lists referenced in the query. For example, if there is a subquery to list B for every row of list A, the query is inefficient. The LINQ to SharePoint provider comes with a restriction. Such queries are not supported. If you require such a style of execution, use nested loops (and accept that it is suboptimal).

Queries that assume an implicit join between two SharePoint lists will be supported if and only if the joining field is configured as a lookup field in the SharePoint list.

Restrictions of LINQ to SharePoint Provider

The provider does not supported two LINQ operators:

- `ElementAt`
- `ElementAtOrDefault`

Some queries cannot be completely translated into CAML. However, it is possible to execute such a query by downloading the entire SharePoint list to the client and enumerating through it to carry out the non-CAML parts of the query. You can specify whether to allow such queries by setting the `DataContext.AllowInefficientQueries` property to `true`. It is obvious that this is not an efficient way to retrieve data.

Assume you have a LINQ select clause like the following:

```
select new { c.Name, c.ZipCode }
```

This query would translate into CAML as a `<ViewFields>` tag with two `<FieldRef>` child elements. But the following `select` clause contains a mathematical function that is not supported in CAML:

```
select new { c.Price*2, c.Orders, c.Customer }
```

A query that contains a mathematical function or another unsupported aggregator function clause is considered inefficient. If inefficient queries have been enabled, the query will be executed, but only up to the `select` clause, by LINQ to SharePoint on the server. Then the results that are received from the CAML query are sent to the client as an `IEnumerable` object. A new LINQ query on the client will then execute the `select` clause projection on the object by using the `System.Linq.Enumerable.Select` method. From here on, the LINQ to Object provider takes over and finishes the querying. It's obvious that this handover is less efficient.

The following LINQ operators are semi-efficient:

- Aggregate
- All
- Any
- Average
- Distinct
- Except
- Intersect
- Join
- Max
- Min
- Reverse
- SequenceEqual
- Skip
- SkipWhile
- Sum

Semi-efficient means that the provider will probably additionally to the CAML query one or more LINQ to Object operations to fulfill the task. That means additional memory consumption and CPU resources. Such queries are also called *two-stage queries*.

Entity Classes and the SPMetal Tool

As the LINQ to SharePoint provider gives typed access to list data, there must be a way to retrieve the column information. Reading it at runtime would decrease performance appreciably. As with other LINQ providers, the solution is a proxy class. To create such a class, a command-line tool is used. This tool, called `SPMetal`, reads the SharePoint list's definition and generates a proxy class. This autogenerated class could look like the following:

```
[List(Name="Customers")]
partial public class Customer
{
   [Column(Id=true)]
   public int CustomerId;

   [Column]
   public string City;
}
```

You can of course write such classes by hand, but using the tool is very helpful. It's part of the SDK for SharePoint 2010. (Refer to the section "Creating the Layer with SPMetal.exe" later in this chapter.)

■ **Note** To ensure that the proxy classes are up-to-date, you should plan to call `SPMetal` in a prebuild event and read the most current list definitions.

Creating list proxies is probably not the most efficient way. It is of course a way that will work just fine out of the box.

Writing Data

You can use the gateway class, `DataContext`, to write changes to the SharePoint content database. Simply call the `DataContext.SubmitChanges` method. The following is an example demonstrating how to add an item to a list and save the changes to the database:

```
Customer customer = new Customer();
DataContext data = new DataContext(SPContext.GetContext(this.Context).Web.Url);
EntityList<Customer> Customers = data.GetList<Customer>("Lists/Customers");
// write data into "customer" object
Customers.Add(customer);
data.SubmitChanges();
```

Entity Identity

The LINQ to SharePoint provider keeps track of all entities that are returned by queries and all changes to those entities. When a specified entity is returned more than once, the provider will always return the same instance of the entity that it returned the first time. This behavior ensures that an application is always working with the same instance of a specified entity and that it never works with an entity that has been changed by another application.

When `SubmitChanges` executes, it compares the current state of the entity in the database with the state of the entity when it was first returned. If there is a discrepancy, then some other application has changed the entity after the first return. You can configure the behavior of `SubmitChanges` to stop writing more changes when it finds the first discrepancy, or you can set it to continue writing, regardless of discrepancies.

Creating the Layer with SPMetal.exe

`SPMetal` is a command-line tool that generates entity classes, which provide an object-oriented interface to the content databases. These classes are primarily used in LINQ to SharePoint queries; but they are also be used to add, delete, and change list items with protection against concurrency conflicts. They can be used as an alternative to the regular SharePoint object model for accessing data.

Where to Get SPMetal?

The tool is included with SharePoint Foundation and is usually located here:

```
%ProgramFiles%\Common Files\Microsoft Shared\web server extensions\14\bin
```

You can use this tool in any kind of batch file, typically as a prebuild command in Visual Studio. The generated code should be placed somewhere in the project to make it available for subsequent building steps.

How to Use SPMetal?

SPMetal reads the custom lists found in the specified site and creates a class. The class is marked partial so that you can add members without worrying that your code could be overwritten by subsequent building steps. SPMetal has several options to modify the code generation:

- /web:<site>. The URL of the <site> from which you want to retrieve the lists.
- /code:<file.cs>. The name of the output file for the generated code. If omitted, the code is emitted to the console.
- /language:<lang>. Either csharp or vb—if omitted, the language is used that fits the output file extension.
- /namespace:<ns>. The namespace that wraps around the code.
- /user:<user> and /password:<pass>. User and password credentials for the site.
- /serialization:<none|unidirectional>. If the value unidirectional is used, the generated code is serializable. The default is none.

A typical command with parameters looks like this:

```
SPMetal /web:http://sharepointserve /code:Authors.cs /namespace:Apress.Sp2010.Linq
```

This call will generate the code in C# within the current directory.

■ **Tip** If a parameter for an SPMetal option contain spaces, you must enclose it in quotes.

Advanced Configuration

SPMetal has a few parameters, as described earlier. Several defaults apply for the process of code generation. To override those values, parameters can be supplied via an XML file. A typical file looks like this:

```
<?xml version="1.0" encoding="utf-8"?>
<Web AccessModifier="Internal"
     xmlns="http://schemas.microsoft.com/SharePoint/2009/spmetal">
  <ContentType Name="Contact" Class="Contact">
    <Column Name="ContId" Member="ContactId" />
    <Column Name="ContactName" Member="ContactName1" />
    <Column Name="Category" Member="Cat" Type="String"/>
    <ExcludeColumn Name="HomeTelephone" />
  </ContentType>
  <ExcludeContentType Name="Order"/>
  <List Name="Team Members" Type="TeamMember">
    <ContentType Name="Item" Class="TeamMember" />
  </List>
</Web>
```

The <Web> element is always the root. It supports two attributes:

- AccessModifier: Modifies the access modifier that defaults to public. The only allowed values are Internal and Public.
- Class: Name of the generated class (overwrites the "xxxDataContext" name).

Within the <Web> element, several other elements can be used to modify the behavior. Use the <List> element to manage lists. It supports two operations. First, you can include lists that SPMetal would not model by default, such as hidden lists. Second, you can change the name SPMetal uses—by default, the list's name. Supported attributes are as follows:

- Name: The name of the list—this attribute is mandatory.
- Member: Specifies an alternate name.
- Type: Alternate type used as the list's base type. You can define the type in your custom code, and this type is used as the parent to the list's type. This is to allow custom base classes that expose additional functionality.

While <List> can include lists, <ExcludeList> excludes lists SPMetal would normally model by default. The only attribute is Name. If you want to exclude all lists and include only a few specific ones, add an empty <ExcludeOtherLists /> element and use the appropriate <List> elements. If you want to include all hidden lists, add the <IncludeHiddenLists /> element. This element cannot be used together with <ExludeOtherLists />.

Lists are made of columns, and several columns are defined in content types. The <ContentType> element can be used globally (under <Web>) or within the scope of a list (under <List>). Two attributes are supported:

- Name: Name of the content type. Use Item as the basic type the Foundation provides.
- Class: The alternate class name.

To modify the <ContentType> element, columns can be added to or removed from the model using the <Column> and <ExcludeColumn> elements, respectively. An empty <ExcludeOtherColumns /> element can exclude all columns. If you want to include all hidden columns the <IncludeHiddenColumns /> element is used. To have the same function for the whole content type, the <ExcludeOtherContentType /> element can exclude all, and <IncludeHiddenContentType /> includes those with the Hidden attribute.

Once the XML file is created with the appropriate values, you can use the following syntax to assign the file:

```
spmetal /parameters:<path>\params.xml
```

The basic parameters are still required and must be provided as described earlier.

What SPMetal Generates

SPMetal has some basic rules that apply (except where the particular default rule has been overridden). First, any class is marked public by default. You can override this with the AccessModifier attribute of the <Web> element. Second, the class is named FileNameDataContext, where FileName is the name of the file without the file extension that is specified by the /code option on the SPMetal command. For example, if /code:Personnel.cs is on the command line, the class is called PersonnelDataContext. You can override this with the Class attribute of the <Web> element. A property is generated in the DataContext-derived class for every nonhidden list in the web site. This can be overridden with the <ExcludeList> or <ExcludeOtherLists> elements. The type of the property is EntityList<(Of <(TEntity>)>). These properties are marked public. No property is generated for hidden lists. The

<IncludeHiddenLists> element or a <List> element whose Name attribute is assigned to a hidden list can be used to override this behavior. A property that represents a list has the same name as the list with three exceptions. First, if there are spaces in the list name, they are removed from the property name. Note that this is different from the behavior SharePoint uses internally, such as replacing spaces with the _x0020_ string. Second, if the first letter of the list name is lowercase, it is capitalized in the property name. Third, if SPMetal judges the list name to be an English singular term, it attempts to give the property a plural version of the name. In several common cases, this is doomed, because the complex and arbitrary English pluralization rules such as child/children are not recognized correctly. We suggest overriding any tricky names with suitable values in the XML parameter file, as described earlier.

The type parameter, T, of the EntityList<(Of <(TEntity>)>)<T> property is the content type class generated for the list. If there is more than one content type associated with the list, T is the class that represents the basic Item content type of SharePoint. Use the Type attribute of the <List> element to override this.

A content type class named Item is generated to represent the basic SharePoint content type. You can override this with the <ExcludeContentType> element for that content type. For any list that has not been excluded, a content type class is generated for every defined content type assigned to the list. Again, overriding this behavior is possible using the <ExcludeContentType> or <ExcludeOtherContentTypes> element. For any defined content type, including the basic Item content type, the generated class has the same name as the content type. You can override with the Class attribute of a <ContentType> element. For any list that does not use a defined content type but to which one or more columns have been added, a class is generated to represent the implied content type. This means that the generator assumes a generic content type to use the same rules. The class that represents an implied content type will be named listpropertynameItem, where listpropertyname is the name of the property that represents the list.

If a content type inherits from another, the generator creates the same hierarchy for the classes. The classes are marked both partial and public. Use the AccessModifier attribute of a <ContentType> element to override this behavior. There is no way to suppress the partial modifier.

The class that represents the basic Item content type implements ITrackEntityState, ITrackOriginalValues, INotifyPropertyChanged, and INotifyPropertyChanging interfaces. A property is generated in a content type class for every nonhidden field. You can override this with the <ExcludeColumn> or <ExcludeOtherColumns> element. The property is marked public. It has the same name as the column it represents, but spaces in a column name are removed.

If the first letter in the column name is lowercase, it is made uppercase in the property name. The type of a column property is determined from the property of the field in accordance with the mapping presented in SharePoint to .NET Type Mapping. You can override this with the Type attribute of a <Column> element. No property is generated for columns that are on the list, but not in the content type. The same applies to hidden columns, except the hidden Id and Version columns, which are always present.

For every Choice field that does not allow Fill-in choices, an enumerated class is generated. For every MultiChoice field that does not allow Fill-in choices and has fewer than 31 choices, an enumerated class decorated with the [Flags] attribute is generated. The values Invalid and None are added as possible values to the enumerations. Additionally, a sealed class is generated with a String constant for each defined value.

To represent lookup list relationship fields' names, EntityRef, EntitySet, and LookupList are generated. For every column that is a lookup to a field on another list and that does not allow multiple values, the property that represents the column wraps a private field of type EntityRef<(Of <(TEntity>)>)<T>, where T is the content type of the lookup list. If the lookup to a field allows multiple values, the property that represents the column wraps a private field of type EntitySet<(Of <(TEntity>)>)<T>, where T is the content type of the lookup list.

When talking about the content type and its representation in .NET classes, the type mapping is worth a closer look. Table 4–11 shows the complete mapping list.

Table 4–11. Type Mapping Between Field Types and Common Type System (CTS)

Field Type	CTS Type
AllDayEvent	Boolean.
Attachments	Boolean.
Boolean	Boolean.
Calculated	Type of the returned value,
Choice	Enum or String. The enum has values -1 and 0 for Invalid and None added to the choices. The enums name is <FieldName>Choice. (For fill-in choices see MultiChoice.)
Computed	Object
ContentTypeId	Byte[]
Counter	Int32
CrossProjectLink	Boolean
Currency	Double
DateTime	DateTime
File	String
GridChoice	Object
Guid	Guid
Integer	Int32
Lookup	EntityRef<T> for single lookups and EntitySet(T)<T> for multilookups.
MaxItems	Object
ModStat	Object
MultiChoice	Flagged Enum or String. If fill-in choices are allowed, strings are used. Constant string values are stored in a class as a set of constants. Strings are also used if there are more than 31 values in the choice.
Note	String

Field Type	CTS Type
Number	Double
PageSeparator	Object
Recurrence	Boolean
Text	String
ThreadIndex	Object
Threading	Object
URL	String
User	String for a single user. IList<String> if multiple are values allowed.
WorkflowEventType	Object
WorkflowStatus	Object

With this information in mind, using LINQ with SharePoint seems to be easy and smart.

Using LINQ

All LINQ to SharePoint code begins with the data context. In this section all examples use the same context, stored in the variable *ctx*. The context is created on a per-site basis, so it doesn't make sense to refer to specific lists.

```
DatacontextDataContext ctx = new DatacontextDataContext("http://sharepointserve");
```

The examples are in one console application and use simple console output to show data.

Example: Reading Data

Assuming that a proxy class created by SPMetal exists, the following example (see Listing 4–32) shows the entries of items in the list named Authors.

Listing 4–32. *Complete Example That Retrieves Data Using LINQ*

```
using System;
using System.Linq;
using Microsoft.SharePoint;

namespace Apress.SP2010.Linq
{
    class Program
    {
```

```
        static void Main(string[] args)
        {
            using (SPSite site = new SPSite("http://sharepointserve"))
            {
                using (SPWeb web = site.OpenWeb())
                {
                    DatacontextDataContext ctx =
                       new DatacontextDataContext("http://sharepointserve/");
                    var authors = from a in ctx.Authors
                                  select a;
                    foreach (var ac in authors)
                    {
                        Console.WriteLine("{0}, {1}, {2}",
                                          ac.Company,
                                          ac.FirstName,
                                          ac.EMail);
                    }
                    Console.ReadLine();

                }
            }
        }
    }
}
```

The DatacontextDataContext class is generated with SPMetal using the default settings. The LINQ query does not have any options and fetches the complete list. The object is retrieved directly using the syntax select *a*, where *a* is the loop variable defined in the LINQ query. In the foreach statement, the current author is held in the loop variable ac. The type defined by the context is AuthorsContact, the name constructed from the current list (Author) and the base content type (Contact). The loop could also look like this:

```
foreach (AuthorsContact ac in authors)
```

However, the var type is both short and type-safe and is the preferred way to express variables and to improve readability. Instead of accepting the type defined by the list, you can easily create a new anonymous type that fits your needs, as shown in Listing 4–33.

Listing 4–33. *Different Version of the Query Shown in Listing 4–32*

```
var authors2 = from a in ctx.Authors
               select new
               {
                   Firm = a.Company,
                   Name = a.FullName,
                   Mail = a.EMail
               };
foreach (var ac in authors2)
{
    Console.WriteLine("{0}, {1}, {2}", ac.Firm, ac.Name, ac.Mail);
}
```

The type created by select new is anonymous and contains three public properties (*Firm*, *Name*, *Mail*). The properties types are determined from the source type (*a.Company* and so on). This is still type-safe, but you don't have to care about the types.

Example: Read Joined Data

To read a joined list, you can use the `join` operator. The order of the join is vital. Creating an output type is a common technique to get exactly what you want (see Listing 4–34).

***Listing 4–34.** Retrieve Joined Data*

```
EntityList<AuthorsContact> authorsj = ctx.GetList<AuthorsContact>("Authors");
EntityList<BooksItem> booksj = ctx.GetList<BooksItem>("Books");
var result5 = from book in booksj
              join author in authorsj on book.LeadAuthor.Id equals author.Id
              select new
              {
                  Book = book.Title,
                  Author = author.FullName
              };
result5.ToList().ForEach(ab => Console.WriteLine("{0} was written by {1}",
    ab.Book,
    ab.Author));
```

The code produces the output shown in **Figure 4–17**. The conversion with `ToList` was used only to get access to the `ForEach` method for easy output.

```
ASP.NET Extensibility was written by Joerg Krause
ASP.NET: Tips, Tutorial, and Code was written by Scott Mitchell
Real World SharePoint 2007 was written by Scott Hillier
Pro InfoPath 2007 was written by Philo Janus
Pro ASP.NET 3.5 in C# 2008 was written by Matthew MacDonald
SharePoint 2010 as a Development Platform was written by Joerg Krause
SharePoint Server 2007 was written by Bill English
SharePoint 2007 Development was written by Steve Fox
.NET WCF was written by Joerg Krause
Programming Microsoft Office Business Applications was written by Steve Fox
ASP.NET 3.5 was written by Joerg Krause
```

***Figure 4–17.** Output produced by the join example*

Example: Inserting Items Using EntityList<T>

Another strategy is to use `EntityList` to get a list representation, to which you can add new elements (see Listing 4–35).

***Listing 4–35.** Using the EntityList Class*

```
EntityList<AuthorsContact> list = ctx.GetList<AuthorsContact>("Authors");
foreach (var ac in list)
{
   Console.WriteLine("{0}, {1}, {2}", ac.Company, ac.FullName, ac.EMail);
}
EntityList<AuthorsContact> list2 = ctx.GetList<AuthorsContact>("Authors");
AuthorsContact newAuthor = new AuthorsContact();
newAuthor.FirstName = "Bernd";
newAuthor.Title = "Pehlke";
newAuthor.EMail = "bpehlke@computacenter.com";
```

```
newAuthor.Company = "Computacenter";
list2.InsertOnSubmit(newAuthor);
ctx.SubmitChanges();
foreach (var ac in list2)
{
    Console.WriteLine("{0}, {1}, {2}", ac.Company, ac.FullName, ac.EMail);
}
```

The foreach loop is merely to show that the element has been successfully added. The new item is created using the type AuthorsContact and its default constructor. Once all required properties are filled in with appropriate values, the element can be added using the InsertOnSubmit method. As the name implies, the SubmitChanges method invoked on the data context writes the data into the SharePoint database.

■ **Caution** Notice carefully the internal field names that are used. For instance, the Contact content type does not have a field Last Name. The mandatory Title field is used instead, and expressed with the DisplayName Last Name. Consequently, in code you must use item.Title instead of item.LastName. To make your code safer, use the SPField object and retrieve the InternalName property for a particular field.

Example: Deleting Items

Deleting an item is similar to the insertion procedure. The item is part of a list. Hence, the DeleteOnSubmit method can be found in the list's class, Authors, as in Listing 4–36.

Listing 4–36. *Delete an Item*

```
var authors3 = from a in ctx.Authors
               where a.Title.Equals("Pehlke")
               select a;
foreach (var ac in authors3)
{
   ctx.Authors.DeleteOnSubmit(ac);
   Console.WriteLine("Delete: {0}, {1}, {2}", ac.Company, ac.FullName, ac.EMail);
}
ctx.SubmitChanges();
```

The context class sends the delete task to the list with the SubmitChanges call. Instead of deleting an item, you can use RecycleOnSubmit to remove the item and put it into the Recycle Bin list (see Listing 4–37).

Listing 4–37. *Recycling an Item*

```
var authors4 = from a in ctx.Authors
               where a.Title.Equals("Pehlke")
               select a;
foreach (var ac in authors4)
{
   ctx.Authors.RecycleOnSubmit(ac);
```

```
    Console.WriteLine("Recycled: {0}, {1}, {2}",
                      ac.Company, ac.FullName, ac.EMail);
}
ctx.SubmitChanges();
```

Example: Updating Properties Using the ForEach Pattern

Updating an item is similar and simply requires access to a single item to change its properties and call the SubmitChanges method.

When changing or accessing all items, a foreach loop is the only way. All previous examples use this pattern. However, the extensibility model allows a custom definition of such a ForEach pattern, in the same style as ForEach method supported by the List<T> and Array<T> types.

```
ctx.Authors.ForEach<AuthorsContact>(ac => ac.Company = "Microsoft");
ctx.SubmitChanges();
ctx.Authors.ForEach<AuthorsContact>(ac => Console.WriteLine("{0} at {1}",
                                           ac.FirstName, ac.Company));
```

In this example, a generic ForEach method is used to invoke an Action<T>. Each element of the collection is used to call the action defined in the lambda expression. System.Action is a predefined delegate that has no return value. The definition encapsulates the foreach statement:

```
public static class Extensions
{
    public static void ForEach<T>(this IQueryable<T> source, Action<T> func)
    {
        foreach (var item in source)
            func(item);
    }
}
```

This defines the *ForEach* extension method for the commonly used type IQueryable. The Action parameter takes any lambda expression. A return value—if any—is thrown away. In the previous example, the method is used to change a property and to write the content to the console. Assuming the extension method is defined once somewhere in your project, the LINQ lines are obviously shorter and nonetheless perfectly readable.

Sometimes you deal with detached data. That happens if you serialize an object and send it over the wire to some other application. If you work with Windows Communication Foundation (WCF) connections, Workflow Foundation (WF), or web services at all, this can happen. You receive back, according to the previous examples, an object of type AuthorsContact, but it is not generated in the context of the previous class. Inserting such an object using the InsertOnSubmit method is risky. If the same object already exists, the tracking does not matter. If all properties are not unique, this will work, but the object is now in the list twice. If the list requires unique properties, such as an ID, an exception is thrown. To avoid such behavior, you can use the Attach method. Attaching means that the item is inserted with tracking. (See the section "Track Changes" to read more about how the conflict resolver works internally to deal with such situations.)

Advanced List Examples

The basic techniques to retrieve data from lists are not sufficient in all cases in real-life projects. Sooner or later you will encounter the limitations of LINQ to SharePoint.

Handle Queries Containing Functions

As shown at the beginning of the chapter, the LINQ to SharePoint provider translates the LINQ query into CAML. (The CAML query is converted again into SQL clauses.) As a result, you need to be aware of what CAML is able to express efficiently. Simple select constructs, whether they use anonymous or typed objects, are always efficient. However, if the statement contains a formula you can't express with CAML but is allowed in LINQ, the query is rejected. You can, however, take advantage of another LINQ provider—LINQ to Objects. LINQ to Objects is not recommended if the amount of data retrieved from a list is high. If you access a list's item collection directly, the whole list is held in memory. If this is on a per-session basis, it could have a detrimental effect on performance. If you put a result set into the cache, this might work, but you lose the ability to issue per-user queries.

To overcome such limitations, you can retrieve the data first using either CAML directly or LINQ to SharePoint. This should reduce the number of items drastically. The result is then copied to an `IEnumerable` type that you can easily filter using LINQ to Objects. Copy your results using a method such as `ToList<T>` (see Listing 4–38), `ToDictonary<T>`, `ToArray<T>`, or `Cast<T>`.

***Listing 4–38.** Combining LINQ to SharePoint with LINQ to Objects*

```
DataContext data = new DataContext("http://sharepointserve");
DataContext subData = new DataContext("http://sharepointserve/SubTeamSite");

EntityList<Announcement> announcement =
                        data.GetList<Announcement>("Announcements");
EntityList<Announcement> subannouncements =
                        subData.GetList<Announcement>("Announcements");
List<Announcement> annsList = (from ann in announcements
                               select ann).ToList();
List<Announcement> annsSubList = (from ann in subannouncements
                                  select ann).ToList();

IEnumerable<Announcement> allAnnotations = annsSubList.Union(annsAnns);

foreach (Announcement ann in allAnnotations)
{
    Console.WriteLine(ann.Title);
}
```

This example uses the LINQ to SharePoint provider to get two result sets from lists. Both results are copied to `List<T>` objects. They are combined using the `Union` method, which SharePoint does not support directly.

Splitting queries into two parts can be cumbersome work. Fortunately, some of such operations are done internally. Such operations are called *semi-efficient queries.*

Customize the Mapping

The generation of the LINQ layer is a onetime process. If you run your layer in an environment where users can add fields or where custom field types are used, the layer can't handle this. The reason for the good performance of the LINQ provider is at the same time its biggest weakness—the statically generated classes.

Apart from custom fields, the generator oversees public properties too. Internally `SPMetal` reads the content type and its fields. Properties that the list provides by default, such as Attachments, are not recognized.

To overcome this limitation, you can use a custom mapping that provides new public properties and handle the calls to the provider's internal data handling. To attach new properties, the generated class is marked as `partial`. The first step is to create a new class with the same name and is also marked as `partial`. This new class implements the `ICustomMapping` interface. The methods the interface requires and the properties you add create the mapping.

```
public partial class Book : ICustomMapping
{
  [CustomMapping(Columns = new String[] { "ISBN", "UPCA" })]
  public void MapFrom(object listItem)
  {
    SPListItem item = (SPListItem)listItem;
    this.ISBN = item["ISBN"];
    this.UPCA = item["UPCA"];
  }

  public void MapTo(object listItem)
  {
    SPListItem item = (SPListItem)listItem;
    item["ISBN"] = this.ISBN;
    item["UPCA"] = this.UPCA;
  }

  public void Resolve(RefreshMode mode,
                      object originalListItem,
                      object databaseObject)
  {
  }

    // New property declarations go here.

}
```

The custom mapping is managed by the `CustomMapping` attribute. The `Columns` array contains the mapped columns.

■ **Caution** The public methods `MapTo` and `MapFrom` are not intended to be called directly from your code.

This does not address how to handle columns added by users after your code has been deployed. To handle "any" column, you can use a placeholder such as the following:

```
[CustomMapping(Columns = new String[] { "*" })]
```

The next example shows how to handle such columns properly:

```
[CustomMapping(Columns = new String[] { "*" })]
public void MapFrom(object listItem)
{
    SPListItem item = (SPListItem)listItem;
    foreach (var field in item.Fields)
    {
```

```
            this.Properties[field.InternalName] = item[field.InternalName];
        }
    }

    public void MapTo(object listItem)
    {
        SPListItem item = (SPListItem)listItem;
        foreach (var kvp in this.Properties)
        {
            item[kvp.Key] = this.Properties[kvp.Key];
        }
    }
```

The ICustomMapping methods can also be used to map properties to hash table entries of the Properties property the generated class provides:

```
[CustomMapping(Columns = new String[] { "*" })]
public void MapFrom(object listItem)
{
    this.PreviousManager = ((SPListItem)listItem).Properties["PreviousManager"];
}

public void MapTo(object listItem)
{
    ((SPListItem)listItem).Properties["PreviousManager"] = this.PreviousManager;
}
```

Managing Concurrency Conflicts for the New Columns

To ensure that your properties are participating in the object change tracking system, check that the set accessor of the properties is calling the content type class's OnPropertyChanging and OnPropertyChanged methods, as shown in the following example. These methods are part of the code generated by SPMetal. They handle the PropertyChanging and PropertyChanged events, respectively. The following is an example for one of the columns discussed earlier in this topic that uses a custom field type. Note the custom field type is ISBNField in this example.

```
public ISBNField ISBN
{
    get
    {
        return iSBN;
    }
    set
    {
        if ((value != iSBN))
        {
            this.OnPropertyChanging("ISBN", iSBN);
            iSBN = value;
            this.OnPropertyChanged("ISBN");
        }
    }
}
```

Track Changes

The LINQ to SharePoint provider checks changes made in the database against its current state. This is the default behavior. If you access the lists in a read-only manner, the tracking can be suppressed to optimize performance:

```
ctx.ObjectTrackingEnabled = false;
```

As a developer, you must always be aware of changes made by other applications, including the standard SharePoint UI. LINQ to SharePoint uses so-called optimistic concurrency to resolve conflicts. If a discrepancy has been found, the provider stops writing data back to the database. The `SubmitChanges` method has a parameter `ConflictMode` to control the behavior:

```
ctx.SubmitChanges(ConflictMode.ContinueOnConflict);
ctx.SubmitChanges(ConflictMode.FailOnFirstConflict);
```

In either case, data is written, but if the option opts to continue any further, the same data record is tried again. *Optimistic* means that the operation does not fail definitely. The user can decide how to proceed and any possible actions are allowed—cancel the change or overwrite existing data. That means that your code must provide a way to inform the user and let them decide what to do or assume a default action. To help you to do the right thing, the `EntityState` property is used. In a proxy class created by `SPMetal`, it looks like this:

```
[Microsoft.SharePoint.Linq.ContentTypeAttribute(Name="Item", Id="0x01")]
public partial class Item : ITrackEntityState, ITrackOriginalValues,
                            INotifyPropertyChanged, INotifyPropertyChanging
{
    private EntityState _entityState;

    private IDictionary<string, object> _originalValues;

    EntityState EntityState
    {
        get
        {
            return this._entityState;
        }
        set
        {
            this._entityState = value;
        }
    }

    IDictionary<string, object> OriginalValues
    {
        get
        {
            return this._originalValues;
        }
        set
        {
            this._originalValues = value;
        }
    }

    public Item()
```

```
    {
        this._entityState = EntityState.Unchanged;
        this.OnCreated();
    }
}
```

As shown in the exhibit from SPMetal-generated code, the EntityState property is private. You may wonder how to get the information directly from the code. The state is relevant only during a conflict. Such a conflict throws a ChangeConflictException. The exception details expose some information that's internally retrieved from EntityState and OriginalValues properties. The following example triggers the exception by writing values to the same item using two different data contexts:

```
AuthorDataContext ctx2 = new AuthorDataContext(ctx.Web);
var a1 = (from a in ctx2.Authors where a.Title.Equals("Krause") select a).First();
a1.Title = "Krause (LastName)";
// Change same with another value in default context
var a2 = (from a in ctx.Authors where a.Title.Equals("Krause") select a).First();
a2.Title = "Krause (Title)";
try
{
   ctx2.SubmitChanges();
   ctx.SubmitChanges();
}
catch (Microsoft.SharePoint.Linq.ChangeConflictException ce)
{
   foreach (var cc in ctx.ChangeConflicts)
    {
        Console.WriteLine("Conflict for {0}", cc.Object);
        if (cc.MemberConflicts.Count() > 0)
        {
            foreach (MemberChangeConflict mcc in cc.MemberConflicts)
            {
                Console.WriteLine(" Current: {0}, Database: {1}, Original: {2}",
                    mcc.CurrentValue,
                    mcc.DatabaseValue,
                    mcc.OriginalValue);
            }
        }
    }
}
```

Using a second data context, the same LINQ query ensures that the same item is fetched from the database twice. The Title property is changed to two different values within the two separate contexts. The conflict occurs when the second SubmitChanges method is called. This throws the ChangeConflictException, which is caught. The ChangeConflict property of the second context (*ctx*) exposes all the information you need in order to decide how to proceed (see Figure 4–18).

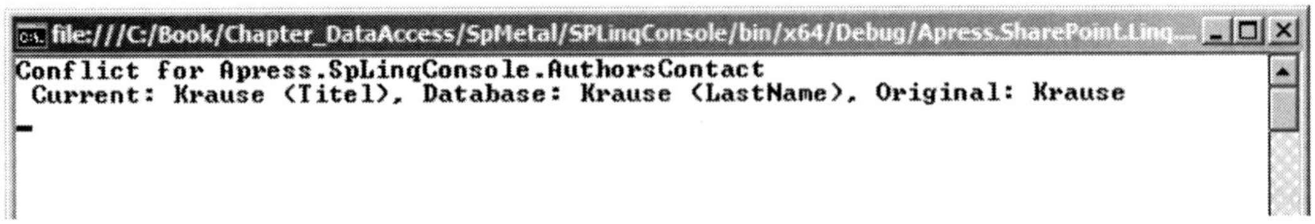

```
file:///C:/Book/Chapter_DataAccess/SpMetal/SPLinqConsole/bin/x64/Debug/Apress.SharePoint.Linq...
Conflict for Apress.SpLinqConsole.AuthorsContact
 Current: Krause (Titel), Database: Krause (LastName), Original: Krause
```

Figure 4–18. Investigating conflict information reveals current, old, and original values

As shown in the previous example, you can easily use multiple data context objects against the same site. As long as all contexts but one are read-only, there should be no conflicts. The read-only contexts could also be optimized by switching off the tracking:

```
ctx.ObjectTrackingEnabled = false;
```

Resolving Conflicts

If writing from multiple contexts is necessary for your business layer or if changes from other parties are expected, the `ChangeConflict` property (of `MemberChangeConflict` type) provides everything you need. Within the object, the property `MemberConflicts` resolves the conflict separately for each field (see Table 4–12).

Table 4–12. Properties of MemberChangeConflict Type to Investigate a Conflict

Property	Description
`OriginalValue`	What it was before any change
`DatabaseValue`	The value currently found in the database, written by another user
`CurrentValue`	The value set by the current operation
`IsModified`	The value was modified
`IsResolved`	The conflict has been resolved by calling the `Resolve` method (see below)
`Member`	`MemberInfo` object of the property

To resolve a conflict, call the `Resolve` method for each item in `MemberConflicts` collection. The parameter expects a value from `RefreshMode` enumeration:

- `KeepChanges`: The current value is kept, but all others changed values are updated.
- `KeepCurrentValues`: No value is modified— keeps what is already in the database.
- `OverwriteCurrentValues`: This overwrites all current values with those found in the database.

It is worth noting that all changed properties are exposed in this collection, even if only one property throws the exception. That's necessary to resolve conflicts, because returning to the original value of the conflicting item may require doing so for all or some other properties. But it's up to you to resolve multiple conflicts.

Declare Your Own Type Classes

Using SPMetal is powerful and provides a great set of features to access SharePoint lists with type-safe objects. However, under rare circumstances, it may be necessary to define your own classes. This is, typically, the case if the lists are themselves based on an external definition. Such a definition might use XML Schema (XSD) to define lists and their data types. The schema can be distributed with the feature, and it should support both the list creation as well as the data access layer using LINQ to SharePoint. At least two attributes are required to decorate the classes and properties appropriately:

```
[ContentType(Name="Announcement", Id="0x0104")]
public partial class Announcement
{
    [Column(Name = "Title", FieldType = "Text", IsId=true)]
    public String Title { get; set; }
}
```

In this example, the only field you can retrieve is Title. Consequently, you are not limited to the fields defined by the underlying content type in both directions. You can add more fields, and you can leave columns you don't need. However, if a column is not defined as a property, it is not available from the LINQ provider.

Examine Relationships

When you create a lookup, you can choose to enforce referential integrity between elements in the related lists, as shown in Figure 4–19.

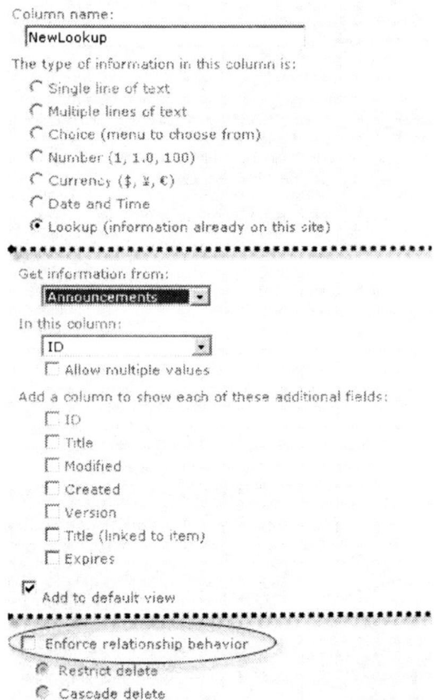

***Figure 4–19.** Enforcing referential integrity*

There are two options available here: Restrict Delete and Cascade Delete. The Restrict Delete option enables you to enforce that you cannot delete from the list any item that has related data. For example, if the item you are trying to delete has one or more child items, you cannot delete the item. Cascade Delete, on the other hand, means that when you're trying to delete an item with related data, it will delete the item and the related items as well. If there is no such option, the related data becomes orphaned.

When working with such lists, it's sometimes helpful to know about the current settings before starting a particular action (see Listing 4–39).

***Listing 4–39.** Investigate List Settings*

```
using (SPSite site = new SPSite("http://sharepointserve"))
{
    using (SPWeb web = site.OpenWeb())
    {

        SPRelatedFieldCollection RelatedFields =
                                      web.Lists["Authors"].GetRelatedFields();
        foreach (SPRelatedField RelatedField in RelatedFields)
        {
            Console.WriteLine("Field <{0}>{5}   ↵
                               bound to <{1}>{5}  ↵
                               lookup on <{2}>{5}   ↵
```

```
                                SPRelationshipDeleteBehavior.{3}{5}Web <{4}>",

                web.Lists[RelatedField.ListId].
                                Fields[RelatedField.FieldId].InternalName,
                web.Lists[RelatedField.ListId].Title,
                RelatedField.LookupList,
                RelatedField.RelationshipDeleteBehavior,
                site.AllWebs[RelatedField.WebId].Title,
                Environment.NewLine);
        }

    }
}
```

In this code, the `GetRelatedFields` method is used to get access to the current related data. The `SPRelatedField` type returns mostly GUIDs of the particular objects. These are used to resolve the names. The code produces the output shown in **Figure 4–20**.

```
Field <Books>
   bound to <Authors>
   lookup on <Authors>
   SPRelationshipDeleteBehavior.None
Web <Home>
Field <LeadAuthor>
   bound to <Books>
   lookup on <Authors>
   SPRelationshipDeleteBehavior.Restrict
Web <Home>
```

Figure 4–20. *Show a list's relationships.*

You can use the same approach to establish a relationship programmatically. This is typically part of a complete list creation process (see Listing 4–40). Usually, you do this as part of a feature to configure an existing SharePoint site properly.

Listing 4–40. *Create Two Lists and Add a Relationship with Referential Integrity*

```
string lookupFieldName = "RelatedField";
using (SPSite site = new SPSite("http://sharepointserve"))
{
    using (SPWeb web = site.OpenWeb())
    {
        SPListCollection lists = web.Lists;
        Guid SourceListId = lists.Add("Parent List",
            "",
            SPListTemplateType.GenericList);
        Console.WriteLine("Parent List Done...");
        Guid TargetListId = lists.Add("Child List",
            "",
            SPListTemplateType.GenericList);
        Console.WriteLine("Child List Done...");
        SPList SourceList = lists[SourceListId];
        SPList TargetList = lists[TargetListId];
```

```
            SPFieldCollection Fields = TargetList.Fields;
            Fields.AddLookup(lookupFieldName, SourceList.ID, true);
            Console.WriteLine("Lookup Field Created");
            SPFieldLookup NewLookupField = Fields[lookupFieldName] as SPFieldLookup;
            NewLookupField.Indexed = true;
            NewLookupField.LookupField = "Title";
            NewLookupField.RelationshipDeleteBehavior =
                                   SPRelationshipDeleteBehavior.Restrict;
            NewLookupField.Update();
            Console.WriteLine("Lookup field integrity enforced");
            SPListItem NewSourceItem = SourceList.Items.Add();
            NewSourceItem["Title"] = "Parent Data";
            NewSourceItem.Update();
            Console.WriteLine("Source listitem created");
            SPListItem NewTargetItem = TargetList.Items.Add();
            NewTargetItem["Title"] = "Child Data";
            NewTargetItem[lookupFieldName] = new SPFieldLookupValue(1, "Source Data");
            NewTargetItem.Update();
            Console.WriteLine("Parent listitem created");
            TargetList.Update();
            SourceList.Update();
        }
}
```

You can test the relationship by deleting an item in the parent list either from code or from the UI. In code, use a try...catch clause to catch the exception and get an error description, as shown in Figure 4–21.

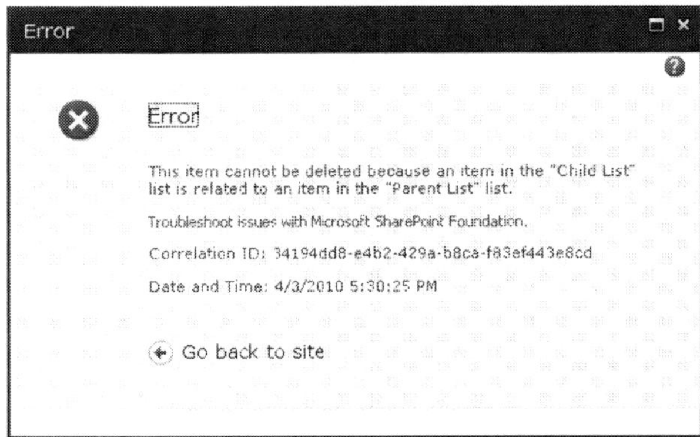

***Figure 4–21.** Error shown if a user tries to delete an item with relational integrity turned on*

Furthermore, some properties exist to control the remaining aspects of a list. These definitions are set in the SPField object. Assume you have an SPField object called myField. To activate indexing on this column, you can write the following:

```
myField.Indexed = true;
```

To enforce unique values, set this property:

```
myField.AllowDuplicateValues = false;
```

In both cases you must call `myField.Update()` to effect the change.

Understanding LINQ to CAML Conversion

The world of LINQ is much bigger than we can convey here. You are sure to find several ways to work with LINQ to SharePoint in real-life projects. To deal with errors or unexpected behavior, you need to know what CAML code is produced from your LINQ code. This is straightforward using the data context's `Log` property, as shown in Listing 4–41.

Listing 4–41. *Retrieve the CAML Created Internally*

```
StringBuilder sb = new StringBuilder();
TextWriter tw = new StringWriter(sb);
ctx.Log = tw;
// Any LINQ activity goes here
EntityList<AuthorsContact> authorsj2 = ctx.GetList<AuthorsContact>("Authors");
EntityList<BooksItem> booksj2 = ctx.GetList<BooksItem>("Books");
var result6 = from book in booksj2
              join author in authorsj2 on book.LeadAuthor.Id equals author.Id
              select new
              {
                  Book = book.Title,
                  Author = author.FullName
              };
result6.ToList().ForEach(ab => Console.WriteLine("{0} was written by {1}",
    ab.Book,
    ab.Author));
// End of LINQ activity
Console.WriteLine(sb.ToString());
tw.Dispose();
```

In this example, a joined list is queried, and this will produce the following CAML:

```
<View>
  <Query>
    <Where>
      <And>
        <BeginsWith>
          <FieldRef Name="ContentTypeId" />
          <Value Type="ContentTypeId">0x0100</Value>
        </BeginsWith>
        <BeginsWith>
          <FieldRef Name="LeadAuthorContentTypeId" />
          <Value Type="Lookup">0x010600</Value>
        </BeginsWith>
      </And>
    </Where>
    <OrderBy Override="TRUE" />
   </Query>
   <ViewFields>
     <FieldRef Name="Title" />
     <FieldRef Name="LeadAuthorFullName" />
   </ViewFields>
```

```
  <ProjectedFields>
    <Field Name="LeadAuthorFullName" Type="Lookup" List="LeadAuthor"
           ShowField="FullName" />
    <Field Name="LeadAuthorContentTypeId" Type="Lookup" List="LeadAuthor"
           ShowField="ContentTypeId" />
  </ProjectedFields>
  <Joins>
    <Join Type="INNER" ListAlias="LeadAuthor">

      <!--List Name: Authors-->
      <Eq>
        <FieldRef Name="LeadAuthor" RefType="ID" />
        <FieldRef List="LeadAuthor" Name="ID" />
      </Eq>
    </Join>
  </Joins>
  <RowLimit Paged="TRUE">2147483647</RowLimit>
</View>
```

If you're speaking LINQ more fluently than CAML, it's a good way to learn CAML. However, there are some verbose parts in this query, such as the restriction to a specific content type.

Summary

In this chapter, you learned about the basic object model and API regarding lists, libraries, folders, and document sets. Lists contain data in a structured form. Views are used to retrieve filtered and sorted data. Libraries contain files, and several methods are available to store and download them. Document sets are highly customized content types. The Document Sets API provides a way to group items into packages.

While storing data is relatively simple, retrieving data can be more complex. CAML allows queries against lists and libraries to fetch a subset of data. LINQ to SharePoint adds another layer on top of the CAML query layer to give type-safe access. Using SPMetal, you can create a data context class and embed it into your application to have instant access from a rich type model.

CHAPTER 5

■ ■ ■

External Data Access

This chapter describes external data access techniques. They include using REST-based URLs via WCF Data Services. This is a common way to read and write data provided by SharePoint from remote locations where the API is not available.

The opposite scenario allows SharePoint to gather data from external systems—principally line-of-business (LOB) applications or native databases. Business Connectivity Services (BCS) smoothly integrates with SharePoint, making external data available as if it were a regular SharePoint list.

This chapter covers the following:

- Querying data using WCF Data Services
- Accessing external data using Business Connectivity Services
- Highly efficient data access using the SharePoint database

The basic protocols and techniques used to access data are also examined in this chapter.

Introducing External Data Access

Accessing SharePoint via its object model API is widely covered in this book. However, there are often requirements to access SharePoint data from other platforms, through Internet connections, or simply from a remote location. In all those instances, you cannot use the API directly, because the necessary assemblies are either not available or not applicable. The new client object model, while advantageous for developers who are fluent with the programming style and object model hierarchy, is not always a viable alternative, either. (We cover this model in depth in Chapter 12.) Since it is limited to platforms and technologies explicitly supported by the current client object model, eventually you encounter situations that need other ways to access SharePoint data. A powerful, easy, standardized approach is needed. There are several options, as shown in Figure 5–1.

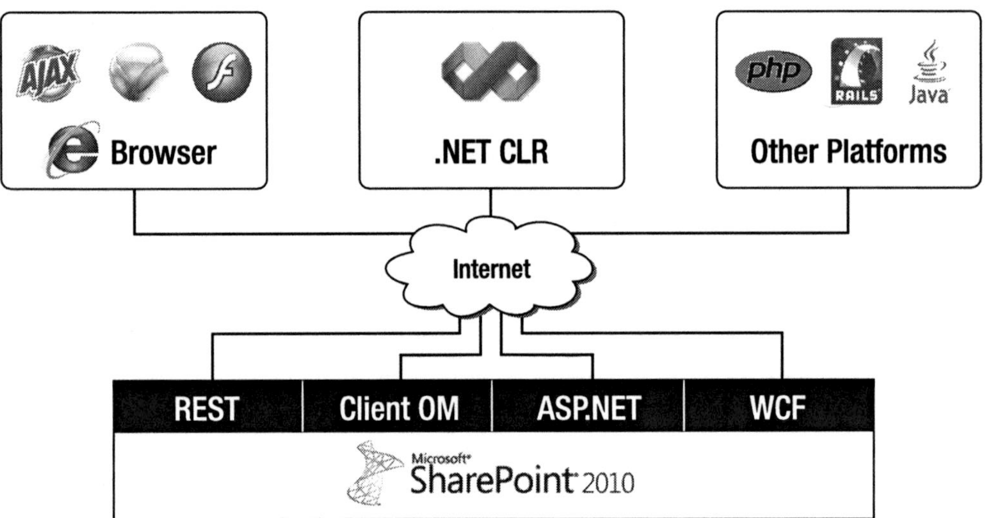

Figure 5–1. Accessing SharePoint remotely

The SharePoint Representational State Transfer (REST) interface plays an outstanding role in this picture. Some readers may recall the period when Internet protocols arose and gained wide acceptance. The secret behind their amazing success was their simplicity. Indeed, today they still have few architectural weaknesses, while a full-blown architecture, as perfect as it might have been at the time, would not have had such an enduring achievement. A simple architecture is fast to implement, it's cheap to create applications, and it's easy to understand. REST is repeating history and makes data access as simple and straightforward as possible. It's not fully defined, and anything superfluous to establishing a connection has been jettisoned. However, it is powerful enough for most daily tasks.

For a more structured alternative, SharePoint still supports web services using Simple Object Access Protocol (SOAP) to transmit and receive data. This is a much more comprehensive standard compared with REST.

Whichever data access strategy you choose, external data access is the key to opening up SharePoint to other worlds and keeping it at the heart of an enterprise infrastructure.

Query Data Using Data Services

WCF Data Services enables REST-based access to data stored on a SharePoint server. REST-based access uses a simple URL-based API to fetch data from lists using HTTP GET requests. The simple access opens up the server as a data source to a wide range of clients from all platforms. The technical foundation is provided by the WCF Data Services Framework.

The WCF Data Services Framework

WCF Data Services (formerly known as ADO.NET Data Services) is a platform that is actually a combination of a runtime service and a web service. The final version appeared with .NET 3.5 Service

Pack 1. It is not specific to SharePoint—rather, it's a new unified way to access a data source using nonproprietary standards. The standards involved are as follows:

- HTTP to transport the web service
- Plain Old XML (POX), JavaScript Object Notation (JSON), or Resource Description Framework (RDF) as the preferred data transport layer
- REST as the access and addressing method

It's obvious that the SharePoint web services used to access data can easily be replaced with WCF Data Services. ASP.NET applications, SharePoint, and WCF share the same data access technology, simplifying the development of data-driven web services.

Introducing REST

Representational State Transfer is an architectural style that is a hybrid of existing network-based protocols and technologies to address sources.

REST FOR EXPERTS

Using REST seems easy and powerful. The theory behind it and the reasons for its existence are more challenging. Roy Thomas Fielding published his doctoral dissertation in 2000 explaining the background, structure, and motivation behind REST.

You can read more about REST here:

`www.ics.uci.edu/~fielding/pubs/dissertation/rest_arch_style.htm`

Wikipedia provides a more down-to-earth introduction:

`http://en.wikipedia.org/wiki/REST`

This section explains the elementary aspects of REST so that you can comprehend the later sections.

A common term for systems using REST is *RESTful*—meaning that the system supports accessing endpoints using REST. Referring to web services, the underlying protocol is usually HTTP. Technically, other transport protocols on layer 7 (see the ISO/OSI reference model at `http://en.wikipedia.org/wiki/OSI_model`)—such as File Transfer Protocol (FTP), Simple Mail Transfer Protocol (SMTP), and others—are RESTful, too. REST uses the existing vocabulary of such protocols to express queries and receive results.

What About SOAP?

In contrast, SOAP is another protocol usually defined to support data access and transfer. It's quite powerful and widely used. However, it's anything but simple. The drawback is that SOAP encourages the developer to reinvent a common set of access methods for each application. Furthermore, it disregards the basic features the underlying transport protocol provides, such as authentication and caching. The intention was to have a more independent protocol, but the reality is that all implementations actually use HTTP and ignore the designated features. This is where REST shines. There is, by the way, a major difference. While SOAP is a standardized protocol, REST is merely an architecture using existing protocols. Hence, there is no "REST standard."

Constraints and Opportunities

The REST architecture defines some constraints. The actual implementation is not part of the standard and another reason for its wide acceptance. These constraints are as follows:

- Clients are separated from servers by a uniform interface (decoupled architecture).
- The communication is stateless.
- The responses are cacheable.
- A layered system exists between the client and server routing requests independently.
- A server may expose code to transfer logic in addition to data.

Routing data independently in a layered system means that each routing device operates as if it were alone. It's not looking back (no session tracking) and handling the request as a single operation. This ensures that changing the routing by removing or adding components has no influence on the other components in the chain.

The last point sounds odd, but a RESTful system could indeed respond by sending a piece of code—think JavaScript—and let the code execute on the client. This is where JSON as a data container comes to mind. JSON is more compact than XML—while still human-readable—but it needs a script engine to be processed properly. Once the data block is in the scripting environment, further processing is much easier because the data is converted into business objects again. Clearly, adding JavaScript code to help the client process the data is just the next step.

Addresses for Resources

REST uses Uniform Resource Identifiers (URIs) to address endpoints. An *endpoint* is a combination of an address (where to get), a binding (protocol to access), and a contract (data schema transferred). The term *resource* is a central feature. In a hypermedia world, everything is a resource—something out there. A resource is both a piece of information and the physical container storing this information in a transmissible way (read "a document").

In SharePoint, you use REST to address web services. These addresses contain the whole path to a specific resource. This could be a collection of data such as the following:

```
http://sharepoint/_vti_bin/listdata.svc/calendar
```

It's even possible to add more specific information and filter the result set:

```
http://sharepoint/_vti_bin/listdata.svc/calendar('Cal2')/Entries?$filter=Name eq 'Joerg'
```

(See the section "Querying Data" later in this chapter for details about the URL-based syntax.)

Operations can map to several HTTP verbs, such as GET, POST, PUT, or DELETE. For reading data, GET is obviously the most common. When you navigate to an address in your browser, you are executing a GET query.

Reading the Response

By default, WCF Data Services respond with a XML called the Atom Publishing Protocol (AtomPub). JSON is an alternative method. An AtomPub response could look like this:

```
<?xml version="1.0" encoding="utf-8" standalone="yes" ?>
```

```
<entry xml:base="http://myserver/data.svc/"
    xmlns:ads="http://schemas.microsoft.com/ado/2007/08/dataservices"
    xmlns:adsm="http://schemas.microsoft.com/ado/2007/08/dataservices/metadata"
    adsm:type="NorthwindModel.Customers"
    xmlns="http://www.w3.org/2005/Atom">
  <id>http://myserver/data.svc/Customers('Computacenter')</id>
  <updated />
  <title />
   http://localhost:61243/nw.svc/Customers('Computacenter')
   <author>
    <name />
  </author>
  <link rel="edit" href="//myserver/data.svc/Customers('Computacenter')"
        title="Customers" />
        http://localhost:61243/nw.svc/Customers('Computacenter')
       <content type="application/xml">
    <ads:CustomerID>Computacenter</ads:CustomerID>
    <ads:CompanyName>A. Computacenter AG & Co. oHG</ads:CompanyName>
    <ads:ContactName>Joerg Krause</ads:ContactName>
    <ads:ContactTitle>Senior Consultant</ads:ContactTitle>
    <ads:Address>Mariendorfer Damm 1-3</ads:Address>
    <ads:City>Berlin</ads:City>
    <ads:Region ads:null="true" />
    <ads:PostalCode>12099</ads:PostalCode>
    <ads:Country>Germany</ads:Country>
    <ads:Phone>0172-2302633</ads:Phone>
    <ads:Fax>030-70785505</ads:Fax>
  </content>
  <link rel="related" title="Orders"
        href="Customers('Computacenter')/Orders"
        type="application/xml;type=feed" />
  <link rel="related" title="Demographics"
        href="Customers('Computacenter')/ Demographics"
        type="application/xml;type=feed" />
</entry>
```

AtomPub is the key to reading such data with an ordinary feed reader. Figure 5–2 shows Internet Explorer accessing a SharePoint list.

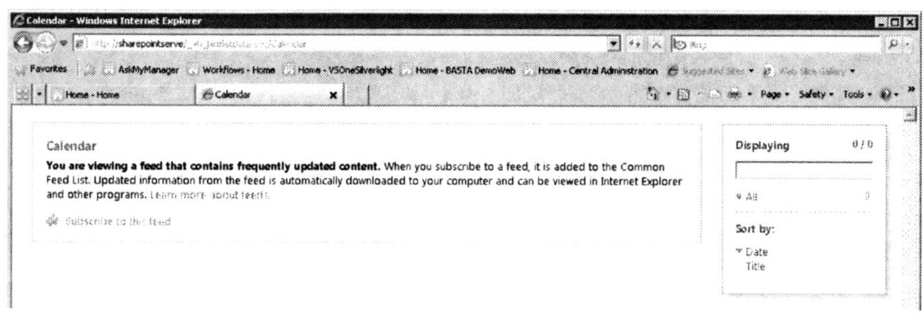

Figure 5–2. *Accessing a SharePoint list as a feed*

Setting the Accept request header to the application/json MIME type forces the WCF Data Services server to respond in JSON format. A sample response follows:

```
{
   "d":{
    __metadata: {
        uri: "Customers(\'Computacenter\')",
        type: "NorthwindModel.Customers"
    },
    CustomerID: "COMPUTACNT",
    CompanyName: "Computacenter AG & Co. oHG",
       ContactName: "Joerg Krause",
       ContactTitle: "Senior Consultant",
    Address: "Mariendorfer Damm 1-3",
    City: "Berlin",
    Region: null,
    PostalCode: "12099",
    Country: "Germany",
    Phone: "0172-2302633",
    Fax: "030-700855505",
    Orders: {
        __deferred: {
            uri: "Customers(\'COMPUTACNT\')/Orders"
        }
    }
   }
}
```

When accessing data from a client application with low bandwidth, the JSON format is preferable. It is compact and not as verbose as AtomPub's XML.

Install and Use WCF Data Services

The WCF Data Services implementation SharePoint provides supports all the basic operations. You can add, modify, and delete data using the framework. As shown earlier, the response contains strongly typed data. That's one of the big advantages compared with the SharePoint API's most common element, SPListItem. WCF Data Services uses object-relational mapping for the internal representation, which creates a type for each list. While this is powerful and easy to use, it's limited to lists as the fundamental data container. However, lists are a basic concept in SharePoint and considered to be the preferred data store.

WCF Data Services enables access to SharePoint lists for client applications. They are applications that do not normally run on a SharePoint server. Such an application would be any sort of console application, Windows Forms or Windows Presentation Foundation (WPF) application, or even Silverlight.

CONFUSING NAME HELPER

The version of WCF Data Services you use with SharePoint is provided by an update to .NET Framework 3.5 SP1, called the Data Services Update for .NET 3.5 SP1. This download replaces the former ADO.NET Data Services v1.5. While this renaming takes the chaotic versioning a step further, the move to WCF makes absolute sense. The services are exactly what WCF is for—communication between endpoints. Windows Communication Foundation is now the source for building services and n-tier applications.

When you download the package as explained in the next section, you'll find that it's still called ADO.NET Data Services. This is, according to some WCF Data Services team members, to make it consistent within the current .NET Framework 3.5 we are forced to use with SharePoint. However, the road map takes it forward to .NET 4, where the name changes.

In this book, we use the name *WCF Data Services*, since it is the most recent one. If you follow the instructions and occasionally encounter the old name, don't stress—just remember that both names refer to the same thing, and proceed.

Download the Data Services Update

WCF Data Services is not part of either current operating system. For Windows Server 2008 R2 and Windows 7, you can find the download here:

```
http://www.microsoft.com/downloads/details.aspx?
      familyid=79d7f6f8-d6e9-4b8c-8640-17f89452148e&displaylang=en
```

For Windows Server 2008 and Windows Vista, the download is here:

```
http://www.microsoft.com/downloads/details.aspx?
      familyid=4B710B89-8576-46CF-A4BF-331A9306D555&displaylang=en
```

Double-check that you select the 64-bit version to use the services with SharePoint 2010 if you intend to run it within your SharePoint development environment, as suggested in Chapter 1.

Installing the Package

The package is a hotfix and doesn't require any further action except for a system restart to get the service up and running.

▩ **Caution** It's strongly recommended to install this package before you install SharePoint. If it is too late, you should at least rerun the SharePoint 2010 Products Configuration Wizard.

Programming WCF Data Services with SharePoint

SharePoint 2010 simply uses WCF Data Services, and hence the access method is not specific to SharePoint. The URI for all such services has the following form:

```
http://<server>/<site>/_vti_bin/listdata.svc
```

Replace `<server>` with your machine's name and replace `<site>` with the site containing the data to be retrieved. The `<site>` fragment is not required if you run your code in the root site. Most of the examples in this chapter run in the root site, and thus the `<site>` fragment is omitted. To create an application to retrieve data from a SharePoint list, follow the steps explained in Chapter 4 "Data Access". Figure 5–3 illustrates a typical response from the service to a request without any additional parameters.

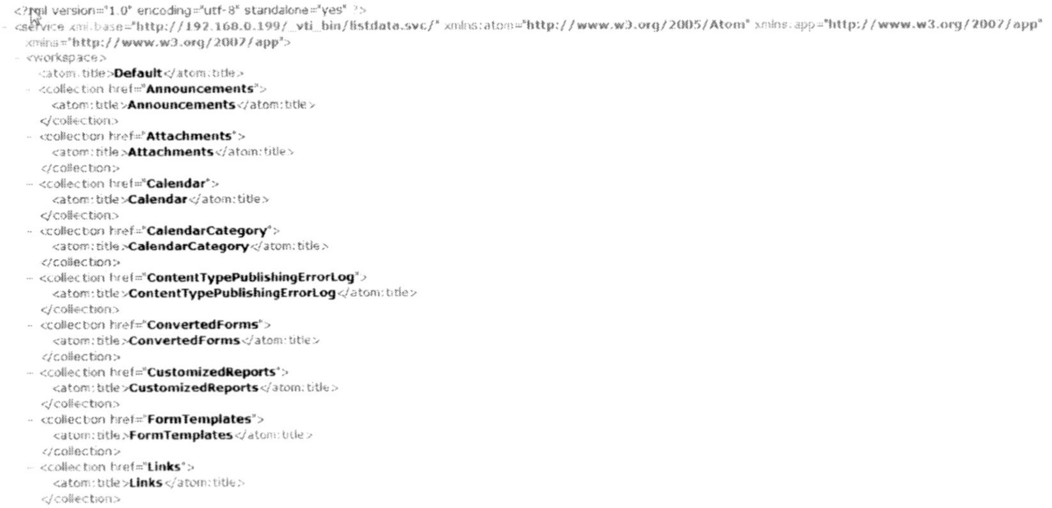

```
<?xml version="1.0" encoding="utf-8" standalone="yes" ?>
- <service xml:base="http://192.168.0.199/_vti_bin/listdata.svc/" xmlns:atom="http://www.w3.org/2005/Atom" xmlns:app="http://www.w3.org/2007/app"
  xmlns="http://www.w3.org/2007/app">
- <workspace>
    <atom:title>Default</atom:title>
  - <collection href="Announcements">
      <atom:title>Announcements</atom:title>
    </collection>
  - <collection href="Attachments">
      <atom:title>Attachments</atom:title>
    </collection>
  - <collection href="Calendar">
      <atom:title>Calendar</atom:title>
    </collection>
  - <collection href="CalendarCategory">
      <atom:title>CalendarCategory</atom:title>
    </collection>
  - <collection href="ContentTypePublishingErrorLog">
      <atom:title>ContentTypePublishingErrorLog</atom:title>
    </collection>
  - <collection href="ConvertedForms">
      <atom:title>ConvertedForms</atom:title>
    </collection>
  - <collection href="CustomizedReports">
      <atom:title>CustomizedReports</atom:title>
    </collection>
  - <collection href="FormTemplates">
      <atom:title>FormTemplates</atom:title>
    </collection>
  - <collection href="Links">
      <atom:title>Links</atom:title>
    </collection>
```

Figure 5–3. *listdata.svc without parameters returns all available resources.*

To further investigate the source and retrieve data, you can add a list's name after the base URL. You'll see some examples of how this looks later in this chapter. If the client acts as a feed reader (as in Figure 5–2), you will see the reader's view. Otherwise, the feed data is displayed. The source XML would look similar to this:

```
<?xml version="1.0" encoding="utf-8" standalone="yes"?>
<feed xml:base="http://sharepointserve/_vti_bin/listdata.svc/"
      xmlns:d="http://schemas.microsoft.com/ado/2007/08/dataservices"
      xmlns:m="http://schemas.microsoft.com/ado/2007/08/dataservices/metadata"
      xmlns="http://www.w3.org/2005/Atom">
  <title type="text">Authors</title>
  <id>http://sharepointserve/_vti_bin/listdata.svc/Authors/</id>
  <updated>2010-03-26T12:58:33Z</updated>
  <link rel="self" title="Authors" href="Authors" />
  <entry m:etag="W/&quot;2&quot;">
    <id>http://sharepointserve/_vti_bin/listdata.svc/Authors(1)</id>
    <title type="text">Krause</title>
    <updated>2010-03-26T13:57:02+01:00</updated>
    <author>
      <name />
    </author>
    <link rel="edit" title="AuthorsItem" href="Authors(1)" />
    <link rel="http://schemas.microsoft.com/ado/2007/
             08/dataservices/related/CreatedBy"
          type="application/atom+xml;type=entry"
          title="CreatedBy" href="Authors(1)/CreatedBy" />
    <link rel="http://schemas.microsoft.com/ado/2007/
             08/dataservices/related/ModifiedBy"
          type="application/atom+xml;type=entry"
          title="ModifiedBy" href="Authors(1)/ModifiedBy" />
```

```
    <link rel="http://schemas.microsoft.com/ado/2007/
              08/dataservices/related/Attachments"
          type="application/atom+xml;type=feed"
          title="Attachments" href="Authors(1)/Attachments" />
    <category term="Microsoft.SharePoint.DataService.AuthorsItem"
             scheme="http://schemas.microsoft.com/ado/2007/
                   08/dataservices/scheme" />
    <content type="application/xml">
      <m:properties>
        <d:Id m:type="Edm.Int32">1</d:Id>
        <d:ContentTypeID>0x0106001A6C5BC3D1EED04C97BC134601639F39</d:ContentTypeID>
        <d:ContentType>Contact</d:ContentType>
        <d:LastName>Krause</d:LastName>
        <d:Modified m:type="Edm.DateTime">2010-03-26T13:57:02</d:Modified>
        <d:Created m:type="Edm.DateTime">2010-03-26T13:53:35</d:Created>
        <d:CreatedById m:type="Edm.Int32">1</d:CreatedById>
        <d:ModifiedById m:type="Edm.Int32">1</d:ModifiedById>
        <d:Owshiddenversion m:type="Edm.Int32">2</d:Owshiddenversion>
        <d:Version>1.0</d:Version>
        <d:Path>/Lists/Authors</d:Path>
        <d:FirstName>Joerg</d:FirstName>
        <d:FullName>Joerg Krause</d:FullName>
        <d:EMailAddress>joerg@krause.net</d:EMailAddress>
        <d:Company>Computacenter</d:Company>
        <d:JobTitle>Senior Consultant</d:JobTitle>
        <d:BusinessPhone m:null="true" />
        <d:HomePhone m:null="true" />
        <d:MobileNumber m:null="true" />
        <d:FaxNumber m:null="true" />
        <d:Address m:null="true" />
        <d:City>Berlin</d:City>
        <d:StateProvince m:null="true" />
        <d:ZIPPostalCode m:null="true" />
        <d:CountryRegion m:null="true" />
        <d:WebPage>http://www.joergkrause.de, http://www.joergkrause.de</d:WebPage>
        <d:Notes>&lt;div&gt;&lt;/div&gt;</d:Notes>
      </m:properties>
    </content>
  </entry>
...
```

The retrieved data appears more or less unstructured. The fields follow the requested list's fields, but this is not sufficient to navigate through lists automatically. By adding `$metadata` to the URL, you can retrieve the entity data model description (see Figure 5–4).

```
<?xml version="1.0" encoding="utf-8" standalone="yes" ?>
- <edmx:Edmx Version="1.0" xmlns:edmx="http://schemas.microsoft.com/ado/2007/06/edmx">
  - <edmx:DataServices xmlns:m="http://schemas.microsoft.com/ado/2007/08/dataservices/metadata" m:DataServiceVersion="1.0">
    - <Schema Namespace="Microsoft.SharePoint.DataService" xmlns:d="http://schemas.microsoft.com/ado/2007/08/dataservices"
        xmlns:m="http://schemas.microsoft.com/ado/2007/08/dataservices/metadata" xmlns="http://schemas.microsoft.com/ado/2007/05/edm">
      - <EntityType Name="AuthorsItem">
        - <Key>
            <PropertyRef Name="Id" />
          </Key>
          <Property Name="Id" Type="Edm.Int32" Nullable="false" />
          <Property Name="ContentTypeID" Type="Edm.String" Nullable="true" />
          <Property Name="ContentType" Type="Edm.String" Nullable="true" />
          <Property Name="LastName" Type="Edm.String" Nullable="true" m:FC_TargetPath="SyndicationTitle" m:FC_ContentKind="text"
            m:FC_KeepInContent="true" />
          <Property Name="Modified" Type="Edm.DateTime" Nullable="true" m:FC_TargetPath="SyndicationUpdated" m:FC_ContentKind="text"
            m:FC_KeepInContent="true" />
          <Property Name="Created" Type="Edm.DateTime" Nullable="true" />
          <NavigationProperty Name="CreatedBy" Relationship="Microsoft.SharePoint.DataService.AuthorsItem_CreatedBy" FromRole="AuthorsItem"
            ToRole="CreatedBy" />
          <Property Name="CreatedById" Type="Edm.Int32" Nullable="true" />
          <NavigationProperty Name="ModifiedBy" Relationship="Microsoft.SharePoint.DataService.AuthorsItem_ModifiedBy" FromRole="AuthorsItem"
            ToRole="ModifiedBy" />
          <Property Name="ModifiedById" Type="Edm.Int32" Nullable="true" />
          <Property Name="Owshiddenversion" Type="Edm.Int32" Nullable="true" ConcurrencyMode="Fixed" />
          <Property Name="Version" Type="Edm.String" Nullable="true" />
          <NavigationProperty Name="Attachments" Relationship="Microsoft.SharePoint.DataService.AuthorsItem_Attachments" FromRole="AuthorsItem"
            ToRole="Attachments" />
          <Property Name="Path" Type="Edm.String" Nullable="true" />
          <Property Name="FirstName" Type="Edm.String" Nullable="true" />
          <Property Name="FullName" Type="Edm.String" Nullable="true" />
          <Property Name="EMailAddress" Type="Edm.String" Nullable="true" />
          <Property Name="Company" Type="Edm.String" Nullable="true" />
          <Property Name="JobTitle" Type="Edm.String" Nullable="true" />
          <Property Name="BusinessPhone" Type="Edm.String" Nullable="true" />
          <Property Name="HomePhone" Type="Edm.String" Nullable="true" />
          <Property Name="MobileNumber" Type="Edm.String" Nullable="true" />
          <Property Name="FaxNumber" Type="Edm.String" Nullable="true" />
          <Property Name="Address" Type="Edm.String" Nullable="true" />
          <Property Name="City" Type="Edm.String" Nullable="true" />
          <Property Name="StateProvince" Type="Edm.String" Nullable="true" />
          <Property Name="ZIPPostalCode" Type="Edm.String" Nullable="true" />
          <Property Name="CountryRegion" Type="Edm.String" Nullable="true" />
          <Property Name="WebPage" Type="Edm.String" Nullable="true" />
          <Property Name="Notes" Type="Edm.String" Nullable="true" />
        </EntityType>
```


***Figure 5–4.** The service's metadata description*

The URL looks like this:

```
http://<server>/_vti_bin/listdata.svc/$metadata
```

The entities are described for each list available on the site you're querying. Armed with this, you have everything you need to know about the lists' fields.

Data Services URIs and URI Parameters

As shown in the previous example, the construction of the URI is the key to receiving the expected response. While this is generic WCF Data Services information, you need to be familiar with it when you start working with SharePoint. This section covers the necessary background.

The basic format of the URI is as follows:

```
http://<srv>/_vti_bin/ListData.svc/<EntitySet>[(<Key>)[/<Property>[(<Key>)]]
```

The square brackets, [ ], indicate optional components. The `EntitySet` property is usually the list from which you want to obtain data. The `Property` parameter is optional and returns a related list. The `Key` property specifies filtering or sorting criteria. Table 5–1 describes the options to manipulate the response.

Table 5–1. *Options to Manipulate the Response*

Option	Description
`$expand`	Includes related entities in the result set. These are usually lists joined by a lookup. Multiple lookups are requested as a comma-separated list. Example: `$expand=Authors,Publishers`.
`$orderby`	Includes a sorting instruction using a field name and optionally the keywords `asc` for ascending or `desc` for descending. Ascending sort order is the default. Example: `$orderby:Title desc`.
`$skip`, `$top`	The `$skip` option skips a number of items, while `$top` limits the result set. When they're used together, you can implement paging. Example: `$skip=25&$top=5`. Consider adding `$orderby` too, because only sorted result sets have a predictable order of items.
`$filter`	Adds a filter expression to limit the result set. See the expressions in Table 5–2. Example: `$filter=Title eq 'Apress'`.

To restrict a result set, use the `$filter` options. Because of limitations on allowable characters in URIs, the operators are expressed as abbreviated words, as shown in Table 5–2.

Table 5–2. *Filter Expressions and Operators*

Operator	Description
`eq`	Equal to
`ne`	Not equal to
`gt`	Greater than
`ge`	Greater than or equal to
`lt`	Less than
`le`	Less than or equal to
`and`	Logical and
`or`	Logical or
`not`	Logical negation
`add`	Addition
`sub`	Subtraction
`mul`	Multiplication
`div`	Division
`mod`	Modulo
`( )`	Precedence grouping

In addition to these operators, a set of functions are also defined for use with the filter query string operator. Table 5–3 lists the available functions.

Table 5–3. Functions used in Expressions

Function	Description
bool substringof(string s0, string s1)	Checks whether s0 is within s1
bool endswith(string s0, string s1)	Checks whether s0 ends with s1
bool startswith(string s0, string s1)	Checks whether s0 starts with s1
int length(string s)	Length of string s
int indexof(string s0, string s1)	Index of string s0 within s1
string insert(string s0, int pos, string s1)	Inserts s0 into s1 at position pos.
string remove(string s0, int pos)	Removes characters from position pos in s0
string remove(string s0, int pos, int length)	Removes length characters from position pos in s0
string replace(string s0, string f0, string s1)	Replaces f0 in s0 with s1
string substring(string s0, int pos)	Returns the substring from position pos in s0
string substring(string s0, int pos, int length)	Returns the substring from position pos in s0 with the length characters
string tolower(string s0)	Transforms s0 to lowercase
string toupper(string s0)	Transforms s0 to uppercase
string trim(string s0)	Removes leading and trailing whitespaces
string concat(strings s0, string s1)	Concatenates two strings
int day(DateTime dt)	Day of the date dt
int hour(DateTime dt)	Hour of the date dt
int minute(DateTime dt)	Minute of the date dt
int month(DateTime dt)	Month of the date dt
int second(DateTime dt)	Second of the date dt
int year(DateTime dt)	Year of the date dt
double round(double dbl)	Rounded value of dbl with double precision
decimal round(decimal dec)	Rounded value of dec with decimal precision
double floor(double dbl)	Floor value of dbl with double precision
decimal floor(decimal dec)	Floor value of dec with decimal precision
double ceiling(double dbl)	Ceiling value of dbl with double precision
decimal ceiling(decimal dec)	Ceiling value of dec with double precision
bool IsOf(type T)	Checks whether a value is of type T
bool IsOf(expression ex, type tp)	Checks whether expression ex is of type T
<T> Cast(type T)	Casts to type T using generic syntax
<T> Cast(expression ex, type T)	Casts expression ex to type T using generic syntax

Options for Data Representation

WCF Data Services currently supports exchanging entities in JSON and Atom formats. The same format can be used both to receive information from the data service and to send to it. The choice of format depends mostly on the client. In a JavaScript environment, JSON is preferable. A .NET- or Silverlight-based client will probably find Atom's XML much easier to process. If bandwidth is important, choose JSON.

To specify the format in which information is to be sent from WCF Data Services, set the `Content-Type` HTTP header. The corresponding setting, according to RFC 2616, controlling the format accepted by WCF Data Services is the `Accept` HTTP header. Table 5–4 lists some valid types.

Table 5–4. *Request and Response MIME Types*

Requested MIME Type	Response MIME Type	Serialization Format
`*/*`	`application/atom+xml`	AtomPub
`text/*`	Not supported	Not applicable
`application/*`	Not supported	Not applicable
`text/xml`	`text/xml`	AtomPub
`application/xml`	`application/xml`	AtomPub
`application/atom+xml`	`application/atom+xml`	AtomPub
`application/json`	`application/json`	JSON

Querying Data

The syntax to fetch data using only a URL seems easy at first sight. However, it can become complex if you need to include filtering and sorting instructions.

Examples

To understand how you can retrieve data simply by typing a URL into your browser's address bar, let's examine some examples. To execute these examples, add the expression after the `/_vti_bin/listdata.svc` part. If the service can't execute the expression because of invalid syntax, it will return a Bad Request error (HTTP code 400). When using field names, you must enter the internal names and be aware that the names are case sensitive.

■ **Tip** If Internet Explorer returns the Bad Request error page with no additional information, you can turn off "Show friendly HTTP error messages" in Advanced settings. It will then show the XML message returned from the service (see Figure 5–5). Alternatively, you can use Fiddler to examine the response.

```
<?xml version="1.0" encoding="utf-8" standalone="yes" ?>
- <error xmlns="http://schemas.microsoft.com/ado/2007/08/dataservices/metadata">
    <code />
    <message xml:lang="en-US">No property 'Fullname' exists in type 'Microsoft.SharePoint.Linq.DataServiceEntity' at position 0.</message>
  </error>
```

***Figure 5–5.** Developer-friendly error message*

The filter using the eq operator extracts exactly one element if the filtered element is unique:

```
/Authors?$filter=Id eq 1
```

It is more common to use filter expressions to search for elements:

```
Authors?$filter='Joerg,Krause' eq concat(FirstName, concat(',', LastName))
```

This matches the item from the Authors list with the value of the properties FirstName and LastName equal to Joerg,Krause. The string is built using the concat function twice.

Boolean operators enable even more complex queries:

```
Authors?$filter=City eq 'Berlin' and FirstName eq 'Joerg'
```

Some functions enable you to operate with parts of data, such as the year of the Modified property:

```
Authors?$filter=year(Modified) eq 2010
```

Using functions is not always as straightforward as you might expect. If you filter using functions, the result set must be limited to one item before you can work within a field. This expression works well:

```
Authors?$filter=Id eq 3 and substring(City, 0, 1) eq 'M'
```

It works because the first part extracts exactly one item, and the second expression checks whether it matches a very specific condition (the first letter of City equals M). If you filter just for the second expression, an error occurs. This expression will not work:

```
Authors?$filter=substring(City, 0, 1) eq 'M'
```

While it is syntactically correct, the function cannot apply to "many."

Work with Data Services

Typing the filter expression into the browser's address bar is easy and provides immediate feedback. However, it is a "no code" approach that isn't very useful. To work with this data, you need a more versatile method of accessing the data services layer.

Adding a reference to the service from any kind of Visual Studio 2010 project creates an object-relational mapping to the list. The mapping is generated code in reference.cs, and these classes build the data context. The name is predefined as <sitename>DataContext. It inherits from the DataServiceContext base class. Each list found on the site creates a property of generic type DataServiceQuery<T>. The type parameter T is the list item type for that particular list. The name is autogenerated using the pattern <listname>Item. Figure 5–6 shows this using the namespace MyServiceReference.

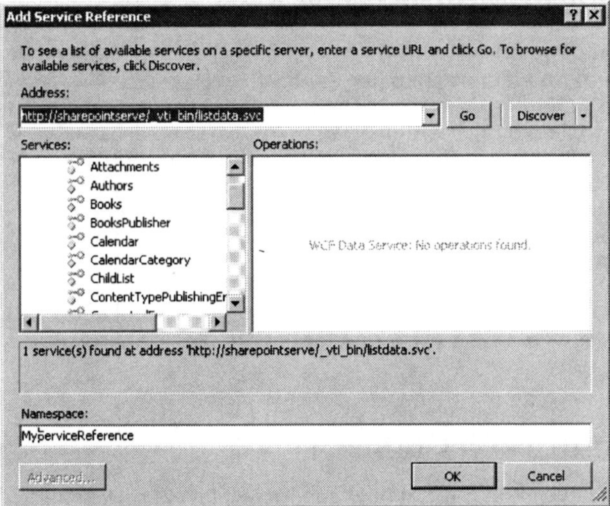

Figure 5–6. Adding a reference to the service

To use this service, add a using statement with the project's default namespace and the namespace you entered in the Add Service Reference dialog:

```
using Apress.SP2010.ListService.MyServiceReference
```

In this example, the site is called Home. It is the root site, so we don't need another path section. The data context is automatically named HomeDataContext. The data context exposes all the lists, and you can use standard LINQ expressions to retrieve data, change it, and save it to SharePoint.

The next example retrieves the Authors list. If the site does not allow anonymous access, you must provide the credentials to access the service. To execute the code, add the System.Net namespace to your using statements.

In this example (Listing 5–1), the service returns all the Authors data, and LINQ is used to select it. Clearly, you can filter further using the full power of LINQ. (You can find many examples of using LINQ in Chapter 4.)

Listing 5–1. *Retrieve Data Using a Service (As Part of a Console Application)*

```
Uri uri = new Uri("http://sharepointserve/_vti_bin/listdata.svc", UriKind.Absolute);
HomeDataContext ctx = new HomeDataContext(uri);
ctx.Credentials = new NetworkCredential("username", "password");

var authors = from a in ctx.Authors select a;

foreach (var ac in authors)
{
   Console.WriteLine("{0} works at {1}",
                     ac.FullName,
                     ac.Company);
}
```

External Data: Business Connectivity Services

Business Connectivity Services (BCS) is the successor to the Business Data Catalog (BDC) introduced in SharePoint 2007. It is an awesome refinement and much more than just another new version. The previous section showed how to access SharePoint data from external client applications. In real life scenarios, there are good reasons to access external data from within SharePoint. External data includes legacy databases. For various reasons—from performance to the need to have a native relational data model to lack of time or budget to migrate data to within SharePoint—the data must be accessed outside the SharePoint ecosystem. BCS is the primary path to connect LOB systems into a SharePoint portal.

BCS achieves this and presents the data in such a way as to make it as accessible as internal data. The advantages over the BDC implementation move it more into the focus of the developer. While BDC made it easy to read data, writing data back to the external storage was cumbersome. The challenging XML that mapped the external data to internal structures was even harder to manage because of the lack of an appropriate designer. Several new components in BCS make it much easier to create SharePoint applications using external data.

Business Connectivity Architecture at a Glance

The basic architecture, shown in Figure 5–7, reveals that BCS is not only an abstract layer for external data. It also tightly integrates into the world of Microsoft Office.

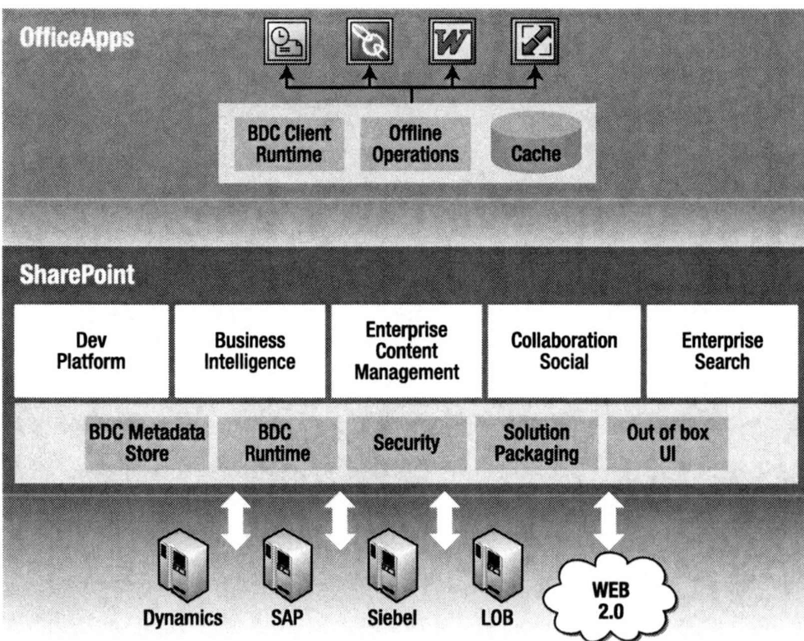

Figure 5–7. BCS architecture

■ **Note** The acronym BDC can still be found in descriptions of BCS. However, it now refers to a set of services that provide the connectivity to an external data store, and therefore it becomes a component of BCS.

The core components are as follows:

- *The BDC Metadata Store*: This store provides a collection of external content types. Such external content types are a fundamental part of BCS. They describe how the data is actually connected.
- *BDC Server Runtime*: The runtime is responsible for connecting to the external source or data store.
- *BDC Client Runtime*: Similar to the server runtime, but this adopts the principles of the client object model to allow clients to access SharePoint.
- *Security*: BCS comes with its own security model and integrates with the Secure Store Service (SSS).
- *Design Tools*: The needs of both power users and professional developers are addressed using BCS. Power users get support via SharePoint Designer 2010, and professional developers gain templates in Visual Studio 2010.
- *User Interface*: SharePoint provides Web Parts and a deep integration using lists for external data.

Using well-known and mature technologies such as content types and lists to manage and use external data makes the data connectivity available to all developers. It's now incredibly easy to reach external data. This is even true for smart client applications, which can now use the client access and a local data cache based on SQL Server Compact. Managing external data offline is an integral part of real-life solutions.

External Content Types

Content types are a fundamental concept in SharePoint. External content types (ECT) are the equivalent feature for BCS. A content type describes a schema for list data. An ECT extends this by adding a description of where the data originates and how the data source behaves. The ECT defines the primary mapping of data between SharePoint and the external data store. The metadata definition of an ECT is specified in XML and is deployed to the BDC Metadata Store.

For your first foray into BCS, we recommend you start with SharePoint Designer. It makes creating and deploying an ECT easy. In advanced scenarios, you'll find that SharePoint Designer supports only a subset of available features. While it's a large subset, if you want to use all the bells and whistles, Visual Studio 2010 is the tool of choice.

Create an External Content Type Using SharePoint Designer

The SharePoint Designer can create ECTs for these data sources:

- SQL Server
- Windows Communication Foundation (WCF) services
- .NET Types

For a first walk-through, let's assume that the Northwind database is available and that you want to retrieve some data from it.

GET SAMPLE DATA

If the sample databases are not installed on your system, you can download the files from here:

`www.codeplex.com/Wikipage?ProjectName=SqlServerSamples`

All samples are now hosted at CodePlex. On this page, scroll down to the Sample Databases section, and click SQL Server 2000 Sample Databases. This package includes the Northwind sample database.

The `.msi` package extracts into the folder `c:\SQL Server 2000 Sample Databases`. Don't worry about the "2000" label. The package is quite old but still a good source even if attached to a SQL Server 2008 instance.

Open SQL Server Management Studio, and attach the `Northwind.mdf` from this folder to your current connection.

To create an ECT, open a site using SharePoint Designer 2010, and click External Content Types (see Figure 5–8).

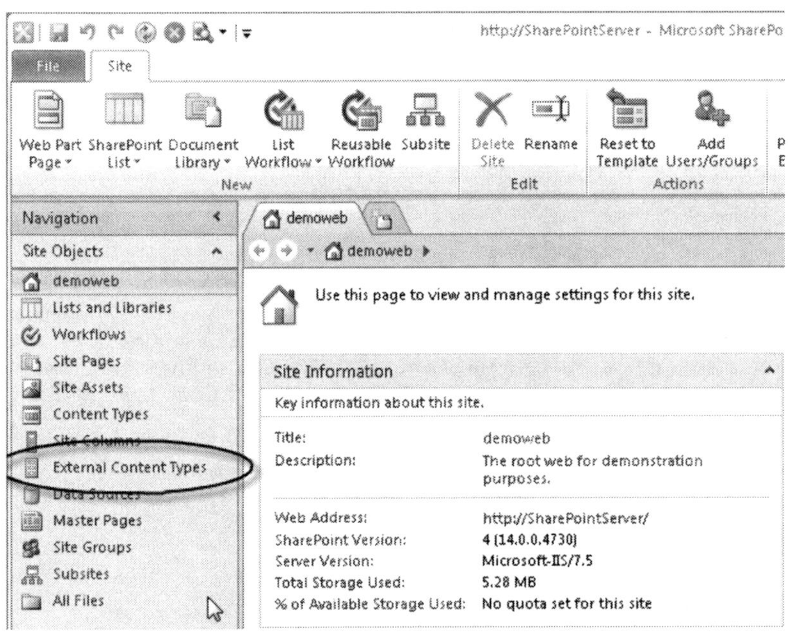

***Figure 5–8.** Add an ECT using SharePoint Designer*

The front page of the newly created type allows you to assign a name and a description. In this example, the name is NorthwindProducts, and the description is Northwind Products. Next, click the link “Click here to discover external data sources and …” (see Figure 5–9 at the bottom of the center area External Content Type Information).

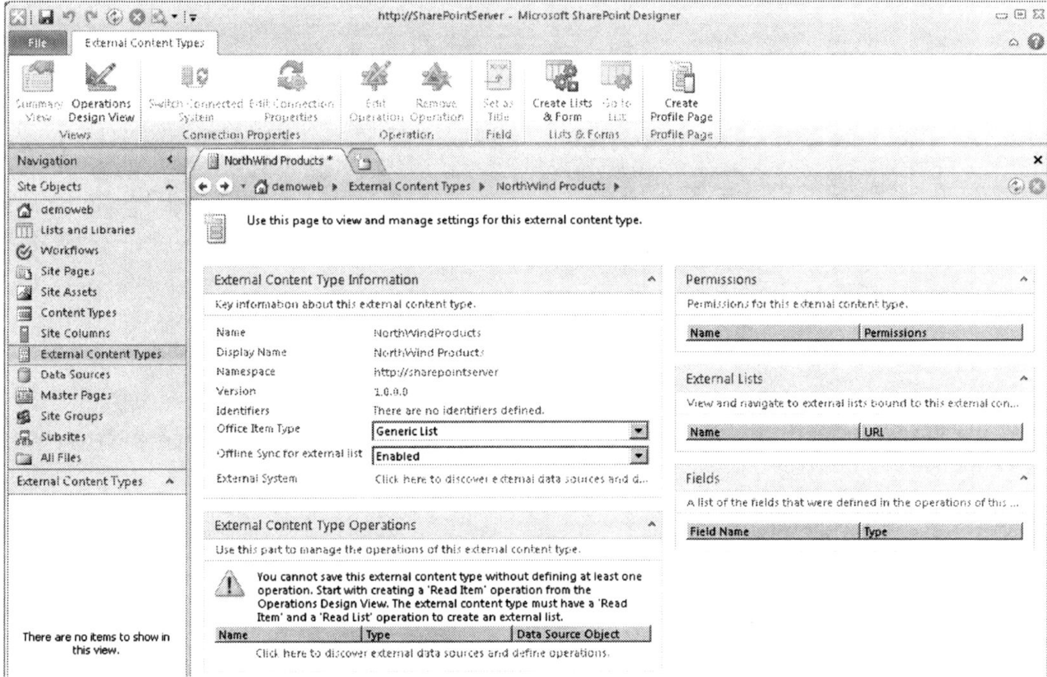

Figure 5–9. *Create a new ECT.*

The wizard jumps to the next page where you can add the connection. First, select the connection type. As shown in Figure 5–10, for this example you should choose SQL Server.

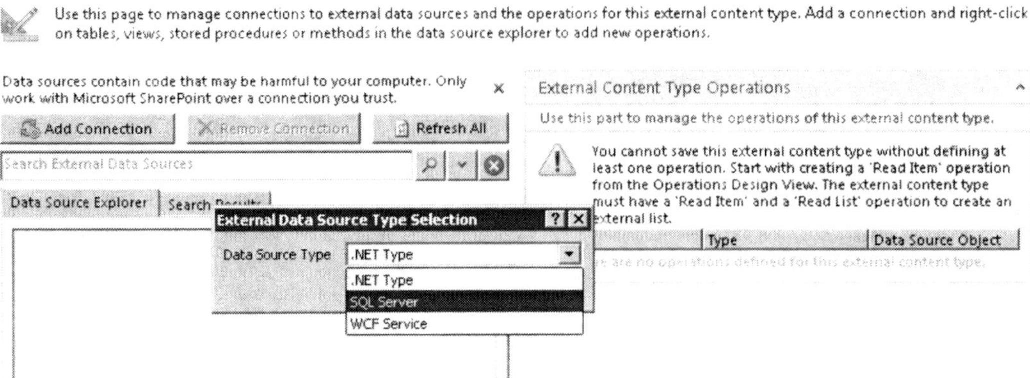

Figure 5–10. Select the appropriate connection type.

For the SQL Server, enter the database server, database name, and the identity that connects to this server (see Figure 5–11).

Figure 5–11. Connection details for a SQL Server connection

The Data Source Explorer should now show all tables in the chosen database (see Figure 5–12). Right-click the table you want to access in order to display the context menu with available operations. For read access, you need at least New Read Item Operation and New Read List Operation. After selecting both—one after another—they appear in the right column named External Content Type Operations.

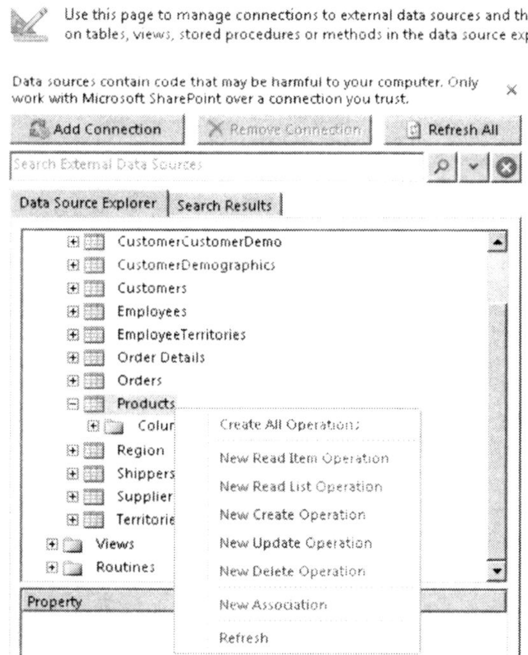

Figure 5–12. Create the operations used to access the data source.

Each operation uses its own configuration wizard (see Figure 5–13) that allows you to limit the data by choosing specific columns and filter the result sets with specific conditions. For this example, click Finish to get all the data available in this table.

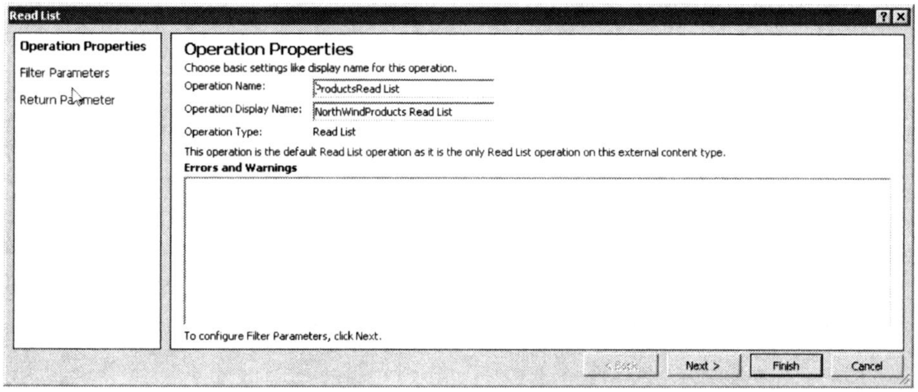

Figure 5–13. Configure the selected operation.

Finally, click the Create Lists & Form icon in the ribbon to create the forms associated with the ECT. That makes the external data appear like a regular list. With the Enterprise license, you can choose to create InfoPath forms, too.

Manage Appropriate Security Settings

By default the external data is not yet available because there are no access permissions set in the metadata catalog. To correct this, you will need access to the Central Administration (see Figure 5–14).

Figure 5–14. *Select "Manage service applications."*

On the next screen, click the Business Data Connectivity Service link. The freshly created ECT should appear there as shown in Figure 5–15. Next, open the context menu from the link in the Name column, and select Set Permissions.

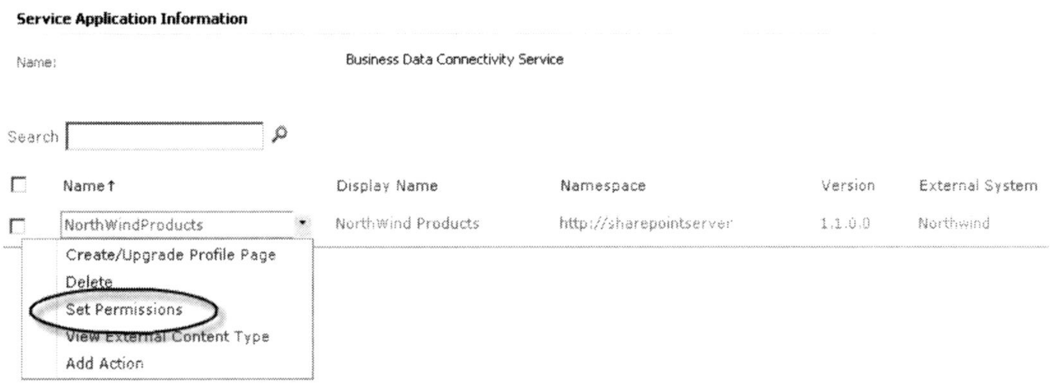

Figure 5–15. The ECT

You can now select the user and assign the permissions for this user. Click OK and close the dialog (see Figure 5–16).

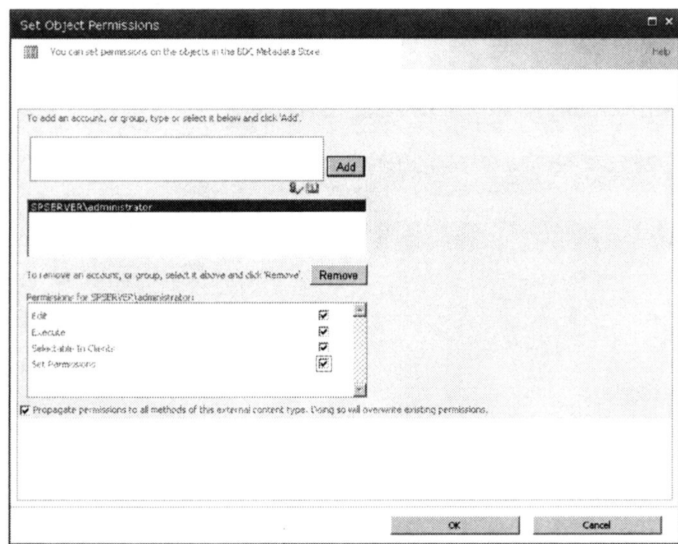

Figure 5–16. Set a user and assign particular permissions.

Access External Data

When the External Content Type is created and forms and permissions are assigned, the data appears as if it were internal data. If you refresh the site's front page, the list should appear in the navigation, and you can simply click and view the data (see Figure 5–17).

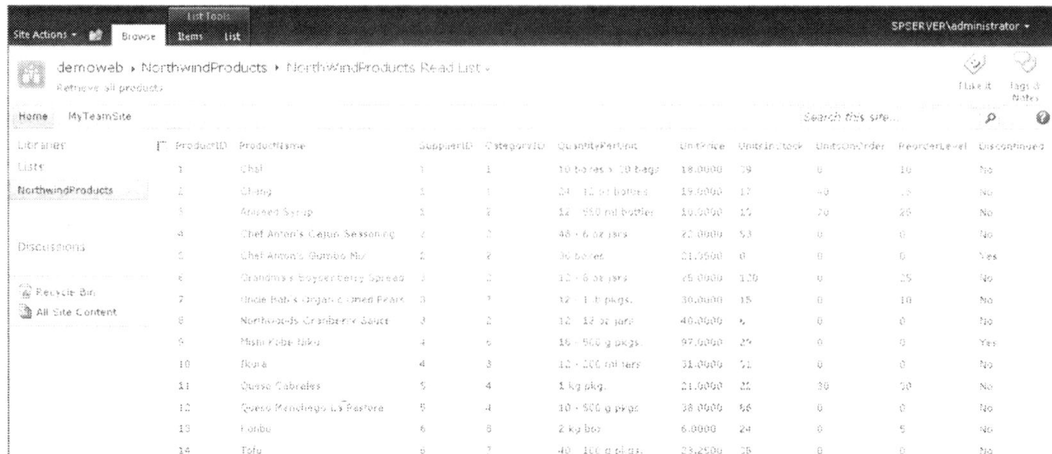

Figure 5–17. External data appears just like any other internal list.

Create an External List Using the Browser UI

If you have the appropriate rights, you can add an external list using the UI. Select More Options from the site menu and External List from the Create dialog, as shown in Figure 5–18.

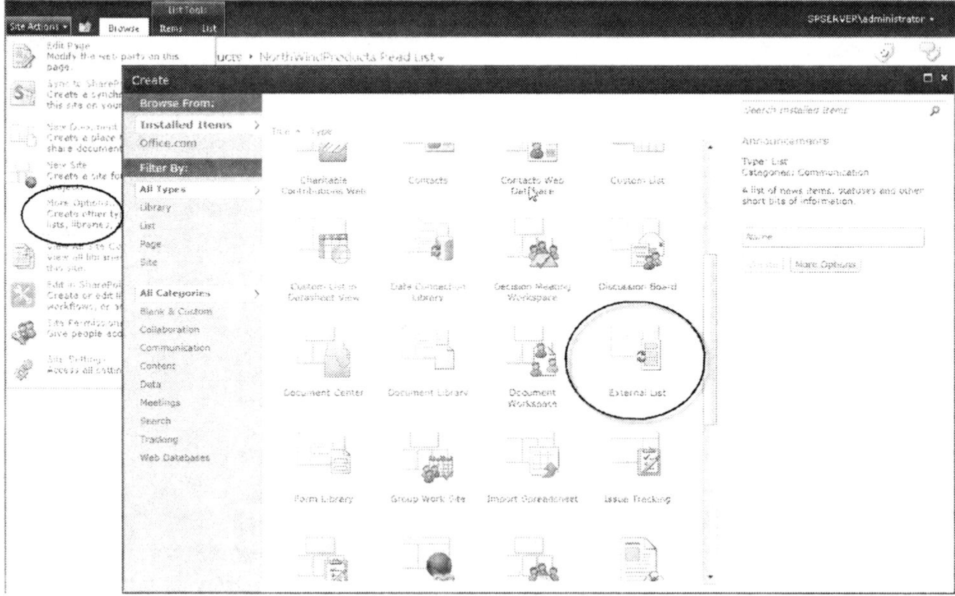

Figure 5–18. Create an external list using the Browser UI (composition).

After this, you can enter a name and select the ECT that must already exist in the Business Metadata Catalog.

Whichever way you used to access the external data, it's now time to get programmatic access using the SharePoint object model.

Access External Data Through the Object Model

First, the good news. The external list does not only *appear* like an internal list. Even the API is able to access it the same way. This means that, as with almost all the previous examples, the data access relies heavily on the SPList class. Listing 5–2 shows a simple console application that retrieves some data using a CAML query.

Listing 5–2. *A Console Application That Selects Some External Data*

```
using System;
using System.Collections.Generic;
using System.Linq;
using System.Text;
using Microsoft.SharePoint;
using System.Xml.Linq;

namespace RetrieveExternalDataConsole
{
    class Program
    {
        static void Main(string[] args)
        {
            using (SPSite site = new SPSite("http://sharepointserve"))
            {
                using (SPWeb web = site.OpenWeb())
                {
                    SPList list = web.Lists["NorthwindProducts"];
                    SPQuery query = new SPQuery();
                    var xml = new XElement("Where",
                                new XElement("Equals",
                                    new XElement("FieldRef",
                                        new XAttribute("Name", "CategoryID")),
                                    new XElement("Value", 1)));
                    query.Query = xml.ToString();
                    SPListItemCollection items = list.GetItems(query);
                    foreach (SPListItem item in items)
                    {
                        Console.WriteLine(item.DisplayName);
                    }
                }
            }
            Console.ReadLine();
        }
    }
}
```

This code opens the given site's root web and links to the NorthwindProducts list created in the previous section. The XML builds a CAML query to access items whose CategoryID equals 1.

Access External Data Through the Client Object Model

The client object model allows you to access SharePoint data from a remote location. The client libraries emulate the object model similar to the API and use web services internally to access the farm. The client object model is explained in depth in Chapter 12 for .NET applications and JavaScript and in Chapter 13 for Silverlight applications. External data is available just like internal lists if it is set up as described earlier.

Highly Efficient Data Access

The common data access methods, based on CAML and LINQ to SharePoint, are usually fast enough for most data access. However, when collecting a vast amount of data, creating reports, or filling in data rows into chart controls (see Chapter 11), it is never "fast enough." Officially, Microsoft discourages direct access to the database. However, read-only access to data seems less of an issue for large performance gains. In this section, we explain how to access data the most direct way.

Using LINQ to SQL

Please note that this scenario directly accesses the SharePoint content database and thus is not a supported scenario by Microsoft. But if you require very fast queries over large SharePoint lists, this may be a solution for you.

The concept is to create SQL views for every SharePoint list directly within the SharePoint content database. Queries can then be executed either with LINQ to SQL or—for the ultimate performance possible—with pure SQL.

Understanding the Content Database

The SharePoint content database is where SharePoint stores nearly all its data. All content that is uploaded or produced through the web UI, over web services, or via the SharePoint API is stored in the content database. A detailed description of the whole content database is beyond the scope of this section. Instead, let's focus on the SQL table AllUserData as the place where all data that has to do with list items is stored. This important table has 192 (!) columns, and all list items (remember that documents in document libraries are also list items) including their history are stored in this single table. Table 5–5 describes the most important columns.

***Table 5–5.** Most Important Columns of Table AllUserData*

Column Name	DataType	Description
tp_ID	int	The identifier for the list item, uniquely identifying it within the AllUserData table.
tp_GUID	uniqueid	The list item identifier uniquely identifying this list item.
tp_ListId	uniqueid	The list identifier of the list or document library containing the list item.
tp_SiteId	uniqueid	The site collection identifier of the site collection containing the list item.

Column Name	DataType	Description
tp_RowOrdinal	tinyint	The zero-based ordinal index of this row in the set of rows representing the list item. Additional rows are used to represent list items that have more application-defined columns of one or more datatypes than can fit in a single row in the AllUserData table.
tp_Version	int	A counter incremented any time a change is made to the list item, used for internal conflict detection. Because of the mapping of application properties to the generic columns schema in this table, changes to application schema as well as property values can affect a version increment.
tp_Author	int	The user identifier for the user who created the list item.
tp_Editor	int	The user identifier for the user who last edited the list item.
tp_Modified	datetime	The date and time (in UTC format) when this list item was last modified.
tp_Created	datetime	The date and time (in UTC format) when this list item was created.
tp_DeleteTransactionId	varbinary	An identifier for use with the Windows SharePoint Services implementation-specific deleted items recycle bin. This *must* equal 0x if the list item is nondeleted.
tp_ContentType	nvarchar	The user-friendly name of the content type associated with the list item.
tp_IsCurrentVersion	bit	A bit indicating whether this row corresponds to a current version or an historical version of the list item. This value *must* be 1 if this row contains a current version. Otherwise, it *must* be 0.
nvarchar1..64	nvarchar	Columns for application-defined fields that hold values of type nvarchar. The 64 columns are named nvarchar1 to nvarchar64. If the column does not contain data, this value *must* be `NULL`.
ntext1..32	ntext	Columns for application-defined fields that hold values of type ntext. The 32 columns are named ntext1 to ntext32. If the column does not contain data, this value *must* be `NULL`.
bit1..16	bit	Columns for application-defined fields that *must* values of type bit. The 16 columns are named bit1 to bit16. If the column does not contain data, this value *must* be `NULL`.
datetime1..8	datetime	Columns for application-defined fields that hold values of type datetime. The 8 columns are named datetime1 to datetime8. If the column does not contain data, this value *must* be `NULL`.
float1..12	float	Columns for application-defined fields that hold values of type float. The 12 columns are named float1 to float12. If the column does not contain data, this value *must* be `NULL`.
int1..16	int	Columns for application-defined fields that hold values of type int. The 16 columns are named int1 to int16. If the column does not contain data, this value *must* be `NULL`.

Column Name	DataType	Description
sql_variant1..8	sql_variant	Columns for application-defined fields that hold values of type sql_variant. The eight columns are named sql_variant1 to sql_variant8. If the column does not contain data, this value *must* be NULL.

■ **Note** For a complete list of all columns in the AllUserData table, see the MSDN documentation at `http://msdn.microsoft.com/en-us/library/cc704499.aspx`.

As you can see in Table 5–5, there are groups of columns in which the values of SharePoint lists are stored (including nvarchar#, ntext#, bit#, datetime#, float#, int#, and sql_variant#). Every time you create a new column in a SharePoint list, either by calling the API or over the UI, the new SharePoint list column is automatically mapped to a "free" column of the desired type in the table AllUserData. For example, if you add a column Publisher of type Single Line to your SharePoint list, an unused database column in the range from nvarchar1 to nvarchar64 will automatically be assigned (see Figure 5–19).

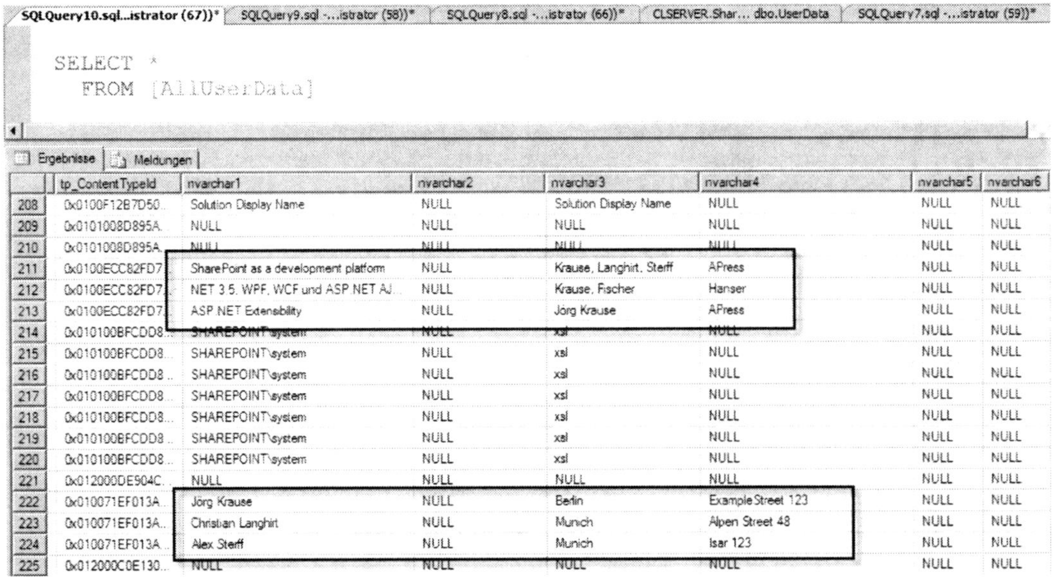

	tp_ContentTypeId	nvarchar1	nvarchar2	nvarchar3	nvarchar4	nvarchar5	nvarchar6
208	0x0100F12B7D50...	Solution Display Name	NULL	Solution Display Name	NULL	NULL	NULL
209	0x0101008D895A...	NULL	NULL	NULL	NULL	NULL	NULL
210	0x0101008D895A...	NULL	NULL	NULL	NULL	NULL	NULL
211	0x0100ECC82FD7...	SharePoint as a development platform	NULL	Krause, Langhirt, Sterff	APress	NULL	NULL
212	0x0100ECC82FD7...	NET 3.5, WPF, WCF und ASP.NET AJ...	NULL	Krause, Fischer	Hanser	NULL	NULL
213	0x0100ECC82FD7...	ASP.NET Extensibility	NULL	Jörg Krause	APress	NULL	NULL
214	0x010100BFCDD8...	SHAREPOINT\system	NULL	xsl	NULL	NULL	NULL
215	0x010100BFCDD8...	SHAREPOINT\system	NULL	xsl	NULL	NULL	NULL
216	0x010100BFCDD8...	SHAREPOINT\system	NULL	xsl	NULL	NULL	NULL
217	0x010100BFCDD8...	SHAREPOINT\system	NULL	xsl	NULL	NULL	NULL
218	0x010100BFCDD8...	SHAREPOINT\system	NULL	xsl	NULL	NULL	NULL
219	0x010100BFCDD8...	SHAREPOINT\system	NULL	xsl	NULL	NULL	NULL
220	0x010100BFCDD8...	SHAREPOINT\system	NULL	xsl	NULL	NULL	NULL
221	0x012000DE904C...	NULL	NULL	NULL	NULL	NULL	NULL
222	0x010071EF013A...	Jörg Krause	NULL	Berlin	Example Street 123	NULL	NULL
223	0x010071EF013A...	Christian Langhirt	NULL	Munich	Alpen Street 48	NULL	NULL
224	0x010071EF013A...	Alex Sterff	NULL	Munich	Isar 123	NULL	NULL
225	0x012000C0E130...	NULL	NULL	NULL	NULL	NULL	NULL

Figure 5–19. *Query result for table AllUserData (showing Books list items and LeadAuthors list items)*

Figure 5–19 makes the column assignment clear. Here, you can see three items of the list Books and three items of the list LeadAuthors. The SharePoint column Title is mapped to the database column nvarchar1 for both lists. The Publisher column from Books is mapped to nvarchar4, and also the Street column of LeadAuthors is mapped to nvarchar4.

The next thing to understand regarding the table AllUserData is how to identify an item correctly. You need the ID of your current site collection (`SPSite.ID` = tp_SiteId) and the ID of the list you want to query (`SPList.ID` = tp_ListId). To identify a particular list item, it is not sufficient to have the ID of this item. There could be more than one row with the same ID (`SPListItem.ID` = tp_ID) because every version is stored in the table. So, you also need to query the flag `tp_IsCurrentVersion` to be sure it is the latest version. Furthermore, you must ensure that the item has not been deleted. Therefore, you need to check if the `tp_DeleteTransactionId` is null.

There is one final pitfall. Check that the column `tp_RowOrdinal` is 0. This column was designed for the special case that the provided 156 fields are insufficient, for at least one type (for example, if the `datetime` type is required more than eight times in one list). In this case, an additional row with `tp_RowOrdinal=1` is added to the table and contains the "overflowing" fields. Although the probability of running into this issue is very low, you need to remember that this case can occur. Especially with our custom view implementation, we have to keep that in mind.

The simplest approach for satisfying all the query restrictions mentioned earlier is to use the built-in view, called UserData (see Listing 5–3).

Listing 5–3. *SharePoint Built-in SQL View: UserData*

```
SELECT * FROM AllUserData
WHERE
     tp_IsCurrentVersion = CONVERT(bit,1)
     AND tp_CalculatedVersion = 0
     AND tp_DeleteTransactionId = 0x
```

This view serves as the foundation for our own views. It ensures that always the current version is returned and that this list item has not been deleted. Let's build a SQL SELECT query for the list Books that returns all the items and only the fields we need (see Figure 5–20).

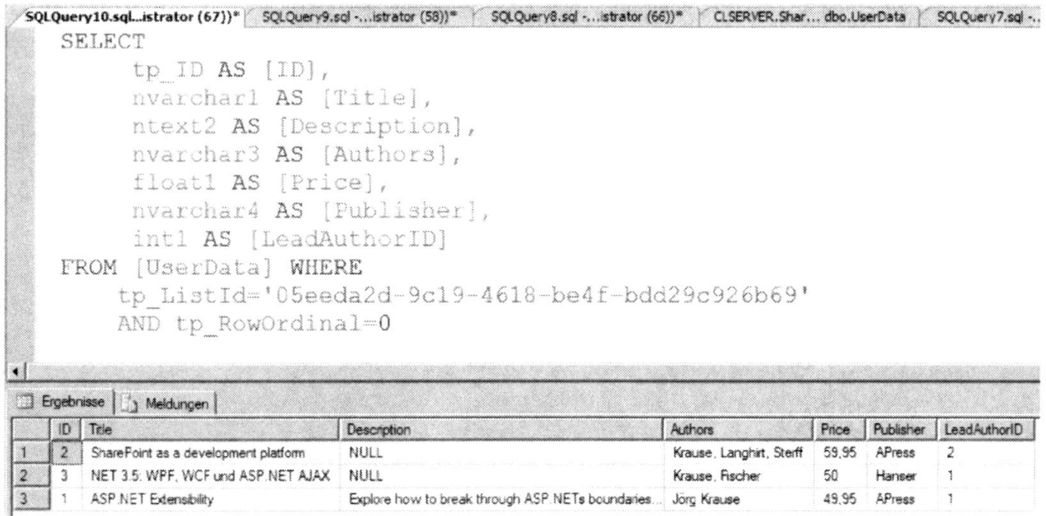

	ID	Title	Description	Authors	Price	Publisher	LeadAuthorID
1	2	SharePoint as a development platform	NULL	Krause, Langhirt, Sterff	59,95	APress	2
2	3	NET 3.5: WPF, WCF und ASP.NET AJAX	NULL	Krause, Fischer	50	Hanser	1
3	1	ASP.NET Extensibility	Explore how to break through ASP.NETs boundaries...	Jörg Krause	49,95	APress	1

Figure 5–20. *SQL SELECT query that returns all books*

The only two things needed for this query are the list ID and the column assignments. To find the ID of a list, you can simply get it programmatically:

```
SPContext.Current.Web.Lists["Books"].ID
```

The next challenge is to get the name of the mapped database columns from a SharePoint list. Unfortunately, the SPField class offers no suitable public property containing that data. To overcome this, we use reflection to interrogate a private property called ColName containing the mapped column's name (see Listing 5–4).

Listing 5–4. *Method for Getting the Mapped Column Name of an SPField Object*

```
private static String GetColName(SPField field)
{
    PropertyInfo pi = field.GetType().GetProperty("ColName",
                      BindingFlags.Instance | BindingFlags.NonPublic);
    return (string) pi.GetValue(field, null);
}
```

The next section shows how to dynamically create SQL views for your SharePoint lists.

Creating SQL Views for SharePoint Lists

In the previous section, the fundamental approach for querying the content database has been established. But before you start with your own custom SQL views, there is one further consideration: all datetime values in the database are stored in Universal Time Coordinated (UTC). Consequently, if you want to include a datetime value in your queries, the database values have to be converted from UTC to local time.

To achieve this, let's write a SQL function to automatically convert datetime values on the database server (see Listing 5–5).

Listing 5–5. *SQL Function Script for Converting UTC Time to Local Time*

```
CREATE FUNCTION [fn_FromUtcToLocalDateTime] (@DateTimeToConvert datetime)
RETURNS datetime
AS BEGIN
     -- Convert a UTC Time to a Local Time
     DECLARE @UTCDate datetime
     DECLARE @LocalDate datetime
     DECLARE @TimeDiff int
     -- Figure out the time difference between UTC and Local time
     SET @UTCDate = GETUTCDATE()
     SET @LocalDate = GETDATE()
     SET @TimeDiff = DATEDIFF(hh, @UTCDate, @LocalDate)
     -- Convert UTC to local time
     DECLARE @DateYouWantToConvert datetime
     DECLARE @ConvertedLocalTime datetime
     SET @ConvertedLocalTime = DATEADD(hh, @TimeDiff, @DateTimeToConvert)
     -- Check Results
     RETURN @ConvertedLocalTime
END
```

Now you have everything you need for creating SQL views. The SQL function fn_FromUtcToLocalDateTime that converts UTC datetime values into the local time of the SQL Server can be integrated directly into the SELECT statement of the CREATE VIEW, and as a result, the results of querying your SQL views will always contains the correct `datetime`. Listing 5–6 shows the complete `CREATE VIEW` script for the SharePoint list Books.

Listing 5–6. *SQL View Creation Script for the SharePoint List Books*

```
CREATE VIEW [BooksView_d832061a-57e9-473a-b9a5-623d78c0950e]
AS SELECT
     ud.tp_ID AS [ID],
     ud.nvarchar1 AS [Title],
     ud.ntext2 AS [Description],
     ud.nvarchar3 AS [Authors],
     ud.float1 AS [Price],
     ud.nvarchar4 AS [Publisher],
     ud.int1 AS [LeadAuthorID],
     dbo.fn_FromUtcToLocalDateTime(ud.tp_Modified) AS [LastModified] ,
     ui.tp_Title AS [LastModifiedBy]
FROM UserData ud, UserInfo ui
WHERE
     ud.tp_Editor=ui.tp_ID
     AND ud.tp_SiteId=ui.tp_SiteID
     AND ud.tp_ListId='05eeda2d-9c19-4618-be4f-bdd29c926b69'
     AND ud.tp_RowOrdinal=0
```

This view contains one extra feature. As you can see, a SQL JOIN on the table UserInfo is integrated that resolves the user ID of the Editor (ud.tp_Editor=ui.tp_ID) and adds a column containing the login name of the user who last modified the list item (see Figure 5–21).

	ID	Title	Description	Authors	Price	Publisher	LeadAuthorID	LastModified	LastModifiedBy
1	2	SharePoint as a development platform	NULL	Krause, Langhirt, Sterff	59.95	APress	2	2009-10-29 10:57:01.000	CLSERVER\administrator
2	3	NET 3.5: WPF, WCF und ASP.NET AJAX	NULL	Krause, Fischer	50	Hanser	1	2009-10-29 10:57:22.000	CLSERVER\administrator
3	1	ASP.NET Extensibility	Explore hot to break through AS...	Jörg Krause	49.95	APress	1	2009-10-29 10:56:36.000	CLSERVER\administrator

Figure 5–21. *Query result for SQL view BooksView*

Similar to the Books list, the view for the list LeadAuthors can be created (see Listing 5–7).

Listing 5–7. *SQL View Creation Script for the SharePoint List LeadAuthors*

```
CREATE VIEW [LeadAuthorsView_d832061a-57e9-473a-b9a5-623d78c0950e]
AS SELECT
     ud.tp_ID AS [ID],
     ud.nvarchar1 AS [Title],
     ud.nvarchar3 AS [City],
     ud.nvarchar4 AS [Street],
     dbo.fn_FromUtcToLocalDateTime(ud.tp_Modified) AS [LastModified] ,
     ui.tp_Title AS [LastModifiedBy]
FROM UserData ud, UserInfo ui
WHERE
     ud.tp_Editor=ui.tp_ID
```

```
AND ud.tp_SiteId=ui.tp_SiteID
AND ud.tp_ListId='12286c78-ef39-425e-a5da-27b86ff87455'
AND ud.tp_RowOrdinal=0
```

Figure 5–22 shows the result.

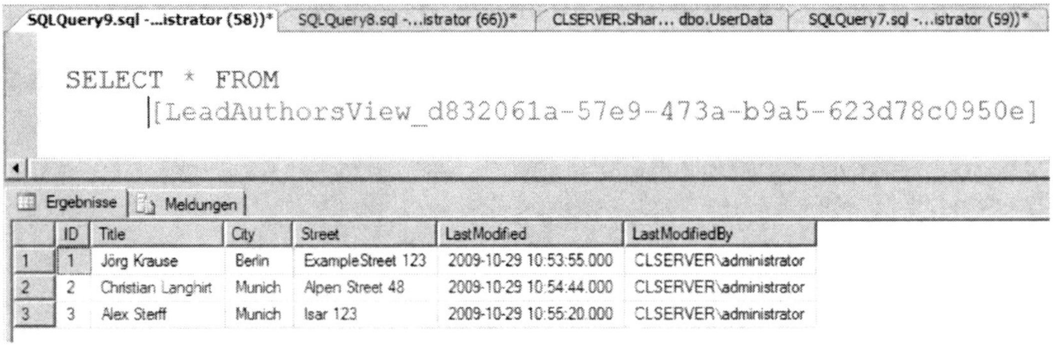

SQLQuery9.sql -...istrator (58))* | SQLQuery8.sql -...istrator (66))* | CLSERVER.Shar... dbo.UserData | SQLQuery7.sql -...istrator (59))*

```
SELECT * FROM
    [LeadAuthorsView_d832061a-57e9-473a-b9a5-623d78c0950e]
```

Ergebnisse | Meldungen

	ID	Title	City	Street	LastModified	LastModifiedBy
1	1	Jörg Krause	Berlin	ExampleStreet 123	2009-10-29 10:53:55.000	CLSERVER\administrator
2	2	Christian Langhirt	Munich	Alpen Street 48	2009-10-29 10:54:44.000	CLSERVER\administrator
3	3	Alex Sterff	Munich	Isar 123	2009-10-29 10:55:20.000	CLSERVER\administrator

Figure 5–22. *Query result for SQL view LeadAuthorsView*

You may wonder why both SQL views do not have normal names but contain a `GUID` string in their names. This is because the views are created automatically by a script. In the examples, the ID of the `SPWeb` containing the lists is added to the SQL view name. Listing 5–8 presents the generic method `CreateViewSql` that generates an `SQL CREATE VIEW` script for the `SPList` instance passed in as a parameter.

Listing 5–8. *Method That Creates an SQL CREATE VIEW Command for an SPList*

```
public string CreateViewSql(SPList list)
{
  string listName = list.Title.Replace(" ", "");
  string viewName = "[" + listName + "View_" + list.ParentWeb.ID + "]";
  StringBuilder sb = new StringBuilder();
  sb.Append("CREATE VIEW " + viewName + " AS ");
  sb.Append(" SELECT ud." + GetColName(list.Fields["ID"]) + " AS [ID], ");
  sb.Append("ud." + GetColName(list.Fields.GetFieldByInternalName("Title"))
                        + " AS [Title], ");

  String del = "";
  foreach (SPField f in list.Fields)
  {
      if (IsAllowedField(f))
      {
          if (f.Type == SPFieldType.DateTime)
          {
             sb.Append(del + "dbo.fn_FromUtcToLocalDateTime(ud."
                           + GetColName(f) + ") AS [" + f.InternalName + "]");
           }
           else if (f.Type == SPFieldType.Lookup)
           {
              sb.Append(del + "ud." + GetColName(f)
                            + " AS [" + f.InternalName + "ID]");
```

```
            }
            else
            {
                sb.Append(del + "ud." + GetColName(f)
                          + " AS [" + f.InternalName + "]");
            }
            del = ", ";
        }
    }

    //added LastModified / LastModifiedBy
    sb.Append(del +
            "dbo.fn_FromUtcToLocalDateTime(ud.tp_Modified) AS [LastModified] ");
    sb.Append(del + "ui.tp_Title AS [LastModifiedBy] ");
    sb.Append(" FROM UserData ud, UserInfo ui ");
    sb.Append(" WHERE ud.tp_Editor=ui.tp_ID AND ud.tp_SiteId=ui.tp_SiteID
              AND ud.tp_ListId='" + list.ID.ToString() + "'
              AND ud.tp_RowOrdinal=0");

     return sb.ToString();
}
```

To differentiate between important fields and fields that are intended only for internal use, the private method IsAllowedField decides this based on the internal name of the SPField instance. In the actual implementation (see Listing 5–9), 52 fields are disallowed from the SQL view.

Listing 5–9. *Method That Indicates Whther a SPField Should be Included into the SQL View*

```
private bool IsAllowedField(SPField field)
{
    if (field.Type == SPFieldType.Computed) return false;

    List<String> permittedNames = new List<string>();
    permittedNames.AddRange(new String[]
    {
        "ID",
        "Title",
        "ContentTypeId",
        "ContentType",
        "Modified",
        "Created",
        "Author",
        "Editor",
        "_HasCopyDestinations",
        "_CopySource",
        "owshiddenversion" ,
        "WorkflowVersion",
        "_UIVersion",
        "_UIVersionString",
        "Attachments",
        "_ModerationStatus",
        "_ModerationComments",
        "Edit",
        "LinkTitleNoMenu",
```

```
        "LinkTitle",
        "SelectTitle",
        "InstanceID",
        "Order",
        "GUID",
        "WorkflowInstanceID",
        "FileRef",
        "FileDirRef",
        "Last_x0020_Modified",
        "Created_x0020_Date",
        "FSObjType",
        "PermMask",
        "FileLeafRef",
        "UniqueId",
        "ProgId",
        "ScopeId",
        "File_x0020_Type",
        "HTML_x0020_File_x0020_Type",
        "_EditMenuTableStart",
        "_EditMenuTableEnd",
        "LinkFilenameNoMenu",
        "LinkFilename",
        "DocIcon",
        "ServerUrl",
        "EncodedAbsUrl",
        "BaseName",
        "MetaInfo",
        "_Level",
        "_IsCurrentVersion",
        "SortBehavior",
        "SyncClientId",
        "ItemChildCount",
        "FolderChildCount"
    });
    return (!permittedNames.Contains(field.InternalName));
}
```

This concludes the foundation work. While there are many things to take into account when building these queries, as you will see in the next section, the performance gains should more than compensate for the effort spent on SQL view generation.

Querying with LINQ to SQL

The next step after creating the SQL views for the SharePoint lists is to implement model classes. These classes are intended to ensure type-safe access to the SQL views. You need a model class for each list. Listing 5–10 shows the classes `BooksDbItem` and `LeadAuthorsDbItem` for the lists Books and LeadAuthors, respectively.

Listing 5–10. *Model Classes for the Two SQL Views to Use with LINQ*

```
namespace Apress.SP2010.DbModel
{
    public class BooksDbItem
```

```
    {
        public int ID { get; set; }
        public String Title { get; set; }
        public String Description { get; set; }
        public String Authors { get; set; }
        public decimal Price { get; set; }
        public String Publisher { get; set; }
        public int LeadAuthorID { get; set; }
        public DateTime LastModified { get; set; }
        public String LastModifiedBy { get; set; }
    }

    public class LeadAuthorsDbItem
    {
        public int ID { get; set; }
        public String Title { get; set; }
        public String City { get; set; }
        public String Street { get; set; }
        public DateTime LastModified { get; set; }
        public String LastModifiedBy { get; set; }
    }
}
```

Both classes contain exactly the same properties as the SQL views of the SharePoint lists. You can now use these model classes with LINQ, as shown in Listing 5–11. This method needs a `using` reference to `System.Linq` namespace.

Listing 5–11. *Querying the Number of Books per Lead Author with Type-Safe and Very Efficient LINQ to SQL Query*

```
public DataTable QueryBooksOfLeadAuthorsByLinqToSql()
{
    //create result DataTable
    DataTable dataTable = new DataTable("BooksOfLeadAuthors");
    dataTable.Columns.Add(new DataColumn("FullName", typeof(String)));
    dataTable.Columns.Add(new DataColumn("NumberOfBooks", typeof(int)));

    String conStr = SPContext.Current.Web.Site.ContentDatabase.DatabaseConnectionString;
    String xml = GetXmlMapping(new String[] {"Books", "LeadAuthors"});

    DataContext ctx = new DataContext(conStr, XmlMappingSource.FromXml(xml));
    var results = from book in ctx.GetTable<BooksDbItem>()
                  join leadAuthor in ctx.GetTable<LeadAuthorsDbItem>()
                  on book.LeadAuthorID equals leadAuthor.ID
                  group leadAuthor by leadAuthor.Title into grp
                  select new
                  {
                     FullName = grp.Key,
                     NumOfBooks = grp.Count()
                  };

     //add new row to DataTable
     foreach (var obj in results)
```

```
        dataTable.Rows.Add(obj.FullName, obj.NumOfBooks);

     return dataTable;
}
```

The implementation of this method uses the DataContext class of LINQ to SQL. But instead of using the default attribute mapping that requires code attributes in the model classes describing the mapping to the database columns, a custom XML mapping is used. In Listing 5–12 is an example of a dynamically generated XML file, defining the mapping from the SQL view columns to the properties of the model class. The code for the method that generates the XML is shown in Listing 5–13.

Listing 5–12. *Dynamically Generated XML Mapping for Use with LINQ to SQL*

```
<Database Name="SharePoint" xmlns="http://schemas.microsoft.com/linqtosql/mapping/2007">

  <Table Name="[BooksView_d832061a-57e9-473a-b9a5-623d78c0950e]"
         Member="Apress.SP2010.DbModel.BooksDbItem">

    <Type Name="Apress.SP2010.DbModel.BooksDbItem">
      <Column Name="ID" Member="ID" />
      <Column Name="Title" Member="Title" />
      <Column Name="Description" Member="Description" />
      <Column Name="Authors" Member="Authors" />
      <Column Name="Price" Member="Price" />
      <Column Name="Publisher" Member="Publisher" />
      <Column Name="LeadAuthorID" Member="LeadAuthorID" />
      <Column Name="LastModified" Member="LastModified" />
      <Column Name="LastModifiedBy" Member="LastModifiedBy" />
    </Type>

  </Table>

  <Table Name="[LeadAuthorsView_d832061a-57e9-473a-b9a5-623d78c0950e]"
         Member="Apress.SP2010.DbModel.LeadAuthorsDbItem">

    <Type Name="Apress.SP2010.DbModel.LeadAuthorsDbItem">
      <Column Name="ID" Member="ID" />
      <Column Name="Title" Member="Title" />
      <Column Name="City" Member="City" />
      <Column Name="Street" Member="Street" />
      <Column Name="LastModified" Member="LastModified" />
      <Column Name="LastModifiedBy" Member="LastModifiedBy" />
    </Type>

  </Table>

</Database>
```

Listing 5–13. *Method for Dynamic Generation of Mapping XML*

```
private String GetXmlMapping(String[] listNames)
{
  string assembly = @"Apress.SP2010, Version=1.0.0.0, Culture=neutral,
                      PublicKeyToken=4113b8ec9b28df52";
```

```
    StringBuilder sb = new StringBuilder();

    //add xml header
    sb.Append("<Database Name=\"SharePoint\""
            + " xmlns=\"http://schemas.microsoft.com/linqtosql/mapping/2007\">\r\n");
    using (SPWeb web = SPContext.Current.Web)
    {
       foreach (String listName in listNames)
       {
           String viewName = "[" + listName + "View_" + web.ID + "]";
           String modelClass = "Apress.SP2010.DbModel." + listName + "DbItem";

           sb.Append("<Table Name=\"" + viewName + "\" Member=\""
                                     + modelClass + "\">\r\n");
           sb.Append("<Type Name=\"" + modelClass + "\">");
           Type t = Type.GetType(modelClass + "," + assembly);

           foreach (PropertyInfo pi in t.GetProperties())
           {
              sb.Append("<Column Name=\"" + pi.Name + "\" Member=\""
                                         + pi.Name + "\" />");
           }
           sb.Append("</Type>\r\n</Table>\r\n");
       }
     }
     sb.Append("</Database>");
     return sb.ToString();
}
```

The GetXmlMapping method dynamically generates a mapping XML that is used by the LINQ to SQL DataContext to resolve the mapping of SQL view columns to SharePoint list columns (see Listing 5–13). The method takes a String array of list names (such as Books, LeadAuthors) as a parameter. Each individual name, with the suffix *DbItem* appended and the namespace APress.SP2010.DbModel as a prefix (such as Apress.SP2010.DbModel.BooksDbItem), is assumed to exist as a model class implementation. The Type.GetType() call returns the type of the model class and is used for iterating through all the existing properties. These properties are written as XML Column elements that assign the property name to both mapping attributes: Name (the name of the SQL view column) and Member (the property name).

Limitations of This Method

Accessing the content database directly is not supported by Microsoft. It is possible that the structure of the content database could be changed in one of the next updates, breaking the custom SQL views. Although the probability of a major change in the structure is not high (SharePoint 2007 and SharePoint 2010 have nearly the same database structure for storing list items), it is a possibility you should always remember.

Another limitation concerns the Business Connectivity Services introduced with SharePoint 2010. BCS supports retrieving, editing, updating, and deleting data from external systems. External content types integrate external data sources, such as databases, web, or WCF services and other custom data sources. These external data sources can be used like normal SharePoint lists. Using SQL views for accessing SharePoint lists is valid only for normal SharePoint lists and not for SharePoint lists that are connected through BCS. Hence, the data to be queried by SQL views has to be fully stored within the content database—BCS-based lists or fields are not supported.

Conclusion

With SQL views, the performance problems arising from inefficient LINQ or CAML queries are mainly resolved. However, before you can use SQL views, you have to expend some effort to make it work. It's not sufficient to manually create SQL views once only. Instead, you need to implement functionality to re-create your SQL views automatically, such as if columns are added or removed.

But if, for your requirements, the performance of your queries is of topmost importance then you should use direct SQL access. It offers the very best performance for complex queries over large SharePoint lists.

A great advantage of using LINQ in general is the ability to change your data access method at any time with very low effort. For example, you can start with LINQ to SharePoint, and if you notice that your performance degrades, then you can quickly switch to direct access with LINQ to SQL. The changes required in your code are quite minimal because the LINQ queries are largely unchanged. You simply have to substitute the `DataContext` instance and the model classes (for example, change `BooksItem` to `BooksDbItem`).

■ **Caution** Using SQL views for displaying list items of SharePoint lists is not a scenario supported by Microsoft! Although it works very well, you have to be very careful with future updates and service packs. Also, only use direct database access for reading data. *Never* write data back without using the SharePoint object model. Otherwise, this could cause integrity problems and damage the SharePoint content database.

Efficient Access to Huge Lists

If a list contains more items than, say, a grid can handle, you need to access the data in chunks. In UI terms, this is called *paging*. Paging requires two separate parameters—the size of the page (a chunk of data from a source) and the number of the current page.

The following code (see Listing 5–14) example reads a list in chunks of ten items. This is set by defining the `RowLimit` property of the `SPQuery` object. `GetItems` executes the query, which has no further limitation but the number of rows returned. The items are written to the console.

Listing 5–14. *Access a Complete List Page by Page*

```
SPQuery q = new SPQuery();
q.RowLimit = 10;
int intIndex = 1;
do
{
    Console.WriteLine("## Page: " + intIndex);
    SPListItemCollection listItems = hugeList.GetItems(q);

    foreach (SPListItem listItem in collListItems)
    {
        Console.WriteLine(listItem["Title"].ToString());
    }
    // Assign the list's current paging position
    q.ListItemCollectionPosition = listItems.ListItemCollectionPosition;
    intIndex++;
```

```
} while (q.ListItemCollectionPosition != null);
```

The actual pagination is accomplished via the `ListItemCollectionPosition` property of the `SPQuery` class. The property returns an object of type `SPListItemCollectionPosition`. This class has one property: `PagingInfo`. The containing string looks like this:

```
Paged=TRUE&p_ID=20
```

This looks a bit crude because there is no obvious need to write and parse strings just to provide paging. However, if you notice some URLs while flipping through a paged list, you'll find that this string is used to manage paging through query strings. Fortunately, the list's `ListItemCollectionPosition` contains the object with the current settings ready to use. If you use it as the query's current position, the query is "automatically" paging. The *`intIndex`* variable in Listing 5–14 exists only to display the current page number in the output—the actual paging is a copy of the `SPListItemCollectionPosition` object.

The *`p_ID`* parameter in `PagingInfo` points to the ID of the first item of the next page. To skip six pages, you have to calculate the target by evaluating RowLimit * Page. However, this is true only if the ID of the items is in order (requires an `OrderBy` clause), complete (not interrupted by previously deleted items), and the list does not contains folders.

Using Paging in Advanced Scenarios

We treat as advanced any scenario that has a list that is ordered by anything other than ID, that has incomplete IDs, or whose items are not part of the regular paging process, such as folders. The complete paging management is done by parameters (see Table 5–6) in the `PagingInfo` string.

Table 5–6. *URL Parameters Used in the PagingInfo Property*

Parameter	Example	Description
`Paged`	`TRUE`	Indicates that the list is paged. This parameter is mandatory for paged lists.
`PagedPrev`	`TRUE`	This element appears when the previous page is visited.
`p_`*`<FieldName>`*	`p_Created`	The first sort by parameter, which is `Created` prefixed with `p_`. The right hand is the encoded universal date and time.
`p_ID`	`20`	The ID of the previous page's last item's ID. This parameter is mandatory.
`View`	`Guid`	This is the encoded GUID for the current list. See examples below.
`PageFirstRow`	`4`	The ID of the current page's first item.
`p_FSObjType`	`0|1`	The object's type that the paging refers to, 0 = items, 1 = folders. Refers to the internal FSObjType field in any item.

Some paging examples taken from actual sites look like these:

- First Page
    - `AllItems.aspx`
- Next page
    - `AllItems.aspx?Paged=TRUE&p_Created=20100307%1964%3a26%3a05&p_ID=3&View=%7BA1ED7B16%2D7524%2D41B2%2D83A9%2DDFC4219161BE%7D&PageFirstRow=4`
- Next page
    - `AllItems.aspx?Paged=TRUE&p_Created=20100307%1964%3a26%3a05&p_ID=6&View=%7BA1ED7B16%2D7524%2D41B2%2D83A9%2DDFC4219161BE%7D&PageFirstRow=7`
- Previous page
    - `AllItems.aspx?Paged=TRUE&PagedPrev=TRUE&p_Created=20100307%1964%3a26%3a05&p_ID=7&View=%7BA1ED7B16%2D7524%2D41B2%2D83A9%2DDFC4219161BE%7D&PageLastRow=6`

The information what sort parameter is currently used looks a bit weird, because the field's name is the parameter (p_Created, p_Modified, p_Title, and so on) while the value is the current element's—the first element on the page—field value. In the example, the list is sorted by the Created field, and the date is part of the query. This way you can browse through a sorted list page by page.

The code snippet in Listing 5–12 can be extended by adding sorting:

```
q.Query = "<OrderBy><FieldRef Name='Created' Ascending='FALSE' /></OrderBy>";
```

If you retrieve the internally created PageInfo property, the value now has an additional parameter:

```
Paged=TRUE&p_Created=20100306%2012%3a37%3a58&p_ID=2938
```

Since the intention of the PageInfo property is to produce the pagination portion of the URL, the values must be encoded. If you construct the content and insert values, we recommend you use the SPEncode.UrlEncode method to encode values.

Summary

In this chapter, you learned about using WCF Data Services to retrieve SharePoint data from any remote client. The powerful REST API filters data on the server and sends back to the client exactly the data you need. Using a service reference, you can extend this to the LINQ layer and retrieve data using LINQ expressions. It's even possible to save data back to the underlying list.

With Business Connectivity Services, you can retrieve and present data from external sources so that it appears just like internal SharePoint data. Several new components in BCS make it much easier to create SharePoint applications using external data, such as line-of-business systems.

If you need highly efficient data access, you might consider direct database support. This is not supported by Microsoft, but ultimately it's a solution for ultra-fast read-only access to a huge database. If you don't need all data at once, consider using paging to get chunks of data quickly.

CHAPTER 6

Web Parts

Most developers take their first steps into SharePoint development with Web Parts. If you work with ASP.NET, you might already know about Web Parts—though it's unlikely you've had a project that requires Web Parts. There is a good reason why Web Parts are used heavily in SharePoint but have never attained popularity in other projects. SharePoint is not only the application that best shows the power of Web Parts, it's the reason Web Parts exist. Users can use the personalization framework to create their own view of a page and arrange parts to suit their personal preferences.

For these reasons, the Web Part programming style plays a lead role in this book. In this chapter we cover

- The constituent elements of SharePoint Web Parts
- An introduction to the ASP.NET Web Part framework
- Personalizing Web Parts and modifying the editor pane
- Creating connectable Web Parts

Furthermore, a comprehensive collection of best practices helps you build Web Parts with sophisticated features.

Fundamentals

During SharePoint 2007 development, the developer team was rewriting the Web Parts module. They did a great job on top of .NET 1.1, and the ASP.NET team was asked to incorporate the Web Parts functionality into the core ASP.NET library. In doing so, the ASP.NET team expanded the model and added many advanced features to ensure widespread support in SharePoint. Thus, ASP.NET Web Parts are heavily influenced by the needs of SharePoint. In SharePoint, some configuration options have been added, and an impressive number are available out of the box.

Web Parts are a basic building block for the UI. They integrate well with the UI, the administration, and with each other. End users can add Web Parts to pages, configure them, and use them without seeing a single line of code.

In this section we'll explain the basics of Web Parts.

Usage Scenarios

Let's start with some of the benefits of using custom Web Parts:

- Creating custom properties you can display and modify in the UI.

- Implementing proprietary code without disclosing the source code.
- Controlling access to content. With a custom Web Part, you can determine the content or properties to display to users, regardless of their permissions.
- Interacting with the SharePoint object model.
- Controlling the cache for the Web Part by using built-in cache tools.
- Creating a base class for other Web Parts to extend.

With all these benefits, Web Parts provide great flexibility and customization in a modularized manner.

Distinctions Between SharePoint and ASP.NET Web Parts

A Web Part is an ASP.NET user control that derives from the `System.Web.UI.WebControls.WebPart` class. This is an assembly that's provided by the framework as part of ASP.NET. The Web Part supports the management of the UI layout via zones. A zone is an area on the page where the Web Part can reside. If configured appropriately, an end user can drag Web Parts from a catalog into a zone, drag Web Parts from one zone to another, or remove the Web Part completely from any zone. Web Parts can be opened, closed, and hidden. You can consider a Web Part as a loosely coupled control. Web Parts support data connections between each other—meaning that one Web Part can raise an action within another. A control called `WebPartManager` holds all the active Web Part instances and the zone definitions. It acts like a director for the page.

WHERE MICROSOFT.SHAREPOINT.WEBPARTPAGES.WEBPART HAS GONE

Deriving the Web Part from `Microsoft.Sharepoint.WebPartPages.WebPart` is not recommended. The preferred way is to use the most basic infrastructure available because it reduces the complexity at least slightly. However, a small subset of features are exclusively available in this type. If you need some of these, it's OK to use the more specific implementations. These features include

- Cross-page connections
- Connections between Web Parts that are outside of a zone
- Client-side connections through the WPSC (Web Part Page Services Component) object model
- Data caching infrastructure, including the ability to cache to the database

You can find more about these features in the "Advanced Web Part Development" section later in the chapter.

SharePoint supports ASP.NET Web Parts directly. There is no need to derive from any SharePoint class to create a SharePoint Web Part. Instead, SharePoint supports a custom implementation of `WebPartManager` named `SPWebPartManager`. In addition, there is an `SPLimitedWebPartManager` class that supports environments that have no `HttpContext` or `Page` available. The reason for SharePoint-specific managers is, as for pages, that Web Parts are stored in serialized form in the content database. To read the stream from the database, the Web Part manager must provide the appropriate support. Building a

Web Part is straightforward. Start by creating a class that inherits from the WebPart base class, as shown in Listing 6–1.

Listing 6–1. *A Very Basic WebPart Class*

```
using System;
using System.ComponentModel;
using System.Runtime.InteropServices;
using System.Web;
using System.Web.UI;
using System.Web.UI.WebControls;
using System.Web.UI.WebControls.WebParts;
using Microsoft.SharePoint;
using Microsoft.SharePoint.WebControls;

namespace Apress.SP1010WebPartProject.WebParts
{
    [ToolboxItemAttribute(false)]
    public class WebPart1 : WebPart
    {

        public WebPart1()
        {
        }

        protected override void CreateChildControls()
        {
            Label1 control = new Label();
            control.Text = "Dynamic Label";
            Controls.Add(control);
            base.CreateChildControls();
        }

        protected override void RenderContents(HtmlTextWriter writer)
        {
            base.RenderContents(writer);
        }
    }
}
```

In the example, you can see that the content is created by overriding the CreateChildControls method. By default the Web Part is empty, so you're responsible for writing whatever content you need. This can be done using controls, as shown in the example. Another method writes directly into the output stream, using the RenderContents method parameter, HtmlTextWriter. This is usually more appropriate if a large amount of text or HTML is being written.

Web Part Primer

In this section you'll learn how to create your first elementary Web Part.

Creating a Simple Web Part

The following exercise shows how to create a basic Web Part using the appropriate template.

CREATING A SIMPLE WEB PART

1. Start a new Project using the Visual Web Part template.
2. Name the project and attach it to a SharePoint web for debugging purposes using the wizard. Visual Studio will create the project's files.
3. Open the ASCX file and add code as shown in Listing 6–2. In this example only the Label element has been added.
4. Open the `.webpart` file and change the settings as shown in Listing 6–3.
5. Edit the `.package` file.
6. Deploy to your local server. Once completed, the Web Part can be activated on an appropriate web page that supports Web Parts.

In the ASCX file you can now proceed as with any user control. There is a visual designer and a code editor window. There are no Web Part–specific modifications—you can program against the SharePoint API, and you can add ASP.NET as well as SharePoint controls.

***Listing 6–2.** ASCX File of a Simple Web Part*

```
<%@ Assembly Name="$SharePoint.Project.AssemblyFullName$" %>
<%@ Assembly Name="Microsoft.Web.CommandUI, Version=14.0.0.0,
                   Culture=neutral, PublicKeyToken=71e9bce111e9429c" %>
<%@ Register Tagprefix="SharePoint" Namespace="Microsoft.SharePoint.WebControls"
             Assembly="Microsoft.SharePoint, Version=14.0.0.0, Culture=neutral,
                       PublicKeyToken=71e9bce111e9429c" %>
<%@ Register Tagprefix="Utilities" Namespace="Microsoft.SharePoint.Utilities"
             Assembly="Microsoft.SharePoint, Version=14.0.0.0, Culture=neutral,
                       PublicKeyToken=71e9bce111e9429c" %>
<%@ Register Tagprefix="asp" Namespace="System.Web.UI"
             Assembly="System.Web.Extensions, Version=3.5.0.0, Culture=neutral,
                       PublicKeyToken=31bf3856ad364e35" %>
<%@ Import Namespace="Microsoft.SharePoint" %>
<%@ Register Tagprefix="WebPartPages" Namespace="Microsoft.SharePoint.WebPartPages"
             Assembly="Microsoft.SharePoint, Version=14.0.0.0, Culture=neutral,
                       PublicKeyToken=71e9bce111e9429c" %>
<%@ Control Language="C#" AutoEventWireup="true"
            CodeBehind="VisualWebPart1UserControl.ascx.cs"
    Inherits="VisualWebPartProject1.VisualWebPart1.VisualWebPart1UserControl" %>
<asp:Label runat="server" ID="lbl1" Font-Size="Large">Hello World</asp:Label>
```

In this example, only the Label element has been added.

Listing 6–3. .webpart File with Basic Settings

```
<?xml version="1.0" encoding="utf-8"?>
<webParts>
  <webPart xmlns="http://schemas.microsoft.com/WebPart/v3">
    <metaData>
      <type name="VisualWebPartProject1.VisualWebPart1.VisualWebPart1,
                 $SharePoint.Project.AssemblyFullName$" />
      <importErrorMessage>$Resources:core,ImportErrorMessage;</importErrorMessage>
    </metaData>
    <data>
      <properties>
        <property name="Title" type="string">My First VisualWebPart</property>
        <property name="Description" type="string">My First WebPart</property>
      </properties>
    </data>
  </webPart>
</webParts>
```

In this example the properties `Title` and `Description` has been changed.

Built-In Web Parts

As mentioned several times in this book, pages must derive from a master page supported by SharePoint. Web Part pages are no exception. Using the `default.master` page as the basis for internal pages ensures that `SPWebPartManager`'s sole instance is present, if required. There are no further settings or actions needed.

If additional zones are required, we use a slightly different approach. SharePoint defines its own zone model, which derives from the `WebPartZone` class. Employ the `Microsoft.SharePoint.WebPartPages` namespace instead of the one provided with ASP.NET. (Note that contrary to the standard SharePoint namespace naming convention, the type does not have the `SP` prefix.)

SharePoint Web Parts are an integral part of a SharePoint web site. There are many built-in Web Parts a developer may use. Also, there are many Web Parts available on the Internet that could meet your requirements. The various built-in SharePoint Web Parts are categorized as follows:

- *List and Library Web Parts*: These include special lists such as Announcements and Calendar, as well as any other list in the site.
- *Filter Web Parts*: These are used to filter the data based on user requirements, and include the Data Catalog Filter, User Filter, Date Filter, and Text Filter.
- *Outlook Web Parts*: These display content in Microsoft Outlook using Microsoft Exchange Server.
- *Search Web Parts*: These are used to provide search facilities on your site. Examples are Advanced Search, People Search, and Search Summary.
- *Miscellaneous Web Parts*: These Web Parts include Content Editor Web Parts, Page Viewer Web Parts, and Form Web Parts.

Almost all the built-in SharePoint Web Parts are generic. That means that they have properties you can modify in SharePoint.

Web Part Properties

Consider the *Content Editor Web Part*, which, when in Edit mode, provides an option called *Rich Text Editor*, which allows the user to enter and format content. Another option is *Source Editor*, which allows you to edit the raw HTML that the Content Editor will render.

Similarly, in the *Page Viewer Web Part*, the user can set the link to display a web page, folder, or file in the Web Part. Therefore, the advantage of generic Web Parts is that users can configure them to suit their own requirements.

The method of creating a generic Web Part is more or less the same as creating an ASP.NET Web Part—the difference comes when you want to provide the user with the means to set some values or fields in the Web Part.

The developer has to set the fields as properties in the code to enable the user to edit the desired values. Apart from setting the fields as properties, you have to add several attributes to the property that are visible to the user when editing the Web Part. Apart from one for the category (`SPWebCategoryName`), all attributes are from the common ASP.NET namespace.

```
private string _name;

[
System.Web.UI.WebControls.WebParts.WebBrowsable(true),
System.Web.UI.WebControls.WebParts.Personalizable(PersonalizationScope.User),
System.Web.UI.WebControls.WebParts.WebDescription("Enter your name"),
Microsoft.SharePoint.WebPartPages.SPWebCategoryName("Custom Properties"),
System.Web.UI.WebControls.WebParts.WebDisplayName("Name")]
public string Name
{
   get { return _name; }
   set { _name = value; }
}
```

Several attributes, as shown in the example `Name` property, modify the design-time behavior of the Web Part. Here, *design-time* means both the control shown in a designer environment such as SharePoint Designer or Visual Studio 2010, and a Web Part page in Edit mode.

In the “Advanced Web Part Development” section later in the chapter, you’ll find a complete description and further usage scenarios for these and other, more essential attributes.

■ **Note** The attributes from `System.ComponentModel`, such as `Category` and `Browsable`, are deprecated.

Web Part in a Chrome

All Web Parts render inside a *chrome*. The term refers to common UI elements such as titles and borders. You may interpret *chrome* as *frame style*. This style is simple but provides a consistent look and feel to all Web Parts. Primarily, it’s designed to support the basic functionality that the SharePoint environment needs, such as the context menu that allows editing (which appears at the upper-right corner of the Web Part). The chrome functionality is part of the Web Part framework, which consists primarily of the `WebPartZoneManager`. If the Web Part is used as a simple control, without being in any zone, the chrome will not render. The Web Part will still be usable, but you’re responsible for providing editing capabilities, if needed.

Securing Web Parts

Web Parts provide a powerful way to extend the UI by adding features that have access to the API and allowing full control over parts of default pages. The security model protects you from just inserting a Web Part and letting it do something. This makes sense, because otherwise even end users could under certain conditions upload a Web Part and activate it. There are two ways to add a Web Part you trust to your installation. The first way is to use Code Access Security (CAS), or just adopt the corresponding settings from the built-in security models, such as `WSS_Minimal` or `WSS_Medium`. The other approach is to explicitly register a Web Part as *safe*, if you know exactly what it does. The second way is the default because it allows developers to gain control over the procedure. However, administrators will still have to execute the primary installation of a Web Part—and so, ultimately, they know what's going on. The methods described simplify the installation procedure.

Registering a Web Part as Safe

Whether you use the Visual Web Part or the regular Web Part project template, the procedure to register it as a safe control is somewhat automated. The file that contains the `SafeControl` instruction is named `<webpart>.spdata`. It is hidden by default. Usually you edit it by using the `PropertyGrid` and modifying the safe control entries file by file (see Figure 6–1). However, sometimes it's easier to edit the file directly, either if Visual Studio fails or you want to change several items at once. You must unhide all files in the project to view it. Usually there is no need to edit it—however, for example, if you change a namespace, the changes will not be tracked and the registration can fail. In these rare circumstances, you can use the property grid to edit the file.

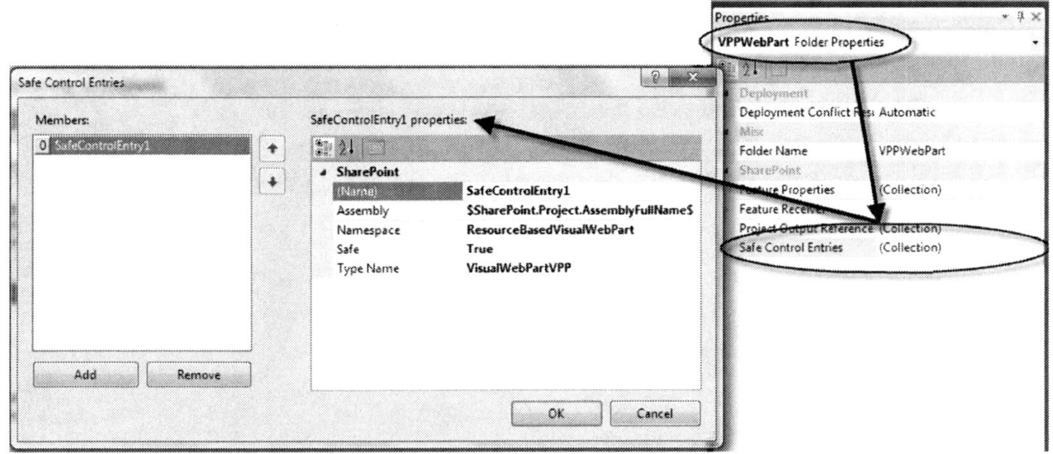

Figure 6–1. *Edit the safe control entries using the Properties Editor.*

The properties defined here are specific to the Web Part. Select the Web Part item in Solution Explorer, press F4, and select the ellipses button in the Safe Control Entries row. Typically, the file these entries refer to looks like that shown in Listing 6–4.

Listing 6–4. *The Project Item That Defines the Files and Security Instructions*

```
<?xml version="1.0" encoding="utf-8"?>
<ProjectItem Type="Microsoft.VisualStudio.SharePoint.WebPart"
```

```
            DefaultFile="CustomWebPart.cs" SupportedTrustLevels="All"
            SupportedDeploymentScopes="Site"
            xmlns="http://schemas.microsoft.com/VisualStudio/2010/
                  SharePointTools/SharePointProjectItemModel">
  <Files>
    <ProjectItemFile Source="Elements.xml" Target="CustomWebPart\"
                     Type="ElementManifest" />
    <ProjectItemFile Source="CustomWebPart.webpart" Target="CustomWebPart\"
                     Type="ElementFile" />
  </Files>
  <SafeControls>
    <SafeControl Name="CustomWebPart"
                 Assembly="$SharePoint.Project.AssemblyFullName$"
                 Namespace="WebPartPageProject.MyWebParts"
                 TypeName="*" IsSafe="true" />
  </SafeControls>
</ProjectItem>
```

The `<SafeControl>` element at the end is responsible for the setting copied to `web.config`. You can modify this to reapply settings not applied automatically.

Dealing with Built-In Security

There are three configuration files in the SharePoint root under the subfolder `CONFIG`: `wss_minimaltrust.config`, `wss_mediumtrust.config`, and `wss_usercode.config`. The latter, `wss_usercode.config`, is specifically for sandboxed solutions. When code runs in the sandbox, the `web.config` file that references the trust file in the subfolder \UserCode is used. This typically contains the following:

```
<trustLevel name="WSS_Sandbox" policyFile="..\config\wss_usercode.config" />
```

Regular solutions use the common trust files. These come with a specific set of restrictions. The default configuration is `wss_miminaltrust`, which is quite limited. Table 6–1 outlines the permissions available.

Table 6–1. Limitations for Web Parts Concerning Specific Trust Levels

Permission	Medium Trust	Minimal Trust
`AspNetHostingPermission`	Medium	Minimal
`DirectoryServicesPermission`	None	None
`DnsPermission`	Unrestricted	None
`EnvironmentPermission`	Read access to `TEMP`, `TMP`, `OS`, `USERNAME`, and `COMPUTERNAME` (environment variables)	None
`EventLogPermission`	None	None
`FileIOPermission`	Read, write, append, and `PathDiscovery` permissions to current application directory	None
`IsolatedStoragePermission`	`IsolatedStorageContainment.AssemblyIsolationByUser`, `IsolatedStoragePermissionAttribute.UserQuota` unrestricted	None
`MessageQueuePermission`	None	None
`OleDBPermission`	None	None
Performance counters	None	None
`PrintingPermission`	Default printing	None
`ReflectionPermission`	None	None
`RegistryPermission`	None	None
`SecurityPermission`	`Execution`, `Assertion`, `ControlPrincipal`, `ControlThread`, and `RemotingConfiguration` (`SecurityPermissionFlag` enum)	
`ServiceControllerPermission`	None	None
`SharePointPermission`*	`ObjectModel` property equals `true`	None
`SocketPermission`	None	None
`SqlClientPermission`	`AllowBlankPassword` property equals `false`	None
`WebPermission`	Connect to origin host (if configured)	None

* *Declared in the `Microsoft.SharePoint.Security` namespace*

This means that if you use any of the disallowed permissions mentioned in the table, the execution engine will reject the attempt with a security exception (see Figure 6–2).

Figure 6–2. *Unexpected exception during Web Part import due to security violations*

In the following example, the Web Part has code that attempts to write to the event log:

```
protected override void CreateChildControls()
{
    base.CreateChildControls();
    Label l = new Label();
    EventLog log = new EventLog("Application");
    log.WriteEntry("WebPart was Displayed", EventLogEntryType.Information,
                   10000, 4);
    l.Text = "Hello Security Web Part";
    Controls.Add(l);
}
```

Because the error message is not very instructive, and could be difficult even for an administrator to decipher, you should add a security permission attribute to your code:

```
[ToolboxItemAttribute(false)]
[EventLogPermission(System.Security.Permissions.SecurityAction.Demand)]
public class WebPartMinimalTrust : WebPart
{
    // Code removed for sake of clarity
}
```

In this case, the error occurs earlier (see Figure 6–3), and SharePoint can catch it before the Web Part is added.

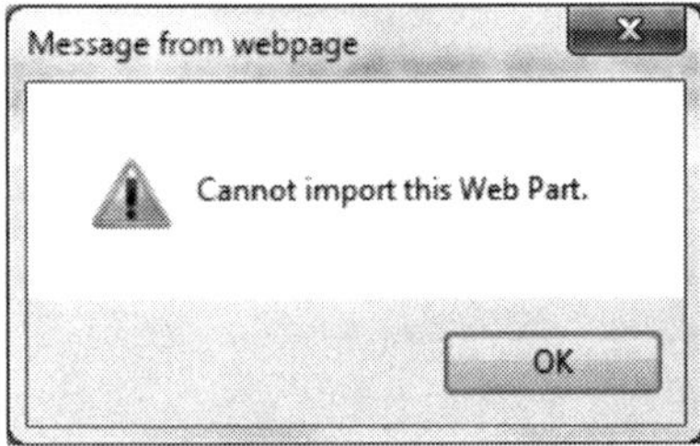

Figure 6–3. *Still an uninformative dialog for the security error*

In fact, the error message from SharePoint is no better. But instead of an unexpected error being generated, the process is stopped by the permission check and the Web Part is not added.

■ **Tip** If your Web Part requires a particular permission, always add the corresponding permission attribute to aid the runtime in checking the permissions before the class is instantiated.

If medium trust is sufficient, you can consider setting it as the default trust level. However, for Web Parts requiring classes you can't access with medium trust, you must provide a custom code access policy. Sandboxed solutions do not allow overwriting the CAS policy.

Providing Web Part–Specific CAS Policy

If a Web Part needs some specific CAS policy, you can add the information to the deployment package. In addition, the administrator must provide the `-allowCasPolicies` parameter when installing the solution using the `stsadm` tool. This ensures that the administrator has ultimate control over what a new Web Part can do.

To use a custom CAS policy, do the following:

1. Change the installation target to `WebApplication`.
2. Add the CAS policy XML to the package.
3. Set the assembly attribute, `AllowPartiallyTrustedCallers`.

Using the same Web Part as before and Visual Studio 2010 to create the package, this is very easy. First, set the Assembly Deployment property of the current Web Part project to `WebApplication` (see Figure 6–4). This deploys the assembly—not into the GAC, but into a less trusted file location of your project target.

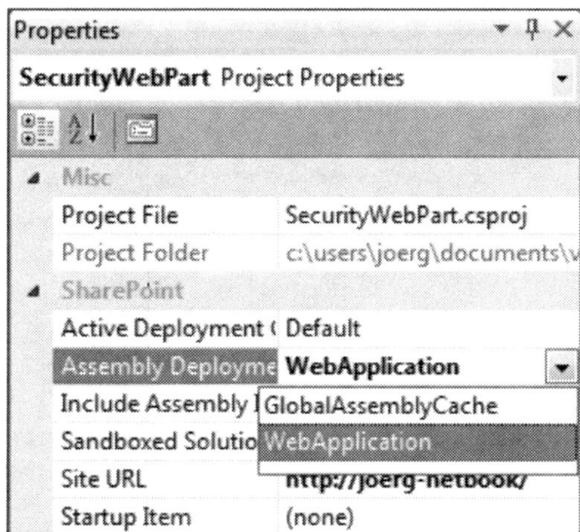

Figure 6–4. *Setting the Assembly Deployment property*

Second, add the custom policy to the package designer. Open the package designer by double-clicking Package.package. Then select the Manifest tab and enter the CAS data into the template windows. The content is merged into the package file shown in the preview pane, as shown in Figure 6–5.

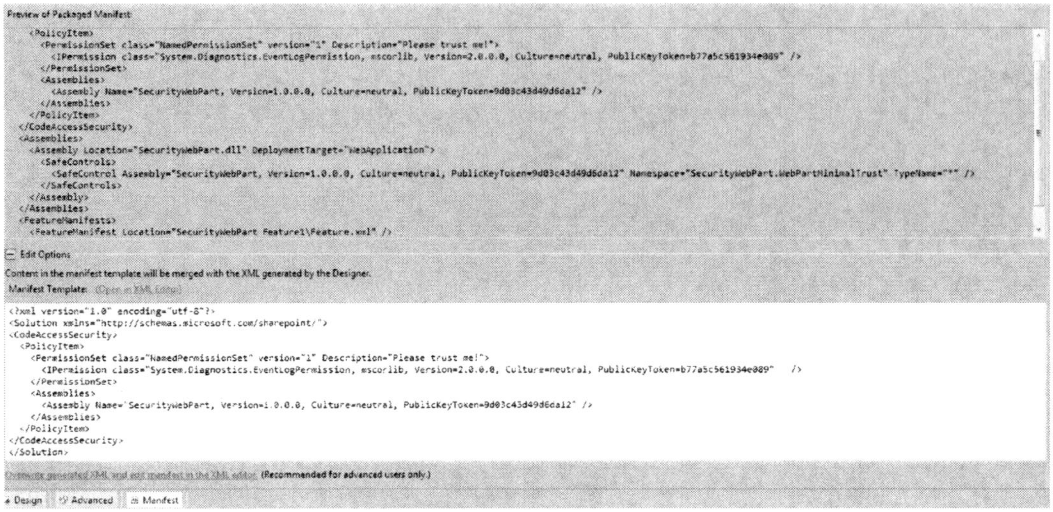

Figure 6–5. *Adding the CAS policy to the current project's package*

Third, add the required attribute to the `assemblyinfo.cs` file:

```
[assembly: AllowPartiallyTrustedCallers()]
```

Finally, build and deploy the package again. You can now add it to the current installation and use the formerly blocked classes. The CAS policy should be completed to allow at least the typical permissions a Web Part demands. The XML would then look as shown in Listing 6–5.

Listing 6–5. *Definition for a Custom CodeAccessSecurity Section*

```
<CodeAccessSecurity>
 <PolicyItem>
  <PermissionSet class="NamedPermissionSet" version="1"
                 Description="Permission set for my Web Part">
  <IPermission class="AspNetHostingPermission" version="1" Level="Minimal" />
  <IPermission class="SecurityPermission" version="1"
               Flags="Execution,ControlPrincipal,
                      ControlAppDomain,ControlDomainPolicy,
                      ControlEvidence,ControlThread" />
  <IPermission class="Microsoft.SharePoint.Security.SharePointPermission,
               Microsoft.SharePoint.Security, Version=14.0.0.0, Culture=neutral,
               PublicKeyToken=71e9bce111e9429c"
               version="1" ObjectModel="True" />
  <IPermission class="System.Security.Permissions.EnvironmentPermission, mscorlib,
                      Version=2.0.0.0, Culture=neutral,
                      PublicKeyToken=b77a5c561934e089" version="1"
               Read="UserName" />
```

```
<IPermission class="System.Security.Permissions.FileIOPermission, mscorlib,
                      Version=2.0.0.0, Culture=neutral,
                      PublicKeyToken=b77a5c561934e089" version="1"
              Read="$AppDir$ "
              Write="$AppDir$"
              Append="$AppDir$"
              PathDiscovery="$AppDir$" />
 </PermissionSet>
 <Assemblies>
  <Assembly Name="VisualWebPartProject1" />
 </Assemblies>
</PolicyItem>
</CodeAccessSecurity>
```

It's necessary to add all these permissions because the custom CAS file does not merge. Instead, it replaces the common definitions. Thus, the definition must contain all permissions required to execute the Web Part.

The settings in the CAS file depend on the permissions you need. That's why the `IPermission` element is not described elsewhere. The only common attribute is the `class` attribute that specifies the fully qualified name of the permission class. In the next example, this is the `EventLogPermissionAttribute`. All the other attributes are extracted from the named parameters. Figure 6–6 illustrates how to view all the named parameters at once in Visual Studio.

```
[EventLogPermission(System.Security.Permissions.SecurityAction.Demand,)]
▲ 2 of 2 ▼ EventLogPermissionAttribute.EventLogPermissionAttribute(System.Security.Permissions.SecurityAction action,
           Named Parameters...)
Initializes a new instance of the System.Diagnostics.EventLogPermissionAttribute class.
Named Parameters:   Action = System.Security.Permissions.SecurityAction
                    MachineName = string
                    PermissionAccess = EventLogPermissionAccess
                    Unrestricted = bool
```

Figure 6–6. *Check the code editor to view the named parameters.*

If you add `enum` values, the value is sufficient; the `enum` type does not need to be explicitly stated. The engine will extract it from the property's type.

Visual Web Parts

Writing controls or text directly into a Web Part's body seems an odd approach for a complex UI. A visual designer tool would make the task much easier. In Visual Studio 2010, there is a new project template, *Visual Web Part*, to fulfill that role. This is, however, not that new. The template simply scaffolds a conglomeration of files that consists of a traditional Web Part and an ASP.NET user control (ASCX). The user control designer appears as the Visual Web Part designer. This is the way it worked before, except that now the template saves you a few seconds when you start developing. A skeleton of the main class file is shown in Listing 6–6.

Listing 6–6. *Skeleton of a Visual Web Part*

```
using System;
using System.ComponentModel;
using System.Runtime.InteropServices;
using System.Web;
```

```
using System.Web.UI;
using System.Web.UI.WebControls;
using System.Web.UI.WebControls.WebParts;
using Microsoft.SharePoint;
using Microsoft.SharePoint.WebControls;

namespace Apress.SP2010.VisualWebPart
{
    [ToolboxItemAttribute(false)]
    public class VisualWebPart1 : WebPart
    {
        // Visual Studio might automatically update this path
        // when you change the Visual Web Part project item.
        private const string _ascxPath = @"~/_CONTROLTEMPLATES/VisualWebParts/
                                VisualWebPart1/VisualWebPart1UserControl.ascx";

        public VisualWebPart1()
        {
        }

        protected override void CreateChildControls()
        {
            Control control = this.Page.LoadControl(_ascxPath);
            Controls.Add(control);
            base.CreateChildControls();
        }

        protected override void RenderContents(HtmlTextWriter writer)
        {
            base.RenderContents(writer);
        }
    }
}
```

The Visual Web Part contains a constant value that points to the control's relative path. The `CreateChildControls` method has been overwritten to load the control dynamically using the `LoadControl` method provided by the Page class. All of your Web Part UI design is applied to the user control.

■ **Caution** Renaming a path such as the `_ascxPath` variable requires you to carefully check related files, such as `element.xml`. There are several tight connections between these files that Visual Studio does not track completely.

However, when you create controls that load their content in a different way, as Silverlight controls do, there is no need to use the Visual Web Part template. Remember that the Visual Web Part requires you to add an additional file to the deployment package. This means that it ends up deployed to the `CONTROLTEMPLATES` folder or one of its subfolders. That might be permissible for most projects, but you would have to check whether it violates any conditions imposed by a server administrator. Deploying files into the SharePoint root (14 hive) prevents you from creating a sandboxed solution. That's why Visual Web Parts can't be used in a project that has the Sandboxed Solution property set to True.

The Visual Web Part template creates everything you need to deploy it as a feature. When you deploy the Web Part, the feature is installed and activated. You can add and debug the Web Part immediately, which makes for a great developer experience. However, if you plan to deploy the Web Part as part of a project or as a standalone solution, you have to consider the various settings in the Visual Studio template.

Understanding the Project Structure

The project provides several files that create the Web Part and define its appearance within the SharePoint site. By default, the feature is deployed to the referenced site collection. Figure 6–7 shows the standard structure that is created.

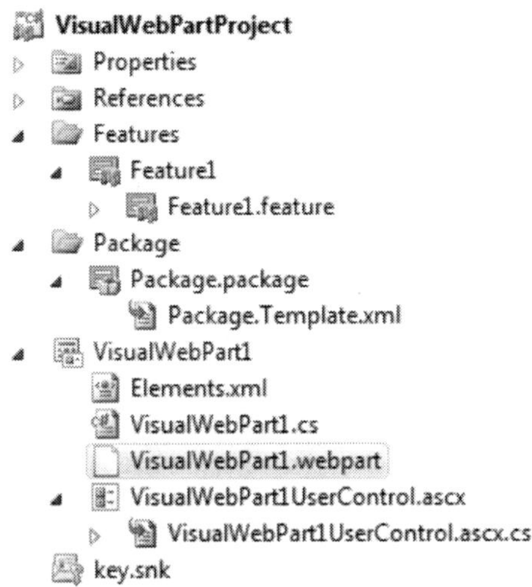

Figure 6–7. *Structure of a Visual Web Part project*

The folder VisualWebPart1 contains the Web Part itself. VisualWebPart1UserControl.ascx is the markup file (see Listing 6–7), which when first created contains the code shown in Listing 6–8.

Listing 6–7. *Markup of the "Visual" Part*

```
<%@ Assembly Name="$SharePoint.Project.AssemblyFullName$" %>
<%@ Assembly Name="Microsoft.Web.CommandUI, ..." %>
<%@ Register Tagprefix="SharePoint" Namespace="Microsoft.SharePoint.WebControls"
             Assembly="Microsoft.SharePoint, ..." %>
<%@ Register Tagprefix="Utilities" Namespace="Microsoft.SharePoint.Utilities"
             Assembly="Microsoft.SharePoint, ..." %>
<%@ Register Tagprefix="asp" Namespace="System.Web.UI"
             Assembly="System.Web.Extensions, ..." %>
<%@ Import Namespace="Microsoft.SharePoint" %>
<%@ Register Tagprefix="WebPartPages" Namespace="Microsoft.SharePoint.WebPartPages"
             Assembly="Microsoft.SharePoint, ..." %>
```

```
<%@ Control Language="C#" AutoEventWireup="true"
            CodeBehind="VisualWebPart1UserControl.ascx.cs"
Inherits="VisualWebPartDashboard.VisualWebPart1.VisualWebPart1UserControl" %>
```

This is simply time-saving and housekeeping code. The first line references the assembly that is created by your project, via a placeholder. The assembly is usually deployed to the GAC, and the line references it at runtime. The second line contains a reference to `Microsoft.Web.CommandUI`, the assembly that contains the ribbon support. The next few lines reference and import the corresponding namespaces to get access to the SharePoint controls. The last line defines the control itself and references the code-behind file.

The code-behind (see Listing 6–8) file is essentially empty, except for the `Load` event handler to get you started.

Listing 6–8. *The Code-Behind for the User Control*

```
using System;
using System.Web.UI;
using System.Web.UI.WebControls;
using System.Web.UI.WebControls.WebParts;
using Microsoft.SharePoint;
using Microsoft.SharePoint.Utilities;

namespace Apress.SP2010.VisualWebPartProject
{
    public partial class VisualWebPart1UserControl : UserControl
    {
        protected void Page_Load(object sender, EventArgs e)
        {
        }
    }
}
```

In the same folder, the Web Part definition (`.webpart`) describes what you see within SharePoint when adding the Web Part to a page (Listing 6–9).

Listing 6–9. *Web Part Definition File with Basic Properties*

```
<?xml version="1.0" encoding="utf-8"?>
<webParts>
  <webPart xmlns="http://schemas.microsoft.com/WebPart/v3">
    <metaData>
      <type name="Apress.SP2010.VisualWebPartProject.VisualWebPart1,
                  $SharePoint.Project.AssemblyFullName$" />
      <importErrorMessage>$Resources:core,ImportErrorMessage;</importErrorMessage>
    </metaData>
    <data>
      <properties>
        <property name="Title" type="string">VisualWebPart1</property>
        <property name="Description" type="string">My Visual WebPart</property>
      </properties>
    </data>
  </webPart>
</webParts>
```

The metadata describes the class's name and the assembly's full name, again using the placeholder. The `<importErrorMessage>` element contains a message that appears if an end user can't import a Web Part previously exported by somebody else. Users can—if they have the appropriate permissions—export a Web Part as a file and import it elsewhere. That means that users can move Web Parts across site and server boundaries.

If there are Web Part dependencies that are not found on the target SharePoint system, the error message is displayed. In the preceding example, the message extracted from the resources of the core RESX file via the `$Resources` expression is the default one. You could replace it with any useful text here. Inside the `<data>` element, some properties are defined. (See the "Understanding Properties" section later in the chapter for more information regarding what you can write in here.) We recommend you provide at least a title and a short description, as these are helpful when dealing with the Web Part later.

▒ **Note** Using `.dwp` files instead of `.webpart` files is deprecated, and is supported for backward compatibility only.

The features manifest contains the manifest file `elements.xml` (see Listing 6–10). It specifies where to store the Web Part (Web Part catalog) and where the Web Part itself is defined (`VisualWebPart1.webpart` file, as shown previously).

Listing 6–10. *The elements.xml File*

```
<?xml version="1.0" encoding="utf-8"?>
<Elements xmlns="http://schemas.microsoft.com/sharepoint/" >
  <Module Name="VisualWebPart1" List="113" Url="_catalogs/wp">
    <File Path="VisualWebPart1\VisualWebPart1.webpart"
          Url="VisualWebPartDashboard_VisualWebPart1.webpart"
          Type="GhostableInLibrary" >
      <Property Name="Group" Value="Custom" />
    </File>
  </Module>
</Elements>
```

In addition, the solution package and the feature definition are part of the template. This aspect is common to all deployable projects and explained in greater depth in Chapter 7. Primarily, it contains the name and description, and optionally an icon that represents the feature. It also contains the settings that define the scope in which the feature becomes visible.

As with any other class project, you are supposed to edit the `AssemblyInfo.cs` file. Because the project's assembly is deployed as part of the feature, someone can inspect the file, looking for metadata. Editing the `AssemblyInfo.cs` file is equivalent to editing the settings of the project's Properties pane. You can edit either of these to set the appropriate file data, such as copyright notice, file title and description, and company information.

```
[assembly: AssemblyTitle("My VisualWebPart")]
[assembly: AssemblyDescription("Something really useful")]
[assembly: AssemblyConfiguration("")]
[assembly: AssemblyCompany("Apress")]
[assembly: AssemblyProduct("VisualWebPart Product")]
[assembly: AssemblyCopyright("Copyright © Apress 2009")]
[assembly: AssemblyTrademark("")]
[assembly: AssemblyCulture("")]
```

The settings are preset when the project is created but are not updated to match your changes. The assembly title, for example, follows the project's name. However, if you change the project name later, the corresponding assembly title attribute remains unchanged.

To put an assembly into the GAC, it must have a strong name. The project template comes with a predefined `key.snk` file that contains a key to sign the assembly. We strongly recommend replacing this key file with one key file common to all your projects so that you have a unique token for all assemblies created as part of a project.

Running Visual Web Parts in a Sandbox

If you create a new Visual Web Part project, the Sandbox option appears disabled. That's a significant impediment. Loading a file from the root folder of the SharePoint installation—the 14 hive—is not allowed in a sandboxed solution. This is reasonable, as you can imagine what would happen if a hosting provider or Microsoft SharePoint Online installation allowed everybody to deploy such Web Parts to a shared host. However, that's exactly what the Visual Web Part project template does. Visual Studio knows this, so you cannot create a sandboxed Web Part. Even trying to fool it by creating an empty sandboxed solution and adding a Web Part to it will fail once you try to create the package (see Figure 6–8).

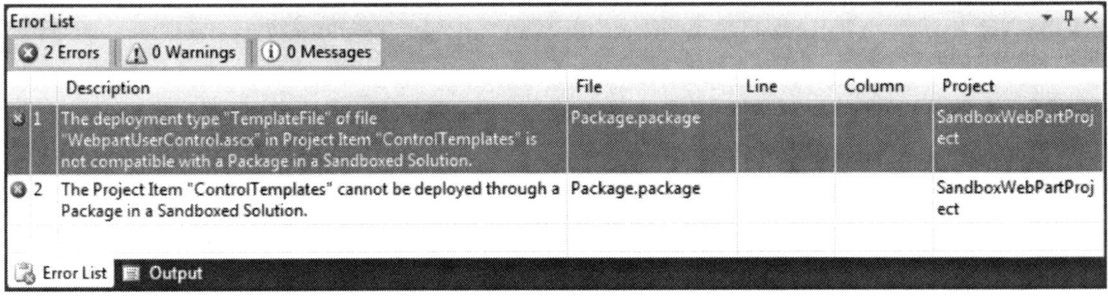

***Figure 6–8.** Sandboxed solutions can't contain files that deploy into the 14 hive.*

If you really need a Web Part running in a sandboxed solution, you are supposed to use a regular (not Visual) Web Part. Create a new, empty SharePoint solution, add a Web Part to it, and you're done. However, the visual experience has gone—you are limited to building the UI via code only.

Creating Visual Web Parts

Creating Visual Web Parts using Visual Studio 2010 is relatively easy. The project template includes everything you need for a designer surface and the required deployment elements. Compared with SharePoint 2007, there is nothing special or new. The template simply follows the best practices. It creates a custom control (ASCX) file and uses Visual Studio's built-in designer to scaffold the control. It overrides the `CreateChildControl` method and loads the control dynamically.

The complete solution consists of the following Web Part–related elements:

- User control file (`.ascx`)
- User control code-behind file (`.ascx.cs`)
- Hidden user control designer file (`.ascx.designer.cs`)
- Web Part code-behind file (`.cs`)

- Web Part file (.webpart)
- Elements.xml

For deployment support, the solution also contains the feature and solution package files. (See Chapter 9 for more information.) The deployment determines the way how a Web Part becomes part of a SharePoint application.

The basic code used to load a custom control is as shown in Listing 6–11.

Listing 6–11. *A Visual Web Part Class That Loads a User Control*

```
using System;
using System.Runtime.InteropServices;
using System.Web.UI;
using System.Web.UI.WebControls;
using System.Web.UI.WebControls.WebParts;
using Microsoft.SharePoint;
using Microsoft.SharePoint.WebControls;

namespace SimpleWebPart.VisualWebPart1
{
    public class VisualWebPart1 : WebPart
    {
        protected const string _ascxPath = ↵
            @"~/_CONTROLTEMPLATES/SimpleWebPart/VisualWebPart1/  ↵
              VisualWebPart1UserControl.ascx";

        public VisualWebPart1()
        {
        }

        protected override void CreateChildControls()
        {
            try
            {
                Control control = this.Page.LoadControl(_ascxPath);
                Controls.Add(control);
            }
            finally
            {
                base.CreateChildControls();
            }
        }

        protected override void Render(HtmlTextWriter writer)
        {
            base.Render(writer);
        }
    }
}
```

This code implies that the Web Part's content is deployed as a custom control to the virtual CONTROLTEMPLATES folder. That makes the Web Part global to the server. To reiterate, Web Parts are reusable components that can be used in many applications on a server, so this is the most robust strategy for your controls. Of course, you can also use other methods, such as writing HTML to the output stream, to create the content.

Two additional XML files control how the Web Part is deployed. The Web Part appears in the Web Part gallery, as well as in several dialogs that end users access to add elements. The `.webpart` file provides additional information, as shown in Listing 6–12.

Listing 6–12. *Namespace and Property Definition in the .webpart File*

```
<?xml version="1.0" encoding="utf-8"?>
<webParts>
  <webPart xmlns="http://schemas.microsoft.com/WebPart/v3">
    <metaData>
      <type name="SimpleWebPart.VisualWebPart1.VisualWebPart1,
                  $SharePoint.Project.AssemblyFullName$" />
      <importErrorMessage>$Resources:core,ImportErrorMessage;</importErrorMessage>
    </metaData>
    <data>
      <properties>
        <property name="Title" type="string">VisualWebPart1 Title</property>
        <property name="Description" type="string">VisualWebPart1
                                                   Description</property>
      </properties>
    </data>
  </webPart>
</webParts>
```

The `<property>` element overrides the default settings of the corresponding property from the `WebPart` base class. That means you can either override these properties in code or set values in the `.webpart` file. The declarative way using the XML file is the preferred technique.

MSDN LOOKUP

See `http://msdn.microsoft.com/en-us/library/ms227561.aspx` for a complete reference to the XML used in `.webpart`.

See `http://msdn.microsoft.com/en-us/library/system.web.ui.webcontrols.webparts.webpart_properties.aspx` for a complete list of available properties.

If a text portion begins with `$Resources`, it references an assembly containing compiled resource data. Here it's the core assembly that SharePoint comes with. You can replace this string with any hard-coded one or assign your own resource file. (For more information, see the Chapter 8.) Using resource files is the preferred way to implement localization.

Understanding ASP.NET Web Parts

Web Parts in SharePoint are ASP.NET Web Parts. This means that the programming methods are similar. The code-behind might use the SharePoint API and the chrome ensures a consistent look and feel, but everything you can do is provided by ASP.NET.

Web Part controls support the personalization of a page. The page developer can decide what parts of the page are editable. If you have only static pages and no part is reusable, a Web Part does not make much sense. But you can also use Web Parts to make the work of a page developer easier. By developing Web Parts you enable the page developer to use these modules and decide later where on the page they can appear. Once the layout is fixed, the editing option can be disabled.

Web Parts can come from any third-party supplier. Web Parts are sold by many companies, and many more are free or available as open source. That makes it easy to add them to your pages or replace them with newer or improved versions any time. All this is possible without recompiling and redeploying your application. That adds a significant level of flexibility to your application design.

How It Works

As with any other aspect of ASP.NET, understanding the control's life cycle is crucial to understanding its behavior. There are four life cycle steps that allow you to add custom code: `OnInit`, `OnLoad`, `OnPrerender`, and `OnUnload`.

`OnInit` occurs first, and allows you to access the uninitialized elements that have been added by the designer to the Web Part. It calls `CreateChildControls` implicitly to ensure that all elements render themselves. Overriding this method is the most robust way to add content programmatically. This ensures that you don't disturb the life cycle events and that the elements appear at the correct time.

`OnLoad` signals that the control is properly loaded and initialized. Any programmatic manipulation of existing elements should be placed here. It's safe to add synchronous operations here, such as database access or SharePoint list access.

For launching asynchronous processing, the best practice is to override the `OnPreRender` event. (Asynchronous processing is covered in depth in the section "Asynchronous Web Parts," later in this chapter.) A long-running external call, such as data retrieval from a web service or a database, blocks the current thread and will slow down the application if the thread pool runs out of threads. This can happen even if the CPU load is low. Asynchronous programming of long-running external calls frees the threads faster. When the external call returns, the runtime requests the thread again, processes the changes—for example, by populating a `Gridview` with the data—and completes rendering the page. That's best done in the `PreRender` step. The `PreRenderComplete` step is available at the page level only.

Closing and disposing of any connections made and other garbage collection tasks are best placed in the `OnUnload` step. In this step there is no more access to the controls because the rendering is done. All life cycle events are explained in Table 6–2. Figure 6–9 explains the relations between the events.

Table 6–2. Life Cycle Events for Web Parts

Event	Source	Description
`OnInit`	Control	Fired after initialization.
`OnLoad`	Control	Fired after loading is completed.
`CreateChildControls`	Control	Creates child controls.
`EnsureChildControls`	Control	Called to ensure that `CreateChildControls` has executed.
`OnPreRender`	Control	Fired after all internal processing and before the controls render. This is the last step you can use to modify controls.
`PreRenderComplete`	Page	Fires if the page is executed asynchronously, and shows that rendering can be completed.
`Render`	Control	Renders the Web Part, including the outer elements and chrome.
`RenderContents`	Control	Renders the Web Part inside the outer elements and with styles, but no chrome.

There are five segments in the event model chart, from left to right:

- `Page`: Events and methods happening in the page (`System.Web.UI.Page` derivatives).
- `WebPartManager`: Events and methods in the `SPWebPartManager` (inherited from `WebPartManager`).
- `WebPartZone`: Methods called in `WebPartZone` that render the `WebPart` controls.
- `WebPart`: Events that occur during a normal view of a `WebPart`.
- `WebPart` *postback*: Postback-specific event flow, which is a bit different from the normal `WebPart` flow. (Note that `CreateChildControls` occurs before the `OnLoad` and connections.)

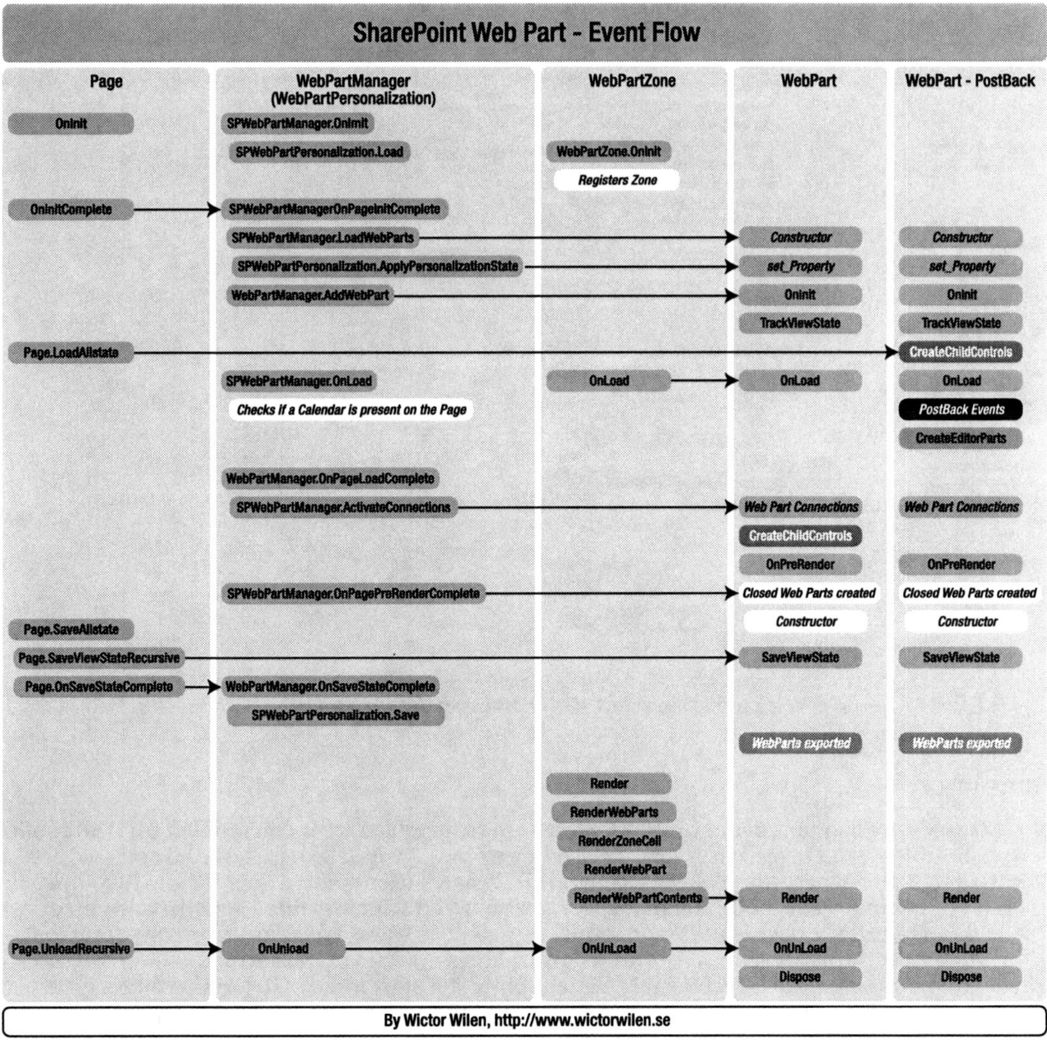

***Figure 6–9.** Web Part event model chart*

Some events and methods are not specific to Web Parts. Instead, they are inherited from base classes. Understanding these base classes is vital for Web Part development.

The inheritance from `Control` and the implementation of the `IComponent` interface build the foundation of a Web Part. As you can see, there is no dependency on SharePoint. Consequently, you can create Web Parts in any ASP.NET-aware environment and use them in SharePoint. In the hierarchy (in Figure 6–10), notice the `Panel` class toward the middle. A `Panel` renders as a `<div>` element in HTML, implying a rectangular surface. Hence, all Web Parts have a `Width` and `Height` property. The Web Part–specific behavior originates with the `WebPart` base class. This base class's elements are implementations of the `IWebPart`, `IWebEditable`, and `IWebActionable` interfaces.

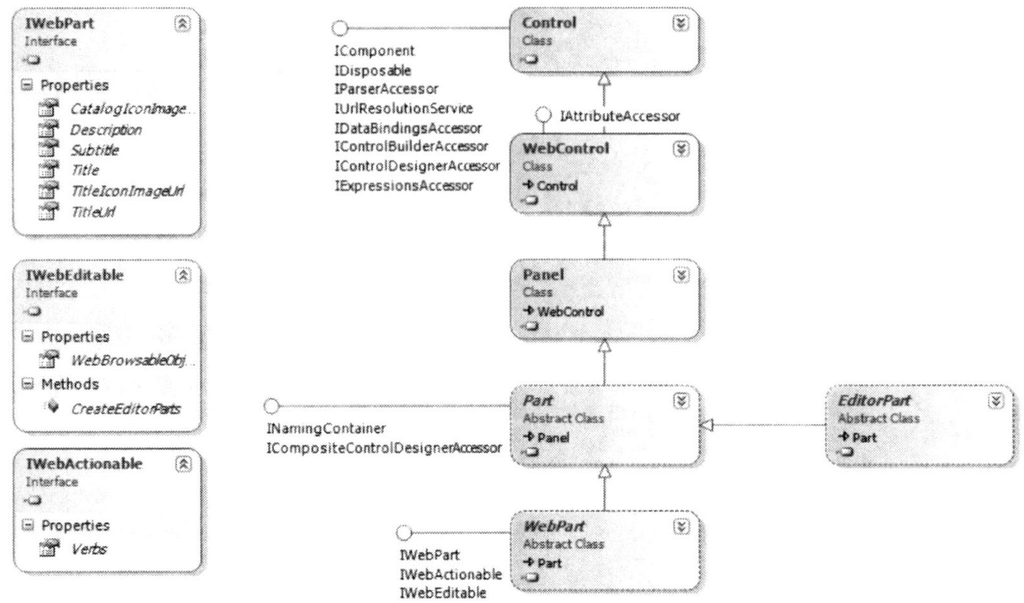

***Figure 6–10.** Class diagram of the base classes and Web Part–specific interfaces*

The Zone Concept

The `WebPartManager` enables any layout of zones. Zones are rectangular areas constructed from any valid HTML—usually tables—and tagged with `<asp:webpartzone>` tags. Inside the tag, the `<contenttemplate>` element is used to define where the Web Part can appear. When a user opens a page for the first time, all the Web Parts appear in *Browse* mode. Technically, each Web Part supports three actions: minimize, maximize, and remove. If the page is in *Design* mode, the user can move Web Parts from one zone to another. In *Edit* mode, the user can modify the customizable properties of the currently selected Web Part. A predefined property zone is responsible for rendering the appropriate UI. *Catalog* mode gives access to currently invisible Web Parts so that a user can add them to the page. The five modes are

- *Browse*: This is default mode, showing the final page layout.
- *Design*: In this mode, you can minimize or move Web Parts.
- *Edit*: In this mode, you can edit the properties of the currently selected Web Part.
- *Catalog*: This mode shows additional Web Parts that you can add to any zone.
- *Connect*: This mode allows you to add data connections between Web Parts.

Structure of a Web Part Page

SharePoint provides several predefined Web Part pages. Adding such a page means that you add an ASPX page that has a layout with zones arranged in some way. You may want to add your own page if you create custom application pages or if you desire a different layout. (See Chapter 8 for more details on programming such pages.)

In the following exercise, an application page contains the Web Part zones. To create the project, perform the following steps.

ADDING A PRIVATE WEB PART PAGE

1. Create a new Empty SharePoint Solution project.
2. Add the `LAYOUTS` folder by right-clicking in the Solution Explorer tree and choosing Add ➤ SharePoint "Layouts" Mapped Folder.
3. Right-click the folder and choose Add ➤ "New item."
4. Select Application Page from Template Explorer.
5. Add the code shown in Listing 6–13.

When you're done coding the page, deploy it using Visual Studio. Open the page directly from the `_layouts/`*<project>* folder, where *<project>* is a placeholder for your project's name.

Listing 6–13 shows a page with embedded code that allows two modes: Design and Browse.

Listing 6–13. *A Custom Web Part Page*

```
<%@ Assembly Name="$SharePoint.Project.AssemblyFullName$" %>
<%@ Import Namespace="Microsoft.SharePoint.ApplicationPages" %>
<%@ Register TagPrefix="SharePoint" Namespace="Microsoft.SharePoint.WebControls"
    Assembly="Microsoft.SharePoint, ..." %>
<%@ Register TagPrefix="SharePoint" Namespace="Microsoft.SharePoint.WebPartPages"
    Assembly="Microsoft.SharePoint, ..." %>
<%@ Register TagPrefix="Utilities" Namespace="Microsoft.SharePoint.Utilities"
    Assembly="Microsoft.SharePoint, ..." %>
<%@ Register TagPrefix="asp" Namespace="System.Web.UI"
    Assembly="System.Web.Extensions, ..." %>
<%@ Register TagPrefix="asp" Namespace="System.Web.UI.WebControls.WebParts"
    Assembly="System.Web.Extensions, ..." %>
<%@ Import Namespace="Microsoft.SharePoint" %>
<%@ Assembly Name="Microsoft.Web.CommandUI, ..." %>

<%@ Page Language="C#" AutoEventWireup="true" CodeBehind="WebPartPage.aspx.cs"
         Inherits="WebPartPageProject.Layouts.WebPartPageProject.WebPartPage"
         DynamicMasterPageFile="~masterurl/default.master" %>

<asp:Content ID="PageHead"
             ContentPlaceHolderID="PlaceHolderAdditionalPageHead" runat="server">
```

```
</asp:Content>
<asp:Content ID="Main" ContentPlaceHolderID="PlaceHolderMain" runat="server">
    <h1>
        Webpart Introduction</h1>
    <table width="100%" border="1">
        <tr>
            <td colspan="2">
                <asp:WebPartZone runat="server" ID="headerZone"
                                 HeaderText="Header Zone">
                </asp:WebPartZone>
            </td>
        </tr>
        <tr>
            <td style="width:50%">
                <asp:WebPartZone runat="server" ID="leftZone"
                                 HeaderText="Left Zone">
                </asp:WebPartZone>
            </td>
            <td style="width:50%">
                <asp:WebPartZone runat="server" ID="rightZone"
                                 HeaderText="Right Zone">
                </asp:WebPartZone>
            </td>
        </tr>
        <tr>
            <td colspan="2">
                <asp:CatalogZone runat="server" ID="catZone">
                    <ZoneTemplate>
                        <asp:PageCatalogPart runat="server" ID="catalogZonePart"
                                             Title="Page Parts">
                        </asp:PageCatalogPart>
                        <asp:DeclarativeCatalogPart runat="server"
                                  ID="declarativeZonePart" Title="Catalogue">
                            <WebPartsTemplate>
                                <SharePoint:ListViewWebPart runat="server"
                                  id="listView1" Title="Authors"
                                  ListName="32AF232D-375A-4504-9076-261F347448CF" />
                                <SharePoint:ListViewWebPart runat="server"
                                  id="listView2" Title="Tasks"
                                  ListName="4F6DEED2-3A62-49EE-A3F7-080E5BCBAB82" />
                            </WebPartsTemplate>
                        </asp:DeclarativeCatalogPart>
                    </ZoneTemplate>
                </asp:CatalogZone>
            </td>
        </tr>
        <tr>
            <td colspan="2">
                <asp:LinkButton runat="server" ID="lnkMode"
                      Text="Browse Mode" OnClick="lnkMode_Click"></asp:LinkButton>
                <asp:LinkButton runat="server" ID="lnkCatM"
                      Text="Catalog Mode"
                      OnClick="lnkCatMode_Click"></asp:LinkButton>
            </td>
```

```
        </tr>
    </table>
</asp:Content>
<asp:Content ID="PageTitle" ContentPlaceHolderID="PlaceHolderPageTitle"
             runat="server">
    Application Page
</asp:Content>
<asp:Content ID="PageTitleInTitleArea" ContentPlaceHolderID="PlaceHolderPageTitleInTitleArea"
    runat="server">
    My WebPart Page
</asp:Content>
```

This page contains several zones to place Web Parts and a Catalog zone where the user can select more Web Parts. In the example, a table defines the position of the zones. This is usually the easiest way to place Web Parts at particular locations. (All styles and descriptive aspects are omitted for the sake of clarity. Consider adding more useful error-checking and validation code to extend the user experience when defining private Web Part pages, such as shown in Listing 6–14.)

Listing 6–14. *Code-Behind for the Custom Web Part Page*

```
using System;
using Microsoft.SharePoint;
using Microsoft.SharePoint.WebControls;
using Microsoft.SharePoint.WebPartPages;
using System.Web.UI.WebControls.WebParts;

namespace WebPartPageProject.Layouts.WebPartPageProject
{
    public partial class WebPartPage : LayoutsPageBase
    {
        SPWebPartManager spWebPartManager;
        protected void Page_Load(object sender, EventArgs e)
        {
            spWebPartManager = WebPartManager.GetCurrentWebPartManager(this)
                               as SPWebPartManager;

            if (spWebPartManager.SupportedDisplayModes.Contains(
                                WebPartManager.CatalogDisplayMode))
            {
                lnkCatM.Visible = true;
            }
            else
            {
                lnkCatM.Visible = false;
            }
        }

        protected void lnkCatMode_Click(object sender, EventArgs e)
        {
            spWebPartManager.DisplayMode = WebPartManager.CatalogDisplayMode;
        }

        protected void lnkMode_Click(object sender, EventArgs e)
        {
```

```
                if (spWebPartManager != null)
                {
                    if (lnkMode.Text == "Design Mode")
                    {
                        spWebPartManager.DisplayMode = WebPartManager.BrowseDisplayMode;
                        lnkMode.Text = "Browse Mode";
                    }
                    else
                    {
                        spWebPartManager.DisplayMode = WebPartManager.DesignDisplayMode;
                        lnkMode.Text = "Design Mode";
                    }
                }
            }

        }
}
```

The code-behind class contains only the LinkButton event handlers to change the zone modes. The SPWebPartManager is retrieved in the page's Load event. If Catalog mode is currently supported, the appropriate LinkButton is made visible (see Figure 6–11).

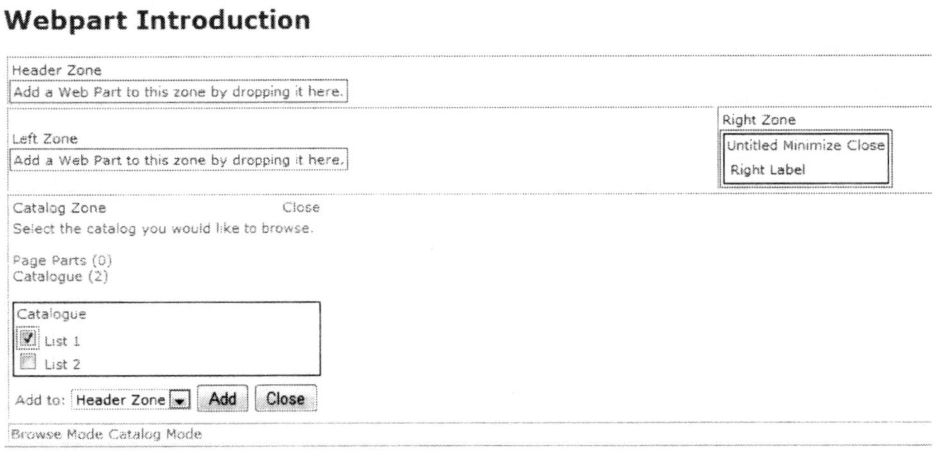

Figure 6–11. *A simple custom Web Part page*

On clicking the LinkButton control, the page switches into Design mode. You can now move Web Parts around—from zone to zone. This is performed by JavaScript that supports drag-and-drop operations. In the example, the current text displayed by LinkButton is set dynamically to represent the available state, determined from the SPWebPartManager control.

This merely demonstrates that it's possible to build Web Part–enabled application pages. When you use the predefined templates for Web Part pages, you simply develop the Web Part itself. The remaining section explains in depth the capabilities of Web Part development.

SPWebPartManager

SPWebPartManager manages all Web Parts on a page. It is defined in the default master page and has the ID m. To get a reference, you can use the WebPartManager class:

```
var m = WebPartManager.GetCurrentWebPartManager(this) as SPWebPartManager;
```

(The preceding code assumes that you're on an application page. If the code runs inside a Web Part or a user control, use this.Page, instead of this.) To get the currently supported modes, use m.SupportedDisplayModes, which returns a value of the WebPartDisplayModes enumeration. Under certain circumstances—such as when no HttpContext is available—SPLimitedWebPartManager is used. It supports only a subset of the features available in SPWebPartManager.

WebPartZone

WebPartZone is a container that holds the Web Parts. Web Parts can't exist outside such a container. You can define Web Parts within a ZoneTemplate statically or let the user add one or more dynamically.

EditorZone

EditorZone allows for the editing of a Web Part's properties. To activate the Edit mode, set SPWebPartManager's DisplayMode property:

```
m.DisplayMode = WebPartManager.EditDisplayMode;
```

If the user has set something that makes the page no longer work properly, you can offer a reset option. This invokes the following method:

```
m.Personalization.ResetPersonalizationState();
```

CatalogZone

CatalogZone can contain several catalogs. Catalogs allows users to select Web Parts from a predefined selection. User can remove Web Parts. To add a Web Part to the page again, a catalog is required, too. To switch to Catalog mode, use the following call:

```
m.DisplayMode = WebPartManager.CatalogDisplayMode;
```

There are three catalog controls available:

- PageCatalogPart: All removed Web Parts are listed here. By default this catalog is empty. If you don't provide a PageCatalogPart control, then the user won't be able to readd removed Web Parts. You can omit this control if closing of Web Parts is disabled, too.
- DeclarativeCatalogPart: This catalog contains a list of statically defined Web Parts available on the page.
- ImportCatalogPart: This zone allows the user to upload and import Web Part definition files.

ConnectionsZone

ConnectionsZone allows the definition of connections between data Web Parts. Typically, this creates a parent/child relationship or a list/details view using two different Web Parts.

WebPart's Class Hierarchy

A Web Part is a user control that implements at least the abstract WebPart base class. This includes several base classes and interfaces that the Web Part manager employs to interact with a custom Web Part (see Figure 6–12).

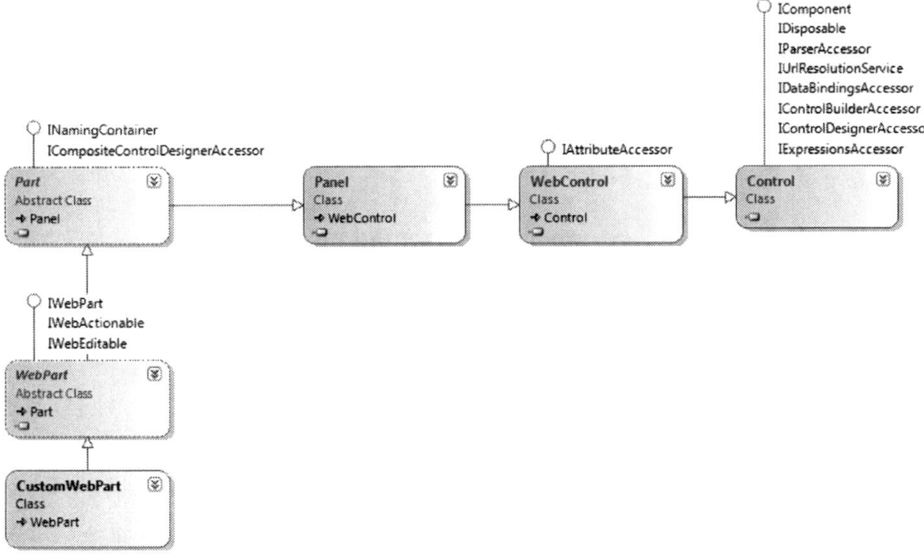

***Figure 6–12.** Base classes and interfaces for a custom Web Part*

The WebControl class provides the basic behavior of a user control. The Panel class, next in the hierarchy, ensures that the control appears as a rectangle. The IWebPart interface provides the descriptive aspects, with such properties as Title, Description, and TitleIconImageUrl. IWebActionable provides the Verbs property, a collection of so-called *verbs*. A verb defines an action and usually appears in the context menu of the Web Part as a menu item. The WebPartVerb class is a Web Part–specific implementation that supports a checked state (Checked property), a ClientScriptHandler and ServerClickHandler to launch the action, and menu item–specific properties such as Enabled, Text, Visible, and ImageUrl.

Along with the Web Part's properties, many attributes can be used to modify the design-time experience. Remember that a Web Part's design time is when the user adds it to a Web Part page. The attributes decorating the Web Part properties are responsible for

- Personalizing behavior
- Customizing the property pane and the properties' behavior
- Controlling the connectivity between Web Parts

Table 6–3 summarizes the attributes available.

***Table 6–3.** Web Part Attributes to Modify Properties*

Name	Description
`WebBrowsable`	Controls whether the property is visible in the property grid.
`Personalizable`	Activates the per-user settings.
`WebDisplayName`	Provides a friendly name for the property grid.
`ConnectionProvider`	Identifies the callback method that acts as the control's data provider.
`ConnectionConsumer`	Identifies the callback method that acts as the control's data consumer.
`WebPartStorage`	Determines in what scope the property data is stored. It is normally set to `Storage.Personal` so that settings are user-specific. However, you should set the storage to `None` if the Web Part contains constant values.
`WebDescription`	Provides a description that appears as a tooltip in the property grid.
`SPWebCategoryName`	Defines the category under which the property appears.

The first five attributes are standard ASP.NET attributes found in the `System.Web.UI.WebControls.WebParts` namespace, while the others are SharePoint-specific attributes from the `Microsoft.SharePoint.WebPartPages` namespace.

Advanced Web Part Development

Web Parts support many features and sophisticated customization options. This section explains more advanced techniques for the SharePoint page editor, SharePoint Designer, and the design-time experience.

Personalizing Web Parts

SharePoint Web Parts are intended to enable personalized versions of a page. The ASP.NET Web Part framework supports this via the `Personalizable` attribute. Internally, the location of a Web Part, the current state (closed or open), and other personalizable settings are stored in the database.

```
[Personalizable(true)]
public string myProperty
{
  ...
}
```

The attribute has several overloads. Either you simply turn the personalization on (`true`) or use one of the following two options: `PersonalizationsScope.User` or `PersonalizationsScope.Shared`. You can decide for each property whether each user is allowed to store his or her own value. If the property is shared, the user needs additional rights to change the value. From the perspective of SharePoint, he or she must be permitted to edit the shared version of the page.

For a property to be made personalizable, it must meet the following requirements:

- It must be public.
- It must have both public getter and setter accessors.
- It must not be decorated with the `ReadOnlyAttribute`.
- It must not be an indexer.

A property marked with `ReadOnly` is still visible in the property pane.

Customizing the Property Pane

Web Parts are intended to be used by end users. That increases the expectations of your components. Web Parts are—barring extremely simple ones—highly configurable components. SharePoint users normally cannot access `web.config` or Central Administration. Therefore, you have to provide any required configuration settings and keep in mind that inexperienced users will use your component, too.

As shown in the previous sections, you can use attributes on properties to add metainformation that supports the design-time experience. For the end user, the time they add or move a Web Part is the design time. The property pane is what appears at the right-hand side of the page. It's a simplified way—using HTML—to present properties in much the same style as the property grid in Visual Studio. The property grid uses reflection to gather information about properties (both the underlying data type and any custom attributes) and manage the UI.

■ **Note** The term *property* is used intentionally. You cannot use public fields or methods to show settings in the property pane. The reflection mechanism looks only for public properties, and further investigates attributes solely on those public properties.

The metainformation needed for each property in the property pane is

- The name (e.g., "Alternative Text" in Figure 6–13)
- The type that controls the UI element (e.g., `TextBox` for `String`)
- An optional description (e.g., the "To link to an image . . ." text)
- A category that manages where the element appears (e.g., Layout or Advanced)

To have full control of the property pane, you need a complete grasp of how properties work.

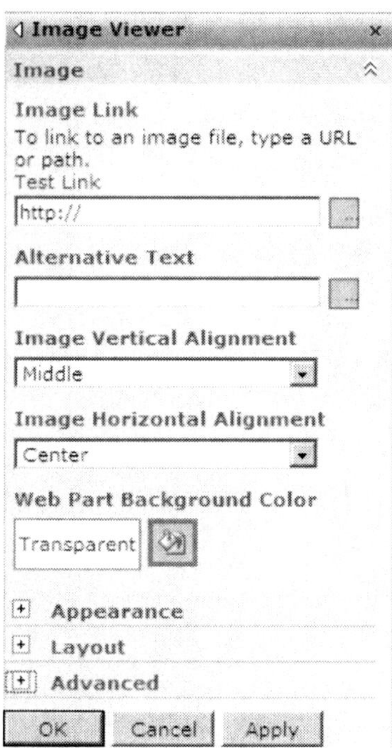

Figure 6–13. *The property pane for Web Parts with some custom properties*

Understanding Properties

Properties of a programming language like C# seem to be a simple thing. However, when a property controls the design of the property pane and the behavior in code, it's more than just a simple property.

A property consists of

- *A name*: This is the name that appears by default in the pane and is used in code.
- *A type*: This is the type used in code. To support a UI, the type must be converted into another type that a specific control supports.
- *A description*: This is a descriptive name shown in the UI and managed by an attribute. It has no meaning in code and is an optional element. Use `WebDescriptionAttribute` to decorate the property.
- *A category*: The property pane is divided in categories. This element is managed by an attribute. It's optional because the property pane provides a default category. Use `WebCategoryAttribute` to decorate the property.
- *A type converter*: This is optional if the editable type and the internal type differ. If the internal type is complex, such as a color (`System.Drawing.Color`), and the UI provides a simple text box (returns `System.String`), a conversion is necessary. Using a type converter is the standard .NET way to convert values between types using custom code.

- *A readonly flag*: This disables user access to publicly visible properties. The property is still writable from code and is still visible in the property pane. Mark a property with the ReadOnlyAttribute to put the input control into the disabled state.
- *A browsable flag*: Turns on or off visibility in the pane without affecting public access to the property via code. Use the WebBrowsable attribute to make the property visible in the property pane.
- *An editor flag*: HtmlDesignerAttribute provides a custom editor page for a value and appears as a pop-up window, extending the property's UI.

A Web Part can control more of its own behavior by overriding properties and methods. For some functions, the implementation of additional classes is required.

■ **Note** FriendlyNameAttribute, which was used in previous versions, is deprecated. Use WebDescriptionAttribute instead.

Depending on their type, properties can create specific controls in the property pane. Table 6–4 shows the default mapping between types and controls.

Table 6–4. *Types That Show as a Particular Control (All Other Types Create a TextBox)*

Type	Control
Boolean	Checkbox
String	TextBox
Enum	DropDown
Int, Float	TextBox
DateTime	TextBox
Unit	TextBox

You may wonder how the Height and Width properties in Figure 6–14 render with the more sophisticated control. The editing zone at the right of a Web Part page in Edit mode is indeed a <EditZone> control. There are several predefined editors that handle a subset of the default properties exposed by a Web Part (inherited from either a WebPart or Part class).

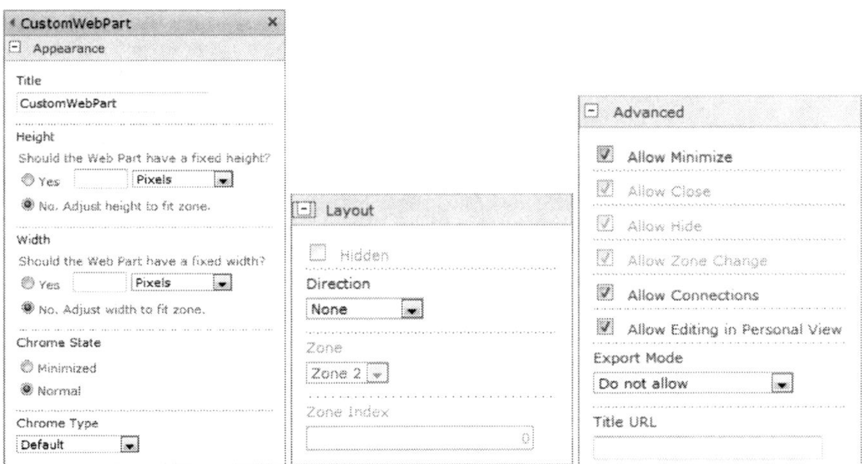

***Figure 6–14.** Predefined Web Part editor parts (from left to right: AppearanceEditorPart, LayoutEditorPart, and BehaviorEditorPart)*

If you scroll down the editor pane, you'll find the categories you defined using the `WebCategoryAttribute`, and probably a section called Miscellaneous that contains all the editable properties that don't have a category. As shown in Figure 6–14, the internally used editors provide a more impressive user experience. (In the next section, you'll find more information about custom editor panes.)

Global Settings

There are a few attributes you can use to decorate a Web Part. `ToolboxItemAttribute` should be set to `false` to prevent the Web Part from being added to the Visual Studio toolbox:

```
[ToolboxItemAttribute(false)]
```

Editing Complex Properties with Editor Parts

Storing more complex values than just strings or integers is more complicated. Editing these properties with the standard generated interface using the `WebBrowsable` and `Personalizable` attributes does not work, since it only accepts basic types, as shown earlier. To make these properties editable, you have to build an editor part and control the properties in the `SyncChanges` and `ApplyChanges` methods.

Using Editor Parts to Edit Properties

Using the standard approach of marking properties using specific attributes, you can make a Web Part editable as required. But the default user experience for editing is still suboptimal. Firstly, the properties to be edited are located in their own category at the bottom of the list—not easy to find for inexperienced or untrained users. Secondly, the properties often have dependencies and require validation.

ASP.NET contains an abstract class called EditorPart. This class is used with the ASP.NET WebPart class to create customized tool panes. By inheriting from this control, you can customize the appearance and functionality of the tool pane and use standard ASP.NET constructs such as auto postbacks and validations. Start with a new class that inherits from System.Web.UI.WebControls.WebParts.EditorPart. In this class, you have to override two abstract methods and add the controls that you want to use.

The custom editing section exists once per Web Part. Other than for common editor controls, you don't need an attribute to decorate a property. Instead, you must override the CreateEditorParts method. This method returns an EditorPartCollection that contains all EditorPart objects presented in the editor pane. That includes but is not limited to the standard parts explained previously. However, by default all properties get a generic input control. To avoid duplicate controls, you must exclude the property you wish to be editable in the customized part. This can be done by removing the WebBrowsable attribute or setting its initial value to false. The latter approach is recommended so that others reading the code can see that this is a publicly editable property with some controls found elsewhere:

```
[WebBrowsable(false)]
```

You can add one or more controls to a custom editor pane. If you have just one property, it's very simple:

```
public override EditorPartCollection CreateEditorParts()
{
    List<EditorPart> editorParts = new List<EditorPart>();
    EditorPart part = new CustomEditorPart();
    part.ID = this.ID + "_stateEditorPart";
    editorParts.Add(part);
    EditorPartCollection coll = base.CreateEditorParts();
    return new EditorPartCollection(coll, editorParts);
}
```

This method returns a merge of the existing EditorParts and the custom ones. In this example only one additional EditorPart, named CustomEditorPart, has been added. The ID property must be explicitly set to some unique name. Because only one instance of the EditorPart is usually present on a page, a static suffix is adequate. The skeleton of such a control looks as shown in Listing 6–15.

Listing 6–15. *Skeleton of an EditorPart Control*

```
using System;
using System.Collections.Generic;
using System.Linq;
using System.Text;
using System.Web.UI.WebControls;
using System.Web.UI.WebControls.WebParts;

namespace Apress.SP2010.WebPartPageProject.MyWebParts
{
    public class CustomEditorPart : EditorPart
    {

        public CustomEditorPart()
            : base()
        {
        }

        protected override void CreateChildControls()
        {
```

```
            base.CreateChildControls();
        }

        public override bool ApplyChanges()
        {
            EnsureChildControls();
            return true;
        }

        public override void SyncChanges()
        {
            EnsureChildControls();
        }
    }
}
```

The controls that appear in the editor must be added to the control collection in either the `CreateChildControls` or the `Render` method. This is similar to the way you create the content of a Web Part. In this example, the custom editor creates a list of `RadioButton` elements instead of a `DropDown` control. This requires some conversion between the underlying `Enum` type and the string types used for list items. A reference to the `WebPart` control gives access to the values to create the appropriate controls and write the values back:

```
private CustomWebPart webPart;
private readonly Type enumType = typeof(CustomWebPart.States);
```

Adding Controls

The controls are added in the `CreateChildControls` method. This is where you should place most of your control logic in editor parts, Web Parts, and so on.

```
private RadioButtonList rbl;

protected override void CreateChildControls()
{
    base.CreateChildControls();
    // Instead of a drop-down list, create a couple of radio buttons
    rbl = new RadioButtonList();
    webPart = (CustomWebPart)this.WebPartToEdit;

    var items = from i in Enum.GetNames(enumType)
                select new ListItem(i)
                {
                    Selected = Enum.GetName(enumType,
                                     webPart.ControlStatesDrop).Equals(i)
                };
    rbl.Items.AddRange(items.ToArray());
    base.Controls.Add(rbl);
}
```

This method creates the `RadioButtonList`, in which each item represents an `Enum` value. The LINQ statement converts the `Enum` values into `ListItem` controls and sets the currently selected item. The complete list appears with the current value set. Now you need to retrieve and apply changes.

Syncing Changes

The SyncChanges method is used by the EditorPart to get the values from the Web Part into the editor part.

```
public override void SyncChanges()
{
    EnsureChildControls();
    rbl.Items.FindByValue(Enum.GetName(enumType,
                          webPart.ControlStatesDrop)).Selected = true;
}
```

Firstly, the method ensures that all the controls are present. This calls the CreateChildControls method if required. Then the RadioButton element is retrieved, which matches the currently selected value. Again, the enumType field helps, using the Enum class to transform an enumeration value into a string representation.

Applying Changes

The ApplyChanges method is executed when you click OK or Apply, and sets the property values of your Web Part. SyncChanges is always called directly after the ApplyChanges method to make sure that the properties are in sync.

```
public override bool ApplyChanges()
{
    EnsureChildControls();
    if (rbl.SelectedIndex >= 0)
    {
        webPart.ControlStatesDrop = (CustomWebPart.States)Enum.Parse(enumType,
                                                          rbl.SelectedValue);
        return true;
    }
    else
    {
        return false;
    }
}
```

Again, the EnsureChildControls method call ensures that the controls are properly loaded. The currently selected value is parsed and written back to the Web Part's property.

Handling Validation Errors

In the previous examples we assumed that users don't make any mistakes. We accept any incoming value. That's far from real-world experience, and therefore some validation has to be added. As the properties render automatically, there must be some way to expose an error message. That's done by throwing a WebPartPageUserException.

```
[Personalizable(true)]
[WebBrowsable(true)]
public States ControlStatesDrop
{
     get
     {
         if (ViewState["States"] == null)
         {
```

```
                ViewState["States"] = States.State2;
            }
            return (States) Enum.Parse(typeof(States), ViewState["States"].ToString());
        }
        set
        {
            if (value == States.State3)
            {
              throw new WebPartPageUserException("State 3
                                                    is currently not supported");
            }
            ViewState["States"] = value;
        }
}
```

The exception puts a red message from the constructor's parameter into the editor pane and a generic message on top (see Figure 6–15).

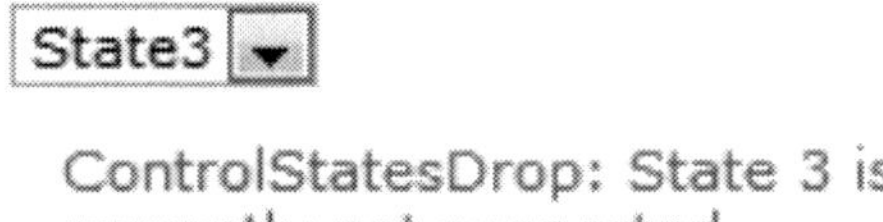

Figure 6–15. *An error message that is autogenerated from the exception*

The message appears when the page is posted back, when either OK or Apply is clicked. The message appears above the controls if a custom `EditorPart` is used as shown in Figure 6–16.

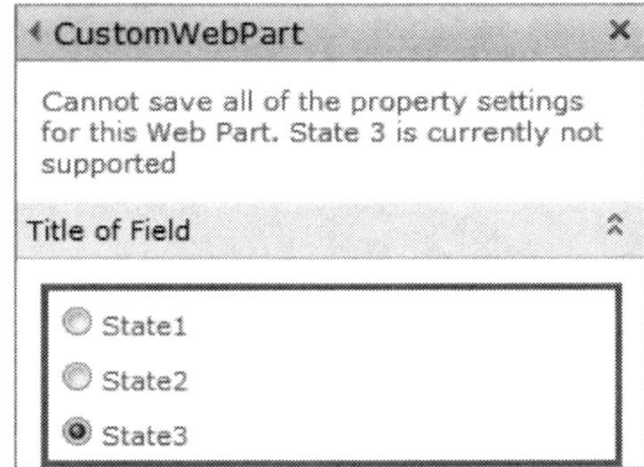

Figure 6–16. *An error message that is autogenerated within a custom EditorPart*

Creating a Custom Editor Part Example

The previous sections explained the basic tasks required to customize the editable section of a Web Part. In this section is an example of a complete Web Part together with a custom editor—putting all the pieces of the puzzle together. Custom editors are often advantageous if you deal with custom types, such as geographic coordinates. The Web Part explained here creates a little map using the Bing client library, and the custom editor allows the setting of the region as well as the coordinates of a *pushpin*—a specific location within the map. The error handler checks whether the coordinates of the pushpin are within the map region.

HOW TO DISPLAY A MAP

The Bing map library comes with an online SDK that makes learning and testing easy. The SDK is at `www.microsoft.com/maps/isdk/ajax`. Google Maps is an alternative with similar features. The SDK can be found at `http://code.google.com/intl/en-US/apis/maps`. We recommend building some test pages outside of SharePoint first, to get familiar with such libraries and integrate the results later into a Web Part.

The project consists of

- A Web Part file, `BingWebPart.cs`
- A Web Part definition, `BingWebPart.webpart`
- A user control (consisting of `BingWebPartUserControl.ascx` and `BingWebPartUserControl.cs`) that defines the visual part of the Web Part and loads the map libraries
- `Coordinates.cs`, which defines the geographical type
- A user control (consisting of `CoordinatesEditor.ascx` and `CoordinatesEditor.cs`) that defines the coordinate input fields
- `CoordinatesEditorPart.cs`, which defines the editor part

All these files are shown in the next three code listings. The results produced by the example are shown in Figure 6–17.

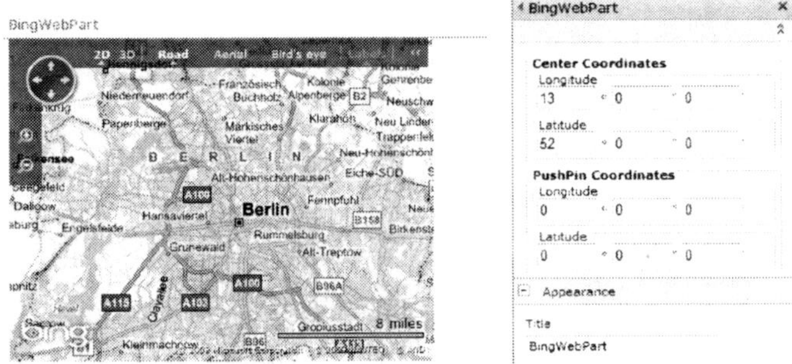

***Figure 6–17.** The Bing map with a default location, and the custom editor*

The Web Part itself defines the minimum required properties. `WebBrowsable` is set to `false` to suppress the generic editors (Listing 6–16).

***Listing 6–16.** The WebPart Class with a Call to the User Control*

```
using System;
using System.ComponentModel;
using System.Runtime.InteropServices;
using System.Web;
using System.Web.UI;
using System.Web.UI.WebControls;
using System.Web.UI.WebControls.WebParts;
using Microsoft.SharePoint;
using Microsoft.SharePoint.WebControls;
using System.Collections.Generic;

namespace Apress.SP2010.WebPartPageProject.BingWebPart
{
    [ToolboxItemAttribute(false)]
    public class BingWebPart : WebPart
    {
        private const string _ascxPath =
             @"~/_CONTROLTEMPLATES/WebPartPageProject/
                BingWebPart/BingWebPartUserControl.ascx";

        public BingWebPart()
        {
        }

        protected override void CreateChildControls()
        {
            BingWebPartUserControl control = this.Page.LoadControl(_ascxPath)
                                             as BingWebPartUserControl;
            Controls.Add(control);
            base.CreateChildControls();
        }

        protected override void RenderContents(HtmlTextWriter writer)
        {
            base.RenderContents(writer);
        }

        public override EditorPartCollection CreateEditorParts()
        {
            List<EditorPart> parts = new List<EditorPart>();
            EditorPart edit = new CoordinatesEditorPart();
            edit.ID = this.ID + "_coordEditor";
            parts.Add(edit);
            return new EditorPartCollection(base.CreateEditorParts(), parts);
        }

        [WebBrowsable(false)]
        [Personalizable(true)]
        public Coordinates CenterCoordinate
        {
            get;
```

```
            set;
        }

        [WebBrowsable(false)]
        [Personalizable(true)]
        public Coordinates PushPin
        {
            get;
            set;
        }

    }
}
```

This code defines the properties that center the map and define a pushpin (marker) that you can set into the map. The code to manage the map is based on JavaScript and defined in the Web Part's markup section (see Listing 6–17).

***Listing 6–17.** The User Controls Markup Part*

```
%@ Assembly Name="$SharePoint.Project.AssemblyFullName$" %>
<%@ Assembly Name="Microsoft.Web.CommandUI, Version=14.0.0.0, Culture=neutral,
             PublicKeyToken=71e9bce111e9429c" %>
<%@ Register Tagprefix="SharePoint" Namespace="Microsoft.SharePoint.WebControls"
             Assembly="Microsoft.SharePoint, ..." %>
<%@ Register Tagprefix="Utilities" Namespace="Microsoft.SharePoint.Utilities"
             Assembly="Microsoft.SharePoint, ..." %>
<%@ Register Tagprefix="asp" Namespace="System.Web.UI"
             Assembly="System.Web.Extensions, ..." %>
<%@ Import Namespace="Microsoft.SharePoint" %>
<%@ Register Tagprefix="WebPartPages" Namespace="Microsoft.SharePoint.WebPartPages"
             Assembly="Microsoft.SharePoint, ..." %>
<%@ Control Language="C#" AutoEventWireup="true"
    CodeBehind="BingWebPartUserControl.ascx.cs"
   Inherits="WebPartPageProject.BingWebPart.BingWebPartUserControl" %>
<script type="text/javascript"
        src="http://dev.virtualearth.net/mapcontrol/mapcontrol.ashx?v=6.2">
</script>
<script type="text/javascript">

/// <reference path="http://dev.virtualearth.net/mapcontrol/mapcontrol.ashx?v=6.2" />
function GetMap() {
    var map = new VEMap('<% = spBingMap.ClientID %>');
    var lat = document.getElementById('<% = latField.ClientID  %>').value;
    var lng = document.getElementById('<% = lngField.ClientID  %>').value;
    var latlng = new VELatLong(lat, lng);
    map.LoadMap(latlng, 10, 'r', false);
}
window.onload = function () {
    GetMap();
}
</script>
<div id="spBingMap" runat="server" style="position:relative; width:400px; height:300px"></div>
<asp:HiddenField runat="server" ID="latField" Value="52.222" />
```

```
<asp:HiddenField runat="server" ID="lngField" Value="13.297" />
```

Even this user control has a code-behind to set or get the values from hidden fields and the dimensions of the <div> container (see Listing 6–18).

Listing 6–18. *The User Control's Code-Behind*

```
using System;
using System.Web.UI;
using System.Web.UI.WebControls;
using System.Web.UI.WebControls.WebParts;
using System.Globalization;

namespace Apress.SP2010.WebPartPageProject.BingWebPart
{
    public partial class BingWebPartUserControl : UserControl
    {
        protected void Page_Load(object sender, EventArgs e)
        {
        }

        public Unit Width
        {
            get { return Unit.Parse(spBingMap.Style[HtmlTextWriterStyle.Width]); }
            set { spBingMap.Style[HtmlTextWriterStyle.Width] = value.ToString(); }
        }

        public Unit Height
        {
            get { return Unit.Parse(spBingMap.Style[HtmlTextWriterStyle.Height]); }
            set { spBingMap.Style[HtmlTextWriterStyle.Height] = value.ToString(); }
        }

        public decimal Longitude
        {
            get { return Convert.ToDecimal(latField.Value); }
            set { latField.Value = value.ToString(CultureInfo.InvariantCulture); }
        }

        public decimal Latitude
        {
            get { return Convert.ToDecimal(lngField.Value); }
            set { lngField.Value = value.ToString(CultureInfo.InvariantCulture); }
        }

    }
}
```

Using the Unit type is just a suggestion. Use the strongest possible type to simplify testing and validation.

Next, the user control is loaded within the CreateChildControls method. By overriding the CreateEditorParts method, the custom editor is shown to support the Coordinates type. This type is used to deal flexibly with complex values, like geographical coordinates (see Listing 6–19).

***Listing 6–19.** A Helper Class That Supports Private Types*

```
using System;
using System.Collections.Generic;
using System.Linq;
using System.Text;
using System.Globalization;
using System.Web.UI;

namespace Apress.SP2010.WebPartPageProject.BingWebPart
{

    public struct DegMinSec
    {
        public int Deg { get; set; }
        public int Min { get; set; }
        public int Sec { get; set; }
    }

    public struct Coordinates
    {

        public Coordinates(DegMinSec lat, DegMinSec lng) : this()
        {
            SetLongitude(lng);
            SetLatitude(lat);

        }

        public static Coordinates Empty
        {
            get
            {
                return new Coordinates();
            }
        }

        public static bool operator ==(Coordinates c1, Coordinates c2)
        {
            return (c1.Latitude == c2.Latitude && c1.Longitude == c2.Longitude);
        }

        public static bool operator !=(Coordinates c1, Coordinates c2)
        {
            return (c1.Latitude != c2.Latitude || c1.Longitude != c2.Longitude);
        }

        public decimal Latitude { get; set; }
        public decimal Longitude { get; set; }

        public bool IsInRange(Coordinates from, Coordinates to)
        {
            return (
```

```
            this.Longitude > from.Longitude && this.Latitude > from.Latitude &&
            this.Longitude < to.Longitude && this.Latitude < to.Latitude);
        }

        public DegMinSec LatitudeDegrees
        {
            get
            {
                return GetDegMinSec(Latitude);
            }
        }

        public DegMinSec LongitudeDegrees
        {
            get
            {
                return GetDegMinSec(Longitude);
            }
        }

        private static DegMinSec GetDegMinSec(decimal longlat)
        {
            int deg = (int)Math.Truncate(longlat);
            decimal mins = (longlat - deg) * 60;
            int min = (int)Math.Truncate(mins);
            int sec = (int)(mins - min) * 60;
            return new DegMinSec()
            {
                Deg = deg,
                Min = min,
                Sec = sec
            };
        }

        public void SetLongitude(DegMinSec t)
        {
            Longitude = t.Deg + t.Min + t.Sec;
        }

        public void SetLatitude(DegMinSec t)
        {
            Latitude = t.Deg + t.Min + t.Sec;
        }

        public override string ToString()
        {
            return String.Format(CultureInfo.CurrentCulture, "{0}:{1}",
                                 Latitude, Longitude);
        }

    }
}
```

The operator overloads make it easier when later checking the values. It makes sense to deal with business data objects like this instead of scalar types. The DegMinSec struct defined at the beginning simplifies converting values between the degrees/minutes/seconds format and the decimal format, which map libraries like Bing prefer. This makes designing the user controls simpler. The first user control is the definition for one triplet of data (see Listing 6–20).

Listing 6–20. *The Markup of the Custom Editor*

```
<%@ Assembly Name="$SharePoint.Project.AssemblyFullName$" %>
<%@ Assembly Name="Microsoft.Web.CommandUI, Version=14.0.0.0, Culture=neutral,
             PublicKeyToken=71e9bce111e9429c" %>
<%@ Register TagPrefix="SharePoint" Namespace="Microsoft.SharePoint.WebControls"
             Assembly="Microsoft.SharePoint, ..." %>
<%@ Register TagPrefix="Utilities" Namespace="Microsoft.SharePoint.Utilities"
             Assembly="Microsoft.SharePoint, ..." %>
<%@ Register TagPrefix="asp" Namespace="System.Web.UI"
             Assembly="System.Web.Extensions, ..." %>
<%@ Import Namespace="Microsoft.SharePoint" %>
<%@ Register TagPrefix="WebPartPages" Namespace="Microsoft.SharePoint.WebPartPages"
    Assembly="Microsoft.SharePoint, ..." %>
<%@ Control Language="C#" AutoEventWireup="true"
            CodeBehind="CoordinatesEditor.ascx.cs"
            Inherits="WebPartPageProject.BingWebPart.CoordinatesEditor" %>
<fieldset>
    <legend>
        <asp:Label runat="server" ID="lblControl" Font-Bold="true"></asp:Label></legend>
    <fieldset title="Longitude">
        <legend>Longitude </legend>
        <asp:TextBox ID="TextBoxDegLng" runat="server" Width="50px"></asp:TextBox>
        &deg;
        <asp:TextBox ID="TextBoxMinLng" runat="server" Width="50px"></asp:TextBox>"
        <asp:TextBox ID="TextBoxSecLng" runat="server" Width="50px"></asp:TextBox>'
    </fieldset>
    <fieldset title="Latitude">
        <legend>Latitude </legend>
        <asp:TextBox ID="TextBoxDegLat" runat="server" Width="50px"></asp:TextBox>
        &deg;
        <asp:TextBox ID="TextBoxMinLat" runat="server" Width="50px"></asp:TextBox>"
        <asp:TextBox ID="TextBoxSecLat" runat="server" Width="50px"></asp:TextBox>'
    </fieldset>
</fieldset>
```

The code-behind file (see Listing 6–21) sets or gets the values.

Listing 6–21. *The Code-Behind Class of the Custom Editor*

```
using System;
using System.Web.UI;
using System.Web.UI.WebControls;
using System.Web.UI.WebControls.WebParts;
using WebPartPageProject.BingWebPart;

namespace Apress.SP2010.WebPartPageProject.BingWebPart
{
```

```
    public partial class CoordinatesEditor : UserControl
    {
        protected void Page_Load(object sender, EventArgs e)
        {
        }

        public Coordinates Coordinate
        {
            set
            {
                DegMinSec lat = value.LatitudeDegrees;
                DegMinSec lng = value.LongitudeDegrees;
                TextBoxDegLat.Text = lat.Deg.ToString();
                TextBoxMinLat.Text = lat.Min.ToString();
                TextBoxSecLat.Text = lat.Sec.ToString();
                TextBoxDegLng.Text = lng.Deg.ToString();
                TextBoxMinLng.Text = lng.Min.ToString();
                TextBoxSecLng.Text = lng.Sec.ToString();
            }
            get
            {
                DegMinSec lat = new DegMinSec();
                DegMinSec lng = new DegMinSec();
                lat.Deg = Int32.Parse(TextBoxDegLat.Text);
                lat.Min = Int32.Parse(TextBoxMinLat.Text);
                lat.Sec = Int32.Parse(TextBoxSecLat.Text);
                lng.Deg = Int32.Parse(TextBoxDegLng.Text);
                lng.Min = Int32.Parse(TextBoxMinLng.Text);
                lng.Sec = Int32.Parse(TextBoxSecLng.Text);
                return new Coordinates(lat, lng);
            }
        }

        public string Title
        {
            get { return lblControl.Text; }
            set { lblControl.Text = value; }
        }
    }
}
```

There is nothing ambitious here. The code does not contain any validation or error checking, for the sake of clarity. Consider adding the necessary validator controls and exposing error messages to the Web Part control. This user control is used twice to define the custom editor for the coordinates and the pushpin value. This is done in the `EditorPart` implementation shown in Listing 6–22.

Listing 6–22. *The Editor Part That References Custom Controls*

```
using System;
using System.Collections.Generic;
using System.Linq;
using System.Text;
using System.Web.UI.WebControls.WebParts;
using System.Web.UI.WebControls;
```

```
namespace Apress.SP2010.WebPartPageProject.BingWebPart
{
    public class CoordinatesEditorPart : EditorPart
    {

        private const string _ascxPath = @"~/_CONTROLTEMPLATES/WebPartPageProject/
                                          BingWebPart/CoordinatesEditor.ascx";

        public CoordinatesEditorPart()
            : base()
        {
        }

        BingWebPart webPart;
        CoordinatesEditor center;
        CoordinatesEditor pushp;

        protected override void CreateChildControls()
        {
            center = this.Page.LoadControl(_ascxPath) as CoordinatesEditor;
            center.Title = "Center Coordinates";
            pushp = this.Page.LoadControl(_ascxPath) as CoordinatesEditor;
            pushp.Title = "PushPin Coordinates";
            Controls.Add(center);
            Controls.Add(pushp);
            base.CreateChildControls();
            webPart = (BingWebPart)this.WebPartToEdit;
            center.Coordinate = webPart.CenterCoordinate;
            pushp.Coordinate = webPart.PushPin;
        }

        public override bool ApplyChanges()
        {
            EnsureChildControls();
            if (pushp.Coordinate != Coordinates.Empty)
            {
                webPart.CenterCoordinate = center.Coordinate;
                webPart.PushPin = pushp.Coordinate;
            }
            return true;
        }

        public override void SyncChanges()
        {
            EnsureChildControls();
            webPart.CenterCoordinate = center.Coordinate;
            webPart.PushPin = pushp.Coordinate;
        }
    }
}
```

The CreateChildControls method creates the two sections that comprise the user control. They are bound to the Web Part by the SyncChanges and ApplyChanges methods. It's recommended that you add the appropriate error-checking code to ApplyChanges to avoid invalid values being saved. Now all the pieces of a complex Web Part with a custom editor are available. The two user controls can be saved to the CONTROLTEMPLATES folder. In the Visual Studio project, the XML in Listing 6–23 defines the target.

Listing 6–23. *The Project Item File for the Bing Map Web Part*

```
<?xml version="1.0" encoding="utf-8"?>
<ProjectItem Type="Microsoft.VisualStudio.SharePoint.VisualWebPart"
             SupportedTrustLevels="FullTrust" SupportedDeploymentScopes="Site"
             xmlns="http://schemas.microsoft.com/VisualStudio/2010/
                    SharePointTools/SharePointProjectItemModel">
  <Files>
    <ProjectItemFile Source="Elements.xml" Target="BingWebPart\"
                     Type="ElementManifest" />
    <ProjectItemFile Source="BingWebPart.webpart" Target="BingWebPart\"
                     Type="ElementFile" />
    <ProjectItemFile Source="..\BingWebPart\BingWebPartUserControl.ascx"
                     Target="CONTROLTEMPLATES\WebPartPageProject\BingWebPart\"
                     Type="TemplateFile" />
    <ProjectItemFile Source="..\BingWebPart\CoordinatesEditor.ascx"
                     Target="CONTROLTEMPLATES\WebPartPageProject\BingWebPart\"
                     Type="TemplateFile" />
  </Files>
  <SafeControls>
    <SafeControl Name="SafeControlEntry1"
                 Assembly="$SharePoint.Project.AssemblyFullName$"
                 Namespace="WebPartPageProject.BingWebPart" TypeName="*"
                 IsSafe="true" />
  </SafeControls>
</ProjectItem>
```

The entries correspond with the settings for the path to the ASCX file defined in the user control.

■ **Caution** Using visual controls that install ASCX files in the CONTROLTEMPLATES folder precludes you from using sandboxed solutions.

With all this, you can create and deploy the Web Part and get the results, as shown previously in Figure 6–17.

Editing Complex Properties Using a Pop-Up

Even if it is possible to use a custom editor pane, it is sometimes better to hook into SharePoint's client framework. This is especially true if the data types become more complex. For the pop-up that appears when the ellipses button (...) is clicked, you have to provide a regular web page.

To accomplish this, decorate the property you want to edit with such a pop-up with HtmlDesignerAttribute. It's defined in the Microsoft.SharePoint.WebPartPages namespace. Adding this with the using statement is not recommended, because in this namespace several classes have the same name as in System.Web.UI.WebControls.WebParts, and name resolution conflicts will result. Instead, use the using statement with a named assignment:

```
using WPP = Microsoft.SharePoint.WebPartPages;
```

The property is decorated as shown in the prior sections. There is just one new attribute:

```
[WebBrowsable(true)]
[Personalizable(true)]
[WebDisplayName("Complex Url")]
[WPP.HtmlDesignerAttribute(@"/_layouts/VisualWebPartEditor/PopupEditor.aspx",
     DialogFeatures = "center:yes; dialogHeight:40px",
     HtmlEditorBuilderType = BrowserBuilderType.Dynamic)]
public string ComplexUrl
{
    get;
    set;
}
```

The attribute requires at least a URL for the pop-up. This can be any folder to which your SharePoint web has access. In the example, the LAYOUTS folder is used. The attribute cannot resolve the ~ token, so you must provide a completely resolved relative name here. The DialogFeatures parameter takes JavaScript values that are similar to those used in the window.open() function. Finally, set the HtmlEditorBuilderType to the Dynamic option—the only one supported in this context.

This is sufficient to make the page pop up on demand. The page requires some JavaScript code to retrieve the current value and return the modified one. In addition, you can use the very simple dialog.master master page to ensure a consistent look and feel. This master page provides head and body sections, as well as predefined buttons to close and cancel.

A minimal but complete page could look like Listing 6–24.

Listing 6–24. *Pop-Up Editor Using the dialog.master Master Page*

```
<%@ Assembly Name="$SharePoint.Project.AssemblyFullName$" %>
<%@ Import Namespace="Microsoft.SharePoint.ApplicationPages" %>
<%@ Register TagPrefix="SharePoint" Namespace="Microsoft.SharePoint.WebControls"
    Assembly="Microsoft.SharePoint, ..." %>
<%@ Register TagPrefix="Utilities" Namespace="Microsoft.SharePoint.Utilities"
    Assembly="Microsoft.SharePoint, .." %>
<%@ Register TagPrefix="asp" Namespace="System.Web.UI"
    Assembly="System.Web.Extensions, ..." %>
<%@ Import Namespace="Microsoft.SharePoint" %>
<%@ Assembly Name="Microsoft.Web.CommandUI, ..." %>

<%@ Page Language="C#" AutoEventWireup="true" CodeBehind="PopupEditor.aspx.cs"
         Inherits="VisualWebPartEditor.Layouts.VisualWebPartEditor.PopupEditor"
         MasterPageFile="~/_layouts/dialog.master" %>

<asp:Content runat="server" ContentPlaceHolderID="PlaceHolderAdditionalPageHead">
    <script language="javascript" type="text/javascript">

    var isOkay = false;
    var oldValue = "";

    function addOnLoadEvent(func) {
        var oldonload = window.onload;
```

```
        if (typeof window.onload != 'function') {
            window.onload = func;
        } else {
            window.onload = function () {
                if (oldonload) {
                    oldonload();
                }
                func();
            }
        }
    }

    function addOnUnLoadEvent(func) {
        var oldonunload = window.onunload;
        if (typeof window.onunload != 'function') {
            window.onunload = func;
        } else {
            window.onunload = function () {
                if (oldonunload) {
                    oldonunload();
                }
                func();
            }
        }
    }

    addOnLoadEvent(function () {
        var input = window.dialogArguments;
        var field = document.getElementById("<%= urlField.ClientID %>");
        oldValue = input;
        field.value = input;
    });

    addOnUnLoadEvent(function () {
        var field = document.getElementById("<%= urlField.ClientID %>");
        window.returnValue = (isOkay) ? field.value : oldValue;
    });

    function CloseOkButton() {
        isOkay = true;
        doCancel();
    }
    </script>
</asp:Content>
<asp:Content runat="server" ContentPlaceHolderID="PlaceHolderDialogDescription">
    Edit the URL field.
</asp:Content>
<asp:Content runat="server" ContentPlaceHolderID="PlaceHolderDialogBodyMainSection">
    Please enter a valid URL:
   <asp:TextBox runat="server" ID="urlField" />
</asp:Content>
```

The major part is the script code required to add the `window.onload` and `window.onunload` events to take over the current parameter and write back to the Web Part. Two helper functions ensure that the events are added to probably existing events. The load event function reads `window.dialogArguments`, a string passed to the pop-up internally via the `showModalDialog` function. It is written into the `TextBox` control. For more ambitious solutions, consider writing the value into a hidden field for further reference. During the `unload` event, the current value is written into `window.returnValue`. The Web Part receives this internally and without further coding.

One final step is required to change the behavior of the supplied OK button from the `dialog.master` page. In the page's code-behind, the client click event is changed to invoke a private function, `CloseOkButton`. It sets the variable `isOkay` to indicate that the value should be taken and then forces the dialog to close. The default behavior is to simply post back the page and leave it open.

```
namespace VisualWebPartEditor.Layouts.VisualWebPartEditor
{
    public partial class PopupEditor : LayoutsPageBase
    {
        protected void Page_Load(object sender, EventArgs e)
        {
            ((Microsoft.SharePoint.WebControls.DialogMaster)Master).
                          OkButton.OnClientClick = "CloseOkButton();";
        }
    }
}
```

The code assumes that you indeed use the `dialog.master` page and the associated code from the `DialogMaster` class. Here you have access to the controls defined on this page.

If everything is deployed and run, it creates a dialog with some predefined styles taken from the master page. The result is shown in Figure 6–18.

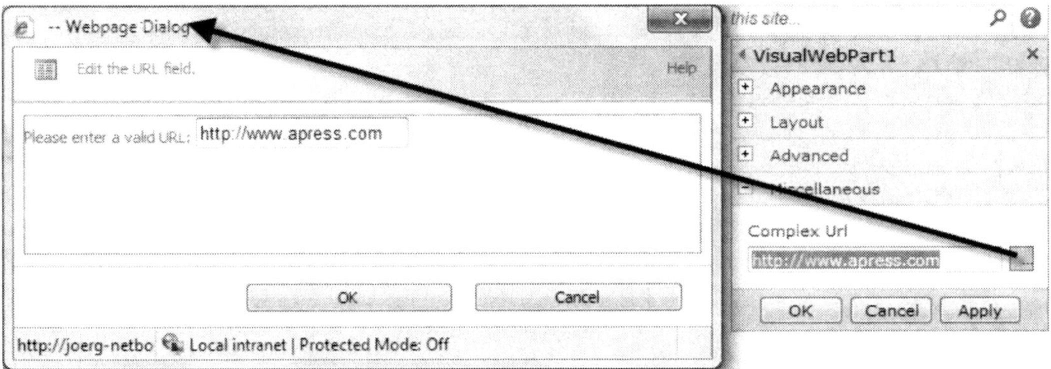

Figure 6–18. *Clicking the ellipses button in the property pane opens an attractive dialog.*

The example page is an ASPX page that allows you to use the master page. However, you can create a simple page using plain HTML and code the complete active portion on the client side using JavaScript. Consider using web services or other advanced scripting techniques for more comprehensive tasks.

Connectable Web Parts

The SharePoint Web Part infrastructure supplies a standardized set of interfaces called *connection interfaces* that allow Web Parts to exchange information with each other at runtime. For example, SharePoint's built-in List Web Part can provide a row of data to any other Web Part that can consume that row. Technically, this becomes a send/receive pipeline.

The interfaces ensure a high level of abstraction. Developers can create connectable Web Parts using data connection without knowing anything about the other connecting Web Parts—only these interfaces. As for the other Web Part classes and interfaces, the technique is completely taken from ASP.NET; no SharePoint-specific interfaces or classes are used.

Understanding Data Connections

To connect anything, two pieces are required. This requires a little extra effort for the initial steps with data connections. However, several built-in Web Parts provide data connections and can be used as data providers. Generally, the provider is the *sending* component while the consumer is the *receiving* component. Sending and receiving implies a communication channel. However, the connection is made via callbacks instead. To create a provider and a consumer, you need methods decorated with the `ConnectionProvider` and `ConnectionConsumer` attributes, respectively. Both methods use one common interface that is shared between the controls. The interface is used to transfer a specific data structure.

In the first example that follows, the interface is used to transfer the state of a `RadioButton` group and show the selection in another Web Part:

```
public interface ICurrentSelection
{
   int SelectionID { get; }
}
```

The provider implements this interface and sends it using a public method:

```
[ConnectionProvider("Selection ID", AllowsMultipleConnections = true)]
public ICurrentSelection GetMyProvider()
{
  return this;
}
```

The consumer receives the data from the provider:

```
private ICurrentSelection myProvider;

[ConnectionConsumer("Selection ID")]
public void RegisterMyProvider(ICurrentSelection provider)
{
  this.myProvider = provider;
}
```

During the render process, the Web Part accesses the object to retrieve the transferred data:

```
protected override RenderContents(HtmlTextWriter writer)
{
  if (this.myProvider != null)
  {
    lblSelection.text = myProvider.SelectionID;
  }
  else
```

```
  {
    lblSelection.text = "";
  }
}
```

While this works well with private interfaces, you will find that the types of data being transferred often have similar schemas. ASP.NET provides three predefined generic interfaces for the common types of data. (An example using these interfaces is in the section "Advanced Connection Scenarios.")

Developing Connected Web Parts

The predefined generic interfaces are ideal for lists and similar common data. If you want to transfer private data, such as business objects, you have to define your own interface. This is straightforward. In this section is a simple pair of Web Parts that connect and interact. This is a complete example, composed of the following files:

- The source Web Part (the provider), consisting of
  - `SourceWebPart.webpart`: The Web Part definition file
  - `Elements.xml`: The manifest file
  - `SourceWebPart.cs`: The Web Part itself (not visual, only code)
  - `ImageSelectorProvider.cs`: The interface used by the provider and consumer
- The target Web Part (the consumer), consisting of
  - `TargetWebPart.webpart`: The Web Part definition file
  - `Elements.xml`: The manifest file
  - `TargetWebPart.cs`: The Web Part itself (not visual, only code)
- `Feature.xml`: Combines both Web Parts into one installable feature
- `Package.xml`: Makes the feature a deployable package

The feature can be defined either directly or by using the property grid of the particular solution item. In this example, the packaging is using the manually edited files, as shown next.

Creating the Web Part Definition Files

The package defines what SharePoint receives as a solution. This includes the assembly, as well as the settings for `web.config` (as shown in Listing 6–25).

Listing 6–25. *Definition File for Connected Web Parts*

```
<Solution xmlns="http://schemas.microsoft.com/sharepoint/"
          SolutionId="62ad2e91-9449-45ca-a42d-42f7762fad72">
  <Assemblies>
    <Assembly Location="WebPartPageProject.dll"
              DeploymentTarget="GlobalAssemblyCache">
      <SafeControls>
        <SafeControl Assembly="WebPartPageProject, ..."
```

```
                    Namespace="WebPartPageProject.ConnectedWebPart"
                    TypeName="SourceWebPart"
                    SafeAgainstScript="True" Safe="True" />
        <SafeControl Assembly="WebPartPageProject, ..."
                    Namespace="WebPartPageProject.ConnectedWebPart"
                    TypeName="TargetWebPart"
                    SafeAgainstScript="True" Safe="True" />
      </SafeControls>
    </Assembly>
  </Assemblies>
  <FeatureManifests>
    <FeatureManifest Location="WebPartPageProject_Feature1\Feature.xml" />
  </FeatureManifests>
</Solution>
```

The file contains the instructions to register the Web Parts as "safe," along with the feature definition file:

```
<Feature xmlns="http://schemas.microsoft.com/sharepoint/"
        Title="WebPartPageProject Feature1"
        Id="cd61bb69-d05b-4572-8532-de6a2b0ea90d" Scope="Site">
  <ElementManifests>
    <ElementManifest Location="TargetWebPart\Elements.xml" />
    <ElementFile Location="TargetWebPart\TargetWebPart.webpart" />
    <ElementManifest Location="SourceWebPart\Elements.xml" />
    <ElementFile Location="SourceWebPart\SourceWebPart.webpart" />
  </ElementManifests>
</Feature>
```

This includes the manifest files and the Web Part definitions. For the sake of clarity, these files are simplified as much as possible. The source Web Part's manifest file is shown in Listing 6–26.

Listing 6–26. *The Source Web Part Definition*

```
<?xml version="1.0" encoding="utf-8"?>
<Elements xmlns="http://schemas.microsoft.com/sharepoint/" >
  <Module Name="SourceWebPart" List="113" Url="_catalogs/wp">
    <File Path="SourceWebPart\SourceWebPart.webpart" Url="SourceWebPart.webpart"
          Type="GhostableInLibrary">
      <Property Name="Group" Value="Custom" />
    </File>
  </Module>
</Elements>
```

The `*.webpart` definition referenced there is shown in Listing 6–27.

Listing 6–27. *The Web Part Property Definition*

```
<?xml version="1.0" encoding="utf-8"?>
<webParts>
  <webPart xmlns="http://schemas.microsoft.com/WebPart/v3">
    <metaData>
      <type name="WebPartPageProject.ConnectedWebPart.SourceWebPart,
                 $SharePoint.Project.AssemblyFullName$" />
      <importErrorMessage>$Resources:core,ImportErrorMessage;</importErrorMessage>
```

```
    </metaData>
    <data>
      <properties>
        <property name="Title" type="string">SourceWebPart</property>
        <property name="Description" type="string">Source of a connected WebPart</property>
      </properties>
    </data>
  </webPart>
</webParts>
```

The target Web Part is very similar. First, Listing 6–28 shows the manifest file.

Listing 6–28. *The Manifest File for the Target Web Part*

```
<?xml version="1.0" encoding="utf-8"?>
<Elements xmlns="http://schemas.microsoft.com/sharepoint/" >
  <Module Name="TargetWebPart" List="113" Url="_catalogs/wp">
    <File Path="TargetWebPart\TargetWebPart.webpart" Url="TargetWebPart.webpart"
Type="GhostableInLibrary">
      <Property Name="Group" Value="Custom" />
    </File>
  </Module>
</Elements>
```

Second, Listing 6–29 shows the `*.webpart` definition file.

Listing 6–29. *The Manifest File for the Source*

```
<?xml version="1.0" encoding="utf-8"?>
<webParts>
  <webPart xmlns="http://schemas.microsoft.com/WebPart/v3">
    <metaData>
      <type name="WebPartPageProject.ConnectedWebPart.TargetWebPart,
                  $SharePoint.Project.AssemblyFullName$" />
      <importErrorMessage>$Resources:core,ImportErrorMessage;</importErrorMessage>
    </metaData>
    <data>
      <properties>
        <property name="Title" type="string">TargetWebPart</property>
        <property name="Description" type="string">Target of a connected WebPart
        </property>
      </properties>
    </data>
  </webPart>
</webParts>
```

Now we have all the definitions to get the Web Parts deployed and running. Next, let's inspect the code.

Coding a Connected Web Part

The goal for the pair of Web Parts in the preceding example is an image selector. The source part should show a list of images from which the user can select one. Once selected, the second (target) Web Part should display the selected image. The data transferred from one component to the other is the file name. This is exactly what you have to define in the interface as part of your project:

```
using System;

namespace WebPartPageProject.ConnectedWebPart
{
    public interface IImageSelectorProvider
    {
        string ImageName { get; }
    }
}
```

The source Web Part uses some SharePoint controls, especially the `SPGroupedDropDownList`. This simplifies the selection process by grouping the images using their file extensions.

■ **Tip** For more information about using SharePoint controls, refer to Chapter 10.

The code for the complete sender control is shown in Listing 6–30.

Listing 6–30. *The Sender WebPart's Complete Code*

```
using System;
using System.IO;
using System.ComponentModel;
using System.Web.UI;
using System.Web.UI.WebControls;
using System.Web.UI.WebControls.WebParts;
using Microsoft.SharePoint;
using Microsoft.SharePoint.WebControls;
using Microsoft.SharePoint.Utilities;
using System.Web.UI.HtmlControls;

namespace Apress.SP2010.WebPartPageProject.ConnectedWebPart
{
    [ToolboxItemAttribute(false)]
    public class SourceWebPart : WebPart, IImageSelectorProvider
    {

        private GroupedDropDownList list;

        public SourceWebPart()
        {
        }

        protected override void CreateChildControls()
        {
            base.CreateChildControls();
            try
            {
```

```
            // Few controls with IDs sent to target
            string path = SPUtility.GetGenericSetupPath("TEMPLATE\\IMAGES");
            // Group Drop Box
            SPHtmlSelect dlGroup = new SPHtmlSelect();
            dlGroup.ID = this.ID + "dlGroup";
            dlGroup.Height = 22;
            dlGroup.Width = 100;
            Controls.Add(dlGroup);
            SPHtmlSelect dlCandidate = new SPHtmlSelect();
            dlCandidate.ID = this.ID + "dlCandidate";
            dlCandidate.Height = 22;
            Controls.Add(dlCandidate);
            Button b = new Button();
            b.Text = "Select Image";
            Controls.Add(b);
            Controls.Add(new HtmlGenericControl("br"));
            HtmlGenericControl lblText = new HtmlGenericControl("span");
            lblText.ID = this.ID + "lblText";
            lblText.InnerText = "No image selected";
            Controls.Add(lblText);
            list = new GroupedDropDownList();
            list.GroupControlId = dlGroup.ID;
            list.CandidateControlId = dlCandidate.ID;
            list.DescriptionControlId = lblText.ID;
            string filter = (Page.IsPostBack && dlGroup.Items.Count > 0) ?
                            dlGroup.Items[dlGroup.SelectedIndex].Value : "*.*";
            foreach (string file in Directory.GetFiles(path, filter))
            {
                list.AddItem(
                    Path.GetFileName(file),
                    Path.GetFileNameWithoutExtension(file),
                    file,
                    Path.GetExtension(file).ToLowerInvariant());
            }
            Controls.Add(list);
        }
        catch
        {
        }
    }

    protected override void RenderContents(HtmlTextWriter writer)
    {
        base.RenderContents(writer);
    }

    public string ImageName
    {
        get
        {
            return (list == null) ? null : list.Value;
        }
    }
```

```
        [ConnectionProvider("Image Name", AllowsMultipleConnections=false)]
        public IImageSelectorProvider GetCustomerProvider()
        {
            return this;
        }

    }
}
```

To make the Web Part into a connected one, you have to implement the `IImageSelectorProvider` interface. (Actually, as mentioned earlier, any interface that defines the data object you wish to transfer will do.) Furthermore, one method must be decorated with the `ConnectionProvider` attribute. In the preceding example, the `ConnectionProvider` attribute is defined with a name, "Image Name," which appears in the connection dialog.

As you can see in Figure 6–19, the connection menu dialog creates a virtual item named Send <*Provider Name*> To (in this example, it's Send Image Name To). Keep this in mind when naming the provider so that you create useful and self-explanatory menu items. The `ConnectionProvider` attribute has several properties. The most important ones are

- `AllowMultipleConnections`: If set to `false`, only one other Web Part can connect.
- `DisplayName`: This overrides the value used in the constructor.
- `ConnectionPointType`: This is the type of the connection interface, if a callback is used (see the "Advanced Connection Scenarios" section for more information).

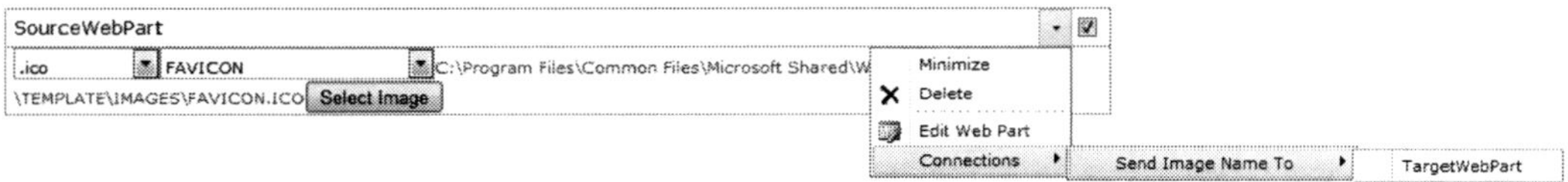

***Figure 6–19.** Establish a connection between two Web Parts.*

Our example Web Part uses the `GroupedDropDownList` control. This control creates a client-side environment to select values using a two-stage drop-down list. This requires two `<select>` elements created by `HtmlSelect` and a `<span>` element that shows the final selection. The span is created using the `HtmlGenericControl` class. Once the appropriate IDs have been set to associate the drop-down lists with the `GroupedDropDownList` control, the UI appears as shown in Figure 6–19. The control itself has no UI. You must perform all layout changes with HTML elements. At a minimum, you should set the element's height, as the default value is inappropriate.

The advantage of the `GroupedDropDownList` control is how easily you can fill it with items. Merely define a group as a string value, and the items get grouped in the first drop-down and filtered automatically in the second.

Because the Web Part appears in two stages—after the first call and after a regular postback—you must recognize this and set the filters appropriately:

```
string filter = (Page.IsPostBack && dlGroup.Items.Count > 0) ?
                              dlGroup.Items[dlGroup.SelectedIndex].Value : "*.*";
```

In this code, the current selection is taken to use the value of the group drop-down to filter the selection drop-down. A simple `GetFiles` call applies the filter:

```
foreach (string file in Directory.GetFiles(path, filter))
```

```
{
  list.AddItem(
    Path.GetFileName(file),
    Path.GetFileNameWithoutExtension(file),
    file,
    Path.GetExtension(file).ToLowerInvariant());
}
```

The whole grouping is done internally. A `foreach` loop adds all values using the `GetExtension` method to create the grouping instruction.

That's all you need to add the Web Part to a page. It will start interrogating the images folder and create a UI, as shown in Figure 6–20.

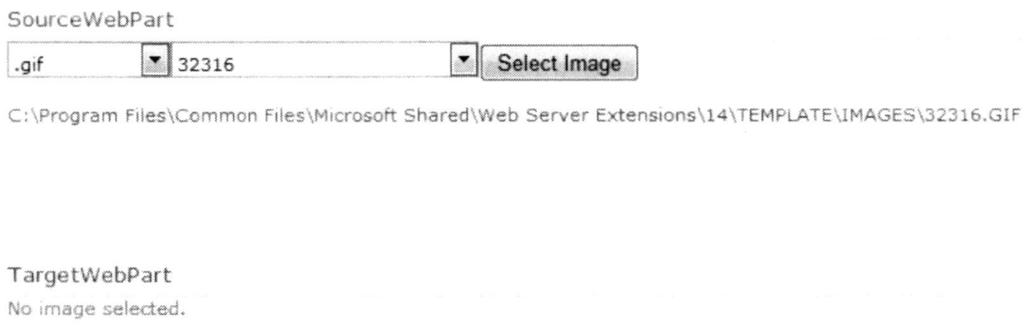

SourceWebPart

.gif | 32316 | Select Image

C:\Program Files\Common Files\Microsoft Shared\Web Server Extensions\14\TEMPLATE\IMAGES\32316.GIF

TargetWebPart

No image selected.

Figure 6–20. *The source Web Part is fully functional.*

Next, we require the target Web Part to receive the selection. This Web Part is much easier to build and simply displays either an error message or an image (see Listing 6–31).

Listing 6–31. *The Target WebPart's Complete Code*

```
using System;
using System.ComponentModel;
using System.Web.UI;
using System.Web.UI.WebControls;
using System.Web.UI.WebControls.WebParts;
using Microsoft.SharePoint;
using Microsoft.SharePoint.Utilities;

namespace Apress.SP2010.WebPartPageProject.ConnectedWebPart
{
    [ToolboxItemAttribute(false)]
    public class TargetWebPart : WebPart
    {

        private IImageSelectorProvider customerProvider;

        public TargetWebPart()
        {
```

```
        }

        [ConnectionConsumer("Image Name")]
        public void RegisterCustomerProvider(IImageSelectorProvider provider)
        {
            this.customerProvider = provider;
        }

        protected override void CreateChildControls()
        {
            base.CreateChildControls();
            Image img = new Image();
            if (customerProvider != null && customerProvider.ImageName != null)
            {
                string path = "/_layouts/images/";
                img.ImageUrl = SPContext.Current.Web.Url + path
                             + customerProvider.ImageName;
                Controls.Add(img);
            }
            else
            {
                Label l = new Label();
                if (customerProvider == null)
                {
                    l.Text = "No Connection established.";
                }
                else
                {
                    l.Text = "No image selected.";
                }
                l.ForeColor = System.Drawing.Color.Red;
                Controls.Add(l);
            }
        }

        protected override void RenderContents(HtmlTextWriter writer)
        {
            base.RenderContents(writer);
        }
    }
}
```

The vital code is the method decorated with the `ConnectionConsumer` attribute. It must match the name of the `ConnectionProvider` attribute. The transferred object matches the interface. The name of the method doesn't matter—something self-explanatory is always recommended. Once the provider control is present, the consumer control has access to it. You must check in the `CreateChildControls` method whether the provider is already present. The first time, when the page loads and nothing is selected, the provider returns `null`. If the page loads again and the postback source is not the provider Web Part, the source property will return `null` again. Both values are used to create an appropriate error message, as shown in Figure 6–20. If everything works, the transferred image name is used to construct an absolute path and the image is displayed on the page (see Figure 6–21).

Figure 6–21. *The target Web Part shows the image selected in the source.*

The established connection can now interact between the two Web Parts, wherever they are on the page. Imagine that such a channel can be established between one source and many targets, allowing the user to choose a Web Part from several that display the same data in different forms and styles, all from the same source. This greatly improves the flexibility and power of Web Parts at little cost.

Advanced Connection Scenarios

One of the classic connection scenarios is the *master-detail pattern*. It's made up of a master view, such as a list that appears as a grid, and a detail view that shows the details for the currently selected row in some customized format. It's a straightforward pattern that is followed by several built-in Web Parts.

If you need to build a customized solution for a similar scenario, with both master and detail parts, you can use the predefined data providers designed to transport the selection. That adds a quasipattern to your Web Part and enables connection to Web Parts developed by others using the same pattern.

Using Generic Interfaces

ASP.NET's Web Part support includes three interfaces that support generic connections:

- `IWebPartTable`
- `IWebPartField`
- `IWebPartRow`

All three interfaces (see Figure 6–22) provide a callback method and a delegate to support it.

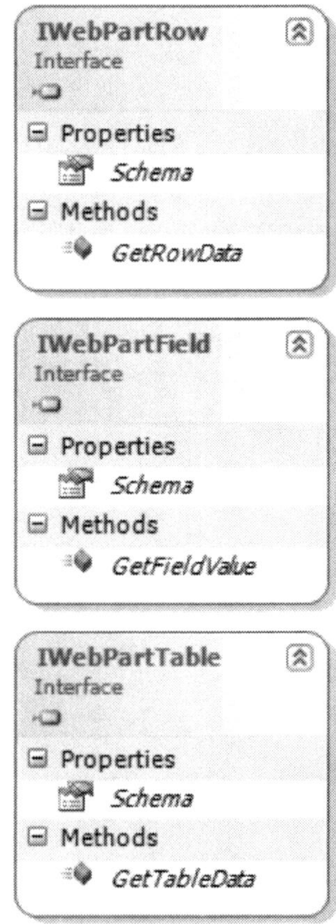

Figure 6–22. *Generic data connection interfaces*

The delegates are `FieldCallback`, `RowCallBack`, and `TableCallback`, respectively. `TableCallback` accepts an `ICollection` type to support multiple tables, while the others accept any `object`. The following example shows a Web Part that contains a list of data. The user's current selection is provided by the `IWebPartField` interface to a consuming Web Part.

The next example retrieves all the lists from the current web and exposes a connection using the `IWebPartField` interface to trigger another Web Part to consume this connection. The master Web Part, created first, displays the data using an `SPGridView` control (see Listing 6–32).

Listing 6–32. *A WebPart That Implements IWebPartField*

```
using System;
using System.ComponentModel;
using System.Web.UI;
```

```
using System.Web.UI.WebControls;
using System.Web.UI.WebControls.WebParts;
using Microsoft.SharePoint;

namespace Apress.SP2010.WebPartPageProject.ConnectedWebParts
{
    [ToolboxItemAttribute(false)]
    public class MasterWebPart : WebPart, IWebPartField
    {

        private SPGridView webLists;
        public string ListName { get; set; }

        public MasterWebPart()
        {
        }

        protected override void CreateChildControls()
        {
            base.CreateChildControls();
            SPWeb web = SPContext.Current.Web;
            var lists = web.Lists.Cast<SPList>();
            webLists = new SPGridView();
            webLists.AutoGenerateColumns = false;
            webLists.DataSource = lists;
            webLists.Columns.Add(new BoundField()
            {
                DataField = "Title",
                HeaderText = "List Name"
            });
            webLists.Columns.Add(new BoundField()
            {
                DataField = "ItemCount",
                HeaderText = "No Items"
            });
            webLists.Columns.Add(new CommandField()
            {
                HeaderText = "Action",
                ControlStyle = { Width = new Unit(70) },
                SelectText = "Show Items",
                ShowSelectButton = true
            });
            webLists.DataKeyNames = new string[] { "Title" };
            webLists.DataBind();
            Controls.Add(webLists);
            webLists.SelectedIndexChanged +=
                new EventHandler(webLists_SelectedIndexChanged);
        }

        void webLists_SelectedIndexChanged(object sender, EventArgs e)
        {
            ListName = webLists.SelectedValue.ToString();
        }
```

```
        public void GetFieldValue(FieldCallback callback)
        {
            callback(Schema.GetValue(this));
        }

        public PropertyDescriptor Schema
        {
            get
            {
                PropertyDescriptorCollection props =
                                TypeDescriptor.GetProperties(this);
                return props.Find("ListName", false);
            }
        }

        [ConnectionProvider("List Name Selection Provider")]
        public IWebPartField GetFieldInterface()
        {
            return this;
        }

    }
}
```

The SPGridView is constructed with three columns, and uses the Title field as the key to retrieve the selected value. The grid shows just the Title and the ItemCount properties. A command field is used to create a callback that retrieves the current value and sends it to the connected detail Web Part (shown next). There are three crucial parts in the master Web Part:

- The GetFieldInterface method, which exposes the interface. Again, the name doesn't matter; it's the return value that the Web Part manager is looking for. The attribute decorating the method ensures that the Web Part manager can find it.
- The Schema property, which exposes the value's source. This requires the source to be a property (a public field will not suffice); it must be declared public, and it must return a serializable value. Here, the ListName method of type string is eminently suitable.
- The GetFieldValue method, exposed by the IWebPartField interface, which receives the callback used in the consumer to retrieve the value. The FieldCallback delegate is predefined, but any similar construct will suffice.

Once the connection details are completed, the consumer Web Part can be constructed. Since it is only a consumer, its code is less complicated, as shown in Listing 6–33.

Listing 6–33. *A Web Part That Receives an Object of Type IWebPartField*

```
using System;
using System.ComponentModel;
using System.Web.UI;
using System.Web.UI.WebControls;
using System.Web.UI.WebControls.WebParts;
using Microsoft.SharePoint;

namespace Apress.SP2010. WebPartPageProject.ConnectedWebParts
```

```
{
    [ToolboxItemAttribute(false)]
    public class DetailWebPart : WebPart
    {
        public DetailWebPart()
        {
            dataLabel = new Label();
        }

        private Label dataLabel;

        protected override void CreateChildControls()
        {
            base.CreateChildControls();
            Controls.Add(dataLabel);
        }

        [ConnectionConsumer("List Name Consumer",
                            AllowsMultipleConnections = false)]
        public void SetFieldInterface(IWebPartField field)
        {
            field.GetFieldValue(new FieldCallback(SetLabel));
        }

        private void SetLabel(object fieldData)
        {
            if (fieldData != null)
            {
                SPList list = SPContext.Current.Web.Lists[fieldData.ToString()];
                dataLabel.Text = String.Format("List {0} with {1} items.",
                    list.Title,
                    list.ItemCount);
            }
        }

    }
}
```

The `SetFieldInterface` method is again needed to inform the Web Part manager to which Web Part it can connect. The attribute is again the key—the name doesn't matter. The method can now use the predefined callback that it hands over to the producer Web Part. This means that the master calls the `SetLabel` method implicitly. The `fieldData` parameter is whatever the master exposes. It's of type `object`, which is both easy to use (since you can transfer any value) and problematic (because users might connect to Web Parts that expose values your code can't handle). Consider adding error-checking routines here, or at least put a `try...catch` clause around the consumer's methods. In the examples, all such code is stripped out for the sake of clarity. Figure 6–23 shows the result the example code produces.

MasterWebPart

List Name	No Items	Action
Announcements	1	Show Items
Authors	0	Show Items
Calendar	0	Show Items
fpdatasources	0	Show Items
Links	0	Show Items
List Template Gallery	1	Show Items
Master Page Gallery	3	Show Items
Shared Documents	0	Show Items
Site Assets	1	Show Items
Site Pages	2	Show Items
Solution Gallery	3	Show Items
Style Library	0	Show Items
Tasks	0	Show Items
Team Discussion	0	Show Items
Telephone	0	Show Items
Theme Gallery	**20**	**Show Items**
User Information List	6	Show Items
Web Part Gallery	17	Show Items

DetailWebPart

List Theme Gallery with 20 items.

Figure 6–23. *Master and detail Web Part in action*

The other predefined interfaces come with similar object relationships that make advanced connection scenarios easy to build. We won't include any examples, as they would simply repeat the preceding example, with minor changes.

Enhancing Web Parts Using Ajax

In the previous examples, you saw how to connect Web Parts. Transferring the value the classic way via postbacks is well known and available out of the box. Users might expect today that things are becoming more "magical"—with Ajax being used in the background. SharePoint 2010 uses Ajax at many points, and a well-developed custom Web Part designed for such an environment should use it as well. In Chapter 2, you got a first insight into Ajax as a base technology. Based on that knowledge, you can now enhance the Web Parts to make them Ajax-driven.

■ **Note** For an introduction to Ajax, refer to *Foundations of ASP.NET AJAX*, by Robin Pars, Laurence Moroney, and John Grieb (Apress, 2007).

Ajax-enabled Web Parts are quite similar to their non-Ajax counterparts. However, they require three fundamental changes:

- The source Web Part must invoke an action in the background.
- The target Web Part must receive the event and have an updatable region.
- The interface that connects both must define some kind of callback event.

The easiest way to do this is to use controls that support Ajax out of the box. In the following example, an UpdatePanel encapsulates both the control that invokes the callback and the region that is updated silently. The following project does exactly the same as the last example—it retrieves some images from a folder and updates another Web Part to display the selected image. For the sake of brevity, the initial steps and configuration files are skipped. The required changes are in the interface definition, its implementation, and the additional controls created in the CreateChildControls method.

The interface looks like this:

```
public interface IEventWebPartField
{
   event EventHandler ImageChanged;
   string ImageName { get; }
}
```

The event is necessary to invoke the update in the target, called from the source when the user changes the selected image. Listing 6–34 shows the implementation.

Listing 6–34. *A WebPart That Exposes Data via Ajax (using Statements Have Been Removed for Readibility)*

```
[ToolboxItemAttribute(false)]
public class AjaxSourceWebPart : System.Web.UI.WebControls.WebParts.WebPart,
                                 IEventWebPartField
{

    private GroupedDropDownList list;

    public AjaxSourceWebPart()
    {
    }

    protected override void OnInit(EventArgs e)
    {
        base.OnInit(e);
        WebPartManager.ConnectionsActivated +=
              new EventHandler(WebPartManager_ConnectionsActivated);
    }

    void WebPartManager_ConnectionsActivated(object sender, EventArgs e)
    {
        if (!Page.IsPostBack)
        {
            //
        }
    }

    protected override void CreateChildControls()
    {
         base.CreateChildControls();
         try
         {

             // Few controls with IDs sent to target
             string path = SPUtility.GetGenericSetupPath("TEMPLATE\\IMAGES");
```

```
    // Group Drop Box
     SPHtmlSelect dlGroup = new SPHtmlSelect();
     dlGroup.ID = this.ID + "dlGroup";
     dlGroup.Height = 22;
     dlGroup.Width = 100;
     Controls.Add(dlGroup);
     SPHtmlSelect dlCandidate = new SPHtmlSelect();
     dlCandidate.ID = this.ID + "dlCandidate";
     dlCandidate.Height = 22;
     Controls.Add(dlCandidate);
     // Put the button into the panel
     UpdatePanel panel = new UpdatePanel()
     {
         ID = this.SkinID + "updatePanel",
         ChildrenAsTriggers = false,
         UpdateMode = UpdatePanelUpdateMode.Conditional
     };
     Button b = new Button();
     b.Text = "Select Image";
     b.Click += new EventHandler(Button_OnClick);
     panel.ContentTemplateContainer.Controls.Add(b);
     Controls.Add(panel);
     // Register for async
     ScriptManager sc = ScriptManager.GetCurrent(Page);
     if (sc != null)
     {
         sc.RegisterAsyncPostBackControl(b);
     }
     //
     Controls.Add(new HtmlGenericControl("br"));
     HtmlGenericControl lblText = new HtmlGenericControl("span");
     lblText.ID = this.ID + "lblText";
     lblText.InnerText = "No image selected";
     Controls.Add(lblText);
     list = new GroupedDropDownList();
     list.GroupControlId = dlGroup.ID;
     list.CandidateControlId = dlCandidate.ID;
     list.DescriptionControlId = lblText.ID;
     string filter = (Page.IsPostBack && dlGroup.Items.Count > 0) ?
                     dlGroup.Items[dlGroup.SelectedIndex].Value : "*.*";
     foreach (string file in Directory.GetFiles(path, filter))
     {
        list.AddItem(
            Path.GetFileName(file),
            Path.GetFileNameWithoutExtension(file),
            file,
            Path.GetExtension(file).ToLowerInvariant());
     }
     Controls.Add(list);
}
catch
{
```

```
        }
    }

    protected void Button_OnClick(object sender, EventArgs e)
    {
         OnImageChanged();
    }


    protected override void RenderContents(HtmlTextWriter writer)
    {
        base.RenderContents(writer);
    }

    public string ImageName
    {
        get
        {
            return (list == null) ? null : list.Value;
        }
    }

    [ConnectionProvider("Image Name", AllowsMultipleConnections=false)]
    public IEventWebPartField GetCustomerProvider()
    {
        return this;
    }

    public event EventHandler ImageChanged;

    protected void OnImageChanged()
    {
        if (ImageChanged != null)
        {
            ImageChanged(this, EventArgs.Empty);
        }
    }
}
```

The first thing you need is an `UpdatePanel`, added in `CreateChildControls`. It contains the button that used to post back the form. To capture the button click as a server event instead, the button (`b`) is registered as an asynchronous source within the `ScriptManager`:

```
ScriptManager sc = ScriptManager.GetCurrent(Page);
if (sc != null)
{
    sc.RegisterAsyncPostBackControl(b);
}
```

It's nice to know that SharePoint 2010 is Ajax-enabled by default, and you don't need to register, configure, or enable anything to get it working. The button's `Click` event invokes the private event defined through the interface. The target Web Part hooks its handler to this event and receives the click (see Listing 6–35). Thus, as it did in the last example, it can retrieve the image's file name.

Listing 6–35. *A WebPart That Receives Data via Ajax (using Statements Have Been Removed for Readibility)*

```
[ToolboxItemAttribute(false)]
public class AjaxTargetWebPart : WebPart
{

        private IEventWebPartField customerProvider;
        private UpdatePanel panel;

        public AjaxTargetWebPart()
        {
        }

        [ConnectionConsumer("Image Name")]
        public void RegisterCustomerProvider(IEventWebPartField provider)
        {
            this.customerProvider = provider;
            this.customerProvider.ImageChanged += new
                  EventHandler(customerProvider_ImageChanged);
        }

        void customerProvider_ImageChanged(object sender, EventArgs e)
        {
            panel.Update();
        }

        private string ImageName
        {
            get
            {
                return customerProvider.ImageName;
            }
        }

        protected override void CreateChildControls()
        {
            base.CreateChildControls();
            Image img = new Image();
            panel = new UpdatePanel();
            if (customerProvider != null && ImageName != null)
            {
                string path = "/_layouts/images/";
                img.ImageUrl = SPContext.Current.Web.Url + path + ImageName;
                panel.ContentTemplateContainer.Controls.Add(img);
            }
            else
            {
                Label l = new Label();
                if (customerProvider == null)
                {
                    l.Text = "No Connection established.";
                }
```

```
                else
                {
                    l.Text = "No image selected.";
                }
                l.ForeColor = System.Drawing.Color.Red;
                panel.ContentTemplateContainer.Controls.Add(l);
            }
            Controls.Add(panel);
        }

        protected override void RenderContents(HtmlTextWriter writer)
        {
            base.RenderContents(writer);
        }

}
```

The Image element is also placed in another UpdatePanel. There is nothing to register here. The click event from source Web Part is finally routed through to the Update method of the UpdatePanel. The registration happens within the RegisterCustomerProvider method, which is called when the connection is established. That's all you need to get two Web Parts working smoothly together.

The Web Part Page Services Component

The Web Part Page Services Component (WPSC) adds more dynamic capabilities. Some services and events can be used to interact between the client and the server.

Only Web Parts that inherit directly from the Microsoft.SharePoint.WebPartPages.WebPart class can access the WPSC object model. The SharePoint-specific Web Part adds the necessary script code. However, this capability is related to client-side programming, which we cover in greater depth in Chapter 12.

Creating Private Actions Using Verbs

Properties are used to set values for a Web Part, and a Web Part's appearance can be customized using attributes. To execute actions, the user must click a link somewhere on the page. In SharePoint Web Parts, these action links are part of the drop-down menu each Web Part possesses. The technique to create custom action links uses so-called verbs.

Adding Entries to the Web Part Drop-Down Menu

To get one or more entries in the drop-down menu, you must override the Verbs property and return a WebPartVerbCollection, which contains WebPartVerb objects. The WebPartVerb type has several settings to control the appearance of the menu item, as shown in Table 6–5.

Table 6–5. WebPartVerb Settings That Modify the Context Menu Items

Property	Description
Checked	If set to true, the item appears as checked (activated) to represent some state.
Description	This is the description used as a tooltip.
Enabled	This enables or disables the item.
ImageURL	This is the URL to an icon, which appears in front of the item.
Text	This is the text on the item.

The constructor of the verb object has three overloads. It takes either a client script event handler, a server script handler, or both. While the client script is a JavaScript method, the server-side handler is a callback of the type WebPartEventHandler.

Using Client Script to Handle Menu Clicks

The client script can be any JavaScript. To handle the script properly, it's recommended to place just a function call there. Use the ClientScript object of the Page class to add the required script methods. The example code assumes you have a Label named l available and created in CreateChildControls.

```
protected override void OnPreRender(EventArgs e)
{
        base.OnLoad(e);
        if (!Page.ClientScript.IsClientScriptBlockRegistered("ClientVerbScript"))
        {
         Page.ClientScript.RegisterClientScriptBlock(Page.GetType(), "ClientVerbScript",
           String.Format(@"<script>
                      function SetBlueColorOnClient() {{
                      var label = document.getElementById('{0}');
                      label.style.color = 'Blue';
                       }}
                      </script>", l.ClientID));
        }
}
```

Because the Web Part can appear multiple times on a page, it's necessary to check whether the script has already been added using the IsClientScriptBlockRegistered method. Each such block has a specific name that's used internally to reference it. You can register script at the beginning or end of the page. Usually scripts are placed at the beginning of the page. This works well if they get called for the first time after the page is loaded completely. A user can reach a verb that is bound to a menu item once the page is loaded at the earliest; hence, the script is working fine.

For the server-side event, the handler is just an event handler method as it would be for any other event, such as Click.

Adding Server-Side and Client-Side Handlers

The WebPartEventHandler class is used to hold the callback method. For each menu item, exactly one WebPartVerb object is required, and it must be included in the collection returned by the Verbs property. The type returned is WebPartVerbCollection. The collection's constructor takes two parameters: the first parameter ensures that the default Web Part menu items are still present. Theoretically, you could omit this and void the menu. The second parameter takes the new menu items. A generic List<WebPartVerb> object is recommended. The following code adds two verbs: a client-side and a server-side click event handler.

```
public override WebPartVerbCollection Verbs
{
    get
    {
        List<WebPartVerb> verbs = new List<WebPartVerb>();
        // Client-Side Handler
        WebPartVerb verbClient = new WebPartVerb(this.ID + "clientVerb1",
                                 "SetBlueColorOnClient()");
        verbClient.Text = "Set Blue Color (Client)";
        verbClient.Description = "Invokes a JavaScript Method";
        verbs.Add(verbClient);
        // Server-Side Handler
        WebPartEventHandler handler = new
                                    WebPartEventHandler(SetRedColorServerClick);
        WebPartVerb verbServer = new WebPartVerb(this.ID + "serverVerb1", handler);
        verbServer.Text = "Set Red Color (Server)";
        verbServer.Description = "Invokes a post back";
        verbs.Add(verbServer);
        // add
        return new WebPartVerbCollection(base.Verbs, verbs);
    }
}
```

The server event handler has easy access to the SharePoint object model. For the client event handler, using the client object model is makes it possible to access the server. This is explained in-depth in Chapter 12. JavaScript allows you to directly access the server quite easily. The server side works in the same way. You have to ensure that the controls already exist:

```
private void SetRedColorServerClick(object sender, WebPartEventArgs e)
{
    EnsureChildControls();
    l.ForeColor = System.Drawing.Color.Red;
}
```

The context menu is available at the designated position and exposes the menu items in the same order as the verbs appear in the collection (see Figure 6–24).

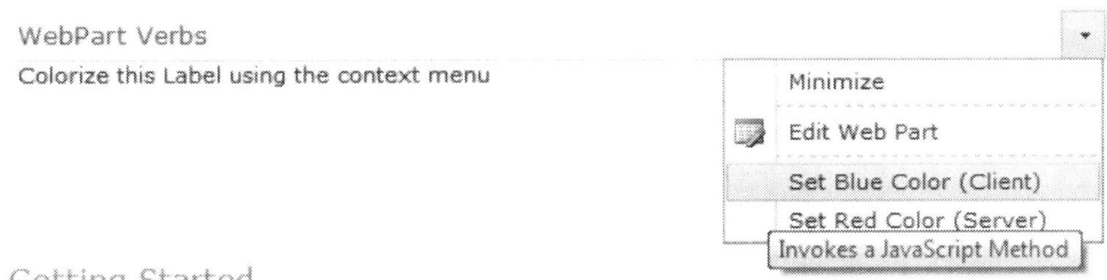

Figure 6–24. *The Web Part with custom context menu entries*

Asynchronous Web Parts

Using the asynchronous pattern to create application pages is common in ASP.NET sites. To understand why it is often appropriate to program asynchronously, remember how the worker process handles requests.

To handle as many parallel incoming requests as possible, the ASP.NET engine creates a thread pool that makes a number of threads available to handle requests. This thread pool is limited and usually set to a number that the processor architecture can handle efficiently. If there are more incoming requests than threads, IIS starts queuing up requests, dramatically slowing down the response time. The internal page-processing time is not that critical. Using the Developer Dashboard, you'll find that they range from a few milliseconds to a few hundred milliseconds. Thus, each thread is being freed after several milliseconds and becomes available for the next request. If the pool has 20 threads, then around 100 requests per second can be handled. For most installations, at least for an intranet, this is perfectly adequate—especially because it's for just one server.

However, things deteriorate rapidly if the page-processing time increases significantly. It may not be because the code is slow, but because of calls to external components. For example, a database call for some reporting or analysis services can take several seconds to respond. Even a web service call, an RSS feed, or another similar external connection can prolong the page-processing time. During the time the code waits for an answer, the CPU runs in idle mode. However, the thread is still blocked, and eventually IIS starts queuing requests because the pool runs out of threads.

Asynchronous programming is a simple pattern that starts an external operation in wait mode while the original thread is returned to the pool. Once the external source responds—with or without a result—the thread is requested again from the pool, and the page is processed up to the end. The total page-processing time is still the same. For a single user, the whole asynchronous pattern changes nothing. But while the page is idle (awaiting the response from the external call), the CPU can serve dozens of requests from other users. That discharges the thread pool, which is the reason to program asynchronously.

Making a Web Part Asynchronously

There is no asynchronous Web Part pattern by design. Only pages can be handled asynchronously. However, this is a *per-task* action. This means that you can register tasks on a page that the page handler can process asynchronously. Registering such tasks can be performed at any time during the `PreRender` step. This step is accessible through the `OnPreRender` event handler even from a Web Part, and this is where you can add the Web Part's tasks as part of the page's tasks.

An asynchronous task uses a callback pattern that consists of three methods: one called at the beginning, one at the end, and one, optionally, if a timeout occurs. The timeout method is optional, but you can treat it as mandatory, because all external calls might fail. The basic code to create such a task looks like this:

```
protected override void OnPreRender(EventArgs e)
{
   this.Page.RegisterAsyncTask(
      new PageAsynchTask(
        new BeginEventHandler(BeginMethod),
        new EndEventHandler(EndMethod),
        new EndEventHandler(TimeOutMethod),
        null,
        true)
      );
}
```

The fourth parameter is a private value that is transferred to the handler. It's set to `null` if the parameter is not required. The fifth parameter ensures that the task runs in parallel, if other tasks are registered on the same page at the same time. This happens if you add the same Web Part more than once.

In this example, you don't see any particular call invoking the methods. However, there is such a call—the `ExecuteRegisteredAsyncTasks` method. Under some circumstances, it might be necessary to know when the threads start. If there is no such call, the ASP.NET engine launches `ExecuteRegisteredAsyncTasks` immediately before the `PreRenderComplete` event.

USING THE ADDONPRERENDERCOMPLETEASYNC METHOD

If you have some experience with asynchronous pages, you might wonder why we don't use the simpler pattern based on the `AddOnPreRenderCompleteAsync` method. This method just accepts the `Begin` and `End` callback methods, and you're done. However, for Web Parts, this method has some serious drawbacks. Firstly, the missing timeout parameter can cause problems because the page may hang endlessly. In that situation, even removing the Web Part can be fraught with difficulty.

More critical is the internal behavior of this method. It does not track the state and current context. If your Web Part is the only one on the page, the method might work. But if other controls use the same pattern, then you have no indication at the `End` method where the call came from. The method is designed to handle only one task per page. Having no context also prevents you from using impersonation or manipulating culture settings. Even if these are not typical tasks for a Web Part, you might experience unexpected behavior.

To avoid potential headaches, we recommend that you follow the `RegisterAsyncTask` pattern instead.

When you call the external source, you must use a method that supports asynchronous access. Mimicking this by starting another thread will not help; any thread requested in a .NET application can only come from the solitary thread pool. Fortunately, asynchronous requests are widely supported in the framework.

In the next example (see Listing 6–36), the `WebRequest` class from the `System.Net` namespace is used to retrieve an RSS feed from a remote—and possibly slow—server.

Listing 6–36. *An Asynchronous WebPart*

```
using System;
using System.ComponentModel;
```

```
using System.Runtime.InteropServices;
using System.Web.UI;
using System.Web.UI.WebControls;
using System.Web.UI.WebControls.WebParts;
using Microsoft.SharePoint;
using Microsoft.SharePoint.WebControls;
using System.Net;
using System.IO;
using System.Xml.Linq;
using System.Xml;
using System.Web.UI.HtmlControls;

namespace Apress.SP2010.WebParts.AsynchWebPart
{
    [ToolboxItemAttribute(false)]
    public class FeedWebPart : WebPart
    {
        public FeedWebPart()
        {
            currentState = State.Undefined;
        }

        private enum State
        {
            Undefined,
            Loading,
            Loaded,
            Timeout,
            NoAsync
        }

        private WebRequest rssRequest;
        private WebResponse rssResponse;
        private XDocument xml;
        private State currentState;

        protected override void OnPreRender(EventArgs e)
        {
            base.OnPreRender(e);
            if (String.IsNullOrEmpty(FeedUrl))
                return;
            if (WebPartManager.DisplayMode == WebPartManager.DisplayModes["Design"])
                return;
            Page.AsyncTimeout = TimeSpan.FromSeconds(10); // 10 sec
            Page.RegisterAsyncTask(
                new PageAsyncTask(
                    new System.Web.BeginEventHandler(BeginRSSRead),
                    new System.Web.EndEventHandler(EndRSSRead),
                    new System.Web.EndEventHandler(TimeOutRSSRead),
                    null,
                    true));
        }

        private IAsyncResult BeginRSSRead(object sender, EventArgs e,
```

```
                                    AsyncCallback cb, object state)
{
    currentState = State.Loading;
    rssRequest = HttpWebRequest.Create(FeedUrl);
    return rssRequest.BeginGetResponse(cb, state);
}

private void EndRSSRead(IAsyncResult ar)
{
    rssResponse = rssRequest.EndGetResponse(ar);
    Stream response = rssResponse.GetResponseStream();
    XmlReader reader = XmlReader.Create(response);
    xml = XDocument.Load(reader);
    currentState = State.Loaded;
    WriteControls();
}

private void TimeOutRSSRead(IAsyncResult ar)
{
    currentState = State.Timeout;
    WriteControls();
}

private void WriteControls()
{
    switch (currentState)
    {
        case State.Loaded:
            HtmlGenericControl ctrl = new HtmlGenericControl("pre");
            ctrl.InnerText = xml.ToString();
            Controls.Add(ctrl);
            break;
        case State.Timeout:
            Label lt = new Label();
            lt.Text = "RSS Feed timed out";
            lt.ForeColor = System.Drawing.Color.Red;
            Controls.Add(lt);
            break;
        case State.NoAsync:
            Label nl = new Label();
            nl.Text = "Asynch not supported.";
            Controls.Add(nl);
            break;
        default:
            Label ll = new Label();
            ll.Text = "Loading...";
            Controls.Add(ll);
            break;
    }
}

[Personalizable(true)]
[WebBrowsable(true)]
[WebDescription("RSS Feed URL")]
```

```
        [WebDisplayName("Feed URL")]
        [Category("Feed Properties")]
        public string FeedUrl
        {
            get;
            set;

        }

    }
}
```

The asynchronous tasks are defined in OnPreRender. This is the last opportunity in the pipeline to do so, because the methods are invoked in the following PreRenderComplete state. The code that writes the output is very simple. It checks the state of the control, (e.g., Undefined, Loading, or Loaded) using the internal enumeration, State. The only property defined for this Web Part is FeedUrl, which stores the selected RSS feed.

The example demonstrates the basic tasks required to invoke an asynchronous call. It starts with the BeginGetResponse call to retrieve the data:

```
rssRequest.BeginGetResponse(cb, state);
```

The output is plain XML, written to the page—not very useful, but this is a simplistic example to make the code as easy to read as possible.

A more challenging task is the creation of an asynchronous call if the framework does not explicitly support this. This is discussed in the following section.

Creating an Asynchronous Data Source

As long as you have some predefined classes that support the asynchronous pattern, the implementation is relatively easy. You just need to call the Begin... and End... methods respectively, and hand over the IAsyncResult object. If your underlying source does not support this pattern, you must implement your own stack. The next example reads the data off a feed from the local hard disk. The file stream reader does not support asynchronous access. The challenge here is to implement such access using the common pattern around the IAsyncResult interface (see Listing 6–37).

Listing 6–37. *An Asynchronous Data Source*

```
using System;
using System.Collections.Generic;
using System.Linq;
using System.Text;
using System.Xml.Linq;
using System.IO;

namespace Apress.SP2010.WebParts.AsynchWebPart
{

    public abstract class AsyncTask<T> where T : new()
    {
        public T Result { get; protected set; }
        private Action task;
        private Action taskFinished;
```

```
    public AsyncTask()
    {
    }

    public AsyncTask(Action finishHandler)
    {
        taskFinished = finishHandler;
    }

    public virtual IAsyncResult OnBegin(object sender, EventArgs e,
                                        AsyncCallback cb, object data)
    {
        task = new Action(Execute);
        return task.BeginInvoke(cb, data);
    }

    public virtual void OnEnd(IAsyncResult result)
    {
        if (taskFinished != null)
        {
            taskFinished.Invoke();
        }
        task.EndInvoke(result);
    }

    public virtual void OnTimeout(IAsyncResult result)
    {
        Result = default(T);
    }

    public abstract void Execute();

}


public class ReadFileAsync : AsyncTask<XDocument>
{

    public string FileName { get; set; }

    public ReadFileAsync(string fileName, Action finishCallback)
        : base(finishCallback)
    {
        if (String.IsNullOrEmpty(fileName))
            throw new ArgumentException("fileName");
        if (!File.Exists(fileName))
            throw new FileNotFoundException();
        FileName = fileName;
    }

    public override void Execute()
    {
        XDocument xdoc = XDocument.Load(FileName);
```

```
            Result = xdoc;
        }

    }
}
```

For the Begin and End calls, you need a delegate. Because these are simple triggers that do not return anything, the predefined Action class is the optimal choice. The Execute method is where the file is actually read from disk. That's bit nonsensical, because this is the End phase of the asynchronous call, and that means the time is not consumed in the background, but just later in the phase. It would make more sense if you had to prepare the call, for instance, by reading a number of folders first, or by doing some authentication in the Begin phase, to get the results later in the End phase, as shown. That would indeed free the thread while something is being waited for. However, the pattern shown is perfectly adequate to demonstrate how to create an asynchronous call.

Best Practices for Developing Web Parts for SharePoint

This section contains a number of recommended best practices for Web Part developers. They are intended to improve the performance and usability of the Web Parts, and to assist you in creating Web Parts that integrate well with other components of a Web Part page.

Avoiding Error-Prone Web Parts

There are several common techniques known to ASP.NET developers that aid with building stable and reliable components. Because Web Parts run in the more complex context of SharePoint, some additional action should be taken to deal with this environment as well.

Handling All Exceptions to Prevent Web Part Page Failures

Your Web Part should handle all exceptions, rather than risk the possibility of causing the Web Part page to stop responding. If an exception is not handled properly, it could prevent the user from using the editing mode of the page, and as a last resort, remove the Web Part. SharePoint 2010 provides some techniques to restore a previous version of the page or remove a nonfunctional Web Part. However, maintaining control over what happens with your code is preferable.

You can achieve this by placing the sections of code that might throw exceptions in a try block and writing code to handle these exceptions in a catch block:

```
private void SetSaveProperties()
{
   if (this.Permission !=
      Microsoft.SharePoint.WebPartPages.Permissions.None)
   {
      try
      {
         SaveProperties = true;
      }

      catch (Exception ex)
      {
      // Setting SaveProperties can throw many exceptions.
      // Two examples are:
```

```
        // 1) SecurityException if the user doesn't have the "ObjectModel"
        //    SharePointPermission or the "UnsafeSaveOnGet"
        //    SharePointPermission
        // 2) WebPartPageUserException if the user doesn't have sufficient
        //    rights to save properties (e.g., the user is a Reader)
           errorText = ex.Message;
        }
    }
}
```

Checking Permissions Before Rendering Your Web Part

Because Web Parts are managed by the user at runtime, you should render your Web Part with a UI that is appropriate for each user's permissions. To do this, always check the `Permissions` property before rendering the Web Part—if the value is `None`, you should suppress the portions of your Web Part UI that require certain permissions. For example, if a Web Part displays a Save button, you can disable or hide it if the user does not have permissions to save changes. Catching the exception that the runtime will throw if you launch an action without proper permissions is not a good practice. An exception is not intended for handling foreseeable situations. Missing permissions can occur, and therefore you should handle them explicitly in code.

If a user is unable to use your Web Part as you designed it, two things could be happening:

- The user is in the Reader role, and the Web Part is not in a Web Part zone. Although the Web Part may be designed to be dynamic, if a user adds it to a blank page, it becomes a static Web Part. Static Web Parts cannot save changes in either shared or personal view.
- The user is anonymous. Without proper authentication, the Web Part will not work.

Validating Properties Before Saving Changes to the Database

You can edit property values in a number of places outside of your Web Part's UI:

- In the Web Part description (`.webpart`) file
- In the tool pane
- In an HTML editor compatible with SharePoint, such as SharePoint Designer

Because of this, whenever you attempt to save changes to the database, you should not make assumptions about the state of your properties. For example, you cannot assume that properties are unchanged because you disabled them in the UI, or that properties are valid because you validated them when they were entered in the UI.

To ensure that you account for all the different places those properties can be set; we recommend that you place your validation code in the property's setter method.

Specifying Custom Error Messages When Appropriate

By default, when an exception occurs, the Web Part infrastructure redirects the user to an error page and renders a generic error message. To specify your own error message to the end user, use the `WebPartPageUserException` class:

```
if (ex is WebPartPageUserException)
```

```
{
    errorText.Text = ex.Message;
}
```

Validating All User Input

As with any web control or application, you should thoroughly validate all user-supplied data before performing operations with that data. This validation can help to protect your code, not only against accidental misuse, but also from deliberately malicious attacks that use the UI to target the code.

Optimizing Performance

As an integral part of the SharePoint platform, Web Parts need careful development regarding performance and power.

Registering the Client-Side Script Shared by Multiple Web Parts to Improve Performance

There are some ways to render client-side script for a Web Part page:

- Place the script in an external file and register the script for the page.
- Place the script as a resource in the assembly and use web references.
- Send the code to the client for each request.

If you have multiple Web Parts that share client-side script, you can improve performance and simplify maintenance by placing the script in an external file or web reference and registering the script for the page. In this way, the code is cached on the client computer on first use and does not need to be resent to the client for each subsequent request. In addition, the page registration ensures that the code is only added once to the page, even if the same Web Part is used several times.

To register client-side script shared by multiple Web Parts via a web reference, proceed as shown in the next exercise.

ADDING CLIENT SCRIPT AS WEB REFERENCE

1. Place the script in a separate file in your project. It's recommended to use a specific folder, such as `ScriptResources`.
2. Open the properties pane for the file and choose Reference as the option for Build Action.
3. Open the `AssemblyInfo.cs` file of the project and add the following attribute (replace the placeholder names with whatever your project requires):

   [assembly: WebResource("*Namespace.Folders.Folder.Filename.ext*")]
4. Register the script by using the following code snippet:

```
if ()
{
   RegisterClientScriptBlock
}
```

5. Compile and deploy. Storing the JavaScript client code in the assembly simplifies the deployment and centralizes the file management.

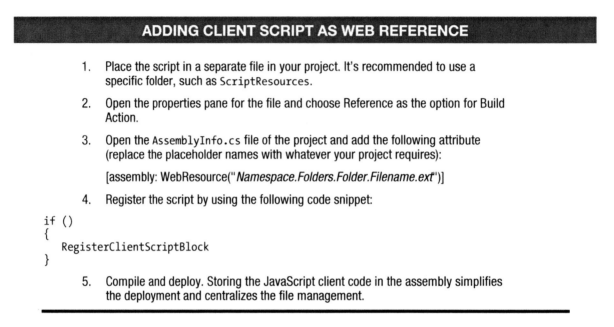

Techniques to Improve Web Part Performance

If your Web Part is working with large amounts of data, you can significantly improve its performance by using the following techniques in your code.

Asynchronous Data Fetching

Use an asynchronous pattern for any external operation that could take a significant amount of time. In particular, if a database or HTTP request is made, an asynchronous fetch allows other parts to continue processing without being blocked. (See the "Asynchronous Web Parts" section earlier in the chapter for more information.)

Caching

Use a Web Part cache to store property values and to expedite data retrieval. Values are stored in the Web Part cache on a per-part or per-user basis by specifying the storage type in the call to the `PartCacheRead` and `PartCacheWrite` methods. You can also determine the type of cache to use—either the content database or the ASP.NET `Cache` object—by setting the value of the `WebPartCache` element in the `web.config` file. The cache objects must be serializable.

Supporting the End User

Web Parts are intended to be used by end users, and this isn't limited to working with the UI that the Web Part exposes. Moreover, a user can personalize a Web Part, move it around, change its appearance, and create connections. The explicit support requires far more effort than creating just a plain control. It is this extra effort that allows you to unleash the true power of Web Parts.

Specifying Whether Web Part Properties Can Be Exported

When you export a Web Part, you create a Web Part description (`.webpart`) file automatically. The `.webpart` file is an XML document that represents the Web Part and its property values. Users can import this file to add the Web Part with all the properties set.

By default, each property is included in the `.webpart` file whenever you export a Web Part. However, you may have properties that contain sensitive information (e.g., a date of birth). The Web Part infrastructure enables you to identify a property as controlled, allowing you or the user to choose to exclude the value if the Web Part is exported. Only properties that are exported when the user is in personal view can be controlled; in shared view, all property values are exported because it is unlikely that sensitive information would be included on a shared page.

There are two properties that cooperate to provide this functionality:

- *The* `ControlledExport` *property of the* `WebPartStorageAttribute` *class*: If set to `true`, the property is specified as a controlled property. The default value is `false`.
- *The* `ExportControlledProperties` *property of the* `WebPart` *class*: This is used at runtime to determine whether controlled properties are exported when the user is in personal view. The default value is `false`, which prevents controlled properties from being exported while in personal view.

```
[WebPartStorage (Storage.Personal, ControlledExport=true)]
```

The `ExportControlledProperties` property maps directly to the Export Mode drop-down in the Advanced category of the tool pane (see Figure 6–25), enabling the user to set this value at runtime. By default, this check box is not selected, which prevents controlled properties from being exported. The user has to explicitly select this check box to allow different behavior. This option applies only to controlled properties.

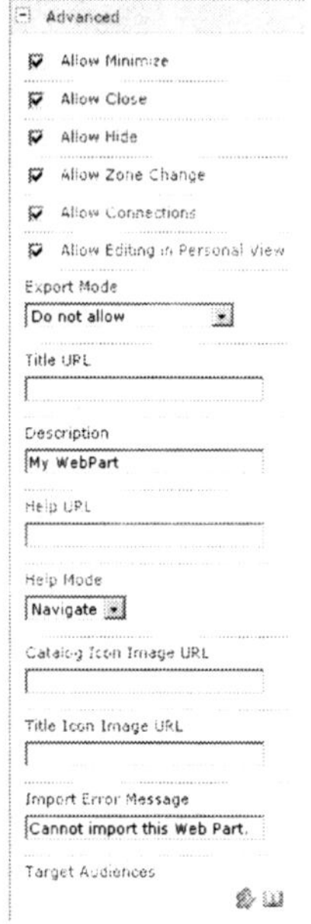

Figure 6–25. *The Advanced category as viewed in the tool pane*

The Advanced category in the tool pane appears only in the view in which the Web Part was added. For example, if the Web Part is added in shared view, the Advanced section appears in the tool pane only when you are modifying properties in the shared page. If it is added in personal view, the Advanced section of the tool pane appears only when you are modifying properties in personal page of a My Site scenario. In either case, the setting determines how properties are exported only when the user is exporting in personal view.

Supporting SharePoint Designer and the Visual Studio Design-Time Experience

Implement the `IDesignTimeHtmlProvider` interface in your Web Part to ensure correct rendering on designer surfaces. If you do not implement this interface, and a user opens a Web Part page in design view, your part appears only as the message, "There is no preview available for this part."

Following is an example of a simple `IDesignTimeHtmlProvider` implementation:

```
namespace Apress.SP2010.WebParts.MyWebParts
{
   [XmlRoot(Namespace = "MyNamespace")]
   public class DesignTimeHTMLSample :
      Microsoft.SharePoint.WebPartPages.WebPart, IDesignTimeHtmlProvider
   {
      private string designTimeHtml = "This is the design-time HTML.";
      private string runTimeHtml = "This is the run-time HTML.";

      public string GetDesignTimeHtml()
      {
         return SPEncode.HtmlEncode(designTimeHtml);
      }
      protected override void RenderWebPart(HtmlTextWriter output)
      {
         output.Write(this.ReplaceTokens(runTimeHtml));
      }
   }
}
```

Making Properties User-Friendly in the Tool Pane

Because the tool pane is where users modify Web Part properties, you should be aware of how your properties appear in it. Following are some attributes (see Table 6–6) you should use to ensure that your users can work with your Web Part properties easily in the tool pane.

Table 6–6. Attributes to Control the Property Pane

Name	Description
FriendlyNameAttribute	Controls how the property name is displayed. This name should be user-friendly. For example, a property named MyText should have a friendly name of My Text (notice the space between the two words).
Description	Specifies the tooltip shown when the mouse pointer lingers over the property. Write the property description so that a user can figure out how and why they should set the property. Try to minimize users having to navigate away from your UI and seek help in the documentation to set a property.
Category	Describes the general section in which the property appears: Advanced, Appearance, Layout, or Miscellaneous. If possible, avoid the Miscellaneous category, which is used if no category is assigned for a property. Because this category title is not descriptive, your user has no indication of what is included in Miscellaneous without expanding it.

A custom property is also placed in the Miscellaneous category if you attempt to include it in the Appearance, Layout, or Advanced categories. These categories are reserved for base class properties only.

For example, the following statements demonstrate the attributes for a custom property that is a string displayed as a text box in the tool pane.

```
// Create a custom category in the tool pane.
[Category("Custom Properties")]
// Assign the default value.
[DefaultValue(c_MyStringDefault)]
// Make the property available in both Personalization
// and Customization modes.
[WebPartStorage(Storage.Personal)]
// The caption that appears in the tool pane.
[FriendlyNameAttribute("My Custom String")]
// The tooltip that appears when pausing the mouse pointer over
// the friendly name in the tool pane.
[Description("Type a string value.")]
// Display the property in the tool pane.
[Browsable(true)]
```

You can customize the appearance of your properties in the tool pane in several ways. You can expand or collapse specific categories when the pane opens. Use the Expand method of either the WebPartToolPart or CustomPropertyToolPart class to expand selected categories.

You can also hide base class properties. Use the Hide method of the WebPartToolPart class to hide selected properties. To control the order of tool parts within a tool pane, use the array passed to the GetToolParts method of the WebPart class.

Encoding All User Input Rendered to the Client

Use the HTMLEncode method of the SPEncode class as a security precaution to help prevent malicious script blocks from being able to execute in applications that execute across sites. You should use

HTMLEncode for all input that is rendered to the client. This will convert dangerous HTML tags to more secure escaped characters.

Following is an example of using the HTMLEncode method to render HTML to a client computer:

```
protected override void RenderWebPart(HtmlTextWriter output)
{
   output.Write("<font color='" + SPEncode.HTMLEncode(this.Color) + "'>"
      + "Your custom text is: <b>" + SPEncode.HTMLEncode(this.Text)
      + "</b></font><hr>");
}
```

Checking Web Part Zone Properties Whenever You Attempt to Save Changes

Web Part zones have properties that control whether a user can persist changes. If you attempt to save changes to a Web Part without the correct permissions, it could result in an unhandled exception. For this reason, you should account for any combination of permissions for your Web Part.

Following are the properties in the WebPartZone class that determine whether a Web Part can save properties:

- AllowCustomization: If false, and the user is viewing the page in shared view, the Web Part cannot persist any changes to the database.
- AllowPersonalization: If false, and the user is viewing the page in personal view, the Web Part cannot persist any changes to the database.
- LockLayout: If true, changes to the AllowRemove, AllowZoneChange, Height, IsIncluded, IsVisible, PartOrder, Width, and ZoneID properties are not persisted to the database, regardless of the current view.

Fortunately, the Web Part infrastructure does a lot of the work. You can check the Permissions property, which takes into account the values of the zone's AllowCustomization and AllowPersonalization properties. If, however, your UI permits changes to the properties controlled by the LockLayout property, you must explicitly check this value, typically in the property setter.

The following code illustrates how you can get a reference to a Web Part's containing zone to check the LockLayout property:

```
WebPartZone myParent = (this.Page.FindControl(this.ZoneID));
```

Using Simple Types for Custom Properties You Define

Web Part property values can be specified in one of two ways. One way is as XML elements contained in the Web Part. For example:

```
<WebPartPage:ContentEditorWebPart runat=server>
<WebPart>
   <title>My content Web Part</title>
   <description>This is cool</description>
</WebPart>
</WebPartPages:ContentEditorWebPart>
```

The other way, commonly used for ASP.NET controls, uses attributes of the Web Part:

```
<WebPartPage:ContentEditorWebPart runat=server title="My content Web Part" description="this
is cool" />
```

Because of how the Web Part infrastructure handles property values, we recommend that you define your properties as simple types so that they work correctly if specified as attributes of the Web Part. As shown in the examples, the editor can handle the attributes as strings only. Any type other than `System.String` would need a serialization/deserialization round trip. For numbers or colors this might be effortless, but for more complex types this could become painful for the user of the Web Part. If your code requires a value to be a complex type, you can convert the string value to a complex type as required by your program.

Making Properties Independent of Each Other If They Both Appear in the Tool Pane

There is no guarantee of the order that properties are displayed in the tool pane. For this reason, you should avoid writing Web Part properties that are dependent on each other and that both appear in the tool pane.

Making Web Parts Easily Searchable in the Galleries

Web Part galleries can contain numerous custom Web Parts, so the Web Part infrastructure provides search functionality to help users quickly find the Web Part they need (see Figure 6–26).

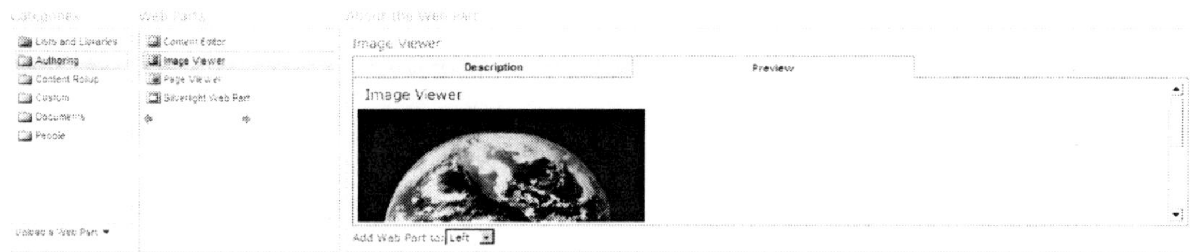

Figure 6–26. *Adding a Web Part to a page*

The search function uses the `Title` and `Description` properties of your Web Part to build the response, so you should provide comprehensive information in these fields to increase the chance of your Web Part being discovered by Search. In addition, each Web Part in the Web Part list has an icon that appears on the left. By default, the Web Part infrastructure uses generic icons for each Web Part; however, you can customize this icon using the `PartImageLarge` property.

Providing a Preview of Your Web Part for the Web Part Gallery

Be sure to create previews for your Web Parts so that administrators are able to review the parts included in the Web Part gallery.

In your `RenderWebPart` method, you can determine whether you are in preview mode using the following code:

```
if (this.Parent.GetType().Fullname = "Microsoft.SharePoint.WebPartPages.WebPartPreview")
```

If you are in preview mode, you should render the HTML for the content you want to appear in the preview—typically an image. The chrome and title bar are provided by the infrastructure, with the Web Part title appearing in the title bar. The next exercise explains how to display the Web Part preview.

HOW TO PREVIEW A WEB PART

1. On the top-level site, select Site Settings, and then go to Site Administration.
2. Select Manage Web Part Gallery to see the list of available Web Parts.
3. Click the Web Part name, and the preview will be displayed if one is available.

Localizing Your Custom Properties

We recommend that you localize the `FriendlyName`, `Title`, and `Description` attributes. By planning for localization in the development phase, you can provide a more customer-friendly UI and save on the costs associated with localizing your Web Part after development. The Web Part infrastructure provides a simple way to localize certain attributes (`FriendlyName`, `Category`, and `Description`) of your custom properties, making it easier for users to work with them in the tool pane. (See Chapter 8 for more information.)

Supporting Anonymous Access

Ensure that when anonymous access is on, the user can view the Web Part page without logging in. You do not want to prompt users for a login if the site has anonymous access enabled. You can determine whether anonymous access is enabled by querying the `AllowAnonymousAccess` property of the `SPWeb` class. If this value is `true`, anonymous access is enabled, and you should not perform any action that requires credentials.

Help Using Resources

If you use resources, it's possible to get confused regarding the exact names of the embedded data. Even using the formula *`Namespace + Path + File`*, you don't always get the whole string correct. If you are in a debug session and are able to use the Immediate window, you can read all the names of the embedded resources using the code shown in Figure 6–27.

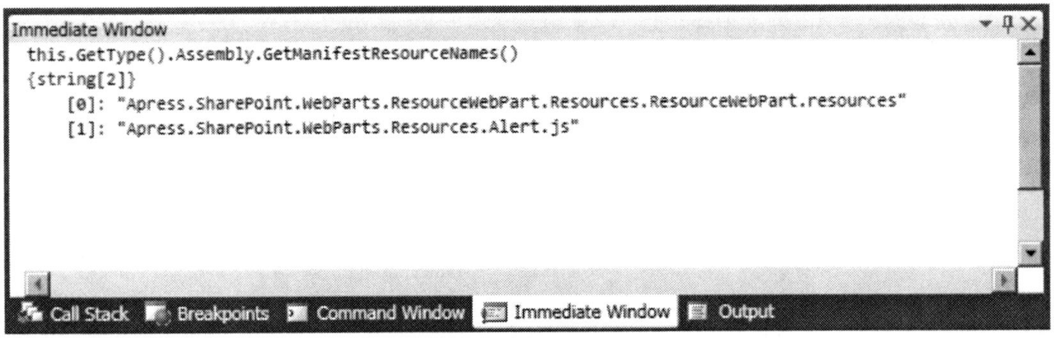

```
Immediate Window
this.GetType().Assembly.GetManifestResourceNames()
{string[2]}
    [0]: "Apress.SharePoint.WebParts.ResourceWebPart.Resources.ResourceWebPart.resources"
    [1]: "Apress.SharePoint.WebParts.Resources.Alert.js"

Call Stack | Breakpoints | Command Window | Immediate Window | Output
```

Figure 6–27. *You can retrieve embedded resource names using the Immediate window.*

If it is not displayed here, it is not an embedded resource in this assembly. First check the build action (as shown in Figure 6–28) and the `AssemblyInfo.cs` file to make sure that the resource is embedded as a web resource. If it is present and your code still doesn't work, double-check the string—it's case sensitive.

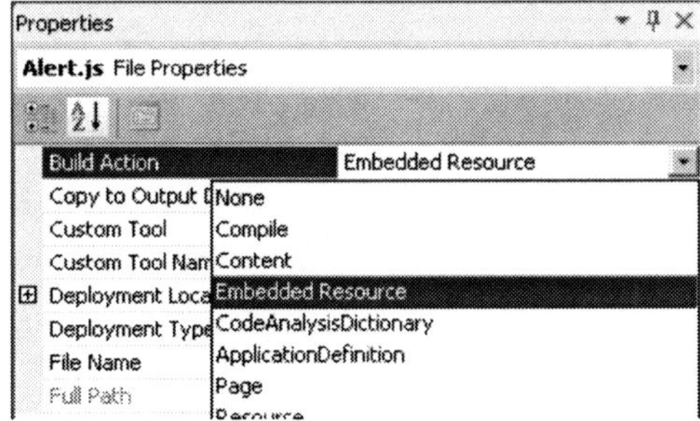

Figure 6–28. *Declare an item as an embedded resource.*

Summary

In this chapter, you learned the basics of Web Part development, plus several methods to extend them. On top of the Web Part UI that SharePoint provides, you saw how to add custom editor panes, pop-up dialogs, and error-checking methods. Using verbs, you can extend the default Web Part context menu.

Connectable Web Parts provide a well-defined pattern to form master/detail relationships. Using callbacks, you can make such connections via Ajax calls, and let Web Parts talk silently to each other.

All this is mostly covered by ASP.NET-driven Web Parts. However, the integration in SharePoint has some bells and whistles you need to know to get access to Web Parts as one of the most powerful extensibility concepts SharePoint provides.

CHAPTER 7

■ ■ ■

Templates

Templates form the bedrock of most professionally developed SharePoint applications. They are more flexible and extensible than customized solutions built using the SharePoint UI or SharePoint Designer. There are different types of templates within the SharePoint framework. The range includes the following:

- Column templates
- List templates, including those for content types, fields, and views
- Site templates

Working with templates enables you to develop solutions for custom columns, lists, content types, and complete SharePoint applications. Furthermore, they are highly reusable and deployable in order to create instances from your template on every SharePoint environment. In this context, we describe the new tools and opportunities introduced with Visual Studio 2010.

First this chapter describes how you can easily build a column template. This is followed by an explanation of the purpose and context for list templates. By constructing a sample list template, you'll learn how list definitions are structured, what kind of custom extensions you can build, and how to integrate such a template into your SharePoint application landscape.

The chapter also deals with the creation of templates for a SharePoint site or site collection. A simple example explains each component you need to construct your own custom site template.

By the end of this chapter, you should be able to build your own custom templates that can be used in nearly every SharePoint environment (depending on the SharePoint version you are using—Foundation, Standard, or Enterprise).

Templates Overview

In SharePoint 2010, different templates are available. This section describes each one in turn (Table 7–1 gives an overview).

Table 7–1. SharePoint 2010 Templates

Template	Description
Column templates	Can be created either using the Web UI or using an XML field definition
Custom field types	Are reusable and can be used as templates
List templates	Can be created using the SharePoint UI (List Settings ➤ Save list as template)
List definitions	List definition in XML format that provides a list template
Site template	Can be created using the SharePoint UI (Site Settings ➤ Save site as template)
Site definitions	Site definitions in XML format providing a site template

All these elements, except for custom field types, are covered in this chapter. Custom field types are explored in Chapter 11.

Column Templates

One of the easiest templates that you can create is a template for a site column. Templates for columns are often used if you require the same column in different lists—or even sites—over and over again. Consider, for example, a project management site that needs a Choice column called Status in every project-related list, and every instance has the same choice options. Simply build a feature once, defining a template for this specific column, and instantiate it many times.

To specify, deploy, and use such a column template, you need to build a SharePoint feature. Features in SharePoint are components with various contents, such as custom code, list definitions, event handlers, and Web Parts. They can be installed and activated separately in an existing SharePoint web site, or they can be integrated in a SharePoint solution (`.wsp` file). (Features are introduced in more detail in Chapter 9.)

The element manifest file of a feature specifies the column, as shown in Listing 7–1.

Listing 7–1. *Column Template Elements.xml*

```
<?xml version="1.0" encoding="utf-8"?>
<Elements xmlns="http://schemas.microsoft.com/sharepoint/">
    <Field ID="{2FAB9B49-1A3A-47b3-174C-8A84F0D322AB}"
      Name="Status"
      Group="MyProjectColumns"
      Type="Choice"
      DisplayName="Project Status"
      SourceID="http://schemas.microsoft.com/sharepoint/v4/fields"
      StaticName="Status"
      FillInChoice="FALSE">
        <CHOICES>
```

```
            <CHOICE>Not Started</CHOICE>
            <CHOICE>Running</CHOICE>
            <CHOICE>Closed</CHOICE>
        </CHOICES>
        <Default>Not Started</Default>
    </Field>
</Elements>
```

The attributes of the Field element specify the parameters of the template:

- `ID`: Specifies the unique ID of the field
- `Name`: Specifies the name of the field
- `Group`: Specifies the group in which the custom column appears
- `Type`: Specifies the field type of this column
- `DisplayName`: Specifies the display name of the column
- `SourceID`: References the SharePoint base field definitions
- `StaticName`: Specifies the static name of the column
- `FillInChoice`: Specifies whether an additional value can be entered in a choice field
- `Choices`: Specifies the available choices and default choice of this field

(For details on creating a custom field type, see Chapter 11.)

Features can be deployed to a SharePoint environment with a specific scope. Some features may be used only on a concrete site, and others may be used for a whole SharePoint farm.

There are four possible values for the feature's `Scope` attribute:

- `Web`: Single web site
- `Site`: Site collection
- `WebApplication`: Web application
- `Farm`: SharePoint Farm

To deploy a custom site column definition on every web site separately (`Web`-scoped), you use the feature definition shown in Listing 7–2.

Listing 7–2. *Column Template Feature.xml*

```
<?xml version="1.0" encoding="utf-8"?>
<Feature Id="1F7BD552-10B1-1B54-85B5-5ED1D39C12F5"
  Title="ProjectStatusField"
  Description="Provides a custom project status choice column for lists."
  Version="1.0.0.0"
  Scope="Web"
  xmlns="http://schemas.microsoft.com/sharepoint/">

    <ElementManifests>
        <ElementManifest Location="elements.xml"/>
    </ElementManifests>
</Feature>
```

The first attributes `ID`, `Title`, `Description`, `Version`, and `Scope` of the Feature element define mandatory data. The ElementManifest element references the `Elements.xml` file you created earlier (Listing 7–1).

As a result, you should have the target folder called `ProjectStatus`, as shown in Figure 7–1.

Figure 7–1. *Custom column feature folder*

For deploying and activating, you can use the SharePoint administration command-line tool `stsadm.exe`.

DEPLOYING AND ACTIVATING A FEATURE USING STSADM.EXE

1. Copy the feature folder to `%SharePointRoot%\TEMPLATE\FEATURES`.
2. Open a command-line window with administrator rights.
3. Enter **stsadm.exe –o installfeature –name projectstatus**.
4. The next step is to activate the feature (except in farm-scoped features that are activated automatically). Enter `C:\stsadm.exe -o activatefeature -name projectstatus -url http://myserver`.
5. Click OK to create an instance from your custom list template.

(For more details about features, see Chapter 9.) After deployment and activation of this feature, you can see your status column in the "Available column types" list on the Column Creation page (see Figure 7–2).

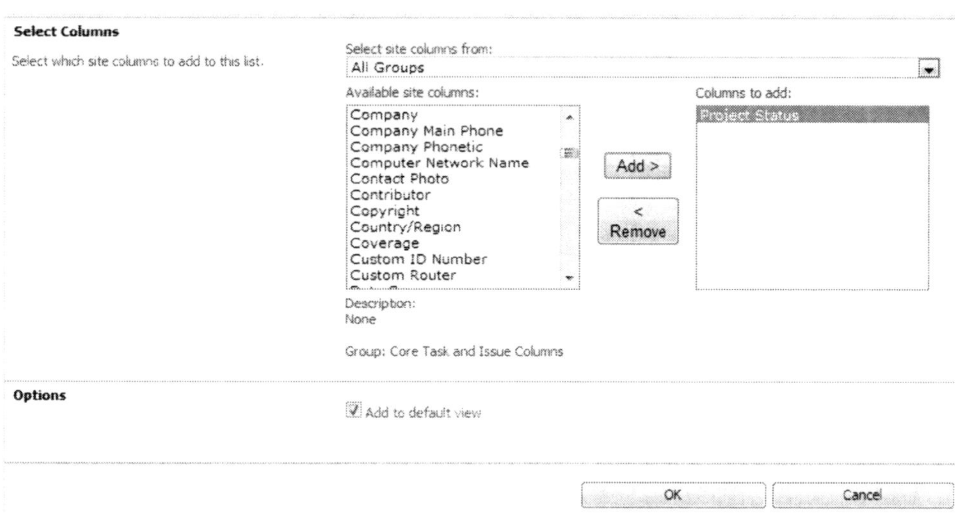

Figure 7-2. Column Creation page

The other approach to constructing a column template is to use the SharePoint UI. The following exercise demonstrates how to create a reusable site column.

CREATING A REUSABLE SITE COLUMN

1. Go to the Site Settings page.
2. Open the site columns gallery.
3. Create a new column, and specify a group where the column should be stored.
4. Click OK to create the column. The column is now available to use in a list.
5. Go to the List Settings page for a list. Click "Add from existing site columns," and add the column.

List Templates

Templates for lists make sense in many scenarios. For example, if you need several instances from the same list type, including the same columns, views, and so on, on multiple web sites, you don't want to repeatedly build the same list. In such a scenario you would create a list template or definition once and reuse it.

List Definitions vs. List Templates

There are two types of list templates: list definitions and list templates. List templates can be created in the SharePoint UI. Simply go to the List Settings page of a list, and click "Save list as template." The template will be stored in the list template gallery. But this method has several disadvantages. When SharePoint creates the list template, there can be references to other lists and fields, if, for instance, you have used lookup fields. If you try to build a new list instance from this template in another SharePoint system, SharePoint may throw an exception because some of the references that are defined in the list definition file using GUIDs cannot be resolved. Another disadvantage is the limited extensibility. You can use only the fields and options that you can configure through the UI or SharePoint Designer.

List definitions, on the other hand, are specified in XML and are provided through a feature or site definition. Using list definitions, you have a greater scope for customization. For example, you can add event handlers for list events such as `ItemAdded`, and you can add custom actions that extend list context menus or toolbar buttons.

Custom List Definitions

To create a custom list definition, use the List Definition Visual Studio 2010 project template (Figure 7–3).

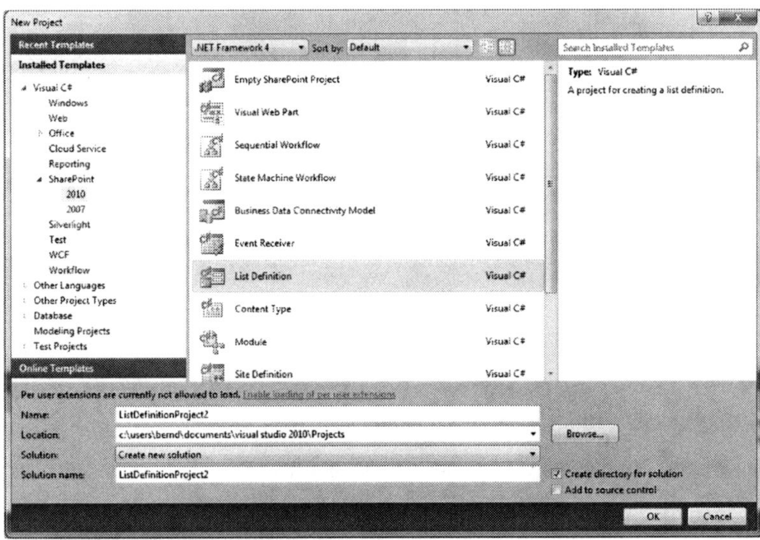

***Figure 7–3.** SharePoint project templates in Visual Studio 2010*

This project template offers a wizard where you can add a list instance feature based on the list definition you want to create. That could be confusing, because that is more than you need at this point. If you activate this feature, it will create a concrete list instance.

The presentation of these files in Solution Explorer shown in Figure 7–4 is even more confusing since the physical files that are deployed look different from this. You have to decide whether you can work more efficiently with the Visual Studio 2010 project template support for features, packages, and so forth, or whether you want to use the conventional method of building features, solutions, and so on. These conventional methods are, for instance, writing features and list definitions from scratch directly into XML files and using a folder layout in Solution Explorer such as the one illustrated in Figure 7–4.

For a pared-down list template, you only need a feature containing the list definition file. Thus, the target folder would have the structure and contents as in Figure 7–5.

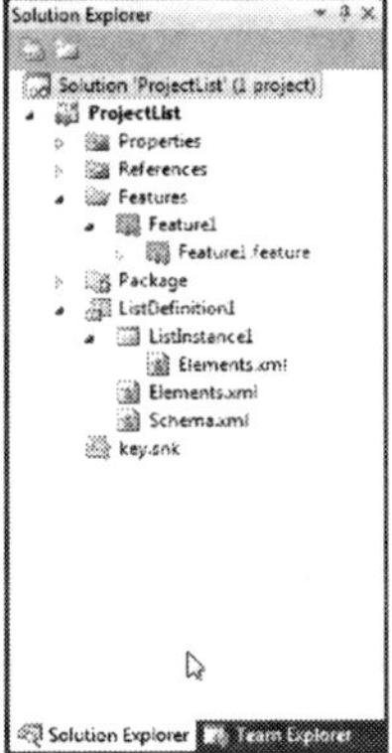

Figure 7–4. Basic structure of the List Definition template

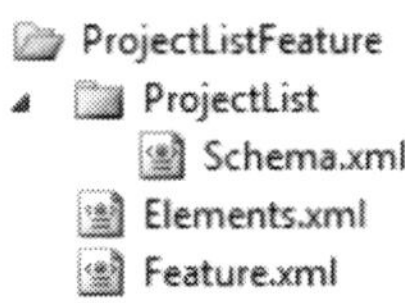

Figure 7–5. Contents of the target folder

To build our example list definition, remove the list instance related files so that you end up with the structure shown in Figure 7–6 in the Solution Explorer window.

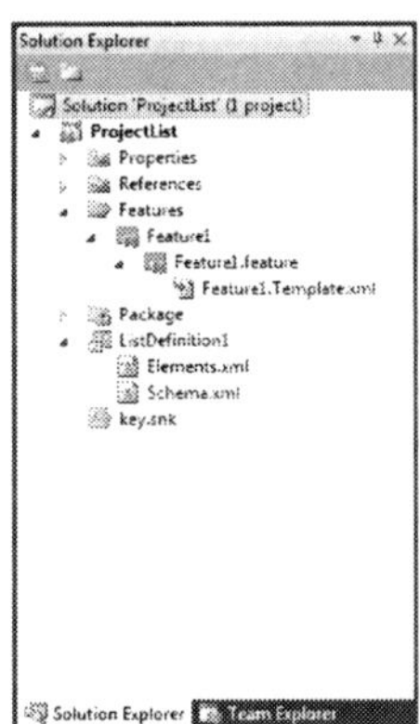

Figure 7–6. Reduced structure for a list defintion without a list instance

For a list definition, you only need an XML list definition file called `schema.xml` and, according to the base type of your new list definition, different list forms. For a list based on the custom list template, you need no more files. Nevertheless, you have to specify four list forms inside the list definition file. The first three basic forms are derived from the %SharePoint Root%\TEMPLATE\Pages\form.aspx template file. The AllItems.aspx page uses the viewpage.aspx page at the same location.

- NewForm.aspx
- EditForm.aspx
- DispForm.aspx
- AllItems.aspx

These four files are merely placeholders for the real content that will be loaded from SharePoint at runtime. Thus, these four files are identical for all list types that are derived from the custom list template or similar definitions. The list forms, especially the view forms, for the calendar or picture library list types use additional view forms that need to be delivered with the list definition.

You need to define a feature that acts as a container that can be deployed and that provides the custom list template in a SharePoint environment. A feature providing the list definition looks like Listing 7–3.

Listing 7–3. *Feature.xml*

```
<?xml version="1.0" encoding="utf-8"?>
<Feature xmlns="http://schemas.microsoft.com/sharepoint/"
         Id="2de7fd2d-da5a-499d-860e-5e2b70374631"
         ImageUrl=""
         Scope="Web"
         Title="ProjectListFeature">
  <ElementManifests>
    <ElementManifest Location="Elements.xml" />
    <ElementFile Location="ProjectList\Schema.xml" />
  </ElementManifests>
</Feature>
```

In addition to the standard feature attributes—ID, Title, Scope, and Description—you can define an assembly and class attribute for a custom feature receiver to handle the FeatureActivated and FeatureDeactivated events.

```
ReceiverAssembly="ProjectList, Version=1.0.0.0, Culture=neutral,
PublicKeyToken=64f6d54d1d6e09cd"
ReceiverClass="Core.Feature.ListFeatureReceiver"
```

■ **Tip** You can find a full reference for all feature attributes at http://msdn.microsoft.com/en-us/library/ms475601(office.14).aspx.

In a feature receiver FeatureActivated event, you can execute custom initializations when the feature is activated. For instance, create a list from the template you provide in this feature, and create initial list items.

A feature receiver class that implements event handlers for these events could look like the example in Listing 7–4.

Listing 7–4. *FeatureReceiver Class*

```
using System;
using System.Collections.Generic;
using System.Text;
using Microsoft.SharePoint;
using System.Collections;

namespace Core.Feature
{
    public class ListFeatureReceiver : SPFeatureReceiver
    {

        public override void FeatureActivated(
                            SPFeatureReceiverProperties properties)
        {
            //feature is scoped at Web, so the parent type is SPWeb
            using (SPWeb web = properties.Feature.Parent as SPWeb)
            {
                //For Example print Url of the Web
                Response.Write(web.Url);
            }
         }
        public override void FeatureDeactivating(
                                   SPFeatureReceiverProperties properties)
        {
                //do nothing
        }
      }
}
```

The element <ElementManifest> specifies which element files are deployed for the list definition. In the example, the list definition file schema.xml and the elements.xml file contain the real list template declaration (see Listing 7–5).

Listing 7–5. *Elements.xml for List Definition Deployment*

```
<?xml version="1.0" encoding="utf-8"?>
<Elements xmlns="http://schemas.microsoft.com/sharepoint/">
    <ListTemplate
        Name="ProjectList"
        Type="12099"
        BaseType="0"
        OnQuickLaunch="TRUE"
        SecurityBits="11"
        Hidden="TRUE"
        Sequence="410"
        DisplayName="ProjectList - My custom list"
        Description=""
        Image="/_layouts/images/itgen.gif"/>
</Elements>
```

Be careful that the value for the list template's name attribute and the subdirectory name shown in Figure 7–5 containing the list definition are exactly the same. Otherwise, SharePoint may not find the referenced files if you want to create a list instance from this template.

The other attributes define basic properties of the list template.

In any case, you must set a type attribute. The value should be greater than 10,000 in order to prevent conflicts with existing template types from SharePoint. Furthermore, you can control the visibility with the `hidden` attribute, set a base type, and enter values for the display name, description, and icon for the list template. Base types range from 0 to 4, where 0 refers to a list type and, for instance, 1 refers to a document library.

List Template Definition Files

The `schema.xml` file defines the final appearance of the list. The basic elements such as fields, views, and content types are defined in this file.

Listing 7–6 shows the basic structure.

***Listing 7–6.** Basic List Definition Structure in schema.xml*

```
<List>
    <MetaData>
<ContentTypes/>
<Fields/>
<Views>
  <View>
    <Joins/>
    <Projections/>
    <ViewFields/>
    <Query/>
  </View>
<Forms/>
</MetaData>
</List>
```

The following sections explain these basic elements of a list definition file and show how to build the example template step-by-step by defining the necessary attributes, fields, views, and so on.

The List Element

The List element specifies basic attributes such as list `Title`, `Type`, `BaseType`, and `Url` (see Listing 7–7).

***Listing 7–7.** List Element in schema.xml*

```
<List
  xmlns:ows="Microsoft SharePoint"
  Title="ProjectList"
  FolderCreation="FALSE"
  Direction="$Resources:Direction;"
  Url="Lists/ProjectList"
  BaseType="0">
```

The Url property is generally overwritten by the settings inside the onet.xml file of a site definition. Furthermore, you need to specify a BaseType ID from which your custom list template is derived. At this point, you can also define, for instance, whether to enable versioning.

■ **Note** Additional attributes are optional; you can find them at http://msdn.microsoft.com/en-us/library/ms459356(office.14).aspx.

The ContentTypes Element

In the ContentTypes section, you define a new content type for your list template based on the base type of your list template. If you have used the Visual Studio list definition project template, it has created the section shown in Listing 7–8 inside your schema.xml file.

Listing 7–8. *ContentTypes Element in schema.xml*

```
<ContentTypes>
    <ContentTypeRef ID="0x01">
        <Folder TargetName="Item" />
    </ContentTypeRef>
    <ContentTypeRef ID="0x0120" />
</ContentTypes>
```

Change this initial declaration to the one shown in Listing 7–9, since you're creating your own content type:

Listing 7–9. *ContentType Declaration*

```
<ContentType ID="0x0100443C8F5ED3211f01ACC2EC3F262E51F6"
             Name="$Resources:Item"
             Group="$Resources:List_Content_Types"
             Description="$Resources:ItemCTDesc"
             Version="1">
<FieldRefs>
</FieldRefs>
</ContentType>
```

In this ContentType declaration, specify a unique ID, which must be in a particular format based on a hexadecimal inheritance schema (starting with 0x01) in combination with a unique ID. In addition, specify the Name, a Description, and a Group for your content type. (For more information about creating content types, see Chapter 4.)

After specifying custom fields in the next section, you can add these fields to your custom content type at this section. The content type section of the example will be completed later in the chapter.

■ **Note** You can find explanations and a full reference to content types at http://msdn.microsoft.com/en-us/library/aa544130(office.14).aspx.

The Fields Element

In the Fields section of the list definition file, you define the fields that you want to use for your list. The field definitions are based on the `fldtypes.xml` file located in the `%SharePoint Root%\TEMPLATE\XML\` folder. For example, if you want to add a simple text field, you would use the following line:

```
<Field
    Type="Text"
    Description="Name of the customer "
    DisplayName="Customer"
    Required="TRUE"
    MaxLength="255"
    ID="{1185203c-4916-47f9-af3f-d5ac6cbaf676}"
    Name="Customer"/>
```

Each field definition has standard attributes such as `Name`, `Type`, `ID`, `Description`, `DisplayName`, and `Required`, as well as some additional type-specific attributes, such as `MaxLength` for a text field. You have to supply some of these attributes such as `Name`, `ID`, and `Type` since they are required attributes.

■ **Note** Other field attributes are optional and may be related to a field type. You can find a full reference of field attributes at `http://msdn.microsoft.com/en-us/library/ms437580(office.14).aspx`.

The `ID` attribute specifies a GUID to identify the field. You can add this ID to the previous content type definition if you want to use this field in your content type.
For the example with the project scenario, you need to define some fields for the project list (see Listing 7–10).

Listing 7–10. *Field Specification in schema.xml*

```
<Field
    Type="Text"
    Description="Name of the Project"
    DisplayName="ProjectName"
    Required="TRUE"
    MaxLength="255"
    ID="{ce7ac62b-d584-48b6-8022-524b7bbaa83e}"
    StaticName="ProjectName"
    Name="ProjectName" />
<Field
    Type="Choice"
    DisplayName="Phase"
    ReadOnly="TRUE"
    Required="TRUE"
    Format="Dropdown"
    FillInChoice="FALSE"
    ID="{eeb87858-0017-46c3-8bba-31caa0abc9fa}"
    StaticName="Phase"
    Name="Phase">
        <Default>Presales</Default>
```

```
        <CHOICES>
          <CHOICE>Presales</CHOICE>
          <CHOICE>Initiation</CHOICE>
          <CHOICE>Execution</CHOICE>
          <CHOICE>Close</CHOICE>
        </CHOICES>
 </Field>
<Field
    Type="Boolean"
    Description="Is the project manager contract owner?"
    DisplayName="ContractOwner"
    ID="{1a72202d-fcbe-40e7-9571-e59cfc4b4cc6}"
    StaticName="ContractOwner"
    Name="ContractOwner"
    RowOrdinal="0">
        <Default>0</Default>
</Field>
<Field
    Type="Currency"
    Description="Total Product Revenue"
    DisplayName="Volume Product"
    Required="FALSE"
    LCID="1033"
    ID="{6f5f2e54-2314-43de-9bd2-231ce4e984fb}"
    StaticName="VolumeProduct"
    Name="VolumeProduct" />
<Field
    Type="Currency"
    Description="Total costs for products"
    DisplayName="Cogs Products"
    Required="FALSE"
    LCID="1031" ID="{f4df0519-1cff-4fab-afa1-56591997a134}"
    StaticName="CogsProducts"
    Name="CogsProducts" />
```

Lookup Fields

You can define a lookup field that looks up a field in another list. For this, you need to supply the name of the lookup field, the target list, and the field from the target list that is to be displayed. You can even specify additional fields that come from that target list and show supplementary values—but they are read-only. Figure 7–7 shows how a lookup field refers to a Greetings list and displays two extra fields from that Greetings list.

Title	ProjectName	ProjectPhase	ContractOwner	Cogs Product	Volume Product	Greetings	Greetings:My Column	Greetings:MyColumn2
Special Project	SharePoint Project List	Execution	Windows?Dev\Bernd	$1,234,567.00	$1,234,567.00	Hello	Hi	What's up

Add new item

Figure 7–7. List with lookup fields

The first field declaration specifies a normal lookup field called Greetings. The two subsequent fields are read-only and display additional data related to the first lookup field (see Listing 7–11).

Listing 7–11. Lookup Field Specification in schema.xml

```
<Field Type="Lookup" DisplayNam="Greetings" Required="FALSE" List="Lists/Greetings"
ShowField="Title" ID="{f76e5a46-83eb-480a-8e62-d99c67d3f9e9}" StaticName="Greetings"
Name="Greetings" />

<Field Type="Lookup" DisplayName="Greetings:My Column" List="Lists/Greetings"
ShowField="My_Column" FieldRef="f76e5a46-83eb-480a-8e62-d99c67d3f9e9" ReadOnly="TRUE"
ID="{4f152f23-c6a2-4375-8de2-77df143b8bdc}"  StaticName="Greetings_x003a_My_Column "
Name="Greetings_x003a_My _Column" />

<Field Type="Lookup" DisplayName="Greetings:MyColumn2" List="Lists/Greetings"
ShowField="MyColumn2" FieldRef="f76e5a46-83eb-480a-8e62-d99c67d3f9e9" ReadOnly="TRUE"
ID="{251798c2-95f6-451e-bd06-df9191774477}" StaticName="Greetings_x003a_MyColumn2"
Name="Greetings_x003a_MyColumn2" />
```

■ **Note** Defining lookup fields always presumes that the target list exists at runtime. Especially in templates and list definitions, you cannot be sure that the target list exists while instantiating a list from this template.

After specifying all fields, you can add them to your sample content type specification (see Listing 7–12).

Listing 7–12. ContentType Specification in schema.xml

```
<ContentType ID="0x0100443C8F5ED3211f01ACC2EC3F262E51F6" Name="$Resources:Item"
             Group="$Resources:List_Content_Types"
             Description="$Resources:ItemCTDesc" Version="1" >
    <FieldRefs>
       <FieldRef ID="{ec70c353-343a-4d20-9532-29ce0150680b}" Name="ProjectName" />
       <FieldRef ID="{84c56f39-3d3f-4cf4-8be4-203cb94be296}" Name="Phase"/>
       <FieldRef ID="{fa564e0f-0c70-4ab9-b863-0177e6ddd247}" Name="Title" />
       <FieldRef ID="{f4df0519-1cff-4fab-afa1-56591997a134}" Name="ContractOwner"/>
       <FieldRef ID="{9f5f2e54-61ba-43de-9bd2-231ce4e984fc}" Name="CogsProducts" />
       <FieldRef ID="{6f5f2e54-2314-43de-9bd2-231ce4e984fb}" Name="VolumeProduct" />
       <FieldRef ID="{f76e5a46-83eb-480a-8e62-d99c67d3f9e9}" Name="Greetings" />
       <FieldRef ID="{4f152f23-c6a2-4375-8de2-77df143b8bdc}"
                 Name="Greetings_x003a_My_Column" ReadOnly="TRUE" />
       <FieldRef ID="{251798c2-95f6-451e-bd06-df9191774477}"
                 Name="Greetings_x003a_MyColumn2" ReadOnly="TRUE" />
    </FieldRefs>
</ContentType>
```

The Views Element

The Views section is one of the most important ones in the schema.xml file. Here you define how many views you need, which fields are displayed, and any other options such as filtering, grouping, and sorting.

To create a view for the list, you use the default view as a starting point (see Listing 7–13).

Listing 7–13. *Default View Specification*

```
<Views>
    <View DisplayName="All Items" DefaultView="TRUE" BaseViewID="1" Type="HTML"
          MobileView="TRUE" MobileDefaultView="TRUE" XslLink="main.xsl"
          ImageUrl="/_layouts/images/generic.png" WebPartZoneID="Main"
          WebPartOrder="1" Url="AllItems.aspx" SetupPath="pages\viewpage.aspx">

        <XslLink>main.xsl</XslLink>
            <Query>
                <OrderBy>
                    <FieldRef Name="ID" />
                </OrderBy>
            </Query>
        <ViewFields>
            <FieldRef Name="Attachments" />
            <FieldRef Name="LinkTitle" />
            <FieldRef Name="Date" />
        </ViewFields>
        <RowLimit Paged="TRUE">30</RowLimit>
    </View>
</Views>
```

The View element specifies common properties:

- `DisplayName`: Sets the name of the view
- `DefaultView`: Sets the default view property
- `BaseViewID`: Sets the ID of the base view
- `Type`: Sets the type (the default is `HTML`; could be `Chart` or `Pivot`)
- `MobileView`: Specifies whether it is a mobile view
- `MobileDefaultView`: Sets the default for mobile view
- `ImageUrl`: Sets the image at the `ViewSelector`
- `XslLink`: Sets the path to the XSL rendering file
- `WebPartZoneID`: Specifies the Web Part zone in which the list view is to be inserted
- `WebPartOrder`: Sets the Web Part order inside the specified zone
- `Url`: Sets the Url URL the Web Part Page that hosts the list view
- `SetupPath`: Specifies a parent view page from which the actual (`AllItem.aspx`) page is derived

XSL-Based Rendering

The first element of the view references the XSL file that is used for rendering the view. The XSL-based rendering replaces the CAML-based approach from SharePoint 2007 that contained about 3,000 lines of rendering information inside the `schema.xml` file. With SharePoint 2010, you can now customize the rendering by editing the referenced `main.xsl`. There is a new element inside the view section called `ViewStyle` that controls the appearance of list items in a view. By inserting a specific `ViewStyle` ID, you can, for instance, display the list items in a tile arrangement instead of the standard list view. The next exercise demonstrates how you can change this design using SharePoint Designer.

USING SHAREPOINT DESIGNER TO CHANGE LIST RENDERING

1. Start SharePoint Designer 2010, and select the list you want to edit on the left.
2. Select the view you want to change, such as All Items.
3. Now select the XSLT list view Web Part, and click Design in the ribbon.
4. Here you can select a different list item arrangement.
5. Click the Save button to preserve the changes.

Another new feature of SharePoint 2010 is the XSLT List View Web Part that replaces the existing list view Web Part.

We recommend that you use SharePoint Designer 2010 to customize the rendering of a list in these XSLT list view Web Parts, for instance, by creating conditional formatting. With SharePoint Designer, you can add rules to show or hide content; to change the format, fonts, or colors; and even to reorder the whole list item arrangement.

If you add a conditional formatting rule, SharePoint Designer adds the required XSLT code to the view page such as `AllItems.aspx`. Examine the changed contents of `AllItems.aspx` in order to reuse the XSLT specifications for your custom list definition. This procedure is much easier than writing the XSL transformation from scratch.

Joins and Projections

In SharePoint 2010, you can use CAML-based joins and projections to build views based on joining two lists connected via an existing lookup relationship. In essence, projections are like lookup fields that show one or more fields from the target list.

One or more joins are defined inside the Joins element within the View element. There are two types of joins: inner joins and left joins. You can define joins only between two lists, but you can build a chain of joins. Therefore, you have to use at least the parent list of the view, called the *primary list*. The other list for the join is called the *foreign list*. An additional join can be built from that foreign list joining to another foreign list, which in turn can join another foreign list, and so forth.

The following excerpt—not included in our sample project list definition—shows how it works.

The example scenario needs to display which projects are located at what location. So, the view needs to join the projects list with an existing project partner list and, in the next step, the project partner list with the list of locations. Define a lookup field named ProjectPartnerName in a Project list that looks up to a ProjectPartner list, as shown in Figure 7–8. This list has a lookup field called LocationName that looks up data from a Locations list, as shown in Figure 7–9 and Figure 7–10.

Figure 7–8. Project list view including Project Partner

Figure 7–9. Project partners list

Figure 7–10. Locations list

The joins defined within the schema look like Listing 7–14.

Listing 7–14. Specification of Joins in schema.xml

```
<Joins>
  <Join Type="LEFT" ListAlias="ProjectPartner">
    <Eq>
      <FieldRef Name="ProjectPartnerName" RefType="Id" />
      <FieldRef List="ProjectPartner" Name="ID" />
    </Eq>
  </Join>

  <Join Type="LEFT" ListAlias="partnersLocations">
    <Eq>
      <FieldRef List="ProjectPartner" Name="LocationName" RefType="Id" />
      <FieldRef List="partnersLocations" Name="ID " />
    </Eq>
  </Join>
</Joins>
```

The type of join can be either left or inner. If you have more than one join from one list to another, they have to be distinguished using the `ListAlias` attribute in order to identify them individually. For the first `Join` element, the `ListAlias` attribute equals the name of the list. The next `Join` elements can have individually aliases. In the `List` attribute of the `FieldRef` element, you always have to use the value from the `ListAlias` attribute. The `FieldRef` parameter specifies the "join on" fields, where the first one is the lookup field from the primary list, and the second one is the field from the foreign list. The field from the foreign list must always be the `ID` field.

■ **Note** You cannot use a multilookup field as a base for a join relationship.

If you have a `Where` clause in the `Query` section of the view that uses a field from a foreign list—for instance, LocationName—you need to specify this field in the `ProjectedFields` element (see Listing 7–15).

Listing 7–15. *Specification of Projected Fields in Schema.xml*

```
<ProjectedFields>
  <Field
    Name="LocationName"
    Type="Lookup"
    List="partnerLocations"
    ShowField="Title" />
</ProjectedFields>
```

Should you want to show one or more fields from another list inside your view, you can define these fields inside the `ProjectedFields` element. You also have to insert these fields in the `ViewFields` section of the `View` element and in the content type specification.

The `Name` attribute refers to the name of the lookup field. The `Type` attribute must always be `Lookup` since the joins and projected fields mechanism is built on an existing lookup relationship between the two lists. The `List` attribute refers to the list alias specified in the corresponding join section. The final attribute, `ShowField`, defines the field from the foreign list that should be displayed in the view.

To distinguish a projected field from the normal lookup field that you can specify in the fields section, remember that projected fields always relate to joined lists, whereas lookup fields in the field section do not require a join relation.

■ **Note** Not all lists can be joined, and not every field can be used as a "join on" parameter. Furthermore, the total number of join elements in a view cannot exceed the `MaxQueryLookupFields` property from the `SPWebApplication` object (the default is six).

The ViewFields Element

In the ViewFields section of a view, you can specify which fields should be visible in the list view. Listing 7–16 shows how you can define fields to be shown in a view.

Listing 7–16. *Specification of ViewFields in schema.xml*

```
<ViewFields>
    <FieldRef Name="LinkTitle"/>
    <FieldRef Name="Phase" />
    <FieldRef Name="ProjectName" />
    <FieldRef Name="ContractOwner" />
</ViewFields>
```

You only need to supply the internal name of the field using a FieldRef attribute. In addition to the fields you have specified in the Fields section, you can refer to the base fields that exist in every list. For example, you can add the Title field to your view fields. That would add the Title text column. But you can also add LinkTitle if you want to add the title field with the context menu.

The Query Element

In this section, you can define a CAML-based query that sorts or filters your list elements in this view. Listing 7–17 gives an example.

Listing 7–17. *Query Specification in a View*

```
<Query>
    <Where>
        <Eq>
            <FieldRef Name="Phase" />
            <Value Type="Text">Execution</Value>
        </Eq>
    </Where>
    <OrderBy>
        <FieldRef Name="ID"></FieldRef>
    </OrderBy>
</Query>
```

This query filters the list items by comparing the Phase field value with Execution and orders the list items by ID. Using CAML, you can build complex queries in this section.

Forms

Inside the <Forms> element, you define which forms are used for creating a new list item, editing an item, or displaying an item. If your list definition is based on the custom list template, you can use a master form, specified by the SetupPath attribute, from which your forms are derived (see Listing 7–18).

Listing 7–18. *Specification of Forms in schema.xml*

```
<Form Type="DisplayForm" Url="DispForm.aspx"
      SetupPath="pages\form.aspx" WebPartZoneID="Main" />

<Form Type="EditForm" Url="EditForm.aspx"
      SetupPath="pages\form.aspx" WebPartZoneID="Main" />

<Form Type="NewForm" Url="NewForm.aspx"
      SetupPath="pages\form.aspx" WebPartZoneID="Main" />
```

You can also provide your own custom forms through this feature containing the list definition file and form files that are referenced through the Url attribute. Don't forget to include these custom forms inside the element manifest of the list definition feature. You create custom forms by simply copying the referenced form's .aspx file and renaming it to, for example, EditForm.aspx (Listing 7–19).

Listing 7–19. Feature.xml for List Definition Using Custom Forms

```
<?xml version="1.0" encoding="utf-8"?>
<Feature xmlns="http://schemas.microsoft.com/sharepoint/"
         Id="2de7fd2d-da5a-499d-860e-5e2b70374631"
         ImageUrl=""
         Scope="Web"
         Title="ProjectListFeature">
    <ElementManifests>
        <ElementManifest Location="Elements.xml" />
        <ElementFile Location="ProjectList\Schema.xml" />
        <ElementFile Location="ProjectList\NewForm.aspx" />
        <ElementFile Location="ProjectList\DispForm.aspx" />
        <ElementFile Location="ProjectList\EditForm.aspx" />
        <ElementFile Location="ProjectList\AllItems.aspx" />
    </ElementManifests>
</Feature>
```

Using List Templates

There are several different approaches to actually using your custom list templates. After deploying and activating the feature containing the list definition files—either built manually from scratch or autogenerated from Visual Studio—you can create a list from this list definition.

The following exercises describe four ways to create an instance from a list template, assuming the list definition is installed properly.

USING THE SHAREPOINT UI

1. Click the "View All site content" button on the quick launch bar.
2. Click the Create button.
3. On the Create page shown in Figure 7–11, select your custom list template from the custom lists group.
4. Enter a list name and a description, and decide whether to add a link to the quick launch bar.
5. Click OK to create an instance from your custom list template.

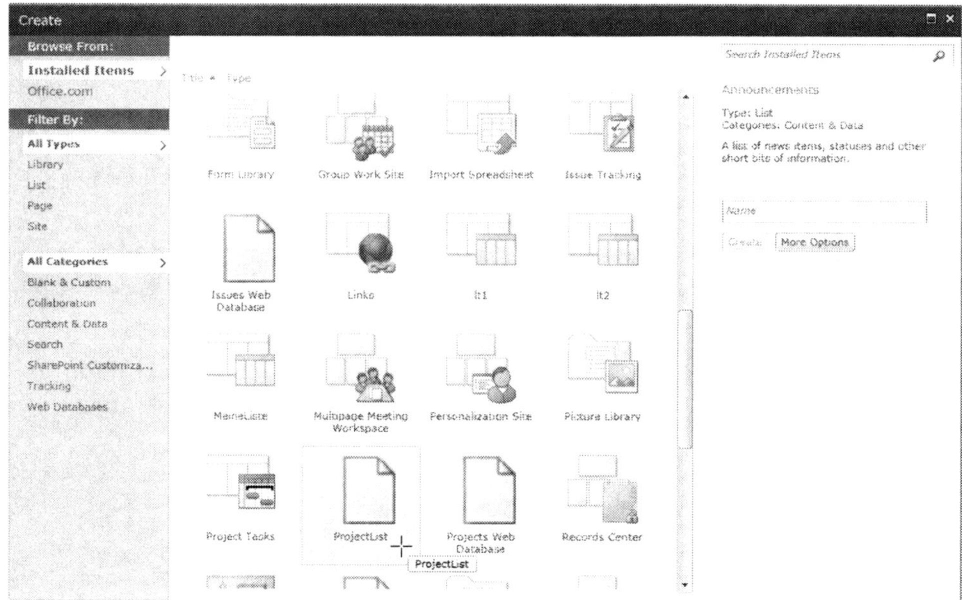

Figure 7–11. Custom list template on the Create page

The following exercise includes a list definition in a custom site definition.

USING A CUSTOM SITE DEFINITION

1. Open the `onet.xml` file for your custom site definition.
2. To provide your custom list template for a site template, edit the `<ListTemplates>` section, and add the following line:

```
<ListTemplate  Name="ProjectList" Type="13001" Hidden="FALSE" BaseType="0"
SecurityBits="11" DisplayName="ProjectList" Description="This list contains common
project details." Image="/_layouts/images/itgen.gif"/>
```

The `SecurityBits` attribute controls the general read and write access to the list. The first 1 means users can read all items; the second 1 means users can edit all items. Users with the ManageList permission can read and write list items, regardless of the `SecurityBits` value. Document libraries are not affected by this attribute.

3. To instantiate a list from this list template, you need to add a `<List>` element to the `<Lists>` element of a `<Configuration>` section:

```
<List FeatureId="7346F629-03E1-436D-B2A2-80E2744FD8BC" Type="12001" Title="ProjectList"
Url="Lists/ProjectList" />
```

4. Provide the feature containing the list definition in the `<WebFeatures>` or `<SiteFeatures>` element of the `<Configuration>` section.
5. Deploy your custom site definition, and create a site from this site template.

Another way of creating a new list is using the SharePoint API. In contrast to the preceding example, using the SharePoint API enables you to create a new list directly from a template without building a whole new site.

USING THE SHAREPOINT API

1. Open the class or `.aspx.cs` file for a web page that should contain the code to create a new list from an installed template.
2. Insert the following lines to create a new list from the installed template:

```
SPWeb web = SPContext.Current.CurentSite.OpenWeb(http://myserver);
web.AllowUnsafeUpdates = true;
Guid guid = web.Lists.Add("MyList", "MyListDescription",
web.ListTemplates["ProjectList"]);
SPList myList = web.Lists.GetList(guid, true);
//do something
...
myList.Update();
web.Update();
```

The final exercise shows how to use SharePoint Designer to create a new list from an installed list template.

USING SHAREPOINT DESIGNER

1. Open the Site Actions menu, and click Edit Site in SharePoint Designer. Or, open SharePoint Designer and then open the current web site.
2. On the Site Objects panel on the left side, choose Site Objects.
3. On the ribbon, click SharePoint Lists. Click ProjectList, and fill out the configuration form.
4. Click OK to create a new list from this template.

Site Templates

By using templates for SharePoint sites, you can build complete SharePoint applications that can be instantiated over and over again. For example, if you need a SharePoint site for managing projects including custom lists, Web Parts, and so forth, you can define a site template that you can reuse for every project by instantiating a site from it. But, like list templates, site templates can be created in different ways, as you will learn in a moment.

■ **Note** Almost every component that can be defined in a site definition can also be defined as a feature. Site definitions and features both use the SharePoint Foundation XML schema located in the SharePoint root in the `XML/Schema` subdirectory.

Visual Studio 2010 Support

Visual Studio 2010 includes a project template for a SharePoint site definition. By creating a new project from this project template, Visual Studio 2010 provides the necessary files and skeleton content (see Figure 7–12).

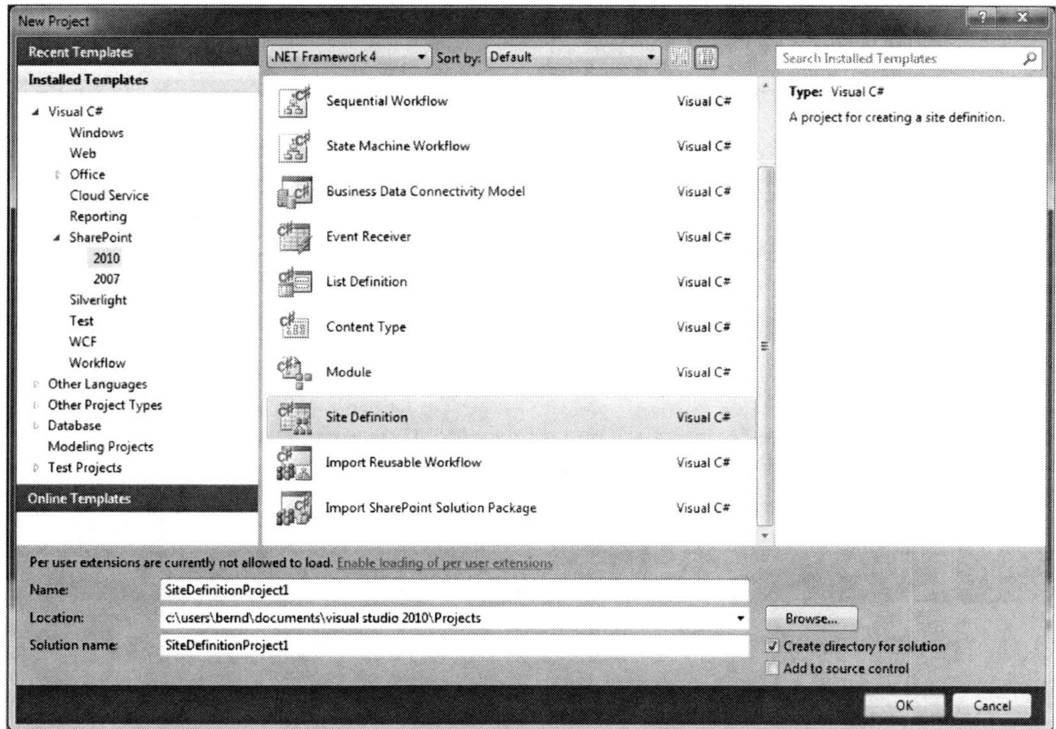

Figure 7–12. *Site definition project template in Visual Studio2010*

You can now use the new Visual Studio 2010 tools for SharePoint to complete your site definition. In the following sections, we explain how to use and extend the files that are generated by the Visual Studio 2010 project template.

SiteTemplate vs. SiteDefinition

SharePoint distinguishes between a site template and a site definition. You can create a site template by building a SharePoint application including lists, Web Parts, and such elements, using the SharePoint UI and the SharePoint Designer. Afterward, you can save the complete site as a template in a SharePoint solution (`.wsp` file) that can be imported to the site template gallery.

CREATE A SITE TEMPLATE

1. Build your SharePoint site by using the SharePoint UI and SharePoint Designer.
2. After finishing your site, click SiteActions ➤ SiteSettings.
3. Go to the Save Site as Template page.
4. Enter a file name, a template name, and a description, and decide whether to include content.
5. Click OK to create a template from your SharePoint site.

Site templates built this way are using their base template, such as team site or blank site, including such components as lists, Web Parts, and language settings. It follows that you need to be careful to provide the same preconditions as in the source SharePoint environment. If, for instance, the target SharePoint system uses a different language, the template wouldn't even appear in the template selection box of the target site's Create page. Although the algorithm was improved in SharePoint 2010, because SharePoint now builds `.wsp` solution files instead of `.stp` files (that only stored a delta of customizations compared to its base template), you still can't guarantee that your template will work in another SharePoint environment. To avoid surprises, you should consider the language and whether there were any customizations in the template's source site that can lead to missing references on the target site.

Site definitions, on the other hand, are defined in XML files and can contain all the necessary components—with no surprises. They are packaged in SharePoint solution files (`.wsp`) and are easy to transport since everything you need is packaged into a single file. Thus, site definitions are preferred by professional developers because they are more dependable and extensible.

The following exercise explains how to create a minimal site definition using Visual Studio 2010.

CREATE A SITE DEFINITION

1. Start Visual Studio 2010, and select New Project.
2. Select Site Definition Template, from the SharePoint ➤ 2010 section.
3. Enter a name, location, and solution name, and click OK. Figure 7–13 shows the basic site definition structure of the project template.

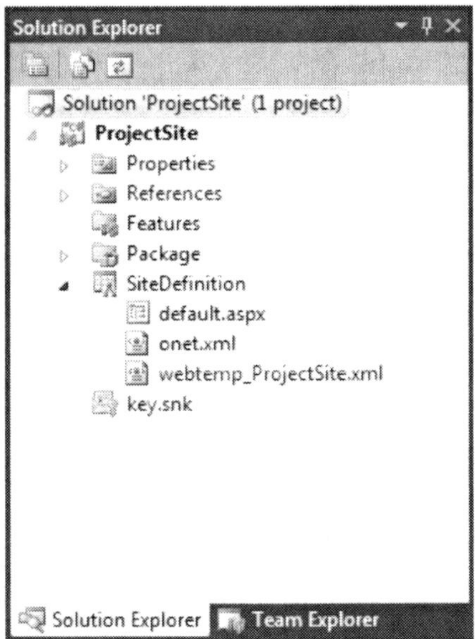

Figure 7–13. *Basic site definition structure of the project template*

Site Definition Structure

A bare-bones site definition contains three files:

- `webTemp.xml`: Created for every language version and contains the entries for the template selection box on the site creation page
- `onet.xml`: Contains one or more configurations for a site template, including specification of all components used, such as features, lists, and Web Parts
- `default.aspx`: Empty page

In the following subsections, these files are detailed. You will learn their purpose and which attributes are most important.

■ **Note** For a full site definition reference and extending the examples, see the official MSDN reference at `http://msdn.microsoft.com/en-us/library/aa978512(office.14).aspx`.

---

webTemp.xml

Usually site definitions are deployed as SharePoint solutions. Although you could alternatively copy your site definition files to the SharePoint Root (14 hive), you gain much more control of your solutions by deploying it as a solution file (.wsp) using Central Administration or by uploading it to the solution gallery. (For more information about solution deployment, see Chapter 9.)

To use a site definition (by creating sites from a template), you must first specify a declaration of the template as an XML file in order to make it available in the template selection box of the New SharePoint Site page. This requires an XML file called webTemp*.xml. Insert your unique name in place of the asterisk to avoid overwriting internal template files. The path for these template declaration files is SharePoint Root\Template\LocaleCodeID\XML\. In the Visual Studio 2010 Solution Explorer, these files appear beneath the locale ID, such as en-US.

To demonstrate the creation of a simple site definition, we will reuse the project management scenario from the list template chapter. Therefore, a simple template declaration file, called webTempProject.xml, looks like Listing 7–20.

Listing 7–20. *A webTempProject.xml File*

```
<Templates xmlns:ows="Microsoft SharePoint">
  <Template Name="ProjectSite" ID="12099" >
     <Configuration ID="0" Title="SharePoint Project Management DB Site"
                   Description="" Hidden="FALSE"
                   ImageUrl="/_layouts/images/Project/logo.bmp"
                   DisplayCategory="CustomSharePoint" RootWebOnly=”false” />
  </Template>
</Templates>
```

This short declaration contains the following elements and attributes:

- Template element attributes:
    - * Name: Specifies the name of the template and the folder where the site definition is located inside the %SharePointRoot%\TEMPLATE\Site Definition folder.
    - * ID: Specifies a unique ID for this template. Use IDs greater than 10,000 to avoid conflicts with existing SharePoint templates.
- Configuration element attributes:
    - * ID: References the ID inside the onet.xml file of this site definition
        - * Title: Title of the new site
        - * Description: Description text of the new site
        - * Hidden: Flag indicating whether the configuration appears on the site creation page
        - * ImageUrl: URL to a picture that is displayed on the site creation page as a preview picture
        - * DisplayCategory: The category under which the configuration appears inside the template selection box of the site creation page
        - * RootWebOnly: Flag indicating whether the configuration can only be used for root sites (site collections)

■ **Tip** If you have created a site definition using the Visual Studio 2010 site definition project template, you can easily locate the `webTemp*.xml` file in Solution Explorer under SiteDefinition ➤ LocaleCode and customize it as shown earlier.

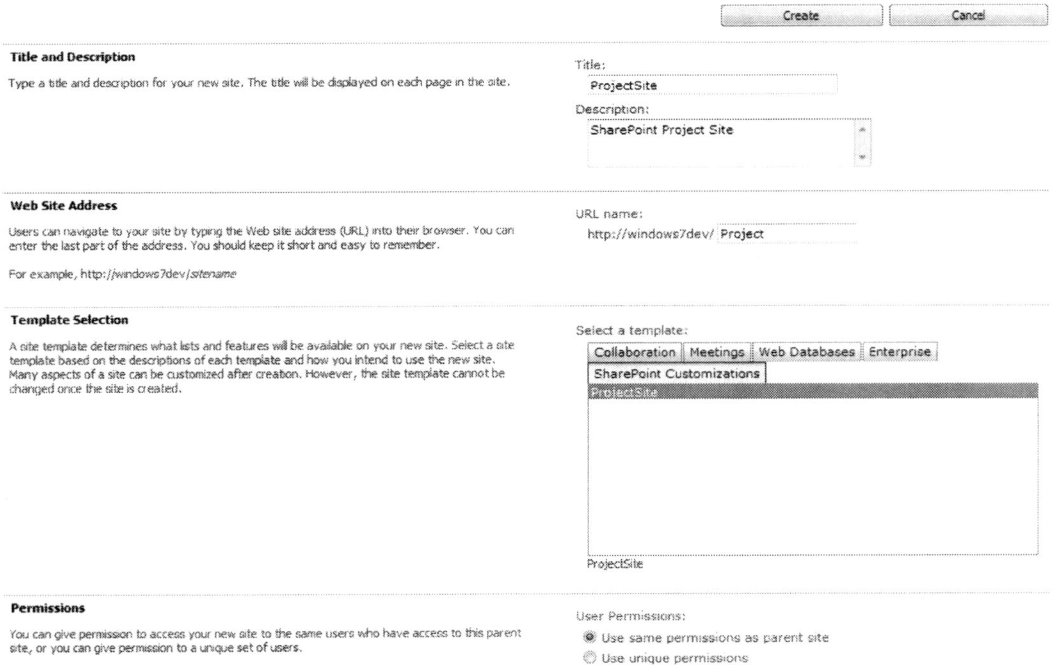

***Figure 7–14.** Template selection box of the New SharePoint Site page*

This is a small example that creates an additional entry in the New SharePoint Site page template selection box in the specified group, as shown in Figure 7–14. But first you have to deploy this file by copying the file into the `%SharePoint Root%\TEMPLATE\LocaleID\XML` folder and resetting IIS or using the Visual Studio 2010 built-in deployment by pressing F5.

In the `webTemp*.xml` file, you can specify much more than a single site template. For example, the SharePoint basic site definitions that are defined in the `webtemp.xml` file located in the same folder contain different configurations for such sites as team sites, meeting spaces, and blog sites.

To achieve this, you can specify multiple Template elements that reference different site definitions in the `%SharePointRoot%\TEMPLATE\Site Definition` folder. Each of the Template elements can contain multiple configurations that are specified inside an `onet.xml` file of a site definition. An example of using multiple configurations is shown next. We also explain the structure of an `onet.xml` file and how the configurations work.

Site Provisioning Provider

Using a site provisioning provider, you can execute custom code in the provisioning event of a site. In the event handler method, you can directly customize the new site—for instance, by creating new subsites or lists.

In the Configuration element of the `webTempProject.xml` file, simply add two additional attributes (see Listing 7-21).

Listing 7-21. *webTempProject.xml*

```
<Templates xmlns:ows="Microsoft SharePoint">
  <Template Name="ProjectSite" ID="12099" >
    <Configuration ID="0" Title="SharePoint Project Management DB Site"
                   Description="" Hidden="FALSE"
                   ImageUrl="/_layouts/images/Project/logo.bmp"
                   DisplayCategory="CustomSharePoint" RootWebonly="false"
                   ProvisionAssembly="Project, Version=1.0.0.0, Culture=neutral,
                   PublicKeyToken=xxxxxxxx"
                   ProvisionClass="Project.ProvisioningProvider"
                   ProvisionData="Custom Project Site"/>
  </Template>
</Templates>
```

In addition to the assembly and the class that implements the provisioning provider, you can also pass data, which is then available for further use in the event-handling method.

Listing 7-22 shows how the class `ProvisioningProvider` and the event-handling method for the `Provision` event are implemented.

Listing 7-22. *Custom Provisioning Provider*

```
using System;
using Microsoft.SharePoint;

namespace Project
{

    public class ProvisioningProvider : SPWebProvisioningProvider
    {
        public override void Provision(SPWebPovisioningProperties props)
        {
            //Apply Site Template
            properties.Web.ApplyWebTemplate("Project#0");

            //for further use of the site you need to elevate privileges
            SPSecurity.RunWithElevatedPrivileges(delegate() {
                using (SPWeb web = properties.Web)
                {
                    web.Title=properties.Data;
                    web.Update;
                }
            });
        }
    }
}
```

As a result, when a new site from the actual site definition is created, the Provision event handler automatically applies the first configuration of the project site definition and sets the Title of the site to the ProvisionData value you specified in the webTempProject.xml file. In the Properties.Web.ApplyWebTemplate method, the first part of the string Project#0 references the site definition, whereas the portion after the # defines the configuration.

You can use such a provisioning provider to automatically create subsites using a particular site definition. Doing it this way, you can even create sites from site definitions and their configurations that are marked as hidden and are not visible in the SharePoint Create Site page.

default.aspx

For a minimalist site definition, you need at least a start page for your new site. This start page is a page called default.aspx. It uses the default master page of SharePoint, and consequently you must supply all content in Content controls.

Tip If you created a site definition using the Visual Studio 2010 site definition project template, a minimal default.aspx has already been created. Now you can easily extend it.

A skeleton default.aspx page, such as Visual Studio 2010, created with the site definition project template looks like Listing 7–23.

Listing 7–23. *Minimal default.aspx File*

```
<%@ Page language="C#" MasterPageFile="~masterurl/default.master"
Inherits="Microsoft.SharePoint.WebPartPages.WebPartPage,Microsoft.SharePoint,Version=14.0.0.0,
Culture=neutral,PublicKeyToken=71e9bce111e9429c"  %>
<%@ Register Tagprefix="SharePoint" Namespace="Microsoft.SharePoint.WebControls"
Assembly="Microsoft.SharePoint, Version=14.0.0.0, Culture=neutral,
PublicKeyToken=71e9bce111e9429c" %>
<%@ Register Tagprefix="Utilities" Namespace="Microsoft.SharePoint.Utilities"
Assembly="Microsoft.SharePoint, Version=14.0.0.0, Culture=neutral,
PublicKeyToken=71e9bce111e9429c" %>
<%@ Import Namespace="Microsoft.SharePoint" %>
<%@ Assembly Name="Microsoft.Web.CommandUI, Version=14.0.0.0, Culture=neutral,
PublicKeyToken=71e9bce111e9429c" %>
<%@ Register Tagprefix="WebPartPages" Namespace="Microsoft.SharePoint.WebPartPages"
Assembly="Microsoft.SharePoint, Version=14.0.0.0, Culture=neutral,
PublicKeyToken=71e9bce111e9429c" %>
<asp:Content ContentPlaceHolderId="PlaceHolderPageTitle" runat="server">
    <SharePoint:ProjectProperty Property="Title" runat="server"/>
</asp:Content>
<asp:Content ID="Content1" ContentPlaceHolderId="PlaceHolderMain" runat="server">
    <h1>
<asp:Literal ID="Literal1" runat="server"
Text="<%$Resources:ProjectSite,Greeting%>"></asp:Literal>
    <font color="red">ProjectSite</font>
    </h1>
```

```
</asp:Content>
```

Besides the usual @Page, @Assembly, and @Register directives, a sample page title in the Content control with the ID Content1 is defined in the code. For our actual example, we will extend this to become a dual-zone Web Part page.

Add two WebPartZone controls to this Content control (Listing 7–24).

***Listing 7–24.** Extended default.aspx*

```
<asp:Content ID="Content1" ContentPlaceHolderId="PlaceHolderMain" runat="server">
    <h1>

        <font color="red"> ProjectSite</font>
    </h1>
         <table width="100%" cellpadding=0 cellspacing=0
               style="padding: 5px 10px 10px 10px;">
            <tr>
                <td valign="top" width="70%">
                    <WebPartPages:WebPartZone runat="server"
                         FrameType="TitleBarOnly" ID="Left" Title="loc:Left" />
                  </td>
                  <td> </td>
                  <td valign="top" width="30%">
                      <WebPartPages:WebPartZone runat="server"
                         FrameType="TitleBarOnly" ID="Right" Title="loc:Right" />
                  </td>
                      <td> </td>
                  </tr>
        </table>
</asp:Content>
```

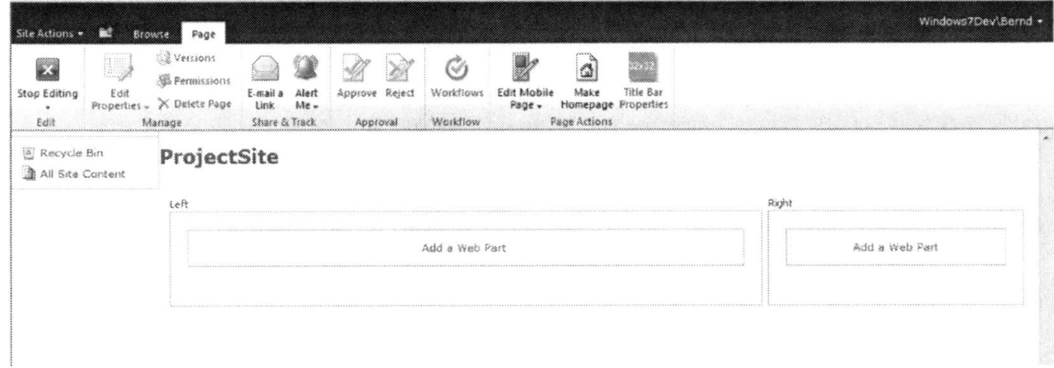

***Figure 7–15.** Web Part zones at the default.aspx page*

These are empty Web Part zones whose contents can be filled by modules specified in the onet.xml file. This is a big advantage because you can provide one empty start page (containing only a page title and empty Web Part zones) that can be used for different configurations. The next section explains how this works.

Onet.xml

The core of a site definition is the onet.xml file that specifies all the components that the site contains, such as lists, Web Parts, and pages.

To allow SharePoint to find the onet.xml and any files referenced in it while creating an instance from a site template, it is essential that the file is located in a subfolder of %SharePoint Root%\Template\SiteTemplates. The folder's name must be the same as the one specified in the webTemp*.xml's template name attribute. In our example, the folder's name is ProjectSite.

Thus, the ProjectSite folder must hold a default.aspx file and a subfolder called XML containing the onet.xml file. Figure 7–16 shows the target folder.

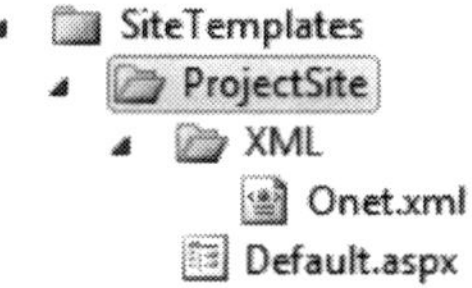

Figure 7–16. Site template target folder

The basic structure for the onet.xml looks like Listing 7–25.

Listing 7–25. Basic Structure of onet.xml

```
<Project Title="ProjectSite">
    <NavBars/>
    <ListTemplates/>
    <DocumentTemplates/>
    <Configurations>
        <Configuration ID>
            <Lists/>
            <Modules/>
            <SiteFeatures/>
            <WebFeatures/>
        </Configuration>
    </Configurations>
    <Modules>
        <Module/>
    </Modules>
</Project>
```

■ **Tip** If you have created a site definition using the Visual Studio 2010 site definition project template, a basic onet.xml file has been generated automatically. You can easily extend this onet.xml file.

The project element is the root element. The value of the title attribute must once again match with the subfolder's name under %SharePointRoot%\14\Template\SiteDefinition and the entry in the webTempProject.xml file.

- `NavBars`: This defines the top and quick launch navigation statically so that when creating a new page, the desired navigation is available directly.
- `ListTemplates`: This defines list templates that are provided for use in the new site.
- `Document Templates`: This provides document templates for list types and document.
- `Configurations`: Each configuration is a set of lists, modules, and features.
- `Modules`: This specifies one or more modules that are used within configurations and contain a Web Part page's content, sites, and auxiliary files.

The following sections explain each element with an example and incrementally build a complete definition for a sample project site.

The NavBars Element

In this section, we define several entries for the top-navigation and quick launch bar. With little effort you can define a complete navigation structure for the site.

Listing 7–26 shows the common format for two-level navigation.

Listing 7–26. *Basic NavBar Structure*

```
<NavBar Name=""  ID="" Url="">
    <NavBarLink Name="" Url=""/>
</NavBar>
```

■ **Tip** All `NavBarLink` elements that are defined in `onet.xml` are static links that appear in the UI regardless of whether the user has the right to visit the link's target page. A more flexible solution is to change the navigation bars programmatically—in a feature receiver, for instance.

The top navigation bar must start with ID 1002. This is because the top node for the top navigation starts with 1002 in the content database. You can copy and paste the entry from the STS site definition in order to get an empty top navigation bar containing a home link button only (see Listing 7–27).

Listing 7–27. *Specification for Top-Navbar (Watch That the Body Attribute Contains HTML)*

```
<NavBar Name="$Resources:core,category_Top;"
        Separator="&amp;nbsp;&amp;nbsp;&amp;nbsp;"
        Body="&lt;a ID='onettopnavbar#LABEL_ID#' href='#URL#'
                 accesskey='J'&gt;#LABEL#&lt;/a&gt;"
        ID="1002" />
```

For the quick launch bar on the left side, you can define `<NavBar>` elements for your project site from ID 1025 because that's the start node for the quick launch bar in the content database (see Listing 7–28).

***Listing 7–28.** Specification of Quick Launch Bar*

```
<NavBar Name="Project" ID="1025" Url="default.aspx">
    <NavBarLink Name="ProjectDetails" Url="details.aspx"/>
    <NavBarLink Name="FinancialDetails" Url="financials.aspx"/>
    <NavBarLink Name="Overview" Url="overview.aspx"/>
</NavBar>
<NavBar Name="Reports"ID="1026" Url=„reports.aspx"">
    <NavBarLink Name="DetailsReport" Url="detailsreport.aspx"/>
    <NavBarLink Name="ProjectManagement Cockpit" Url="pmcockpit.aspx"/>
    <NavBarLink Name="FinancialReport" Url="financialreport"/>
</NavBar>
<NavBar Name="Project Team" ID="1027" Url="team.aspx"/>
```

The result of this NavBar specification looks like Figure 7–17 if you have created a new site from the site definition examples up to this point.

***Figure 7–17.** Navigation structure in the quick launch bar*

■ **Tip** At this point, if you want, you can configure the quick launch bar to have a two-tier appearance. If you want a two-tier top navigation bar, you must use the administration pages (which requires the publishing feature to be activated) or use the SharePoint API.

The ListTemplates Element

In the ListTemplates section, you define list templates to be available on the Create page of the new site. At this point, you use list definition features and `element.xml` files to define these list templates. For the list definition example that you created earlier, the ListTemplate element looks like Listing 7–29.

Listing 7–29. List Template Declaration in the onet.xml

```
<ListTemplate
    Name="ProjectList"
    Type="13001"
    Hidden="FALSE"
    BaseType="0"
    SecurityBits="11"
    Sequence="1410"
    DisplayName="Project List"
    Description="This list contains common project details."
    Image="/_layouts/images/itgen.gif" />
```

Document Templates

The DocumentTemplates element is used to define templates for document libraries that are available if you click the New button in the document libraries toolbar. We recommend you copy and paste the section from the team site definition, located in the `%SharePointRoot%\Template\SiteTemplate\STS\XML` folder, and, if necessary, extend or replace it with your own document templates. The section can also be left blank, but the user cannot create any new documents when they click the New button on the document libraries toolbar.

Modules

In the Modules section, you define one or more modules that can be used by configurations. A *module* is a container that can contain different files or content. This content could be as follows, for instance:

- Master pages
- Web pages
- Web Part content

The next example defines two modules that are used in the configuration elements that are specified later.

The first module contains the `default.aspx` that is needed at least for a bare-bones site definition. Add the lines in Listing 7–30 to the `onet.xml` file.

Listing 7–30. Module Specification in onet.xml

```
<Module Name="Default" Url="" Path="">
      <File Url="default.aspx" NavBarHome="True">
```

These lines merely name the module and reference the corresponding file. The `NavBarHome` attribute makes it the start page, available in the root of the site that is linked to the home button. Next, define two Web Parts for the left and right Web Part zones you added earlier to the `Content` control in `default.aspx` named Content1. The first one is a `ContentEditorWebPart` containing a "Hello World" message, located at the left `WebPartZone` (see Listing 7–31).

Listing 7–31. Content Editor Web Part Specification in a Module

```
<AllUsersWebPart WebPartZoneID="TopLeftZone" WebPartOrder="1">
    <![CDATA[
```

```
        <WebPart xmlns:xsi="http://www.w3.org/2001/XMLSchema-instance"
                xmlns:xsd="http://www.w3.org/2001/XMLSchema"
                xmlns="http://schemas.microsoft.com/WebPart/v2">
            <Title>Hello World</Title>
            <FrameType>TitleBarOnly</FrameType>
            <Description>Hello World</Description>
            <IsIncluded>true</IsIncluded>
            <ZoneID>Left</ZoneID>
            <PartOrder>1</PartOrder>
            <FrameState>Normal</FrameState>
            <Height />
            <Width />
            <AllowRemove>true</AllowRemove>
            <AllowZoneChange>true</AllowZoneChange>
            <AllowMinimize>true</AllowMinimize>
            <IsVisible>true</IsVisible>
            <Hidden>false</Hidden>
            <DetailLink />
            <HelpLink />
            <Dir>Default</Dir>
            <PartImageSmall />
            <MissingAssembly />
            <PartImageLarge>/_layouts/images/mscontl.gif</PartImageLarge>
            <IsIncludedFilter />
            <Assembly>Microsoft.SharePoint, Version=14.0.0.0, …</Assembly>
            <TypeName>Microsoft.SharePoint.WebPartPages.ContentEditorWebPart
            </TypeName>
            <ContentLink
               xmlns="http://schemas.microsoft.com/WebPart/v2/ContentEditor" />
            <Content xmlns="http://schemas.microsoft.com/WebPart/v2/ContentEditor">
               Hello World!
            </Content>
            <PartStorage
               xmlns="http://schemas.microsoft.com/WebPart/v2/ContentEditor" />
        </WebPart>
    ]]>
</AllUsersWebPart>
```

The Web Part's content needs to be in CDATA encoding, such as < instead of a < character.

In the right Web Part zone, you specify the standard SharePoint Foundation Logo Image Web Part (see Listing 7–32).

Listing 7–32. *Image Web Part Specification in onet.xml*

```
<AllUsersWebPart WebPartZoneID="Right" WebPartOrder="1">
<![CDATA[
    <WebPart xmlns="http://schemas.microsoft.com/WebPart/v2"
            xmlns:iwp="http://schemas.microsoft.com/WebPart/v2/Image">
        <Assembly>Microsoft.SharePoint, Version=14.0.0.0, …</Assembly>

        <TypeName>Microsoft.SharePoint.WebPartPages.ImageWebPart</TypeName>
        <FrameType>None</FrameType>
        <Title>$Resources:wp_SiteImage;</Title>
        <iwp:ImageLink>/_layouts/images/homepage.gif</iwp:ImageLink>
```

```
        <iwp:AlternativeText>$Resources:core,sitelogo_wss;</iwp:AlternativeText>
    </WebPart>
]]>
</AllUsersWebPart>
```

For the example report module, simply copy the `default.aspx` file, rename it to `report.aspx`, edit the `NavBarHome` attribute to `false`, and put it into the same folder as the `default.aspx` file. Specify a new module called Reports that contains a list view Web Part showing a project list that is an instance from the project list definition created earlier. This list is instantiated in the Configuration section shown in Listing 7–33.

Listing 7–33. *List View Web Part Specification in onet.xml*

```
<Module Name="Reports" Url="" Path="">
    <File Url="Report.aspx" NavBarHome="False">
        <View List="12001" BaseViewID="0" WebPartZoneID="Left" WebPartOrder="1">
            <![CDATA[
                <WebPart xmlns="http://schemas.microsoft.com/WebPart/v2">
                    <Assembly>Microsoft.SharePoint, Version=14.0.0.0, …</Assembly>
                    <TypeName>Microsoft.SharePoint.WebPartPages.ListViewWebPart
                    </TypeName>
                    <TitleProjectMasterData</Title>
                    <FrameType>TitleBarOnly</FrameType>
                </WebPart>
            ]]>
        </View>
    </File>
</Module>
```

Configurations

In this section, you can define one or more configurations for your site definition. Why should you define more than one configuration?

Imagine that you have built a site definition and want to use it on a developer system, a staging system for testing, and a production system. You want to integrate some kind of feedback or bug-tracking list, but this shouldn't appear in a production environment. Configurations give you the ability to build different templates that vary slightly from each other. For example, you can build three different configurations that contain largely the same content but with a "bug-tracking" list added for the developer configuration and a feedback list included in the staging configuration. The production environment has no extras. You can control the visibility of these configurations in the `webTempProject.xml` file via three different configuration sections.

There are essentially three types of components can you define in an `onet.xml` configuration section:

- Lists
- Modules
- Features

Extend your project site definition example by adding the three different configurations outlined earlier.

Start by defining the production configuration that contains the base components (Listing 7–34).

Listing 7–34. Configuration Specification in onet.xml

```
<Configuration ID="0" Name="Production"
               CustomMasterUrl="_catalogs/masterpage/cc.master"
               MasterUrl="_catalogs/masterpage/cc.master">
    <Lists>
        <List FeatureId="00BFEA71-E717-4E80-AA17-D0C71B360101"
              Type="101"
              Title="$Resources:core,shareddocuments_Title;"
              Url="$Resources:core,shareddocuments_Folder;"
                 QuickLaunchUrl="$Resources:core,shareddocuments_Folder;
                              /Forms/AllItems.aspx" />
        <List FeatureId="7346F629-03E1-436D-B2A2-80E2744FD8BC"
              Type="12001"
              Title="ProjectList" Url="Lists/ProjectList" />
    </Lists>
    <Modules>
        <Module Name="Default" />
        <Module Name="Reports" />
    </Modules>
    <SiteFeatures>
        <!-- BasicWebParts Feature -->
        <Feature ID="00BFEA71-1C5E-4A24-B310-BA51C3EB7A57" />
        <!-- Three-state Workflow Feature -->
        <Feature ID="FDE5D850-671E-4143-950A-87B473922DC7" />
    </SiteFeatures>
    <WebFeatures>
        <!-- Custom ProjectList Feature -->
        <Feature ID="7346F629-03E1-436D-B2A2-80E2744FD8BC" />
        <!-- TeamCollab Feature -->
        <Feature ID="00BFEA71-4EA5-48D4-A4AD-7EA5C011ABE5" />
        <!-- MobilityRedirect -->
        <Feature ID="F41CC668-37E5-4743-B4A8-74D1DB3FD8A4" />
    </WebFeatures>
</Configuration>
```

In the Lists section, two lists are defined: a shared documents library for storing project-related documents and an instance from the project list definition built earlier in this chapter. It also references the two modules that you defined earlier.

The next step is to define which features should be used within this template. You need to specify site-scoped and web-scoped features separately. For the site-scoped features, use the basic Web Part feature and three-state workflow that comes with SharePoint and that enables basic functionalities. At the web-scoped section, you first reference the project list feature containing the list definition. The next two features are SharePoint standard elements that contain several list templates, such as custom list or calendar and the mobility redirect feature.

To create the configuration for the development environment, copy the configuration you've just built, change the configuration ID to 1, rename it to Developer, and add a bug-tracking list (issue-tracking list) to the list section (Listing 7–35).

Listing 7–35. Add an Issue Tracking List in the Lists Section of onet.xml

```
<List FeatureId="00bfea71-5932-4f9c-ad71-1557e5751100"
      Type="1100" Title="BugTrackingList"
      Url="Lists/BugTrackingList" />
```

For the third configuration, you again copy the configuration for the production environment, change the configuration ID to 2, rename it to Staging, and add another list for collecting feedback (discussion board) in the staging environment (Listing 7–36).

Listing 7–36. Add a Discussion Board in the Lists Section of onet.xml

```
<List FeatureId="00bfea71-6a49-43fa-b535-d15c05500108"
      Type="108"
      Title="Feedback"
      Url="Lists/Feedback" />
```

To use these configurations, you need to extend the `webTempProject.xml` file you specified earlier. Simply add the two extra configurations (Listing 7–37).

Listing 7–37. Extend webTempProject.xml

```
<Templates xmlns:ows="Microsoft SharePoint">
    <Template Name="ProjectSite" ID="12099" >
        <Configuration ID="0" Title="SharePoint Project Site Production Environment"
Description="" Hidden="FALSE" ImageUrl="/_layouts/images/Project/logo.bmp"
DisplayCategory="CustomSharePoint" RootWebOnly="false" />
        <Configuration ID="1" Title="SharePoint Project Site Development Environment"
Description="" Hidden="FALSE" ImageUrl="/_layouts/images/Project/logo.bmp"
DisplayCategory="CustomSharePoint" RootWebOnly="false" />
        <Configuration ID="2" Title="SharePoint Project Site Staging Environment"
Description="" Hidden="FALSE" ImageUrl="/_layouts/images/Project/logo.bmp"
DisplayCategory="CustomSharePoint" RootWebOnly="false" />
    </Template>
</Templates>
```

As a result, you have these configurations available at the template selection box of the Create page, after deploying your solution package (see Figure 7–18).

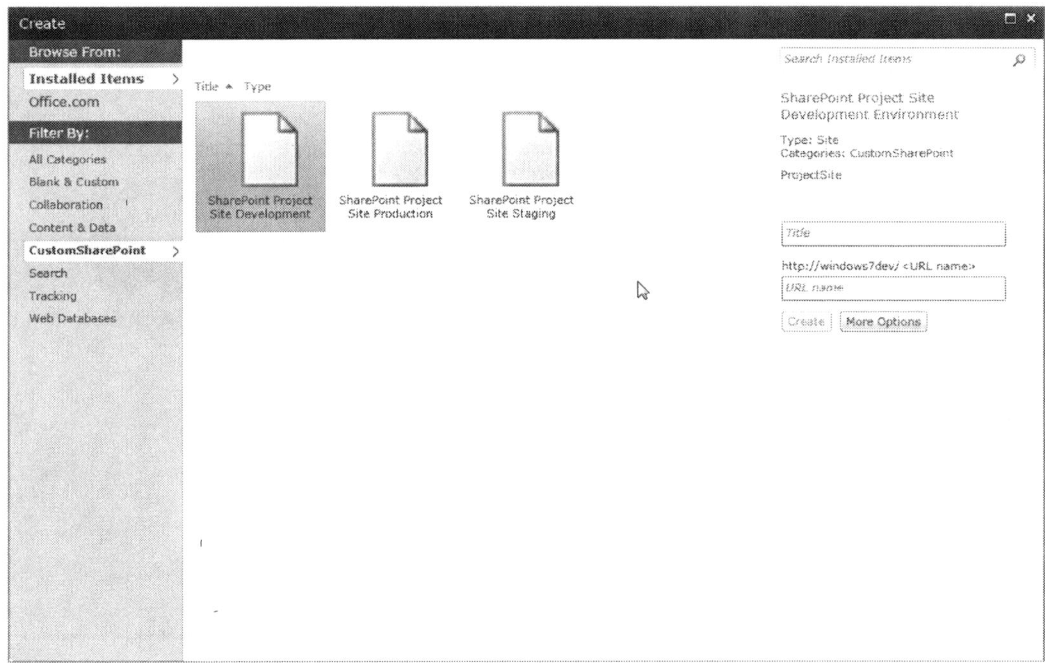

Figure 7–18. Custom site template at the site creation page

The site definition specification in `onet.xml` is finished, and you can now deploy this site definition, either by pressing F5 in Visual Studio or by copying all the necessary files to the `%SharePointRoot%\Template\SiteTemplates` folder and recycling the application pool (IIS reset). You can now use the custom site definition.

Using a Site Definition

You have different options to create a new site from a site definition. Three of them are as follows:

- `stsadm.exe`
- SharePoint UI's Create Workspace/Site Collection
- Custom code

stsadm.exe

You can create a new site via the `stsadm.exe` command-line tool by specifying, at a minimum, the `Url` attribute, the `ownerlogin`, the `owneremail`, and the site template to use:

```
STSADM.EXE -o createsite -url http://projectserver.com -ownerlogin ProjectServer\bpehlke -
owneremail bpehlke@projectserver.com -sitetemplate Project#0
```

The first part of the site template parameter refers to the template name. The number preceded by the # specifies the configuration ID.

Create Workspace or Site Collection via the UI

To create a new site from a site definition using the browser interface of SharePoint, you can use either Central Administration or the site settings of a SharePoint site.

CENTRAL ADMINISTRATION

1. Go to the Central Administration home page.
2. Select Application Management ➤ Create Site Collection.
3. Enter the new site's name and description.
4. Enter the URL that refers to the new site.
5. Select a language and template from a category, such as SharePoint Project Management DB Site.
6. Enter at least a primary site administrator, and click Create.

The second option to create a site from a site definition is to use the SharePoint Create pages, like in Figure 7–19.

SITE SETTINGS

1. Click the Site Actions button on an existing SharePoint site.
2. Open the Create dialog, and select Create Site and Workspace.
3. Enter the new site's name and description.
4. Enter the URL that refers to the new site.
5. Select a language and template from a category, such as SharePoint Project Management DB Site.
6. Select user permissions options, and fill out the navigation settings.
7. Click Create to create a new subsite.

■ **Note** If you don't see your template in the template selection box, you may have selected the wrong language or defined your template as `RootWebOnly=true` in your `webTemp*.xml` file.

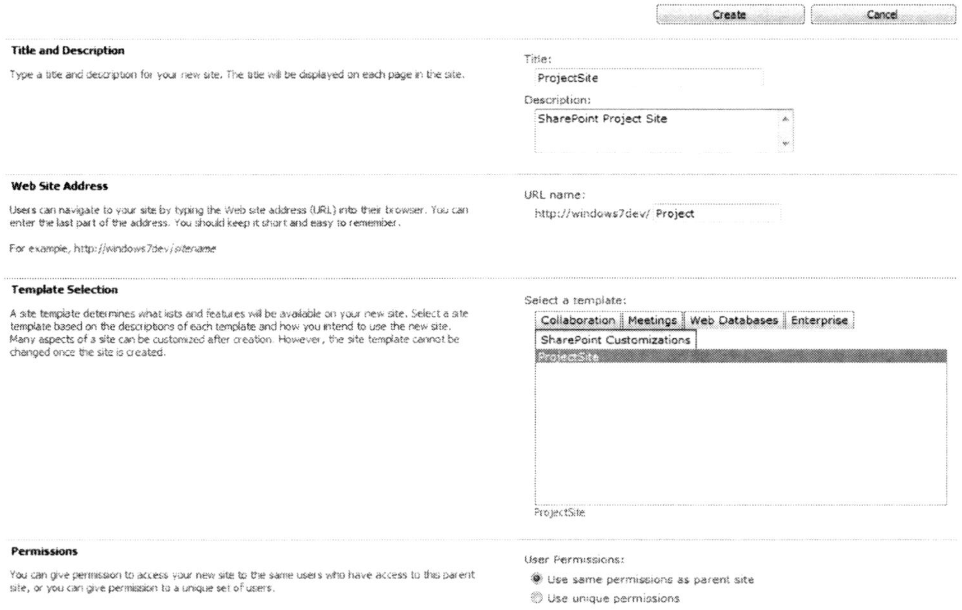

Figure 7–19. Site creation page

Custom Code

You can build a console application, an application page, or even a feature that creates subsites by implementing a custom `FeatureActivated` event handler in a feature receiver class (or any other program code, such as a web page). A class that meets these requirements looks like Listing 7–38.

Listing 7–38. Create a New Subsite

```
using System;
using Microsoft.SharePoint;

namespace project.feature
{
    class projectFeatureReceiver : SPFeatureReceiver
    {
        public override void FeatureActivated(SPFeatureReceiverProperties props)
        {
            using (SPWeb web = props.Feature.Parent as SPWeb)
```

```
                {
                    web.Webs.Add("SubSite1", "Sub Site 1", "",
                                  1033, "Project#0", false, false);
                }
            }
        }
}
```

Summary

Using templates enables you to extend your custom solution with many features that would not be possible simply using the SharePoint UI or SharePoint Designer. These templates increase the reusability of components in your custom SharePoint applications and make them more structured.

A combination of different templates and contents such as list definitions, site definitions, Web Parts, features, images, and application pages in a custom SharePoint solution (`.wsp` file) can form a template for a whole SharePoint application that can be instantiated over and over again in different SharePoint environments.

CHAPTER 8

Application Techniques

Regarding SharePoint as both a platform and a framework presumes that you can create any kind of application on top of it. In this chapter we cover some advanced techniques you can use when you create such applications. These include

- Using application pages to create SharePoint applications
- Localization techniques for globalized applications
- Using the event model at a feature and site level to create interactive solutions
- Sending e-mail from custom code
- Creating managed extensions for SharePoint applications and using LINQ

Creating SharePoint applications, and particularly application pages, combines almost everything you know from ASP.NET, and adds the SharePoint API together with some special features and controls. We assume that you're familiar with ASP.NET and can create ASPX pages, and add controls and code.

Application Pages

Application pages are the most powerful way to program and extend SharePoint. In theory, it is easy to add ASPX pages and write anything at all within the scope of ASP.NET. However, isolated pages that run in their own context do not integrate seamlessly with SharePoint. To create and deploy application pages we recommend you use the appropriate project template within Visual Studio 2010. The pages can be deployed either directly into a subdirectory of the `_layouts` folder or as a component in a feature. As part of a feature they are copied to the very same folder when the feature is activated. Regardless of the deployment scenario, we explain the basics of application pages in this section. There are two fundamental requirements for creating application pages:

1. The page should derive from the correct base class.
2. The page should use the appropriate master page.

Creating Application Pages Using Visual Studio

Visual Studio 2010 has an item template specifically for SharePoint application pages (see Figure 8–1). It supports the conventional settings, including master pages and basic references.

In the following exercise you'll create a new SharePoint project and add an application page to add sophisticated functionality using Visual Studio 2010.

CREATING A PROJECT USING APPLICATION PAGES

1. Choose Empty SharePoint Project from the New Project dialog. Enter a name and click OK.
2. In the ensuing SharePoint Customization wizard, select Deploy as a Farm Solution, and click Finish. The project will be empty and there should be no editing area visible.
3. Right-click the project in Solution Explorer and choose Add ➤ New Item.
4. In the subsequent dialog, select Application Page, and name the page appropriately.
5. Click Add. This may take a little while, but Visual Studio will add the SharePoint "Layouts" Mapped Folder and create in it a subfolder named after your project. The new application page will be saved within this subfolder. The page will open in the editor, and you can start working on it.

Application pages deploy into the `_layouts` folder—that is, under the SharePoint root (the 14 hive within the `TEMPLATE` folder). Consequently, you cannot choose a sandboxed solution because the usage of shared areas of the installation violates the conditions for sandboxed solutions.

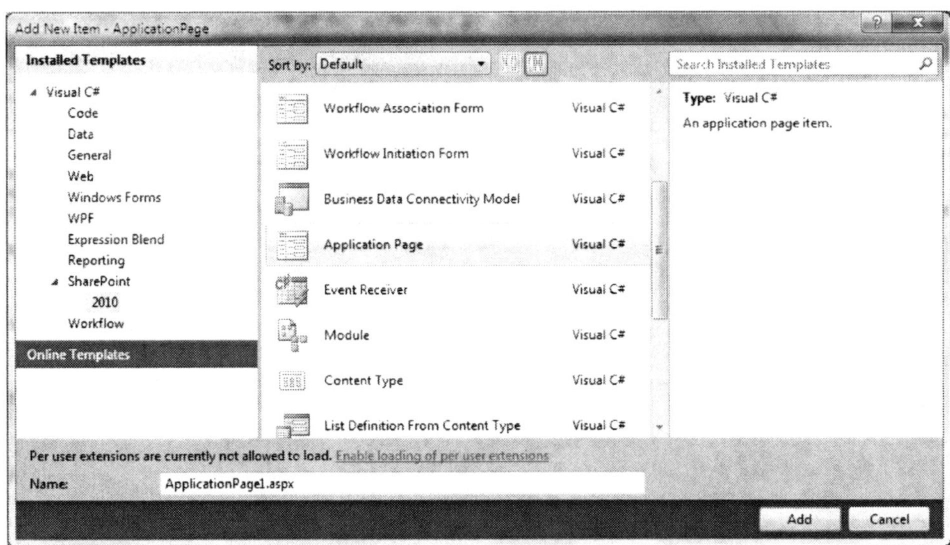

Figure 8–1. Adding an application page to a SharePoint project

You can check the settings first using the Properties window (F4). To get the instant F5 experience—that is, launching directly into the debugger by pressing the F5 key—you should set the Startup Item property to the application page of your choice (see Figure 8–2).

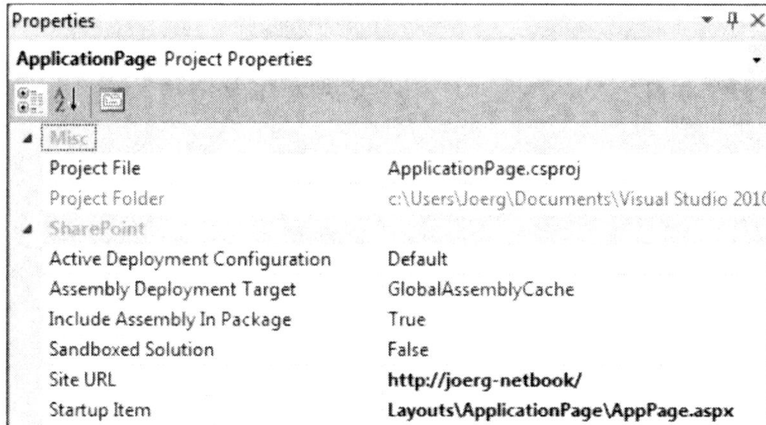

Figure 8–2. *Settings for an application page project*

Check that Sandboxed Solution is set to False and Startup Item is set to a suitable ASPX page to start debugging. Active Deployment Configuration will be set to Default as long as you don't create other configurations. You can find a comprehensive description in Chapter 9 regarding how to set and configure customized deployment settings.

Each new application page is created with at least these placeholder sections to edit in the master page:

- `PlaceHolderAdditionalPageHead`: The `<head>` element where you can add script references, styles, inline script, meta tags, and the like
- `PlaceHolderMain`: The main area for content
- `PlaceHolderPageTitle`: The page title that appears in the browser's Window title bar
- `PlaceHolderPageTitleInTitleArea`: Page title in the title area

There are many more placeholders (see Figure 8–3) available to modify individual parts of the master page.

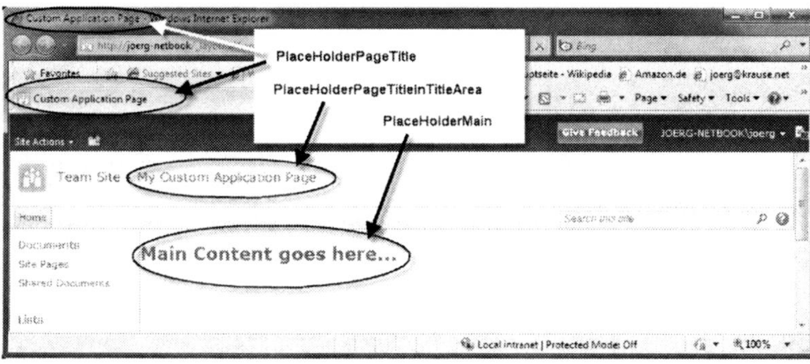

Figure 8–3. *The main placeholders included by default*

This page is not yet part of the navigation tree and must be either linked somewhere or manually added. If it is part of an application, consider adding custom navigation or add the page's structure programmatically to the site. (The section entitled "The Event Model" later in the chapter thoroughly explains the use of events to manipulate a site when adding and activating a feature. You can find more about master pages in Chapter 10.)

Using the Base Class

ASP.NET pages usually derive from the `Page` class. Even though it is feasible to continue using the `Page` class within SharePoint, another base class is more appropriate: `LayoutsPageBase`. This type is defined in the `Microsoft.SharePoint` assembly and found in the `Microsoft.SharePoint.WebControls` namespace. Internally, it ultimately derives from `Page`, so as an ASP.NET developer you should find this class familiar. The full class diagram is shown in Figure 8–4.

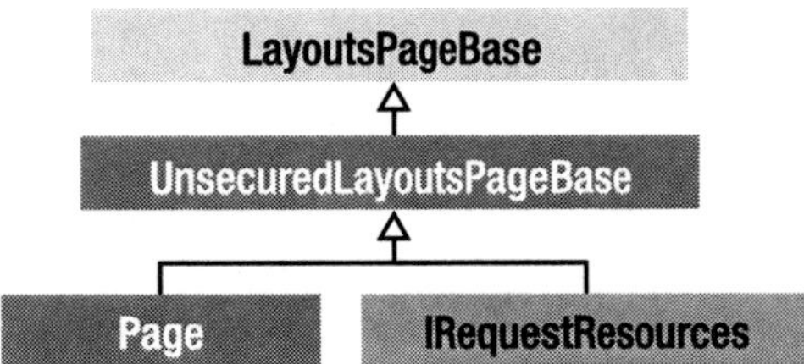

Figure 8–4. *Class diagram for the LayoutsPageBase class*

The base class performs security checks and provides access to the fundamental objects. In particular, from the `UnsecuredLayoutsPageBase` base class, the properties `Site` and `Web` are vital. `Site` returns an object of type `SPSite` that represents the site, and `Web` returns an object of type `SPWeb`. All internal layout pages derive from this base class. While it is not necessary to do so for private application pages, we recommend that you adhere to the same practice to ensure that your pages match with the SharePoint environment.

As mentioned, the `LayoutsPageBase` class provides several security checks. You should derive your pages from this class if the pages are accessible only by authenticated users. For pages intended for unauthenticated users, the parent class `UnsecuredLayoutsPageBase` is appropriate.

Using Inline Code

When deriving from either class, you have to decide whether to program inline or with code-behind. Listing 8–1 shows how to create a simple layout page with inline code.

Listing 8–1. *An Application Page with Inline Code*

```
<%@ Assembly Name="Microsoft.SharePoint, ..." %>
<%@ Page Language="C#" MasterPageFile=" ~masterurl/default.master "
         Inherits="Microsoft.SharePoint.WebControls.LayoutsPageBase" %>
<%@ Import Namespace="Microsoft.SharePoint" %>

<script runat="server">
   ... inline code goes here
</script>
```

```
<asp:Content id="main" ContentPlaceHolderID="PlaceHolderMain" runat="server">
 ...
</asp:Content>
<asp:Content>
  ...
<asp:Content>
</asp:Content>
  ...
</asp:Content>
```

There are two crucial things here. First, the Inherits attribute of the @Page directive ensures the right base class. Second, the @Assembly directive is required, and it needs to point to the assembly that contains the base class type.

Furthermore, the MasterPageFile attribute is used to load the default master page and supply Content controls for the content you will furnish. (In the "Using the Master Page" section later in the chapter, you'll find out more about the appropriate settings for the MasterPageFile attribute.) Note that the example in Listing 8–1 shows three Content controls. The master page contains several placeholders for placing content on the page. This includes but is not limited to the main area, the page's title, and page title's description.

The script block shown is simply to give the page a modicum of dynamic output. It makes use of the Site and Web properties derived from the base page. The access is equivalent to the static methods of the SPControl class. Both use the current context of the request internally to retrieve the objects.

As mentioned previously, the base classes provide different support for user access rights. LayoutsPageBase overrides the OnPreInit method and calls the CheckRights method internally, which performs several checks. If any check fails, an Access Denied exception is thrown. The UnsecuredLayoutsPageBase class does not perform these checks, and lets anyone requesting the page execute it.

Table 8–1 shows several important and useful properties and methods provided by the base classes.

Table 8–1. *Properties and Methods Available from the Page Base Classes*

Name	Base Class	Description
GetResourceString	UnsecuredLayoutsPageBase	Returns an internal resource from SharePoint, defined with the leading ID wss
StopRequestIfClientIsNotValid	UnsecuredLayoutsPageBase	Same as the static method in the SPUtility class. It stops further processing if client is no longer connected. This is used to improve performance. If longer operations are unavoidable, consider using the SPLongOperation class to show an animated wait icon.
Site	UnsecuredLayoutsPageBase	Returns the current site of type SPSite.
Web	UnsecuredLayoutsPageBase	Returns the current web of type SPWeb.
CheckRights	LayoutsPageBase	Checks whether the current user has appropriate rights
MakeImageUrl	LayoutsPageBase	Adds _layout/images before the given string

The other virtual properties and methods are inconsequential unless you override them. Some control the minimum rights required to execute the page. For example, you can require the user to have the right to access the _layouts folder by overriding the RequireDefaultLayoutRights property to return true. Via the RequireSiteAdministrator property you can restrict the page to administrative usage only. On the opposite end of the spectrum, you can set AllowAnonymousAccess to open the page to everybody.

Using Code-Behind

When developing ASP.NET pages you may prefer using the code-behind approach. The separation of markup and code is the key to a clean and maintainable project structure. To use code-behind you simply need to provide the right attributes to the @Page directive. However, SharePoint 2010 also supports the code-behind method. Instead of deriving from one of the base classes, you can inherit from your own base class. As shown in the following code snippet, a private class, MyPageBase, is used.

```
<%@ Assembly Name="Microsoft.SharePoint, ..." %>
<%@ Page Language="C#" DynamicMasterPageFile=" ~masterurl/default.master "
         Inherits="Apress.SP2K10.ApplicationPages.MyPageBase" %>
<%@ Import Namespace="Microsoft.SharePoint" %>
```

The definition of MyPageBase is straightforward:

```
namespace Apress.SP2010.ApplicationPages
{
   class MyPageBase : LayoutsPageBase
   {
   }
 }
```

If you examine the markup portion, it's almost identical to the previous example. However, the Inherits attribute points to the private class, and this in turn derives from one of the base classes. The assembly that contains the MyPageBase type must be compiled and installed in the GAC (Global Assembly Cache).

SharePoint 2010 also supports the common pattern of attaching a code file to an application page to add code-behind. Instead of inheriting a type, the CodeBehind attribute in the application page defines a path to the file that contains the code. If you follow the standard ASP.NET pattern, which is strongly recommended, the file is named after the markup file, with an appended .cs extension to indicate a C# file.

```
<%@ Assembly Name="Microsoft.SharePoint, ..." %>
<%@ Page Language="C#"
         MasterPageFile=" ~masterurl/default.master "
         CodeBehind="Page1.aspx.cs" %>
<%@ Import Namespace="Microsoft.SharePoint" %>
```

The page parser recognizes the file, reads its contents, and compiles the code on the fly. In a precompiled project it would create a hidden assembly and make it available. That happens behind the scenes and is no different from any other kind of ASP.NET application. The only disparity here is the base page: the LayoutsPageBase class is used instead of the Page class.

Using the Master Page

The previous examples already refer to a master page. The default master is managed on a per-site basis. It's crucial to use this master. If the administrator or an end user with suitable permissions changes the master page, your application pages must reflect that change. Hard-coding the markup or adding navigation controls or other functionality that's typically part of the master page directly into your own application pages is not recommended. Creating pop-up dialogs that are based on ASPX pages a special base class and another master is the preferred method. Coding a whole page without one of the built-in master pages is not permitted.

In Chapter 10 we explain in depth how to work with master pages and what options are available to use in application pages. For now, the reference to the `~masterurl/default.master` token is the best way to accomplish the integration of your pages within a SharePoint site. The reference is made using the `DynamicMasterPageFile` attribute. You might wonder where this comes from, as ASP.NET does not support it. The `@Page` directive can be extended simply by adding public properties to the base class. Once an attribute is used, the value is stored against the base property. To understand how to deal with the property, a further examination of the `DynamicMasterPageFile` property in the `UnsecuredLayoutPageBase` class will be helpful. See the section "Master Page Tokens for Application Pages" in Chapter 10 for more details.

Integrating Application Pages

In order for you to work with application pages, they need to be reachable, usually within the context of the site. That means you must provide a way for the pages to be called. In addition, the caller may supply context variables, such as the ID of the item or list initiating the call.

Linking to an application page is easy. Either you create a direct link on another page or you add an entry to the navigation control. More sophisticated methods include adding a custom action to the Site Actions menu or to a list's context menu.

New in SharePoint 2010 is the ribbon-style menu, which is extensible. Adding a menu item is usually part of a feature. A feature definition might contain a custom action item. In the section "The Event Model" later in this chapter, we elaborate on this further.

Security Considerations

Custom application pages can supply features that are intended for administrators only. As you saw earlier, the base classes provide support to either authenticated or unauthenticated users. If authenticated, you can distinguish users with administrative rights. Application pages often extend the administration of a site, and thus it is desirable to have an easy way to restrict access. SharePoint takes care of the menu item by adding the `RequireSiteAdministrator` attribute to the custom action definition:

```
<CustomAction RequireSiteAdministrator="true">
  ...
</CustomAction>
```

However, this does not prevent users from calling the page directly. It only removes the menu item if the current user does not have sufficient permissions. To ensure that your application page is locked down well, you need to override the virtual property `RequireSiteAdministrator`:

```
class MyPageBase : LayoutsPageBase
{
    protected override bool RequireSiteAdministrator
    {
        get { return true; }
    }
}
```

If the page is called by users that are curious about hidden pages, a security exception is thrown, and the Access Denied page will appear.

Resources and Localization

Multilanguage support, localization with culture-specific resources, and centralized resource management are key concepts for globalization, localization, and localizability. Resources include everything that supports the basic content stream (HTML), such as replaceable text portions, images, and scripts. By making those parts dynamic you can replace them with language-specific versions. It's also common practice to support target device–specific content, such as for devices that are connected via a low-bandwidth connection.

In this section you will learn about the common .NET techniques for handling resources that have evolved since the first release of ASP.NET within the context of Web Parts and SharePoint. (However, this section is not intended to provide basic information about resource management).

MSDN LOOKUP

For complete documentation concerning .NET 3.5 resource management, see the following link in the MSDN library: `http://msdn.microsoft.com/en-us/library/h6270d0z.aspx`.

In this section we cover

- Using the `ResourceManager` class to retrieve resources
- Using resources to deploy static data within an assembly
- Localizing properties and other parts of a Web Part
- Using resources for linked (external) data to be consumed by a Web Part

Resource Primer

In countries where English is not the native tongue, localization can be important. Localization within SharePoint is achieved using resources and resource files in a similar manner to ASP.NET sites. Although the use of resources is not mandatory, it's usually best practice to incorporate them anyway. Hard-coding strings is generally undesirable, whether or not you plan to support localization. However, setting up and using resources within SharePoint can be confusing.

Resources are stored within XML-based RESX files. Usually you can equate "resource" with "string." Nonetheless, a resource file can store any serializable data, including images and other binary data converted into a Base64-encoded stream. Windows forms in particular utilize such embedded data. For web pages, it's more involved to extract data from resources using handlers.

Every resource in a resource file is identified by a fixed name. A typical RESX file looks like this:

```
<root>
  <data name="FieldManagerPageDescription">
    <value>Manage the field of this application.</value>
  </data>
</root>
```

For every culture your localization project supports, you need a unique RESX file with the same key names. Usually, you simply copy the original RESX file and translate the original values within each value tag into the new language. The new resource file has to be named as follows: *<original_name>*.*<culture>*.resx. Several example names follow:

- `myresource.resx`
- `myresource.en-US.resx`
- `myresource.fr-FR.resx`
- `myresource.de-DE.resx`

The culture's name is either the complete combination of language and country, or simply a language-specific fallback to the parent culture. The reason is that in several countries people speak more than one language, and the same language is spoken in several countries. It depends on your project's requirements whether the parent culture will suffice.

Defining Resources in SharePoint

SharePoint defines two kinds of resource files: runtime resources (also called application resources) and provisioning resources. Application resources are used within the normal execution of a SharePoint application. Normal SharePoint execution includes application pages, Web Parts, and controls, as discussed in this chapter. SharePoint also distinguishes between application resources used in normal web applications and those used in Central Administration. Provisioning resources, on the other hand, are used when provisioning elements. You use them within features, site definitions, and list definitions. This means you need to be aware of the deployment and usage scenarios.

Provisioning Resources

Provisioning resources are used to localize solutions. This includes

- Descriptions for solutions, features, Web Parts, lists, sites, and so on
- Options presented in choice fields (`SPFieldChoice` controls)
- Base names of files used in the solution, such as "images" and "template"
- String resources used in the definition files

Resources encapsulate and abstract data from logic and design. This makes sense in larger projects involving many developers. Resources are mainly, but not exclusively, used for localization. Localizing all this data can be a challenging task. It makes sense to think about what parts really need to be localized. Remember that in addition to the various kinds of resource files, the localized version requires you to include one file for each supported culture for each of these files. Such projects tend to have an exploding number of files requiring maintenance and deployment.

Resource Locations

Resource files in SharePoint are located in different folders, including these:

- `C:\Inetpub\wwwroot\wss\VirtualDirectories\<port>\App_GlobalResources\`
- `$SharePointRoot$\14\Resources\`
- `$SharePointRoot$\14\CONFIG\Resources\`
- `$SharePointRoot$\14\CONFIG\AdminResources\`
- `$SharePointRoot$\14\TEMPLATE\FEATURES\<feature>\Resources\`

The target folder you use depends on what kind of resource you want to deploy. Every type of resource has its own folder. Provisioning resources are part of either a solution package or a feature. They land in these folders:

- `$SharePointRoot$\14\TEMPLATE\FEATURES\<feature>\Resources\Resources.<culture>.resx`
- `$SharePointRoot$\14\TEMPLATE\FEATURES\<feature>\Resources\`
- `$SharePointRoot$\14\Resources\`

Every feature uses the resources file located in its `Resources` folder. You can, however, use another resource file or even shared resources. To share resource files you have to put them in the `14\Resources\` folder. This is the default option that is used when you add an item of type Global Resource File to your current solution. Site definitions and list definitions also get their resources from this folder.

Application resources can appear in these folders:

- `$SharePointRoot$\14\CONFIG\Resources\`
- `C:\Inetpub\wwwroot\wss\VirtualDirectories\<port>\App_GlobalResources\`

Application resources are located in the `CONFIG\Resources` folder. For a web application to use those resources, they must be copied to their own `App_GlobalResources` folder. This is standard practice for global resources in any conventional ASP.NET project. On creation of the web application, the resources are initially copied to the `App_GlobalResources` folder. When you add new resources to the `CONFIG\Resources` folder, the resources need to be copied to existing web applications. You can do this manually or use the `stsadm` command `copyappbincontent`. Alternatively, you can automate this by including the following in your `FeatureActivated` event in your feature receiver. For Central Administration resources and site maps, call

```
SPWebService.AdministrationService.ApplyApplicationContentToLocalServer();
```

For regular application page resources and site maps, this code snippet applies:

```
SPFarm.Local.Services.GetValue().ApplyApplicationContentToLocalServer();
```

■ **Tip** Refer to the section "The Event Model" for more information about how to add and activate event receivers for features.

For administrative purposes, application resources use different folders. Administrative extensions add UI elements for features to Central Administration, allowing administrators to manage your code. Chapter 17 contains more information regarding these tasks. The appropriate folders are

- `$SharePointRoot$\14\CONFIG\AdminResources\`
- `C:\Inetpub\wwwroot\wss\VirtualDirectories\<port>\App_GlobalResources\`

Application resources for Central Administration work the same way as normal application resources, except that the base folder is `CONFIG\AdminResources`.

Usage Scenarios in SharePoint

Now you need to know how to use resources within SharePoint elements. It doesn't really matter which kind of resource you are using. SharePoint will retrieve the data from any of the resources available through the current context. A global resource for an application page can be read from the current context:

```
HttpContext.GetGlobalResourceObject("MyResource", "MyName").ToString();
```

Any property within a markup file can use the expression builder syntax:

```
<%$Resources:MyResource, MyName%>
```

For a regular ASP.NET or SharePoint element, this would read

```
<asp:literal runat="server" Text="<%$Resources:MyResource, MyName%>" />
```

In XML configuration files (CAML) that SharePoint can read, you use this syntax:

```
$Resources:MyResource, MyName
```

In XML features, you use the default resource of the feature and access it like this:

```
$Resources:MyName
```

The next section contains a more detailed description of common usage scenarios in Web Parts and application pages.

Using Resources in Web Parts

To localize properties such as `FriendlyName`, `Title`, and `Description`, the attributes can be localized. Resources can be part of any .NET assembly. You can create either an assembly dedicated to resources only or add the resources to the current assembly. Assemblies that contain resources for a specific culture only are called *satellite assemblies*. An assembly can contain any kind of resources for any number of cultures. Using satellite assemblies allows you to add more languages to the project later without having to recompile the core assembly. It also allows language packs to be updated independently of the project assemblies. Using resources is the best practice for localization; however, they can be used to hold any static content used in the control too. It's better to use a dedicated technique to deal with such data than to use constants spread throughout your code.

Access to resources always follows the same strategy; content declared as a resource in the project is added to the assembly and becomes part of the manifest. If the source is an XML file with a `.resx` extension, then the content is compiled into a `.resource` file—a binary representation of the content. A naming scheme is used to address the content in a unique way:

```
Namespace.Folder.File.Element
```

The namespace is defined in the project's properties. If the content is in a folder structure, the folders define the middle part. A folder chain such as `\Resources\Global\Webparts` translates into `Resources.Global.Webparts`. Then the RESX file name follows. The complete name will look like this, for example:

```
Apress.SP2010.Resources.Global.Webparts.MenuItems
```

In this example the namespace is `Apress.SP2010`, the folder chain is as shown before, and the name of the files is `MenuItems.resx`. Such an element is resolved by the `ResourceManager` class.

Using Resources for Static Data in Web Parts

Static data can be defined at the assembly level and per element or class within an assembly, such as a Web Part class.

Defining a Static Resource per Solution

For static data you need a resource file. Visual Studio 2010 provides an item for this in the General section of the Installed Templates window. Simply add a resource file by using the Resources File project template (see Figure 8–5). The name must be unique within the project. The RESX file is compiled internally into a `.resource` file and stored in the assembly as part of the metadata. It does not become part of the package or feature definition files.

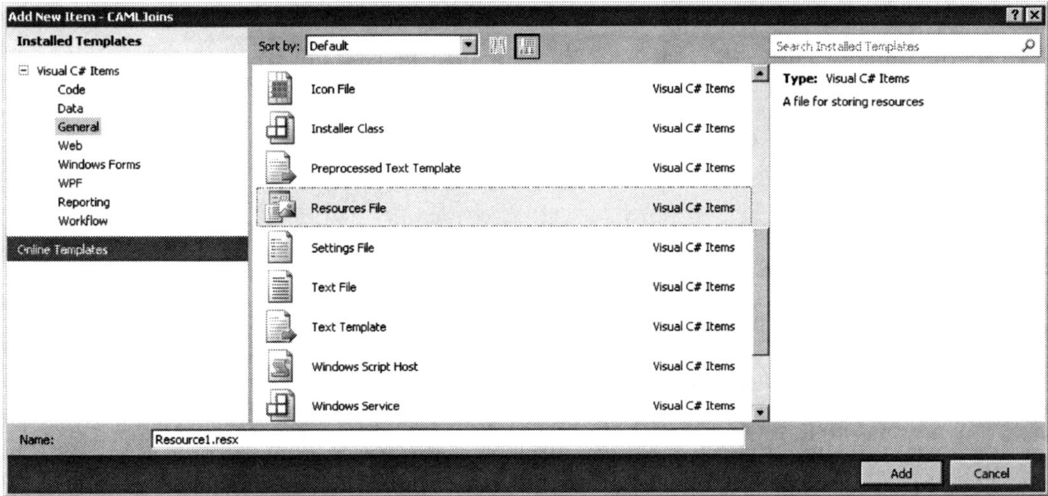

Figure 8–5. Adding a global resource file from the General tab

Defining a Static Resource per Item

To create a global resource that is dedicated to supporting a specific Web Part within your solution, you can choose the project item template Global Resources File from SharePoint ➤ 2010 in the Installed Templates tree (see Figure 8–6). It will appear only if you select a Web Part within Solution Explorer.

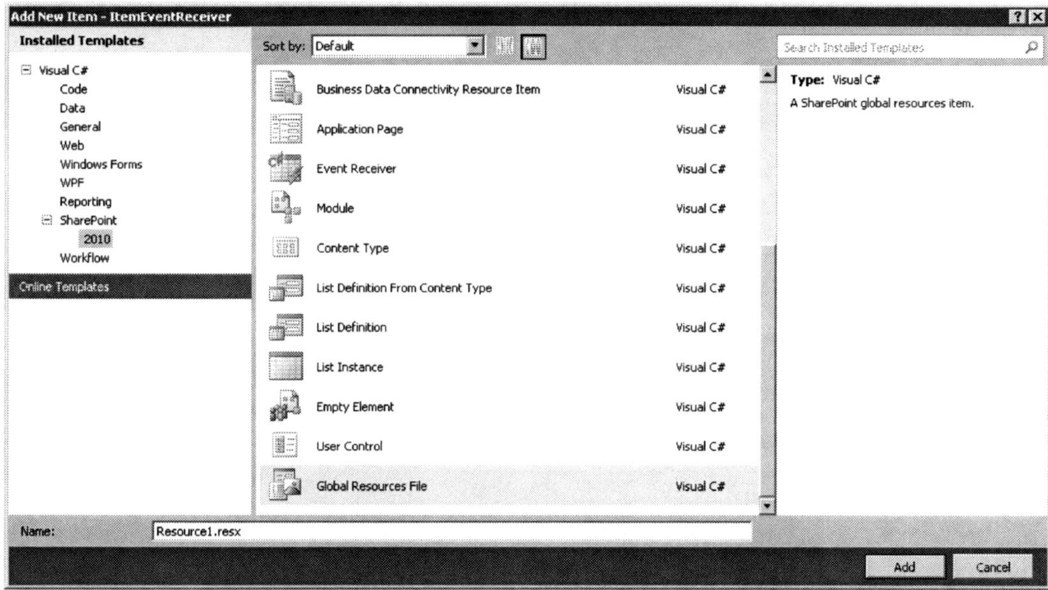

***Figure 8–6.** Adding a global resource file from SharePoint ➤ 2010 within a Web Part*

The result is much the same as with the common resource item—a RESX file. After choosing this template, you'll be asked whether you wish to create a culture-invariant file or a culture-specific file. This simply affects whether a culture shortcut is included within the file name (such as `en-us` for US culture) or whether one is omitted altogether.

SharePoint has its own resource management. This does not prevent you from using the common ASP.NET model, but it's useful to know what the differences are and why they exist. If you add a global resource file to any item in the project, Visual Studio adds the resource to the package at a global level. That's confusing, as the relative path to the file in the solution does not match the position in the SharePoint root. Moreover, resources that are created for SharePoint this way are not compiled. They become part of the package as original files. They are deployed to the `\Resources` folder directly under the `14\TEMPLATE` folder. Let's examine first how this works internally before looking into modification options.

When you add a global resource file, it is assigned the deployment type `RootFile` and placed directly under `14\TEMPLATE\Resources`, as shown in Figure 8–7.

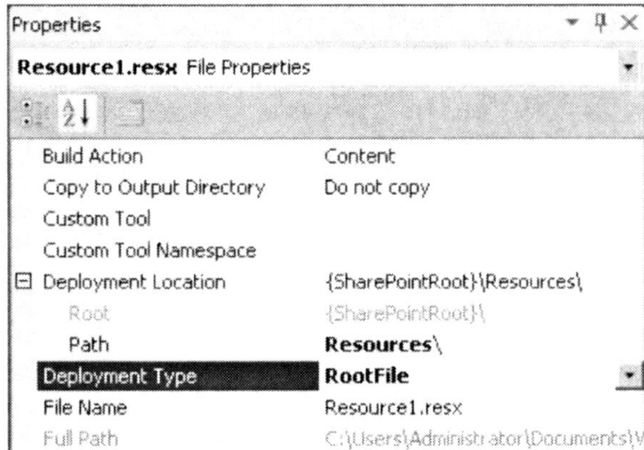

Figure 8–7. SharePoint resources are deployed as is to a special folder.

In the package this looks like this:

```
<Solution ...>
   <RootFiles>
      <RootFile Location="Resources\VisualGlobalResource.resx" />
   </RootFiles>
</Solution>
```

Changing the properties of the file changes the package definition, too. There are good reasons that this is the case. Placing all files into the root can cause naming conflicts with other packages. Such resources are accessible through the resource expression builder syntax. You may be familiar with the `$Resources: core...` snippets, which access the internal resources. The `core.resx` file, together with the installed language packs, is stored in the `\Resources` folder, too. Consequently, you can access your own global resource files the same way from any markup file, including visual Web Parts and ASPX application pages, and within CAML markup files.

Using Static Resource Files

After choosing either template, you can assign the file to a specific culture, or leave it culture invariant. If you simply wish to store static data, use the invariant culture. Once added, you can edit the file with the resource editor. Alternatively, use the XML editor to edit the data directly.

You can access the resources from markup using expressions if you create a visual Web Part. That uses expressions based on the `Resources` expression builder:

```
<%$ Resources:StaticResources,Help.Text %>
```

The expression must appear within a specific attribute, such as

```
<asp:label runat="server" Text="<%$ Resources:StaticResources,Help.Text %>" />
```

The name `StaticResources` is the resource's file name. Nonvisual (regular) Web Parts don't have any markup. To use the data in code, you can use the `ResourceManager` of the current `Page` that is available through any Web Part.

Using Resources for Localization with Embedded Resource Files

Using resources for localization requires some preliminary work, as described in the following exercise.

PREPARING RESOURCES FOR LOCALIZATION

1. Add a default resource file for your Web Part, named `WebPartName.resx`. For example, if your Web Part is named `MyVisualWebPart`, the RESX file will be named `MyVisualWebPart.resx`.
2. Copy the default file once for each supported language. Rename each file according the schema `MyVisualWebPart.culture.resx`. Use either the global cultures, such as `En` or `De`, or specific ones like `En-Us`, or `De-de`. These strings are not case sensitive; uppercase letters are used to improve readability only. You should end up with several files, named `MyVisualWebPart.en.resx`, `MyVisualWebPart.de.resx`, and so on.
3. Tag each file as an embedded resource via the Build Action property. Refer to the first property shown in Figure 8–7.

You can now compile the project and add the resource calls to your code, as shown next.

The RESX files are similar to the following XML snippet (the schema and type definition have been omitted for clarity):

```
<data name="Button.Text" xml:space="preserve">
    <value>Click me</value>
</data>
<data name="Button.Tooltip" xml:space="preserve">
    <value>Click me tooltip</value>
</data>
```

The following code can be used to retrieve the resource:

```
protected override void CreateChildControls()
{
   Button b = new Button();
   ResourceManager rm = new ResourceManager("Apress.SP2010.WebParts.
                                            ResourceWebPart.NonVisualWebPart",
                                                 this.GetType().Assembly);
   b.Text = rm.GetString("Button.Text");
   b.OnClientClick = "ShowAlert(this)";
   Controls.Add(b);
   base.CreateChildControls();
}
```

The `ResourceManager` class is defined in the `System.Resources` namespace and stored in the `System.Configuration.dll` assembly, which must be referenced in the project. The resource manager requires a string that defines the full name to the embedded resource. As shown in Figure 8–8, you can attach RESX files directly to the Web Part itself (the first constructor call of `ResourceManager`) or use any folder structure that's appropriate (the second call; `rm2`).

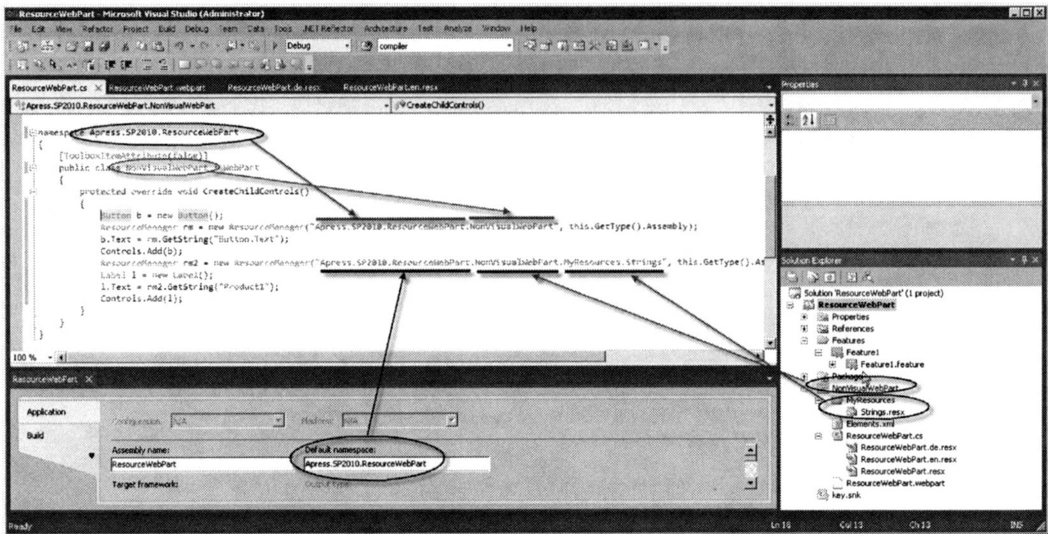

Figure 8–8. The name of the resource is built from the namespace, path, and file name.

The GetString method uses the current culture, if one is specified, to retrieve the correct resource. There is an overloaded GetString method that also accepts a CultureInfo object to force a specific culture.

Using Resources to Localize Web Part Attributes

If you are building a reusable Web Part, localization for the content is straightforward, as shown previously. However, localizing the attributes is not supported the same way. In all the previous examples, the strings were hard-coded:

```
[WebBrowsable]
[Category("Look and feel")]
[WebDisplayName("Use custom palette")]
[WebDescription("Check this to use a custom palette")]
[Personalizable(PersonalizationScope.Shared)]
public bool UseCustomPalette {
   get;
   set;
}
```

All these attribute values are hard-coded into your assembly, and you have to build different assemblies for different languages. Fortunately the .NET Framework is extensible, allowing these attributes (Category, WebDisplayName, and WebDescription) to be extended to take advantage of the localization features. To do so, create derived classes, such as LocalizedCategoryAttribute, LocalizedWebDisplayNameAttribute, and LocalizedWebDescriptionAttribute.

They essentially look the same. Code for the LocalizedWebDisplayNameAttribute looks like this:

```
[AttributeUsage(AttributeTargets.Property, AllowMultiple = false, Inherited = true)]
public sealed class LocalizedWebDisplayNameAttribute
    : WebDisplayNameAttribute
{

     bool m_isLocalized ;

     public LocalizedWebDisplayNameAttribute(string displayName)
         : base(displayName)
     {
     }

     public override string DisplayName
     {
         get
         {
             if (!m_isLocalized)
             {
                 this.DisplayNameValue =
                     Resources.ResourceManager.GetString(
                         base.DisplayName, Resources.Culture);
                 m_isLocalized = true;
             }
             return base.DisplayName;
         }
     }
}
```

To change the attributes' behavior, this code overrides the `DisplayName` property; and instead of only returning the value, it uses the `ResourceManager` object to retrieve the value from your localized resources. Subsequently, you can change the original property code to something like this:

```
[WebBrowsable]
[LocalizedCategory("LookAndFeel")]
[LocalizedWebDisplayName("UseCustomPalette")]
[LocalizedWebDescription("UseCustomPaletteDesc")]
[Personalizable(PersonalizationScope.Shared)]
public bool UseCustomPalette
{
   get;
   set;
}
```

To make this work, simply add the three attribute values (`LookAndFeel`, `UseCustomPalette`, and `UseCustomPaletteDesc` in this example) to resource files—one for each language you want support.

Using Resources for Linked Data

In addition to the resources retrieved from an assembly, some elements of an HTML page may require file-based data. JavaScript files are usually linked this way. Assuming your Web Part needs some custom JavaScript, it makes sense to hold it in a separate file. The browser caches this file, and if the Web Part is added several times, the script is only loaded once.

ASP.NET has a concept dedicated to this situation, called *web references*. Similar to the resources explained previously, web references add resources to the project's assembly. These resources are global, and there is a specific way to call them directly using an HTTP GET request. There is a handler responsible to resolve such calls. The handler is bound to the file name `WebResource.axd`. In HTML, such a call would look like this:

```
<script src="WebResource.axd?d=SbXSD3uTnhYsK4gMD8..." />
```

The unique parameter `d` provided in the request is built dynamically during the render process. Additionally, a time stamp using the parameter `t` can be set to allow the resource to time out. This happens when a new assembly is built, to force reloading of the cache.

To support the web resource, you need to prepare the project with the steps shown in the following exercise.

PREPARING WEB RESOURCES

1. Note the namespace of your project.
2. Add your resources in a dedicated folder, such as `/Resources/Alert.js`.
3. Right-click your resource file and set Build Action to Embedded Resource, as shown in Figure 8–9.
4. Add the following code line in the `AssemblyInfo.cs` file (replace `NameSpace` with the namespace of the project, as noted in step 1):

```
[assembly: System.Web.UI.WebResource("NameSpace.Resources.Alert.js",
                                      "text/javascript")]
```

5. Recompile the project.

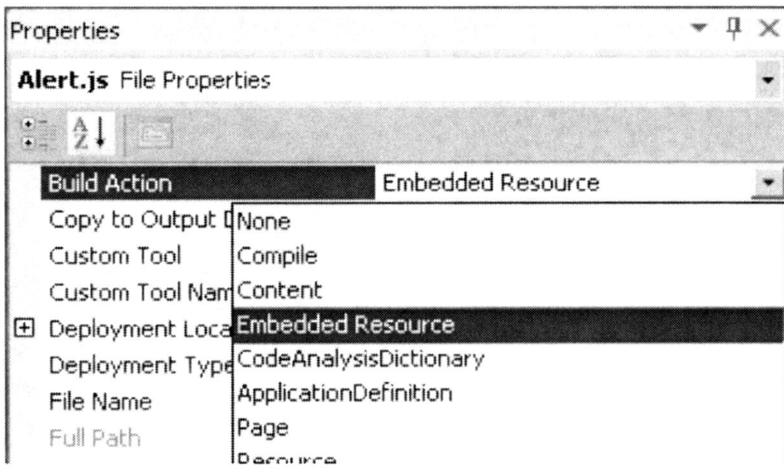

***Figure 8–9.** Set the Build Action property to add the file to the assemblies manifest.*

The file is now part of the assembly and can be used using the `WebResource.axd` syntax.

To use the file, you must retrieve the ID that's created dynamically for each request. Depending on what kind of file is used, you need to add the appropriate HTML element to your Web Part. The next example uses a simple JavaScript file. It adds a button dynamically to the Web Part and invokes a method in that file. First, here's the JavaScript snippet that's responding to the button's click:

```
function ShowAlert(val) {
    alert("Value: " + val);
}
```

The Web Part itself makes use of the embedded resource, as shown in Listing 8–2.

Listing 8–2. *The Complete Web Part Code*

```
using System;
using System.Runtime.InteropServices;
using System.Web.UI;
using System.Web.UI.WebControls;
using System.Web.UI.WebControls.WebParts;
using Microsoft.SharePoint;
using Microsoft.SharePoint.WebControls;

namespace SimpleWebPart.ResourceWebPart
{
    public class ResourceWebPart : WebPart
    {
        public ResourceWebPart()
        {
        }

        protected override void OnInit(EventArgs e)
        {
            base.OnInit(e);
            string script = "Apress.SP2010. ↵
                            ResourceWebPart.NonVisualWebPart.MyResources. ↵
                            Alert.js";
            if (!Page.ClientScript.IsClientScriptBlockRegistered(script))
            {
                Page.ClientScript.RegisterClientScriptResource(this.GetType(), ↵
                                                               script);
            }
        }

        protected override void CreateChildControls()
        {
            Button b = new Button();
            b.Text = "Click me!";
            b.OnClientClick = "ShowAlert(this)";
            Controls.Add(b);
            base.CreateChildControls();
        }

    }
}
```

The `script` variable contains the string defined in the `AssemblyInfo.cs` file shown in the previous instruction. The code registers a script block on the page and ensures that the script is linked only once. When you now build, deploy, and add the Web Part to a page, the HTML code is produced and creates the output shown in Figure 8–10.

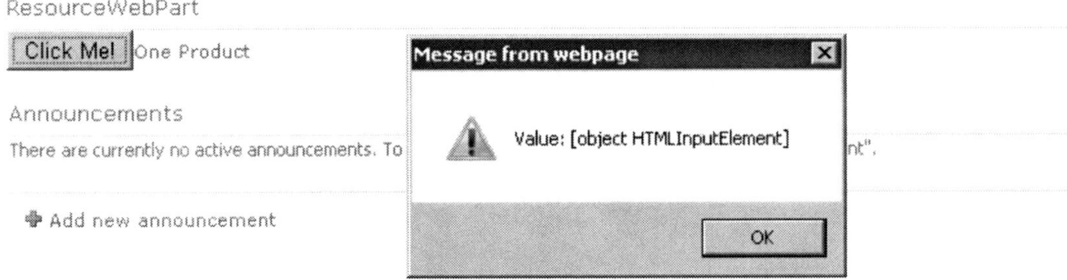

Figure 8–10. *A Web Part using embedded resources in the page's edit view*

The Resource Manager

The resource manager loads the resources from files and retrieves the desired element for a specific culture. A culture is a combination of a country and a language. The country defines the currency—for instance, while the language defines the number format and month names. Several types can be formatted dynamically using different cultures. Cultures are defined in a *`language-country`* format, such as `En-Us` or `De-de`. Cultures form a hierarchy. If the current culture is not found (e.g., `De-de`), then the resource manager tries to fall back to the parent—De in this case. If this fails, a default resource is used instead. If there is no default resource, an exception is thrown.

■ **Note** If the `ResourceManager` is used in the default way, it will always retrieve resources from the assembly's embedded files.

The explicit usage of file-based resources is not the common way to provide such additional data. However, under specific circumstances it may make sense to have resources distributed separately. Adding the files as a module to the package makes the deployment easier. Extracting the data from those files requires two steps:

1. Adding a reference to the `System.Configuration` assembly to your project
2. Calling the `System.Resources.ResourceManager` class

The resource manager reads the contents of the `.resources` files (compiled RESX files) and provides instant access:

```
System.Resources.ResourceManager rm;
rm = ResourceManager.CreateFileBasedResourceManager("Global", "ResourceDir", null);
lbl.Text = rm.GetString("Help.Text");
```

The parameters require a base name as the first parameter—usually the name of the compiled file. If the file name is `Global.en-us.resx`, then it compiles to `Global.en-us.resources` (the base name is `Global`). The resource manager is smart enough to look for all files of that name in the target folder (`ResourceDir`) whether or not they have a culture segment in their name. The resulting type is `ResourceSet` by default—that's what the third parameter specifies. In advanced scenarios you could create a type that behaves differently here in the way it is reading the resources. If set to `null` the default type is used. The resource manager accesses resources by their key, using the `GetString` or `GetObject` method. In the case of an object, you need to determine the type and cast the returned value appropriately.

Using Resources to Localize a Feature

While Web Parts are very common and usually the only part of your application that requires localization, you might occasionally need to localize a feature, too. This means that the feature's description and common resources would get localized.

Using Visual Studio 2010 you can easily add a feature resource. Simply right-click the feature in Solution Explorer and choose Add Feature Resource... (see Figure 8–11). The resulting dialog asks for the culture of the new resource. Choose Invariant Culture if you only need to create a fallback file. A fallback file is used if the resource manager cannot resolve the currently active culture—for this reason such a file is strongly recommended. If there is no fallback, an exception is thrown instead.

■ **Tip** If you need to handle all supported cultures explicitly and there is no fallback strategy, you should still create a fallback file. Add error information to every resource—for example, include an error message such as "ERR:" as a prefix to all data. Then, if you mistype a resource's name (key) accidentally, the message will appear somewhere on the page, and you can fix it.

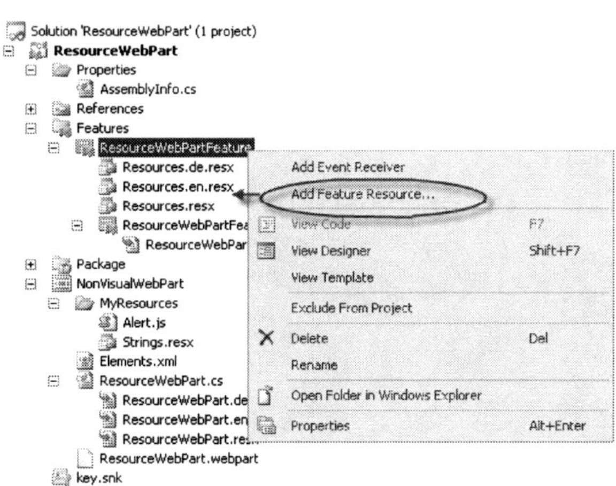

Figure 8–11. *A feature with several feature resources added in Solution Explorer*

Using these files follows the standard pattern that SharePoint uses for its internal resources stored in the core.resx files:

```
$Resources:ResourceKey
```

The $Resources part calls the expression builder. Everything after the colon defines the resource. The file's base name is Resources by default, whereas ResourceKey is the key within the file. The resource manager evaluates the correct language depending on the current context. For a feature definition, this looks like

```
<feature xmlns:dm0="http://schemas.microsoft.com/VisualStudio/2008/DslTools/Core"
         dslVersion="1.0.0.0" Id="244d3ced-8f88-49ac-8846-ebc8de430e0f"
         description="$Resources:Description"
         featureId="244d3ced-8f88-49ac-8846-ebc8de430e0f"
         imageUrl=""
         scope="Site"
         solutionId="00000000-0000-0000-0000-000000000000"
         title="$Resources:Title"
         version=""
           deploymentPath="$SharePoint.Project.FileNameWithoutExtension$"
           xmlns="http://schemas.microsoft.com/...">
</feature>
```

To change the settings in Visual Studio, open the Feature Designer, click in the manifest definition section, and open the Properties pane (by pressing F4) (see Figure 8–12).

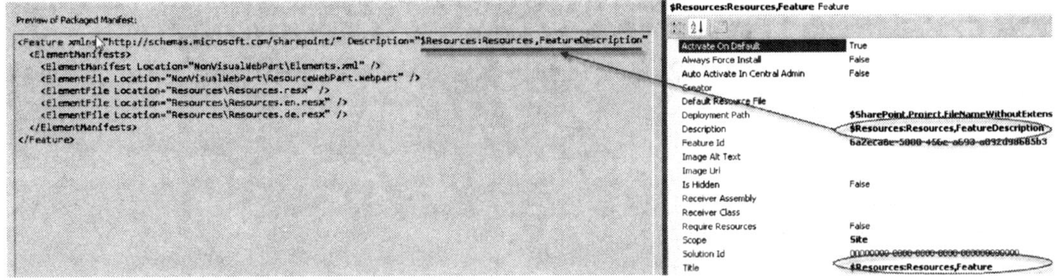

***Figure 8–12.** In the features manifest, press F4 to open the properties editor*

Simply create and deploy the package, and you'll have a localized feature. The content of the files deployed with the feature is shown in Figure 8–13.

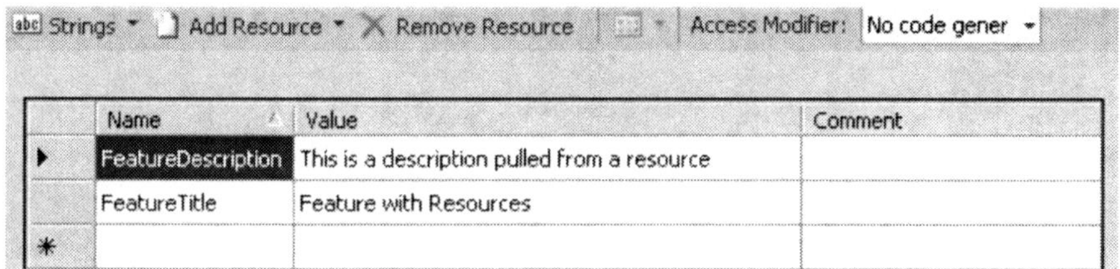

***Figure 8–13.** The resource file used in the feature resource example*

The Event Model

Events are a core concept for SharePoint developers. SharePoint is a user-driven platform. Users work with the sites, pages, lists, items, and more. Monitoring their activities and launching actions when a particular condition arises is flexible and enhances the capabilities immensely. Instead of writing whole applications, you merely hook into internal events and modify the behavior to suit your specific needs.

Events occur on several levels and under many conditions. In this section, we extensively cover the feature and site levels.

■ **Tip** See Chapter 4 for list- and item-level events in more detail.

The following introduction gives an overview and has several references to the events explained later.

The Event Receiver Principles

Event handling is based on event receiver base classes. You inherit from those base classes and override the event handlers you need to invoke specific tasks. The base classes are public in the object model. A reference to `Microsoft.SharePoint.dll` is required. Visual Studio even supports feature receivers with particular tasks.

Events at a Glance

Events appear at virtually all levels of SharePoint objects. Table 8–2 shows the base classes for the event definitions. Handlers that receive event notifications are not simply event handler methods, but predefined methods you can override within the inheriting class.

Table 8–2. Basic Event Classes

Class	Description
`SPListEventReceiver`	Provides events when users add, change, or remove columns for a list definition
`SPItemEventReceiver`	Provides events when users modify items within a list or documents within a document library
`SPWebEventReceiver`	Provides events when users move or delete a site collection or a site
`SPEmailEventReceiver`	Provides events when users send e-mail to an e-mail–enabled list
`SPFeatureReceiver`	Provides access to events that occur when a user activates or deactivates a feature

In this chapter we cover the more global, deployment-aware events at a feature level.

Events at the Deployment Stage: Feature Receivers

A feature receiver allows you to control a significant moment in the deployment process. Any time a user with appropriate rights activates or deactivates a feature, the associated event receiver is called. Table 8–3 shows the available events.

Table 8–3. Feature Receiver Events

Event	Description
`FeatureActivated`	Invoked when the user activates a deactivated feature. Remember that the feature is active by default after installation (if the settings are left unmodified) and therefore the event is invoked after installing the first time.
`FeatureDeactivating`	Invoked before the feature gets deactivated.
`FeatureInstalled`	Invoked after installation.
`FeatureUninstalling`	Invoked before uninstallation. This includes the deactivation.
`FeatureUpgrading`	Invoked if a new version of the feature is deployed through the upgrade option.

All methods receive a parameter of type `SPFeatureReceiverProperties`, which gives access to the underlying feature by exposing `SPFeatureDefinition`, `SPFeature`, and `SPSite` via the `Definition`, `Feature`, and `UserCodeSite` properties, respectively.

CREATING A FEATURE RECEIVER PROJECT

A feature receiver project creates an assembly that deploys into the GAC and adds the necessary registration files to connect the event with the receiver class. To create a feature receiver, you first of all need a feature.

1. Select your feature in Solution Explorer and right-click it.
2. Select Add Event Receiver from the context menu (see Figure 8–14).

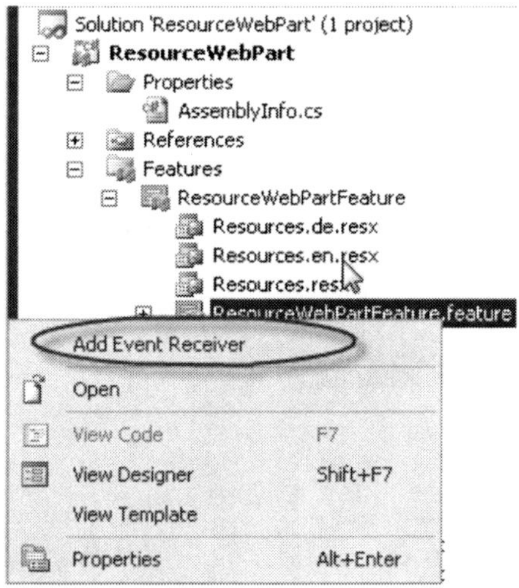

Figure 8–14. Adding a feature event receiver

3. The class will be created in the feature definition tree near the XML files. Within the created file, uncomment the events you'd like to implement.

Feature receivers are named after the feature. For example, if the feature is called "Feature1," the name is "Feature1EventReceiver." We recommend you name the feature appropriately before creating any dependent objects.

Typical examples for features are the creation of lists, adding default data to existing lists, and adding application pages to the navigation. The next example shows how to hook into the navigation and add an application page structure there. This requires two steps. First, when activating, the items must be added. Second, when deactivating, the items must be removed. Because something could go wrong, you must check in both steps whether the expected conditions are fulfilled—in this example, the expected items must exist after activating and must not exist after deactivating.

Creating a Feature with the Application Page's Navigation

A feature can contain items published to the configuration database (e.g., lists, data, and event receivers). It cannot contain elements copied to a target folder. These items must be part of the package. In the example, the navigation is defined in a `web.sitemap` file that is common for ASP.NET projects. To edit it easily, you can add an XML file to the current project and name it `web.sitemap`. Then add the correct schema to it, and IntelliSense will support you (see Figure 8–15).

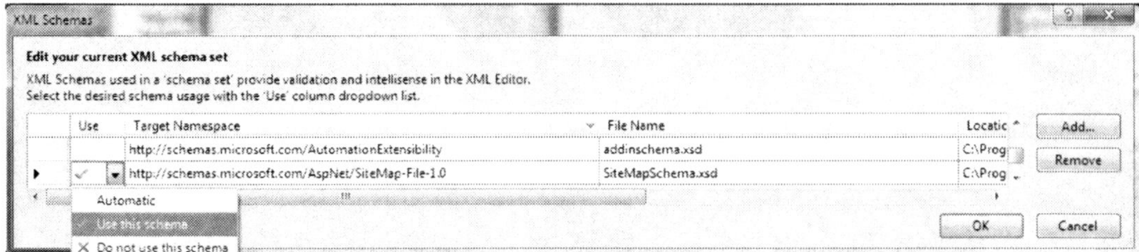

Figure 8–15. *Add the appropriate schema to get IntelliSense.*

Once IntelliSense is operating you can edit the file, as shown in Figure 8–16.

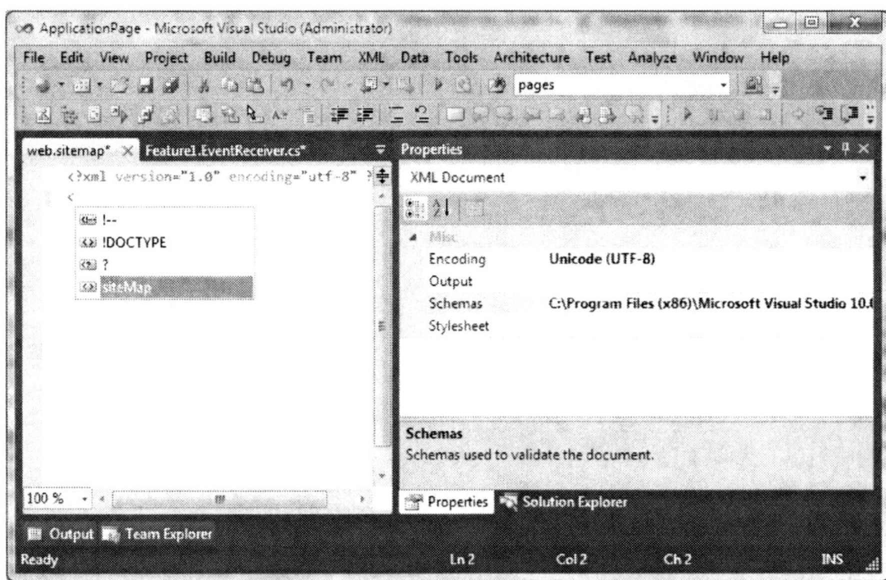

Figure 8–16. *Editing an embedded XML file using the schema*

The `web.sitemap` file in this example is embedded in the assembly by setting Build Action to Embedded Resource. This makes deployment easier and prevents users from modifying the contents.

Creating the Feature Receiver

Next, the feature receiver can be added to the project. Listing 8–3 shows the complete code.

***Listing 8–3.** A Feature Receiver Class*

```
using System;
using System.Runtime.InteropServices;
using System.Security.Permissions;
using Microsoft.SharePoint;
using Microsoft.SharePoint.Security;
using Microsoft.SharePoint.Navigation;
using System.Xml.Linq;
using System.Linq;
using System.IO;
using System.Xml;
using Microsoft.SharePoint.Utilities;

namespace ApplicationPage.Features.Feature1
{
    [Guid("9f3e821a-1e27-425f-b3f6-93a2847f6544")]
    public class Feature1EventReceiver : SPFeatureReceiver
    {

        string PATH = @"/_layouts/";

        public override void FeatureActivated(
                             SPFeatureReceiverProperties properties)
        {
            if (properties.Feature.Parent is SPSite)
            {
                // Cannot activate this feature at site level
                return;
            }
            SPWeb web = (SPWeb)properties.Feature.Parent;
            SPNavigationNodeCollection topNavi = web.Navigation.TopNavigationBar;
            // Check existing top element. If present remove first
            CheckAndRemove(topNavi);
            // Read navigation instruction
            using (Stream st = GetType().Assembly.
                        GetManifestResourceStream("ApplicationPage.web.sitemap"))
            {
                using (XmlReader tr = new XmlTextReader(st))
                {
                    try
                    {
                        XElement siteMap = XElement.Load(tr);
                        // Add nodes
                        var root = from r in siteMap.Descendants()
                                   where r.Attribute("title").
                                           Value.Equals("HR Department")
                                   select r;
                        // Found
                        if (root.Count() == 1)
                        {
                            XElement rootElement = root.First();
                            string rootPath = web.Url + PATH;
```

```
                    // Create and add root node
                    SPNavigationNode rootNode = new SPNavigationNode(
                        rootElement.Attribute("title").Value,
                        rootPath + rootElement.Attribute("url").Value,
                        true);
                    SPNavigationNode topNode = topNavi.AddAsLast(rootNode);
                    AddNodes(rootElement, topNode, rootPath);

                }
            }
            catch (Exception ex)
            {
            }
        }
    }
}

private void AddNodes(XElement currentFrom, SPNavigationNode currentTo,
                      string rootPath)
{
    foreach (XElement r in currentFrom.Elements())
    {
        SPNavigationNode n = new SPNavigationNode(
                             r.Attribute("title").Value,
                             rootPath + r.Attribute("url").Value);
        SPNavigationNode newnode = currentTo.Children.AddAsLast(n);
        if (r.HasElements)
        {
            AddNodes(r, newnode, rootPath);
        }
    }
}

private void CheckAndRemove(SPNavigationNodeCollection topNavi)
{
    var nodes = from n in topNavi.Cast<SPNavigationNode>()
                where n.Title.Equals("HR Department")
                select n;
    if (nodes.Count() == 1)
    {
        topNavi.Delete(nodes.First());
    }
}

public override void FeatureDeactivating(
                     SPFeatureReceiverProperties properties)
{
    SPWeb web = (SPWeb)properties.Feature.Parent;
    SPNavigationNodeCollection topNavi = web.Navigation.TopNavigationBar;
    CheckAndRemove(topNavi);
}

    }
}
```

This code checks first whether the parent object is an SPSite or SPWeb. This feature receiver supports SPWeb only, and therefore does nothing if SPSite appears. This is because there is no navigation object at the site level. You should set the feature's properties appropriately, as shown in Figure 8–17.

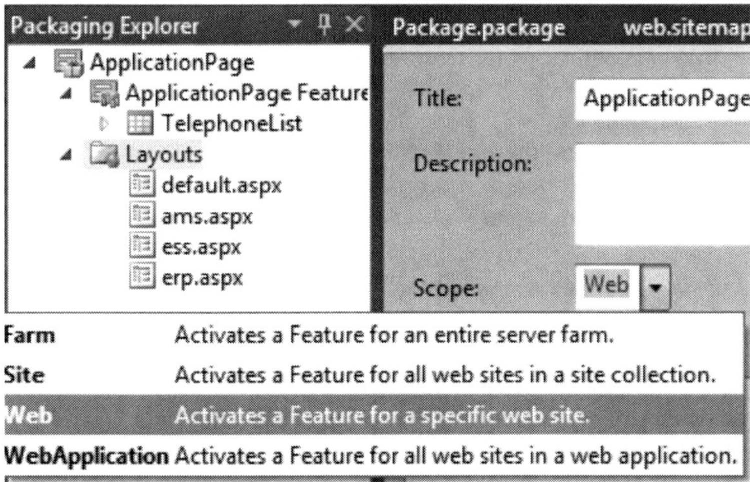

Figure 8–17. *Set the right scope for the feature to have access to scope-specific data.*

There are two private methods to create the node collection and remove it later. The creation method is recursive to allow for an unlimited number of node levels. The elements in Top Navigation and Quick Launch are SPNavigationNode objects. These objects require valid paths before being added to the parent node's collection. The URL is set to the URL of the current web, and the _layouts folder is hard-coded. This example also assumes that the root folder is named HRDepartment, and even this is hard-coded. You can easily extend the code to be more flexible. The options available for the navigation are explained in more detail in Chapter 10.

Registering the Event

The feature you deploy must contain the information about the receiver. This requires two settings:

- ReceiverAssembly: The assembly containing the code of your event receiver
- ReceiverClass: The actual class that defines the receiver

If you create the feature and feature receiver as explained previously using Visual Studio 2010, the necessary information is built automatically. If you plan to create your feature's manifest file manually or edit it later, you will need to define this information. Such a file looks like this:

```
<Feature xmlns="http://schemas.microsoft.com/sharepoint/"
         Title="ApplicationPage Add Menuitems"
         Id="4e8fed7b-0acf-48f9-9b60-4584b5bcd4bc"
         ReceiverAssembly="ApplicationPage, Version=1.0.0.0, Culture=neutral,
                           PublicKeyToken=791a6f2c4cde1076"
         ReceiverClass="ApplicationPage.Features.Feature1.Feature1EventReceiver"
         Scope="Web">
</Feature>
```

The `ReceiverAssembly` and `ReceiverClass` tags must be set to the appropriate values. The receiver class entry must define the whole namespace. The feature itself may be used only to transport the event receiver information—meaning that you can leave it empty if you don't have anything to add there.

The `feature.xml` file has several more properties that also influence the receiver:

- `Hidden`: Set to `true` to make the feature invisible in the Site Properties dialog. This prevents users from activating or deactivating the feature. This is usually an option that helps to manage dependent features, such as base features used by others. The default value is `false`.
- `ActivateOnDefault`: Set to `false` to prevent the feature from activating immediately. The default value is `true`.
- `AlwaysForceInstall`: Forces the feature to install even if code execution fails. The default value is `false`.

Please refer to Chapter 9 to read more about the various settings.

Events at the Site and Site Collection Levels

SharePoint 2010 supports events fired when you add, move, or delete a site or site collection. You can add these events as event receivers through a project template (see Figure 8–18).

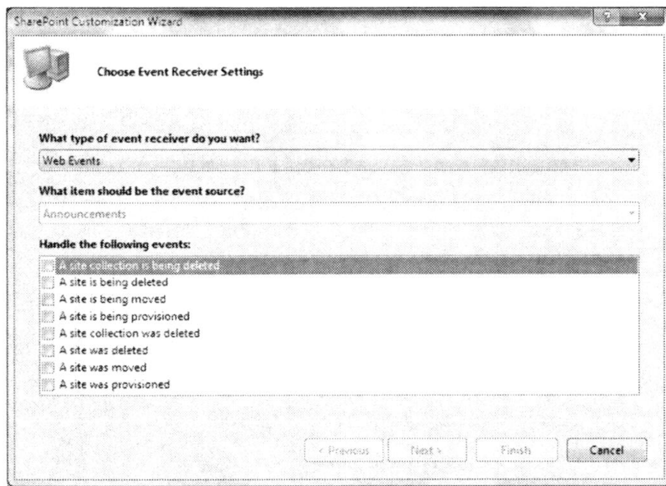

Figure 8–18. *Events supported by sites and site collections*

Event receivers are usually deployed at a site or site collection level as part of a feature. Therefore it doesn't make sense to have site collection events such as adding. For site collections there are two events (the corresponding terms used in the wizard are in parentheses):

- `SiteDeleting` *(being deleted)*: Fired before the site collection is deleted
- `SiteDeleted` *(was deleted)*: Fired after the site collection is deleted

These and several more events available for sites are defined in `SPWebEventReceiver`:

- `WebDeleting`: Fired before the site is deleted (synchronous)
- `WebDeleted`: Fired after the site is deleted (asynchronous)
- `WebMoving`: Fired before the site has been renamed or moved (synchronous)
- `WebMoved`: Fired after the site has been moved to another collection (asynchronous)
- `WebAdding`: Fired before the site has been created (synchronous)
- `WebProvisioned`: Fired after the site has been created and is fully provisioned (asynchronous)

The provisioning procedure is—as all "after" events—asynchronous by default. This means that when the event executes, the site is probably not yet completely installed. To ensure that the event fires synchronously, you must set the `Synchronization` attribute to `true`.

Defining the Event Receiver

The event receiver manifest file `elements.xml` controls this behavior. An example is shown in Listing 8–4.

Listing 8–4. *Definition of Site Receivers*

```
<?xml version="1.0" encoding="utf-8"?>
<Elements xmlns="http://schemas.microsoft.com/sharepoint/">
  <Receivers >
    <Receiver>
      <Name>SiteEventReceiverWebDeleting</Name>
      <Type>WebDeleting</Type>
      <Assembly>$SharePoint.Project.AssemblyFullName$</Assembly>
      <Class>WebProvisioning.SiteEventReceiver.SiteEventReceiver</Class>
      <SequenceNumber>10000</SequenceNumber>
    </Receiver>
    <Receiver>
      <Name>SiteEventReceiverWebAdding</Name>
      <Type>WebAdding</Type>
      <Assembly>$SharePoint.Project.AssemblyFullName$</Assembly>
      <Class>WebProvisioning.SiteEventReceiver.SiteEventReceiver</Class>
      <SequenceNumber>10000</SequenceNumber>
    </Receiver>
    <Receiver>
      <Name>SiteEventReceiverWebProvisioned</Name>
      <Type>WebProvisioned</Type>
      <Assembly>$SharePoint.Project.AssemblyFullName$</Assembly>
      <Class>WebProvisioning.SiteEventReceiver.SiteEventReceiver</Class>
      <SequenceNumber>10000</SequenceNumber>
      <Synchronization>Synchronous</Synchronization>
    </Receiver>
  </Receivers>
</Elements>
```

For elements that support asynchronous behavior, you can force a synchronous call by using the `<Synchronization>` element. The receiver itself needs the assembly where the class is stored, the full class name including the namespace, a name that's used internally only, and the type, which is the internal event name listed in the preceding bullet points.

If there are several event handlers attached to the same event, you can use the sequence number element to define the order. If you create the file using Visual Studio 2010, the `$SharePoint.Project.AssemblyFullName$` placeholder is used to reference the current project's assembly. If you create the file manually, you must enter the fully qualified assembly name in the `<Assembly>` element.

Creating a Web Event Receiver Class

The event receiver for sites and webs is defined in the `Microsoft.SharePoint.SPWebEventReceiver` class. The example in Listing 8–5 modifies the title of the created site after provisioning.

***Listing 8–5.** A Web Event Receiver*

```
using System;
using System.Security.Permissions;
using Microsoft.SharePoint;
using Microsoft.SharePoint.Security;
using Microsoft.SharePoint.Utilities;
using Microsoft.SharePoint.Workflow;

namespace WebProvisioning.SiteEventReceiver
{

    public class WebEventReceiver : SPWebEventReceiver
    {

       public override void WebDeleting(SPWebEventProperties properties)
       {
           try
           {
               if (properties.Web.Lists["Data"] != null)
               {
                   properties.Cancel = true;
               }
           }
           catch
           {
           }
           base.WebDeleting(properties);
       }

       public override void WebAdding(SPWebEventProperties properties)
       {
           base.WebAdding(properties);
       }

       public override void WebProvisioned(SPWebEventProperties properties)
       {
           properties.Web.Title += String.Format(" [Created By: {0}]",
                                   properties.UserDisplayName);
```

```
            properties.Web.AllowUnsafeUpdates = true;
            properties.Web.Update();
            base.WebAdding(properties);
        }

    }
}
```

The code simply adds the current user's full name (including the domain) to the site's title (see Figure 8–19). In the web-deleting event it tries to prevent the action from being processed if a list named `Data` still exists. This is a common technique to prevent users from accidentally removing a site along with crucial data. Imagine backing up this data before the user will be able to remove the site and all containing lists. To abort the process, simply set the `Cancel` property to `true`.

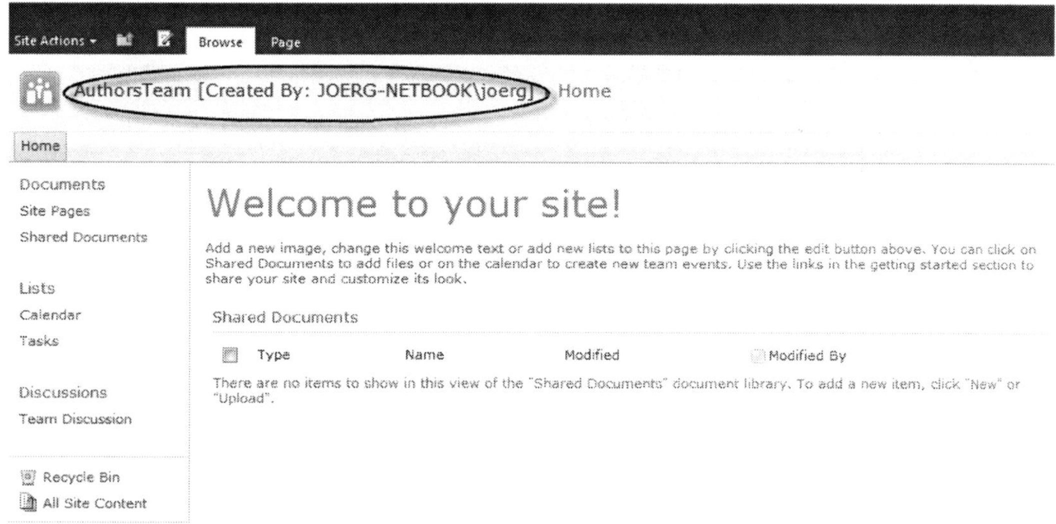

***Figure 8–19.** A site title modified by a site collection feature's web event receiver*

If you don't want to let users deactivate a feature that's dedicated to such basic tasks, you can set the feature state to "hidden." While it is invisible, it is still working. When the feature is deployed as a solution, normally administrators will still be able to remove the solution to deactivate and remove the feature.

Dealing with Error Conditions

The cancellation of the web deletion is probably not obvious to the user, because from their perspective nothing happens. You can write to the event log or in some private log, but an end user with limited rights is unlikely to access either of those. To force SharePoint to display a message, you can throw an exception, as demonstrated in the following modified `WebDeleting` method:

```
public override void WebDeleting(SPWebEventProperties properties)
{
   try
```

```
    {
       if (properties.Web.Lists["Data"] != null)
       {
          properties.Cancel = true;
        }
     }
     catch
     {
         throw new SPException("Cannot delete the site because it
                                has user data in it");
      }
      base.WebDeleting(properties);
}
```

Now the exception is caught at a higher level and presented via an error message box. (It's not very aesthetic, but the text is communicated (see Figure 8–20).

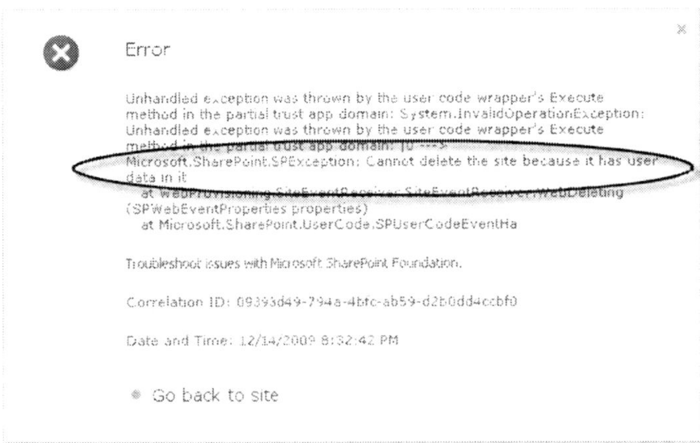

Figure 8–20. A slightly customized error message

The exception aborts the procedure internally, so you don't need to explicitly set the `Cancel` property.

Sending E-mail

Transmitting messages via e-mail is widely supported in SharePoint. While .NET supports SMTP, you also have the option of choosing a delivery framework. Using SharePoint ensures that the required settings are maintained by Central Administration. However, both techniques have their specific pros and cons. Hence we show two examples.

Sending E-mail Using ASP.NET

Sending e-mail via ASP.NET uses the `SmtpClient` class, as shown in Listing 8–6.

Listing 8–6. *Sending E-Mail Using .NET*

```
public static bool SendMail(string Subject, string Body,
             bool IsBodyHtml, string From, string To, string Cc, string Bcc)
{
    bool mailSent= false;
    try
    {
        SmtpClient smtpClient = new SmtpClient();
        smtpClient.Host = SPContext.Current.Site.WebApplication.
                          OutboundMailServiceInstance.Server.Address;
        MailMessage mailMessage = new MailMessage(From, To, Subject, Body);
        if (!String.IsNullOrEmpty(Cc))
        {
            MailAddress CCAddress = new MailAddress(Cc);
            mailMessage.CC.Add(CCAddress);
        }
        if (!String.IsNullOrEmpty(Bcc))
        {
            MailAddress BCCAddress = new MailAddress(Bcc);
            mailMessage.Bcc.Add(BCCAddress);
        }

        mailMessage.IsBodyHtml = IsBodyHtml;
        smtpClient.Send(mailMessage);
        mailSent = true;
    }
    catch (Exception) { return mailSent; }

    return mailSent;
}
```

Note that the code retrieves the SMTP host's address from the SharePoint configuration database. This ensures that you get the advantages of.NET-style mail delivery while keeping your configuration in Central Administration.

If you are not working in a SharePoint context, you can get the `SPWebApplication` reference from a new `SPSite` object:

```
public static string GetSharePointMailService(string mysite)
{
    string address;
    using (SPSite site = new SPSite(mysite))
    {
      address = site.WebApplication.OutboundMailServiceInstance.Server.Address;
    }
    return address;
}
```

Using SharePoint's Mail-Sending Classes

The embedded SharePoint function has fewer capabilities, but is as straightforward as possible, and is the preferred approach if you simply want to send e-mail:

```
SPUtility.SendEmail(web, useHtml, htmlEncode, to, subject, htmlBody)
```

The static method has three more overloads. One has an additional Boolean parameter that adds a footer. The other two use a StringDictionary to add additional headers to the mail. An example is shown in Listing 8–7.

Listing 8–7. *Sending E-mail Using SendMail from a Layout Page*

```
try
{
   SPWeb thisWeb = this.Web;  // Requires LayoutsPageBase
   string to = "someone@apress.com";
   string subject = "Book Message";
   string body = "A message from SharePoint";
   bool success = SPUtility.SendEmail(thisWeb, true, true, to, subject, body);
}
catch (Exception ex)
{
  // Exception handling skipped for clarity
}
```

The parameters are shown in Table 8–4.

Table 8–4. *Parameters of the SendMail Method*

Name	Type	Description
web	SPWeb	An object that represents the site
headers	StringDictionary	A collection of additional headers
useHtml	bool	Used to append an HTML tag to the message (true)
htmlEncode	bool	Encodes the message and replaces characters in HTML tags with entities
to	string	The address to which to send the e-mail
subject	string	Contains the subject for the e-mail message
htmlBody	string	Contains the body of the e-mail message
addFooter	bool	Used if there is a footer to be appended to the e-mail

The headers parameter is used instead of the to and subject parameters. It allows you to set all possible mail headers and forces you to add at least the to header that way. An example follows:

```
StringDictionary headers = new StringDictionary();
headers.add("to","authors@apress.com");
headers.add("cc","joerg@krause.net");
headers.add("bcc","checkthis@apress.com");
headers.add("from","sp2010@apress.com");
```

```
headers.add("subject","Send an EMail from SPUtility");
headers.add("content-type","text/html");
string bodyText ="This is an <b>html</b> formatted message.";
SPUtility.SendEmail(web, headers, bodyText);
```

Note that `StringDictionary` is defined in the `System.Collections.Specialized` namespace.

■ **Tip** You can read more about mail headers at Wikipedia: `http://en.wikipedia.org/wiki/E-mail#Message_header`.

Sending E-Mail from a WCF Service

Sending an e-mail from a service when `SPContext` is not available could fail. As a workaround, you have to prevent the mail function from reading the current context by using `HttpContext.Current = null`. If it can't, it will retrieve the right context and it will then work. The example in Listing 8–8 shows this.

Listing 8–8. *Sending E-mail Using SendMail from a WCF Service*

```
try
{
   using (SPSite site = new SPSite("http://sharepointserve"))
   {
     SPWeb thisWeb = site.RootWeb;
     {
        string to = "someone@apress.com";
        string subject = "Book Message";
        string body = "A message from SharePoint";
        HttpContext curCtx = HttpContext.Current;
        HttpContext.Current = null;
        bool success = SPUtility.SendEmail(thisWeb, true, true, to, subject, body);
        HttpContext.Current = curCtx;
     }
   }
}
catch (Exception ex)
{
  // Exception handling skipped for clarity
}
```

The current context is set to `null` to force the context to be retrieved again. Saving the current context ensures that the service works properly after the method has been executed.

■ **Note** ASMX Web Services require the same procedure.

Custom Helper Classes

Aside from the utilities and helper classes included within the SharePoint namespaces, it's useful to encapsulate some functions. In particular, there are common object access methods that are used often in an application. If you decompose the helper classes into the subjects they address, you arrive at four areas, each encapsulated into its own manager class:

- `DataManager`
- `SiteManager`
- `SecurityManager`
- `Extensions`

We suggest using at least two of these classes for your projects to include your own useful methods. In this section we show some examples of functions that such classes might contain. We focus only on the `DataManager` and `Extensions` classes here, as these two are usually the most helpful.

Data Manager Functions

A data manager encompasses all functions required to access sites, webs, and lists. These functions are nondeterministic and therefore declared `static`.

Getting a Web with Elevated Privileges

In previous chapters we explained how to raise the access rights by elevating privileges. It makes sense to encapsulate this in a method that returns an elevated web, as shown in Listing 8–9. Note that the caller is responsible for disposing the object afterward to free up memory properly.

Listing 8–9. *Creating an SPWeb Object with Elevated Privileges*

```
public static SPWeb GetElevatedWeb()
{
    SPWeb web = null;
    try
    {
        SPSecurity.RunWithElevatedPrivileges(
            () =>
            {
                if (SPContext.Current != null)
                {
                    using (SPSite site = new SPSite(SPContext.Current.Web.Url))
                    {
                        web = site.OpenWeb();
                    }
                }
            });
    }
    catch
    {
        if (web != null)
        {
```

```
            web.Dispose();
            web = null;
        }
    }
    return web;
}
```

The code uses the current context to retrieve the current web and returns the same web with the System Account as the current user.

Getting a List Instance

You can obtain a list instance from the current SPWeb via the Lists property. A custom method results in cleaner code. Listing 8–10 demonstrates one way to make small improvements to simplify the higher-level calling code.

Listing 8–10. *Two Overloads of a Method That Retrieves a List*

```
public static SPList GetList(string title, SPWeb web)
{
    return web.Lists.Cast<SPList>().FirstOrDefault(list => list.Title == title);
}

public static SPList GetList(Guid id, SPWeb web)
{
    return web.Lists[id];
}
```

As well as using either the list's Title or its Guid to get the list instance, you can modify this code to use any other property to select a list, such as RootFolder.Name to use the internal name.

Getting a List with a Data Model Behind the Scenes

When working with list data you should use a strongly typed data model. With SPMetal you can create a LINQ to SharePoint layer for existing lists. In a distributed environment, however, this is not generally the best solution. A "self-made" data context and a hand-written data model are sometimes better options than using SPMetal. Such a data layer is thin, easy to create, and fast.

First, assume you want to get a list instance, not just as an SPList object, but as something more type-safe. Such a method could look like this:

```
public static SPList GetList<T>(SPWeb web) where T : BaseSPListItem
{
    return GetList(ApplicationResources.ResourceManager.GetString(typeof(T).Name),
                   web);
}
```

The GetList call leads to the method shown in Listing 8–11. The lists the application actually uses are stored in an application resource. The crucial thing is the type T and the base class used to constrain the generic. The SPWeb object is used explicitly to allow the caller to decide whether it's a regular object or one with elevated privileges.

Second, the BaseSPListItem class plays a vital role. It encapsulates access to a list item and provides serialization. Serializing SharePoint objects can be messy, because the underlying COM objects prevent you from doing so. The base class in Listing 8–11 uses methods for direct SharePoint object access to avoid serialization. Serializing here means that the object is destroyed on serializing—only the list's ID and item's ID survive. The deserializer calls the default constructor and re-creates the object.

Listing 8–11. *Serializable Base Class with Standard Fields*

```
public static class BaseSPListItemFields
{
    public const string ID = "ID";
    public const string UniqueID = "UniqueID";
    public const string Title = "Title";
    public const string Name = "Name";
    public const string Author = "Author";
    public const string Editor = "Editor";
    public const string Created = "Created";
    public const string Modified = "Modified";
}

[Serializable()]
public abstract class BaseSPListItem
{

    private SPListItem _item;

    public SPListItem GetListItem()
    {
        return _item;
    }

    public void SetListItem(SPListItem item)
    {
        _item = item;
    }

    public SPList GetBaseList()
    {
        return _item.ParentList;
    }

    protected BaseSPListItem()
    {
        if (ID != Guid.Empty)
        {
            SPList list = DataManager.GetList(ParentList, SPContext.Current.Web);
            _item = list.GetItemByUniqueId(ID);
        }
    }

    protected BaseSPListItem(SPListItem listItem)
        : this()
    {
        this._item = listItem;
        this.ParentList = _item.ParentList.Title;
        this.ID = _item.UniqueId;
```

```
    this.ParentWeb = _item.Web.Title;
}

public Guid ID
{
    get;
    set;
}

public string ParentList
{
    get;
    set;
}

public string ParentWeb
{
    get;
    set;
}

/// <summary>
/// Internal ID of the ListItem
/// </summary>
public int GetID()
{
    return _item.ID;
}

public Guid GetUniqueID()
{
    return _item.UniqueId;
}

public String Title
{
    get { return (String)GetValue(BaseSPListItemFields.Title); }
    set { SetValue(BaseSPListItemFields.Title, value); }
}

public String Name
{
    get { return (String)GetValue(BaseSPListItemFields.Name); }
    set { SetValue(BaseSPListItemFields.Name, value); }
}

public SPFieldLookupValue GetAuthor()
{
    return new SPFieldLookupValue(
            (String)GetValue(BaseSPListItemFields.Author));
}

public SPFieldLookupValue GetEditor()
{
```

```
        return new SPFieldLookupValue(
                    (String)GetValue(BaseSPListItemFields.Editor));
    }

    public DateTime? GetModified()
    {
        return GetValue(BaseSPListItemFields.Modified) as DateTime?;
    }

    public DateTime? GetCreated()
    {
        return GetValue(BaseSPListItemFields.Created) as DateTime?;
    }

    public virtual void EnsureTitle()
    {

    }

    public object GetValue(Guid fieldID)
    {
        object retVal = null;
        if (_item != null)
        {
            try
            {
                retVal = _item[fieldID];
            }
            catch { }
        }
        return retVal;
    }

    public void SetValue(Guid fieldID, object value)
    {
        if (_item != null)
        {
            _item[fieldID] = value;
        }
    }

    public object GetValue(String propertyName)
    {
        object retVal = null;
        if (_item != null)
        {
            try
            {
                retVal = _item[propertyName];
            }
            catch { }
        }
        return retVal;
    }
```

```
public void SetValue(String propertyName, object value)
{
    if (_item != null)
    {
        _item[propertyName] = value;
    }
}

public bool DoesFieldExist(String fieldName)
{
    return _item.Fields.ContainsField(fieldName);
}

public override string ToString()
{
    StringBuilder sb = new StringBuilder();
    String del = "";
    sb.Append(this.GetType().Name + "[");
    foreach (PropertyInfo pi in this.GetType().GetProperties())
    {
        if (pi.GetGetMethod() != null)
        {
            object obj = pi.GetValue(this, null);
            sb.Append(del + pi.Name + "=" +
                      ((obj == null) ? "NULL" : obj.ToString()));
            del = ", ";
        }
    }
    sb.Append("]");
    return sb.ToString();
}

public void Update()
{
    if (_item != null)
    {
        _item.Update();
    }
}
public void UpdateUnsafe()
{
    if (_item != null)
    {
        using (SPWeb web = this._item.Web)
        {
            bool allow = web.AllowUnsafeUpdates;
            web.AllowUnsafeUpdates = true;
            _item.Update();
            web.AllowUnsafeUpdates = allow;
        }
    }
}
public void SystemUpdate()
```

```
    {
        if (_item != null)
        {
            _item.SystemUpdate();
        }
    }
    public void SystemUpdateUnsafe()
    {
        if (_item != null)
        {
            using (SPWeb web = this._item.Web)
            {
                bool allow = web.AllowUnsafeUpdates;
                web.AllowUnsafeUpdates = true;
                _item.SystemUpdate();
                web.AllowUnsafeUpdates = allow;
            }
        }
    }
    public void Delete()
    {
        if (_item != null)
        {
            _item.Delete();
        }
    }
    public void DeleteUnsafe()
    {
        if (_item != null)
        {
            using (SPWeb web = this._item.Web)
            {
                bool allow = web.AllowUnsafeUpdates;
                web.AllowUnsafeUpdates = true;
                _item.Delete();
                web.AllowUnsafeUpdates = allow;
            }
        }
    }
}
```

Several methods give direct access to common operations, such as saving and deleting. This is all possible using the "unsafe" operation (`AllowUnsafeUpdates`).

Using this base class is straightforward. Any class in the data model simply implements this class and adds the field access properties. This can look like Listing 8–12.

***Listing 8–12.** Sample Class That Provides Type-Safe ListItem Access*

```
public static class RequestListFields
{
    public const string MainCategory = "MainCategory";
    public const string SubCategory = "SubCategory";
    public const string DetailCategory = "DetailCategory";
}

[Serializable]
public class RequestList : BaseSPListItem
{
    public RequestList() : base() { }
    public RequestList(SPListItem listItem) : base(listItem) { }

    public SPFieldLookupValue ParentRequest
    {
        get { return new SPFieldLookupValue(
              base.GetValue(RequestListFields.ParentRequest) as string); }
        set { base.SetValue(RequestListFields.ParentRequest, value); }
    }

    public string MainCategory
    {
        get { return base.GetValue(RequestListFields.MainCategory) as string; }
        set { base.SetValue(RequestListFields.MainCategory, value); }
    }
    public string SubCategory
    {
        get { return base.GetValue(RequestListFields.SubCategory) as string; }
        set { base.SetValue(RequestListFields.SubCategory, value); }
    }
    public string DetailCategory
    {
        get { return base.GetValue(RequestListFields.DetailCategory) as string; }
        set { base.SetValue(RequestListFields.DetailCategory, value); }
    }
}
```

This is merely a suggestion of how to deal with data. You could also extend existing classes using extension methods to simplify the access.

Extension Methods Elaborated

Sometimes you need to get a list by its internal name. This requires retrieving the complete collection of lists and checking the `RootFolder.Name` property. Using LINQ makes this easy, and using an extension method hides the implementation from the developer. This method reads the complete collection of lists into memory, but not the lists' items.

```
public static SPList GetListByInternalName(this SPWeb web, string internalname)
{
```

```
    return web.Lists.Cast<SPList>().FirstOrDefault(
                                     list => list.RootFolder.Name == internalname);
}
```

Once you have a list, you can do many things with it and its items. Extending the SPList object is a clever way of encapsulating common operations within simple method calls. The CanCreateItems method checks whether the current user has the appropriate permissions to add items to the list:

```
public static bool CanCreateItems(this SPList list)
{
    return list != null && (list.EffectiveBasePermissions &
           SPBasePermissions.AddListItems) != SPBasePermissions.EmptyMask;
}
```

The next two methods perform a similar check to determine whether the user has read or write permissions, respectively:

```
public static bool CanReadItems(this SPList list)
{
    return list != null && (list.EffectiveBasePermissions &
           SPBasePermissions.ViewListItems) != SPBasePermissions.EmptyMask;
}
public static bool CanWriteItems(this SPList list)
{
    return list != null && (list.EffectiveBasePermissions &
           SPBasePermissions.EditListItems) != SPBasePermissions.EmptyMask;
}
```

The CanDeleteItems method retrieves all the items of a list as an enumerable collection, enabling you to run LINQ to Object queries against the items. However, use this method with caution, as the entire list is read into memory, even if a subsequent LINQ clause extracts a single item.

```
public static bool CanDeleteItems(this SPList list)
{
    return list != null && (list.EffectiveBasePermissions &
           SPBasePermissions.DeleteListItems) != SPBasePermissions.EmptyMask;
}
```

The next method performs a query first and then returns the list of items. This call does not read the complete list in case of GetItemsByFieldEquals. The CAML instructions ensure that it's the fastest way to get a filtered list of items. GetItems does not use any filter, and returns all items.

```
public static IEnumerable<SPListItem> GetItems(this SPList list)
{
    return list.GetItemsByQuery(String.Empty);
}
public static IEnumerable<SPListItem> GetItemsByFieldEquals(this SPList list,
                                                            string value,
                                                            string field)
{
    var query = new XElement("Where",
                    new XElement("Eq",
                        new XElement("FieldRef",
                            new XAttribute("Name", field)),
                        new XElement("Value", value)
                        )
                    );
```

```
    return list.GetItemsByQuery(query.ToString(SaveOptions.DisableFormatting));
}
```

The next method closely corresponds to the previous one, but it uses the Contains operator instead of Eq:

```
public static IEnumerable<SPListItem> GetItemsByFieldContains(this SPList list, string value,
string field)
{
    var query = new XElement("Where",
                    new XElement("Contains",
                        new XElement("FieldRef",
                            new XAttribute("Name", field)),
                        new XElement("Value", value)
                        )
                    );
    return list.GetItemsByQuery(query.ToString(SaveOptions.DisableFormatting));
}
```

Lookup fields need slightly different treatment. Setting the LookupId="true" attribute ensures that the CAML query works as expected:

```
public static IEnumerable<SPListItem> GetItemsByFieldLookupId(this SPList list,
                                                               int lookupId,
                                                               string field)
{
    var query = new XElement("Where",
                    new XElement("Eq",
                        new XElement("FieldRef",
                            new XAttribute("LookupId", "true"),
                            new XAttribute("Name", field)),
                        new XElement("Value", value)
                        )
                    );
    return list.GetItemsByQuery(query.ToString(SaveOptions.DisableFormatting));
}
```

If a simple Eq or Contains operator is inadequate, you can pass a query. The following example accepts CAML as a string:

```
public static IEnumerable<SPListItem> GetItemsByQuery(this SPList list, string caml)
{
    if (list != null)
    {
        if (list.ItemCount <= Constants.PaginationThreshold)
        {
            SPQuery query = new SPQuery();
            query.ViewAttributes = "Scope=\"Recursive\"";
            query.Query = caml;
            SPListItemCollection items = list.GetItems(query);
            foreach (SPListItem item in items)
            {
                yield return item;
            }
        }
        else
```

```
        {
            SPQuery query = new SPQuery();
            query.ViewAttributes = "Scope=\"Recursive\"";
            query.Query = caml;
            query.RowLimit = Convert.ToUInt32(Constants.RowLimit);
            do
            {
                SPListItemCollection items = list.GetItems(query);
                foreach (SPListItem item in items)
                {
                    yield return item;
                }
                query.ListItemCollectionPosition = items.ListItemCollectionPosition;
            } while (query.ListItemCollectionPosition != null);
        }
    }
}
```

This code assumes you have a constant defined in `Constants.PaginationThreshold`, which determines from what number of items the method starts using paging. (For more information about paging, refer to Chapter 4.)

The following method uses a similar approach to return just one item. If the query returns more items, the first in the collection is taken.

```
public static SPListItem GetItemByQuery(this SPList list, string caml)
{
    SPQuery query = new SPQuery();
    query.ViewAttributes = "Scope=\"Recursive\"";
    query.Query = caml;
    query.RowLimit = 1;
    SPListItemCollection items = list.GetItems(query);
    return items.Cast<SPListItem>().FirstOrDefault();
}
```

Creating an item is easy. This extension simply improves code readability:

```
public static SPListItem CreateItem(this SPList list)
{
    return list.Items.Add();
}
```

While the methods shown previously create or return items, the subsequent methods deal with existing items. These two methods set and get a value using a field's internal name:

```
public static void SetValue(this SPListItem item, string internalname, object value)
{
    SPField field = item.Fields.GetFieldByInternalName(internalname);
    item[field.Id] = value;
}
public static object GetValue(this SPListItem item, string internalname)
{
    SPField field = item.Fields.GetFieldByInternalName(internalname);
    return item[field.Id];
}
```

Getting a lookup value is often a pain, because the object type cannot be cast directly. Instead, a constructor call is required. This is what the GetLookup method encapsulates:

```
public static SPFieldLookupValue GetLookup(this SPListItem item)
{
    return item != null ? new SPFieldLookupValue(item.ID, String.Empty) : null;
}
```

Updating an item can either be done by the Update method, which sets the current user and processes attached workflows and events, or by SystemUpdate, which internally sets the system account and suppresses security validation on GET requests. Quite often, internal checks need to be suppressed, and to do so the AllowUnsafeUpdates property must be set to true.

```
public static void UpdateUnsafe(this SPListItem item)
{
    if (item != null)
    {
        bool allow = item.Web.AllowUnsafeUpdates;
        item.Web.AllowUnsafeUpdates = true;
        item.Update();
        item.Web.AllowUnsafeUpdates = allow;
    }
}

public static void SystemUpdateUnsafe(this SPListItem item)
{
    if (item != null)
    {
        bool allow = item.Web.AllowUnsafeUpdates;
        item.Web.AllowUnsafeUpdates = true;
        item.SystemUpdate();
        item.Web.AllowUnsafeUpdates = allow;
    }
}
public static void DeleteUnsafe(this SPListItem item)
{
    if (item != null)
    {
        bool allow = item.Web.AllowUnsafeUpdates;
        item.Web.AllowUnsafeUpdates = true;
        item.Delete();
        item.Web.AllowUnsafeUpdates = allow;
    }
}
```

The two extension methods shown next are simplifications for lazy coders. They replace the LookupId and LookupValue properties of the SPFieldLookupValue type with Id and Value properties:

```
public static int Id(this SPFieldLookupValue lookup)
{
    return lookup != null ? lookup.LookupId : 0;
}
public static string Value(this SPFieldLookupValue lookup)
{
    return lookup != null ? lookup.LookupValue : String.Empty;
```

```
}
```

Caching Queries to Improve Performance

Caching is a common technique to avoid unnecessary calls to a database. The previous examples showed that it is possible to extend SharePoint types to support LINQ to Objects. Remember that this will consume a lot of memory if you have very large lists. Most projects do not have more than a few thousand items in a list, and with a dozen gigabytes of memory or more available on a server, it seems a good idea to store lists in RAM. Using the `Cache` object, the requested data is shared between the users, and the list is retrieved once only.

```
public static class LinqCacheExtensions
{
    public static IEnumerable<T> Cache<T>(this IEnumerable<T> source,
                                           string key,
                                           DateTime absoluteExpiration)
    {
        var items = HttpRuntime.Cache.Get(key) as List<T>;
        if (items == null)
        {
            items = source.ToList();
            HttpRuntime.Cache.Add(key, items, null, absoluteExpiration,
                                  System.Web.Caching.Cache.NoSlidingExpiration,
                                  CacheItemPriority.Normal, null);
        }
        foreach (var item in items)
        {
            yield return item;
        }
    }

    public static IEnumerable<T> Cache<T>(this IEnumerable<T> source, string key,
                                          TimeSpan slidingExpiration)
    {
        var items = HttpRuntime.Cache.Get(key) as List<T>;
        if (items == null)
        {
            items = source.ToList();
            HttpRuntime.Cache.Add(key, items, null,
                                  System.Web.Caching.Cache.NoAbsoluteExpiration,
                                  slidingExpiration,
                                  CacheItemPriority.Normal, null);
        }
        foreach (var item in items)
        {
            yield return item;
        }
    }
}
```

A LINQ query that uses the `Cache<T>` method will be cached using the `HttpRuntime.Cache` store. The method extends `IEnumerable`, a type that the method `GetItemsByQuery` will return, for example.

Summary

In this chapter, you were introduced to a powerful aspect of SharePoint programming: the application page programming style. Programming application pages extends the world of SharePoint to whatever you like. Any ASP.NET-like application can run in the context of SharePoint and get instant access to the object model's API.

SharePoint programming is mostly ASP.NET programming. However, regarding resources and localization, there are some differences. In this chapter, this was covered along with several usage scenarios.

Furthermore, the event model is an outstanding programming area. Events fired at the site and feature levels were explained in this chapter. Such global events allow developers to have comprehensive influence on what happens if end users activate or deactivate features, or create new sites somewhere deep in the structure.

Sending e-mail is a vital part of any collaboration solution. In this chapter, you saw how to use the standard .NET mail function properly, as well as how to use the dedicated mail function that SharePoint provides.

For real-life applications, extension methods make your life as a developer easier. Custom helper classes encapsulate repetitive operations into extensions. In particular, LINQ queries are well supported by LINQ to Object operations, if LINQ to SharePoint is not appropriate for some reason.

CHAPTER 9

Solution Deployment

This book has shown you how to customize and extend SharePoint using templates, Web Parts, and other techniques. If you wish to move your development efforts to another SharePoint farm, there is a mechanism provided, which enables a smooth transfer and installation—SharePoint solution packages.

In this chapter you'll learn about SharePoint solution packages and features, and how to create them. You will also see how Visual Studio 2010 supports developing for SharePoint 2010. After a deeper look at sandboxed solutions—a new feature of SharePoint 2010—you will learn how to deploy a solution package using `stsadm` and the new PowerShell cmdlets for SharePoint. If you have created your own solution packages for SharePoint 2007, the last section may be of relevance—it describes how to upgrade your existing solutions to SharePoint 2010, and how to integrate the new features of SharePoint 2010 in your solutions.

At a glance this chapter covers

- SharePoint solution packages and features
- An introduction to sandboxed solutions
- How to create SharePoint solution packages and features
- How to deploy SharePoint solutions using `stsadm` and PowerShell cmdlets
- How to upgrade existing solution packages to SharePoint 2010

SharePoint Features

SharePoint features enable you to deploy applications and functions to a SharePoint site. Features are typically deployed as part of a solution package.

Features can contain templates, list definitions, event handlers, workflows, customizations, and other items. On the front-end web server, each feature is stored in its own subfolder within the folder `%SharePointRoot%\TEMPLATE\FEATURES` (see Figure 9–1).

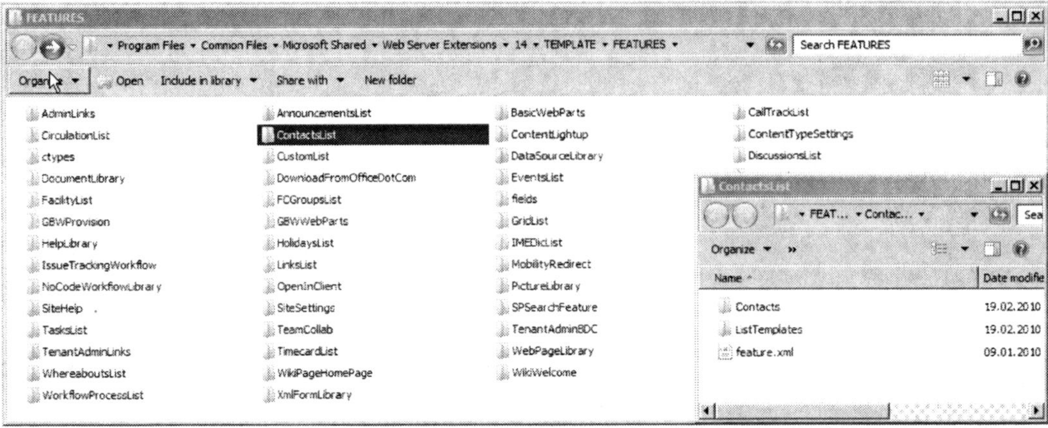

***Figure 9–1.** SharePoint's Feature folder*

When you open a features folder (e.g., `ContactsList`) in Windows Explorer, you can explore the typical structure of a feature. In the root of a feature is a file named `feature.xml`, which defines the feature. Listing 9–1 shows a simple example of a `feature.xml` file.

***Listing 9–1.** Example of a feature.xml File*

```
<?xml version="1.0" encoding="utf-8" ?>
<Feature  xmlns="http://schemas.microsoft.com/sharepoint/"
          Id="A7CEA23C-A1FD-4c1a-A62E-1F523FBE3D5A"
          Scope="Web"
          Title="Msdn Links List"
          Description="Creates a List for MSDN links"
          Version="1.0.0.0">
   <ElementManifests>
     <ElementManifest Location="elements.xml"/>
   </ElementManifests>
</Feature>
```

Table 9–1 describes the elements in this file.

Table 9–1. Elements and Attributes of the feature.xml File

Element or Attribute	Description
`Feature`	The root node
`xmlns`	The namespace of the XML
`ID`	The GUID that identifies the feature in SharePoint
`Scope`	The scope of the feature (see Table 9–2)
`Title`	The title of the feature shown in the feature list
`Description`	Explains what the feature does
`Version`	The version of the feature
`ElementManifests`	Node for the referenced `elements.xml` files
`ElementManifest`	References an `elements.xml` file
`Location`	Defines where the referenced `elements.xml` (see Listing 9–2) is located

Features can provide their functions to different scopes, as listed in Table 9–2.

Table 9–2. Scopes of a Feature

Scope	Description
`Farm`	The feature will be available in the entire server farm.
`WebApplication`	The feature will be available for all web sites in a web application.
`Site`	The feature will be available for all web sites in a site collection.
`Web`	The feature will be available on a single web site.

In the `feature.xml`, another file is referenced in the `ElementManifest` node: `elements.xml`. Listing 9–2 shows an example of an `elements.xml` file.

Listing 9–2. Example of an elements.xml File

```
<?xml version="1.0" encoding="utf-8" ?>
<Elements xmlns="http://schemas.microsoft.com/sharepoint/">
<ListInstance
               Url="Lists/MsdnLinks"
               Title="MsdnLinks"
```

```
                TemplateType="103"
                FeatureId="00BFEA71-2062-426C-90BF-714C59600103"
                OnQuickLaunch="TRUE"/>
</Elements>
```

This elements.xml defines a ListInstance for links. When you activate the feature, a new list will be created, as defined in the elements.xml. Table 9–3 explains the nodes and attributes in the example elements.xml:

***Table 9–3.** Elements and Attributes of the Example elements.xml File*

Element or Attribute	Description
Elements	The file's root node
xmlns	The namespace of the XML
ListInstance	A SharePoint item to be deployed through the feature
Url	The URL relative to the URL of the site collection
Title	The title displayed in the UI
TemplateType	The type of ListTemplate (e.g., the value 103 defines a list based on the link list template)
FeatureId	The GUID that identifies the feature containing the template
OnQuickLaunch	Element that, if set to true, displays a link to the list on the Quick Launch menu

The elements.xml file in the example contains the element ListInstance, which creates a new list when you activate the feature. There are many other feature element types you can use. Table 9–4 summarizes the options.

***Table 9–4.** Feature Element Types*

Type	Description
ListTemplate	Specifies a list definition that is available as an option for creating lists
ListInstance	Creates a list instance using a list template
Field	Defines the properties of a site column
ContentType	Defines a content type
Module	Specifies files with which to provision SharePoint web sites within an element manifest

Type	Description
`CustomAction`	Defines an extension to the UI, such as a button on a ribbon or a link on a site settings page
`CustomActionGroup`	Contains the core definition for a grouping of custom actions
`Receiver`	Describes an event receiver for handling list item events
`Workflow`	Defines a workflow

The section "How To: Creating a Solution Package Step by Step" examines in detail the individual steps required to create a feature. In addition, Chapter 7 includes several examples using the different element types.

Solution Packages

If you create customizations and extensions for SharePoint, there are many items that need to be deployed: assemblies, resource files, features, images, application pages, site definitions, and so on. Imagine a scenario with three systems: development, staging, and production. There needs to be an easy way to deploy these files to the different systems.

SharePoint 2007 introduced solution packages, a powerful deployment tool. Using solution packages enables a developer or SharePoint administrator to transport and install extensions and customizations to other SharePoint servers. Solution packages can be deployed using the command-line tool `stsadm` or PowerShell cmdlets (see Figure 9–2).

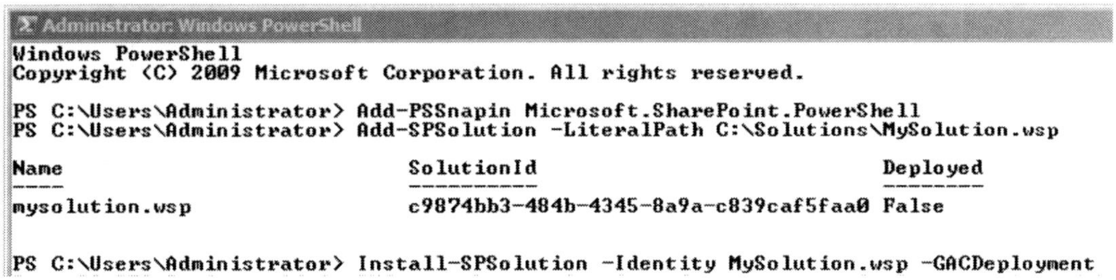

```
Administrator: Windows PowerShell
Windows PowerShell
Copyright (C) 2009 Microsoft Corporation. All rights reserved.

PS C:\Users\Administrator> Add-PSSnapin Microsoft.SharePoint.PowerShell
PS C:\Users\Administrator> Add-SPSolution -LiteralPath C:\Solutions\MySolution.wsp

Name                         SolutionId                            Deployed
----                         ----------                            --------
mysolution.wsp               c9874bb3-484b-4345-8a9a-c839caf5faa0  False

PS C:\Users\Administrator> Install-SPSolution -Identity MySolution.wsp -GACDeployment
```

Figure 9–2. *Deploying a solution using PowerShell*

A solution package is stored as a cabinet (CAB) file, with the file extension `.wsp`. This file contains all the files to be deployed. If you rename the file extension to `.cab`, you can open the solution and explore its content. Figure 9–3 shows the files and folders of an example WSP solution file.

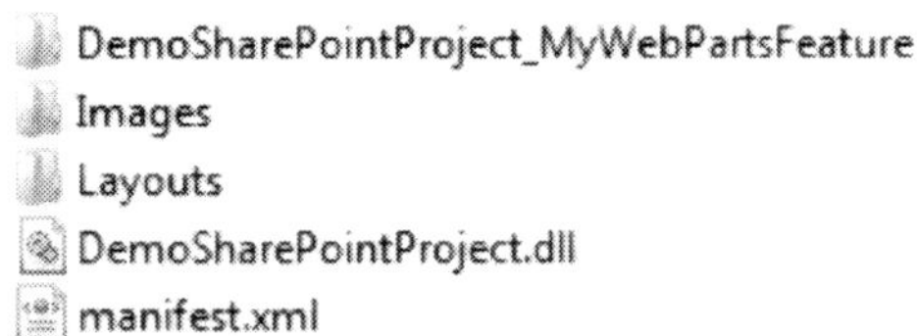

Figure 9–3. Example WSP solution package

- In general, a solution package has the following structure, as illustrated in Figure 9–4:
- A manifest file is in the root, where normally a .NET assembly is located too.
- Subdirectories contain features, deployment files, definitions, and configurations.

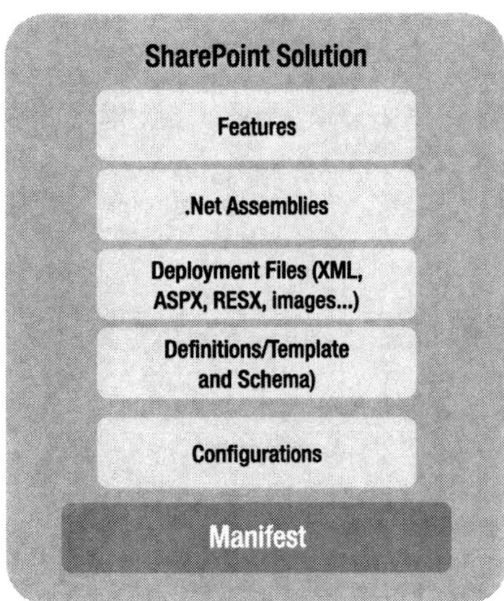

Figure 9–4. Contents of a SharePoint solution

The structure inside the WSP file defines the final structure in the file system of your SharePoint solution. The manifest file defines the inner structure of the solution. The manifest file is a XML file named `manifest.xml`. See Listing 9–3 for an example.

Listing 9–3. Example of a manifest.xml file

```
<?xml version="1.0" encoding="utf-8"?>
<Solution
```

```
        xmlns="http://schemas.microsoft.com/sharepoint/"
        SolutionId="c6bee3ac-bc38-48f3-9adf-7a5c8b97eaa7">
  <Assemblies>
    <Assembly
        Location="SharePointProject15.dll" DeploymentTarget="GlobalAssemblyCache">
      <SafeControls>
        <SafeControl Assembly="SharePointProject15, Version=1.0.0.0,
        Culture=neutral, PublicKeyToken=ce72b677bc54dfc7"
        Namespace="SharePointProject15.VisualWebPart2" TypeName="*" />
      </SafeControls>
    </Assembly>
  </Assemblies>
  <TemplateFiles>
    <TemplateFile Location="CONTROLTEMPLATES\SharePointProject15\VisualWebPart2\
        VisualWebPart2UserControl.ascx" />
  </TemplateFiles>
  <FeatureManifests>
    <FeatureManifest Location="SharePointProject15_WebParts\Feature.xml" />
     </FeatureManifests>
</Solution>
```

Table 9–5 describes each node of the `manifest.xml` file shown in Listing 9–3.

Table 9–5. *Elements and Attributes of the Example manifest.xml File*

Element or Attribute	Description
`Solution`	Specifies the top-level element for a solution manifest file
`xmlns`	Specifies the XML namespace
`SolutionId`	Specifies the GUID of the solution identifying the package in SharePoint
`Assemblies`	Specifies the assemblies to include in the solution
`Assembly`	Specifies an assembly to include in the solution
`SafeControls`	Specifies the safe controls of an assembly that are included in a solution
`SafeControl`	Adds or removes a control assembly from the safe controls list for a solution
`TemplateFiles`	Specifies the template files to include in the solution
`TemplateFile`	Specifies a template file to include in the solution
`FeatureManifests`	Specifies the features to include in the solution
`FeatureManifest`	Specifies a feature to include in the solution

Because a solution package is stored as a cabinet file, you can use the utility `makecab.exe` to create such a cab (WSP) file. A data definition file (DDF) contains the instructions required by `makecab` to create the WSP file. This includes

- The name of the WSP file
- The location of the source files
- The location of the new WSP file
- All files that are in the solution package

Listing 9–4 gives an example of a DDF. The comments in the listing explain the usage of the commands.

Listing 9–4. *An Example DDF*

```
.OPTION EXPLICIT                              ; Generate errors on variable typos
;
.Set CabinetNameTemplate=MsdnLinkList.wsp ; The name of the WSP file
.set DiskDirectoryTemplate=CDROM              ; All cabinets go in a single directory
.Set CompressionType=MSZIP                    ;
.Set Cabinet=on                       ;
.Set Compress=on                              ;
.Set DiskDirectory1=.                 ; Use the specified directory for output
;
;*** Disable size limits for wsp (cab) files ;
;
.Set CabinetFileCountThreshold=0
.Set FolderFileCountThreshold=0
.Set FolderSizeThreshold=0
.Set MaxCabinetSize=0
.Set MaxDiskFileCount=0
.Set MaxDiskSize=0
;
;*** Files to zip                              ;
;
"D:\SolutionExample\14\TEMPLATE\FEATURES\MsdnLinkList\elements.xml"
"MsdnLinkList\elements.xml"
"D:\SolutionExample\14\TEMPLATE\FEATURES\MsdnLinkList\feature.xml" "MsdnLinkList\feature.xml"
"D:\SolutionExample\manifest.xml" "manifest.xml"
```

Solution packages can deploy the following items:

- Site definitions
- Feature definitions and their corresponding element definitions and files
- Web Part files
- Template files and root files
- Resource files
- Assemblies
- Code access security policies

Farm administrators deploy solution packages to a web server. These solutions have full access to the server object model, and there are no usage limits. SharePoint 2010 introduces an additional type of solution package called sandboxed solution. A sandboxed solution can be deployed by a site collection admin to a site Solution Gallery. These solutions have limited access to the server object model—they can be validated and monitored.

Sandboxed Solutions

Before SharePoint 2010, the farm administrator had to trust custom code running on the server. That meant having to perform lengthy tests and code reviews before custom code was allowed to run on the server, which cost a lot of time and money.

With SharePoint 2010, Microsoft introduced the concept of sandboxing user code, which allows for isolation and resource limitations regarding memory, CPU, database query count, and time. This means that users can add and consume custom solutions safely without impacting overall farm performance and stability. This new solution type addresses key scenarios that include the ability to use custom Web Parts and event receivers.

Sandboxed solutions run with lower trust for hosted environments, for testing foreign solutions, and for secured production servers. A sandboxed solution cannot access the full SharePoint object model; it is limited to a subset of the `Microsoft.SharePoint` namespace. Sandboxed solutions run in a safe and monitored process with restricted access to resources. A SharePoint admin is enabled to monitor and validate these solutions. Sandboxed solutions address hosted SharePoint solutions, such as SharePoint Online, which is hosted in the cloud. They enable you to extend a hosted SharePoint solution with your own secure code. A SharePoint installation contains a *Solution Gallery*, which stores sandboxed solutions for further installation and activation. To peruse this gallery, click Site Settings on the Site Actions menu. On the settings page, click Solutions under the Galleries section (see Figure 9–5).

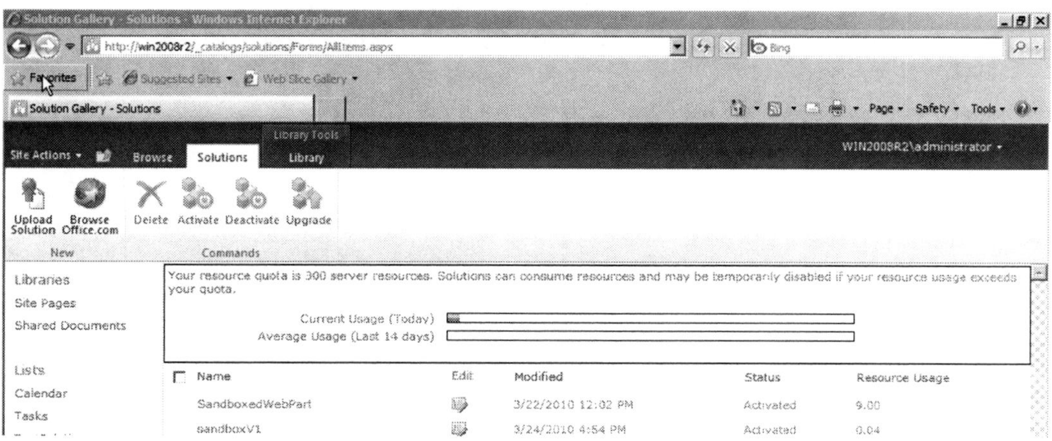

Figure 9–5. *Solution Gallery for sandboxed solutions*

Restrictions of Sandboxed Solutions

You are restricted with regard to the SharePoint items you can deploy with a sandboxed solution and the code you can write in it.

Using a sandboxed solution you can deploy the following SharePoint items:

- Web Parts (code only; not visual Web Parts)
- Event receivers
- Content types
- List templates
- List instances
- Custom actions
- InfoPath forms

In general, with a sandboxed solution you can't deploy files to disk. This means you can't deploy the following SharePoint items:

- Visual Web Parts (they contain web controls that have to be deployed to disk)
- Business data connectivity models
- Application pages
- User controls
- Files included in mapped folders, such as `IMAGES` or `LAYOUTS`

You can do the following things with your code in a sandboxed solution:

- Read and write to lists and libraries within the same site collection
- Access a large subset of the `Microsoft.SharePoint` namespace. All the classes below `SPSite` are available: `SPSite`, `SPWeb`, `SPList`, and `SPListItem`.
- Run client-side code (i.e., Silverlight and JavaScript—including usage of jQuery library)

Some aspects of custom code are *not* allowed in the sandbox:

- Call web services in an intranet or over the Internet
- Access data outside the site collection where the solution has been deployed
- Read and write files with your code
- Run code that is not marked to allow partially trusted callers (code with restricted rights may call full-trust code if it is marked with the appropriate attribute)
- Use objects above `SPSite` (e.g., `SPFarm`)
- Use security-related functions (`RunWithElevatedPreviledges` and other `SPSecurity` methods)

■ **Tip** For a complete reference to the sandboxed API, see `www.microsoft.com/downloads/details.aspx?FamilyID=f0c9daf3-4c54-45ed-9bde-7b4d83a8f26f&displaylang=en`.

The Sandbox Architecture

The structure of a sandboxed solution is very similar to a farm solution. The main differences lie in the way the solution is deployed.

A sandboxed solution can run with full trust when it is deployed as full trust, or with partial trust when the solution is deployed at the site collection scope. Depending on how the solution is deployed, it can be hosted by different services. The Microsoft SharePoint Foundation Sandboxed code execution host service (SPUserCodeV4) executes the user code (code in your sandboxed solution) in the sandbox. This service consists of the following three processes:

- Microsoft SharePoint Foundation Sandboxed code execution host service (`SPUCHostService.exe`)
- Microsoft SharePoint Foundation Sandboxed Code Execution Worker Process (`SPUCWorkerProcess.exe`)
- Microsoft SharePoint Foundation Sandboxed Code Execution Worker Process Proxy (`SPUCWorkerProcessProxy.exe`)

The user code service (`SPUCHostService.exe`) decides whether you can run sandboxed solutions on the server on which this service is running. Your sandboxed solution code runs in the sandboxed worker process (`SPUCWorkerProcess.exe`). This is in contrast to having the code of a full-trust solution run inside of `w3wp.exe`. `SPUCWorkerProcessProxy` exposes a subset of the SharePoint API. If a method is not exposed, you cannot use it in the sandboxed solutions.

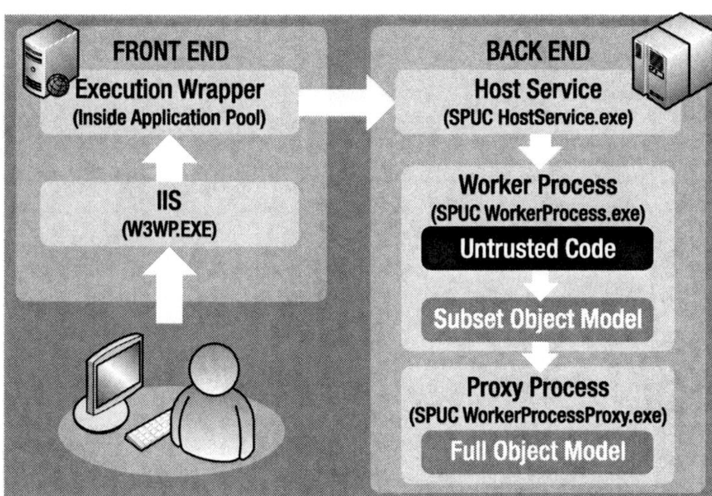

Figure 9–6. *Sandbox architecture*

Life Cycle of a Sandboxed Solution

The life cycle of a sandboxed solution consists of the following stages: *upload*, *activation*, *deactivation*, and *deletion* (as shown in Figure 9–7), as well as an optional stage, *upgrade*.

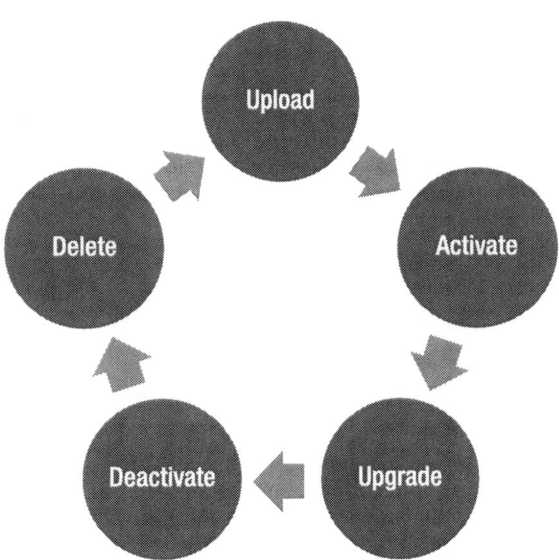

Figure 9–7. *Life Cycle of a Sandboxed Solution*

Table 9–6 describes each stage:

Table 9–6. *Stages in the Life Cycle of a Sandboxed Solution*

Stage	Description
Upload	Uploads the WSP file to the Solution Gallery.
Activate	Validates the selected solution is validated. If this is successful, the solution is activated to run the code it contains and make its features available for activation. Features with a scope of `SiteCollection` are autoactivated.
Deactivate	Disables the code of the solution and ensures that the contained features are no longer available.
Delete	Removes the solution from the Solution Gallery.
Upgrade	Uses the selected solution to upgrade a previously installed version of the solution that is still active.

To manage sandboxed solutions in your site collection, open the Solution Gallery by clicking Site Settings from the Site Actions menu. Then, on the settings page, click Solutions in the Galleries section, and the Solution Gallery will appear (see Figure 9–5, shown previously). In the Solution Gallery, you can upload, activate, upgrade, deactivate, and delete your solutions.

Deploying a Sandboxed Solution

To upload a WSP file, select the Solution tab and click the Upload button. Choose the location of your file and upload it, as shown in Figure 9–8. The next step is to activate the solution, at which point your solution is validated through the solution validators. Once it is validated, the solution will be activated to run the code that it contains, and the site-scoped features will be activated automatically. (You need to activate web-scoped features on each web site separately.)

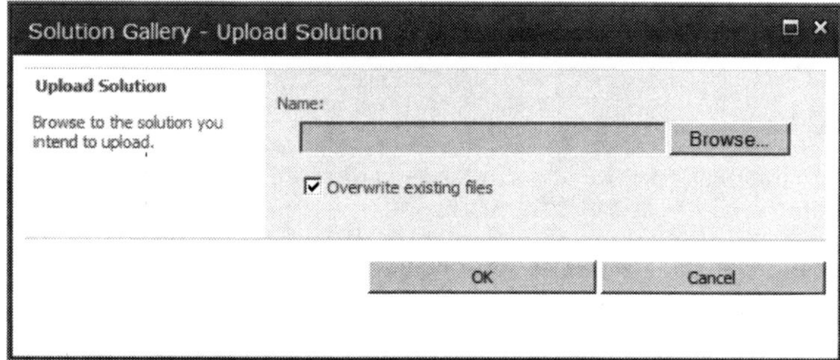

Figure 9–8. Uploading a WSP file to the Solution Gallery

Upgrading a Sandboxed Solution

When you create a new version of an active solution running in your site collection, you can easily upgrade the previous version to the newer one.

For a successful upgrade, two things are important:

- Both the old and new versions must contain the same solution ID
- The solution files must have different names, such as `solution-v1.wsp` and `solution-v2.wsp`.

If version 1 is active and you upload version 2, SharePoint will recognize the new version of the solution (because both solutions have the same ID, but different hash codes) and ask if you want to upgrade. Alternatively, you can just upload version 2 and choose Upgrade at a later date. Interesting, you can also switch back to version 1 after version 2 has been installed, meaning that you can perform a downgrade as well. When you upgrade a solution, it is validated through the solution validators, too.

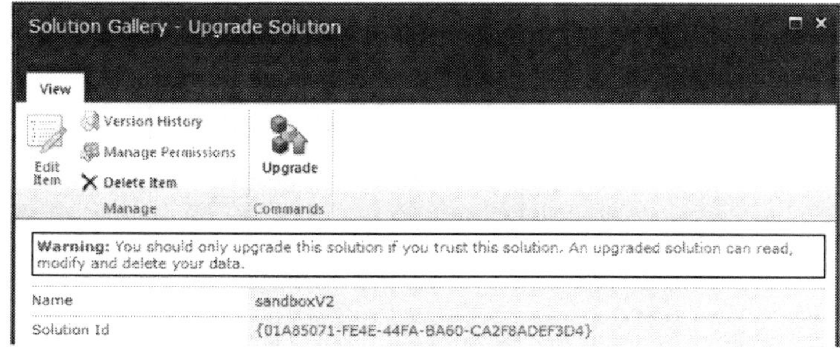

Figure 9–9. Upgrading a solution in the Solution Gallery

■ **Note** You can also use PowerShell to manage sandboxed solutions via command-line scripts. For instance, the `Add-SPUserSolution` cmdlet uploads a new user solution package to the Solution Gallery:

```
Add-SPUserSolution -LiteralPath C:\MySandboxedSolution.wsp -Site http://DemoSite
```

Unfortunately, `stsadm` does not support the new sandboxed solutions feature.

Monitoring Sandboxed Solutions

A SharePoint administrator can measure the performance of a sandboxed solution. SharePoint administrators can assign resources with the UI in Central Administration.

You can access the quotas from the Application Management page. In the site collection section, click Configure Quotas and Locks (see Figure 9–10). First, select the site collection you wish to edit. In the site quota section, you can set the user resource quota properties.

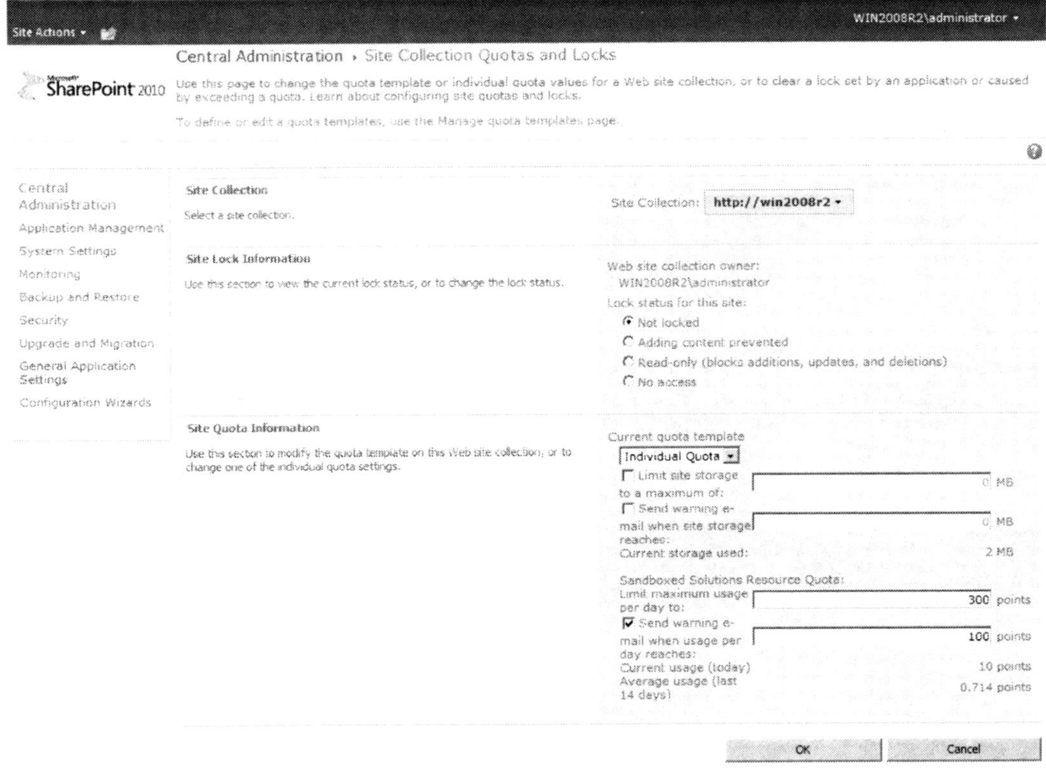

Figure 9–10. Setting site collection quotas and locks for sandboxed solutions

You can limit the site storage and enable a daily resource use limit in points. Points are calculated based on a number of performance indicators such as CPU execution time, memory usage, database query time, abnormal termination, critical exceptions, unhandled exceptions, and data marshalling size. For a detailed view of the performance indicators, enter the command `[Microsoft.SharePoint.Administration.SPUserCodeService]::Local.ResourceMeasures` at the SharePoint management shell. Alternatively, you can use PowerShell, if you load the SharePoint snap-in (`Add-PSSnapin Microsoft.SharePoint.PowerShell`) before entering your command (see Figure 9–11).

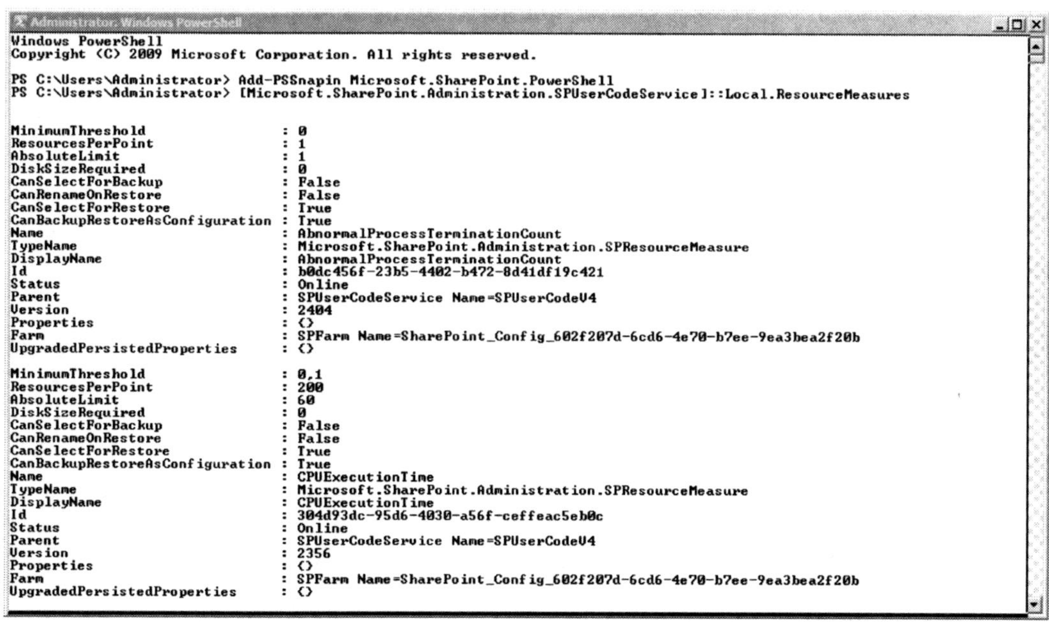

Figure 9–11. *Getting the local resource measures for sandboxed solutions*

This will show the details on each indicator. Table 9–7 lists these performance indicators.

Table 9–7. *Performance Indicators*

Indicator	Resources per Point	Description
`AbnormalProcessTerminationCount`	1	Number of abnormally terminated sandboxed solution processes
`CPUExecutionTime`	3600	Amount of time the CPU spends executing instructions
`CriticalExceptionCount`	3600	Number of fatal errors
`InvocationCount`	100	Number of solution invocation events

Indicator	Resources per Point	Description
PercentProcessorTime	85	Percent of CPU usage by solution
ProcessCPUCycles	100000000000	Number of solution CPU cycles
ProcessHandleCount	10000	Number of Windows handles
ProcessIOBytes	10000000	Memory consumed for input/output (I/O)
ProcessThreadCount	10000	Thread count in the overall processes
ProcessVirtualBytes	100000000	Memory consumed
SharePointDatabaseQueryCount	20	Number of SharePoint database queries
SharePointDatabaseQueryTime	120	Elapsed time to execute query
UnhandledExceptionCount	50	Number of unhandled exceptions
UnresponsiveProcessCount	2	Number of unresponsive processes

If a sandboxed solution hits the defined resource limits, it is shut down.

If a special solution uses too many resources or causes too many errors, the SharePoint farm administrator may want to block the solution. In order to block it, go to Central Administration ➤ System Settings ➤ Manage User Solutions, and add a solution to the Blocked Solutions list.

Sandboxed Solution Validators

The monitoring and blocking of a solution is used for already deployed solutions. Another line of defense is the validation of sandboxed solutions before execution.

Farm administrators can deploy solution validators to their farm. These validators always run when a sandboxed solution is activated or upgraded. When a solution fails validation, an error message is shown to the user and the solution is not activated (see Figure 9–12). If a validator is added after solution has been activated, the solution validator will be called the next time the solution is executed. For more information on how to develop and deploy your own validators, see the section "How-to for creating a Sandboxed Solution".

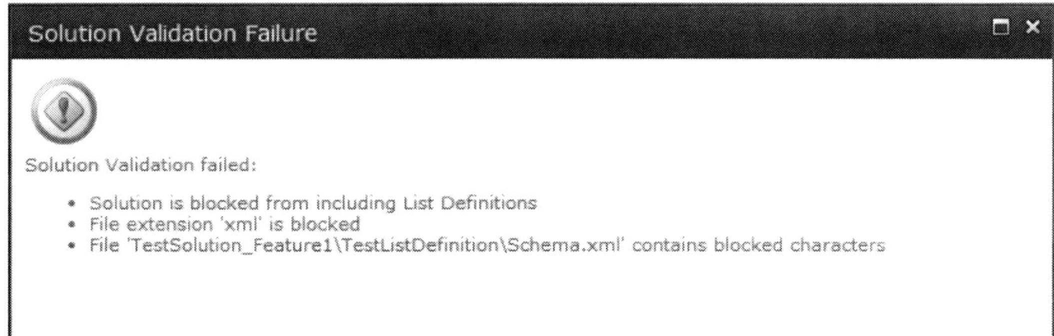

Figure 9–12. *Example of solution validation failure*

Sandboxed Solution Full-Trust Proxies

The sandbox provides sufficient functionality for most applications required at a site collection level. But what if you need to perform a function that exceeds the security restrictions of a sandbox? If you want your application to reach outside the sandbox for such operations as web service calls and database access, you have the option of creating a *full-trust proxy*.

A full-trust proxy enables you to extend the boundaries of a sandboxed solution when necessary. It is a special class library that's deployed to the GAC and runs under full trust.

Since the assembly runs under full trust, you can create a proxy operation that calls a web service or has access to other data sources that are not accessible for a sandboxed solution. Your proxy exposes a method that can be called by the sandboxed user code to perform a specific task, such as reading data from data sources outside the site collection of your sandboxed solution.

The purpose of a full-trust proxy is to break your architecture down into two major pieces:

- One part that runs completely as a sandboxed solution (limited by the sandbox to the usual list definitions, fields, content types, Web Parts, and so forth).
- A custom API you build using full-trust proxies that the sandbox solutions can use (providing access to web services and other data, and permitted to use the full SharePoint API).

Figure 9–13 illustrates this architecture.

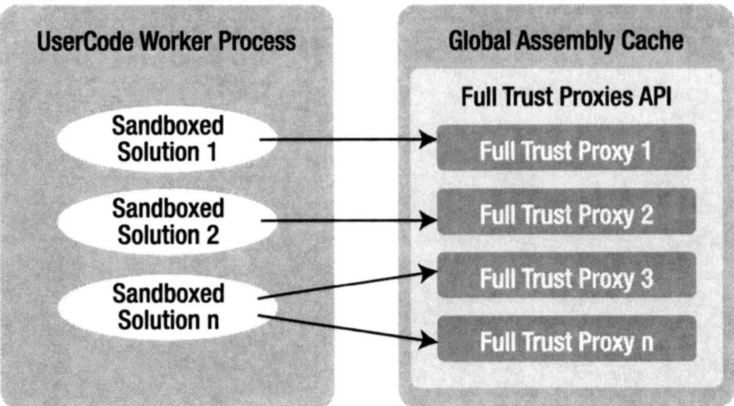

Figure 9–13. *Full-Trust Proxies API Architecture*

Using Full-trust proxies, you weaken slightly the security of sandboxed solutions, but you still have much more control over the called code than you do with normal full-trust solutions.

■ **Caution** The proxy has to be registered by a farm administrator and is accessible to the whole farm, which means that all developers who know about the assembly, class, and method can use the method. You need to be cognizant of this when considering the methods to expose in the proxy. Try to keep them to a minimum.

You can write your own full-trust proxies by creating one or two class libraries containing the following classes:

- A class that inherits from `Microsoft.SharePoint.UserCode.SPProxyOperation`: This class will be used to execute operations that are normally disqualified for sandboxed solutions.
- A second class that inherits from `Microsoft.SharePoint.UserCode.SPProxyOperationsArgs`: This class will be passed to the `Execute` method of the `SPProxyOperation` class.

Both classes have to be deployed to the GAC and registered in SharePoint.
Then you can call the class that inherits from `SPProxyOperation` from your sandboxed code.
Figure 9–14 illustrates this approach.

■ **Tip** Create your full-trust proxies as farm solutions, which are registered using feature activation and unregistered using deactivation of the feature. Then the farm administrators can enable and disable them.

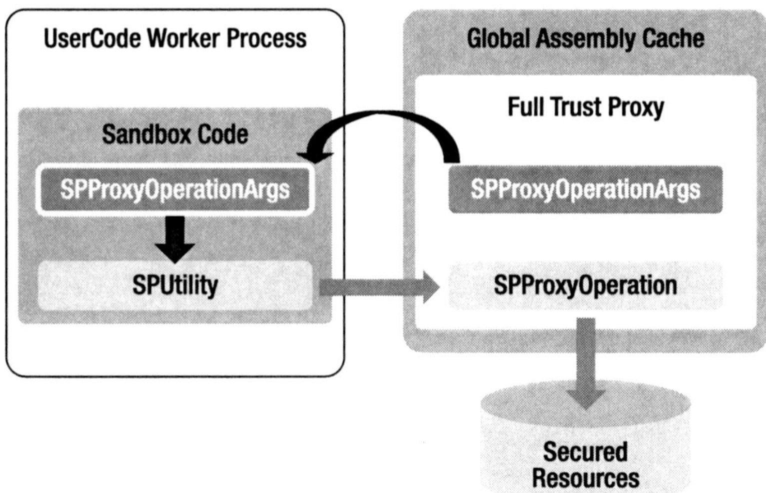

***Figure 9–14.** Full-trust proxy architecture*

Later, in the section "Creating a Sandboxed Solution using Visual Studio 2010," you will learn how to construct such a full-trust proxy.

Deploying Solution Packages Using PowerShell Cmdlets

Windows PowerShell is the command-line interface and scripting language that was developed specifically for system administration and is used for SharePoint 2010 administration (see Figure 9–15).

With Windows PowerShell, administrators have a powerful tool for scripting and shell administration. PowerShell follows a completely new paradigm as compared to other shells like bash or cmd.exe. While those shells accept and return text, Windows PowerShell uses .NET objects as input and output, since it is based on an object model supported by the .NET Common Language Runtime (CLR). This is an immense change that offers more control, efficiency, and productivity to developers and administrators.

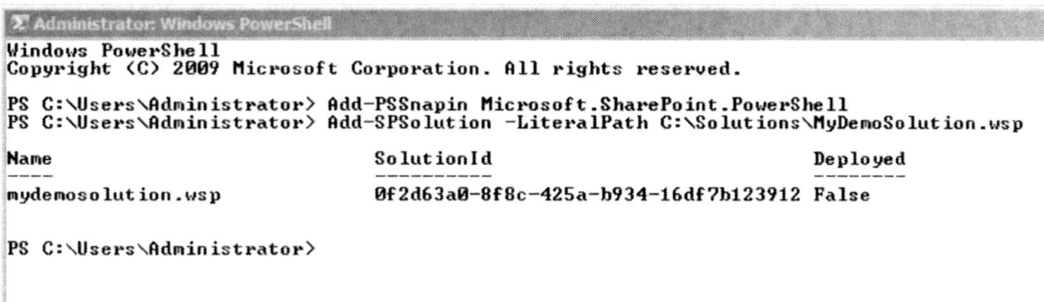

Administrator: Windows PowerShell
Windows PowerShell
Copyright (C) 2009 Microsoft Corporation. All rights reserved.
PS C:\Users\Administrator> Add-PSSnapin Microsoft.SharePoint.PowerShell
PS C:\Users\Administrator> Add-SPSolution -LiteralPath C:\Solutions\MyDemoSolution.wsp
Name SolutionId Deployed
---- ---------- --------
mydemosolution.wsp 0f2d63a0-8f8c-425a-b934-16df7b123912 False
PS C:\Users\Administrator>

***Figure 9–15.** Adding a solution using Windows PowerShell*

Cmdlets

Windows PowerShell introduces the concept of cmdlets (aka commandlets). A cmdlet is a simple command-line tool that is integrated into the shell and executes a single function. You can use a single cmdlet, but their power is more obvious when used together to perform complex tasks or automated administration.

PowerShell comes with a large collection of built-in cmdlets. A cmdlet is a simple command used for interaction with a managed application (including the operating system). PowerShell runs cmdlets as instances of .NET classes focused on the simple cmdlet model. Cmdlets return objects instead of text. The output can be forwarded (piped) to other cmdlets. This way you can combine cmdlets. You provide the parameters, validate the values, and set details for objects and layout; and PowerShell does the remaining work—parsing parameters, binding values, and formatting and displaying the output. You can create your own cmdlets and share them with others as needed.

■ **Tip** For more information about developing custom cmdlets, visit `http://msdn.microsoft.com/en-us/magazine/cc163293.aspx`.

An Interactive Environment

Windows PowerShell supports a completely interactive environment, similar to other shells. If you enter a command at the input prompt, the command will be processed and the output displayed in the shell window. You can send the output from a command to a file or printer, or you can use a pipe operator (`|`) to send it to another command. For example, you can use the command `Get-Command -Noun SP*` to get all commands containing a noun starting with `SP`. Then you can use the pipe operator to send it to the cmdlet `measure-object` to count the number of search results.

The PowerShell Scripting Language

A new language, the PowerShell scripting language, has been introduced for PowerShell for the following reasons:

- Windows PowerShell needed a language to manage .NET objects
- The language had to support complex tasks
- The language had to meet the conventions for other languages used in .NET programming, such as C#

Scripting with PowerShell and the PowerShell Integrated Scripting Environment

If you repeat the same commands frequently, it is useful to save the commands in a file and execute the file. Such a file is called a *script*.

Windows PowerShell offers complete script support. You can run a script by entering the name of the script at the prompt. The file extension for PowerShell scripts is `.ps1`.

Although scripts are very useful, they can also be used to spread harmful code. Execution policies in PowerShell specify which scripts may be run and whether they must be digitally signed. For security reasons, PowerShell does not allow you to execute a script by double-clicking the file, as you can with `.bat` or `.vbs` files.

For scripting purposes, PowerShell 2.0 comes with the PowerShell Integrated Scripting Environment (ISE). This application enables you to run commands, and write, test, and debug scripts in a user-friendly environment. ISE is a WPF application and requires .NET 3.5.

ISE offers the following:

- A command pane for running interactive commands, just as in the Windows PowerShell console. Simply type a command and press Enter, and the output will appear in a separate output pane.
- A script pane to compose, edit, debug, and run functions and scripts.
- Multiple tabs, each with its own command and script pane to allow you to work on several tasks independently.
- The ability to edit text in complex scripts.
- The ability to extend every aspect of ISE through its underlying scripting object model with your own code.
- Separate profiles. You can create a PowerShell profile and add aliases, functions, and variables to it. Every time PowerShell starts, these settings are loaded.

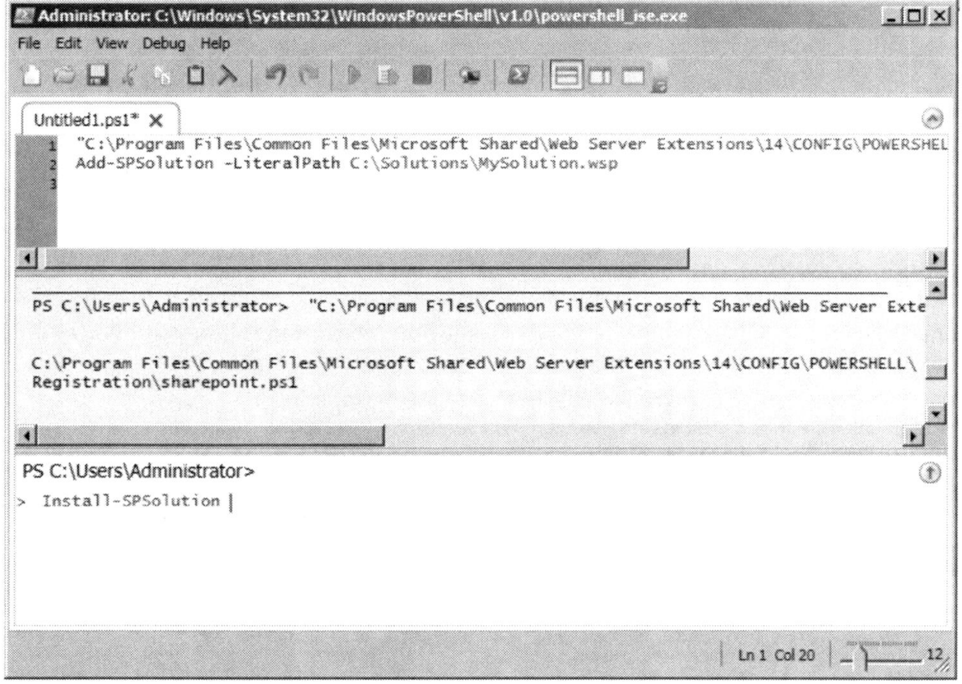

Figure 9–16. *PowerShell ISE*

PowerShell and SharePoint 2010

To start administering SharePoint 2010 with PowerShell, launch the SharePoint 2010 management shell (see Figure 9–17) from the Start menu, under All Programs ➤ Microsoft SharePoint 2010 Products.

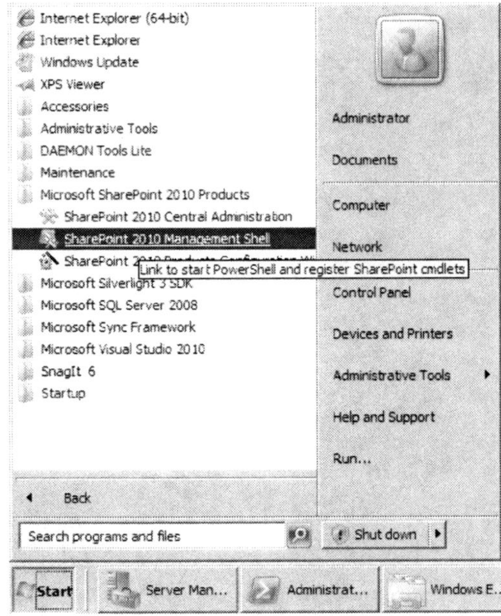

Figure 9–17. Starting the SharePoint 4.0 management shell

The management shell is actually just a PowerShell console that preloads the SharePoint PowerShell snap-in. When you look at the target for the shortcut, you should see the following:

```
C:\Windows\System32\WindowsPowerShell\v1.0\PowerShell.exe -NoExit  "
& ' C:\Program Files\Common Files\Microsoft Shared\Web Server
Extensions\14\CONFIG\POWERSHELL\Registration\\sharepoint.ps1 ' "
```

A peek inside the SharePoint.ps1 file (see Figure 9–18) reveals the secret:

```
SharePoint.ps1 - Notepad
File  Edit  Format  View  Help
$ver = $host | select version
if ($ver.Version.Major -gt 1)  {$Host.Runspace.ThreadOptions = "ReuseThread"}
Add-PsSnapin Microsoft.SharePoint.PowerShell
Set-location $home

# SIG # Begin signature block
# MIIXUAYJKoZIhvcNAQcCoIIXQTCCFz0CAQExCzAJBgUrDgMCGgUAMGkGCisGAQQB
```

Figure 9–18. SharePoint.ps1

The SharePoint.ps1 script runs the Add-PsSnapin cmdlet to load the new SharePoint 2010 cmdlets, as shown in Figure 9–19. It also changes the threading model of PowerShell so that commands are processed in the same thread. This is important for the disposal of disposable objects, which is important when you are working with SharePoint objects such as SPWeb. Knowing the sharePoint.ps1 script and its contents, you can easily load any PowerShell console (i.e., either the native PowerShell console or another editor such as the PowerShell ISE) and administer SharePoint 2010. To do so, run the sharepoint.ps1 script or enter the following commands:

```
$ver = $host | select version
if ($ver.Version.Major -gt 1)  {$Host.Runspace.ThreadOptions = "ReuseThread"}
Add-PsSnapin Microsoft.SharePoint.PowerShell
Set-location $home
```

PowerShell Cmdlets for SharePoint 2010 Overview

SharePoint ships with hundreds of SharePoint PowerShell commands out of the box. To compile a list of these cmdlets, enter the following at the shell:

```
Get-Command -PSSnapin Microsoft.SharePoint.PowerShell | select Name
```

This command returns the names of all the installed SharePoint PowerShell cmdlets. As usual, the naming convention for the commands is: *[Verb]*-SP*[Noun]*. To obtain the exact number of cmdlets, use the following command:

```
Get-Command -PSSnapin Microsoft.SharePoint.PowerShell | measure-object
```

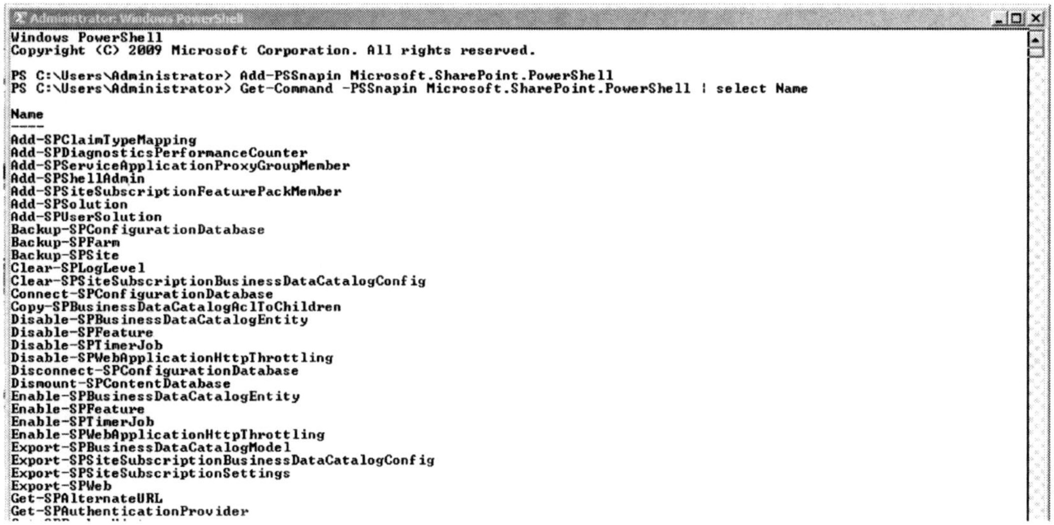

```
Windows PowerShell
Copyright (C) 2009 Microsoft Corporation. All rights reserved.

PS C:\Users\Administrator> Add-PSSnapin Microsoft.SharePoint.PowerShell
PS C:\Users\Administrator> Get-Command -PSSnapin Microsoft.SharePoint.PowerShell | select Name

Name
----
Add-SPClaimTypeMapping
Add-SPDiagnosticsPerformanceCounter
Add-SPServiceApplicationProxyGroupMember
Add-SPShellAdmin
Add-SPSiteSubscriptionFeaturePackMember
Add-SPSolution
Add-SPUserSolution
Backup-SPConfigurationDatabase
Backup-SPFarm
Backup-SPSite
Clear-SPLogLevel
Clear-SPSiteSubscriptionBusinessDataCatalogConfig
Connect-SPConfigurationDatabase
Copy-SPBusinessDataCatalogAclToChildren
Disable-SPBusinessDataCatalogEntity
Disable-SPFeature
Disable-SPTimerJob
Disable-SPWebApplicationHttpThrottling
Disconnect-SPConfigurationDatabase
Dismount-SPContentDatabase
Enable-SPBusinessDataCatalogEntity
Enable-SPFeature
Enable-SPTimerJob
Enable-SPWebApplicationHttpThrottling
Export-SPBusinessDataCatalogModel
Export-SPSiteSubscriptionBusinessDataCatalogConfig
Export-SPSiteSubscriptionSettings
Export-SPWeb
Get-SPAlternateURL
Get-SPAuthenticationProvider
```

Figure 9–19. *Getting a list of SharePoint cmdlets in PowerShell*

■ **Note** In order to use PowerShell for SharePoint operations, you need to be a site collection administrator and a `db_owner` of the content database.

Getting Help: What Are Cmdlets Good For?

If you want to get more information about a cmdlet, you can use the built-in help:

```
Get-Help <cmdlet>
```

To get more information, add the parameters `-full` or `-detailed` (see Figure 9–20).

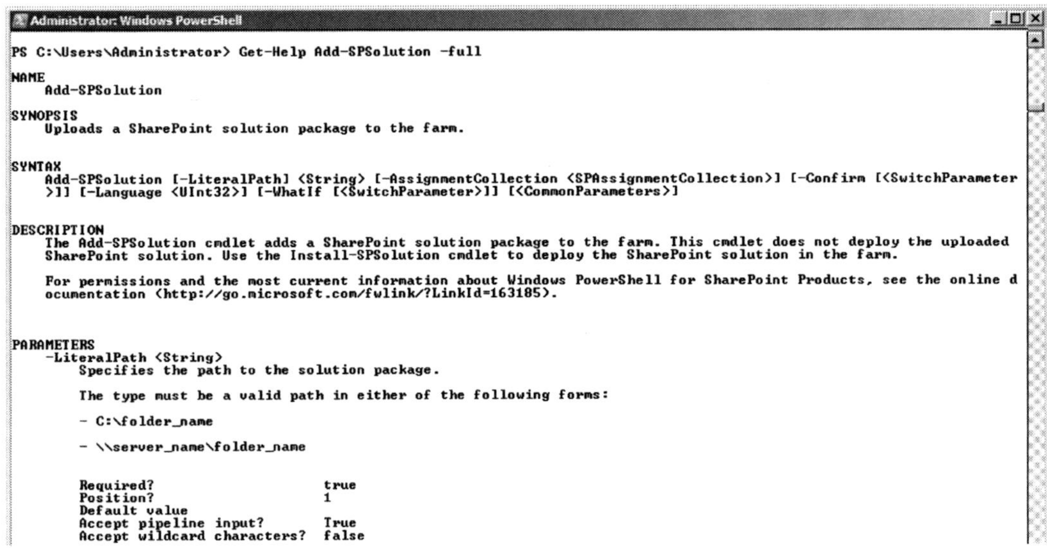

***Figure 9–20.** A summary of the Get-Help command*

Deploying a Farm Solution Package

To deploy a farm solution, you first need to upload the solution to the farm. This is accomplished with the `Add-SPSolution` cmdlet:

```
Add-SPSolution -LiteralPath C:\MySolution.wsp
```

Now the solution package is in the solution store of the farm, but it is not yet deployed. To deploy it, execute the command as shown in Figure 9–21:

```
Install-SPSolution -Identity MySolution.wsp -GACDeployment
```

Eventually it will become necessary to remove the solution from the farm. To achieve this, you will have to first have to uninstall the solution:

```
Uninstall-SPSolution -Identity SolutionName
```

Then you can remove the solution:

```
Remove-SPSolution -Identity SolutionName
```

This deletes the solution package from the solution store.

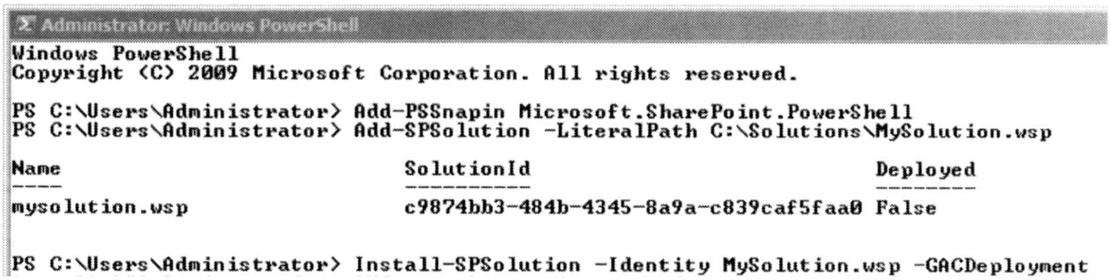

```
Administrator: Windows PowerShell
Windows PowerShell
Copyright (C) 2009 Microsoft Corporation. All rights reserved.

PS C:\Users\Administrator> Add-PSSnapin Microsoft.SharePoint.PowerShell
PS C:\Users\Administrator> Add-SPSolution -LiteralPath C:\Solutions\MySolution.wsp

Name                           SolutionId                           Deployed
----                           ----------                           --------
mysolution.wsp                 c9874bb3-484b-4345-8a9a-c839caf5faa0 False


PS C:\Users\Administrator> Install-SPSolution -Identity MySolution.wsp -GACDeployment
```

Figure 9–21. *Installing a solution using PowerShell*

Deploying a Sandboxed Solution using PowerShell

As an alternative to using `stsadm`, you can use SharePoint PowerShell cmdlets for sandboxed solution deployment.

You can use the `Add-SPUserSolution` cmdlet to upload a new user solution package to the Solution Gallery as follows:

```
Add-SPUserSolution -LiteralPath C:\MySandboxedSolution.wsp -Site http://DemoSite
```

However, this cmdlet does not activate the uploaded user solution. Use the `Install-SPUserSolution` cmdlet to activate the user solution in the site collection, like this:

```
Install-SPUserSolution -Identity MySandboxedSolution -Site http://DemoSite
```

The `Install-SPUserSolution` cmdlet activates a user solution in a site collection.

If you have to remove a solution from the Solution Gallery, the user solution must be inactive. To handle this, you can use the `Uninstall-SPUserSolution` cmdlet, which deactivates a user solution on a site collection. It also removes the included features from the site collection features.

You can use the `Remove-SPUserSolution` cmdlet to remove a user solution from the Solution Gallery as follows:

```
Remove-SPUserSolution -Identity MySandboxedSolution.wsp -Site sitename
```

Deploying Solution Packages Using stsadm

After creating a WSP solution package file, you can deploy it onto a SharePoint server. One option for this task is the command-line tool `stsadm`.

By default you can find the SharePoint admin tool `stsadm.exe` in the folder `%SharePointRoot%\Bin`. `stsadm` enables a SharePoint administrator to manage administrative tasks for SharePoint via the command line and write batch files and scripts for these tasks. `stsadm` offers access to operations and parameters that are not accessible via Central Administration. Important examples of this are the following operations:

- addcontentdb
- addsolution
- upgradesolution
- setadminport
- renameserver

There are two major requirements for running stsadm:

- You must run stsadm on the server you are managing.
- You have to be a member of the local group Administrators.

■ **Note** If you are already familiar with stsadm and like it, you can continue using it for SharePoint 2010. But note that since Microsoft's introduction of the new PowerShell cmdlets for SharePoint administration, stsadm exists only for backward compatibility.

Adding a Solution Package

To deploy a solution package, you need to add the WSP file to the configuration database. You can do this with the stsadm operation addsolution:

```
stsadm -o addsolution -filename C:\MySolution.wsp
```

This command adds the solution to the configuration database, but does not deploy it. To deploy the solution package, you have to execute the deploysolution command:

```
stsadm -o deploysolution -name MySolution.wsp -immediate -allowGacDeployment -force
```

When you issue deployment commands to stsadm, these commands are executed asynchronously via a timer job. This way, solution packages can be deployed to several servers in a farm. After the deployment of a solution, SharePoint forces a reset of IIS. Because this causes problems when the server is used, you can set a parameter to schedule the deployment for a period when demand is low (such as nighttime). If you create a deployment script, you may prefer to run the tasks synchronously, such as addsolution and deploysolution. To do this, you can use the command execadmsvcjobs. This command executes all commands immediately instead of waiting for execution by the timer job, as shown in Listing 9–5 and Figure 9–22.

Listing 9–5. *Adding and Deploying a Solution*

```
SET STSADM="C:\Program Files\Common Files\Microsoft Shared\web server
extensions\14\BIN\stsadm.exe"
%STSADM% -o addsolution -filename c:\ MySolution.wsp
%STSADM% -o execadmscvjobs
%STSADM% -o deploysolution -name MySolution.wsp -immediate -allowGacDeployment -force
%STSADM% -o execadmscvjobs
```

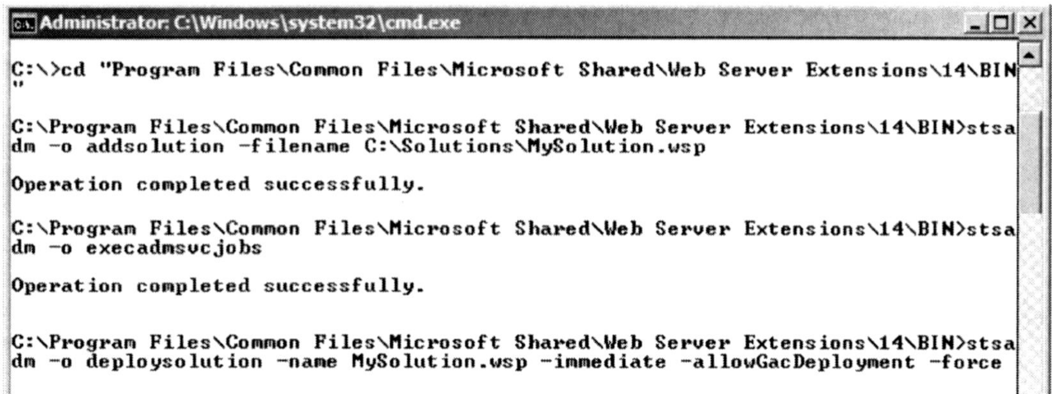

Figure 9–22. Deploying a solution using stsadm

Removing Solutions

Particularly during development, but also for normal deployments, it can become necessary to remove a deployed solution. You can achieve this with the `stsadm` operations `retractsolution` and `deletesolution`, as shown in Listing 9–6.

Listing 9–6. Removing a solution

```
SET STSADM="C:\Program Files\Common Files\Microsoft Shared\web server
extensions\14\BIN\stsadm.exe"
%STSADM% -o retractsolution -name MySolution.wsp -immediate
%STSADM% -o execadmscvjobs
%STSADM% -o deletesolution -name MySolution.wsp -override
%STSADM% -o execadmsvcjobs
```

Installing Features

When deploying the solution package the included features are installed, too. However, you have to activate the features in a separate step. To do this, execute the `activatefeature` operation of `stsadm`, as follows:

```
stsadm -o activatefeature
```

You can also install a feature without activating it, as follows:

```
stsadm -o installfeature
```

■ **Tip** See `http://technet.microsoft.com/en-us/library/cc263384.aspx` for a complete reference for `stsadm` operations and properties.

Creating a Solution Package Step by Step

The following example shows the steps needed to build a solution package. This example creates a simple solution package for deploying a feature that creates a list called `MsdnLinks`, which contains interesting MSDN links.

■ **Note** Visual Studio is not used for this example. Since Visual Studio generates many XML files in the background, it can be difficult to understand in detail how it actually creates a solution package. Instead, in this example, every step is performed manually so that you can better understand what happens. This example is designed to show you the individual steps required to assemble a solution package.

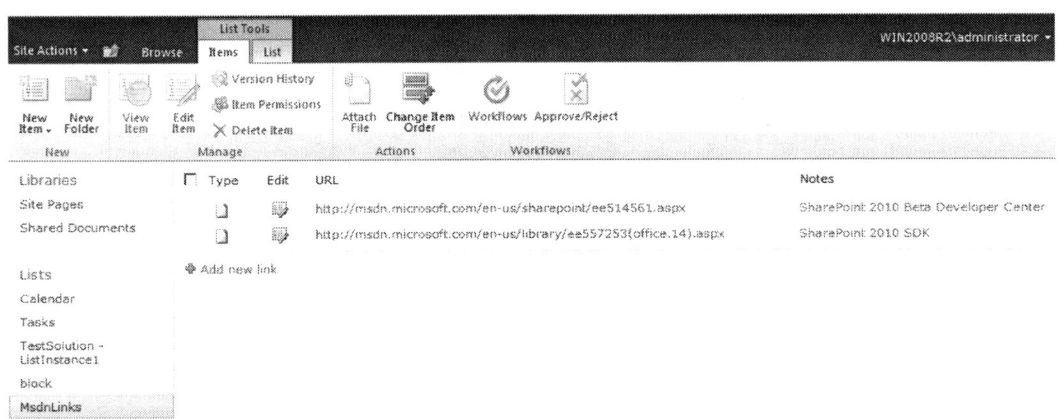

Figure 9–23. List for MSDN links

Step 1: Creating the Folder Structure

Begin by constructing a folder structure in a working folder, as shown in Figure 9–24. This structure should be similar to the structure of the SharePoint folders in `%SharePoint Root%`.

Figure 9–24. *Folder structure for the example solution*

Step 2: Building the Feature

The list for the MSDN links will be created when you activate the `MsdnLinks` list. To do this, you must first build a feature that creates a list based on the SharePoint list type `linksList` (TemplateType="103").

Go to the `MsdnLinksList` folder and create two XML files: `feature.xml` and `element.xml`. `feature.xml` is the main file (see Listing 9–7). The attribute ID contains a unique GUID, which identifies the feature in the farm. The `Scope` attribute specifies the level at which you can activate and use the feature. In this case it is `Web`, for deployment on a single web site. `feature.xml` references the element manifest file (see Listing 9–8) containing the real function of the feature.

Listing 9–7. *feature.xml*

```
<?xml version="1.0" encoding="utf-8" ?>
<Feature
        xmlns="http://schemas.microsoft.com/sharepoint/"
        Id="A7CEA23C-A1FD-4c1a-A62E-1F523FBE3D5A"
        Scope="Web"
        Title="Msdn Links List"
        Description="Creates a List for MSDN links"
        Version="1.0.0.0">
        <ElementManifests>
                <ElementManifest Location="elements.xml"/>
        </ElementManifests>
</Feature>
```

■ **Tip** SharePoint uses GUIDs to identify features, solutions, and so forth. To this end, the GUID generator tool in the Windows SDK is very useful for creating valid GUIDs (see Figure 9–25). Always click New GUID to be sure the GUID is really unique.

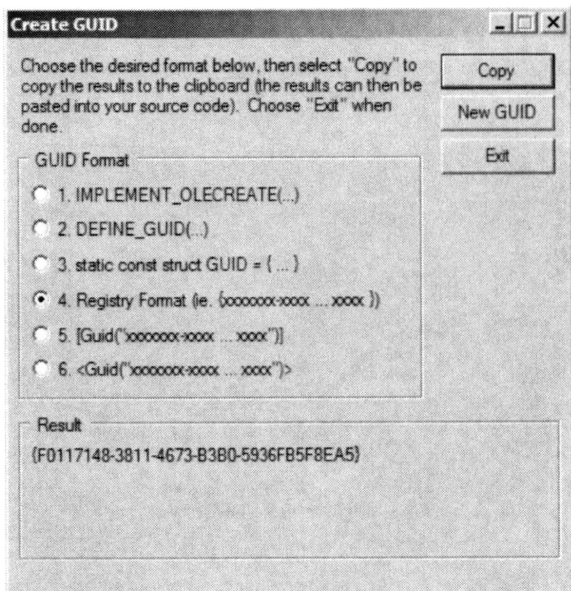

Figure 9–25. GUID generator

In our example, the element manifest forces SharePoint to create a new link list called `MsdnLinks`. The attributes `TemplateType` and `FeatureID` point to the link list that is the template for the list. Setting the attribute `OnQuickLaunch` to `true` makes the list visible in the Quick Launch menu of your web site.

Listing 9–8. elements.xml

```
<?xml version="1.0" encoding="utf-8" ?>
<Elements xmlns="http://schemas.microsoft.com/sharepoint/">
<ListInstance
                Url="Lists/MsdnLinks"
                Title="MsdnLinks"
                TemplateType="103"
                FeatureId="00BFEA71-2062-426C-90BF-714C59600103"
                OnQuickLaunch="TRUE"/>
</Elements>
```

Step 3: Creating a Solution Definition

After you've built the feature, you can create the `manifest.xml` file in the `SolutionExample` folder. The `manifest.xml` file (see Listing 9–9) is an installation instruction for SharePoint. It informs SharePoint how to use and where to install the files contained in the solution package. The ID of the solution identifies your solution package as unique in SharePoint.

In this example, the feature manifest references the `feature.xml` file to deploy the new feature.

Listing 9–9. manifest.xml

```
<?xml version="1.0" encoding="utf-8"?>
<Solution
xmlns:xsi="http://www.w3.org/2001/XMLSchema-instance"
xmlns:xsd="http://www.w3.org/2001/XMLSchema"
xmlns="http://schemas.microsoft.com/sharepoint/"
SolutionId="05FB6131-4714-403b-B3AA-C73C5C535AC3">
  <FeatureManifests>
    <FeatureManifest Location="MsdnLinkList\feature.xml" />
  </FeatureManifests>
 </Solution>
```

Step 4: Creating a DDF

The next step is to write the SolutionExample.ddf file (see Listing 9–10) in the SolutionExample folder. This file contains all the instructions for makecab.exe to create your WSP file.

Listing 9–10. The DDF

```
.OPTION EXPLICIT                                ; Generate errors on variable typos
;
.Set CabinetNameTemplate=MsdnLinkList.wsp   ; The name of the WSP file
.set DiskDirectoryTemplate=CDROM                ; All cabinets go in a single directory
.Set CompressionType=MSZIP                      ;
.Set Cabinet=on                             ;
.Set Compress=on                                ;
.Set DiskDirectory1=.                   ; Use the specified directory for output
;
;*** Disable size limits for wsp (cab) files ;
;
.Set CabinetFileCountThreshold=0
.Set FolderFileCountThreshold=0
.Set FolderSizeThreshold=0
.Set MaxCabinetSize=0
.Set MaxDiskFileCount=0
.Set MaxDiskSize=0
;
;*** Files to zip                                ;
;
"D:\SolutionExample\14\TEMPLATE\FEATURES\MsdnLinkList\elements.xml"
"MsdnLinkList\elements.xml"
"D:\SolutionExample\14\TEMPLATE\FEATURES\MsdnLinkList\feature.xml" "MsdnLinkList\feature.xml"
"D:\SolutionExample\manifest.xml" "manifest.xml"
```

Step 5: Creating the Solution Package

Now you have created all the files to build the solution package. To create the CAB-based solution package, run the command-line tool makecab.exe.

The DDF is needed for the creation of the WSP file using makecab.

At the command line, enter the following command to create the WSP:

```
makecab -f SolutionExample.ddf
```

MakeCAB generates three files:

- setup.rpt
- setup.inf
- MsdnLinkList.wsp

The setup.rpt file contains information about the total files included in the WSP file, how much data was compressed, and the time taken to compress the data. The setup.inf file contains information about the cabinet file that was created, and also contains a list of the files included in the WSP file. The MsdnLinkList.wsp file the your solution package you can deploy to SharePoint. The setup.rpt and setup.inf files are not important for your solution package, so you can delete them.

To make the MakeCAB step easier and repeatable, write a batch file, as shown in Listing 9–11.

***Listing 9–11.** MakeCAB.bat*

```
makecab -f makecab.ddf
del setup.inf
del setup.rpt
pause
```

The output is shown in Figure 9–26.

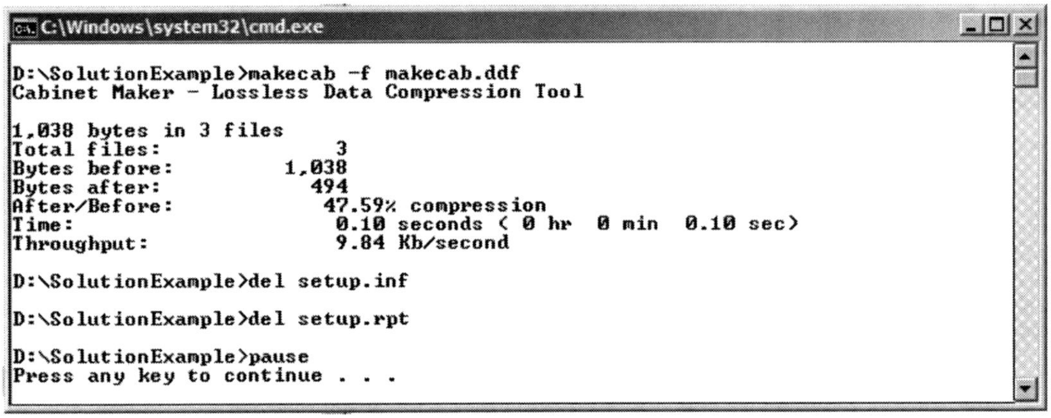

```
C:\Windows\system32\cmd.exe

D:\SolutionExample>makecab -f makecab.ddf
Cabinet Maker - Lossless Data Compression Tool

1,038 bytes in 3 files
Total files:              3
Bytes before:         1,038
Bytes after:            494
After/Before:            47.59% compression
Time:                     0.10 seconds ( 0 hr  0 min  0.10 sec)
Throughput:               9.84 Kb/second

D:\SolutionExample>del setup.inf

D:\SolutionExample>del setup.rpt

D:\SolutionExample>pause
Press any key to continue . . .
```

***Figure 9–26.** The MakeCAB tool creates the WSP file.*

The WSP file MsdnLinkList.wsp should now exist in the SolutionExample folder. Now the solution package is ready for deployment using stsadm or PowerShell cmdlets.

How To: Creating a Solution Package Using Visual Studio 2010

The previous example outlined the necessary steps to create a solution package. However, if you want to create a solution package containing many features, assemblies, and so on, this process will become quite complex and difficult. Therefore, Visual Studio 2010 aids the developer in building flexible SharePoint solution packages.

Using the Project Templates

You can easily start assembling SharePoint solutions using Visual Studio 2010, provided that you have set up a SharePoint 2010 development environment with the following:

- A 64-bit operating system (Windows Server 2008, Windows 7, or Windows Vista)
- SharePoint Foundation or SharePoint Server 2010
- Visual Studio 2010

Start Visual Studio 2010 and create a new project. Visual Studio 2010 includes many project templates for SharePoint solutions, as shown in Figure 9–27. The result of every project template is a WSP solution package. In this example, choose the Empty SharePoint Project template. Set the name, location, and solution name of your project and click OK. This starts the SharePoint Customization wizard, as shown in Figure 9–28.

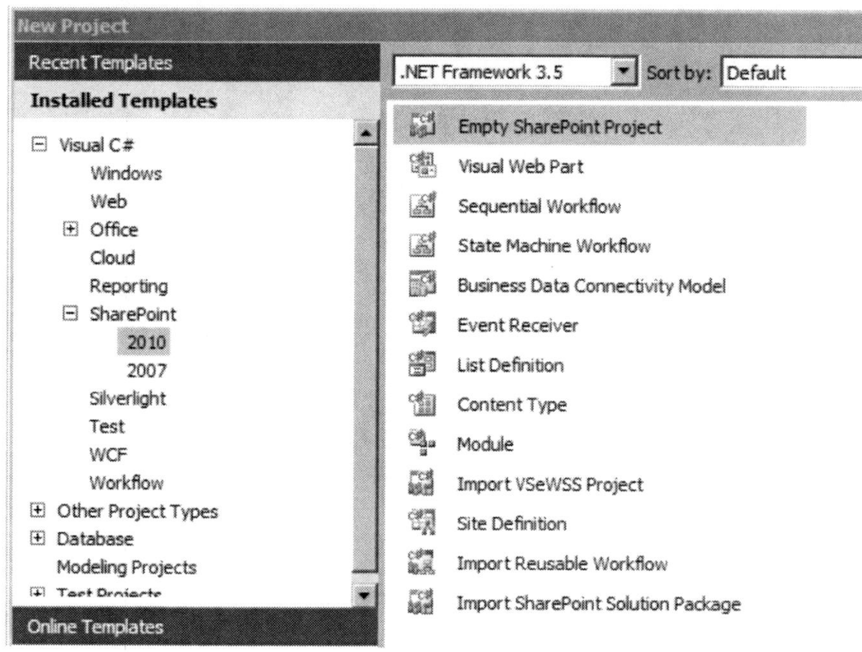

Figure 9–27. SharePoint project templates in Visual Studio 2010

Site and Security Level for Debugging

The wizard (Figure 9–28) asks for the URL of a SharePoint you can use for debugging your new solution. By default, Visual Studio proposes your local SharePoint installation. Click Validate to check that the URL is valid and the SharePoint site is available.

The security level for your solution is also configurable. In this instance, choose "Deploy as a farm solution," and click Finish to initialize your project in Visual Studio.

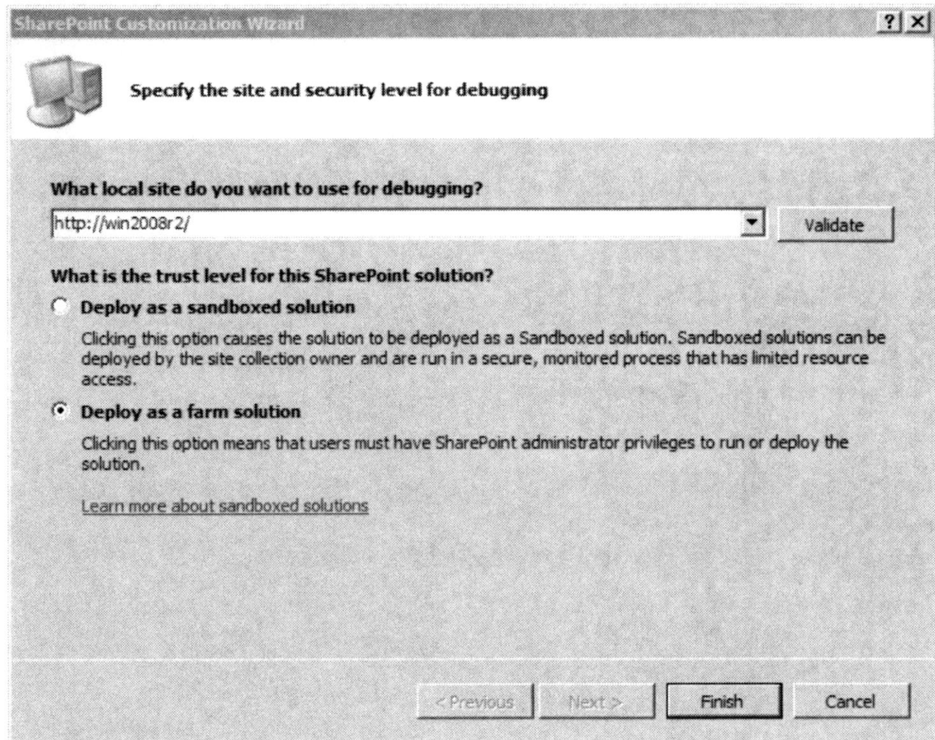

Figure 9–28. *The SharePoint Customization wizard*

Adding SharePoint Items and Features to Your Project

Once the project is established, you will see its predefined structure—there is a folder for the features and one for the package (see Figure 9–29).

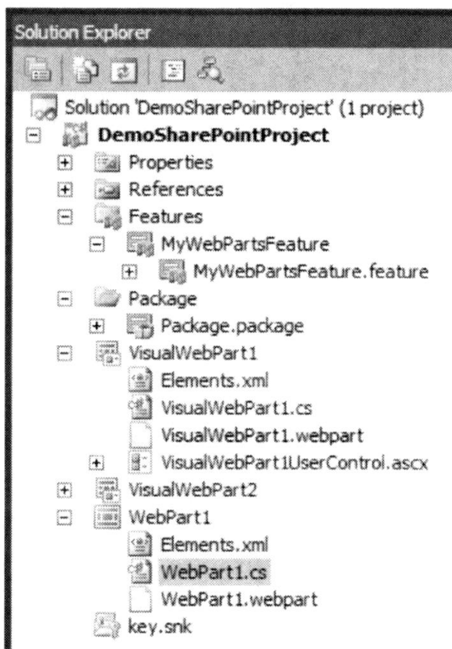

Figure 9–29. *The project structure in Solution Explorer*

You can extend your project with

- SharePoint items, such as Web Parts and list definitions
- Mapped folders, such as layouts (for application pages and more) and images
- Additional features and feature receivers

To add a new SharePoint item, right-click the Project and choose Add ➤ New Item, as shown in Figure 9–30. Now you can add such SharePoint items as Web Parts and list definitions. For this example, pick a visual Web Part, set its name, and click Add.

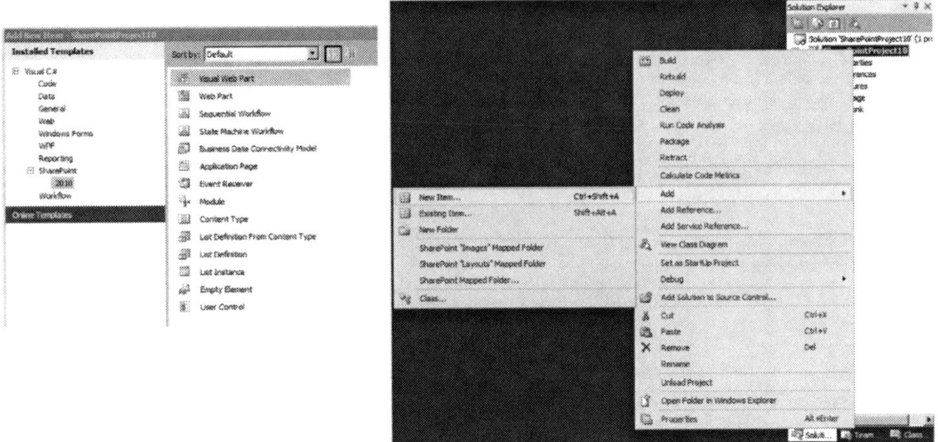

Figure 9–30. Adding a new item

Add two more Web Parts using the same approach. Now you should have three Web Parts in your project.

Each Web Part has its own folder. A feature named Feature 1 was automatically created when you added the first Web Part, and all subsequent SharePoint items were added to this feature. (For more information about using the different SharePoint items in your project, review Chapter 7.)

Perhaps you would prefer to use more than one feature to deploy your SharePoint items, though. You can add a new feature by right-clicking the features folder and selecting Add Feature. When you right-clicking the features folder, you can add an event receiver or resource to the feature (as explained in Chapter 3).

The name Feature 1 doesn't provide much information about the content of a features folder. Right-click the `Feature 1` folder, choose Rename, and enter a more descriptive name, such as MyWebPartsFeature.

Editing Your Features

Double-click a features folder to open the Feature Designer, as illustrated in Figure 9–31. In the Feature Designer are three zones: the header, a middle part, and the footer. In the header you can edit the following general information:

- The title and description of your feature, which are displayed in the feature administration.
- The scope of your feature. Depending on the scope, you can see the appropriate SharePoint items in your solution.

In the center pane of the Feature Designer you can add items to or remove items from your feature. In the footer are advanced options—here you can specify a list of features on which the activation of the current feature depends. Clicking the + to the left of Feature Activation Dependencies opens a menu to define these. Click Add to add a dependency. You can choose a dependency on a feature in your solution, or add a custom feature activation dependency by entering the title, feature ID, and description. In the dependency list you can select a dependency and remove it. If it is a custom one, you can also edit it. If you want to look behind the scenes, you can switch from design view to manifest view.

Here you'll see a preview of the generated manifest, and you'll have the opportunity to edit the template for the generated manifest. Advanced users can ignore the generated XML and edit the manifest directly in the XML editor, as shown in the following exercise.

EDITING THE MANIFEST MANUALLY

1. Double-click your feature in the features folder in Solution Explorer to open the Feature Designer.
2. Click the button marked "Manifest" at the bottom of the window. Once you see a preview of the generated manifest, you can edit the `template.xml` file for the manifest.
3. Click the + button next to Edit Options.
4. Click the link "Overwrite generated XML and edit manifest in the XML editor" at the bottom. Now Visual Studio will display a warning box, checking whether you really want to disable the designer.
5. Click Yes.
6. Click the link "Edit manifest in the XML Editor." You also have the option to reenable the designer.

The next time you double-click your feature, you can choose again if you wish to edit the XML or reenable the designer. You can choose for each feature whether you want to use the designer or edit the XML manually.

To edit the next feature, double-click the next features folder in Solution Explorer, or double-click the feature in the Packaging Explorer next to the Feature Designer (see Figure 9–31).

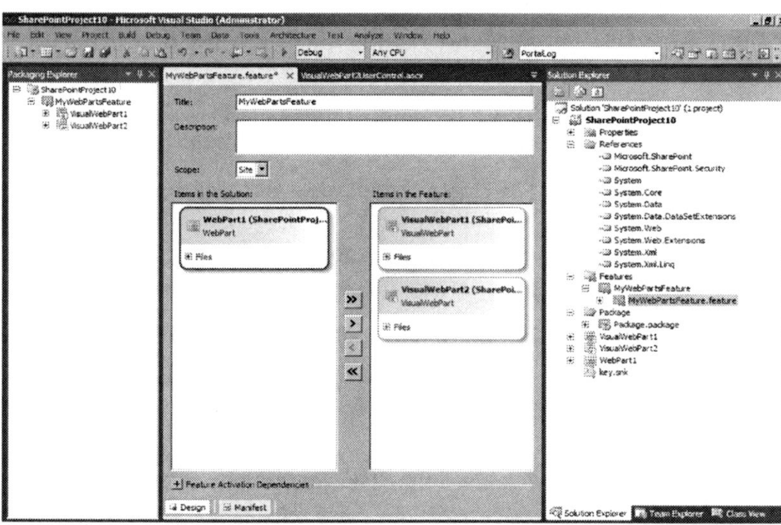

Figure 9–31. *Feature Designer and Packaging Explorer*

If the Feature Designer is enabled, you can also edit the feature properties when you opened the designer. In the Property window you can edit the Properties shown in Table 9–8. If the window is not open, press F4 to display it.

Table 9–8. Feature Properties

Property	Description
Activate on Default	Indicates whether the feature is activated during installation.
Always Force Install	Indicates whether the feature should be installed by force, even if the feature is already installed.
Auto Activate in Central Admin	Indicates whether the feature is activated by default for administrators.
Creator	The developer who created the feature.
Default Resource File	The central resource file for retrieving feature resources.
Deployment Path	The path within the package to which the feature will be deployed.
Description	Indicates what the feature does.
Feature Id	The SharePoint ID of the feature.
Image Alt Text	The text for the image associated with the feature.
Image Url	The relative URL of the image associated with the feature.
Is Hidden	Indicates whether the feature is visible in the list of available features to activate.
Receiver Assembly	The fully qualified name of the assembly that contains the event receiver for the feature.
Receiver Class	The class name of the event receiver for the feature.
Require Resources	Indicates whether SharePoint checks for resources for a particular language and culture.
Scope	The context in which a feature is activated.
Solution Id	Specifies the ID of the SharePoint server where the feature will be installed (Microsoft internal use only)
Title	The title of the feature (limited to 255 characters)
UIVersion	Specifies a string that indicates the compatible versions of the site.

Property	Description
Upgrade Actions Receiver Assembly	The fully qualified name of the assembly containing the feature event receiver that handles custom upgrade actions.
Upgrade Actions Receiver Class	The class name of the feature event receiver that handles custom upgrade actions.
Version	Specifies a `System.Version`–compliant representation of the version of the feature. This can be up to four numbers delimited by decimal points.

Editing Your Solution Package

When you double-click the root node in the Packaging Explorer or the package folder in Solution Explorer, you open the designer for your package, as shown in Figure 9–32.

Here you can enter the name of your package (WSP) file and force a reset of the web server after deployment. As described previously, from the Feature Designer you can assign items in your solution such as mapped folders and features to your package.

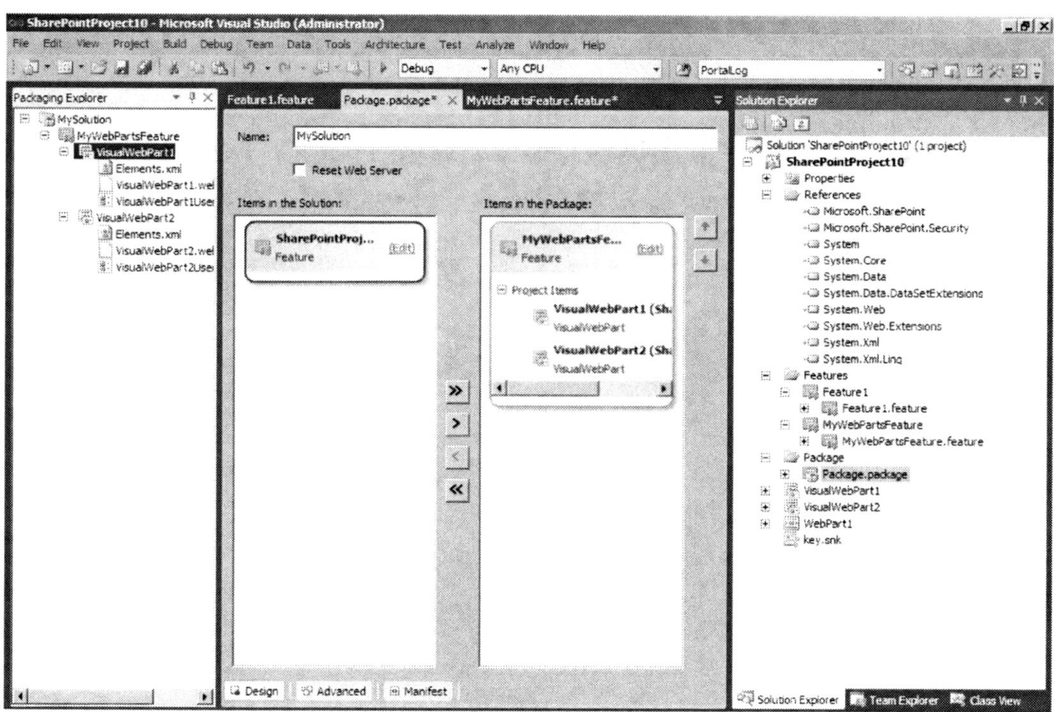

Figure 9–32. Editing your solution in the package designer

At the bottom of the designer are three buttons: Design, Advanced, and Manifest.

From the Advanced menu, you can add, edit, or delete additional assemblies, as shown in Figure 9–33. You have to decide whether to deploy the assembly to the GAC or the `bin` folder of the web application. Here you can also add safe controls and class resources.

When you click the Manifest button, you can preview the generated manifest, edit the template, or edit the complete manifest. You should be familiar with this procedure from the Feature Designer. You can also edit the manifest manually, as described in the previous exercise. If the package designer is enabled, you can also edit the package properties when you open the designer. In the Properties window (which you can open by pressing F4), you can edit the properties shown in Table 9–9.

Table 9–9. Package Properties

Property	Description
Deployment Server Type	The type of server that will host the package: `WebFrontEnd` or `ApplicationServer`
Description	The description of the package
Name	The name of the package (WSP) file
Receiver Assembly	The fully qualified name of the assembly that contains the event receiver for the package
Receiver Class	The class name of the event receiver for the package
Reset Web Server	Indicates whether IIS will be restarted after installing the package
Reset Web Server Mode On Upgrade	Indicates how IIS will be restarted after upgrading the package: `StartStop` or `Recycle`
Solution Id	The ID of the package
Title	The title of the package

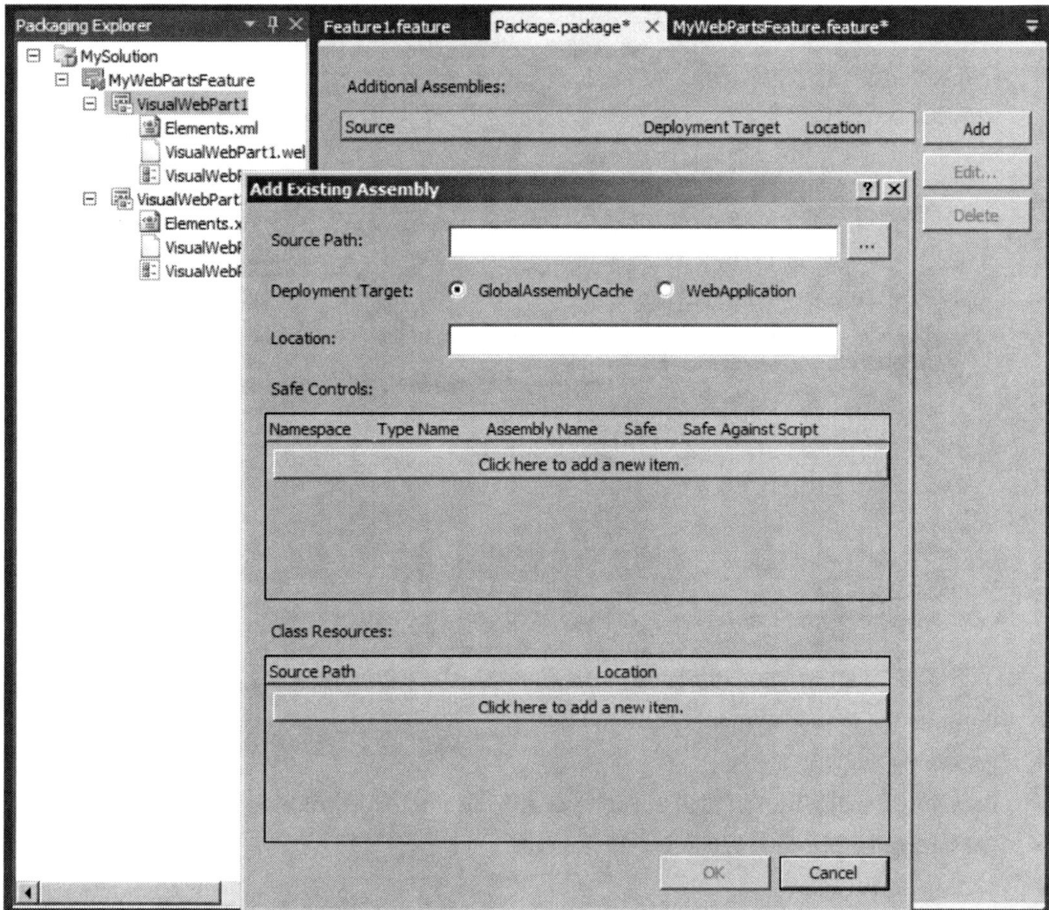

Figure 9–33. Adding assemblies in the package designer

Project Properties and Deployment Configuration

To set the project properties, select the project's root node in Solution Explorer, right-click, and select Properties. Alternatively, you can select the node and press Alt+Enter. You should be familiar with most of the tabs, except the new SharePoint tab. Select this tab now. As shown in Figure 9–34, you can enter pre- and post-commands to run on the command line—these include commands to copy files, start or stop services, and force an `iisreset` call. More interesting is the Active Deployment Configuration selection. Out of the box, Visual Studio comes with two configuration options: Default and No Activation. Select an entry and click View to explore these configurations.

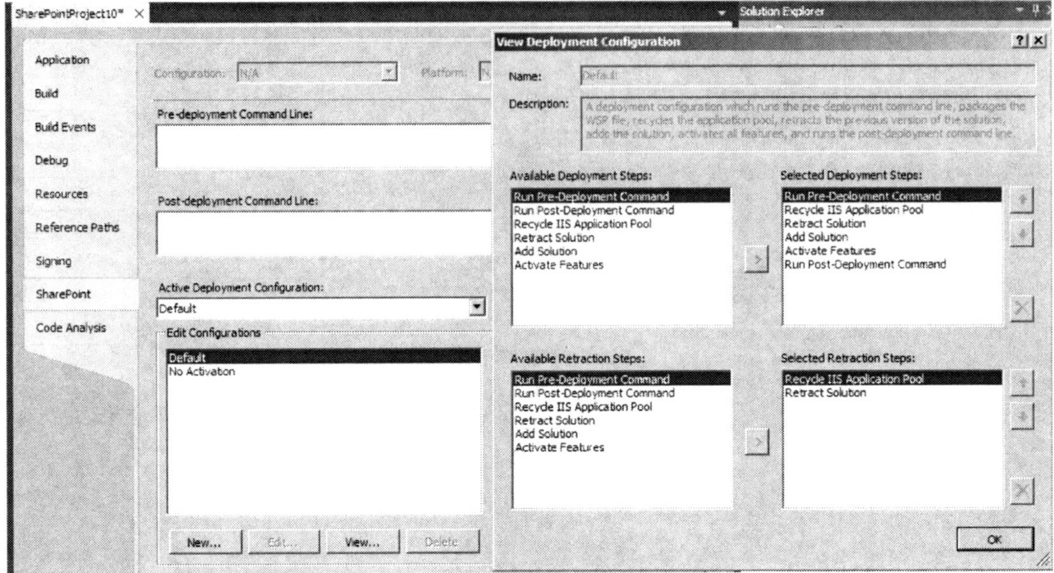

***Figure 9–34.** Deployment configuration*

The No Activation deployment configuration executes the following steps:

- Running the predeployment command line
- Packaging the WSP file
- Recycling the application pool (if you're deploying a full-trust solution)
- Retracting the previous version of the solution
- Adding the solution
- Running the postdeployment command line

The Default configuration does the same and also activates all features.

If you don't want to use the existing static configurations, click New to add your own deployment configuration. In general, the build and package steps are performed before every configuration—you can't edit this. Table 9–10 lists the available deployment and retraction steps. Using the pre- and postdeployment commands, you can extend these steps with your own custom actions. If this is insufficient, you can develop your own steps and add them using Visual Studio Extensions.

■ **Tip** If you want to create your own deployment steps, there is a helpful walkthrough on MSDN at `http://msdn.microsoft.com/en-us/library/ee256698(VS.100).aspx`.

Table 9–10. Available Deployment and Retraction Steps for Deployment Configuration

Step	Description
Run Pre-Deployment Command	Runs any specified commands before the deployment starts
Run Post-Deployment Command	Runs any specified commands after the deployment ends
Recycle IIS Application Pool	Recycles the application pool of your SharePoint web application in IIS
Retract Solution	Retracts a previously installed version of your solution by deactivating, retracting, and deleting it from the local SharePoint site
Add Solution	Adds and installs your solution to the local SharePoint site
Activate Features	Activates all features in your solution for the local SharePoint site

In the Properties window you can also set some properties for your project. Here you can choose the active deployment configuration, too. Other properties you can edit include

- Assembly deployment target: GAC or bin folder
- Include assembly in package
- Startup item

Do you recall the wizard at the beginning of the How-To where you specified the local site for debugging and where you decided whether you want to deploy the solution as full trust or sandboxed? Here in the Properties window you can also change those settings.

Debugging the Solution

To debug, press F5, click the Debug button, or click Debug on the build menu. This will build your project. Once the build has completed, the solution package will be created and deployed onto your development SharePoint site. You set the URL of this server in the wizard at the beginning of the project or in the project Properties window. You can follow the process in the Output window of Visual Studio.

Visual Studio will start Internet Explorer, which loads the URL of your SharePoint for debugging. You can now test your newly developed features inside SharePoint. The debugger is automatically attached to the IIS process `w3wp.exe` and Internet Explorer so that you can debug your solution. Your deployment configuration affects whether all features are activated by default, or whether you have to activate them manually. If you want to debug your code in a feature receiver when a feature is activated, set a breakpoint on the relevant line. When the feature is activated, the debugger will stop at this breakpoint. If you want to debug code that is already deployed, you can similarly set a breakpoint, and then click Attach to Process in the Tools menu of Visual Studio. Then select the `w3wp.exe` process to debug your solution in SharePoint, as shown in Figure 9–35.

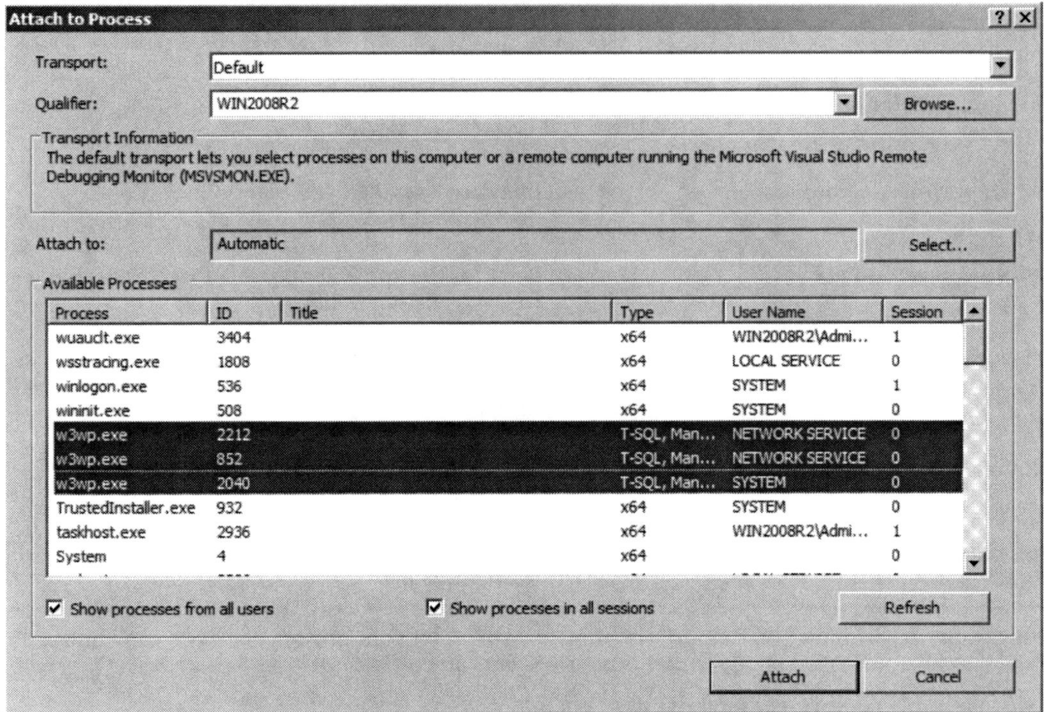

Figure 9–35. Attach to the w3wp process to debug your code for SharePoint

Packaging the Solution

To provide the solution package for deployment on other systems, you need to pass the newly generated WSP file to these systems.

In the debugging process, you have already created a solution file. Examine the Output window or the project properties output path to find the location of the file. Alternatively, you can force Visual Studio to create a solution package. To do so right-click the project and click Package, or click Package in the build menu. If you want the WSP file copied to a special folder, you can change the output path in the build settings, or better still, insert a copy command as a predeployment command line in the SharePoint tab of your project properties:

```
xcopy "$(TargetDir)*.wsp" C:\Solutions /Y
```

To customize this packaging step further, you can define your own deployment configuration (as described previously in the "Project Properties and Deployment Configuration" section). The solution package is now ready for deployment using `stsadm`, PowerShell cmdlets, or the object model.

How To: Creating a Sandboxed Solution Using Visual Studio 2010

When you create a new SharePoint 2010 Project in Visual Studio 2010, the wizard will ask whether you want to create a sandboxed solution or a full-trust solution.

By default, Sandboxed is selected if the type of solution can be deployed as sandboxed.

You can also set this project property later, in the project properties window (see Figure 9–36).

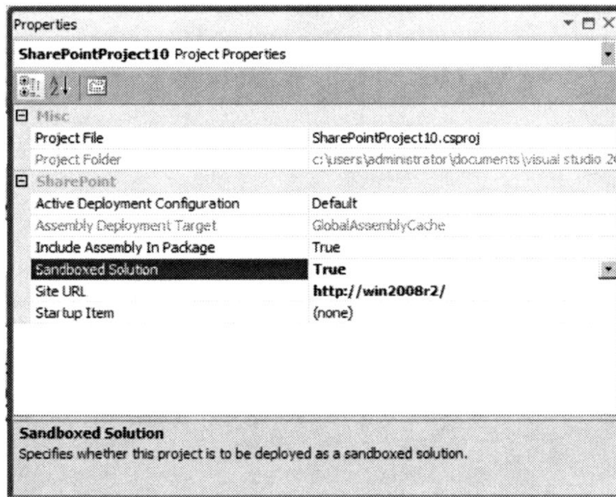

Figure 9–36. *Project properties*

While developing your sandboxed solution, remember the restrictions mentioned earlier. Visual Studio supports the writing valid code for sandboxed solutions by filtering IntelliSense.

■ **Tip** Visual Studio compiles your code against the full version of SharePoint API, but at runtime your code runs against the reduced, sandboxed API. To ensure that your solution only contains valid code for a sandboxed solution you can use a workaround for compile-time checking: delete the `Microsoft.SharePoint.dll` reference on `[SharePoint Root]\UserCode\assemblies\Microsoft.SharePoint.dll`. However, please note that this workaround is only for checking; remember to reset the reference when building the solution package for deployment.

To create your first sandboxed solution, choose the Empty SharePoint Project template in Visual Studio 2010. Set the name to, say, SandboxedWebPart and the solution name to SandboxedSolutionDemo. Next, choose "deploy as sandboxed solution." For this demo, add a Web Part to your solution—right-click the project and add a Web Part named `SandboxDemoWebPart`.

■ **Caution** Take care you don't select a visual Web Part. You can't use visual Web Parts in a sandboxed solution. They contain web controls, which have to be deployed to disk. This is not allowed for sandboxed solutions.

Open the .cs code file of your Web Part to edit it. Listing 9–12 shows sample code.

This code enables your Web Part to show all lists in your site collection in a bulleted list. When completed, the final Web Part should appear similar to Figure 9–37.

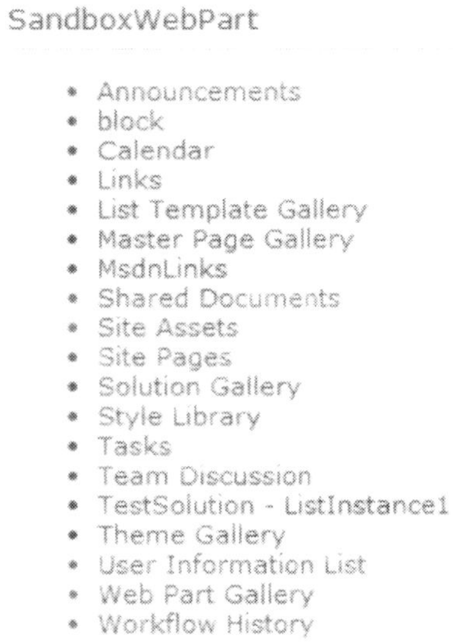

SandboxWebPart

- Announcements
- block
- Calendar
- Links
- List Template Gallery
- Master Page Gallery
- MsdnLinks
- Shared Documents
- Site Assets
- Site Pages
- Solution Gallery
- Style Library
- Tasks
- Team Discussion
- TestSolution - ListInstance1
- Theme Gallery
- User Information List
- Web Part Gallery
- Workflow History

Figure 9–37. *Sandbox Web Part*

Listing 9–12. *Web Part Code*

```
using System;
using System.Diagnostics;
using System.ComponentModel;
using System.Web.UI.WebControls;
using System.Web.UI.WebControls.WebParts;
using Microsoft.SharePoint;
using Microsoft.SharePoint.Utilities;

namespace Apress.SP2010.SandboxedWebPart.SandboxWebPart
{
    [ToolboxItemAttribute(false)]
    public class SandboxWebPart : WebPart
    {
```

```
        private ListBox myListsBox = new ListBox();
        private Label result = new Label();
        public SandboxWebPart()
        {
            try
            {
                using (SPWeb site = SPContext.Current.Site.RootWeb)
                {
                    SPListCollection lists = site.Lists;
                    foreach (SPList list in lists)
                    {
                       myListsBox.Items.Add(list.Title);
                    }
                }


            }
            catch (Exception ex)
            {
                result.Text = ex.Message;
              }
        }
        protected override void CreateChildControls()
        {
            this.Controls.Add(myListsBox);
            this.Controls.Add(result);
            base.CreateChildControls();
        }
    }
}
```

Debugging the Solution

During development, Visual Studio 2010 automatically builds the solution package, deploys it, and activates it in the Solution Gallery when you start debugging by pressing F5.

If you browse to the Solution Gallery, you can see your new solution activated (see Figure 9–38). When you start debugging, Visual Studio automatically attaches the debugger to `SPUCWorkerProcess.exe` to debug your solution.

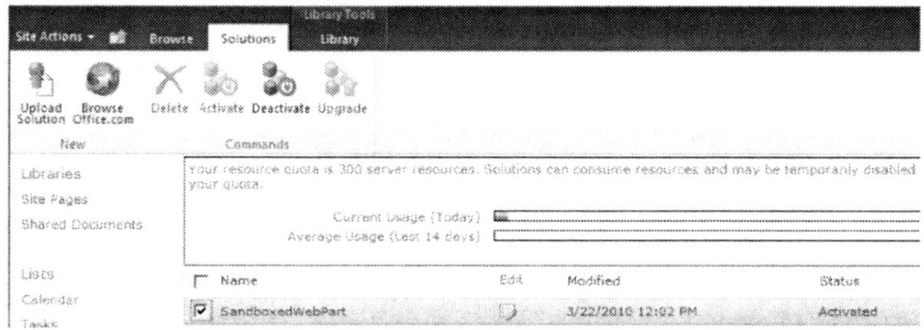

Figure 9–38. Solution Gallery

If you want to debug an already deployed sandboxed solution, you need to attach to `SPUCWorkerProcess.exe` manually, as shown in Figure 9–39.

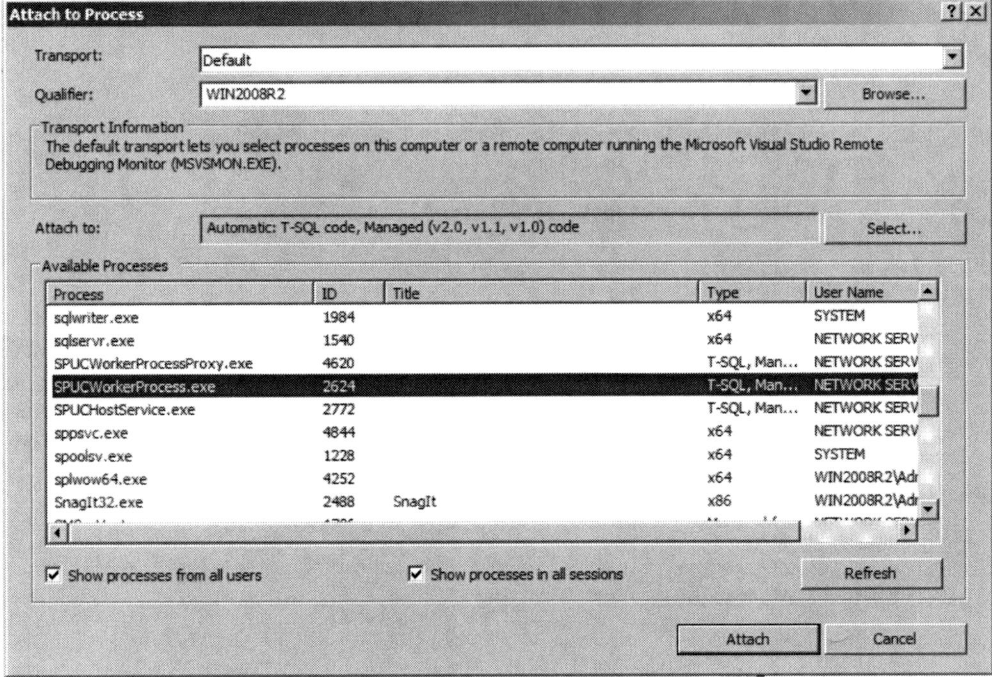

Figure 9–39. Attaching to the SPUCWorkerProcess.exe process

Creating a Full-Trust Proxy

If you want to extend the capabilities of your sandbox, you can create a full-trust proxy for your sandboxed solution. The full-trust proxy in the following example extends the previous sandboxed Web Part example. The proxy writes the names of the lists in your site collection to a log file (see Figure 9–40) on disk.

Figure 9–40. *Text file created by the full-trust proxy*

To do so, you need to

- Create a full-trust proxy class library
- Deploy this DLL to the GAC
- Register the full-trust proxy in SharePoint
- Extend the sandboxed solution with the full-trust proxy

The full-trust proxy is a DLL you have to deploy to the GAC. To build one, add a class library project to the existing SharePoint solution you started earlier for the sandboxed Web Part. Call it, for example, FullTrustProxy. The default framework for a new class library project is the new .NET 4.0 Framework, so you need to set the target framework to .NET 3.5 in the project properties. Otherwise, you'll be unable to reference the project in your SharePoint 2010 projects, because SharePoint 2010 is based on .NET 3.5. The assembly has to be signed when you deploy it to the GAC. To sign it, go to the Signing tab in the project properties (see Figure 9–41) and check the "Sign the assembly" check box. In the window that appears, enter a name for the key file, uncheck "Protect my key file with password," and click OK. Then add a reference to `Microsoft.SharePoint.dll`.

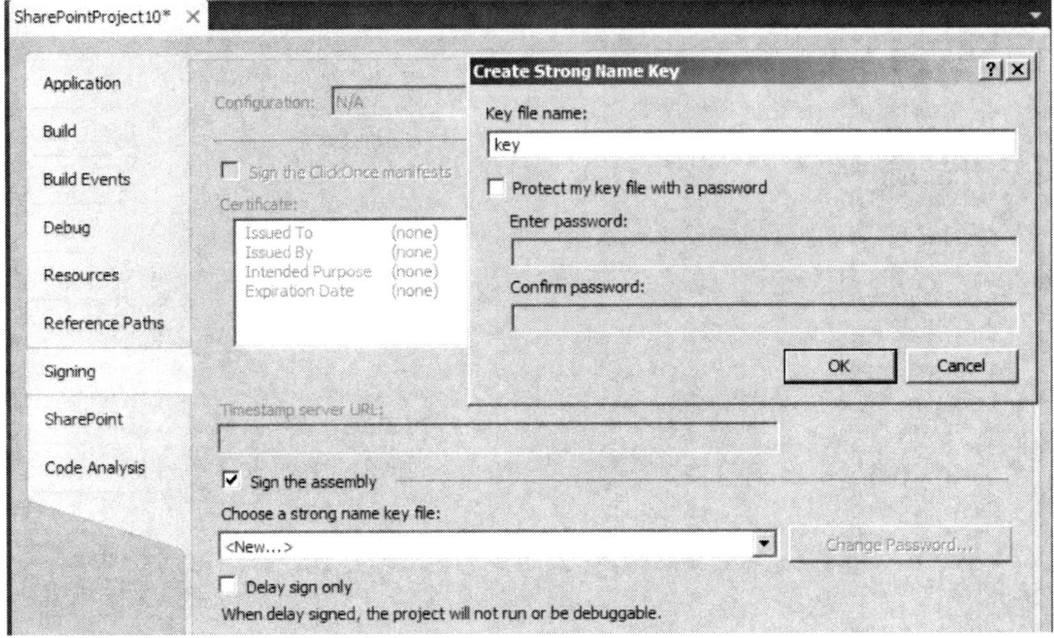

Figure 9–41. *The DLL has to be signed for GAC deployment.*

The next step is to add two class files:

- `FullTrustProxyArgs.cs`, a class that inherits from `Microsoft.SharePoint.UserCode.SPProxyOperationsArgs` (this just passes arguments)
- `FullTrustProxyOps.cs`, which inherits from `Microsoft.SharePoint.UserCode.SPProxyOperation` and does the work

The `FullTrustProxyArgs` class delivers the parameters needed by the `FullTrustProxyOps` class, as shown in Listing 9–13.

Listing 9–13. *FullTrustProxyArgs Class*

```
using System;
using System.Reflection;
using Microsoft.SharePoint.UserCode;

namespace Apress.SP2010.FullTrustProxy
{
    [Serializable]
    public class FullTrustProxyArgs : SPProxyOperationArgs
    {
        public string FileContents { get; set; }
```

```
        public string FullTrustProxyOpsAssemblyName
        {
            get
            {
                 // Return the full assembly name, like "FullTrustProxy,
                //  Version=1.0.0.0, Culture=neutral,
                //  PublicKeyToken=29d96910438b4111";
                return Assembly.GetExecutingAssembly().FullName;
            }
        }
        public string FullTrustProxyOpsTypeName
        {
            get
            {
               return "Apress.SP2010.FullTrustProxy.FullTrustProxyOps";
            }
        }

        public FullTrustProxyArgs()
        {
        }
        public FullTrustProxyArgs(string fileContents)
        {
            this.FileContents = fileContents;
        }
    }
}
```

The FullTrustProxyOps class implements the operations to be executed by the full-trust proxy.

In the example, in Listing 9–14 the proxy writes a string to a log file in the temp folder. Figure 9–40 shows the output of the proxy operation. It is important to allow partially trusted callers for the assembly so that the sandboxed code can call the proxy.

Listing 9–14. *FullTrustProxyOps Class*

```
using System;
using System.IO;
using System.Security;
using Microsoft.SharePoint.UserCode;

[assembly: AllowPartiallyTrustedCallers()]
namespace Apress.SP2010.FullTrustProxy
{
    public class FullTrustProxyOps : SPProxyOperation
    {
        public override object Execute(SPProxyOperationArgs args)
        {
            if (args != null)
            {
        string tempPath = Environment.GetEnvironmentVariable("TEMP",
        EnvironmentVariableTarget.Machine);

                FullTrustProxyArgs fileArgs = args as FullTrustProxyArgs;
                FileStream fStream =
```

```
                    new FileStream(tempPath + @"\SPFullTrustProxyLog.txt",
                                   FileMode.Append);
                fStream.Write(System.Text.ASCIIEncoding.ASCII.GetBytes(
                             fileArgs.FileContents), 0,
                 fileArgs.FileContents.Length);
                fStream.Flush();
                fStream.Close();
                return fileArgs.FileContents;
            }
            else return null;
        }
    }
}
```

Deploying the Full-Trust Proxy DLL to the GAC

Your first full-trust proxy is now complete. But before you can use it, you need to deploy it to the GAC.

Add a new empty SharePoint project called DeployFullTrustProxy to your open Visual Studio solution. It must be deployed as full trust. Set a reference to the project output of the class library project. The solution is used to deploy and register the DLL. Open the package designer and click the Advanced button. Here, you add the project output of the class library project, as shown in Figure 9–42.

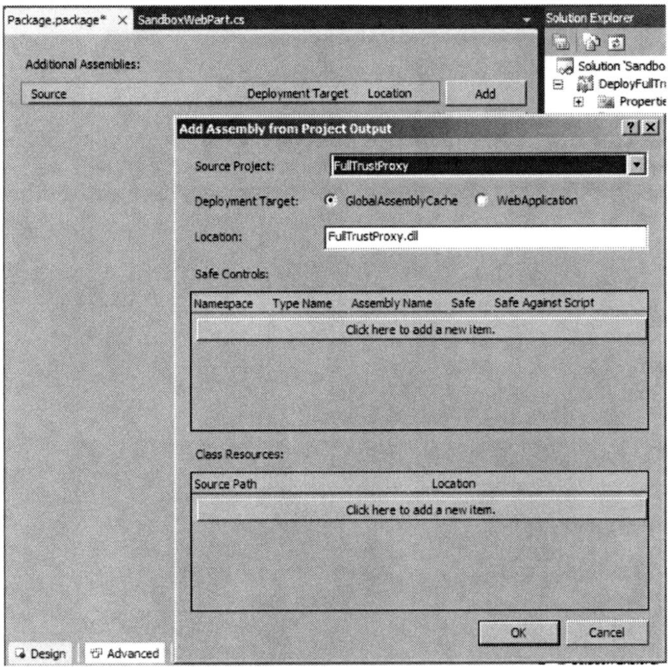

Figure 9–42. *Deploy the Full-Trust Proxy DLL to the GAC*

Registering the Full-Trust Proxy Using a Feature Receiver

Before you can use the full-trust proxy, you need to register the DLL in SharePoint.

The best way to do this is to use a feature receiver so that the farm administrator can activate and deactivate the full-trust proxy in Central Administration, as shown in Figure 9–43.

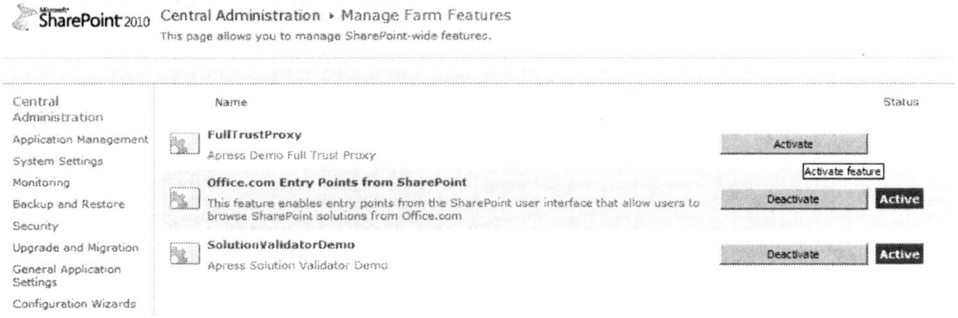

Figure 9–43. *Managing the full-trust proxy via a feature in Central Administration*

Add a feature with the scope of `Farm`, and a feature event receiver to the project. The feature will be used to register your proxy as `SPProxyOperationType` in SharePoint (see Listing 9–15).

Listing 9–15. *Feature Event Receiver*

```
using System;
using System.Runtime.InteropServices;
using Microsoft.SharePoint;
using Microsoft.SharePoint.Administration;
using Microsoft.SharePoint.UserCode;
using Apress.SP2010.FullTrustProxy;

namespace Apress.SP2010.DeployFullTrustProxy.Features.Feature1
{
    [Guid("65a428e1-c14a-4f9c-b7fe-9dbac8e830d4")]
    public class Feature1EventReceiver : SPFeatureReceiver
    {
        // Handle the event raised after a feature has been activated
        public override void FeatureActivated(SPFeatureReceiverProperties
                                                         properties)
        {
            try
            {
                SPUserCodeService userCodeService = SPUserCodeService.Local;
                if (userCodeService != null)
                {
                    SPProxyOperationType operation =
                        new SPProxyOperationType(
                            new FullTrustProxyArgs().FullTrustProxyOpsAssemblyName,
                            new FullTrustProxyArgs().FullTrustProxyOpsTypeName);
```

```
                    userCodeService.ProxyOperationTypes.Add(operation);
                    userCodeService.Update();
                }
            }
            catch
            {
              // Exception handling
            }
        }
        // Handle the event raised before a feature is deactivated
        public override void FeatureDeactivating(
                             SPFeatureReceiverProperties properties)
        {
            try
            {
                SPUserCodeService userCodeService = SPUserCodeService.Local;
                if (userCodeService != null)
                {
                    SPProxyOperationType operation = null;
                    foreach (SPProxyOperationType operationType in
                             userCodeService.ProxyOperationTypes)
                    {
                        if (operationType.AssemblyName.Equals(new
                            FullTrustProxyArgs().FullTrustProxyOpsAssemblyName,
                            StringComparison.CurrentCultureIgnoreCase))
                        {
                            operation = operationType;
                            break;
                        }
                    }
                    if (operation != null)
                    {
                        userCodeService.ProxyOperationTypes.Remove(operation);
                        userCodeService.Update();
                    }
                }
            }
            catch
            {
                // Exception handling
            }
        }
    }
}
```

Now the proxy is completed. You could build, package, and deploy the solution containing your full-trust proxy. However, the proxy is only one half of the scenario; it's just a tool to achieve the goal of extending the boundaries of a sandboxed solution, which we'll describe next.

Using the Full-Trust Proxy to Extend a Sandboxed Solution

In the next step, you will extend your sandboxed solution to use the proxy.

Add a reference in the SandboxedWebPart project named to the project output of the proxy class library project. In the next step, edit the code of the existing Web Part (see Listing 9–12) in the project. Listing 9–16 shows the new code of the Web Part in bold. The proxy call consists of two simple lines: first you create a new instance of FullTrustProxyArgs and deliver the parameter string as the argument for the proxy, and then you call the proxy operation with SPUtility.ExecuteRegisteredProxyOperation. That's it.

Listing 9–16. *Web Part Code*

```
using System;
using System.Diagnostics;
using System.ComponentModel;
using System.Web.UI.WebControls;
using System.Web.UI.WebControls.WebParts;
using Apress.SP2010.FullTrustProxy;
using Microsoft.SharePoint;
using Microsoft.SharePoint.Utilities;

namespace Apress.SP2010.SandboxedWebPart.SandboxWebPart
{
    [ToolboxItemAttribute(false)]
    public class SandboxWebPart : WebPart
    {
        private string myLists;
        private ListBox myListsBox = new ListBox();
        private Label result = new Label();
        public SandboxWebPart()
        {
            try
            {
                using (SPWeb site = SPContext.Current.Site.RootWeb
                {
                   SPListCollection lists = site.Lists;
                   foreach (SPList list in lists)
                   {
                           myListsBox.Items.Add(list.Title);
                           myLists += list.Title + Environment.NewLine;
                   }
                }
                  FullTrustProxyArgs proxyArgs = new FullTrustProxyArgs(myLists);
                  SPUtility.ExecuteRegisteredProxyOperation(
                       proxyArgs.FullTrustProxyOpsAssemblyName,
                        proxyArgs.FullTrustProxyOpsTypeName,
                        proxyArgs);

            }
            catch (Exception ex)
            {
                result.Text = ex.Message;
          }

        }
        protected override void CreateChildControls()
```

```
            {
                this.Controls.Add(myListsBox);
                this.Controls.Add(result);
                base.CreateChildControls();
            }
        }
}
```

Now you are ready for a test flight. Deploy both solutions to your development SharePoint.

If you want to check that your full-trust proxy is registered correctly in SharePoint, you can enter the following command at the SharePoint management shell or PowerShell:

`[Microsoft.SharePoint.Administration.SPUserCodeService]::Local.ProxyOperationTypes.`

If your full-trust proxy was registered, your output should look similar to that shown in Figure 9–44.

Insert the Web Part into a web site and test the full-trust proxy. The Web Part should display all the lists in the site collection. In addition, you will find a file called `SPFullTrustProxyLog.txt` created by the proxy in the `temp` folder.

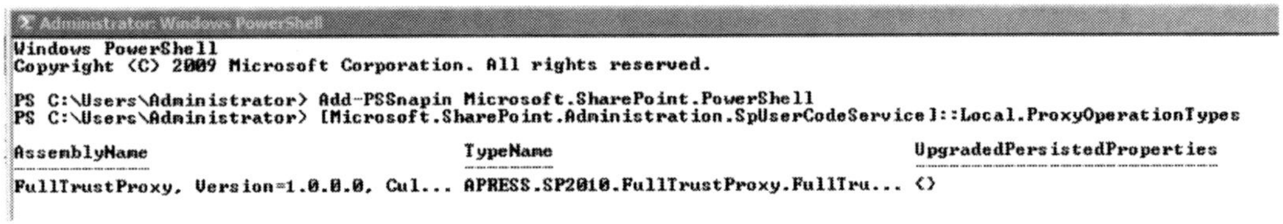

```
Administrator: Windows PowerShell
Windows PowerShell
Copyright (C) 2009 Microsoft Corporation. All rights reserved.

PS C:\Users\Administrator> Add-PSSnapin Microsoft.SharePoint.PowerShell
PS C:\Users\Administrator> [Microsoft.SharePoint.Administration.SpUserCodeService]::Local.ProxyOperationTypes

AssemblyName                          TypeName                                UpgradedPersistedProperties
------------                          --------                                ---------------------------
FullTrustProxy, Version=1.0.0.0, Cul... APRESS.SP2010.FullTrustProxy.FullTru... {}
```

Figure 9–44. *Check whether your full-trust proxy was registered in SharePoint.*

Creating a Solution Validator

Farm administrators can proactively deploy solution validators to their farms. These validators always run when a sandboxed solution is activated or upgraded. You can easily create your own solution validator by performing the following steps:

- Writing a solution validator class
- Creating an error page
- Deploying the solution validator to the GAC
- Registering the solution validator in SharePoint

Start with a new Empty SharePoint project and name it `SolutionValidatorDemo`. Choose “Deploy as farm solution” in the wizard. Then add a class with the name `SolutionValidator` to your project. This file will contain your validator, as shown in Listing 9–17. It shows the general structure of a solution validator and gives examples of how to validate. You can validate an assembly and a solution.

Listing 9–17. *Solution Validator*

```
using System;
using System.Collections.ObjectModel;
using System.Reflection;
using System.Runtime.InteropServices;
using System.Text;
using Microsoft.SharePoint;
```

```
using Microsoft.SharePoint.Administration;
using Microsoft.SharePoint.UserCode;

namespace Apress.SP2010.SolutionValidatorDemo
{
    [Guid("481823F5-75A7-4EF8-8A4B-11C4D52D1014")]
    public class SolutionValidator : SPSolutionValidator
    {
        private const string strValidatorName = "My Solution Validator";
        // Help method to validate the content of files in the solution
        private byte[] LoadBytes(ReadOnlyCollection<byte> bytes)
        {

            byte[] fileBytes = new byte[bytes.Count];
            int count = 0;
            foreach (byte b in bytes)
            {
                fileBytes[count] = b;
                count++;
            }

            return fileBytes;
        }
        // Help method to validate features in the solution
        private bool CheckForFeature(string fileContents, string type)
        {
            string EorF = "<Elements";

            if (type.Equals("ReceiverAssembly"))
                EorF = "<Feature";

            if (fileContents.Contains(EorF) && fileContents.Contains("<" + type))
            {
                return true;
            }

            return false;
        }

        public SolutionValidator()
        {

        }

        public SolutionValidator(SPUserCodeService userCodeService)
            : base(strValidatorName, userCodeService)
        {
            this.Signature = 1983;
        }

        public override void ValidateAssembly(
             SPSolutionValidationProperties properties, SPSolutionFile assembly)
        {
            properties.ValidationErrorUrl =
```

```
        "/_layouts/SolutionValidatorDemo/SolutionValidationErrorPage.aspx";
    bool valid = true;
// Block Solutions containing assemblies named "TestSolution"
    string blockAssemblyName ="TestSolution";
   // Block Solutions containing assemblies with the Public Key Token
   string blockPKT = "29d96910438b4111";

    byte[] fileBytes = LoadBytes(assembly.OpenBinary());
    Assembly a = Assembly.Load(fileBytes);
    string[] assemblyFullName = a.FullName.ToLower().Split(',');
    string assemblyName = assemblyFullName[0];
    string version = assemblyFullName[1].Replace("version=", "").Trim();
    string culture = assemblyFullName[2].Replace("culture=", "").Trim();
    string publicKeyToken = assemblyFullName[3].
                              Replace("publickeytoken=", "").Trim();

    // Validate AssemblyName
    if (assemblyName.Equals(blockAssemblyName.ToLower()))
    {
        valid = false;
        properties.ValidationErrorMessage += "Assembly name '"
                                      + assemblyName + "' not valid. ";
    }
    // Validate PublicKeyToken
    if (publicKeyToken.Equals(blockPKT.ToLower()))
    {
        valid = false;
        properties.ValidationErrorMessage += "Assembly PublicKeyToken '"
                                  + publicKeyToken + "' not valid. ";
    }


    if (!valid)
    {
        properties.ValidationErrorUrl += "?ErrorMessage="
                                  + properties.ValidationErrorMessage;
    }

        properties.Valid = valid;

}

public override void ValidateSolution(
                     SPSolutionValidationProperties properties)
{
    properties.ValidationErrorUrl =
       "/_layouts/SolutionValidatorDemo/SolutionValidationErrorPage.aspx";
    bool valid = true;
    string blockSolutionID = "{3CCB9CAF-54A7-42FF-A03F-F6D6D881BC70}";
    string[] blockFileName = {"SandboxedWebPart","Test"};
    string[] blockFileExt = { "xml", "jpg","webpart" };
    string[] blockFileContent = { "Sand", "box"};

   ReadOnlyCollection<SPSolutionFile> files = properties.Files;
```

```
foreach (SPSolutionFile file in files)
{

    // Block Filenames
    foreach (string filename in blockFileName)
    {
        if (file.Location.ToLower().Equals(filename))
        {
            valid = false;
            properties.ValidationErrorMessage += "Filename '"
                                     + filename + "' is blocked. ";

        }
    }

    // Block FileExtensions
    foreach (string ext in blockFileExt)
    {
        if (file.Location.ToLower().EndsWith(ext))
        {
            valid = false;
            properties.ValidationErrorMessage += "File extension '"
                                         + ext + "' is blocked. ";
        }
    }

    if (file.Location.ToLower().EndsWith("xml"))
    {
        byte[] fileBytes = LoadBytes(file.OpenBinary());

        string fileContents = ASCIIEncoding.ASCII.GetString(fileBytes);

        // Check for file content
        foreach (string content in blockFileContent)
        {
            if (fileContents.ToLower().Contains(content))
            {
                valid = false;
                properties.ValidationErrorMessage += "File '"
                  + file.Location + "' contains blocked characters. ";

            }
        }

        // Check for features like ContentType, CustomAction, Workflow,
        // Receivers, ReceiverAssembly, ListTemplate, Module,
        // Field, and WebPart

        if (CheckForFeature(fileContents, "ListTemplate"))
        {
           valid = false;
           properties.ValidationErrorMessage = "Solution is blocked
                                from including List Definitions. ";
        }
```

```
                }
            }
            // Block SolutionID
            if (properties.SolutionId.Equals(new Guid(blockSolutionID)))
            {
                 valid = false;
                 properties.ValidationErrorMessage += "SolutionID is not valid. ";
            }

            // Block SolutionID stored in SharePoint list
            string strListName = "block";

            using (SPSite site = properties.Site)
            {
               SPList list = site.OpenWeb().Lists.TryGetList(strListName);
               if (list!=null)
               {
                  SPListItemCollection items = list.GetItems();
                  foreach (SPListItem item in items)
                  {
                     if (properties.SolutionId.Equals(new Guid(item.Title)))
                     {
                        valid = false;
                        properties.ValidationErrorMessage += "SolutionID is not
                                                              valid. ";
                        break;
                     }


                  }
               }
            }
            if (!valid)
            {
                 properties.ValidationErrorUrl += "?ErrorMessage=" +
                                           properties.ValidationErrorMessage;
            }

            properties.Valid = valid;
        }
    }
}
```

Creating an Error Page for the Solution Validation

If a solution is not valid, you can display an error message. If you wish, you can define your own custom error page, such as the one shown in Figure 9–45.

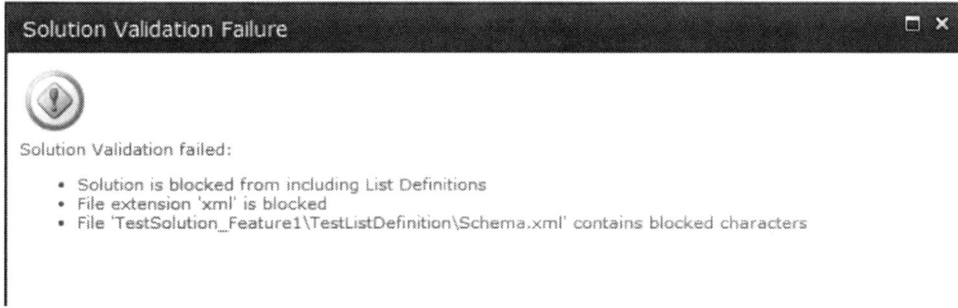

Figure 9–45. *Solution validator error page*

To construct this, add a new application page called SolutionValidationErrorPage.aspx to your project. Listing 9–18 shows example code for your error page.

Listing 9–18. *Custom Error Page: SolutionValidationErrorPage.aspx*

```
<asp:Content ID="Main" ContentPlaceHolderID="PlaceHolderMain" runat="server">
     Solution Validation failed: <%= this.ErrorMessage %>
</asp:Content>
<asp:Content ID="PageTitle" ContentPlaceHolderID="PlaceHolderPageTitle"
            runat="server">
      Solution Validation Failure
</asp:Content>
<asp:Content ID="PageTitleInTitleArea"
            ContentPlaceHolderID="PlaceHolderPageTitleInTitleArea" runat="server" >
      Solution Validation Failure
</asp:Content>
```

To display the error message of the validator, retrieve the message from the url parameter, as shown in Listing 9–19.

Listing 9–19. *Custom Error Page CodeBehind*

```
using System;
using Microsoft.SharePoint.WebControls;
namespace Apress.SP2010.SolutionValidatorDemo.Layouts.SolutionValidatorDemo
{
    public partial class SolutionValidationErrorPage : LayoutsPageBase
    {
        public string ErrorMessage= String.Empty;

        protected void Page_Load(object sender, EventArgs e)
        {
            if (Request.QueryString["ErrorMessage"] != null)
            {
                this.ErrorMessage = Request.QueryString["ErrorMessage"].ToString();
            }
        }
```

```
    }
}
```

Deploying and Registering the Solution Validator

When you have finished developing your validator, you can deploy it as a farm feature as follows:

1. Add a new feature to your SharePoint project.
2. Set the scope to `Farm`.
3. Add a feature event receiver. Once the receiver contains code like that shown in Listing 9–20, you can simply activate and deactivate your solution validator with the feature using Central Administration (see Figure 9–43).

■ **Caution** When you deploy a restrictive solution validator to your development machine, remember to deactivate it when you want to resume developing sandboxed solutions.

Listing 9–20. *Feature Event Receiver*

```
using System;
using System.Runtime.InteropServices;
using System.Security.Permissions;
using Microsoft.SharePoint;
using Microsoft.SharePoint.Security;

using Microsoft.SharePoint.Administration;

namespace Apress.SP2010.Features.SolutionValidatorFeature
{
    [Guid("2a4d3a6b-ab9c-4008-9408-26dd4cd1f6d8")]
    public class SolutionValidatorFeatureEventReceiver : SPFeatureReceiver
    {
        public override void FeatureActivated(
                          SPFeatureReceiverProperties properties)
        {
            SPUserCodeService.Local.SolutionValidators.Add(
                          new SolutionValidator(SPUserCodeService.Local));
        }
        public override void FeatureDeactivating(
                          SPFeatureReceiverProperties properties)
        {
            SPUserCodeService.Local.SolutionValidators.Remove(
                          new Guid("481823F5-75A7-4EF8-8A4B-11C4D52D1014"));
        }
    }
}
```

Now you are ready to test this. Deploy your solution to your development machine.

If you want to check whether your solution validator was registered in SharePoint, you can enter the following command at the SharePoint management shell or PowerShell:

`[Microsoft.SharePoint.Administration.SPUserCodeService]::Local.SolutionValidators.`

If your solution validator was registered correctly, the output should appear similar to that shown in Figure 9–46.

```
Administrator: Windows PowerShell
Windows PowerShell
Copyright (C) 2009 Microsoft Corporation. All rights reserved.

PS C:\Users\Administrator> Add-PSSnapin Microsoft.SharePoint.PowerShell
PS C:\Users\Administrator> [Microsoft.SharePoint.Administration.SpUserCodeService]::Local.SolutionValidators


Signature                          : 1
ProviderId                         : 80e10941-c4fe-4f93-9709-0153ae69a91e
DiskSizeRequired                   : 0
CanSelectForBackup                 : False
CanRenameOnRestore                 : False
CanSelectForRestore                : False
CanBackupRestoreAsConfiguration    : True
Name                               : Default solution validator
TypeName                           : Microsoft.SharePoint.UserCode.SPDefaultSolutionValidator
DisplayName                        : Default solution validator
Id                                 : be77903d-2599-4acd-8ad7-5c2fb8809a3c
Status                             : Online
Parent                             : SPUserCodeService Name=SPUserCodeV4
Version                            : 2444
Properties                         : {}
Farm                               : SPFarm Name=SharePoint_Config_602f207d-6cd6-4e70-b7ee-9ea3bea2f20b
UpgradedPersistedProperties        : {}

Signature                          : 1983
ProviderId                         : 481823f5-75a7-4ef8-8a4b-11c4d52d1014
DiskSizeRequired                   : 0
CanSelectForBackup                 : False
CanRenameOnRestore                 : False
CanSelectForRestore                : False
CanBackupRestoreAsConfiguration    : True
Name                               : My Solution Validator
TypeName                           : APRESS.SP2010.SolutionValidatorDemo.SolutionValidator
DisplayName                        : My Solution Validator
Id                                 : 9e669373-2b63-44d6-872a-bbc07629819b
Status                             : Online
Parent                             : SPUserCodeService Name=SPUserCodeV4
Version                            : 24408
Properties                         : {}
Farm                               : SPFarm Name=SharePoint_Config_602f207d-6cd6-4e70-b7ee-9ea3bea2f20b
UpgradedPersistedProperties        : {}
```

Figure 9–46. *Check whether your solution validator was registered in SharePoint*

■ **Tip** On CodePlex is the Generic Solution Validator at `http://spgenericvalidator.codeplex.com/`. You can install this validator on your SharePoint 2010 server to set solution validation settings on a config page in your site collection.

Upgrading Custom Developed Solutions to SharePoint 2010

If you have already customized and extended SharePoint 2007, you have probably created your own solutions. If you want to use your solutions in SharePoint 2010, one option is to use *backward compatibility mode*. If you wish to edit your solutions in Visual Studio 2010, however, we recommend you upgrade them.

Backward Compatibility Mode

SharePoint 2010 comes with a UI compatibility mode for SharePoint 2007 for backward compatibility.

If you upgrade your SharePoint 2007 farm to SharePoint 2010, backward compatibility mode is active by default. If you want to use the SharePoint 2010 UI, you can activate the new experience for every site collection, or for a single site in the site settings (Site Collection Administration\Supported User Experiences). You can also activate backward compatibility mode via the API; set the UI version to 3 for compatibility mode and to 4 for the SharePoint 2010 UI, as shown in Listing 9–21.

Listing 9–21. *Activating Backward Compatibility Mode*

```
public class UIModeFeatureEventReceiver : SPFeatureReceiver
{
   public override void FeatureActivated(SPFeatureReceiverProperties properties)
   {
            // Feature is scoped at Web, so the parent type is SPWeb
            using (SPWeb web = properties.Feature.Parent as SPWeb)
            {
                web.UIVersion = 3;
                web.Update();
            }
    }
   public override void FeatureDeactivating(
                                       SPFeatureReceiverProperties properties)
   {
       // Feature is scoped at Web, so the parent type is SPWeb
            using (SPWeb web = properties.Feature.Parent as SPWeb)
            {
                web.UIVersion = 4;
                web.Update();
            }
   }
}
```

Reasons for Upgrading

If you wish to use the new SharePoint 2010 features and develop your solutions with Visual Studio 2010, it is necessary to upgrade your existing solutions. The following are some important reasons to upgrade:

- New APIs (`Microsoft.SharePoint.Linq.dll`, `Microsoft.SharePoint.Client.dll`, `Microsoft.SharePoint.Taxonomy.dll`) vs. old API (`Microsoft.SharePoint.dll`)
- Deprecated APIs
- LINQ to SharePoint
- Client APIs
- New technologies available: Silverlight, AJAX, and JSON
- New UI: ribbon, pop-ups, CSS
- Business Connectivity Services (BCS)
- Changed paths (14 hive instead of 12 hive)

- Large list query throttling
- Sandboxed solutions

Depending on how you created your existing solutions, there are different options for migrating them to Visual Studio 2010 and SharePoint 2010:

- Upgrading a Visual Studio Extensions for Windows SharePoint Services (VSeWSS) 2005/2008 solution
- Upgrading a WSP package
- Upgrading a custom solution

Upgrading a VSeWSS Solution

For SharePoint 2007 development with Visual Studio 2005 or 2008, Microsoft offered VSeWSS 3.0. If you have created your solutions with VSeWSS, you can upgrade them to a Visual Studio 2010 solution.

Unfortunately, you can't open a VSeWSS project directly with Visual Studio 2010. If you try to do so, you'll get the following error message: "The project type is not supported by this installation." However, Microsoft offers an additional project template as an extension for Visual Studio 2010 (VSIX) that allows the importing of existing VSeWSS projects. You have to download and install this tool separately, as described in the next exercise.

INSTALLING THE IMPORT VSEWSS PROJECT VISUAL STUDIO TEMPLATE

1. Download the `VSeWSS_Upgrade_Sample_Beta_20100108.msi` installer from `http://download.microsoft.com/download/3/0/2/3022725B-53C6-413A-B624-B3DBC480E3BA/VSeWSS_Upgrade_Sample_Beta_20100108.msi`.
2. Install the package.
3. If Visual Studio 2010 is open, close it.
4. By default, a second installer package and a readme file will be installed to `C:\Program Files (x86)\Microsoft\VSeWSS Upgrade`. Run the second package from this folder.
5. Open a command prompt as administrator and switch to the Visual Studio 2010 IDE folder (the default location is `C:\Program Files (x86)\Microsoft Visual Studio 10.0\Common7\IDE`), and then run `devenv /installvstemplates`.
6. Open Visual Studio 2010 and create a new SharePoint 2010 Project. The Import VSeWSS Project template should be available now (see Figure 9–47).

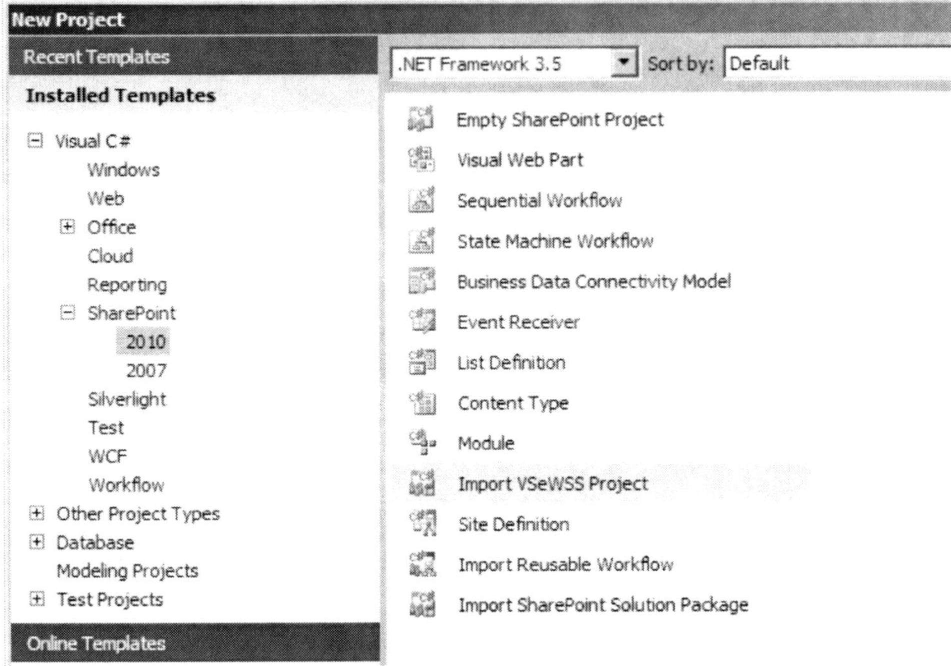

***Figure 9–47.** Importing the VSeWSS project*

This additional template enables you to import VSeWSS projects version 1.1 and above into a new Visual Studio 2010 SharePoint project, including your Visual Basic or C# code.

The import process converts the existing structure of your VSeWSS project as closely as possible to the new Visual Studio 2010 layout. This also means that you'll have one SharePoint item per feature, because VSeWSS had a one-to-one approach. Since Visual Studio 2010 is more flexible, allowing you to arrange multiple artifacts per feature, you can rearrange the features later.

When you choose the template, the wizard will also ask you for the security level setting. This time, full trust is the default. You should take this option, because the old solutions were also full trust. If you want to deploy your imported solution as a sandboxed solution in the future, you can change this setting in the project properties, as shown in the "Sandboxed Solutions" section earlier in the chapter (also see Figure 9–36). However, remember the restrictions of sandboxed solutions before taking this step.

IMPORTING A VSEWSS PROJECT

1. Open Visual Studio 2010 and create a new project. Choose the Import VSeWSS Project template.
2. Set the name, location, and solution name of the project. Then click OK.
3. Choose or enter the URL of the local site for debugging, and keep "Deploy as a farm solution" as the trust level for the solution.
4. Browse to the path of the existing VSeWSS project and choose the project file (`*.csproj` or `*.vbproj`). Click Finish to start the import.

Visual Studio will create the new project and import the old VSeWSS project. When this process is complete, Visual Studio should prompt you that the import was successful, and you should see all the items of your old VSeWSS project in Solution Explorer for your new Visual Studio 2010 project.

When the import has finished, take a look at the Output window and the error list in Visual Studio 2010. In the Output window, choose Show Output from SharePoint Tools

to display a log of the import process and some extra information. This includes advice about what you need to do next. In the error list, you may also find messages and warnings concerning the import.

The import process handles a number of problems that can occur while importing the source project:

- The source solution can contain artifacts whose handling has changed in SharePoint 2010, such as themes.
- The source solution can be corrupt in many ways. The readme file delivered with the VSeWSS Import tool describes several scenarios.

For example, when you import a SharePoint 2007 theme, the import process detects this theme and displays a message explaining that the handling of themes has been changed in SharePoint 2010 and providing a pointer to solve the problem. You should check and fix the following:

- The assembly name and default namespace of your project
- Referenced assemblies or projects
- Web references (ASMX) and service references (WCF)

During the import the default namespace of your old project is also imported. But the assembly name can differ from the source assembly name if your new project does not have the same name. Check this in the project properties, too.

The VSeWSS import process converts only the VSeWSS project. It does not import referenced projects that were part of the source solution. You need to add the referenced projects again to the solution and reference the output in the SharePoint project, or reference the resulting assemblies. References to `Microsoft.SharePoint.*` and `Microsoft.Office.*` assemblies are automatically updated from version 12 to version 14.

If your VSeWSS project contains web or service references, the files created by adding and updating these references are imported and the project will still build. But they are not added as web or service references to the project, so you can't update them. Hence, you should remove the files and add the web and service references again manually.

Visual Studio 2010 enables you to redesign the structure of your package and your features. Using the Package Explorer, features and assemblies can be easily added to or removed from your package. With the Feature Designer you can add multiple SharePoint items to one feature, remove them, and rename them. (The previous section "How To: Creating a Solution Package Using Visual Studio 2010" contains the details.)

Upgrading a WSP Package

For all other projects deployed via WSP files, upgrading a WSP package may be the best option. To upgrade a WSP-packaged solution, import it into Visual Studio 2010. This option can also be used to import and edit solutions created with SharePoint Designer 2010.

The import wizard gives you the option to choose which items of the solution you want to import (see Figure 9–48). Based on the chosen parts, Visual Studio creates a new project structure and inserts the chosen items. The tool only imports the XML files, images, and other files that are included in your WSP file. Since a WSP file doesn't contain your source code, you have to import your code manually and set the correct namespaces. The following exercise will guide you through the WSP import process.

IMPORTING A WSP FILE

1. Open Visual Studio 2010 and create a new project using the Import SharePoint Solution Package template.
2. Set the name, location, and solution name of the project. Then click OK.
3. Choose or enter the URL of the local site for debugging, and choose "Deploy as a farm solution" as the trust level for the solution.
4. Browse to the path of the existing WSP file and choose it. Click Next.
5. Select the items from the WSP file you want to import. Click Finish to start the import.

Visual Studio should indicate the progress of the import and that the import was successful. Now you should see all the selected items of your old WSP file in Solution Explorer for your new Visual Studio 2010 project.

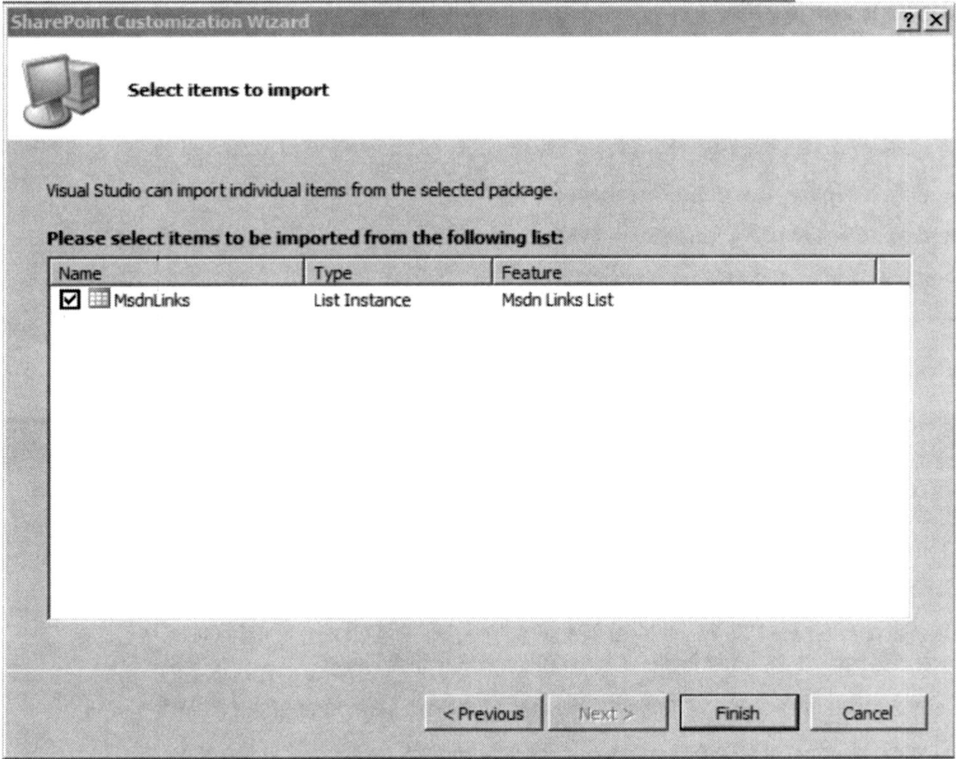

Figure 9–48. *Selecting the items to import from the WSP file*

When the import has finished, examine the Output window and the error list as described in the previous section. Since your code is not imported from a WSP file, it needs to be imported manually.

In this context, you should check and fix the following:

- The assembly name and default namespace of your project
- Referenced assemblies or projects
- Web references (ASMX) and service references (WCF)
- Your custom code import

You can redesign your solution easily using the Package Explorer and the Feature Designer. After the import, the features folders will be named `Feature 1`, `Feature 2`, and so on. You should rename them in Solution Explorer.

Upgrading Custom Solutions

Although importing VSeWSS projects and WSP packages can help greatly, in some cases you may have to explore other ways of upgrading your solutions to Visual Studio 2010 and SharePoint 2010.
This will become necessary in the following scenarios:

- If you haven't used VSeWSS
- If you didn't deploy your solutions through WSP files
- If you don't want to use a VSeWSS or WSP import
- If you have used your own installer or script

In these cases you need to create an empty SharePoint 2010 solution project and insert the items from the old project, as shown in the following exercise. (The section "How to: Creating a Solution Package Using Visual Studio 2010" may help you, too.)

MANUAL UPGRADE OF A SOLUTION

1. Open Visual Studio 2010 and create a new project using the Empty SharePoint Project template.
2. Set the name, location, and solution name of the project. Then click OK.
3. Choose or enter the URL of the local site for debugging, and choose "Deploy as a farm solution" as the trust level for the solution. Then click Finish.
4. Set the assembly name and default namespace to match your preupgrade project.
5. Build the skeleton of your project: right-click your project, select Add ➤ New Item, and add SharePoint items such as Web Parts, list definitions, or mapped folders.
6. Organize the SharePoint items of your solution with the Feature Designer and the Package Explorer.
7. Add assemblies, assembly references, or references to project output, web, or service references.
8. Copy the content, such as images and other resources, from the source mapped folders to the new ones.
9. Import your code.

Using Existing SharePoint 2007 Code in SharePoint 2010

In general your custom assemblies for SharePoint 2007 also run in SharePoint 2010. There are three different types:

- Code that runs within IIS
- Code that runs within the timer service
- Code that runs outside of IIS

Code for SharePoint 2007 that runs within IIS will work in SharePoint 2010 without recompilation. If your code runs within the timer service (such as workflows, feature receivers, and timer jobs), you have to compile it for SharePoint 2010. It's the same with code that utilizes the SharePoint object model and runs outside of IIS in a service or console application: you need to recompile or provide binding redirects. Thinking of deprecated APIs, it's recommended that you always import your source code into your SharePoint/Visual Studio 2010 projects and recompile it.

Deprecated APIs

In SharePoint 2010, numerous APIs of previous versions have been deprecated. But don't worry: most deprecated types and methods are still available in SharePoint 2010. Microsoft will not invest in these APIs in the future, so you should use the newer alternatives. While recompiling your code in Visual Studio 2010, compiler warnings will tell you which elements are deprecated and which newer alternatives are available. When you edit your code, IntelliSense will also indicate deprecated types and methods, as shown in Figure 9–49.

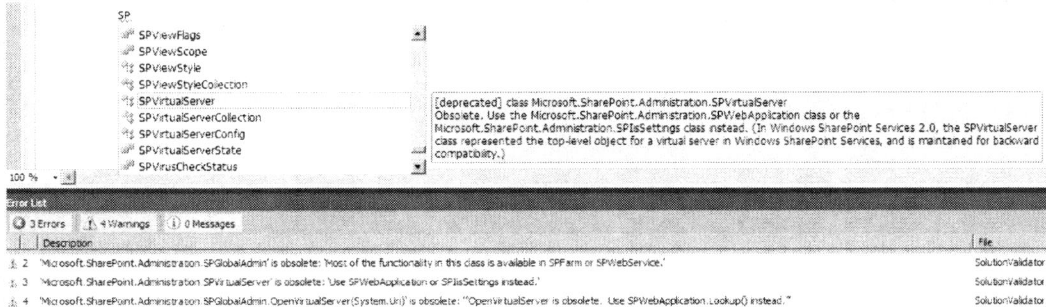

Figure 9–49. *Compiler warnings and IntelliSense indicate deprecated types and methods.*

Most deprecated types and methods are in the `Microsoft.SharePoint.Portal` namespace. In fact, with a few exceptions, the entire namespace has been made obsolete. Other examples of deprecated types and methods are shown in Table 9–11.

Table 9–11. *Examples of Deprecated Types and Methods*

Namespace	Deprecated Type or Method
`Microsoft.SharePoint.Administration`	`SPVirtualServer`
`Microsoft.SharePoint`	`SPCheckoutStatus`
`Microsoft.SharePoint`	`SPRights`
`Microsoft.SharePoint`	`SPPermission`
`Microsoft.SharePoint.Webcontrols`	`RaisePostbackEvent`
`Microsoft.Office.Server`	`Get Context`

You can find a complete list of deprecated types and methods in SharePoint 2010 at `http://code.msdn.microsoft.com/sps2010deprecated`. (For more information about the API see Chapters 2 and 3 of this book.)

■ **Tip** Microsoft published a whitepaper entitled "Redeploying Customizations and Solutions in SharePoint Foundation 2010 and SharePoint Server 2010," which you can find at `http://msdn.microsoft.com/en-us/library/ee662217%28office.14%29.aspx`.

Summary

This chapter introduced SharePoint solution packages provided with SharePoint to deploy customizations and extensions. You learned about solution packages and features and how to create and use them, including the different ways you can deploy a solution package (via `stsadm`, PowerShell, or the UI). This chapter also introduced the new SharePoint 2010 feature of sandboxed solutions. Finally, you got an overview on how to upgrade your existing solution packages from SharePoint 2007 to SharePoint 2010.

PART 2

■■■

User Interface

CHAPTER 10

Extending the User Interface

The SharePoint user interface (UI) provides a professional look and feel for modern business applications. In this chapter you will gain deep insight into the SharePoint UI. It includes standard UI elements required to build custom applications, as well as custom extensions to existing SharePoint functionality. The many developer tips in this chapter reveal fast and efficient ways to build sophisticated applications on top of the SharePoint framework.

This chapter includes

- Insights into the different types of master pages
- A look into SharePoint navigation
- The concepts behind SharePoint theming
- Opportunities to extend the SharePoint UI

SharePoint offers a collection of interdependent UI artifacts:

- Master pages
- Navigation providers
- Themes
- UI extensions

This chapter provides a walkthrough for each of these mechanisms, which can extend a SharePoint environment and aid in developing custom application pages. With master pages and the placeholder concept, an ASP.NET developer can modify existing pages or create his or her own pages. The differences between the various types of navigation are highlighted in this chapter, and you will learn how to create custom navigation providers. Furthermore, the concept of theming is explained. UI extensions include custom actions (added to context and regular menus), and the new ribbon and its various features.

A good technical understanding of these base types will give you a strong foundation—and a head start—for developing your own custom SharePoint applications.

Master Pages

Master pages were introduced in version 2.0 of ASP.NET. Master pages are templates that other pages can use to maintain a consistent layout and functionality throughout an application. Single master pages define the standard look and feel for all pages or a group of pages. Hence, master pages ease the manageability of web-based applications.

The architecture of master pages uses the concept of *merging*. A page refers to a master page, and the ASP.NET Framework merges the two together to build one page, as illustrated in Figure 10–1.Technically, a master page is an ASPX page that inherits from `System.UI.MasterPage`. It usually consists of code, web controls, and one or more placeholders. The placeholders are regions whose content is specified in each ASPX page that utilizes the master page. An example of a basic master page follows:

```
<%@Master language="C#"%>
<%@ Import Namespace="Microsoft.SharePoint" %>
<%@ Import Namespace="Microsoft.SharePoint.ApplicationPages" %>

<html id="HTML1" runat="server">
<head id="HEAD1" runat="server">
     <link rel="stylesheet" type="text/css" href="/_layouts/1031/styles/core.css" />
</head>
<body>
     <form id="Form1" runat="server" >
     <div>
          <asp:ContentPlaceHolder id="MyPlaceHolder" runat="server">
               Hello World - I am a Master Page
          </asp:ContentPlaceHolder>
     </div>
...
```

A master page is identified by three main characteristics:

- Its file extension is `.master`—for example, `default.master`.
- It begins with the `@Master` directive—`<%@Master language="C#" %>`. Note that ASPX pages usually begin with the `@Page` directive.
- It contains one or more `ContentPlaceHolder` tags.

A master page is almost the same as an ordinary ASP.NET page. The difference is that a master page can have special sections built with `ContentPlaceHolder` controls that allow content pages to replace them with their own content.

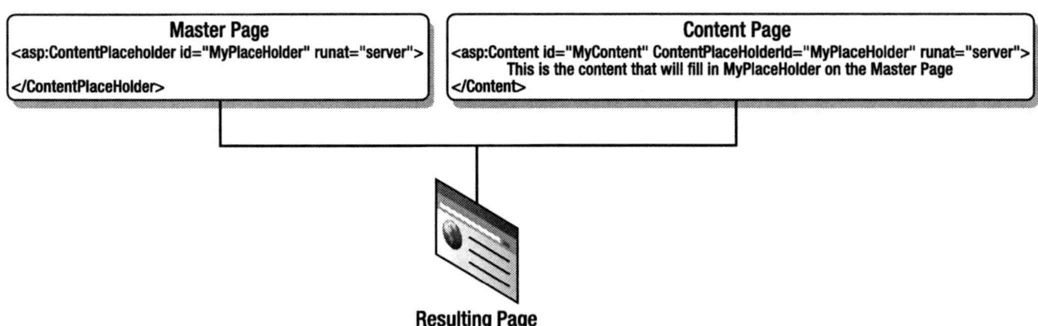

Figure 10–1. *Merging a master page and a content page*

Content pages in ASP.NET are pages that reference a master page. They contain an attribute that instructs the compiler to merge the page with the referenced master page. This attribute is part of the `@Page` directive tag and is called `MasterPageFile`.

```
<%@ Page Language="C#" AutoEventWireup="true"
         MasterPageFile="~/MyMasterPage.Master"
         CodeBehind="Default.aspx.cs" Inherits="WebApp._Default" %>
```

Content pages implement `<content>` tags to inform the compiler to override specified `ContentPlaceHolder` controls in the master page.

```
<asp:Content ID=""MyContent" ContentPlaceHolderId="MyPlaceHolder" runat="server">
     Hello World - I am a content page and I have overwritten the master page content
</asp:Content>
```

Content pages are not required to supply unique content for all the ContentPlaceHolder controls in a master page. If a content page does refer to a ContentPlaceHolder, then the code inside the particular content tag will override the corresponding ContentPlaceHolder section in the master page. If a content page does not implement a particular ContentPlaceHolder, the markup defined on the master page for that ContentPlaceHolder will be rendered.

Master Page Types

SharePoint is based entirely on the concept of master pages. Almost all of the built-in ASP.NET pages in SharePoint inherit from a master page. Thus, if you want to modify the look and feel of all the SharePoint pages, you can do this by customizing the referenced master pages. This defines a centralized place for customizations instead of modifying every web page in the entire SharePoint portal. There are several types of master pages in SharePoint:

- System master page (default master page)
- Site master page (custom master page)
- Application master page
- Dialog master page
- Specific master pages (minimal.master, simple.master)

System Master Page (Default Master Page)

The system master page—also known as the default master page—is used for most of the built-in ASPX pages within SharePoint. It's typically used for pages related to lists and libraries on existing SharePoint sites (see pages such as DispForm.aspx, EditForm.aspx, NewForm.aspx, and AllItems.aspx). It's also used for common pages like default.aspx and application pages residing in the _layouts directory (see Figure 10–2).

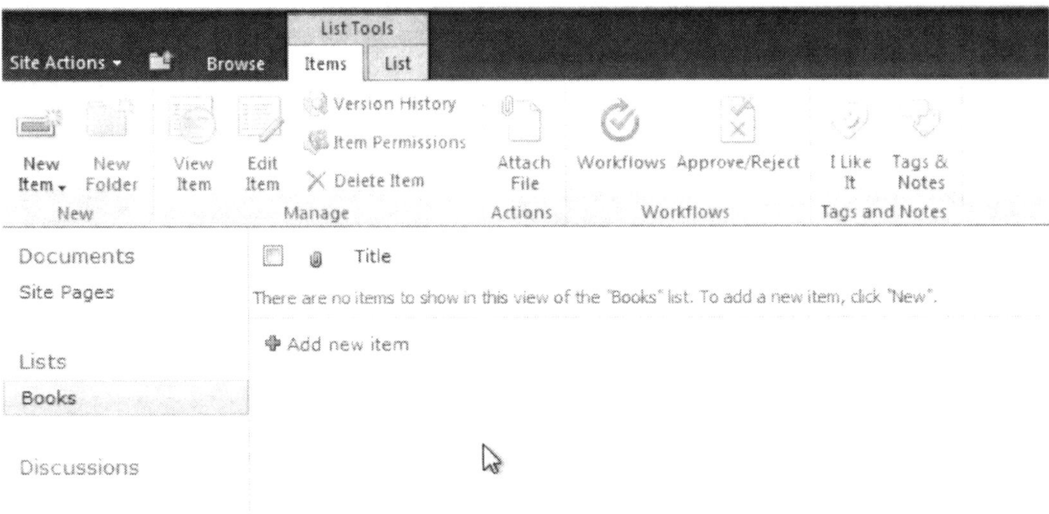

Figure 10–2. System master page used for a list view page (AllItems.aspx)

A system master page is referenced by a predefined token, `~masterurl/default.master`, in the ASP.NET `@Page` directive, as shown in Figure 10–3.

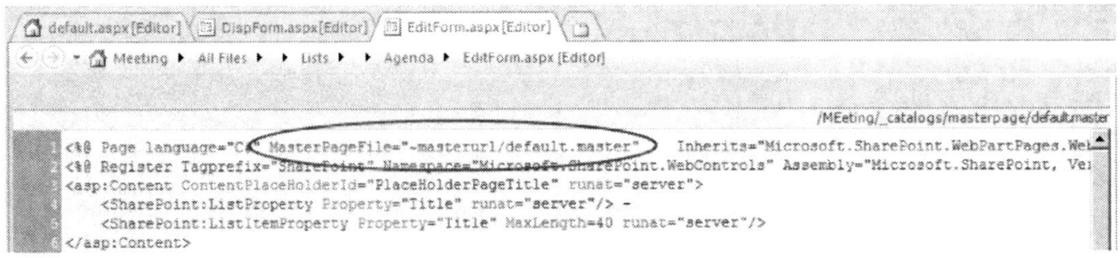

Figure 10–3. System master page token

Site Master Page (Custom Master Page)

A site master page—also known as a custom master page—is mostly used when one or more pages are required to have a master page that is different from the system master page. An example for this is the Meeting Workspace site definition, which contains a `default.aspx` page based on a site master page.

A site master page is referenced by the token `~masterurl/custom.master` in the ASP.NET `@Page` directive (see Figure 10–4).

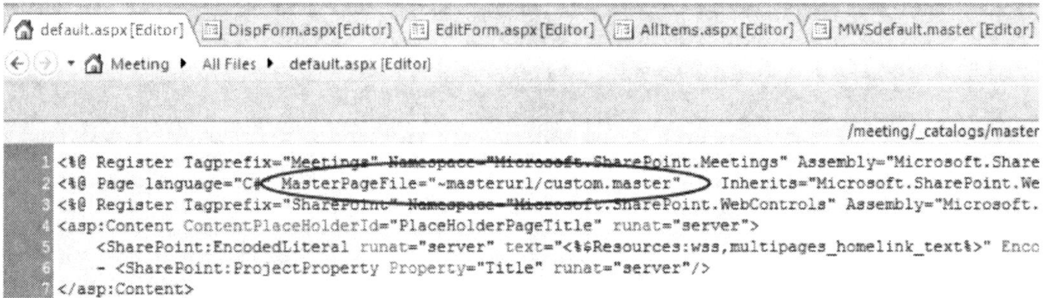

Figure 10–4. Site master page token

Application Master Pages

Application master pages are used for application pages. Application pages are SharePoint administrative pages that are usually used during site administration. They are static ASP.NET pages stored on the file system, unlike most other pages in SharePoint that are stored in the database. Application master pages can be found in the same directory as the application pages: `%Program Files\Common Files\Microsoft Shared\web server extensions\14\TEMPLATE\LAYOUTS` (see Figure 10–5).

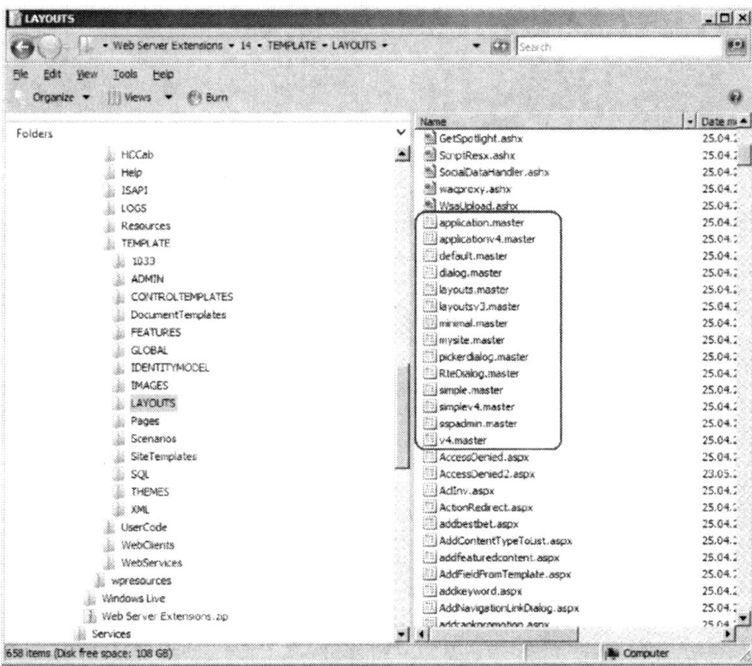

Figure 10–5. Application pages in the LAYOUTS folder

The most important master page for developing application pages, especially in previous versions of SharePoint, is `application.master`. This page has been used in nearly all application pages within the `LAYOUTS` folder. SharePoint 2010 has introduced the new concepts of site and system master pages within your own application pages. These are described later in this chapter, in the "Master Page Tokens" section.

In SharePoint 2007, the placeholders used in the various master page types were different, especially between site and system master pages and application pages. With SharePoint 2010, the placeholders for the site and system master pages and those for the application master pages have been standardized. Table 10–1 gives an overview of the most important placeholders.

***Table 10–1.** Placeholder IDs in Master Pages*

Content Placeholder	Description
`PlaceHolderAdditionalPageHead`	Additional content that needs to be within the `<head>` tag of the page—for example, references to script in stylesheets
`PlaceHolderBodyAreaClass`	Additional body styles in the page header
`PlaceHolderBodyLeftBorder`	Border element for the main page body
`PlaceHolderBodyRightMargin`	Right margin of the main page body
`PlaceHolderCalendarNavigator`	A date picker for navigating in a calendar when a calendar is visible on the page
`PlaceHolderFormDigest`	The form digest security control, which generates a security validation or message digest to help prevent the type of attack whereby a user is tricked into posting data to the server without knowing it.
`PlaceHolderGlobalNavigation`	The global navigation breadcrumb trail
`PlaceHolderHorizontalNav`	Top navigation menu for the page
`PlaceHolderLeftActions`	Bottom of the left navigation area
`PlaceHolderLeftNavBar`	Left navigation area
`PlaceHolderLeftNavBarBorder`	Border element on the left navigation bar
`PlaceHolderLeftNavBarDataSource`	Data source for the left navigation menu
`PlaceHolderLeftNavBarTop`	Top of the left navigation area
`PlaceHolderMain`	The page's main content
`PlaceHolderMiniConsole`	A place to show page-level commands—for example, wiki commands such as Edit Page, History, and Incoming Links

Content Placeholder	Description
`PlaceHolderPageDescription`	Description of the page contents
`PlaceHolderPageImage`	Page icon in the upper-left area of the page
`PlaceHolderPageTitle`	The page `<title>` that is shown in the browser's title bar
`PlaceHolderPageTitleInTitleArea`	Page title shown immediately below the breadcrumb trail.
`PlaceHolderSearchArea`	Search box area
`PlaceHolderSiteName`	Site name
`PlaceHolderTitleAreaClass`	Additional styles in the page header
`PlaceHolderTitleAreaSeparator`	Shadows for the title area
`PlaceHolderTitleBreadcrumb`	Main content breadcrumb area
`PlaceHolderTitleLeftBorder`	Left border of the title area
`PlaceHolderTitleRightMargin`	Right margin of the title area
`PlaceHolderTopNavBar`	Top navigation area
`PlaceHolderUtilityContent`	Extra content that needs to be at the bottom of the page
`SPNavigation`	Empty by default in Windows SharePoint Services (can be used for additional page-editing controls)
`WSSDesignConsole`	The page-editing controls when the page is in Edit mode (after clicking Site Actions ➤ Edit Page)

Figure 10–6 illustrates the layout of the placeholders within the master page.

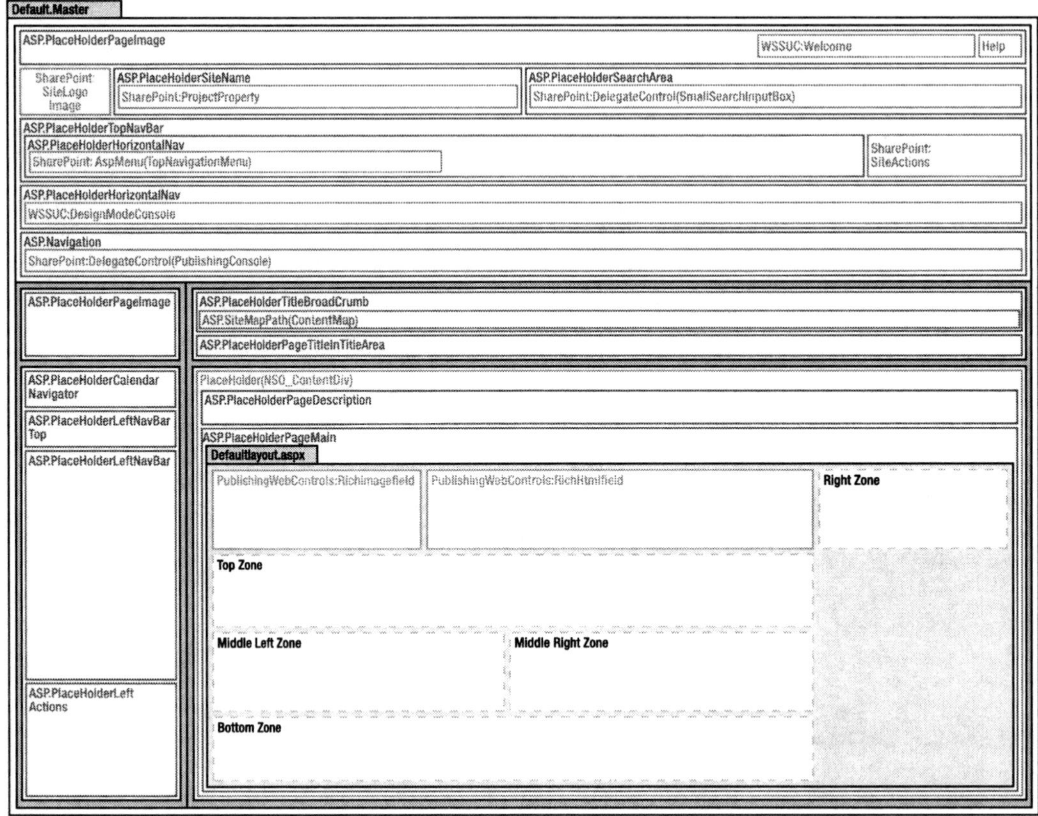

Figure 10–6. Layout of placeholders in a SharePoint master page

Improvements with SharePoint 2010

Master pages in SharePoint 2010 allow much more control over customization and branding of application pages. In previous versions, site administrators were forced to leave users with an inconsistent look and feel between content and application pages, mainly because the master page of the application pages (`application.master`) could only be modified by a system administrator. The largest weakness was the uncertainty about changes in the next SharePoint update or hotfix. There was a slight chance that changes to `application.master` would be overwritten by such an update, and there was no safe way of changing the application pages included in the `LAYOUTS` folder. In order to eliminate this inconsistency, the following matters have been addressed in SharePoint 2010:

- Application pages now use the same master page as content pages.
- Administrators can turn off custom master pages for application pages.
- Content and application pages now contain the same content placeholders.
- Default application pages can be easily redirected.

Master Page Tokens for Application Pages

In previous SharePoint versions, application pages and content pages used different master pages with different content placeholders. The master pages for the application pages could not be changed easily. Most of the application pages used the application.master master page contained in the LAYOUTS folder. The inability to change the master page for application pages created an inconsistent look and feel. With SharePoint 2010, application pages use the same master page as content pages. Hence, the long-awaited support for the ~masterurl/default.master and ~masterurl/custom.master tokens in application pages has been added. This allows a site designer to change the master page for the content pages and have the application pages automatically reflect the same master page appearance.

For example, the @Page directive of the ASP.NET page that shows all lists of a site (_layouts/viewlsts.aspx) now references the system master page (~masterurl/default.master). In the previous SharePoint version, the file viewlsts.aspx started with this directive:

```
<%@ Page Language="C#"
         Inherits="Microsoft.SharePoint.ApplicationPages.ViewListsPage"
         MasterPageFile="~/_layouts/application.master" ...   %>
```

In SharePoint 2010 this has been changed to the following:

```
<%@ Page Language="C#"
         DynamicMasterPageFile="~masterurl/default.master"
         Inherits="Microsoft.SharePoint.ApplicationPages.ViewListsPage" ... %>
```

In order to support referencing the site's master pages, all application pages had to be changed. The tag that referenced the original master page file was removed from the ASPX file. A code-behind file, specifying the site master page, was added. Individual page code was changed to comply with the new master pages as well.

Content placeholder differences between master pages are taken into account by SharePoint 2010. Content placeholders can be inserted or removed, depending on how the master pages use the placeholder. The goal is to maintain as much of the same look and feel as possible.

The content placeholders in custom application pages will need to conform to the site master page. A new DynamicMasterPageFile attribute replaces the old MasterPageFile reference as well.

A deeper look inside that implementation shows that the class Microsoft.SharePoint.WebControls.UnsecuredLayoutsBasePage has been extended with the DynamicMasterPageFile property. This class serves as a base class for LayoutsBasePage, which itself is the base class for most of the application pages, such as ViewListsPage (LAYOUTS/viewlsts.aspx). Examining this class with .NET Reflector shows that during the page initialization (OnPreInit), a new master page handling has been implemented. If the old MasterPageFile property exists, the two common master pages, application.master and simple.master, will be replaced by applicationv4.master and simplev4.master. This enhances compatibility with pages formerly made with SharePoint 2007.

```
string masterPageUrl = this.MasterPageFile.ToLowerInvariant();
if (masterPageUrl != null)
{
    if (!(masterPageUrl == "/_layouts/application.master"))
    {
        if (masterPageUrl == "/_layouts/simple.master")
        {
            this.MasterPageFile = "/_layouts/simplev4.master";
        }
    }
    else
    {
        this.MasterPageFile = "/_layouts/applicationv4.master";
```

```
    }
}
```

In the other case, which is the default for SharePoint, the `MasterPageFile` property is `null` and the new `DynamicMasterPageFile` property contains a dynamic token, such as `~masterurl/default.master`. In this case, the code looks like this:

```
if ((ver <= 3) || !SPControl.GetContextWeb(this.Context).MasterPageReferenceEnabled)
{
    customMasterUrl = this.DetermineMasterPage(ver);
}
else if (((this.DynamicMasterPageFile != null) &&
           SPControl.GetContextWeb(this.Context).MasterPageReferenceEnabled) &&
           ((this.DynamicMasterPageFile.Length > 1) &&
           (this.DynamicMasterPageFile[0] == '~')))
      {
           string str6;
           string str3 = null;
           int index = this.DynamicMasterPageFile.IndexOf('/');
           if (index >= 0)
           {
               str3 = this.DynamicMasterPageFile.Substring(0, index);
           }
           if (((str6 = str3.ToUpperInvariant()) == null)
              || !(str6 == "~MASTERURL"))
           {
               customMasterUrl = null;
           }
           else
           {
               string str7 = this.DynamicMasterPageFile.
                             Substring("~MASTERURL".Length).ToUpperInvariant();
               if (str7 != null)
               {
                  if (!(str7 == "/DEFAULT.MASTER"))
                  {
                     if (str7 == "/CUSTOM.MASTER")
                     {
                        customMasterUrl = SPControl.GetContextWeb(this.Context).
                                          CustomMasterUrl;
                     }
                  }
                  else
                  {
                     customMasterUrl = SPControl.GetContextWeb(this.Context).
                                       MasterUrl;
                  }
               }
           }
}
```

The tokens work as expected. For `~masterurl\default.master`, `SPWeb.MasterUrl` is returned, and for `~masterurl/custom.master`, `SPWeb.CustomMasterUrl` is returned.

Of interest in this code snippet is that, if the SharePoint version is 3 or below (2007 or 2003) or the property MasterPageReferenceEnabled is set to false, the method DetermineMasterPage is called. It looks like this:

```
protected internal string DetermineMasterPage(int ver)
{
   switch (ver)
   {
      case 1:
      case 2:
      case 3:
          return "/_layouts/layoutsv3.master";
   }
    return "/_layouts/v4.master";
}
```

That's the mechanism to use default layout master pages for application pages.

Safeguards for Application Pages

The DetermineMasterPage method is also used for a new SharePoint feature to "autorepair" master pages that contain errors. If, for instance, a custom control within a user-defined master page throws an exception, all the application pages that use this master page will become broken and inaccessible. To overcome this, a detection mechanism for master page errors is implemented that switches automatically to a working master page if such an error occurs.

However, allowing application pages to reference dangerous master pages that can contain any custom code has potential security implications. There are some critical pages that have safeguards for broken master pages. If a broken master page is detected, the application page will automatically use the default master page. Pages implementing this feature include

- RecycleBin.aspx
- ReGhost.aspx
- ReqAcc.aspx
- Settings.aspx

These files will try to load the dynamic master page and fall back to a ghosted version of the default master page if an error occurs. If the default master page fails to load, the user will be notified of the error to aid further investigation. This behavior is disabled for postback events. If you want to use this safeguard functionality for your own application pages, you merely set the UnsecuredLayoutsBasePage.RequiresHighReliability property to true.

Turning Off Dynamic Master Page Support

Dynamic master pages can be turned off at the web application level. This new option is controlled by the MasterPageReferenceEnabled property of the SPWeb object. It returns the value from the current web application. A code snippet for this property follows:

```
public bool MasterPageReferenceEnabled
{
    get
    {
        return this.Site.WebApplication.MasterPageReferenceEnabled;
    }
}
```

Compiled application pages can now reference user-customized master pages, which are untrusted and may be compiled or not. By introducing the dynamic master page handler (the DynamicMasterPageFile attribute of the page), the master page is evaluated in a way that is transparent to the page parser filter, which usually prohibits referencing uncompiled and therefore untrusted master pages. Hence, by using the MasterPageReferenceEnabled property in conjunction with the DynamicMasterPageFile property, application pages are allowed to reference any master pages.

Redirecting Default Application Pages

Imagine you wish to implement a custom error page or need to change the layout of the default login page. For such needs, SharePoint 2010 introduces the ability to redirect the seven default application pages to custom application pages. The seven pages are

- /_LAYOUTS/AccessDenied.aspx
- /_LAYOUTS/Confirmation.aspx
- /_LAYOUTS/Error.aspx
- /_LAYOUTS/Login.aspx
- /_LAYOUTS/ReqAcc.aspx
- /_LAYOUTS/SignOut.aspx
- /_LAYOUTS/WebDeleted.aspx

In order to replace those existing application pages, a replacement page must be created and stored in the LAYOUTS directory on the server. This can be accomplished by deploying a replacement page within a feature and a feature event receiver that sets the mapping, for instance. For implementation, the SPWebApplication class provides a method called UpdateMappedPage. By using this method, you can map the default application pages to custom ones:

```
using (SPWeb web = SPContext.Current.Web)
{
    web.Site.WebApplication.UpdateMappedPage(
        SPWebApplication.SPCustomPage.AccessDenied,"/_LAYOUTS/MyAccessDenied.aspx");
}
```

This example maps the default page for AccessDenied to a custom application page MyAccessDenied.aspx. The UpdateMappedPage method expects the enumeration type SPWebApplication.SPCustomPage as its first parameter. This enumeration has the following possible values: AccessDenied, Confirmation, Error, Login, None, RequestAccess, Signout, and WebDeleted. To retrieve custom mappings, you can use the method SPWebApplication.GetMappedPage. The redirection itself is located within the application runtime inside the Microsoft.SharePoint.ApplicationRuntime.SPVirtualPathProvider class. The SPVirtualPathProvider.GetFile method calls the SPLayoutsMappedFile.GetFile method that looks up the custom page mappings. Here's a snippet of the SPVirtualPathProvider.GetFile method:

```
public override VirtualFile GetFile(string virtualPath)
{
    VirtualFile file = null;
    if ((virtualPath == null) || SPRequestModule.IsExcludedPath(virtualPath))
    {
        file = SPLayoutsMappedFile.GetFile(virtualPath, base.Previous);
        if (file == null)
        {
```

```
                file = base.Previous.GetFile(virtualPath);
            }
            return file;
        }
    }
```

The SPLayoutsMappedFile.GetFile method calls the private method MapLayoutsVirtualPath, which looks up the requested virtual path by using the GetMappedPage method of the SPWebApplication class. The implementation of GetMappedPage used here takes the page URL as a parameter and ensures that the mapped URL will be returned. For example, if /_LAYOUTS/AccessDenied.aspx is the first parameter, it returns /_LAYOUTS/MyAccessDenied.aspx if this mapping exists.

```
private static string MapLayoutsVirtualPath(string virtualPath)
{
    string str = null;
    if (virtualPath == null)
    {
        return str;
    }
    SPWebApplication context = SPWebApplication.Context;
    if (context == null)
    {
        return null;
    }
    return context.GetMappedPage(virtualPath);
}
```

Dialog Master Pages

Dialog master pages (dialog.master) reside in the LAYOUTS folder, too. They are commonly used for pop-up dialogs, such as the various picker dialogs used to select data.

An example is the Select People and Groups dialog, shown in Figure 10–7.

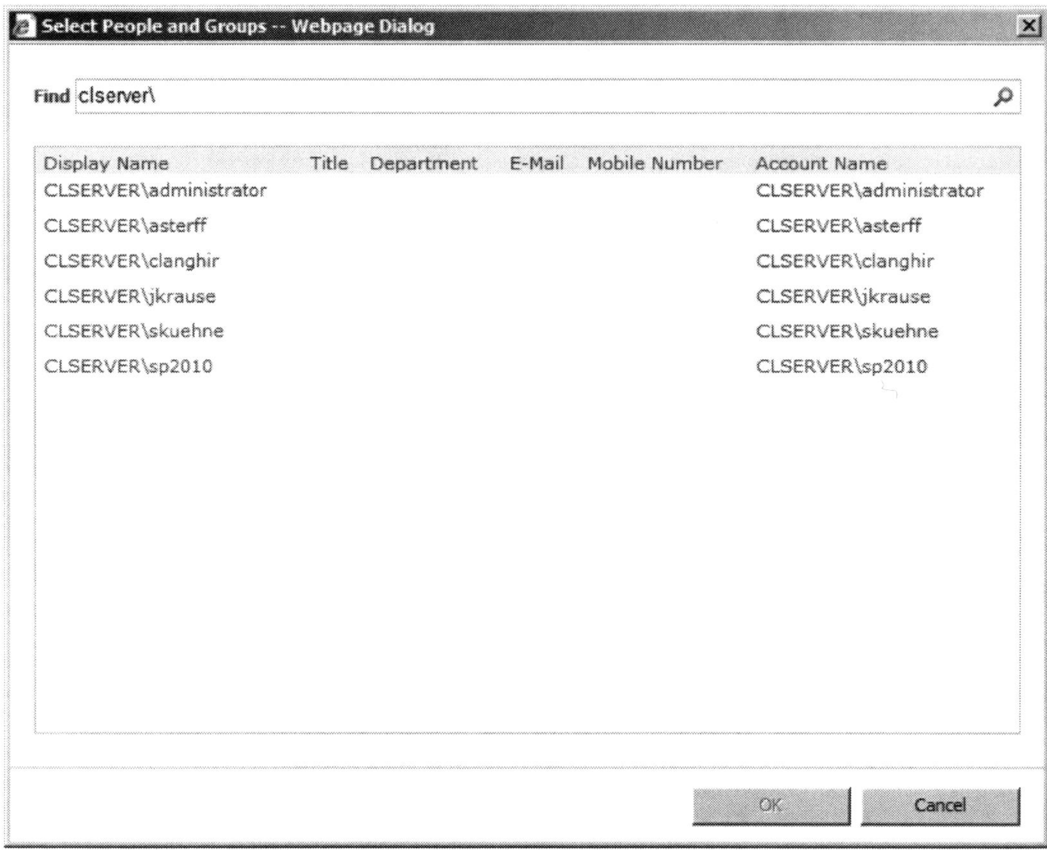

Figure 10–7. *The Select People and Groups dialog is based on dialog.master*

If you need to build a custom dialog for your SharePoint application, you should reference the `dialog.master` page. It contains several relevant ASP.NET content placeholders for your use depending on your specific requirements (see Table 10–2).

Table 10–2. Placeholders in dialog.master

Placeholder	Description
PlaceHolderDialogHeaderSectionMaster	Contains the dialog header, including the three placeholders for an image, a description, and a help link.
PlaceHolderDialogImage	Contains the dialog image in the upper-left corner.
PlaceHolderDialogDescription	Contains the description text for the dialog.
PlaceHolderHelpLink	Contains the help link in the upper-right corner.
PlaceHolderDialogBodySection	Contains the dialog body.
PlaceHolderDialogBodyHeaderSection	Contains the header within the dialog body.
PlaceHolderDialogBodyAreaClass	Contains the class name for the main body section. The default value is ms-dialogBodyMain.
PlaceHolderDialogBodyMainSection	Contains the main content. For developers, this is the placeholder to insert content.
PlaceHolderDialogBodyFooterMainSection	Contains the footer within the dialog body.
PlaceHolderDialogPrebuttonSection	Contains content that is displayed to the left of the buttons at the bottom.
PlaceHolderAdditionalPreButton	Contains additional buttons to the left of the default buttons.
PlaceHolderAdditionalButton	Contains additional buttons to the right of the default buttons.

In addition to PlaceHolderDialogBodyMainSection, the placeholders at the bottom of the dialog are also important. As shown in the following simplified extract of dialog.master, there are various placeholders, such as PlaceHolderAdditionalPreButton and PlaceHolderAdditionalButton, next to the OkButton and CancelButton placeholders.

```
<!-- Dialog Button Section Begins -->
<tr id="buttonRow">
     <td width="100%" height="0%" class="ms-dialogButtonSection" style="">
          <table id='Buttons' cellspacing="0" cellpadding="0"
                width="100%" border="0">
               <tr height="10"><td colspan="3"></td></tr>
               <tr >
                    <td width="100%" colspan="3">
                         <asp:ContentPlaceHolder
                              id="PlaceHolderDialogPrebuttonSection"
```

```
                                        runat="server"/>
                              </td>
                         </tr>
                         <tr>
                              <td width="100%">
                                   <asp:ContentPlaceHolder
                                           id="PlaceHolderAdditionalPreButton"
                                           runat="server">
                                         
                                   </asp:ContentPlaceHolder>
                              </td>
                              <td class="ms-dialogButtonCell" style="padding-right:15px">
                                   <asp:Button UseSubmitBehavior="false" runat="server"
                                        class="ms-ButtonHeightWidth"
                                        OnClick="OkButton_Click" Text="Ok" id="OkButton"/>
                              </td>
                              <td class="ms-dialogButtonCell" style="padding-right:10px">
                                   <input type="button" id="CancelButton"
                                          class="ms-ButtonHeightWidth"
                                          value="Cancel" onclick="doCancel();" />
                              </td>
                              <td class="ms-dialogButtonCell" style="padding-right:10px">
                                   <asp:ContentPlaceHolder
                                          id="PlaceHolderAdditionalButton" runat="server"/>
                              </td>
                         </tr>
                         <tr height="10"><td colspan="3"></td></tr>
                    </table>
          </td>
     </tr>
<!-- Dialog Button Section Ends -->
```

The following example for a custom dialog page inherits from System.Web.UI.Page. Since the OK button belongs to dialog.master, it is not directly accessible within the page. You have to first cast the master page property to DialogMaster before you can access the OK button. Then you can attach a Click event and write your own custom actions for it.

```
public class MyCustomDialog : System.Web.UI.Page
{
    protected override void OnInit(EventArgs e)
    {
        ((DialogMaster)this.Page.Master).OkButton.Click += btnOk_Click;
        base.OnInit(e);
    }
    protected void btnOk_Click(object sender, EventArgs e)
    {
        // do something
    }
}
```

Content Pages vs. Application Pages

ASP.NET pages within SharePoint that use site or system master pages are commonly known as content pages. In addition to these content pages, there are application pages that focus on special functions for the SharePoint application rather than content.

Content pages are designed to be customizable. SharePoint users with appropriate rights (designer) are allowed to modify those pages according to their needs using SharePoint Designer. For security reasons, those pages are not permitted to contain inline code or unsafe controls. A designer is only allowed to change basic settings, such as the alignment or some attributes of placeholders. In addition, you may insert custom web controls (inherited from `System.Web.UI.WebControls.WebControl`) that are explicitly marked as `SafeControl` in `web.config`. Content pages are saved directly into the content database.

In contrast to content pages, application pages may use inline code. Nearly all application pages shipped with SharePoint contain a reference to a class that is defined in the `Microsoft.SharePoint.ApplicationPages.dll` assembly (`%SharePointRoot%\14\CONFIG\BIN`). The following excerpt is from the file `LAYOUTS/viewlsts.aspx`:

```
<%@ Page Language="C#"
    DynamicMasterPageFile="~masterurl/default.master"
    Inherits="Microsoft.SharePoint.ApplicationPages.ViewListsPage"
    EnableViewState="false"
    EnableViewStateMac="false"    %>
```

The page class `ViewListsPage` is derived from the `Microsoft.SharePoint.WebControls.LayoutsBasePage` class. A detailed description of how to create your own application pages can be found in Chapter 3.

Conclusion

SharePoint 2010 provides two master pages that are used in different scenarios. While master pages are designed for using with the old and new UIs, there are also some simplified master pages, namely `minimal.master` and `simple.master`.

The most important master page for SharePoint 2010 is `v4.master`. This master page can be found in the directory `%SharePointRoot%\14\TEMPLATE\GLOBAL` and also in the directory `%SharePointRoot%\14\TEMPLATE\LAYOUTS`. The two files are identical copies, where the first one is used as the default master page (e.g., for blank sites or team sites) and the second one is intended to be used by application pages. The master page `v4.master` provides the ribbon bar and other web controls, such as menus, navigations, stylesheets, and JavaScript references.

An additional master page, used for example by Office web applications and the search site, is `minimal.master`, which is likewise stored in both the `GLOBAL` and the `LAYOUTS` directories. It is, as the name implies, a very minimalistic master page that has next to nothing on it. It doesn't even have navigation. Very similar to `minimal.master`, SharePoint offers the `simple.master` and the `simplev4.master` pages. These master pages are used particularly for login and error application pages residing in the `LAYOUTS` directory. The second one (`simplev4.master`) is automatically used with SharePoint 2010, even if the first one is referenced explicitly (look at section "Master Page Tokens for Application Pages" in this chapter for more information).

■ **Tip** A good starting point to get a better understanding of master pages is the CodePlex project Starter Master Pages for SharePoint 2010, published by Randy Drisgill. Check this URL: `http://startermasterpages.codeplex.com`.

Master Page Tokens

SharePoint content pages usually refer to master pages from the SharePoint master page gallery. You might assume that there would be hard-coded paths inside each content page to the master page. However, it would be suboptimal if the whole master page needed to be changed (e.g., from `default.master` to `mycompany.master`)—every content page would have to be modified. To avoid this, SharePoint uses tokens, which are dynamically replaced at runtime.

Dynamic Tokens

SharePoint offers two tokens that are dynamically replaced by the appropriate values of the current `SPWeb` object: `SPWeb.MasterUrl` and `SPWeb.CustomMasterUrl` (see Table 10–3).

Table 10–3. SharePoint Dynamic Master Page Tokens

Token	Object Property	Synonyms
`~masterurl/default.master`	`SPWeb.MasterUrl`	Default master page, system master page
`~masterurl/custom.master`	`SPWeb.CustomMasterUrl`	Custom master page, site master page

The dynamic token `~masterurl/default.master` is usually used in the forms and views of a site. In contrast to the previous SharePoint versions, SharePoint 2010 uses this dynamic token heavily—it is in most of the application pages, such as `viewlsts.aspx`. The token is embedded in the `@Page` directive as follows:

```
<%@Page language="C#" MasterPageFile="~masterurl/default.master" ... @>
```

When calling an ASP.NET page, SharePoint automatically replaces the token `~masterurl/default.master` at runtime with the value of the property `MasterUrl` of the `SPWeb` object. If you want to change the master page for this token with the SharePoint GUI, navigate to Site Settings ➤ Look and Feel ➤ Site Master Page.

■ **Note** The menu item Site Settings ➤ Look and Feel ➤ Master Page is not available if you use SharePoint Foundation only, since this feature is one of the publishing features provided by SharePoint Server. Developers particularly need to know this, because not all SharePoint applications are based on the standard or enterprise versions of SharePoint Server. The only way to change the master page when using SharePoint Foundation is via the object model (`SPWeb.MasterUrl`).

The following example shows how to access the `SPWeb.MasterUrl` property using the object model:

```
using (SPWeb web = SPContext.Current.Web)
{
   web.MasterUrl = "/_catalogs/masterpage/mysystem.master";
   web.Update();
}
```

Figure 10–8 shows how to change the `SPWeb.MasterUrl` property through the SharePoint UI.

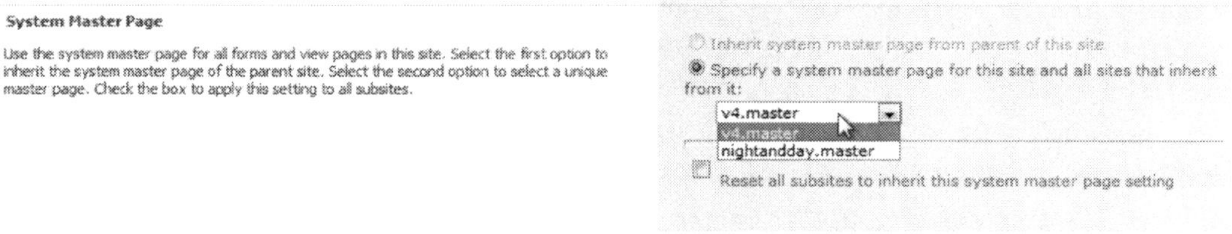

Figure 10–8. *Choosing a system master page (only possible if the Publishing feature is activated)*

The second dynamic token, `~masterurl/custom.master`, works in a similar manner to `default.master`. The `@Page` directive of an ASP.NET page looks like this:

```
<%@Page language="C#" MasterPageFile="~masterurl/custom.master" ... @>
```

At runtime, this token is replaced with the contents of the `CustomMasterUrl` property of the `SPWeb` object. You can change the master page specified for this token by browsing to Site Settings ➤ Look and Feel ➤ Master Page (see Figure 10–9), or by using the object model, as follows:

```
using (SPWeb web = SPContext.Current.Web)
{
    web.CustomMasterUrl = "/_catalogs/masterpage/mysite.master";
    web.Update();
}
```

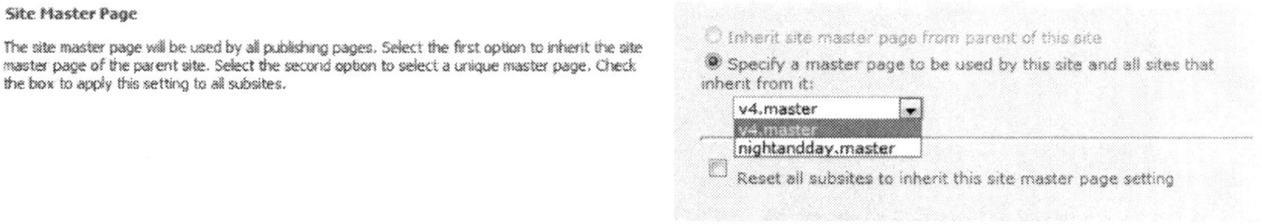

Figure 10–9. *Choosing a site master page (only possible if the Publishing feature is activated)*

Static Tokens

Static tokens are direct references to master pages. This means that SharePoint will replace these tokens with the corresponding URL paths (see Table 10–4).

Table 10–4. SharePoint Static Master Page Tokens

Token	Replacement Example
`~site/mycompany.master`	`http://mySiteCollection/mySite/mycompany.master`
`~sitecollection/mycompany.master`	`http://mySiteCollection/mycompany.master`

Assuming your ASPX page is at `http://mySiteCollection/mySite/default.aspx` and your static token is `~sitecollection/mycompany.master`, then your master page file has to be stored at this URL:

```
http://mySiteCollection/mycompany.master
```

On the other hand, if your static token is `~site/mycompany.master`, then your master page has to be stored here:

```
http://mySiteCollection/mySite/mymaster.master
```

Master Page Gallery

SharePoint master pages have their own library, called the *master page gallery*. This is a location on the site where a site administrator can access and modify SharePoint master pages. To access a SharePoint master page gallery, go to a SharePoint site collection, and then to the site settings, and click "Master pages," as shown in Figure 10–10.

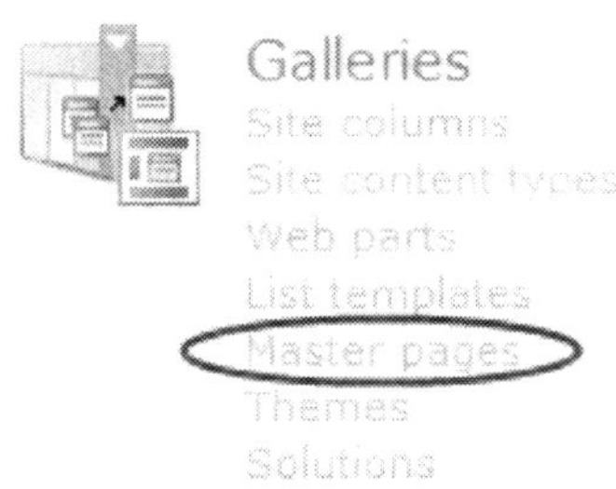

Figure 10–10. Browsing to the master page gallery of a site collection

The advantage of storing master pages in the SharePoint master page gallery is that you have easy access to the master pages. Furthermore, you can make changes to a master page and upload it to the master page gallery when you are done. If your content page already refers to that master page, the end user will see your master page changes as soon as it is checked in.

In a standalone ASP.NET application (without SharePoint), the master page typically lives on the file system, and a direct reference is made to the physical file. In SharePoint there are two different places where master pages are stored:

- Site and system master pages are stored in the master page gallery (within the content database).
- Application master pages are stored in the file system under `%SharePointRoot%\14\TEMPLATE\LAYOUTS`.

■ **Note** Master pages in the master page gallery are not allowed to use code at all. Only layout changes and web controls that are marked as `SafeControls` in the `web.config` file are allowed, for security reasons.

To reference master pages that reside in master page galleries, you have to use static and dynamic master page tokens.

Example: Applying a Master Page Recursively

You'll often need to apply a custom master page to your SharePoint site and all the sites within it. Sometimes you'll even need to apply your master page to all the site collections contained within all your web applications operating within a farm. This is easy to accomplish when you are customizing a site for the first time, since most subwebs are set up to inherit from their parent site.

Consequently, when you customize the parent site, it will apply to all the children. It's more challenging, however, when a site collection has already been in use, and you want to create a new custom page that applies to all the child sites, even if someone has explicitly declared not to inherit the master page from the parent site. Furthermore, you have to consider what happens when you deactivate the feature, assuming you realize this functionality is a feature. When the feature is deactivated, does that mean that you have to reset all the sites back to the `default.master` master page, thereby erasing all the customizations people have made?

This is exactly what the following example illustrates. It creates a custom master page as a feature. It includes code that applies the master page to all the child sites, ensures that the feature can be successfully uninstalled, and reverts all the sites back to their original master page.

```
public override void FeatureActivated(SPFeatureReceiverProperties properties)
{
    SPSite site = properties.Feature.Parent as SPSite;
    if (site == null) return;
    String customizedMasterUrl = "/_catalogs/masterpage/MyCustomMasterPage.master";

    SPWeb rootWeb = site.RootWeb;
    rootWeb.AllProperties["OldMasterUrl"] = rootWeb.MasterUrl;
    rootWeb.AllProperties["OldCustomMasterUrl"] = rootWeb.CustomMasterUrl;
    rootWeb.MasterUrl = customizedMasterUrl;
    rootWeb.CustomMasterUrl = customizedMasterUrl;
    rootWeb.Update();
    foreach (SPWeb subWeb in rootWeb.Webs)
    {
        ProcessSubWebs(subWeb, true);
    }
}

private void ProcessSubWebs(SPWeb web, bool isActivation)
{
    if (isActivation)
    {
        web.AllProperties["OldMasterUrl"] = web.MasterUrl;
        web.AllProperties["OldCustomMasterUrl"] = web.CustomMasterUrl;
        web.MasterUrl = web.Site.RootWeb.MasterUrl;
        web.CustomMasterUrl = web.Site.RootWeb.MasterUrl;
```

```
    }
    else
    {
        DeactivateWeb(web);
    }
    web.Update();

    foreach (SPWeb subWeb in web.Webs)
    {
        ProcessSubWebs(subWeb, isActivation);
    }
}
```

The example code ensures that the feature's parent (in this case, site collection) exists. If not, it exits having done nothing. The next step is to record the current master and custom master pages for the top-level site. Properties are added to SPWeb to persist this information.

■ **Note** You should not use the `SPWeb.Properties` property, as this will return only a subset of properties. Instead, make sure you use `SPWeb.AllProperties`. When adding a property to the property bag, if it doesn't exist, it will be created, and if it already exists, it will be overwritten.

Next, the root-level site's `MasterUrl` and `CustomMasterUrl` properties can be reset. After that, call `SPWeb.Update` to save the changes. Then you need to recursively iterate through all the child sites and point them to this top-level site's master page.

The next step is to write code to deactivate the feature. This is slightly more complicated because there are several manual checks to implement. To revert the deployment of the solution package back to the original state, you have to manually set all the subsites back to their original master pages (after you've determined if that master page still exists), and then ensure that the custom master page is deleted correctly.

```
public override void FeatureDeactivating(SPFeatureReceiverProperties properties)
{
    SPSite site = properties.Feature.Parent as SPSite;
    if (site == null) return;

    SPWeb rootWeb = site.RootWeb;
    DeactivateWeb(rootWeb);
    rootWeb.Update();

    foreach (SPWeb subWeb in rootWeb.Webs)
    {
        ProcessSubWebs(subWeb, false);
    }

    if (rootWeb.MasterUrl != customizedMasterUrl)
    {
        try
        {
            bool fileExists = rootWeb.GetFile(customizedMasterUrl).Exists;
```

```
            SPFile file = rootWeb.GetFile(customizedMasterUrl);
            SPFolder masterPageGallery = file.ParentFolder;

            SPFolder temp = masterPageGallery.SubFolders.Add("Temp");
            file.MoveTo(temp.Url + "/" + file.Name);
            temp.Delete();
        }
        catch (ArgumentException)
        {
            return;
        }
    }
}

private void DeactivateWeb(SPWeb web)
{
    String defaultMasterUrl = "/_catalogs/masterpage/default.master";

    if (web.AllProperties.ContainsKey("OldMasterUrl"))
    {
        string oldMasterUrl = web.AllProperties["OldMasterUrl"].ToString();
        try
        {
            bool fileExists = web.GetFile(oldMasterUrl).Exists;
            web.MasterUrl = oldMasterUrl;
        }
        catch (ArgumentException)
        {
            web.MasterUrl = defaultMasterUrl;
        }

        string oldCustomUrl = web.AllProperties["OldCustomMasterUrl"].ToString();
        try
        {
            bool fileExists = web.GetFile(oldCustomUrl).Exists;
            web.CustomMasterUrl =
                    web.AllProperties["OldCustomMasterUrl"].ToString();
        }
        catch (ArgumentException)
        {
            web.CustomMasterUrl = defaultMasterUrl;
        }

        web.AllProperties.Remove("OldMasterUrl");
        web.AllProperties.Remove("OldCustomMasterUrl");
    }
    else
    {
        web.MasterUrl = defaultMasterUrl;
        web.CustomMasterUrl = defaultMasterUrl;
    }
}
```

Begin by checking that the parent site collection exists. Next, deactivate the top-level site. Inside `DeactivateWeb`, check if the `OldMasterUrl` property still exists in the web's properties collection. If it doesn't, there is no alternative but to revert back to `default.master`. If the `OldMasterUrl` property exists, you have to make sure that the file it points to still exists.

■ **Note** Although it may seem intuitive that accessing the `SPFile.Exists` property would return `True` or `False`, in fact, if a file doesn't exist, it throws an `ArgumentException` error.

As previously described, you need to follow the same procedure for the `OldCustomMasterUrl` property. If either original master page doesn't exist in SharePoint any longer at its old location, revert it back to `default.master`. Finally, you can delete the custom properties because they are no longer needed. Then you can iterate through this same process for every child site.

Going back to the `DeactivateFeature` method, the next step is to delete the custom master page from the `/_catalogs/masterpage` directory. Unfortunately, there seems to be a bug in SharePoint where you cannot delete a master page that was installed by a feature, even if no reference to that master page exists. It will throw an error saying, "This item cannot be deleted because it is still referenced by other pages." A quick workaround is to move the master page to another folder and then delete that folder.

Navigation

SharePoint comes with several navigation artifacts, all of which are aimed at ensuring a great end-user experience. For developers, it is especially important to understand the underlying SharePoint navigation concepts, in case one day you need to build your own navigation control or extend the existing controls. On the next few pages you'll be introduced to the different navigation elements and their usage.

Navigation Controls

SharePoint provides several navigation controls that are usually defined within master pages. There are four main navigation controls that are rendered on pages by default (see Figure 10–11):

- Top link bar navigation
- Quick launch navigation
- Breadcrumb navigation
- Tree view navigation

■ **Note** Tree view navigation is turned off by default. Site administrators can show or hide it by going to Site Settings ➤ Look and Feel ➤ "Tree view."

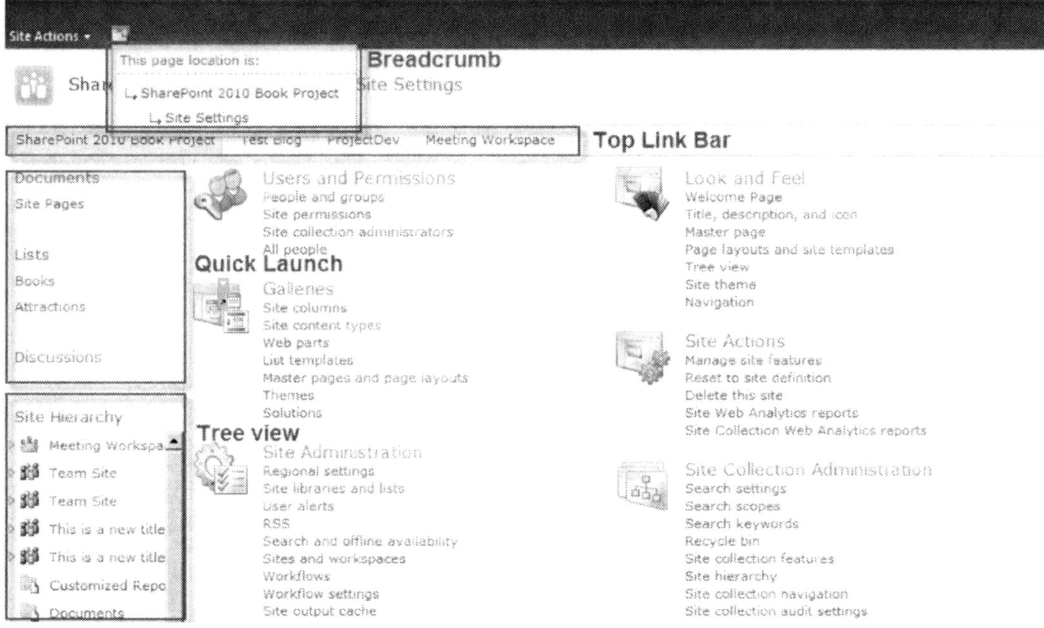

Figure 10–11. SharePoint navigation controls

The SharePoint navigation controls are fully based on the data-driven navigation concepts from ASP.NET. Hence, a navigation control requires a site map provider that supplies the data structure to be filtered and displayed.

Top Link Bar Navigation

The top link bar normally appears at the top of each page. If the page contains a ribbon tab, the top link bar is placed within the Browse tab of the ribbon bar. From a technical perspective, the top link bar is a navigation menu containing links usually to sites that are at least one level below the current site in the site hierarchy. Each SharePoint site (`SPWeb`) can either have its own top link bar or inherit the top link bar from its parent site.

Site administrators are able to customize the navigation links in the top link bar. New navigation link items can be added and existing ones can be modified and sorted (see Figure 10–12).

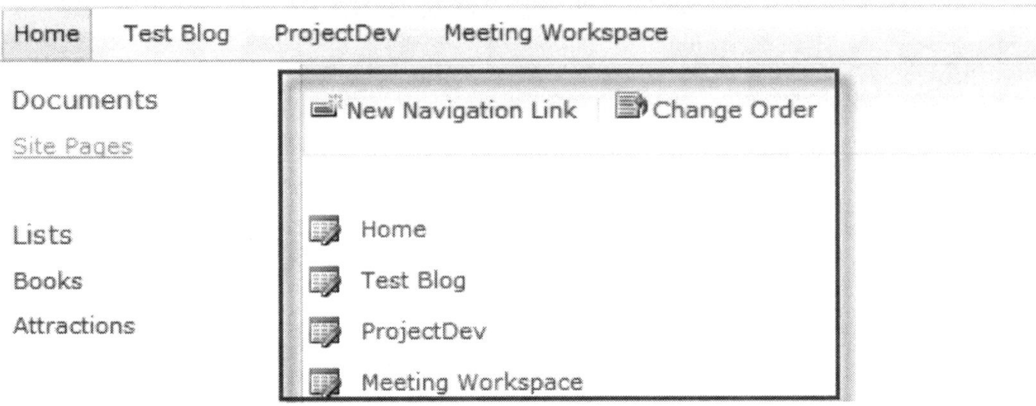

Figure 10–12. *Customizing the top link bar using the UI*

When adding navigation link items, those items are treated internally as *external links.* Otherwise, if you create a new site and it is added automatically to the top link bar by SharePoint, then it is regarded as an *internal link*. The difference between external and internal links is in the security-trimming functionality. External links are always displayed, regardless of whether the user is authorized to view the page or not. In contrast, internal links are security-trimmed. That means that internal links are only displayed if the user is authorized to view the link's destination page. It is not possible to create internal links manually by using the SharePoint UI, but you can easily overcome that by using the API, as shown in Listing 10–1.

Listing 10–1. *Adding Internal and External Links to the Top Link Bar*

```
using (SPWeb web = SPContext.Current.Web)
{
        SPNavigationNode newInternalNode =
                new SPNavigationNode("New Home", "default.aspx", false);

        SPNavigationNode newExternalNode =
                new SPNavigationNode("BING", "http://www.bing.com", true);

        web.Navigation.TopNavigationBar.AddAsLast(newInternalNode);
        web.Navigation.TopNavigationBar.AddAsLast(newExternalNode);

        web.Update();
}
```

As shown in Listing 10–1, the constructor of the `SPNavigationNode` class requires `linkTitle`, `URL`, and a Boolean value for `isExternal`, which indicates whether the navigation link should be internal (`false`) or external (`true`).

■ **Tip** The default UI for SharePoint Foundation sites does not allow managing a top navigation hierarchy. Only a flat list of navigation links is supported. To work around this, you can use the object model and nest a couple of `SPNavigationNode` instances to build a hierarchy. The web control itself supports hierarchies and displays them using flyout menus.

Within the `v4.master` master page, the top link bar is, by default, defined as follows:

```
<SharePoint:AspMenu
        Id="TopNavigationMenuV4"
        Runat="server"
        EnableViewState="false"
        DataSourceID="topSiteMap"
        UseSimpleRendering="true"
        UseSeparateCss="false"
        Orientation="Horizontal"
        StaticDisplayLevels="2"
        MaximumDynamicDisplayLevels="1"
        SkipLinkText=""
        CssClass="s4-tn" />
```

The properties `StaticDisplayLevels` and `MaximumDynamicDisplayLevels` specify how the navigation control renders hierarchies. The first property defines how many hierarchy levels should be rendered without flyout menus. The second property defines that, beginning from the third level (`StaticDisplayLevels+1`), one level (the third) will be rendered within a flyout menu. Another interesting property is `UseSimpleRendering`. When this property is set to `true`, the SharePoint navigation menu is rendered using a simple HTML list (with `UL` and `LI` elements) instead of using complex nested `<div>` and `<table>` tags. The resulting HTML is clean, short, and easy to understand.

The data source that defines the SharePoint navigation provider and the starting node ID looks like this:

```
<asp:SiteMapDataSource
        ShowStartingNode="False"
        SiteMapProvider="SPNavigationProvider"
        Id="topSiteMap"
        runat="server"
        StartingNodeUrl="sid:1002"/>
```

The `StartingNodeUrl` property points to the top link bar, which is represented by the hard-coded value `sid:1002`.

Quick Launch Navigation

The quick launch is intended for navigation within a site and usually contains links to lists and libraries. The quick launch navigation usually appears on the left of each page in a site.

To customize the quick launch navigation, you can use the SharePoint UI (see Figure 10–13).

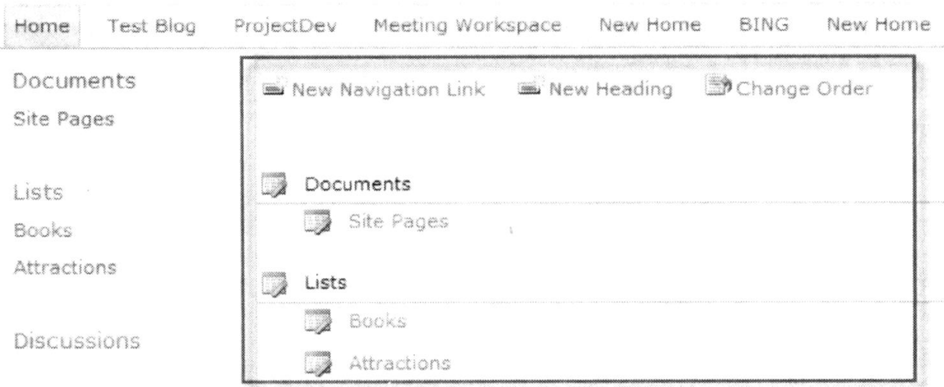

***Figure 10–13.** Customize the quick launch navigation through the SharePoint UI.*

The quick launch navigation works in a very similar manner to the top link bar navigation, as described previously. In comparison to the top link bar, the SharePoint UI supports at least two hierarchy levels: *heading* and *navigation link*. Internally, these two levels are just normal, nested `SPNavigationNode` elements. To access the quick launch programmatically, you can use the following line:

```
SPNavigationNodeCollection allNodes = web.Navigation.QuickLaunch;
```

As with the top link bar, you can easily add, modify, or remove navigation link items. You can also overcome the limitation of two hierarchy levels by working with nested `SPNavigationNode` instances. The web control definition in the `v4.master` master page is quite similar to that for the top link bar. The differences are shown in bold in the following code.

```
<SharePoint:AspMenu
        Id="V4QuickLaunchMenu"
        Runat="server"
        EnableViewState="false"
        DataSourceID="QuickLaunchSiteMap"
        UseSimpleRendering="true"
        UseSeparateCss="false"
        Orientation="Vertical"
        StaticDisplayLevels="2"
        MaximumDynamicDisplayLevels="0"
        SkipLinkText=""
        CssClass="s4-ql"/>
```

The property `MaximumDynamicDisplayLevels` is set to `0`. This means that flyout menus are deactivated by default. You have to manually modify this property in the master page (e.g., via SharePoint Designer) to use flyout menus.

The data source for the quick launch navigation points to the `StartingNodeUrl` value `sid:1025`, which represents the quick launch, as shown here:

```
<asp:SiteMapDataSource
       ShowStartingNode="False"
       SiteMapProvider="SPNavigationProvider"
```

```
        Id="QuickLaunchSiteMap"
        runat="server"
        StartingNodeUrl="sid:1025"/>
```

Breadcrumb Navigation

The breadcrumb navigation displays a hierarchical path from the current navigation position to the root. In the v4.master page, the breadcrumb trail is defined using a PopoutMenu web control:

```
<SharePoint:PopoutMenu
        runat="server"
        ID="GlobalBreadCrumbNavPopout"
        IconUrl="/_layouts/images/fgimg.png"
        IconOffsetX=0
        IconOffsetY=112
        IconWidth=16
        IconHeight=16
        AnchorCss="s4-breadcrumb-anchor"
        AnchorOpenCss="s4-breadcrumb-anchor-open"
        MenuCss="s4-breadcrumb-menu">

<div class="s4-breadcrumb-top">
   <asp:Label runat="server" CssClass="s4-breadcrumb-header" Text="This page location is:" />
</div>

<asp:ContentPlaceHolder id="PlaceHolderTitleBreadcrumb" runat="server">
        <SharePoint:ListSiteMapPath
             runat="server"
             SiteMapProviders="SPSiteMapProvider,SPContentMapProvider"
             RenderCurrentNodeAsLink="false"
             PathSeparator=""
             CssClass="s4-breadcrumb"
             NodeStyle-CssClass="s4-breadcrumbNode"
             CurrentNodeStyle-CssClass="s4-breadcrumbCurrentNode"
             RootNodeStyle-CssClass="s4-breadcrumbRootNode"
             NodeImageOffsetX=0
             NodeImageOffsetY=321
             NodeImageWidth=16
             NodeImageHeight=16
             NodeImageUrl="/_layouts/images/fgimg.png"
             HideInteriorRootNodes="true"
             SkipLinkText="" />
</asp:ContentPlaceHolder>

</SharePoint:PopoutMenu>
```

As you can see, the breadcrumb navigation is built up from the two site map providers SPSiteMapProvider and SPContentMapProvider. These providers are explained later on in this chapter.

Modifying the breadcrumb navigation is only recommended if you plan to implement your own navigation provider.

■ **Note** Usually, the built-in SharePoint application pages in the `LAYOUTS` folder override the `PlaceHolderTitleBreadcrumb` placeholder and provide a `ListSiteMapPath` control with a small change to the `SiteMapProviders` property: `SiteMapProviders="SPSiteMapProvider,SPXmlContentMapProvider"`. The `SPXmlContentMapProvider` class ensures the correct breadcrumb navigation within application pages. (Also see the section "The SPXmlContentMapProvider Class" later in this chapter.)

Tree View Navigation

The tree view navigation displays the site contents—such as lists, libraries, and sites—that are below the current site in a hierarchical structure. It usually appears under the quick launch navigation on the left of a page. Notice that the tree view navigation is turned off by default. Site administrators can control the visibility of the tree view under Site Settings ➤ Look and Feel ➤ "Tree view." An excerpt of the `v4.master` master page contains the following definition for the tree view navigation:

```
<SharePoint:SPHierarchyDataSourceControl
 runat="server"
 id="TreeViewDataSourceV4"
 RootContextObject="Web"
 IncludeDiscussionFolders="true"
/>

  <Sharepoint:SPTreeView
        id="WebTreeViewV4"
        runat="server"
        ShowLines="false"
        DataSourceId="TreeViewDataSourceV4"
        ExpandDepth="0"
        SelectedNodeStyle-CssClass="ms-tvselected"
        NodeStyle-CssClass="ms-navitem"
        SkipLinkText=""
        NodeIndent="12"
        ExpandImageUrl="/_layouts/images/tvclosed.png"
        CollapseImageUrl="/_layouts/images/tvopen.png"
        NoExpandImageUrl="/_layouts/images/tvblank.gif" />
```

The `SPTreeView` web control is populated with the data source `TreeViewDataSourceV4`, which provides the property `RootContextObject="Web"`. The tree view initially renders all the subsites of the current site (`SPWeb.Webs`), followed by the libraries and lists, and finishing with the content pages. No SharePoint navigation provider is required.

Understanding ASP.NET Site Map Providers

ASP.NET features a data-driven navigation system that uses hierarchical data sources and associated controls. It is much easier to create a site navigational system and track the current position of the user if you use the `Menu`, `TreeView`, or `SiteMapPath` control. As is common in ASP.NET, these controls use a provider to obtain data from a specific data source. The objective of ASP.NET's site navigation feature is to allow developers to specify a site map that describes the logical structure of a web site. This structure can be readily displayed with the SiteMapPath, TreeView, and Menu web controls of ASP.NET. Usually, these controls use XmlSiteMapProvider to read site map information from a .sitemap XML file.

If your web project requires a site map data source other than a static XML file, you can implement your own site map provider. This is done by creating a class, which inherits from the abstract System.Web.SiteMapProvider class and implements at least the abstract members described in Table 10-5.

Table 10-5. *Exposed Abstract Members of the SiteMapProvider Class*

Method	Description
FindSiteMapNode	Retrieves an instance of the SiteMapNode class, which represents a page.
GetChildNodes	Retrieves the child nodes of a specific SiteMapNode instance.
GetParentNode	Retrieves the parent node of a specific SiteMapNode instance.
GetRootNodeCore	Retrieves the root node of all the nodes that are managed by the current provider. This method is called internally by various site navigation classes to ensure that the navigation data has been loaded by the provider. This method must not return a null node.

A very simplistic implementation of a site map provider looks like the following snippet:

```
public class MySiteMapProvider : SiteMapProvider
{
    SiteMapNode rootNode = null;

    public MySiteMapProvider()  {}

    public override void Initialize(string name,
              System.Collections.Specialized.NameValueCollection attributes)
    {
        // Initialize static siteMap
        this.rootNode = new SiteMapNode(this, "rootNode", "/default.aspx", "Home");
        this.rootNode.ChildNodes.Add(new SiteMapNode(this, "childNode1",
                                                      "/page1", "SubPage 1"));
        this.rootNode.ChildNodes.Add(new SiteMapNode(this, "childNode2",
                                                      "/page2", "SubPage 2"));
    }

    public override SiteMapNode FindSiteMapNode(string rawUrl)
    {
        switch (rawUrl)
        {
            case "/default.aspx": return this.rootNode;
            case "/page1.aspx": return this.rootNode.ChildNodes[0];
            case "/page2.aspx": return this.rootNode.ChildNodes[1];
            default: return null;
        }
    }

    public override SiteMapNodeCollection GetChildNodes(SiteMapNode node)
    {
```

```
        SiteMapNodeCollection children = new SiteMapNodeCollection();
        if (node != null && node.HasChildNodes)
        {
            foreach (SiteMapNode cNode in node.ChildNodes) children.Add(cNode);
        }
        return children;
    }

    public override SiteMapNode GetParentNode(SiteMapNode node)
    {
        return (node == null) ? null : node.ParentNode;
    }

    protected override SiteMapNode GetRootNodeCore()
    {
        return rootNode;
    }
}
```

This example shows the principles behind ASP.NET site map providers. All the various SharePoint site map providers are based upon this concept, and it's not difficult to write your own provider to meet your particular requirements.

SharePoint Foundation Navigation Providers

SharePoint offers its own site map providers—called navigation providers—which are declared in the `web.config` file in the root directory of the web application (usually `C:\inetpub\WSS\Virtual Directories\80\web.config`). These named navigation providers can be found at the `<SiteMap>` element within the `<System.Web>` section, as shown in Figure 10–14.

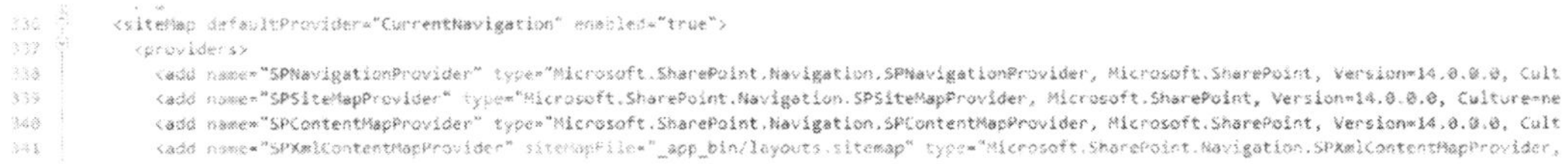

```
<siteMap defaultProvider="CurrentNavigation" enabled="true">
  <providers>
    <add name="SPNavigationProvider" type="Microsoft.SharePoint.Navigation.SPNavigationProvider, Microsoft.SharePoint, Version=14.0.0.0, Cult
    <add name="SPSiteMapProvider" type="Microsoft.SharePoint.Navigation.SPSiteMapProvider, Microsoft.SharePoint, Version=14.0.0.0, Culture=ne
    <add name="SPContentMapProvider" type="Microsoft.SharePoint.Navigation.SPContentMapProvider, Microsoft.SharePoint, Version=14.0.0.0, Cult
    <add name="SPXmlContentMapProvider" siteMapFile="_app_bin/layouts.sitemap" type="Microsoft.SharePoint.Navigation.SPXmlContentMapProvider,
```

Figure 10–14. *SharePoint navigation providers in web.config*

For SharePoint Foundation, the following navigation providers are defined:

- `SPNavigationProvider`
- `SPSiteMapProvider`
- `SPContentMapProvider`
- `SPXmlContentMapProvider`
- `SPXmlAdminContentMapProvider` (only available in a Central Administration web application)

All these providers share the same namespace: `Microsoft.SharePoint.Navigation`. They are included in the assembly `Microsoft.SharePoint.dll`.

The SPNavigationProvider Class

This provider acts as a base class for SharePoint site map providers that are specialized for SharePoint site navigation, such as the top link bar and the quick launch. It is generally used for SharePoint Foundation or SharePoint Server implementations without the Publishing feature enabled.

The SPSiteMapProvider Class

The `SPSiteMapProvider` class is used for default breadcrumb navigation. It provides `SiteMapNode` site objects (`SPWeb`) in the site hierarchy, starting from the underlying site collection (`SPSite`). For example:

- Site collection
    - Site 1
    - Site 2
        - Subsite 2a
        - Subsite 2b
    - Site 3

The SPContentMapProvider Class

This provider is also used for default breadcrumb navigation. It adds content information of the current page to the breadcrumb trail, such as information about lists, folders, items, and list forms.
Consider a practical example. Assume that you have a list named `Books`, and you are viewing the default view, `/Lists/Books/AllItems.aspx`. In this situation, `SPContentMapProvider` would return a navigation node named Books (see Figure 10–15).

Figure 10–15. *SPSiteMapProvider and SPContentMapProvider used for breadcrumb navigation*

The SPXmlContentMapProvider Class

This provider is used for breadcrumb navigation within application pages. The class is derived from `System.Web.XmlSiteMapProvider` and uses an XML file as a data source. The provider uses a `siteMapFile` attribute, which by default points to an XML site map file in the `_app_bin` folder of the current web application. This file contains the site map for most of the application pages in the `LAYOUTS` folder. For example, the application page `mysubs.aspx` contains a section along these lines:

```
<SharePoint:ListSiteMapPath
        runat="server"
        SiteMapProviders="SPSiteMapProvider,SPXmlContentMapProvider" ... />
```

The file `app_bin/layouts` contains a `siteMapNode` hierarchy, as shown in Figure 10–16.

```
- <siteMapNode title="$Resources:wss,people_pagetitle" url="/_layouts/people.aspx">
    <siteMapNode title="$Resources:wss,associatedgroups_pagetitle" url="/_layouts/associatedgroups.aspx" />
    <siteMapNode title="$Resources:wss,editgrp_pagetitle" url="/_layouts/editgrp.aspx" />
    <siteMapNode title="$Resources:wss,grpmbrs_pagetitle" url="/_layouts/grpmbrs.aspx" />
    <siteMapNode title="$Resources:wss,newgrp_pagetitle" url="/_layouts/newgrp.aspx" />
    <siteMapNode title="$Resources:wss,permsetup_pagetitle" url="/_layouts/permsetup.aspx" />
  - <siteMapNode title="$Resources:wss,useredit_pagetitleintitlearea" url="/_layouts/userdisp.aspx">
    - <siteMapNode title="$Resources:wss,mysubs_pagetitle" url="/_layouts/mysubs.aspx">
        <siteMapNode title="$Resources:wss,subchoos_pagetitle" url="/_layouts/SubChoos.aspx" />
      </siteMapNode>
```

__Figure 10–16.__ Section from the file _app_bin/layouts.sitemap

The resulting application page is shown in Figure 10–17.

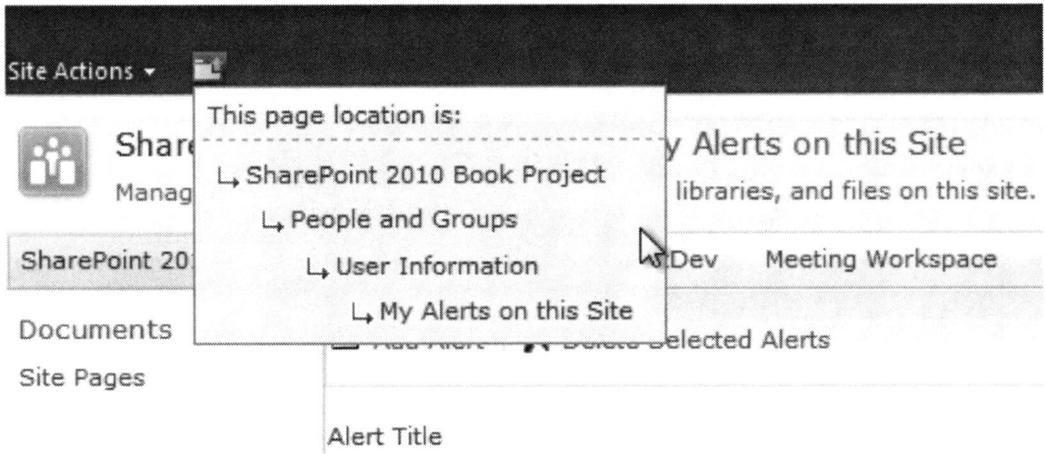

__Figure 10–17.__ Result of SPXmlContentMapProvider on an application page

SharePoint Server Navigation Providers

In addition to those provided by SharePoint Foundation, SharePoint Server adds some further navigation providers to the `web.config` file of a web application. Table 10–6 summarizes the SharePoint Server navigation providers.

__Table 10–6.__ SharePoint Server Navigation Providers

Provider	Description
AdministrationQuickLaunchProvider	Quick launch navigation provider for the Central Administration site
CombinedNavSiteMapProvider	CMS provider for combined navigation
CurrentNavigation	Provider for current navigation
CurrentNavSiteMapProvider	CMS provider for current navigation
CurrentNavSiteMapProviderNoEncode	CMS provider for current navigation; no output encoding
ExtendedSearchXmlContentMapProvider	Provider for navigation in extended search pages
GlobalNavigation	Provider for global navigation
GlobalNavSiteMapProvider	CMS provider for global navigation
MySiteLeftNavProvider	MySite left navigation provider that returns areas and is based on the current user context
MySiteMapProvider	MySite provider that returns areas and is based on the current user context
SharedServicesQuickLaunchProvider	Quick launch navigation provider for shared service administration sites
SiteDirectoryCategoryProvider	Provider for categories of a site directory
UsagePagesSiteMapProvider	Provider for navigation in portal usage pages

The main difference between these additional providers and the SharePoint Foundation navigation providers is the NavigationType property. Most of the SharePoint Server navigation providers use one of three different navigation types (see Table 10–7).

__Table 10–7.__ Navigation Types Used in SharePoint Server Navigation Providers

NavigationType Property	Description
Global	Displays the same navigation as the parent site
Current	Displays only the navigation items below the current site
Combined	Uses a combination of both global and current navigation

Example: Browsing Through Navigation Providers

The results of the different navigation providers are not always transparent and traceable. If you want to test that a navigation provider works as you expect, simply write a small application page that allows you browse through all available navigation providers (see Figure 10–18).

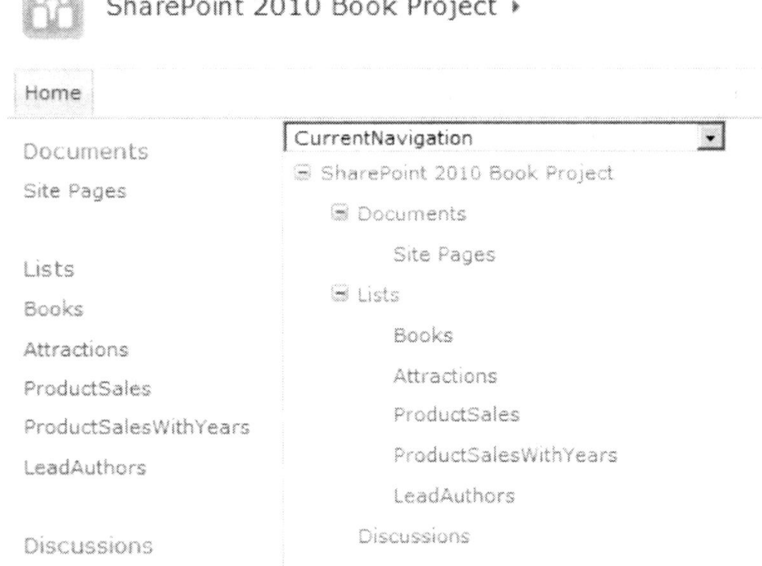

***Figure 10–18.** Example application page for browsing through navigation providers*

The example application page contains a DropDownList and a TreeView element. DropDownList allows you to select a navigation provider and TreeView displays the navigation hierarchy.

```
<%@ Page Language="C#" AutoEventWireup="true"
DynamicMasterPageFile="~masterurl/default.master"
    CodeFile="NavigationProviders.aspx.cs" Inherits="NavigationProviders"
    CodeFileBaseClass="Microsoft.SharePoint.WebControls.LayoutsPageBase" %>

<asp:Content ContentPlaceHolderId="PlaceHolderMain" runat="server">

    <asp:DropDownList id="ddlNavProviders" runat="server" AutoPostBack="True"
        OnSelectedIndexChanged="ddlNavProviders_SelectedIndexChanged" />

    <asp:TreeView id="navTreeView" runat="server"></asp:TreeView>

</asp:Content>
```

The code-behind class first initializes DropDownList with all the navigation providers defined in web.config. By selecting a navigation provider, the SiteMapDataSource pointing to the selected provider is bound to the TreeView.

```
using System;
using System.Web;
using System.Web.UI.WebControls;
using Microsoft.SharePoint;
using Microsoft.SharePoint.WebControls;

public partial class NavigationProviders : LayoutsPageBase
{
    protected void Page_Load(object sender, EventArgs e)
    {
        if (!IsPostBack)
        {
            // Init the DropDown element with all available navigation providers
            ddlNavProviders.DataSource = SiteMap.Providers;
            ddlNavProviders.DataTextField = "Name";
            ddlNavProviders.DataBind();
        }
    }

    protected void ddlNavProviders_SelectedIndexChanged(object sender,
                                                        EventArgs args)
    {
       // Bind the selected navigation provider to the TreeView
       SiteMapDataSource ds = new SiteMapDataSource();
       ds.Provider = SiteMap.Providers[ddlNavProviders.SelectedItem.Text];
       navTreeView.DataSource = ds;
       navTreeView.DataBind();
    }
}
```

This example is useful if you wish to check which navigation providers are currently available in your SharePoint web application. Furthermore, it can be interesting to examine the resulting navigation hierarchy for some navigation providers.

Themes

A theme is a collection of graphics and Cascading Style Sheet (CSS) files that define the look and feel of a web site. Themes serve as an instrument to apply colors and fonts to UI elements on SharePoint sites.

This section provides a high-level overview over the infrastructure of themes, and suggests ways to extend the capabilities of themes by using CSS. This is especially useful to designers who want to use themes as a quick and easy technique to apply colors and fonts to SharePoint sites without any knowledge of CSS or the details of the SharePoint CSS infrastructure.

The themes used in SharePoint 2010 use the same file extension (THMX) and structure as theme files used in Microsoft Office 2007 and Microsoft Office 2010 client applications, such as Microsoft PowerPoint 2010.

■ **Note** SharePoint themes are totally unrelated to (and incompatible with) the themes provided by the ASP.NET Framework.

Understanding Themes

SharePoint 2007 provided several default files and entry points you could customize to change the look and feel and behavior of content pages. Such customizations often required full-scale branding efforts that included customizing code and editing multiple files. Custom styles were supported by using customized, user-defined CSS files, but modifying the look and feel of a site or site collection required deep knowledge of CSS syntax and coding conventions. SharePoint 2010 introduces two new features that make it easier and less code-intensive to customize the UI. A new master file called `v4.master` and the new concept of theming are the foundations for customization.

Customization Levels

As Figure 10–19 shows, there are several customization levels. Each of these features exists along with other design and branding options. These options range from minimal complexity requiring minimal developer involvement to a large degree of complexity, which requires the expertise of a web developer.

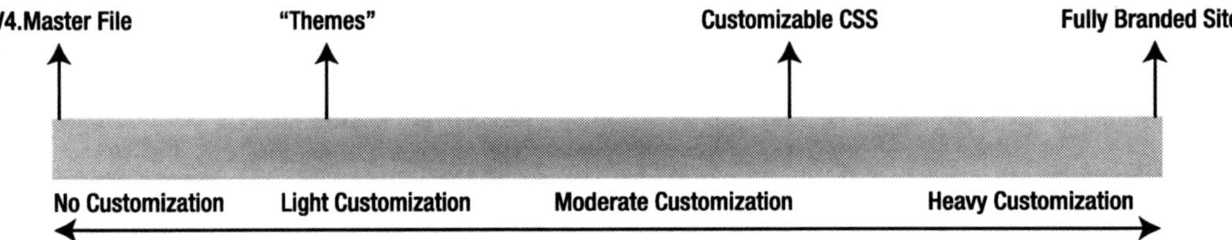

Figure 10–19. *SharePoint customization levels*

You can use the `v4.master` file that is installed by default if you just want to use the SharePoint default colors and fonts. However, if you want to change the look and feel of a SharePoint site, you now have three options with varying degrees of customization depth and flexibility. Table 10–8 explains these options.

Table 10–8. *Customization Levels*

Level	Description
No customization	The `v4.master` file is applied as a master page to all sites by default. No additional work is required by the site user, a designer, or a developer.
Light customization	You can modify fonts and colors of your site by applying a THMX file. You or a designer can apply a theme by using a simple web-based UI that requires no knowledge of CSS. With themes, you get broad and clear control of colors and fonts. Also, recoloring of images is supported.
Moderate to heavy customization	A designer is able to modify all design elements of a page layout that are controlled by CSS, including fonts, font sizes, colors, spacing, and background images. Customizable CSS requires detailed knowledge of CSS and the SharePoint page layout structure.

Level	Description
Heavy customization	If you want to fully brand your SharePoint site, you need skilled and experienced designers and web developers who are deeply familiar with the SharePoint page layout structure and the default CSS files. Full branding provides the most specific and precise control, but it is not straightforward. You have to ensure that all pages are consistent and that all changed UI elements are displayed correctly.

Applying Fonts and Colors

One goal of the SharePoint theming infrastructure is to provide a quick and easy way to uniformly apply combinations of colors and fonts that does not require learning CSS or site-branding intricacies. You simply define some basic colors and fonts through an integrated styling page, as shown in Figure 10–20. You can access this page under Site Settings ➤ Look and Feel ➤ Site Theme.

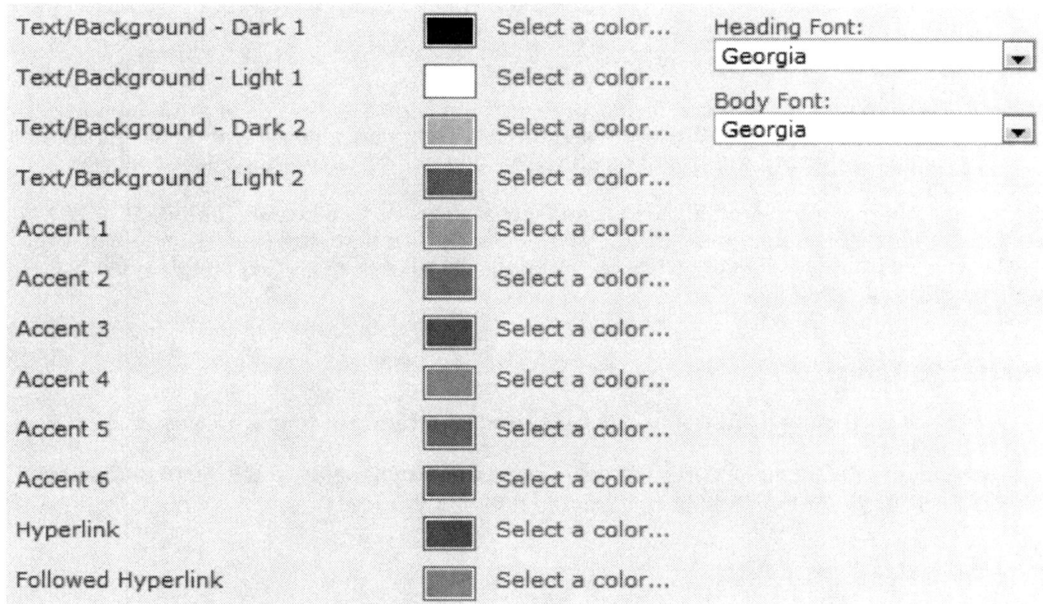

Figure 10–20. *Applying fonts and colors*

Dynamic Stylesheets

The ability to easily change colors and fonts is appealing. If you take it one step further to customizing your CSS styles, you need to know how to use the theme colors within a custom stylesheet. To address this, SharePoint provides a way to dynamically modify styles that are already being used on sites, whereby these styles can then be used in themes. If an existing site has been customized using CSS, you can mark that CSS with a markup syntax that is specifically designed to be used with themes on

SharePoint sites. Elements that are denoted with this CSS syntax will be themed when a theme is applied. An example for a custom CSS file could look like the following:

```
.myCssClass
{
        /*[ReplaceColor(themeColor:"Light2")]*/
        Color:#FFFFFF;
}
```

In this example, the color `#FFFFFF` (white) will be replaced dynamically with `Light2`, the named color of the current theme.

Correlation with Office THMX Files

SharePoint 2010 themes are fully compatible with the Office themes introduced with Microsoft Office 2007. Every theme you create within SharePoint will result in a THMX file, containing collections of colors, fonts, and images. These files can be exported to or imported from Office applications, such as PowerPoint. Such files can be used as starting points for further customization or as default sources of UI styling elements.

Separation of Design and Implementation

Themes offer a way to change the look and feel of a site, without knowledge of CSS or professional web developer skills. Themes are separate from but related to CSS. They work alongside other design options, such as CSS file customization and full-branding initiatives that use the talents of professional web designers and web developers.

While themes afford a way to modify the look and feel of a site, they do not affect how CSS, SharePoint programmability, and branding work. Themes do not interfere with professionals who want to use more advanced or technical approaches for branding SharePoint sites—they simply provide a lighter-weight option for site design.

SharePoint Theming

The infrastructure of the themes feature supports consistent application of colors, images, and fonts across SharePoint sites.

To understand how the themes infrastructure supports this functionality, you need to understand how the themes feature works in Windows SharePoint Foundation.

Themes in SharePoint 2010

SharePoint makes it possible to use themes with both SharePoint Server 2010 sites and SharePoint Foundation 2010 sites. The new approach to themes in this release simplifies the required steps and reduces the number of steps to customize the site design. SharePoint 2010 addresses performance issues of earlier versions by instructing the browser to get only one set of CSS files when applying a theme.

Instead of creating a custom CSS file for a theme, you can annotate the actual CSS file with variables that are unique to themes and translated into valid values within the CSS. These variables are stored as comments in the CSS file, so they are completely supported by web standards. Creating a new theme simply involves defining new values for those variables. All UI elements in SharePoint 2010 can be themed. When you apply a theme, it is applied to all UI elements and controls—the following list provides some examples:

- Ribbon UI elements
- Highlighting for bulk-editing operations
- The Site Actions button and drop-down menu
- Shortcut menus
- Pages available in the `_layouts` folder
- Dialog boxes
- Web Part chrome

Theming Prerequisites

Compared with older SharePoint versions, the theme infrastructure of SharePoint 2010 has completely changed:

- Inline styles in pages have been removed.
- All CSS files to which themes can be applied have been marked up with theme variables.
- All CSS files to which themes can be applied have been moved to themable locations in the product.

Inline styles (i.e., any styles that include `style=""` attributes and the `<font>` tag) cannot be overridden by the CSS that SharePoint Foundation 2010 uses, and therefore you cannot apply a theme to them. Themes apply only to CSS styles that are defined in a CSS file stored in a location that can be themed. These styles contain markup syntax for Web Parts, controls, and the ribbon. Style declarations within a master page or page layout file cannot be themed.

The elements, attributes, and variables defined in a THMX file define the colors, fonts, and image colors that are applied to a site. The THMX file contains all the information that the server needs to correctly apply the style elements defined in this file to the UI elements of a SharePoint site.

You can extend your CSS files so that your controls and Web Parts adhere to the theme. However, if you do not design a control with the requirements of themes in mind, you might, for example, choose to use inline styles. This would create a problem because SharePoint Server cannot override inline styles.

If your control or Web Part uses its own CSS files, then you can override inline styles in a way that makes it possible to apply themes to them. You do this by first determining which styles are used by the control or Web Part, then adding those styles to the site's CSS file, and finally annotating them with the appropriate variables. This ensures that the styles that your control or Web Part uses are processed by the SharePoint themes engine and overridden properly.

Theme Colors and Variations

Generally, themes for Office have 12 color slots. The first four horizontal colors are for text and backgrounds (`Dark1`, `Light1`, `Dark2`, and `Light2`). Text that is created with light colors will be legible over the dark colors, and text that is created with dark colors will be legible over the light colors. The next six colors are accent colors (`Accent1` to `Accent6`) that are visible over the four possible background colors. The last two colors are reserved for hyperlinks and followed hyperlinks. Finally, there are two different fonts: one for headings and one for body content. Figure 10–21 shows the fonts and color slots.

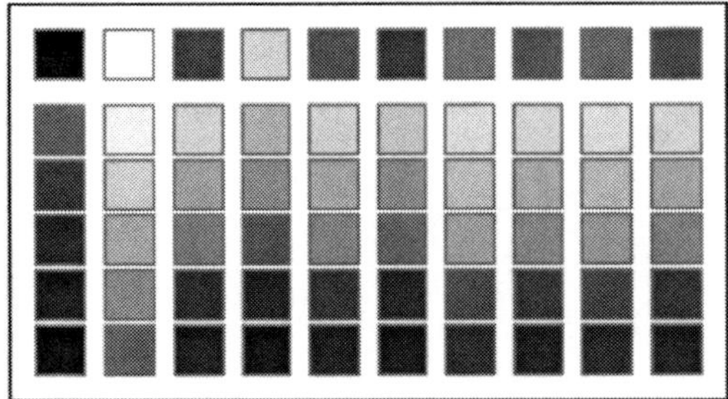

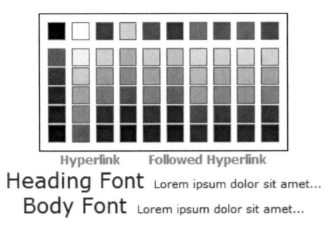

Figure 10–21. Theme color palette

The five subsequent rows beneath the main colors are populated with tints (lighter variations) and shades (darker variations) of the specified theme colors (see Table 10–9). These tints and shades are set automatically, based on the original color, and cannot be altered programmatically.

Table 10–9. Variations with Tints and Shades

Variation	Dark1	Dark2	Light1	Light2	Accent1 to 6
Lightest	`themeTint:0.5`	`themeTint:0.9`	`themeShade:0.05`	`themeShade:0.10`	`themeTint:0.8`
Lighter	`themeTint:0.35`	`themeTint:0.75`	`themeShade:0.15`	`themeShade:0.25`	`themeTint:0.6`
Medium	`themeTint:0.25`	`themeTint:0.50`	`themeShade:0.25`	`themeShade:0.50`	`themeTint:0.4`
Darker	`themeTint:0.15`	`themeTint:0.25`	`themeShade:0.35`	`themeShade:0.75`	`themeShade:0.25`
Darkest	`themeTint:0.05`	`themeTint:0.10`	`themeShade:0.50`	`themeShade:0.90`	`themeShade:0.5`

■ **Tip** Microsoft offers a Theme Builder application that enables you to create your own themes. You can find it at `http://connect.microsoft.com/ThemeBuilder`.

Dynamic Stylesheets

The new dynamic stylesheets use transparent comments to create a relationship between a theme and default CSS values. The next example shows a stylesheet definition, `.myclass`, that is defined with white foreground color. This white default color should be replaced according to the theme that is currently active. To do so, just define a CSS selector for the class:

```
.myclass
{
        Color:#FFFFFF;
}
```

Then add the theme variable above the color:

```
.myclass
{
        /*[ReplaceColor(themeColor:"Light1")]*/
        Color:#FFFFFF;
}
```

The color declaration is replaced by whatever the theme's `Light1` color is. The following example adds 50 percent shading to the color `Light2`:

```
.myclass
{
        /*[ReplaceColor(themeColor:"Light2",themeShade:"0.5")]*/
        Color:#FFFFFF;
}
```

Another way to add 50 percent shading is to add the variation name to the color instead of explicitly adding the shading factor:

```
.myclass
{
        /*[ReplaceColor(themeColor:"Light2-Medium")]*/
        Color:#FFFFFF;
}
```

Theming Attributes

Applying a theme essentially consists of taking unprocessed CSS files and resources such as images and applying the specified theme settings to those files. The theme settings that you specify are stored in a THMX file, and SharePoint applies these to all of the appropriate CSS files and images. SharePoint includes a set of attributes that you can use to specify that certain CSS elements should use a variable that is specified in the THMX file. Table 10–10 lists those attributes.

***Table 10–10.** Theming Attributes*

Name	Description
`ReplaceColor`	Replaces the `color` value of the following CSS rule with the specified color
`ReplaceFont`	Replaces the `font-family` value of the following CSS rule with the specified font family
`RecolorImage`	Recolors an image specified in the following CSS rule

The themes engine reads and executes these statements to apply the specified colors, fonts, and images to a site. To change the value of a CSS attribute, the user specifies a different attribute/value pair in the CSS file.

Theming Attributes of Internal CSS

Most CSS files used in SharePoint are extended with special CSS comments that are interpreted by the themes engine. For instance, the example in Figure 10–22, a screenshot from the `coreV4.css` file, changes some of the colors of the `ms-toolbar` CSS class.

```
.ms-toolbar{
font-family:verdana;
font-size:8pt;
text-decoration:none;
/* [ReplaceColor(themeColor:"Hyperlink")] */ color:#0072BC;
}
a.ms-toolbar:hover{
text-decoration:underline;
/* [ReplaceColor(themeColor:"Accent1",themeShade:"0.8")] */ color:#005e9a;
}
.ms-toolbar-togglebutton-on{
/* [ReplaceColor(themeColor:"Accent3-Darker")] */ border:1px solid #2353b2;
/* [ReplaceColor(themeColor:"Accent4-Lightest")] */ background-color:#fffacc;
}
table.ms-toolbar{
height:45px;
border:none;
/* [RecolorImage(themeColor:"Light2",includeRectangle:{x:0,y:516,width:1,height:42})] */
background:url("/_layouts/images/bgximg.png") repeat-x -0px -516px;
/* [ReplaceColor(themeColor:"Light1")] */ background-color:#fff;
}
```

Figure 10–22. *Stylesheet corev4.css with theme markups*

For example, by applying the theme Municipal Dark, a new preprocessed theme CSS file called `corev4-4159570246.css` is automatically created in the virtual folder `/_themes/Municipal%20Dark.thmx-3258465106` of the web. A random autogenerated number is added as a suffix to the file and directory names. The reference to this themed version of the stylesheet is simple and already implemented in almost all master pages:

```
<!—CSS LINK -->
     <SharePoint:CssLink runat="server" Version="4" />
<!— /CSS LINK -->
```

The rendering result of the tag `<SharePoint:CssLink>` is shown in Figure 10–23. You can see that there are several stylesheets to be included.

```
<!-- CSS LINK -->
    <link rel="stylesheet" type="text/css" href="/_themes/Municipal%20Dark.thmx-3258465106/corev4-4159570246.css?ctag=12"/>
<link rel="stylesheet" type="text/css" href="/_layouts/1033/styles/cuidark.css?rev=VTyIVsmli2tIcbHY%2BkP4QA%3D%3D"/>
<link rel="stylesheet" type="text/css" href="/_themes/Municipal%20Dark.thmx-3258465106/layouts-395646476.css?ctag=12"/>
<link rel="stylesheet" type="text/css" href="/_layouts/1033/styles/menu-21.css?rev=icIJJqeHhpFYhcUA0pceCg%3D%3D"/>
<link rel="stylesheet" type="text/css" href="/_layouts/1033/styles/search.css?rev=5mHWEbODg1zpA0cGDKpt8A%3D%3D"/>
<link rel="stylesheet" type="text/css" href="/_themes/Municipal%20Dark.thmx-3258465106/WPEditMode-1830875387.css?ctag=12"/>
<link rel="stylesheet" type="text/css" href="/_themes/Municipal%20Dark.thmx-3258465106/corev4-4159570246.css?ctag=12"/>

<!-- /CSS LINK -->
```

Figure 10–23. *Result of embedding the default stylesheets*

As you can see, the created file `/_themes/Municipal%20Dark.thmx-3258465106/corev4-4159570246.css` is now automatically used as a CSS reference. Figure 10–24 shows a screenshot of the resultant file.

```
.ms-toolbar{
font-family:verdana;
font-size:8pt;
text-decoration:none;
 color:#F7B615;
}
a.ms-toolbar:hover{
text-decoration:underline;
 color:#588AB4;
}
.ms-toolbar-togglebutton-on{
 border:1px solid #8B7A20;
 background-color:#FDEED3;
}
table.ms-toolbar{
height:45px;
border:none;
 background:url(/_themes/Construct.thmx-3831204095/bgximg-3884107457.png?ctag) repeat-x -0px -516px;
 background-color:#fff;
}
```

Figure 10–24. *Themed stylesheet corev4.css after processing and applying a theme*

Applying Themes

If a theme is to be applied to a site, the THMX file is first read into memory. Then all the CSS and PNG files that are located in themable locations (either in the file system or the content database) are processed. The processing task takes each file and applies the required changes to it. For example, in stylesheets, all themed attributes will be processed, and then the changed file will be copied into a new location. Also, all themable PNG images will be processed and changed according to the applied theme.

▒ **Note** When applying a theme, the included images could also be modified through theming attributes such as `RecolorImage`. Note that currently only PNG images are supported.

Figure 10–25 shows the processing of themes.

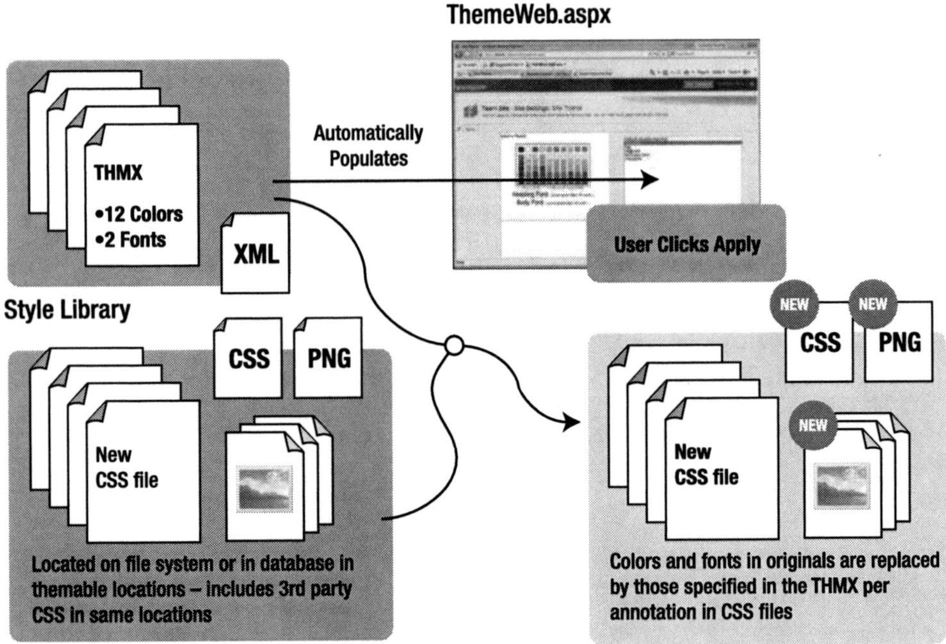

Figure 10–25. Tasks when applying a theme

Creating Themable Application Pages

A common requirement for developers is to design Web Parts, custom controls, and application pages that support theming.

With the new theme infrastructure of SharePoint 2010, this is relatively easy to accomplish. In the example that follows, these steps are accomplished:

1. Creating a stylesheet file with theming attributes
2. Copying the stylesheet file to the `/Themable` directory to mark it themable
3. Applying a theme
4. Creating an application page that uses the stylesheet

Creating a Stylesheet File with Theming Attributes

First, create a stylesheet file and save it as `MyStyleSheet.css` in the 14 hive under `TEMPLATE\LAYOUTS\1033\styles`. It should contain the following style definition:

```
.myStyle
{
        text-decoration:underline;
        /* [ReplaceColor(themeColor:"Accent1")] */ color:#FF0000;
}
```

Copying the Stylesheet File to the /Themable Directory to Mark It Themable

Next, copy this file to the `/Themable` subdirectory (see Figure 10–26). This is necessary because only files within this directory will be processed when applying a theme.

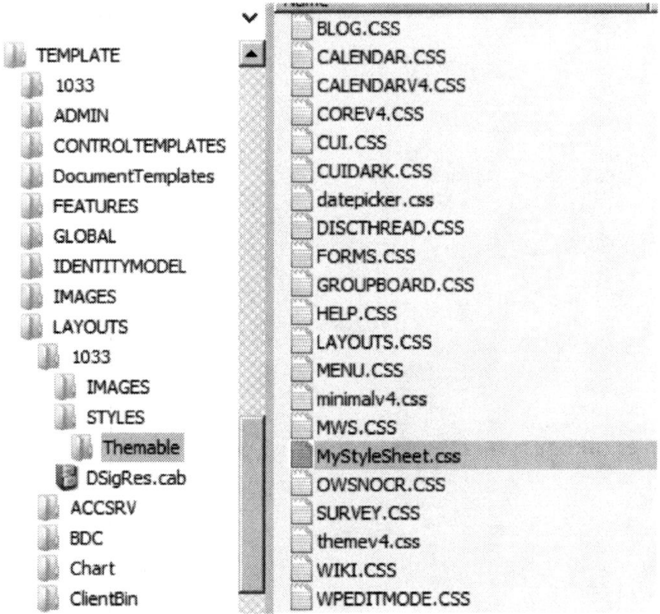

***Figure 10–26.** Contents of the localized, themable style directory*

■ **Note** The stylesheet file must always exist in the `/styles` directory, because if no theme is activated, the file from the style directory is used (without preprocessing the CSS attributes). If the file also exists in the `/Themable` directory, it is automatically used when a theme is activated.

Applying a Theme

Next, activate a theme in your web by choosing Site Actions ➤ Site Settings ➤ Look and Feel ➤ Site Theme and selecting a theme there (see Figure 10–27).

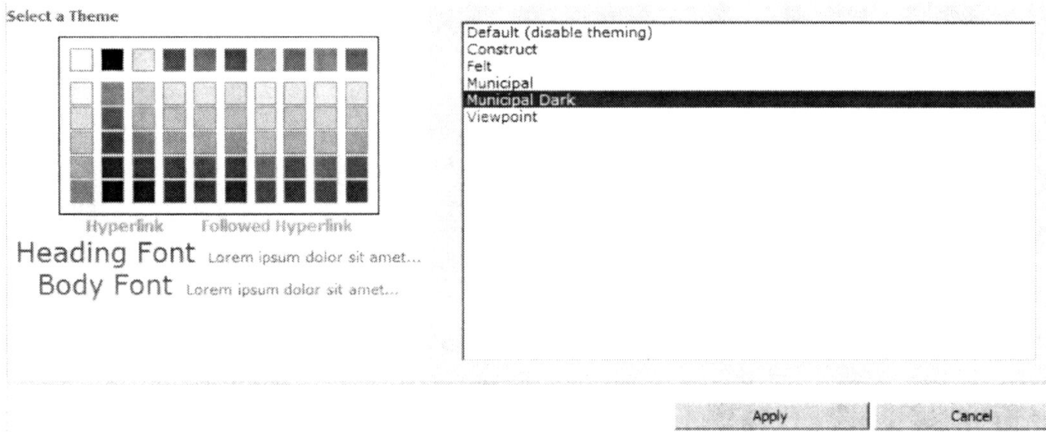

Figure 10–27. *Selecting a theme*

After applying the theme, all the `.css` files of the `styles/themable` directory will be processed and copied to the virtual path *`site/`*`_themes/`*`THEMENAME`* (see Figure 10–28).

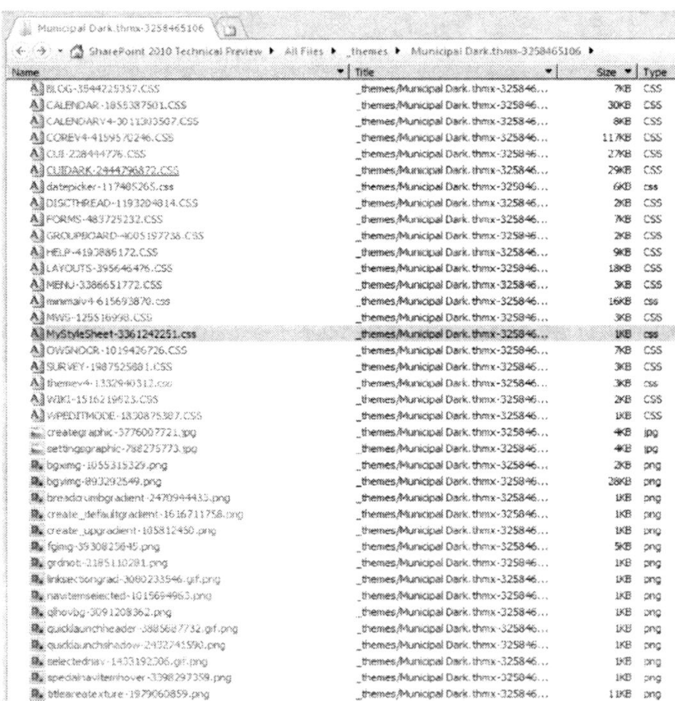

Figure 10–28. *Automatically created virtual folder after applying a theme*

Creating an Application Page That Uses the Stylesheet

Finally, create a simple application page that uses the new stylesheet. In the LAYOUTS folder of the SharePoint root, create an ASPX page that looks like this:

```
<%@ Page Language="C#" AutoEventWireup="true"
    DynamicMasterPageFile="~masterurl/default.master"
    Inherits="Microsoft.SharePoint.WebControls.LayoutsPageBase" %>
<%@ Register Tagprefix="SharePoint" Namespace="Microsoft.SharePoint.WebControls"
    Assembly="Microsoft.SharePoint, Version=14.0.0.0, Culture=neutral,
PublicKeyToken=71e9bce111e9429c" %>
<%@ Import Namespace="Microsoft.SharePoint" %>

<asp:content ID="Content1" ContentPlaceHolderId="PlaceHolderAdditionalPageHead"
            runat="server">
    <SharePoint:CssLink ID="CssLink1" runat="server"
                        DefaultUrl="Themable/MyStyleSheet.css"  />
 </asp:content>

<asp:Content ID="Content2" ContentPlaceHolderId="PlaceHolderMain" runat="server">
    <asp:label ID="Label1" Font-Size="Large" runat="server" CssClass="myStyle" Text="This is
my label" />
</asp:Content>
```

The layout for this page without a theme applied results in a red underlined label (color #FF0000) as shown in Figure 10–29.

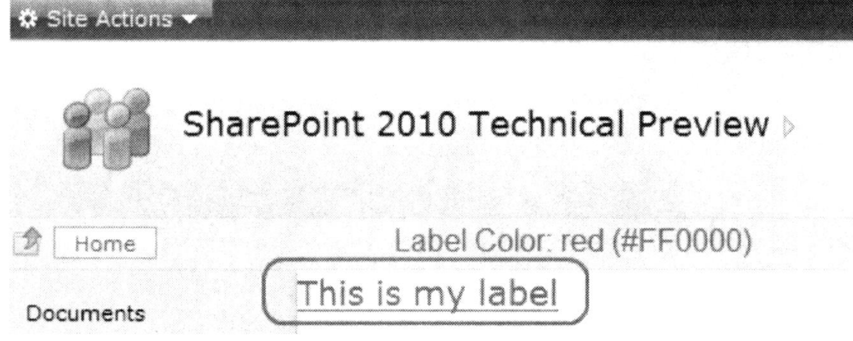

Figure 10–29. *Application page without a theme*

The generated HTML source code for this example shows the link to the (unthemed) stylesheet (Figure 10–30).

```
<link rel="stylesheet" type="text/css" href="/_layouts/1033/styles/Themable/MyStyleSheet.css?
 rev=0m7RGOZFjB0wftXFaWOWZA%3D%3D"/>
```

Figure 10–30. *Stylesheet integration without a theme*

When the Municipal Dark theme is applied, the label is displayed in the theme color Accent1 (color #D34817), as shown in Figure 10–31.

Figure 10–31. Application page with the Municipal Dark theme

In contrast to the stylesheet link in Figure 10–31, the generated HTML source code now shows the link to the themed stylesheet (see Figure 10–32).

```
<link rel="stylesheet" type="text/css" href="/_themes/Municipal%20Dark.thmx-3258465106/MyStyleSheet-
3361242251.css?ctag=14"/>
```

Figure 10–32. Stylesheet integration with the Municipal Dark theme

The stylesheet itself in the themes directory contains only the processed result—all the comments have been eliminated:

```
.myStyle
{
        text-decoration:underline;
         color:#D34817;
}
```

Extending the UI

One of the most obvious UI features of SharePoint 2010 is the context-sensitive ribbon interface, already familiar from Office 2007. There are many extensibility points from which you can customize the built-in functionality. For example, you can extend the ribbon interface to include new menu items. The UI also contains a status bar positioned below the ribbon bar to indicate the status of the current page. This section shows how to use custom actions to extend the SharePoint UI with your own menu items or ribbon elements.

■ **Note** SharePoint 2010 also provides many client-side elements, mostly implemented with JavaScript, to extend the UI. A brief description, including many examples, of the client-side dialog framework and the status bars and notification areas can be found in Chapter 12.

Custom Actions

Using features, you can easily add your custom actions to menus of the SharePoint UI. SharePoint offers specific extension points where you can hook into and extend the standard UI. The implementation of these extension points is usually based on the following web controls:

- `Microsoft.SharePoint.WebControls.FeatureMenuTemplate`
- `Microsoft.SharePoint.WebControls.FeatureLinkSection`

The `FeatureMenuTemplate` control is used as a kind of placeholder for several menu items. Close inspection of the SharePoint default master page reveals that the Site Actions menu contains a `FeatureMenuTemplate` element. This element contains some static menu items (`MenuItemTemplate`) and can be extended by defining custom actions within features.

The `FeatureLinkSection` control is usually used to extend overview pages for SharePoint sites and Central Administration. Figure 10–33 contains an excerpt of the default master page that determines the menu items of the Site Actions menu.

```
<SharePoint:SiteActions runat="server" accesskey="<%$Resources:wss,tb_SiteActions_AK%>"
 PrefixHtml=""
 SuffixHtml=""
 ImageUrl="/_layouts/images/saPegs.png"
 MenuNotVisibleHtml="&amp;nbsp;"
 >
 <CustomTemplate>
 <SharePoint:FeatureMenuTemplate runat="server"
     FeatureScope="Site"
     Location="Microsoft.SharePoint.StandardMenu"
     GroupId="SiteActions"
     UseShortId="true"
     >
     <SharePoint:MenuItemTemplate runat="server" id="MenuItem_EditPage"
         Text="<%$Resources:wss,siteactions_editpage%>"
         Description="<%$Resources:wss,siteactions_editpagedescriptionv4%>"
         ImageUrl="/_layouts/images/EditDocument32.png"
         MenuGroupId="100"
         Sequence="110"
         ClientOnClickNavigateUrl="javascript:ChangeLayoutMode(false);"
         />
```

Figure 10–33. *Definition of the Site Actions menu in the default master page*

The code snippet displayed in Figure 10–33 is responsible for displaying the Site Actions menu shown in Figure 10–34.

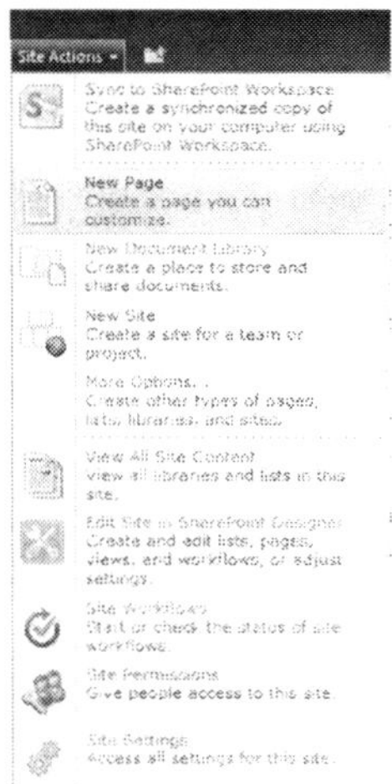

Figure 10–34. *Site Actions menu based on FeatureMenuTemplate*

To understand the behavior of these two web controls, peruse the code of the `FeatureMenuTemplate` control (see Figure 10–35). As you can see in the `CreateChildControls` section, there is a `GetCustomMenuItemActions` method call that returns all available custom actions as `SPCustomActionElement` instances.

```
protected override void CreateChildControls()
{
  base.CreateChildControls();
  if (!string.IsNullOrEmpty(this.Location) && !string.IsNullOrEmpty(this.GroupId))
  {
    SPWeb web = this.RenderContext.Web;
    SPList list = this.RenderContext.List;
    List<SPCustomActionElement> list2 = SPElementProvider.GetAvailableProvider().GetCustomMenuItemActions(web, list, this.Location);
    if (list2.Count > 0)
    {
      foreach (SPCustomActionElement element in list2)
      {
```

Figure 10–35. *Source code of FeatureMenuTemplate*

From this we can conclude that extensions to those web controls can only be created by using SharePoint features containing correctly registered custom actions. Although it is possible to change menu items in code in your application pages, it is bad practice; you should instead use features with custom actions. To define a custom action, you have to build a feature (see Listing 10–2). Features are described in detail in Chapter 7.

Listing 10–2. *Example feature.xml File*

```
<Feature
  Id="7F762A93-2205-499B-84E3-125423D86E31"
  Title="Add a link to user section"
  Description="Feature that adds a link to Welcome User section"
```

```
  Scope="WebApplication"
  xmlns="http://schemas.microsoft.com/sharepoint/">
  <ElementManifests>
    <ElementManifest Location="Elements.xml" />
  </ElementManifests>
</Feature>
```

Listing 10–2 shows a feature definition file (feature.xml) that references the elements.xml file, as displayed in Listing 10–3.

Listing 10–3. *Example elements.xml File with a Custom Action Definition*

```
<Elements xmlns="http://schemas.microsoft.com/sharepoint/">
    <CustomAction
        Id="myCustomAction"
        GroupId="PersonalActions"
        Location="Microsoft.SharePoint.StandardMenu"
        Sequence="1000"
        Title="Open custom page"
        Description="Open my custom page"
        ImageUrl="_layouts/1033/images/KpiListView.png">
        <UrlAction Url="~site/_layouts/myCustomPage.aspx"/>
    </CustomAction>
</Elements>
```

The CustomAction element defined in the elements.xml file adds an additional menu item to the PersonalActions menu, as shown in Figure 10–36.

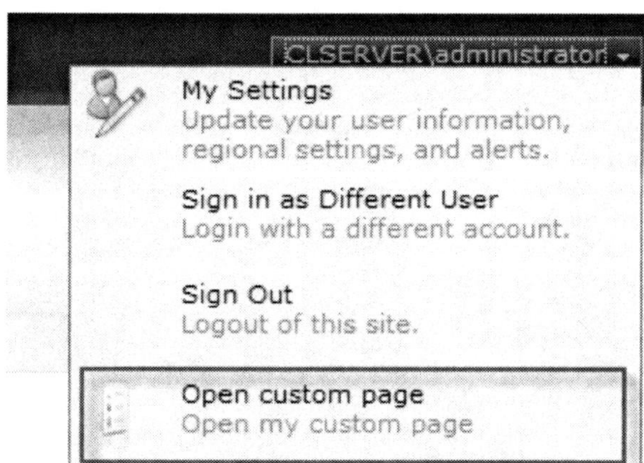

Figure 10–36. *A custom action*

This example shows that it's very easy to extend the SharePoint standard UI. The CustomAction element has some important properties that are only described briefly here. Additional information can be found in the MSDN library or the SharePoint SDK.

To define a custom action for a particular menu, you must first identify the menu. The property Location defines the menu—for example, Microsoft.SharePoint.SiteSettings or

Microsoft.SharePoint.StandardMenu. The GroupID property defines an area within the menu (see Table 10–11 for some examples).

Table 10–11. Location and GroupID Properties for StandardMenu

Location	GroupID	Description
Microsoft.SharePoint.StandardMenu	ActionsMenu	Actions menu in list and document library views
Microsoft.SharePoint.StandardMenu	ActionsMenuForSurvey	Site actions menu for surveys
Microsoft.SharePoint.StandardMenu	NewMenu	New menu in list and document library views
Microsoft.SharePoint.StandardMenu	PersonalActions	Menu showing “Welcome *username*” and usually containing “Sign in” and “Sign out” items.
Microsoft.SharePoint.StandardMenu	SettingsMenu	Settings menu in list and document library views
Microsoft.SharePoint.StandardMenu	SettingsMenuForSurvey	Site settings links for surveys
Microsoft.SharePoint.StandardMenu	SiteActions	Site actions menu
Microsoft.SharePoint.StandardMenu	UploadMenu	Upload menu in list and document library views

The third important property of a custom action is the UrlAction, which usually includes a URL that is opened when clicking an action item. SharePoint supports various URL tokens, described in Table 10–12.

Table 10–12. Supported URL Tokens for Custom Actions

Token	Description
~site	URL relative to the current web site (SPWeb)
~sitecollection	URL relative to the current site collection (SPSite)
{ItemId}	ID that identifies the item within a list
{ItemUrl}	URL of the current item
{ListId}	GUID of the current list
{SiteUrl}	Absolute URL of the current web site (SPWeb)

Custom Action Examples

To give you a better understanding of how to use custom actions, this section will present examples on how to do the following:

- List all custom actions
- Extend site settings
- Add nested menus

Listing All Custom Actions

To give you a look at the UI customization possibilities, this example shows how to build an application page that displays all the custom actions of all the enabled features. This can be very helpful, especially if you aren't sure which `Location` or `GroupId` property you need. It's also very interesting to explore SharePoint and see what custom actions are available (see Figure 10–37).

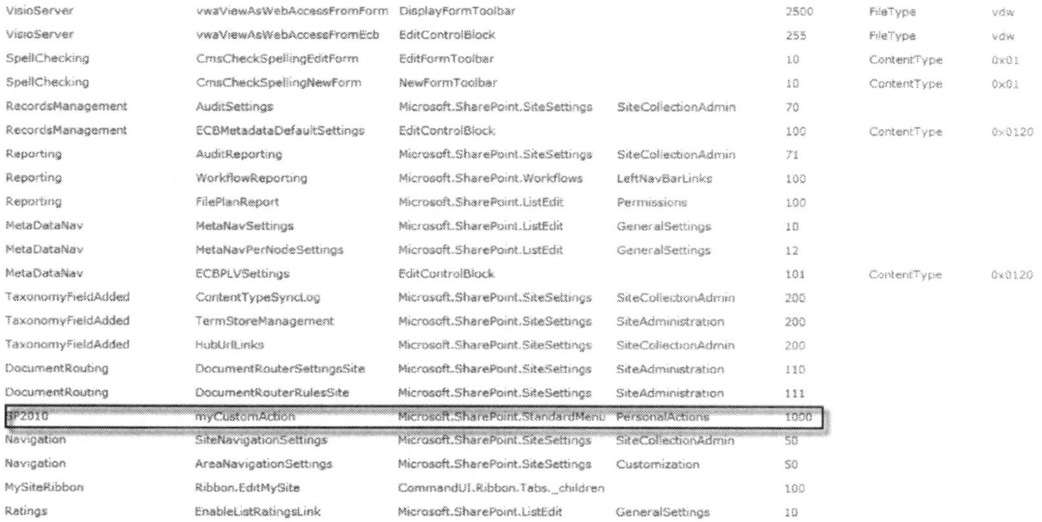

VisioServer	vwaViewAsWebAccessFromForm	DisplayFormToolbar		2500	FileType	vdw
VisioServer	vwaViewAsWebAccessFromEcb	EditControlBlock		255	FileType	vdw
SpellChecking	CmsCheckSpellingEditForm	EditFormToolbar		10	ContentType	0x01
SpellChecking	CmsCheckSpellingNewForm	NewFormToolbar		10	ContentType	0x01
RecordsManagement	AuditSettings	Microsoft.SharePoint.SiteSettings	SiteCollectionAdmin	70		
RecordsManagement	ECBMetadataDefaultSettings	EditControlBlock		100	ContentType	0x0120
Reporting	AuditReporting	Microsoft.SharePoint.SiteSettings	SiteCollectionAdmin	71		
Reporting	WorkflowReporting	Microsoft.SharePoint.Workflows	LeftNavBarLinks	100		
Reporting	FilePlanReport	Microsoft.SharePoint.ListEdit	Permissions	100		
MetaDataNav	MetaNavSettings	Microsoft.SharePoint.ListEdit	GeneralSettings	10		
MetaDataNav	MetaNavPerNodeSettings	Microsoft.SharePoint.ListEdit	GeneralSettings	12		
MetaDataNav	ECBPLVSettings	EditControlBlock		101	ContentType	0x0120
TaxonomyFieldAdded	ContentTypeSyncLog	Microsoft.SharePoint.SiteSettings	SiteCollectionAdmin	200		
TaxonomyFieldAdded	TermStoreManagement	Microsoft.SharePoint.SiteSettings	SiteAdministration	200		
TaxonomyFieldAdded	HubUrlLinks	Microsoft.SharePoint.SiteSettings	SiteCollectionAdmin	200		
DocumentRouting	DocumentRouterSettingsSite	Microsoft.SharePoint.SiteSettings	SiteAdministration	110		
DocumentRouting	DocumentRouterRulesSite	Microsoft.SharePoint.SiteSettings	SiteAdministration	111		
SP2010	myCustomAction	Microsoft.SharePoint.StandardMenu	PersonalActions	1000		
Navigation	SiteNavigationSettings	Microsoft.SharePoint.SiteSettings	SiteCollectionAdmin	50		
Navigation	AreaNavigationSettings	Microsoft.SharePoint.SiteSettings	Customization	50		
MySiteRibbon	Ribbon.EditMySite	CommandUI.Ribbon.Tabs._children		100		
Ratings	EnableListRatingsLink	Microsoft.SharePoint.ListEdit	GeneralSettings	10		

Figure 10–37. *List of custom actions (Feature, Id, Location, GroupId, Sequence, RegistrationType, and RegistrationId)*

Start by building a new application page containing a `Repeater` control to display the custom action properties, as shown in Listing 10–4.

Listing 10–4. *Application Page Containing a Repeater to Display Custom Action Properties*

```
<%@ Page Language="C#" AutoEventWireup="true"
DynamicMasterPageFile="~masterurl/default.master"
    CodeFile="ListAllCustomActions.aspx.cs" Inherits="ListAllCustomActions"
    CodeFileBaseClass="Microsoft.SharePoint.WebControls.LayoutsPageBase" %>
```

```
<asp:Content ID="Content1" ContentPlaceHolderId="PlaceHolderMain" runat="server">

    <asp:Repeater runat="server" ID="rptCustomActions" EnableViewState="false">
           <HeaderTemplate>
            <table>
                <tr>
                    <td class="ms-vh2">Feature</td>
                    <td class="ms-vh2">Id</td>
                    <td class="ms-vh2">Location</td>
                    <td class="ms-vh2">GroupId</td>
                    <td class="ms-vh2">Sequence</td>
                    <td class="ms-vh2">RegistrationType</td>
                    <td class="ms-vh2">RegistrationId</td>
                </tr>
            </tr>
           </HeaderTemplate>
           <ItemTemplate>
            <tr>
                <td class="ms-vb2"><%# Eval("Feature") %></td>
                <td class="ms-vb2"><%# Eval("Id") %></td>
                <td class="ms-vb2"><%# Eval("Location") %></td>
                <td class="ms-vb2"><%# Eval("GroupId") %></td>
                <td class="ms-vb2"><%# Eval("Sequence")%></td>
                <td class="ms-vb2"><%# Eval("RegistrationType")%></td>
                <td class="ms-vb2"><%# Eval("RegistrationId")%></td>
            </tr>

           </ItemTemplate>
           <FooterTemplate>
            </table>
           </FooterTemplate>
    </asp:Repeater>

</asp:Content>
```

Listing 10–4 defines an application page containing a Repeater control with a table for displaying the custom action definitions. The code-behind is shown in Listing 10–5.

***Listing 10–5.** Code-Behind for the Application Page*

```
public partial class ListAllCustomActions : LayoutsPageBase
{
    protected void Page_Load(object sender, EventArgs e)
    {
        List<CustomActionContainer> containers = new List<CustomActionContainer>();
        foreach (SPFeatureDefinition feature in SPFarm.Local.FeatureDefinitions)
        {
            containers.AddRange(FindCustomActionsForFeature(feature));
        }
        rptCustomActions.DataSource = containers;
        rptCustomActions.DataBind();
    }

    protected List<CustomActionContainer>
```

```
            FindCustomActionsForFeature(SPFeatureDefinition feature)
    {
        List<CustomActionContainer> retVal = new List<CustomActionContainer>();
        foreach (SPElementDefinition element in
            feature.GetElementDefinitions(CultureInfo.CurrentCulture))
        {
            if (element.XmlDefinition.Name == "CustomAction")
            {
                CustomActionContainer c = new CustomActionContainer();
                c.Feature = feature.DisplayName;
                c.Id = GetAttributeValue(element.XmlDefinition,"Id");
                c.GroupId = GetAttributeValue(element.XmlDefinition, "GroupId");
                c.Location = GetAttributeValue(element.XmlDefinition, "Location");
                c.Sequence = GetAttributeValue(element.XmlDefinition, "Sequence");
                c.RegistrationType = GetAttributeValue(element.XmlDefinition,
                                                  "RegistrationType");
                c.RegistrationId = GetAttributeValue(element.XmlDefinition,
                                                  "RegistrationId");
                retVal.Add(c);
            }
        }
        return retVal;
    }

    private String GetAttributeValue(XmlNode node, String attributeName)
    {
        String retVal = String.Empty;
        if (node.Attributes[attributeName] != null)
             retVal = node.Attributes[attributeName].Value;
        return retVal;
    }
}

public class CustomActionContainer
{
    public String Feature { get; set; }
    public String Id { get; set; }
    public String GroupId { get; set; }
    public String Location { get; set; }
    public String Sequence { get; set; }
    public String RegistrationType { get; set; }
    public String RegistrationId { get; set; }
}
```

The code in the `Page_Load` method of the code-behind class iterates through all the available features for the current SharePoint farm (`SPFarm.Local.FeatureDefinitions`). Next, for every feature and element definition in it, it checks if there's a custom action element definition. For every custom action definition, it collects the attributes into a helper class (`CustomActionContainer`) and returns a list of `CustomActionContainer` objects, which is bound to the repeater.

The result is a simple HTML table that contains values for the properties `Feature`, `Id`, `GroupId`, `Location`, `Sequence`, `RegistrationType`, and `RegistrationId`.

Extending Site Settings

If you build your own complex SharePoint applications, you are often faced with the need to add some custom administrative pages to offer configuration of various application settings. To do this you can, for example, easily extend the site settings page (`/_layouts/settings.aspx`) with custom sections and links (see Figure 10–38).

You can use the same principle to extend the setting pages of the Central Administration web site.

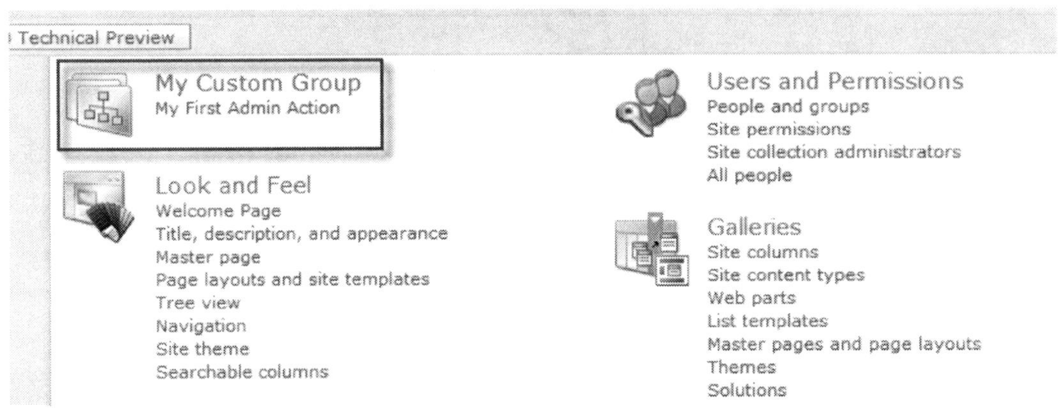

Figure 10–38. *Custom section and link on the site settings page*

Listing 10–6 shows two XML elements: `CustomActionGroup`, which is for a section, and `CustomAction`, which is for displaying a link within this section. `CustomActionGroup` is placed in the location `Microsoft.SharePoint.SiteSettings`; `CustomAction` is also placed in this location, but its `GroupID` points to `CustomActionGroup`.

Listing 10–6. *Adding a Custom Action Group and a Custom Action to the Site Settings (elements.xml)*

```
<CustomActionGroup
    Id="Apress.SP2010.myCustomGroup"
    Title="My Custom Group"
    Description="This is my custom group"
    ImageUrl="_layouts/images/SiteSettings_SiteCollectionAdmin_48x48.png"
    Location="Microsoft.SharePoint.SiteSettings"
    RequiredAdmin="Delegated"
    Sequence="1" />

  <CustomAction
    Id="myFirstAdminAction"
    Title="My First Admin Action"
    Description="This is a short description of my first admin action."
    Location="Microsoft.SharePoint.SiteSettings"
    GroupId="Apress.SP2010.myCustomGroup"
    Sequence="100" >
    <UrlAction Url="~site/_layouts/sp2010/myFirstAdminPage.aspx" />
  </CustomAction>
```

Adding Nested Menus

Using nested menus is a powerful technique for custom actions. For example, you may have seen that the Site Actions menu can have flyout menus (Figure 10–39 contains examples). Normally, you add a single menu item, without any subitems. However, two properties of `CustomAction`—namely, `ControlAssembly` and `ControlClass`—allow us to assemble our own web controls for hierarchical menu structures. Here's how:

1. Create a web control that renders itself in the form of `MenuItemTemplates`.
2. Register this class as a safe control in the `web.config` file.
3. Add a custom action with a web control reference to the `elements.xml` file of your feature.
4. Add custom actions as menu items for your custom implementation.

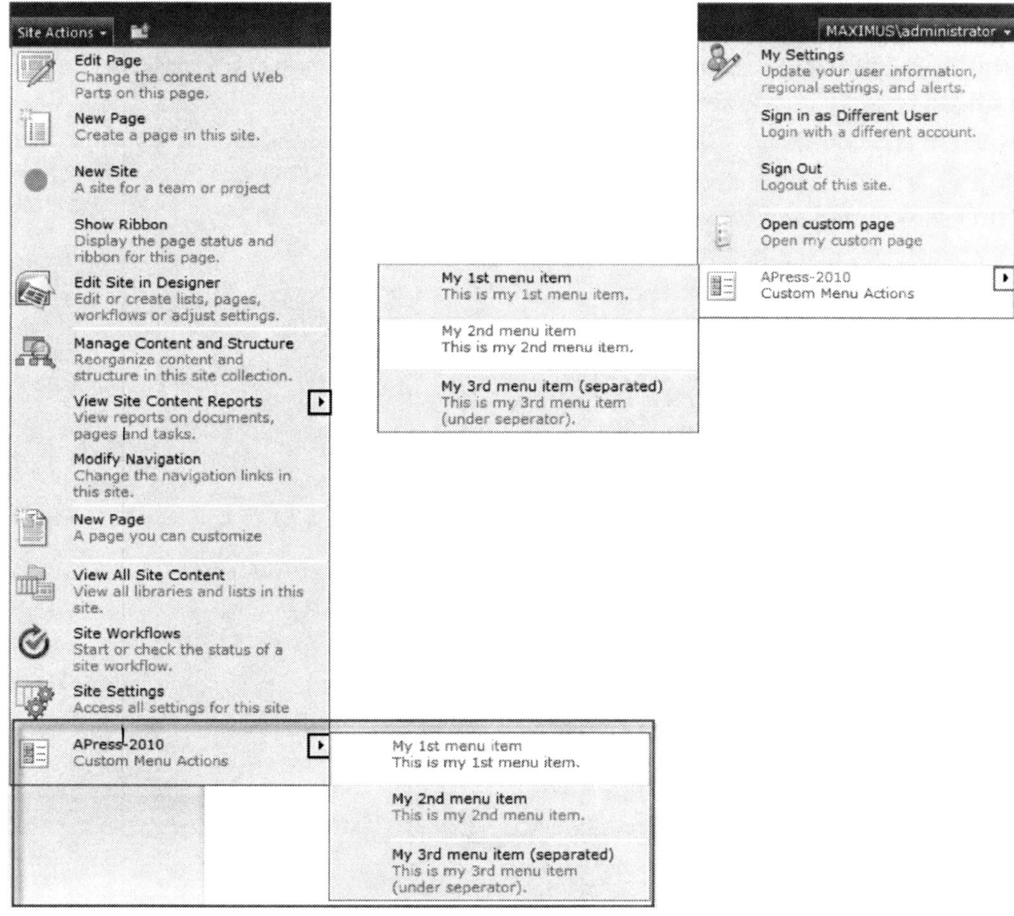

***Figure 10–39.** Nested menus*

Custom Web Controls

The idea is to create a web control containing three child controls: one `SubMenuTemplate` control and two `FeatureMenuTemplate` controls.

All three controls are SharePoint web controls, defined in the namespace `Microsoft.SharePoint.WebControls`. Note that `FeatureMenuTemplate` is a control that renders existing custom actions for a defined `Location` and `GroupId`. You can use these two `FeatureMenuTemplate` instances to dynamically add further menu items through custom actions.

To make this work, you need to use a little trick: in the `OnPreRender` method, you need to ensure that the custom action menu item controls of `FeatureMenuTemplate` are added directly to `SubMenuTemplate`. These menu item controls are automatically initialized in the `CreateChildControls` method of the `FeatureMenuTemplate` class. Then check if there are controls within `FeatureMenuTemplate` and add them to `SubMenuTemplate`. Listing 10–7 shows an example implementation for nested menus.

▒ **Tip** By implementing your custom menu behavior, it is possible to dynamically modify items in the page load event. For example, you could process custom URL tokens for automatic URL rewriting or add additional information to menu items.

Listing 10–7. *CustomAppMenu.cs: Custom Web Control Implementation*

```
namespace Apress.SP2010.NestedMenu
{
    public class CustomAppMenu : WebControl
    {
        protected SubMenuTemplate customSubMenu;
        protected FeatureMenuTemplate customMenuTemplate1;
        protected FeatureMenuTemplate customMenuTemplate2;

        protected override void CreateChildControls()
        {
            customSubMenu = new SubMenuTemplate();
            customSubMenu.Text = "APress-2010";
            customSubMenu.Description = "Custom Menu Actions";
            customSubMenu.ImageUrl = "/_layouts/images/lg_ICASCX.gif";
            this.Controls.Add(customSubMenu);

            customMenuTemplate1 = new FeatureMenuTemplate();
            customMenuTemplate1.FeatureScope = "Site";
            customMenuTemplate1.Location = "APress.CustomMenu";
            customMenuTemplate1.GroupId = "APress";
            this.Controls.Add(customMenuTemplate1);

            customMenuTemplate2 = new FeatureMenuTemplate();
            customMenuTemplate2.FeatureScope = "Site";
            customMenuTemplate2.Location = "APress.CustomMenu";
            customMenuTemplate2.GroupId = "APress2";
            this.Controls.Add(customMenuTemplate2);
        }
```

```
        protected override void OnPreRender(EventArgs e)
        {
            while (customMenuTemplate1.Controls.Count > 0)
            {
                MenuItemTemplate menuItem = customMenuTemplate1.Controls[0]
                                            as MenuItemTemplate;
                if (menuItem!=null) customSubMenu.Controls.Add(menuItem);
            }

            // Separator
            MenuSeparatorTemplate subMenuSep = new MenuSeparatorTemplate();
            customSubMenu.Controls.Add(subMenuSep);

            while (customMenuTemplate2.Controls.Count > 0)
            {
                MenuItemTemplate menuItem = customMenuTemplate2.Controls[0]
                                            as MenuItemTemplate;
                if (menuItem != null) customSubMenu.Controls.Add(menuItem);
            }

            base.OnPreRender(e);
        }
    }
}
```

Registering a Control as Safe

After compiling the preceding class into a strongly named assembly, you need to add it to the GAC or the bin folder of your web application. Then ensure that the namespace of your web control implementation is registered as a safe control within the web.config file (see Listing 10–8).

Listing 10–8. *web.config: Registering the Namespace as a Safe Control*

```
<SafeControl Assembly="Apress.SP2010, Version=1.0.0.0, Culture=neutral,
             PublicKeyToken=4113b8ec9b28df52"
             Namespace="Apress.SP2010.NestedMenu" TypeName="*" Safe="True" />
```

■ **Note** If you use a Visual Studio SharePoint Project Template, the GAC registration is done automatically when deploying the project.

Specifying Custom Actions for Menu Extension

To use the web control implementation, you have to add a CustomAction element to the elements.xml file of the feature. This CustomAction element defines the Location and GroupId properties for the control, and it references the class and assembly names via the ControlAssembly and ControlClass properties (see Listing 10–9).

Listing 10– 9. elements.xml: Custom Action That References a Web Control Class

```
<CustomAction
      Id="Apress_MenuExtension"
      GroupId="SiteActions"
      Sequence="1"
      Location="Microsoft.SharePoint.StandardMenu"
      ControlAssembly="Apress.SP2010, Version=1.0.0.0, Culture=neutral,
PublicKeyToken=4113b8ec9b28df52"
      ControlClass="Apress.SP2010.NestedMenu.CustomAppMenu">
</CustomAction>
```

Specifying Custom Actions for Submenu Items

In the final step, you fill out the `FeatureMenuTemplate` placeholders of the custom class implementation with custom menu items. These placeholders are identified by their `Location` and `GroupId` properties. The sample code shown in Listing 10–10 adds two menu items to the first `FeatureMenuTemplate` (`Location=Apress.CustomMenu, GroupId=APress`) and one item to the second `FeatureMenuTemplate` (`Location=Apress.CustomMenu, GroupID=Apress2`).

Listing 10–10. elements.xml: Adding Menu Items as Custom Actions

```
<CustomAction
    Id="apressMenuItem1"
    Title="My 1st menu item"
    Description="This is my 1st menu item."
    Location="APress.CustomMenu"
    GroupId="APress"
    Sequence="100" >
    <UrlAction Url="~site/_layouts/sp2010/page01.aspx" />
  </CustomAction>

  <CustomAction
    Id="apressMenuItem2"
    Title="My 2nd menu item"
    Description="This is my 2nd menu item."
    Location="APress.CustomMenu"
    GroupId="APress"
    Sequence="200" >
    <UrlAction Url="~site/_layouts/sp2010/page02.aspx" />
  </CustomAction>

  <CustomAction
    Id="apressMenuItem3"
    Title="My 3rd menu item (separated)"
    Description="This is my 3rd menu item (under separator)."
    Location="APress.CustomMenu"
    GroupId="APress2"
    Sequence="100" >
    <UrlAction Url="~site/_layouts/sp2010/page03.aspx" />
  </CustomAction>
```

Using Ribbons

With SharePoint 2010, the ribbon interface of Microsoft Office has been ported to the Web (see Figure 10–40). The ribbon interface is designed to help users quickly find the commands they need to complete a task. Commands are organized in logical groups, which are collected in tabs. Each tab relates to a type of activity, such as editing items or lists. To reduce clutter, some tabs are only displayed when they are needed, based on the current context.

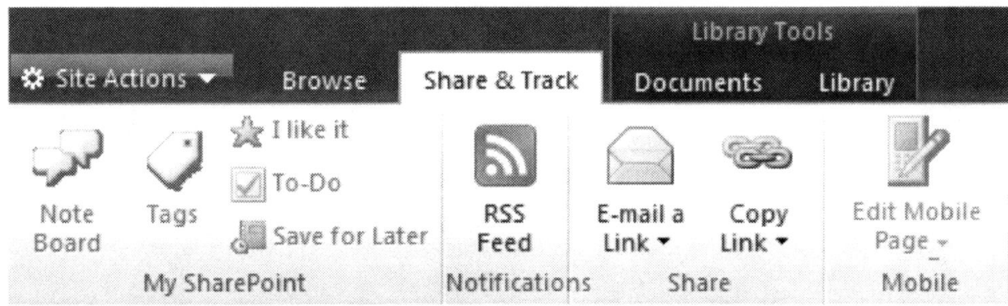

Figure 10–40. Ribbon bar

■ **Note** This section contains only a short overview of the SharePoint Command UI and its ribbon interface. For an in-depth description of programming the Command UI, please take a look at Chapter 11.

The various SharePoint ribbon bars are defined in one XML file under the 14 hive: `/14/TEMPLATE/GLOBAL/XML/CMDUI.XML`. This file contains a definition for the SharePoint Command UI. The simplified XML structure looks like this:

```
<CommandUI>
  <Ribbon>
    <Tabs>
      <Tab ID="Ribbon.TrackTab" Command="TrackTab" ...>
        <Groups>
          <Group ID="Ribbon.TrackTabNotifications"
                 Command="NotifictionsGroup" ...>
            <Controls>
              <Button  ID="Ribbon.TrackTabNotificationsControls.MyButton"
                       Command="MyButton" ...>
```

As the sample shows, each tab contains groups that in turn contain controls, such as buttons and menus. Every element from the tab is identified by an ID and has a command that is executed if the matching event (normally a click) occurs. The example XML excerpt of `CMDUI.XML` in Figure 10–41 shows how ribbon tabs and their related controls are defined.

```
<Tab Id="Ribbon.TrackTab" Command="TrackTab" Description="" Title="$Resources:core,cui_TabTrackTitle;">
  <Scaling Id="Ribbon.TrackTab.Scaling">
    <MaxSize Id="Ribbon.TrackTab.Scaling.Notifications.MaxSize" Sequence="10" GroupId="Ribbon.TrackTab.Notifications" Size="LargeMedium" />
    <MaxSize Id="Ribbon.TrackTab.Scaling.Share.MaxSize" Sequence="10" GroupId="Ribbon.TrackTab.Share" Size="LargeMedium" />
    <MaxSize Id="Ribbon.TrackTab.Scaling.Mobile.MaxSize" Sequence="10" GroupId="Ribbon.TrackTab.Mobile" Size="LargeMedium" />
    <Scale Id="Ribbon.TrackTab.Scaling.Mobile.MediumSmall" Sequence="70" GroupId="Ribbon.TrackTab.Mobile" Size="MediumSmall" />
    <Scale Id="Ribbon.TrackTab.Scaling.Share.Popup" Sequence="70" GroupId="Ribbon.TrackTab.Share" Size="Popup" />
    <Scale Id="Ribbon.TrackTab.Scaling.Mobile.Popup" Sequence="70" GroupId="Ribbon.TrackTab.Mobile" Size="Popup" />
  </Scaling>
  <Groups Id="Ribbon.TrackTab.Groups">
    <Group
      Id="Ribbon.TrackTab.Notifications"
      Sequence="10"
      Command="NotificationsGroup"
      Description=""
      Title="$Resources:core,cui_GrpNotifications;"
      Template="Ribbon.Templates.Flexible2"
    >
      <Controls Id="Ribbon.TrackTab.Notifications.Controls">
        <FlyoutAnchor
          Id="Ribbon.TrackTab.Notifications.AlertMe"
          Alt="$Resources:core,cui_ButAlertMe;"
          ImageArrow="/_layouts/images/menudark.gif"
          Image16by16="/_layouts/images/formatmap16x16.png" Image16by16Class="formatmap16x16_AlertMe16"
          Image32by32="/_layouts/images/formatmap32x32.png" Image32by32Class="formatmap32x32_alertme32"
          LabelText="$Resources:core,cui_ButAlertMe;"
          TemplateAlias="o1">
          <Menu Id="Ribbon.TrackTab.Notifications.AlertMe.Menu">
            <MenuSection Id="Ribbon.TrackTab.Notifications.AlertMe.Menu.Scope" Sequence="10" DisplayMode="Menu">
              <Controls Id="Ribbon.TrackTab.Notifications.AlertMe.Menu.Scope.Controls">
                <Button
                  Id="Ribbon.TrackTab.Notifications.AlertMe.Menu.Scope.AlertPage"
                  Sequence="10"
                  Alt="$Resources:core,cui_ButAlertMePage;"
                  Command="AlertMePage"
                  LabelText="$Resources:core,cui_ddTrackScopePage;"
                  ToolTipTitle="$Resources:core,cui_ButAlertMePage;"
                  ToolTipDescription="$Resources:core,cui_STT_ButAlertMePage;"
                  />
                <Button
                  Id="Ribbon.TrackTab.Notifications.AlertMe.Menu.Scope.AlertLibrary"
                  Sequence="20"
```

Figure 10–41. *Command UI XML defintion in the file, CMDUI.XML*

If you wish to customize the SharePoint ribbons, the straightforward way to do this is using custom actions. You don't need to make any changes to the default `CMDUI.XML`. Instead, you can add new elements, or modify and remove existing elements using normal custom actions and deploy them with a feature.

As mentioned, every control on a ribbon has a command ID. To respond to a command, implement a JavaScript command handler in your custom actions. Such a handler could be implemented like this:

```
<CustomAction>
  ...
  <CommandUIHandlers>
    <CommandUIHandler Command="NewRibbonButtonCommand" *#*
                      CommandAction="javascript:alert('This is my new button!');" />
  </CommandUIHandlers>
  ...
</CustomAction>
```

The following sections show some examples of how to add to and modify existing ribbon bars.

Adding a Button

To add a button, you have to define the location on the ribbon where you want the button to appear. In the following example, a button is added to the List tab of a custom list toolbar (RegistrationID=100).

```
<Elements xmlns="http://schemas.microsoft.com/sharepoint/">

  <CustomAction Id="Ribbon.List.Actions.AddAButton"
                Location="CommandUI.Ribbon"
                RegistrationId="100"
                RegistrationType="List"
                Title="My custom Ribbon Button">
    <CommandUIExtension>
      <CommandUIDefinitions>
        <CommandUIDefinition
        Location="Ribbon.List.Actions.Controls._children">
          <Button Id="Ribbon.List.Actions.NewRibbonButton"
                  Command="MyNewRibbonButtonCommand"
                  Image16by16="/_layouts/images/newtargetapp16.png"
                  Image32by32="/_layouts/images/newtargetapp32.png"
                  LabelText="My custom button"
                  TemplateAlias="o1" />
        </CommandUIDefinition>
      </CommandUIDefinitions>
      <CommandUIHandlers>
        <CommandUIHandler Command="MyNewRibbonButtonCommand"
                          CommandAction="javascript:alert('This is my custom button!');" />
      </CommandUIHandlers>
    </CommandUIExtension>
  </CustomAction>

</Elements>
```

The result of this custom action is shown in Figure 10–42.

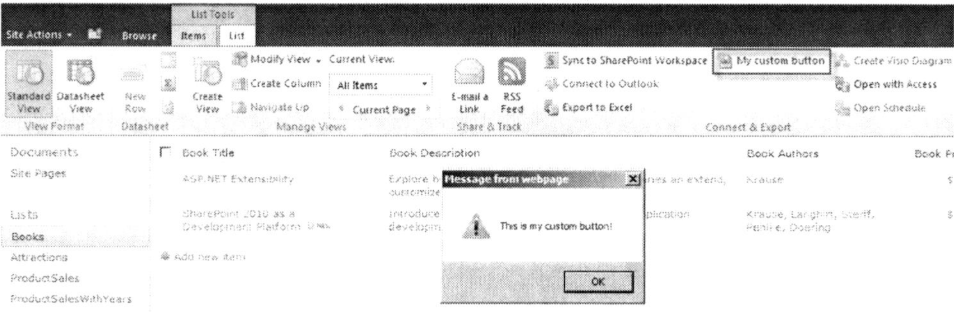

Figure 10–42. Adding a custom button to the List tab of a custom list

Removing a Button

To remove a button from the ribbon, you define the location of the button you want to remove. You use a `HideCustomAction` element to remove a button from the ribbon. The following example removes the Connect to Outlook button from the Library tab in the Actions group for a document library.

```
<HideCustomAction Id="RemoveRibbonButton"
Location="CommandUI.Ribbon.Library.Actions.ConnectToClient">
  </HideCustomAction>
```

Replacing a Button

Replacing a button on the ribbon bar also begins by specifying the button to be replaced. The following procedure replaces the Open with Access button on the List tab in the Actions group for a custom list.

```
<Elements xmlns="http://schemas.microsoft.com/sharepoint/">
<CustomAction Id="Ribbon.List.Actions.ReplacementButton"
                Location="CommandUI.Ribbon"
                RegistrationId="100"
                RegistrationType="List"
                Title="Replace a Ribbon Button">
    <CommandUIExtension>
      <CommandUIDefinitions>
        <CommandUIDefinition Location="Ribbon.List.Actions.OpenWithAccess">
          <Button Id="Ribbon.List.Actions.OpenWithAccess.ReplacementButton"
                  Command="ReplacementButtonCommand"
                  Image16by16="/_layouts/images/msg16.gif"
                  Image32by32="/_layouts/images/msg32.gif"
                  LabelText="Open with Access (replaced)"
                  TemplateAlias="o1" />
        </CommandUIDefinition>
      </CommandUIDefinitions>
      <CommandUIHandlers>
        <CommandUIHandler Command="ReplacementButtonCommand"
                          CommandAction="javascript:alert('You cannot  open this list with
Access.');" />
      </CommandUIHandlers>
    </CommandUIExtension>
  </CustomAction>
</Elements>
```

After activating the feature with the custom action for ribbon button replacement, the ribbon bar will be rendered as shown in Figure 10–43.

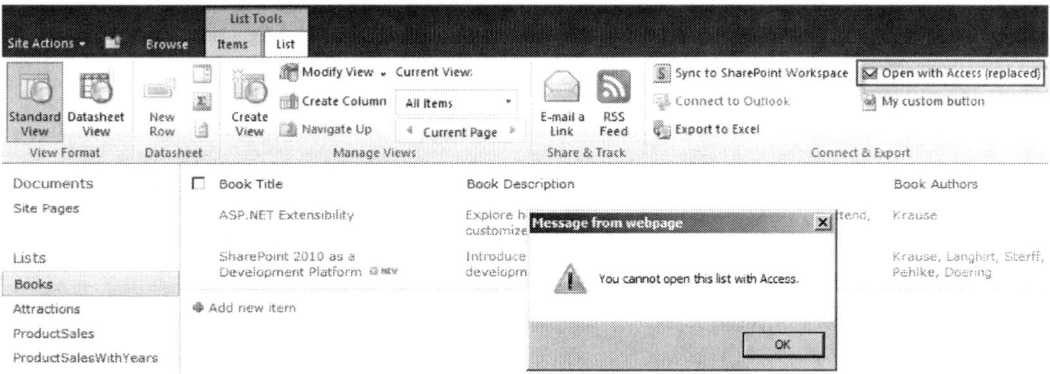

Figure 10–43. *Replacing a button from the toolbar of a custom list*

Summary

This chapter explained the different types of master pages and how to use them in your own application pages. Understanding and using master pages in your own custom web controls and application pages are indispensable skills for every professional SharePoint developer.

This chapter also provided insight into the SharePoint navigation concepts, together with some practical examples.

It also introduced the SharePoint theming infrastructure, including the dramatic changes compared to previous versions of SharePoint, and an in-depth explanation of what is going on under the hood.

Extending the SharePoint UI with your own custom actions is the foundation for building professional SharePoint-based solutions. Finally, you learned how to enhance standard SharePoint menus with custom menu items and customize the ribbon bar.

CHAPTER 11

Using Web Controls

While Web Parts and ASP.NET application pages are easy to create and deploy, experienced SharePoint developers agree that building professional SharePoint applications is anything but trivial.

To address this incongruity, in this chapter we will walk through the most important SharePoint web controls that are needed to build individual custom applications or SharePoint Web Parts.

The main part of this chapter describes the most common SharePoint user interface (UI) controls. They include such powerful controls as the `SPGridView` control and the new `SPRibbon` control—both are highly useful when creating applications with a great user experience.

This chapter covers

- Field controls
- Input form controls
- Picker and selector controls
- Toolbar and ribbon controls
- Data controls (`SPGridView`, `JSGrid`)

With each new version, the SharePoint framework has grown in size. Currently, the `Microsoft.SharePoint.WebControls` namespace alone contains more than 450 public classes and over 370 classes that inherit from `System.Web.UI.Control`.

Overview

This section covers a fraction of all the available controls. Divided into five categories, the most significant controls for developers are each described briefly (see Table 11–1).

Table 11–1. *Web Control Categories*

Category	Description
Field controls	Controls that inherit from `Microsoft.SharePoint.WebControls.BaseFieldControl`. These controls are usually used in the list item forms (Display, Edit, and Add forms).
Input controls	Controls that begin with the prefix `Input` and that work as wrapped controls surrounding the ASP.NET default controls (e.g., `InputFormTextBox`).
Picker controls	Controls for displaying picker boxes and dialogs.

Category	Description
Toolbar and Ribbon controls	Controls that enable the user to control pages.
Data controls	Controls for displaying list data.

Field Controls

Let's start with the field controls that are commonly used to display or edit list items. When you create a custom list and add a column, you can choose between 12 field types, as shown in Figure 11–1.

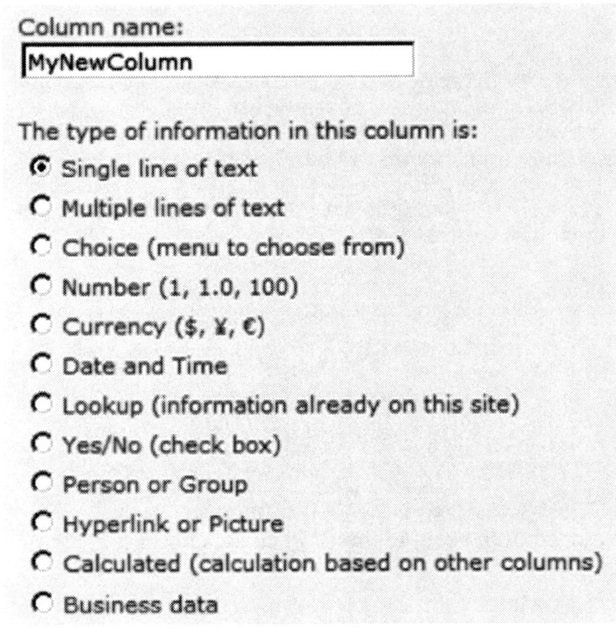

Figure 11–1. *Available default field types for list items*

Each field type is mapped to a SharePoint field control in the `Microsoft.SharePoint.WebControls` namespace. Table 11–2 shows these mappings.

Table 11–2. Field Type Mappings

List Column Type	SharePoint Web Control
Single line of text	TextField
Multiple lines of text (plain text)	NoteField
Multiple lines of text (rich text)	RichTextField
Multiple lines of text (enhanced rich text)	RichTextField
Choice (drop-down)	DropDownChoiceField
Choice (radio button)	RadioButtonChoiceField
Number	NumberField
Currency	CurrencyField
Date and Time	DateTimeField
Lookup (single item)	LookupField
Lookup (multiple items)	MultipleLookupField
Yes/no	BooleanField
Person or group	UserField
Hyperlink or picture	UrlField
Calculated	CalculatedField
Business data	BusinessDataField

Understanding the BaseFieldControl Base Class

As you've learned, SharePoint provides various standard form controls to render each type of column. These controls appear on the standard Display, Add, and Edit forms, and they all inherit from the `BaseFieldControl` class.

In a SharePoint list (class `SPList`), there are a number of fields, and each `SPField` element creates a control based on `BaseFieldControl`. Each control is a composite control consisting of one or more ASP.NET controls.

For a single-line text field, the control is a wrapped `TextBox`. For more advanced fields, such as a multiselect lookup field or a rich text field, you will need some more complex controls, and of course their related JavaScript code.

The BaseFieldControl can be directly connected to a SharePoint SPListItem, and BaseFieldControl.Value will match the format required to fill the SPListItem.

To see the functionality, create a list named MyNewList with the columns LastName, FirstName, and Age. Now you can write an application page that displays a list item with the rendering controls defined for the fields (see Figure 11–2).

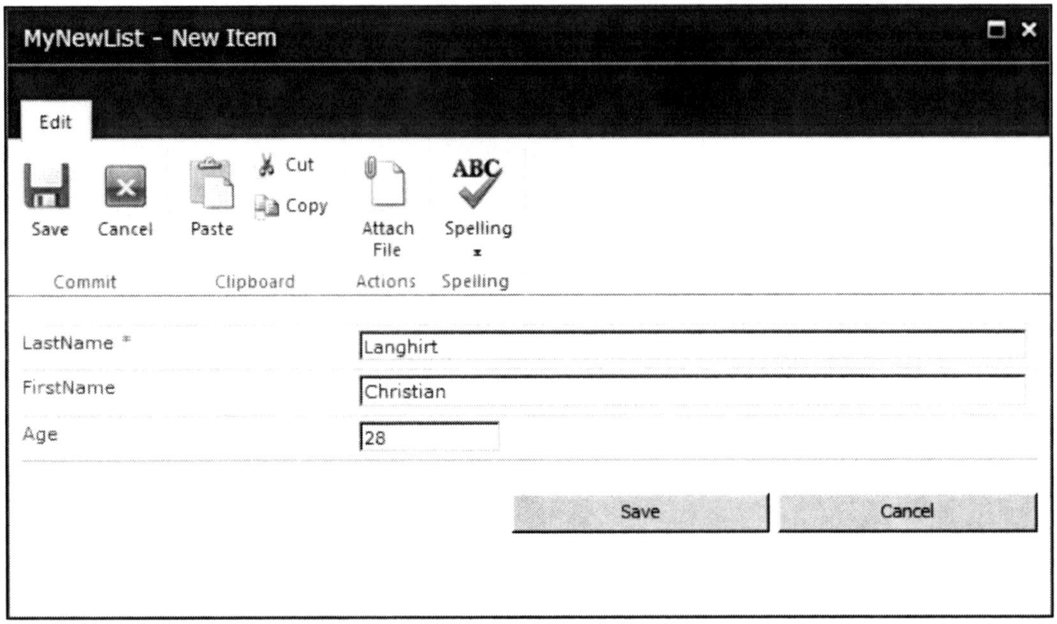

Figure 11–2. *Creating a new list item*

First, build a simple application page (DisplayListItem.aspx) with a code-behind file in the LAYOUTS directory, as shown in Listing 11–1.

Listing 11–1. *Application Page DisplayListItem.aspx*

```
<%@ Page Language="C#" AutoEventWireup="true"
         DynamicMasterPageFile="~masterurl/default.master"
         CodeFile="DisplayListItem.aspx.cs"
         Inherits="DisplayListItem"
         MasterPageFile="v4.master"
         CodeFileBaseClass= "Microsoft.SharePoint.WebControls.LayoutsPageBase" %>

<asp:Content ContentPlaceHolderId="PlaceHolderMain" runat="server">
    <asp:PlaceHolder runat="server" ID="content" />
</asp:Content>
```

Second, implement suitable methods to display the list items' fields, as shown in Listing 11–2.

***Listing 11–2.** Code-Behind Class DisplayListItem.aspx.cs*

```
public partial class DisplayListItem : LayoutsPageBase
{
    protected void Page_Load(object sender, EventArgs e)
    {
        ShowListItem();
    }

    protected void ShowListItem()
    {
        using (SPWeb web = SPContext.Current.Web)
        {
            // Define List and ItemID
            SPList list = web.Lists["MyNewList"];
            int listItemId = 1;

            Table table = new Table();
            table.BorderStyle = BorderStyle.Dotted;

            foreach (SPField f in list.Fields)
            {
                if (!f.Hidden && f.CanBeDisplayedInEditForm)
                {
                    // Render every visible field with a rendering control
                    BaseFieldControl bfc = f.FieldRenderingControl;
                    if (bfc != null)
                    {
                        SPContext renderContext =
                        SPContext.GetContext(this.Context, listItemId,
                                             list.ID, web);

                        bfc.ListId = list.ID;
                        bfc.FieldName = f.InternalName;
                        bfc.ID = f.InternalName;
                        bfc.ControlMode = SPControlMode.Display;
                        bfc.RenderContext = renderContext;
                        bfc.ItemContext = renderContext;
                        bfc.EnableViewState = true;
                        bfc.Visible = true;
                        table.Rows.Add(CreateTR(f,bfc));
                    }
                }
            }
            content.Controls.Add(table);
        }
    }

    private TableRow CreateTR(SPField field, Control ctl)
    {
        TableRow tr = new TableRow();
```

```
            TableCell td1 = new TableCell();
            td1.Text = field.InternalName + " (" + field.Title + ")";

            TableCell td2 = new TableCell();
            td2.Controls.Add(ctl);

            TableCell td3 = new TableCell();
            td3.Text = field.Description;

            TableCell td4 = new TableCell();
            td4.Text = field.FieldRenderingControl.ToString();

            tr.Cells.AddRange(new TableCell[] {td1, td2, td3, td4});
            return tr;
        }
}
```

The example in Listing 11–2 loops through all the visible fields of the SharePoint list `MyNewList`. Within each iteration, the `FieldRenderingControl` property is evaluated, and the assigned `BaseFieldControl` instance of this field is rendered. By populating the `RenderContext` and `ItemContext` properties of the `BaseFieldControl` list item, values for the list item are loaded with `ID=1`. For each field value, a table row instance is created and added to the output table. Thus, the ASP.NET page renders all visible list fields and displays them in a table, as shown in Figure 11–3.

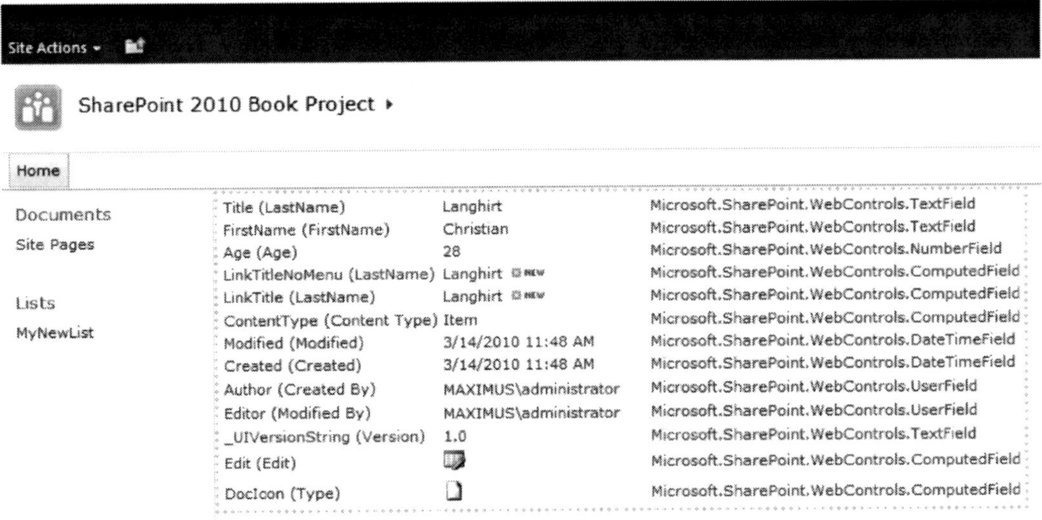

***Figure 11–3.** Rendered list item fields in display mode (including read-only fields)*

You can also set the `ControlMode` property of the rendering controls to `SPControlMode.Edit`. This switches the controls to appear in their editable mode (see Figure 11–4). If you build your own Edit mode forms, be sure to exclude read-only fields (`SPField.ReadOnlyField` is `true`).

Figure 11–4. Rendered list item fields in Edit mode (without read-only fields)

To build a fully functional edit form, place an `<asp:Button>` on the page and add the methods shown in Listing 11–3 to the code-behind file.

Listing 11–3. Postback Event Handler Implementation

```
protected void Button1_Click(object sender, EventArgs e)
{
   SPListItem li = null;
   List<BaseFieldControl> ctls =  FindControls<BaseFieldControl>(content);
   foreach (BaseFieldControl bfc in ctls)
   {
       bfc.UpdateFieldValueInItem();
        li = bfc.ListItem;
   }
   li.Update();
}

private List<T> FindControls<T>(Control rootControl) where T : Control
{
    List<T> retVal = new List<T>();
    if (rootControl.HasControls())
    {
        foreach (Control c in rootControl.Controls)
        {
            if (c.GetType().IsSubclassOf(typeof(T))) retVal.Add((T)c);
            retVal.AddRange(FindControls<T>(c));
        }
    }
    return retVal;
}
```

This example includes a helper method, `FindControls`, which iterates recursively through all the controls of a container control and assembles in a list all the child controls of a particular type. In the example, the `Button1_Click` method uses this function to obtain all the controls of type `BaseFieldControl`. For every control, the code calls the `UpdateFieldValueInItem` method to ensure that the new values are stored within the `ListItem` of the rendering context. The final step is to call the `SPListItem.Update` method to write the list item data back to the database.

Custom Field Controls

The need to create a custom field type for lists is a frequent requirement—but it is unfortunately not as easy as it seems. There are a couple of ways to build your own custom field types; in this section we'll show you a way to do that.

The most important thing is to understand the correlations between the involved elements, as shown in Figure 11–5. First of all, a custom field implementation consists of at least the following elements:

- A *field class*, which inherits from `SPField` and contains the field data
- A *field-rendering control class*, which inherits from `BaseSPFieldControl` and references the field-rendering template
- A *field-rendering template* for adding and editing dialogs (ASCX), which is used within the field-rendering control
- An XML *field type definition* (`fldtypes_[myFieldType].xml`), which defines the custom field type and points to a field class and a field editor user control
- A custom *field type XSL stylesheet*, which renders the field within list views (`fldtypes_[myFieldType].xsl`]). You only need to implement this if you want to customize the rendering output of your custom field.

There is one further element if custom column properties are used:
A *field editor user control* for creating and changing the column settings (ASCX)

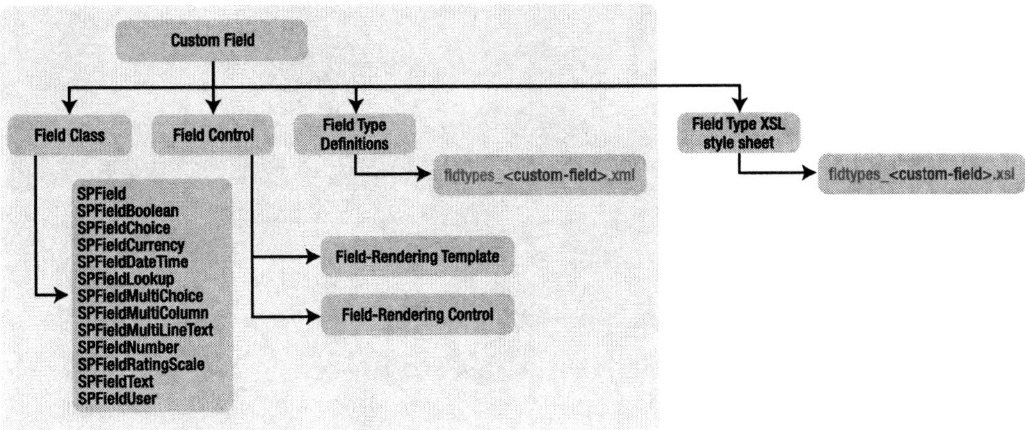

Figure 11–5. *Field elements and their relationships*

The following example demonstrates how to create a custom field that behaves as a number field while it is being edited, and renders as a bar indicator when it is viewed (see Figure 11–6).

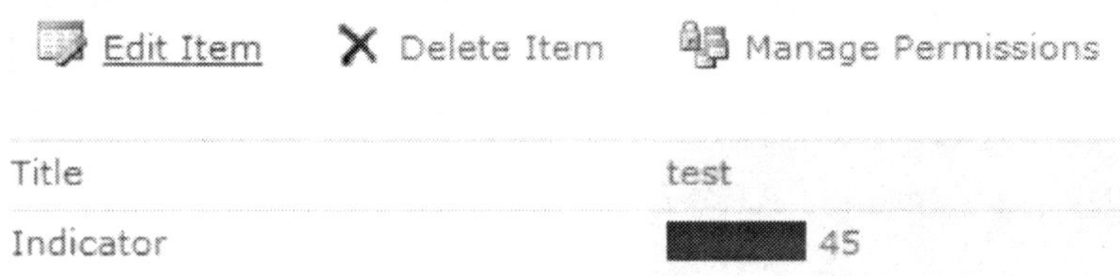

Figure 11–6. *Custom bar indicator field*

Field Type Definition

We start with the XML file for the field type definition. Simply create an XML file, prefix the file name with `fldtypes_` (in this example, it is called `fldtypes_CustomIndicatorField.xml`), and save the file in the `TEMPLATE/XML` directory of the 14 hive, as shown in Listing 11–4.

Listing 11–4. *Field Type Definition: fldtypes_CustomIndicatorField.xml*

```
<?xml version="1.0" encoding="utf-8"?>
<FieldTypes>
  <FieldType>
    <Field Name="TypeName">CustomIndicatorField</Field>
    <Field Name="ParentType">Number</Field>
    <Field Name="TypeDisplayName">Custom Indicator Field</Field>
    <Field Name="TypeShortDescription">Custom Indicator Field Description</Field>
    <Field Name="UserCreatable">TRUE</Field>
    <Field Name="ShowOnListCreate">TRUE</Field>
    <Field Name="ShowOnSurveyCreate">TRUE</Field>
    <Field Name="ShowOnDocumentLibrary">TRUE</Field>
    <Field Name="ShowOnColumnTemplateCreate">TRUE</Field>
    <Field Name="Sortable">TRUE</Field>
    <Field Name="Filterable">TRUE</Field>
    <Field Name="FieldTypeClass">Apress.SP2010.CustomIndicatorField, Apress.SP2010,
           Version=1.0.0.0, Culture=neutral, PublicKeyToken=4113b8ec9b28df52</Field>

   <PropertySchema>
      <Fields>
        <Field Name="ToolTip" DisplayName="ToolTip Text"
               MaxLength="255" Type="Text">
          <Default>-</Default>
        </Field>
        <Field Name="ShowToolTip" DisplayName="Show ToolTip" Type="Boolean">
          <Default>1</Default>
        </Field>
      </Fields>
    </PropertySchema>
   <RenderPattern Name="DisplayPattern" DisplayName="DisplayPattern">
      <HTML>
         <![CDATA[<span><span style='background-color:blue'>
         <img src='/_layouts/images/blank.gif' height='10' width=']]>
```

```
        </HTML>
        <HTML>
          <Column HTMLEncode="TRUE"/>
        </HTML>
        <HTML><![CDATA[' /></span> ]]></HTML>
        <HTML>
          <Column HTMLEncode="TRUE"/>
        </HTML>
        <HTML><![CDATA[</span> ]]></HTML>
      </RenderPattern>

  </FieldType>
</FieldTypes>
```

The first few XML elements define the type and the names of our new field. The `FieldTypeClass` attribute is important, as it has a fully named reference to an assembly containing the field class.

After the field elements, there is a `PropertySchema` section. Here you can define custom properties. Custom properties are column-related values and are stored within the field class (see Figure 11–7). The `RenderPattern` section defines how the field is rendered within HTML. In the preceding example (Listing 11–4), the custom indicator field renders as a transparent image, encapsulated by a `<span>` tag with blue background color. The width of the image in pixels depends on the value of the custom column.

```
<span><span  style='background-color:blue'>
<img src='/_layouts/images/blank.gif' height='10'
     width='[value of the custom indicator column]'/>
<span>[value of the custom indicator column]</span>
```

■ **Note** With SharePoint 2010, the `RenderPattern` section of the field definition by default has no effect on list views. This is because SharePoint 2010 introduces `XsltListViewWebPart`, which simplifies the customizing of list views by using XSLT. If you still want to use `RenderPattern`, you have to add the following code to the field type definition: `<Field Name="CAMLRendering">TRUE</Field>`.

Once the file has been saved and IIS reset, the new column is available for your lists (see Figure 11–7). If you choose the custom column and click Save, an error will be thrown, since the field class does not yet exist.

Column name:

MyIndicatorColumn

The type of information in this column is:

Single line of text
Multiple lines of text
Choice (menu to choose from)
Number (1, 1.0, 100)
Currency ($, ¥, €)
Date and Time
Lookup (information already on this site)
Yes/No (check box)
Person or Group
Hyperlink or Picture
Calculated (calculation based on other columns)
Business data
Custom Indicator Field Description
Managed Metadata

Description:

This is my own custom column

Require that this column contains information:

Yes No

Allow duplicate values:

Yes No

ToolTip Text Here comes my tooltip text
Show ToolTip

Add to default view

Figure 11–7. *Our custom field with two custom properties*

XSL Stylesheets for Custom Fields

As already mentioned, SharePoint 2010 comes with a new `XsltListViewWebPart` architecture (XLV). It ships with a set of shared XSLT files that are used to generate out-of-the-box list views. These files are placed in the `LAYOUTS` folder within the `.xsl` directory (e.g., `main.xsl`, `fldtypes.xsl`, etc.). If you want to add your own customization for your field, you just have to add an XSL file named `fldtypes_`*`yourFieldName`*`.xsl`.

```
<xsl:stylesheet xmlns:x="http://www.w3.org/2001/XMLSchema"
    xmlns:d="http://schemas.microsoft.com/sharepoint/dsp" version="1.0"
    exclude-result-prefixes="xsl msxsl ddwrt"
    xmlns:ddwrt="http://schemas.microsoft.com/WebParts/v2/DataView/runtime"
    xmlns:asp="http://schemas.microsoft.com/ASPNET/20"
    xmlns:__designer="http://schemas.microsoft.com/WebParts/v2/DataView/designer"
    xmlns:xsl="http://www.w3.org/1999/XSL/Transform"
    xmlns:msxsl="urn:schemas-microsoft-com:xslt"
    xmlns:SharePoint="Microsoft.SharePoint.WebControls"
    xmlns:ddwrt2="urn:frontpage:internal">

<xsl:template match="FieldRef[@FieldType='CustomIndicatorField']"
```

```
    mode="Number_body">
    <xsl:param name="thisNode" select="."/>
    <xsl:variable name="value" select="$thisNode/@*[name()=current()/@Name]" />
    <span>
        <span style="background-color:blue">
            <img src="/_layouts/images/blank.gif" height="10" width="{$value}" />
        </span>
        <xsl:value-of select="$value"/>
    </span>
</xsl:template>

</xsl:stylesheet>
```

The XSL template displayed in the preceding code will be used if a field is of type CustomIndicatorField and has a base type of Number. The result of the template is HTML output such as the following:

```
<span><span  style='background-color:blue'>
<img src='/_layouts/images/blank.gif' height='10'
     width='[value of the custom indicator column]'/>
<span>[value of the custom indicator column]</span>
```

The numeric value of the current field instance is assigned to the XSL variable value. Then this variable is used for the width attribute of the image tag and for displaying the value as clear text behind the image.

The Field Class

This class is derived from SPField. It manages the data required by a custom field, such as additional properties. Furthermore, it handles validation, data loading, and saving. In our example, we inherit directly from SPFieldNumber. The only things we have to implement are

- Two constructors that merely call the corresponding constructors of the base class
- Overriding the FieldRenderingControl and returning an instance of our CustomIndicatorFieldControl implementation
- Overriding the GetValidatedString method to serialize the field's value into a string

Listing 11–5 shows the code for the CustomIndicatorField class, with two custom properties (ToolTipCustomProperty and ShowToolTipCustomProperty) added.

Listing 11–5. *Field Class CustomIndicatorField.cs*

```
namespace Apress.SP2010
{
    public class CustomIndicatorField : SPFieldNumber
    {
        public CustomIndicatorField(SPFieldCollection fields, string fieldName)
            : base(fields, fieldName) { Init(); }

        public CustomIndicatorField(SPFieldCollection fields, string typeName,
                                    string displayName)
            : base(fields, typeName, displayName) { Init(); }
```

```
        public String ToolTipCustomProperty { get; set; }
        public bool ShowToolTipCustomProperty { get; set; }

        private void Init()
        {
            // Initialize properties
            this.ToolTipCustomProperty = this.GetCustomProperty("ToolTip") + "" ;
            bool showToolTip = false;
            bool.TryParse(Convert.ToString(GetCustomProperty("ShowToolTip")),
                          out showToolTip);
            this.ShowToolTipCustomProperty = showToolTip;
        }

        public override BaseFieldControl FieldRenderingControl
        {
            get
            {
                BaseFieldControl fieldControl = new CustomIndicatorFieldControl();
                fieldControl.FieldName = this.InternalName;
                return fieldControl;
            }
        }

        public override string GetValidatedString(object value)
        {
            int intValue = 0;
            Int32.TryParse(Convert.ToString(value), out intValue);
            return intValue.ToString();
        }

        public override void Update()
        {
            this.SetCustomProperty("ToolTip", this.ToolTipCustomProperty);
            this.SetCustomProperty("ShowToolTip", this.ShowToolTipCustomProperty);
            base.Update();
        }
    }
}
```

The Field-Rendering Control Class

The field-rendering control renders our custom field. To build one, you need to override some methods (see Listing 11–6):

- Override the `DefaultTemplateName` method and return the name of the custom field-rendering template.
- Override the `CreateChildControls` method to initialize the web controls of the rendering template and assign them to local variables.
- Override the `Value` property and implement your own get and set methods.

- Override the Focus method to set the focus to the correct web control (if using more than one).

Listing 11–6. *Field-Rendering Control Class CustomIndicatorFieldControl.cs*

```
namespace Apress.SP2010
{
    public class CustomIndicatorFieldControl : BaseFieldControl
    {

        protected TextBox txtNumber;

        protected override string DefaultTemplateName
        {
            get { return "CustomIndicatorFieldTemplate"; }
        }

        public override object Value
        {
            get {
                EnsureChildControls();
                return txtNumber.Text;
            }

            set {
                try
                {
                    EnsureChildControls();
                    txtNumber.Text = value.ToString();
                }
                catch { }
            }
        }

        public override void Focus()
        {
            EnsureChildControls();
            txtNumber.Focus();
        }

        protected override void CreateChildControls()
        {

            if (Field == null) return;
            base.CreateChildControls();

            // Don't render the text box if we are just displaying the field
            if (ControlMode == SPControlMode.Display) return;
            txtNumber = (TextBox)TemplateContainer.FindControl("txtNumber");

            if (txtNumber == null)
                            throw new NullReferenceException("txtNumber is null");

            if (ControlMode == SPControlMode.New)
```

```
            {
                txtNumber.Text = "0";
            }
        }

    }
}
```

The Field-Rendering Template

The rendering template is a web user control (in our example it is named CustomIndicatorFieldTemplate.ascx) with at least the following:

- A SharePoint:RenderingTemplate tag with a unique ID
- One or more web controls and HTML elements

Listing 11–7 defines a RenderingTemplate web control, which contains a TextBox and HTML text.

Listing 11–7. *Field-Rendering Template CustomIndicatorFieldTemplate.ascx*

```
<%@ Control Language="C#" AutoEventWireup="false" %>
<%@Assembly Name="Microsoft.SharePoint, Version=14.0.0.0, Culture=neutral,
PublicKeyToken=71e9bce111e9429c" %>
<%@Register TagPrefix="SharePoint" Assembly="Microsoft.SharePoint, Version=14.0.0.0,
Culture=neutral, PublicKeyToken=71e9bce111e9429c"
namespace="Microsoft.SharePoint.WebControls"%>

<SharePoint:RenderingTemplate ID="CustomIndicatorFieldTemplate" runat="server">
    <Template>
        <asp:TextBox runat="server" ID="txtNumber" /><br />
        Enter a number from 0 to 100
    </Template>
</SharePoint:RenderingTemplate>
```

Please note that the ASCX control defines no code-behind class, and thus no server-side code. Don't create a new ASCX control that automatically adds a code-behind class by using Visual Studio. Instead, just create a new text file and rename it with an .ascx extension. In conjunction with the field-rendering control class, the content of the RenderingTemplate is displayed if you edit an item (see Figure 11–8).

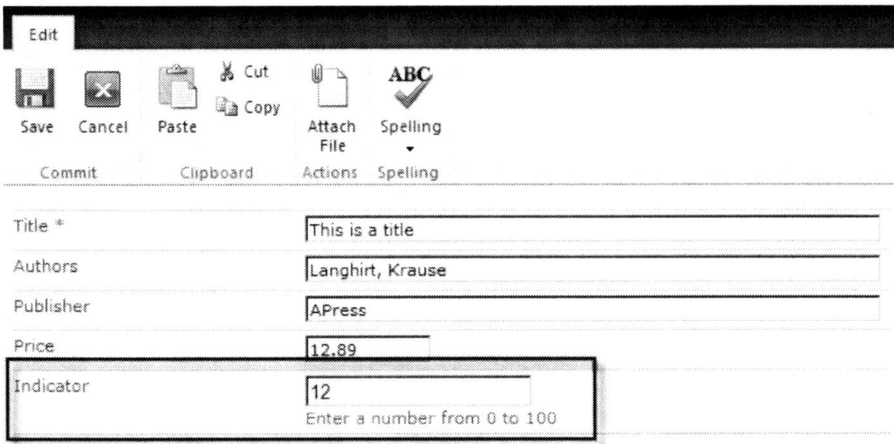

Figure 11–8. *Custom field-rendering control in Edit mode*

Getting the Custom Field to Work

This chapter shows how to rapidly develop and deploy your code. The optimal way to deploy nearly all customizations is to encapsulate the functionalities within a feature and deliver this feature as a SharePoint solution (a WSP file, which by design can be easily deployed to other SharePoint servers).

Getting the custom field working is quickly accomplished:

- Ensure that the field type definition file (`fldtypes_CustomIndicatorField.xml`) is named correctly (it must begin with the prefix `fldtypes_`) and resides under `TEMPLATE/XML` within the 14 hive.
- Ensure that the field-rendering template (`CustomIndicatorFieldTemplate.ascx`) has a unique ID and is stored under `TEMPLATE/CONTROLTEMPLATES` within the 14 hive.
- Ensure that the field class (`CustomIndicatorField.cs`) and the field-rendering control class (`CustomIndicatorFieldControl.cs`) are both compiled for AnyCPU or x64 as the platform target (not for x86!) into an assembly that is signed with a strong name, and that they're both installed into the GAC.
- Restart IIS (or recycle the application pool).

Custom Field Properties

In the previous section, some fields were defined within the `PropertySchema` element of the field type definition file (`fldtypes_CustomIndicatorField.xml`) to store custom properties into a field. The input controls rendering these fields have very limited functionality. Although it is possible to input simple values—such as strings using text boxes and Booleans through check boxes—what if you need a more complex input control? Consider the case where you wish to select another `SPList` from a drop-down menu—for example, to populate values of a custom field control (similar to the lookup field). To achieve this you need to implement a so-called *field editor user control* (see Figure 11–9).

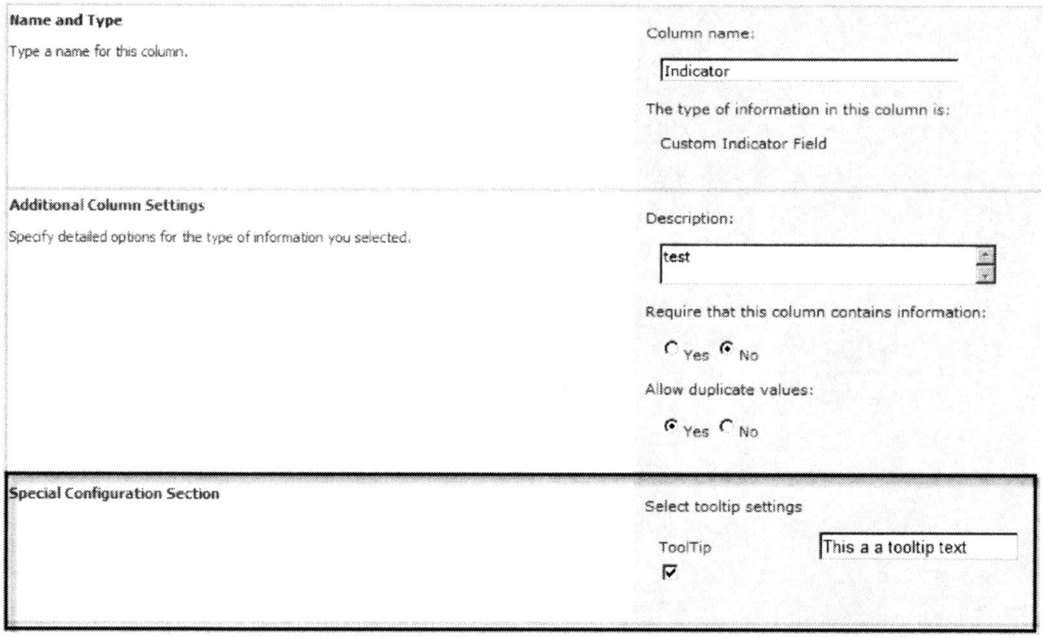

Figure 11–9. Separate configuration section for a custom field

There are several things to do:

- Add a field element containing the path to a `FieldEditorUserControl` to the `fldtypes_[FieldName].xml` file (as shown in Figure 11–10).
- Hide the fields of the property schema so that they are not automatically displayed (however, you still need them to store your custom properties).
- Implement a `FieldEditorUserControl` (ASCX and code-behind).

```
<?xml version="1.0" encoding="utf-8"?>
<FieldTypes>
  <FieldType>
    <Field Name="TypeName">CustomIndicatorField</Field>
    <Field Name="ParentType">Integer</Field>
    <Field Name="TypeDisplayName">Custom Indicator Field</Field>
    <Field Name="TypeShortDescription">Custom Indicator Field Description</Field>
    <Field Name="UserCreatable">TRUE</Field>
    <Field Name="ShowOnListCreate">TRUE</Field>
    <Field Name="ShowOnSurveyCreate">TRUE</Field>
    <Field Name="ShowOnDocumentLibrary">TRUE</Field>
    <Field Name="ShowOnColumnTemplateCreate">TRUE</Field>
    <Field Name="Sortable">TRUE</Field>
    <Field Name="Filterable">TRUE</Field>
    <Field Name="FieldTypeClass">Apress.SP2010.CustomIndicatorField, Apress.SP2010, Version=1.0.0.0, Cult
    <Field Name="FieldEditorUserControl">/_controltemplates/CustomIndicatorFieldEditControl.ascx</Field>
    <PropertySchema>
      <Fields>
        <Field Name="ToolTip" DisplayName="ToolTip Text" Hidden="TRUE" MaxLength="255" Type="Text">
          <Default>-</Default>
        </Field>
        <Field Name="ShowToolTip" DisplayName="Show ToolTip" Hidden="TRUE" Type="Boolean">
          <Default>1</Default>
        </Field>
      </Fields>
    </PropertySchema>
  </FieldType>
</FieldTypes>
```

Figure 11–10. *Modify fldtypes_CustomIndicatorField.xml to support a field editor user control.*

Field Editor User Control: Web Form (ASCX)

The user control for editing custom field properties (see Listing 11–8) consists of

- A reference to a compiled code-behind class (`Inherits=...`)
- An assembly reference to `Microsoft.SharePoint.dll`
- Tag registrations (`InputFormControl`, `InputFormSection`)
- Content, usually enclosed by `InputFormSection` and `InputFormControl`

Listing 11–8. *The CustomIndicatorFieldEditControl.ascx Web User Control*

```
<%@ Control Language="C#" AutoEventWireup="false"
Inherits="Apress.SP2010.CustomIndicatorFieldEditControl, Apress.SP2010, Version=1.0.0.0,
Culture=neutral, PublicKeyToken=4113b8ec9b28df52" %>
<%@ Assembly Name="Microsoft.SharePoint, Version=14.0.0.0, Culture=neutral,
PublicKeyToken=71e9bce111e9429c" %>
<%@ Register TagPrefix="SharePoint" Assembly="Microsoft.SharePoint, Version=14.0.0.0,
Culture=neutral, PublicKeyToken=71e9bce111e9429c"
namespace="Microsoft.SharePoint.WebControls"%>
<%@ Register TagPrefix="wssuc" TagName="InputFormControl"
src="~/_controltemplates/InputFormControl.ascx" %>
<%@ Register TagPrefix="wssuc" TagName="InputFormSection"
src="~/_controltemplates/InputFormSection.ascx" %>
```

```
<%@ Import Namespace="Microsoft.SharePoint" %>

<wssuc:InputFormSection runat="server" id="MySections"
                        Title="Special Configuration Section">
    <Template_InputFormControls>
         <wssuc:InputFormControl runat="server"
                LabelText="Select tooltip settings">
                <Template_Control>
                      <asp:Label ID="lblTooltip" runat="server" Text="ToolTip"
                                 Width="120px" />
                      <asp:TextBox runat="server" ID="txtToolTip" />
                      <br />
                      <asp:CheckBox ID="chkShowToolTip" runat="server" />
                </Template_Control>
         </wssuc:InputFormControl>
    </Template_InputFormControls>
</wssuc:InputFormSection>
```

The web user control in Listing 11–8 defines an `InputFormSection` containing a `Label`, a `TextBox`, and a `CheckBox`. This section is displayed when editing the field in a list (see Figure 11–9).

Field Editor User Control: Code-Behind (CS)

The code-behind class of the field user control derives from `System.Web.UI.UserControl` and implements the interface `IFieldEditor` (see Listing 11–9), containing three methods (see Table 11–3).

***Table 11–3.** Methods of the IFieldEditor Interface*

Method	Description
`DisplayAsNewSection`	This method indicates whether the control renders in a separate section (`true`) or directly in the default section (`false`).
`InitializeWithField`	This is an initialization method that is called automatically when displaying the field properties for the first time. It can be used to get the custom properties of the nominated `SPField` to initialize the web controls.
`OnSaveChange`	This method is called when the user clicks the OK button to save the changes. It must be used to save the values of the web controls into the custom properties of the `SPField`.

***Listing 11–9.** The CustomIndicatorFieldEditControl.cs Code-Behind Class*

```
namespace Apress.SP2010
{
    public partial class CustomIndicatorFieldEditControl : UserControl, IFieldEditor
    {

        CustomIndicatorField _field = null;
```

```
        public bool DisplayAsNewSection
        {
            get { return true; }
        }

        public void InitializeWithField(SPField field)
        {
           this._field = field as CustomIndicatorField;
        }

        public void OnSaveChange(SPField field, bool isNewField)
        {
            CustomIndicatorField myField = field as CustomIndicatorField;
            myField.ShowToolTipCustomProperty =
                     FindControlRecursive<CheckBox>(this, "chkShowToolTip").Checked;
            myField.ToolTipCustomProperty =
                     FindControlRecursive<TextBox>(this, "txtToolTip").Text;
        }

        protected override void CreateChildControls()
        {
            base.CreateChildControls();
            if (!IsPostBack && _field != null)
            {
                FindControlRecursive<TextBox>(this, "txtToolTip").Text =
                       _field.ToolTipCustomProperty;
                FindControlRecursive<CheckBox>(this, "chkShowToolTip").Checked =
                      _field.ShowToolTipCustomProperty;
            }
        }

        protected T FindControlRecursive<T>(Control rootControl, String id)
                   where T : Control
        {
            T retVal = null;
            if (rootControl.HasControls())
            {
                foreach (Control c in rootControl.Controls)
                {
                    if (c.ID == id) return (T)c;
                    retVal = FindControlRecursive<T>(c, id);
                    if (retVal != null) break;
                }
            }
            return retVal;
        }
    }
}
```

The example in Listing 11–9 implements a helper method, `FindControlRecursive`, that recursively finds a control by name in the control tree. You need this for accessing the property controls (`TextBox` and CheckBox). In the OnSaveChange method, you save the control values into appropriate properties of the field. In the overridden CreateChildControls method, you ensure that already saved properties are displayed correctly.

Input Form Controls

SharePoint offers many useful web controls that you can easily use for your own application pages or Web Parts. Obviously, before building a custom control for a specific behavior, it's a good idea to check if SharePoint's repertoire includes something that will do the job already. This section introduces the more significant SharePoint web controls with simple examples of their usage.

Sections

The controls InputFormSection and InputFormControl are mainly responsible for separating input areas, as shown in Figure 11–11.

Figure 11–11. *InputFormSection with InputFormControl including a TextBox*

To use these two controls, you first need to register them in your ASP.NET application page. Remember to surround the InputFormSection element with a <table> tag, because it only generates HTML output starting with <tr> (see Listing 11–10).

Listing 11–10. *Using the InputFormSection and InputFormControl User Controls*

```
<%@ Register TagPrefix="wssuc" TagName="InputFormSection"
src="~/_controltemplates/InputFormSection.ascx" %>
<%@ Register TagPrefix="wssuc" TagName="InputFormControl"
src="~/_controltemplates/InputFormControl.ascx" %>

<asp:Content ID="Content1" ContentPlaceHolderId="PlaceHolderMain" runat="server">

 <table class="propertysheet" border="0" width="100%"
        cellspacing="0" cellpadding="0">
    <wssuc:InputFormSection Title="InputFormSection"
           Description="InputFormSection Description" runat="server">
        <template_inputformcontrols>
            <wssuc:InputFormControl runat="server"
                                    LabelText="InputFormControl Text">
                <Template_Control>
                    <asp:TextBox runat="server" CssClass="ms-input" />
                </Template_Control>
            </wssuc:InputFormControl>
        </template_inputformcontrols>
```

```
    </wssuc:InputFormSection>
 </table>
 </asp:Content>
```

Listing 11-10 defines a simple InputFormSection that includes an InputFormControl with a TextBox (see Figure 11-11).

Text Controls

The InputFormTextBox control is derived directly from System.Web.UI.WebControls.TextBox and also implements the System.Web.UI.IValidator interface. Several methods for supporting rich text input fields are also implemented (see Listing 11-11):

Listing 11-11. *Properties for Rich Text Support in InputFormTextBox*

```
public bool AllowHyperlink { get; set; }
public bool RichText { get; set; }
public SPRichTextMode RichTextMode { get; set; }
```

Figure 11-12 contains two InputFormTextBox controls, one without and one with rich-text support. The code example for Figure 11-12 is shown in Listing 11-12.

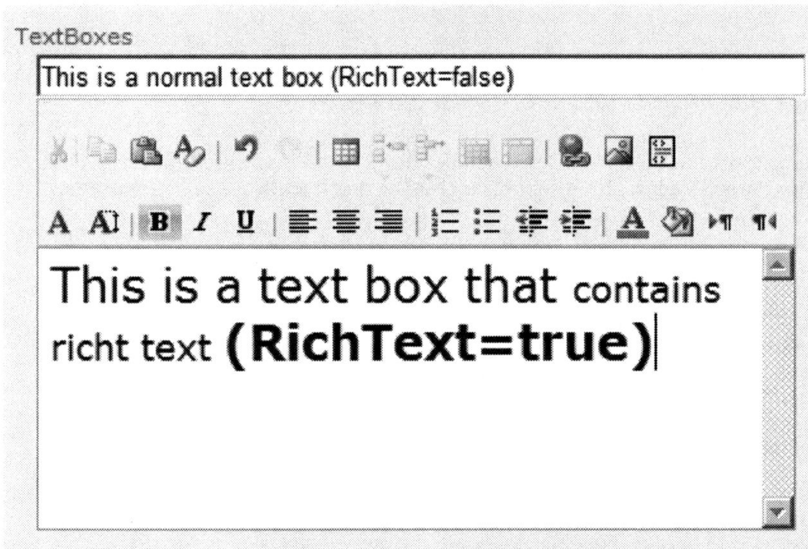

Figure 11-12. *Two InputFormTextBox controls*

Listing 11-12. *Example of Using InputFormTextBox Controls*

```
<wssuc:InputFormControl runat="server" LabelText="TextBoxes">
    <Template_Control>
       <SharePoint:InputFormTextBox ID="Subject" RichText="false" runat="server"
              Width="100%"/>
```

```
        <SharePoint:InputFormTextBox ID="Body" RichText="true"
                     RichTextMode="FullHtml"
                     runat="server"
                     TextMode="MultiLine"
                     Rows="10"/>
    </Template_Control>
</wssuc:InputFormControl>
```

Check Boxes and Radio Buttons

The SharePoint controls InputFormCheckBox, InputFormCheckBoxList, and InputFormRadioButton all derive from their corresponding web controls in the System.Web.UI.WebControls namespace (CheckBox, CheckBoxList, and RadioButton).

The InputFormCheckbox includes three additional properties:

```
public int ButtonSpacing { get; set; }
public string LabelText { get; set; }
public bool ToggleChildren { get; set; }
```

For the InputFormRadioButton class, the extra properties are

```
public int ButtonSpacing { get; set; }
public string LabelText { get; set; }
```

Listing 11–13 demonstrates how to use both web controls.

***Listing 11–13.** Example of Using Check Boxes and Radio Buttons*

```
<wssuc:InputFormControl runat="server" LabelText="Radio button list">
    <Template_Control>
        <SharePoint:InputFormRadioButton runat="server" ID="rbtn01"
                GroupName="myGroup" LabelText="High" />
        <SharePoint:InputFormRadioButton runat="server" ID="rbtn02"
                GroupName="myGroup" LabelText="Middle" />
        <SharePoint:InputFormRadioButton runat="server" ID="rbtn03"
                GroupName="myGroup" LabelText="Low" />
    </Template_Control>
</wssuc:InputFormControl>

<wssuc:InputFormControl runat="server" LabelText="Single Checkbox">
    <Template_Control>
        <SharePoint:InputFormCheckBox ID="chkBox"
                LabelText="Do you want to show a tooltip?" runat="server" />
    </Template_Control>
</wssuc:InputFormControl>

<wssuc:InputFormControl runat="server" LabelText="CheckBox list">
    <Template_Control>
       <SharePoint:InputFormCheckBoxList ID="chkBoxList"
                LabelText="Color" runat="server">
            <asp:ListItem Text="Red" Value="Red" />
            <asp:ListItem Text="Green" Value="Green" />
            <asp:ListItem Text="Blue" Value="Blue" />
```

```
        </SharePoint:InputFormCheckBoxList>
    </Template_Control>
</wssuc:InputFormControl>
```

The example in Listing 11–13 defines three `InputFormControl` objects. The first one has three `InputFormRadioButton` controls; the second has a single `InputFormCheckBox`, and the last has an `InputFormCheckBoxList` with three `ListItem` values. Figure 11–13 shows the rendered output.

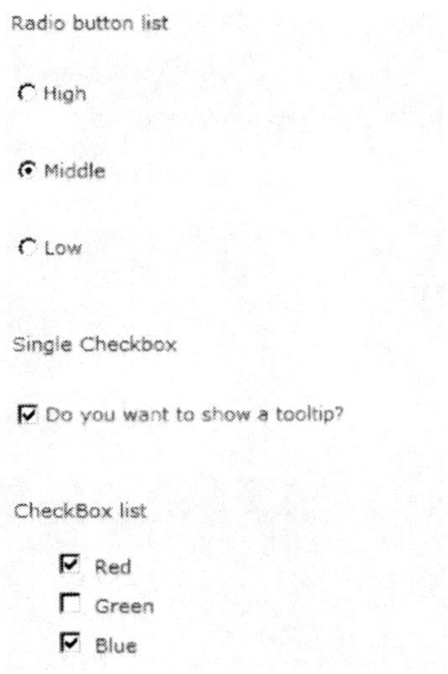

***Figure 11–13.** Check boxes and radio buttons*

Using Validator Controls

For validation of user input fields, you can use the standard ASP.NET validator controls. Better still, you can use the SharePoint `InputField` validator controls. SharePoint comes with six controls that are derived from the standard validator controls from ASP.NET:

- `InputFormCheckBoxListValidator`
- `InputFormCompareValidator`
- `InputFormCustomValidator`
- `InputFormRangeValidator`
- `InputFormRegularExpressionValidator`
- `InputFormRequiredFieldValidator`

All of the validation controls inherit from the base class `System.Web.UI.BaseValidator`, so they all have properties and methods that are common to all validation controls. Table 11–4 shows the standard properties of `System.Web.UI.BaseValidator`.

Table 11–4. Standard ASP.NET Validation Control Properties from BaseValidator

Property	Description
`ControlToValidate`	This is the control to which the validator is applied.
`ErrorMessage`	This is the error message that will be displayed in the validation summary.
`IsValid`	This takes a Boolean value for whether or not the control is valid.
`Validate`	This is a method to validate the input control and update the `IsValid` property.
`Display`	This controls how the error message is shown. The possible options are `None`: The validation message is never displayed. `Static`: Space for the validation message is allocated in the page layout. `Dynamic`: Space for the validation message is dynamically added to the page if the validation fails.

The derived SharePoint input validation controls add three properties that primarily influence the rendering of the error message:

```
public bool BreakAfter { get; set; }
public bool BreakBefore { get; set; }
public string ErrorImageUrl { get; set; }
```

InputFormRequiredFieldValidator

The first control is the `InputFormRequiredFieldValidator` control. It ensures that a user inputs a value. Here is how it is used:

```
<SharePoint:InputFormTextBox ID="txtBox" runat="server" CssClass="ms-input" />
<SharePoint:InputFormRequiredFieldValidator runat="server"
    ControlToValidate="txtBox" ErrorMessage="Please enter a value"
    ErrorImageUrl="/_layouts/images/cell-error.png" />
```

Figure 11–14 shows the result of the preceding code.

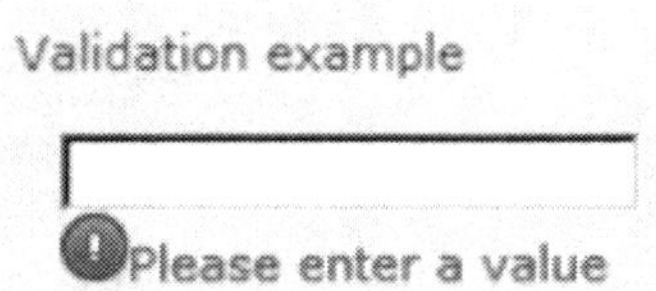

***Figure 11–14.** InputFormRequiredFieldValidator in action*

InputFormCompareValidator

Next, have a look at the InputFormCompareValidator control. Use this control for such tasks as confirming that new passwords match or checking whether a departure date is before an arrival date (see Figure 11–15).

```
<SharePoint:InputFormTextBox ID="txt01" runat="server" CssClass="ms-input" />
<SharePoint:InputFormTextBox ID="txt02" runat="server" CssClass="ms-input" />
<SharePoint:InputFormCompareValidator runat="server" ControlToValidate="txt01"
    ControlToCompare="txt02" ErrorMessage="The values are not equal" />
```

Validation example

test | test2

The values are not equal

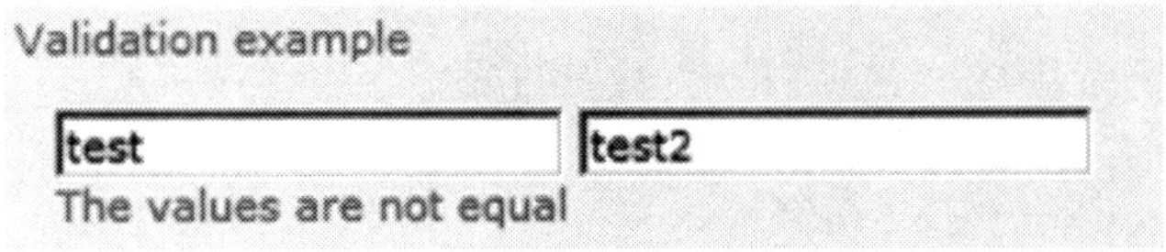

Figure 11–15. InputFormCompareValidator in action

■ **Tip** By using the validator properties ValueToCompare, Type, and Operator, you can easily compare an entered value with a predefined value (e.g., if you want to check if an entered number is greater than *X*).

InputFormRangeValidator

The InputFormRangeValidator control checks whether a control value is within a valid range. The required attributes for this control are MaximumValue, MinimumValue, and Type.

The following code shows how to use the InputFormRangeValidator web control:

```
Enter your age between 18 and 99:
<SharePoint:InputFormTextBox ID="txt3" runat="server" CssClass="ms-input" />
<SharePoint:InputFormRangeValidator runat="server"
    ControlToValidate="txt3" Type="Integer" MinimumValue="18"
    MaximumValue="99" ErrorMessage="Your age is not valid" />
```

The result is displayed in Figure 11–16.

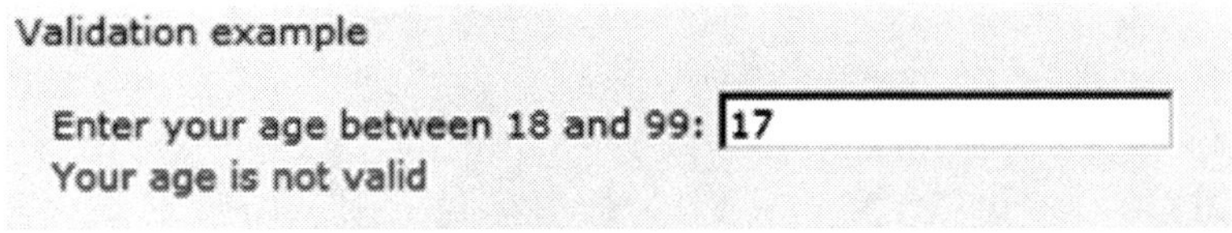

Validation example

Enter your age between 18 and 99: 17

Your age is not valid

Figure 11–16. InputFormRangeValidator in action

InputFormRegularExpressionValidator

The regular expression validator is one of the more powerful features of ASP.NET. While many developers don't enjoy building their own regular expressions, there are many examples to be found on the Web. The resulting regular expressions can be somewhat cryptic. The following example checks whether an e-mail address is valid (see Figure 11–17):

```
Enter your email address:
<SharePoint:InputFormTextBox ID="txtMail" runat="server" CssClass="ms-input" />
<SharePoint:InputFormRegularExpressionValidator runat="server" ControlToValidate="txtMail"
ValidationExpression="^([a-zA-Z0-9_\-\.]+)@((\[[0-9]{1,3}\.[0-9]{1,3}\.[0-9]{1,3}\.)|(([a-zA-
Z0-9\-]+\.)+))([a-zA-Z]{2,4}|[0-9]{1,3})(\]?)$" ErrorMessage="Your email address is not valid"
/>
```

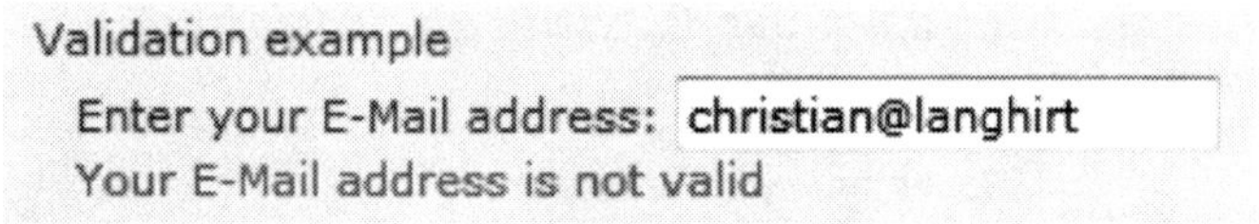

Figure 11–17. *InputFormRegularExpressionValidator in action*

InputFormCustomValidator

The `InputFormCustomValidator` control adds great flexibility because it enables developers to write their own validation methods (server- or client-side). This is useful if, for example, an entered value has to be checked against a database.

```
Enter your new username:
<SharePoint:InputFormTextBox ID="txt4" runat="server" CssClass="ms-input" />
<SharePoint:InputFormCustomValidator runat="server" ControlToValidate="txt4"
    OnServerValidate="OnServerValidate"
    ErrorMessage="Your username is already in use" />
```

In your code-behind class, implement the `OnServerValidate` method as follows:

```
protected void OnServerValidate(object source, ServerValidateEventArgs e)
{
    e.IsValid = (e.Value != "chris");
}
```

The result is shown in Figure 11–18.

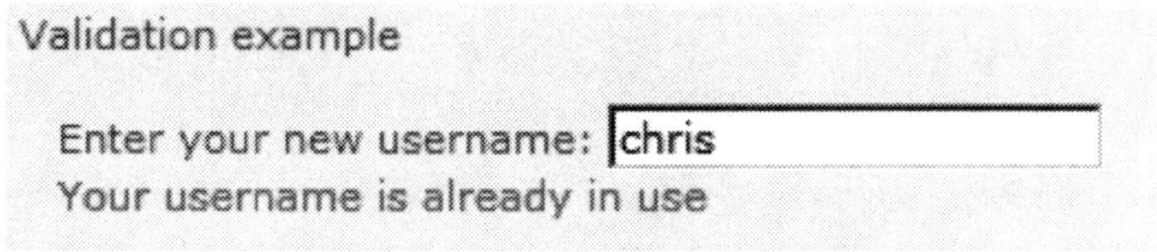

Figure 11–18. *InputFormCustomValidator in action*

Security Trimming

Security is always an issue to keep in mind when developing custom application pages or Web Parts. The `SPSecurityTrimmedControl` class is a web control that selectively displays content or controls depending on the current user's SharePoint permissions. Irrespective of the inner content of the control, it will not be shown if the user lacks the nominated permissions—for example:

```
<SharepointWebControls:SPSecurityTrimmedControl runat="server"
                                                Permissions="ManageWeb">
    This is only visible to users who can manage the current web...
</SharepointWebControls:SPSecurityTrimmedControl>
```

In addition to the Permissions property, which is an enumeration of type SPBasePermission, you can also use the PermissionsString property to specify a comma-separated list of required permissions. There are other ways to define who may view the controls (see the properties in Table 11–5).

Table 11–5. *Properties of SPSecurityTrimmedControl*

Property	Default Value	Values
AuthenticationRestrictions	AllUsers	AllUsers, AnonymousUsersOnly, AuthenticatedUsersOnly
PageModes	All	All, Design, Normal
PermissionContext	CurrentSite	CurrentSite, CurrentList, CurrentItem, RootSite, CurrentFolder
PermissionMode	All	All, Any
Permissions	EmptyMask	AddAndCustomizePages, AddDelPrivateWebParts, AddListItems, ApplyStyleSheets, ApplyThemeAndBorder, ApproveItems, BrowseDirectories, BrowseUserInfo, CancelCheckout, CreateAlerts, CreateGroups, CreateSSCSite, DeleteListItems, DeleteVersions, EditListItems, EditMyUserInfo, EmptyMask, EnumeratePermissions, FullMask, ManageAlerts, ManageLists, ManagePermissions, ManagePersonalViews, ManageSubwebs, ManageUnsafeContent, ManageWeb, Open, OpenItems, UpdatePersonalWebParts, UseClientIntegration, UseRemoteAPIs, ViewFormPages, ViewListItems, ViewPages, ViewUsageData, ViewVersions
PermissionsString	n/a	Comma-separated list of permissions (e.g., ViewPages,ManageWeb)

■ **Caution** Some property combinations, especially combinations with AuthenticationRestriction, PageModes, and PermissionContext, don't always work as expected. If you use the Permissions and PermissionsString properties only, they will work without ambiguity.

Deriving from SPSecurityTrimmedControl

When developing your own web controls, it is not always optimal to wrap your content with SPSecurityTrimmedControl. Instead, you can derive from this class and thus include security-trimming behavior directly within your web control.

A good example is the SPLinkButton class, which is directly derived from the SPSecurityTrimmedControl class. The SPLinkButton control is used within the default master page to display the link to the recycle bin. This link is security-trimmed and only visible for users with the right to delete list items:

```
<SharePoint:SPLinkButton runat="server"
                         NavigateUrl="~site/_layouts/recyclebin.aspx"
                         ImageUrl="/_layouts/images/recycbin.gif"
                         Text="Recycle Bin"
                         PermissionsString="DeleteListItems" />
```

Looking inside the SPSecurityTrimmedControl class using .NET Reflector (see Figure 11–19) reveals a very simple implementation—overriding the Visible property of the control. All permission-related code is encapsulated within the private method ShouldRender, which simply returns true or false.

```
public override bool Visible
{
  [SharePointPermission(SecurityAction.Demand, ObjectModel=true)]
  get
  {
    return (base.Visible && this.ShouldRender);
  }
  [SharePointPermission(SecurityAction.Demand, ObjectModel=true)]
  set
  {
    base.Visible = value;
  }
}
```

Figure 11–19. *Overridden method of SPSecurityTrimmingControl*

Pickers and Selector Controls

A collection of controls are available for selecting data using particular pop-up dialogs.

Useful Controls

In this section we'll introduce several interesting SharePoint web controls for selecting data.

Selectors for WebApplication, SiteCollection, Site, and List

SharePoint comes with four selector controls to choose destination elements for operations:

- `WebApplicationSelector` to select a web application
- `SiteAdministrationSelector` to select a site collection
- `WebAdministrationSelector` to select a site
- `ListAdministrationSelector` to select a list or document library

These selector controls are normally used within the SharePoint administration pages. You can easily integrate the controls with the following lines (see Figure 11–20):

```
<SharePoint:WebApplicationSelector runat="server" ID="webAppSelector" />
<SharePoint:SiteAdministrationSelector runat="server" ID="siteColSelector" />
<SharePoint:WebAdministrationSelector runat="server" ID="webSelector" />
<SharePoint:ListAdministrationSelector runat="server" ID="listSelector" />
```

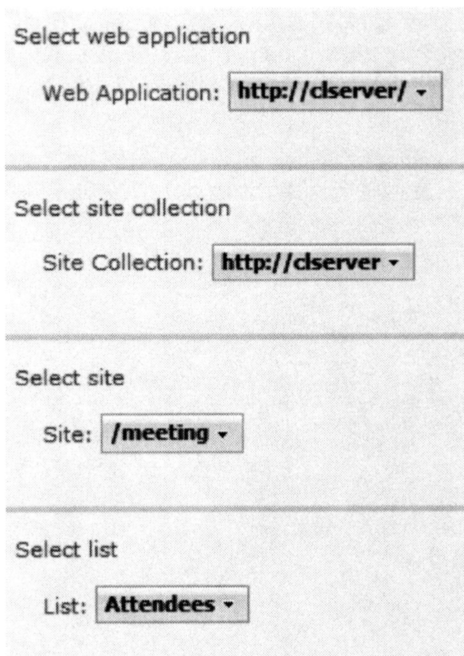

Figure 11–20. Rendering of the selector web controls

To connect the controls, include the following code during page initialization:

```
protected void Page_Load(object sender, EventArgs e)
{
    this.webSelector.SiteSelector = this.siteSelector;
    this.listSelector.SiteSelector = this.siteSelector;
    this.listSelector.WebSelector = this.webSelector;
}
```

After clicking the selection field, a pop-up dialog with a list of items to choose will be displayed (see Figure 11–21).

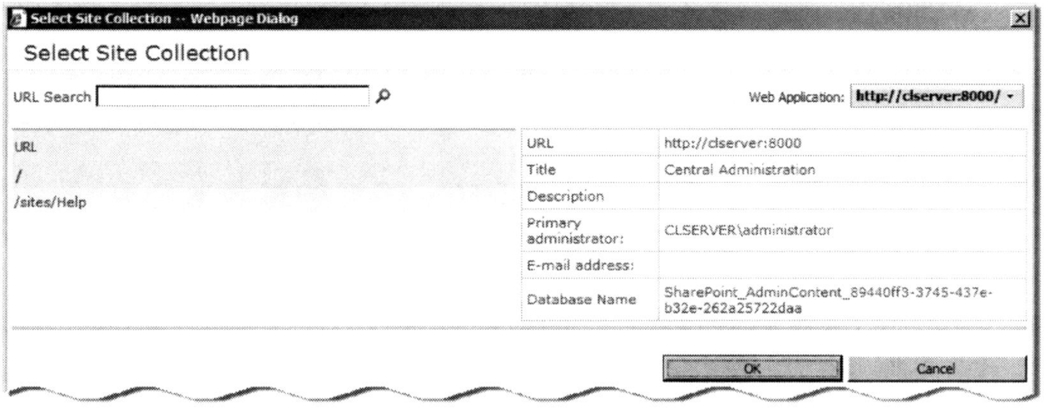

Figure 11–21. Site collection selection pop-up dialog

However, if you want to get the selected values, just use the `CurrentItem` property of the selector controls:

```
SPWebApplication webApplication = webAppSelector.CurrentItem
SPSiteAdministration siteAdmin = siteColSelector.CurrentItem
SPWeb web = webSelector.CurrentItem
SPList list = listSelector.CurrentItem
```

SharePoint Central Administration itself uses these controls on the Site Or List Export page (`/_admin/SiteAndListExport.aspx`; see Figure 11–22).

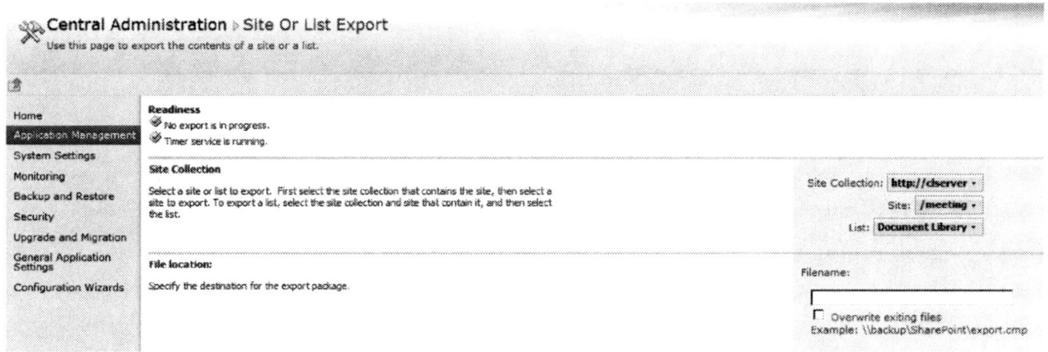

Figure 11–22. Site Or List Export page in Central Administration

The internal implementation of the selector controls shows that all are derived from the generic class `Microsoft.SharePoint.WebControls.ContextSelector<T>`. If you need to write your own selector, you can inherit this class with the object type you want to return. You simply have to override some methods and properties, as shown in Figure 11–23, and build a custom pop-up dialog page to select items.

```
public sealed class WebAdministrationSelector : ContextSelector<SPWeb>
{
    // Fields
    private SiteAdministrationSelector m_SiteSelector;

    // Methods
    public WebAdministrationSelector();
    protected override string DefaultSelectionId();
    protected override SPWeb GetItem();

    // Properties
    public override string CurrentName { get; }
    protected override string Key { get; }
    protected override string NavigateUrl { get; }
    public SiteAdministrationSelector SiteSelector { get; set; }
    protected override string TypeName { get; }
}
```

Figure 11–23. *Contents of the WebAdministrationSelector class as a starting point for your own implementation*

Schedule Picker

Another useful control is `SPSchedulePicker`, which allows a user to define recurring events to use for timer jobs. Several Boolean properties control the rendering of the `SPSchedulePicker` control:

- `Minutes`
- `Hourly`
- `Daily`
- `Weekly`
- `Monthly`

If one or more of these properties are set to `true`, they will be rendered as radio button elements. After you select a radio button, further settings are displayed. Figures 11–24 through 11–28 show the various properties and their settings for recurring events.

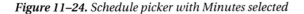

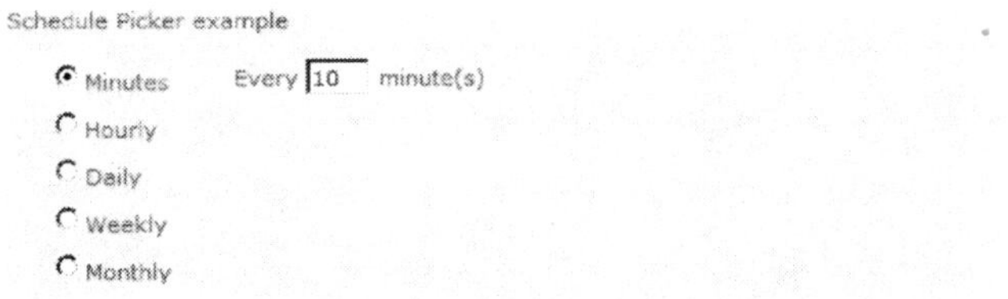

Figure 11–24. *Schedule picker with Minutes selected*

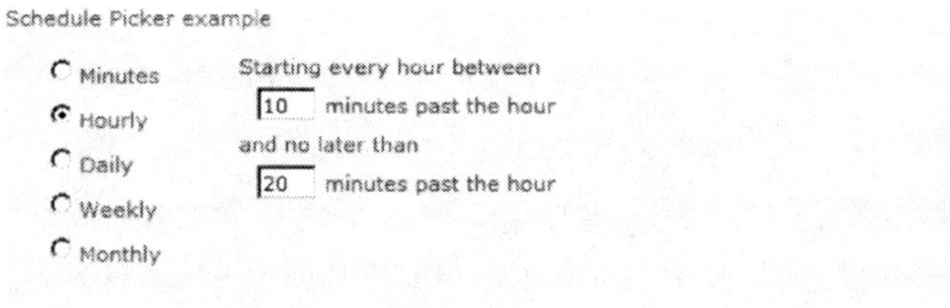

Figure 11–25. Schedule picker with Hourly selected

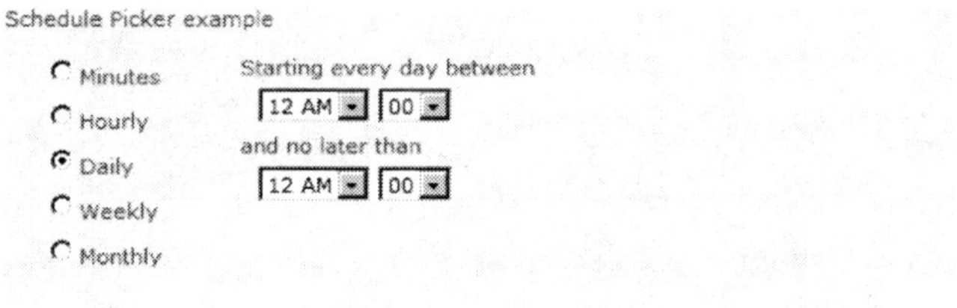

Figure 11–26. Schedule picker with Daily selected

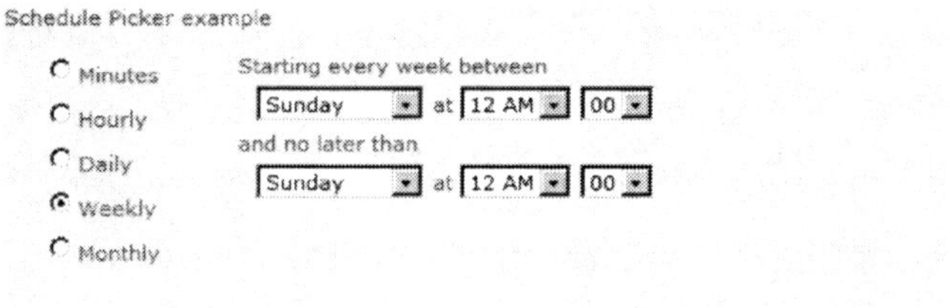

Figure 11–27. Schedule picker with Weekly selected

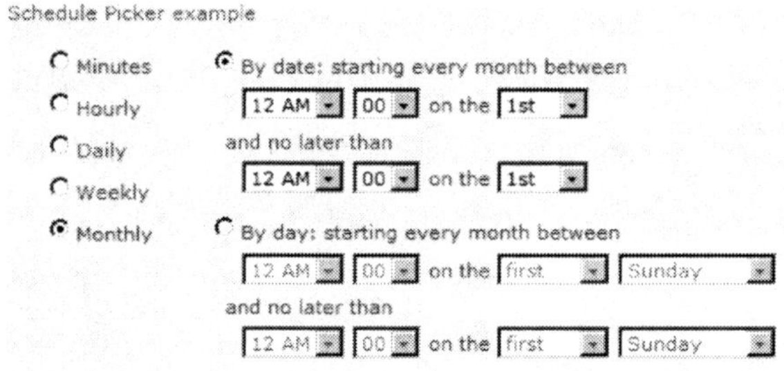

Figure 11–28. Schedule picker with Monthly selected

Utilizing the schedule picker is straightforward. First, register the user control at the top of your ASP.NET application page:

```
<%@ Register TagPrefix="wssuc" TagName="SchedulePicker"
           src="~/_controltemplates/SchedulePicker.ascx" %>
```

Second, call it using this format:

```
<wssuc:SchedulePicker id="schedulePicker" Minutes="True" Hourly="True" Daily="True"
Weekly="True" Monthly="True" Enabled="True" EnableStateView="True" runat="server" />
```

As you can see, there are several properties for configuring the selectable picker time spans. After the user fills out a schedule, you get the result from the Schedule property:

```
protected void btnOk_Click(object sender, EventArgs e)
{
     SPWebApplication webApp = webAppSelector.CurrentItem;
     CustomTimerJob customTimerJob = new CustomTimerJob("MyCustomJob",  webApp);
     customTimerJob.Schedule =  schedulePicker.Schedule;
     customTimerJob.Update();
}
```

If you need to display the current schedule for a timer job, you can use the following schedule picker example:

```
protected override void OnLoadComplete(EventArgs e)
{
    SPWebApplication webApp = webAppSelector.CurrentItem;
    if (!Page.IsPostBack)
    {
        foreach (SPJobDefinition job in webApp.JobDefinitions)
        {
            if (job.Name == "MyCustomJob" )
            {
                schedulePicker.ScheduleString = job.Schedule.ToString();
            }

        }
    }
}
```

People Picker

The people picker is one of the most important and commonly used controls in SharePoint. The people picker allows users to search for and select users defined at some specified scope. This control is normally associated with the Person or Group field in a SharePoint list.

This is another simple control to implement in your own code. The people picker is actually a `PeopleEditor` control, and is in the `Microsoft.SharePoint.WebControls` namespace (see Figure 11–29). Insert the following line into your application page:

```
<SharePoint:PeopleEditor runat="server" />
```

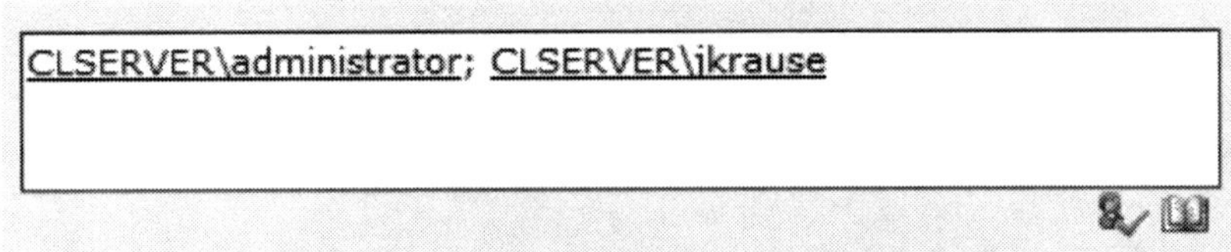

Figure 11–29. *People picker text box to select multiple persons*

The control consists of three child controls:

- A text box where you can enter partial or complete usernames
- An image button to check the filled-out names
- A browse image button to search for a username

When you click the browse image button, a dialog opens where you can search for specific users or groups, as shown in Figure 11–30.

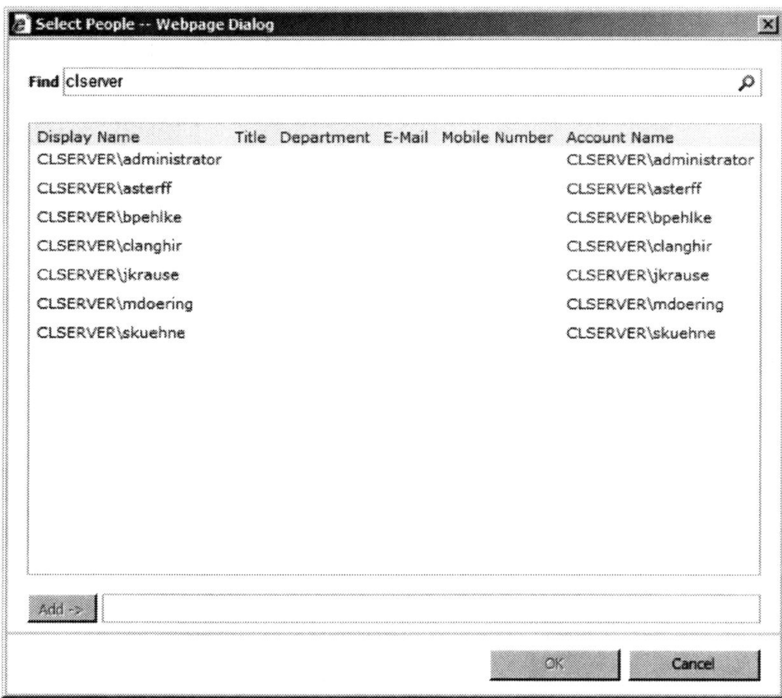

Figure 11–30. People picker pop-up dialog

There are several properties available for the people picker (see Table 11–6):

Table 11–6. Most Important Properties of the PeopleEditor Web Control

Property	Description
`Accounts`	Retrieves the accounts associated with the `PeopleEditor` control as an `ArrayList`.
`AllowEmpty`	Sets or retrieves whether the user must fill in at least one entry.

Property	Description
`AllowTypeIn`	Sets or retrieves whether the user can type the desired user or group name into the text box or whether the search pop-up has to be used.
`CommaSeparatedAccounts`	Initializes the control with predefined login names separated by commas.
`EntitySeparator`	Specifies the character that separates entities. The default value is a semicolon (`;`).
`ErrorMessage`	Sets or retrieves a custom error message.
`MultiSelect`	Indicates whether the user can select multiple people.
`NoMatchesText`	Sets or retrieves the warning text if a search returns no results.
`PlaceButtonsUnderEntityEditor`	Indicates whether the check names and browse image buttons will be on the same line as the text box or beneath it.
`SharePointGroup`	Sets or retrieves a SharePoint group of the site from which people can be selected.
`ShowButton`	Indicates whether to display the check names and browse image buttons.
`ShowCreateButtonInActiveDirectoryAccountCreationMode`	Indicates whether to display a Create button when creating an Active Directory service account.
`PrincipalSource`	Defines where to look up users. Allowed values are `All`, `MembershipProvider`, `None`, `RoleProvider`, `UserInfoList`, and `Windows`.
`ResolvedEntities`	Contains an `ArrayList` of selected entities.
`SelectionSet`	Defines the type of selectable entities as a comma-separated string. Valid values are `User` (single user), `DL` (Active Directory distribution list), `SecGroup` (Active Directory security group), and `SPGroup` (SharePoint group).
`ValidatorEnabled`	Specifies that an error message should be displayed if the input is invalid.

Property	Description
ValidateResolvedEntity	Validates the resolved entry when set to true (the default value). Setting the value to false prevents entity validation.

If you are developing a Web Part, you need to create the PeopleEditor control completely in code:

```
private PeopleEditor peopleEditor;

private void EnsureChildControls()
{
    peopleEditor = new PeopleEditor();
    peopleEditor.AutoPostBack = true;
    peopleEditor.ID = "MyPeopleEditor";
    peopleEditor.AllowEmpty = false;
    peopleEditor.MultiSelect = true;
    peopleEditor.SelectionSet = "User,SPGroup" ;
    MyPanel.Controls.Add(peopleEditor);
}
```

If you wish to populate the PeopleEditor with the username of the current user, this can be accomplished in code, as shown in Listing 11–14.

Listing 11–14. *Populating the PeopleEditor with the Current User*

```
protected void initPeopleEditor()
{
    PickerEntity entity = new PickerEntity();
    entity.Key = SPContext.Current.Web.CurrentUser.LoginName;

    // Make sure the entity is correct
    entity = peopleEditor.ValidateEntity(entity);

    ArrayList entityArrayList = new ArrayList();
    entityArrayList.Add(entity);
    peopleEditor.UpdateEntities(entityArrayList);
}
```

The line peopleEditor.ValidateEntity(entity) can be omitted if you are sure that the entity is correct. The code simply creates a new PickerEntry instance with the LoginName as the key. This PickerEntity is added to an ArrayList and finally passed to the UpdateEntites method of the PickerEditor. The result is shown in Figure 11–31.

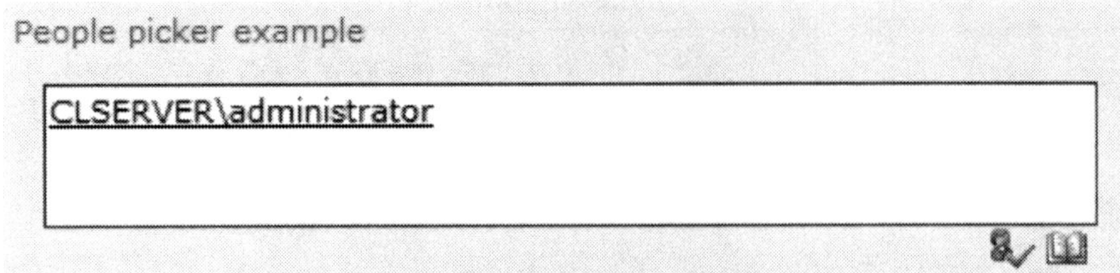

Figure 11–31. The people picker automatically populated with the current user

Now let's go a step further and get the typed in names after a postback. First, define the `PeopleEditor` control with a customized `SelectionSet` property:

```
<SharePoint:PeopleEditor runat="server" id="peopleEditor"
   SelectionSet="User,SecGroup,SPGroup" />
```

Then add a Submit button with a server-side click event that gets the property `ResolvedEntities` of the `PickerEditor` and displays the `entity.EntityData` hashtable for each entity:

```
protected void OnBtnSubmit_Click(object sender, EventArgs args)
{
     lblPickerResult.Text = "";
    foreach (PickerEntity entity in peopleEditor.ResolvedEntities)
    {
        lblPickerResult.Text += "--------------------------------<br>";
        foreach (object key in entity.EntityData.Keys)
        {
            lblPickerResult.Text += key + " -> " + entity.EntityData[key] + "<br>";
        }
    }
}
```

■ **Caution** It is not recommended to use the `Entities` property to get the selected entities, because using this sometimes causes unexpected behavior. It's much more reliable to use `ResolvedEntities` instead.

The result of the preceding example is shown in Figure 11–32.

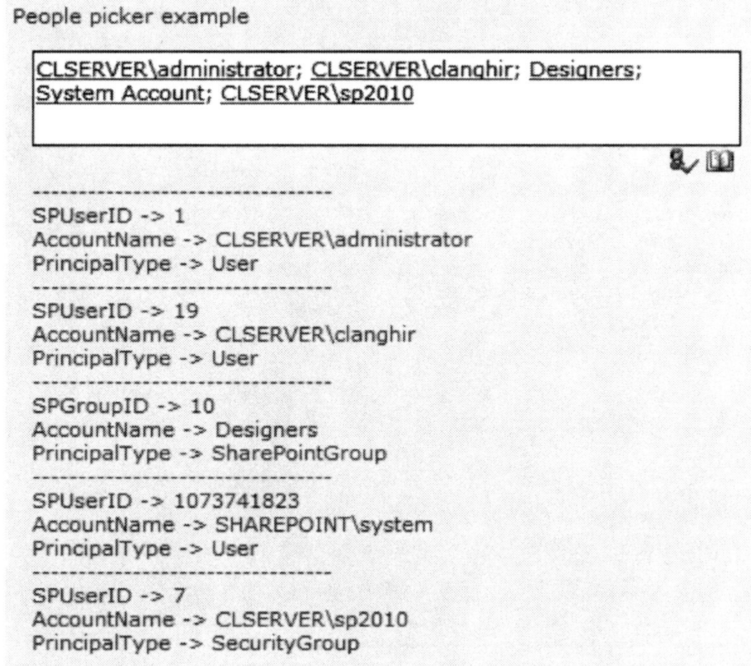
People picker example
CLSERVER\administrator; CLSERVER\clanghir; Designers; System Account; CLSERVER\sp2010

SPUserID -> 1
AccountName -> CLSERVER\administrator
PrincipalType -> User

SPUserID -> 19
AccountName -> CLSERVER\clanghir
PrincipalType -> User

SPGroupID -> 10
AccountName -> Designers
PrincipalType -> SharePointGroup

SPUserID -> 1073741823
AccountName -> SHAREPOINT\system
PrincipalType -> User

SPUserID -> 7
AccountName -> CLSERVER\sp2010
PrincipalType -> SecurityGroup

Figure 11–32. *The people picker with the output of resolved entities*

The default behavior and styling of the `PeopleEditor` control is adequate for most situations. However, if you need to do more than the very basics with the control, then it is strongly recommended that you subclass the control so that you can hook into the behavior at a much deeper level.

Implementing Custom Pickers

The requirement to select one or more items from a list is most commonly met by using a simple drop-down list. But what happens if this list is very long and becomes a performance issue for your page? (Even if you overcome the performance issue, the user experience is poor if a user has to scroll through hundreds or thousands of items.) The `DialogPicker` classes enable you to easily build usable custom pickers. SharePoint provides base classes for this purpose. This section shows how to implement a dialog for picking items from a list (see Figures 11–33 and 11–34).

Custom book picker example
ASP.NET Extensibility (Jörg Krause)

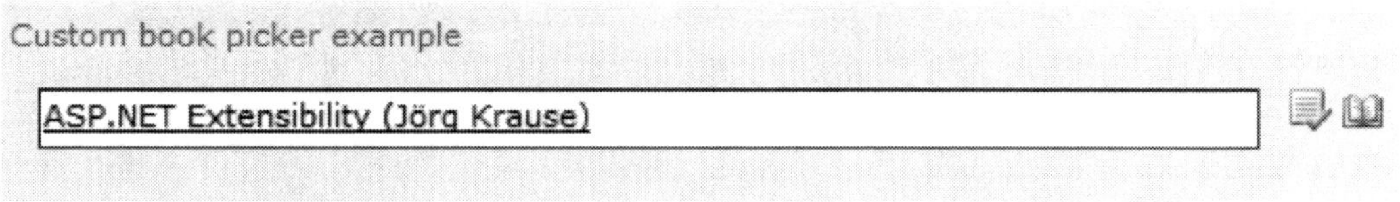

Figure 11–33. *Custom editor dialog for books*

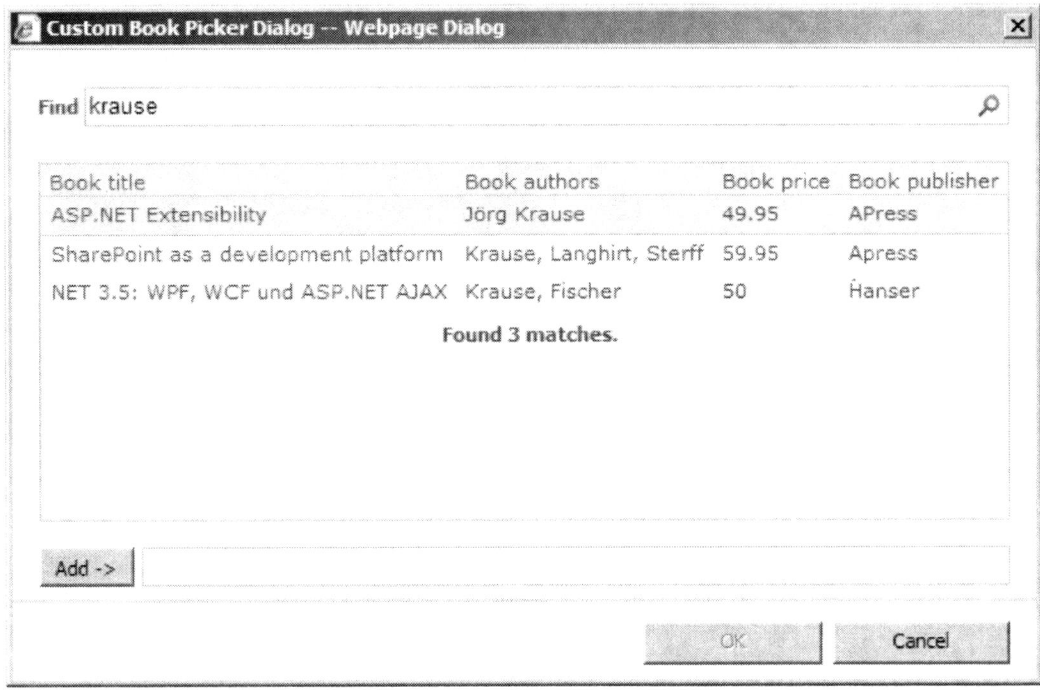

Figure 11–34. *Custom picker dialog for books*

Our custom picker implementation consists of the following elements:

- A data source from which the data to select can be queried. For our example we use a simple SharePoint list.
- An editor class that inherits from `Microsoft.SharePoint.WebControls.EntityEditorWithPicker`.
- A dialog picker class that inherits from `Microsoft.SharePoint.WebControls.PickerDialog`.
- A query control class that inherits from `Microsoft.SharePoint.WebControls.SimpleQueryControl`.

The Data Source

The data source for our example picker implementation is a custom SharePoint list called `Books`. This list has five columns: Title, Description, Authors, Price, and Publisher (see Figure 11–35).

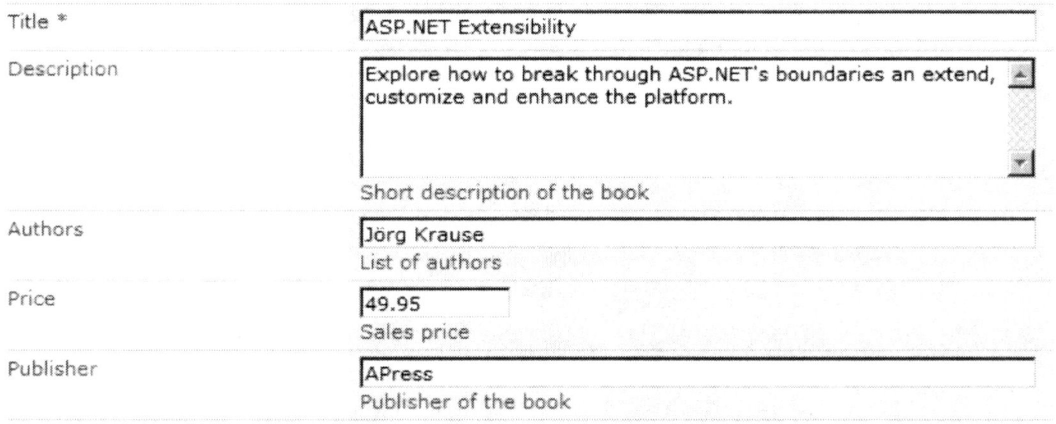

Figure 11–35. A custom Books list

To query your data source, build a simple manager class with static methods as shown in Listing 11–15.

Listing 11–15. Implementation of BookDataManager.cs

```
namespace Apress.SP2010.Picker
{
    public class BookDataManager
    {

        protected static SPList BookList
        {
            get { return SPContext.Current.Web.Lists["Books"]; }
        }

        public static DataTable ValidateBook(String key)
        {
            SPQuery query = new SPQuery();
            query.Query = "<Where><Eq><FieldRef Name=\"Title\"/>" +
                          "<Value Type=\"Text\">{0}</Value></Eq></Where>";
            query.Query = String.Format(query.Query, key);
            return BookList.GetItems(query).GetDataTable();
        }

        public static DataTable SearchForBooks(String keyword)
        {
            SPQuery query = new SPQuery();
            query.Query = "<Where><Or><Contains><FieldRef Name=\"Title\"/>" +
                          "<Value Type=\"Text\">{0}</Value></Contains>" +
                          "<Contains><FieldRef Name=\"Authors\"/>" +
                          "<Value Type=\"Text\">{0}</Value></Contains></Or>" +
                          "</Where>";
            query.Query = String.Format(query.Query, keyword);
```

```
            DataTable dt = BookList.GetItems(query).GetDataTable();
            return dt;
        }

        public static PickerEntity ConvertFromDataRow(DataRow dataRow,
                                                      PickerEntity entity)
        {
            if (entity == null) entity = new PickerEntity();
            entity.Key = Convert.ToString(dataRow["Title"]);
            entity.DisplayText = Convert.ToString(dataRow["Title"]) + " (" +
                                 Convert.ToString(dataRow["Authors"]) + ")";
            entity.Description = Convert.ToString(dataRow["Description"]);

            // Fill hashtable with item values
            entity.EntityData = new Hashtable();
            foreach (DataColumn dc in dataRow.Table.Columns)
            {
                entity.EntityData[dc.ColumnName] = dataRow[dc.ColumnName];
            }

            return entity;
        }
    }
}
```

This class contains in the first stage three static methods and one static property. The property `BookList` simply returns an `SPList` instance of your data source. The two methods `ValidateBook` and `SearchForBooks` execute various CAML queries—`ValidateBook` looks for a single entry with the specified title, and `SearchForBooks` looks up multiple entries where the Title or Authors fields contain a specified search string.

The third method, `ConvertFromDataRow`, is a helper method that converts a `DataRow` into a `PickerEntity`. It also fills a `Hashtable` called `EntityData` with all columns from the data row. This method is used by several methods of the following picker classes, and therefore it makes sense to extract that functionality to a single place.

Dialog Editor Class

The dialog editor class inherits from the base class `EntityEditorWithPicker`, and is mainly responsible for the look and feel of the input text box (see Figure 11–36).

***Figure 11–36.** Result of a custom dialog editor class*

To build such a class, set the property `PickerDialogType` to a custom dialog type. (In Listing 11–16 we specify the type as `BookPickerDialog`, a class we cover in the next section.) Then override the `ValidateEntity` method to suit your requirements.

Listing 11–16. Implementation of BookEditor.cs

```
namespace Apress.SP2010.Picker
{
    public class BookEditor : EntityEditorWithPicker
    {
        public BookEditor()
        {
            PickerDialogType = typeof(BookPickerDialog);
            ValidatorEnabled = true;
        }

        public override PickerEntity ValidateEntity(PickerEntity needsValidation)
        {
            DataTable tblItem = BookDataManager.ValidateBook(needsValidation.Key);
            needsValidation.IsResolved = false;
            if (tblItem != null && tblItem.Rows.Count > 0)
            {
                needsValidation = BookDataManager.ConvertFromDataRow(
                                               tblItem.Rows[0], needsValidation);
                needsValidation.IsResolved = true;
            }
            return needsValidation;
        }

    }
}
```

As you can see, the PickerDialogType property is set within the constructor. This property is important because the autogenerated JavaScript code in the page uses this property to open the dialog window:

```
function __Dialog__ctl00_PlaceHolderMain_ctl08_ctl00_bookEditor(defaultSearch)
{
    if(defaultSearch==undefined)
    defaultSearch='';
    var sDialogUrl = '/_layouts/Picker.aspx?MultiSelect=True&CustomProperty=&
            PickerDialogType=Apress.SP2010.Picker.BookPickerDialog, Apress.SP2010,
            Version=1.0.0.0, Culture=neutral,PublicKeyToken=3D4113b8ec9b28df52&
            EntitySeparator=;'
    sDialogUrl = sDialogUrl + '&DefaultSearch=' + escapeProperly(defaultSearch);
    var sFeatures='resizable: yes; status: no; scroll: no; help: no; center: yes;
            dialogWidth : 575px; dialogHeight : 500px;';

    var rv=commonShowModalDialog(sDialogUrl, sFeatures,
            CallbackWrapperctl00_PlaceHolderMain_ctl08_ctl00_bookEditor);
}
```

To display the picker pop-up, the fully qualified class name (including the assembly) is added as a query string parameter to the dialog picker URL (/_layouts/picker.aspx).

Dialog Picker Class

The dialog picker class is referenced by the property `PickerDialogType` of the dialog editor class mentioned previously. It is used by the code-behind implementation of the `picker.aspx` application page. Figure 11–37 shows an excerpt of the class `Microsoft.SharePoint.ApplicationPages.Picker` using .NET Reflector.

```
protected override void OnLoad(EventArgs e)
{
    base.OnLoad(e);
    bool flag = false;
    m_strPeoplePicker = "false";
    if (string.IsNullOrEmpty(m_strJSONInitialData))
    {
        m_strJSONInitialData = "{}";
    }
    Type type = Utility.GetTypeFromAssembly(base.Request["PickerDialogType"], true, false);
    if (type == typeof(PeoplePickerDialog))
    {
        flag = true;
        m_strPeoplePicker = "true";
    }
    SPWeb contextWeb = SPControl.GetContextWeb(this.Context);
    string unsafeErrorMessage = null;
    if (!type.IsSubclassOf(typeof(PickerDialog)) || !contextWeb.SafeControls.IsSafeControl(type, out unsafeErrorMessage))
    {
        throw new SPInvalidPropertyException(SPResource.GetString("InvalidPropertyDialogControl", new object[0]), "PickerDia
    }
    if (flag && (m_strJSONInitialData != "{}"))
    {
        this.DialogControl = new PeoplePickerDialog(false);
    }
    else
    {
        this.DialogControl = (PickerDialog) Activator.CreateInstance(type);
    }
    this.DialogControl.CustomProperty = base.Request["CustomProperty"];
    this.DialogControl.EditorControl.CustomProperty = this.DialogControl.CustomProperty;
```

Figure 11–37. *OnLoad method of class Microsoft.SharePoint.ApplicationPages.Picker*

The request property `PickerDialogType` is resolved, and there are two checks to ensure that the class is a subclass of `PickerDialog` and is registered as a safe control within the `web.config` file. The property `DialogControl` is then set to a new instance of the dialog picker class (here, `BookPickerDialog`). For this example, the class looks like Listing 11–17.

Listing 11–17. *Implementation of BookPickerDialog.cs*

```
namespace Apress.SP2010.Picker
{
    public class BookPickerDialog : PickerDialog
    {
        public BookPickerDialog() :
            base(new BookQueryControl(),new TableResultControl(), new BookEditor())
        {
```

```
            this.DialogTitle = "Custom Book Picker Dialog";
            this.Description = "Please select one more more books";
            this.MultiSelect = true;
        }

        protected override void OnPreRender(EventArgs e)
        {
            TableResultControl resultControl = (TableResultControl)ResultControl;

            ArrayList columnDisplayNames = resultControl.ColumnDisplayNames;
            ArrayList columnNames = resultControl.ColumnNames;
            ArrayList columnWidths = resultControl.ColumnWidths;

            columnDisplayNames.Clear();
            columnNames.Clear();
            columnWidths.Clear();

            columnDisplayNames.AddRange(new String[] {
                  "Book title","Book authors","Book price","Book publisher"});
            columnNames.AddRange(new String[] {
                  "Title", "Authors", "Price", "Publisher" });
            columnWidths.AddRange(new String[] { "40%", "20%", "10%", "30%" });

            base.OnPreRender(e);
        }
    }
}
```

Some associated objects are defined in the constructor (the picker query control, the picker result control, and the editor control). In addition to modifying several properties in the constructor, you need to override the `OnPreRender` method to define the columns to be displayed. You do this by setting the `ColumnNames`, `ColumnDisplayNames`, and `ColumnWidths` properties of the `ResultControl` property from the `PickerDialog` base class. The result is shown in Figure 11-38.

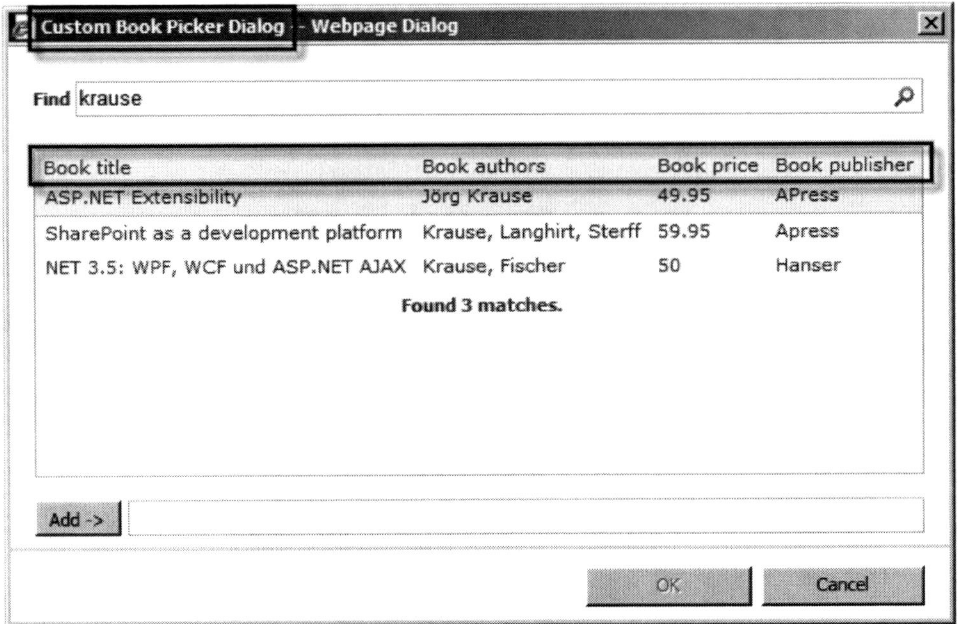

Figure 11–38. Picker dialog with custom columns

Query Control Class

This class is referenced by the dialog picker class. It is mainly responsible for executing search queries in the picker dialog (see Figure 11–39).

Figure 11–39. Picker dialog search

There's also one special feature to mention. By default, the Find row consists of two parts: a drop-down list to select a group/category or similar, and a text field for entering search text (see Figure 11–40).

Figure 11–40. *Picker dialog search with drop-down*

To initialize the drop-down field, override the `OnLoad` method:

```
protected override void OnLoad(EventArgs e)
{
    base.OnLoad(e);

    EnsureChildControls();
    mColumnList.Items.Clear();
    mColumnList.Items.Add("red");
    mColumnList.Items.Add("yellow");
    mColumnList.Items.Add("blue");
}
```

In our example in Listing 11–18, we don't use the drop-down field, and therefore we set the `Visible` property to `false`.

Listing 11–18. *Implementation of BookQueryControl.cs*

```
namespace Apress.SP2010.Picker
{
    public class BookQueryControl : SimpleQueryControl
    {
        protected override void OnLoad(EventArgs e)
        {
            base.OnLoad(e);

            // Hide search drop-down
            EnsureChildControls();
            mColumnList.Visible = false;
        }


        public override PickerEntity GetEntity(DataRow entityDataRow)
        {
            if (entityDataRow == null)
                throw new ArgumentNullException("entityDataRow==null");

            PickerEntity entity = BookDataManager.ConvertFromDataRow(
                                                    entityDataRow,null);
            entity.IsResolved = true;

            return entity;
        }
```

```
        protected override int IssueQuery(string search, string groupName,
                                 int pageIndex, int pageSize)
        {

            DataTable dt = BookDataManager.SearchForBooks(search);
            if (dt !=null && dt.Rows.Count != 0)
            {
                PickerDialog.Results = dt;
                PickerDialog.ResultControl.PageSize = dt.Rows.Count;
                return dt.Rows.Count;
            }
            else
            {
                return 0;
            }
        }

    }
}
```

The two main methods to override are `GetEntity` and `IssueQuery`. The `GetEntity` method simply converts a `DataRow` instance into a `PickerEntity` instance. The `IssueQuery` method executes a query with the entered search string. Also notice the `groupName` parameter, which contains the selected value from the drop-down list. (In our example we don't use this parameter.) After the search query returns the `DataTable`, this `DataTable` is bound to the `Results` property of the `PickerDialog`. The `PageSize` is set to the total count of results.

Getting the Custom Picker to Work

To get the custom picker to work, you have to ensure that

- All classes (`BookDataManager`, `BookEditor`, `BookPickerDialog`, and `BookQueryControl`) are properly implemented, compiled into a strongly named assembly, and installed into the GAC.
- The namespace of your picker classes (in our example, `Apress.SP2010.Picker`) is explicitly registered as a safe control in the `web.config` file.

To register your implementation under the `SafeControls` section of the `web.config` file, add your assembly and namespace as follows:

```
<SafeControl Assembly="Apress.SP2010, Version=1.0.0.0, Culture=neutral,
             PublicKeyToken=xxxxxxxxxxxx" Namespace="Apress.SP2010.Picker"
             TypeName="*"
             Safe="True" />
```

After registering your assembly as a safe control, integrate your custom editor class into an application page:

```
<Apress:BookEditor runat="server" ID="bookEditor"
                   AllowTypeIn="true" MultiSelect="true" />
```

To test your implementation, add a submit button and a label, and write the following event handler code for your button:

```
protected void OnBtnSubmit_Click(object sender, EventArgs args)
{
    lblBookPickerResult.Text = "";
    foreach (PickerEntity entity in bookEditor.ResolvedEntities)
    {
        lblBookPickerResult.Text += "--------------------------------<br>";
        foreach (object key in entity.EntityData.Keys)
        {
             lblBookPickerResult.Text +=
                             key + " -> " + entity.EntityData[key] + "<br>";
        }
    }
}
```

This outputs all the hashtable values of the selected `PickerEntity` instances into the label `lblBookPickerResult`, as shown in Figure 11–41.

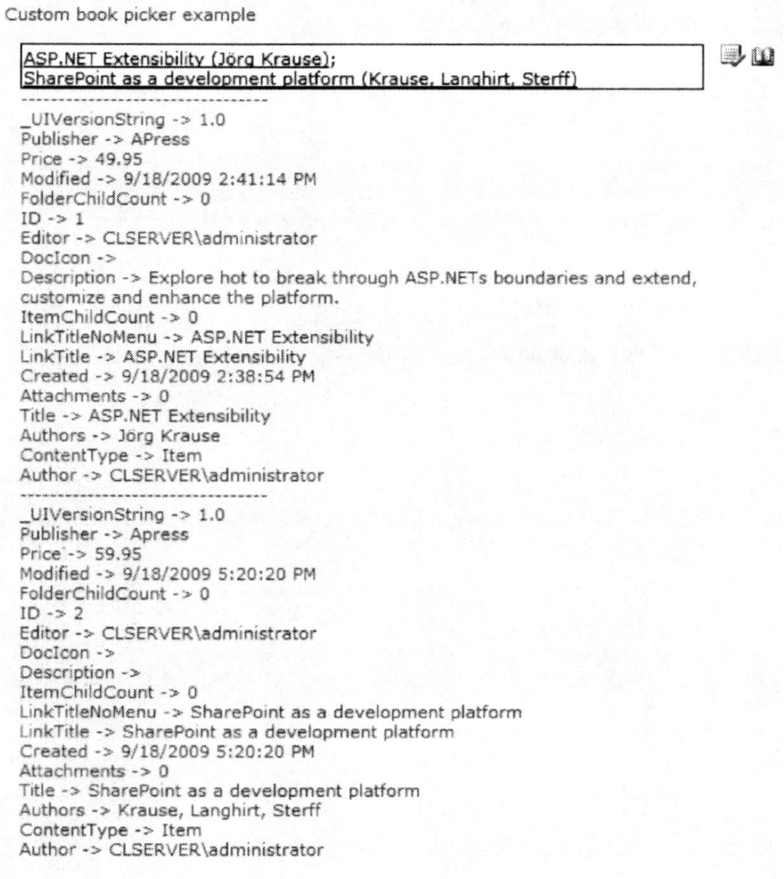

Custom book picker example

ASP.NET Extensibility (Jörg Krause);
SharePoint as a development platform (Krause, Langhirt, Sterff)

_UIVersionString -> 1.0
Publisher -> APress
Price -> 49.95
Modified -> 9/18/2009 2:41:14 PM
FolderChildCount -> 0
ID -> 1
Editor -> CLSERVER\administrator
DocIcon ->
Description -> Explore hot to break through ASP.NETs boundaries and extend, customize and enhance the platform.
ItemChildCount -> 0
LinkTitleNoMenu -> ASP.NET Extensibility
LinkTitle -> ASP.NET Extensibility
Created -> 9/18/2009 2:38:54 PM
Attachments -> 0
Title -> ASP.NET Extensibility
Authors -> Jörg Krause
ContentType -> Item
Author -> CLSERVER\administrator

_UIVersionString -> 1.0
Publisher -> Apress
Price -> 59.95
Modified -> 9/18/2009 5:20:20 PM
FolderChildCount -> 0
ID -> 2
Editor -> CLSERVER\administrator
DocIcon ->
Description ->
ItemChildCount -> 0
LinkTitleNoMenu -> SharePoint as a development platform
LinkTitle -> SharePoint as a development platform
Created -> 9/18/2009 5:20:20 PM
Attachments -> 0
Title -> SharePoint as a development platform
Authors -> Krause, Langhirt, Sterff
ContentType -> Item
Author -> CLSERVER\administrator

***Figure 11–41.** The custom picker control after a postback with all picker entity data*

Toolbar and Ribbon Controls

This section describes the following controls:

- The old (but still useful) toolbar control
- The new SharePoint 2010 ribbon control

Toolbar Control

A toolbar control is typically a control containing one or more buttons (see Figure 11–42). Each button, when clicked by a user, executes an action. In SharePoint, toolbars are used in many pages, generally at the top of the content area. With SharePoint 2010 and its new ribbon control, toolbars will be pushed into the background. However, you can regard ribbons as modern toolbars. Nevertheless, toolbars still make sense, and should be used to improve the user experience in custom SharePoint application pages or Web Parts. The advantage of toolbars over ribbons is their simplicity and rapid implementation. It's very easy to implement a toolbar with a few buttons compared with the effort required to do the same thing using a ribbon. In this section, toolbars are covered first.

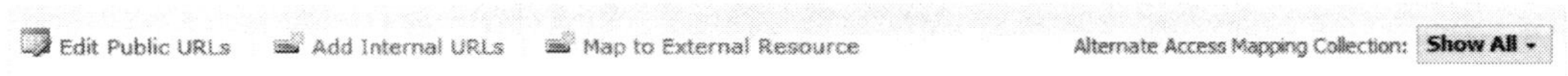

Figure 11–42. Toolbar with three buttons and a menu

SharePoint comes with two web user controls in the /_CONTROLTEMPLATES directory:

- ToolBar.ascx
- ToolBarButton.ascx

These two controls can be used in custom application pages if you register them at the top of your page:

```
<%@ Register TagPrefix="wssuc" TagName="ToolBar" src="~/_controltemplates/ToolBar.ascx" %>
<%@ Register TagPrefix="wssuc" TagName="ToolBarButton"
src="~/_controltemplates/ToolBarButton.ascx" %>
```

To display a basic toolbar, simply define some buttons in it:

```
<wssuc:ToolBar runat="server" id="ToolBar" CssClass="ms-menutoolbar">
    <Template_Buttons>

       <wssuc:ToolBarButton runat="server" Text="First button"
                            NavigateUrl="/_admin/EditOutboundUrls.aspx"
                            ImageUrl="/_layouts/images/edit.gif" Padding="2px" />

       <wssuc:ToolBarButton runat="server" Text="Second button"
                            OnClick="SecondButton_Click"
                            ImageUrl="/_layouts/images/edit.gif" Padding="2px" />

    </Template_Buttons>
</wssuc:ToolBar>
```

The result is shown in Figure 11–43.

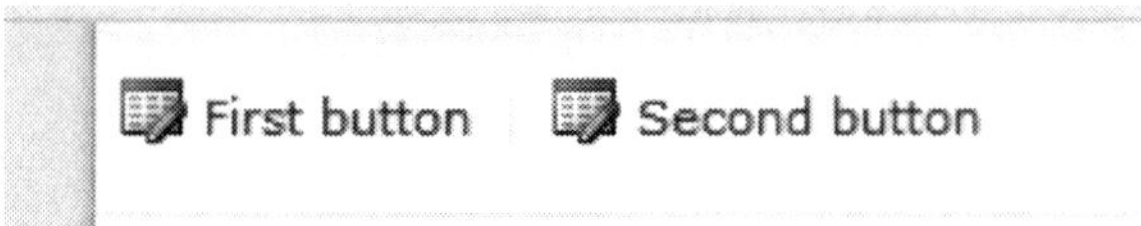

Figure 11–43. Toolbar with two buttons

In our example, the NavigateUrl property of the first button is set to a URL, which after rendering results in an HTTP link. The second button uses a server-side event handler. To handle the postback event from clicking the button, implement the methods referenced in the OnClick attributes in the code-behind class:

```
protected void SecondButton_Click(object sender, EventArgs args)
{
   // Do something
}
```

SharePoint toolbars usually use ASCX user controls to direct the HTML rendering and layout. This is great if you have an ASPX page, but presents an interesting challenge when you want to create toolbars in code only.

Notice that there's no constructor for the two useful classes Toolbar and ToolbarButton in the Microsoft.SharePoint.WebControls namespace. To include a toolbar in, say, your Web Part, you need to create a control using the Page.LoadControl method, pointing to the relevant user control and casting the result. It's relatively straightforward, as Listing 11–19 demonstrates.

Listing 11–19. *Creating a Toolbar Programmatically*

```
private void CreateToolbar()
{
        ToolBarButton myToolbarButton1 =
          (ToolBarButton)Page.LoadControl("~/_controltemplates/ToolBarButton.ascx");
        myToolbarButton1.Text = "First button";
        myToolbarButton1.ImageUrl = "/_layouts/images/edit.gif";
        myToolbarButton1.NavigateUrl = "/_admin/EditOutboundUrls.aspx";

        ToolBarButton myToolbarButton2 =
          (ToolBarButton)Page.LoadControl("~/_controltemplates/ToolBarButton.ascx");
        myToolbarButton2.Text = "Second button";
        myToolbarButton2.ImageUrl = "/_layouts/images/edit.gif";
        myToolbarButton2.Click += new EventHandler(myToolbarButton2_Click);

        ToolBar toolbar =
          (ToolBar)Page.LoadControl("~/_controltemplates/ToolBar.ascx");
        toolbar.Buttons.Controls.Add(myToolbarButton1);
        toolbar.Buttons.Controls.Add(myToolbarButton2);

        myToolBar.Controls.Add(toolbar);
}

void myToolbarButton2_Click(object sender, EventArgs e)
{
    throw new NotImplementedException();
}
```

This code programmatically produces the exact toolbar shown in Figure 11–43.

Ribbon Control

As mentioned in the previous chapter, with SharePoint 2010, the already well-known ribbon interface of Microsoft Office has been ported to the Web. The ribbon interface is designed to help users quickly find the commands they need to complete a task (see Figure 11–44).
It creates a consistent user interface for working with SharePoint objects. You can extend the ribbon to add new functionality.

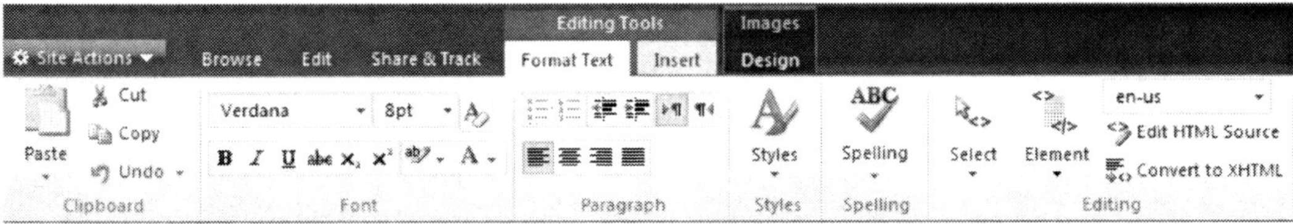

Figure 11–44. Complex ribbon bar

Ribbon Basics

The top-level elements in the ribbon are tabs. Tabs appear across the top of the page in a SharePoint site. Each tab organizes a set of groups. These groups contain sets of controls. Each group can contain multiple controls and has a label to identify each group. The controls inside the group include buttons, drop-down menus, check boxes, combo boxes, split buttons, and galleries (see Figure 11–45). Each of these controls is tied to a unique command.

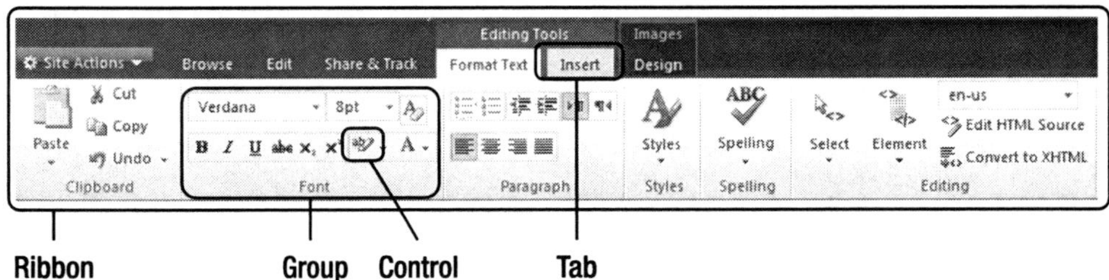

Figure 11–45. Ribbon elements

The ribbon is defined in XML in a feature manifest or a user custom action. The XML used for the ribbon defines each tab, group, and control. The `Tab` element contains one `Groups` element. Each `Groups` element has multiple `Group` elements. Inside the `Group` element is a single `Controls` element containing multiple types of controls. A sample XML snippet is shown following for all of the basic levels in the ribbon:

```
<Tab Id="Ribbon.Custom_Tab" Description="A new tab" Title="Custom Tab">
  <Groups Id="Ribbon.Custom_Tab.Groups">
    <Group Id="Ribbon.Custom_Tab.Custom_Group"
     Title="Custom Commands">
      <Controls Id="Ribbon.Custom_Tab.Custom_Group.Controls">
```

```
        <Button
         Id="Ribbon.Custom_Tab.Custom_Group.CustomCommand"
         Command="CustomCommand"
         Image16by16=""
         Image32by32=""
         Alt=""
         TemplateAlias=""
         LabelText="Custom Command"
         ... />
      </Controls>
    </Group>
  </Groups>
</Tab>
```

Ribbon Communication

The ribbon interface, also known as the command UI, uses multiple objects to interact with the rest of the page. It requires information about the following:

- Which controls are enabled/disabled
- The current state of the controls
- When to refresh

The ribbon communicates using the `CommandDispatcher`, `PageManager`, and `PageComponent` objects, among others. Each of these objects plays an important role in interacting with the ribbon. The communication is largely done on the client side—thus, all objects are implemented in JavaScript (see Figure 11–46).

The `PageManager` initializes all of the controls and registers the `PageComponent` objects for the ribbon. Exactly one instance of the `PageManager` lives on the page and can be accessed in JavaScript via the method `SP.Ribbon.PageManager.get_instance`.

```
/////////////////////////////////////////////////////////////////////////////
// CUI.Page.PageManager

CUI.Page.PageManager = function() {
    CUI.Page.PageManager.initializeBase(this);
    this._components = [];
    this._componentIds = {};
    this._commandDispatcher = new CUI.Page.CommandDispatcher();
    this._focusManager = new CUI.Page.FocusManager(this);
    this._undoManager = new CUI.Page.UndoManager(this);
    this._roots = [];
    this._onPageUnloadHandler = Function.createDelegate(this, this.onPageUnload);
    Sys.UI.DomEvent.addHandler(window, 'unload', this._onPageUnloadHandler);
}
CUI.Page.PageManager.initialize = function() {
    if (!CUI.ScriptUtility.isNullOrUndefined(CUI.Page.PageManager._instance)) {
        return;
    }
    CUI.Page.PageManager._instance = CUI.Page.PageManager.createPageManager();
    CUI.Page.PageManager._instance.initializeInternal();
}
CUI.Page.PageManager.createPageManager = function() {
    return new CUI.Page.PageManager();
}
CUI.Page.PageManager.get_instance = function() {
    if (!CUI.Page.PageManager._instance) {
        CUI.Page.PageManager.initialize();
    }
    return CUI.Page.PageManager._instance;
}
```

Figure 11–46. *PageManager class written in JavaScript (/_layouts/CUI.js.debug)*

The CommandDispatcher handles all of the PageComponent objects and the commands they can handle. When a command is received on the page, the CommandDispatcher receives the command and passes it to the correct PageComponent.

A PageComponent is created in JavaScript, too, and handles commands passed by the CommandDispatcher. After the PageComponent is added to the page, you use JavaScript to create an instance of your PageComponent and register it with the PageManager. The PageComponent can then respond to the commands you defined in XML.

As you can see in Listing 11–20, the client-side class CUI.Page.PageComponent defines a kind of abstract class for further implementations.

Listing 11–20. *JavaScript Code for the PageComponent Class from File /_layouts/CUI.js.debug*

```
/////////////////////////////////////////////////////////////////////////////
// CUI.Page.PageComponent

CUI.Page.PageComponent = function() {
}
CUI.Page.PageComponent.prototype = {

    init: function() {
    },
```

```
    getGlobalCommands: function() {
        return null;
    },

    getFocusedCommands: function() {
        return null;
    },

    handleCommand: function(commandId, properties, sequence) {
        return false;
    },

    canHandleCommand: function(commandId) {
        return false;
    },

    isFocusable: function() {
        return false;
    },

    receiveFocus: function() {
        return false;
    },

    yieldFocus: function() {
        return true;
    },

    getId: function() {
        return 'PageComponent';
    }
}
```

This class also implements the JavaScript pseudointerface ICommandHandler.

```
CUI.Page.PageComponent.registerClass('CUI.Page.PageComponent', null,
CUI.Page.ICommandHandler);
```

This class needs to be implemented if you want to extend the command UI with your controls. An example implementation for a custom PageComponent class could look like Listing 11–21.

Listing 11–21. *Example JavaScript Implementation of a Custom PageComponent*

```
////////////////////////////////////////////////////////////////////////////////
// SP.Ribbon.MyCustomPageComponent

SP.Ribbon.MyCustomPageComponent = function() {
    SP.Ribbon.MyCustomPageComponent.initializeBase(this);
}

/// Singleton implementation for getting only one instance
SP.Ribbon.MyCustomPageComponent.get_instance = function() {
        if (!SP.Ribbon.MyCustomPageComponent.s_instance) {
```

```
            SP.Ribbon.MyCustomPageComponent.s_instance = new SP.Ribbon.MyCustomPageComponent
();
        }
        return  SP.Ribbon.MyCustomPageComponent.s_instance;
    }

SP.Ribbon.MyCustomPageComponent.prototype = {

    init: function() {
    },

    getGlobalCommands: function() {
        return ['CommandX', 'CommandY', 'CommandZ']
    },

    getFocusedCommands: function() {
        return null;
    },

    handleCommand: function(commandId, properties, sequence) {
        if (commandId == 'CommandX') { alert('CommandX:' + commandId); }
        else if (commandId == 'CommandY') { alert(commandId); }
        else if (commandId == 'CommandZ') { alert('->' + commandId); }
        else return false;
        return true;
    },

    canHandleCommand: function(commandId) {
        if ((commandId == 'CommandX')
        || (commandId == 'CommandY')
        || (commandId == 'CommandZ')) {  return true; }
        return false;
    },

    isFocusable: function() {
        return false;
    },

    receiveFocus: function() {
        return false;
    },

    yieldFocus: function() {
        return true;
    },

    getId: function() {
        return 'MyCustomPageComponent';
    }
}

/// Register class and ensure it "inherits" from CUI.Page.PageComponent
```

```
SP.Ribbon.MyCustomPageComponent.registerClass(SP.Ribbon.MyCustomPageComponent ',
CUI.Page.PageComponent);
```

This example implementation handles three commands: CommandX, CommandY, and CommandZ. If a matching command of the getGlobalCommands array is triggered, first the canHandleCommand method is executed to check whether this command should ever be handled. If the return value is true, then the handleCommand method is executed. In our example, an alert box is displayed.

Before a PageComponent class can be active, it must be registered by the PageManager. This is achieved with the following code:

```
var pageMgr = SP.Ribbon.PageManager.get_instance();
pageMgr.addPageComponent(SP.Ribbon.MyCustomPageComponent.get_instance());
```

Now our PageComponent (MyCustomPageComponent) is registered and able to receive the defined commands from the command UI. It is the CommandDispatcher, implemented as the class CUI.Page.CommandDispatcher in JavaScript, that receives all the commands and distributes them among the registered PageComponent instances. For a clearer understanding, look through the source code excerpt shown in Figure 11–47. As you can see, there is a local property called _registrations that contains one or more command handlers that can handle a command. Because the PageComponent class itself implements the pseudointerface ICommandHandler, it is possible to detect this interface and execute the method callCommandHandler for every registered PageComponent. This method simply invokes the handleCommand method of the PageComponent.

```
executeCommandInternal: function(commandId, properties, sequenceNumber) {
    var rec = this._registrations[commandId];
    if (CUI.ScriptUtility.isNullOrUndefined(rec)) {
        return false;
    }
    else if (CUI.Page.ICommandHandler.isInstanceOfType(rec)) {
        return this.callCommandHandler(rec, commandId, properties, sequenceNumber);
    }
    else {
        var handlers = rec;
        var success = false;
        for (var i = 0; i < handlers.length; i++) {
            var handler = handlers[i];
            if (this.callCommandHandler(handler, commandId, properties, sequenceNumber)) {
                success = true;
            }
        }
        return success;
    }
},

isCommandEnabled: function(commandId) {
    var rec = this._registrations[commandId];
    if (CUI.ScriptUtility.isNullOrUndefined(rec)) {
        return false;
    }
    else if (CUI.Page.ICommandHandler.isInstanceOfType(rec)) {
        return this.callCommandHandlerForEnabled(rec, commandId);
    }
```

Figure 11–47. *Source code of class CUI.Page.CommandDispatcher (/_layouts/CUI.js.debug)*

■ **Caution** Elements of a ribbon (tabs, groups, controls) are only active and clickable if the appropriate command is handled by a registered `PageComponent`. If only the commands of the controls (e.g., buttons) are implemented, but not the commands for the enclosed tab or group of the controls, they will not fire any events. Your elements will appear to be deactivated.

Ribbon Controls Overview

The ribbon contains many types of controls. These can include simple controls, such as check boxes, buttons, and combo boxes, and also more advanced controls, such as split buttons or flyout anchors. The controls described in Table 11–7 are available in the ribbon.

***Table 11–7.** Available Ribbon Controls for SharePoint 2010*

Control Type	Description	Image
`Button`	A simple button used to perform an action.	 Make Homepage
`Checkbox`	A check box used to select an option.	 Lock Aspect Ratio
`ColorPicker`	A grid used to select colors.	 Standard Colors
`ComboBox`	A list used to select a value by clicking or typing.	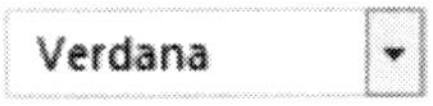 Verdana
`DropDown`	A list used to select a value by clicking.	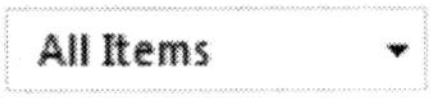 All Items
`FlyoutAnchor`	A button with a down arrow used to open a menu.	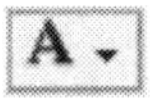 A
`Gallery`	A container used to show custom pop-ups containing `GalleryButton` elements.	 Examp Example Headline Subhead

`GalleryButton`	A button within a `Gallery` element that consists of custom HTML.	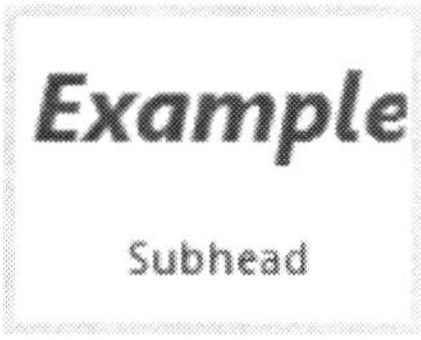
`InsertTable`	A ten-by-ten grid used to specify the dimensions of a table.	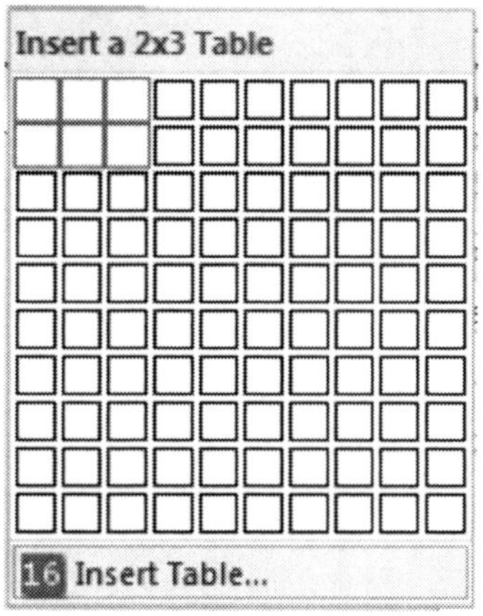
`Label`	A line of text, with an optional image, used to provide information.	
`Menu`	A container used to show pop-up menus.	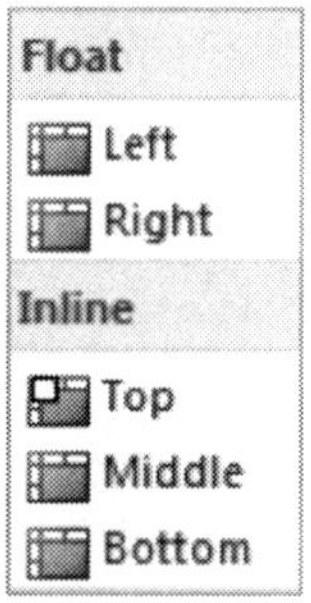
`MenuSection`	A section used to divide a menu. A menu section can have a title and contain controls.	

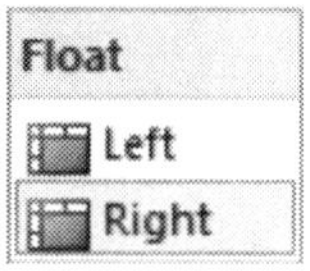

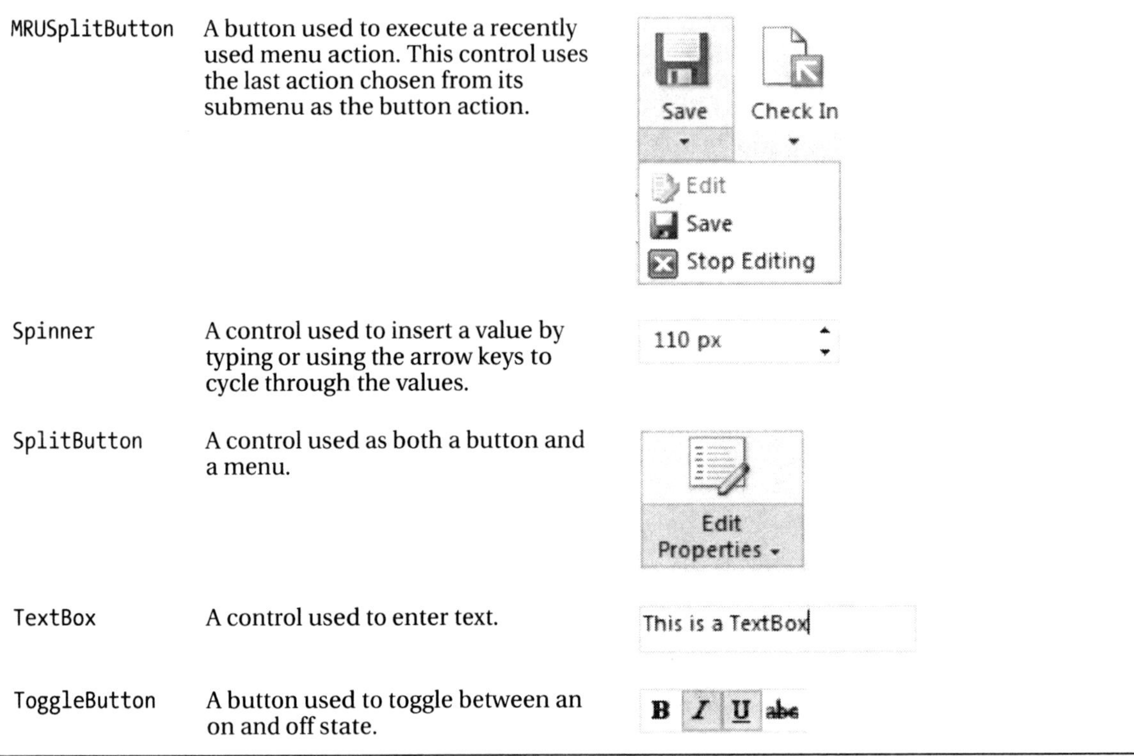

`MRUSplitButton`	A button used to execute a recently used menu action. This control uses the last action chosen from its submenu as the button action.	Save / Check In / Edit / Save / Stop Editing
`Spinner`	A control used to insert a value by typing or using the arrow keys to cycle through the values.	110 px
`SplitButton`	A control used as both a button and a menu.	Edit Properties
`TextBox`	A control used to enter text.	This is a TextBox
`ToggleButton`	A button used to toggle between an on and off state.	B *I* U abc

The implementation of the ribbon interface is very dynamic, and the client-side JavaScript plays a large role. For example, controls such as the `FlyoutAnchor` or `ComboBox` have so-called "population properties" that begin with the prefix `Populate` and support generating the necessary submenus dynamically in JavaScript. These properties control how menus are loaded and displayed. An example for this is the `ComboBox` to select fonts shown in Figure 11–48.

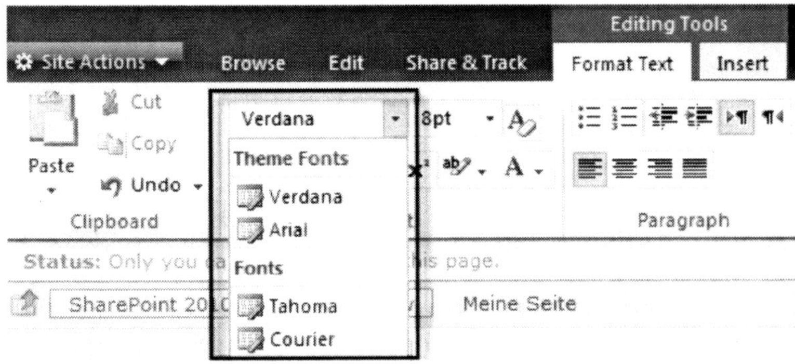

Figure 11–48. *ComboBox control for selecting a font*

This ComboBox is defined in the file /TEMPLATE/GLOBAL/XML/CMDUI.XML:

```
<ComboBox
    Id="Ribbon.FormatText.Font.Fonts"
    Command="FontFamilyStyleValue"
    QueryCommand="QueryFontFamily"
    AllowFreeForm="true"
    PopulateDynamically="true"
    PopulateOnlyOnce="false"
    PopulateQueryCommand="GetFontFamilyMenuXml"
    Width="75px"
    ImageArrow="/_layouts/images/Menu1.gif"
    TemplateAlias="font">
</ComboBox>
```

The three properties beginning with Populate determine that if a user clicks the right arrow of the ComboBox, the menu that appears will be generated on every click (PopulateOnlyOnce=false) by the JavaScript function GetFontFamilyMenuXml (PopulateQueryCommand). The implementation can be found in the file /_layouts/SP.UI.rte.debug.js:

```
commandHandlerRibbonGetFontFamilyMenuXml: function(commandId, properties, sequence) {ULS_SP();
    var props = properties;
    props.PopulationXML = SP.UI.Rte.FontCommands.initFontFamilyDropDownMenu();
    return true;
},
```

The called function, initFontSizeDropDownMenu, which in turn calls the function populateFontFamilyDropDownMenu, can also be found in the same JavaScript file (see Listing 11–22).

Listing 11–22. *JavaScript Functions from SP.UI.rte.debug.js*

```
SP.UI.Rte.FontCommands.initFontFamilyDropDownMenu = function() {ULS_SP();
    var sb = new Sys.StringBuilder();
    SP.UI.Rte.FontCommands.populateFontFamilyDropDownMenu(sb);
    return sb.toString();
}
SP.UI.Rte.FontCommands.populateFontFamilyDropDownMenu = function(sb) {ULS_SP();
    var prefix = SP.UI.Rte.Canvas.getCurrentStyleSheetPrefix();
    var prefixWithClasses = [ prefix + 'ThemeFontFace', prefix + 'FontFace' ];
    var standardFontInfo = SP.UI.Rte.StyleRuleUtility.getStyleRules(prefixWithClasses[1]);
    var themeFontInfo = SP.UI.Rte.StyleRuleUtility.getStyleRules(prefixWithClasses[0]);
    var firstMenuDisplayName = null;
    var groupDisplayNames = [ SP.Res.themeFonts, SP.Res.fonts ];
    var commands = [ 'FontFamilyThemeClass', 'FontFamilyCssClass' ];
    var commandsPreview = [ 'FontFamilyThemeClassPreview', 'FontFamilyCssClassPreview' ];
    var commandsRevert = [ 'FontFamilyThemeClassPreviewRevert',
'FontFamilyCssClassPreviewRevert' ];
    sb.append('<Menu Id=\'');
    sb.append('Ribbon.EditingTools.CPEditTab.Font.FontSize.Menu');
    sb.append('\'>');
    for (var groupIndex = 0; groupIndex < groupDisplayNames.length; groupIndex++) {
        var infos;
        if (!groupIndex) {
            infos = themeFontInfo;
        }
```

```
        else {
            infos = standardFontInfo;
        }
        if (!infos || !infos.length) {
            continue;
        }
        sb.append('<MenuSection Id=\'');
        sb.append('msFontFamily-' + groupIndex.toString());
        sb.append('\' Title=\'');
        sb.append(SP.Utilities.HttpUtility.escapeXmlText(groupDisplayNames[groupIndex]));
        sb.append('\' Description=\'');
        sb.append('\' Scrollable=\'false\' >');
        sb.append('<Controls>');
        for (var i = 0; i < infos.length; i++) {
            var info = infos[i];
            var selectorText = info.rule.selectorText;
            var className =
SP.UI.Rte.StyleRuleUtility.getClassNameFromSelectorText(selectorText);
            var suffix = SP.UI.Rte.StyleRuleUtility.getSuffix(selectorText,
prefixWithClasses[groupIndex] + '-');
            var displayName = SP.UI.Rte.StyleRuleUtility.getRuleDisplayName(info, suffix,
'fontFamily');
            if (!firstMenuDisplayName) {
                firstMenuDisplayName = displayName;
            }
            sb.append('<Button id=\'');
            sb.append('fseaFont-' + groupIndex.toString() + '-' + i.toString());
            sb.append('\' LabelText=\'');
            sb.append(SP.Utilities.HttpUtility.escapeXmlText(displayName));
            sb.append('\' LabelStyle=\'');
            sb.append(className);
            sb.append('\' Image32by32=\'/_layouts/images/actionscreate.gif\'
Image16by16=\'/_layouts/images/edit.gif\' MenuItemId=\'');
            sb.append(SP.Utilities.HttpUtility.escapeXmlText(displayName));
            sb.append('\' CommandValueId=\'');
            sb.append(className);
            sb.append('\' Command=\'');
            sb.append(commands[groupIndex]);
            sb.append('\' CommandPreview=\'');
            sb.append(commandsPreview[groupIndex]);
            sb.append('\' CommandRevert=\'');
            sb.append(commandsRevert[groupIndex]);
            sb.append('\' />');
        }
        sb.append('</Controls>');
        sb.append('</MenuSection>');
    }
    sb.append('</Menu>');
    return firstMenuDisplayName;
}
```

The result is returned into the property `props.PopulationXML` as plain XML. In the example it defines a `Menu` containing two `MenuSection` elements, each with two `Button` elements:

```
<Menu Id='Ribbon.EditingTools.CPEditTab.Font.FontSize.Menu'>
  <MenuSection Id='msFontFamily-0' Title='Theme Fonts' Description='' Scrollable='false' >
    <Controls>
      <Button id='fseaFont-0-0' LabelText='Verdana'
              LabelStyle='ms-rteThemeFontFace-1'
              Image32by32='/_layouts/images/actionscreate.gif'
              Image16by16='/_layouts/images/edit.gif'
              MenuItemId='Verdana'
              CommandValueId='ms-rteThemeFontFace-1'
              Command='FontFamilyThemeClass'
              CommandPreview='FontFamilyThemeClassPreview'
              CommandRevert='FontFamilyThemeClassPreviewRevert' />

      <Button id='fseaFont-0-1' LabelText='Arial'
              LabelStyle='ms-rteThemeFontFace-2'
              Image32by32='/_layouts/images/actionscreate.gif'
              Image16by16='/_layouts/images/edit.gif'
              MenuItemId='Arial'
              CommandValueId='ms-rteThemeFontFace-2'
              Command='FontFamilyThemeClass'
              CommandPreview='FontFamilyThemeClassPreview'
              CommandRevert='FontFamilyThemeClassPreviewRevert' />
    </Controls>
  </MenuSection>
  <MenuSection Id='msFontFamily-1' Title='Fonts' Description='' Scrollable='false' >
    <Controls>
      <Button id='fseaFont-1-0' LabelText='Tahoma' LabelStyle='ms-rteFontFace-1'
              Image32by32='/_layouts/images/actionscreate.gif'
              Image16by16='/_layouts/images/edit.gif'
              MenuItemId='Tahoma'
              CommandValueId='ms-rteFontFace-1'
              Command='FontFamilyCssClass'
              CommandPreview='FontFamilyCssClassPreview'
              CommandRevert='FontFamilyCssClassPreviewRevert' />
      <Button id='fseaFont-1-1' LabelText='Courier' LabelStyle='ms-rteFontFace-2'
              Image32by32='/_layouts/images/actionscreate.gif'
              Image16by16='/_layouts/images/edit.gif'
              MenuItemId='Courier'
              CommandValueId='ms-rteFontFace-2'
              Command='FontFamilyCssClass'
              CommandPreview='FontFamilyCssClassPreview'
              CommandRevert='FontFamilyCssClassPreviewRevert' />
    </Controls>
  </MenuSection>
</Menu>
```

As you can see, there are new, very flexible concepts introduced with the new command UI ribbon interface. The idea of separation between the UI definition and its implementation is obvious. But for real developers, this doesn't necessarily make things easier, because we are now faced with two worlds: the new client-side JavaScript world and the old, familiar world of server-side code. To facilitate the beginning of ribbon development, the next section outlines a practical way to integrate the ribbon UI interface in your own application pages.

Customizing the Ribbon

As you've learned already in Chapter 10, you can easily customize the existing ribbon interface by adding, removing, or hiding various ribbon controls. This can be done using XML and JavaScript. The XML defines the controls on the ribbon and the JavaScript performs actions on the page or object. You can, for example, create buttons and use JavaScript to implement your own handlers.

When customizing the ribbon, you can add, replace, and remove controls, groups, and tabs. Customizations to the ribbon are defined using a custom action in a feature, and can be deployed in a solution package (WSP file). Ribbon customizations can be scoped to a particular list type via the `RegistrationId` and `RegistrationType` attributes. Customizations can also be scoped to a site or a particular web through the `Scope` attribute in the `feature.xml` file.

In this section we use the ribbon interface to extend the user experience of our custom application pages. We want to use ribbons as a contemporary replacement for toolbars. Step by step we will develop a modern ribbon interface and demonstrate how to use both client-side and server-side event handlers to process user actions.

Prerequisites for a Custom Ribbon

The steps to building your own custom ribbon in an application page are as follows:

1. Create a feature with a ribbon definition.
2. Create an application page and render the ribbon.
3. Create client-side JavaScript code for a `PageHandler`.
4. Implement event handlers (client side and server side).

Creating a Feature with a Ribbon Definition

To provide a custom ribbon in your application pages, you have to define it in an element manifest file within a feature. Such a `feature.xml` file follows:

```
<?xml version="1.0" encoding="utf-8" ?>
<Feature
  Id="7F762A93-2205-499B-84E3-125423D86E32"
  Title="Provides a ribbon"
  Description="Feature that provides a ribbon definition"
  Scope="Site"
  xmlns="http://schemas.microsoft.com/sharepoint/">
  <ElementManifests>
    <ElementManifest Location="MyCustomRibbon.xml" />
  </ElementManifests>
</Feature>
```

This feature references the file `MyCustomRibbon.xml` which describes the ribbon and all of its elements (tabs, groups, and controls; see Listing 11–23).

***Listing 11–23.** MyCustomRibbon.xml Defines a Tab and a Group Containing a Button Control*

```
<Elements xmlns="http://schemas.microsoft.com/sharepoint/">

  <CustomAction
        Id="Ribbon.CustomTab.CA"
```

```
      Location="CommandUI.Ribbon.Tabs._children"
      Sequence="100"
      Title="My Custom Tab">
    <CommandUIExtension>
      <CommandUIDefinitions>
        <CommandUIDefinition>
           <Tab Id="Ribbon.Tabs.MyCustomTab" Sequence="200" Command="MyCustomTab"
                Description="desc" Title="My Custom Actions">
            <Scaling Id="Ribbon.Tabs.MyCustomTab.Scaling">
              <MaxSize Id="Ribbon.Tabs.MyCustomTab.maxsize"
                       GroupId="Ribbon.Tabs.MyCustomTab.Actions"
                       Sequence="20" Size="LargeLarge" />
            </Scaling>

            <Groups Id="Ribbon.Tabs.MyCustomTab.Groups">
              <Group Id="Ribbon.Tabs.MyCustomTab.Actions"
                     Command="MyCustomTabActions"
                     Sequence="10"
                     Description=""
                     Title="Group X"
                     Template="Ribbon.Templates.Flexible2">

                <Controls Id="Ribbon.Tabs.MyCustomTab.Actions.Ctrls">

                  <Button Id="Ribbon.Tabs.MyCustomTab.Actions.Save"
                    Command="MyCustomSave"
                    Image16by16="/_layouts/images/formatmap16x16.png"
                    Image16by16Class="formatmap16x16_rbsavehs"
                    Image32by32="/_layouts/images/formatmap32x32.png"
                    Image32by32Class="formatmap32x32_rbsavehh"
                    LabelText="My Save" Alt="My Safe Tooltip" TemplateAlias="o1"
                          />
                </Controls>
              </Group>
            </Groups>
          </Tab>
        </CommandUIDefinition>
      </CommandUIDefinitions>
    </CommandUIExtension>
  </CustomAction>
</Elements>
```

Creating an Application Page and Displaying the Ribbon Bar

After deploying the preceding feature, create an application page in which you can render the defined ribbon tab. The necessary code-behind C# code is very simple, as Listing 11–24 shows.

Listing 11–24. *Overriding the OnPreRender Method to Show the Ribbon*

```
protected override void OnPreRender(EventArgs e)
{
    SPRibbon current = SPRibbon.GetCurrent(this);
    if (current != null)
```

```
    {
        current.CommandUIVisible = true;
        current.MakeTabAvailable("Ribbon.Tabs.MyCustomTab");
        current.InitialTabId = "Ribbon.Tabs.MyCustomTab";
        current.Minimized = false;
        current.Visible = true;
        current.ServerRendered = true;
    }
    base.OnPreRender(e);
}
```

The preceding code gets the current ribbon (`SPRibbon.GetCurrent(this)`), which automatically exists because it has previously been defined in the associated master page.

The property `CommandUIVisible` shows or hides the ribbon section at the top of the application page. For example, if you have an application page that doesn't need a ribbon, you can hide the ribbon section to increase the space for your content. By using an `ID` parameter, the `MakeTabAvailable` method ensures that a tab will be available for the current page. If you need more than one tab, call this method for each required tab. To ensure that our single tab is displayed at page load, set the `InitialTabId` property to the ID of a tab that you've already defined via the `MakeTabAvailable` method.

To correctly render the ribbon, as shown in Figure 11–49, set three more properties: set `Minimized` to `false`, `Visible` to `true`, and `ServerRendered` to `true`.

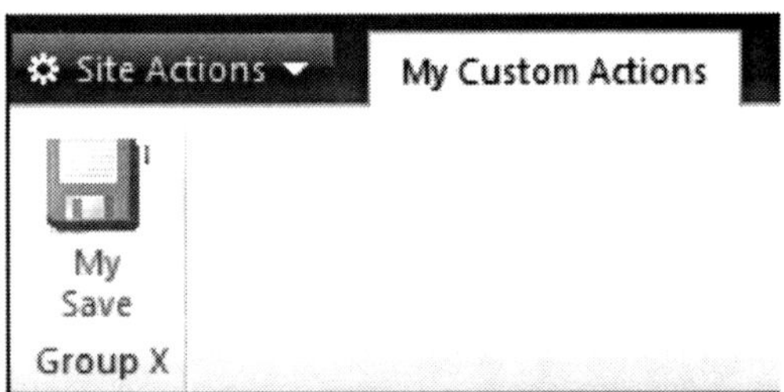

Figure 11–49. The custom ribbon with a tab, a group, and a button

When testing your application page, you will find that the button cannot be clicked. It seems to be disabled. The problem is that there's no way to set an enabled/disabled property for this button. At this point—if not earlier—you'll need a deeper understanding of how the ribbon implementation works.

Recall the explanation of the client-side `PageComponent` a few paragraphs earlier. To enable our button we have to implement a `PageComponent` class in JavaScript that is responsible for the ribbon tab group and handles the commands of all the elements. But instead of hard-coding all the commands in JavaScript, we use a combination of client- and server-side code (see Listing 11–25).

Listing 11–25. Enabling Custom Commands on the Ribbon

```
protected override void OnPreRender(EventArgs e)
{
    SPRibbon current = SPRibbon.GetCurrent(this);
    if (current != null)
    {
        current.CommandUIVisible = true;
        current.MakeTabAvailable("Ribbon.Tabs.MyCustomTab");
        current.InitialTabId = "Ribbon.Tabs.MyCustomTab";
```

```
        current.Minimized = false;
        current.Visible = true;
        current.ServerRendered = true;

        SPRibbonScriptManager manager = new SPRibbonScriptManager();
        List<IRibbonCommand> commands = new List<IRibbonCommand>();
        commands.Add(new SPRibbonCommand("MyCustomTab", ""));
        commands.Add(new SPRibbonCommand("MyCustomTabActions", ""));
        commands.Add(new SPRibbonCommand("MyCustomSave", "alert(commandId)"));

        manager.RegisterGetCommandsFunction(this, "getGlobalCommands", commands);
        manager.RegisterCommandEnabledFunction(this, "commandEnabled", commands);
        manager.RegisterHandleCommandFunction(this, "handleCommand", commands);

        String script = "<script type=\"text/javascript\" defer=\"true\"> //
                   <![CDATA[ \r\n function InitPageComponent() {
                    SP.Ribbon.UsageReportPageComponent.initialize(); }
                    \r\nExecuteOrDelayUntilScriptLoaded(InitPageComponent, \"SP.Ribbon.js\");
\r\n
                  //]]\r\n</script>";


        this.Page.ClientScript.RegisterClientScriptBlock(this.GetType(),
                "InitPageComponent", script, false);

    }
    base.OnPreRender(e);
}
```

In this extended code version, we create an instance of SPRibbonScriptManager that offers some very useful register methods. Initially, we traverse our CommandID chain (the tab command equals MyCustomTab, the group command equals MyCustomTabActions, and the button command equals MyCustomSave) and add a new SPRibbonCommand instance for each CommandID. Then we register these commands with all three registration methods of the SPRibbonScriptManager. The JavaScript output of those methods is shown in Figure 11–50.

The last thing to do is assign a PageComponent. To do this, we can use an existing PageComponent implementation of the UsageReportPage for our example. The registered script block (InitPageComponent) is also shown in Figure 11–50.

```
//]]>
</script><script type="text/javascript" defer="true">
//<![CDATA[
function getGlobalCommands() {
 return ['MyCustomTab', 'MyCustomTabActions', 'MyCustomSave'];
}
//]]
</script>
<script type="text/javascript" defer="true">
//<![CDATA[
function commandEnabled(commandId) {
 if ((commandId === 'MyCustomTab') || (commandId === 'MyCustomTabActions') || (commandId
 === 'MyCustomSave')) {
  return true; }
 return false;
}
//]]
</script>
<script type="text/javascript" defer="true">
//<![CDATA[
function handleCommand(commandId, properties, sequence) {
 if (commandId === 'MyCustomTab') { ; }
 else if (commandId === 'MyCustomTabActions') { ; }
 else if (commandId === 'MyCustomSave') { alert(commandId); }
 else return false;
 return true;
}
//]]
</script>
<script type="text/javascript" defer="true"> //<![CDATA[
 function InitPageComponent() { SP.Ribbon.UsageReportPageComponent.initialize(); }
ExecuteOrDelayUntilScriptLoaded(InitPageComponent, "SP.Ribbon.js");
 //]]
</script>
```

Figure 11–50. *Generated JavaScript from the SPRibbonScriptManager*

This JavaScript code becomes clear if you look at the PageComponent implementation that uses our generated functions to detect which commands should be handled and how (see Listing 11–26).

Listing 11–26. *Extracting from UsageRibbonPageComponent in File SP.Ribbon.js*

```
...
   getGlobalCommands: function() {ULS_SP();
        return getGlobalCommands();
    },

    canHandleCommand: function(commandId) {ULS_SP();
        return commandEnabled(commandId);
    },

    handleCommand: function(commandId, properties, sequence) {ULS_SP();
        return handleCommand(commandId, properties, sequence);
    }
...
```

After executing the application page with the new code enhancements, our button is enabled, and thus clickable. After clicking the button, internally the PageComponent validates via the commandEnabled function if the command (MyCustomSave) is valid. It then executes handleCommand, which displays an alert box containing the command ID, as shown in Figure 11–51.

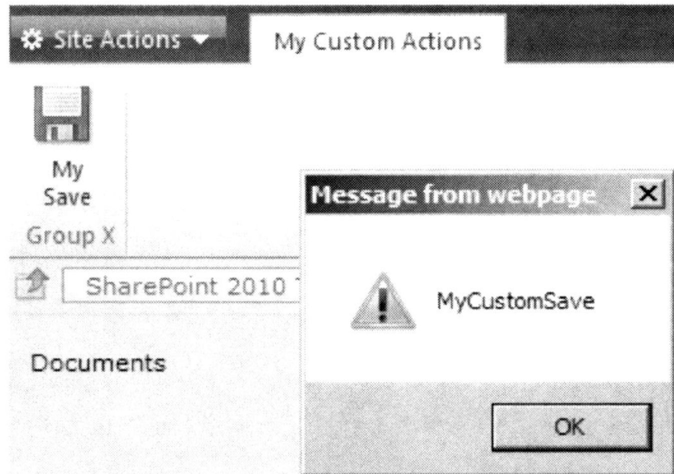

Figure 11–51. *Our custom ribbon with an enabled button and client event (alert box with commandID)*

Creating Client-Side JavaScript Code for a PageComponent Implementation

Although it is possible to use the UsageRibbonPageComponent that already exists in the built-in script file SP.Ribbon.js, this is not recommended. The reason for this is because the implementation could be changed with the next SharePoint update. Instead, you should create your own custom PageComponent implementation, as shown in Listing 11–27.

Listing 11–27. *Custom PageComponent Implementation in File SP.UI.MyCustomRibbon.debug.js*

```
Type.registerNamespace('MyCustom.Ribbon');

///////////////////////////////////////////////////////////////////////////////
// MyCustom.Ribbon.RibbonComponent

MyCustom.Ribbon.RibbonComponent = function() {
    MyCustom.Ribbon.RibbonComponent.initializeBase(this);
}

    MyCustom.Ribbon.RibbonComponent.get_instance = function() {
        if (!MyCustom.Ribbon.RibbonComponent.s_instance) {
            MyCustom.Ribbon.RibbonComponent.s_instance =
                 new MyCustom.Ribbon.RibbonComponent();
        }
        return MyCustom.Ribbon.RibbonComponent.s_instance;
    }

    MyCustom.Ribbon.RibbonComponent.prototype = {
        focusedCommands: null,
```

```
        globalCommands: null,

        registerWithPageManager: function() {
            SP.Ribbon.PageManager.get_instance().addPageComponent(this);

SP.Ribbon.PageManager.get_instance().get_focusManager().requestFocusForComponent(this);
        },

        unregisterWithPageManager: function() {
            SP.Ribbon.PageManager.get_instance().removePageComponent(this);
        },

        init: function() {
        },

        getFocusedCommands: function() {
            return [];
        },

        getGlobalCommands: function() {
            return getGlobalCommands();
        },

        canHandleCommand: function(commandId) {
            return commandEnabled(commandId);
        },

        handleCommand: function(commandId, properties, sequence) {
            return handleCommand(commandId, properties, sequence);
        },

        isFocusable: function() {
            return true;
        },

        receiveFocus: function() {
            return true;
        },

        yieldFocus: function() {
            return true;
        }
    }

////////////////////////////////////////////////////////////////////////////////

MyCustom.Ribbon.RibbonComponent.registerClass('MyCustom.Ribbon.RibbonComponent',
CUI.Page.PageComponent);
NotifyScriptLoadedAndExecuteWaitingJobs("sp.ui.mycustomribbon.debug.js");
```

To embed your own PageComponent implementation, you need to change the code of the PreRender method (see Listing 11–28). Add the script link to your custom JavaScript code file (SP.UI.MyCustomRibbon.debug.js), which has to be stored relative to the LAYOUTS folder. Also, ensure that the CUI.js and SP.Ribbon.js script files are registered. The function InitPageComponent must be executed after the custom script file is loaded. Within this function, retrieve the singleton instance of this `PageComponent` and call the function `registerWithPageManager` to register the `PageComponent` at the `PageManager`.

Listing 11–28. *Extended OnPreRender Method for Using a Custom PageComponent*

```
...
manager.RegisterGetCommandsFunction(this, "getGlobalCommands", commands);
manager.RegisterCommandEnabledFunction(this, "commandEnabled", commands);
manager.RegisterHandleCommandFunction(this, "handleCommand", commands);

ScriptLink.RegisterScriptAfterUI(this.Page, "CUI.js", false, true);
ScriptLink.RegisterScriptAfterUI(this.Page, "SP.Ribbon.js", false, true);
ScriptLink.RegisterScriptAfterUI(this.Page, "SP.UI.MyCustomRibbon.debug.js", false,
                                 true);

String script = "<script type=\"text/javascript\" defer=\"true\"> //<![CDATA[ \r\n
                            function InitPageComponent() {
                            MyCustom.Ribbon.RibbonComponent.
                            get_instance().registerWithPageManager()}
                             \r\nExecuteOrDelayUntilScriptLoaded(InitPageComponent,
                              \"SP.UI.MyCustomRibbon.debug.js\"); \r\n //]]\r\n</script>";

this.Page.ClientScript.RegisterClientScriptBlock(this.GetType(),"InitPageComponent",
                                                 script, false);
...
```

As you see, it's not trivial, but it is feasible to integrate your own page component.

Implementing Server-Side Event Handlers

You may have already asked yourself how it would be possible to handle click events on the server side instead of the client side. If you understand the complex examples of the last two subsections, this should be a very simple exercise.

Just replace the following line in the `PreRender` method with the second one, and the `SPRibbonPostBackCommand` will do everything you need (see Figure 11–52).

```
commands.Add(new SPRibbonCommand("MyCustomSave", "alert(commandId)"));
commands.Add(new SPRibbonPostBackCommand("MyCustomSave", this));
```

```
function handleCommand(commandId, properties, sequence) {
 if (commandId === 'MyCustomTab') { ; }
 else if (commandId === 'MyCustomTabActions') { ; }
 else if (commandId === 'MyCustomSave') { __doPostBack('__Page','{\"id\":\"MyCustomSave\"}'); }
 else return false;
 return true;
}
```

Figure 11–52. *Rendering of postback events in JavaScript code*

In the JavaScript code that is automatically generated, the command `MyCustomSave` executes the `__doPostBack` function, which causes a postback of the current page. To handle this postback event, you have to implement the interface `IPostBackEvent` and the corresponding method `RaisePostBackEvent`, as shown in Listing 11–29.

Listing 11–29. Postback Handler Implementation for Ribbon Postbacks

```
void IPostBackEventHandler.RaisePostBackEvent(string eventArgument)
{
        SPRibbonPostBackEvent event2 =
                 SPRibbonPostBackCommand.DeserializePostBackEvent(eventArgument);
        if (event2 != null) {
            Response.Write("-->" + event2.Id + " -> " + event2.Arguments);
        }
}
```

Finally, after a postback, you have to deserialize the event arguments before you can use them. The output, after clicking the button, looks like Figure 11–53.

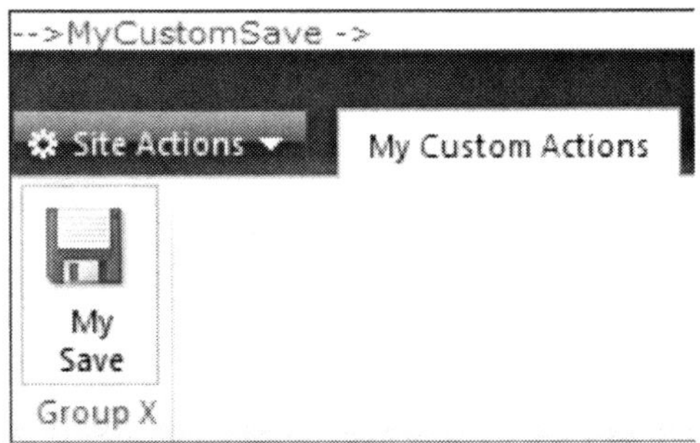

Figure 11–53. Response output of a postback event

Data Controls

In this section, two important SharePoint web controls used to display list data are covered:

- The SPGridView control
- The JS Grid control

Both controls provide powerful functionality to deal with list data, but both also come with incredible complexity. This section explains how to use the controls in your own application pages or Web Parts.

Working with the SPGridView Control

One of the most complex SharePoint web controls is the SPGridView control. Many developers fear it because of its complexity and lack of good documentation. In this section you'll get a practical introduction to this web control and some good reproducible examples of customizing this control for your own needs.

When you create custom application pages, you often need to display data from SharePoint list items in a grid consisting of rows and columns. One way to do that is to build an HTML table programmatically. Although this is the easiest and fastest approach for displaying data, it offers only very limited functionality. For example implementing filtering, sorting, or paging isn't possible with a pure HTML table.

With ASP.NET, the recommended approach for displaying a grid is to use the `GridView` control introduced with ASP.NET 2.0. SharePoint Foundation offers a grid control named `SPGridView` that inherits from the ASP.NET `GridView` control and provides a good alternative for displaying grid data in SharePoint application pages or Web Parts.

One significant advantage of the `SPGridView` control is that it automatically supports the SharePoint stylesheets, and you don't need to worry about the look and feel of your grid. The `SPGridView` control is widely used in standard application pages and Web Parts that are built into SharePoint Foundation. That means that your custom solutions can have the same look and feel as other aspects of the standard SharePoint user interface.

Let's look at some examples of how to use the control. Keep the following steps in mind:

1. Add a `Register` directive to your application page.
2. Add an `SPGridView` tag to your application page.
3. Define bound fields for your grid.
4. Retrieve data and bind it to the `DataSource` property of the `SPGridView`.

■ **Caution** The `SPGridView` control does not support the automatic generation of columns. You always have to set the property `AutoGenerateColumns` to `false` and explicitly bind your columns using `SPBoundField`. Otherwise you will receive an exception.

Example: Implementing a Grid for a SharePoint List

In this first example, we query a SharePoint list named `Books` and display all the items in an `SPGridView` control (see Figure 11–54).

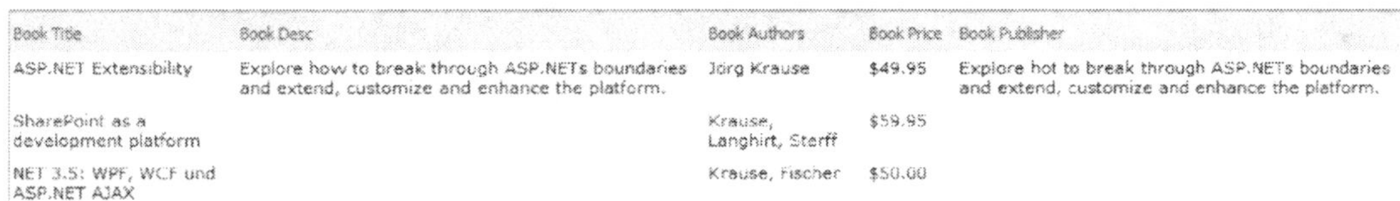

Book Title	Book Desc	Book Authors	Book Price	Book Publisher
ASP.NET Extensibility	Explore how to break through ASP.NETs boundaries and extend, customize and enhance the platform.	Jörg Krause	$49.95	Explore hot to break through ASP.NETs boundaries and extend, customize and enhance the platform.
SharePoint as a development platform		Krause, Langhirt, Sterff	$59.95	
NET 3.5: WPF, WCF und ASP.NET AJAX		Krause, Fischer	$50.00	

***Figure 11–54.** Simple grid with five columns*

In the code-behind class of our application page, we define the model class `Book` that is later bound to the `SPGridView`. The class contains five properties and a constructor, as shown in Listing 11–30.

***Listing 11–30.** Example Class Book with Five Properties and a Constructor*

```
public class Book
{
    public Book(String title, String desc, String authors, double price,
                String publisher)
    {
        this.Title = title;
        this.Description = desc;
```

```
        this.Authors = authors;
        this.Price = price;
        this.Publisher = publisher;
    }

    public String Title { get; set; }
    public String Description { get; set; }
    public String Authors { get; set; }
    public double Price { get; set; }
    public String Publisher { get; set; }
}
```

Next, we query the data from a SharePoint list and populate the Book instances, as shown in Listing 11–13.

***Listing 11–31.** Querying the SharePoint Books List and Returning the Values as Instances of Type Book*

```
/// <summary>
/// Query all books and convert the list item properties to the book object
/// </summary>
protected List<Book> GetAllBooks()
{
    List<Book> allBooks = new List<Book>();
    using (SPWeb web = SPContext.Current.Web)
    {
        foreach (SPListItem li in web.Lists["Books"].GetItems(new SPQuery())) {
            Book b = new Book(
                Convert.ToString(li["Title"]),
                Convert.ToString(li["Description"]),
                Convert.ToString(li["Authors"]),
                Convert.ToDouble(li["Price"]),
                Convert.ToString(li["Publisher"])
                );
            allBooks.Add(b);
        }
    }
    return allBooks;
}
```

You can now bind the list of Book objects to the SPGridView during the page load:

```
protected void Page_Load(object sender, EventArgs e)
{
    myGrid.DataSource = GetAllBooks();
    myGrid.DataBind();
}
```

So far it is straightforward. To display the properties of the Book instances, define bound fields with at least two properties: HeaderText and DataField. The HeaderText property contains the column title, and the DataField property contains the name of the property to display from the bound data source (in this case, Book; see Listing 11–32).

***Listing 11–32.** Application Page Containing an SPGridView with Bound Column Definitions*

```
<%@ Page Language="C#" AutoEventWireup="true"
DynamicMasterPageFile="~masterurl/default.master"
    CodeFile="GridViewExample.aspx.cs" Inherits="GridViewExample" MasterPageFile="v4.master"
    CodeFileBaseClass="Microsoft.SharePoint.WebControls.LayoutsPageBase" %>

<%@ Register Tagprefix="SharePoint" Namespace="Microsoft.SharePoint.WebControls"
    Assembly="Microsoft.SharePoint, Version=14.0.0.0, Culture=neutral,
PublicKeyToken=71e9bce111e9429c" %>

<asp:Content ContentPlaceHolderId="PlaceHolderMain" runat="server">

    <SharePoint:SPGridView runat="server" ID="myGrid" AutoGenerateColumns="false">
        <Columns>
            <asp:BoundField HeaderText="Book Title" DataField="Title" />
            <asp:BoundField HeaderText="Book Desc" DataField="Description" />
            <asp:BoundField HeaderText="Book Authors" DataField="Authors" />
            <asp:BoundField HeaderText="Book Price" DataField="Price"
                            DataFormatString="{0:c}" />
            <asp:BoundField HeaderText="Book Publisher" DataField="Publisher" />
        </Columns>
    </SharePoint:SPGridView>

</asp:Content>
```

Example: Using the DataTable Class

The preceding example is rather cumbersome—it requires an object model to be built and the list items to be converted. But there is a much easier approach—the SharePoint `SPListItemCollection` object can return `DataTable` instances. The complete code-behind implementation can now be done in only two lines and without the need for a separate object model and its conversion methods:

```
protected void Page_Load(object sender, EventArgs e)
    {
        myGrid.DataSource =  SPContext.Current.Web.Lists["Books"].GetItems(
                             new SPQuery()).GetDataTable();
        myGrid.DataBind();
    }
```

The `SPList.GetItems` method takes an `SPQuery` object, which defines the CAML query to run against the SharePoint list. Instead of querying only one list, you can use the `SPWeb.GetSiteData` method, which takes an `SPSiteDataQuery` parameter. With such site queries, it is possible to query several lists in one call. Imagine you wish to display the latest documents (say, modified within the last seven days) across multiple document libraries in one grid view (see Listing 11–33).

***Listing 11–33.** SPSiteDataQuery Example for All Documents in All Document Libraries Modified Within the Last Seven Days*

```
SPSiteDataQuery Query = new SPSiteDataQuery();
String str7DaysBackDateTime = (DateTime.Now.Add(
        new TimeSpan(-7, 0, 0, 0, 0))).ToString("yyyy-MM-ddThh:mm:ssZ");
```

```
string strQuery = String.Format("<Where><Gt><FieldRef Name=\"Modified\" />"
            +"<Value Type=\"DateTime\">{0}</Value></Gt></Where>"
            +"<OrderBy><FieldRef Ascending=\"FALSE\" Name=\"Modified\"/></OrderBy>",
            str7DaysBackDateTime);
Query.Query = strQuery;
Query.RowLimit = 25;
StringBuilder sb = new StringBuilder();
sb.Append("<Lists>");
foreach (SPList list in web.Lists)
{
    if (list.BaseType == SPBaseType.DocumentLibrary)
    {
        sb.Append("<List ID=\"" + list.ID.ToString() + "\"/>");
    }
}
sb.Append("</Lists>");
Query.Lists = sb.ToString(); // the lists on which you want your query to run
DataTable dt = web.GetSiteData(Query);
```

Example: Adding Custom Menus

The previously presented grid view implementation is static and does not allow any user interaction. The default interactions of grids or tables are simple hyperlinks that can easily be constructed, for example, by using the asp:HyperLink field. SharePoint offers an enhanced method to expose several actions on single items within the SPGridView: the SPMenuField. A per-item menu could look like Figure 11–55.

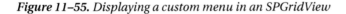

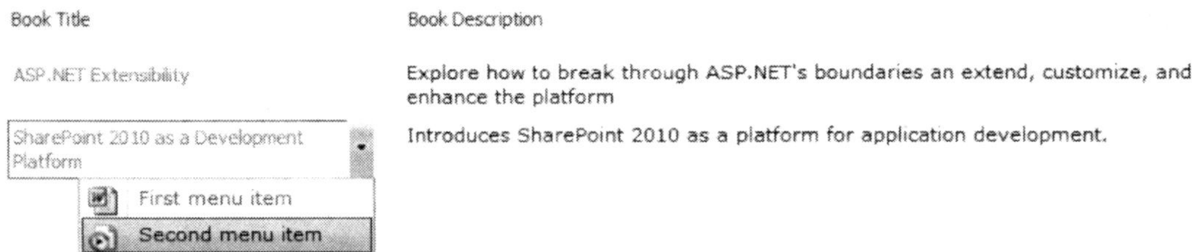

***Figure 11–55.** Displaying a custom menu in an SPGridView*

You construct such a menu by adding a menu definition (consisting of MenuTemplate and MenuItemTemplate; see Listing 11–34) and using an SPMenuField within the SPGridView that references a menu definition (see Listing 11–35).

***Listing 11–34.** Declarative Menu Definition*

```
<SharePoint:MenuTemplate runat="server" ID="myMenu">
    <SharePoint:MenuItemTemplate ID="mit1" runat="server"
         Text="First menu item" ImageUrl="/_layouts/images/ICDOC.gif"
         ClientOnClickNavigateUrl="page.aspx?ID=%MYID%&title=%NAME%" />

    <SharePoint:MenuItemTemplate ID="mit2" runat="server"
```

```
        Text="Second menu item" ImageUrl="/_layouts/images/ICWM.gif"
        ClientOnClickNavigateUrl="page2.aspx?ID=%MYID%&title=%NAME%" />
</SharePoint:MenuTemplate>
```

Listing 11–35. Declarative SPGridView Definition with SPMenuField

```
<SharePoint:SPGridView runat="server" ID="myGrid" AutoGenerateColumns="false">
    <Columns>
        <SharePoint:SPMenuField HeaderText="Book Title" TextFields="Title"
                                MenuTemplateId="myMenu"
                                TokenNameAndValueFields="MYID=ID,NAME=Title" />
        <asp:BoundField HeaderText="Book Desc" DataField="Description" />
        <asp:BoundField HeaderText="Book Authors" DataField="Authors" />
        <asp:BoundField HeaderText="Book Price" DataField="Price"
                        DataFormatString="{0:c}" />
        <asp:BoundField HeaderText="Book Publisher" DataField="Publisher" />
    </Columns>
</SharePoint:SPGridView>
```

The most interesting part here is the token syntax that is passed to the menu items. In our example, the token MYID is assigned to the ID property of the data column, and the token NAME is assigned to the Title property. These two tokens can be used, encapsulated in percent signs, in the ClientOnClickNavigateUrl of the MenuItemTemplate. A click on the second list item (which has an ID of 2) calls the link: page.aspx?ID=2&title=SharePoint as a development Platform.

■ **Tip** If you need to add different menu items to your list items (e.g., for different content types), you can change the bound fields programmatically for every row, by using the event onRowDataBound. With this event you get access to the current row instance, and you are able to modify the controls bound to this row. By casting, for example, a menu control with (Microsoft.SharePoint.WebControls.Menu) e.Row.Cells[n].Controls[n], you get access to the menu properties, such as HiddenMenuItems, where you can hide menu items that should not be displayed for this row.

Example: Enabling Sorting

A modern grid view in SharePoint needs to be able to sort and filter the columns. Fortunately, this nontrivial functionality is built in, so it's very easy to implement.

There are three steps to enable sorting:

1. Set the SPGridView property AllowSorting to true.
2. Implement the SPGridView event OnSorting.
3. Add a SortExpression to every bound column.

The following code shows the declarative implementation of the three steps:

```
<SharePoint:SPGridView runat="server" ID="myGrid"
               AutoGenerateColumns="false"
```

```
                AllowSorting="true"
                OnSorting="myGrid_Sorting">
    <Columns>
        <SharePoint:SPMenuField HeaderText="Book Title"
                        SortExpression="Title"
                        TextFields="Title"
                        MenuTemplateId="myMenu"
                        TokenNameAndValueFields="MYID=ID,NAME=Title" />
        <asp:BoundField HeaderText="Book Desc"
                            SortExpression="Description"
                            DataField="Description" />
...
```

The sorting itself has to be implemented programmatically in the method `myGrid_Sorting`. To understand what's happening under the hood, you need to be familiar with the `DataTable` and `DataView` classes. The `DataView` class can be customized to present a subset of data from a `DataTable`. This allows you to have more than one control bound to the same data table. Hence, you can bind different views of the data table to several web controls. Imagine you bind a `DataTable` to the `DataSource` property of an `SPGridView` like this:

```
myGrid.DataSource = myDataTable
```

This is what happens under the covers:

```
myGrid.DataSource = myDataTable.DefaultView
```

The `SPGridView` binds to the `DataTable.DefaultView` property, which returns all columns and rows in your table with a `DataRowState` equal to `CurrentRows`. Remember, we merely wish to implement basic sorting for our columns. As you can see in Listing 11–36, we need the `DataView.Sort` property to make use of the built-in sorting methods. This property takes an SQL-like sort expression and, in our example, the value of the `SortExpression` property of the bound fields.

Listing 11–36. *Custom Sorting Implementation Using DataView*

```
protected void myGrid_Sorting(object sender, GridViewSortEventArgs e)
{
    string lastExpression = "";
    if (ViewState["SortExpression"] != null)
        lastExpression = ViewState["SortExpression"].ToString();

    string lastDirection = "asc";
    if (ViewState["SortDirection"] != null)
        lastDirection = ViewState["SortDirection"].ToString();

    string newDirection = "asc";
    if (e.SortExpression == lastExpression)
        newDirection = (lastDirection == "asc") ? "desc" : "asc";

    ViewState["SortExpression"] = e.SortExpression;
    ViewState["SortDirection"] = newDirection;

    ((DataTable)myGrid.DataSource).DefaultView.Sort =
                                    e.SortExpression + " " + newDirection;
    myGrid.DataBind();
}
```

In this listing, the SortExpression is saved into the view state and the SortDirection (either ascending or descending) is calculated. Then the new SortExpression is set to the Sort property of the DefaultView of the DataTable. Figure 11–56 shows the sorting arrow of the first column, Book Title.

Book Title ↓
Book Description
SharePoint 2010 as a Development Platform
Introduces SharePoint 2010 as a platform for application development.
ASP.NET Extensibility
Explore how to break through ASP.NET's boundaries an extend, customize, and enhance the platform

Figure 11–56. *Sorting enabled in an SPGridView*

Example: Enabling Sorting and Filtering Using a LINQ Data Source

The next step is to integrate filtering capabilities. Unfortunately, filtering is not as easy as it seems, and can be a very frustrating issue. To enable filtering you have to follow these steps:

1. Set the SPGridView property AllowFiltering to true.
2. Define a DataSource declaratively and set the DataSourceID property.
3. Set additional SPGridView properties: FilterDataFields, FilteredDataSourcePropertyName, and FilteredDataSourcePropertyFormat.

```
<SharePoint:SPGridView runat="server" ID="myGrid"
        AutoGenerateColumns="false"
        AllowSorting="true"
        AllowFiltering="true"
        FilterDataFields="Title,,Authors,,Publisher"
        DataSourceID="linqDS"
        FilteredDataSourcePropertyName="Where"
        FilteredDataSourcePropertyFormat='{1} == "{0}"'
>...
```

The property FilterDataFields specifies to the SPGridView which columns filtering should be enabled on. This is a comma-separated string of column names. In our example, we want to filter for Title, Authors, and Publisher, but not Description or Price, so we leave the unwanted fields empty.

The next step is to declaratively define a data source and assign the DataSourceID property to it. In this example we use a LINQ data source:

```
<asp:LinqDataSource runat="server"
            ID="linqDS"
            OnSelecting="linqDS_Selecting"  />
```

The implementation of this data source is relatively easy. We simply query all the list items and return them in the LINQ syntax (see Listing 11–37).

Listing 11–37. *Implemenation of a LINQ Data Source*

```
protected void linqDS_Selecting(object sender, LinqDataSourceSelectEventArgs e)
{
    SPList list = SPContext.Current.Web.Lists["Books"];
    IEnumerable<SPListItem> books =
```

```
                                list.GetItems(new SPQuery()).OfType<SPListItem>();
    e.Result = from book in books
               select new
               {
                   ID = book.ID,
                   Title = Convert.ToString(book["Title"]),
                   Description = Convert.ToString(book["Description"]),
                   Authors = Convert.ToString(book["Authors"]),
                   Price = Convert.ToDouble(book["Price"]),
                   Publisher = Convert.ToString(book["Publisher"])
               };
}
```

The values of the filter properties (`FilteredDataSourcePropertyName` and `FilteredDataSourcePropertyFormat`) depend on the data source. Usually, a data source has a property for a filter string that is used by executing queries. For example, the `ObjectDataSource` has a property called `FilterExpression`, and for our `LinqDataSource` the property is called `Where` (see Figure 11–57). The format of the property contains two tokens (`{0}` and `{1}`) that are both automatically replaced by the column name (`{1}`) and the filter value (`{0}`).

```
linqDS.Where = "Publisher == \"APress\"";
```

string LinqDataSource.Where
Gets or sets a value that specifies what conditions must be true for a record to be included in the retrieved data.

Figure 11–57. The Where property of the LINQ data source

The result of this very simple implementation is a grid that can be sorted and filtered with only a few lines of code, as shown in Figure 11–58.

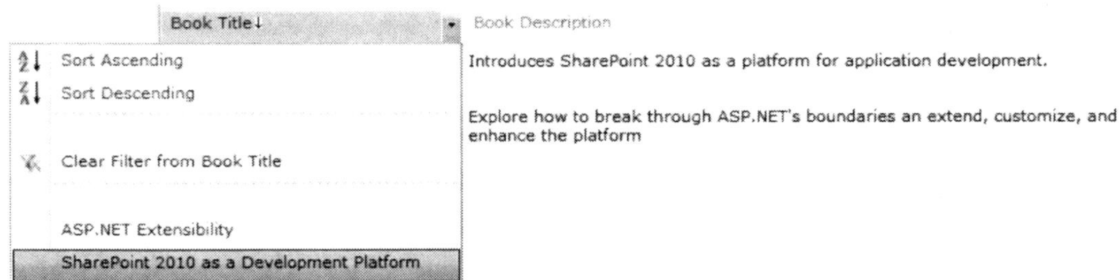

Figure 11–58. Sorting and filtering with LinqDataSource

Working with the JS Grid Control

The JS Grid control is new in SharePoint 2010. It allows Excel-like editing and rendering of tabular data, and replaces the ActiveX-based datasheet of Windows SharePoint Services 3.0 with a richer, more extensible UI. It also supports the Access Services grid and offers a Gantt chart view, familiar to users of Microsoft Project (see Figure 11–59).

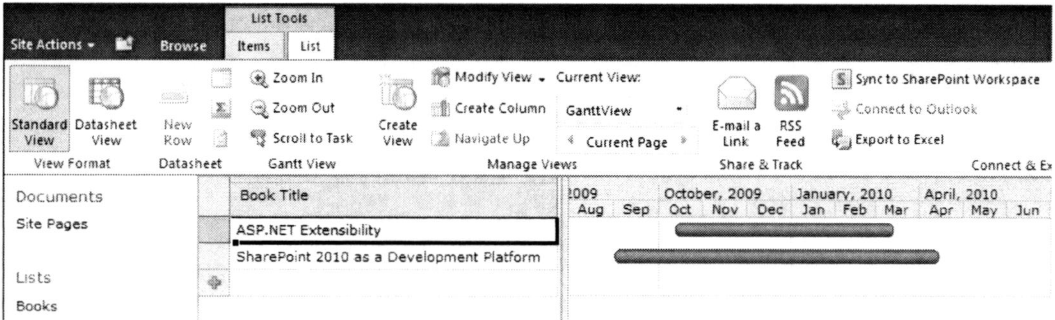

***Figure 11–59.** The JS Grid control in action (left: grid pane; right: Gantt pane)*

From a technical perspective, the JS Grid control is a grid manager component hosting one or two panes. The *grid pane* is the pane that renders tabular data. The *Gantt pane* is the surface on which charts are rendered.

The grid is extensible and offers developers a rich environment in which to create interactive and responsive applications in a browser. Developers can create a control that behaves more like one in a desktop application. The client-side rendering provides the user more immediate feedback because a round trip to the server is not required.

Features

The JS Grid control offers a broad variety of functions similar to a desktop application. The following features are supported:

- Copy, paste, undo, redo, fill-down, and export-to-Excel operations
- Asynchronous validation
- Control/widget display and edit capabilities
- Multiple views, in the form of grid, Gantt, and pivot charts

First of all, the JS Grid control supports the default copy and paste operations, as well as undo and redo. The undo/redo functionality is implemented as a multilevel operation, which means that changes are stored in a stack with up to 20 levels of undo/redo.

Even more complex operations such as fill-down (better known from Excel; Ctrl+U) and exporting data to Excel are supported. If paged data is exported, the JS Grid control requests all pages of data from the server to send to the client. The update status indicator displays the message "Preparing data for export." When all the data is in memory, the control automatically transforms the datasheet into spreadsheet XML.

Another important feature is asynchronous validation. Errors from the server need to be displayed to the user so that the user can correct them. Because dynamic grid implementations use asynchronous updates, the reporting of errors can be complicated. For instance, the user can make a change that is invalid and scroll that change out of view before the server returns an error. Or the user can make several invalid changes (through fill-down or copy/paste operations) that each need separate attention. In the JS Grid control errors are highlighted with red exclamation mark icons. The error message is displayed if the user clicks the icon (see Figure 11–60).

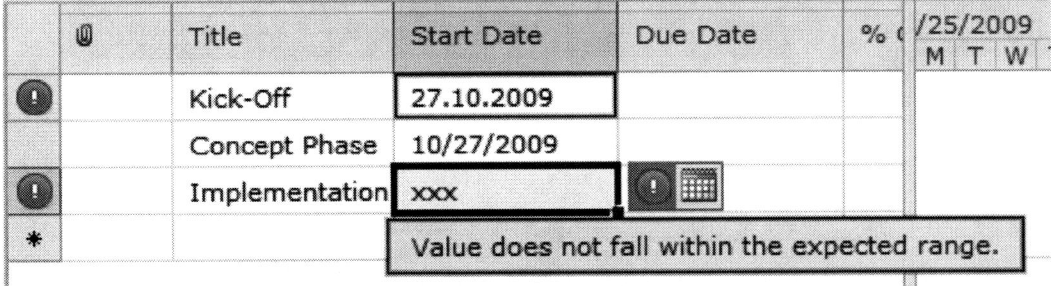

Figure 11–60. Error messages for date fields

The JS Grid control supports data validation by using a widget framework and infrastructure. Widgets can be complex controls that can be built by developers with their own icons and click actions. Some built-in widgets include

- Date picker
- People picker
- Edit control

When working with the JS Grid control, the precedence of edit mode is important to understand. The default order of precedence is cell, row, column, and then the grid itself. That means the user can type directly in a grid cell if the edit mode of the cell permits. The `EditMode` enumeration specifies whether the cells contained in a grid should allow editing. The enumeration values are as follows:

- `ReadOnly`
- `ReadWrite`
- `ReadOnlyDefer`
- `ReadWriteDefer`
- `Defer`

To use the JS Grid control in your custom pages or controls, you must write a new controller. The controller tells the grid how to render content (i.e., which panes or columns to display). The controller enables the data source and controller to understand how to handle unrelated rows, allowing edits to occur without having all the data.

■ **Note** Implementing a JS Grid control in your own application pages or Web Parts is possible, but not necessarily recommended. At the time of writing this chapter, the functionality is poorly documented, and although it is possible to write custom JavaScript grid controller classes, it seems to be a very complex and error-prone endeavor. In particular, if you want to use editing, sorting, filtering, and paging functionalities, you will have to implement a large amount of JavaScript code to handle this.

Despite this, anyone who wishes to explore this grid implementation deeply should not be discouraged. Soon there will be many interesting blog articles with very clever solutions describing how to use the JS Grid in your own application pages and Web Parts.

Perhaps with the next edition of this book you will also find new examples using the JS Grid control in this section.

Example: Using the JS Grid Control

In this example, the JS Grid control is used to display data from a data source. Integrating the JS Grid control to display read-only data from a data table is not very complicated. Just follow these steps:

- Embed the grid control either by adding a `<SharePoint:JSGrid>` tag to your application page or user control, or by creating a new instance programmatically.
- Implement a JavaScript grid controller class for your grid.
- Implement server-side code to feed the `GridSerializer` with the necessary data (data table, data columns, data fields).
- Set grid properties, such as `JSControllerClassName`, and bind the `GridSerializer` to the grid.

To embed the JS Grid control, add the following line to your application page:

```
<SharePoint:JSGrid ID="myGrid" runat="server" />
```

Then implement a basic grid controller class with JavaScript:

```
Type.registerNamespace("MyGridManager");
MyGridManager = function() {
     this.Init = function(jsGridControl, initialData, props) {
          var dataSource = new SP.JsGrid.StaticDataSource(initialData);
          var jsGridParams = dataSource.InitJsGridParams();
          jsGridControl.Init(jsGridParams);
     }
};
```

The only thing this minimal controller implementation does is initialize the grid control with the data source and additional parameters.

Now let's turn to the server side. The next step is to provide all the mandatory parameters for the `GridSerializer`. The code for the `Page_Load` method looks like Listing 11–38.

***Listing 11–38.** Example for Displaying a JS Grid Control in an Application Page*

```
protected void Page_Load(object sender, EventArgs e)
{
    DataTable dataTable = GetBookDataTable();
    SerializeMode serializeMode = SerializeMode.Full;
    String keyColumnName = "ID";
    FieldOrderCollection sortedColumns = new FieldOrderCollection(
                                          new String[] { "Title" });
    IEnumerable<GridField> gridFields = GetGridFields(dataTable);
    IEnumerable<GridColumn> gridColumns = GetGridColumns(dataTable);

    // Create a grid serializer to connect to data
    GridSerializer gds = new GridSerializer(serializeMode, dataTable,
        keyColumnName, sortedColumns, gridFields, gridColumns);

    // Point this at the grid serializer data
    myGrid.GridDataSerializer = gds;

    // Tell the grid which JavaScript controller it should listen to
    myGrid.JSControllerClassName = "MyGridManager";
}
```

As you can see, the GridSerializer needs six properties for the grid to display data. These properties are explained in Table 11–8.

***Table 11–8.** Constructor Parameters for Microsoft.SharePoint.JSGrid.GridSerializer*

Parameter	Type	Description
serializeMode	SerializeMode	The type of data serialization (e.g., SerializeMode.Full)
dataTable	DataTable	An instance of DataTable containing the data to be displayed
keyColumnName	String	A column with a unique key as the identifier (e.g., ID)
sortedColumns	FieldOrderCollection	Names of columns to be sorted by
gridFields	IEnumarable<GridField>	Field definitions for grid fields
gridColumns	IEnumerable<GridColumn>	Column definitions for grid columns

You start by querying the data and storing it in a DataTable instance. For the example, use the SharePoint list Books, as shown in Figure 11–61.

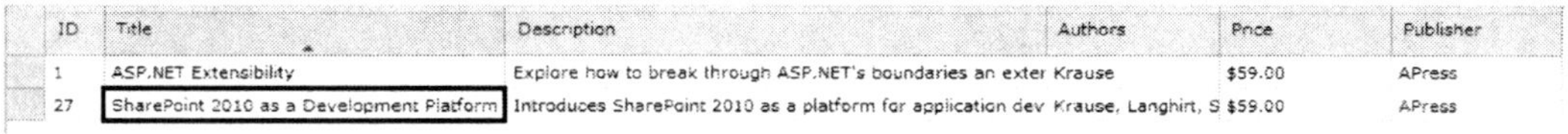

ID	Title	Description	Authors	Price	Publisher
1	ASP.NET Extensibility	Explore how to break through ASP.NET's boundaries an exter	Krause	$59.00	APress
27	SharePoint 2010 as a Development Platform	Introduces SharePoint 2010 as a platform for application dev	Krause, Langhirt, S	$59.00	APress

Figure 11–61. *SharePoint list displayed in a JS Grid control*

To query the data, you can use the `SPList.GetItems.GetDataTable` method. The disadvantage of this is that if your `SPQuery` parameter doesn't limit the view fields, you get all fields back. When displaying in a grid, you have to filter out the unwanted fields. To overcome this, use a LINQ query and convert the result to a `DataTable` instance (see Listing 11–39). For this conversion, a separate extension method called `Linq2DataTable` is provided (see Listing 11–40).

Listing 11–39. *Querying the SharePoint Books List and Return the Selected Fields in a DataTable*

```
public DataTable GetBookDataTable()
{
        SPList list = SPContext.Current.Web.Lists["Books"];
        IEnumerable<SPListItem> books = list.GetItems(
                                        new SPQuery()).OfType<SPListItem>();
        var query = from book in books
                    select new
                    {
                        ID = book.ID,
                        Title = Convert.ToString(book["Title"]),
                        Description = Convert.ToString(book["Description"]),
                        Authors = Convert.ToString(book["Authors"]),
                        Price = Convert.ToDouble(book["Price"]),
                        Publisher = Convert.ToString(book["Publisher"])
                    };

        return query.Linq2DataTable();
 }
```

Listing 11–40. *Extension Method for Converting Results of a LINQ Query to a DataTable*

```
public static class Extensions
{
    public static DataTable Linq2DataTable<T>(this IEnumerable<T> list)
    {
        DataTable dt = new DataTable(Guid.NewGuid().ToString());
        PropertyInfo[] cols = null;

        if (list == null) return dt;

        foreach (T item in list)
        {
            if (cols == null)
            {
                cols = item.GetType().GetProperties();
                foreach (PropertyInfo pi in cols)
                {
```

```
                    Type colType = pi.PropertyType;

                    if (colType.IsGenericType &&
                        colType.GetGenericTypeDefinition() == typeof(Nullable<>))
                        colType = colType.GetGenericArguments()[0];

                    dt.Columns.Add(new DataColumn(pi.Name, colType));
                }
            }

            DataRow dr = dt.NewRow();
            foreach (PropertyInfo pi in cols)
                dr[pi.Name] =
                    pi.GetValue(item, null) ?? DBNull.Value;

            dt.Rows.Add(dr);
        }

        return dt;
    }
}
```

The next step is the implementation method to convert the `DataTable` data into grid columns and fields automatically (see Listing 11–41 and Listing 11–42).

Listing 11–41. *GetGridColumns Iterates Through a DataTable and Creates GridColumns*

```
public virtual IList<GridColumn> GetGridColumns(DataTable table)
{
      List<GridColumn> r = new List<GridColumn>();
      foreach (DataColumn iterator in table.Columns)
      {
             GridColumn col = new GridColumn();
             col.FieldKey = iterator.ColumnName; //unique key
             col.Name = iterator.ColumnName; //column title
             col.Width = 110;    //column width
             r.Add(col);
      }
      return r;
}
```

Listing 11–42. *GetGridFields Iterates Through a DataTable and Creates GridFields*

```
public virtual IList<GridField> GetGridFields(DataTable table)
{
     List<GridField> r = new List<GridField>();
     foreach (DataColumn dc in table.Columns)
     {
            GridField field = new GridField();
            field.FieldKey = dc.ColumnName;

            if (dc.DataType == typeof(string))
            {
                field.PropertyTypeId = "String";
```

```
                field.Localizer = (ValueLocalizer)delegate(DataRow row,
                                  object toConvert)
                {
                    return toConvert.ToString();
                };
            }
            else if (dc.DataType == typeof(int) || dc.DataType == typeof(double))
            {
                field.PropertyTypeId = "JSNumber";
                field.Localizer = (ValueLocalizer)delegate(DataRow row,
                                   object toConvert)
                {
                    if (dc.ColumnName == "ID") return toConvert.ToString();
                    return String.Format("{0:C}", toConvert);
                };
            }
            else
                throw new Exception("No PropTypeId defined for this datatype: "
                                    + dc.DataType);

            r.Add(field);
        }
        return r;
    }
```

The GetGridColumns method is very simple because it merely iterates through all the columns of the DataTable and creates GridColumn instances. The GetGridFields method, on the other hand, does extra work. For every DataColumn, the DataType property is evaluated and the GridField.PropertyTypeId is set. Using this ID, the client-side controller determines the appropriate rendering method. Also, an anonymous Localizer delegate that converts values to the right format has to be implemented.

Summary

This chapter has given detailed insight into many different web controls supplied with SharePoint. It introduced the most significant SharePoint web controls for building custom applications and SharePoint Web Parts.

We covered the base field controls for working with list fields, as well as the creation of custom field controls. To arrange the field controls, knowledge about some common input form controls is required. These controls were described in the second section.

If you need to build user-friendly interfaces, you cannot avoid integrating pickers and selector controls into your user interface. The third section introduced those controls and gave examples of how to implement your own custom picker controls.

With SharePoint 2010, the toolbar is replaced with the new ribbon bar. Nevertheless, it is feasible in some scenarios to still use the toolbar control. This chapter showed how both the toolbar and the ribbon bar can be customized to meet your custom requirements.

Finally, the last section showed how to use more complex controls to display list item data: the SPGridView control and the JS Grid control.

CHAPTER 12

■ ■ ■

Client Programming

In this chapter we focus on the client object model introduced in SharePoint Foundation 2010. There are three new object models for interacting with SharePoint sites in different scenarios: the two managed code models for .NET and Silverlight, and the JavaScript object model. We cover two basic techniques in this chapter:

- Using JavaScript that executes in the browser
- Using code that executes in a .NET managed application

With these new object model implementations, it is much easier to build fast and robust applications that interact with SharePoint sites. Imagine you want to build a Silverlight application that displays data from SharePoint lists. In previous SharePoint versions, the only way to access SharePoint list items was to implement a web service call and handle all the asynchronous data retrieval via hand-coded routines. With SharePoint 2010 you get a client object model, specially customized for use in Silverlight applications, to access SharePoint list data. A similar situation arises if you are using JavaScript (Ajax) in your application and you want to access list items from a SharePoint site. There is a JavaScript object model equivalent to the other client models, and you don't have to deal directly with web services and their internal implementation.

The client object model can be used in much the same manner as the well-known server object model—get an `SPWeb` object instance and access its properties, such as `SPWeb.Lists` and `SPWeb.Users`.

The examples within this chapter are mainly focused on the .NET managed code and the JavaScript object models. Code that executes in a Microsoft Silverlight application (for Silverlight version 2.0 onward) works similarly to the managed code that the regular .NET Framework provides. However, the current development stage of the client libraries seems to be far behind the .NET Framework. To express the differences explicitly, we dedicate a whole chapter (Chapter 13) to Silverlight and the client object model support available there.

Understanding the Client Object Model

The new JavaScript, .NET managed, and Silverlight client object models each provide a subset of the server object model that is defined in `Microsoft.SharePoint.dll`.

There are objects that correspond to the major objects in the server-side object model. Because the primary goal is to improve the security and performance, the client object model focuses on the most relevant APIs for client-side development, and does not contain all the types and properties that are implemented in the server-side model. The limited scope of the client object model reduces the size of the client libraries and thus reduces the download time in the Silverlight and JavaScript contexts.

The new object models are designed to minimize the number of round trips that must be implemented for custom actions, such as web service requests. The object model provides a consistent, easy-to-use, object-oriented system for interoperating with SharePoint data from a remote client or server.

Figure 12–1 shows three ways to access SharePoint data. In the left pane, a SharePoint application page or Web Part runs on the server and interacts with the server object model directly. This is the traditional server-side approach. In previous SharePoint versions—without the client object model—you had to use web services to access SharePoint data, as you can see in the middle of the figure. The client object model is illustrated in the right pane. It allows .NET managed applications, Silverlight applications, and browser-based JavaScript applications to interact with a SharePoint site.

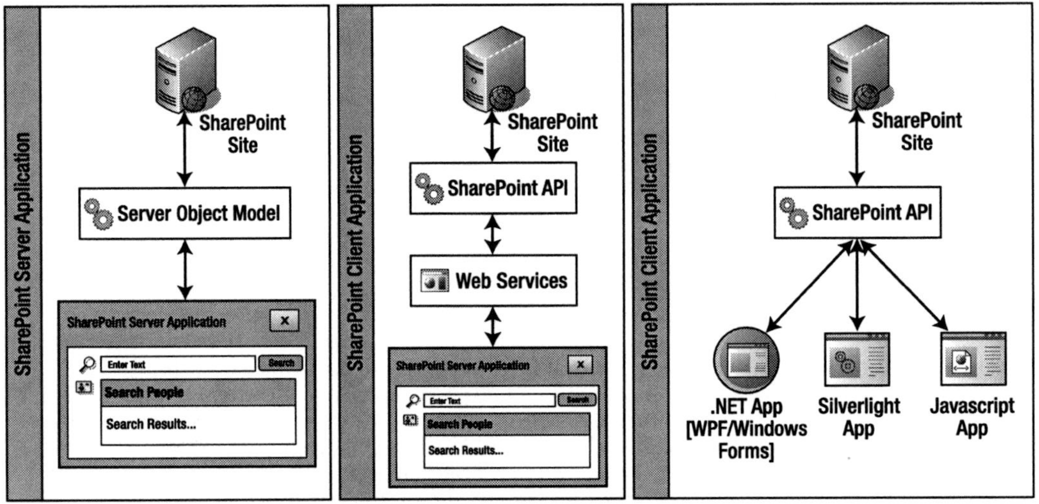

Figure 12–1. Evolution of client access to SharePoint data

All three client object models are very similar. They offer the same object model hierarchy, data retrieval semantics, client objects, and exception-handling methods. If you are already familiar with the server-side SharePoint API, you can quickly adapt to using the client object model in your own applications.

To use the client object models, you need to reference certain proxy files: JS files for JavaScript, and managed DLL files for Silverlight or .NET client applications. The raw data requested from the server is returned in compacted JavaScript Object Notation (JSON) format. The proxy classes parse the JSON data and deserialize it into appropriate objects. As a developer, you merely utilize the client object model. It transparently uses asynchronous data access to optimize the performance of complex operations and queries. An overview of the client object model architecture is illustrated in Figure 12–2.

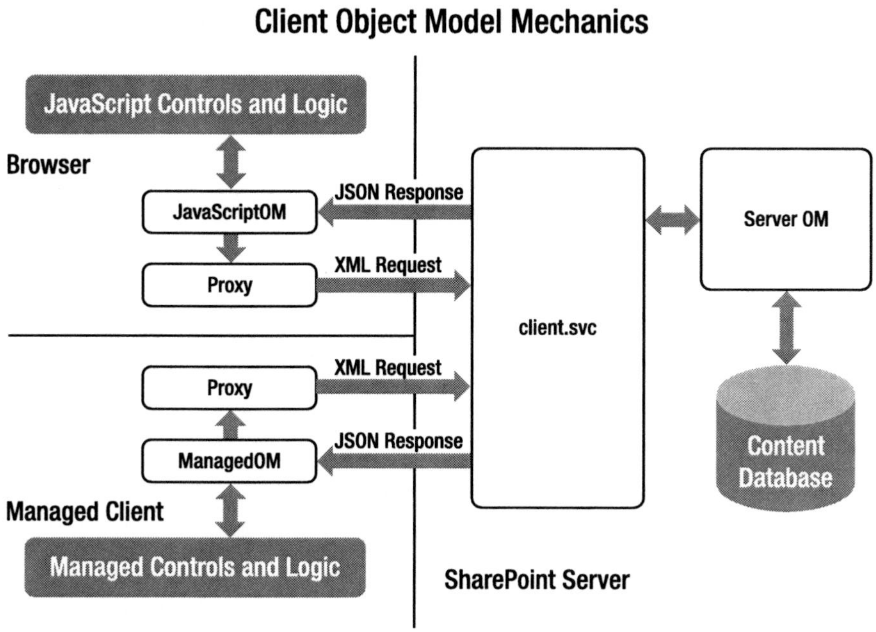

Figure 12–2. Client object model architecture

Getting Started

The first task with the client object model is to reference local copies of the DLL or JS files. Of course, this can also be performed on a remote computer on which SharePoint 2010 is not installed.

.NET Managed Applications

To develop a custom Windows application, you need to reference two DLLs:

- `Microsoft.SharePoint.Client.dll`
- `Microsoft.SharePoint.Client.Runtime.dll`

These files are usually installed into this directory:

```
%ProgramFiles%\Common Files\Microsoft Shared\web server extensions\14\ISAPI
```

In Figure 12–3, the two referenced .NET managed code libraries are shown for a new Windows console application.

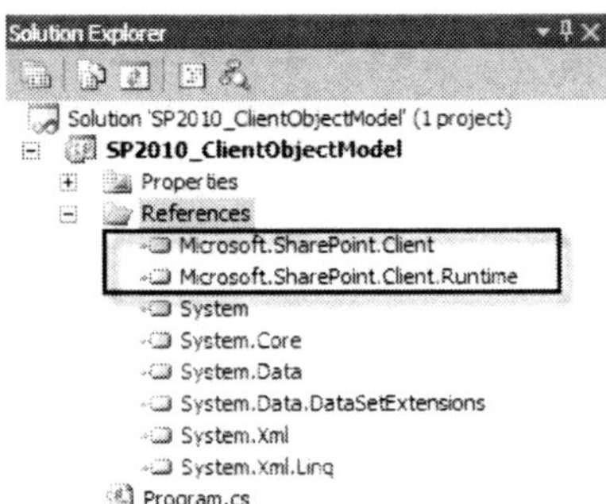

Figure 12–3. *Referencing the client object model DLLs in a Windows application*

Silverlight Applications

To develop a Silverlight application, you need to use the following two assemblies:

- `Microsoft.SharePoint.Client.Silverlight.dll`
- `Microsoft.SharePoint.Client.Silverlight.Runtime.dll`

The SharePoint installer puts these files into a special scripts folder, which is the standard folder for hosting assemblies used in Silverlight:

```
%ProgramFiles%\Common Files\Microsoft Shared\web server
extensions\14\TEMPLATE\LAYOUTS\ClientBin
```

Figure 12–4 shows a Silverlight project with referenced client libraries in Solution Explorer in Visual Studio 2010. For the cases in which the statements are not valid for both .NET and Silverlight, we give the Silverlight statements as well. The examples and code snippets, however, require different techniques to get them running under the particular framework. For more information on how to deal specifically with the Silverlight client object model, see Chapter 13.

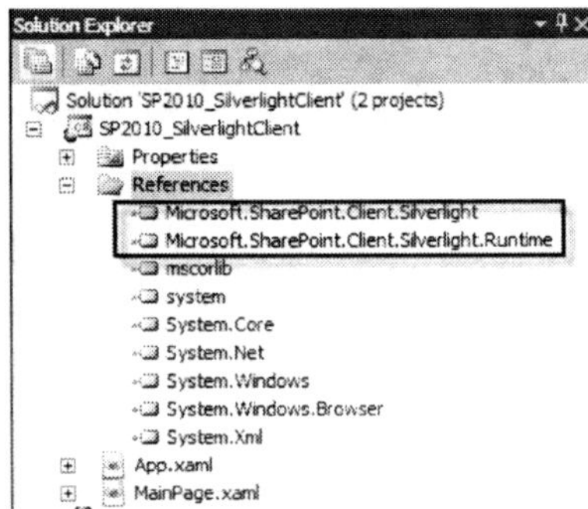

Figure 12–4. *Referencing the client object model DLLs in a Silverlight application*

JavaScript Applications

The JavaScript client object model consists of several JS files that are all installed into the `LAYOUTS` folder under the path `%ProgramFiles%\Common Files\Microsoft Shared\web server extensions\14\TEMPLATE\LAYOUTS`:

- `SP.js/SP.debug.js`
- `SP.Core.js/SP.Core.debug.js`
- `SP.Runtime.js/SP.Runtime.debug.js`
- `SP.Ribbon.js/SP.Ribbon.debug.js`
- `JsGrid.js/JsGrid.debug.js`
- `JSGrid.Gantt.js/JSGrid.Gantt.debug.js`

All JavaScript files are available in two versions: one with compressed files for production use and one with a `.debug.js` extension for development and debugging. The files for debugging are readable and thus larger in size than the files for production use. Compression involves removing all line breaks and replacing several longer variable names with shorter ones to optimize the overall size of the files. For example, the file `SP.js` (380KB) is nearly 40 percent smaller than `SP.debug.js` (559KB).

To use these JavaScript files in your SharePoint application pages or Web Parts, you need to include these scripts by using the tag `<SharePoint:ScriptLink>`, as follows:

```
<SharePoint:ScriptLink runat="server" Name="sp.js" Localizable="false" LoadAfterUI="true" />
```

The web control ensures that the JavaScript file is loaded, including all dependencies. Note that the client computer using the JavaScript object model must support the minimum set of requirements needed for ASP.NET AJAX and SharePoint 2010. The supported browsers (with their minimum version numbers) are Microsoft Internet Explorer 7, Firefox 3.5, and Safari 4.0.

■ **Tip** The "Development Best Practices" section later in this chapter explains how to set up Visual Studio 2010 to work with JavaScript and how to use IntelliSense.

Namespaces Overview

There are two core namespaces for the client object model. The `Microsoft.SharePoint.Client` namespace is used for the .NET managed and Silverlight APIs. `SP` is the core namespace for the JavaScript object model.

In addition to the core namespaces, SharePoint provides the namespaces shown in Table 12–1.

Table 12–1. Additional SharePoint Client Object Namespaces

.NET Managed Code and Silverlight	JavaScript
Microsoft.SharePoint.Client.Application	SP.Application.UI
	SP.Ribbon
	SP.Ribbon.PageState
	SP.Ribbon.TenantAdmin
	SP.UI
	SP.UI.ApplicationPages
	SP.UI.ApplicationPages.Calendar
Microsoft.SharePoint.Client.Utilities	SP.Utilities
Microsoft.SharePoint.Client.WebParts	SP.WebParts

Clearly, Table 12–1 shows that the JavaScript client object model contains more elements than the .NET managed code and Silverlight APIs. The additional namespaces in JavaScript mostly cover functionality to access SharePoint UI elements such as the ribbon bar.

Table 12–2 compares the more important client objects and their corresponding classes.

Table 12–2. Comparison of SharePoint Main Objects Between Client Object Models

Server	.NET Managed Code and Silverlight	JavaScript
Microsoft.SharePoint.SPContext	Microsoft.SharePoint.Client.ClientContext	SP.ClientContext
Microsoft.SharePoint.SPSite	Microsoft.SharePoint.Client.Site	SP.Site
Microsoft.SharePoint.SPWeb	Microsoft.SharePoint.Client.Web	SP.Web
Microsoft.SharePoint.SPList	Microsoft.SharePoint.Client.List	SP.List
Microsoft.SharePoint.SPListItem	Microsoft.SharePoint.Client.ListItem	SP.ListItem
Microsoft.SharePoint.SPField	Microsoft.SharePoint.Client.Field	SP.Field

Table 12–2 shows that the SharePoint administration objects (e.g., `Microsoft.SharePoint.Administration`) are not supported by the client API. Only the basic objects to work with site collections (`Site`), sites (`Web`), lists (`List`), list items (`ListItem`), and fields (`Field`) are supported. But that's sufficient to access SharePoint data.

The Client Context

The ClientContext class is the entry point for programming with the client object model. It behaves very similarly to the server-side SPContext object, and it ensures that there is a single object as a starting point for working with the client object model. The following examples demonstrate the use of the ClientContext class with .NET managed code (marked with [.NET]), Silverlight (marked with [Silverlight]), and JavaScript (marked with [JavaScript]).

```
[.NET]
ClientContext clientContext = new ClientContext("http://servername");

[Silverlight]
ClientContext clientContext = new ClientContext("http://servername");

[JavaScript]
var clientContext = new SP.ClientContext("/siteCollection/site");
```

The examples create an instance of the ClientContext class for a specific site. Usually, the ClientContext constructor takes a URL parameter to get the connection to a web site or site collection. In the Silverlight managed code implementation, it is also possible to ignore the URL and instead access the ClientContext.Current property to get the ClientContext of the current site. This instantiation only works if the Silverlight application runs directly within SharePoint, such as within a Web Part. In JavaScript, this works in much the same way, and you have two options to get a ClientContext of the current site: either via the SP.ClientContext.get_current property or through the empty version of the SP.ClientContext constructor:

```
[.NET]
ClientContext clientContext = new ClientContext.Current;

[Silverlight]
var clientContext = SP.ClientContext.get_current();

[JavaScript]
var clientContext = new SP.ClientContext();
```

Authentication Modes

A very important subject when using the ClientContext class is authentication. There are three possible authentication modes:

- Default
- Anonymous
- FormsAuthentication

By default, the managed client object models authenticate users via their current Windows credentials (NTLM and Kerberos). Optionally, you can define another authentication mode (e.g., Anonymous) to access a SharePoint site that needs no authentication or FormsAuthentication if the SharePoint site uses form-based authentication. When using form-based authentication, you have to supply a username and a password to the ClientContext instance. Internally, SharePoint first calls the Authentication web service to obtain the authentication cookie before making the requested object model calls. When using JavaScript, you don't have to worry about the correct authentication mode because JavaScript itself already runs in an authenticated page.

If you want to use anonymous authentication from .NET managed code, you have to set the AuthenticationMode property of the client context instance:

```
clientContext.AuthenticationMode = ClientAuthenticationMode.Anonymous
```

When connecting to a SharePoint site with Forms Authentication enabled, you also have to set the FormsAuthenticationLoginInfo property:

```
clientContext.AuthenticationMode = ClientAuthenticationMode.Anonymous
clientContext.FormsAuthenticationLoginInfo =
                                 new FormsAuthenticationLoginInfo("user","password")
```

■ **Caution** The Silverlight object model does not offer the property ClientContext.AuthenticationMode. If you build a Silverlight application that runs within the SharePoint context, it automatically uses the information of the current user, and it works well. However, it is not possible to use the Silverlight client object model with anonymous authentication. Also, building standalone Silverlight applications that connect to SharePoint sites is not supported. For more details, see Chapter 13.

Client and Value Objects

When working with ClientContext instances, you are also working with client objects. A *client object* is any object that inherits from Microsoft.SharePoint.Client.ClientObject (.NET managed code and Silverlight) or SP.ClientObject (JavaScript). All SharePoint objects on the client side (e.g., Site, Web, List, and ListItem) are inherited from ClientObject.

It is important to know that client objects initially have no data—they are essentially empty objects. To populate them with data, you first have to define what data should be retrieved. After this you can query the server for the defined data. The response populates the client objects with this data. Using the client object model to load and query data is explained in detail in the next two sections: "Working with Data" and "Data Loading and Querying."

In contrast to client objects, there are *value objects* that inherit from Microsoft.SharePoint.Client.ClientValueObject (.NET managed code and Silverlight) and SP.ClientValueObject (JavaScript). As mentioned, objects such as Site, Web, List, and ListItem are client objects; however, values of list items, such as FieldLookupValue, are value objects. You can view value objects as simple model classes that contain properties but no methods. Value objects behave like C# structs and usually contain a set of primitive types, such as string or int.

Automatically Obtaining Object Identity

As you will see in the examples that follow, the SharePoint client object model has a built-in "intelligence" for dealing with objects. The aim was to make using the client object model as easy as possible. For example, consider a client-side process that creates a list and then adds a new list item to that list. Normally you would do that with two separate operations: one that creates a list and another that adds an item to that list (where the list is identified by a newly generated ID). The client object model allows you to load these dependent operations into a single batch queue that is executed with only one call to the SharePoint server.

The client object model handles the complexity of retrieving and using the new object identity (in the example of creating a new list, this is the newly assigned ListID). You don't have to worry about creating a list, getting the ListID, and adding an item to that list. The result is that using the client object model is very much like the more familiar server-side object model. Thus, you can write more complex operations before starting a round trip to the server.

The only thing you have to remember is that such chained operations are only possible within the same `ClientContext` instance. Separate contexts do not automatically handle the object identity. This means that you should, as much as possible, ensure that only one `ClientContext` instance exists in your code.

Working with Data

Using the client object model to retrieve data from SharePoint is not difficult, but first you need to understand the underlying principles. Client-side data retrieval is not as straightforward as when using the server-side object model. Listings 12–1 and 12–2 illustrate this.

Listing 12–1. *Retrieving the Web Object and Printing Out the Title*

```
class Program
{
    static void Main(string[] args)
    {
        ClientContext ctx = new ClientContext("http://clserver");
        Web web = ctx.Web;
        ctx.Load(web);
        ctx.ExecuteQuery();
        Console.WriteLine(web.Title);
    }
}
```

The example in Listing 12–1 uses the .NET managed code client object model to access a specific SharePoint site. It loads the `Web` object, executes a query, and finally writes out the `Title` property of the retrieved `Web` object. Listing 12–2 shows the equivalent code for the JavaScript API.

Listing 12–2. *Retrieving the Web Object and Displaying the Title in an Alert Box*

```
<script type="text/javascript">
    var web = null;
    function showWebTitle() {
        var ctx = new SP.ClientContext.get_current();
        web = ctx.get_web();
        ctx.load(web);
        ctx.executeQueryAsync(onSucceededCallback, onFailedCallback)
    }

    function onSucceededCallback(sender, args) {
        alert('Title: ' + web.get_title());
    }

    function onFailedCallback(sender, args) {
        alert('Request failed. ' + args.get_message() + '\n' + args.get_stackTrace());
    }

</script>
```

Listing 12–2 uses asynchronous methods (ClientContext.executeQueryAsync) to retrieve the data from SharePoint. Asynchronous data retrieval is always necessary when using the JavaScript client object model, because otherwise the browser would freeze until the server responded or timed out. In contrast to the JavaScript object model, the .NET managed code client object model only offers a synchronous method, ClientContext.executeQuery. If you want asynchronous calls in your Windows client applications, you can easily accomplish this by implementing your own thread handling. When using asynchronous data retrieval, you have to define two delegates (Silverlight) or callback methods (JavaScript) that are executed when the request to the remote server finishes (see onSucceededCallback and onFailedCallback).

Data Loading and Querying

The most important point to understand is the combination of loading and querying data. These are two separate tasks that comprise one operation:

- *Loading data* means you inform the client object model about operations that you want to perform. Operations include, for example, accessing properties of objects (such as Site, Web, List, ListItem, or Field), defining CAML queries that you want to run, and manipulating (inserting, updating, or deleting) list items.
- *Querying data* takes your loaded operations and sends them to the SharePoint server. Note that no network access occurs until you call ExecuteQuery or ExecuteQueryAsync. Until that point, data loading only registers requests without executing them.

The loading method for objects or collections uses the LINQ lambda expression syntax. To load objects, collections, or data, you use the Load and LoadQuery methods:

```
void Load<T>(T clientObject, params
           System.Linq.Expressions.Expression<Func<T,object>>[] retrievals)
```

The LoadQuery method returns an IEnumerable and is defined with your choice of two constructors:

```
IEnumerable<T> LoadQuery<T>(IQueryable<T> clientObjects)
IEnumerable<T> LoadQuery<T>(ClientObjectCollection<T> clientObjects)
```

For the JavaScript client object model, the two corresponding methods are

```
Load(clientObject)
LoadQuery(clientObjectCollection, expression)
```

The LoadQuery method works in much the same way as the Load method, but it allows the client to process the queries more efficiently. As the preceding definitions indicate, the LoadQuery method has a syntax that differs from the Load method. The main difference is that the Load method populates the client object or client object collection that is passed into it. (In the examples shown in Listings 12–1 and 12–2, the Load method simply populates the properties of the Web object.) The LoadQuery method instead returns an entirely new collection of client objects. To get a clarification of these differences, examine the following examples for .NET managed code. They both write the same result to the console.
In Listing 12–3, the Load method is initialized with the instance ctx.Web.Lists. After the query execution, the client object instance ctx.Web.Lists is populated with data and can be directly accessed.

***Listing 12–3.** Retrieving the Number of Lists via the Load Method*

```
class Program
{
```

```
    static void Main(string[] args)
    {
       ClientContext ctx = new ClientContext("http://server");
       ctx.Load(ctx.Web.Lists);
       ctx.ExecuteQuery();
       Console.WriteLine("" + ctx.Web.Lists.Count);
       Console.ReadLine("Press RETURN...");
    }
}
```

Listing 12–4, which follows, uses the LoadQuery method, which is also initialized with the ctx.Web.Lists object. However, after the query is executed, the lists are returned as a completely new client object collection. If you try to directly access the property ctx.Web.Lists.Count, a CollectionNotInitialized exception is raised. This implies that, unlike in Listing 12–3, the original ctx.Web.Lists property has not been populated. Instead, a new allLists collection has been created and populated.

Listing 12–4. *Retrieving the Number of Lists via the LoadQuery Method*

```
class Program
{
    static void Main(string[] args)
    {
       ClientContext ctx = new ClientContext("http://server");
       IEnumerable<List> allLists = ctx.LoadQuery(ctx.Web.Lists);
       ctx.ExecuteQuery();
       Console.WriteLine("" + allLists.Count());
       Console.ReadLine("Press RETURN...");
    }
}
```

The advantage of LoadQuery over the Load method is its flexibility, especially when working with more than one query. It gives you better control over memory consumption, and query processing is more efficient. Consider garbage collection: the Load method populates objects that reside within the ClientContext instance. Those objects can only be cleaned up when the ClientContext instance is destroyed. Conversely, objects created by LoadQuery are separate from the ClientContext instance and can be destroyed much more readily, for example by setting them to NULL. In addition, if you want to query the same object collection multiple times and retain separate results for each query, this query will fail when using the Load method. To examine this point, try to query for all unhidden lists and then query all hidden lists (see Figure 12–5).

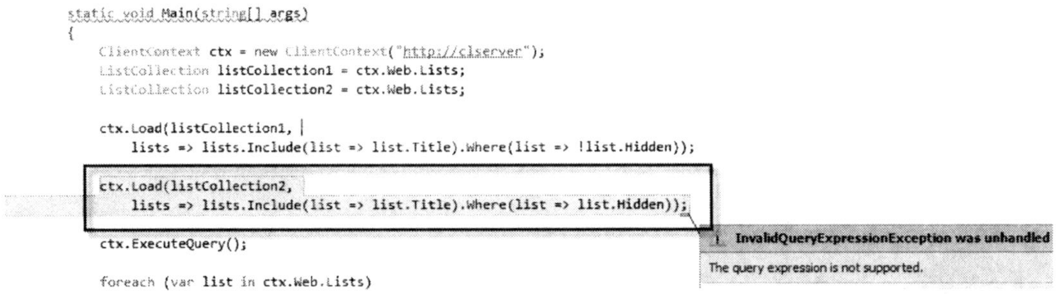

```
static void Main(string[] args)
{
    ClientContext ctx = new ClientContext("http://clserver");
    ListCollection listCollection1 = ctx.Web.Lists;
    ListCollection listCollection2 = ctx.Web.Lists;

    ctx.Load(listCollection1,
        lists => lists.Include(list => list.Title).Where(list => !list.Hidden));

    ctx.Load(listCollection2,
        lists => lists.Include(list => list.Title).Where(list => list.Hidden));

    ctx.ExecuteQuery();

    foreach (var list in ctx.Web.Lists)
```

InvalidQueryExpressionException was unhandled

The query expression is not supported.

Figure 12–5. *Error while trying to load two queries on the same underlying object*

To overcome this issue you have to use LoadQuery, as shown in Listing 12–5.

Listing 12–5. *Querying the Same Lists with Two Different Queries*

```
class Program
{
    static void Main(string[] args)
    {
        ClientContext ctx = new ClientContext("http://clserver");

        IEnumerable<List> shownLists = ctx.LoadQuery(
            ctx.Web.Lists.Include(list => list.Title).Where(list => !list.Hidden));

        IEnumerable<List> hiddenLists = ctx.LoadQuery(
            ctx.Web.Lists.Include(list => list.Title).Where(list => list.Hidden));

        ctx.ExecuteQuery();

        foreach (var list in shownLists)
            Console.WriteLine("shown list -> " + list.Title);
        foreach (var list in hiddenLists)
            Console.WriteLine("hidden list -> " + list.Title);
    }
}
```

The example in Listing 12–5 defines two queries on the ctx.Web.Lists collection. One query queries all lists where the Hidden property is false, and the other returns all lists where the Hidden property is true. Finally, the Title property of the lists is written out to the console.

Differences and Limitations

When using the various client object models, be aware that there are some small differences, especially between the managed code and JavaScript implementations.

Absolute and Relative URLs Within the Constructors

The constructors of the ClientContext class are different among the three client object models. For JavaScript you have to provide a server-relative URL:

```
[JavaScript]
var clientContext = new SP.ClientContext("/mySiteCollection/mySite");
```

When working with the managed object models for Windows or Silverlight applications, you need to use either an absolute URL or an object of type System.Uri:

```
[.NET]
ClientContext clientContext = new ClientContext("http://servername");

[Silverlight]
ClientContext clientContext = new ClientContext("http://servername");
```

Different Data Types

Keep in mind that between the managed object model and the JavaScript object model, there are some differences regarding the data types. Most of the data types behave similarly to each other, but there are some language-specific particularities, like the NaN (Not a Number) value in JavaScript, which has no equivalent in managed code. On the other hand, complex list objects like StringCollection in managed code do not exist on the JavaScript side and therefore are implemented as normal arrays—in our example, as string[].

Specifying the Authentication Mode

When using JavaScript you do not need to worry about authentication because the page that runs your JavaScript is already authenticated either by Windows Authentication or Forms Authentication. If you are using the managed object models and you want to use Forms Authentication instead of Windows Authentication, use code like this:

```
[.NET]
clientContext.FormsAuthenticationLoginInfo = new
                         FormsAuthenticationLoginInfo("user","password");
```

Using the Digest Web Control

Before you can use the JavaScript object model on a page, you have to ensure that the page contains the FormDigest web control. This web control inserts a security validation token within the form of an ASPX page. When making a call to the server—for example, to retrieve data—this token will also be included and validated by the server. A security token is specific to a user, site, and time period—thus, it expires after a configurable time interval.

```
<SharePoint:FormDigest runat="server" />
```

The output of the FormDigest control in a rendered ASPX page looks like:

```
<input type="hidden" name="__REQUESTDIGEST" id="__REQUESTDIGEST"
value="0x2FCF84AE7A97855C64D0A9620C39B3ECA66695C4A1B087A570C01DD1EE0E
426B6B3D9B716E9D8128B86D9E28FE6BA7B16BDB13F5C7991DFA830285453A9E6103,
20 Dec 2009 16:35:48 -0000" />
```

Using the FormDigest to validate requests prevents attacks wherein a user is tricked into posting data to the server.

Summary

As you have learned in this section, there are a few differences between the managed object models used for Windows and the JavaScript object model. The main differences are summarized in Table 12–3.

Table 12–3. *Main Differences Between SharePoint Objects Models*

Category	.NET Managed Code	JavaScript
Constructor URL	Absolute URL	Server-relative URL
Data types	StringCollection, null, and infinity	string[] array, NaN, positive infinity, and negative infinity
Forms authentication	Explicit	Integrated
Form digest	Not required	Needs <SharePoint:FormDigest />

Using the Dialog Framework

Within the JavaScript client object model, there is an important framework introduced with SharePoint 2010: the Dialog framework. This framework is a set of JavaScript classes that are used for displaying dialogs.

Working with Modal Pop-Up Dialogs

Modal pop-up dialogs are an integral component of the SharePoint 2010 user interface. They allow users to perform actions without losing the underlying information. For example, if you are working with items, the display, edit, and new forms are displayed in a pop-up dialog (see Figure 12–6). The background appears darkened (creating a *lightbox effect*) and thus inactive, so the user is forced to deal first with the dialog before returning to the original page.

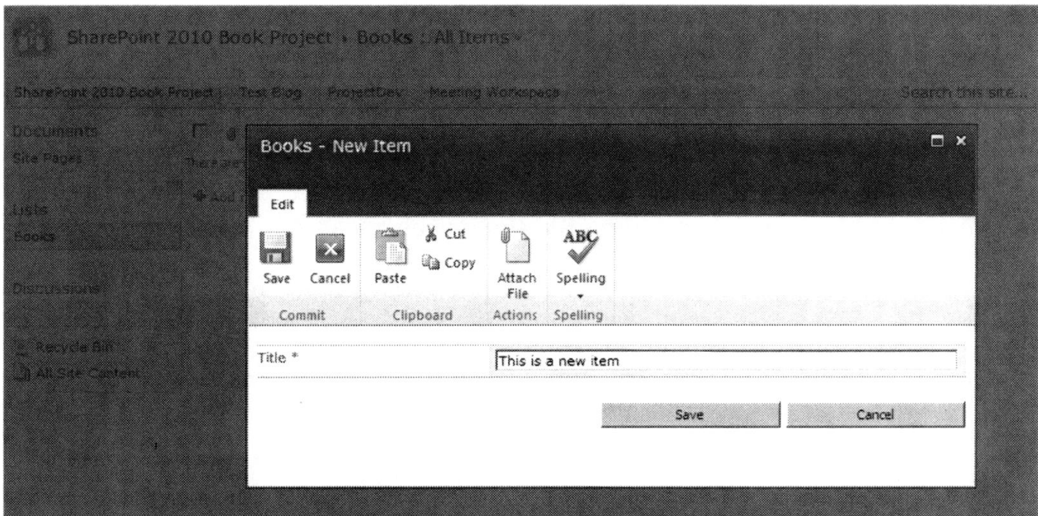

Figure 12–6. Dialog for adding a new item to a list

Some important usability improvements with the SharePoint 2010 user interface include

- Reduced page transitions and postbacks to keep the user in context
- Heavy use of modal dialogs
- Improved use of modal dialogs (e.g., offering the ability to maximize, close, and move them)

Modal pop-up dialogs are easily created using JavaScript. From a technical perspective, the Dialog framework consists of a single JavaScript library, `SP.UI.Dialog.js`. (The corresponding fully readable library is `SP.UI.Dialog.debug.js`.) Listing 12–6 shows how to display an external web page as pop-up dialog.

Listing 12–6. Opening an External Web Page as a Pop-Up Dialog with JavaScript

```
function showDialog() {

    var options = {
                url: 'http://sharepoint2010.microsoft.com',
                width: 700,
                title: 'Microsoft SP2010',
                allowMaximize: true,
                showClose: true
    }

    SP.UI.ModalDialog.showModalDialog(options);
}
```

Before you call SP.UI.ModalDialog.showModalDialog, you have to define some options, such as the URL, dialog width, dialog title, and behavior of the maximize and close buttons. The result is shown in Figure 12–7.

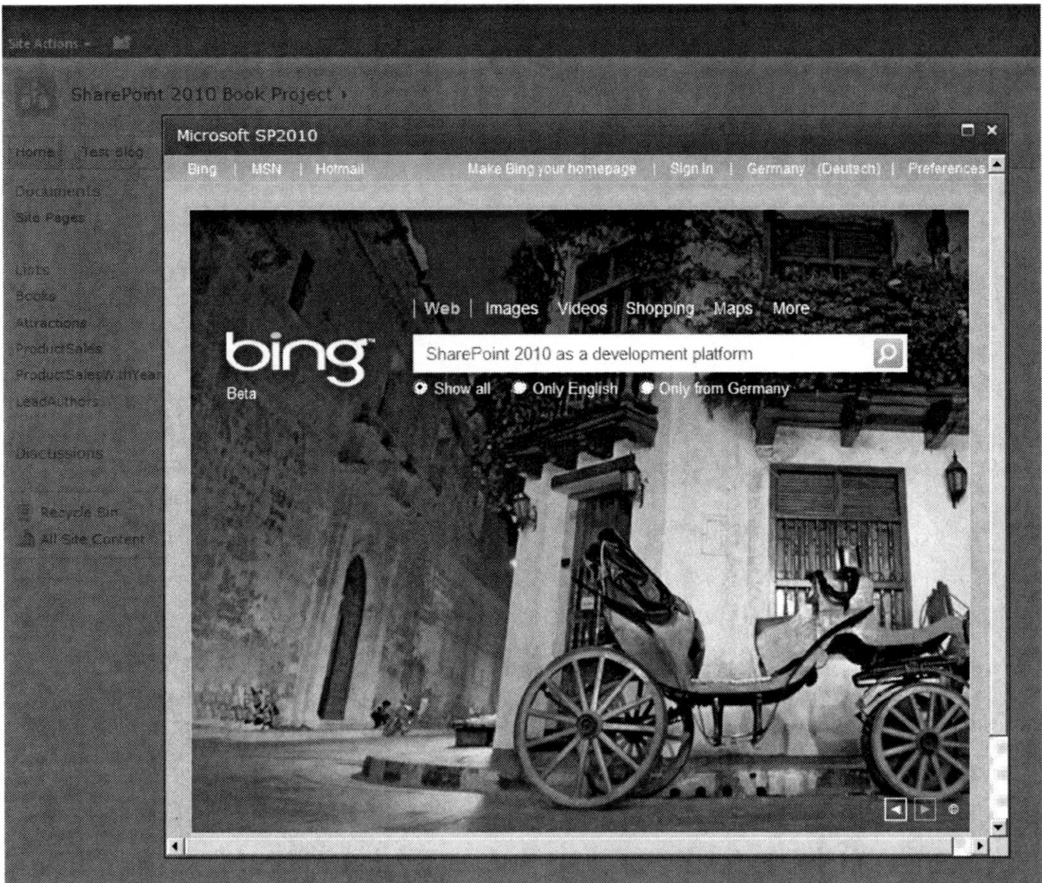

Figure 12–7. *Pop-up dialog containing an external web page*

The possible options that can be passed to the function SP.UI.ModalDialog.showModalDialog are summarized in Table 12–4.

Table 12–4. Options for Function showModalDialog

Option	Description
url	Specifies the absolute or relative URL for the page to be displayed within the pop-up
html	Contains HTML content to be displayed within the pop-up if the url parameter is not set
title	Defines the title of the dialog
width	Defines the dialog width in pixels
height	Defines the dialog height in pixels
allowMaximize	Indicates whether the dialog can be maximized (true/false)
showMaximized	Indicates whether the maximize box in the upper-right corner should be displayed (true/false)
showClose	Indicates whether the close box in the upper-right corner should be displayed (true/false)
dialogReturnValueCallback	Points to a function that should be called when the dialog is closed

Using Callback Functions and Return Values

To interact with the data or the result of a dialog, the Dialog framework provides callback mechanisms. Listing 12–7 shows an example of using callbacks.

Listing 12–7. Using Callbacks with JavaScript

```
function myCallback(dialogResult, returnValue) {
     alert('I am back!')
}

function showDialog() {

     var options = {
               url: 'http://sharepoint2010.microsoft.com',
               width: 700,
               title: 'Microsoft SP2010',
               allowMaximize: true,
               showClose: true,
               dialogReturnValueCallback:myCallback
     }

     SP.UI.ModalDialog.showModalDialog(options);
}
```

The options instance that is used for calling the showModalDialog function contains a reference (dialogReturnValueCallback) to the function myCallback. Immediately after the dialog is closed, this function will be called and an alert box displayed.

The example in Listing 12–7 uses a very simple callback without utilizing the two callback parameters dialogResult and returnValue. These two parameters are very important for interacting with the data of a dialog. The SP.UI.DialogResult enumeration used for the dialogResult parameter is defined as follows:

```
SP.UI.DialogResult.prototype = {
    invalid: -1,
    cancel: 0,
    OK: 1
}
```

The returnValue parameter can contain any value. For example, if you edit an item within a pop-up dialog, you could return the ID of that item when leaving the dialog. Then the underlying callback handler would be able to update the display of this item. To control the dialog via JavaScript, you need to use the property window.frameElement. This property is automatically stored by the Dialog framework in the window context. The reason for this is that this context is also accessible by external pages loaded within an IFRAME element. Those pages don't have to implement SharePoint JavaScript files because they can simply access the window.frameElement and its functions. Some important functions for finishing dialogs are listed in Table 12–5.

***Table 12–5.** Functions of window.frameElement for Finishing Dialogs*

Function	Parameters	Description
cancelPopUp	--	Closes the dialog and returns SP.UI.DialogResult.cancel (0) as the dialog result.
commitPopup	returnValue	Closes the dialog and returns SP.UI.DialogResult.OK (1) as the dialog result. Additionally, the return value property is set.
commitPopupAndRedirect	redirectUrl	Closes the dialog with SP.UI.DialogResult.cancel (0) as the dialog result and redirects to a URL.
commonModalDialogClose	dialogResult, returnValue	Closes the dialog with a dialog result and a return value.
navigateParent	--	Navigates to the parent page.

For a demonstration of the functions listed in Table 12–5, take a look at Listing 12–8. There is a very simple HTML page that contains several links with JavaScript. This HTML page can be opened from within SharePoint by using SP.UI.ModalDialog.showModalDialog (see Figure 12–8).

***Listing 12–8.** Working with Dialogs and Return Values*

```
<html>
  <body>
    Working with dialogs
    <br />
```

```
    <a href="javascript:window.frameElement.cancelPopUp()">cancelPopUp()</a><br />
    <a href="javascript:window.frameElement.commitPopup('myReturnValue')">
               commitPopup('myReturnValue')</a><br />
    <a href="javascript:window.frameElement.commitPopupAndRedirect('http://www.bing.com')">
               commitPopupAndRedirect('http://www.bing.com')</a><br />
    <a href="javascript:window.frameElement.commonModalDialogClose(1,'myReturnValue')">
               commonModalDialogClose(1,'myReturnValue')</a><br />
    <a href="javascript:window.frameElement.navigateParent()">navigateParent()</a><br />

  </body>
</html>
```

After clicking a link, the defined callback function is executed, and depending on the called function, the parameters `dialogResult` and `returnValue` are filled and passed to the callback function.

Figure 12–8. *HTML page of Listing 12–8 displayed as a pop-up dialog*

Building Dialog Pages

The Dialog framework enables you to build SharePoint application pages that can be opened both as normal ASPX pages and also as pop-up dialog pages. Good examples of this behavior are the form pages for lists and document libraries: `NewForm.aspx`, `EditForm.aspx`, and `DispForm.aspx`. If you open the forms page directly by typing in the URL, it looks like Figure 12–9.

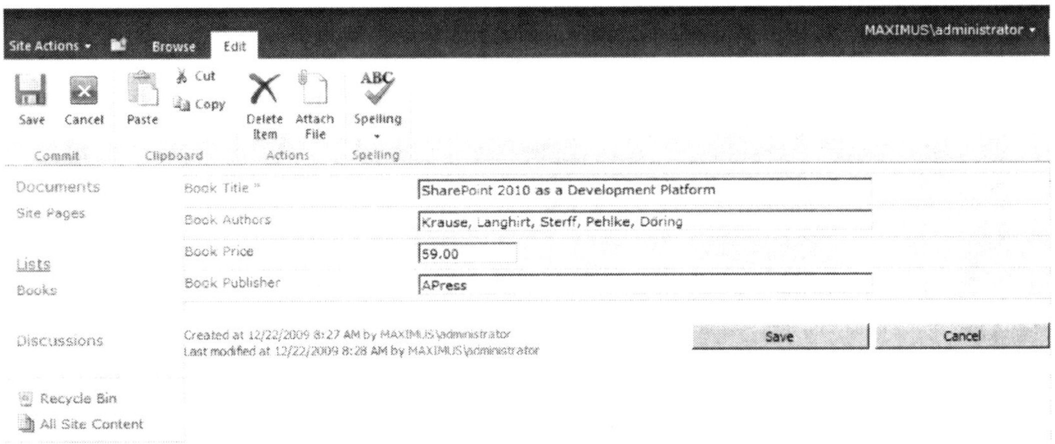

Figure 12–9. *EditForm.aspx as a normal ASPX page*

Notice the navigation column on the left side and also the information about the current user in the upper-right corner. If you open the same page within a pop-up dialog, its appearance changes slightly, as you can see in Figure 12–10.

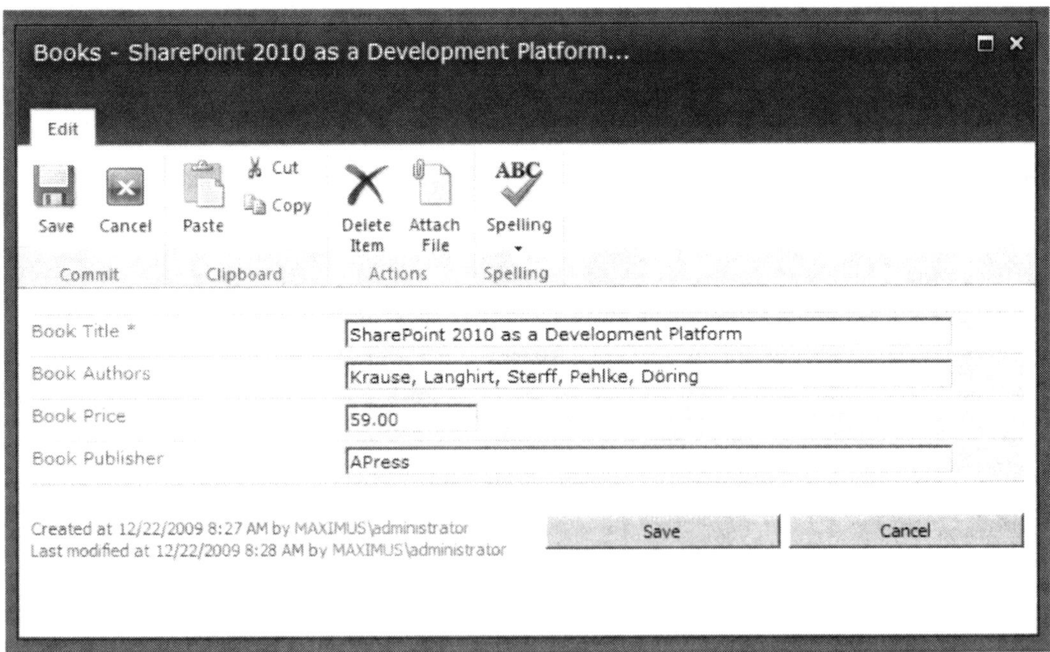

Figure 12–10. *EditForm.aspx as a pop-up dialog*

The difference between Figures 12–9 and 12–10 is the omission of the left navigation and the current user information. The page detects whether it is being opened directly or within a pop-up dialog. The detection is based on the query string parameter that is automatically added by the Dialog framework when opening a new dialog via its URL. The complete URL for the dialog in Figure 12–10 is

```
http://[servername]/Lists/Books/EditForm.aspx?ID=1&IsDlg=1
```

The URL query string parameter `IsDlg` passes the information to the ASPX page. The evaluation of this parameter is encapsulated in the central `SPContext` class as the property `IsPopUI`, and can be used as follows:

```
SPContext.Current.IsPopUI
```

With this property, it is easy to implement different behaviors. The example in Listing 12–9 shows the assignment of different JavaScript code to the `OnClientClick` event of a cancel button.

Listing 12–9. *Implementing Different Behavior for Pop-Up Dialogs (C#)*

```
String redirectUrl = "http://www.bing.com";
if (SPContext.Current.IsPopUI)
{
     button.OnClientClick = "window.frameElement.cancelPopUp();return false;";
}
else
{
      button.OnClientClick = "STSNavigate(redirectUrl);return false;";
}
```

You can also perform a similar test using plain JavaScript, either by parsing the query string parameter `IsDlg` directly from the `document.location.search` property, or by checking whether the `window.frameElement` object exists (see Listing 12–10).

Listing 12–10. *Implementing Different Behavior for Pop-Up Dialogs (JavaScript)*

```
var redirectUrl = "http://www.bing.com";
var button = document.getElementById('myButton');

if (window.frameElement)
{
     button.onclick = new Function("window.frameElement.cancelPopUp();return false;");
}
else
{
      button.onclick = new Function("STSNavigate(redirectUrl);return false;");
}
```

In addition to its ability to modify the behavior of existing elements, such as button events, the Dialog framework has built-in functionality to automatically hide complete sections when displaying a page through a pop-up dialog. You can design your pages to display either inside a dialog or as a normal application page. The visibility for HTML elements is controlled by a CSS class called `s4-notdlg`. This class can be used to hide some HTML sections when a page is shown within a dialog. The preceding example of `EditForm.aspx` (see Figure 12–10) uses that to hide the left navigation and the information about the current user. Inspecting the assigned master page (`v4.master`) shows that the CSS class `s4-notdlg` is used in several lines to hide particular regions (see Figure 12–11).

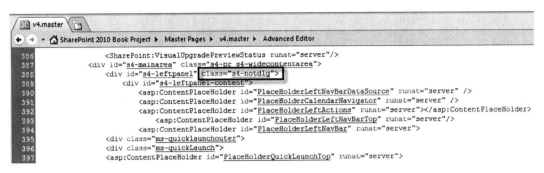

```
v4.master
SharePoint 2010 Book Project ▶ Master Pages ▶ v4.master ▶ Advanced Editor
            <SharePoint:VisualUpgradePreviewStatus runat="server"/>
        <div id="s4-mainarea" class="s4-pr s4-widecontentarea">
            <div id="s4-leftpanel" class="s4-notdlg">
                <div id="s4-leftpanel-content">
                    <asp:ContentPlaceHolder id="PlaceHolderLeftNavBarDataSource" runat="server" />
                    <asp:ContentPlaceHolder id="PlaceHolderCalendarNavigator" runat="server" />
                    <asp:ContentPlaceHolder id="PlaceHolderLeftActions" runat="server"></asp:ContentPlaceHolder>
                        <asp:ContentPlaceHolder id="PlaceHolderLeftNavBarTop" runat="server"/>
                    <asp:ContentPlaceHolder id="PlaceHolderLeftNavBar" runat="server">
            <div class="ms-quicklaunchouter">
            <div class="ms-quickLaunch">
            <asp:ContentPlaceHolder id="PlaceHolderQuickLaunchTop" runat="server">
```

Figure 12–11. Master page v4.master with the s4-notdlg CSS class attribute

Internally, the implementation is very simple. The `SharePoint:CssLink` web control, which is usually used in SharePoint master pages, ensures that in dialogs, the CSS file `dlgframe.css` is included. This CSS file defines some classes that override the default properties. For `s4-notdlg`, it contains the following line:

```
.ms-dialog .s4-notdlg { display:none !important}
```

This line hides all HTML elements that are assigned to the CSS class `s4-notdlg`. Simply use this CSS class in your own master pages or application pages to control the visibility of your pop-up dialogs. You don't have to implement your own logic to show and hide elements depending on the context in which a page is loaded.

Working with Status Information and Notifications

With SharePoint 2010, two new user interface elements have been introduced: the status bar and the notification area. The objective with those two elements is to give users information without distracting them (see Figure 12–12).

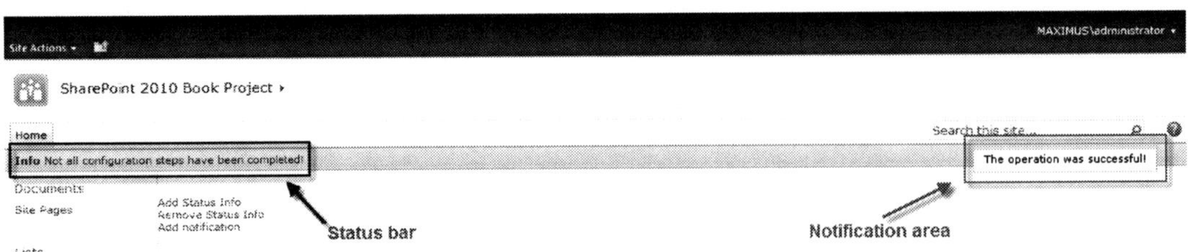

Figure 12–12. Status bar and notification area

Status API

The status bar is intended to display persistent information, such as messages about state. For example, the status bar would be the appropriate place to display warning messages regarding the configuration of your SharePoint application. Table 12–6 contains a list of functions for working with the status bar.

Table 12–6. Functions of the Status API (SP.UI.Status)

Function	Parameters	Description
addStatus	strTitle, strHtml, atBeginning	Adds a status line to the status bar. The parameter strTitle contains the title of the status message and the parameter strHtml contains HTML code containing the message. The parameter atBeginning (true/false) controls whether the new status should be added as the first entry or the last entry. The function returns a generated statusId for the new status.
updateStatus	statusId, strHtml	Updates the content of an existing status line. The status line is identified by the statusId parameter.
removeStatus	statusId	Removes a status line identified by statusId.
removeAllStatus	hide	Removes all status lines and hides the status bar if the hide parameter is true.
setStatusPriColor	statusId, color	Sets the primary color of a status line identified by statusId to color. The color parameter can contain valid colors, such as #FF0000 or red.

The example in Listing 12–11 shows how to use the status API. It assumes you have an application page and use the PlaceHolderMain content placeholder for your code.

***Listing 12–11.** Application Page That Uses the Status API*

```
<asp:Content ContentPlaceHolderId="PlaceHolderMain" runat="server">

    <script language="javascript" type="text/javascript">
        function addStatusInfo() {
            var myStatusId = SP.UI.Status.addStatus("Info", "Not all configuration steps have
been completed!",true);
        }

        function removeStatusInfo() {
            SP.UI.Status.removeAllStatus(true);
        }
    </script>

    <br /><br />
    <a href="javascript:addStatusInfo()">Add Status Info</a> <br />
    <a href="javascript:removeStatusInfo()">Remove Status Info</a> <br />

</asp:Content>
```

The code declares two JavaScript functions, one to add a new status line and one to remove all status lines. Both of these functions can simply be called through HTML links (see Figure 12–13).

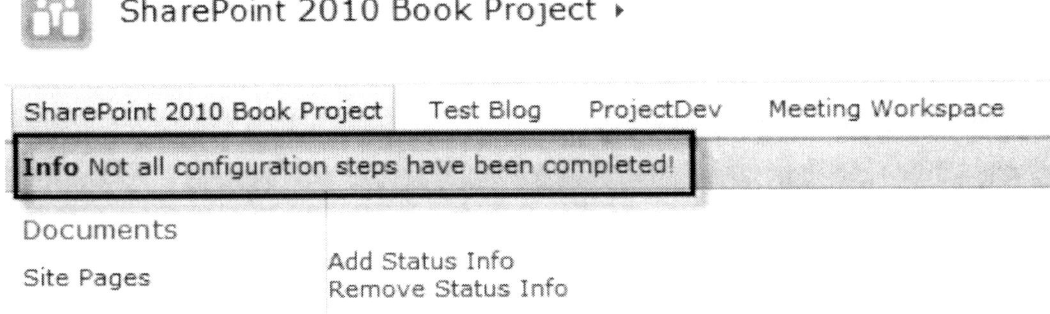

***Figure 12–13.** Status information on a custom application page*

Notification API

The notification area is intended to be used for transient messages such as messages that occur after an operation. An example would be the message "The item has been saved" after a saving operation. Table 12–7 contains a list of functions for using the notification bar.

***Table 12–7.** Functions of the Notification API (SP.UI.Notify)*

Function	Parameters	Description
`addNotification`	`strHtml`, `isSticky`	Adds a notification to the notification area. The notification message is contained in the parameter `strHtml` as HTML code. The Boolean parameter `isSticky` defines whether the notification disappears automatically after some seconds (`false`) or if you have to call the `removeNotication` function to hide it (`true`). The function returns a generated `notificationId` for the new notification.
`removeNotification`	`notificationId`	Removes a notification by its `notificationId`.

Using the notification API is quite similar to using the status API. The example in Listing 12–12 contains code to add a notification within a custom application page.

***Listing 12–12.** Application Page That Uses the Notification API*

```
<asp:Content ContentPlaceHolderId="PlaceHolderMain" runat="server">

  <script language="javascript" type="text/javascript">
```

```
    function addNotify() {
      var myNotifyId = SP.UI.Notify.addNotification("The operation was successful!", false);
    }

  </script>

  <br /><br />
  <a href="javascript:addNotify()">Add notification</a>

</asp:Content>
```

The code adds a notification to the page if the user clicks the "Add notification" link. The notification appears on the screen with a small animation from the right-hand side. After 3 seconds it disappears automatically because the `isSticky` parameter is set to `false`. If the `isSticky` parameter were set to `true`, the notification would remain visible until removed via the `removeNotification` function. Figure 12–14 shows the custom application page containing the notification.

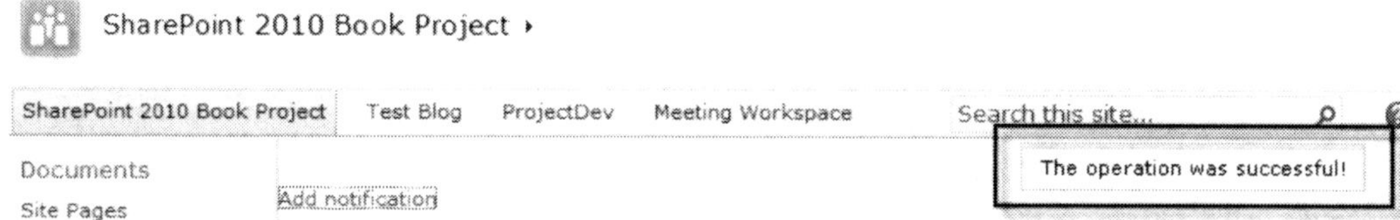

Figure 12–14. *Notification on a custom application page*

Development Best Practices

At first glance, client-side development seems to be quite simple. The examples are mostly easy to understand and follow. But using the SharePoint client object model requires both a good understanding of the concept and of some rules and best practices. The concept behind the client object model can be compared to SQL-like programming: first you define a query, and after that you can execute it. Only then are you able to access the data. The main difference here is that you are working with the object model instead of writing a SQL query string. Many developers are not familiar with that concept, so there may be a learning curve before they're able to adopt the client object model and write clean and efficient code.

This section tries to shine a light on the client object model development. Wrapped into many useful examples, a lot of best practices are explained.

Preparing Visual Studio for JavaScript

If you wish to develop a Windows or Silverlight application using the managed client object model, it's no challenge to set up the project within Visual Studio. The problems arise if you want to use the JavaScript client object model, for example, within your custom application pages or Web Parts. The vital factor is the lack of support for SharePoint JavaScript IntelliSense within Visual Studio. Visual Studio of course has built-in support for JavaScript IntelliSense, but only when it can access the necessary files.

One reason for Visual Studio's ignorance of the JavaScript files is the lack of support for the SharePoint web control `<SharePoint:ScriptLink>`, which enables JavaScript files to be loaded.

When Visual Studio encounters the following code line, it is unaware that the referenced file should be used to provide IntelliSense support:

```
<SharePoint:ScriptLink runat="server" Name="sp.js" Localizable="false" LoadAfterUI="true" />
```

Visual Studio only supports normal HTML tags for JavaScript, such as the following:

```
<script type="text/javascript" src="sp.js" />
```

Hence, if you want IntelliSense support in your application pages, you have to make sure that Visual Studio gets what it expects.

Workaround to Enable JavaScript IntelliSense in Custom Application Pages

Because Visual Studio needs normal HTML script tags for its JavaScript background compiler to generate IntelliSense information, simply place all the necessary JavaScript files within appropriate script tags (notice the absolute path to the 14 hive in Listing 12–13). Because SharePoint does not like JavaScript files to be referenced multiple times, you need to ensure that those development-environment-only script tags are not visible after rendering the ASPX page. This can be accomplished by wrapping the script tags in a PlaceHolder control that is invisible at runtime.

Listing 12–13. *Enabling IntelliSense for SharePoint's JavaScript Client Object Model*

```
<asp:PlaceHolder runat="server" Visible="false">
        <script type="text/javascript"
                   src="file://{path to 14 hive}\TEMPLATE\LAYOUTS\MicrosoftAjax.js" />
        <script type="text/javascript"
                   src="file:// {path to 14 hive}\TEMPLATE\LAYOUTS\SP.Runtime.debug.js" />
        <script type="text/javascript"
                   src="file:// {path to 14 hive} \TEMPLATE\LAYOUTS\SP.debug.js" />
        <script type="text/javascript"
                    src="file:// {path to 14 hive}\TEMPLATE\LAYOUTS\SP.Core.debug.js" />
        <script type="text/javascript"
                    src="file:// {path to 14 hive} \TEMPLATE\LAYOUTS\SP.Ribbon.debug.js" />
</asp:PlaceHolder>
```

As you can see in Listing 12–13, along with the SharePoint JavaScript files, you also have to reference the file MicrosoftAjax.js. It is also very important to take care with the order of the JavaScript files, because some have dependencies on others. For example, the file SP.Runtime.debug.js contains base classes that are used within SP.debug.js. If you change the loading order of these files, your IntelliSense output will contain only a subset of all the functions and properties. Figure 12–15 shows the working IntelliSense support for SharePoint 2010 in Visual Studio 2010.

```
<script type="text/javascript">
    var web = null;

    function showWebTitle() {
        var ctx = new SP.ClientContext.get_current();
        web = ctx.get_web();
        ctx.load(t  executeQueryAsync
        ctx.execut  get_applicationName                       nFailedCallback)
    }               get_hasPendingRequest
                    get_pendingRequest
    function onSuc  get_serverLibraryVersion
        alert('Tit  get_serverSchemaVersion
    }               get_serverVersion
                    get_site
    function onFai  get_staticObjects
        alert('Req  get_url                                   ) + '\n' + args.get_stackTrace());
    }               get_web
                    hasOwnProperty
</script>           isPrototypeOf

<a href="javascrip  load
                    loadQuery
```

Figure 12–15. *JavaScript IntelliSense support within Visual Studio 2010*

It's also important to reference the `.debug.js` files, because these files contain more readable information than their compressed versions. This is especially helpful if you call functions with named parameters. A comparison of Figures 12–16 and 12–17 demonstrates this point. In Figure 12–16, IntelliSense proposes the two parameters `succeededCallback` and `failedCallback` for the method `executeQueryAsync`.

```
ctx.executeQueryAsync(
    executeQueryAsync(succeededCallback, failedCallback)
```

Figure 12–16. *JavaScript IntelliSense support when using the .debug JavaScript files*

In Figure 12–17, the compressed JavaScript files without the `.debug.js` extension are used. IntelliSense proposes only the parameters `b` and `c` for the same method call. This is not useful at all.

```
ctx.executeQueryAsync(
    executeQueryAsync(b, c)
```

Figure 12–17. *JavaScript IntelliSense when not using the .debug JavaScript files*

Using JavaScript IntelliSense Within JS Files

The previous section described a workaround for enabling JavaScript IntelliSense within ASPX application pages. But you don't always develop JavaScript directly within an application page. Imagine that you're writing a JavaScript library that encapsulates the data access for your application and you wish to use this library in more than one custom application page. Usually you'd write your library in a JS file. Unfortunately, the problem with using IntelliSense arises here, too.

To overcome that, you can use the reference directive that enables Visual Studio to establish a relationship between the script you are currently editing and other scripts. One or more `<reference>` directives have to be added to the top of your JavaScript library (see Listing 12–14).

Listing 12–14. *Using the Reference Directive in a JavaScript Library (.js)*

```
/// <reference path="MyScript.js" />
function test() {
        ...
}
```

This basic example tells the Visual Studio IntelliSense background compiler to process the script `MyScript.js` so that all declared functions are recognized and can be used within the example function `test`. Because of the three prefixed slashes, the JavaScript interpreter recognizes the `<reference>` directives as comments and ignores them.

With this strategy, it's very easy to integrate full Visual Studio IntelliSense support for SharePoint client object libraries. Just add references to the SharePoint JavaScript libraries, as described in the previous section (see Listing 12–15).

Listing 12–15. *Using the Reference Directive in a JavaScript Library (.js) for SharePoint 2010*

```
/// <reference path="{path to 14 hive}\TEMPLATE\LAYOUTS\MicrosoftAjax.js" />
/// <reference path="{path to 14 hive}\TEMPLATE\LAYOUTS\SP.Runtime.debug.js" />
/// <reference path="{path to 14 hive} \TEMPLATE\LAYOUTS\SP.debug.js" />
/// <reference path="{path to 14 hive}\TEMPLATE\LAYOUTS\SP.Core.debug.js" />
/// <reference path="{path to 14 hive} \TEMPLATE\LAYOUTS\SP.Ribbon.debug.js" />
```

Now you have full IntelliSense support in your custom JavaScript libraries too, as shown in Figure 12–18.

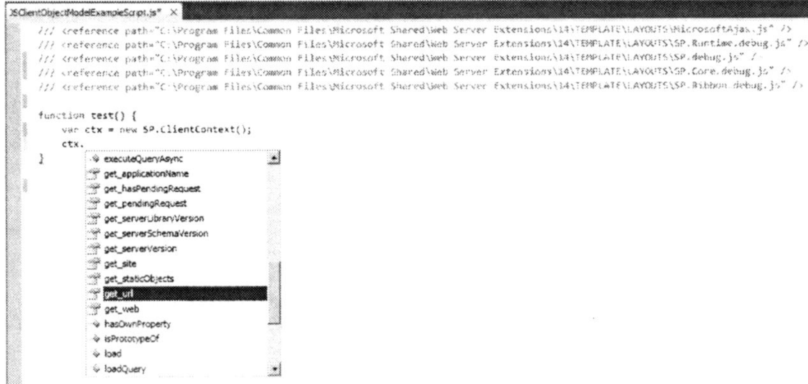

Figure 12–18. *JavaScript IntelliSense support within a JavaScript library via <reference> directives*

Programming Examples

This section provides a number of real-world code examples using the SharePoint client object model. All the examples are explained and presented in both managed C# and JavaScript code.

Common Pitfalls

When working with the client object model, most developers soon face some strange and unexpected error messages thrown by their own code. Those developers are usually very familiar with the server-side object model and they try to write code in the same style. The client object model has a different philosophy, and this requires different programming techniques. Simply keep cognizant of one key concept of the client model: every object is empty and its data has to be loaded first, before any properties can be accessed.

This section describes some of the common pitfalls when working with the client object model.

Objects Cannot Be Accessed Until They Are Loaded

Developers coming from the server side tend to forget the load-query-access cycle for the client object model. Look at the incorrect code in Listing 12–16.

Listing 12–16. *Incorrect Code: Accessing a Property That Has Not Been Loaded (C#)*

```
public void Example01_Incorrect()
{
     ClientContext ctx = new ClientContext("http://clserver");
     Web oWeb = ctx.Web;
     Console.WriteLine(oWeb.Title + " " + oWeb.Description);
}
```

This code throws an exception (PropertyOrFieldNotInitializedException) because the property oWeb.Title has not been loaded yet. Remember that you have to tell the client object model what you want, via the Load method. Then you need to initiate a round trip to the server to query for the data by using the executeQuery method. A working version of the code is displayed in Listing 12–17.

Listing 12–17. *Correct Code: Accessing a Property (C#)*

```
public void Example01()
{
   ClientContext ctx = new ClientContext("http://clserver");
   Web oWeb = ctx.Web;
   ctx.Load(oWeb, w => w.Title, w => w.Description);
   ctx.ExecuteQuery();
   Console.WriteLine(oWeb.Title + " " + oWeb.Description);
}
```

The Load method is initialized with the oWeb object and a lambda expression that selects the Title and Description properties to be loaded. When you call ExecuteQuery, the requested data is retrieved from the server. The Title and Description properties of the oWeb object are populated with the data from the server and can be accessed. The corresponding JavaScript code is shown in Listing 12–18.

Listing 12–18. Correct Code: Accessing a Property (JavaScript)

```
<script type="text/javascript">
    var web = null;

    function showWebTitle() {
        var ctx = new SP.ClientContext.get_current();
        web  = ctx.get_web();
        ctx.load(web, "Title", "Description");
        ctx.executeQueryAsync(
            Function.createDelegate(this, this.onSucceededCallback),
            Function.createDelegate(this, this.onFailedCallback));
    }

    function onSucceededCallback(sender, args) {
        alert('Title: ' + this.web.get_title());
    }

    function onFailedCallback(sender, args) {
        alert('Request failed. ' + args.get_message() + '\n' + args.get_stackTrace());
    }
</script>
```

The JavaScript example in Listing 12–18 uses an asynchronous pattern, so you need to implement the two callback functions: onSucceededCallback and onFailedCallback. JavaScript does not support C# lambda expressions, so the syntax to select single properties is a little different. The JavaScript load function supports multiple parameters containing field names. To retrieve the Title and Description properties, you can use the following code:

```
ctx.load(web, "Title", "Description")
```

To better understand what happens behind the scenes, use tools like Fiddler to inspect the HTTP protocol. The XML that is passed by the executeQuery or executeQueryAsync method to the client.svc service on the server looks like Listing 12–19.

Listing 12–19. XML Request to Retrieve Two Properties of a Web Object

```
<Request xmlns="http://schemas.microsoft.com/sharepoint/clientquery/2009"
        SchemaVersion="14.0.0.0" LibraryVersion="14.0.4536.1000"
        ApplicationName="Javascript Library">
  <Actions>
    <Query Id="6" ObjectPathId="2">
      <Query SelectAllProperties="false">
        <Properties>
          <Property Name="Description" ScalarProperty="true" SelectAll="true" />
          <Property Name="Title" ScalarProperty="true" SelectAll="true" />
        </Properties>
      </Query>
    </Query>
  </Actions>
  <ObjectPaths>
    <Identity Id="2" Name="740c6a0b-85e2-48a0-a494-e0f1759d4aa7:web:1039552e-a1b2-4ddd-b1e7-
cbe9bab90a1c" />
  </ObjectPaths>
</Request>
```

The XML requests the two properties Title and Description for the web with ID 1039552e-a1b2-4ddd-b1e7-cbe9bab90a1c. The response from the client.svc service is sent back in JSON format, as shown in Listing 12–20.

Listing 12–20. *JSON Response Containing Two Properties of a Web Object*

```
[{
"SchemaVersion":"14.0.0.0",
"LibraryVersion":"14.0.4536.1000",
"ErrorInfo":null
},6,{
"_ObjectType_":"SP.Web",
"_ObjectIdentity_":"740c6a0b-85e2-48a0-a494-e0f1759d4aa7:web:1039552e-a1b2-4ddd-b1e7-cbe9bab90a1c",
"Description":"Start page for the SharePoint 2010 development book project",
"Title":"SharePoint 2010 Book Project"
}]
```

The JSON response contains the values of the two requested properties (Title and Description) and is used by the JavaScript client object model to populate the oWeb object.

Not All Values Are Retrieved

Instead of defining only the properties you wish to retrieve, it is also possible to retrieve all the properties of an object. After retrieving a whole object, without defining explicitly which properties should be retrieved, you would usually expect that all available properties of the retrieved object contain values. But unfortunately this is not the case. The main client objects such as Site and Web have some properties that have to be explicitly requested in order for them to be retrieved by a query (see Listing 12–21).

Listing 12–21. *Example for Retrieving All Properties of a Web Object*

```
public void Example02()
{
    ClientContext ctx = new ClientContext("http://clserver");
    Web oWeb = ctx.Web;
    ctx.Load(oWeb);
    ctx.ExecuteQuery();
    Console.WriteLine(oWeb.Title + " " + oWeb.Description);
}
```

After looking at this code, a developer might assume that the oWeb object has been populated with all available properties. But, if you try, for example, to access the property HasUniqueRoleAssignments, a PropertyOrFieldNotInitializedException exception will be thrown. When trying the same with JavaScript and using Fiddler to detect what happens in the background, you will get an XML request such as that shown in Listing 12–22.

Listing 12–22. *XML Request for All Properties of a Web Object*

```
<Request xmlns="http://schemas.microsoft.com/sharepoint/clientquery/2009"
                SchemaVersion="14.0.0.0" LibraryVersion="14.0.4536.1000"
                ApplicationName="Javascript Library">
<Actions>
```

```
        <ObjectPath Id="1" ObjectPathId="0" />
        <ObjectPath Id="3" ObjectPathId="2" />
        <Query Id="4" ObjectPathId="2">
            <Query SelectAllProperties="true">
                <Properties />
             </Query>
         </Query>
</Actions>
<ObjectPaths>
        <StaticProperty Id="0" TypeId="{3747adcd-a3c3-41b9-bfab-4a64dd2f1e0a}"
               Name="Current" />
        <Property Id="2" ParentId="0" Name="Web" />
</ObjectPaths>
</Request>
```

The XML requests all properties (`SelectAllProperties=true`) of the `oWeb` object. The JSON response is shown in Listing 12–23.

Listing 12–23. *JSON Response Containing All Properties of a Web Object*


```
[{
"SchemaVersion":"14.0.0.0",
"LibraryVersion":"14.0.4536.1000",
"ErrorInfo":null
},1,{
"IsNull":false
},3,{
"IsNull":false
},4,{
"_ObjectType_":"SP.Web",
"_ObjectIdentity_":"740c6a0b-85e2-48a0-a494-e0f1759d4aa7:web:1039552e-a1b2-4ddd-b1e7-
cbe9bab90a1c",
"Description":"Start page for the SharePoint 2010 development book project",
"Created":"\/Date(1258929292000)\/",
"LastItemModifiedDate":"\/Date(1261475758000)\/",
"RecycleBinEnabled":true,
"Title":"SharePoint 2010 Book Project",
"ServerRelativeUrl":"\u002f",
"Id":"\/Guid(1039552e-a1b2-4ddd-b1e7-cbe9bab90a1c)\/",
"SyndicationEnabled":true,
"AllowRssFeeds":true,
"QuickLaunchEnabled":true,
"TreeViewEnabled":false,
"Language":1033,
"UIVersion":4,
"UIVersionConfigurationEnabled":false,
"AllowRevertFromTemplateForCurrentUser":true,
"AllowMasterPageEditingForCurrentUser":true,
"ShowUrlStructureForCurrentUser":true
}]
```


At first glance, the JSON response contains all properties of the Web object. But on closer inspection, it is apparent that at least two properties are missing: `EffectiveBasePermissions` and

HasUniqueRoleAssignments. To retrieve these two properties, you have to explicitly declare them in the Load method.

Table 12–8 lists the properties that are not retrieved by default. The difference between .NET managed code and Silverlight properties and the JavaScript properties is only the first letter of the property names (lowercase in JavaScript and uppercase in .NET managed code).

***Table 12–8.** Objects and Properties Not Retrieved by Default*

Object	.NET/Silverlight Properties	JavaScript Properties
Site	Usage	usage
Web	EffectiveBasePermissions, HasUniqueRoleAssignments	effectiveBasePermissions, hasUniqueRoleAssignments
List	BrowserFileHandling, DataSource, EffectiveBasePermissions, HasUniqueRoleAssignments, IsSiteAssetsLibrary, OnQuickLaunch, RoleAssignments, SchemaXml, ValidationFormula, ValidationMessage	browserFileHandling, dataSource, effectiveBasePermissions, hasUniqueRoleAssignments, isSiteAssetsLibrary, onQuickLaunch, roleAssignments, schemaXml, validationFormula, validationMessage
Folder	ContentTypeOrder, UniqueContentTypeOrder	contentTypeOrder, uniqueContentTypeOrder
ListItem	DisplayName, EffectiveBasePermissions, HasUniqueRoleAssignments, RoleAssignments	displayName, effectiveBasePermissions, hasUniqueRoleAssignments, roleAssignments

The Difference Between Value Objects and Client Objects

As explained earlier, there are client objects and value objects. Client objects are Site, Web, List, and ListItem. Value objects have properties but do not have methods. SharePoint treats all primitive types, such as string or int, as value objects.

It's very important to recall that the client object model treats these objects differently. There are two important things to remember in this regard:

- Client objects can be used across methods in a query.
- Value objects cannot be used across methods in a query.

To understand the first statement, consider a simple scenario where you need to get a list item from a list via a client object model (see Listing 12–24).

Listing 12–24. Using Client Objects Across Methods

```
public void Example03()
{
    ClientContext ctx = new ClientContext("http://clserver");
    Web oWeb = ctx.Web;
    List oList = oWeb.Lists.GetByTitle("Books");
    ListItem oListItem = oList.GetItemById(1);
    ctx.Load(oListItem);
    ctx.ExecuteQuery();

    Console.WriteLine(oListItem["Title"] + " " + oListItem["Book_Authors"]);
}
```

The code in Listing 12–24 obtains a `Web` client object, then a `List` client object, and then a `ListItem` client object. Although it may seem that those objects call real functions (`GetByTitle` and `GetItemById`), the returned client objects are empty and all their properties are uninitialized. Only when the `oListItem` client object is loaded and executed does the `oListItem` object contain real values or value objects. To clarify this quite intelligent behavior of the client object model, you don't have to make a server round trip to get the `Web` object, another round trip to get the `List`, and another to get the `ListItem`. Instead, you only make one call to the server.

In contrast, here is another example for value objects. Assume you want to get a list item from a list that is named like the `Title` property of the `Web` object. For example, the title of the `Web` object is Books, and you want to get a list with the name `Books`. Listing 12–25 shows an invalid effort to code this.

Listing 12–25. Incorrect: Using Value Objects Across Methods

```
public void Example04_Incorrect()
{
    ClientContext ctx = new ClientContext("http://clserver");
    Web oWeb = ctx.Web;
    List oList = oWeb.Lists.GetByTitle(oWeb.Title);
    ListItem oListItem = oList.GetItemById(1);
    ctx.Load(oListItem);
    ctx.ExecuteQuery();

    Console.WriteLine(oListItem["Title"] + " " + oListItem["Book_x0020_Authors"]);
}
```

While executing this code, the familiar `PropertyOrFieldNotInitializedException` is thrown at the line `List oList = oWeb.Lists.GetByTitle(oWeb.Title)`. This happens because you try to access a property or value object that has not been loaded and queried. It is not possible to use such value objects across methods. To overcome this issue, you have to put in a server round trip to populate the `Title` property of the `oWeb` object before you can use it for the second server call as shown in Listing 12–26:

Listing 12–26. Correct: Using Value Objects Across Methods

```
public void Example04_Correct()
{
    ClientContext ctx = new ClientContext("http://clserver");
    Web oWeb = ctx.Web;
    ctx.Load(oWeb, w => w.Title);
```

```
    ctx.ExecuteQuery();

    List oList = oWeb.Lists.GetByTitle(oWeb.Title);
    ListItem oListItem = oList.GetItemById(1);
    ctx.Load(oListItem);
    ctx.ExecuteQuery();

    Console.WriteLine(oListItem["Title"] + " " + oListItem["Book_x0020_Authors"]);
}
```

Both examples (Listings 12–25 and 12–26) demonstrate the use of client objects and value objects. As a developer you always have to take care about the loading and executing sequence of the client object model.

Accessing Webs and Sites

This section demonstrates the client-side use of the SPWeb object, best known from the server-side:

- How to retrieve site and web properties
- How to retrieve certain properties only
- How to update properties
- How to create new web sites

How to Retrieve Site and Web Properties

A basic example of retrieving all properties of the Web and Site objects passes the two objects to the Load method and then initiates the query execution via ExecuteQuery or executeQueryAsync (see Listings 12–27 and 12–28).

Listing 12–27. *Retrieving Site and Web Properties (C#)*

```
public void Example05()
{
    ClientContext ctx = new ClientContext("http://clserver");
    Site oSite = ctx.Site;
    Web oWeb = ctx.Web;
    ctx.Load(oSite);
    ctx.Load(oWeb);
    ctx.ExecuteQuery();

    Console.WriteLine(oSite.Url + " " + oWeb.Title);
}
```

Listing 12–28. *Retrieving Site and Web Properties (JavaScript)*

```
function example05() {
    var ctx = new SP.ClientContext.get_current();

    this.site = ctx.get_site();
    this.web = ctx.get_web();
```

```
    ctx.load(this.site);
    ctx.load(this.web);

 ctx.executeQueryAsync(
        Function.createDelegate(this, this.onSucceededCallback),
        Function.createDelegate(this, this.onFailedCallback));
}

function onSucceededCallback(sender, args) {
    alert('Site-URL: ' + this.site.get_url() + '\r\nWeb-Title: ' + this.web.get_title());
}

function onFailedCallback(sender, args) {
    alert('Request failed. ' + args.get_message() + '\n' + args.get_stackTrace());
}
```

■ **Caution** Keep in mind that not all available properties are populated with values. There are some properties that have to be requested explicitly. Check Table 12–8 for an overview of properties that are not populated with values by default.

How to Retrieve Specific Properties Only

To reduce the amount of data transferred from server to client, you can specify precisely the properties you want to be populated with data. Listings 12–29 and 12–30 both return only the `Url` and `Id` properties of the `Site` object and the `Title` property of the `Web` object.

Listing 12–29. *Retrieving Only Some Site and Web Properties (C#)*

```
public void Example06()
{
    ClientContext ctx = new ClientContext("http://clserver");
    Site oSite = ctx.Site;
    Web oWeb = ctx.Web;
    ctx.Load(oSite, s => s.Id, s => s.Url);
    ctx.Load(oWeb, w => w.Title);
    ctx.ExecuteQuery();

    Console.WriteLine("Site-ID: " + oSite.Id + "\r\nSite-URL: " + oSite.Url
      + "\r\nWeb-Title: " + oWeb.Title);
}
```

The console output of Listing 12–29 looks like this:

```
Site-ID: ff845efa-f800-41ec-8349-d26d3fb4063b
Site-URL: http://clserver
Web-Title: SharePoint 2010 Book Project
```

Instead of lambda expressions, with JavaScript you have to define the properties as function parameters, as shown in Listing 12–30.

Listing 12–30. Retrieving Only Some Site and Web Properties (JavaScript)

```
function example06() {
    var ctx = new SP.ClientContext.get_current();
    this.site = ctx.get_site();
    this.web = ctx.get_web();
    ctx.load(this.site, "Id", "Url");
    ctx.load(this.web, "Title");
    ctx.executeQueryAsync(
        Function.createDelegate(this, this.onSucceededCallback),
        Function.createDelegate(this, this.onFailedCallback));
}

function onSucceededCallback(sender, args) {
    alert('Site-ID: ' + this.site.get_id() + '\r\nSite-URL: ' + this.site.get_url()
     + '\r\nWeb-Title: ' + this.web.get_title());
}
```

The resulting alert box for Listing 12–30 is shown in Figure 12–19.

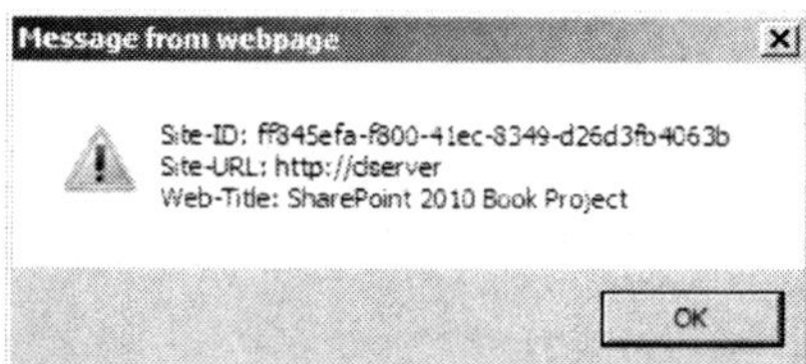

***Figure 12–19.** JavaScript alert box displaying the site and web properties*

How to Update Properties

Modifying the properties of a web site or another client object is similar to retrieving data. Instead of using the Load or LoadQuery methods, you call the Update method. After that, remember that the modification will not be sent back to the server until ExecuteQuery or ExecuteQueryAsync is executed (see Listings 12–31 and 12–32).

Listing 12–31. Updating Web Site Properties (C#)

```
public void Example07()
{
    ClientContext ctx = new ClientContext("http://clserver/blog");
    Web oWeb = ctx.Web;
    oWeb.Title = "This is a new title";
    oWeb.Description = "This is a new description";
    oWeb.Update();
    ctx.ExecuteQuery();
}
```

Listing 12–32. Updating Web Site Properties (JavaScript)

```
function example07() {
    var ctx = new SP.ClientContext.get_current();
    this.web = ctx.get_web();
    this.web.set_title("This is a new title");
    this.web.set_description("This is a new description");
    this.web.update();
    ctx.executeQueryAsync(
        Function.createDelegate(this, this.onSucceededCallback),
        Function.createDelegate(this, this.onFailedCallback));
}
```

How to Create a New Web Site

To create a new web site, you need a client object called `WebCreationInformation` that contains a set of properties for the new web site. Listing 12–33 creates a new team site using the team site web template STS#0.

Listing 12–33. Creating a New Web Site (C#)

```
public void Example08()
{

    string siteUrl = "http://clserver";
    string tsDescription = "A new Team site.";
    int tsLanguage = 1033;
    string tsTitle = "Team Site";
    string tsUrl = "teamSite";
    bool tsInheritPermissions = false;
    string webTemplate = "STS#0";

    ClientContext ctx = new ClientContext(siteUrl);
    Web oWebsite = ctx.Web;

    WebCreationInformation webCreateInfo = new WebCreationInformation();
    webCreateInfo.Description = tsDescription;
    webCreateInfo.Language = tsLanguage;
    webCreateInfo.Title = tsTitle;
    webCreateInfo.Url = tsUrl;
    webCreateInfo.UseSamePermissionsAsParentSite = tsInheritPermissions;
    webCreateInfo.WebTemplate = webTemplate;

    Web oNewWeb = oWebsite.Webs.Add(webCreateInfo);

    ctx.Load(oNewWeb,
           website => website.ServerRelativeUrl,
           website => website.Created);

    ctx.ExecuteQuery();
```

```
    Console.WriteLine("Web-Url: {0} Web-Created: {1}",
        oNewWeb.ServerRelativeUrl, oNewWeb.Created);

}
```

The creation of a new site requires an instance of the WebCreationInformation class that is passed as a parameter to the Web.Webs.Add method. After the site creation is executed using the ExecuteQuery method, the two properties of the oNewWeb object, ServerRelativeUrl and Created, are populated with values, as shown in Listing 12–34.

Listing 12–34. *Creating a New Web Site (JavaScript)*

```
function example08() {

    var siteUrl = '/';
    var tsDescription = 'A new Team site.';
    var tsLanguage = 1033;
    var tsTitle = 'Team Site';
    var tsUrl = 'teamSite';
    var tsInheritPermissions = false;
    var webTemplate = 'STS#0';

    var ctx = new SP.ClientContext(siteUrl);
    this.oWeb = ctx.get_web();

    var webCreateInfo = new SP.WebCreationInformation();
    webCreateInfo.set_description(tsDescription);
    webCreateInfo.set_language(tsLanguage);
    webCreateInfo.set_title(tsTitle);
    webCreateInfo.set_url(tsUrl);
    webCreateInfo.set_useSamePermissionsAsParentSite(tsInheritPermissions);
    webCreateInfo.set_webTemplate(webTemplate);

    this.oNewWeb = this.oWeb.get_webs().add(webCreateInfo);
    clientContext.load(this.oNewWeb, 'ServerRelativeUrl', 'Created');

    ctx.executeQueryAsync(
        Function.createDelegate(this, this.onSucceededCallback),
        Function.createDelegate(this, this.onFailedCallback));
}

function onSucceededCallback(sender, args) {
    alert('Web-Title: ' + this.oNewWeb.get_title() + " created at " +
this.oNewWeb.get_created());
}
```

The JavaScript example is very similar to the C# example. There are no major differences to be taken into account.

Accessing Lists

Various tasks concerning lists are demonstrated in this section:

- How to retrieve all the SharePoint lists in a web site
- How to retrieve list schema information
- How to create a new SharePoint list
- How to modify an existing SharePoint list
- How to delete a SharePoint list

How to Retrieve All SharePoint Lists in a Web Site

You can retrieve all the lists for a web site using the property `Web.Lists`. You just have to load and query the list collection and iterate through the lists (see Listing 12–35).

***Listing 12–35.** Retrieving All the Lists for a Web Site (C#)*

```
public void Example09()
{
    ClientContext ctx = new ClientContext("http://clserver");
    ListCollection oListColl = ctx.Web.Lists;

    ctx.Load(oListColl);
    ctx.ExecuteQuery();

    foreach (List oList in oListColl)
    {
        Console.WriteLine("Title: " + oList.Title);
    }
}
```

The corresponding JavaScript implementation in Listing 12–36 is similar to the managed code example. The main difference is the iteration through the results. Because JavaScript has no built-in mechanism to handle enumerations, the client object model extends JavaScript so that you can access the lists through an iterator.

***Listing 12–36.** Retrieving All the Lists for a Web Site (JavaScript)*

```
function example09() {
    var ctx = new SP.ClientContext.get_current();
    this.oListColl = ctx.get_web().get_lists();
    ctx.load(this.oListColl);

    ctx.executeQueryAsync(
        Function.createDelegate(this, this.onSucceededCallback),
        Function.createDelegate(this, this.onFailedCallback));
}

function onSucceededCallback(sender, args) {
```

```
    var listEnum = this.oListColl.getEnumerator();
    while (listEnum.moveNext()) {
        var oList = listEnum.get_current();
        alert(oList.get_title());
    }
}
```

Both examples return all the lists containing all properties. To reduce the number of properties, you should explicitly define only those properties you really need. For collections this can be done using LINQ in combination with the Include expression:

```
[C#]
ctx.Load(oListColl, lists => lists.Include(list => list.Title, list => list.Id));
```

Because LINQ is not available in JavaScript, there is a LINQ-like syntax implemented for including selected properties:

```
[JavaScript]
ctx.load(this.oListColl, 'Include(Title, Id)');
```

How to Retrieve List Field Information

Information about the various fields of a list is obtained via the List.Fields property (see Listings 12–37 and 12–38).

Listing 12–37. *Retrieving List Schema Information (C#)*

```
public void Example10()
{
    ClientContext ctx = new ClientContext("http://clserver");
    FieldCollection oFldColl = ctx.Web.Lists.GetByTitle("Books").Fields;
    ctx.Load(oFldColl);
    ctx.ExecuteQuery();

    foreach (Field oFld in oFldColl)
    {
        Console.WriteLine("InternalName: " + oFld.InternalName
                +  ", DataType: " + oFld.FieldTypeKind);
    }
}
```

Listing 12–38. *Retrieving List Schema Information (JavaScript)*

```
function example10() {
    var ctx = new SP.ClientContext.get_current();
    this.oFldColl = ctx.get_web().get_lists().getByTitle('Books').get_fields();
    ctx.load(this.oFldColl);
    ctx.executeQueryAsync(
            Function.createDelegate(this, this.onSucceededCallback),
            Function.createDelegate(this, this.onFailedCallback));
}

function onSucceededCallback(sender, args) {
    var fieldEnum = this.oFldColl.getEnumerator();
```

```
    while (fieldEnum.moveNext()) {
        var oField = fieldEnum.get_current();
        alert("InternalName: " + oField.get_internalName()
             + ", DataType: " + oField.get_fieldTypeKind());
    }
}
```

How to Create a New SharePoint List

Creating a new SharePoint list requires an instance of the `ListCreationInformation` class. At a minimum, you need to define the `Title` and the `TemplateType` properties. Furthermore, the list fields have to be added. In the following examples, the fields are defined in XML and added to the list using the `AddFieldAsXml` method (see Listings 12–39 and 12–40).

***Listing 12–39.** Creating a New List (C#)*

```
public void Example11()
{
    ClientContext ctx = new ClientContext("http://clserver");
    Web oWeb = ctx.Web;

    ListCreationInformation listCreationInfo = new ListCreationInformation();
    listCreationInfo.Title = "MyBooks";
    listCreationInfo.TemplateType = (int)ListTemplateType.GenericList;

    List oList = oWeb.Lists.Add(listCreationInfo);
    ctx.Load(oList);

    String fldAuthorsXml = "<Field DisplayName='Authors' Type='Text' />";
    String fldPublisherXml = "<Field DisplayName='Publisher' Type='Text' />";
    String fldPriceXml = "<Field DisplayName='Price' Type='Currency' />";

    oList.Fields.AddFieldAsXml(fldAuthorsXml, true, AddFieldOptions.DefaultValue);
    oList.Fields.AddFieldAsXml(fldPublisherXml, true, AddFieldOptions.DefaultValue);
    oList.Fields.AddFieldAsXml(fldPriceXml, true, AddFieldOptions.DefaultValue);
    oList.Update();

    ctx.ExecuteQuery();
    Console.WriteLine("List " + oList.Title + " has been created successfully.");
}
```

***Listing 12–40.** Creating a New List (JavaScript)*

```
function example11() {
    var ctx = new SP.ClientContext.get_current();
    this.oWeb = ctx.get_web();

    var listCreationInfo = new SP.ListCreationInformation();
    listCreationInfo.set_title('MyBooks');
    listCreationInfo.set_templateType(SP.ListTemplateType.genericList);

    this.oList = this.oWeb.get_lists().add(listCreationInfo);
    ctx.load(this.oList);
```

```
    var fldAuthorsXml = "<Field DisplayName='Authors' Type='Text' />";
    var fldPublisherXml = "<Field DisplayName='Publisher' Type='Text' />";
    var fldPriceXml = "<Field DisplayName='Price' Type='Currency' />";

    this.oList.get_fields().addFieldAsXml(fldAuthorsXml, true,
           SP.AddFieldOptions.defaultValue);
    this.oList.get_fields().addFieldAsXml(fldPublisherXml, true,
           SP.AddFieldOptions.defaultValue);
    this.oList.get_fields().addFieldAsXml(fldPriceXml, true, SP.AddFieldOptions.defaultValue);
    this.oList.update();

    ctx.executeQueryAsync(
            Function.createDelegate(this, this.onSucceededCallback),
            Function.createDelegate(this, this.onFailedCallback));
}

function onSucceededCallback(sender, args) {
    alert("List " + this.oList.get_title() + " has been created successfully.");
}
```

How to Modify an Existing SharePoint List

Modifying a property of an existing SharePoint list can be accomplished easily by setting the property to a new value and calling Update. The examples in Listing 12–41 and 12–42 demonstrate how to update list properties, and also how to add a new field to a list and customize its field properties. If you examine the source code you will notice the use of the `ClientContext.Cast` method. After calling this method, the field that has been added as XML can be used a type of class `FieldMultiLineText`. A normal cast does not work.

Listing 12–41. *Modifying Existing Lists (C#)*

```
public void Example12()
{
    ClientContext ctx = new ClientContext("http://clserver");
    List oBooksList = ctx.Web.Lists.GetByTitle("MyBooks");

    // Update list description
    oBooksList.Description = "This is a new description";
    oBooksList.Update();

    // Add a field and change its properties
    String fldCommentXml = "<Field DisplayName='Comment' Type='Note' />";
    Field fldComment = oBooksList.Fields.AddFieldAsXml(
                                         fldCommentXml,
                                         true,
                                         AddFieldOptions.DefaultValue);

    FieldMultiLineText fldCommentCasted =
                          ctx.CastTo<FieldMultiLineText>(fldComment);
    fldCommentCasted.RichText = false;
```

```
        fldCommentCasted.NumberOfLines = 10;
        fldCommentCasted.Update();

        ctx.Load(fldCommentCasted);
        ctx.ExecuteQuery();

        Console.WriteLine(fldCommentCasted.Title);
}
```

The JavaScript code also requires an explicit casting of the newly added field. Only after using the `clientContext.castTo` function can the specific properties, such as `set_richText` and `set_numberOfLines`, be accessed (see Listing 12–42). Otherwise JavaScript throws the following error: "Object doesn't support this property or method."

Listing 12–42. *Modifying Existing Lists (JavaScript)*

```
function example12() {

    var ctx = new SP.ClientContext.get_current();
    this.oBooksList = ctx.get_web().get_lists().getByTitle("MyBooks");

    // Update list description
    this.oBooksList.set_description = "This is a new description2";
    this.oBooksList.update();

    // Add a field and change its properties
    var fldCommentXml = "<Field DisplayName='Comment' Type='Note' />";
    this.fldComment = oBooksList.get_fields().addFieldAsXml(fldCommentXml, true,
            SP.AddFieldOptions.defaultValue);

    this.fldCommentCasted = ctx.castTo(this.fldComment, SP.FieldMultiLineText);
    this.fldCommentCasted.set_richText(false);
    this.fldCommentCasted.set_numberOfLines(10);
    this.fldCommentCasted.update();

    ctx.load(this.fldCommentCasted);

    ctx.executeQueryAsync(
    Function.createDelegate(this, this.onSucceededCallback),
    Function.createDelegate(this, this.onFailedCallback));

}

function onSucceededCallback(sender, args) {
    alert("Field " + this.fldComment.get_title() + " has been created successfully.");

}
```

How to Delete a SharePoint List

Deleting objects is quite simple—you just need to call `DeleteObject` and execute the server round trip. The examples in Listings 12–43 and 12–44 demonstrate the deletion of a list called `MyBooks`.

Listing 12–43. *Deleting a List (C#)*

```
public void Example13()
{
    ClientContext ctx = new ClientContext("http://clserver");
    List oBooksList = ctx.Web.Lists.GetByTitle("MyBooks");
    oBooksList.DeleteObject();
    ctx.ExecuteQuery();
    Console.WriteLine("List deleted!");
}
```

Listing 12–44. *Deleting a List (JavaScript)*

```
function example13() {
    var ctx = new SP.ClientContext.get_current();
    var oList = ctx.get_web().get_lists().getByTitle('MyBooks');
    oList.deleteObject();
    ctx.executeQueryAsync(
            Function.createDelegate(this, this.onSucceededCallback),
            Function.createDelegate(this, this.onFailedCallback));
}

function onSucceededCallback(sender, args) {
    alert('List deleted!');
 }
```

Accessing List Items

Querying and accessing list items is one of the most common scenarios when working with the SharePoint client object model. The examples in this section demonstrate a number of operations with list items:

- How to retrieve all the items in a SharePoint list
- How to retrieve list items using CAML queries
- How to create new list items
- How to update list items
- How to delete list items

How to Retrieve All Items in a SharePoint List

The retrieval of all items in a list is generally not recommended for performance reasons, especially if the list contains many items. Only if you access a very small list, such as a list containing a few configuration items, is it reasonable to use an empty `CamlQuery` instance, as shown in Listing 12–45.

Listing 12–45. *Retrieving All the Items in a List (C#)*

```
public void Example14()
{
    ClientContext ctx = new ClientContext("http://clserver");
```

```
    List oBooksList = ctx.Web.Lists.GetByTitle("Books");

    CamlQuery caml = new CamlQuery();
    ListItemCollection allBooks = oBooksList.GetItems(caml);
    ctx.Load(allBooks);

    ctx.ExecuteQuery();

    foreach (ListItem li in allBooks)
    {
        Console.WriteLine("ID: " + li.Id + ", Title=" + li["Title"]);
    }
}
```

The JavaScript code in Listing 12–46 looks very similar. The only real difference concerns reading the list item properties. For managed C# code you can simply use `ListItem["propertyName"]`, whereas in JavaScript you have to use an extra function get_item: `ListItem.get_item("propertyName")`.

***Listing 12–46.** Retrieving All the Items in a List (JavaScript)*

```
function example14() {
    var ctx = new SP.ClientContext.get_current();
    var oBooksList = ctx.get_web().get_lists().getByTitle('Books');
    var caml = new SP.CamlQuery();
    this.allBooks = oBooksList.getItems(caml);
    ctx.load(this.allBooks);

    ctx.executeQueryAsync(
            Function.createDelegate(this, this.onSucceededCallback),
            Function.createDelegate(this, this.onFailedCallback));
}

function onSucceededCallback(sender, args) {
    var enumerator = this.allBooks.getEnumerator();
    while (enumerator.moveNext()) {
        var listItem = enumerator.get_current();
        alert("ID: " + listItem.get_id() + ", Title: " +
                       listItem.get_item("Title"));
    }
}
```

How to Retrieve List Items Using CAML Queries

Using CAML queries to retrieve list items is the best practice. The filtering of list items is performed on the server, and you can be sure that only relevant data is transmitted to the client. The following example goes a step further and defines, beyond the CAML query, which properties should be returned. This is accomplished using the `Include` clause of the LINQ expression within the `Load` method (see Listing 12–47).

***Listing 12–47.** Retrieving List Items Using CAML (C#)*

```
public void Example15()
{
    ClientContext ctx = new ClientContext("http://clserver");
```

```
    List oBooksList = ctx.Web.Lists.GetByTitle("Books");

    CamlQuery caml = new CamlQuery();
    caml.ViewXml = "<View><Query><Where><Eq><FieldRef Name='Publisher'/>" +
        "<Value Type='Text'>APress</Value></Eq></Where></Query></View>";

    ListItemCollection allBooksFromAPress = oBooksList.GetItems(caml);
    ctx.Load(allBooksFromAPress, books => books.Include(
            book => book.Id,
            book => book["Title"],
            book => book["Publisher"]
        ));

    ctx.ExecuteQuery();

    foreach (ListItem li in allBooksFromAPress)
    {
        Console.WriteLine("ID: " + li.Id + ", Title=" + li["Title"] + ",
                             Publisher: "
                + li["Book_x0020_Publisher"]);
    }
}
```

The examples in Listings 12–47 und 12–48 query for all list items whose Publisher field contains the value APress. Only three properties are retrieved and displayed: `Id`, `Title`, and `Publisher`. Although it is not possible to use LINQ in JavaScript, you can use the implemented `Include` expression to define which fields you do want to be populated.

***Listing 12–48.** Retrieving List Items Using CAML (JavaScript)*

```
function example15() {
    var ctx = new SP.ClientContext.get_current();
    var oBooksList = ctx.get_web().get_lists().getByTitle('Books');
    var caml = new SP.CamlQuery();
    caml.ViewXml = "<View><Query><Where><Eq><FieldRef Name='Publisher'/>" +
        "<Value Type='Text'>APress</Value></Eq></Where></Query><View>";

    this.allBooksFromAPress = oBooksList.getItems(caml);
    ctx.load(this.allBooksFromAPress, "Include(Id, Title, Publisher)");

    ctx.executeQueryAsync(
            Function.createDelegate(this, this.onSucceededCallback),
            Function.createDelegate(this, this.onFailedCallback));
}

function onSucceededCallback(sender, args) {
    var enumerator = this.allBooksFromAPress.getEnumerator();
    while (enumerator.moveNext()) {
        var li = enumerator.get_current();
        alert("ID: " + li.get_id() + ", Title: " + li.get_item("Title")
                + ", Publisher: " + li.get_item("Publisher"));
    }
}
```

How to Create a New List Item

To create a new list item with the client object, use the `List.AddItem` method. As with creating webs and lists, a list item also has its own `ListItemCreationInformation` class (see Listings 12–49 and 12–50).

***Listing 12–49.** Creating a New List Item (C#)*

```
public void Example16()
{
    ClientContext ctx = new ClientContext("http://clserver");
    List oBooksList = ctx.Web.Lists.GetByTitle("Books");

    ListItemCreationInformation itemCreationInfo =
                                new ListItemCreationInformation();
    ListItem newListItem = oBooksList.AddItem(itemCreationInfo);

    newListItem["Title"] = "SharePoint 2010 Book";
    newListItem["Authors"] = "Krause, Langhirt, Sterff, Pehlke, Doering";
    newListItem["Publisher"] = "APress";
    newListItem["Price"] = 59;

    newListItem.Update();

    ctx.ExecuteQuery();
    Console.WriteLine("Book added successfully!");
}
```

In JavaScript you need to use the `set_item` function instead of directly accessing an item in an array, as shown in Listing 12–50.

***Listing 12–50.** Creating a New List Item (JavaScript)*

```
function example16() {
    var ctx = new SP.ClientContext.get_current();
    var oBooksList = ctx.get_web().get_lists().getByTitle('Books');

    var itemCreationInfo = new SP.ListItemCreationInformation();
    this.newListItem = oBooksList.addItem(itemCreationInfo);

    this.newListItem.set_item("Title","SharePoint 2010 Book");
    this.newListItem.set_item("Authors",
                              "Krause, Langhirt, Sterff, Pehlke, Doering");
    this.newListItem.set_item("Publisher","APress");
    this.newListItem.set_item("Price", 59);

    this.newListItem.update();

    ctx.executeQueryAsync(
            Function.createDelegate(this, this.onSucceededCallback),
            Function.createDelegate(this, this.onFailedCallback));
}
```

```
function onSucceededCallback(sender, args) {
    alert('Book added successfully');
}
```

How to Update a List Item

Updating a list item works in exactly the same way (see Listings 12–51 and 12–52).

Listing 12–51. *Updating a List Item (C#)*

```
public void Example17()
{
    ClientContext ctx = new ClientContext("http://clserver");
    List oBooksList = ctx.Web.Lists.GetByTitle("Books");
    ListItem listItem = oBooksList.GetItemById(2);

    listItem["Title"] = "SharePoint 2010 Bookx";
    listItem["Authors"] = "Krause, Langhirt, Sterff, Pehlke, Doering";
    listItem["Publisher"] = "APress";
    listItem["Price"] = 59;

    listItem.Update();
    ctx.ExecuteQuery();

    Console.WriteLine("Book updated successfully!");
}
```

Listing 12–52. *Updating a List Item (JavaScript)*

```
function example17() {
    var ctx = new SP.ClientContext.get_current();
    var oBooksList = ctx.get_web().get_lists().getByTitle('Books');
    this.listItem = oBooksList.getItemById(2);

    this.listItem.set_item("Title", "SharePoint 2010 Book2");
    this.listItem.set_item("Authors", "Krause, Langhirt, Sterff, Pehlke, Doering");
    this.listItem.set_item("Publisher", "Apress");
    this.listItem.set_item("Price", 59);

    this.listItem.update();

    ctx.executeQueryAsync(
            Function.createDelegate(this, this.onSucceededCallback),
            Function.createDelegate(this, this.onFailedCallback));
}

function onSucceededCallback(sender, args) {
    alert('Book updated successfully');
}
```

How to Delete a List Item

Deleting a list item also works in the same manner as the previous examples (see Listings 12–53 and 12–54).

Listing 12–53. *Deleting a List Item (C#)*

```
public void Example18()
{
    ClientContext ctx = new ClientContext("http://clserver");
    List oBooksList = ctx.Web.Lists.GetByTitle("Books");
    ListItem listItem = oBooksList.GetItemById(3);
    listItem.DeleteObject();

    ctx.ExecuteQuery();

    Console.WriteLine("Book item deleted successfully!");
}
```

Listing 12–54. *Deleting a List Item (JavaScript)*

```
function example18() {
    var ctx = new SP.ClientContext.get_current();
    var oBooksList = ctx.get_web().get_lists().getByTitle('Books');
    var listItem = oBooksList.getItemById(2);
    listItem.deleteObject();

    ctx.executeQueryAsync(
            Function.createDelegate(this, this.onSucceededCallback),
            Function.createDelegate(this, this.onFailedCallback));
}

function onSucceededCallback(sender, args) {
    alert('Book deleted successfully');
}
```

Accessing Users and Roles

Working with users, groups, and roles, and dealing with their permissions for SharePoint elements, can be quite complex. In former SharePoint versions, the only way to affect the security was to use the provided security web services. With SharePoint 2010, the client object model dramatically simplifies working with security settings. For third-party applications, no matter if they are written as Windows or Silverlight applications, it's very easy to access the SharePoint security model and to build extended functionality on it. This section contains examples of how the client object model can deal with security.

- How to add users to a SharePoint group
- How to retrieve members of a SharePoint group
- How to create a role
- How to add a user to a role
- How to create a new SharePoint group and assign the group to a role
- How to break the security inheritance

How to Add Users to a SharePoint Group

Adding a user to a SharePoint group is a common task, particularly in conjunction with creating a web site. The following example shows two ways to add a user to a group. The first one uses the `Group.Users.AddUser` method, which expects a `User` instance of an existing user. The second method adds a new user to a group by using the `UserCreationInformation` class. The new user is identified by its `LoginName`. If the user already exists in the site collection, the user is added to the group anyway. The examples in Listings 12–55 and 12–56 require a valid group within the property `Web.AssociatedMemberGroup` to exist; thus, the default group at the time of the web site creation has not been removed.

Listing 12–55. *Adding Users to a SharePoint Group (C#)*

```
public void Example19()
{
    ClientContext ctx = new ClientContext("http://clserver");
    Group membersGroup = ctx.Web.AssociatedMemberGroup;

    // Add existing user to membersGroup
    User currentUser = membersGroup.Users.AddUser(ctx.Web.CurrentUser);

    // Add new user to membersGroup
    UserCreationInformation userCreationInfo = new UserCreationInformation();
    userCreationInfo.Email = "joerg@krause.de";
    userCreationInfo.LoginName = @"MAXIMUS\jkrause";
    userCreationInfo.Title = "Joerg Krause";
    User newUser = membersGroup.Users.Add(userCreationInfo);

    ctx.Load(currentUser);
    ctx.Load(newUser);
    ctx.Load(membersGroup);
    ctx.ExecuteQuery();

    Console.WriteLine("The users " + currentUser.LoginName
        + " and " + newUser.LoginName
        + " have been added to group '" + membersGroup.Title
        + "'.");
}
```

Listing 12–56. *Adding Users to a SharePoint Group (JavaScript)*

```
function example19() {
    var ctx = new SP.ClientContext.get_current();
    this.membersGroup = ctx.get_web().get_associatedMemberGroup();

    // Add existing user to membersGroup
    this.currentUser = this.membersGroup.get_users().
                                addUser(ctx.get_web().get_currentUser());

    // Add new user to membersGroup
    this.userCreationInfo = new SP.UserCreationInformation();
    this.userCreationInfo.set_email("joerg@krause.de");
    this.userCreationInfo.set_loginName("MAXIMUS\\jkrause");
```

```
    this.userCreationInfo.set_title("Joerg Krause");
    this.newUser = this.membersGroup.get_users().add(this.userCreationInfo);

    ctx.load(this.currentUser);
    ctx.load(this.newUser);
    ctx.load(this.membersGroup);

    ctx.executeQueryAsync(
    Function.createDelegate(this, this.onSucceededCallback),
    Function.createDelegate(this, this.onFailedCallback));
}

function onSucceededCallback(sender, args) {

    alert("The users " + this.currentUser.get_loginName()
        + " and " + this.newUser.get_loginName()
        + " have been added to group '" + this.membersGroup.get_title()
        + "'.");
}
```

How to Retrieve Members of a SharePoint Group

To get a list of all users that are members of a specified group, you can use the `Group.Users` collection (see Listings 12–57 and 12–58).

Listing 12–57. *Retrieving Group Members (C#)*

```
public void Example20()
{
    ClientContext ctx = new ClientContext("http://clserver");
    Group membersGroup = ctx.Web.AssociatedMemberGroup;
    UserCollection allUsersOfGroup = membersGroup.Users;
    ctx.Load(allUsersOfGroup);

    ctx.ExecuteQuery();

    foreach (User user in allUsersOfGroup)
    {
        Console.WriteLine("ID: " + user.Id + ", LoginName=" + user.LoginName);
    }
}
```

Listing 12–58. *Retrieving Group Members (JavaScript)*

```
function example20() {
    var ctx = new SP.ClientContext.get_current();
    var membersGroup = ctx.get_web().get_associatedMemberGroup();
    this.allUsersOfGroup = membersGroup.get_users();
    ctx.load(allUsersOfGroup);

    ctx.executeQueryAsync(
            Function.createDelegate(this, this.onSucceededCallback),
```

```
            Function.createDelegate(this, this.onFailedCallback));
}

function onSucceededCallback(sender, args) {

    var enumerator = this.allUsersOfGroup.getEnumerator();
    while (enumerator.moveNext()) {
        var user = enumerator.get_current();
        alert("ID: " + user.get_id() + ", LoginName: " + user.get_loginName());
    }
}
```

How to Create a Role

Defining your own roles, also known as *permission levels,* is a common task when dealing with complex security requirements. With the client object model, you can easily define your own roles and assign them to SharePoint users or groups. The examples in Listings 12–59 and 12–60 show how to create a new role.

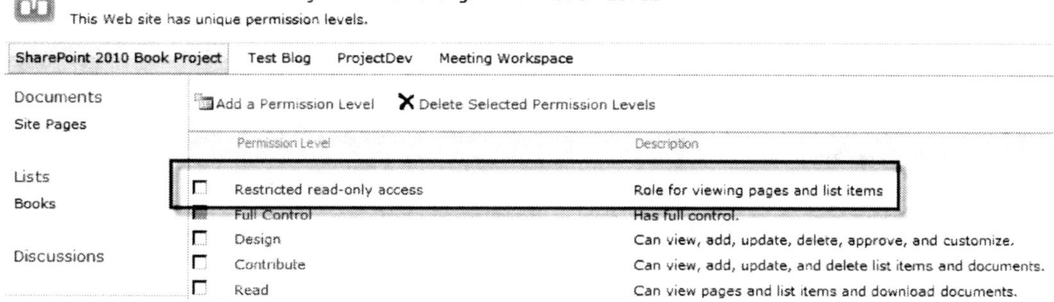

***Figure 12–20.** Newly created role (permission level)*

***Listing 12–59.** Creating a Role (C#)*

```
public void Example21()
{
    ClientContext ctx = new ClientContext("http://clserver");
    Web oWeb = ctx.Web;

    BasePermissions basePerms = new BasePermissions();
    basePerms.Set(PermissionKind.ViewListItems);
    basePerms.Set(PermissionKind.ViewPages);

    RoleDefinitionCreationInformation roleCreationInfo =
            new RoleDefinitionCreationInformation();
    roleCreationInfo.BasePermissions = basePerms;
    roleCreationInfo.Description = "Role for viewing pages and list items";
    roleCreationInfo.Name = "Restricted read-only access";
```

```
    RoleDefinition roleDef = oWeb.RoleDefinitions.Add(roleCreationInfo);
    Ctx.Load(roleDef);
    ctx.ExecuteQuery();

    Console.WriteLine("New role '" + roleDef.Name +
                      "' has been successfully created.");
}
```

Listing 12–60. Creating a Role (JavaScript)

```
function example21() {
    var ctx = new SP.ClientContext.get_current();
    this.oWeb = ctx.get_web();

    var basePerms = new SP.BasePermissions();
    basePerms.set(SP.PermissionKind.viewListItems);
    basePerms.set(SP.PermissionKind.viewPages);

    var roleCreationInfo = new SP.RoleDefinitionCreationInformation();
    roleCreationInfo.set_basePermissions(basePerms);
    roleCreationInfo.set_description("Role for viewing pages and list items");
    roleCreationInfo.set_name("Restricted read-only access");
    roleCreationInfo.set_order(1);

    this.roleDef = this.oWeb.get_roleDefinitions().add(roleCreationInfo);
    ctx.load(this.roleDef);

    ctx.executeQueryAsync(
            Function.createDelegate(this, this.onSucceededCallback),
            Function.createDelegate(this, this.onFailedCallback));
}

function onSucceededCallback(sender, args) {
    alert("New role '" + this.roleDef.get_name() +
          "' has been successfully created.");
}
```

How to Add Users or Groups to Roles

Assigning SharePoint users or groups to roles is shown in Listings 12–61 and 12–62.

Listing 12–61. Adding a User or Group to a Role (C#)

```
public void Example22()
{
    ClientContext ctx = new ClientContext("http://clserver");
    Web oWeb = ctx.Web;

    Principal oUser = oWeb.CurrentUser;

    RoleDefinition oRoleDef =
```

```
        oWeb.RoleDefinitions.GetByName("Restricted read-only access");
    RoleDefinitionBindingCollection roleDefinitionBindingColl =
        new RoleDefinitionBindingCollection(ctx);
    roleDefinitionBindingColl.Add(oRoleDef);

    RoleAssignment oRoleAssignment =
        oWeb.RoleAssignments.Add(oUser, roleDefinitionBindingColl);

    ctx.Load(oUser, user => user.Title);
    ctx.Load(oRoleDef, role => role.Name);

    ctx.ExecuteQuery();

    Console.WriteLine("User '" + oUser.Title +
                      "' assigned to role '" + oRoleDef.Name + "'.");
}
```

***Listing 12–62.** Adding a User or Group to a Role (JavaScript)*

```
function example22() {
    var ctx = new SP.ClientContext.get_current();
    this.oWeb = ctx.get_web();

    this.oUser = oWeb.get_currentUser();
    this.oRoleDef =
        this.oWeb.get_roleDefinitions().getByName("Restricted read-only access");

    var roleDefinitionBindingColl =
                            SP.RoleDefinitionBindingCollection.newObject(ctx);
    roleDefinitionBindingColl.add(this.oRoleDef);

    var oRoleAssignment = this.oWeb.get_roleAssignments().add(
                                      this.oUser, roleDefinitionBindingColl);

    ctx.load(this.oUser, "Title");
    ctx.load(this.oRoleDef, "Name");

    ctx.executeQueryAsync(
            Function.createDelegate(this, this.onSucceededCallback),
            Function.createDelegate(this, this.onFailedCallback));
}

function onSucceededCallback(sender, args) {
    alert("User '" + this.oUser.get_title() + "' assigned to role '" +
          this.oRoleDef.get_name() + "'.");
}
```

As you can see, the `RoleAssignments.Add` (in JavaScript, `RoleAssignments.add`) method takes a `Principal` object as a parameter. The `Principal` class serves as the base class for both users (`User`) and groups (`Group`). So, you can assign either a user or a group to a role.

■ **Caution** When using JavaScript, the instantiation for the class `SP.RoleDefinitionBindingCollection` is done through the static function `SP.RoleDefinitionBindingCollection.newObject(ClientContext)`, which takes the current client context as a parameter.

How to Create a New SharePoint Group and Assign the Group to a Role

The examples in this section demonstrate the creation of a new SharePoint group, using the `GroupCreationInformation` class. The Contributors role is then assigned to this new group (see Listings 12–63 and 12–64).

***Listing 12–63.** Creating a New SharePoint Group and Assigning It to a Role (C#)*

```
public void Example23()
{
    ClientContext ctx = new ClientContext("http://clserver");
    Web oWeb = ctx.Web;

    GroupCreationInformation groupCreationInfo = new GroupCreationInformation();
    groupCreationInfo.Title = "My Custom Contributor Group";
    groupCreationInfo.Description = "This group has contributor rights.";
    Group oGroup = oWeb.SiteGroups.Add(groupCreationInfo);

    RoleDefinitionBindingCollection roleDefinitionBindingColl =
        new RoleDefinitionBindingCollection(ctx);
    RoleDefinition oRoleDefinition =
        oWeb.RoleDefinitions.GetByType(RoleType.Contributor);

    roleDefinitionBindingColl.Add(oRoleDefinition);
    oWeb.RoleAssignments.Add(oGroup, roleDefinitionBindingColl);

    ctx.Load(oGroup, group => group.Title);
    ctx.Load(oRoleDefinition, role => role.Name);

    ctx.ExecuteQuery();

    Console.WriteLine("Group " + oGroup.Title + " created and assigned to role "
        + oRoleDefinition.Name);
}
```

***Listing 12–64.** Creating a New SharePoint Group and Assigning It to a Role (JavaScript)*

```
function example23() {
    var ctx = new SP.ClientContext.get_current();
    this.oWeb = ctx.get_web();

    var groupCreationInfo = new SP.GroupCreationInformation();
    groupCreationInfo.set_title("My Custom Contributor Group");
    groupCreationInfo.set_description("This group has contributor rights.");
```

```
    this.oGroup = oWeb.get_siteGroups().add(groupCreationInfo);

    var roleDefinitionBindingColl =
                          SP.RoleDefinitionBindingCollection.newObject(ctx);
    this.oRoleDefinition =
        oWeb.get_roleDefinitions().getByType(SP.RoleType.contributor);
    roleDefinitionBindingColl.add(this.oRoleDefinition);

    this.oWeb.get_roleAssignments().add(this.oGroup, roleDefinitionBindingColl);

    ctx.load(this.oGroup, "Title");
    ctx.load(this.oRoleDefinition, "Name");

    ctx.executeQueryAsync(
            Function.createDelegate(this, this.onSucceededCallback),
            Function.createDelegate(this, this.onFailedCallback));
}

function onSucceededCallback(sender, args) {

    alert("Group '" + this.oGroup.get_title() + "' created and assigned to role '"
        + this.oRoleDefinition.get_name() + "'.");

}
```

How to Break the Role Inheritance

In SharePoint, by default all elements (such as Web, List, and ListItem) rely on role inheritance. That means that permissions are inherited from top to bottom. A user has the same permissions on a list item as on a list, because the list item inherits its permissions from the list. There are scenarios, though, in which this default role inheritance is not desirable and has to be broken—for example, if you want a list item to be accessed only by special users or groups. The example in this section shows how to break the role inheritance of a list item and assign special permissions to it. Figures 12–21 and 12–22 show the list item permissions before and after breaking the role inheritance.

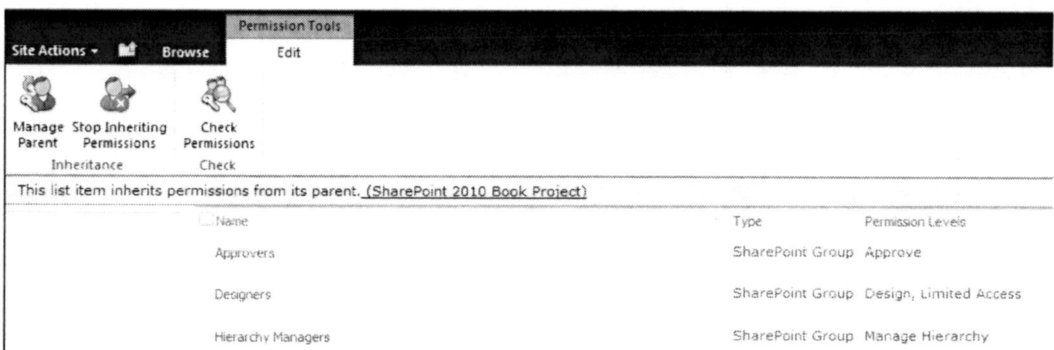

***Figure 12–21.** List item permissions before breaking the inheritance (default)*

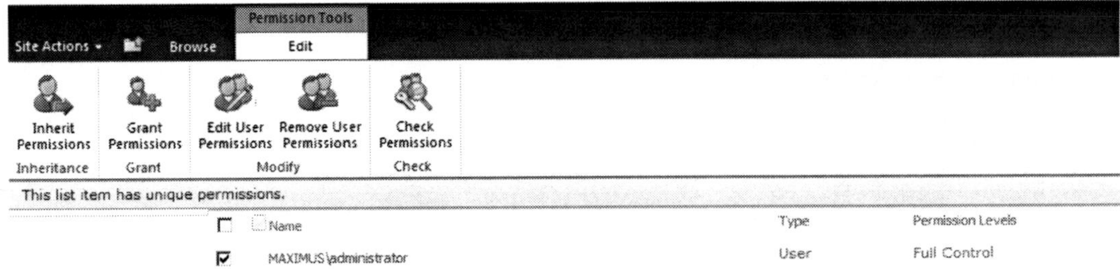

Figure 12–22. *List item permissions after breaking the inheritance and adding a user (MAXIMUS\administrator) with full control to the list item*

The examples shown in Listings 12–65 and 12–66 get a list item with `ID=1` from the list `Books` and break its role inheritance without copying the inherited permissions or clearing the child scope.

Listing 12–65. *Breaking the Role Inheritance (C#)*

```
public void Example24()
{
    ClientContext ctx = new ClientContext("http://clserver");
    Web oWeb = ctx.Web;

    List booksList = oWeb.Lists.GetByTitle("Books");
    ListItem bookToSecure = booksList.GetItemById(1);

    // Break role inheritance for this list item and
    // don't copy the inherited permissions
    bookToSecure.BreakRoleInheritance(false, false);

    // Assign the current user as Administrator
    RoleDefinitionBindingCollection roleDefinitionBindingColl =
        new RoleDefinitionBindingCollection(ctx);
    roleDefinitionBindingColl.Add(
        oWeb.RoleDefinitions.GetByType(RoleType.Administrator));

    bookToSecure.RoleAssignments.Add(oWeb.CurrentUser, roleDefinitionBindingColl);

    ctx.ExecuteQuery();
}
```

The method `BreakRoleInheritance` takes two Boolean parameters: `copyRoleAssignments` and `clearSubScopes`. The first parameter indicates whether all permissions from the parent object should be copied to the element on which the `BreakRoleInheritance` method is executed. The second parameter specifies whether unique permissions of the child elements should be cleared.

Listing 12–66. *Breaking the Role Inheritance (JavaScript)*

```
function example24() {
    var ctx = new SP.ClientContext.get_current();
    this.oWeb = ctx.get_web();
```

```
    var booksList = this.oWeb.get_lists().getByTitle("Books");
    var bookToSecure = booksList.getItemById(1);

    // Break role inheritance for this list item and
    // don't copy the inherited permissions
    bookToSecure.breakRoleInheritance(false, false);

    // Assign the current user as Administrator
    var roleDefinitionBindingColl =
                   SP.RoleDefinitionBindingCollection.newObject(ctx);
    roleDefinitionBindingColl.add(
        oWeb.get_roleDefinitions().getByType(SP.RoleType.administrator));

    bookToSecure.get_roleAssignments().add(
        oWeb.get_currentUser, roleDefinitionBindingColl);

    ctx.executeQueryAsync(
            Function.createDelegate(this, this.onSucceededCallback),
            Function.createDelegate(this, this.onFailedCallback));
}
```

Accessing Web Parts

There are a few reasons for accessing Web Parts via the client object model. A good example is a Windows application, such as SharePoint Designer, that provides surfaces for modifying or adding Web Parts to existing pages. Another scenario, using the JavaScript client object model, could be the implementation of a custom ribbon control for inserting predefined Web Parts to pages. Offering some practical examples, this section provides a good entry into the interaction of the client object model and Web Parts.

- How to update the title of a Web Part
- How to add a Web Part to a page
- How to delete a Web Part from a page

How to Update the Title of a Web Part

To access a Web Part, you need an instance of the `LimitedWebPartManager` class. You get it for a defined SharePoint Web Part page (such as `default.aspx`) via the `Web.GetFileByServerRelativeUrl` method. The following example shows how to access a Web Part on a page and how to update the `Title` property. Figure 12–23 shows the example Web Part on the page before updating the title. In Figure 12–24 the title has been updated.

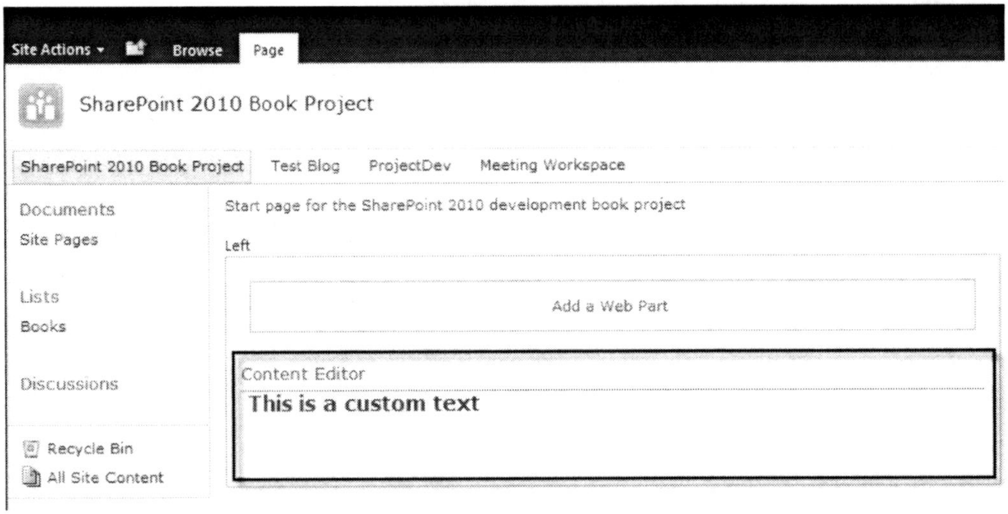

Figure 12–23. Content Editor Web Part in the default.aspx page

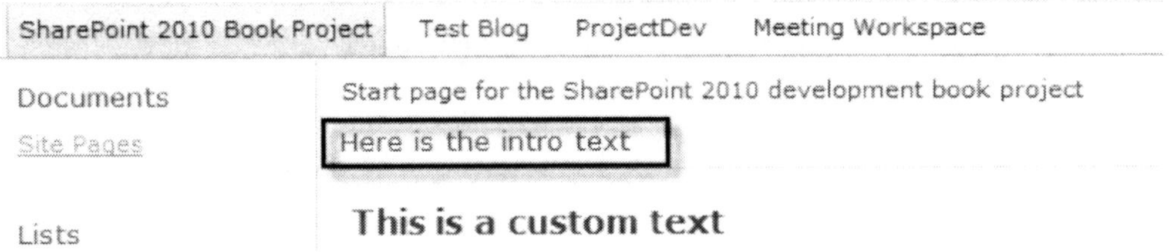

Figure 12–24. Content Editor Web Part after changing the title of the Web Part

To modify Web Parts you first have to load a page containing Web Parts. Then you can change a Web Part and its properties as needed. Finally, call the `SaveWebPartChanges` method on the `WebPartDefinition` object to persist your changes (see Listing 12–67).

***Listing 12–67.** Updating a Web Part Title (C#)*

```
public void Example25()
{
    ClientContext ctx = new ClientContext("http://clserver");
    Web oWeb = ctx.Web;

    File oFile = oWeb.GetFileByServerRelativeUrl("/default.aspx");
    LimitedWebPartManager limitedWebPartManager =
        oFile.GetLimitedWebPartManager(PersonalizationScope.Shared);

    ctx.Load(limitedWebPartManager.WebParts,
             wps => wps.Include(wp => wp.WebPart.Title));
```

```
    ctx.ExecuteQuery();

    if (limitedWebPartManager.WebParts.Count == 0)
        throw new Exception("No web parts found");

    WebPartDefinition oWebPartDef = limitedWebPartManager.WebParts[0];
    oWebPartDef.WebPart.Title = "Here is the intro text";

    oWebPartDef.SaveWebPartChanges();

    ctx.ExecuteQuery();
}
```

The JavaScript code works similarly, but there is one difference to accommodate: you need two callback methods, as shown in Listing 12–68. One is called first to update the title property (changeWebPartTitle), and the other is called after updating the property (onSucceededCallback).

Listing 12–68. *Updating a Web Part Title (JavaScript)*

```
function example25() {
    this.ctx = new SP.ClientContext.get_current();
    this.oWeb = ctx.get_web();

    var oFile = oWeb.getFileByServerRelativeUrl("/default.aspx");
    this.limitedWebPartManager =
        oFile.getLimitedWebPartManager(SP.WebParts.PersonalizationScope.shared)

    this.ctx.load(this.limitedWebPartManager.get_webParts(),
                  "Include(WebPart.Title)");

    this.ctx.executeQueryAsync(
            Function.createDelegate(this, this.changeWebPartTitle),
            Function.createDelegate(this, this.onFailedCallback));
}

function changeWebPartTitle() {

    if (this.limitedWebPartManager.get_webParts().get_count() == 0) {
        alert("No web parts found"); return;
    }

    var oWebPartDef = this.limitedWebPartManager.get_webParts().get_item(0);
    oWebPartDef.get_webPart().set_title("Here is the intro text 2");
    oWebPartDef.saveWebPartChanges();

    this.ctx.executeQueryAsync(
            Function.createDelegate(this, this.onSucceededCallback),
            Function.createDelegate(this, this.onFailedCallback));
}

function onSucceededCallback(sender, args) {

}
```

■ **Caution** The client object model currently only allows changing common Web Part properties such as `Title`, `TitleUrl`, `Subtitle`, and `Hidden`. Actually, there is no way to change specific Web Part properties such as the `Content` property of a Content Editor Web Part. Those changes can only be done using server-side code.

How to Add a Web Part to a Page

Adding a Web Part to a page is straightforward, and again requires an instance of `LimitedWebPartManager`. The new Web Part has to be added via its XML definition. To extract the XML for an existing Web Part, you can use the export function, as shown in Figure 12–25.

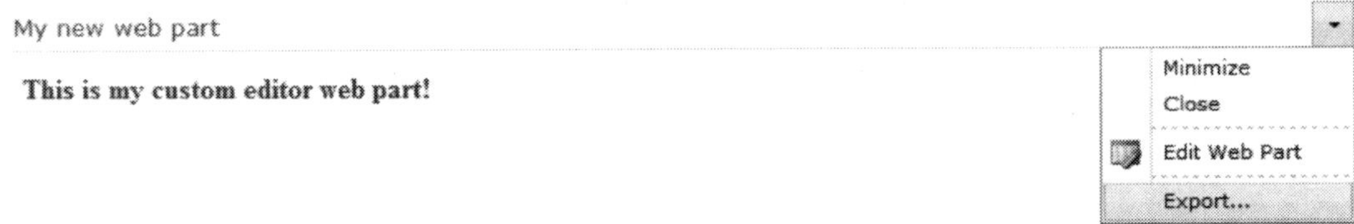

Figure 12–25. To get a Web Part XML definition, use the export function.

■ **Note** In contrast to the server side, the client object model does not know the Web Part classes available on the server. When working with the client object model, you have to use the XML Web Part definition to add a new Web Part to a page. There are no Web Part classes implemented on the client side.

This examples shown in Listings 12–69 and 12–70 add a new Content Editor Web Part to the `default.aspx` page.

Listing 12–69. Adding a Web Part to a Page (C#)

```
public void Example26()
{
    ClientContext ctx = new ClientContext("http://clserver");
    Web oWeb = ctx.Web;

    File oFile = oWeb.GetFileByServerRelativeUrl("/default.aspx");
    LimitedWebPartManager limitedWebPartManager =
        oFile.GetLimitedWebPartManager(PersonalizationScope.Shared);

    string xml = @"
    <?xml version=""1.0"" encoding=""utf-8""?>
    <WebPart xmlns:xsi=""http://www.w3.org/2001/XMLSchema-instance""
             xmlns:xsd=""http://www.w3.org/2001/XMLSchema""
             xmlns=""http://schemas.microsoft.com/WebPart/v2"">
```

```
        <Title>My new web part</Title>
        <FrameType>Default</FrameType>
        <Description></Description>
        <IsIncluded>true</IsIncluded>
        <ZoneID></ZoneID>
        <PartOrder>0</PartOrder>
        <FrameState>Normal</FrameState>
        <Height />
        <Width />
        <AllowRemove>true</AllowRemove>
        <AllowZoneChange>true</AllowZoneChange>
        <AllowMinimize>true</AllowMinimize>
        <AllowConnect>true</AllowConnect>
        <AllowEdit>true</AllowEdit>
        <AllowHide>true</AllowHide>
        <IsVisible>true</IsVisible>
        <DetailLink />
        <HelpLink />
        <HelpMode>Modeless</HelpMode>
        <Dir>Default</Dir>
        <PartImageSmall />
        <MissingAssembly>Cannot import this Web Part.</MissingAssembly>
        <PartImageLarge>/_layouts/images/mscontl.gif</PartImageLarge>
        <IsIncludedFilter />
        <Assembly>Microsoft.SharePoint, Version=14.0.0.0, Culture=neutral,
        PublicKeyToken=71e9bce111e9429c</Assembly>
        <TypeName>Microsoft.SharePoint.WebPartPages.ContentEditorWebPart
        </TypeName>
        <ContentLink
                  xmlns=""http://schemas.microsoft.com/WebPart/v2/ContentEditor"" />
         <Content xmlns=""http://schemas.microsoft.com/WebPart/v2/ContentEditor"">
           <![CDATA[<b>This is my custom editor web part!</b>]]>
         </Content>
         <PartStorage
                  xmlns=""http://schemas.microsoft.com/WebPart/v2/ContentEditor""/>
    </WebPart>";

    WebPartDefinition oWebPartDef = limitedWebPartManager.ImportWebPart(xml);
    limitedWebPartManager.AddWebPart(oWebPartDef.WebPart, "Left", 1);

    ctx.ExecuteQuery();
}
```

Listing 12–70. *Adding a Web Part to a Page (JavaScript)*

```
function example26() {

    this.ctx = new SP.ClientContext.get_current();
    this.oWeb = ctx.get_web();

    var oFile = oWeb.getFileByServerRelativeUrl("/default.aspx");
    this.limitedWebPartManager =
        oFile.getLimitedWebPartManager(SP.WebParts.PersonalizationScope.shared);
```

```
    var xml = "<?xml version=\"1.0\" encoding=\"utf-8\"?>" +
            "<WebPart xmlns:xsi=\"http://www.w3.org/2001/XMLSchema-instance\"" +
            " xmlns:xsd=\"http://www.w3.org/2001/XMLSchema\"" +
         " xmlns=\"http://schemas.microsoft.com/WebPart/v2\">" +
         "<Title>My new web part</Title>" +
         "<FrameType>Default</FrameType>" +
         "<Description></Description>" +
         "<IsIncluded>true</IsIncluded><ZoneID></ZoneID><PartOrder>0</PartOrder>" +
         "<FrameState>Normal</FrameState><Height />" +
         "<Width /><AllowRemove>true</AllowRemove>" +
         "<AllowZoneChange>true</AllowZoneChange>" +
         "<AllowMinimize>true</AllowMinimize>" +
         "<AllowConnect>true</AllowConnect><AllowEdit>true</AllowEdit>" +
         "<AllowHide>true</AllowHide><IsVisible>true</IsVisible>" +
         "<DetailLink /><HelpLink />" +
         "<HelpMode>Modeless</HelpMode><Dir>Default</Dir><PartImageSmall />" +
         "<MissingAssembly>Cannot import this Web Part.</MissingAssembly>" +
         "<PartImageLarge>/_layouts/images/mscontl.gif</PartImageLarge>" +
         "<IsIncludedFilter />" +
         "<Assembly>Microsoft.SharePoint, Version=14.0.0.0, Culture=neutral, " +
         "PublicKeyToken=71e9bce111e9429c</Assembly>" +
         "<TypeName>Microsoft.SharePoint.WebPartPages.ContentEditorWebPart" +
         "</TypeName>" +
         "<ContentLink " +
            "xmlns=\"http://schemas.microsoft.com/WebPart/v2/ContentEditor\" />" +
         "<Content " +
            "xmlns=\"http://schemas.microsoft.com/WebPart/v2/ContentEditor\">" +
         "<![CDATA[<b>This is my custom editor web part!</b>]]></Content>" +
         "<PartStorage " +
            "xmlns=\"http://schemas.microsoft.com/WebPart/v2/ContentEditor\" />" +
         "</WebPart>";

    var oWebPartDef = this.limitedWebPartManager.importWebPart(xml);
    this.limitedWebPartManager.addWebPart(oWebPartDef.get_webPart(), "Left", 1);

    this.ctx.executeQueryAsync(
            Function.createDelegate(this, this.onSucceededCallback),
            Function.createDelegate(this, this.onFailedCallback));
}

function onSucceededCallback(sender, args) {

}
```

How to Delete a Web Part from a Page

The examples in this section show how to remove a Web Part from a page (see Listings 12-71 and 12-72).

Listing 12-71. *Deleting a Web Part from a Page (C#)*

```
public void Example27()
```

```
{
    ClientContext ctx = new ClientContext("http://clserver");
    Web oWeb = ctx.Web;

    File oFile = oWeb.GetFileByServerRelativeUrl("/default.aspx");
    LimitedWebPartManager limitedWebPartManager =
        oFile.GetLimitedWebPartManager(PersonalizationScope.Shared);

    ctx.Load(limitedWebPartManager.WebParts);
    ctx.ExecuteQuery();

    if (limitedWebPartManager.WebParts.Count == 0)
        throw new Exception("No web parts found");

    WebPartDefinition oWebPartDef = limitedWebPartManager.WebParts[0];
    oWebPartDef.DeleteWebPart();

    ctx.ExecuteQuery();
}
```

Accomplishing this in JavaScript is similar to changing Web Part properties. Again, you need two callback functions: one for querying the Web Parts on a page and another for deleting a Web Part (see Listing 12–72).

***Listing 12–72.** Deleting a Web Part from a Page (JavaScript)*

```
function example27() {
    this.ctx = new SP.ClientContext.get_current();
    this.oWeb = ctx.get_web();

    var oFile = oWeb.getFileByServerRelativeUrl("/default.aspx");
    this.limitedWebPartManager =
        oFile.getLimitedWebPartManager(SP.WebParts.PersonalizationScope.shared)

    this.ctx.load(this.limitedWebPartManager.get_webParts());

    this.ctx.executeQueryAsync(
            Function.createDelegate(this, this.deleteWebPart),
            Function.createDelegate(this, this.onFailedCallback));
}

function deleteWebPart() {

    if (this.limitedWebPartManager.get_webParts().get_count() == 0) {
        alert("No web parts found"); return;
    }

    var oWebPartDef = this.limitedWebPartManager.get_webParts().get_item(0);
    oWebPartDef.deleteWebPart();

    this.ctx.executeQueryAsync(
          Function.createDelegate(this, this.onSucceededCallback),
          Function.createDelegate(this, this.onFailedCallback));
```

```
}

function onSucceededCallback(sender, args) {

}
```

Advanced Examples

The previous sections contain many basic examples of working with the client object model. When developing professional applications, you quickly come to a point where you have to handle more complex requirements. This section some contains advanced coding examples that may help you in such situations:

- How to use exception-handling scope
- How to use conditional scope
- How to access large lists

How to Use Exception-Handling Scope

Dealing with exceptions can become very complex. The example in Listing 12–73 shows how you might use exceptions when working with the client object model. The example queries a list named `NonExistentList` and updates its `Description` property. When executing this code for the first time and assuming that the list does not exist, an exception will be thrown when calling `ExecuteQuery`. This exception will be caught, and within the `catch` block, this list will be created. Then, in the `finally` block, the list description property will be updated again.

Listing 12–73. *Using Normal Exception Handling—Not Recommended! (C#)*

```
public void Example28a()
{
    ClientContext ctx = new ClientContext("http://clserver");

    // Get list NonExistingList and update its description
    List myList = ctx.Web.Lists.GetByTitle("NonExistentList");
    myList.Description = "This is a new description";
    myList.Update();

    try
    {
        ctx.ExecuteQuery();
    }
    catch (Exception)
    {
        // Create new list NonExistingList
        ListCreationInformation listCreationInfo = new ListCreationInformation();
        listCreationInfo.Title = "NonExistingList";
        listCreationInfo.Description = "Created within catch block";
        listCreationInfo.TemplateType = (int)ListTemplateType.GenericList;
        List oList = ctx.Web.Lists.Add(listCreationInfo);

        ctx.ExecuteQuery();
```

```
    }
    finally
    {
        // Update description of list NonExistingList
        myList = ctx.Web.Lists.GetByTitle("NonExistingList");
        myList.Description = "This is a description created by the final block";
        myList.Update();

        ctx.ExecuteQuery();
    }
}
```

In the worst case, this example needs three server requests: one to query for the list, another to create the list, and a final one to update the description of this list. To overcome the need for multiple server requests, depending on exceptions, an `ExceptionHandlingScope` class has been introduced. This class includes methods to wrap code in a scope and handle exceptions that occur within the batch processing of the commands given to the `ClientContext` instance. Take a look at Listing 12–74. It is functionally equivalent to Listing 12–73, but requires only a single request to the server.

Listing 12–74. *Using Exception-Handling Scope (C#)*

```
public void Example28b()
{

    ClientContext ctx = new ClientContext("http://clserver");
    ExceptionHandlingScope exScope = new ExceptionHandlingScope(ctx);

    using (exScope.StartScope())
    {
        using (exScope.StartTry())
        {
            // Get list NonExistingList and update its description
            List myList = ctx.Web.Lists.GetByTitle("NonExistingList");
            myList.Description = "This is a new description";
            myList.Update();
        }

        using (exScope.StartCatch())
        {
            // Create new list NonExistingList
            ListCreationInformation listCreationInfo =
                                            new ListCreationInformation();
            listCreationInfo.Title = "NonExistingList";
            listCreationInfo.Description = "Created within catch block";
            listCreationInfo.TemplateType = (int)ListTemplateType.GenericList;
            List oList = ctx.Web.Lists.Add(listCreationInfo);
        }

        using (exScope.StartFinally())
        {
            // Update description of list NonExistingList
            List myList = ctx.Web.Lists.GetByTitle("NonExistingList");
            myList.Description = "This is a description created by the final block";
```

```
                myList.Update();
            }
        }

        ctx.ExecuteQuery();
}
```

The code looks much cleaner than Listing 12–73. The whole client code block is wrapped within an `ExceptionHandlingScope.StartScope` method, which defines the beginning of the client object operations. Then, each logical block (i.e. the blocks that retrieve, create, and update the list) is wrapped into its own scope operation (`StartTry`, `StartCatch`, and `StartFinally`). Only if an exception occurs within the `StartTry` code block will the `StartCatch` block be executed. The `StartFinally` code block will always be executed, irrespective of whether an exception occurs. In JavaScript code the exception handling looks quite similar, as shown in Listing 12–75.

■ **Caution** The program code wrapped in `ExceptionHandlingScope` methods such as `StartTry`, `StartCatch`, or `StartFinally` is always executed. Because the client object model collects the operations to be executed in a kind of queue, the `ExceuteQuery` method will decide internally whether to execute some client object operations.

Listing 12–75. *Using Exception-Handling Scope (JavaScript)*

```
function example28()
{
    this.ctx = new SP.ClientContext.get_current();
    var exScope = new SP.ExceptionHandlingScope(this.ctx);

    var startScope = exScope.startScope();

        var tryScope = exScope.startTry();
            // Get list NonExistingList and update its description
            var myList = ctx.get_web().get_lists().getByTitle("NonExistingList");
            myList.set_description("This is a new description");
            myList.update();
        tryScope.dispose();

        var catchScope = exScope.startCatch();
            // Create new list NonExistingList
            var listCreationInfo = new SP.ListCreationInformation();
            listCreationInfo.set_title("NonExistingList");
            listCreationInfo.set_description("Created within catch block");
            listCreationInfo.set_templateType(SP.ListTemplateType.genericList);
            ctx.get_web().get_lists().add(listCreationInfo);
        catchScope.dispose();

        var finallyScope = exScope.startFinally();
            // Update description of list NonExistingList
            var myList = ctx.get_web().get_lists().getByTitle("NonExistingList");
```

```
            myList.set_description("This is a description created
                                   by the final block");
            myList.update();
        finallyScope.dispose();

    startScope.dispose();

     this.ctx.executeQueryAsync(
            Function.createDelegate(this, this.onSucceededCallback),
            Function.createDelegate(this, this.onFailedCallback));
}
```

The usage of the ExceptionHandlingScope in JavaScript is nearly the same as in C#. Because there is no using construct in JavaScript, you have to dispose of the scope objects manually by calling scope.dispose.

How to Use Conditional Scope

In addition to ExceptionHandlingScope, the client object model provides another helpful construct: ConditionalScope. This scope is created using a Boolean LINQ expression. The client object model operations, wrapped in the scope, are only executed if the Boolean LINQ expression is true.

■ **Note** The JavaScript client object model does not include an equivalent for the ConditionalScope class in the .NET managed and Silverlight client object models.

The example in Listing 12–76 retrieves a list and then creates a ConditionalScope instance with the following condition:

```
oList.BaseTemplate == (int)ListTemplate.GenericList
```

Consequently, the code within the scope.StartScope method block is only executed if the list is of type ListTemplateType.GenericList.

Listing 12–76. Using Conditional Scope (C#)

```
public void Example29()
{
    ClientContext ctx = new ClientContext("http://clserver");
    Web oWeb = ctx.Web;
    List oList = oWeb.Lists.GetByTitle("Books");

    ConditionalScope scope = new ConditionalScope(ctx,
        () => oList.BaseTemplate == (int)ListTemplateType.GenericList);

    using (scope.StartScope())
    {
        // This code executes only if the list Books is of BaseType GenericList
        ctx.Load(oList, list => list.Title);
    }
```

```
    ctx.ExecuteQuery();

    if (scope.TestResult.Value == true)
    {
        Console.WriteLine("List '" + oList.Title + "' is of type 'GenericList'");
    }

}
```

Finally, by using the Boolean result value in `scope.TestResult.Value`, you can access the loaded list property `Title`. The `ConditionalScope` construct is intended for scenarios where you want to minimize the server round trips, and where it is possible to determine, prior to retrieving values, whether or not queries should be executed.

■ **Caution** Some actions, such as setting properties or invoking methods, are not allowed inside a conditional scope.

How to Access Large Lists

Handling lists containing several thousand list items has become quite normal in professional SharePoint usage scenarios. A common problem when working with large lists is the number of items to return in one query. The example in this section demonstrates how a paging mechanism with CAML can be implemented so that only a manageable quantity of items is returned. The first code section adds 20 items to the `Books` list. Multiple CAML queries are then executed within a loop (`while(true)`). The loop is executed until the `ListItemCollectionPosition` property of the returned `ListItemCollection` is `NULL`, indicating that there are no more results (see Listing 12–77).

***Listing 12–77.** Paging a Large List (C#)*

```
public void Example30()
{
    ClientContext ctx = new ClientContext("http://clserver");
    Web oWeb = ctx.Web;
    List oList = oWeb.Lists.GetByTitle("Books");

    // Adding some items to the list
    ListItemCreationInformation newItem = new ListItemCreationInformation();
    for (int i = 0; i < 20; i++)
    {
        ListItem listItem = oList.AddItem(newItem);
        listItem["Title"] = "New Book " + i;
        listItem.Update();
    }
    ctx.ExecuteQuery();


    ListItemCollectionPosition itemPosition = null;
    while (true)
```

```
    {
        CamlQuery camlQuery = new CamlQuery();

        // Setting the item position
        camlQuery.ListItemCollectionPosition = itemPosition;

        // Creating a CAML query with RowLimit=3
        camlQuery.ViewXml = @"<View>"
        + "<ViewFields><FieldRef Name='Title'/></ViewFields>"
        + "<RowLimit>3</RowLimit>"
        + "</View>";

        // Query and retrieve data
        ListItemCollection listItems = oList.GetItems(camlQuery);
        ctx.Load(listItems);
        ctx.ExecuteQuery();

        // Store position for next iteration
        itemPosition = listItems.ListItemCollectionPosition;

        // Print book titles to the console
        foreach (ListItem listItem in listItems)
            Console.WriteLine("  Book: " +  listItem["Title"]);

        // Exit this loop when no more pages are available
        if (itemPosition == null) break;

        Console.WriteLine(itemPosition.PagingInfo);
        Console.WriteLine();
    }
}
```

The console output of Listing 12–77 is reproduced in Figure 12–26. The JavaScript implementation works very similarly.

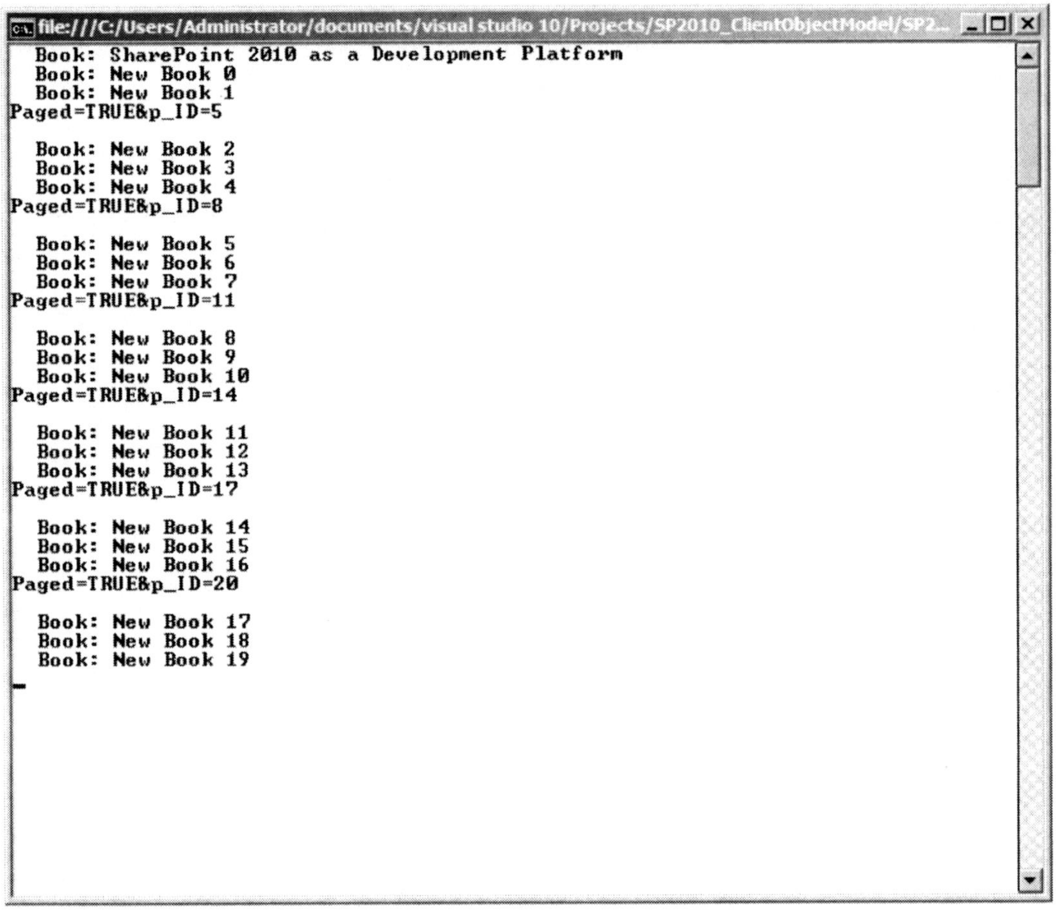

```
file:///C:/Users/Administrator/documents/visual studio 10/Projects/SP2010_ClientObjectModel/SP2...
   Book: SharePoint 2010 as a Development Platform
   Book: New Book 0
   Book: New Book 1
Paged=TRUE&p_ID=5

   Book: New Book 2
   Book: New Book 3
   Book: New Book 4
Paged=TRUE&p_ID=8

   Book: New Book 5
   Book: New Book 6
   Book: New Book 7
Paged=TRUE&p_ID=11

   Book: New Book 8
   Book: New Book 9
   Book: New Book 10
Paged=TRUE&p_ID=14

   Book: New Book 11
   Book: New Book 12
   Book: New Book 13
Paged=TRUE&p_ID=17

   Book: New Book 14
   Book: New Book 15
   Book: New Book 16
Paged=TRUE&p_ID=20

   Book: New Book 17
   Book: New Book 18
   Book: New Book 19
```

Figure 12–26. *Console output of the paging example*

Summary

This chapter covered the SharePoint 2010 client object model. It showed how client applications can be built using the .NET managed code model for .NET Windows applications or Silverlight applications. It also described in detail the use of the client object model for JavaScript.

You also learned about the two important frameworks for JavaScript: the Dialog framework and the Status and Notification framework. More than 30 real-world detailed examples and code snippets demonstrated how to develop code with the client object model.

CHAPTER 13

Integrating Silverlight

In this chapter we focus on the extension of SharePoint's UI using Silverlight. Silverlight is a platform and browser-independent implementation similar to WPF (Windows Presentation Foundation). Primarily, it's a browser plug-in that executes XAML (Extensible Application Markup Language) and code in a sandbox-like environment. The power and programming model of Silverlight together with the tight integration in SharePoint make it a first-choice tool to create business applications that were formerly built as Windows Forms programs.

In this chapter you will learn

- The architecture of Silverlight and the common programming style
- How to host Silverlight and deal with security issues
- How to integrate Silverlight projects into your SharePoint development experience
- How to access SharePoint data from Silverlight using the client object model

This chapter is not intended to teach Silverlight from the ground up, nor is it dedicated to the client object model. (For the latter, refer to Chapter 12.)

Introducing Silverlight

Strictly speaking, Silverlight is an autonomous technology that is independent of .NET. Silverlight uses its own runtime, which is available as a browser plug-in and a standalone runtime. Silverlight is a UI technology that far exceeds what you know from HTML, DHTML, and JavaScript. It has no dependencies on a specific browser, operating system, or processor architecture.

Common elements and the UI framework are based on XAML and use a similar approach to WPF. However, it is not a subset of WPF, and it is independent of it. From a developer's point of view, though, WPF and Silverlight are closely related technologies—if you know one, you know much about the other.

Note Even though Silverlight 4 is currently available, in this chapter we'll focus on the basic features available in version 3, too. Version 3 is the first version that is sufficiently complete to create real business applications, so we don't need to focus on the enhancements in version 4 with respect to SharePoint integration. However, version 4 has a number of significant features, such as printing and client device support, that make it the best choice for your project.

Being Prepared for Silverlight

Most of the support you need to work with Silverlight is provided by Visual Studio 2010 out of the box. Moreover, you don't need to install anything additional to host and use applications created with Visual Studio within SharePoint.

For a professional Silverlight development experience, we recommend you take a look at the free Silverlight Toolkit at `http://silverlight.codeplex.com/`. Microsoft posts new development cycles in early stages here regularly. Some of the controls appear later in the next release. This has happened already during the move from Silverlight 3, where some of the toolkit's controls are now available in the Silverlight 4 release.

The Architecture of Silverlight

Silverlight is not just a technology. It's also a way to interactively access content and media. You can create rich, platform-independent applications. Integrating Silverlight with SharePoint enables you to create Windows-like applications with comprehensive UIs, and still benefit from zero deployment. All this is built from a single development environment and with one set of programming languages (i.e., C#, and for certain tasks JavaScript). The big picture of the architecture is shown in Figure 13–1.

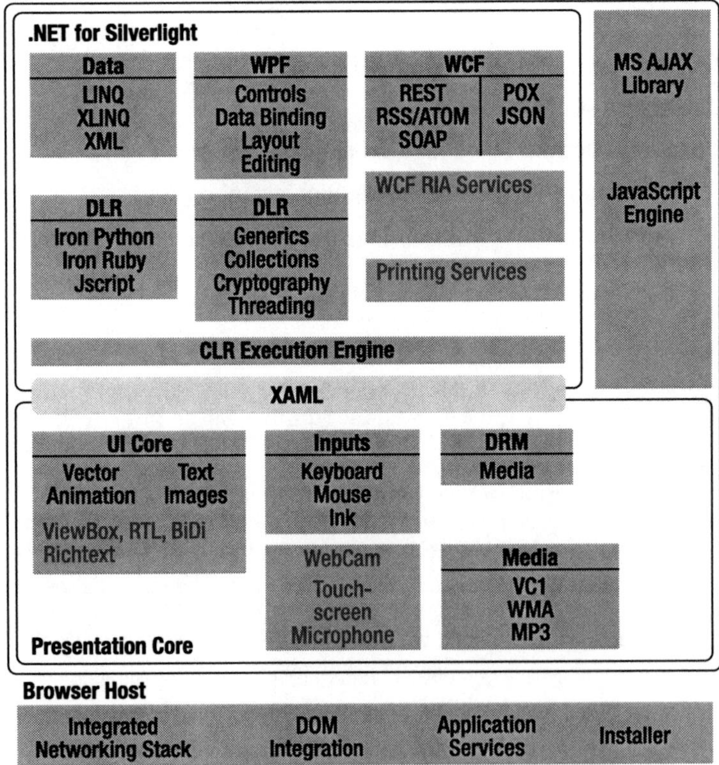

Figure 13–1. Silverlight architecture overview

The Client Library

At first glance, the client libraries appear to be merely a condensed version of the .NET Framework. However, the selection is quite clever, and you'll rarely miss anything you know from .NET. There are a few differences that can be annoying, and these differences highlight the fact that it's not a subset—it is in fact an independent framework.

The Silverlight framework is installed on the client as a plug-in. Some assemblies are only loaded when first requested from the server, to minimize the size of the initial download. The client now includes core components for Windows controls, network functions, base class libraries, garbage collection, and of course a CLR. Additional and optional components include assemblies from the SDK, LINQ to XML, syndication (RSS/Atom) support, XML serializing, and support for dynamic languages through the Dynamic Language Runtime (DLR). The DLR supports client programming using languages such as IronPython and IronRuby.

Essentially, the Silverlight CLR looks the same as the .NET CLR. Memory management, garbage collection, exception handling, and type safety are all handled in the same general manner.

The Core Libraries

The core libraries contain functions for string manipulation, regular expressions, input and output operations, reflection, collections, and localization. Some special libraries accompany this:

- *LINQ to XML*: This allows you to access XML files using LINQ, serialize objects as XML, and deserialize such data back into objects.
- *RSS/Atom*: This provides support for WCF services using HTTP or HTTPS. This includes RSS, Atom, JSON, POX (Plain Old XML), and SOAP services.
- *UI controls*: These are very similar to WPF and use the same XAML dialect for a declarative programming style. Controls such as `Button`, `Calendar`, `CheckBox`, `DataGrid`, `DatePicker`, `HyperlinkButton`, `ListBox`, `RadioButton`, and `ScrollViewer` are included.
- *Windows Media components*: There are several powerful controls within the presentation core to manage media, such as video and audio streams, on the client.

The Presentation Core

Silverlight has strong support for media and can access human interface devices, such as a mouse. Silverlight 4 has added support for webcam, microphone, and printer devices.

- *VC1, WMV, WMA, and MP3*: The presentation core renders images in various formats, and handles vector graphics, animations, and text. Furthermore, you can play videos and audio in such formats as VC1 and WMV, and play back audio encoded with WMA or MP3.
- *XAML*: The language that defines controls, a layout manager, and data binding support to create rich UIs. If you know XAML from WPF, it's easy to work with Silverlight.
- *DRM (digital rights management)*: The integrated media player supports rights management so that media can be played with such restrictions.

Silverlight and XAML

There is no Silverlight without XAML. Silverlight pushes the UI envelope and enables creating sophisticated UIs. (From the user's perspective, the success of each enhancement you build will be judged on your UI design.) This section introduces creating a UI for SharePoint, such as a Web Part.

■ **Tip** If you need more detailed information, please refer to a book dedicated to Silverlight, such as *Pro Silverlight 3 in C#*, by Matthew MacDonald (Apress, 2009).

Describing a Silverlight UI Using XAML

In simple terms, you can consider XAML to be a method to serialize objects with all their properties. It provides a way to divide the business logic from the UI. XAML is based on XML and describes a UI declaratively. It extends XML in a way as well, as the inner structure of attributes and the naming schema of elements have special meaning that's well defined. Technically, XAML represents an object hierarchy, which means it can express whatever you can describe using classes and properties in classic programming languages such as C#.

XAML is used to describe the appearance, behavior, and properties of UI elements such as buttons. Everything you see is an element. That includes, for instance, such things as simple text. You often have two ways to describe elements: either declaratively as a single element, or through extended attributes.

The declarative approach looks like elements in HTML:

```
<Button >
</Button>
```

Many elements can contain other elements. A grid can contain buttons, for instance. If an element has no child elements, the short syntax is equally valid:

```
<Grid>
   <Button />
</Grid>
```

The attribute syntax uses attributes to further describe an element. To name an element, the `Name` or `x:Name` attribute is employed. Naming techniques are briefly described in the sidebar "Confusing Name vs. x:Name Resolver," later in this section.

As another example, the attribute `Background` defines the background:

```
<Grid Name="LayoutRoot" Background="White">
   <Button Name="NiceButton" Background="Green" />
</Grid>
```

However, elements such as a grid can be amazingly complex. With dozens of attributes, grids can be hard to read and impossible to format properly. Therefore, you can use the element property syntax that expresses attributes with complex values as child elements:

```
<Rectangle  Width="100"  Height="100">
  <Rectangle.Fill>
    <SolidColorBrush Color="Blue"/>
  </Rectangle.Fill>
</Rectangle>
```

This example creates a 100-by-100-pixel rectangle. It is filled with a solid brush. The property Fill is assigned the color blue. This format is optional for simple attributes and mandatory for complex values that you can't express as strings. This syntax avoids using impractical object formatters serializing .NET objects in ways that humans reading the code can't interpret well.

Some of these attributes accept collections. For example, gradients may accept more than one value. A gradient collection includes all stop points where the value changes.

```
<LinearGradientBrush>
  <LinearGradientBrush.GradientStops>
    <GradientStop Offset="0.0" Color="Red" />
    <GradientStop Offset="1.0" Color="Blue" />
  </LinearGradientBrush.GradientStops>
</LinearGradientBrush>
```

The parser will implicitly recognize the collection. However, you can also explicitly add the appropriate collection element:

```
<LinearGradientBrush>
  <LinearGradientBrush.GradientStops>
    <GradientStopCollection>
      <GradientStop Offset="0.0" Color="Red" />
      <GradientStop Offset="1.0" Color="Blue" />
    </GradientStopCollection>
  </LinearGradientBrush.GradientStops>
</LinearGradientBrush>
```

This simply improves readability; it does not change the code produced by the parser. In the same way, designer tools may output different markup than what you would write by hand. This sometimes makes it hard to read and understand code you did not write.

The previous sample looks rather verbose. Since all the values are unambiguous, you may presume that there is an implicit way to create elements, which is true:

```
<LinearGradientBrush>
  <GradientStop Offset="0.0" Color="Red" />
  <GradientStop Offset="1.0" Color="Blue" />
</LinearGradientBrush>
```

For experienced developers, the next example looks better because it is clearly laid out. A StackPanel element creates a stack of elements—one above another. The explicit and complete declaration looks like this:

```
<StackPanel>
  <StackPanel.Children>
    <UIElementCollection>
       <TextBlock>Hello</TextBlock>
       <TextBlock>World</TextBlock>
    </UIElementCollection>
  </StackPanel.Children>
</StackPanel>
```

However, the implicit declaration is cleaner:

```
<StackPanel>
  <TextBlock>Hello</TextBlock>
  <TextBlock>World</TextBlock>
</StackPanel>
```

You have to know while writing XAML code that a `StackPanel` does not have a child element or property that takes a collection of `TextBlock` elements. The earlier code reveals that it has a property `Children` that takes an object of type `UIElementCollection`, which is obviously a parent in the `TextBlock`'s inheritance hierarchy. IntelliSense is not so much help during your coding experience either, as it gives often far more options than you need.

CONFUSING NAME VS. X:NAME RESOLVER

In the examples in this chapter, we use both `Name` and `x:Name` to name elements. The support of two naming schemas for Silverlight elements may sound confusing. While this is an advanced Silverlight topic that's beyond the scope of this book, you should at least know when you have to use what name attribute and when it doesn't matter.

The `Name` attribute is exposed by some elements as a dependency property (a property type that's routed through the element hierarchy). In most cases, the `Name` attribute satisfies the need to give an element a unique name to make it accessible in code. However, some elements, such as those used for animations and storyboards, require having no name. Internally, the property is used by the animation code to address the element. If you need programmatic access anyway, `x:Name` is the alternative method. However, finding elements based on its name using a method such as `FindName`, is based upon `Name`, not `x:Name`.

For beginners, there are few simple rules. First, you can't use both for the same element. Either use `Name` or `x:Name`. Second, for most elements covered in this chapter, it doesn't matter what you use. (Advanced scenarios where it matters are not discussed here.) Third, you can only set the `x:Name` attribute in XAML. The MSBuild preprocessor that creates the elements uses this attribute to name the object that represents the element. `Name`, on the other hand, is a property you can set a value to if you create such an element at runtime. However, modifying the `Name` property at runtime for elements that exists in XAML results in unpredictable behavior.

Because the `Name` and `x:Name` literals are finally object names, they follow the naming rules of .NET objects. They must begin with a letter or underscore, followed by letters, digits, or underscores. They should never be localized. Finally, you should never read and use the `Name` property as part of your UI—treat it as internal only.

Events

There is no UI without interaction. Interaction means that events are fired from user operations—most commonly mouse clicks and key presses—and that handlers perform some custom action in direct response. You can declare the standard click event for a `Button` element like this:

```
<Button x:Name="MyButton" Width="60" Height="20" Click="MyButton_Click">
      <TextBlock x:Name="MyButtonCaption">Click Me</TextBlock>
</Button>
```

Just like in ASP.NET, you need to add code to the code-behind file associated with your XAML to create the handler:

```
private void MyButton_Click(object sender, RoutedEventArgs e)
{
   MyButtonCaption.Text = "Clicked";
}
```

Alternatively, you could add the same handler in your code, in the same style as any .NET event handler:

```
public Page()
{
   InitializeComponent();
   MyButton.Click +=new RoutedEventHandler(MyButton_Click);
}
```

Routed Events

The Silverlight event model is more sophisticated than the event model in ASP.NET. Some events support so-called *routing*. To understand this, you need to know that UI elements can form a stack—elements within elements, many levels deep. For example, a `Canvas` can contain a `Grid`, which may have some cells that have `TextBox` and `Button` elements. Each element may have the ability to receive a left mouse button click, for instance. The element next to the surface receives an event, such as a mouse click. This element may route the event to the elements underneath it. It depends on what you want to do and what, if any, element in the hierarchy handles this event. Not all events support routing. In Silverlight, support for routing is provided by these events:

- `KeyDown`
- `KeyUp`
- `GotFocus`
- `LostFocus`
- `MouseLeftButtonDown`
- `MouseLeftButtonUp`
- `MouseMove`
- `BindingValidationError`

The routing of events from the surface (canvas) to the top element is called *bubbling up*—just like a bubble in water. Since several elements in a sequence of events can typically handle a particular event, the `Handled` property is there to inform the other elements that the event has been handled—it stops events from bubbling up. Following is an example:

```
private void BubbleUp_MouseMove(object sender, MouseButtonEventArgs e)
{
   e.Handled = true;
   string msg = "x:y = " + e.GetPosition(null).ToString();
   msg += " from " + (e.OriginalSource as FrameworkElement).Name;
   StatusText.Text = msg;
}
```

If there are no other handler methods, there is no need to cancel bubbling. Thus, routed events are easier than you might imagine at first.

The Layout Manager

Laying out elements on a screen may sound easy. But when you consider the vast number of properties you can set for each element, it quickly becomes complex. A layout manager is used to arrange the elements. Silverlight has three such managers: the canvas layout manager, the grid layout manager, and the stack panel manager. You can nest these within each other to create complex layouts.

Grid Layout

Grid layout has the appearance and behavior of a table. If you understand HTML tables, then you should easily understand the essentials of grid layout. When you first define a grid, it has one cell. The basic template for a new Silverlight application within Visual Studio uses exactly this approach to produce a simple layout container, as follows:

```
<Grid x:Name="LayoutRoot" Background="White">
   <Button x:Name="MyButton" Width="60" Height="20" Click="MyButton_Click" >
   </Button>
</Grid>
```

Of course, you can also define any number of rows and columns. Extended attributes such as Grid.ColumnSpan used in child elements modify the layout.

```
<Grid ShowGridLines="True" x:Name="LayoutRoot" Background="White" >
   <Grid.RowDefinitions>
     <RowDefinition />
     <RowDefinition />
     <RowDefinition />
   </Grid.RowDefinitions>
   <Grid.ColumnDefinitions>
     <ColumnDefinition />
     <ColumnDefinition />
   </Grid.ColumnDefinitions>
   <Button x:Name="MyButton" Width="60" Height="20" Content="Click Me"
           Click="MyButton_Click" Grid.Column="1" Grid.Row="1" />
   <TextBlock x:Name="StatusText" Grid.ColumnSpan="2" />
</Grid>
```

Column and row definitions add elements within the grid. The ShowGridLines property is very helpful—it reveals the layout, even at design time (see Figure 13–2). You can remove the gridlines later when the page layout is completed.

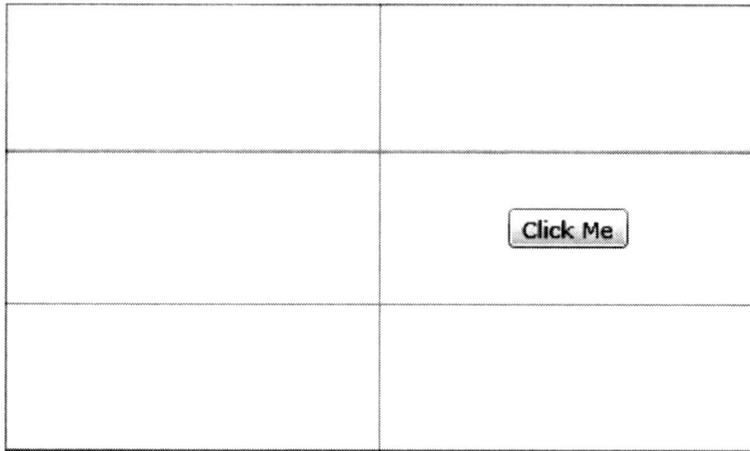

Figure 13–2. The grid layout with visible gridlines

The previous examples have cells of uniform size. However, you can set the cell size relative to its neighbors or to absolute values. Child elements can be defined in any order. The specific cell in which they appear is determined using the `Grid.Row` and `Grid.Column` attributes.

The next example shows how to specify explicit widths and heights:

```
<Grid>
  <Grid.RowDefinitions>
      <RowDefinition />
      <RowDefinition Height="20" />
      <RowDefinition />
    </Grid.RowDefinitions>
    <Grid.ColumnDefinitions>
      <ColumnDefinition Width="40"/>
      <ColumnDefinition />
    </Grid.ColumnDefinitions>
</Grid>
```

The rows and columns that do not have assigned values use the remaining space equally. Using the explicit value `Auto` ensures that the cell is extended until all elements fit into it. Relative values use an asterisk to express relationships:

```
<Grid ShowGridLines="True" x:Name="LayoutRoot" Background="White" >
    <Grid.RowDefinitions>
      <RowDefinition Height="3*" MinHeight="30" MaxHeight="600"/>
      <RowDefinition Height="20" />
      <RowDefinition Height="*"/>
    </Grid.RowDefinitions>
    <Grid.ColumnDefinitions>
      <ColumnDefinition Width="40"/>
      <ColumnDefinition />
    </Grid.ColumnDefinitions>
</Grid>
```

The value 3* means that this row takes a space that is three times what it would take if the space were shared equally. A single * simply indicates "the remaining space" (see Figure 13–3).

Figure 13–3. Grid layout with relative values

Canvas Layout

A canvas is used to arrange elements in absolute positions. The tricky aspect is that each element passes its positional data to the layout manager instead of having its own properties, such as Top and Left. Instead, Canvas.Top and Canvas.Left are used:

```
<Canvas Background="White">
    <Rectangle Canvas.Left="50" Canvas.Top="50" Width="120" Height="60" >
      <Rectangle.Fill>
        <LinearGradientBrush>
          <GradientStop Offset="0.0" Color="White" />
          <GradientStop Offset="1.0" Color="Black" />
        </LinearGradientBrush>
      </Rectangle.Fill>
    </Rectangle>
</Canvas>
```

You can read this syntax as "layout manager, place me at x,y." The result is displayed in Figure 13–4.

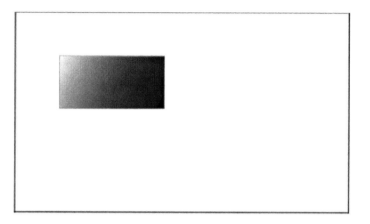

Figure 13–4. A gradient brush placed somewhere in the middle of a canvas

The StackPanel Layout

This is the simplest manager. It forms a stack of elements, one after another. The stack starts at the top border.

```
<StackPanel Orientation="Vertical" >
    <Button Width="90" Content="Hello World 1"></Button>
    <Button Width="90" Content="Hello World 2"></Button>
    <Button Width="90" Content="Hello World 3"></Button>
</StackPanel>
```

The `Orientation` attribute can orient the stack from left to right, instead of the default, top to bottom (the default is shown in Figure 13–5).

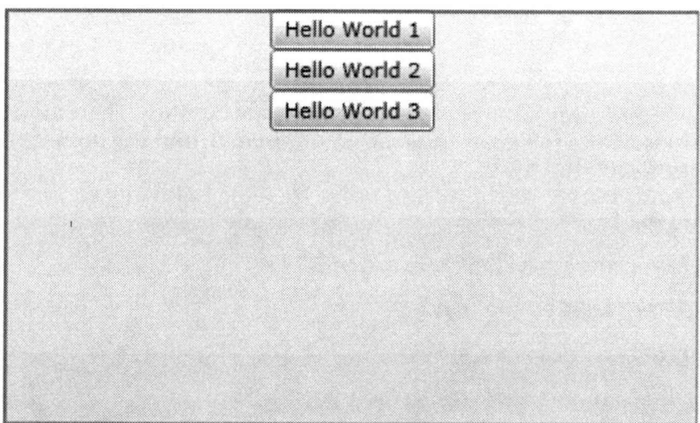

Figure 13–5. StackPanel with three buttons

Silverlight Hosting and Distribution

Silverlight applications are independent of the .NET Framework. As a result, you can use the Silverlight version you prefer. Currently, Silverlight 3 and the next major release, Silverlight 4, are both available. Whether you use .NET 3.5 for your SharePoint applications is immaterial. The following description and examples run equally well with Silverlight 3 and Silverlight 4.

Setup and Deployment

There is no explicit configuration step for Silverlight. SharePoint uses Silverlight internally, and you can use it without configuring any further settings. However, there are some security settings to consider, because Silverlight applications run on the client, and you need to ensure that it has appropriate access rights.

Treat Silverlight as an External Application

One of the first things you should decide upon when using Silverlight is where to place the XAP files, which are the files by which Silverlight applications are deployed. XAP files are zipped containers that contain the XAML code, the compiled assembly, any additional assemblies you have referenced in your project, and a manifest file. XAP files are usually placed in one of the following:

- A document library
- The 14 hive, somewhere in the `LAYOUTS` folder
- A local directory (within `C:\inetpub\wwwroot\wss\VirtualDirectories\`) or the global `ClientBin` directory (within the `LAYOUTS` folder)

Putting the XAP files in a document library is usually the most flexible option, as you have a simple UI to manage the XAP files used within all your applications. In the 14 hive, you should place the files in `TEMPLATE\LAYOUTS`, within a separate folder to avoid conflicts with other applications. Placing them in the `ClientBin` directory is best practice, however, as it gives the XAP files a distinct location.

Cross-Domain Security

By default, you can call from your Silverlight application to services within the same domain. This can cause problems, because the current domain is where the executable (XAP) originated, and the domain where the service is running may not necessarily be the same.

If your XAP file is placed at `http://sharepointserve/XapFiles/app1.xap`, then the following service locations will result in cross-domain security issues:

- `https://sharepointserve`: Different protocol (HTTPS instead of HTTP)
- `http://my.sharepointserve`: Different subdomain (`my`)
- `http://sharepointserver`: Different host (`serve` vs. `server`)
- `http://sharepointserve:8080`: Different port (80 is the default port)

Managing the Client-Access Policy

Silverlight clients are powerful applications. Even if you intend to support your own clients only, technically any Silverlight application can potentially access your services. The cross-domain access, outlined previously, can be benign—or malicious, if an attacker tries to get access. A client-access policy file is used to control what particular actions clients are allowed to perform to what specific addresses. The client-access file is read by the client and probably cached. If you plan to change the settings, we recommend that you switch off browser caching to prevent the browser from persisting an out-of-date version. If you wish to host services with different security claims, consider placing them in different domains. This allows you to use different domain-based security policies (see Listing 13–1).

Listing 13–1. *A clientaccesspolicy.xml File That Allows Access to Services From Any Domain*

```
<?xml version="1.0" encoding="utf-8"?>
<access-policy>
  <cross-domain-access>
    <policy>
      <allow-from http-request-headers="*">
        <domain uri="*"/>
      </allow-from>
      <grant-to>
        <resource path="/" include-subpaths="true"/>
      </grant-to>
    </policy>
  </cross-domain-access>
</access-policy>
```

■ **Tip** The complete schema of the `clientaccesspolicy.xml` can be found at `http://msdn.microsoft.com/en-us/library/cc645032(v=VS.95).aspx.`

Listing 13–2 shows a sample client-access policy file from Microsoft's Contoso samples that illustrates several interesting points.

Listing 13–2. *A ClientAccessPolicy.xml File That Supports Two Policies*

```
<?xml version="1.0" encoding="utf-8"?>
  <access-policy>
    <cross-domain-access>
      <policy>
        <allow-from http-request-headers="SOAPAction">
          <domain uri="*"/>
        </allow-from>
        <grant-to>
          <resource path="/services/" include-subpaths="true"/>
        </grant-to>
     </policy>
      <policy >
        <allow-from http-methods="*">
          <domain uri="www.contoso.com"/>
```

```
      </allow-from>
      <grant-to>
        <resource path="/services/" include-subpaths="true"/>
      </grant-to>
    </policy>
  </cross-domain-access>
</access-policy>
```

The example has two policies. The first enables GET and POST requests from all callers to the path within the current domain. The `Content-type` header of each request must be set to `SOAPAction`. This is a common way to restrict calls to only the specific headers your application supports. The second policy permits all HTTP verbs to access the specified domain including the service path. As shown, several attributes allow wildcards. Wildcards are allowed on each level. If you want to allow all protocols, * will accomplish that, while `http://*` will allow all domains with the HTTP protocol. Even a subdomain can be expressed by using something like `http://*.mydomain.com`.

■ **Note** You may have heard that you should add a similar file to manage client access policies called `crossdomain.xml`. This file indeed has the same intention; however, it is dedicated to supporting Adobe Flash applications. If you plan to create a pure Silverlight environment, you won't need such a file.

Placing the ClientAccessPolicy.xml

The first question arises when you try to copy the `clientaccesspolicy.xml` file somewhere. The position of the XAP files is unimportant, as it is the page that calls them. Silverlight establishes its own request channel to the server. This goes to the root of that web if the page that hosts your application is running within a specific web. To reach this, you need to deploy your `clientaccesspolicy.xml` file to the virtual directory—for example:

```
c:\inetpub\wwwroot\wss\virtualdirectories\80
```

If you receive a security exception when running a Silverlight application, you can use *Fiddler* to check the requests your client made. This usually reveals where the plug-in is looking for the file.

Creating an HTTP Request Forwarder

As explained earlier, Silverlight cannot make cross-domain requests. If your application needs to communicate with a server on another domain, its requests must first be sent to a request-forwarding handler that is in the same domain as the application. The handler can then repackage the request and send it to the destination in the external domain.
Creating a request forwarder is a common task. Most of the logic needed by the handler is in the `RequestForwarder` class. The handler class you create is a kind of wrapper around this class. A handler can be built using the Generic Http Handler template. The complete code is shown in Listing 13–3.

Listing 13–3. *A Forwarder Handler to Overcome Cross-Domain Blocking*

```
<%@ WebHandler Language="C#" Class="SharePointForwarder" %>
using System;
using System.Web;
using Microsoft.SharePoint.Client;
```

```
public class ToSharePointForwarder : IHttpHandler
{

  public bool IsReusable
  {
    get { return false; }
  }
  public void ProcessRequest (HttpContext context)
  {
    RequestForwarder forwarder = new RequestForwarder(context);
    if (!String.IsNullOrEmpty(forwarder.Url))
    {
        forwarder.WebRequest.Credentials
            = new System.Net.NetworkCredential("MySilverlightApp",
                                               "username",
                                               "password");
        forwarder.ProcessRequest();
    }
  }
}
```

In fact, the only operation the handler performs is adding proper network credentials—Silverlight isn't permitted to add these to the requests automatically. The handler must now be activated using External Application XML through the External Application Provider (EAP). The `RequestForwarder` class is defined in `Microsoft.SharePoint.Client.dll`. Hence, this assembly must be referenced in the project.

Activating the Handler Using an External Application Provider

The markup that controls the EAP provides information to SharePoint about a Silverlight application that is hosted in a Web Part. It is only required if the Silverlight application is hosted on a different domain and accesses data from the SharePoint web site, as shown in the previous section. The information in the markup consists of

- Information about the Silverlight application and the credentials it uses to retrieve data from the SharePoint web sites services
- Properties that describe the Web Part that hosts the Silverlight application
- Custom information that can be used if you provide a custom EAP

There are several ways to assign the markup to the Web Part. If you plan to deploy the Web Part to end users, the EAP XML file must be deployed as a file. The users will need some instruction on how to modify and add it using the SharePoint UI. This might require local modifications to this file. You can also use the Application XML property within the Web Part markup of a module, available in a feature definition (`elements.xml`) or site definition (`onet.xml`) file respectively. You can set the `ApplicationXml` property programmatically in a `FeatureInstalled` or `FeatureActivated` event handler, which provides the most flexibility but requires the most effort. It is, however, the preferred method for developers.

The basic structure of an EAP XML file is shown in Listing 13–4.

Listing 13–4. *A Typical EAP XML File (from MSDN/Contoso Project)*

```
<?xml version='1.0' encoding='utf-16'?>
<applicationParts xmlns='http://schemas.microsoft.com/sharepoint/2009/fluidapp'>
```

```
  <applicationPart>
    <metaData>
      <applicationId>00000000-0000-0000-0000-000000000000</applicationId>
      <applicationUrl>http://www.contoso.com/someapplication.xap</applicationUrl>
      <principal>domain\username</principal>
      <sharepointRequestHandlerUrl>/sp.ashx</sharepointRequestHandlerUrl>
    </metaData>
    <data>
      <webPartProperties>
        <property name='Title'>Title</property>
        <property name='Description'>Description</property>
        <property name='WindowlessMode'>TRUE</property>
        <property name='Height'>200px</property>
        <property name='Width'>100px</property>
        <property name='HelpUrl'>
           http://www.contoso.com/someapplication/help.aspx
        </property>
        <property name='HelpMode'>Modal</property>
        <property name='Direction'>NotSet</property>
        <property name='MinRuntimeVersion'>3.0</property>
      </webPartProperties>
      <customProperties>
        <property name='CustomPropertyName'>CustomPropertyInfo </property>
      </customProperties>
    </data>
  </applicationPart>
</applicationParts>
```

If you plan to add this as part of either element.xml or onet.xml, you must treat it as embedded XML. That means that the tags do not match the CAML schema, and must be escaped using the < and > literal entities within a CDATA section, as shown in Listing 13–5.

Listing 13–5. *An Embedded EAP XML File*

```
<AllUsersWebPart WebPartZoneID="Top_Right" WebPartOrder="2">
<![CDATA[
<webParts>
  <webPart xmlns="http://schemas.microsoft.com/WebPart/v3">
    <metaData>
      <type name="Microsoft.SharePoint.WebPartPages.SilverlightWebPart,
                  Microsoft.SharePoint, Version=14.0.0.0, Culture=neutral,
                  PublicKeyToken=94de0004b6e3fcc5" />
      <importErrorMessage>Cannot import this Web Part.</importErrorMessage>
    </metaData>
    <data>
      <properties>
        <property name="ChromeType" type="chrometype">Default</property>
        <property name="Height" type="unit">600px</property>
        <property name="Url" type="string" />
        <property name="HelpMode" type="helpmode">Navigate</property>
        <property name="ApplicationXml" type="string">
&lt;?xml version="1.0" encoding="utf-8"?&gt;
&lt;applicationParts xmlns="http://schemas.microsoft.com/sharepoint/2009/fluidapp"&gt;
  &lt;applicationPart&gt;
```

```
      &lt;metaData&gt;
        &lt;applicationId&gt;
            00000000-0000-0000-000000000000-0000
        &lt;/applicationId&gt;
        &lt;applicationUrl&gt;
           http://server/ClientBin/SomeApplication.xap
        &lt;/applicationUrl&gt;
        &lt;principal&gt;domain\ContosoApp&lt;/principal&gt;
        &lt;sharepointRequestHandlerUrl&gt;
            /ReqForwarder.ashx
        &lt;/sharepointRequestHandlerUrl&gt;
      &lt;/metaData&gt;
    &lt;/applicationPart&gt;
&lt;/applicationParts&gt;</property>
          <property name="Hidden" type="bool">False</property>
          <property name="Title" type="string" />
        </properties>
      </data>
    </webPart>
</webParts>
]]>
</AllUsersWebPart>
```

While this may look strange, it's a common technique you can find in several `onet.xml` files that ship with SharePoint. A description of each of the EAP XML file's elements is given in Table 13–1.

***Table 13–1.** The EAP XML file's Elements*

Element	Description
`applicationId`	GUID of the application
`applicationPart`	Element that defines one external application
`applicationParts`	Root element
`applicationUrl`	Absolute URL to the Silverlight XAP file
`customProperties`	Properties that a custom EAP supports
`data`	Root element for additional data
`metadata`	Container for metadata
`principal`	User account including the domain name, such as `apress.com\jkrause`
`property`	Any public property that the Web Part base class provides
`sharepointRequestHandlerUrl`	The HTTP handler that forwards the request from the outside world into SharePoint
`webPartProperties`	Root element for the Web Part configuration section

Integrating Silverlight

Once your Silverlight application (XAP file) is completed and deployed where a client can read it, you need to decide where to use it. What sort of project type you use for the Silverlight project (refer to Figure 13–6) doesn't matter. Hence, none of the options shown have any advantage for SharePoint projects. You don't even need to host the XAP file. However, it's sometimes helpful to debug your code outside of SharePoint.

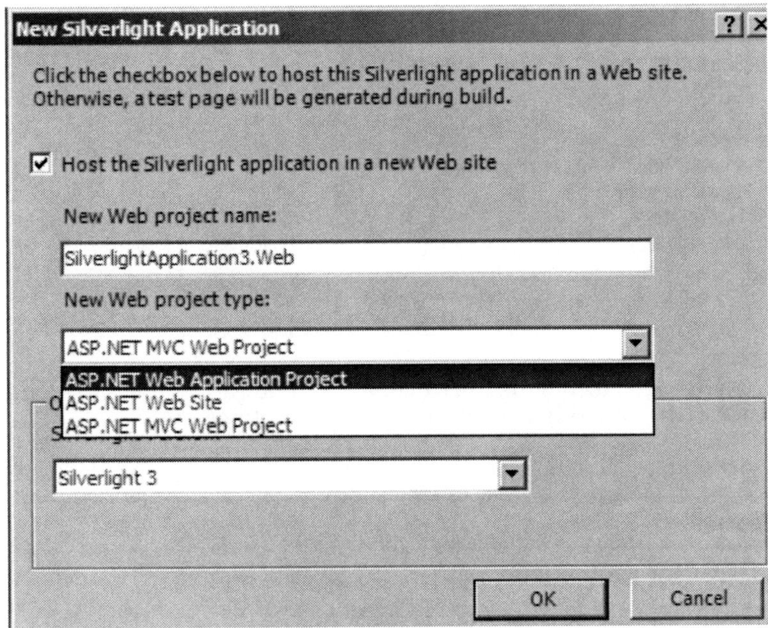

Figure 13–6. Options available for Silverlight projects

For pure Silverlight projects, it's OK to uncheck the "Host the Silverlight application in a new Web site" option shown in Figure 13–6. If you debug such a project, Visual Studio will use a static HTML file to host the control. Hosting and debugging in the context of a static HTML file is a lean and fast way to develop isolated Silverlight applications. In the project settings, you should additionally consider changing the output path that the XAP file is copied to or adding a postbuild command that copies the file where SharePoint can find it. For hosting purposes, these three options are available:

- In an application page
- In a Web Part
- As a list object/control or custom field type

Using the Silverlight Web Part is the easiest way to integrate Silverlight with SharePoint. It's new in SharePoint 2010 and provides simple integration without any additional effort. However, it does have some limitations. The underlying class is marked `sealed`, so you can't extend the existing class. We'll examine some ways in this chapter to overcome this limitation.

Using Silverlight in an Application Page

Using Silverlight within a Web Part is good for small solutions. It is even good if you want your users have the power to use one or another piece of Silverlight. For a complete application made with Silverlight an application page is the better choice. Because the built-in Web Part can't be used you must create a few lines of code to get your application running as shown in Listing 13–6.

Listing 13–6. *An Application Page Skeleton*

```
<%@ Assembly Name="$SharePoint.Project.AssemblyFullName$" %>
<%@ Import Namespace="Microsoft.SharePoint.ApplicationPages" %>
<%@ Register TagPrefix="SharePoint" Namespace="Microsoft.SharePoint.WebControls"
             Assembly="Microsoft.SharePoint, Version=14.0.0.0, Culture=neutral,
                       PublicKeyToken=71e9bce111e9429c" %>
<%@ Register TagPrefix="Utilities" Namespace="Microsoft.SharePoint.Utilities"
             Assembly="Microsoft.SharePoint, Version=14.0.0.0, Culture=neutral,
                       PublicKeyToken=71e9bce111e9429c" %>
<%@ Register TagPrefix="asp" Namespace="System.Web.UI"
             Assembly="System.Web.Extensions, Version=3.5.0.0, Culture=neutral,
                       PublicKeyToken=31bf3856ad364e35" %>
<%@ Import Namespace="Microsoft.SharePoint" %>
<%@ Assembly Name="Microsoft.Web.CommandUI, Version=14.0.0.0, Culture=neutral,
                    PublicKeyToken=71e9bce111e9429c" %>

<%@ Page Language="C#" AutoEventWireup="true" CodeBehind="SilverlightPage.aspx.cs"
         Inherits="Apress.SP2010.SilverlightApps.
                    Layouts.SilverlightAppPage.SilverlightPage"
         DynamicMasterPageFile="~masterurl/default.master" %>

<asp:Content ID="PageHead" ContentPlaceHolderID="PlaceHolderAdditionalPageHead"
             runat="server">
    <script type="text/javascript" src="Silverlight.js"></script>
    <script type="text/javascript">
        function onSilverlightError(sender, args) {
            var appSource = "";
            if (sender != null && sender != 0) {
                appSource = sender.getHost().Source;
            }

            var errorType = args.ErrorType;
            var iErrorCode = args.ErrorCode;

            if (errorType == "ImageError" || errorType == "MediaError") {
                return;
            }

            var errMsg = "Unhandled Error in Silverlight Application "
                     + appSource + "\n";

            errMsg += "Code: " + iErrorCode + "    \n";
            errMsg += "Category: " + errorType + "       \n";
            errMsg += "Message: " + args.ErrorMessage + "     \n";

            if (errorType == "ParserError") {
```

```
                errMsg += "File: " + args.xamlFile + "     \n";
                errMsg += "Line: " + args.lineNumber + "     \n";
                errMsg += "Position: " + args.charPosition + "     \n";
            }
            else if (errorType == "RuntimeError") {
                if (args.lineNumber != 0) {
                    errMsg += "Line: " + args.lineNumber + "     \n";
                    errMsg += "Position: " + args.charPosition + "     \n";
                }
                errMsg += "MethodName: " + args.methodName + "     \n";
            }

            throw new Error(errMsg);
        }
    </script>
</asp:Content>
<asp:Content ID="Main" ContentPlaceHolderID="PlaceHolderMain" runat="server">
   <div id="silverlightControlHost">
      <object data="data:application/x-silverlight-2,"
              type="application/x-silverlight-2" width="100%" height="100%">
         <param name="source" value="ClientBin/HelloWorld.xap"/>
         <param name="onError" value="onSilverlightError" />
         <param name="background" value="white" />
         <param name="minRuntimeVersion" value="3.0.40818.0" />
         <param name="autoUpgrade" value="true" />
         <a href="http://go.microsoft.com/fwlink/?LinkID=149156&v=3.0.40818.0"
            style="text-decoration:none">
           <img src="http://go.microsoft.com/fwlink/?LinkId=161376"
                alt="Get Microsoft Silverlight"
                style="border-style:none"/>
         </a>
    </object>
    <iframe id="_sl_historyFrame"
            style="visibility:hidden;height:0px;width:0px;border:0px">
    </iframe>
  </div>
</asp:Content>
<asp:Content ID="PageTitle" ContentPlaceHolderID="PlaceHolderPageTitle"
             runat="server">
    Application Page Silverlight HelloWorld
</asp:Content>
<asp:Content ID="PageTitleInTitleArea"
             ContentPlaceHolderID="PlaceHolderPageTitleInTitleArea"
             runat="server">
    Application Page Silverlight HelloWorld
</asp:Content>
```

To run Silverlight, you need a container to host the plug-in. This is the `<div>` container with the ID of `silverlightControlHost`. The JavaScript in the head area serves as an interface to the browser's UI, while the `Silverlight.js` file is responsible for loading and invoking the code. The JavaScript shown exposes error messages to the browser. This is necessary in case the plug-in can't produce any useful UI. The link around the `<img>` element with the URL pointing to `go.microsoft.com` produces the alternative HTML shown when the Silverlight plug-in is not present, and offers the user the option to download the plug-in. However, you can place any HTML here, such as another version of your application not using Silverlight.

■ **Caution** Downloading the Silverlight plug-in from any source other than Microsoft is not permitted. This ensures that users get the latest version at any time, including the most recent security updates.

The XAP file (`ClientBin/HelloWorld.xap` in the example) is defined in a `<param>` element. The `<object>` tag inside the `<div>` element passes parameters to the application. Table 13–2 shows the available options.

***Table 13–2.** Parameter Options to Control the Silverlight Plug-In*

Parameter	Description
`allowHtmlPopupWindow`	Allows the creation of new pop-up windows from Silverlight.
`autoUpgrade`	Upgrades the Silverlight plug-in if a newer version is required.
`background`	The background color of the rectangle the plug-in appears in.
`enableautozoom`	Enables zoom controlled by the host (browser's zoom).
`enableCacheVisualization`	Creates a colored overlay to check what parts are GPU (Graphics Processing Unit, the processor on the graphics board) accelerated. This is for development purposes only and should never be used in production environments.
`enableGPUAcceleration`	Enables GPU acceleration on client.
`enablehtmlaccess`	Enables access to the HTML page's content.
`enableNavigation`	Enables the user to navigate to other URLs using hyperlinks.
`initparams`	Static parameters sent to the Silverlight application on load.
`maxframerate`	Maximum frame rate for media.
`minRuntimeVersion`	Minimum runtime version required to run the application.
`onfullscreenchanged`	Name of a JavaScript method invoked when the browser changes to full-screen mode.
`onload`	Name of a JavaScript method invoked when browser loads the page's DOM.

Parameter	Description
onresize	Name of a JavaScript method invoked when the browser is being resized.
onsourcedownloadcomplete	Name of a JavaScript method invoked when the browser finishes downloading the sources.
onsourcedownloadprogresschanged	Name of a JavaScript method invoked when the browser has downloaded another chunk of source data. It's used to create a progress bar. Huge downloads invoke this event a few thousand times.
onzoom	Name of a JavaScript method invoked when the browser changes the zoom level.
source	Name and path of the XAP file.
splashscreensource	Path to a splash screen displayed while the plug-in loads additional assemblies or resources.
windowless	Makes the plug-in rectangle windowless.

The table shows all the parameters the `<object>` tag accepts. There are several more you can use through JavaScript. If you plan to create Silverlight applications professionally, you should learn more about these details using the official reference at MSDN.

■ **Tip** To learn more, *we recommend Pro Silverlight 3 in C#*, by Matthew MacDonald (Apress, 2009).

Using Silverlight in a Web Part

To get an idea of what's possible with the built-in Web Part, you can examine the definition of the `SilverlightWebPart` class. Listing 13–7 shows the public methods and properties.

Listing 13–7. *Public Methods and Properties of the Silverlight Web Part*

```
public sealed class SilverlightWebPart : ClientApplicationWebPartBase
{
    public SilverlightWebPart();

    [WebBrowsable(true)]
    [Personalizable(PersonalizationScope.Shared)]
     public string CustomInitParameters { get; set; }
```

```
    [WebBrowsable(false)]
    [Personalizable(PersonalizationScope.Shared)]
     public string CustomProperties { get; set; }
     public override Unit Height { get; set; }

    [Personalizable(PersonalizationScope.Shared)]
     public string MinRuntimeVersion { get; set; }

    [Personalizable(PersonalizationScope.Shared)]
     public bool WindowlessMode { get; set; }
}
```

The `MinRuntimeVersion` property can be set to the lowest Silverlight version your XAP requires. It is a string in the format of 3.0.50106.0 (the public RTM version for Silverlight 4 was 4.0.50401.0). Unlike the .NET Framework, many builds of Silverlight are publicly available. Setting the lowest possible number enables more clients to launch your application without downloading a new runtime. If you deploy a Silverlight application using Silverlight 3, with a minimum requirement of Silverlight 3, and users have Silverlight 4 installed, your application will run well.

The `CustomInitParameters` property can be set to any string, and the value will become available in the Silverlight application during startup. All other properties are defined in the abstract base class `ClientApplicationWebPartBase`:

```
public abstract class ClientApplicationWebPartBase :
                      System.Web.UI.WebControls.WebParts.WebPart,
                      ITrackingPersonalizable
{
   protected ClientApplicationWebPartBase();

   [Personalizable(PersonalizationScope.Shared)]
    public string ApplicationXml { get; set; }
    protected string SourceUrl { get; }
    public bool TracksChanges { get; }
   [Personalizable(PersonalizationScope.Shared)]
   [ManagedLink]
    public string Url { get; set; }

    public void BeginLoad();
    public void BeginSave();
    public void EndLoad();
    public void EndSave();
    protected string GetInitParams();
}
```

Here the `Url` property is crucial; it is the address where you have copied the XAP file. That are all parameters you can use additionally to those regular Web Parts provide.

■ **Tip** If you need several Silverlight Web Parts, you can just change the XAP file (`Url` property) and use the same Web Part again.

Accessing SharePoint Data

Running Silverlight does not automatically imply that you have direct access to SharePoint data. Instead, you must build support in your Silverlight application to use client-based access. That is limited to web services. However, the client object model is available for Silverlight, too. This encapsulates the services and exposes them as an API-like layer. You can find a thorough introduction in Chapter 12.

Using the SharePoint Client Object Model

To use the SharePoint client object model, you need to reference two assemblies (see Figure 13–7):

- `Microsoft.SharePoint.Client.Silverlight.dll`
- `Microsoft.SharePoint.Client.Silverlight.Runtime.dll`

Both are located in the `%SharePointRoot%\TEMPLATE\LAYOUTS\ClientBin` folder, and are available by default. All the following examples assume that you have a Silverlight project with references to these two assemblies. To execute the code, deploy the XAP file the project builds to one of the locations recommended previously. You can use the Silverlight Web Part to take this XAP file and execute your Silverlight application within your site.

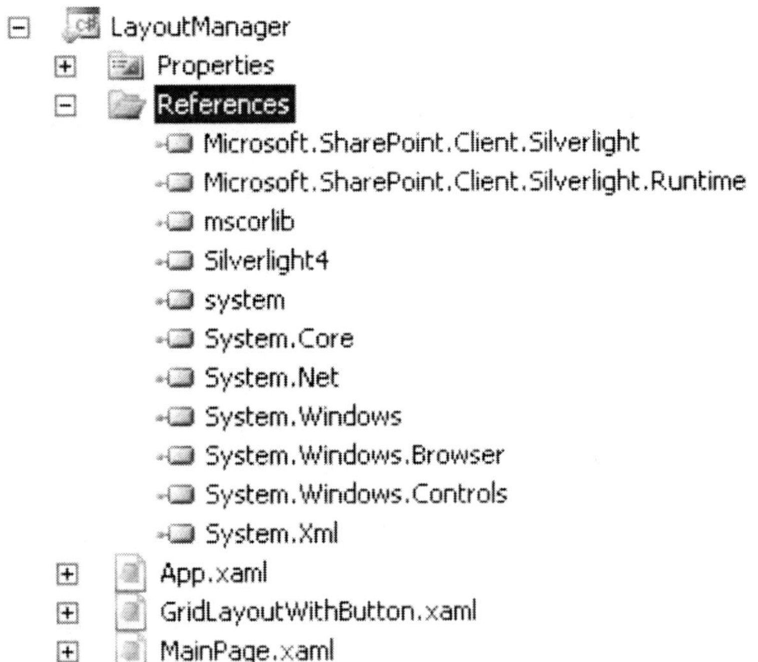

***Figure 13–7.** Silverlight project with references to SharePoint's client object assemblies*

▒ **Note** Remember that even if you load your Silverlight application within a Web Part, it's still executed on the client computer. You can't use a server-side API to access SharePoint from a remote location like this.

Executing Queries

The Silverlight client object model provides both a synchronous ExecuteQuery method and an asynchronous ExecuteQueryAsync method. The first method is intended to be called from threads that do not modify the UI, whereas the second approach is for threads that do. Both methods actually send the query to the server. Nothing is transmitted over the wire before that call. All preparatory steps are cached and held in the objects provided by the client object model.

Example: Reading List Data from SharePoint and Writing Changes Back

The example in Listing 13–8 shows how to retrieve and change data in a SharePoint list using a Silverlight Grid control.

Listing 13–8. *The XAML of a Silverlight Application (MainPage.xaml)*

```
<UserControl x:Class="SilverlightClientApp.MainPage"
    xmlns="http://schemas.microsoft.com/winfx/2006/xaml/presentation"
    xmlns:x="http://schemas.microsoft.com/winfx/2006/xaml"
    xmlns:d="http://schemas.microsoft.com/expression/blend/2008"
    xmlns:mc="http://schemas.openxmlformats.org/markup-compatibility/2006"
    mc:Ignorable="d"
    d:DesignHeight="300" d:DesignWidth="400"
      xmlns:data="clr-namespace:System.Windows.Controls;
                  assembly=System.Windows.Controls.Data">

    <Grid x:Name="LayoutRoot" Background="White">
        <TextBlock Height="15" HorizontalAlignment="Left" Margin="29,12,0,0"
                   Name="textBlock1" Text="Web Name:" VerticalAlignment="Top"
                   Width="76" FontWeight="Bold" />
        <TextBlock Height="37" HorizontalAlignment="Left" Margin="111,12,0,0"
                   Name="txtWebName" Text="TextBlock" VerticalAlignment="Top"
                   Width="277" DataContext="{Binding}" TextWrapping="Wrap" />
        <Button Content="Retrieve" Height="26" HorizontalAlignment="Left"
                Margin="280,57,0,0" Name="button1" VerticalAlignment="Top"
                Width="108" Click="button1_Click" />
        <data:DataGrid AutoGenerateColumns="True"
                       HeadersVisibility="All"
                       RowBackground="Cornsilk"
                       AlternatingRowBackground="LemonChiffon"
                       Height="151"
                       HorizontalAlignment="Left" Margin="12,89,0,0"
                       Name="dataGridXAPFiles" VerticalAlignment="Top" Width="376">
        </data:DataGrid>
        <Button Content="Save" Height="23" HorizontalAlignment="Left"
                Margin="281,258,0,0" Name="button2"
```

```
                VerticalAlignment="Top" Width="107" Click="button2_Click" />
    </Grid>
</UserControl>
```

It's not a very impressive application, but it's sufficient to check the complete data round trip. See Figure 13–8 for the result.

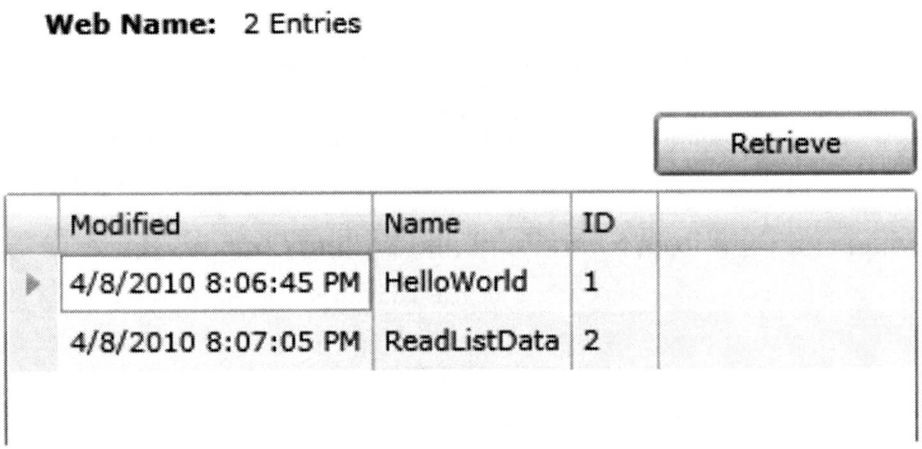

Web Name: 2 Entries

Retrieve

Modified	Name	ID
4/8/2010 8:06:45 PM	HelloWorld	1
4/8/2010 8:07:05 PM	ReadListData	2

Figure 13–8. *The Silverlight application in action*

You can't do much solely with XAML. Hence, you need a code-behind file, as shown in Listing 13–9. This application needs a reference to `System.Windows.Controls.Data.dll` to support the `Grid` control.

Listing 13–9. *The Code-Behind of the XAML File (MainPage.xaml.cs)*

```
using System;
using System.Collections.Generic;
using System.Linq;
using System.Net;
using System.Windows;
using System.Windows.Controls;
using System.Windows.Documents;
using System.Windows.Input;
using System.Windows.Media;
using System.Windows.Media.Animation;
using System.Windows.Shapes;
using Microsoft.SharePoint.Client;

namespace SilverlightClientApp
{
    public partial class MainPage : UserControl
    {
        public MainPage()
        {
```

```
        InitializeComponent();
    }

    Web web;
    ListItemCollection allItems;

    public class BoundItem
    {
        public string Modified { get; set; }
        public string Name { get; set; }
        public int ID { get; set; }
    }

    private void ClientSuccessWeb(object sender,
                                  ClientRequestSucceededEventArgs e)
    {
        Dispatcher.BeginInvoke(() => txtWebName.Text = web.Title);
    }

    private void ClientSuccessFiles(object sender,
                                    ClientRequestSucceededEventArgs e)
    {
        try
        {
            List<BoundItem> items = new List<BoundItem>();
            foreach (ListItem item in allItems)
            {
                items.Add(new BoundItem()
                    {
                        Modified = item["Modified"].ToString(),
                        Name = item.DisplayName,
                        ID = item.Id
                    });
            }
            Dispatcher.BeginInvoke(() => txtWebName.Text =
                        String.Format("{0} Entries", items.Count()));
            Dispatcher.BeginInvoke(() => dataGridXAPFiles.ItemsSource = items);
        }
        catch (Exception ex)
        {
            Dispatcher.BeginInvoke(() => txtWebName.Text = ex.Message);
        }
    }

    private void ClientSaveFiles(object sender,
                                 ClientRequestSucceededEventArgs e)
    {
        Dispatcher.BeginInvoke(() => txtWebName.Text = success);
    }


    private void ClientFailed(object sender, ClientRequestFailedEventArgs e)
    {
        Dispatcher.BeginInvoke(() => txtWebName.Text = "Fehler: "
```

```
                                                    + e.Exception.Message);
        }

        private void button1_Click(object sender, RoutedEventArgs e)
        {
            using (ClientContext ctx =
                new ClientContext("http://sharepointserve/sites/silverlight/"))
            {
                try
                {
                    web = ctx.Web;
                    ctx.Load(web);
                    ctx.ExecuteQueryAsync(
                       new ClientRequestSucceededEventHandler(ClientSuccessWeb),
                       new ClientRequestFailedEventHandler(ClientFailed));

                    xapList = web.Lists.GetByTitle("XAPFiles");
                    CamlQuery caml = new CamlQuery();
                    allItems = xapList.GetItems(caml);
                    ctx.Load(allItems,
                        files => files.Include(
                            file => file.Id,
                            file => file.DisplayName,
                            file => file["Modified"])
                            );
                    ctx.ExecuteQueryAsync(
                       new ClientRequestSucceededEventHandler(ClientSuccessFiles),
                       new ClientRequestFailedEventHandler(ClientFailed));
                }
                catch (Exception ex)
                {
                    txtWebName.Text = "Execution error: " + ex.Message;
                }
            }
        }

        List xapList;
        string success;

        private void button2_Click(object sender, RoutedEventArgs e)
        {
            // Save
            using (ClientContext ctx =
                  new ClientContext("http://sharepointserve/sites/silverlight/"))
            {
                try
                {
                    xapList = ctx.Web.Lists.GetByTitle("XAPFiles");
                    foreach (ListItem item in allItems)
                    {
                        int id = item.Id;
                        ListItem serverItem = xapList.GetItemById(item.Id);
                        serverItem["Title"] = "Modified at "
                                            + DateTime.Now.ToLongTimeString();
```

```
                    serverItem.Update();
                }
                xapList.Update();
                success = "Saved";
                ctx.ExecuteQueryAsync(
                  new ClientRequestSucceededEventHandler(ClientSaveFiles),
                  new ClientRequestFailedEventHandler(ClientFailed));
            }
            catch (Exception ex)
            {
                MessageBox.Show(ex.Message + ex.StackTrace);
            }
        }

    }


  }
}
```

Access to the server is always asynchronous. The application has two buttons: one to load data from the server and the other to write changes back. The `button1_Click` handler method loads the data by issuing a simple list request to the list `XAPFiles`: `web.Lists.GetByTitle("XAPFiles")`. This is the list we defined to store the XAP files. The vital part is the selection and filtering of the files retrieved from server:

```
files => files.Include(
     file => file.Id,
     file => file.DisplayName,
     file => file["Modified"]
```

This is not a true LINQ statement. Instead, the lambda expressions provide a typed way to define property names. You cannot add any other expression code here. In the example, the properties `Id` and `DisplayName`, and the `Modified` field are retrieved. The `ExecuteQueryAsync` method then invokes the web service call. The `allItems` variable is filled with data when the `ClientSuccessFiles` callback method is executed. The remaining part of this method copies the data into a type that Silverlight can bind.

The save method works similarly. The data is gathered from the grid and written back to the list. Because this is another request, invoked by the `button2_Click` handler method, you need to create another context object. The code is simple—it reads the entire list and assumes that there are changes in most rows. (It would be more sophisticated to note changes and select only the rows with changes, using an appropriate CAML statement.) After writing all the changes to the list, you call the `Update` method. This is still a preparation step. The `ExecuteQueryAsync` method actually calls the web service to send the data to the server.

The `ClientSaveFiles` method outputs a suitable message to inform the user that the operation was successful. Because you have a worker thread that is not the UI thread, the UI controls must be modified asynchronously, too. This is why writing to the screen involves the `Dispatcher` object:

```
Dispatcher.BeginInvoke(() => txtWebName.Text = success)
```

Limitations

As you examine this code, you might see where there is room for improvement. (Perhaps not, if you have recently started coding with Silverlight. But if you have years of .NET experience, you'll begin to spot the limitations.)

One very annoying aspect is that data binding does not work with anonymous types. The following code snippet will not work:

```
var items1 = from item in allItems
             select new BoundItem()
             {
                ID = item.Id,
                Modified = item["Modified"],
                Name = item.DisplayName
             };
```

This is a valid collection, and ASP.NET and even WPF would bind this properly. Silverlight, however, does not. You have to copy it to a `List<T>` type first.

■ **Note** If you develop with Silverlight 3 and wonder whether this has been fixed in Silverlight 4, you will be disappointed. However, there is a difference: in Silverlight 3 the code will silently fail, while in Silverlight 4 you'll get a `NotSupportedException`. (This is not really what one would call progress, is it?)

Example: Accessing Lists

Various tasks concerning lists are demonstrated in this section:

- How to retrieve all the SharePoint lists in a web site
- How to retrieve list schema (field) information
- How to create a new SharePoint list
- How to retrieve an existing SharePoint list using a CAML query

Retrieving All SharePoint Lists in a Web Site

You can retrieve all the lists for a web site using the property `Web.Lists`. Simply load and query the list collection and iterate through the lists. The code starts immediately after loading the XAP file by calling the `GetAllLists` method (see Listing 13–10).

***Listing 13–10.** Retrieving All Lists for a Web Site (MainPage.cs)*

```
public partial class MainPage : UserControl
{
    public MainPage()
    {
        InitializeComponent();
        GetAllLists();
    }

    ListCollection listColl;

    private void ClientSuccess(object sender,
```

```
                                ClientRequestSucceededEventArgs e)
    {
        Dispatcher.BeginInvoke(() =>
        {
            lbAllLists.DataContext = listColl;
        });
    }

    private void ClientFailed(object sender,
                               ClientRequestFailedEventArgs e)
    {
        MessageBox.Show(e.Exception.Message, "Exception", MessageBoxButton.OK);
    }

    private void GetAllLists()
    {
        using (ClientContext ctx = new ClientContext("http://sharepointserve/"))
        {
            try
            {
                listColl = ctx.Web.Lists;
                ctx.Load(listColl);
                ctx.ExecuteQueryAsync(
                   new ClientRequestSucceededEventHandler(ClientSuccess),
                   new ClientRequestFailedEventHandler(ClientFailed));
            }
            catch (Exception ex)
            {
                MessageBox.Show(ex.Message, "Exception", MessageBoxButton.OK);
            }
        }
    }
}
```

The corresponding XAML implementation in Listing 13–11 simply uses a `ListBox` element to expose the collection through data binding. The list displays the title and description. The binding uses the `ListCollection` class and the `List` elements it contains to bind the properties `Title` and `Description`, respectively.

***Listing 13–11.** Retrieving All the Lists for a Web Site (XAML)*

```
<UserControl x:Class="RetrieveAllLists.MainPage"
    xmlns="http://schemas.microsoft.com/winfx/2006/xaml/presentation"
    xmlns:x="http://schemas.microsoft.com/winfx/2006/xaml"
    xmlns:d="http://schemas.microsoft.com/expression/blend/2008"
    xmlns:mc="http://schemas.openxmlformats.org/markup-compatibility/2006"
    mc:Ignorable="d"
    d:DesignHeight="300" d:DesignWidth="400">

    <Grid x:Name="LayoutRoot" Background="White">
        <TextBlock >Shows all Lists of the current root Web:</TextBlock>
        <ListBox x:Name="lbAllLists" Margin="5,25,5,5" ItemsSource="{Binding}" >
            <ListBox.ItemTemplate>
                <DataTemplate>
```

```
                    <StackPanel Orientation="Horizontal">
                        <TextBlock Text="{Binding Title}" Margin="5"></TextBlock>
                        <TextBlock Text="{Binding Description}" Margin="5">
                        </TextBlock>
                    </StackPanel>
                </DataTemplate>
            </ListBox.ItemTemplate>
        </ListBox>
    </Grid>
</UserControl>
```

The example returns all the lists containing all their properties. To reduce the number of properties, you should explicitly define only those properties you really need. For collections, this can be done using LINQ in combination with the `Include` expression:

```
ctx.Load(listColl,
        lists => lists.Include(list => list.Title, list => list.Description));
```

The result of the example code is shown in Figure 13–9.

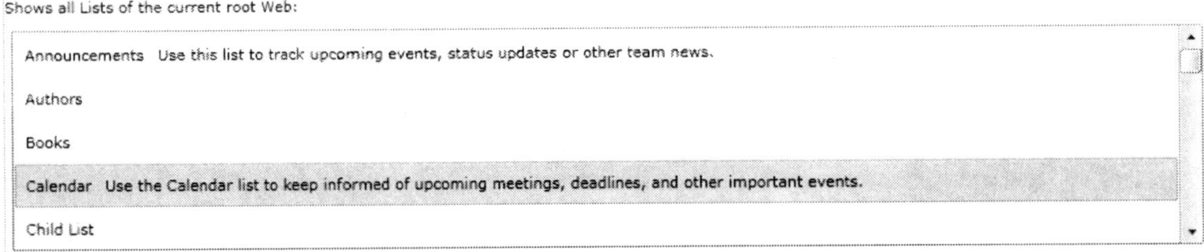

***Figure 13–9.** A ListBox showing the root web's lists*

Retrieving List Field Information

Information about the various fields of a list is obtained via the `List.Fields` property, as shown in Listing 13–12.

***Listing 13–12.** Retrieving List Schema Information (MainPage.cs)*

```
public partial class MainPage : UserControl
{
    public MainPage()
    {
        InitializeComponent();
    }

    FieldCollection fieldColl;

    private void ClientSuccess(object sender,
                               ClientRequestSucceededEventArgs e)
    {
        Dispatcher.BeginInvoke(() =>
        {
```

```
            lbAllFields.DataContext = fieldColl;
        });
    }

    private void ClientFailed(object sender,
                              ClientRequestFailedEventArgs e)
    {
        MessageBox.Show(e.Exception.Message, "Exception", MessageBoxButton.OK);
    }

    private void GetAllFields(string list)
    {
        using (ClientContext ctx = new ClientContext("http://sharepointserve/"))
        {
            try
            {
                fieldColl = ctx.Web.Lists.GetByTitle(list).Fields;
                ctx.Load(fieldColl);
                ctx.ExecuteQueryAsync(
                   new ClientRequestSucceededEventHandler(ClientSuccess),
                   new ClientRequestFailedEventHandler(ClientFailed));
            }
            catch (Exception ex)
            {
                MessageBox.Show(ex.Message, "Exception", MessageBoxButton.OK);
            }
        }
    }

    private void btnRetrieve_Click(object sender, RoutedEventArgs e)
    {
        string list = txtList.Text;
        if (!String.IsNullOrEmpty(list))
        {
            GetAllFields(list);
        }
    }
}
```

The XAML defines a TextBox and a Button to invoke the call. This is a very rudimentary solution—if the user types the wrong name, an exception is thrown. The XAML binds the InternalName and FieldTypeKind properties (see Listing 13–13).

***Listing 13–13.** Retrieving List Schema Information (XAML)*

```
<UserControl x:Class="RetrieveFieldInformation.MainPage"
    xmlns="http://schemas.microsoft.com/winfx/2006/xaml/presentation"
    xmlns:x="http://schemas.microsoft.com/winfx/2006/xaml"
    xmlns:d="http://schemas.microsoft.com/expression/blend/2008"
    xmlns:mc="http://schemas.openxmlformats.org/markup-compatibility/2006"
    mc:Ignorable="d"
    d:DesignHeight="300" d:DesignWidth="400">

    <Grid x:Name="LayoutRoot" Background="White">
```

```
        <TextBlock >Shows all Fields of the this list:</TextBlock>
        <ListBox x:Name="lbAllFields" Margin="5,30,5,5" ItemsSource="{Binding}" >
            <ListBox.ItemTemplate>
                <DataTemplate>
                    <StackPanel Orientation="Horizontal">
                        <TextBlock Text="{Binding InternalName}" Margin="5">
                        </TextBlock>
                        <TextBlock Text="{Binding FieldTypeKind}" Margin="5">
                        </TextBlock>
                    </StackPanel>
                </DataTemplate>
            </ListBox.ItemTemplate>
        </ListBox>
        <TextBox Height="23" HorizontalAlignment="Left" Margin="201,1,0,0"
                 Name="txtList" VerticalAlignment="Top" Width="105" />
        <Button x:Name="btnRetrieve" Content="Retrieve" Height="28"
                HorizontalAlignment="Left" Margin="320,-1,0,0"
                VerticalAlignment="Top" Width="75" Click="btnRetrieve_Click" />
    </Grid>
</UserControl>
```

While the binding limits the output, the whole list of properties is obtained from the server. To limit the transferred data to only what is needed, replace the Load method with a filtered version:

```
ctx.Load(fieldColl, fields => fields.Include(
                    field => field.InternalName, field => field.FieldTypeKind));
```

The result of this example is shown in Figure 13–10.

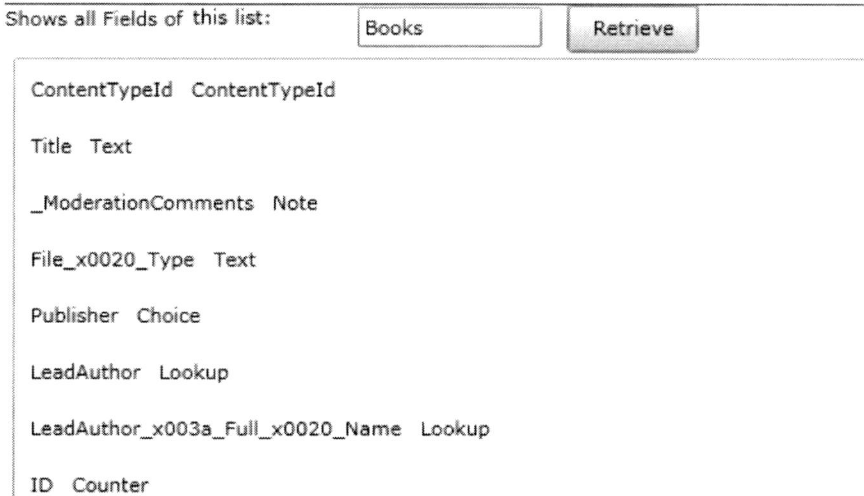

Figure 13–10. *A ListBox displays a list's field definitions*

Creating a New SharePoint List

Creating a new SharePoint list requires an instance of the `ListCreationInformation` class. At a minimum, you need to define the `Title` and the `TemplateType` properties, and add the list fields. In Listing 13–14, the fields are defined in XML and added to the list using the `AddFieldAsXml` method.

Listing 13–14. *Creating a New List (MainPage.xaml.cs)*

```
public partial class MainPage : UserControl
{
    public MainPage()
    {
        InitializeComponent();
    }

    class NewField
    {
        public string Name { get; set; }
        public bool Integer { get; set; }
    }

    List<NewField> newFields;

    private void CreateList()
    {
        using (ClientContext ctx = new ClientContext("http://sharepointserve/"))
        {
            try
            {
```

```
                Web web = ctx.Web;

                ListCreationInformation listCreationInfo =
                                    new ListCreationInformation();
                listCreationInfo.Title = txtName.Text;
                listCreationInfo.TemplateType = (int)ListTemplateType.GenericList;

                List oList = web.Lists.Add(listCreationInfo);
                ctx.Load(oList);

                foreach (NewField newField in newFields)
                {
                    XElement fld = new XElement("Field",
                                    new XAttribute("Authors", newField.Name),
                                    new XAttribute("Type", newField.Integer ?
                                                   "Currency" : "Text"));
                    oList.Fields.AddFieldAsXml(fld.ToString(), true,
                                               AddFieldOptions.DefaultValue);
                }

                oList.Update();

                ctx.ExecuteQuery();
                MessageBox.Show("List successfully created.", "Done",
                                MessageBoxButton.OK);
            }
            catch (Exception ex)
            {
                MessageBox.Show(ex.Message, "Exception", MessageBoxButton.OK);
            }
        }
    }

    private void btnCreate_Click(object sender, RoutedEventArgs e)
    {
        CreateList();
    }

    private void slider1_ValueChanged(object sender,
                                      RoutedPropertyChangedEventArgs<double> e)
    {
        int fields = Convert.ToInt32(slider1.Value);
        newFields = new List<NewField>(fields);
        for (int i = 0; i < fields; i++)
        {
            newFields.Add(new NewField() { Name = "[Type Name]" });
        }
        dgFields.DataContext = newFields;
    }
}
```

The XAML (see Listing 13–15) defines a DataGrid in which the user can edit a field's name and change the field's type from String to Currency. The user can enter the name of the list and invoke the list creation by pressing the button. A two-way binding ensures that the business object bound to the grid is filled properly. The number of fields is defined by a `Slider` control that has a range of zero to ten.

Listing 13–15. *Creating a New List (XAML)*

```
<UserControl x:Class="CreateList.MainPage"
    xmlns="http://schemas.microsoft.com/winfx/2006/xaml/presentation"
    xmlns:x="http://schemas.microsoft.com/winfx/2006/xaml"
    xmlns:d="http://schemas.microsoft.com/expression/blend/2008"
    xmlns:mc="http://schemas.openxmlformats.org/markup-compatibility/2006"
    mc:Ignorable="d"
    d:DesignHeight="300" d:DesignWidth="400"
    xmlns:data="clr-
    namespace:System.Windows.Controls;assembly=System.Windows.Controls.Data">

    <Grid x:Name="LayoutRoot" Background="White">
        <Button Content="Create a new List using this name:" Height="23"
                HorizontalAlignment="Left" Margin="12,21,0,0" Name="btnCreate"
                VerticalAlignment="Top" Width="231" Click="btnCreate_Click" />
        <TextBox Height="23" HorizontalAlignment="Left" Margin="268,21,0,0"
                 Name="txtName" VerticalAlignment="Top" Width="120" />

        <data:DataGrid ItemsSource="{Binding}" AutoGenerateColumns="False"
                       IsReadOnly="False" Height="200" HorizontalAlignment="Left"
                       Margin="12,72,0,0" Name="dgFields"
                       VerticalAlignment="Top" Width="376">
    <data:DataGrid.Columns>
        <data:DataGridTemplateColumn Header="Name" Width="200">
            <data:DataGridTemplateColumn.CellTemplate>
                <DataTemplate>
                    <TextBlock Text="{Binding Name}"
                               Foreground="Green"
                               FontWeight="Bold"
                               VerticalAlignment="Center"/>
                </DataTemplate>
            </data:DataGridTemplateColumn.CellTemplate>
            <data:DataGridTemplateColumn.CellEditingTemplate>
                <DataTemplate>
                    <Grid>
                        <Grid.ColumnDefinitions>
                            <ColumnDefinition Width="Auto" />
                            <ColumnDefinition Width="*" />
                        </Grid.ColumnDefinitions>
                        <TextBlock Text="Edit: " Grid.Column="0" />
                        <TextBox Text="{Binding Name, Mode=TwoWay}"
                                 Grid.Column="1" />
                    </Grid>
                </DataTemplate>
            </data:DataGridTemplateColumn.CellEditingTemplate>
        </data:DataGridTemplateColumn>
        <data:DataGridCheckBoxColumn Binding="{Binding Mode=TwoWay, Path=Type}"
              IsReadOnly="False" CanUserReorder="True" CanUserResize="True"
              CanUserSort="True" Header="Type (Check for 'Currency')"
              Width="Auto" />
```

```
    </data:DataGrid.Columns>
</data:DataGrid>
        <Slider Height="23" HorizontalAlignment="Left" Margin="268,43,0,0"
                Name="slider1" VerticalAlignment="Top" Width="120"
                ValueChanged="slider1_ValueChanged" SmallChange="1"
                LargeChange="2" />
        <TextBlock Height="23" HorizontalAlignment="Left" Margin="12,47,0,0"
                   Name="textBlock1" Text="Use slider to define the
                   number of fields:" VerticalAlignment="Top" Width="231" />
    </Grid>
</UserControl>
```

This is a simple example that shows how to use several Silverlight controls to manage various administrative options (see Figure 13–11).

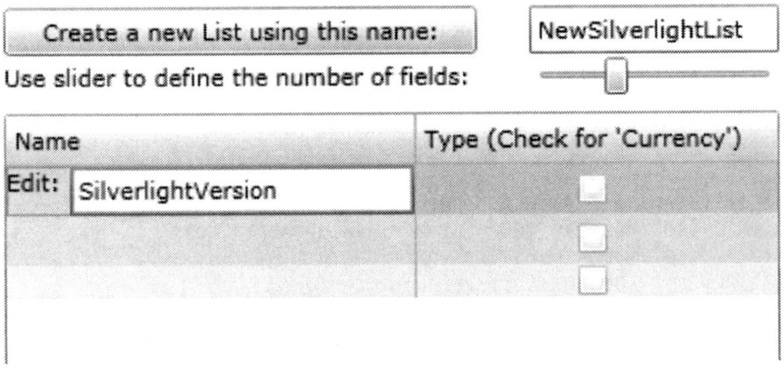

Figure 13–11. *Creating a list using a fancier UI*

Modifying a list follows a similar pattern. You merely call the `Update` method on the field object. Even deleting is equally simple using the `DeleteObject` method:

```
List oBooksList = ctx.Web.Lists.GetByTitle("MyBooks");
oBooksList.DeleteObject();
ctx.ExecuteQuery();
```

Retrieving List Items Using CAML Queries

Using CAML queries to retrieve list items is the best practice. The filtering of list items is performed on the server, and as a result, only relevant data is transmitted to the client. The following example goes a step further and defines, beyond the CAML query, which properties should be returned. This is accomplished using the `Include` clause of the LINQ expression within the `Load` method, as shown in Listing 13–16.

Listing 13–16. *Retrieving List Items Using CAML (Excerpt from Silverlight Code-Behind)*

```
CamlQuery caml = new CamlQuery();
caml.ViewXml = @"<View>
                   <Query>
                     <Where>
```

```
                        <Eq>
                          <FieldRef Name='Publisher'/>
                          <Value Type='Text'>APress</Value>
                        </Eq>
                      </Where>
                    </Query>
                  </View>";

ListItemCollection allBooksFromAPress = booksList.GetItems(caml);
ctx.Load(allBooksFromAPress, books => books.Include(
            book => book.Id,
            book => book["Title"],
            book => book["Publisher"]
));
```

In this example the booksList variable contains the List object you retrieve, as shown in the previous examples. The CAML syntax is the same as you would write for the server-side API.

Example: Accessing Users and Roles

Working with users, groups, and roles, and dealing with their permissions for SharePoint elements can be quite complex. In former SharePoint versions, the only way to alter the security was to use the provided security web services. With SharePoint 2010, the client object model dramatically simplifies working with security settings. The listings in this section are included in a Silverlight application you can find in the download package associated with this book.

How to Add Users to a SharePoint Group

Adding a user to a SharePoint group is a common task, particularly in conjunction with creating a web site. The example in Listing 13–17 shows two ways to add a user to a group. The first approach uses the Group.Users.AddUser method, which expects a User instance of an existing user. The second method adds a new user to a group via the UserCreationInformation class. The new user is identified by its LoginName. If the user already exists in the site collection, the user is added to the group anyway. The example requires that a valid group within the property Web.AssociatedMemberGroup exists; thus, the default group at the time of web site creation has not been removed.

Listing 13–17. *Adding Users to a SharePoint Group (Excerpt from Silverlight Code-Behind)*

```
ClientContext ctx = new ClientContext("http://sharepointserve");
Group membersGroup =  ctx.Web.AssociatedMemberGroup;

// Add existing user to membersGroup
User currentUser = membersGroup.Users.AddUser(ctx.Web.CurrentUser);

// Add new user to membersGroup
UserCreationInformation userCreationInfo = new UserCreationInformation();
userCreationInfo.Email = "joerg@krause.de";
userCreationInfo.LoginName = @"MAXIMUS\jkrause";
userCreationInfo.Title = "Joerg Krause";
User newUser = membersGroup.Users.Add(userCreationInfo);
```

```
ctx.Load(currentUser);
ctx.Load(newUser);
ctx.Load(membersGroup);
ctx.ExecuteQuery();
```

To get a list of all users that are members of a specified group, you can interrogate the Group.Users collection, as shown in Listing 13–18.

***Listing 13–18.** Retrieving Group Members (Excerpt from Silverlight Code-Behind)*

```
ClientContext ctx = new ClientContext("http://sharepointserve");
Group membersGroup = ctx.Web.AssociatedMemberGroup;
UserCollection allUsersOfGroup = membersGroup.Users;
ctx.Load(allUsersOfGroup);
ctx.ExecuteQuery();
```

Defining your own roles (aka permission levels) is a common task when dealing with complex security requirements (see Figure 13–12). With the client object model you can easily define your own roles and assign them to SharePoint users or groups.

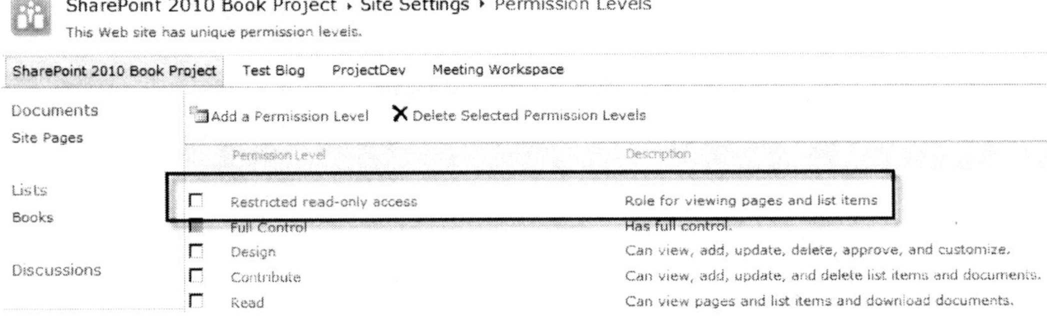

***Figure 13–12.** Newly created role (permission level)*

The example in Listing 13–19 reveals how to create a new role.

***Listing 13–19.** Creating a Role (Excerpt from Silverlight Code-Behind)*

```
ClientContext ctx = new ClientContext("http://sharepointserve");
Web oWeb = ctx.Web;

BasePermissions basePerms = new BasePermissions();
basePerms.Set(PermissionKind.ViewListItems);
basePerms.Set(PermissionKind.ViewPages);

RoleDefinitionCreationInformation roleCreationInfo =
            new RoleDefinitionCreationInformation();
roleCreationInfo.BasePermissions = basePerms;
roleCreationInfo.Description = "Role for viewing pages and list items";
roleCreationInfo.Name = "Restricted read-only access";
```

```
RoleDefinition roleDef = oWeb.RoleDefinitions.Add(roleCreationInfo);
Ctx.Load(roleDef);
ctx.ExecuteQuery();
```

Assigning SharePoint users or groups to roles is shown in Listing 13–20.

Listing 13–20. Adding a User or Group to a Role (Excerpt from Silverlight Code-Behind)

```
ClientContext ctx = new ClientContext("http://sharepointserve");
Web oWeb = ctx.Web;

Principal oUser = oWeb.CurrentUser;

RoleDefinition oRoleDef =
          oWeb.RoleDefinitions.GetByName("Restricted read-only access");
RoleDefinitionBindingCollection roleDefinitionBindingColl =
        new RoleDefinitionBindingCollection(ctx);
roleDefinitionBindingColl.Add(oRoleDef);

RoleAssignment oRoleAssignment =
        oWeb.RoleAssignments.Add(oUser, roleDefinitionBindingColl);

ctx.Load(oUser, user => user.Title);
ctx.Load(oRoleDef, role => role.Name);

ctx.ExecuteQuery();
```

As you can see, the `RoleAssignments.Add` method takes a `Principal` object as a parameter. The `Principal` class serves as the base class for both users (`User`) and groups (`Group`). Thus, you can assign either a user or a group to a role.

The next example (see Listing 13–21) demonstrates the creation of a new SharePoint group, using the `GroupCreationInformation` class. The Contributors role is then assigned to this new group.

Listing 13–21. Creating a New SharePoint Group and Assigning It to a Role (Excerpt from Silverlight Code-Behind)

```
ClientContext ctx = new ClientContext("http://sharepointserve");
Web oWeb = ctx.Web;

GroupCreationInformation groupCreationInfo = new GroupCreationInformation();
groupCreationInfo.Title = "My Custom Contributor Group";
groupCreationInfo.Description = "This group has contributor rights.";
Group oGroup = oWeb.SiteGroups.Add(groupCreationInfo);

RoleDefinitionBindingCollection roleDefinitionBindingColl =
        new RoleDefinitionBindingCollection(ctx);
RoleDefinition oRoleDefinition =
        oWeb.RoleDefinitions.GetByType(RoleType.Contributor);

roleDefinitionBindingColl.Add(oRoleDefinition);
oWeb.RoleAssignments.Add(oGroup, roleDefinitionBindingColl);
```

```
ctx.Load(oGroup, group => group.Title);
ctx.Load(oRoleDefinition, role => role.Name);

ctx.ExecuteQuery();
```

In SharePoint, by default all elements (e.g., Web, List, and ListItem) rely on role inheritance. Consequently, permissions are inherited from top to bottom. For instance, a user has the same permissions on a list item as on a list, because the list item inherits its permissions from the list. There are scenarios, though, in which this default role inheritance is not desirable and has to be broken—for example, if you want a list item to be accessed only by particular users or groups. The example in this section shows how to break the role inheritance of a list item and assign special permissions to it. Figure 13–13 and Figure 13–14 show the list item permissions before and after breaking the role inheritance.

Figure 13–13. List item permissions before breaking the inheritance (default)

Figure 13–14. List item permissions after breaking the inheritance and adding a user (MAXIMUS\administrator) with full control to the list item

The example in Listing 13–23 obtains a list item with an ID of 1 from the list Books and breaks its role inheritance without copying the inherited permissions and without clearing the child scope.

Listing 13–22. Breaking the Role Inheritance (Excerpt from Silverlight Code-Behind)

```
ClientContext ctx = new ClientContext("http://sharepointserve");
Web oWeb = ctx.Web;

List booksList = oWeb.Lists.GetByTitle("Books");
```

```
ListItem bookToSecure = booksList.GetItemById(1);

// Break role inheritance for this list item and
// don't copy the inherited permissions
bookToSecure.BreakRoleInheritance(false, false);

// Assign the current user as Administrator
RoleDefinitionBindingCollection roleDefinitionBindingColl =
        new RoleDefinitionBindingCollection(ctx);
roleDefinitionBindingColl.Add(
        oWeb.RoleDefinitions.GetByType(RoleType.Administrator));

bookToSecure.RoleAssignments.Add(oWeb.CurrentUser, roleDefinitionBindingColl);
ctx.ExecuteQuery();
```

The method `BreakRoleInheritance` takes two Boolean parameters: `copyRoleAssignments` and `clearSubScopes`. The first parameter indicates whether all permissions from the parent object should be copied to the element on which the `BreakRoleInheritance` method is executed. The second parameter specifies whether unique permissions of the child elements should be cleared.

Summary

In this chapter you learned about Silverlight and how to use it to create sophisticated UIs that break the HTML barrier but deploy like any browser-based application. Some basic steps introduced the core features of Silverlight. You examined the security model and saw how to create Silverlight applications using either Web Parts or application pages.

Using the client object model, you can use a SharePoint API style of access from any remote location based on web services. Several examples showed how to create simple XAML-based UIs with code that accesses the SharePoint back end to retrieve and change data from SharePoint lists. Using simple expressions you can limit the amount of data retrieved while obtaining exactly what you want. This improves performance and aids in creating fast UIs.

CHAPTER 14

Integrating Charts and Maps

In this chapter we will focus on extending SharePoint by using UI elements that are not directly part of the SharePoint Foundation framework. The following topics are covered:

- Developing custom charts
- Using map services to display geospatial data

For integrating complex charts or dashboards, we will introduce various data access scenarios, ranging from basic CAML queries to direct database access with LINQ to SQL. Furthermore, we will give you an overview of the features within the Microsoft Chart Control framework. The final section of this chapter examines map services and shows how to integrate these services into SharePoint.

Data Access Scenarios

Before you can start to implement your own charts, dashboards, or maps, you need to decide on the most appropriate data access strategy for the situation. It's important that you have a clear view of your requirements, because the wrong choice of data access method could result in a nasty surprise later. You should ask yourself the following questions:

- *Data location*: Where is the source of the data to be queried? Is it only in basic SharePoint lists? Or is there additional data, possibly connected by business data services?
- *Data size*: How many items do you expect in your lists? How much will the lists grow over time?
- *Query complexity*: How complex will the queries be? Do you have to join many lists together? Are you heavily using grouping and aggregation (`GROUP BY`)?
- *Performance*: How many queries do you expect on a typical (dashboard) page? How many users are accessing this page in a given interval (e.g., queries per hour)? What should the maximum page load time be?

There are several ways to query data from the SharePoint database that we will briefly recap here. For in-depth coverage of the different data access methods, refer back to Chapter 4. More information about efficient data access can be found in Chapter 5.

Integrating Charts

Up to this stage, we have covered a lot about SharePoint and its customization possibilities. As developers, we can easily build our own Web Parts or application pages using the integrated SharePoint web controls. There is one important aspect we have not mentioned yet, though: the ability to build our own charts, dashboards, and map views. These graphical elements are indispensable for most modern business applications. This section covers several approaches to integrating charting capabilities into your own application pages or Web Parts:

- Microsoft Chart Controls
- Google Chart API
- Google Visualization API

The Microsoft Chart Control can be used to create complex charting scenarios on the server side. In contrast, Google offers some very interesting JavaScript frameworks that can also be used for your custom implementations. The big difference between the two is that the Microsoft Chart Control is a pure server-side .NET library, whereas Google offers its APIs as quasi-services, freely accessible over the Internet, which can be embedded. Depending on your needs and your audience, it can be completely appropriate to use the public Google APIs, such as Google Maps, as we shall explore later in this chapter.

Understanding Microsoft Chart Controls

In recent years, Microsoft has been releasing and evolving the .NET Framework step by step. Many namespaces have been added, and the whole framework has become more powerful. However, no effort had been made to integrate or offer charting components for visualizing data. Developers had to license third-party components from specialized vendors.

This finally changed in 2008, when Microsoft licensed one of the best available charting components on the market. Dundas (`www.dundas.com/`) is one of the leaders in data visualization. It provides well-known chart, gauge, map and other visual controls for different Microsoft development platforms (ASP.NET, Windows Forms, SQL Reporting Services, and SharePoint).

The licensed package resulted in the Microsoft Chart Controls, a free downloadable .NET library for the .NET Framework 3.5 (SP1) with designer support for Visuals Studio 2008 (SP1).

Now the Microsoft Chart Controls (namespace `System.Web.UI.DataVisualization.Charting`) are an integral part of the .NET Framework 4.0 and can be used for web and Windows Forms applications (see Figure 14–1 for some examples).

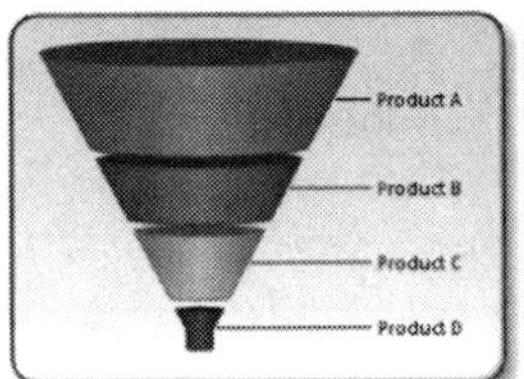

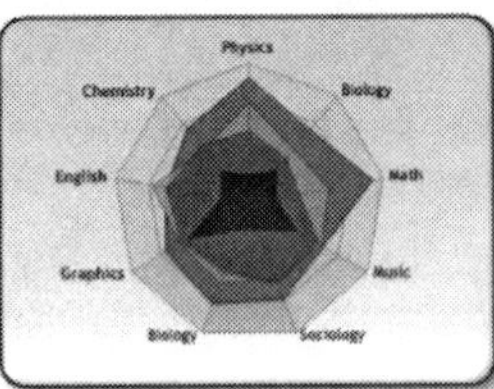

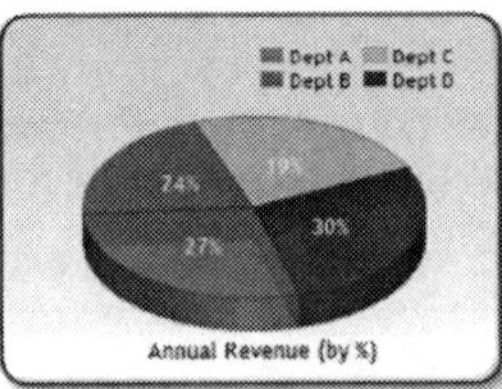

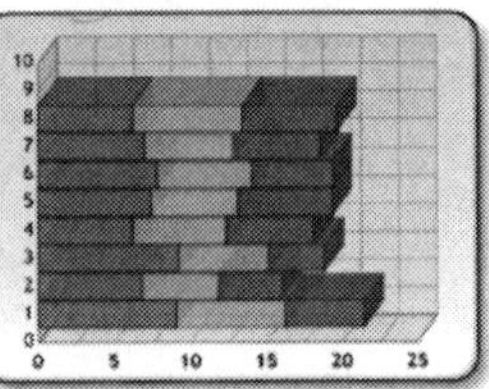

Figure 14–1. Example charts from the Microsoft Chart Controls

Prerequisites

If you want to use the Microsoft Chart Controls with .NET Framework 3.5 SP1 and Visual Studio 2008, you need to download and install the following components (see Table 14–1).

Table 14–1. *Prerequisites for Microsoft Chart Controls on .NET Framework 3.5 SP1*

Component	Downloadable From
Visual Studio 2008 SP1	`www.microsoft.com/downloads/details.aspx?FamilyId=FBEE1648-7106-44A7-9649-6D9F6D58056E&displaylang=en`
.NET Framework 3.5 SP1	`www.microsoft.com/downloads/details.aspx?FamilyID=ab99342f-5d1a-413d-8319-81da479ab0d7&displaylang=en`
Microsoft Chart Controls	`www.microsoft.com/downloads/details.aspx?FamilyID=130f7986-bf49-4fe5-9ca8-910ae6ea442c&DisplayLang=en`
Microsoft Chart Controls add-on for Visual Studio 2008	`www.microsoft.com/downloads/details.aspx?familyid=1D69CE13-E1E5-4315-825C-F14D33A303E9&displaylang=en`
Microsoft Chart Controls documentation	`www.microsoft.com/downloads/details.aspx?FamilyId=EE8F6F35-B087-4324-9DBA-6DD5E844FD9F&displaylang=en`
Microsoft Chart Controls samples	`http://code.msdn.microsoft.com/mschart`

Since the .NET Framework 4.0, the charting controls have been included within `System.Web.DataVisualization.dll`. You can use the chart control from within Visual Studio 2010 if you add a reference to the DLL (see Figure 14–2).

■ **Tip** A good entry point for working with the Microsoft Chart Controls is the MSDN documentation. Start at the following URL: `http://code.msdn.microsoft.com/mschart`.

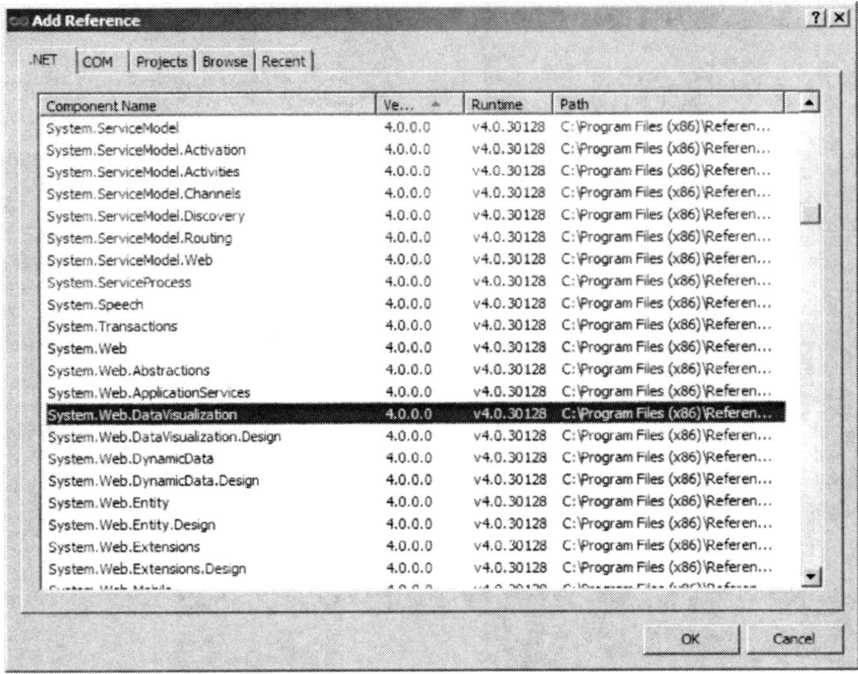

***Figure 14–2.** Adding the new System.Web.DataVisualization namespace to your Visual Studio project*

Both Visual Studio 2008 and 2010 offer design support for charts. For Visual Studio 2008 you first have to download and install the Microsoft Chart Controls add-on for Microsoft Visual Studio. Visual Studio 2010 has built-in design support, and no additional installation is necessary. The design support provides toolbox integration and IntelliSense for ASP.NET and Windows Forms chart controls.

Once installed, the `<asp:chart/>` control appears under the Data tab in the toolbox, and can be declared on any ASP.NET page as a standard server control, as shown in Figure 14–3.

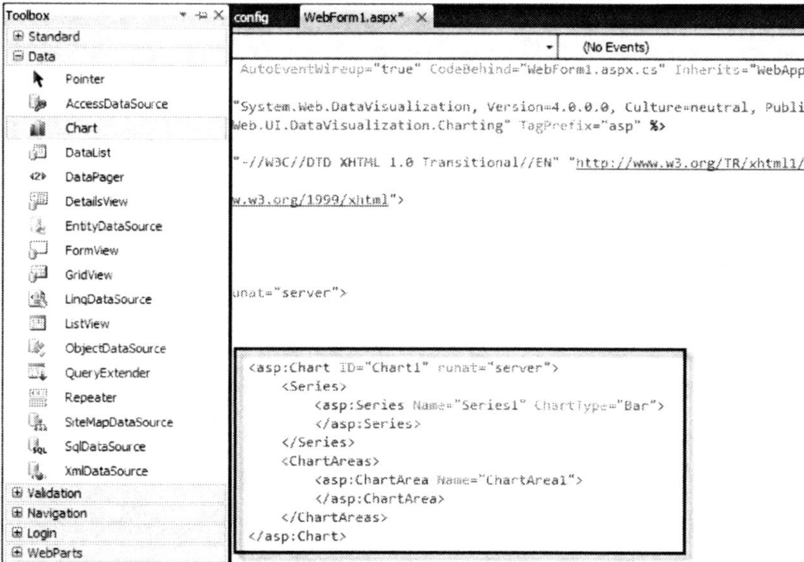

***Figure 14–3.** Visual Studio designer support for the Chart control*

<asp:chart/> supports a rich assortment of chart options, including pie, area, range, point, circular, accumulation, data distribution, Ajax interactive, and doughnut. Figure 14–4 shows the chart web control within the Visual Studio design view.

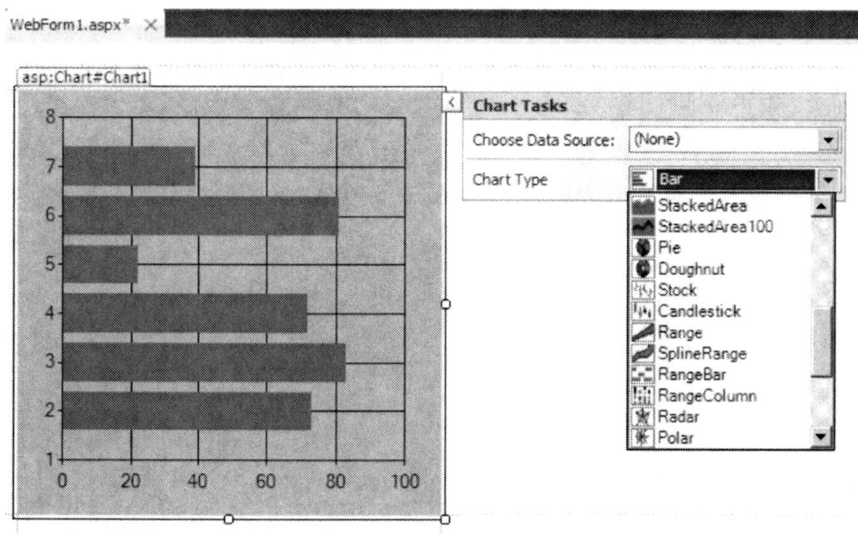

***Figure 14–4.** Customizing charts using the Visual Studio designer*

Features

The chart controls offer the key features shown in Table 14–2 (see also on MSDN at `http://msdn.microsoft.com/en-us/library/dd456632(VS.100).aspx`).

Table 14–2. Key Features for Microsoft Chart Controls

Category	Feature
Development environment	Visual Studio design-time support
Scalability	Support for an unlimited number of chart areas, titles, legends, and annotations Support for an unlimited number of data series and data points
Chart types	Thirty-five distinct chart types
Data	Data binding Data copying, merging, splitting, sorting, searching, grouping, and filtering Data exporting Binary and XML serialization Empty data point handling Support for dates, times, currency, and more More than 50 financial and statistical formulas for data analysis and transformation
Appearance	3D support for most chart types Automatic and manual layout and alignment management 3D customization Fully customizable legends Automatic and manual scaling Logarithmic scaling for any base Intelligent data label positioning Annotations, labels, scale breaks, and interlaced strip lines
Customizations	Real-time chart manipulation Postpaint and prepaint events Drill-down charts and tool tips
Windows Forms specific	Zooming and scrolling Chart printing
ASP.NET specific	Support for Ajax click events State management Binary streaming Animated frame rate control

Setting Up

Several prerequisites must be met before you can use the Microsoft Chart Controls within SharePoint. First, you need to register the chart HTTP handlers for in-memory image generation. To do this, add the following lines (see Figure 14–5) to the root `web.config` file of your SharePoint web application (commonly at `c:\inetpub\VirtualDirectories\PORT\web.config`).

```
<system.webServer>
  <handlers>
    <add name="ChartImageHandler" preCondition="integratedMode" verb="GET,HEAD" path="ChartImg.axd"
         type="System.Web.UI.DataVisualization.Charting.ChartHttpHandler, System.Web.DataVisualization,
         Version=x.x.0.0, Culture=neutral, PublicKeyToken=31bf3856ad364e35"/>
```

Figure 14–5. *Adding ChartHttpHandler under configuration/system.webServer/handlers (for IIS 7)*

After adding ChartImageHandler as shown in Figure 14–5, add an application settings entry to configure your handler to use in-memory storage of your images (see Figure 14–6).

```
<appSettings>
  <add key="ChartImageHandler" value="Storage=memory;Timeout=180;Url=~/tempImages/;"/>
```

Figure 14–6. *Adding the ChartImageHandler settings entry under configuration/appSettings*

Other valid values for the Storage parameter of the application settings entry ChartImageHandler include file and session, though we recommend setting to memory. The last preparatory step is to include the new chart tag, either in the web.config under configuration/system.web/pages/controls or directly within the ASPX page declaration.

```
<add tagPrefix="asp" namespace="System.Web.UI.DataVisualization.Charting"
     assembly="System.Web.DataVisualization, Version=3.5.0.0, Culture=neutral,
     PublicKeyToken=31bf3856ad364e35"/>
```

Having fulfilled all the prerequisites, you can add a simple chart to an ASPX application page by adding code similar to that shown in Listing 14–1.

Listing 14–1. *Simple Chart Declaration*

```
<asp:Chart ID="myChart" runat="server">
    <Series>
        <asp:Series Name="Series1" >
            <Points>
                <asp:DataPoint Label="Joerg" YValues="5" />
                <asp:DataPoint Label="Chris" YValues="7" />
            </Points>
        </asp:Series>
    </Series>
    <ChartAreas>
        <asp:ChartArea Name="ChartArea1">
        </asp:ChartArea>
    </ChartAreas>
</asp:Chart>
```

Figure 14–7 displays the output of the code from Listing 14–1—a simple bar chart.

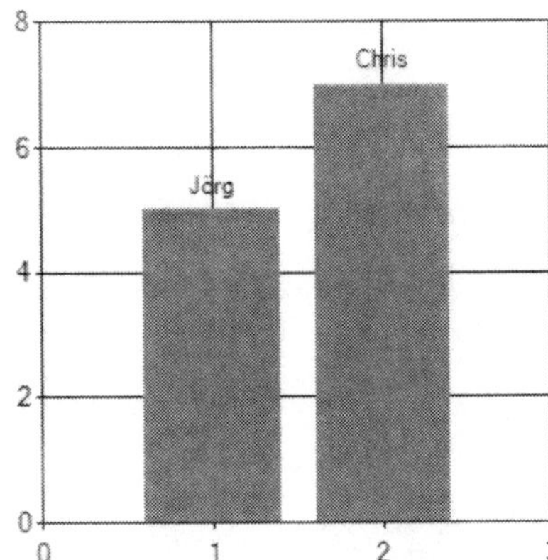

Figure 14–7. Simple bar chart

Using Microsoft Chart Control

The examples and documentation available with the Microsoft Chart Control are helpful and comprehensive. Using the Chart control is very straightforward. Simply drag a chart control onto an ASPX page, set the properties, and bind data to the chart.

You can either statically declare chart data within the control declaration or use data binding to populate it dynamically. At runtime the server control generates an image (e.g., a .PNG file) that is referenced from the client HTML of the page using a `<img/>` element output by the `<asp:chart/>` control. The server control supports caching of the chart image, as well as saving it to disk for persistent caching scenarios. It does not require any other server software to be installed, and will work with any standard ASP.NET page.

Chart Elements

A chart image is composed of various elements, including legends, axes, and series. Each such element is mapped to an object in the Microsoft Chart Control namespace. Figure 14–8 shows the elements of a chart control.

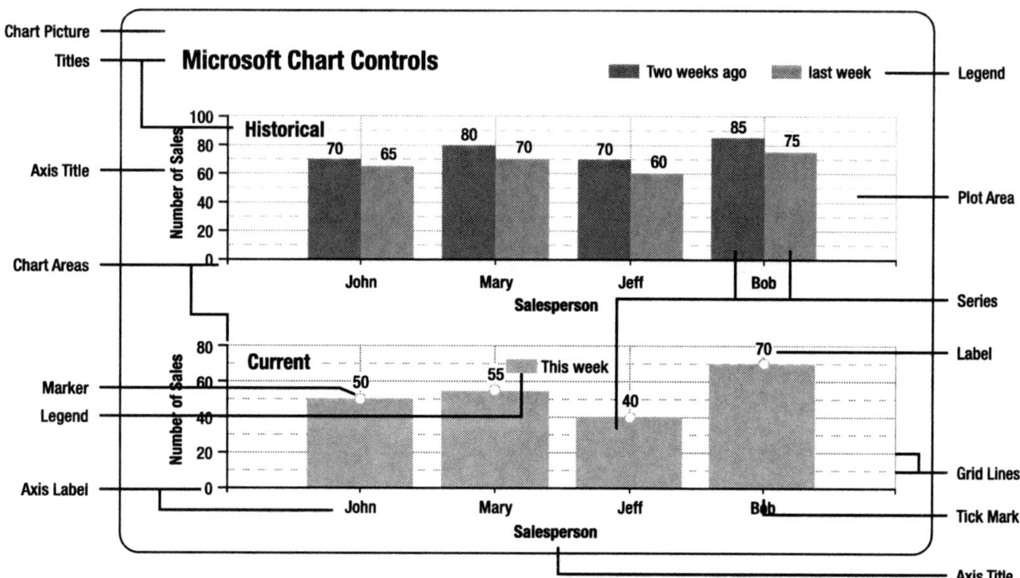

Figure 14–8. Elements of a charting control

The chart control API is object oriented, extensible, and highly flexible. An unlimited number of key chart elements such as data series or data points in a series are supported. Table 14–3 shows a short description of the key elements.

Table 14–3. Description of Charting Control Elements

Element	Description
`ChartArea`	Defines the area where a chart is plotted. Your chart may contain more than one chart area. You may plot more than one chart per render and you may even overlap charts.
`Series`	Consists of the data to plot on your chart area.
`ChartType`	(under the `Series` property) defines how your data series will be displayed on a chart area.
`Axes`	Defines properties for the x and y axes, such as appearance and titles.
`Palette`	Defines the colors set for your chart.
`Titles`	Defines text that may be used to describe a chart, an axis, or any other part of the chart.

Element	Description
Legends	Defines the legends that will display the data series information.
Labels	Defines text that may be displayed, for example, close to an axis or point (includes custom labels).

Working with Data

The Microsoft Chart Control supports various data binding scenarios. It provides a simple and consistent way to visualize data. The most common way to binding data is to use an IEnumerable object, such as a DataView, DataReader, DataTable, DataSet, Array, or List. To understand Chart Control data binding, you first have to be familiar with series and data points. All data for a chart is rendered as a series, and each series consists of data points. Each data point has an X value and one or more Y values, depending on the chart type, that determine where a data point is plotted (DataPoint.XValue, DataPoint.YValues).

There are several data binding methods available (see Table 14–4).

Table 14–4. Data Binding Methods

Method	Description
Chart.DataBindTable	This is a simple binding for X and Y values. It automatically creates series for the columns in the data source.
Chart.DataSource	This method allows data binding at design time.
Chart.DataBindCrossTab	This binds data and offers grouping functionality.
Series.Points.DataBind	This binds complex IEnumerable objects to a series.
Series.Points.DataBind[X]Y	This binds X and Y values to a series.
Series.Points.Add	This method is for manually adding points to a series.

The next few pages show some examples on how to use the various data binding methods in your code.

Chart.DataBindTable

With the Chart.DataBindTable method, you can easily bind a table containing several columns. You can choose one column for the X value, and for each of the other columns a new series will be created automatically.

To demonstrate this, assume there is a SharePoint list called ProductSales. This list contains sales data for several products. Every row has a salesperson name (here, Title) and four article fields (Article1 to Article4) with numeric data (see Figure 14–9).

Title	Article1	Article2	Article3	Article4
Christian	10	12	4	23
Joerg	13	7	6	22
Alex	8	15	5	18

***Figure 14–9.** Example data from a SharePoint list*

Binding this SharePoint list to a chart control is elementary. You define a CAML query that contains at least the required field names for the chart. Then you call the `SPList.GetDataTable` method to execute the query and return a `DataTable` instance. The final step is to bind the `DataTable.DefaultView` using the `Chart.DataBindTable` method (see Listing 14–2).

***Listing 14–2.** Binding a SharePoint List via GetDataTable*

```
private void DataBindTableExample()
{
    SPQuery query = new SPQuery();
    query.ViewFields = "<FieldRef Name='Title'/>" +
         "<FieldRef Name='Article1'/>" +
         "<FieldRef Name='Article2'/>" +
         "<FieldRef Name='Article3'/>" +
         "<FieldRef Name='Article4'/>";

    SPList productSalesList = this.Web.Lists["ProductSales"];
    SPListItemCollectionPosition colPos;

    DataTable dt = productSalesList.GetDataTable(query,
            SPListGetDataTableOptions.None, out colPos);

    myChart.DataBindTable(dt.DefaultView, "Title");
}
```

The example in **Listing 14–2** results in a chart like the one shown in Figure 14–10.

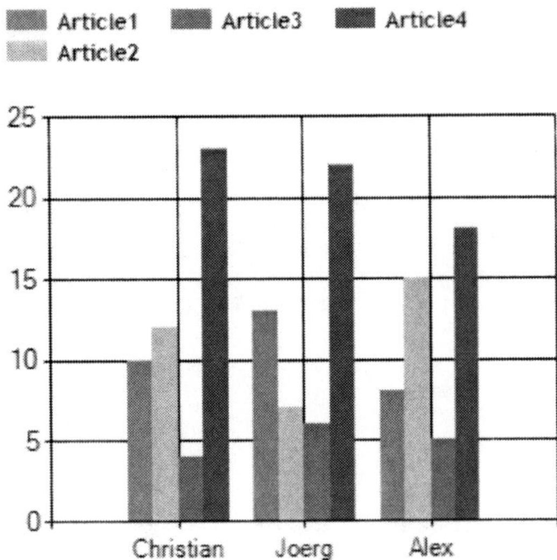

Figure 14–10. Example chart generated from a SharePoint list

Chart.DataSource

To bind data using the `Chart.DataSource` property, you first create one or more series and set their `XValueMember` and `YValueMembers` property names. If multiple Y values are required, they can be bound if you supply a comma-separated list to the `YValueMembers`. The binding itself takes place automatically just before rendering, meaning that you don't need to explicitly call `Chart.DataBind` in your code.

The example in this section uses the same data source as the preceding example (`ProductSales`). Naturally, it also produces the same output as shown in Figure 14–10. The main difference is that it uses a LINQ data source in conjunction with several static series declarations. Listing 14–3 shows the chart series and the LINQ data source declarations.

***Listing 14–3.** Declarartion of Chart Series and a LINQ Data Source*

```
<asp:Chart ID="myChart" runat="server">
    <Series>
        <asp:Series Name="Article1" XValueMember="SalesName" YValueMembers="Article1" />
        <asp:Series Name="Article2" XValueMember="SalesName" YValueMembers="Article2" />
        <asp:Series Name="Article3" XValueMember="SalesName" YValueMembers="Article3" />
        <asp:Series Name="Article4" XValueMember="SalesName" YValueMembers="Article4" />
    </Series>

    <ChartAreas>
        <asp:ChartArea Name="ChartArea1" ></asp:ChartArea>
    </ChartAreas>
</asp:Chart>

<asp:LinqDataSource runat="server" ID="linqDS" OnSelecting="linqDS_Selecting"  />
```

The code-behind for this data binding example also looks straightforward (see Listing 14–4). As you can see, the LINQ data source linqDS is simply assigned to the Chart.DataSource property. The implementation of the data source uses a CAML query to retrieve the list items from the SharePoint list ProductSales, and returns an anonymous type containing the properties SalesName and Article1 to Article4. The X and Y value members of the series take those properties and ensure the correct chart rendering (see Figure 14–10 again).

Listing 14–4. *Data Binding and LINQ Data Source Implementation*

```
protected void Page_Load(object sender, EventArgs e)
{
    // Assign the data source
    myChart.DataSource = linqDS;
}

protected void linqDS_Selecting(object sender, LinqDataSourceSelectEventArgs e)
{
    SPList list = SPContext.Current.Web.Lists["ProductSales"];
    IEnumerable<SPListItem> sales = list.GetItems(
                                        new SPQuery()).OfType<SPListItem>();
    e.Result = from salesItem in sales
       select new
       {
           SalesName = Convert.ToString(salesItem["Title"]),
           Article1 = Convert.ToInt32(salesItem["Article1"]),
           Article2 = Convert.ToInt32(salesItem["Article2"]),
           Article3 = Convert.ToInt32(salesItem["Article3"]),
           Article4 = Convert.ToInt32(salesItem["Article4"])
       };
}
```

Chart.DataBindCrossTab

The Chart.DataBindCrossTab method supports automatic grouping of unique values in a column. Each unique value in the specified grouped column results in the creation of a new data series. Furthermore, you can bind extended data properties, such as AxisLabel, Tooltip, and Label, to the chart.

The example data for this section is shown in Figure 14–11. For every salesperson (Title) and year (Year), a quantity for Article1 complemented by a sales ranking for that year (YearRanking) is included.

Title	Year	Article1	YearRanking
Christian	2008	10	3
Christian	2009	17	2
Christian	2010	25	1
Joerg	2008	18	2
Joerg	2009	15	3
Joerg	2010	21	2
Alex	2008	20	1
Alex	2009	19	1
Alex	2010	14	3

Figure 14–11. Example data of a SharePoint list to use with Chart.DataBindCrossTab

The resulting line chart for this data looks like Figure 14–12. Every salesperson has his or her own series that displays `Article1` on the y axis and the `Year` on the x axis. In addition, the `YearRanking` is rendered as a label.

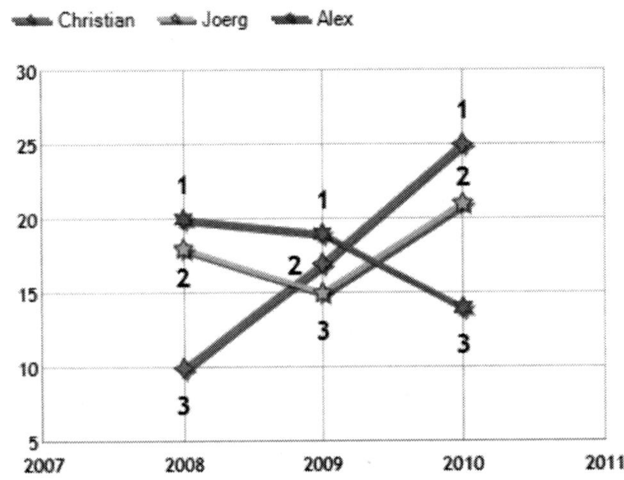

Figure 14–12. Example chart for Chart.DataBindCrossTab

As shown in Listing 14–5, the `DataBindCrossTab` method takes `DataTable.DefaultView` as an input parameter. The series are defined by the second parameter (`Title`) followed by property names for the X and Y values (`Year` and `Article1`). Additionally, the last parameter contains an extended data property definition using this syntax:

In the following example, `Label=YearRanking` is defined, which results in rendering the `YearRanking` value as labels within the chart.

Listing 14–5. Data Binding with Automatic Grouping Using DataBindCrossTab Method

```
private void DataBindCrossTabExample()
{
    SPQuery query = new SPQuery();

    query.ViewFields = "<FieldRef Name='Title'/>" +
         "<FieldRef Name='Year'/>" +
         "<FieldRef Name='Article1'/>" +
         "<FieldRef Name='YearRanking'/>";

    SPList productSalesList = this.Web.Lists["ProductSalesWithYears"];
    SPListItemCollectionPosition colPos;
    DataTable dt = productSalesList.GetDataTable(query,
            SPListGetDataTableOptions.None, out colPos);

    myChart.DataBindCrossTable(dt.DefaultView, "Title", "Year",
          "Article1", "Label=YearRanking");

    // Set series appearance
    MarkerStyle marker = MarkerStyle.Star4;
    foreach (Series ser in myChart.Series)
    {
        ser.ShadowOffset = 2;
        ser.BorderWidth = 3;

        ser.ChartType = SeriesChartType.Line;

        ser.MarkerSize = 12;
        ser.MarkerStyle = marker;
        ser.MarkerBorderColor = Color.FromArgb(64, 64, 64);
        ser.Font = new Font("Trebuchet MS", 12, FontStyle.Bold);
        marker++;
    }
}
```

The code in Listing 14–5 follows a similar style to the other data binding methods. You commence by retrieving data via a CAML query into a `DataTable`. Then you bind the `DataTable.DefaultView` to the chart. Finally, you can modify the autocreated series and assign custom styles, such as chart types, borders, markers, colors, and fonts.

Points.DataBind and Points.DataBind[X]Y

This data binding method allows you to bind X and Y values to a series. Also, the binding syntax enables you to define extended data properties, such as `AxisLabel`, `Tooltip`, `Label`, `LegendText`, and `LegendTooltip`. A simple example looks like:

```
myChart.Series["mySeries"].Points.DataBind(
        dataView, "Year", "Article1", "Tooltip=YearRanking")
```

The usage is similar to `Chart.DataBindCrossTab`, but it is only related to one series, and thus it has no grouping functionality.

Beyond the Points.DataBind method, there are two further methods: Points.DataBindY and Points.DataBindXY. The various methods are defined as follows:

```
DataPointCollection.DataBind(IEnumerable dataSource, string xField,
                             string yFields, string otherFields)
DataPointCollection.DataBindY(IEnumerable yValue, string yFields)
DataPointCollection.DataBindY(params IEnumerable[] yValue)

DataPointCollection.DataBindXY(IEnumerable xValue, params IEnumerable[] yValues)
DataPointCollection.DataBindXY(IEnumerable xValue, string XField,
                              IEnumerable yValue, string yFields)
```

As you can see in the definitions, the main difference between the methods is that DataBind has one data source (IEnumerable dataSource), whereas the other methods may have multiple data sources for X and Y values.

The example in Listing 14–6 demonstrates querying data using LINQ on a data model generated using SPMetal and binding the data with the DataBind method.

Listing 14–6. *Binding an Anonymous Type to a Chart Series Using LINQ*

```
protected void DataBindPointsExample()
{
    SPDataContext ctx = new SPDataContext(SPContext.Current.Web.Url);

    // Create LINQ join query
    var result =
        from sale in ctx.ProductSalesWithYears
        where sale.Title == "Christian"
        select new
        {
            SalesName = sale.Title,
            Year = sale.Year,
            ArticlesSold = sale.Article1,
            TooltipText = sale.Title + " sold " + sale.Article1
                                    + " articles in " + sale.Year,
            LabelText = "Ranking for " + sale.Year + ": "
                                      + sale.YearRanking
        };

    myChart.Series[0].Points.DataBind(result.ToArray(), "Year", "ArticlesSold",
                                      "ToolTip=TooltipText,Label=LabelText");
}
```

SPDataContext contains the SharePoint data model for the list ProductSalesWithYears (shown in Figure 14–13). The example uses a LINQ query to retrieve all items containing Christian as Title. The result is prepared for data binding using a new anonymous type. This type contains the properties SalesName, Year, ArticlesSold, TooltipText, and LabelText, which are directly bound to the chart series. The resulting chart looks like Figure 14–13.

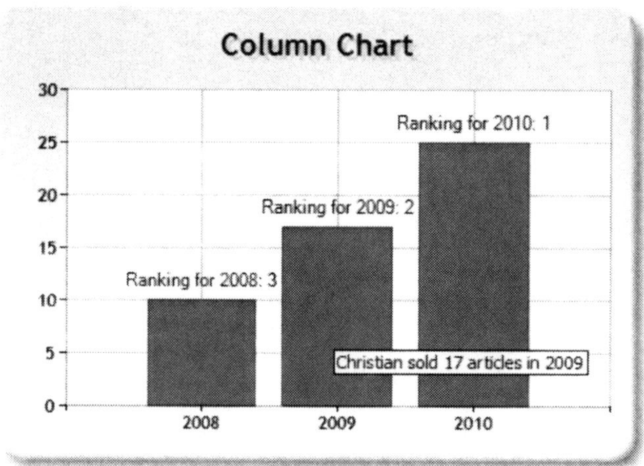

Figure 14–13. Example chart for Point.DataBind

Manual Data Population by Adding Data Points

The data binding methods introduced in the preceding paragraphs are sufficient for many scenarios. But if you are ever faced with more complex requirements and you need full control over the data population process, you can also manually add data points to a series. This approach is also useful if you are working with calculated data. The example in Listing 14–7 shows how to iterate through data received using LINQ, including creating series and adding data points.

Listing 14–7. Manually Populationg Charts Using LINQ and DataPoints

```
private void ManualDataPopulationExample()
{
    SPDataContext ctx = new SPDataContext(SPContext.Current.Web.Url);

    // Query the SharePoint list "ProductSalesWithYears"
    var result = from sale in ctx.ProductSalesWithYears
        select new
        {
            SalesName = sale.Title,
            Year = sale.Year,
            ArticlesSold = sale.Article1,
            TooltipText = sale.Title + " sold " + sale.Article1 +
                                     " articles in " + sale.Year,
            LabelText = "Ranking for " + sale.Year + ": " + sale.YearRanking
        };

    // Getting all sales names (Christian, Joerg, Alex)
    var salesNames = (from s in result select s.SalesName).Distinct();

    // Creating a series for every sales name
    foreach (var seriesName in salesNames)
```

```
    {
        // Create a new series
        Series newSeries = new Series(seriesName);
        newSeries.ChartType = SeriesChartType.Column;
        newSeries.BorderWidth = 2;
        myChart.Series.Add(newSeries);


        var seriesData = from r in result where r.SalesName == seriesName select r;
        foreach (var resultItem in seriesData) {
            // Creating a DataPoint
            DataPoint dp = new DataPoint();

            // Assign X and Y values
            dp.SetValueXY(resultItem.Year, resultItem.ArticlesSold);

            // Assign Label and Tooltip
            dp.Label = resultItem.LabelText;
            dp.ToolTip = resultItem.TooltipText;

            // Add DataPoint to series
            newSeries.Points.Add(dp);
        }
    }
}
```

The code in Listing 14–7 requires an `SPDataContext` and model classes generated using `SPMetal`. A LINQ query retrieves all items from the SharePoint list `ProductSalesWithYears` and creates an anonymous type that consists of some properties. For every different `SalesName`, a new series is created. Therefore, the example uses a distinct LINQ query that returns all the different `SalesName` strings. A loop iterates through the `salesName` strings and creates a new series for each element. A further LINQ query returns all the data for the current `SalesName` within the loop and creates `DataPoint` objects. These `DataPoint` objects are populated with data for X and Y values, and the `Label` and `ToolTip` properties are set. Finally, the `DataPoint` objects are added to the series. The resulting chart is shown in Figure 14–14.

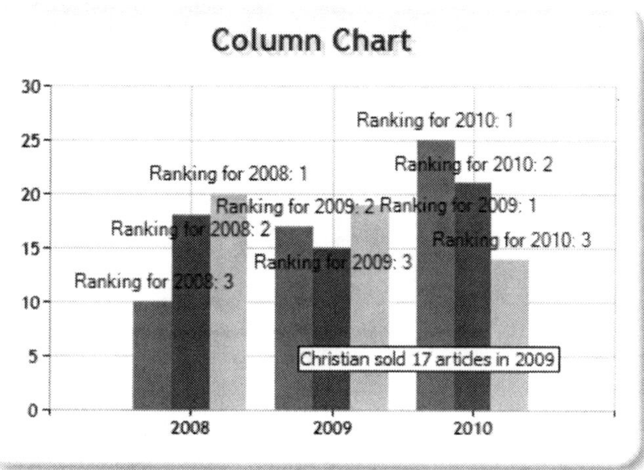

***Figure 14–14.** Example chart for manual data population*

Chart Types and Examples

Microsoft has a samples document for Microsoft Chart Controls available for download at `http://code.msdn.microsoft.com/mschart`). This package contains over 200 chart samples to inspire your own custom charts. To give you a taste of the great visualization possibilities, some well-chosen examples of the chart control sample galleries follow:

- Bar and column charts
- Line charts
- Area charts
- Pie and doughnut charts
- Point charts
- Range charts
- Accumulation charts
- Financial charts

Bar and Column Charts

Bar and column charts (see Figure 14–15) illustrate comparisons among individual items. Bar charts are mostly used for comparing categories by their values, whereas column charts place more emphasis on comparing values over time. Bar and column charts support one Y value per X value. The number of series within one chart is not limited.

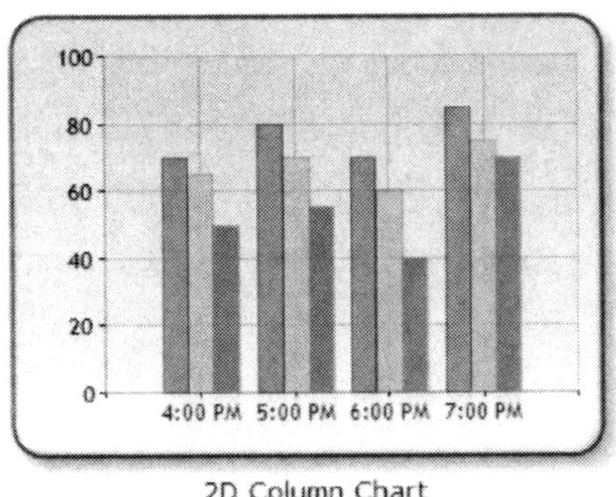

2D Column Chart

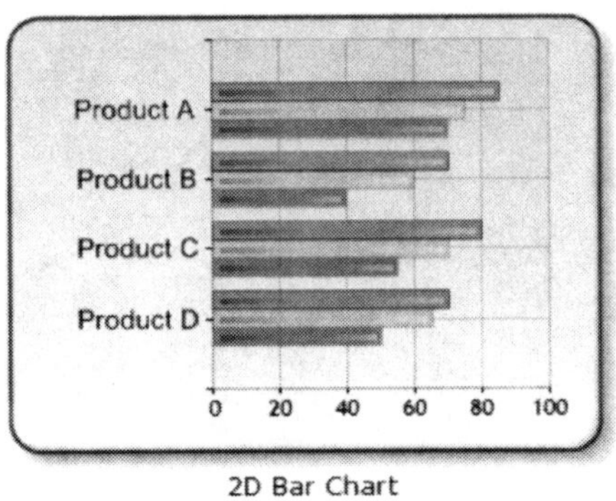

2D Bar Chart

Figure 14–15. Bar and column chart examples

Line Charts

Line charts (see Figure 14–16) can be used to visualize trends along a timeline. Line charts support one Y value per X value. The number of series within one chart is not limited.

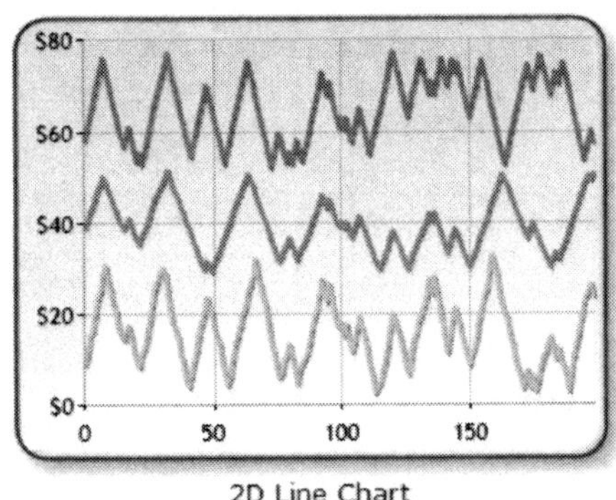

2D Line Chart

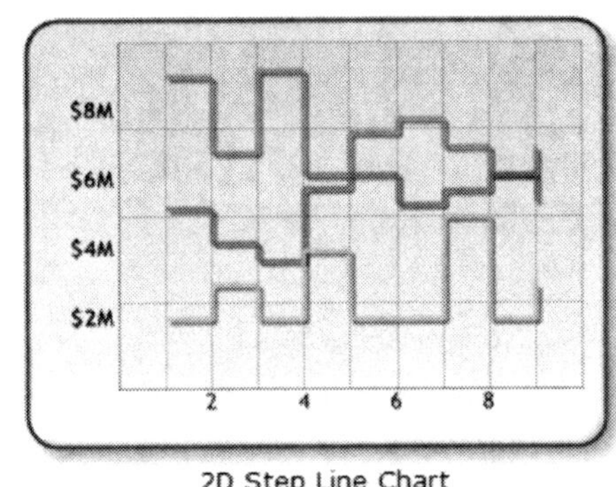

2D Step Line Chart

Figure 14–16. Line chart examples

Area Charts

Area charts (see Figure 14–17) emphasize changes of data over time and show the relationship of different parts to a whole. Area charts support one Y value per X value. The number of series within one chart is not limited.

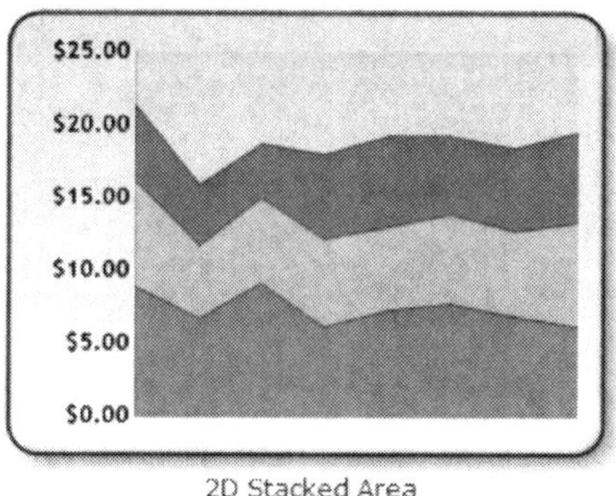

2D Stacked Area

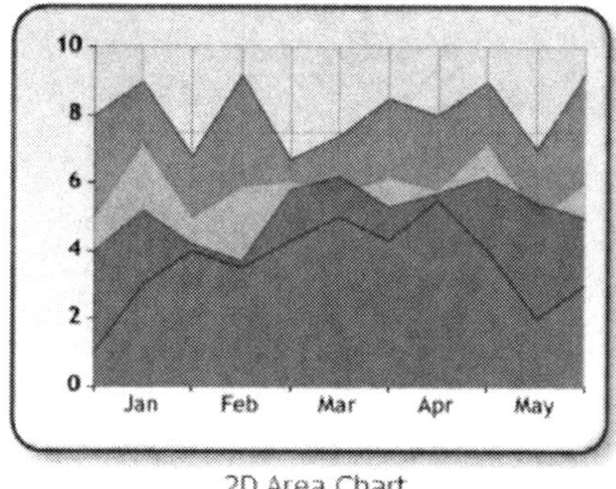

2D Area Chart

Figure 14–17. Area chart examples

Pie and Doughnut Charts

Pie and doughnut charts (see Figure 14–18) show how proportions of data contribute to the data as a whole. They are both shown as pie-shaped pieces. Pie and doughnut charts support one Y value per X value. The number of series is limited to one series per chart.

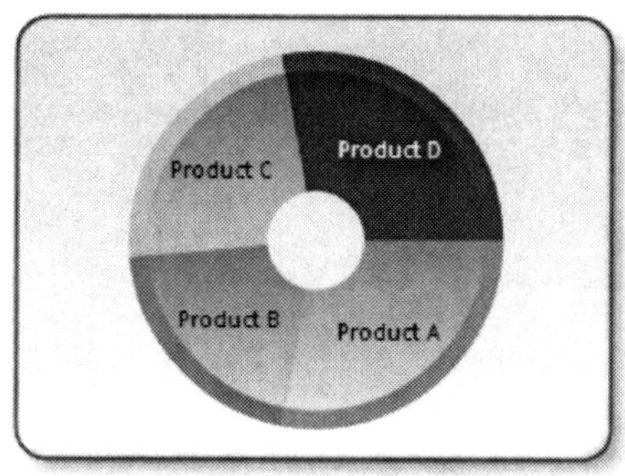

2D Doughnut Chart

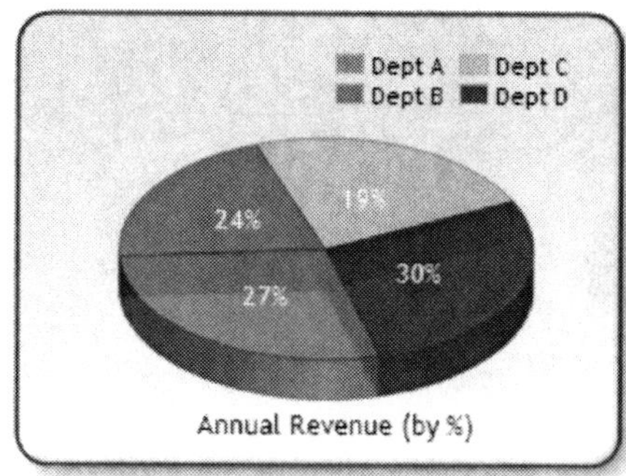

3D Pie Chart

Figure 14–18. Pie and doughnut chart examples

Point Charts

Point charts (see Figure 14–19) use single-value points for displaying data. Point charts support one Y value per X value. The number of series within one chart is not limited.

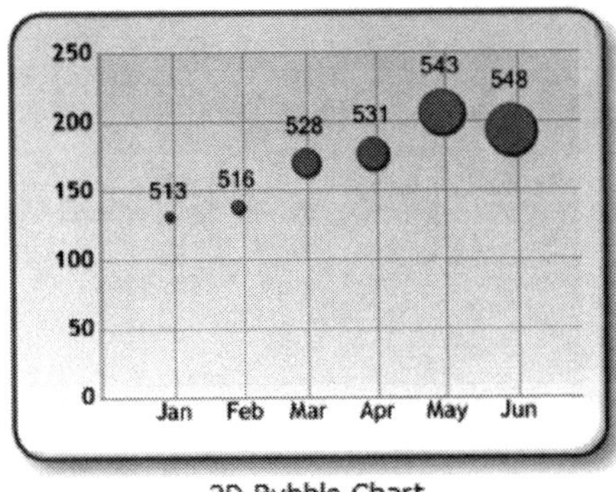

2D Bubble Chart

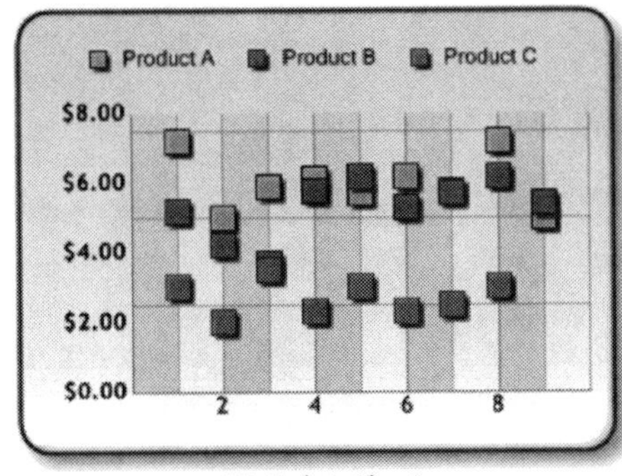

2D Point Chart

Figure 14–19. Point chart examples

Range Charts

Range charts (see Figure 14–20) display a range of data by plotting two Y values per data point. You can imagine those two Y values as two line charts that can be filled with color or an image. The number of series within one chart is not limited.

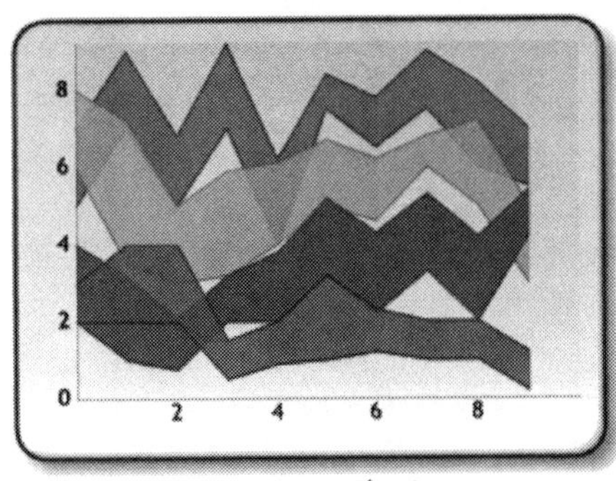

2D Range Chart

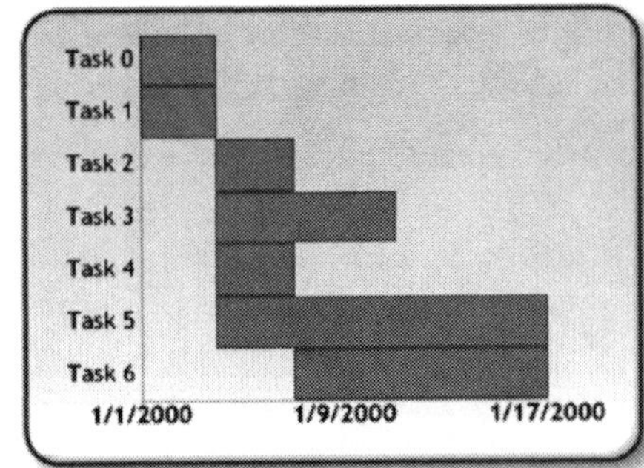

2D Range Bar Chart

Figure 14–20. Range chart examples

Radar Charts

Circular charts (see Figure 14–21), such as radar charts, are primarily used for data comparison. Unlike most other chart types, radar charts have no X values. Nevertheless the X axis is still used for displaying the labels around the chart, as well as spacing between the labels. The number of series within one chart is not limited.

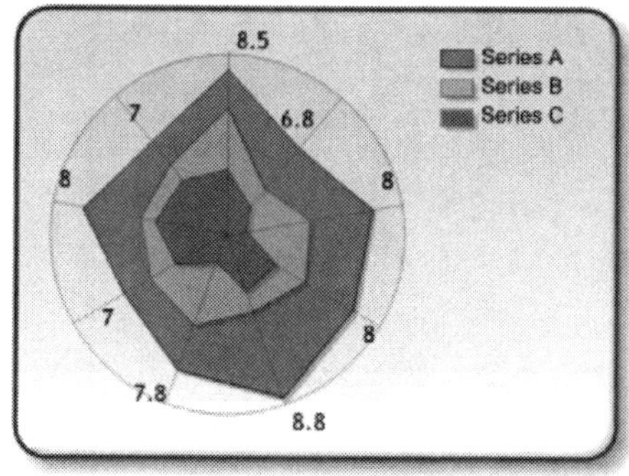

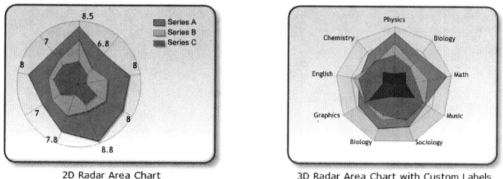

2D Radar Area Chart

3D Radar Area Chart with Custom Labels

Figure 14–21. Circular chart examples

Accumulation Charts

Accumulation charts (see Figure 14–22), such as funnel or pyramid charts, display data that equals 100 percent in total. These chart types have no axes; thus, they support only one Y value per category. The number of series is limited to one per chart.

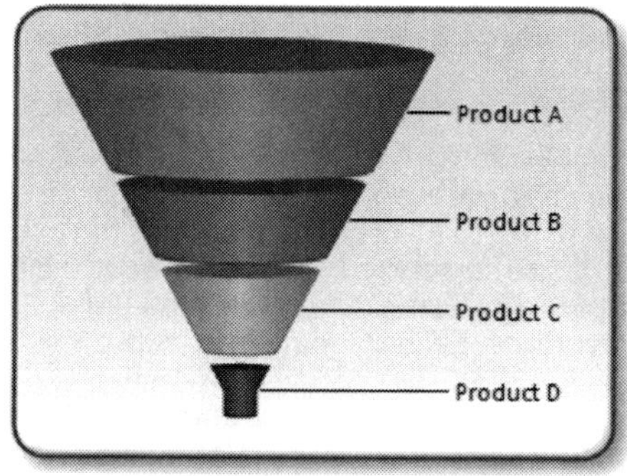

3D Funnel Chart with Point Gaps

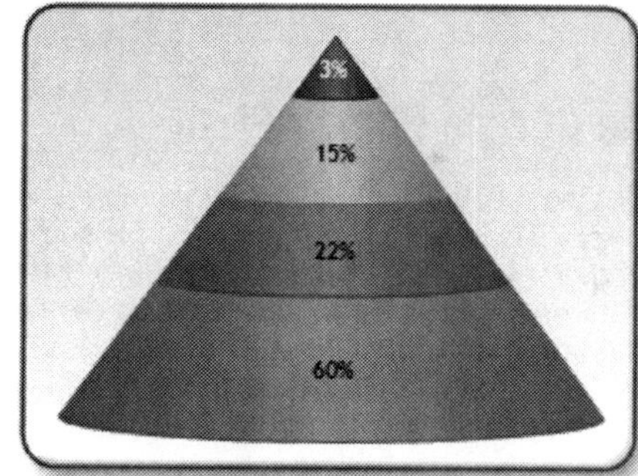

3D Pyramid Chart

Figure 14–22. Accumulation chart examples

Financial Charts

Candlestick and stock charts (see Figure 14–23) are used to display stock information using four values: high, low, open, and close. The height of a line is determined by the high and low values. For a candlestick chart, the size of the bar and whether it is filled or not depend upon the open/close values. In a stock chart, the open/close values are plotted as small markers.

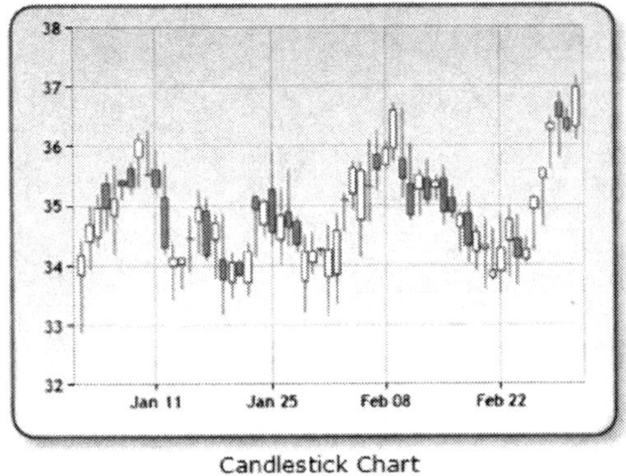

Candlestick Chart

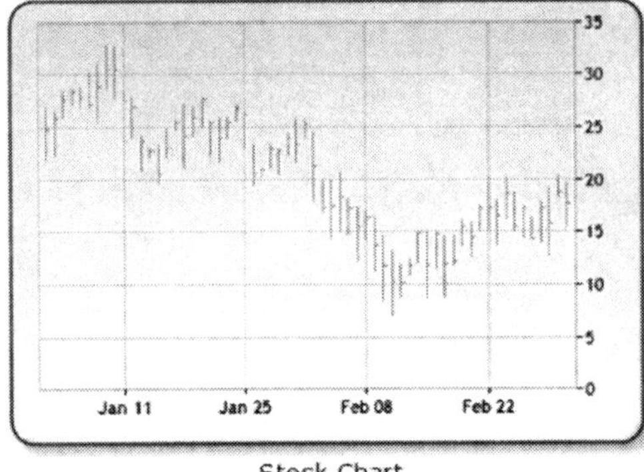

Stock Chart

Figure 14–23. Financial chart examples

Conclusion

The Microsoft Chart Controls offer more than 35 distinct, professional chart types that can be used within application pages and Web Parts. If you are ever faced with implementing custom charts or dashboards, this package should be your first option to consider. With direct support for SharePoint list data and easy-to-use data binding techniques, the Microsoft Chart Control is a powerful toolset.

Using the Google Chart API

The Google Chart API is a charting service offered by Google. The charts are generated completely on Google servers. The data to be charted is passed within the query string to a URL. The response to such an HTTP request is a PNG image of the chart. Many types of charts are supported, and by embedding the URL into an image tag you can simply include the chart in your own application pages or Web Parts. Originally, Google built the Chart API for internal use in its applications. Later, Google opened up the API to web developers. One critical thing to bear in mind when using the Chart API in your own applications is security: all data that is displayed in charts is sent within the openly readable query string over the Internet to Google's servers. We strongly recommend against sending business-critical data, such as brand new revenue figures, over the Internet.

It is extremely easy to use the Google Chart API—simply insert the Chart API URL with some query string parameters into an image tag:

```
<img src="http://chart.apis.google.com/chart?cht=p3&chd=t:35,24,10,3,1&
                 chs=350x150&chl=Krause|Langhirt|Sterff|Pehlke|Doering" />
```

The image URL for the Chart API is `http://chart.apis.google.com/chart`. In addition, there are query string parameters that affect the display of the chart:

- `cht`: Chart type (`p` = pie chart, `p3` = pie chart 3D, etc.)
- `chd`: Chart data (`t` = text encoding; data values are separated by commas)
- `chs`: Chart size (width and height in pixels)
- `chl`: Chart labels (labels corresponding to the chart data values separated by pipes)

The generated chart image looks like Figure 14–24.

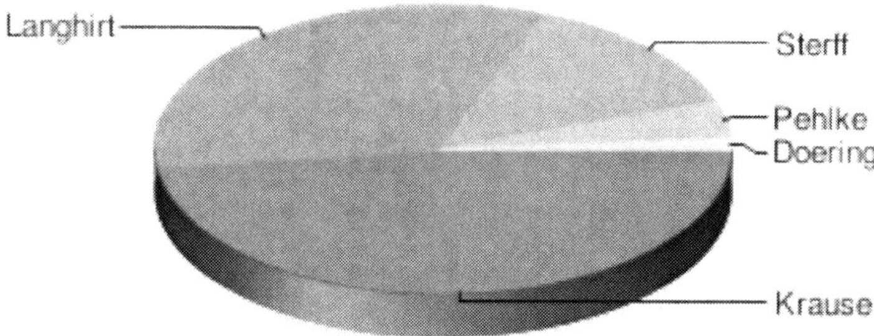

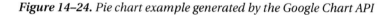

Figure 14–24. *Pie chart example generated by the Google Chart API*

■ **Note** The Google Chart API officially does not support HTTPS/SSL. To overcome this there are two possible workarounds. The first is to simply use the SSL URL `https://www.google.com/chart` instead of `http://chart.apis.google.com/chart`. Although this is not recommended by Google it currently seems to work. A better solution is to retrieve charts as binary HTTP data directly from the server. Therefore, you can, for example, use an ASP.NET web handler file (`.ashx`) that accepts the binary data from the Google URL and returns it to your own page running with SSL.

Chart Types

Google offers many chart types for different scenarios. For a good overview of the different types, visit `http://code.google.com/intl/de/apis/chart/types.html`. Beneath the standard charts, such as line, bar, and pie charts, there are also some extended types. They include Venn diagrams, scatter plots, radar charts, maps, Google-o-Meters, and QR (specialized bar code) charts. Table 14–5 contains some chart examples.

Table 14–5. *Google Chart API Chart Types*

Chart Type	Chart Parameter	Example
Line chart	`cht=[lc|ls|lxy]`	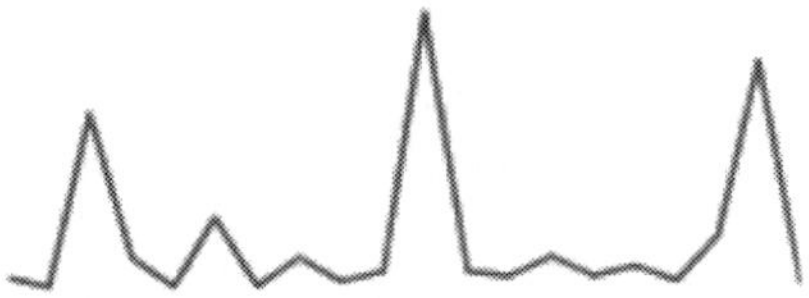
Bar chart	`cht=[bhs|bvs|bhg|bvg]`	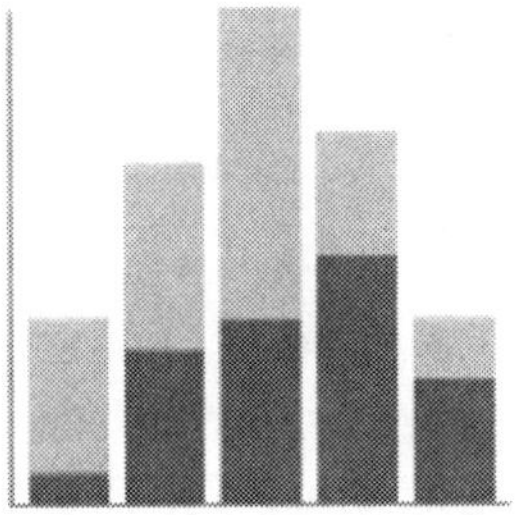
Pie chart	`cht=[p|p3|pc]`	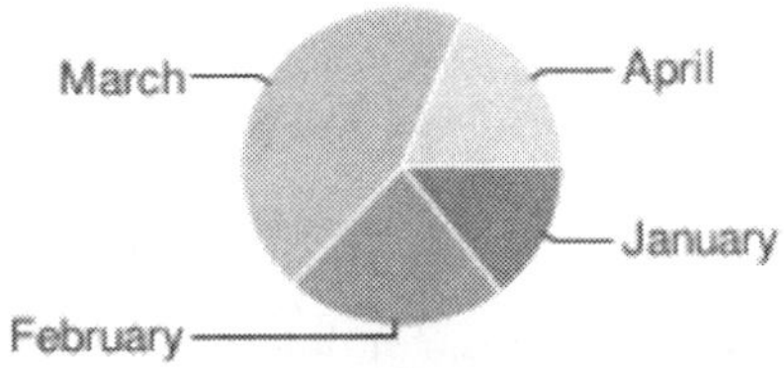
Venn diagram	`cht=v`	

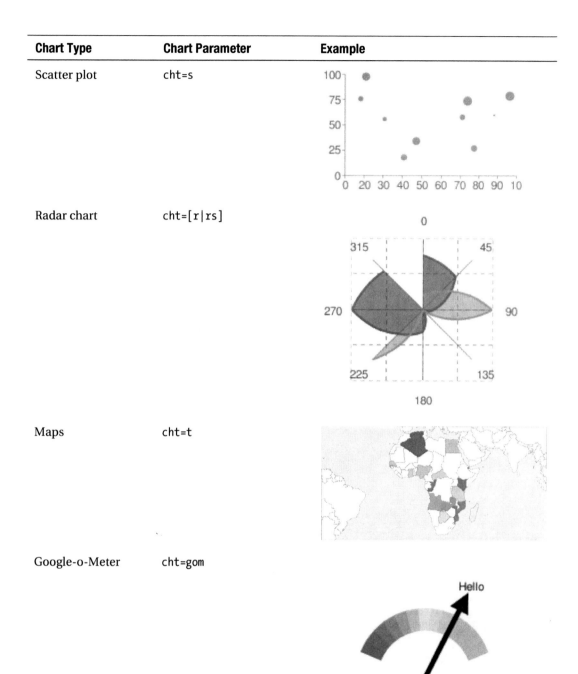

Chart Type	Chart Parameter	Example
Scatter plot	cht=s	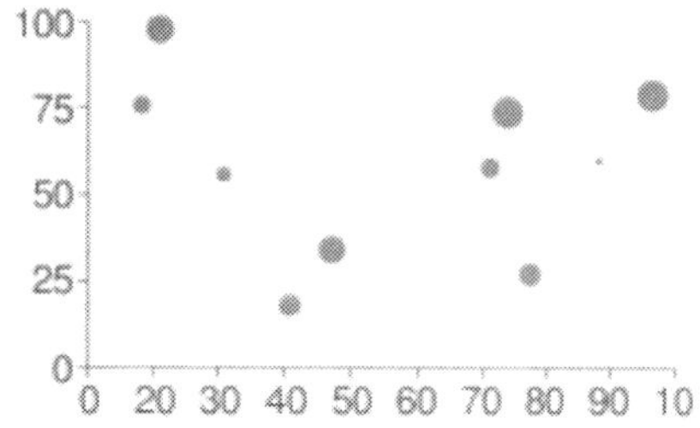
Radar chart	cht=[r|rs]	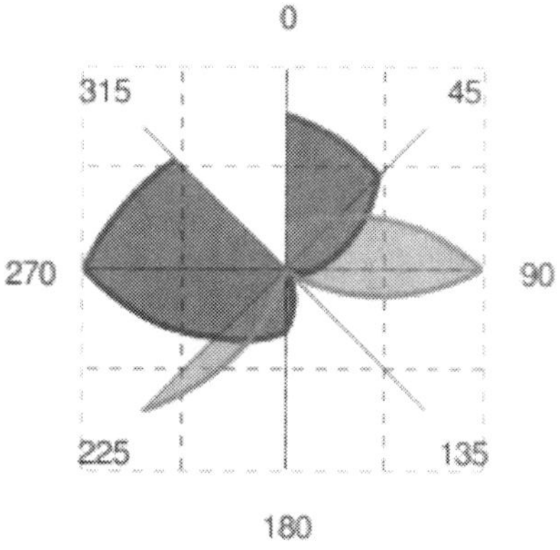
Maps	cht=t	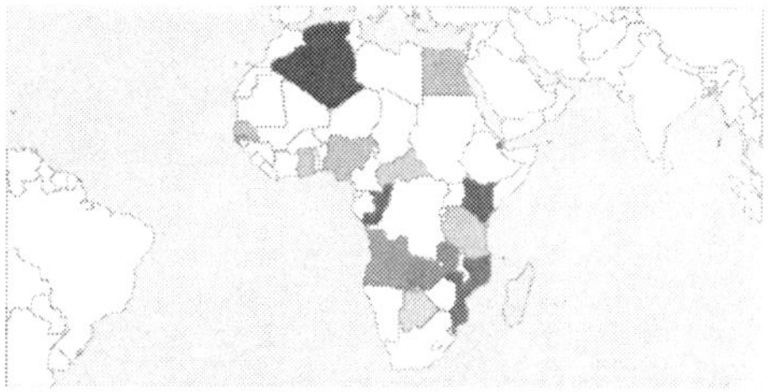
Google-o-Meter	cht=gom	

Chart Type	Chart Parameter	Example
QR codes	cht=qr	

Using the Google Chart API with SharePoint

When generating and displaying Google Charts within SharePoint application pages or Web Parts, we strongly recommend you write classes to encapsulate the building of the complex query strings. The objective is to make displaying a chart as simple as instantiating an object, adding data, and calling a method. For example, if you wish to create a line chart, you should be able to write elementary code in this style:

```
GoogleChart gc = new GoogleChart(ChartTypeEnum.LineLC, 350, 200);
gc.ChartData.AddRange(new int[] {2,50,80,10,40});
gc.ChartLabels.AddRange(new String[] {"A","B","C","D","E" });
imgChart.ImageUrl = gc.BuildUrl();
```

This code creates an instance of a class called GoogleChart that takes the chart type and the output image size as parameters. After passing the data and the labels, call BuildUrl to assign the output to the ImageUrl property of an ASP.NET Image web control. The implementation of the GoogleChart class is shown in Listing 14–8.

Listing 14– 8. *Helper Class for Using Google Charts*

```
public enum ChartTypeEnum
{
    LineLC,
    LineLS,
    LineXY
}

public class GoogleChart
{
    public String ChartBaseUrl = "http://chart.apis.google.com/chart?";

    public ChartTypeEnum ChartType {get; set;}
    public List<int> ChartData { get; set; }
    public List<String> ChartLabels { get; set; }
    public int ChartWidth { get; set; }
    public int ChartHeight { get; set; }

    public GoogleChart(ChartTypeEnum chartType, int width, int height)
    {
        this.ChartType = chartType;
        this.ChartWidth = width;
        this.ChartHeight = height;
        this.ChartData = new List<int>();
```

```
        this.ChartLabels = new List<string>();
    }

    public String BuildUrl()
    {
        StringBuilder sb = new StringBuilder();
        sb.Append(ChartBaseUrl);

        switch (ChartType)
        {
            case ChartTypeEnum.LineLC:
              sb.Append("cht=lc");
              break;
            case ChartTypeEnum.LineLS:
              sb.Append("cht=ls");
              break;
            case ChartTypeEnum.LineXY:
              sb.Append("cht=lxy");
              break;
        }

        // Build data string
        sb.Append("&chd=t:");
        for (int i = 0; i < ChartData.Count; i++)
        {
            if (i>0) sb.Append(",");
            sb.Append(ChartData[i]);
        }

        // Build label string
        sb.Append("&chl=");
        for (int i = 0; i < ChartLabels.Count; i++)
        {
            if (i > 0) sb.Append("|");
            sb.Append(HttpUtility.UrlEncode(ChartLabels[i]));
        }

        // Build chart size
        sb.Append("&chs=" + ChartWidth + "x" + ChartHeight);

        return sb.ToString();
    }
}
```

The code in Listing 14–8 defines a class whose `BuildUrl` method constructs a chart image URL such as the following:

The next big improvement we can make is to implement an ASP.NET web handler that sends chart requests to Google and returns the binary image data. Consequently, the user's browser never connects to Google—only to the SharePoint server. This technique has the advantage that it also works on secured HTTPS/SSL connections. An example for a web handler that requests data from Google is shown in Listing 14–9.

Listing 14–9. *GoogleChartHandler.ashx for Requesting Charts from Google*

```
<%@ WebHandler Language="C#" Class="GoogleChartHandler" %>

using System;
using System.Web;
using System.Net;
using System.IO;

public class GoogleChartHandler : IHttpHandler
{
    public bool IsReusable { get { return true;} }

    public void ProcessRequest(HttpContext context)
    {
        context.Response.ContentType = "image/jpeg";
        context.Response.BufferOutput = false;

        // Get the Google image source
        string googleImage = context.Request.QueryString["GrabUrl"];
        if (googleImage == null) return;

        HttpWebRequest request = (HttpWebRequest)WebRequest.Create(googleImage);
        try
        {
           HttpWebResponse MyResponse = (HttpWebResponse)request.GetResponse();

          if (HttpStatusCode.OK == MyResponse.StatusCode)
          {
             using (Stream MyResponseStream = MyResponse.GetResponseStream())
             {
                // 4K buffer
                byte[] buffer = new byte[4096];
                int bytesRead;
                while (0 < (bytesRead =
                       MyResponseStream.Read(buffer, 0, buffer.Length)))
                {
                   context.Response.OutputStream.Write(buffer, 0, bytesRead);
                }
             }
          }
       }
       catch (Exception ex)
       {
          throw new Exception("Error: " + ex.Message, ex);
       }
    }
}
```

GoogleChartHandler.ashx expects a GrabUrl query string containing the URL of the Google Chart API to grab. The following line shows how to use it:

```
imgChart.ImageUrl = "GoogleChartHandler.ashx?GrabUrl=" +
                                              HttpUtility.UrlEncode(gc.BuildUrl());
```

As a result the image is displayed as if it were received directly from the server. The user is unaware of the source of the image (see Figure 14–25).

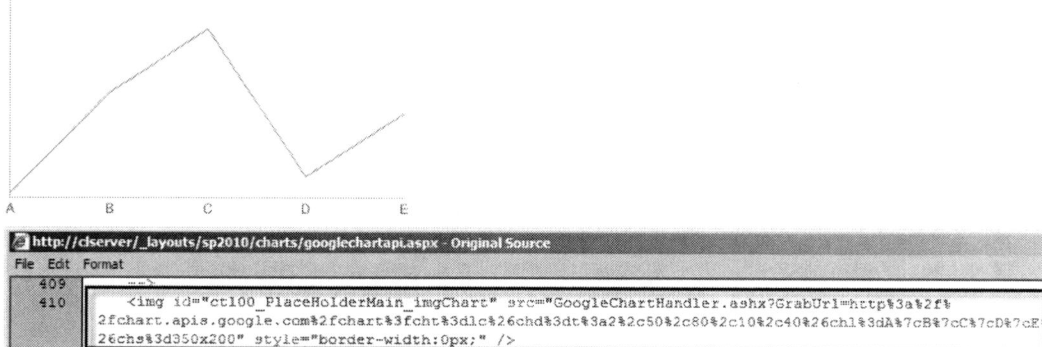

Figure 14–25. Generated Google Chart image and its source code

---

■ **Caution** Be aware that all chart data is sent to Google. Even if you use an ASP.NET web handler, the data is sent over the Internet, and because the query string contains the data, it may be readable within log files of switches, routers, proxies, and such. Don't use the Google Chart API for business-critical data!

Using the Google Visualization API

In 2008 Google released the first version of its Visualization API (see `http://code.google.com/intl/de/apis/visualization/`, and also the examples in Figure 14–26) The API offers a broad range of very useful functions for visualizing data on web pages. From a technical perspective, the API is provided as a JavaScript library that developers use to display charts and graphs in their own custom web pages.

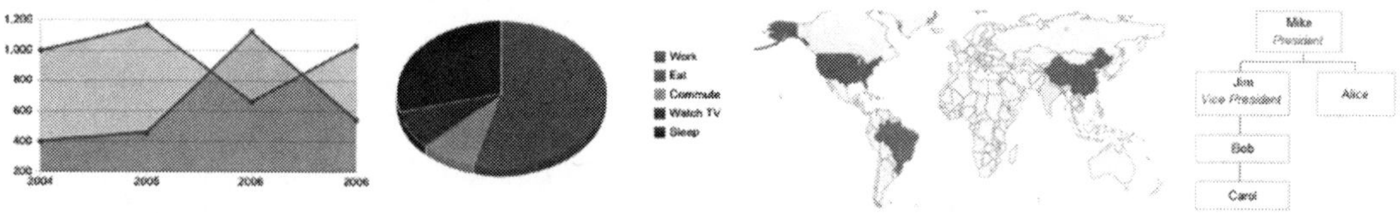

Figure 14–26. Sample visualizations from the Google Visualization API

When building SharePoint applications and Web Parts, developers and power users often need to present data visually. You can simply use the freely offered Google Visualization API, even for use within your intranet or extranet environments.

The big advantage of the Visualization API over the Google Chart API is that the images are rendered within the client, and thus no sensitive data is sent over the network to Google. This makes it viable to use in business-critical scenarios.

The integration of the Google Visualization API is very simple (see Listing 14–10). The following example demonstrates the use of the API within a SharePoint application page.

Listing 14–10. *Displaying a Chart by Using the Google Visualization API on an Application Page*

```
<%@ Page Language="C#" AutoEventWireup="true"
        DynamicMasterPageFile="~masterurl/default.master"
        CodeFile="GoogleVisualizationAPI.aspx.cs"
        Inherits="Charts_GoogleVisualizationAPI"
        CodeFileBaseClass="Microsoft.SharePoint.WebControls.LayoutsPageBase" %>

<asp:Content ContentPlaceHolderID="PlaceHolderMain" runat="server">

    <!-- Load the Google AJAX API -->
    <script type="text/javascript" src="http://www.google.com/jsapi"></script>
    <script type="text/javascript">

    // Load the Visualization API and required chart package(s)
    google.load('visualization', '1', {
        'packages': ['piechart']
      });

    // Set a callback to run after loading
    google.setOnLoadCallback(drawChart);

    function drawChart() {

        // Create a visualization data table
        var data = new google.visualization.DataTable();
        data.addColumn('string', 'Author');
        data.addColumn('number', 'Books');
        data.addRows([
        ['Krause', 35],
        ['Langhirt', 24],
        ['Sterff', 10],
        ['Pehlke', 3],
        ['Doering', 1]
      ]);

        // Draw the chart
        var chart = new
            google.visualization.PieChart(document.getElementById('myChart'));
        chart.draw(data, { width: 400, height: 240, is3D: true,
            title: 'Book authors and their books' });
    }

     </script>

     <div id="myChart"></div>

</asp:Content>
```

The result of Listing 14–10 is shown in Figure 14–27. The example displays a pie chart that contains one value per book author. If you move the mouse pointer over the chart, a balloon tooltip will appear.

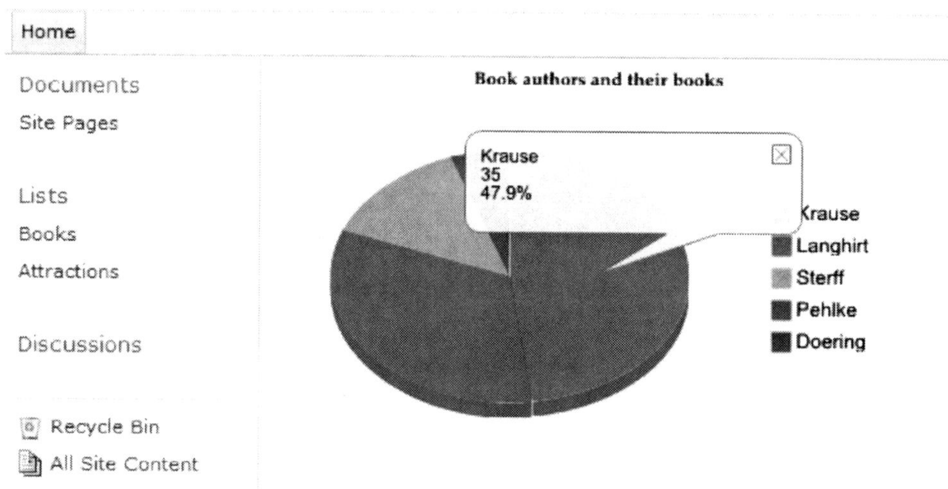

Figure 14–27. Example pie chart from the Google Visualization API embedded in a SharePoint application page

To begin, you have to load the Google AJAX API by referencing the library in your page:

You then load the core visualization libraries and the extra required visualization packages:

After loading, you can define a callback that executes a function after all the requested libraries are loaded:

After loading the Google JavaScript libraries, the callback executes the function that is responsible for drawing the chart. A Google chart usually requires a data table for rendering that has to be passed to the draw function of the relevant chart instance.

```
function drawChart() {

    // Create a visualization data table
    var data = new google.visualization.DataTable();
    data.addColumn('string', 'Author');
    data.addColumn('number', 'Books');
    data.addRows([['Krause', 35],['Langhirt', 24],['Sterff', 10],
                  ['Pehlke', 3],['Doering', 1]]);

    // Draw the chart
    var chart = new google.visualization.PieChart(
                              document.getElementById('myChart'));
    chart.draw(data, { width: 400, height: 240, is3D: true,
                       title: 'Book authors and their books' });
}
```

As you can see, using the Google Visualization API is very straightforward. Also, if you have an environment that runs secured under HTTPS/SSL, the Google Visualization API can be switched to use HTTPS instead of HTTP:

When requesting the core AJAX library with the HTTPS protocol, all additional libraries that are dynamically loaded by the API are also requested from secured URLs. This means that your users are not burdened by browser error messages because of mixed secured and unsecured content.

■ **Tip** The Google AJAX API is also available for use on secure HTTPS/SSL pages. Just use the HTTPS protocol instead of HTTP: `<script type="text/javascript" src="https://www.google.com/jsapi"></script>`.

But despite all this simplicity, there is currently (in version 1.0 of the API) some strange behavior when using Internet Explorer 8. If you move your mouse over the pie segments in the chart, Internet Explorer 8 throws several "Object not found" JavaScript errors. This behavior only occurs if the browser is in Internet Explorer 8 Compatibility View, which is usually the default value for intranet pages. If you manually change the browser mode to Internet Explorer 8, it works perfectly. To overcome this issue, you need to change a `<meta>` tag in the `<head>` section of your master page. Change the value from `IE=8` to `IE=EmulateIE7`, as follows:

■ **Note** There seems to be a bug in version 1.0 of the API when using Internet Explorer 8 involving showing tooltips at mouseover. To overcome this issue, you have to change a META tag in the master page to render the page with IE 7 compatibility: `<meta http-equiv="X-UA-Compatible" content="IE=EmulateIE7" />`.

Chart Types

Google offers a Visualization API Gallery (see `http://code.google.com/intl/de/apis/visualization/documentation/gallery.html`) containing several examples with different chart types. In contrast to the Google Chart API, the Visualizatin API charts are interactive. This means that the charts include hover effects if you move the mouse over the chart. These visual effects can be used in conjunction with an event handling model to interact with the charts. For example, in a bar chart you can catch the click event and show additional information when the user clicks a bar. A selection of the most common chart types is shown in Table 14–6.

Table 14–6. *Google Visualization API Chart Types*

Chart Type	Example
Area chart	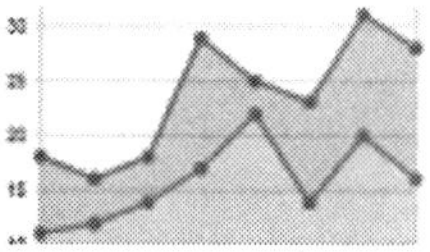
Bar chart	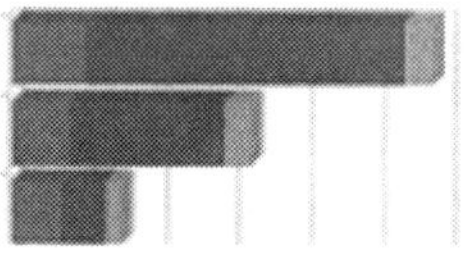
Column chart	
Line chart	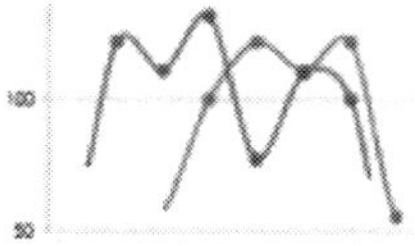
Pie chart	
Gauge	
Geo map	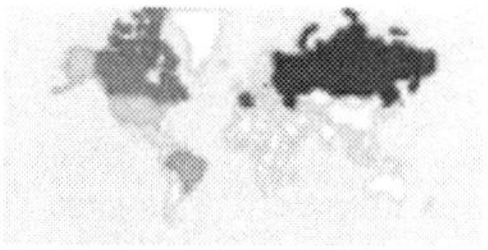
Intensity map	

Chart Type	Example
Organizational chart	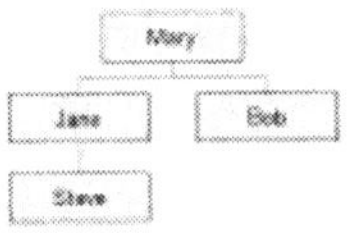 Mary Jane Bob Steve
Scatter chart	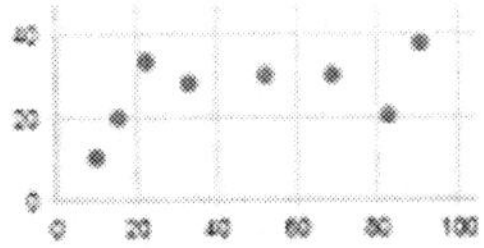 0 20 40 60 80 100

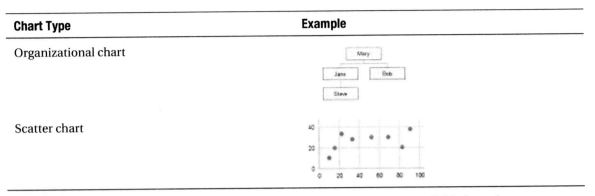

Beyond the chart types displayed in Table 14–6, there are many more available from the Visualization API Gallery page.

Using the Google Visualization API with SharePoint

When using the Google Visualization API within SharePoint, it makes sense to use it in conjunction with the JavaScript client object model. Because all data has to be provided within JavaScript in the form of a `google.visualization.DataTable` instance, the best way to fill the chart with data is by retrieving data using JavaScript.

As mentioned earlier, the rendering of the charts is done on the client side within the user's browser. This enables you to use the Google Visualization API also for displaying business-critical data because the data is not sent over the Internet to Google.

■ **Caution** Although most chart types are rendered on the client by generating SVG images using JavaScript, there are a couple of old chart types that use the Chart API. Those charts are still sending the data over the Internet to the Google Chart API. Don't use these insecure chart for business-critical data.

Integrating Map Services

Interactive maps are becoming increasingly widespread in modern applications. Maps are used to visualize a broad range of data with a geographical background—for example, to display revenues for different locations.

Although many web applications could make good use of integrated mapping software, development teams often shy away from the complexity of integrating a full-fledged geographical database system. Two technologies—Bing Maps from Microsoft and Google Maps—in conjunction with Ajax and the SharePoint client object model, can significantly simplify this area. This chapter explains how you can easily implement dynamic interactive maps in SharePoint applications, using the Bing Maps API and the Google Maps API for the web interface, and the SharePoint client object model to provide real-time interaction with the server.

Bing Maps

Bing Maps from Microsoft belongs to Bing Services, which provides programmatic access to Bing data via APIs. The services include the common Bing API and Bing Maps. The Bing API provides developers easy access to Bing content types such as Images, InstantAnswer, MobileWeb, News, Phonebook, RelatedSearch, Spell, Translation, Video and Web. Technically, the Bing API provides an XML web service through SOAP that enables you to submit queries to and receive results from the Bing search engine.

Bing Maps is an online mapping service that enables users to search, discover, explore, plan, and share information about specific locations. By using traditional road maps, labeled aerial photo views, low-angle high-resolution aerial photos, and proximity-searching capabilities, Bing Maps provides opportunities for developers to incorporate both location and local search features into their applications.

The Bing Maps SDK (available online at `www.microsoft.com/maps/isdk/ajax`) offers hands-on, task-based demonstrations of the features available in the latest version of the map control, including code samples and links back to the reference SDK.

This section demonstrates how to integrate Bing Maps into your own SharePoint application pages and Web Parts. Examples that show how to bind data from SharePoint lists to a map control will demonstrate ways to impress your users and customers.

Integrating Bing Maps into Application Pages

As a developer you will nowadays often be faced with the requirement to implement custom application pages that contain map views based on data that resides in SharePoint lists. Both the server-side API from Bing Maps and the SharePoint client object model make it easy to implement custom map views.

To begin, you need to add a reference to the globally hosted JavaScript file for Bing Maps:

```
<script charset="UTF-8" type="text/javascript"
        src="http://ecn.dev.virtualearth.net/mapcontrol/
             mapcontrol.ashx?v=6.2&mkt=en-us" />
```

Microsoft delivers Bing Maps through the Microsoft Content Delivery Network (CDN), which is a key pillar of Microsoft's cloud computing strategy. CDN is comprised of multiple worldwide datacenters that allow Microsoft to host Bing Maps content closer to end users. This ensures maximum performance when working with Bing Maps. As a developer, you do not have to worry about performance issues due to content delivery—the cloud ensures the best possible performance.

After adding the JavaScript reference to Bing Maps, you can start adding your own map. Define an HTML control (such as a `<div>`) in your application page to contain the map:

Next, add JavaScript code to load the map into the defined `<div>` section:

```
function GetMap()
{
    var map = new VEMap('myMap');
    map.LoadMap();
}
```

To make this code work you have to ensure that it will be executed when the page is loaded. Therefore, you can either add a JavaScript `onLoad` event to the `<body>` tag or use the `Sys.Application.add_init` function from the Microsoft AJAX implementation:

The function passed to this method is executed after all scripts on a page have been loaded. Another approach is to use the SharePoint JavaScript function `ExecuteOrDelayUntilScriptLoaded`. With this function you can ensure that required SharePoint JavaScript libraries, such as the `sp.js` library containing the client object model implementation, are loaded before accessing your map.

The complete code of the ASPX application page is displayed in Listing 14–11.

Listing 14–11. Integrating Bing Maps Within a SharePoint Application Page

```
<%@ Page Language="C#" AutoEventWireup="true"
         DynamicMasterPageFile="~masterurl/default.master"
         CodeFile="BingMap01.aspx.cs"
         Inherits="Maps_BingMap01"
         CodeFileBaseClass="Microsoft.SharePoint.WebControls.LayoutsPageBase"
%>

<asp:Content ContentPlaceHolderID="PlaceHolderMain" runat="server">
    <script charset="UTF-8" type="text/javascript"
              src="http://ecn.dev.virtualearth.net/mapcontrol/
                   mapcontrol.ashx?v=6.2&mkt=en-us" />

    <script type="text/javascript">

        function GetMap() {
            var map = new VEMap('myMap');
            map.LoadMap();
        }


    </script>

    <div id='myMap' style="position: relative; width: 600px; height: 600px;"></div>

</asp:Content>
```

As you can see, the code for integrating Bing Maps is very simple. The example uses the `PlaceHolderMain` section of the system master page (`default.master`) to display the map with a height and width of 600 pixels. The rendered application page is shown in Figure 14–28.

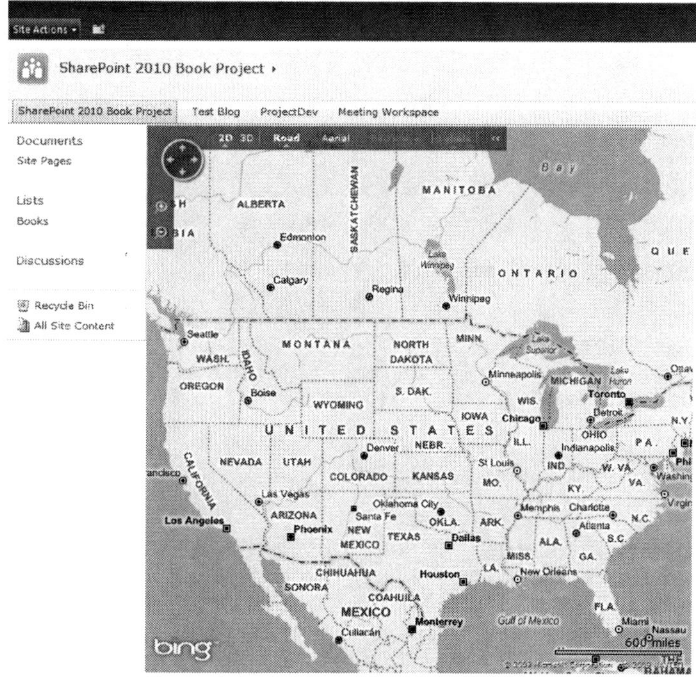

Figure 14–28. SharePoint application page with Bing Maps

Integrating Bing Maps into Web Parts

If you wish to integrate the maps functionality into a Web Part, follow these steps:

- Include a JavaScript reference to Bing Maps (`RegisterClientScriptInclude`).
- Register custom JavaScript code (`RegisterClientScriptBlock`).
- Ensure your code will be started after page load (`RegisterStartupScript`).

An example of implementing a Web Part that contains a Bing map is shown in Listing 14–12.

Listing 14–12. *Implementation of a Bing Maps Web Part*

```
public class BingMapsWebPart : WebPart
{
    private const String mapsLibrary =
      "http://ecn.dev.virtualearth.net/mapcontrol/mapcontrol.ashx?v=6.2&mkt=en-us";

    public BingMapsWebPart () { }

    protected override void OnLoad(EventArgs e)
    {
```

```
            // Add script reference
            this.Page.ClientScript.RegisterClientScriptInclude(this.GetType(),
                    "BingMaps", mapsLibrary);

            // Add loadMap() function
            StringBuilder js = new StringBuilder();
            js.Append("var map = null; ");
            js.Append("function loadMap() { ");
            js.Append("map = new VEMap('myMap'); ");
            js.Append("map.LoadMap(); ");
            js.Append(" }");
            this.Page.ClientScript.RegisterClientScriptBlock(this.GetType(), "JS",
                                                          js.ToString(), true);

            // Add ExecuteOrDelayUntilScriptLoaded function
            this.Page.ClientScript.RegisterStartupScript(this.GetType(), "initMap",
                "ExecuteOrDelayUntilScriptLoaded(loadMap, 'sp.js');", true);
        }

        protected override void RenderContents(HtmlTextWriter writer)
        {
            // Render maps DIV tag
            String width = Convert.ToInt32(this.Width.Value) + "px";
            String height = Convert.ToInt32(this.Height.Value) + "px";
            String div = String.Format("<div id='myMap' style='position: relative; "
                + "width:{0}; height:{1};'></div>", width, height);

            writer.Write(div);
        }
    }
```

In Listing 14–12 the Web Part `OnLoad` method is used to initialize the required Bing Maps JavaScript code. At first the Bing Maps JavaScript library is referenced by using the `ClientScript.RegisterClientScriptInclude` method. Then the client function `loadMap` is registered with `ClientScript.RegisterClientScriptBlock`. The rendered HTML result in the page containing the Web Part looks like this:

```
<script src="http://ecn.dev.virtualearth.net/mapcontrol/
            mapcontrol.ashx?v=6.2&amp;mkt=en-us" type="text/javascript">
</script>
<script type="text/javascript">
//<![CDATA[
  var map = null; function loadMap() { map = new VEMap('myMap'); map.LoadMap();  }//]]>
</script>
```

The final required step is to ensure that the `loadMap` function is called after all the necessary SharePoint JavaScript libraries are loaded. Therefore, the method `ClientScript.RegisterStartupScript` is used to call the `ExecuteOrDelayUntilScriptLoaded` function. The rendered HTML result is placed at the end of the Web Part page together with other function calls that need to be executed during the page load:

```
<script type="text/javascript">
    // <![CDATA[
    var _spFormDigestRefreshInterval =1440000;
    ExecuteOrDelayUntilScriptLoaded(loadMap, 'sp.js');
```

```
    var _fV4UI = true;
...
```

The implemented RenderContents method of the Web Part renders an HTML <div> tag that is intended to contain the Bing Map. The width and height of this <div> are determined by the Width and Height properties of the Web Part. Figure 14–29 shows the Web Part in action.

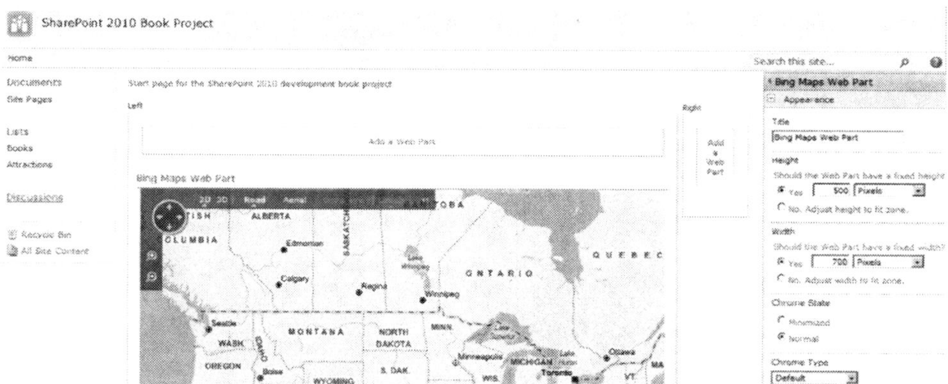

Figure 14–29. Custom Web Part containing Bing Maps

Populating Bing Maps Using the JavaScript Client Object Model

An extension of the example in the previous section could be to read the location data from a SharePoint list. In this situation, you can use the JavaScript client object model to query SharePoint lists and populate the map with this data. First of all, you need to prepare a list containing the location information. The example in this section creates a list containing several tourist attractions—each with a title, description, street, city, and image link (see Figure 14–30).

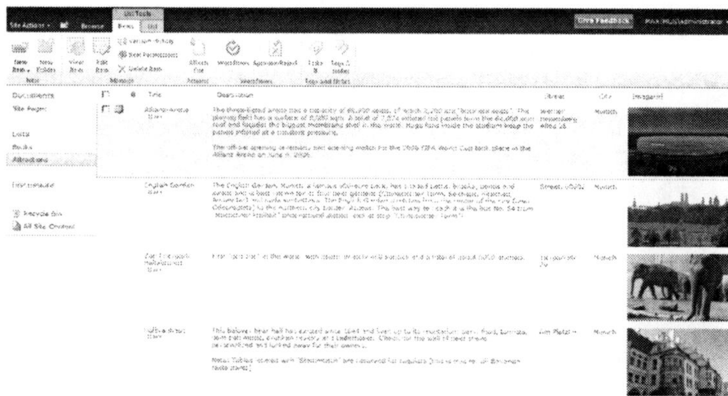

Figure 14–30. SharePoint list for tourist attractions

The JavaScript code to display the items of the `Attractions` SharePoint list as pushpins in a Bing map is shown in Listing 14–13. After loading the page, the `loadMap` function is called. This function uses the client object model to access the `Attractions` list and retrieves all the list items with a CAML query into the `ListItemCollection` `this.allAttractions`. After the successful asynchronous execution of the query, the callback function `onLoadMapCallback` is run. Here, the enumeration `this.allAttractions` is processed, and for every list item a new pushpin will be created (`setPushpin`). The `setPushpin` function is based on the `VEMap.Find` function, which resolves location names (e.g., Tierparkstr. 30, Munich) into map coordinates. The implemented anonymous callback function of the `VEMap.Find` function creates a new `VEShape` instance, populates this instance with data, and finally adds the shape to the map.

Listing 14–13. *Integrating Bing Maps with the JavaScript Client Object Model*

```
<%@ Page Language="C#" AutoEventWireup="true"
        DynamicMasterPageFile="~masterurl/default.master"
        CodeFile="BingMaps02.aspx.cs" Inherits="Maps_BingMaps02"
        CodeFileBaseClass="Microsoft.SharePoint.WebControls.LayoutsPageBase" %>

<asp:Content ContentPlaceHolderID="PlaceHolderMain" runat="server">
    <script charset="UTF-8" type="text/javascript"
        src="http://ecn.dev.virtualearth.net/mapcontrol/mapcontrol.ashx?v=6.2&mkt=en-us" />

    <script type="text/javascript">
        var map = null;
        var allPoints = new Array();


        function loadMap() {
            var ctx = new SP.ClientContext.get_current();
            var oAttractionsList =
                ctx.get_web().get_lists().getByTitle("Attractions");

            var camlQuery = new SP.CamlQuery();
            this.allAttractions = oAttractionsList.getItems(camlQuery);
            ctx.load(this.allAttractions);

             ctx.executeQueryAsync(
                Function.createDelegate(this, this.onLoadMapCallback),
                Function.createDelegate(this, this.onFailedCallback));
        }

        // Callback function to load the map
        function onLoadMapCallback(sender, args) {
            map = new VEMap('myMap');
            map.LoadMap();
            map.SetMapStyle(VEMapStyle.Road);

            var enumerator = this.allAttractions.getEnumerator();
            while (enumerator.moveNext()) {
                var li = enumerator.get_current();
                var location = li.get_item("Street") + ", " + li.get_item("City");
                var title = li.get_item("Title");
                var imageUrl = li.get_item("ImageUrl").get_url();
```

```
            var description = li.get_item("Description");
           setPushpin(map, location, title, description, imageUrl);
        }

    }

    // Callback function for errors
    function onFailedCallback(sender, args) {
        SP.UI.Notify.addNotification('Request failed: ' +
                                    args.get_message() + '\n'
            +  args.get_stackTrace(),false);
    }

    function setPushpin(map, location, title, desc, imageUrl) {
        var result = map.Find(null, location, null, null, 0, 10,
                         true, true, true, false,
                     function (layer, resultsArray, places,
                               hasMore, veErrorMessage) {
                if (places.length > 0) {
                    var shape = new VEShape(VEShapeType.Pushpin,
                                        places[0].LatLong);

                    shape.SetCustomIcon(
                         'http://clserver/_layouts/images/search32x32.png');
                    shape.SetTitle(title);
                    shape.SetDescription(desc + ' <br><br><img src="'
                                        + imageUrl + '"/>');
                    map.AddShape(shape);
                    allPoints.push(places[0].LatLong);
                    map.SetMapView(allPoints)
                }
            }
    );
    }

    ExecuteOrDelayUntilScriptLoaded(loadMap, 'sp.js')
  </script>

  <div id='myMap' style="position: relative; width: 900px; height: 600px;"></div>
</asp:Content>
```

After page loading, the JavaScript function loadMap is called via the ExecuteOrDelayUntilScriptLoaded function. This function call is necessary because the client object model can only be used after the core SharePoint JavaScript library sp.js and its dependencies are loaded.

■ **Caution** When using the client object model for querying data from SharePoint, you have to ensure that all required JavaScript libraries are loaded first. You can only use the client object model if the core library `sp.js` is loaded, including all its dependencies. To do this, you can use the JavaScript function `ExecuteOrDelayUntilScriptLoaded`, which calls a defined function only after the client object model libraries are completely loaded.

Finally, after querying data via the client object model, the Bing map will contain all the tourist attractions defined in the `Attractions` SharePoint list. Every list item is marked with a magnifying glass (image URL: `/_layouts/images/search32x32.png`), and when the mouse pointer is moved over an icon, the information pop-up for the list item is displayed. This information pop-up contains the `Title`, `Description`, and `ImageURL` properties of the list item. Figure 14–31 shows the resulting map for Listing 14–13.

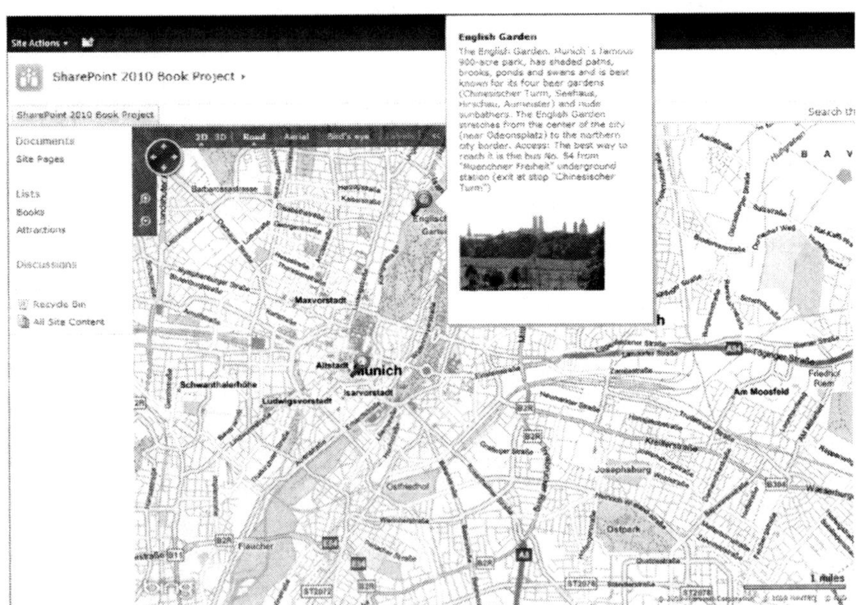

Figure 14–31. Bing map with tourist attractions and information box

Google Maps

Google Maps is a Google service offering powerful, user-friendly mapping technology and local business information. The Google Maps API lets you embed Google maps in your own web application pages with JavaScript. The API provides a number of utilities for manipulating maps and adding content to them through a variety of services, allowing you to create your own custom map applications. A good starting point for working with Google Maps is the API documentation: `http://code.google.com/intl/en/apis/maps`.

Integrating Google Maps into Application Pages

Using Google Maps within custom application pages is very similar to using Bing Maps, as described previously. The first step is to add a reference to the centrally hosted JavaScript file for Google Maps. In older versions of Google Maps, a free Google API key had to be requested and added as a request parameter to the JavaScript library URL. Since version 3 of the Google Maps API, an API key is no longer required. Hence, you can reference the maps library with the following script tag:

```
<script type="text/javascript"
       src="http://maps.google.com/maps/api/js?sensor=false" />
```

■ **Note** Since version 3 of the Google Maps JavaScript API, you no longer need an API key.

As already shown for Bing Maps, Google Maps also needs an HTML element in which to display its map:

```
PointProperty=Field[{Format}] [,PointProperty=Field[{Format}]]
http://chart.apis.google.com/chart?cht=lc&chd=t:2,50,80,10,40&chl=A|B|C|D|E&chs=350x200
<script type="text/javascript" src="http://www.google.com/jsapi"></script>
google.load('visualization', '1', {'packages': ['piechart']});
google.setOnLoadCallback(drawChart);
<script type="text/javascript" src="https://www.google.com/jsapi"></script>
<meta http-equiv="X-UA-Compatible" content="IE=EmulateIE7" />
<div id='myMap' style="position: relative; width: 600px; height: 600px;" />
Sys.Application.add_init(GetMap);
ExecuteOrDelayUntilScriptLoaded(GetMap, 'sp.js');
        ExecuteOrDelayUntilScriptLoaded(GetMap, 'sp.js');
<div id='myMap' style="position: relative; width: 600px; height: 600px;" />
ExecuteOrDelayUntilScriptLoaded(GetMap, 'sp.js');
```

To load and display the map, you have to add initialization JavaScript code that loads the map into the <div> element:

```
function GetMap() {
    var myLatlng = new google.maps.LatLng(39,-77);
    var myOptions = {
        zoom: 3,
        center: myLatlng,
        mapTypeId: google.maps.MapTypeId.ROADMAP
    };
    var mapDiv = document.getElementById("myMap");
    var map = new google.maps.Map(mapDiv, myOptions);
}
```

In contrast to Bing Maps, Google Maps needs a center location for its map. This example sets the variable `myLatlng` to the coordinates of North America. With the `myOptions` property containing information about the zoom level and the map type, a new instance of the `google.maps.Map` class is created and displayed in the `myMap` <div> element.

The `GetMap` function has to be called after page initialization. This can be done by adding the following line:

The complete code for the ASPX application page is displayed in Listing 14–14.

***Listing 14–14.** Integrating Google Maps in a SharePoint Application Page*

```
<%@ Page Language="C#" AutoEventWireup="true"
                DynamicMasterPageFile="~masterurl/default.master"
                CodeFile="GoogleMaps01.aspx.cs" Inherits="Maps_GoogleMaps01"
                CodeFileBaseClass="Microsoft.SharePoint.WebControls.LayoutsPageBase" %>

 <asp:Content ID="Content1" ContentPlaceHolderID="PlaceHolderMain" runat="server">

  <script type="text/javascript"
        src="http://maps.google.com/maps/api/js?sensor=false" >
  </script>

    <script type="text/javascript">

        function getMap() {

            var myLatlng = new google.maps.LatLng(39,-77);
            var myOptions = {
                zoom: 3,
                center: myLatlng,
                mapTypeId: google.maps.MapTypeId.ROADMAP
            };
            var mapDiv = document.getElementById("myMap");
            var map = new google.maps.Map(mapDiv, myOptions);

        }

        ExecuteOrDelayUntilScriptLoaded(getMap, 'sp.js');

    </script>

    <div id='myMap' style="width: 600px; height: 600px;">huhu</div>

</asp:Content>
```

Compared to the Bing Maps integration, using Google Maps (see Figure 14–32) is also very simple. To begin, you reference the Google Maps JavaScript library and then call the function `ExecuteOrDelayUntilScriptLoaded`, which itself calls the `getMap` function to display the map.

■ **Caution** Some very strange behavior occurs when referencing the Bing and Google Maps JavaScript libraries. You must ensure that the script reference tag is always terminated with an end tag (`</script>`). A normal end-of-the-script reference within the `<script>` element does not work. The following example is wrong and leads to JavaScript errors:

```
<script type="text/javascript" src="http://maps.google..." />
```

However, this example will work without problems:

```
<script type="text/javascript" src="http://maps.google..." ></script>
```

This issue occurs with both Internet Explorer and Firefox, neither of which can deal with the shorthand syntax for the script element.

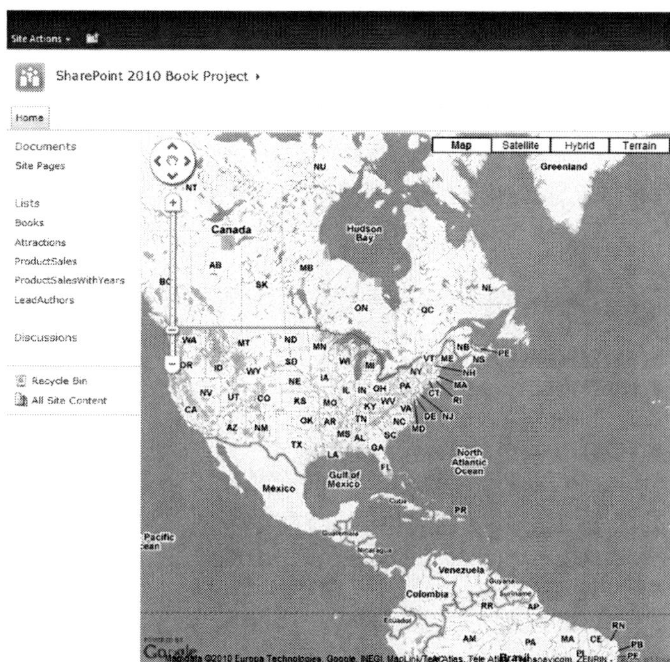

Figure 14–32. SharePoint application page with Google Maps

Integrating Google Maps into Web Parts

The Web Part integration for Google Maps works very similarly to Bing Maps, as shown in Listing 14–15. The only two differences are the JavaScript reference to Google Maps instead of Bing Maps and the different loadMap implementation. In the Google Maps Web Part example in Listing 14–15, the differences are shown in bold.

***Listing 14–15.** Integrating Google Maps with JavaScript Client Object Model*

```
public class GoogleMapsWebPart : WebPart
{
    private const String mapsLibrary =

        " http://maps.google.com/maps/api/js?sensor=false";


    public GoolgeMapsWebPart () { }

    protected override void OnLoad(EventArgs e)
    {
        // Add script reference
        this.Page.ClientScript.RegisterClientScriptInclude(this.GetType(),
                "GoogleMaps", mapsLibrary);

        // Add loadMap() function
        StringBuilder js = new StringBuilder();
        js.Append("var map = null; ");
        js.Append("function loadMap() { ");

        js.Append("var myLatlng = new google.maps.LatLng(39,-77);");
        js.Append("var myOptions = { ");
        js.Append("    zoom: 3,");
        js.Append("    center: myLatlng,");
        js.Append("    mapTypeId: google.maps.MapTypeId.ROADMAP ");
        js.Append("};");
        js.Append("var mapDiv = document.getElementById('myMap');");
        js.Append("map = new google.maps.Map(mapDiv, myOptions);");

        js.Append(" }");
        this.Page.ClientScript.RegisterClientScriptBlock(this.GetType(), "JS",
                                                         js.ToString(), true);

        // Add ExecuteOrDelayUntilScriptLoaded function
        this.Page.ClientScript.RegisterStartupScript(this.GetType(), "initMap",
            "ExecuteOrDelayUntilScriptLoaded(loadMap, 'sp.js');", true);
    }

    protected override void RenderContents(HtmlTextWriter writer)
    {
        // Render maps <div> tag
        String width = Convert.ToInt32(this.Width.Value) + "px";
        String height = Convert.ToInt32(this.Height.Value) + "px";
        String div = String.Format("<div id='myMap' style='position: relative; "
            + "width:{0}; height:{1};'></div>", width, height);
```

```
            writer.Write(div);
        }
}
```

As you can see in Listing 14–15, the integration of Google Maps is very simple. After registering the Google Maps JavaScript library, you have to ensure that the client script for displaying the map (followed by the initial starting script) is run after loading the page by using the `ExecuteOrDelayUntilScriptLoaded` function. The resulting Web Part looks like Figure 14–33.

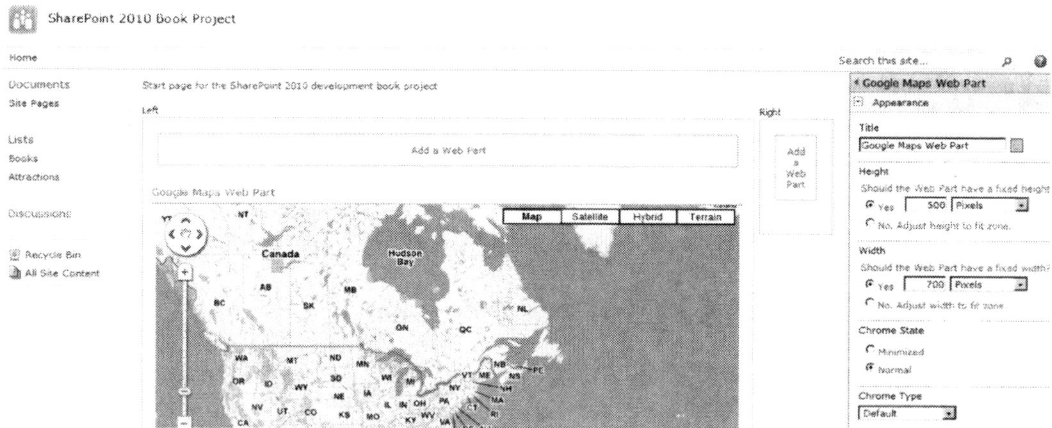

Figure 14–33. Custom Web Part containing Google Maps

Populating Google Maps Using the JavaScript Client Object Model

Based on the example for Bing Maps introduced previously this section shows an example for using Google Maps in conjunction with the client object model. The example again uses the `Attractions` SharePoint list containing several tourist attractions, each with a title, description, street, city, and image link (see Figure 14–34). Every list item is displayed as a marker on the Google map. If you move the mouse over such a marker, a window containing HTML with the description and the image of the attraction comes up (see Figure 14–34).

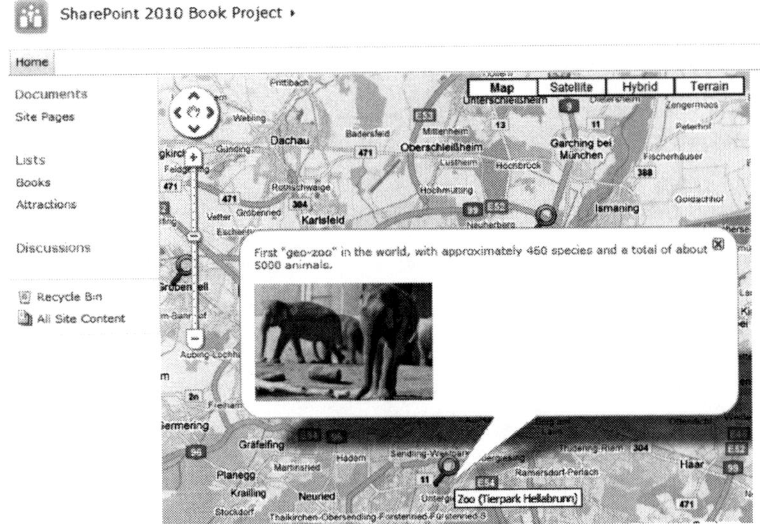

Figure 14–34. Google map with tourist atractions, markers, and an info window

The example code for the SharePoint application page is displayed in Listing 14–16.

Listing 14–16. Implementation of a Google Maps Web Part

```
<%@ Page Language="C#" AutoEventWireup="true"
    DynamicMasterPageFile="~masterurl/default.master"
    CodeFile="GoogleMaps02.aspx.cs"
    Inherits="Maps_GoogleMaps02"
    CodeFileBaseClass="Microsoft.SharePoint.WebControls.LayoutsPageBase" %>

 <asp:Content ID="Content1" ContentPlaceHolderID="PlaceHolderMain" runat="server">
    <script type="text/javascript"
           src="http://maps.google.com/maps/api/js?sensor=false"></script>

    <script type="text/javascript">

    var map = null;

    function loadMap() {

        var ctx = new SP.ClientContext.get_current();
        var oAttractionsList = ctx.get_web().get_lists().getByTitle("Attractions");

        var camlQuery = new SP.CamlQuery();
        this.allAttractions = oAttractionsList.getItems(camlQuery);
        ctx.load(this.allAttractions);

        ctx.executeQueryAsync(
```

```
        Function.createDelegate(this, this.onLoadMapCallback),
        Function.createDelegate(this, this.onFailedCallback));
}

// Callback function to load the map
function onLoadMapCallback(sender, args) {


    var myLatlng = new google.maps.LatLng(39, -77);
    var myOptions = {
        zoom: 3,
        center: myLatlng,
        mapTypeId: google.maps.MapTypeId.ROADMAP
    };
    var mapDiv = document.getElementById("myMap");
    var map = new google.maps.Map(mapDiv, myOptions);


    var enumerator = this.allAttractions.getEnumerator();
    while (enumerator.moveNext()) {
        var li = enumerator.get_current();
        var location = li.get_item("Street") + ", " + li.get_item("City");
        var title = li.get_item("Title");
        var imageUrl = li.get_item("ImageUrl").get_url();
        var description = li.get_item("Description");
        setMarker(map, location, title, description, imageUrl);
    }

}

// Callback function for errors
function onFailedCallback(sender, args) {
    SP.UI.Notify.addNotification('Request failed: ' + args.get_message() + '\n'
      + args.get_stackTrace(), false);
}


function setMarker(map, location, title, description, imageUrl) {
    var geocoder = new google.maps.Geocoder();
    var result = geocoder.geocode({ 'address': location },
                    function (results, status) {
        if (status == google.maps.GeocoderStatus.OK) {
            map.setCenter(results[0].geometry.location);

            // Add marker to map
            var marker = new google.maps.Marker({
                map: map,
                position: results[0].geometry.location,
                icon: "http://clserver/_layouts/images/search32x32.png",
                title: title
            });

            var infoWindow = null;
```

```
                // Show info window on mouseover event on marker
                google.maps.event.addListener(marker, 'mouseover', function () {
                  var html = description + ' <br><br><img src="' + imageUrl + '"/>';
                  infoWindow = new google.maps.InfoWindow({
                      content: html,
                      position: results[0].geometry.location
                  });
                infoWindow.open(map);
                });

                // Hide info window on mouseout event on marker
                google.maps.event.addListener(marker, 'mouseout', function () {
                    if (infoWindow) infoWindow.close();
                });
            }
        });
    }

    ExecuteOrDelayUntilScriptLoaded(loadMap, 'sp.js');

    </script>

     <div id='myMap' style="width: 600px; height: 600px;">
        Loading Google Maps...</div>
     <a href="javascript:loadMap()">loadMap()</a>
     <a href="javascript:initAttractions()">initAttractions()</a>

</asp:Content>
```

After page loading, the JavaScript function `loadMap` is called via the `ExecuteOrDelayUntilScriptLoaded` function. With the client object model and a CAML query, the list items of the `Attractions` list are received. Within the callback function `onLoadMapCallback`, the Google map is initialized. The results of the CAML query are processed within a loop, and for every list item, a marker (`google.maps.Marker`) is added to the map. The marker is displayed with a magnifying class icon. In addition, the markers get the events `mouseover` and `mouseout` attached; these show and hide a `google.maps.InfoWindow` containing the image and the description of an attraction item as HTML.

Bing Maps vs. Google Maps

Both Bing Maps and Google Maps provide very powerful and robust APIs for quickly realizing integration scenarios in custom web applications and SharePoint application pages and Web Parts. This section will outline some of the pros and cons of both services, and the scenarios in which you might use one instead of the other.

Limitations When Using SSL/HTTPS

A very important criterion for using either Bing Maps or Google Maps is the protocol of your SharePoint site that hosts the map. If your site is running secured by SSL (`https://server`), you should ensure that all references in your page (e.g., images, styles, and scripts) are also coming from secured sources. If not, your browser will give users annoying warnings about secure/insecure content on every page reload. Unfortunately, Google Maps does not support SSL in its free API. To access the Google Maps API over a secure (HTTPS) connection, you have to sign up for a Google Maps API Premier account, which is not free. The free Bing Maps API, however, can be accessed by SSL. With Bing Maps, you simply need to change the JavaScript reference from HTTP to HTTPS and add the parameter `s=1` to the query string. The normal, unsecured HTTP reference looks like the following:

```
<script charset="UTF-8" type="text/javascript"
        src="http://ecn.dev.virtualearth.net/mapcontrol/
             mapcontrol.ashx?v=6.2&mkt=en-us" />
```

To use HTTPS, on the other hand, you have to change the `src` attribute of the `script` tag, as follows:

```
<script charset="UTF-8" type="text/javascript"
        src="https://ecn.dev.virtualearth.net/mapcontrol/
             mapcontrol.ashx?v=6.2&mkt=en-us&s=1" />
```

■ **Tip** If your SharePoint site uses maps and will run secured over SSL (HTTPS), you should be aware of the fact that Google Maps currently only supports SSL/HTTPS at additional charge. Bing Maps offers free support for SSL/HTTPS.

Licensing

When using map services, either from Google or Bing, you have to take care of licensing conditions. First of all, the use of map services isn't always as "free" as you might think. Licensing can be a very tricky issue, and the terms for each API are written in pure legalese, so they can be quite difficult for a layperson to understand. Both map services make a distinction between two usage scenarios: *free usage* and *commercial licensing*.

The free usage license is offered for use on *public-facing* web sites. That means you can use map services on web sites that are publicly available on the Internet and that do not charge for access to the maps. There are also limits on how many map loads you can use; Bing maps limits the free usage at 125,000 map page loads per year, whereas Google keeps the limit at its discretion. Also, the terms can change at any time without warning, and uptime is not guaranteed, so you could encounter problems with your maps going offline. It's possible, too, that usage in the future might cease to be free.

If you plan to include map services in your custom business applications, you should consider a commercial license. The commercial license terms contain an uptime service-level agreement (SLA), and remove any unwanted advertisements from your maps. Furthermore, you can use an unlimited number of map loads and features that are not available under the free license.

The price for a commercial license depends upon the traffic, and begins at a few thousand dollars per year. For detailed information, take a look at the licensing conditions and offerings of the map providers.

Summary

This chapter described many graphical visualization UI elements available for extending the functionality of SharePoint. The first part contained an introduction to various data access scenarios, with particular emphasis on strategies for dealing with large lists. Different data access methods, including LINQ to SharePoint and direct SQL access with LINQ to SQL, were explained in depth.

The integration of attractive charts into custom application pages and Web Parts is a common requirement. The chapter described how to use the Microsoft Chart Control, including various data binding examples for SharePoint. Other interesting alternatives—the Google Charts API and the Google Visualization API—were also covered.

In addition to charts, maps are another increasingly important element of modern business applications. Both Bing Maps and Google Maps were explained, including many practical examples on how to embed maps into SharePoint.

PART 3

■■■

Advanced Techniques

CHAPTER 15

Forms Services and InfoPath

Exposing forms to the browser empowers users to leverage one of SharePoint's advanced features. Creating simple forms is easy, even for end users. However, creating more complex forms requires higher-level knowledge. This chapter shows how to build and extend a basic form within InfoPath using code, deploy this to a SharePoint server, and make the form available online. Different ways of deploying InfoPath form templates and integrating forms into complex solutions will be described. Taking it further, you will see how to program InfoPath forms and how to add custom code to forms.

These form templates can be published to a SharePoint server, which can render them in a web browser using InfoPath Forms Services. This enables users without an InfoPath client installed on their computers to fill out InfoPath forms.

`XmlFormView` is a Web Part used to render InfoPath forms in SharePoint and make the form available in the browser. Programming the control extends its behavior and provides enhanced features usually available only to InfoPath clients. In this chapter we explain how to overcome common limitations of the form viewer.

InfoPath uses XML to store user input. With programmatic access to the XML, changes are possible on the fly during the loading and saving processes. Combined with workflows, which are described in the next chapter, this creates powerful applications and makes complex form management possible.

This chapter includes

- How InfoPath files are structured
- How to design browser-enabled forms
- Using data connections to access external data
- Publishing forms to SharePoint and making the forms available in a browser
- Building InfoPath forms with code-behind
- Creating applications with `XmlFormView` and extending its default behavior

Internals of InfoPath Forms

Using line-of-business (LOB) applications on browser-based platforms is a solution in high demand, with many advantages for the enterprise. Often one of the core challenges is to provide users with easy-to-use forms. In many cases, such forms must adhere to corporate design stipulations, and their textual information needs to be adjusted regularly.

SharePoint and InfoPath complement one another and offer a solution to many of these issues. InfoPath provides a very intuitive UI for developing form templates, enabling information workers and even business users to develop and customize forms.

Designing solutions for SharePoint in combination with InfoPath Forms Services requires developers to be familiar with InfoPath. This includes a basic understanding of the internal structure of forms, as well as designing form templates using InfoPath. Since many of the wizards integrated into InfoPath are aimed at ad hoc solutions and lack support for professional development solutions, we will examine the internal structure and functionality of InfoPath form templates.

InfoPath separates layout and data. On one hand, an InfoPath form template describes the layout and behavior of the form. This information is stored within a template file with the extension `.xsn`. On the other hand, the data that is entered by a user into the form's controls is stored in an XML data file. This XML file contains a reference to the corresponding XSN file that is used to display the data. When discussing an InfoPath form, we are generally referring to the form template.

InfoPath Form Template

Despite the attractive InfoPath UI, developers need to understand the internal structure of InfoPath form templates. The XSN file, created by InfoPath when designing a form template, is essentially a *Windows Cabinet Archive (`.cab`)* file containing several different files. You can see those files when you use the option Share ➤ Save Form Template As ➤ Source Files. This allows you to save all the files individually in a local folder. Alternatively, you can rename an XSN file as a CAB file and view the files contained within the archive. Figure 15–1 shows the structure of an XSN file.

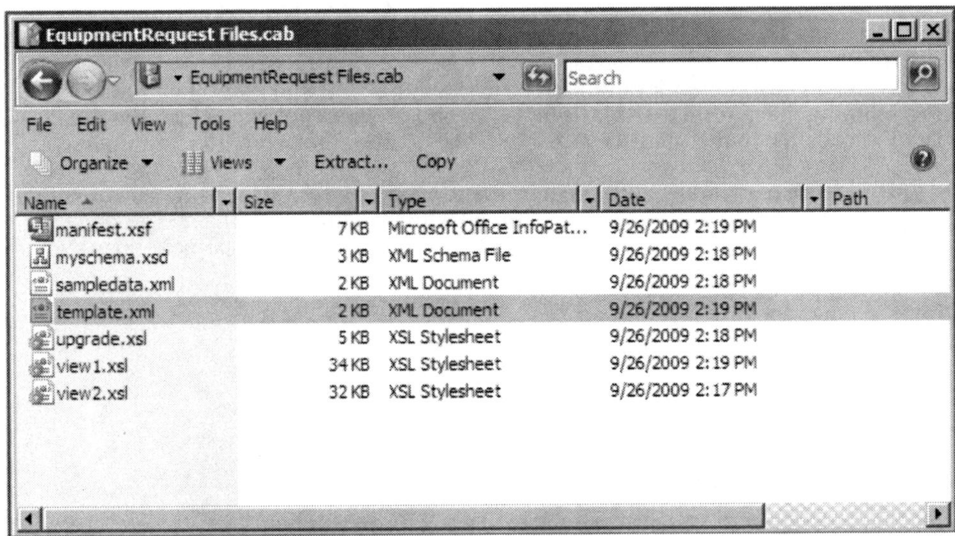

***Figure 15–1.** Structure of InfoPath files*

We will describe the constituent files within an InfoPath form template in more detail. The listings and snippets in this chapter are taken from an example form template called Conference Room Booking. Figure 15–2 shows a form that is used to book conference rooms within a company. Users can enter their names and contact information and reserve a room for a specified date and time period. The form consists of two different views: one for editing the form, and another, marked as read-only, that will be displayed after the document has been submitted.

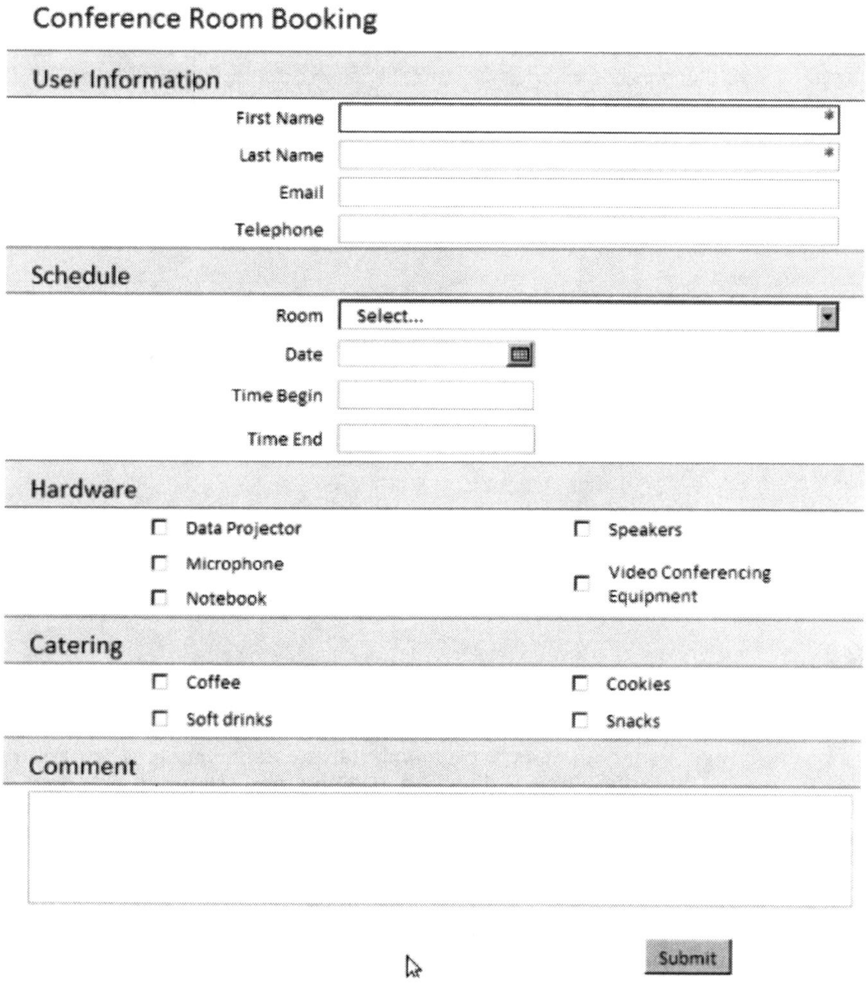

Conference Room Booking

User Information

First Name

Last Name

Email

Telephone

Schedule

Room Select...

Date

Time Begin

Time End

Hardware

Data Projector

Speakers

Microphone

Video Conferencing Equipment

Notebook

Catering

Coffee

Cookies

Soft drinks

Snacks

Comment

Submit

Figure 15–2. Example form template: Conference Room Booking

BUILDING XSN FILES FROM SOURCE FILES

In some scenarios it might be necessary to edit the source files manually, such as when there is a problem with the XSN file, or when you want to edit some of the files programmatically. In these situations you need to add the files to a CAB file and rename the extension to `.xsn`. The command-line utility `makecab.exe`, which is included in all Windows versions since Windows 2000, can assemble CAB archives. This tool is located in the `Windows\System32` folder.

To generate a CAB file, take the following steps:

Copy all files to be included in the cabinet into a folder.

Create a cabinet definition file (`.ddf`) that provides information about the cabinet name, the directory in which the cabinet file should be stored, and a list of files to include, as follows:

```
OPTION EXPLICIT
.Set CabinetNameTemplate=<cabinet filename>.XSN
.set DiskDirectoryTemplate="<directory to save cabinet to>"
.Set Cabinet=on
.Set Compress=on
"<Path to XSN folder> \myschema.xsd"
"<Path to XSN folder>\manifest.xsf"
"<Path to XSN folder>\sampledata.xm"
"<Path to XSN folder>\Template.xml"
"<Path to XSN folder>\upgrade.xsl"
"<Path to XSN folder>\view1.xsl"
"<Path to XSN folder>\view2.xsl"
```

Run the `makecab` command from the command line:

```
Makecab /f <cabinet definition>.ddf
```

Rename the cabinet file extension to `.xsn`.

Form Definition Files

InfoPath stores all the relevant information about a form template in the form definition file, called `manifest.xsf`. This file is the core file of an InfoPath template and holds information about the document schema, views, business logic, event handlers, form metadata, and deployment information.

When viewing the XML structure of this file in a text editor, you will find many elements that hold information you have entered in InfoPath Designer. Listing 15–1 shows a complete XSF file for the Conference Room Booking example form. Some of the subelements have been omitted to increase readability.

Listing 15–1. *Sample XSF File*

```
<?xml version="1.0" encoding="UTF-8"?>
<xsf:xDocumentClass trustSetting="automatic"
                    trustLevel="restricted"
                    solutionFormatVersion="3.0.0.0"
                    solutionVersion="1.0.0.16" productVersion="14.0.0"
                    publishUrl="C:\Forms\EquipmentRequest.xsn"
                    name="urn:schemas-microsoft-com:office:infopath:
                          EquipmentRequest:-myXSD-2009-09-22T18-21-06"
                    xmlns:xsf="http://schemas.microsoft.com/office/
                               infopath/2003/solutionDefinition"... >
    <xsf:package>
        <xsf:files>
            <xsf:file name="myschema.xsd">
               <xsf:property name="namespace" type="string"
                    value="http://schemas.microsoft.com/office/
```

```
                    infoapth/2003/myXSD/2010_01_20T22:54:17"> </xsf:property>
            <xsf:property name="editability" type="string" value="full">
            </xsf:property>
            <xsf:property name="rootElement" type="string" value="RoomBooking">
            </xsf:property>
            <xsf:property name="useOnDemandAlgorithm" type="string" value="yes">
            </xsf:property>
          </xsf:file>
          <xsf:file name="template.xml"></xsf:file>
          <xsf:file name="sampledata.xml">...</xsf:file>
         <xsf:file name="view1.xsl">...</xsf:file>
         <xsf:file name="view2.xsl">...</xsf:file>
         <xsf:file name="upgrade.xsl"></xsf:file>
    </xsf:files>
   </xsf:package>
  <xsf:importParameters enabled="yes"></xsf:importParameters>
  <xsf:documentVersionUpgrade>
      <xsf:useTransform transform="upgrade.xsl" minVersionToUpgrade="0.0.0.0"
                        maxVersionToUpgrade="1.0.0.15"></xsf:useTransform>
  </xsf:documentVersionUpgrade>
  <xsf:extensions>
      <xsf:extension name="SolutionDefinitionExtensions">
          <xsf2:solutionDefinition runtimeCompatibility="client server"
                                   allowClientOnlyCode="no">
              <xsf2:offline openIfQueryFails="yes" cacheQueries="yes">
              </xsf2:offline>
              <xsf2:server isPreSubmitPostBackEnabled="no"
                           isMobileEnabled="no" formLocale="en-US">
             </xsf2:server>
              <xsf2:solutionPropertiesExtension branch="share">
                  <xsf2:share formName="test"
                              path="C:\Users\Administrator\Documents\test.xsn"
                              accessPath="">
                  </xsf2:share>
              </xsf2:solutionPropertiesExtension>
             <xsf2:viewsExtension>
                 <xsf2:viewExtension ref="view2" readOnly="yes" clientOnly="no">
                 </xsf2:viewExtension>
             </xsf2:viewsExtension>
          </xsf2:solutionDefinition>
      </xsf:extension>
  </xsf:extensions>
  <xsf:views default="View 1">
      <xsf:view showMenuItem="yes" name=" View 1" caption=" View 1">
      ...
      </xsf:view>
      <xsf:view showMenuItem="yes" name="Readonly" caption="Readonly">
      ...
      </xsf:view>
  </xsf:views>
  <xsf:applicationParameters application="InfoPath Design Mode">
      <xsf:solutionProperties
fullyEditableNamespace="http://schemas.microsoft.com/office/infopath/2003/myXSD/2009-09-
```

```
22T18:21:06" lastOpenView="view1.xsl"
lastVersionNeedingTransform="1.0.0.15"></xsf:solutionProperties>
    </xsf:applicationParameters>
    <xsf:documentSchemas>
        <xsf:documentSchema rootSchema="yes"
location="http://schemas.microsoft.com/office/infopath /2003/myXSD/2009-09-22T18:21:06
myschema.xsd"></xsf:documentSchema>
    </xsf:documentSchemas>
    <xsf:fileNew>
        <xsf:initialXmlDocument caption="EquipmentRequest" href="template.xml">
        </xsf:initialXmlDocument>
    </xsf:fileNew>
    <xsf:submit caption="Submit" disableMenuItem="no" onAfterSubmit="close"
showStatusDialog="no">
        <xsf:submitToHostAdapter name="Main submit" submitAllowed="yes">
        </xsf:submitToHostAdapter>
        <xsf:errorMessage>The form cannot be submitted because of an error.</xsf:errorMessage>
    </xsf:submit>
    <xsf:ruleSets>
        <xsf:ruleSet name="ruleSet_1">
            <xsf:rule caption="Send" isEnabled="yes">
                <xsf:assignmentAction targetField="my:readonly" expression="&quot;true&quot;">
                </xsf:assignmentAction>
                <xsf:submitAction adapter="Main submit"></xsf:submitAction>
                <xsf:closeDocumentAction promptToSaveChanges="no"></xsf:closeDocumentAction>
            </xsf:rule>
        </xsf:ruleSet>
    </xsf:ruleSets>
</xsf:xDocumentClass>
```

You can find the following important information in the manifest file:

- *Unique identifier for the form*: This identifier is also used within SharePoint to reference the form template. It is provided using the name attribute of the root element <xsf:xDocumentClass>.
- *Global metadata about the form*: The root element <xsf:xDocumentClass> also contains information about document versions, publishing, trust settings, and definitions for the various namespaces that are used within the manifest.
- *Packaging of the XSN file*: The <xsf:package> element lists all the files that are included in the cabinet file using <xsf:files> elements.
- *XML Schema definition of form data*: Within the <xsf:files> section you can see the <xsf:file> element that references the schema XSD file. It contains several <xsf:property> elements, which define the name of the rootElement and whether the schema can be edited. The exact properties that can be specified vary depending on the file type. Later in the manifest file, the element <xsf:documentSchemas> contains a reference to the document schema used in the form.

- *Definition of the different views within the form*: The `<xsf:views>` element contains a child `<xsf:view>` element for each view. Each view element defines the Etensible Stylesheet Language Transformation (XSLT) that is used to display the view. Furthermore, editing components are defined within the `<xsf:editing>` tag. Editing controls are special controls that handle user editing of the nominated data field. In the following example (in Listing 15–2), a calendar control for editing the date field and a control for multiline data are defined. The `<xsf:unboundControls>` element describes additional controls that are not bound to the XML data, such as `Button` controls.

Listing 15–2. *Definition of Views in XSF*

```
<xsf:view showMenuItem="yes" name="View1" caption="Edit View">
    <xsf:mainpane transform="view2.xsl"></xsf:mainpane>
    <xsf:editing>
        <xsf:xmlToEdit name="Date_7" item="/my:RoomBooking/my:Date">
            <xsf:editWith proofing="no" autoComplete="no" component="xField"></xsf:editWith>
        </xsf:xmlToEdit>
        <xsf:xmlToEdit name="Comment_15" item="/my:ConferenceBooking/my:Comment">
            <xsf:editWith type="plainMultiline" component="xField"></xsf:editWith>
        </xsf:xmlToEdit>
    </xsf:editing>
    <xsf:unboundControls>
        <xsf:button name="CTRL18_6">
            <xsf:ruleSetAction ruleSet="ruleSet_1"></xsf:ruleSetAction>
        </xsf:button>
    </xsf:unboundControls>
</xsf:view>
```

- *Actions and rules*: These are defined within the `<xsf:ruleSets>` element as described in Listing 15–3. They define how the rules are bound to controls and what actions are taken. In the following example, a rule is defined that sets the `my:readonly` field to `true`, submits the form using the `Main submit` data source, and closes the document.

Listing 15–3. *Definition of Rules in XSF*

```
<xsf:ruleSet name="ruleSet_1">
    <xsf:rule caption="Send" isEnabled="yes">
        <xsf:assignmentAction targetField="my:readonly"
                              expression="&quot;true&quot;">
        </xsf:assignmentAction>
        <xsf:submitAction adapter="Main submit"></xsf:submitAction>
        <xsf:closeDocumentAction promptToSaveChanges="no"></xsf:closeDocumentAction>
    </xsf:rule>
</xsf:ruleSet>
```

- *Data validation*: In the section `<xsf:CustomValidation>`, all custom validation rules are expressed using `<xsf:ErrorCondition>` elements as shown in Listing 15–4. These describe the fields that are validated using the `match` attribute and the expression to be evaluated. The subelement `<xsf:errorMessage>` contains the `shortMessage` that will be displayed if validation fails.

Listing 15–4. Validation Rules in XSF

```
<xsf:customValidation>
    <xsf:errorCondition match="/my:RoomBooking"/my:Schedule/my:Date"
                        expressionContext="."
                        Expression="msxsl:string-compare(.,xdDate:Today()) &lt; 0">
        <xsf:errorMessage type="modeless" shortMessage="Date must be in the future">
        </xsf:errorMessage>
        <?caption Validate Date?>
    </xsf:errorCondition>
...
</xsf:customValidation>
```

Form Schema File (XSD)

Every form template has a schema file (.xsd) that prescribes the data structure expected by this form template. The schema file is expressed in XML Schema Definition (XSD), as defined by the W3C organization.

InfoPath validates every XML file to be rendered by the specified form template against this schema. This makes designing the schema very important, especially when the XML data files are manipulated outside of the InfoPath and Forms Services environments. If the XML is invalid according to the schema, the form cannot be displayed.

■ **Caution** InfoPath does not support all features of XSD! Please check out the MSDN library for a list of XML schema elements that are not supported by InfoPath: http://msdn.microsoft.com/en-us/library/bb251017.aspx.

Listing 15–5 shows the schema file from the Conference Room Booking example. The second line contains a very important definition: the target namespace. This is the namespace to which all the elements and attributes belong. During validation of XML data files, InfoPath verifies that all the elements and attributes in the XML instance exist within the declared namespace.

In the example form data file (in Listing 15–8), you will see that the namespace declaration for the namespace my is exactly the targetNamespace of the schema. The other namespaces used in the schema define the XML schema namespace that contains all schema elements and some additional InfoPath schema extensions.

InfoPath uses element references to structure the schema. Starting at the root node, InfoPath creates complexType elements containing all elements at that node. Each element is described using element references pointing to elements, which are defined at the root element of the schema. This enhances readability of the schema and reusability of the elements.

Looking at the elements, you can see that InfoPath created some simpleType definitions, such as requiredString. This is used to implement the "Cannot be blank" check box in the field properties dialog in InfoPath Editor. This string extends the basic string format of XML Schema using a restriction, saying that the element has a minimum length of 1. You need to understand the difference between this and the minOccurs attribute used in the element descriptions. minOccurs tells the XML parser how often an element may be present in the XML. If you define the FirstName element with minOccurs=1, you are only specifying that this XML element is mandatory. However, the value of the element could still be empty.

Another important related attribute is the nillable attribute. This is usually used for date and time fields, as it allows an element to set the attribute nillable=true. Because a date element always requires the content to be a valid date, this is the only way to create empty date fields. Otherwise, if you entered an empty string into the date element, the validation of the XML would fail. An empty date can thus be created in the XML as <my:Date nil='true'></my:Date>.

Listing 15–5. *Example Schema*

```
<?xml version="1.0" encoding="UTF-8" standalone="no"?>
<xsd:schema targetNamespace="http://schemas.microsoft.com/office/infopath/2003/myXSD/2009-09-
29T22:54:17" xmlns:xsi="http://www.w3.org/2001/XMLSchema-instance"
xmlns:my="http://schemas.microsoft.com/office/infopath/2003/myXSD/2009-09-29T22:54:17"
xmlns:xd="http://schemas.microsoft.com/office/infopath/2003"
xmlns:xsd="http://www.w3.org/2001/XMLSchema">
    <xsd:element name="RoomBooking">
        <xsd:complexType>
            <xsd:sequence>
                <xsd:element ref="my:UserInformation" minOccurs="0"/>
                <xsd:element ref="my:Schedule" minOccurs="0"/>
                <xsd:element ref="my:Hardware" minOccurs="0"/>
                <xsd:element ref="my:Catering" minOccurs="0"/>
                <xsd:element ref="my:Comments" minOccurs="0"/>
                <xsd:element ref="my:readonly" minOccurs="0"/>
            </xsd:sequence>
            <xsd:anyAttribute processContents="lax"
                              namespace="http://www.w3.org/XML/1998/namespace"/>
        </xsd:complexType>
    </xsd:element>

    <xsd:element name="UserInformation">
        <xsd:complexType>
            <xsd:sequence>
                <xsd:element ref="my:FirstName" minOccurs="0"/>
                <xsd:element ref="my:LastName" minOccurs="0"/>
                <xsd:element ref="my:Email" minOccurs="0"/>
                <xsd:element ref="my:Telephone" minOccurs="0"/>
            </xsd:sequence>
        </xsd:complexType>
    </xsd:element>
    <xsd:element name="FirstName" type="my:requiredString"/>
    <xsd:element name="LastName" type="my:requiredString"/>
    <xsd:element name="Email" type="xsd:string"/>
    <xsd:element name="Telephone" type="xsd:string"/>

    <xsd:element name="Schedule">
        <xsd:complexType>
            <xsd:sequence>
                <xsd:element ref="my:Room" minOccurs="0"/>
                <xsd:element ref="my:Date" minOccurs="0"/>
                <xsd:element ref="my:TimeBegin" minOccurs="0"/>
                <xsd:element ref="my:TimeEnd" minOccurs="0"/>
            </xsd:sequence>
        </xsd:complexType>
```

```
    </xsd:element>
    <xsd:element name="Room" type="xsd:string"/>
    <xsd:element name="Date" nillable="true" type="xsd:date"/>
    <xsd:element name="TimeBegin" nillable="true" type="xsd:time"/>
    <xsd:element name="TimeEnd" type="xsd:string"/>

    <xsd:element name="Hardware">
        <xsd:complexType>
            <xsd:sequence>
                <xsd:element ref="my:DataProjector" minOccurs="0"/>
                <xsd:element ref="my:Microphone" minOccurs="0"/>
                <xsd:element ref="my:Notebook" minOccurs="0"/>
                <xsd:element ref="my:Speakers" minOccurs="0"/>
                <xsd:element ref="my:VideoConferencing" minOccurs="0"/>
            </xsd:sequence>
        </xsd:complexType>
    </xsd:element>
    <xsd:element name="DataProjector" nillable="true" type="xsd:boolean"/>
    <xsd:element name="Microphone" nillable="true" type="xsd:boolean"/>
    <xsd:element name="Notebook" nillable="true" type="xsd:boolean"/>
    <xsd:element name="Speakers" nillable="true" type="xsd:boolean"/>
    <xsd:element name="VideoConferencing" nillable="true" type="xsd:boolean"/>

...

    <xsd:element name="readonly" nillable="true" type="xsd:boolean"/>

    <xsd:simpleType name="requiredString">
        <xsd:restriction base="xsd:string">
            <xsd:minLength value="1"/>
        </xsd:restriction>
    </xsd:simpleType>

    <xsd:simpleType name="requiredAnyURI">
        <xsd:restriction base="xsd:anyURI">
            <xsd:minLength value="1"/>
        </xsd:restriction>
    </xsd:simpleType>

    <xsd:simpleType name="requiredBase64Binary">
        <xsd:restriction base="xsd:base64Binary">
            <xsd:minLength value="1"/>
        </xsd:restriction>
    </xsd:simpleType>
</xsd:schema>
```

GENERATING A CLASS FROM A SCHEMA

The schema definition file can be used to generate .NET classes that represent the XML data elements. Using generated classes makes working with the XML files more convenient and reduces errors.

To generate a C# or VB class from an XSD file, you can use the `xsd.exe` command-line utility, which is part of the .NET Framework. The following command generates a C# class from the input `<schemafile>` and places the generated class into the `<output directory>`:

```
> xsd.exe <schemafile>.xsd /classes /language:CS /outputdir:<output directory>
```

To populate an object with data from an XML instance, you can use the `Deserialize` method of the `XmlSerializer` class as follows:

```
using System.Xml.Serialization;
System.IO.StreamReader str = new System.IO.StreamReader("example.xml");
XmlSerializer xSerializer = new XmlSerializer(typeof(ConferenceBooking));
ConferenceBooking res = (ConferenceBooking) xSerializer.Deserialize(str);
```

In this example we assume that we generated a class called `RoomBooking` based on our example form template.

Form Views (XSL)

Each view in the form template is defined by an XSL stylesheet file, which comprises all the relevant information for displaying the view. To render a view, the selected XML data file will be transformed into an HTML view via XSLT processing.

Listing 15–6 shows the body of such a view definition. For a clearer perspective, the HTML content, style definitions, and namespace definitions have been removed.

Listing 15–6. *Form View Definition in XSL*

```
<?xml version="1.0" encoding="UTF-8"?>
<xsl:stylesheet version="1.0" xmlns:"...">
    <xsl:output method="html" indent="no"/>
    <xsl:template match="my:RoomBooking">
        <html>
            <head>
                <meta content="text/html" http-equiv="Content-Type"></meta>
                <style controlStyle="controlStyle">...</style>
                <style themeStyle="urn:office.microsoft.com:themeOffice">...</style>
                <style languageStyle="languageStyle">...</style>
            </head>
            <body style="BACKGROUND-COLOR: #ffffff; COLOR: #000000">
            ...
            </body>
        </html>
    </xsl:template>
</xsl:stylesheet>
```

The stylesheet defines one template rule that applies to the root element of the XSD schema. In the example you can see that the match attribute points to the RoomBooking node, which is the root element in our example. Within this template, HTML defines the display behavior. To insert the XML information from the data file, XSLT instructions are used within the template. The following snippet (in Listing 15–7) demonstrates how the drop-down list for the room is defined as a table element within the HTML layout. An XSLT select element is inserted, and the attributes value and selected are supplied from the XML data using XSLT instructions.

Listing 15–7. *XSLT Transformation in XSL File*

```
<td class="xdTableComponent" style="PADDING-BOTTOM: 1px; VERTICAL-ALIGN: middle; PADDING-TOP:
1px">
    <div>
        <select class="xdComboBox xdBehavior_Select" title="" size="1" tabIndex="0"
xd:xctname="dropdown" xd:CtrlId="CTRL19" xd:binding="my:Schedule/my:Room" xd:boundProp="value"
style="WIDTH: 100%">
            <xsl:attribute name="value">
                <xsl:value-of select="my:Schedule/my:Room"/>
            </xsl:attribute>
            <option value="">
                <xsl:if test="my:Schedule/my:Room=&quot;&quot;">
                    <xsl:attribute name="selected">selected</xsl:attribute>
                </xsl:if>
            </option>
        </select>
    </div>
</td>
```

As you can see, the structure of XSL views is quite easy to follow and allows you to make changes to the layout or the XSL instructions. Nevertheless, manually editing views is very time consuming and requires you to deal with some Microsoft-specific schemas.

Form XML Template (XML)

Every form template contains two XML files: sampledata.xml and template.xml. The sampledata.xml file contains all the elements of the form with their default values, which were specified when the form was designed. The template.xml file represents an XML template that is used as a template for creating new documents. Although at first sight these files may not seem to be very useful, for developers this is not so. The template file, for example, can be used to create new document instances from custom code. If you wish to dynamically set default values for your forms, you can edit sampledata.xml from within your code.

The structure of the XML files is the same as the structure of form data files, described next.

InfoPath Form Data

The following snippet (see Listing 15–8) shows an example data file for the InfoPath form used in the Conference Room Booking example. In addition to the standard XML structure that complies with the preceding schema definition, InfoPath has added two special processing instructions. Within them are several attributes that define InfoPath metadata, such as version numbers. The most important attribute is the href attribute in the mso-infoPathSolution processing instruction. It links to the InfoPath form template—which is used to render the form—by specifying its location.

Listing 15–8. Sample XML Data File

```
<?xml version="1.0" encoding="UTF-8"?>
<?mso-infoPathSolution solutionVersion="1.0.0.24" productVersion="14.0.0" PIVersion="1.0.0.0"
href="file:///C:\Users\Administrator\AppData\Local\Microsoft\InfoPath\Designer3\70314fc2849b4b
bc\manifest.xsf" ?><?mso-application progid="InfoPath.Document"
versionProgid="InfoPath.Document.3"?>
<my:ConferenceBooking xmlns:xsi="http://www.w3.org/2001/XMLSchema-instance"
xmlns:my="http://schemas.microsoft.com/office/infopath/2003/myXSD/2009-09-22T18:21:06"
xmlns:xd="http://schemas.microsoft.com/office/infopath/2003" xml:lang="en-us">
    <my:UserInformation>
        <my:FirstName>John</my:FirstName>
        <my:LastName>Smith</my:LastName>
        <my:Email>john@smith.com</my:Email>
        <my:Telephone>01234567</my:Telephone>
    </my:UserInformation>
    <my:Schedule>
        <my:Room>Conference Room 1</my:Room>
        <my:RoomNumber>0001</my:RoomNumber>
        <my:Date>2009-12-31</my:Date>
        <my:TimeBegin>12:00:00</my:TimeBegin>
        <my:TimeEnd>14:00:00</my:TimeEnd>
    </my:Schedule>
    <my:Hardware>
        <my:DataProjector>true</my:DataProjector>
        <my:Microphone>false</my:Microphone>
        <my:Notebook>false</my:Notebook>
        <my:Speakers>false</my:Speakers>
        <my:VideoConferencing>true</my:VideoConferencing>
    </my:Hardware>
    <my:Catering>
        <my:Coffee>false</my:Coffee>
        <my:SoftDrinks>false</my:SoftDrinks>
        <my:Cookies>false</my:Cookies>
        <my:Snacks>false</my:Snacks>
    </my:Catering>
    <my:Comments>
        <my:Comment>Some additional comment</my:Comment>
    </my:Comments>
    <my:readonly>false</my:readonly>
</my:RoomBooking>
```

Designing Browser-Enabled Form Templates

Having examined the internal structure of InfoPath form templates, we will now take a closer look at the important steps in building form templates that can be used within SharePoint and Forms Services. Most of the wizards, dialogs, and property windows that can be used throughout these steps are identical in InfoPath 2007 and 2010. Many of the changes made to the InfoPath 2010 UI are concentrated in the reorganized menus on to the ribbon bars. You will find some properties that used to be hidden in cascaded dialogs are now directly available in the ribbon bars, which is a great improvement when designing larger forms.

InfoPath 2010 has been divided into two distinct programs: InfoPath Designer and InfoPath Filler. This separation reflects the two different usage scenarios and with it the two different roles for working with InfoPath. InfoPath Designer is targeted at those who create and design form templates. InfoPath Filler is the client application for filling out forms. The split makes it easier for users to understand InfoPath—in the past this difference was not made clear to new users of InfoPath.

Defining the Data Structure

When using forms in complex business solutions, the most important aspect is the design of your data schema. This is particularly so if you are using the schema throughout a business process where you access the XML contents using custom .NET code or property promotion and demotion in SharePoint lists. Schema design becomes even more complex if you plan to use your schema across different applications (e.g., when using BizTalk to process form data with the BizTalk mapping facilities).

There are two approaches to designing the schema:

- Use the InfoPath client to generate and edit the schema during template design.
- Define your schema first and create a form template based on this schema.

When you begin form creation by selecting a new blank form template, InfoPath will create the schema definition for you. This way you can simply add new controls to your views, or edit the schema in the Fields dialog (see Figure 15–3). Although your control over the schema that is produced is limited in this case, this scenario may be adequate for simple forms.

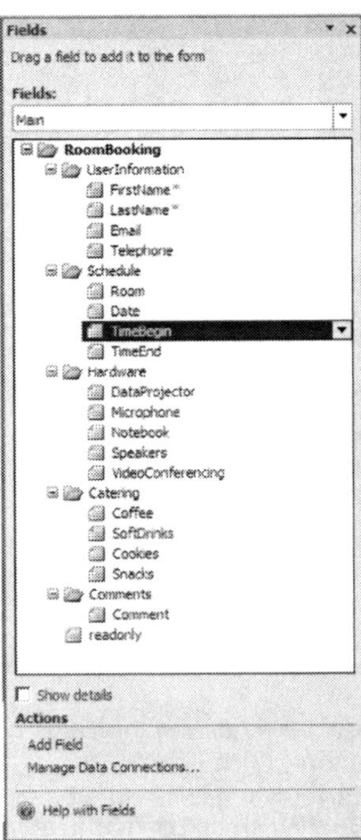

Figure 15–3. The Fields dialog

If you need full control over the XSD schema definition (e.g., when planning to use the XML across different applications), you should first build the XSD schema definition yourself and then create a new form template based on this schema. InfoPath provides a wizard to generate a new form by selecting the XML or Schema template. You merely choose your schema and start designing your form based on that schema.

When you design your own schema, you are able to use some advanced mechanisms of XML Schema, but you should keep in mind the following:

- InfoPath does not support the entire XML Schema syntax.
- If you build your form on an existing schema, you will not be able to change the field properties using the Fields dialog. Instead you will have to use the Data ➤ Refresh Fields option to reload the schema.
- You can use data type restrictions in your schema to limit the allowed values in your form. Since InfoPath validates your XML input against the schema, you have only limited control of the errors that are presented to users when they input data that is invalid according to the schema.
- For suitable user feedback, it may be better to validate input data using rules in InfoPath and displaying meaningful messages to the users.
- Very strict schema definitions can prevent Forms Services from displaying your form at all, since invalid XML, according to the schema, will not be opened. This results in a very general "Form has been closed" message in the UI.
- Overly restrictive data types in the schema make modifying "accepted input" more complex, especially if you intend that not only developers but also information workers should be able to make changes to the form design. For example, if your schema is defined to accept any string for user input, rules can be used to constrain the input to certain values. These rules can be changed by anyone capable of working with InfoPath, whereas a change to the schema would necessitate a complex development change scenario.

Overall, you should create your schema with care and weigh the pros and cons of very strict schemas. Use your schema to define the basic data structure but take care when using strong data type restrictions—you might end up spending a lot of time searching for the reason why your forms can't be displayed.

Designing the Form Templates

To lay out form templates, InfoPath uses different views. Only one view at a time will be displayed when the form is rendered, but users can switch between these views. This allows you to split large forms into different views, which makes it easier to work with the form. Furthermore, views can also be defined as *read-only* or designed with the sole purpose of printing. Read-only views in particular are very useful when forms should be immutable after they have been submitted. To achieve this behavior you simply add a property named `readonly` to your schema that will be set to `true` when the form is submitted. Adding a rule into the form load event, which switches the active view to the read-only view, if this `readonly` property is set to true, will always show the read-only view after the form is submitted.

Within views, layout tables should be used to arrange elements. These layout tables are displayed in InfoPath Editor using dashed lines, but they are not displayed when the form is rendered. These tables result in HTML table elements in the XSL form view. Controls or fields can simply be dragged into the layout table at the desired position. To limit the effort to lay out the form, InfoPath 2010 offers some table and section templates, as shown in Figure 15–4. You can use them to quickly build well-organized form templates.

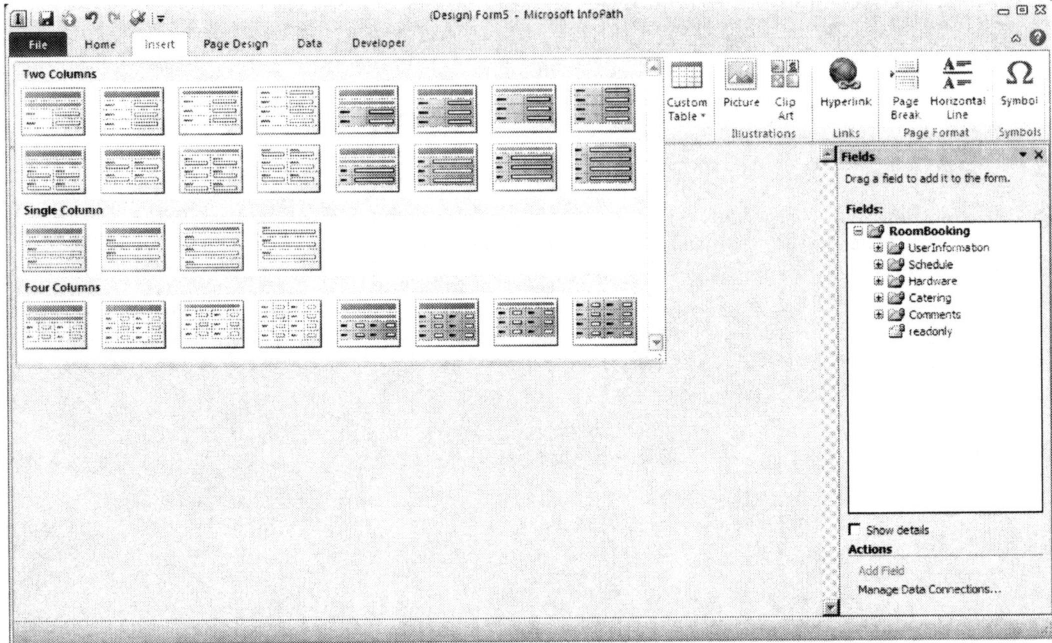

Figure 15–4. Section templates

To edit the behavior of control fields you can use either the context menu or the Properties ribbon bar. Depending on the type of control, different properties will be available. Every control is bound to a field in your document schema. The Change Binding option will change the binding target. Selecting the Control Properties window will allow you to specify data properties, display properties, size properties, and some other advanced properties. For special data types such as integers and dates, on the display tab you can configure the output format—for example, to display an integer as a currency.

Adding Rules and Validation

Rules are used in InfoPath to control form behavior. While in InfoPath 2007 rules are dispersed across multiple menus—rules, data validation, and conditional formatting—InfoPath 2010 merges them together. They can now be action rules, validation rules, or formatting rules, but are all accessible through one editor pane, the Rules dialog (Figure 15–5).

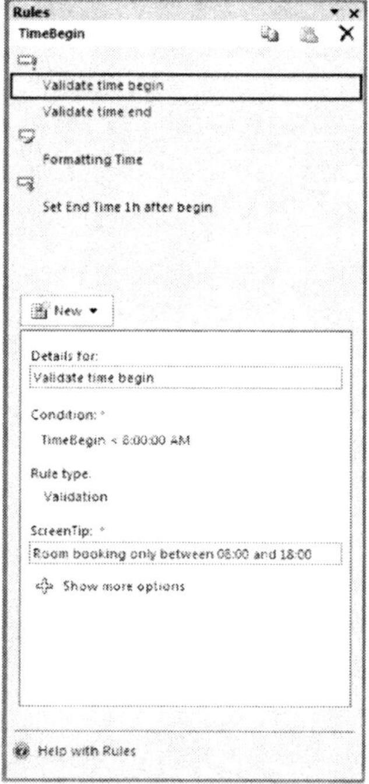

Figure 15–5. *The Rules dialog*

Every rule consists of an entry condition, allowing the form template author to define when the rule applies. Formatting rules specify text formatting to apply to the nominated field. Validation rules will result in a form error when the condition is not met, and the data for the particular control will be flagged as invalid. Whenever a user changes the value of a control, InfoPath checks the entry conditions of all the action rules assigned to that control. If the condition for a rule is fulfilled, the specified actions are executed.

■ **Caution** Action rules will only by evaluated when the value in the field actually changes. Loading a default value does not trigger the change event, even when it meets the condition for the action rule. Formatting and validation rules, on the other hand, will always be applied.

To view all the rules within a form, you can use the Rule Inspector. It shows all the dynamic elements (e.g., rules, calculated default values, and managed code). Figure 15–6 shows the Rule Inspector for the Conference Room Booking example. You can see that data validations have been added for the date and time values, aggregated under Alerts. Also note too the interesting rules shown in the Other Actions section. The Programming section will contain the events raised by your code when you add code to your form template.

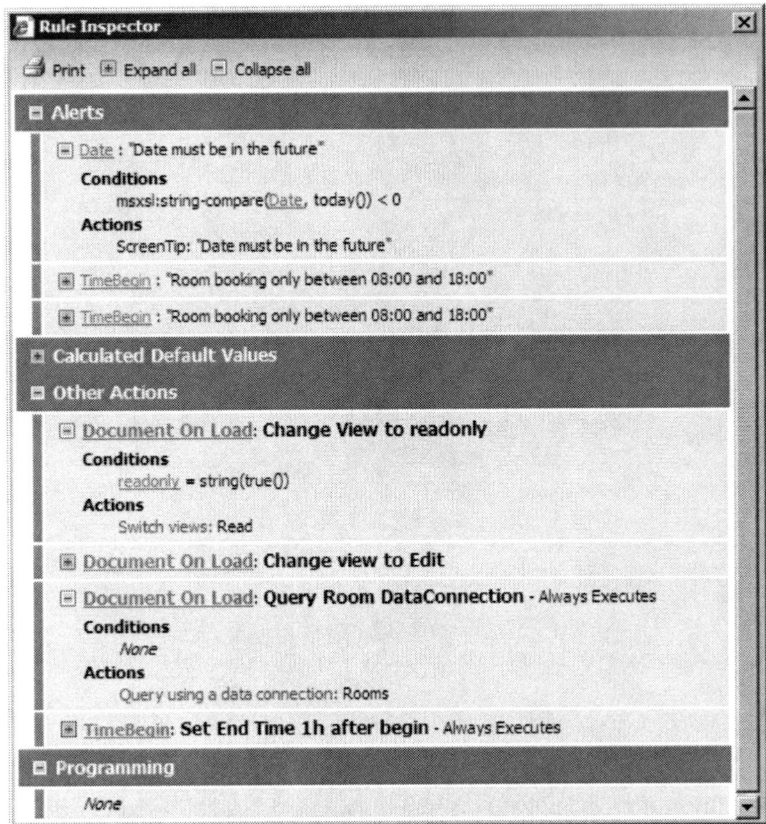

Figure 15–6. The Rule Inspector

Accessing External Data

Designing forms for LOB applications often requires data from external data sources to be included in the form. Typically, such data is retrieved from databases, SharePoint lists, or web services. A drop-down list, for instance, could be populated with values directly within the form. If the values are subject to change, though, you might consider populating them from outside the form. InfoPath accommodates access to external data through the definition of secondary data sources.

Each form consists of one primary data source (also called a data connection) and several secondary data sources. In the previous chapter we described how to define a primary data source using an XSD schema. Data connections can be managed via the `Data` menu. You can add new data connections using the Data Connection wizard. The wizard will prompt for some specific parameters for the data connection, such as the URL of the SharePoint list and the fields that you want to use. Once the data connection is set up, you need to tell InfoPath to load the data from this connection. This is not done automatically, except when you check the box "automatically retrieve data when the form is opened" in the final step of the Data Connection wizard. Otherwise, you will have to add a rule action that queries the data connection, as shown in Figure 15–7, or execute the connection using code.

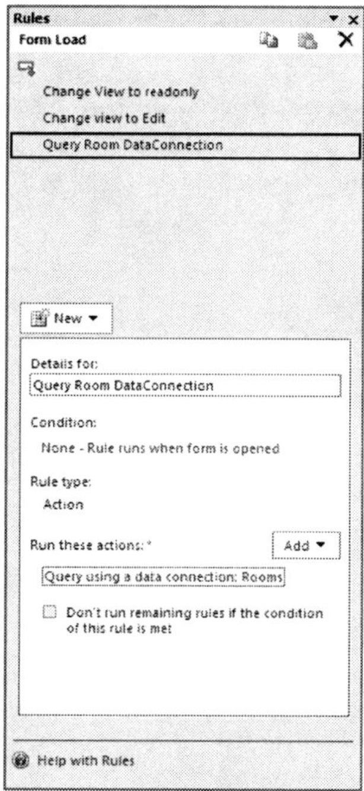

Figure 15–7. Creating a rule to query a data connection

When using web service connections that require query parameters, you need to build a rule that sets the query parameter, queries the connection, and finally returns the result of the web service.

Secondary data connections can be employed in the same ways as primary data connections—in rules and formulas or binding to a control. A common scenario for secondary data connections is to fill a drop-down list with dynamic values, as shown in Figure 15–8.

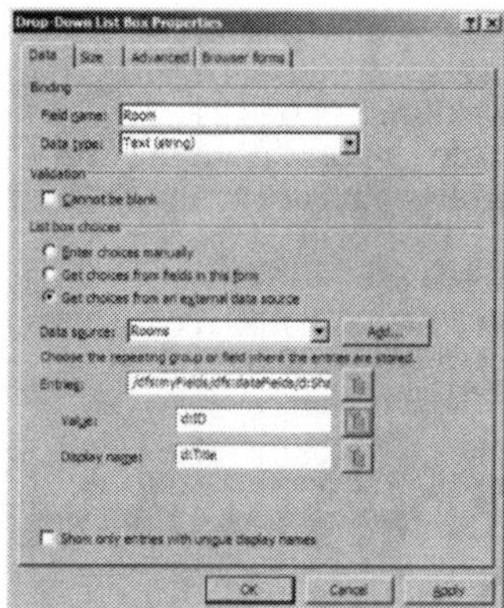

Figure 15–8. Building a drop-down list from a data connection

In this example, the Rooms data source is selected to supply the values in the drop-down list. This data source points to a SharePoint list containing all rooms. The Entries field references the repeating item in the resultant data from the connection, and the list ID and Title are used in the Value and "Display name" fields, respectively.

Data connections can be used for querying data from and submitting data to a data repository. The following table shows a list of data sources you can use and whether they can be used for sending or receiving data.

Table 15–1. *Different Types of Data Connections*

Data Connection	Submit	Receive
Web service	Yes	Yes
SharePoint library or list	No	Yes
SharePoint document library	Yes	No
E-mail message	yes	No
Groove library or list	No	Yes
Microsoft SQL Server database	No	Yes
XML document	No	Yes
Hosting environment	Yes	No

One very useful data repository is the hosting environment. This can be used to send data to the environment that is hosting the InfoPath form, such as the forms service running on SharePoint or a custom application page. We will discuss this topic in the "InfoPath Forms Services" section later in the chapter.

Using the InfoPath wizard to add a data connection strongly binds the form template to the data connection, since all the information about the connection is stored within the form. When working with SharePoint forms within a multilevel development environment—consisting of a development and production environment—or when creating reusable forms, this solution is very inflexible. To add another layer of abstraction for data connections, you should use data connection libraries in SharePoint. They can easily be created like any other library. Select View All Site Content from the Site Actions drop-down menu. Then click Create and select Data Connection Library to create a new data connection library.

Those libraries can hold *Universal Data Description (UDCX)* files, which are used to store connection information. UDCX files can then be used by InfoPath to reference data connections. This decouples the strong binding between the actual data connection and the form template, and thus allows you to supply the same form template with different UDCX files for different SharePoint environments.

UDCX files are XML files adhering to the UDC schema definition. Listing 15–9 shows an example UDCX file for a data connection to SharePoint, to retrieve the rooms for the Conference Room Booking example.

Listing 15–9. Example Universal Data Description File

```
<?xml version="1.0" encoding="UTF-8"?>
<?MicrosoftWindowsSharePointServices
ContentTypeID="0x010100B4CBD48E029A4ad8B62CB0E41868F2B0"?>
<udc:DataSource MajorVersion="2" MinorVersion="0"
xmlns:udc="http://schemas.microsoft.com/office/infopath/2006/udc">
    <udc:Name>Rooms</udc:Name>
    <udc:Description>Format: UDC V2; Connection Type: SharePointList; Purpose: ReadOnly;
Generated by Microsoft Office InfoPath 2007 on 2009-10-05 at 13:46:53 by
WAPPS\moss_service.</udc:Description>
    <udc:Type MajorVersion="2" MinorVersion="0" Type="SharePointList">
        <udc:SubType MajorVersion="0" MinorVersion="0" Type=""/>
    </udc:Type>
    <udc:ConnectionInfo Purpose="ReadOnly" AltDataSource="">
        <udc:WsdlUrl/>
            <udc:SelectCommand>
                <udc:ListId>{68BB674B-85D9-450A-B394-6FD9F08B6959}</udc:ListId>
                <udc:WebUrl>http://winsrv2008as/</udc:WebUrl>
                <udc:ConnectionString/>
                <udc:ServiceUrl UseFormsServiceProxy="false"/>
                <udc:SoapAction/>
                <udc:Query/>
            </udc:SelectCommand>
            <udc:UpdateCommand>
                <udc:ServiceUrl UseFormsServiceProxy="false"/>
                <udc:SoapAction/>
                <udc:Submit/>
                <udc:FileName>Specify a filename or formula</udc:FileName>
                <udc:FolderName AllowOverwrite=""/>
            </udc:UpdateCommand>
            <!--udc:Authentication><udc:SSO AppId='' CredentialType='' />
</udc:Authentication-->
        </udc:ConnectionInfo>
    </udc:ConnectionInfo>
</udc:DataSource>
```

The preceding listing contains a processing instruction for SharePoint with a ContentTypeID attribute, which specifies the ContentType for data connection files within SharePoint. The DataSource element defines the namespace and the version of the UDCX format. The attributes of the data connection are defined within the ConnectionInfo section. The element Type as a subelement of DataSource has an attribute also called Type, which specifies the type of the connection. It can be one of the following values, which match the data connection option in InfoPath Editor:

- SharePointList
- SharePointLibrary
- Database
- XmlQuery
- XmlSubmit
- WebService

The attribute Purpose specifies the direction of the data connection. ReadOnly is used for receive connections, WriteOnly is used for submit connections, and ReadWrite is used for bidirectional connections. Depending on this parameter, SelectCommand and/or UpdateCommand need to be supplied. Both support all the necessary information to set up the connection.

To create a UDCX file, you can edit an existing UDCX file or let InfoPath create the file as follows:

1. Create a data connection library in SharePoint.
2. Configure your data connection using the InfoPath wizard.
3. Select the Data Connection Manager in InfoPath from Data ➤ Data Connections.
4. Choose the particular data connection and click Convert to Connection File...
5. Enter the path to the data connection library you created in step 1, followed by the file name of the UDCX file you want to create.
6. Choose "Relative to site collection" to cause InfoPath to look for the data connection library relative to the site collection, or choose "Centrally managed data connection" if you intend to manage your data connections in Central Administration.
7. If you choose to manage your UDCX files centrally, you need to download the UDCX file, save it locally, and then add it manually to Central Administration.
8. Now you can use this UDCX file in your forms to create a new data connection by selecting "Search for connections on a Microsoft Office SharePoint Server" and entering the URL to the data connection library.

Forms Security

InfoPath form templates support three different levels of security. Each security level defines the allowed level of access to external resources from a form. The required security level for your form depends on the scenario in which you want to use your form. These scenarios range from simple data input scenarios where the form is only used for user input with no programming logic or access to external data sources, to very sophisticated forms that make use of programming facilities and aggregate information from various sources.

You can change the security settings in the Form Options dialog, accessible via File ➤ Info ➤ "Advanced form options," as shown in Figure 15–9.

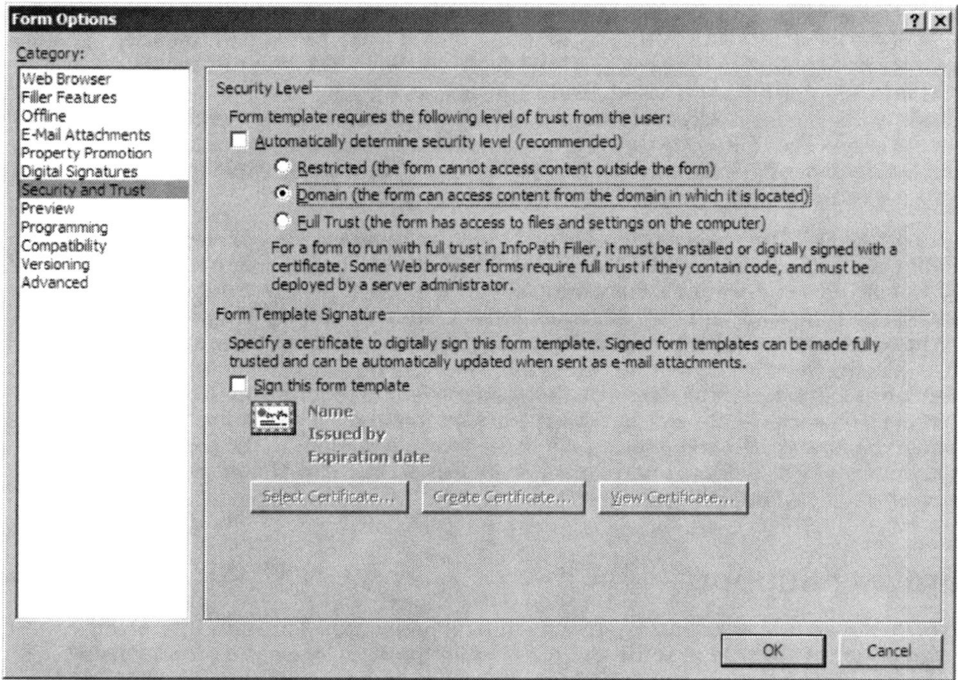

Figure 15–9. *Security options*

By default, the check box "Automatically determine security level" is checked. In this case, InfoPath tries to define the security level based on the features used in the form. Since you should know the scenario for which you are designing the form, it is a good idea to manually select one of the following options. Otherwise, you might run into complications during publishing and deployment, and have to spend extra time searching for the source of your problems.

- *Restricted*: The Restricted security level is used for forms that don't contain any code and don't communicate with external data sources. Forms that are created with restricted access can only be used as a data container to collect information from users. Since communication outside of the form is not permitted and no potentially harmful code can be contained in those forms, restricted forms provide the highest level of security. On the other hand, usage scenarios for these types of forms are very limited. Restricted forms always require InfoPath Filler, because to use them with Forms Services in SharePoint, a minimum security level of Domain is required. However, you could e-mail these forms to the recipients or put them on a network share and have users fill them out with InfoPath Filler.

- *Domain*: The Domain security level restricts the access of a form to a particular domain. The form can contain code and may access data sources within the domain of the form. InfoPath Forms Services requires at least the Domain security level for forms to render in the browser. By default, you will work with this security level when designing browser-based form templates, as they are suitable for most scenarios where the form accesses lists and libraries on the local SharePoint Server but doesn't contain code that accesses local resources. This type of form is also called *sandboxed*, because the form is placed in the local cache while the user is filling it out, and access to system resources is denied.
- *Full Trust*: The Full Trust security level allows the form to access system resources and other components on the computer where the form will be used, or to use cross-domain data connections. For example, fully trusted forms can contain potentially harmful code and use Microsoft ActiveX controls. Having a higher set of permissions requires fully trusted forms to be digitally signed to ensure security when deploying them to SharePoint. Although you could possibly create fully trusted forms without signing the form, this scenario would require you to install the template on each client—not an acceptable solution in most scenarios. We will show you how to sign and deploy fully trusted form templates in the section "Deploying InfoPath Forms to SharePoint." Fully trusted forms in SharePoint need to be approved by a farm administrator.

Enabling Browser Support

InfoPath allows you to design form templates, targeting different scenarios. The most interesting scenario within the context of SharePoint is the ability to render InfoPath forms in a browser using InfoPath Forms Services. Designing browser-based forms requires some special considerations and settings, and poses some limitations compared to designing forms for the InfoPath client.

Setting Form Compatibility

When you start to design a new form, you can choose the type of template you want to design. Some advanced templates will require you to enable browser support in your form template. To enable browser support, go to File ➤ Info ➤ "Advanced form options," and select Compatibility from the Category list. Set the form type to Web Browser Form, as shown in Figure 15–10. This tells InfoPath that this form can be rendered in a browser. You can enter your SharePoint URL in the field beneath to allow InfoPath to validate your browser compatibility directly on the SharePoint server using a web service of InfoPath Forms Services.

Depending on the compatibility setting, some features will be hidden or deactivated in the relevant dialogs. For example, the multiline feature of text boxes is limited when you work with browser-enabled forms. Figure 15–11 shows the different options for templates designed for InfoPath Editor (on the left) and InfoPath Forms Services (on the right). Therefore, you should always set the compatibility before starting to design your form template. This way you ensure that you are only using available features.

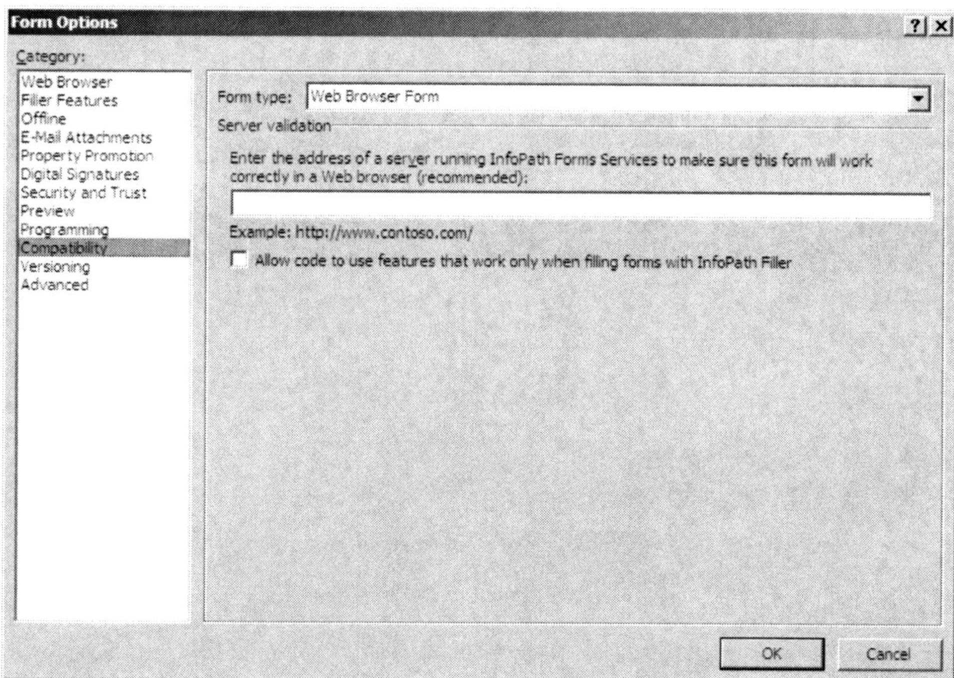

Figure 15–10. Enabling browser compatibility

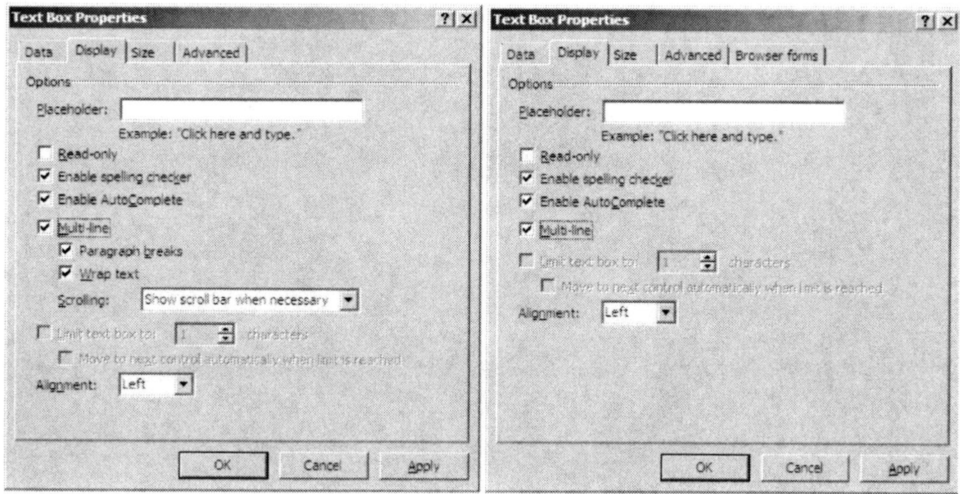

Figure 15–11. Different properties for InfoPath forms (left) and browser-enabled forms (right)

Configuring Interface Options for InfoPath Forms Services

After you have set the compatibility to Web Browser Form, you will find a new category called Web Browser in your Form Options dialog when you reopen it (Figure 15–13). Here you can set advanced options that change the browser interface, which is shown in Figure 15–14. You can select the commands you wish to display to the user when editing the form. Furthermore, you can select alternative toolbars in case the ribbon bar is not available, and set the language that will be used for displaying the commands and dialogs.

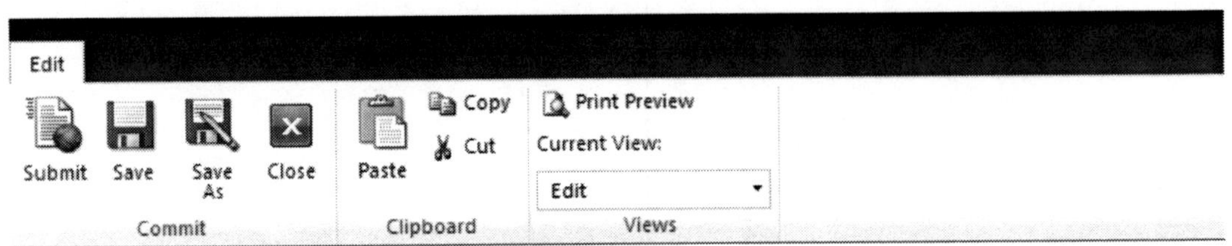

Figure 15–12. UI in InfoPath Forms Services

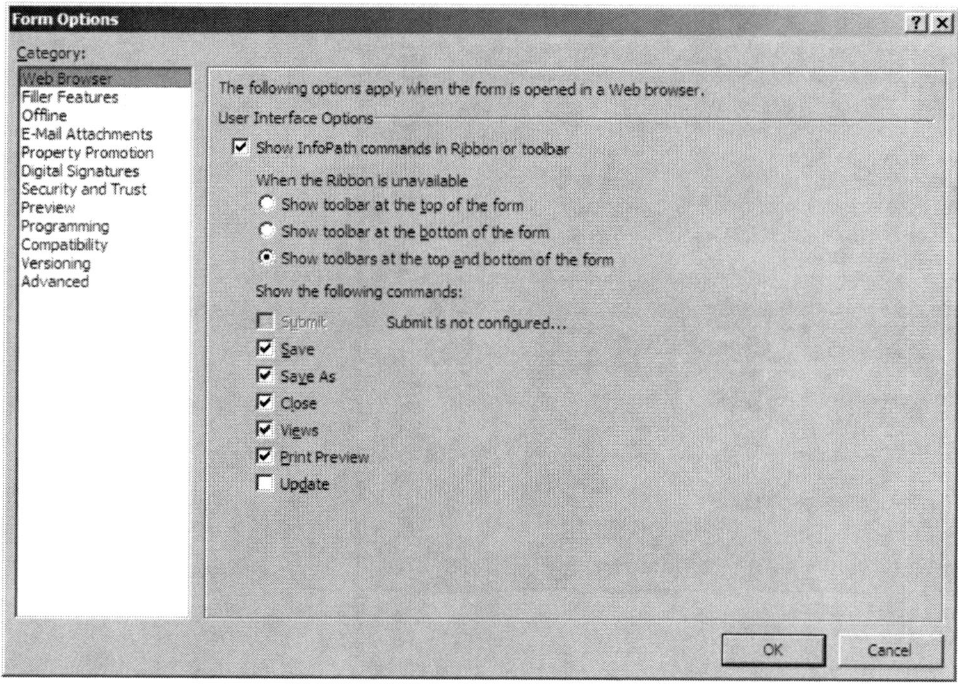

Figure 15–13. Setting UI options

Configuring Submit Options

You need to specify the destination for the data entered into the form. Submitting the form will trigger Forms Services to run the validation checks on the form. All the validation rules must pass before the submit is allowed to proceed.

You can either specify submission using rules (i.e., you can add a button with an action rule and select the submit action) or you can use the submit options from the Data ribbon bar. In either case you need to specify a submit data connection as described previously. Most commonly you will use a connection to a SharePoint library, a SharePoint data connection, or the hosting environment. When specifying a SharePoint library, you need to provide the URL of the library and the file name for saving the form. The file name can be constructed using a formula. The hosting environment will be used when you want to programmatically access the form information from an ASP.NET application such as SharePoint application pages.

The submit options, as shown in Figure 15–14, allow you to specify the submit destination and the corresponding data connection. As an alternative, you could use code to programmatically handle the submit event.

Specifying submit options and using a button with action rules to submit the form differ in the way the submit action will be displayed to the users. If you are using submit options, the submit button will be displayed in the ribbon bar; however, placing a button in the form provides more flexibility and might be more intuitive for many users. You can also make use of the new image buttons, which allow you to customize button layout.

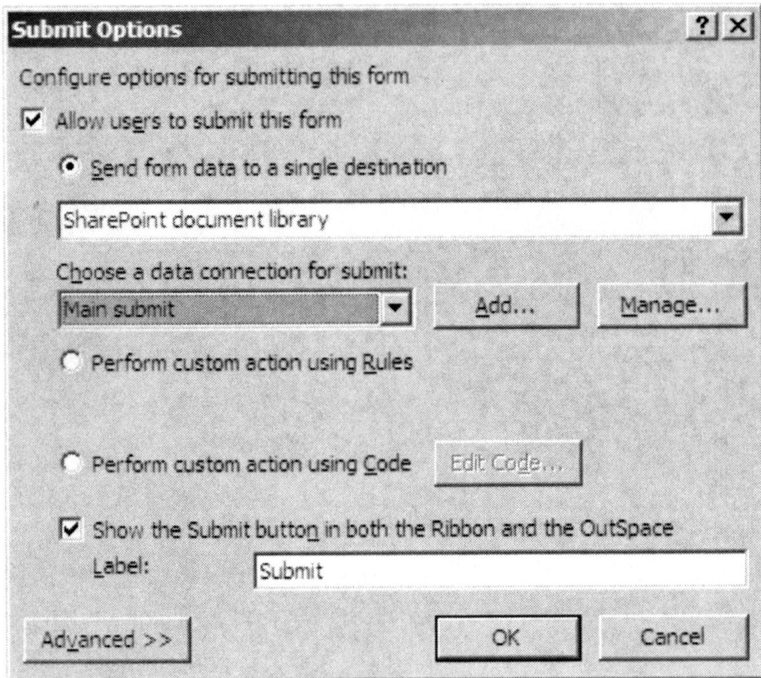

Figure 15–14. Setting submit options

To ensure that browser support is configured correctly, use the following checklist:

- Compatibility is set to Web Browser Form.
- The UI options are set correctly.
- The security level is set to Domain or Full Trust.
- Design Checker shows no compatibility errors.
- The Submit option is set to either SharePoint or Hosting environment.

Deploying InfoPath Forms to SharePoint

Once you have finished designing your InfoPath form template using InfoPath Designer, you need to make the form template available to users so that they can fill out forms based on your form template. Since information about the target location is stored inside the XSN file, you cannot simply copy your form to that location. Instead, InfoPath offers a process called *publishing*, which prepares the form template for its target location. Depending on the targeted scenario, required parameters are set in the `manifest.xml` file inside the XSN archive.

Using InfoPath Forms in SharePoint

Before talking about how publishing works, we will take a closer look at the different ways to use InfoPath forms inside SharePoint. (You can also use your InfoPath forms without SharePoint, but such scenarios will not be covered here.)

The following are some scenarios for using InfoPath forms in SharePoint:

- *Forms in document libraries*: This is probably the most common scenario for using InfoPath forms in SharePoint. You simply create a *forms library*—a special type of document library—in SharePoint and attach form templates to this library. Users are then able to fill out forms based on the provided form templates and submit the results to the forms library. You can easily attach SharePoint workflows to these document libraries to implement simple business processes for your forms.
- *Workflow forms*: When building SharePoint workflows you can use InfoPath forms to gather information from users. Workflows allow you to integrate forms at various stages of workflow execution (e.g., association, initiation, or user tasks). Each of these forms can be handled with InfoPath forms instead of custom ASPX pages. In Chapter 16, we describe workflows in more detail and also show how to deploy and integrate InfoPath forms into workflows.
- *Custom application using InfoPath Forms Services*: Of course, you can also develop your own application pages, built on InfoPath forms and InfoPath Forms Services. You can host the `XmlFormView` control within your own page and use it to display InfoPath forms. We will describe the `XmlFormView` control in more detail later, in the section "InfoPath Forms Services." Creating your own application pages is the most powerful option for using InfoPath forms, because you are barely limited in the solution you build. On the other hand, you have to do more coding, but you gain a significant amount of control!
- *Integrating forms into SharePoint pages using the InfoPath Form Web Part*: In SharePoint 2010 a new Web Part for displaying forms has been added, allowing users to add a form to a SharePoint page without any additional effort. Simply select Insert ➤ Web Part in the editing mode of a page and select the InfoPath Form Web Part. We will describe this Web Part in more detail in the section "InfoPath Forms Services."
- *List item forms*: SharePoint 2010 increases the integration of InfoPath forms and offers the possibility of customizing all forms for creating, editing, and viewing items in SharePoint lists using InfoPath. If you select Customize Form from the List ribbon bar, as shown in Figure 15–15, InfoPath Designer will open, allowing you to create a custom form for viewing, editing, and creating list items. You can also manage these forms under List Settings ➤ General Settings ➤ Form Settings. The created InfoPath forms will be placed in a subfolder of your list, called `Forms`.

Figure 15–15. *Customizing list forms*

Publishing and Deploying Using the InfoPath Wizard

The easiest way to publish your form templates is to use the InfoPath Publishing wizard. You can reach the wizard from File ➤ Share ➤ Publish. In the Publish pane, you will be presented with the following four options to publish your form:

- Publish form to current location
- Publish form to SharePoint Library
- Publish form to a list of E-Mail recipients
- Publish form to a network location or file share

The first option is available as soon as you define a publishing location. You can use this option to quickly publish your form with the settings you entered the last time you published the form. The publish button is also available in the Quick Access Toolbar.

Publishing to e-mail recipients requires each user to have InfoPath Filler installed on their computer, to fill out the form.

To deploy forms directly to SharePoint you can select the second option, "Publish form to SharePoint Library." If you are deploying your form using a special deployment method, such as features, command-line scripts, or uploading your form using Central Administration, you can also use the fourth option and publish your form to a network location. All the InfoPath Publishing wizard does is add some parameters and options to your manifest file. These settings can, of course, also be set by the other publishing methods. Nevertheless, the wizard can be used for prototyping and ad hoc solutions, so we will describe the different publishing options using the wizard first. In the next chapter, we will show how you can use other publishing methods.

When you start to publish a form to SharePoint using the Publishing wizard, the first step requires you to enter the URL of your SharePoint server. After InfoPath contacts the SharePoint web services to gather information about the site, the dialog shown in Figure 15–16 will appear. Some of the options might be disabled based on the security settings of the form. For example, fully trusted forms will only allow the last option to be selected. The three options are discussed following.

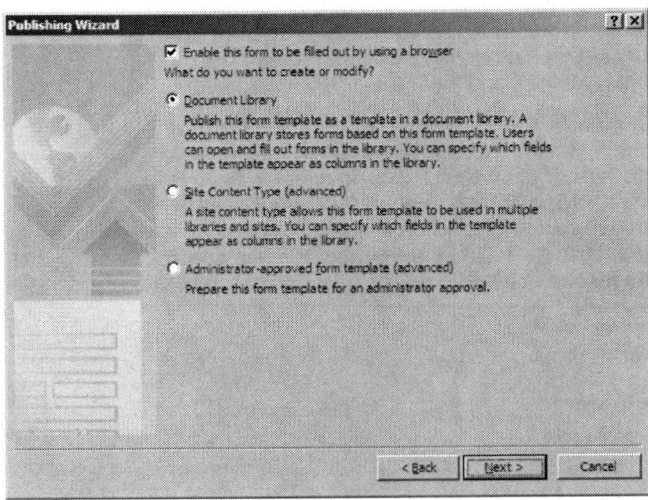

Figure 15–16. Publishing a form template to SharePoint (basic options)

■ **Tip** After you have entered all the relevant information and finished the wizard, InfoPath will use the Forms Services web service to browser-enable the form template. You can use the same web service for your own deployment scenario. The web service is available at `<web application URL>/_vti_bin/FormsServices.asmx`. This web service offers methods for browser-enabling form templates and design-checking forms, and several other methods that are useful for form template deployment. Detailed information is available at `http://msdn.microsoft.com/en-us/library/bb862916.aspx`.

Publishing Form Templates to Document Libraries

When you choose to publish the form template to a document library, the form template will be stored inside the document library in an invisible folder called `Forms`. The form template itself will be called `template.xsn`, irrespective of its original file name. A content type will then be created based on this XSN file, and assigned as a standard content type for the document library in question.

By default, when creating a new document library, either from the wizard or manually, only one content type is allowed per library. During publishing, InfoPath will overwrite this content type and set the form template as the default content type.

You can create new documents based on the published form template by clicking New Document on the library toolbar. Thus, this publishing option offers a quick method to create a document library with one InfoPath form assigned. This way you can provide a single form template per library, and you cannot reuse the published form template across multiple libraries.

■ **Note** Although you can select the "Allow management of multiple content types" option from Form Library Settings ➤ Advanced Settings, publishing a second template to this library using the wizard will still overwrite the existing content type. To publish more than one form to a library, you need to publish the form as a separate content type.

Publishing Form Templates as a Separate Content Type

If you want to use your InfoPath template across multiple libraries, or use multiple form templates within one library, you need to publish your form template as a separate content type. When you do so, InfoPath Forms Services will create a new content type (or update an existing one if you choose this option) based on the form template. You will then be able to select this content type for your library in the list settings page. When you add the new content type to your library, users will be able to create new documents based on this form template by selecting New Document from the Documents ribbon.

In the Publishing wizard you will be asked to specify a location and file name for your form template (Figure 15–17). You can specify any document library within the site to which your content type will be published. However, the best location for your form templates is a library called Form Templates within your site. This library is available in every site and can be accessed by the path `<Site URL>/FormServerTemplates`.

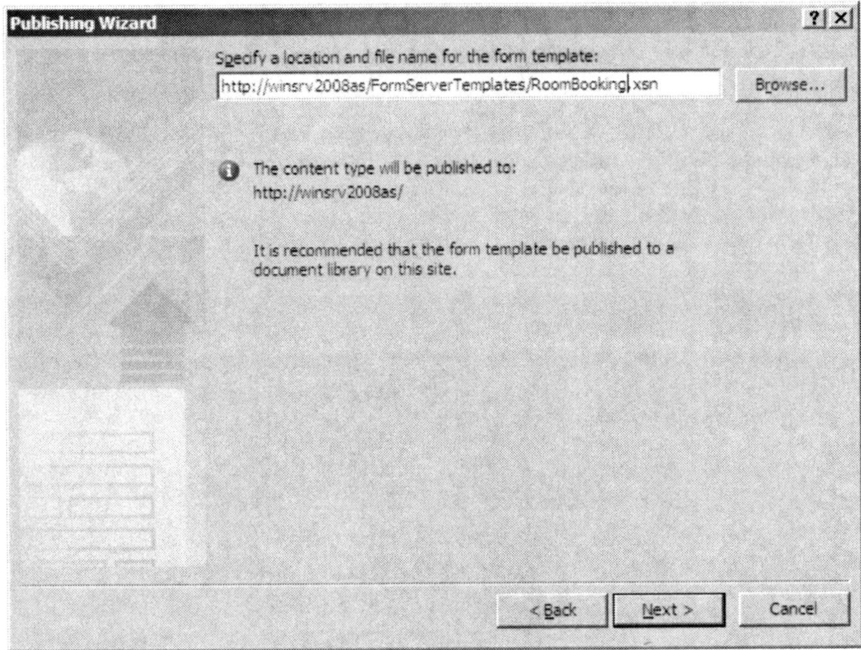

Figure 15–17. Publishing a form template to SharePoint as a content type

Publishing Form Templates as Administrator-Approved Templates

As already mentioned in when talking about forms security earlier, whenever you wish to publish a fully trusted form to SharePoint, the form must be deployed by a farm administrator. Such forms are known as *administrator-approved form templates.* Of course, you can also deploy forms as administrator-approved form templates that don't require administrator approval. You might want to do this to unify your deployment when working with different types of form templates. However, the form templates will have to be deployed by a farm administrator in any case.

During publishing of an administrator-approved template you will be asked to enter the SharePoint URL, which will be saved in the published form template. After that, you must enter a network location or local file name where the template will be saved. A SharePoint administrator can now upload this published form to SharePoint via Central Administration. After uploading, the form must be enabled for the site collections where it is to be used.

In general, using administrator-approved templates requires the following:

- The form template must be published to a location on the network or local file system.
- The template must be uploaded to SharePoint.
- The template must be enabled for a site collection or activated using a script.

In the "InfoPath Forms Services" section we will describe how you can manage form templates in SharePoint Central Administration and how you can deploy and activate your administrator-approved form templates.

Publishing Form Templates to a Network Location

Instead of directly publishing your form template to SharePoint or publishing it as an administrator-approved template, you can publish your template to a network location. In particular, if you are deploying your form template manually to the SharePoint server, or using any other method, such as including your form template into a solution, you can use this publishing method. Since publishing to a network connection does not require you to connect to the SharePoint server, this method will also work when you don't have access to the SharePoint server.

All the relevant settings that allow you to use your form within SharePoint will be established when you enable your template, meaning that you can use this method instead of the more complex SharePoint wizards. In development scenarios, on the other hand, running a wizard allows you to quickly publish new versions of your form. But when using this publishing method, make sure to take one of the following steps to make your form work in Forms Services:

- Manually upload your form using Central Administration.
- Use the Forms Services web service.
- Use `stsadm -activateformtemplate`.
- Use the `Enable-SPInfoPathFormTemplate` cmdlet.
- Use the `XSNFeatureReceiver` class in your feature definition (described next).

■ **Caution** If you are deploying your form to a network location, you must in any case specify no "alternate access path" in the last step of the Publishing wizard (as shown in Figure 15–18). Otherwise, the form will not work, because it will not be browser enabled. When you leave the field empty, InfoPath will show a warning you can ignore by selecting OK.

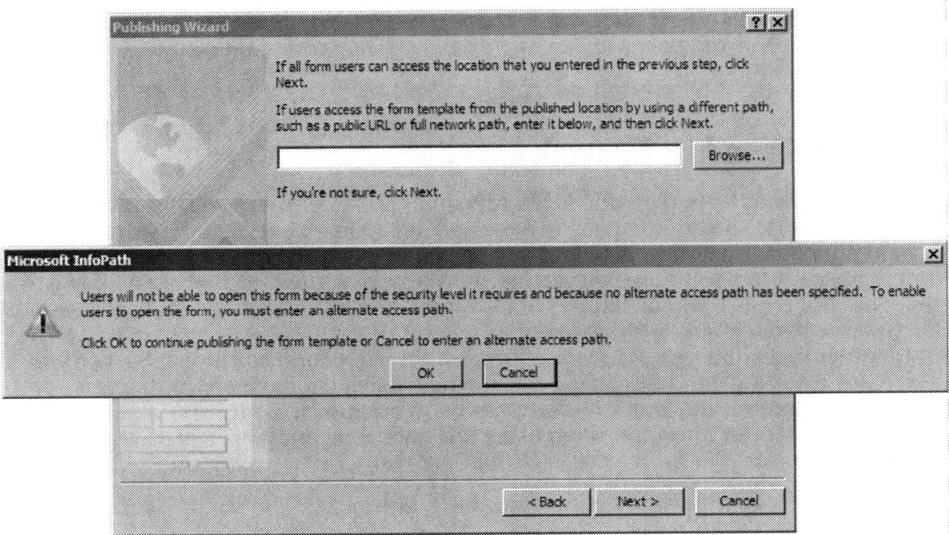

Figure 15–18. *Publishing to a network location: Alternative access path*

Embedding Forms into SharePoint Features

SharePoint features offer a standardized way to package all the relevant elements of a certain scope together and deploy them to a SharePoint farm. When creating a feature you will probably also want to include your form templates to deploy them along with your other elements.

The example in Listing 15–10 demonstrates how to build a feature to deploy your form templates to the Form Template library of a site collection. The feature definition file contains the following important entries that are particular to form template deployment:

- `ReceiverClass`: This attribute of the feature element points to the `XsnFeatureReceiver` class, which provides an implementation of the `SPFeatureReceiver` and handles events that are raised when a feature is installed, uninstalled, activated, or deactivated. It takes actions on the forms according to the feature event, such as registering a form template when the feature is installed. Essentially, the `XsnFeatureReceiver` class takes care of your XSN files when you include them in a feature.
- `ReceiverAssembly`: This refers to the `Microsoft.Office.InfoPath.Server` assembly, which contains the `XsnFeatureReceiver` class.
- `ElementFile`: The `Location` attribute points to the XSN file of your form template relative to your `feature.xml` file.
- `ActivationDependency`: To make sure that the InfoPath Forms Services feature is available, it is good practice to add an activation dependency to this feature. This way, an error will be displayed during feature activation if Forms Services is not available. In the following example, you will see an `ActivationDependency` element referencing the `FeatureId` of the InfoPath Forms Services feature.

■ **Tip** For additional requirements and extreme scenarios, you can also extend the feature receiver and develop your own implementation for deploying XSN files through a SharePoint feature. Please refer to the MSDN documentation for further information: `http://msdn.microsoft.com/en-us/library/microsoft.office.infopath.server.administration.xsnfeaturereceiver(office.14).aspx`.

***Listing 15–10.** Including a Form Template in a Feature: feature.xml*

```
<?xml version="1.0" encoding="utf-8"?>
<Feature  Id="F1C92BB0-61E2-4372-B626-4276BE8A4435"
    Title="RoomBookingFeature"
    Description="RoomBooking form deployed using a feature"
    Version="1.0.0.0"
    Hidden="False"
    Scope="Site"
    DefaultResourceFile="core"
    xmlns="http://schemas.microsoft.com/sharepoint/"
    ReceiverClass="Microsoft.Office.InfoPath.Server.Administration.XsnFeatureReceiver"
    ReceiverAssembly="Microsoft.Office.InfoPath.Server, Version=14.0.0.0, Culture=neutral,
                     PublicKeyToken=71e9bce111e9429c">

    <ElementManifests>
        <ElementManifest Location="elements.xml"/>
        <ElementFile Location="RoomBookingFeature.xsn" />
    </ElementManifests>

    <ActivationDependencies>
        <ActivationDependency FeatureId="C88C4FF1-DBF5-4649-AD9F-C6C426EBCBF5" />
    </ActivationDependencies>

</Feature>
```

The `elements.xml` manifest file contains only one `Module` element (Listing 15–11). `Module` elements are used to provision files to SharePoint. The `Url` attribute of the module element denotes the target URL on the SharePoint server. In this case, the form template will be stored in the form template library relative to the site collection. For each file that needs to be provisioned to SharePoint, one `File` element is required within the `Module` element. You can also provision a collection of files using one module. See the following link for more details on file provisioning: `http://msdn.microsoft.com/en-us/library/ms441170(office.14).aspx`.

***Listing 15–11.** Including a Form Template in a Feature: elements.xml*

```
<?xml version="1.0" encoding="utf-8" ?>
<Elements  xmlns="http://schemas.microsoft.com/sharepoint/">
    <Module Name="RoomBooking" Url="FormServerTemplates" RootWebOnly="TRUE">
        <File Url="RoomBookingFeature.xsn" Name="RoomBookingFeature.xsn"
Type="GhostableInLibrary" />
    </Module>
</Elements>
```

Deploying Forms Using Command-Line Utilities

When you are developing SharePoint applications in a professional environment, you will probably wish to automate deployment and avoid uploading each form template to each environment by hand using the InfoPath UI. There are two options, both of which are command-line utilities to script SharePoint administration tasks: `stsadm.exe` and PowerShell cmdlets.

For either to work correctly, you first need to publish your form to a file on a network share or on the local file system. This step needs to be done manually by the form template designer. When referring to a form template to be deployed, we are always talking about a previously published template.

stsadm.exe

`stsadm.exe` is the command-line utility used in previous SharePoint versions to administer SharePoint from the command line and for scripting batch files. Although its use will diminish in favor of PowerShell cmdlets, it is still supported by SharePoint 2010. Since it is widely used, we will show the most important commands. `stsadm.exe` is located in the `bin` folder of the SharePoint installation path: `C:\Program Files\Common Files\Microsoft Shared\Web Server Extensions\14\bin\stsadm`. To run the utility, you need to pass the parameter `-o` followed by the supported operation you wish to execute.

Working with InfoPath forms, the operations described in Table 15–2 are useful for uploading and installing form templates.

***Table 15–2.** stsadm Operations for InfoPath Form Templates*

Operation	Description
`ActivateFormTemplate`	Activates a form template for a site collection
`AddDataConnectionFile`	Adds a new instance of a `DataConnectionFile` to the `DataConnectionFiles` collection
`DeactivateFormTemplate`	Deactivates a form template for a site collection
`EnumDataConnectionFileDependants`	Enumerates all forms that are dependent on the specified data connection file
`EnumDataConnectionFiles`	Enumerates all of the `DataConnectionFiles` in the collection
`EnumFormTemplates`	Enumerates all form templates
`GetFormTemplateProperty`	Retrieves properties of a form template
`RemoveDataConnectionFile`	Removes specified data connection files from the collection
`RemoveFormTemplate`	Removes the specified form template
`SetDataConnectionFileProperty`	Sets a file property to a data connection file
`SetFormsServiceProperty`	Sets a configuration property of Form Services
`SetFormTemplateProperty`	Sets the properties of an individual form template
`UploadFormTemplate`	Uploads a form template to Forms Services
`VerifyFormTemplate`	Checks whether it's acceptable for the form template to be uploaded to the server

Using the preceding operations you could write a script such as the following to upload a new form template after deactivating and removing the prior version of the form. Instead of the file name, you can also use the `<formid>` to specify the form template.

```
STSADM.EXE -o DeActivateFormTemplate -url http://<servername> -filename <filename.xsn>
STSADM.EXE -o RemoveFormTemplate -filename <filename.xsn>
STSADM.EXE -o VerifyFormTemplate -filename <filename.xsn>
STSADM.EXE -o UploadFormTemplate -filename <filename.xsn>
STSADM.EXE -o ActivateFormTemplate -url http://<servername> -filename <filename.xsn>
```

PowerShell Cmdlets

As described in Chapter 9, SharePoint 2010 relies heavily on PowerShell cmdlets for administration tasks. The following cmdlets are relevant when working with InfoPath form templates. The table also lists the stsadm commands that have similar functions, to give users familiar with `stsadm` a quick cross-reference:

Table 15–3. *PowerShell Cmdlets for InfoPath Form Templates*

Operation Name	Description	stsadm Equivalent
`Disable-SPInfoPathFormTemplate`	Deactivates a form template for a site collection	`DeactivateFormTemplate`
`Enable-SPInfoPathFormTemplate`	Activates a form template for a site collection	`ActivateFormTemplate`
`Get-SPDataConnectionFile`	Enumerates all of the `DataConnectionFiles` in the collection	`EnumDataConnectionFiles`
`Get-SPDataConnectionFileDependent`	Enumerates forms that are dependent on the specified data connection file	`EnumDataConnectionFileDependants`
`Get-SPInfoPathFormTemplate`	Returns an InfoPath form template and its parameters	`GetFormTemplateProperty`, `EnumFormTemplates`
`Install-SPDataConnectionFile`	Installs the provided data connection file	`AddDataConnectionFile`
`Install-SPInfoPathFormTemplate`	Uploads a form template to Forms Services	`UploadFormTemplate`
`Set-SPDataConnectionFile`	Sets properties of a data connection file	`SetDataConnectionFileProperty`
`Set-SPInfoPathFormsService`	Sets parameters for InfoPath Forms Services	`SetFormsServiceProperty`

Operation Name	Description	stsadm Equivalent
`Set-SPInfoPathFormTemplate`	Sets the properties of an individual form template	`SetFormTemplateProperty`
`Test-SPInfoPathFormTemplate`	Validates that a form template can be browser enabled	`VerifyFormTemplate`
`Uninstall-SPDataConnectionFile`	Removes specified data connection files from the collection	`RemoveDataConnectionFile`
`Uninstall-SPInfoPathFormTemplate`	Removes the specified form template from a farm	`RemoveFormTemplate`
`Update-SPInfoPathFormTemplate`	Upgrades all form templates on the farm	

By analogy, with the `stsadm` commands shown in the table, the following script can be used to upload a new version of an InfoPath form, after deactivating and removing the prior version of the form:

```
Uninstall-SPInfoPathFormTemplate -Identity formName.xsn
Install-SPInfoPathFormTemplate -Path C:\Form.xsn
Enable-SPInfoPathFormTemplate -Identity "FormTemplate.xsn" -Site "http://TestSite"
```

Deploying Forms with Code

When using custom code in your InfoPath form template, as described in the next section, you have two deployment options:

- Deploying your form as a sandboxed solution
- Deploying your form as an administrator-approved form

InfoPath forms that contain code will be deployed as sandboxed by default when you use the Publishing wizard to deploy your form to SharePoint. In this case, the code will be run in a sandbox to avoid harm to your SharePoint farm. This publishing method can be chosen by any site administrator and does not require farm administration privileges. Sandboxed form templates are only available to InfoPath 2010 form templates that do not use Web Part connection parameters.

The second option is to deploy your form as an administrator-approved form template, as described earlier. In this case, the code will be granted full trust, since this deployment method is only available to farm administrators.

■ **Tip** To use sandboxed form templates you must ensure that the Microsoft SharePoint Foundation User Code Service is started. This service is responsible for sandboxed solutions. It can be started in Central Administration via System Settings ➤ Manage Services on Server.

Table 15–4 compares the two options for deploying forms with code.

Table 15–4. *Comparing Sandboxed and Administrator-Approved Templates*

Category	Sandboxed Form Template	Administrator-Approved Template
Permission	Site collection administrator	Farm administrator
Publishing	InfoPath Designer wizard	Central Administration
Security	Form code run in sandbox, no harm to farm	Code runs with full trust on the server

Programming InfoPath Forms

InfoPath Designer 2010 features a convenient UI for designing form templates and adding some basic control logic using rules. But as soon as the complexity of your forms grows and interaction with the environment increases, you should take a closer look at the development facilities in InfoPath. Looking at the Developer tab in the ribbon bar (Figure 15–19), you can get an idea of the variety of events that can be used to integrate managed code into your InfoPath form template.

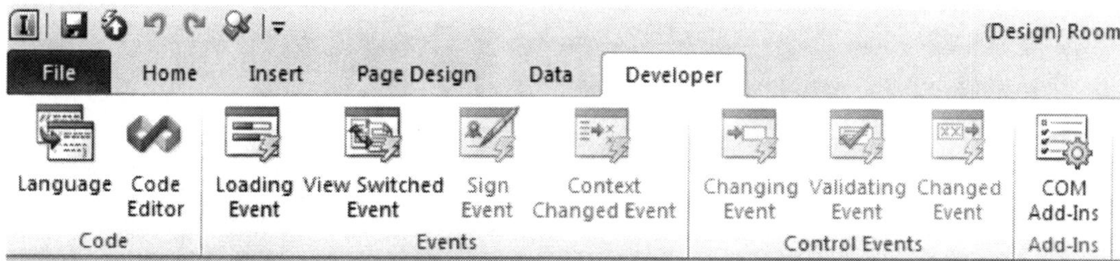

Figure 15–19. *Developer ribbon bar in InfoPath Designer*

Attaching Managed Code

Before you can begin programming your form template, you need to specify the code language and the location for your code project in the Form Options dialog. You can reach this dialog directly using the Language button on the Developer tab. The managed code language options are C# and Visual Basic. In addition, you can nominate the location where the project for your form code will be stored. For every form, a separate project is created. The assembly that is generated when the project is built will also be included in the resulting XSN file.

■ **Note** You can also use InfoPath 2010 to develop forms that are compatible with 2007. You can select "InfoPath 2007 compatible code" from the Form template code language drop-down list. In this case, the project will reference the old library, located by default in `C:\Program files\Microsoft Office\Office14\InfoPathOM\InfoPathFormsServices\InfoPathFormsServicesV12`.

After you have configured these basic development settings, a click on the Code Editor button or one of the events on the Developer tab of the ribbon bar will cause Visual Studio Tools for Applications (VSTA) to start. InfoPath 2010 still uses VSTA 2005, and the resulting projects are based on .NET 2.0. However, VSTA will configure all the required settings for you. The project for your form template will open, and you can start programming your form template. Figure 15–20 shows the basic skeleton of a form project.

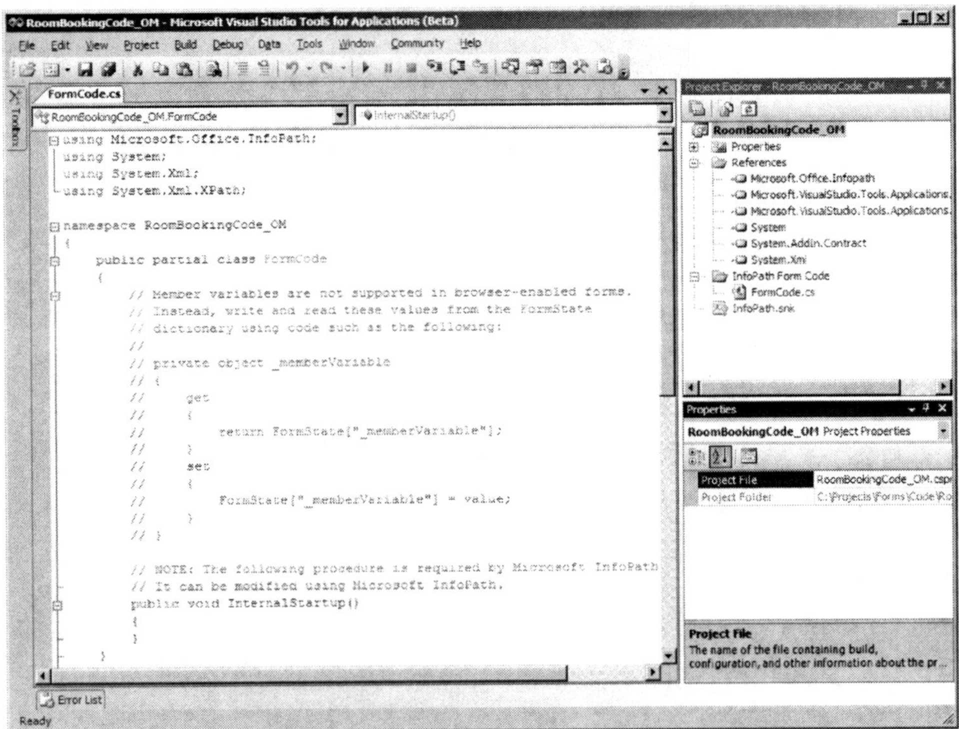

Figure 15–20. Basic InfoPath project with VSTA

■ **Note** The ability to develop script code using JScript or VBScript has been removed in InfoPath 2010. Instead, form templates can use only managed code.

ADDING AN EXISTING PROJECT TO A TEMPLATE

You can add an existing code project to a form template. This can be useful if you accidentally remove the code in the Programming dialog in Form Options. Since you are not able to select a `.csproj` file in the Programming dialog, and since manually entering it will also fail, follow these steps:

1. In Form Options ➤ Programming, select a temporary project location.
2. Click Code Editor on the Developer tab to create a new project.
3. Save your form and close it.
4. Delete the temporary project location.
5. Reopen your form and click Code Editor.
6. InfoPath will display a dialog saying that your project cannot be found. You can select the project file you want to use.

Now you can work with your project. This location will be stored in your form. The next time you open your form template, this project is used.

Depending on the form type that is selected in the form options, the appropriate InfoPath library will be included into the project. Since Forms Services only supports a subset of functionality when designing web browser forms, a different `Microsoft.Office.InfoPath.dll` is loaded from the subfolder `InfoPathOMFormsServices`.

When accessing the form code for the first time, the necessary project will be created automatically. A class named `FormCode` will be autogenerated. This class is derived from `XmlFormHostItem`, which is an abstract class, acting as a wrapper for an `XMLForm`. The `FormCode` class that you will use for programming is implemented as a partial class. All virtual methods that need to be overwritten are implemented in `FormCode.Designer.cs`. From here, the method `InternalStartup` and all the events you implement will be called. This illustrates the basic paradigm for programming InfoPath forms: everything you do must be associated with an event. The only way to execute your code is in reaction to something that happens in the form, such as loading the form, changing a value, or closing the form.

InfoPath Object Model

The InfoPath object model offers programmatic access to the views, data connections, and behavior of the form. Using this object model, you can make your forms highly flexible. As stated earlier in this chapter, Forms Services only supports a subset of the InfoPath object model, which is available to InfoPath Filler forms. Since we are focusing on using InfoPath together with SharePoint, the following descriptions are focused on the object model available to Forms Services.

The `Microsoft.Office.InfoPath.XmlForm` class represents the data of the underlying XML document. Thus, it is one of the key objects for interacting with the XML data of the form. However, when working with browser-compatible forms, you will only have access to the properties and methods of the XmlForm object that are wrapped by the XmlFormHostItem object in the form template code. Since the class that is created for you is a subclass of XmlFormHostItem, you can access the relevant members using the keyword this.

Events

For code in your InfoPath project to be called, it needs to be tied to an event. Events can be added by clicking the event buttons in the development ribbon. Each event will be registered as a delegate in the InternalStartup method. The class EventManager is used to bind event handlers to the different events.

Events are divided into three categories: FormEvents, ControlEvents, and XmlEvents. Each of these categories is represented by an object of the same name. FormEvents are events that occur to the form, such as loading and saving. ControlEvents are events issued by special controls. For example, the ButtonEvent implements the Clicked event, which is handled as a control event. Whenever you add a button and want to handle the Clicked event using code, an event handler will be added to the ControlEvents.

Finally, XmlEvents are used for anything that happens to the underlying XML structure of your form—for example, when a field is changed. When changes are made to the XML data, events will be bubbled up through the data structure. Assume your schema has a group element group1 that contains a field element called test. Figure 15–21 shows the simple data schema for this example.

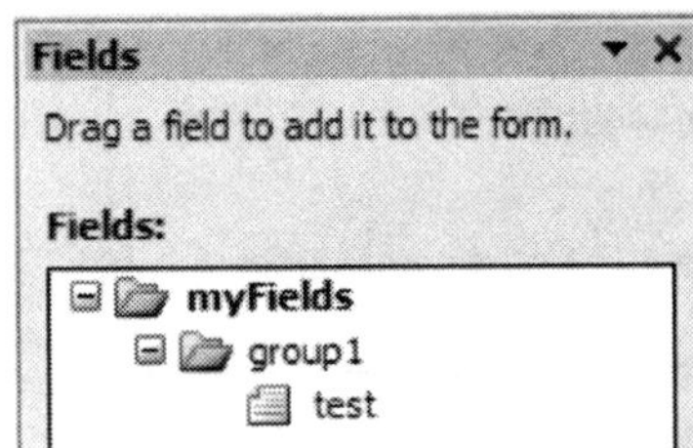

Figure 15–21. Simple data schema used for the events example

When you change the content of the field element test, the event handler of the test element will be called. After that, the Changed event of the group1 element will be raised. When working with XmlChange events, the XmlEventArgs object supplies detailed information about the change. You can retrieve the OldValue, which shows the value before the change, and the NewValue, which contains the value after the change. In addition, the member Site returns an XPathNavigator object that points to the element on which the change event is currently being handled. The element that is responsible for the change (in the preceding example, this is the test element) can be accessed using the sender object. This is also an XPathNavigator object that points to the element that was originally changed and caused the event to be passed upward through the hierarchy. Listing 15–12 shows how these events will be thrown. Each event simply displays a MessageBox that outputs the name of the event along with the name of the Site element and the name of the sender object. This example is built with an InfoPath Filler form template to keep it as simple as possible. The MessageBox is not available to web browser forms.

***Listing 15–12.** Assigning Events in Form Code*

```
public partial class FormCode
{
    public void InternalStartup()
    {
        // Register events
```

```
        EventManager.XmlEvents["/my:myFields"].Changed +=
                             new XmlChangedEventHandler(myFields_Changed);
        EventManager.XmlEvents["/my:myFields/my:group1"].Changed +=
                               new XmlChangedEventHandler(group1_Changed);
        EventManager.XmlEvents["/my:myFields/my:group1/my:test"].Changed +=
                                 new XmlChangedEventHandler(test_Changed);
    }

    public void group1_Changed(object sender, XmlEventArgs e)
    {
        // Show a message box about the changes
        MessageBox.Show("group1_Changed: Site=" + e.Site.Name + " sender=" +
             ((XPathNavigator)sender).Name + "from " + e.OldValue + " -> " +
             e.NewValue);
    }

    public void test_Changed(object sender, XmlEventArgs e)
    {
        MessageBox.Show("test_Changed: Site=" + e.Site.Name + " sender=" +
             ((XPathNavigator)sender).Name);
    }

    public void myFields_Changed(object sender, XmlEventArgs e)
    {
        MessageBox.Show("myFields_Changed: Site=" + e.Site.Name + " sender=" +
             ((XPathNavigator)sender).Name);
    }
}
```

Table 15–5 shows all events that are available in browser-enabled forms. When working with InfoPath Filler, some additional events are available.

***Table 15–5.** Events in Form Templates*

Category	Event	Description
`FormEvents`	`Loading`	Occurs after the form template has been loaded.
`FormEvents`	`Submit`	Occurs when the form is submitted.
`FormEvents`	`ViewSwitched`	Occurs after a view has been switched.
`FormEvents`	`VersionUpgrade`	Occurs when the form needs to be updated, because its version number is older than the form template on which it is based
`ControlEvents`	`Clicked`	Occurs when a `Button` control is clicked. The `ButtonEvent` class implements the `Clicked` event.
`XmlEvent`	`Validating`	Occurs when changes have been made to the XML document and after InfoPath has finished validation.
`XmlEvent`	`Changed`	Occurs after changes have been made to the XML document and after the `Validating` event.

Accessing the Form Data

When discussing events earlier, we encountered a very important class for working with XML data sources: XPathNavigator. This class provides cursor-based access to primary and secondary XML data sources of the InfoPath form and allows modification of the XML data structure. You can use XPathNavigator to navigate over the XML structure using move methods such as MoveToFirstChild or MoveToParent. The cursor of XPathNavigator will then be moved relative to its current node and point to a different node in the XML hierarchy. On the node to which the cursor is currently pointing, you can execute several methods to modify the data or retrieve information about that node. The property Name contains the name of the current node, and OuterXml will return the XML data for the current node from its opening to its closing tags, including its child nodes. InnerXml, on the other hand, returns the XML fragment that is contained within the current node, excluding the node itself. The property Value returns the string of the current node's value item, and the method SetValue allows you to set this value.

When working with InfoPath, navigating through the XML structure along the XPath axes is not very common, since you already know about your data structure. Most of the time you will want to directly select a node or node set to read or write fields in your data source. XPathNavigator offers two very useful methods for selecting nodes: Select and SelectSingleNode. Both methods select nodes according to the given XPath expression, but instead of returning an instance of XPathNodeIterator, SelectSingleNode returns the XPathNavigator object of the first node matching the XPath query. Thus, accessing a node in your form becomes very easy. All you need to do is right-click the node in the Fields pane in InfoPath Designer and select Copy XPath, as shown in Figure 15–22.

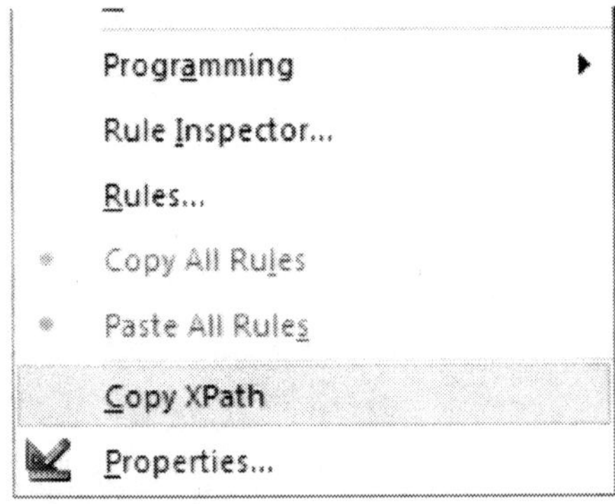

Figure 15–22. Copying the XPath of a field

This will create the XPath expression for selecting the node, which can then be copied into the Select method of the XPathNavigator object. To resolve the namespaces used in the form, the select methods also require an element implementing the IXmlNamespaceResolver interface. Fortunately, the NamespaceManager object of the XmlForm already implements this interface, and you can simply use the NamespaceManager property when calling the Select methods.

To access the XML data using XPathNavigator, you first need access to the data sources. XmlForm offers access to a DataSource through its DataSources property. As mentioned earlier, a form consists of one primary and several secondary data sources. The DataSources property contains all the data sources, including the main data source. In addition, MainDataSource provides direct access to the form's main data source. On any DataSource object, you can call the CreateNavigator method to obtain an XPathNavigator that can be used to access and manipulate the data source.

The following example shows a very common scenario, in which data is loaded from a web service into the main data source using XPathNavigator. A data connection to the SharePoint list Rooms was added to retrieve all the room entries in the list and load them into the Room drop-down list on the InfoPath form, which is shown in Figure 15–23.

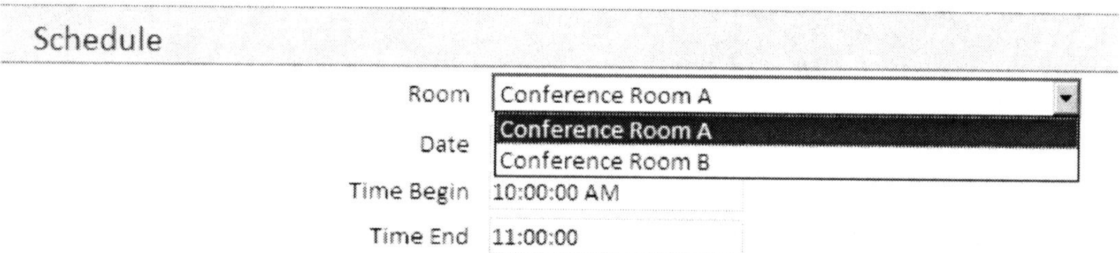

Figure 15–23. *Selecting rooms from a SharePoint list*

The web service will be called during form loading, and a second data connection, called `GetRoom`, will be added. It will be queried when a user selects a room from the drop-down list, and will load the detailed information from the list for the selected room. Then the "RoomNumber" field will be filled from the web service response using `XPathNavigator`. Calling the "GetRoom" data connection and loading the "RoomNumber" will be done in the changed event that is bound to the `Room` field. So whenever someone edits the content of the `Room` field by selecting a room, this code will be executed.

Listing 15–13. *Loading Data from a Web Service into a Form*

```
using Microsoft.Office.InfoPath;
using System;
using System.Xml;
using System.Xml.XPath;

namespace RoomBooking_LoadingWebService
{
    public partial class FormCode
    {

        public void InternalStartup()
        {
            EventManager.XmlEvents["/my:RoomBooking/my:Schedule/my:Room"]
                        .Changed += new XmlChangedEventHandler(Room_Changed);
        }

        public void Room_Changed(object sender, XmlEventArgs e)
        {
            XPathNavigator form = MainDataSource.CreateNavigator();

            // Set parameter for web service request and query connection
            DataSources["GetRoom"].CreateNavigator().SelectSingleNode(
                  "/dfs:myFields/dfs:queryFields/q:SharePointListItem_RW/q:ID",
                  NamespaceManager).SetValue(e.NewValue);
            DataSources["GetRoom"].QueryConnection.Execute();

            // Create navigator on web service response
            XPathNavigator roomdata = DataSources["GetRoom"].CreateNavigator();
```

```
            // Set fields with values from web service response
            XPathNavigator nodeRoomNumber = form.SelectSingleNode(
                "/my:RoomBooking/my:Schedule/my:RoomNumber", NamespaceManager);
            nodeRoomNumber.SetValue(roomdata.SelectSingleNode(
                "/dfs:myFields/dfs:dataFields/d:SharePointListItem_RW/d:RoomNumber",
                NamespaceManager).Value);
        }
    }
}
```

Maintaining State in Browser-Based Forms

To maintain global state in browser-enabled forms, you can use the `FormState` property of `XmlForm`. Working with browser-enabled forms, this is the only way to persist data during a session. As with web pages, you cannot use member variables to maintain state, since they will not be persisted between requests. The `FormState` property will keep its values from the time the form is opened until it is closed.

`FormState` is an `IDictionary` object that holds user-defined key/value pairs of state variables. Both key and value can be any object, but generally strings are used for the key. The value can store objects that hold complex data. For convenience you might consider introducing a global member variable that leverages `FormState` by reading from and writing to `FormState` in the get and set methods. This gives you the ease of use of properties while still persisting data between requests.

Listing 15–14 shows how you can create a member variable using `FormState`, which can persist information across multiple events.

Listing 15–14. *Maintaining State in Forms Using FormState*

```
public string Username
{
    get
    {
        if (FormState["_username"] != null)
        {
            return (string)FormState["_username"];
        }
        else
        {
            return "";
        }
    }
    set
        {
            FormState["_username"] = value;
        }
    }
}
```

Accessing Views

Forms are organized using views. You can also work with views in your form code. As described earlier, you can use the `ViewSwitched` event to react to the change of the current view. The `XmlForm` object contains useful information about views. First of all, you can use the `CurrentView` property to get the view that is currently active. In a web-based form template, the resulting View object contains a ViewInfo member with descriptive information about the view. In web forms, you can only access the Name of the view. To access all the available views for a form template, the ViewInfos member returns a list of ViewInfo objects. In addition, it holds the Default and Init properties, which return the default view and the initial view of the form.

If you wish to programmatically switch the view, you can use the SwitchView method of the ViewInfoCollection returned by ViewInfos to switch the view from the current view to the desired view.

Handling Errors

During validation of a form, several errors in the form data can occur. For example, if you add a validation rule, the field will be displayed in red when the validation fails. In general, errors can arise when a form's XML schema is validated, when a custom validation rule fails, or when the error is added to the collection of errors from code. The XmlForm object keeps in the Errors property a collection of all errors that occurred. You can access individual Error objects from the list of errors, as with any other enumerable collection.

Each Error object contains detailed information about the error, (e.g., in the Name, Message, and DetailedMessage properties). The property FormErrorType specifies how the error was generated: through SchemaValidation, SystemGenerated or, UserDefined. Since an error always belongs to a node in the XML data that caused the error due to a failed validation, the property Site holds an XPathNavigator object that points to the affected node.

You can also add your own errors to the Errors collection using the Add method. This method expects an XPathNavigator pointing to the affected node, a name, and a message. Deleting errors from the list can also be done easily using the Delete method.

Using the Errors collection allows you to manage all the errors in your form that can eventuate during validation.

InfoPath Forms Services

InfoPath Forms Services is part of Microsoft SharePoint Server 2010. It renders InfoPath forms in the browser and allows users to complete InfoPath forms without InfoPath Filler. This section discusses the basic settings for enabling InfoPath Forms Services on SharePoint 2010, how to manage form templates, and how you can use XmlFormView to customize Forms Services. Finally, different ways to integrate forms with SharePoint are presented.

Preparing InfoPath Forms Services Support

Before you can start viewing InfoPath forms in SharePoint, several configuration options need to be set, and the form templates have to be managed appropriately. Compared to SharePoint Server 2007, many of the configuration settings have been simplified, especially because the shared service providers have been replaced by service applications in SharePoint 2010. Many of the settings we will demonstrate using Central Administration can also be adjusted using PowerShell. As far as is practicable, we will also mention corresponding cmdlets.

For Forms Services to work properly, you need to do the following:

- Enable the State Service using the Farm Configuration wizard.
- Configure InfoPath Forms Services in the general application settings.

After you are finished with these settings you can start to deploy your forms and integrate them into your SharePoint solution. But first we will show you in more detail what these settings are about.

State Service

What was a painful configuration hazard in earlier versions of SharePoint has become effortless with SharePoint 2010: configuring the State Service. Since SharePoint relies on service applications to provide shared functionality, you don't have to deal with shared service providers any more. Simply run the Farm Configuration wizard from the Configuration Wizard section. On the second page are many service applications. Select State Service and complete the wizard.

State Service
Provides temporary storage of user session data for Office SharePoint Server components.

Figure 15–24. State Service configuration

The State Service is required to store temporary data between related HTTP requests and thus keep the state of your forms. To store the data, a SQL database is used. By default, the data will be stored in the same database as the content database, and a single State Service instance will be shared among all components that require State Service. You can only change those advanced settings using PowerShell. SharePoint Central Administration does not provide any control other than enabling State Service using default settings.

CONFIGURING STATE SERVICE USING POWERSHELL

Use the following cmdlets to perform additional configuration of State Service, or to enable/disable it:

```
Get-SPStateServiceApplication: Gets a list of State Service applications
New-SPStateServiceApplication: Creates a new State Service application
Set-SPStateServiceApplication: Sets parameters on a State Service application
```

There are many additional cmdlets to manage State Service (e.g., for configuring the databases). For a complete list, type **gcm *spstate*** into PowerShell.

Configuring InfoPath Forms Services

SharePoint Central Administration contains a separate section for managing InfoPath Forms Services. It is located on the General Application Settings page. Besides management of form templates, data connection files, and a proxy for InfoPath forms, it also contains a link to the "Configuration of InfoPath Forms Services" settings.

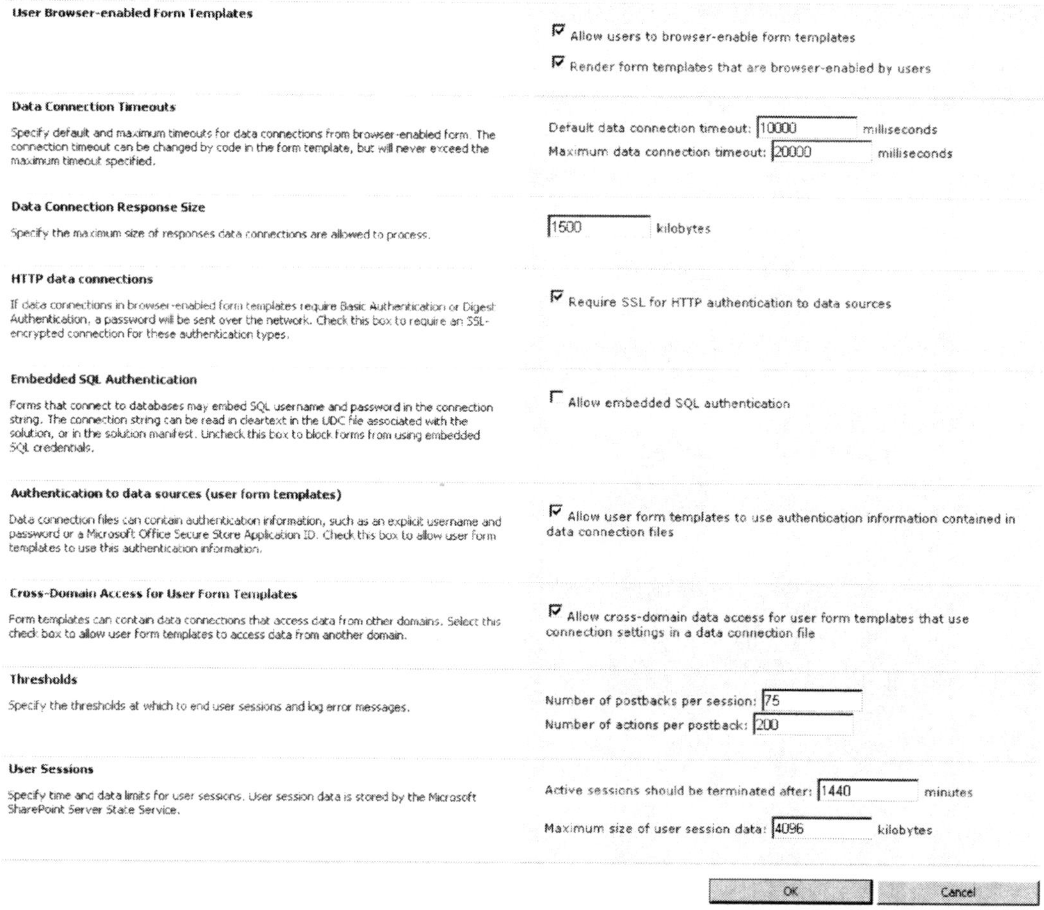

User Browser-enabled Form Templates	☑ Allow users to browser-enable form templates ☑ Render form templates that are browser-enabled by users
Data Connection Timeouts Specify default and maximum timeouts for data connections from browser-enabled form. The connection timeout can be changed by code in the form template, but will never exceed the maximum timeout specified.	Default data connection timeout: 10000 milliseconds Maximum data connection timeout: 20000 milliseconds
Data Connection Response Size Specify the maximum size of responses data connections are allowed to process.	1500 kilobytes
HTTP data connections If data connections in browser-enabled form templates require Basic Authentication or Digest Authentication, a password will be sent over the network. Check this box to require an SSL-encrypted connection for these authentication types.	☑ Require SSL for HTTP authentication to data sources
Embedded SQL Authentication Forms that connect to databases may embed SQL username and password in the connection string. The connection string can be read in cleartext in the UDC file associated with the solution, or in the solution manifest. Uncheck this box to block forms from using embedded SQL credentials.	☐ Allow embedded SQL authentication
Authentication to data sources (user form templates) Data connection files can contain authentication information, such as an explicit username and password or a Microsoft Office Secure Store Application ID. Check this box to allow user form templates to use this authentication information.	☑ Allow user form templates to use authentication information contained in data connection files
Cross-Domain Access for User Form Templates Form templates can contain data connections that access data from other domains. Select this check box to allow user form templates to access data from another domain.	☑ Allow cross-domain data access for user form templates that use connection settings in a data connection file
Thresholds Specify the thresholds at which to end user sessions and log error messages.	Number of postbacks per session: 75 Number of actions per postback: 200
User Sessions Specify time and data limits for user sessions. User session data is stored by the Microsoft SharePoint Server State Service.	Active sessions should be terminated after: 1440 minutes Maximum size of user session data: 4096 kilobytes
	OK Cancel

***Figure 15–25.** Central Administration: Configuring InfoPath Forms Services*

Without going into too much detail, we will briefly describe the most relevant settings in the configuration screen (Figure 15–25). Most of the settings are self explanatory.

The first section defines how browser-enabled forms deployed by users are handled in InfoPath Forms Services. If you select "Allow users to browser-enable form templates," you allow users to deploy browser-enabled forms. The next option allows browser-enabled user form templates to be displayed in the browser. If you don't select "Render form templates that are browser-enabled by users," users will still be able to deploy browser-enabled forms, but the forms will not be displayed in the browser. If you ever have trouble displaying a browser-enabled form, make sure that these options are set correctly.

If you want your users to access data from other domains using data connection files, you should check the "Allow cross-domain data access . . ." check box.

For any other settings, please refer to MSDN for detailed information here: `http://technet.microsoft.com/en-us/library/cc262263(office.14).aspx`.

For many common scenarios, the default settings in this dialog are appropriate.

CONFIGURING INFOPATH FORMS SERVICES USING POWERSHELL

Again, you can also use PowerShell cmdlets for these administrative tasks:

```
Get-SPInfoPathFormsService:  Gets the InfoPath Forms Services settings for the farm
Set-SPInfoPathFormsService:  Sets parameters for InfoPath Forms Services settings
```

`Set-SPInfoPathFormsService` also contains some parameters that are not available to Central Administration.

Configuring Libraries

Each document library has options for displaying browser-based documents and for managing document templates. In addition, settings concerning content types also need to be considered when deploying forms to form libraries. Figure 15–26 shows the most significant options for configuring forms in document libraries.

You can configure separately for each library whether an InfoPath form will be opened in the browser when adding a new form to the library or selecting an existing form in the list. Go to the Library settings page and select Advanced Settings. Among several others, you will be able to change the "Opening Documents in the Browser" setting. You can choose whether you always want your forms to be opened in the browser or on the client using InfoPath Filler.

Depending on how you deploy your forms, and whether you want to use several different forms in one library, you can specify whether the library in question should allow management of content types. Under the Yes option, different forms can be added to the library via content types. This requires you to deploy your form templates as a content type. If you select No, only one template is allowed at a time.

The Document Template setting allows you to specify the URL of the form template used in this library. This option is only available when management of content types is deactivated. If you have InfoPath Designer installed on your computer, you can use the (Edit Template) link to directly edit the form template.

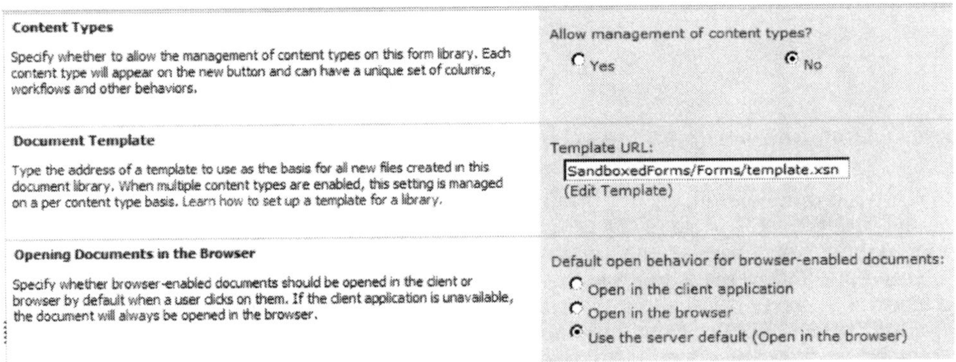

Figure 15–26. *Form options in library settings*

Managing Form Templates

Deploying InfoPath forms to a SharePoint library can easily be done in InfoPath Designer with the help of the Publishing wizards. But if you need to deploy your form template as an administrator-approved template, you must manually upload your template to SharePoint. This can be done in the Central Administration page. Under *General Application Settings, InfoPath Forms Services* is "Manage form templates." On this page (Figure 15–27) you will find all form templates that are available to the farm, which are templates that are either shipped with SharePoint or have been uploaded by an administrator. Those form templates can be activated to a site collection. Doing so will copy these templates to the Form Templates library in the selected site collection. Naturally, you can also deactivate a form template from a site collection, causing the form template to be removed from the Form Templates library of the site collection.

If you don't need your templates to be approved by an administrator, or if you only want to use your forms in the context of a site collection, you can simply upload your form template to the Form Templates library of the site collection.

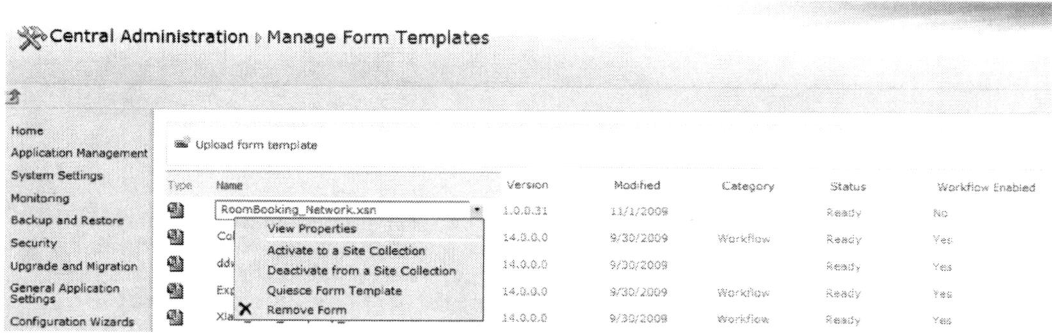

Figure 15–27. Manage form templates in Central Adminstration

Displaying Forms in the InfoPath Form Web Part

Probably the easiest way to display your browser-enabled forms in a web page is by using the InfoPath Form Web Part. This Web Part is new with SharePoint 2010 and allows you to integrate your forms into any page. You can use this Web Part like any other Web Part and simply add it to one of the Web Part zones on your page. Although your influence on form behavior is limited, this Web Part is excellent for rapid prototyping and basic scenarios. For more complex scenarios you might want to look into the possibilities offered by the `XmlFormView` control, described in the next section.

The InfoPath Form Web Part uses the `XmlFormView` control to render InfoPath forms. Many options for configuring the Web Part are available, and the Web Part can handle different sources for the form template and the form data, but form rendering is handled by `XmlFormView`.

To insert the Web Part into your page, you need to switch to Edit mode for the page and select Editing Tools ➤ Insert from the ribbon bar. Now you can select the InfoPath Form Web Part from the Forms category to insert the Web Part, which is shown in Figure 15–28. After you insert the Web Part, a small box is displayed as a placeholder for the InfoPath form. You can now configure your Web Part to display the desired form.

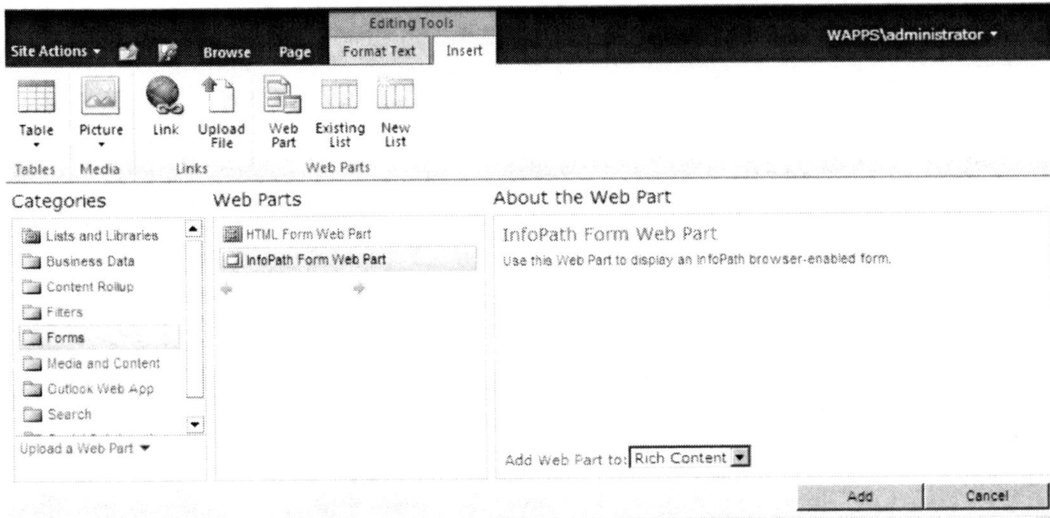

***Figure 15–28.** Inserting the InfoPath Form Web Part*

Use the Edit Web Part option to configure the Web Part. You will find the following settings in the Web Part configuration pane, as shown in Figure 15–29. You can specify the source of your form template to display. Essentially, you can select any form template that is published to a list or library, and is thus available as a content type. Opt for the appropriate list or library and then choose the template. You can also specify the default view to display and the behavior after the form is submitted.

You may be wondering where you configure the destination of the form data when it is submitted. Remember that this is already configured within the form template, and therefore there is no configuration required in the Web Part. However, since you don't have full control over the Web Part, the "Submit to the hosting environment" option cannot be used with this scenario.

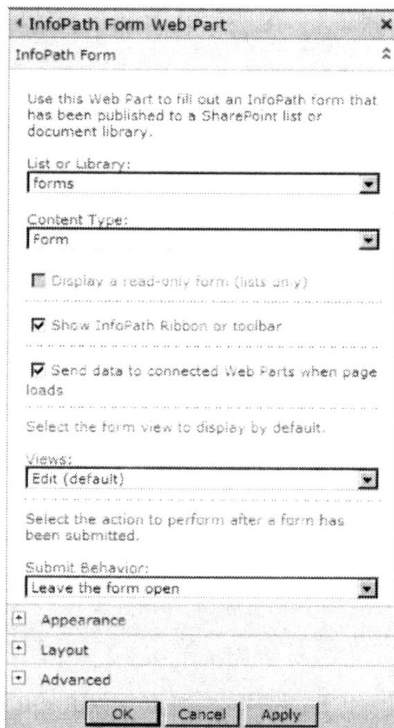

Figure 15–29. *InfoPath Form Web Part configuration dialog*

Customizing the Browser View Using XmlFormView

To display your browser forms within SharePoint you can use the InfoPath Form Web Part to integrate the form with a page, as described earlier. If a form is opened from a form library, it will be displayed by `FormServer.aspx`, which is an application page that hosts a control for displaying forms. If you need more control over the way the form will be displayed and want direct access to events, you can use the `XmlFormView` ASP.NET control in your own application page. This control renders InfoPath forms in the browser and provides several facilities for developers to change its default behavior.

Integrating XmlFormView in an Application Page

To integrate `XmlFormView` with your web page, you need to register the assembly `Microsoft.Office.InfoPath.Server`. Having done that, you can place the `XmlFormView` control in your ASPX markup, set some important parameters for the control, and bind events. The following listing shows the markup for an application page. The `OnSubmitToHost` attribute is bound to a method in the code-behind file. This code will be called when the form sends data to the hosting environment, using a submit data connection. Another attribute to note is the `EditingStatus`. This describes the editing state of the form and has three possible values: `Init`, `Editing`, and `Closed`. Use the `Init` state to hide the form during loading of the form and set it to `Editing` later on. In state `Editing`, the form is visible to the user. This is the only state in which the user can edit or view the form. When the form is closed, the common message "The form has been closed" will be displayed. If you have ever had an error in your form, you will be familiar with this message.

***Listing 15–15.** Integrating XmlFormView into the Markup of an Application Page*

```
<%@ Page Language="C#" AutoEventWireup="true" CodeFile="ShowForm.aspx.cs" Inherits="ShowForm"
EnableSessionState="True" %>
<%@ Register tagprefix="fv" namespace="Microsoft.Office.InfoPath.Server.Controls"
assembly="Microsoft.Office.InfoPath.Server, Version=14.0.0.0, Culture=neutral,
PublicKeyToken=71e9bce111e9429c" %>
<%@ Register tagprefix="Server" namespace="Microsoft.Office.InfoPath"
assembly="Microsoft.Office.InfoPath, Version=14.0.0.0, Culture=neutral,
PublicKeyToken=71e9bce111e9429c" %>
<html xmlns="http://www.w3.org/1999/xhtml">
    <head runat="server">
        <title>FormViews</title>
    </head>
    <body style="margin: 0px;overflow:auto;padding:20px">
        <form id="form1" runat="server" enctype="multipart/form-data">
            <fv:XmlFormView ID="formView" runat="server"
                            EditingStatus="Editing"
                            OnSubmitToHost="FormView_SubmitToHost"
                            Width="700px">
            </fv:XmlFormView>
        </form>
    </body>
</html>
```

To correctly display forms, XmlFormView needs to know the location of the form to display, the location of the form template used to render the form, and finally, the location for saved forms to be stored. The properties XmlLocation, XsnLocation, and SaveLocation are used to pass this information to the XmlFormView object.

■ **Note** You don't need to specify SaveLocation if you don't use the Save method. This may be the case if you deactivate the Save button in the User Interface Options section of the Form Options dialog (see Figure 15–13), or if you implement your own save method.

When opening an existing form, the matching form template is contained in the manifest file and does not need to be specified. But when a new form is created, the form template needs to be specified. You can specify these parameters in the page markup as attributes or set the class properties directly inside your code-behind.

To display an XML form, you can use the following code in the On_Load method in the code-behind file of the previous example. In the following listing, depending on a request parameter, either an existing form will be loaded using the XmlLocation parameter or the template will be assigned by the XsnLocation if the request parameter action equals new.

Listing 15–16. Code-Behind File of an Application Page Hosting XmlFormView

```
using System;
using Microsoft.SharePoint;
using Microsoft.SharePoint.WebControls;
using Microsoft.Office.InfoPath.Server.Controls;

namespace com.apress.formviewdemo
{

    public partial class ShowForm : LayoutsPageBase
    {

        protected void Page_Load(object sender, EventArgs e)
        {
            string action = Request.Params["action"];
            if (action == "new")
            {
                // Set the template location for new forms
                String templateLib = "FormServerTemplates";
                String xsnName = "template.xsn";
                formView.XsnLocation = String.Format("{0}/{1}/{2}",
                             SPContext.Current.Web.Url, templateLib, xsnName);
            }
            else
            {
                // Set the XML location for an existing form
                String lib = "TestForms";
                String name = "example.xml";
                formView.XmlLocation = String.Format("{0}/{1}/{2}",
                                       SPContext.Current.Web.Url, lib, name);
            }
        }

        protected void FormView_SubmitToHost(object sender, SubmitToHostEventArgs e)
        {
            // Will be implemented later
        }
    }
}
```

Accessing the XmlForm Object

Working with `XmlFormView`, you can access the `XmlForm` object and thus all the values and settings of the form described in the "Table 15–6 compares the two options for deploying forms with code.

Table 15–6. Comparing Sandboxed and Administrator-Approved Templates

Category	Sandboxed Form Template	Administrator-Approved Template
Permission	Site collection administrator	Farm administrator
Publishing	InfoPath Designer wizard	Central Administration
Security	Form code run in sandbox, no harm to farm	Code runs with full trust on the server

Programming InfoPath Forms" section. Via the `XmlForm` property you can reach the properties `DataSources`, `ViewInfos`, `FormState`, and such from within the page that is hosting the form. The `XmlForm` object can be accessed whenever the code is run within one of the following event handlers, which enables a form to communicate with its hosting environment:

Table 15–7. Events Available in XmlFormView

Event	Description
`Initialize`	This is called when the form is loaded.
`NotifyHost`	Notification events can pass a parameter to the hosting environment. Call `this.NotifyHost()` in your form template code.
`SubmitToHost`	This is called when the form is submitted using a submit to host data connection.
`Close`	This is called when the form is closed.

If you want to access the `XmlForm` object from another event on your page, you have to first call the method Data Bind of the `XmlFormView objectto` ensure that the `XmlForm` object is adequately populated.

You can directly access fields inside your form using the `XPathNavigator` on the `MainDataSource`. This may be required when implementing your own `OnSubmitToHost` event where you wish to store the XML data into a library and build the file name using information within the form. Listing 15–17 shows how this can be done. To keep things clear, we have only implemented the `OnSubmitToHost` event, which was left blank in the previous example.

Listing 15–17. Saving a Form to a SharePoint Library Using OnSubmitToHost Event

```
protected void FormView_SubmitToHost(object sender, SubmitToHostEventArgs e)
{
    SPWeb web = SPContext.Current.Web;
    web.AllowUnsafeUpdates = true;

    // Load the XML and save it as a byte array
    System.Xml.XPath.XPathNavigator navigator =
                             formView.XmlForm.MainDataSource.CreateNavigator();
```

```
    Byte[] formBytes = System.Text.Encoding.UTF8.GetBytes(navigator.OuterXml);

    // Create XmlDocument from the form XML
    XmlDocument doc = new XmlDocument();
    XmlNamespaceManager nsm = new XmlNamespaceManager(doc.NameTable);
    nsm.AddNamespace("my", "http://schemas.microsoft.com/office/infopath/2003/myXSD/2009-09-
29T22:54:17");
    doc.LoadXml(navigator.OuterXml);

    // Load name information from the XML
    XmlNode nodeLastName = doc.SelectSingleNode(
                    "/my:RoomBooking/my:UserInformation/my:LastName", nsm);
    string name = (nodeLastName != null) ? nodeLastName.InnerText : string.Empty;
    XmlNode nodeFirstName = doc.SelectSingleNode(
                    "/my:RoomBooking/my:UserInformation/my:FirstName", nsm);
    string firstname = (nodeFirstName != null) ?
                                    nodeFirstName.InnerText : string.Empty;

    // Generate file name
    string filename = String.Format("{0}{1}_{2}.xml", name, firstname,
                                      DateTime.Now.ToString("yyyyMMdd"));

    // Open library and save XML
    SPFolder formLibrary = web.GetFolder(LIBRARY_NAME);
    formLibrary.Files.Add(filename, formBytes);

    web.AllowUnsafeUpdates = false;
}
```

Integrating InfoPath Forms with the Environment

InfoPath forms can be developed and designed independently of your SharePoint environment. If you need to load additional information from external sources into your form, you can call a web service or use other data connections. But as soon as your form is part of a more complex business process, you might need some additional information within your form that is provided by the business process, or you may need information from outside of InfoPath that is entered through a form. In some scenarios you will have to pass parameters from your SharePoint application to your form, or vice versa.

Property Promotion and Demotion of XML Documents

Using InfoPath forms in SharePoint and storing the forms in a forms library enables development of complex browser-based applications with a great user experience. The forms are well-integrated into SharePoint with the support of Forms Services, but all the information that was entered by the users is stored within the XML file. There seems to be no easy access from the SharePoint environment to this data. What if you want to create a view that shows all the room bookings for one particular room? Or what if you want to change single values in your XML file from SharePoint? Many of the great features SharePoint offers work with list columns but don't offer extensibility to access information within XML files.

To solve this problem, SharePoint and InfoPath support features called *property promotion* and *property demotion*. SharePoint allows you to define fields in your InfoPath form that will be automatically provided as a column in your SharePoint document library. SharePoint automatically propagates changes that are made in your document to the SharePoint column and vice versa. Property promotion involves extracting fields from XML documents and writing these values to columns in SharePoint document libraries. Property demotion, on the other hand, involves taking changes to the SharePoint column available in your XML form.

Property promotion and demotion work as follows: whenever a new or existing XML file is saved in the document library, SharePoint invokes a built-in XML parser on the XML file. When the document content type contains a column that maps a field in the XML document to a list column (via an XPath expression that is pointing to the XML field), this value will be promoted to the library. In the other situation, where the column in the library is updated, this XPath expression is used to demote the information to the XML file.

In the description of the `XmlFormView` earlier in this chapter, we showed a method to directly manipulate the form's XML structure, which could also be used to access form fields, but requires more effort.

■ **Tip** You can find more details on property promotion and demotion on MSDN at `http://msdn.microsoft.com/en-us/library/aa543481(office.14).aspx`.

Configuring Promotion/Demotion Using InfoPath

When you are using the InfoPath Publishing wizard to publish your form template to SharePoint, you will encounter the dialog shown in Figure 15–30. In this dialog, you can add property promotion and demotion using the Add... button in the upper area of the wizard. In the upcoming dialog you can select a field from your main data source and specify the column name within the document library. InfoPath Forms Services will then create the necessary columns in the document library and store the XPath link to the referenced nodes in the column definition. The lower area is used for Web Part connection parameters (described next).

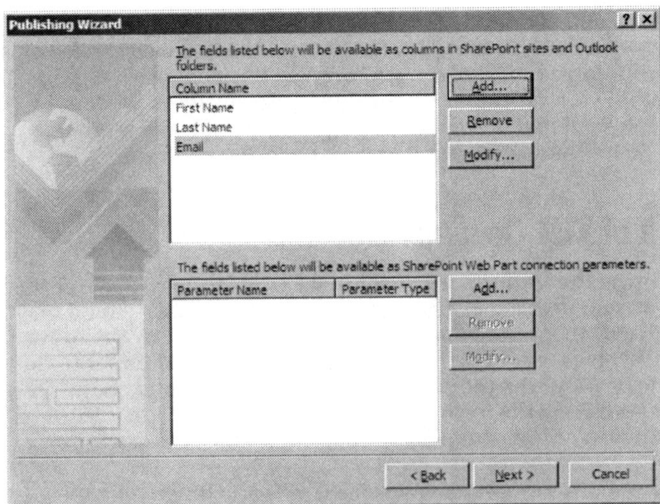

Figure 15–30. Configuring property promotion and demotion

Configuring Promotion/Demotion Within a List Feature

When using InfoPath Designer to manage list propagation, the necessary settings and changes will only be made on the list to which the InfoPath file is published. For any other deployment scenario (such as a multistage development and production environment), you can describe list propagation together with your list using the `schema.xml` file. You can simply nominate the column that should be used for property promotion with an `ID` and `Name` attribute. In addition, you merely need to specify the `Node` attribute. This attribute takes an XPath expression pointing to the field within the XML file. This XPath expression will be used for promotion and demotion of properties. Listing 15–18 shows an example for a list definition that specifies some nodes in the RoomBooking form that will be promoted to the list.

To make sure that you are using the right XPpath expression, you can use InfoPath Designer: right-click the field in the Fields tree and select Copy XPath, which will generate the correct expression for you.

Listing 15–18. *Configuring Property Promotion and Demotion in a Feature Definition*

```
<?xml version="1.0" encoding="utf-8"?>
<List xmlns:ows="Microsoft SharePoint"
    Title="Order Requests"
    Direction="$Resources:Direction;"
    Url="OrderRequests" BaseType="1"
    EnableContentTypes="TRUE"
    AllowMultipleContentTypes="True"
    xmlns="http://schemas.microsoft.com/sharepoint/">
    <MetaData>
        <ContentTypes>
            <ContentType ID="0x01010100B3E78F42234547a580BDE72BCB3E650A" Name="Order Requests"
                         Description="Request a new Order"
                                Group="$Resources:Document_Content_Types" Version="1">
                <FieldRefs>
                    <FieldRef ID="{DDC3C6B7-C34A-4d5a-8355-DC4E81885C8D}"
                              Name="Title" />
        ...
                    <FieldRef ID="{6CE8A87B-0862-4d8d-891F-5CA9C16833D4}"
                              Name="Room" />
                    <FieldRef ID="{05F09611-7D5B-4bae-9FA5-3EC8402F7A00}"
                              Name="Date" />
                    <FieldRef ID="{2C1B30B7-AADC-434b-9F82-D70639B59AB1}"
                              Name="TimeBegin" />
                    <FieldRef ID="{52BBFDF2-3176-43d7-A4D2-EFFA78CCED33}"
                              Name="TimeEnd" />
                </FieldRefs>
                <DocumentTemplate TargetName="/FormServerTemplates/RoomBooking.xsn"
                />
            </ContentType>
        </ContentTypes>
        <Fields>
    ...
            <Field ID="{6CE8A87B-0862-4d8d-891F-5CA9C16833D4}" ShowInNewForm="FALSE"
Type="Text" Name="Room" DisplayName="Room"
SourceID="http://schemas.microsoft.com/sharepoint/v3" StaticName="Room"
Node="/my:RoomBooking/my:Schedule/my:Room" ></Field>
            <Field ID="{05F09611-7D5B-4bae-9FA5-3EC8402F7A00}" ShowInNewForm="FALSE"
Type="DateTime" Name="Date" DisplayName="Date"
```

```
SourceID="http://schemas.microsoft.com/sharepoint/v3" StaticName="Date"
Node="/my:RoomBooking/my:Schedule/my:Date" ></Field>
            <Field ID="{2C1B30B7-AADC-434b-9F82-D70639B59AB1}" ShowInNewForm="FALSE"
Type="DateTime" Name="TimeBegin" DisplayName="TimeBegin"
SourceID="http://schemas.microsoft.com/sharepoint/v3" StaticName="TimeBegin"
Node="/my:RoomBooking/my:Schedule/my:TimeBegin" ></Field>
            <Field ID="{52BBFDF2-3176-43d7-A4D2-EFFA78CCED33}" ShowInNewForm="FALSE"
Type="DateTime" Name="TimeEnd" DisplayName="TimeEnd"
SourceID="http://schemas.microsoft.com/sharepoint/v3" StaticName="TimeEnd"
Node="/my:RoomBooking/my:Schedule/my:TimeEnd" ></Field>
        </Fields>
    </MetaData>
</List>
```

This listing defines common attributes for the list, such as `Title` and `Url`. In the `<MetaData>` section, the content type and fields are specified. The `ID` of the `<ContentType>` element starts with `0x01010`, which is the parent ID for form libraries. The `<FieldRef>` elements refer to the `<Field>` elements that are specified later using their GUIDs. The `<Field>` elements specify an additional attribute, `Node`, which contains the XPath to the field in the XML file of the InfoPath form. This node will be used to perform property promotion and demotion.

Web Part Connection Parameters

Web Parts on a page can be interconnected using connection parameters to pass values between them. Similar to property promotion, InfoPath fields can be promoted as Web Part connection parameters. This allows Web Parts to send data to or get data from a field in an InfoPath form without any further coding. Especially when using the newly introduced InfoPath Form Web Part, these connection parameters enable you to quickly interconnect your form with other SharePoint Web Parts. Figure 15–21, which was already described in connection with property promotion earlier, shows this dialog that allows you to add new Web Part connection parameters.

To specify Web Part connection parameters, you can use the Property Promotion category, accessible either through the Publishing wizard or the Form Options dialog. When adding new Web Part connection parameters, you will be asked to select the field you want to promote and enter a name for the parameter. Finally, you need to choose the parameter type: input, output, or input\output. Input parameters can be used to retrieve data from other Web Parts. Output parameters can send data to other Web Parts. If you want to do both, you must select "input\output."

▒ **Note** Remember that Web Part connection parameters cannot be used with sandboxed form templates, which contain managed code.

Passing Parameters from SharePoint to InfoPath Forms

When your form already exists, you can use property demotion to set fields in your form. But often you want to preload information in your form when a new form is created. In this case, you can pass parameters to your browser form using request parameters. If you write your own application page that hosts the `XmlFormView`, you can access the form's XML data and directly write parameters into the XML. But if you don't, request parameters might be the solution for you.

You can pass your additional parameters as so-called input parameters via HTTP request parameters. There are two ways to access these parameters:

- Using the InfoPath `InputParameters` property
- Directly accessing the HTTP request parameters

InfoPath offers access to input parameters either for InfoPath Filler forms or for browser-based forms. They are handled exactly the same way. In the load event you access the `LoadingEventArgs` parameter e and select the desired parameter using the [ ] selector:

```
String param = e.InputParameters["param"];
```

In this case, you don't have to deal with HTTP request parameters. But since your form is hosted inside a web page you can also read the HTTP request parameters from within your form template in the form code. All you need to do is add a reference to the `System.Web` assembly. Then you can access the `QueryString` collection of the `HttpRequest` to read all the parameters required to load data into the form. Of course, you can also access the other properties of the request (e.g., `Url`, `Headers`, `UserAgent`, `LogonUserIdentity`, and anything else that might be useful when programming your form). You can retrieve the browser session to exchange data between SharePoint and InfoPath. The next example demonstrates both ways to load data into your form using a request parameter. Instead of simply writing the value directly into the form, the parameter will be used to call a web service that is responsible for fetching the data that is required in the form.

To begin, add the following reference to your project, along with the `using` statement, to access the HTTP request:

```
using System.Web;
```

Now you can obtain the request parameters in your form-loading event to retrieve a parameter that identifies an item from the `QueryString`. With this `itemid` parameter, the `GetItemData` web service is called. The results are then stored into the form using `XPathNavigator`.

Listing 15–19. *Accessing Request Parameters in a Form Template*

```
public void FormEvents_Loading(object sender, LoadingEventArgs e)
{
    // Get the request parameter using InputParameters:
    string itemId = e.InputParameters["itemId"];
    // Get the request parameter directly from the request:
    itemId = HttpContext.Current.Request.QueryString["itemId"];

    XPathNavigator form = MainDataSource.CreateNavigator();

    if (!String.IsNullOrEmpty(itemId))
    {
        // Set the parameter for the web service query
        DataSources["GetItemData"].CreateNavigator().SelectSingleNode(
            "/dfs:myFields/dfs:queryFields/tns:GetItemData/tns:itemId",
            NamespaceManager ).SetValue(itemId);

        // Query web service and create navigator
        DataSources["GetItemData"].QueryConnection.Execute();
        XPathNavigator itemdata = DataSources["GetItemData"].CreateNavigator();

        // Fill the Name field with the value from the web service
        XPathNavigator nodeName = form.SelectSingleNode(
```

```
            "/my:ItemForm/my:Name", NamespaceManager);
        nodeName.SetValue(itemdata.SelectSingleNode(
"dfs:myFields/dfs:dataFields/tns:GetItemData/tns:GetItemDataResult/tns:ItemName",
            NamespaceManager).Value);

        // Fill the Price field with the value from the web service
        XPathNavigator nodePrice = form.SelectSingleNode(
            "/my:ItemForm/my:Price", NamespaceManager);
        nodePrice.SetValue(itemdata.SelectSingleNode(
"dfs:myFields/dfs:dataFields/tns:GetItemData/tns:GetItemDataResult/tns:ItemPrice",
            NamespaceManager).Value);
    }
}
```

■ **Caution** As always when working with request parameters, keep in mind that they can be easily modified by users. You must use the same precautions as in any other web page when working with request parameters. Always check the validity of the data passed to your form.

ACCESSING INFOPATH EVENTS IN THE BROWSER

For complex scenarios, working with the `NotifyHost` event can be very frustrating, since you can only pass a string parameter. If you wish to react to InfoPath events in your hosting environment, you can use the following approach, which lets you directly pass events to your server environment from within InfoPath. For example, you can delegate the `ViewSwitched` event to SharePoint by following these steps:

1. Create an Interface and define the methods that will handle the event:

    ```
    public interface IInfoPathEvents
    {
        void OnViewSwitched(object sender, ViewSwitchedEventArgs e);
    }
    ```

2. Implement the interface in a serializable class.
3. Implement the method that will be called by an InfoPath event.
4. Instantiate your class and store the object into the session within your web page.
5. Add a reference to the assembly containing your interface definition to your InfoPath code project.
6. Load your object from the session in the InfoPath event and call the `Interface` method:

    ```
    void FormEvents_ViewSwitched(object sender, ViewSwitchedEventArgs e)
    {
        IInfoPathEvents ev = HttpContext.Current.Session["events"] as
                             IInfoPathEvents;
    ```

```
            if (ev != null)
            {
                ev.OnViewSwitched(this, e);
            }
        }
```

7. If the `ViewSwitched` event is called in the InfoPath form, the events object is loaded from the `Session` object and the method that is offered through the interface is called.

This extended example shows the flexibility of InfoPath and SharePoint working together to bring InfoPath forms to the Web. You can use .NET code to create complex solutions and overcome existing limitations.

Summary

This chapter described how InfoPath forms can be used to create professional SharePoint applications that handle complex user input. InfoPath 2010 has greatly improved browser support and is easier to use when designing forms for the SharePoint environment.

Starting with a description about the internals of the InfoPath form templates, this chapter covered all the topics a developer needs to understand when working with InfoPath forms. Although designing form templates may not be a common developer task, basic information on how to design a browser-enabled form template was provided, together with the different ways to deploy the results to SharePoint.

Programming InfoPath form templates offers developers a powerful way to integrate form templates into complex business processes and develop intelligent form templates. However, not only can you use custom code to enrich business logic within InfoPath form templates, but you can also use it to customize form template–hosting inside SharePoint. Along with some basic configuration tasks, this chapter described the possibilities for programmatically changing the behavior of InfoPath Forms Services within SharePoint.

CHAPTER 16

■ ■ ■

Workflows

For line-of-business applications or portal solutions, the implementation of business processes or simple automated workflows is a crucial and demanding task. When implementing business processes, various stakeholders are involved, and it is a challenge to present workflows in a medium that is comprehensible to both developers and the business.

One of the basic building blocks of SharePoint is its support for workflows on any SharePoint item, such as a list, a site, or a content type. Workflows are an integral asset that can be developed using a variety of tools: Visio 2010, SharePoint Designer 2010, or Visual Studio 2010. All these tools leverage the ability to graphically design workflows that can be enriched using declarative descriptions or code to achieve the desired behavior.

This chapter examines different approaches for constructing workflows within the Microsoft solution stack. Commencing by describing general workflow behavior in SharePoint, we go on to show how to develop and extend workflows using SharePoint Designer. We describe Windows Workflow Foundation (WF) 3.5—the foundation layer for SharePoint workflows—and demonstrate developing custom workflows using Visual Studio. At the end of this chapter, we describe how InfoPath forms can be used to gather workflow-relevant data during workflow execution.

Workflows in SharePoint

SharePoint is a platform that supports collaboration among different people across the enterprise. Within any enterprise, processes are defined to describe the interaction between staff, based on appropriate information. For example, when a new employee is hired, several departments such as HR and IT administration are involved to configure the user's work environment before they can commence work. Equipment needs to be bought, accounts have to be created, and contracts require signatures. All these steps are based on such data as the employee's name, location, and seniority. The process can be completed successfully only if the people involved in the processes collaborate efficiently.

SharePoint contains large quantities of information, stored in lists, libraries, and documents, that is used by various stakeholders to do their work according to the enterprise's processes. To this end, SharePoint supports workflows to organize and execute multiple steps within a business process. Since SharePoint aims at user interaction, most of these workflows tend to be collaborative workflows built around the information made available through SharePoint. This can encompass almost any item in SharePoint, including its complete life cycle within SharePoint.

To inspire you regarding how you can use SharePoint workflows to achieve your business processes, the following section describes the basics of SharePoint workflows. After that, you will see how you can work with SharePoint workflows, and finally the different tools for developing workflows are presented and explained.

SharePoint Workflow Basics

SharePoint 2010 workflows are based on Windows Workflow Foundation 3.5—the same version that underpins the SharePoint 2007 workflows. Therefore, no significant changes have been made to the underlying workflow architecture or the basic workflow functionality. However, many improvements have been made to the way workflows can be developed and used. Furthermore, the tool support for workflows has been enhanced, making porting workflows from previous versions easier. Unfortunately, the new and redesigned WF 4.0 with numerous promising features will not be available to SharePoint 2010 developers.

Workflow Building Blocks

Before studying the details of the SharePoint workflow architecture, it is important to understand the basic building blocks of .NET 3.5 workflows and to comprehend what is special about SharePoint workflows.

Activities

Workflows are constructed from activities. Activities are the basic building blocks for every workflow. Each activity can be regarded as an atomic unit that encapsulates a certain behavior and is designed to fulfill a defined purpose. Some activities, called *composite activities*, contain other activities. They are responsible for the execution of their child activities. Composition of activities brings great flexibility and extensibility to the workflow concept.

During workflow design and creation, you can combine activities by putting them into a sequence or nesting them within each other. This creates the flow of actions that defines your workflow behavior. Depending on the tool you are using for workflow creation, you can specify certain parameters for the activities and even add custom code to influence the behavior of the activities.

Each tool used for workflow creation provides a set of out-of-the-box activities available for inclusion in workflow design. According to the level of abstraction provided by the tool, such activities will either offer very low-level access to WF and SharePoint workflows as in case of Visual Studio workflows, or they offer high-level activities as, for example, in SharePoint Designer. We will show a list of available activities in the following sections where we describe workflow development in detail.

In SharePoint Designer, activities are further classified as actions and conditions. Whereas *conditions* are used for activities that contain conditional behavior, such as `If-Else` statements, *actions* describe any activity that performs any kind of action. However, both types are implemented as WF activities.

Working on Content

SharePoint, by design, works with different contents, such as list items, documents, and sites. You can create content types that aid with structuring the contents within your SharePoint applications. Thus, it is no surprise that workflows are also aimed at dealing with contents. Each workflow you create needs to be assigned to content in your SharePoint application. For any workflow that you use or create, you need to specify a content that your workflow will be assigned to.

A workflow can be directly assigned to a list, to a library, or—new in SharePoint 2010— to a site. To design more flexible workflows and to increase reusability, you can also assign a workflow to a content type. SharePoint Designer 2010 also has the ability to create reusable workflows that are attached to a content type.

A running workflow instance is always tied to one instance of your assigned content type, and you are able to easily access the current content item from within your workflow. For example, when you associate a workflow template with a list, the workflow is connected to one item in that list at runtime.

User Interaction

Any kind of process, especially a SharePoint workflow, requires some sort of user interaction during workflow execution. Since SharePoint offers a standard user interface that is used for collaboration across the enterprise, these existing facilities are also used for human interaction in workflows.

SharePoint tasks are used for user interaction between workflows and humans because they already provide the required functionality. From SharePoint workflows, you can easily assign tasks to users and cause a workflow to wait until these tasks are finished. SharePoint workflows already contain several activities that work with tasks. Using standard SharePoint tasks for user interaction also ensures a tight integration with the SharePoint user experience, since many facilities are aimed at displaying relevant content to the user, such as Web Parts showing the user's tasks. In addition, these tasks also integrate well with Outlook.

Workflow Architecture

SharePoint Foundation 2010 workflows are based on the Windows Workflow Foundation 3.5 to offer workflow support within the SharePoint environment. WF provides a programming model, runtime engine, and tools for building and executing workflow-enabled applications. SharePoint uses the Workflow Designer in Visual Studio for custom workflow development and uses the WF runtime engine to host workflows inside SharePoint.

Workflow Hosting Environment

WF allows any process or application to run workflows by hosting the WF runtime engine, which provides standard services required by any workflow solution, such as persistence, state management, tracking, and transactions. SharePoint also hosts the WF runtime engine, but because of the SharePoint-specific behavior such as its data-centric nature and wide support for human interaction, some implementations of standard WF services have been replaced with custom implementations in SharePoint: transactions, persistence, notifications, roles, tracking, and messaging. Figure 16–1 shows the relationships between WF and SharePoint Foundation. You can use SharePoint Designer and Visual Studio to develop workflow templates that are based on special SharePoint Workflow Activities and work with the SharePoint Workflow Object Model. In addition, these workflow templates are based on the Basic Activity Library of WF. SharePoint Workflow Services uses the WF Runtime and WF Runtime Services to provide a custom workflow runtime environment.

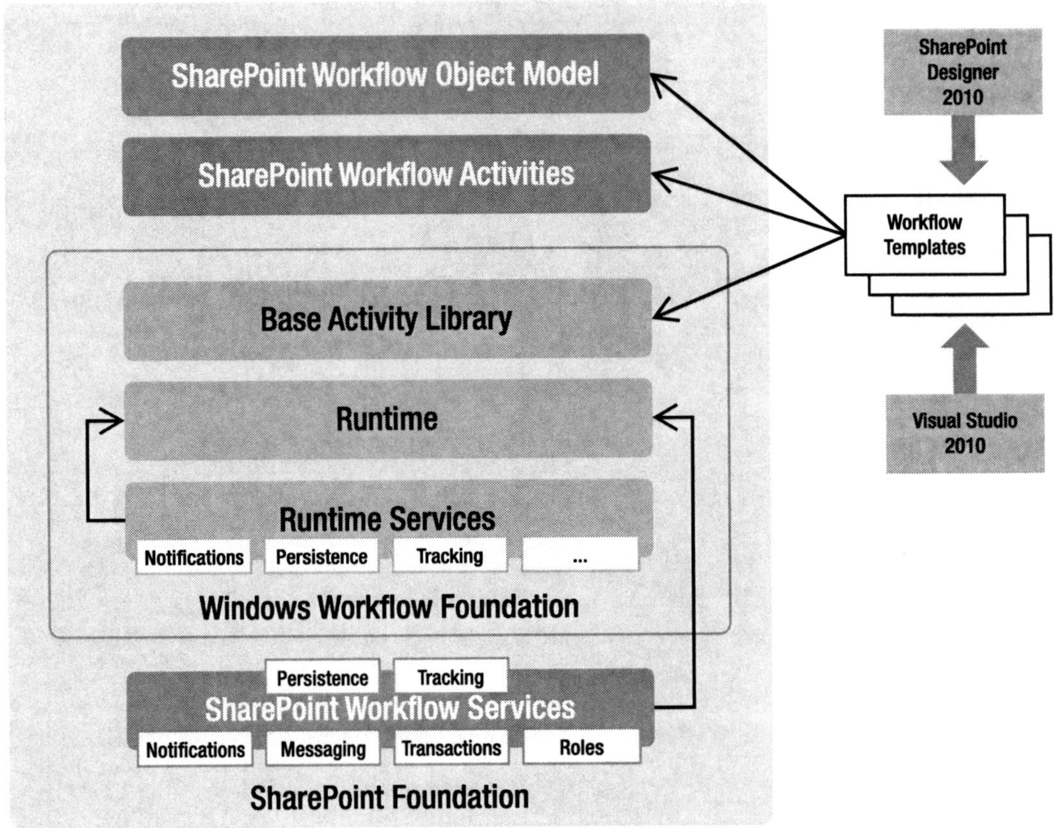

***Figure 16–1.** Workflow architecture in SharePoint Foundation 2010*

The custom implementation of workflow services results in a specific behavior for SharePoint workflows that requires special attention. Since workflows in SharePoint usually incorporate substantial user interaction, persistence of workflows is particularly important. To avoid long-running workflows wasting valuable computing resources, workflows waiting for user input are dehydrated. This means that the workflow object is serialized and stored into the SharePoint database. Hence, the workflow is not wasting memory. Whenever an event occurs, such as when a user updates a task, the dehydrated workflow instance will be reactivated and loaded into the memory to continue its work. To find and associate events to workflows, SharePoint uses *correlation tokens* along with GUIDs. (Refer to the "Custom Workflows with Visual Studio" section for more details on correlation tokens.)

Another important aspect to understand is the way that SharePoint uses transactions to process workflow activities. SharePoint executes a series of workflow activities until a commit point is reached. Changes made in the activities are committed only at the commit point, which is essentially a point where the workflow is serialized to wait for an event to occur. This behavior was chosen to pack all activities into a single batch for increased performance and to allow a rollback if errors occur—but it could result in unexpected behavior. The described batching feature applies only to SharePoint-specific workflow activities, whereas custom code activities will be processed immediately.

Workflow Types

Workflow Foundation supports two different styles of workflow:

- Sequential workflows
- State machine workflows

A *sequential workflow* contains a series of steps that will be executed in the specified order, from the start of the workflow to the end. The individual steps of the workflow will be executed one after the other. To control the flow within a sequential workflow, events and flow structures such as `If-Else`, loops, and parallel branches can modify the workflow execution order. Figure 16–2 shows a simple example that was modeled using the Visual Studio 2010 Workflow Designer. You can see the flow of events from the start, represented by the green arrow symbol at the top, down to the end, which is depicted by the red symbol. Depending on the result of the `CheckValue` shape, either the left or right branch is executed. Sequential workflows are supported by SharePoint Designer workflows as well as by workflows created with Visual Studio.

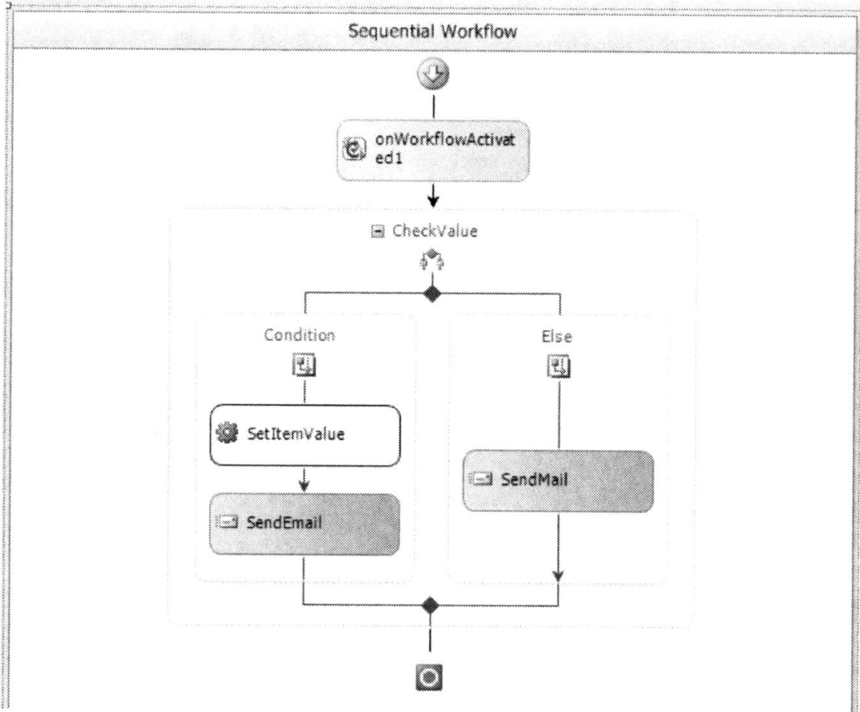

Figure 16–2. *Sequential workflow*

A *state machine workflow* adopts a different approach, because it does not model the flow of activities but instead defines several states that represent the system. It describes the events that transition from one state to another state. Figure 16–3 shows a very simple state machine workflow. You can see the different states represented by rectangles and the arrows denoting transitions from one state to another. SharePoint Designer workflows do not support this workflow type, and thus, state machine workflows can be developed only as custom workflows using Visual Studio.

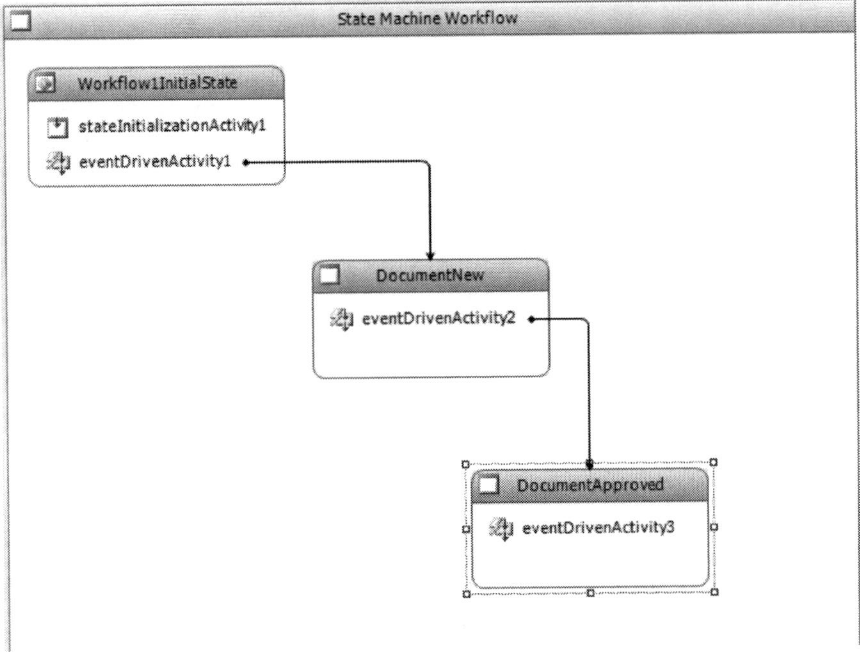

Figure 16–3. *State machine workflow*

Workflow Structure

Workflows for WF consist of several files that contain all the required information about a workflow so that it can be hosted by WF. Similar to ASP.NET, the declarative workflow description can be separated from the code, which encapsulates business logic. The XML dialect Extensible Application Markup Language (XAML) can be used to describe declarative metadata of a workflow within a `.xoml` file. This can be enriched using a separate code-behind file, containing the business logic, or it can be solely used for declarative workflows without additional business logic, as is done by SharePoint Designer. Of course, code files that contain both declarative description as well as business logic can also be used by WF.

Whenever you use code files to develop your workflows, the resulting code will be deployed as a compiled assembly and executed by the WF runtime. Declarative workflows that only use XAML will be deployed as `.xoml` files and compiled at runtime, every time a workflow instance is created. To sum up the options for creating workflows in SharePoint:

- A `.xoml` file containing the declarative description of the workflow. This is used by SharePoint Designer 2010.
- A `.xoml` file in combination with business logic in a separate code-behind file. This is used by Visual Studio 2010 by default.
- Code files that contain declarative and business logic for a workflow.

SharePoint Workflow Life Cycle

The life cycle of SharePoint workflows is very specific to SharePoint, because of its focus on content and the way user interaction is handled. Figure 16–4 illustrates the four stages of the SharePoint workflow life cycle. These stages allow for the assignment of workflows to content type, handle the different ways for starting workflows, and keep the workflow infrastructure flexible during execution. This custom life cycle is provided by the SharePoint-specific workflow hosting environment. During some of the following stages, forms can be used to gather additional user input as parameters, which are required for this stage to execute.

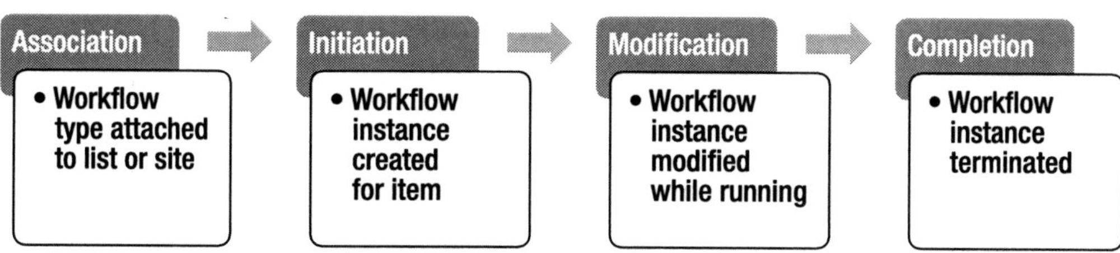

***Figure 16–4.** SharePoint workflow life cycle*

Association

Workflows that have already been deployed to the SharePoint server, as so-called workflow templates, must first be associated with a list, library, content type, or site before they can be run. The site administrator performing the association can also enter various advanced settings for the workflow association: a name, the task list used to store tasks for this particular workflow, and when the workflow should be executed. The resulting association information is stored in the farm-wide workflow association table used by SharePoint to determine the associated workflows for a content item such as lists and sites.

It is possible for workflow developers to assign a workflow association form to a workflow, which will be displayed to the site administrator who performs the association. This form can gather additional workflow-specific data such as default values that have to be entered by the site administrator during association. Later, when an instance of the workflow is started, SharePoint loads the association information from the association table, and this information can be used by the workflow during execution.

Initiation

As soon as a workflow is started—either manually or automatically, depending on its association parameters—it will be initiated. During initiation, a new instance of the workflow is created and assigned to a concrete item, either a list item, a document in a library, or a site. As with the association event shown earlier, workflow developers can add an initiation form to a workflow that will be displayed to the user who triggered the workflow. Parameters entered during initiation can be used to overwrite default parameters or to provide additional information.

Both association and initiation forms can be implemented using either ASP.NET (as an `.aspx` file) or an InfoPath form. We demonstrate how to integrate InfoPath forms into your workflow solutions later in this chapter. Figure 16–5 shows an example form that is used as both an association and an initiation form, for the approval workflow that ships with SharePoint. (This form is based on InfoPath Forms Services; see Chapter 15.)

■ **Caution** If a workflow is started automatically, such as when a new item is created or when an existing item is updated, the initiation form will not be displayed to the user. You should keep this in mind when creating your own workflows. Thus, initiation forms should be used in combination with workflows that are started manually and therefore will always show the initiation form, or they should contain only optional parameters for a workflow.

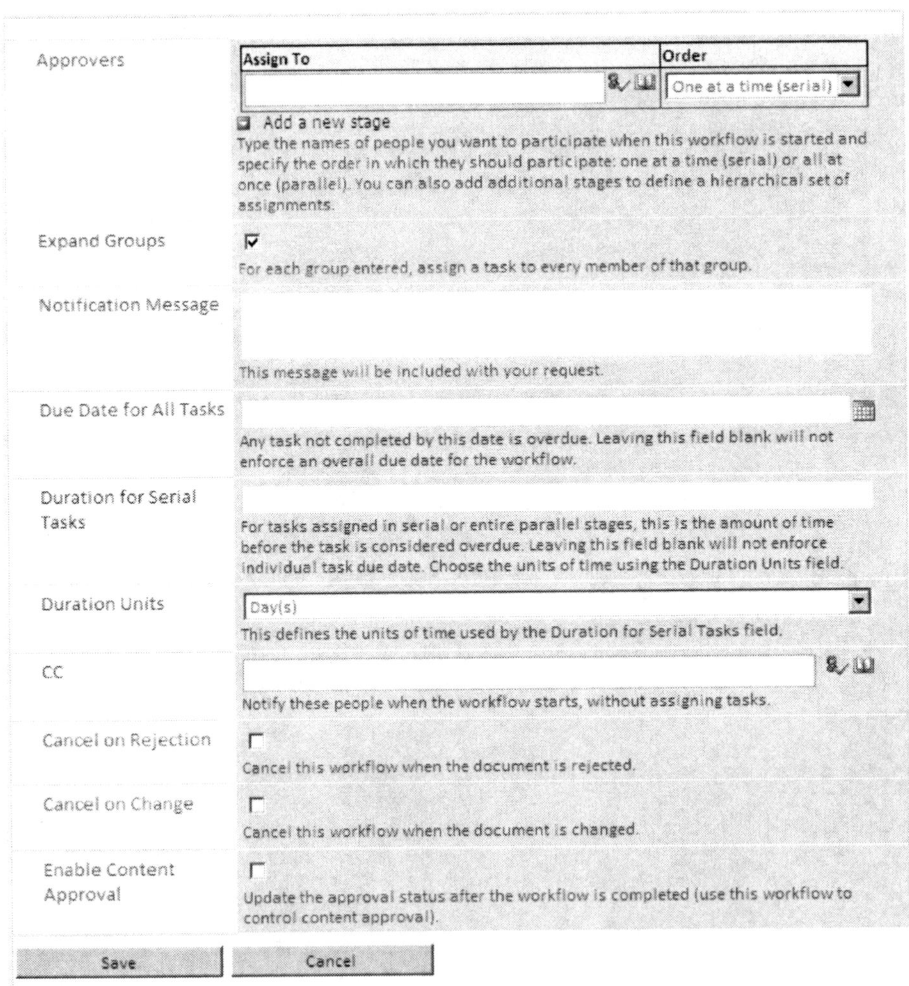

***Figure 16–5.** Example association and initiation form based on InfoPath*

Execution and Modification

While the workflow is running, it processes the different activities and follows the flow by evaluating certain conditions according to the workflow definition. During the execution of a workflow, there are basically two ways for interaction with users:

- *Workflow modification forms*: Modification allows a user to alter the workflow while it is running, such as to delegate their task to someone else. You can add modification forms to your workflow similar to association and initiation forms.
- *Workflow task forms*: Whenever user interaction is required as part of the standard workflow execution, user interaction is handled using tasks. If a workflow requires additional information that should be entered by the user, a task form can be used. You can add a task form to your workflow, which will be displayed to the user when they edit the task.

▒ **Caution** Workflows created with SharePoint Designer do not support modification forms, since those workflows cannot be modified at runtime.

During workflow execution, SharePoint users can view the current status of the workflow in a separate column that is added to the list on which the workflow is running. The first time a workflow of a certain workflow template is started on a list, SharePoint automatically adds a column to that list, which displays the current status for that workflow. All currently running workflow instances will be shown in the workflow overview page of the site or list in the "Running Workflows" section.

Completion

Finally, when all workflow activities are finished or when an activity to stop the workflow is reached, the workflow instance will be terminated. The workflow is then completed, and the workflow status will be updated accordingly and marked as closed. You will be able to view a list of completed workflows in the Workflows Overview page of a list or site. Once a workflow has been completed, you will not be able to make changes to this workflow. You can only start a new instance of that workflow on the same item.

Using Workflows in SharePoint

SharePoint supports different ways to design and build your workflows. However, the result will always be a workflow based on Windows Workflow Foundation that will be hosted in SharePoint. Thus, the way you can use your workflows within SharePoint to leverage the full potential of your SharePoint application is independent of the tool you choose for developing your workflows. Nevertheless, there a number of differences in the way workflows will be treated internally and in the way you can develop and deploy your workflows, which will be shown later in this section. We will also demonstrate some of the basic tasks for working with live workflows, during the different stages of a workflow.

SharePoint Out-Of-the-Box Workflows

This chapter is aimed at developers who want to build their own SharePoint workflows using either SharePoint Designer or Visual Studio. However, SharePoint also provides a small collection of canned out-of-the-box workflows that are shipped with the different versions of SharePoint Foundation and SharePoint Server. Before starting to develop a new workflow from scratch, it is a good idea to examine these workflows first. Even if they do not meet the requirements completely, they might be a head start for development. Since SharePoint 2010, it is possible to edit these out-of-the-box workflows and customize them to meet special requirements. Most of these workflows also offer some additional configuration options through the workflow association form. Table 16–1 lists the available workflows together with the SharePoint version that offers the workflow.

Table 16–1. *SharePoint Out-of-the-Box Workflows*

Workflow Name	Description	Availability
Approval	Routes a document for approval. Approvers can approve or reject the document, reassign the approval task, or request changes to the document.	SharePoint Server 2010
Collect Feedback	Routes a document for review. Reviewers can provide feedback, which is compiled and sent to the document owner when the workflow has completed.	SharePoint Server 2010
Collect Signatures	Gathers signatures needed to complete a Microsoft Office document.	SharePoint Server 2010
Disposition Approval	Manages document expiration and retention by allowing participants to decide whether to retain or delete expired documents.	SharePoint Server 2010
Publishing Approval	Routes a page for approval. Approvers can approve or reject the page, reassign the approval task, or request changes to the page.	SharePoint Server 2010
Three-state	Use this workflow to track items in a list.	SharePoint Foundation 2010

Using some of the out-of-the-box workflows, we demonstrate in the following sections how to use workflows in SharePoint and how to develop your own custom workflows.

Associate Workflows with SharePoint Items

To add a workflow to your SharePoint environment and associate it with a list or library, use the Workflow Settings page (shown in Figure 16–7), which is available through the ribbon bar by selecting List Tools ➤ List from within the particular list (shown in Figure 16–6). This page is also accessible from the List Settings dialog.

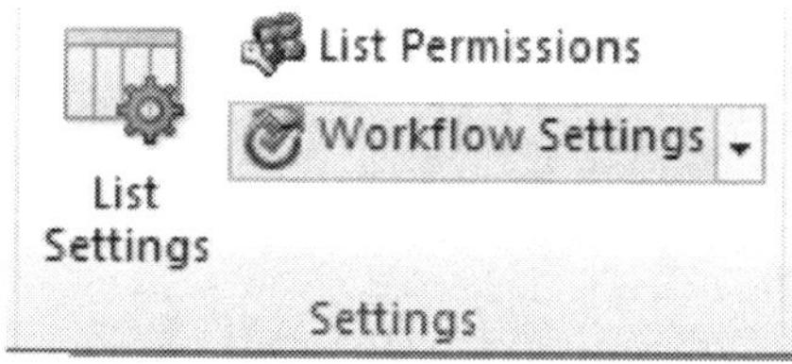

Figure 16–6. List Settings ribbon

To associate a workflow to a content type, navigate to the content type under "Site Settings" and you will also find the "Workflow settings" dialog. (This is analogous to associating a workflow to a site—you find the workflow settings from the Site Settings dialog.)

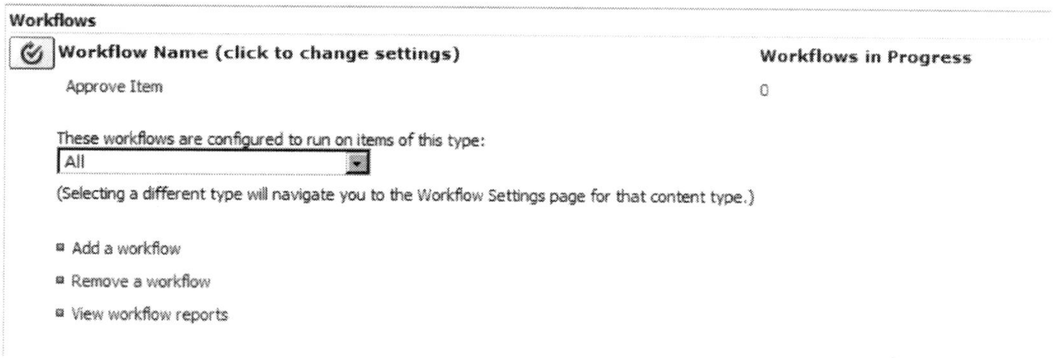

Workflows

Workflow Name (click to change settings) Workflows in Progress

Approve Item 0

These workflows are configured to run on items of this type:

All

(Selecting a different type will navigate you to the Workflow Settings page for that content type.)

- Add a workflow
- Remove a workflow
- View workflow reports

Figure 16–7. Workflow Settings page

On the Workflow Settings page, shown in Figure 16–7, is a summary of the workflows that are currently associated with your list, including the number of currently running workflow instances for each workflow template. You can add workflows to your list, which means associating the workflow to your current list. When you select "Add a workflow" to associate a workflow template with your current list, you will see a dialog similar to Figure 16–8.

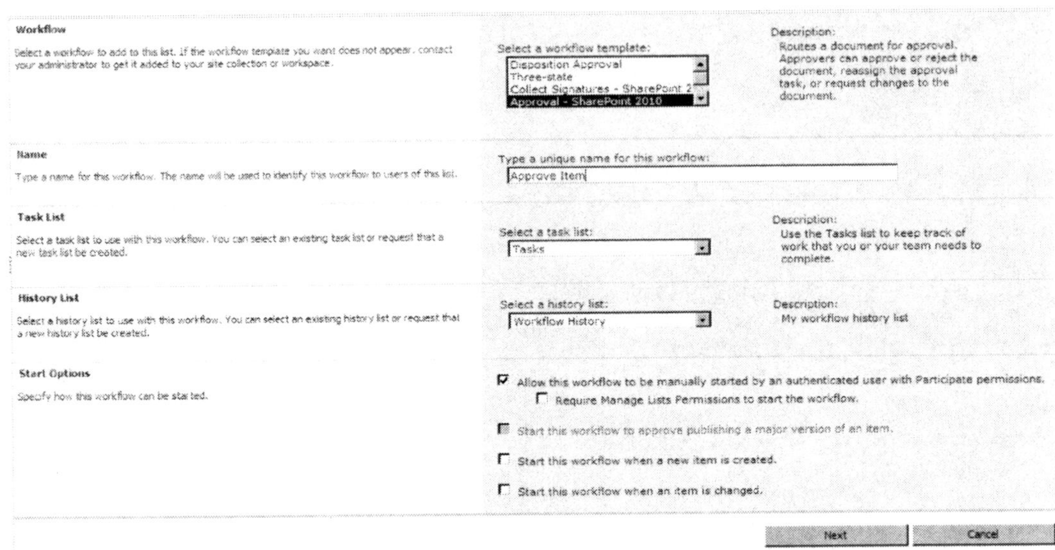

***Figure 16–8.** Adding a workflow to a list*

In the Add a Workflow dialog are some important settings for workflow association:

- *Workflow*: In this section are all the workflows that are deployed to the site collection and available to this list. When you build your own workflow and deploy it to the server, it will be added to this list. Select the workflow template that you want to associate with your content from this list.
- *Name*: Give your workflow association a meaningful name, since this name will be displayed in all the pages used to manage the workflow—from starting up a workflow to the workflow history.
- *Task List*: Specify the task list to be used by the workflow to create tasks for users to complete. You can either use an existing task list or have SharePoint create a new one.
- *History List*: As for the task list, you can specify a history list to be used by the workflow to record information using special activities that write to the workflow history.

- *Start Options*: This option defines which events trigger the workflow to start. You can choose whether you want your workflow to be started manually by users who have at least Participate permission on the list or whether your workflow should start automatically. You could also specify that only users with Manage List permissions are able to manually start a workflow. For automatic workflows, you can choose whether the workflow should start when a new item is created or every time an item is updated. In site workflows, these automatic options are not available. The option that is disabled in Figure 16–8, "Start this workflow to approve publishing a major version of an item," is only available in document libraries where the option "Create major and minor versions" is activated in the Versioning Settings section of the library settings. In addition, it requires either the Approval or the Publishing Approval workflow to be selected.

If an association for the workflow has been specified, this form will be displayed after clicking the Next button. In the case of the Approval workflow in the previous example, the association form as shown in Figure 16–5 will be displayed.

Starting Workflows

After a workflow is associated with a list, library, content type, or site, it may be necessary to manually start the workflow on a specific item, if this option was selected during association. The workflow overview page allows you to start a new workflow and shows you currently running or already finished workflows for an item. It can be reached in different ways:

- For a list or library, you can use the drop-down list of each list item and select workflow as depicted in Figure 16–9, or you can use the Workflow item in the ribbon bar, when the item is selected.
- For a site, use the Site Actions menu and also select Workflows.
- For workflows that are associated to a content type, you will find the workflow in the list or library to which your content type is assigned. You will always need an item of a list or library to start your content type workflow.

■ **Tip** When developing your own workflow, we recommend you check the box that allows the workflow to be started manually. This way, you can stop and restart your workflow in case of an error. After you have finished developing your workflow, you can switch off this option if your workflow should only be started automatically.

The workflow overview page of an item is shown in Figure 16–10. If you have one or more workflows associated, as in the figure, you can start a new workflow instance by simply clicking the workflow. This will set up the workflow, and if an initiation form has been defined, this form will be displayed to the user who started the workflow.

After you have started the workflow, it will appear under Running Workflows. You will not be able to start another instance of this workflow until the running instance has finished. SharePoint allows only one running instance of a workflow template on an item at a time.

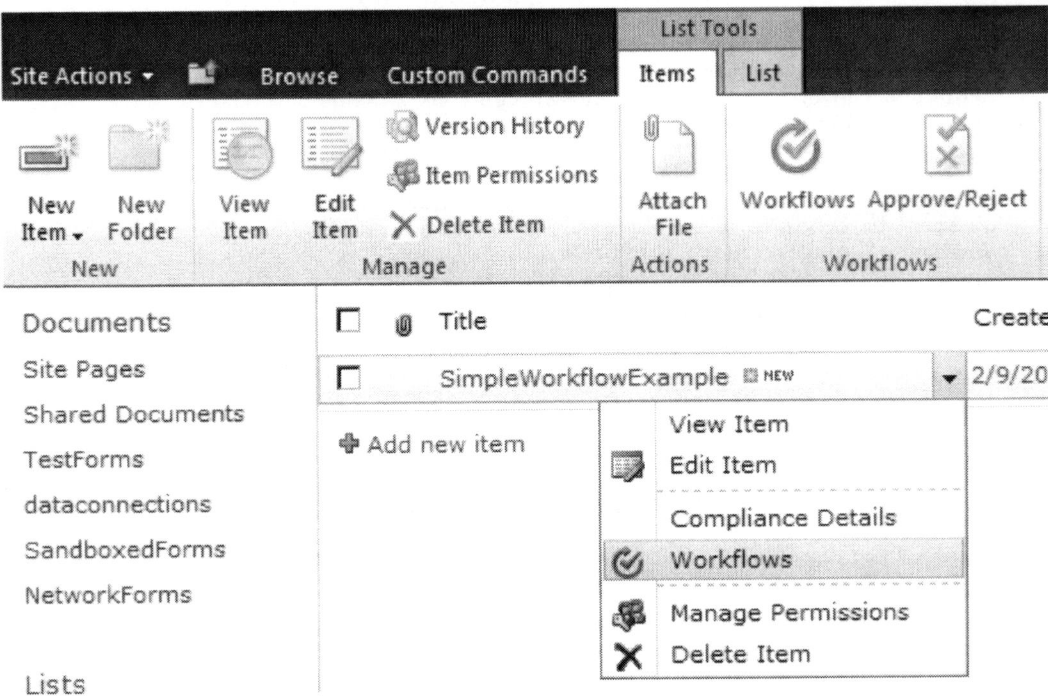

Figure 16–9. Selecting workflow overview page on a list item

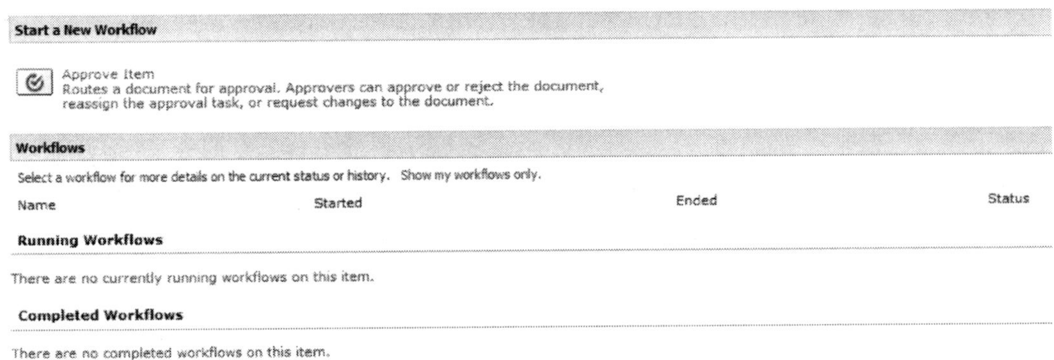

Figure 16–10. Workflow overview: Manually starting a workflow

Managing and Monitoring Running Workflows

SharePoint has many facilities for managing and monitoring running workflows, providing users insight into the current status of their workflows and allowing them to interact with running instances. This information is also helpful to workflow developers. The first place to look for the current status of a workflow is the list or library on which the workflow has been started. Since for each item in the list, a column for each workflow has been added, you can immediately see the status of the workflow in the corresponding column.

From here, or via one of the different ways to access the workflow overview page, you can then reach the workflow overview. If you have running workflow instances for your item, you will see a page similar to the one shown in Figure 16–11.

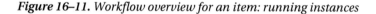

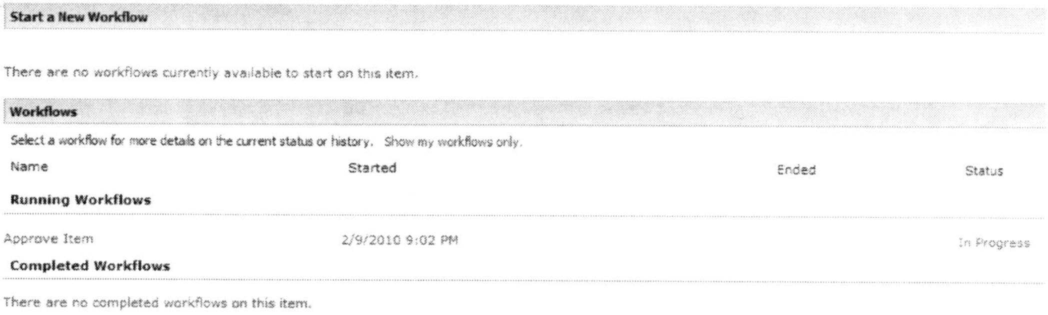

Start a New Workflow

There are no workflows currently available to start on this item.

Workflows

Select a workflow for more details on the current status or history. Show my workflows only.

Name	Started	Ended	Status
Running Workflows			
Approve Item	2/9/2010 9:02 PM		In Progress
Completed Workflows			

There are no completed workflows on this item.

***Figure 16–11.** Workflow overview for an item: running instances*

It displays again the current workflow status and by clicking the link on either the workflow name or the status, you navigate to the detailed workflow information for this workflow instance. The Workflow Information page (see the example in Figure 16–12) lists basic information about the initiator, the time the workflow was started, the current status, and a link to the item on which the workflow is executed.

Below this is a graphical visualization of the workflow, rendered using Visio Web Access. This diagram not only shows a static representation of the workflow but also mirrors the current state of the workflow. Each activity that has been processed is marked by a special symbol. The green tick symbols in Figure 16–12 indicate that the first "Compare date source" activity and the "Set workflow variable" activity at the bottom have already been processed.

Since Visio 2010 supports shapes for SharePoint 2010 workflows and an import for SharePoint workflows into Visio 2010 has been implemented, this is a great example of converting workflows from SharePoint to Visio 2010. Unfortunately, this feature is available only with SharePoint Server 2010 and not with SharePoint Foundation.

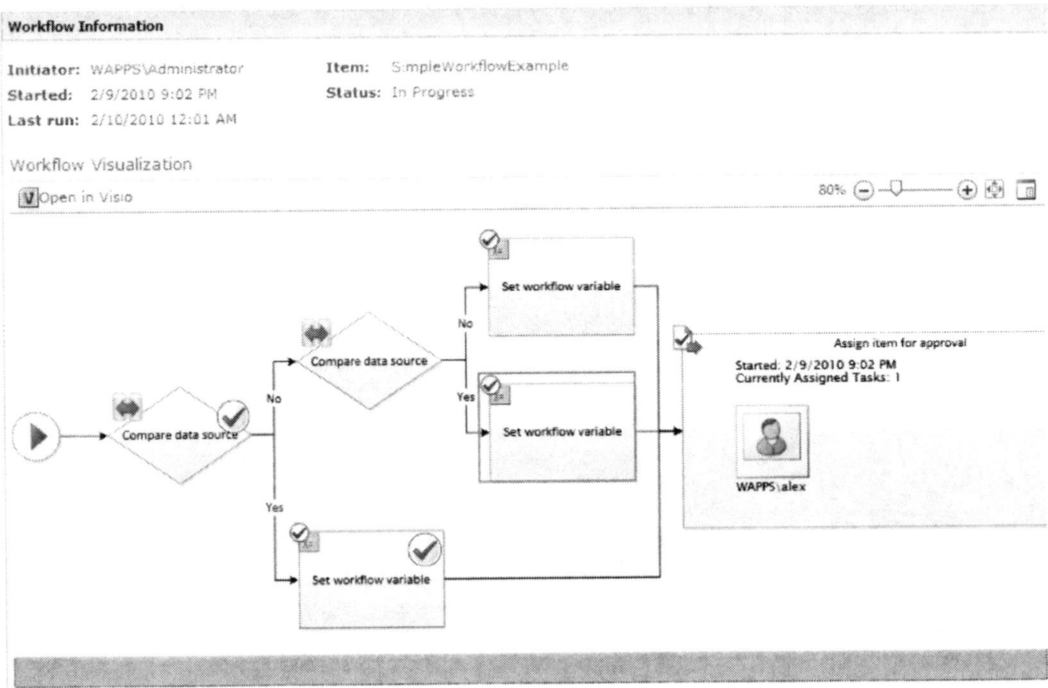

Figure 16–12. Workflow information and Visio visualization

Beneath the workflow visualization, additional information about this workflow is displayed, shown in Figure 16–13. Immediately above the Tasks section are additional commands that can be used to modify the Approval task.

The link "Terminate this workflow now" is displayed in any workflow to users with the required permission. Clicking the link terminates the workflow instance, stopping the workflow in the current state and setting the workflow status to Aborted. This command is useful during workflow development when your workflow errors. Workflows in Error state are incomplete, and you can use this link to terminate your instance, before rerunning the workflow with a new version where your error is fixed. Remember, that you can have only one instance of a workflow running at the same time, so you need to terminate the running instance before you a start a new one.

The Tasks section lists all tasks that have been assigned by this workflow instance. You can see the user assigned to the task, the current status, and the outcome of the tasks. This is a view of the task list that was specified during workflow association that shows all tasks that are related to the current item and the current workflow.

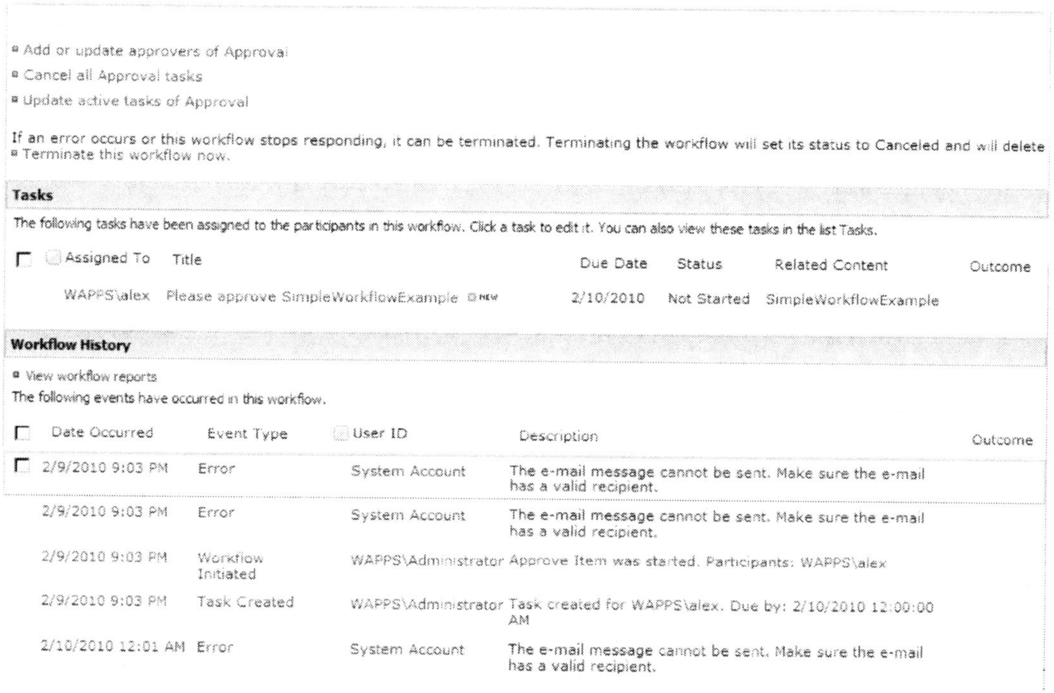

Figure 16–13. *Workflow information: tasks and history*

Finally, the last section of the workflow information page displays the workflow history list containing all entries for this workflow instance. This list summarizes the different actions that were taken throughout this workflow execution and shows you errors and other audit information that is written to the history. You can add activities to your workflow and write information to this history to share information about workflow progress with users and administrators. This is also a good method to debug your workflow during development.

User Interaction Using Tasks

As already mentioned, user interaction during workflow execution is accomplished using tasks. They can be assigned to a user by the workflow and will integrate seamlessly with any other tasks in SharePoint. You can use, for example, the User Tasks Web Part on your page to display all tasks that are assigned to the current user. This allows you to create intuitive solutions that follow your business processes with very little development effort by leveraging existing components.

To gather additional information from users required for your workflow, you can build task forms to display to the user on task completion. Independent of the tool you are using for workflow development, you can use either standard ASP.NET forms or even InfoPath forms as task forms. This again shows the broad application for InfoPath forms and how well they have been integrated into SharePoint 2010. Figure 16–14 shows a sample InfoPath-based workflow task form, which is used in the out-of-the-box Approval workflow.

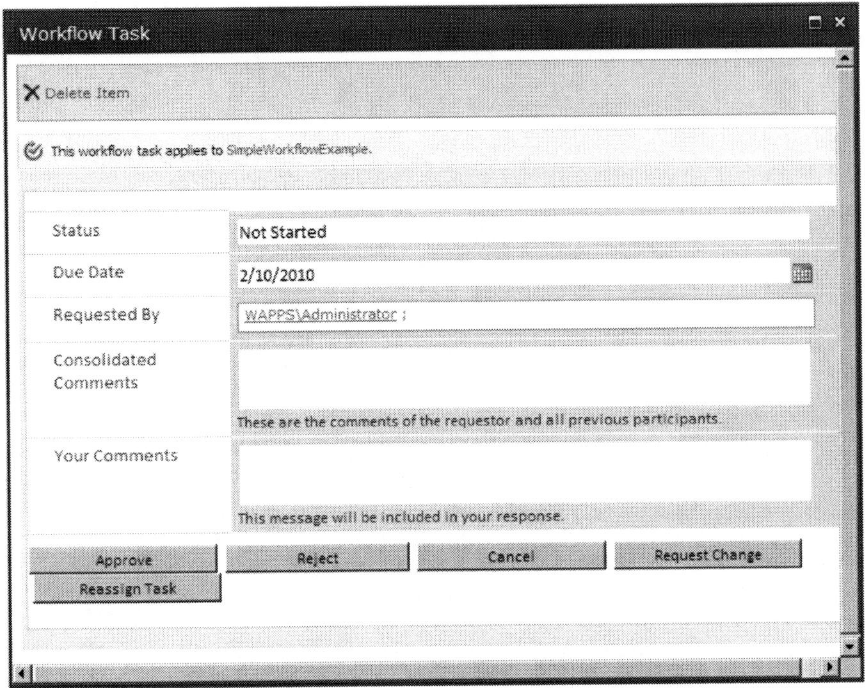

Figure 16–14. Workflow task form using InfoPath

Tools for Workflow Development

The out-of-the-box workflows supplied with SharePoint are very flexible and easy to use, but in most cases they don't fit the diverse and complex business processes in the real world. With SharePoint 2010, the support for constructing custom workflows that exactly fit the business requirements has been greatly improved. In previous versions, developing custom workflows was far more challenging. One of the reasons this task has become much easier lies in the improved tool support.

Not only have the tools been improved to make developing workflow solutions more straightforward, they have also been integrated to allow scalability and extensibility. In contrast, in SharePoint 2007 developing a workflow in SharePoint Designer could lead to a dead end. If you realized at some point that the capabilities of SharePoint Designer were inadequate for your requirements, you would lose all your work, because there was no way of importing a Designer workflow into Visual Studio. This is now possible with SharePoint 2010.

Workflow design usually involves specific knowledge about the business processes, which is only available within business units. Therefore, in Visio 2010, SharePoint workflow shapes have been added that allow business units to design a workflow skeleton, which can be imported into SharePoint Designer. This bridges the gap between business and IT and enables a common understanding of the desired workflows.

Figure 16–15 outlines the tools available across an enterprise to design and develop custom workflows. As you can see, it is possible to import Visio 2010 workflow diagrams into SharePoint Designer and use this skeleton as the basis for workflow development. Further, SharePoint Designer workflows can be exported as Visio 2010 diagrams and thus allow visualization of existing workflows.

Finally, you can now package SharePoint Designer workflows into a WSP solution file, open this solution from Visual Studio 2010, and develop these workflows into custom workflows.

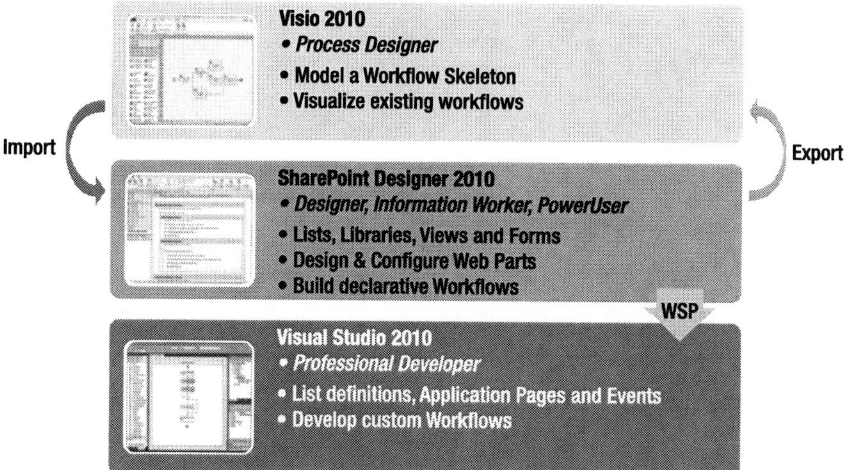

Figure 16–15. *Tool stack for developing Workflows*

ADDITIONAL TOOLS FOR WORKFLOW DEVELOPMENT

This tool stack focuses on the tools provided by Microsoft for developing workflow solutions for SharePoint. In fact, several interesting third-party products allow you to design your workflows within SharePoint using graphical editors. If the Microsoft tools don't fit your requirements, you can check out these products. The following two products are considered the most noteworthy by the authors of this book—however, there may be others:

`Nintex Workflow: www.nintex.com`

`K2 Blackpoint: www.k2.com`

Visio 2010: Process Design

Visio 2010 offers process designers the prospect of designing workflows for SharePoint that can be used directly to develop custom workflows in SharePoint Designer. To design a SharePoint workflow, start a new Visio diagram by selecting the Microsoft SharePoint Workflow template in the Flowchart category. From that, you can design your workflow in the familiar Visio interface using the special SharePoint workflow shapes: SharePoint workflow actions and SharePoint workflow conditions. Figure 16–16 shows an example Visio workflow diagram.

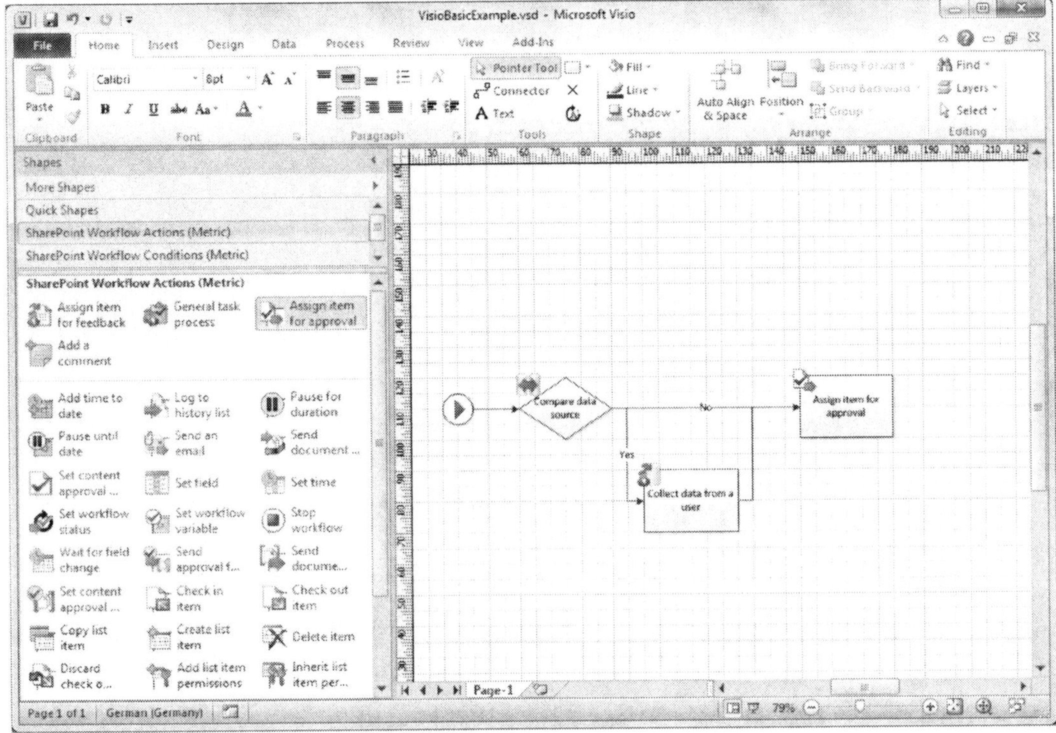

Figure 16–16. *Designing workflows with Visio 2010*

Visio offers the Check Diagram feature in the Process ribbon. This check reports whether your workflow is correctly modeled or if you missed any connections or important shapes. You will also find an option to import and export SharePoint workflows.

SharePoint Designer 2010: Declarative Workflow

SharePoint Designer 2010 allows you to create workflows without writing code, using a declarative workflow description. Usually SharePoint Designer is aimed at designers, information workers, and power users, but since it is now possible to export SharePoint Designer workflows and use them in Visual Studio, SharePoint Designer can also be a useful starting point for developers—especially for prototyping or for simple workflow scenarios. You can even use Visio to design your workflows in cooperation with the business units, import the workflow into the Designer, and later use this workflow to start developing with Visual Studio.

Workflows

After opening a site in SharePoint Designer 2010, you will see all the items of the site in the navigation pane. If you select the Workflows navigation tab, you will see all the workflows that are available to the site. Figure 16–17 shows a sample list of different workflows that are currently available. The workflows are categorized as follows:

- *List Workflow*: These workflows are developed for a particular list and are directly associated with that list. These workflows cannot be reused for any other list because they have direct access to all the columns of the list and thus are strongly tied to that list. Furthermore, list workflows cannot be saved as a template to be imported into Visual Studio, for the same reasons.
- *Site Workflow*: Instead of creating a workflow for a list or a library, with SharePoint 2010 you can also create workflows that can be executed on a site. In SharePoint Designer, you will always be working in the context of a site. When you add a site workflow, it will automatically be available only for the site on which you are working. Like list workflows, site workflows cannot be saved as a template for Visual Studio.
- *Reusable Workflow*: These workflows are not developed for a particular list or library. Instead, they can be associated with any list or library but not to a site. As they are not tied to a list, you can use the option Save as Template to save a reusable workflow to a WSP file, which can be opened in Visual Studio. Because these workflows are independent of lists and content types, you will not have access to any columns other than the base columns inside the workflow. You can use the options Associate to List or Associate to Content Type to associate the workflow from SharePoint Designer, rather than the SharePoint user interface. Reusable workflows, however, are available only to lists within the current site. To make them available to the entire site collection, you can use the option Convert to Globally Reusable.
- *Globally Reusable*: These workflows are reusable workflows that are available to the entire site collection instead of just the site. Unfortunately, these workflows cannot be saved to a template WSP file.

The ribbon bar of the workflows page contains buttons for creating new workflows and editing existing workflows (see Figure 16–17). In addition, the Manage section allows you to export the selected workflow to a WSP template file and to import and export Visio 2010 workflow diagrams. You can also associate workflows to a list or to a content type.

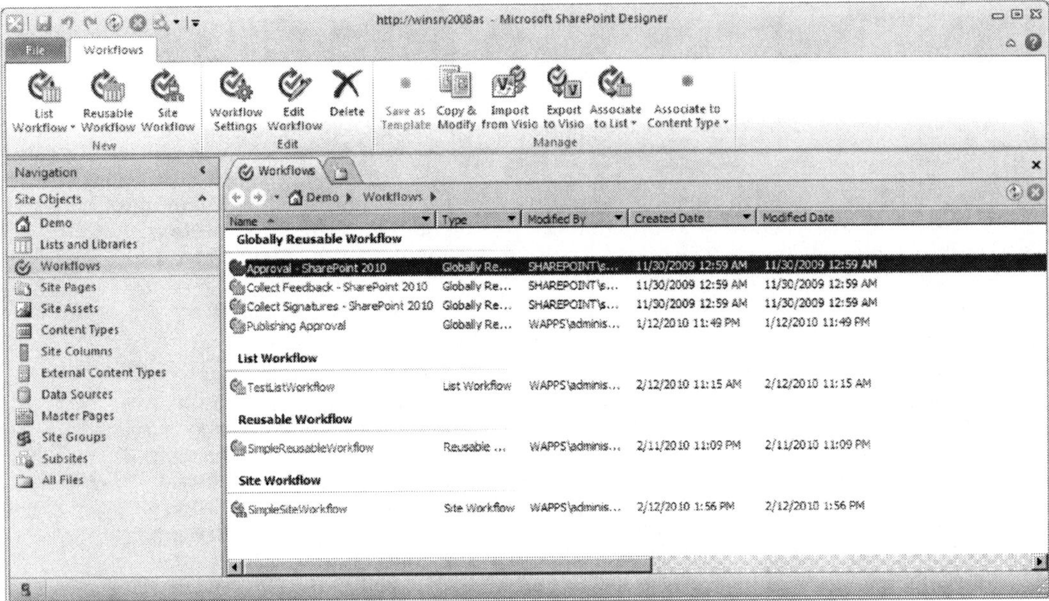

Figure 16–17. List of workflows in SharePoint Designer 2010

Workflow Settings

Clicking a workflow in the overview will take you to the Workflow Settings page for this workflow, as illustrated in Figure 16–18. This page presents all the relevant settings for a workflow, at a glance. Here you can alter similar settings to those exposed in the SharePoint user interface, such as start options and the workflow name. Using the ribbon or the Edit workflow link in the customization section, you can start editing the workflow. In addition to this, you can manage all the variables that are used by the workflow:

- *Initiation Form Parameters*: This allows you to specify variables that will be collected during workflow initiation or association. If not already present, SharePoint Designer will create an initiation form for you, which will appear in the Forms section of the Workflow Settings page. You can access these initiation parameters (and association parameters) within your workflow within conditions and actions.
- *Local Variables*: You can create variables that are available inside the workflow to store information. These variables are accessible throughout the workflow and can be used for conditions and actions. When you add task forms to your workflow, the results can be reached through such variables.

- *Association Columns*: These allow you to add fields to your list or library, when the workflow is associated with this list or library. Association columns enable you to store workflow-related data in the list. This is especially important for reusable workflows because this ensures that required columns are made available in the list to which the workflow will be associated later. Naturally, this is not available to site workflows.

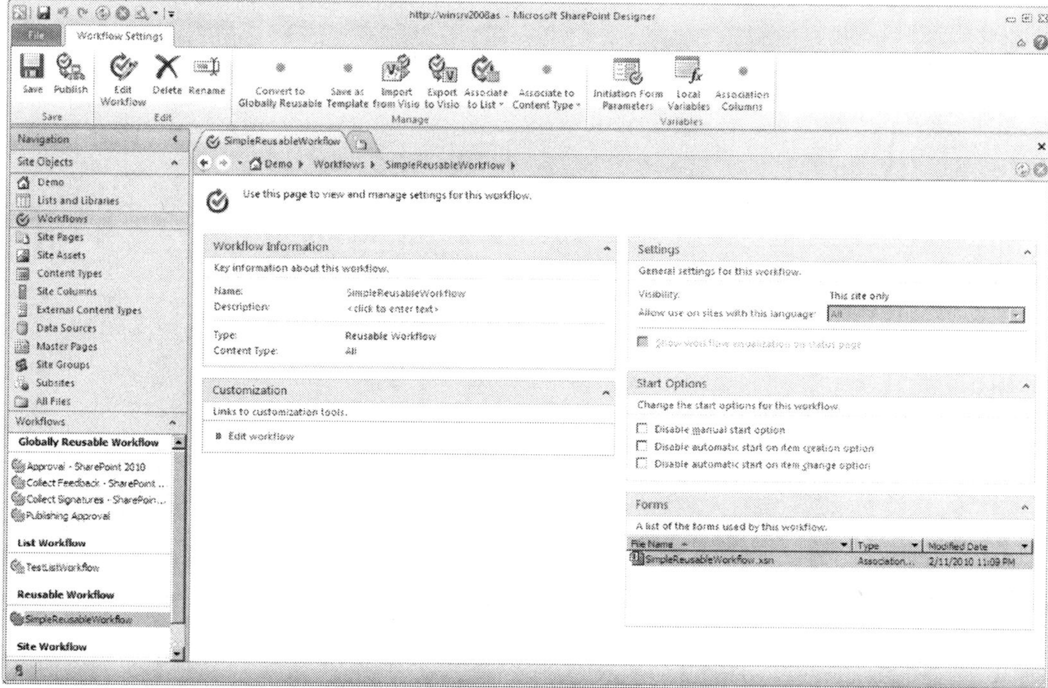

Figure 16–18. *SharePoint Designer 2010: Workflow Settings*

The Forms section contains all the forms used by this workflow, including the initiation form and association form, as well as any task forms. These forms are created automatically by SharePoint Designer as soon as the workflow is published. When InfoPath is available to your SharePoint environment, XSN forms will automatically be created. Otherwise, ASPX forms are produced.

■ **Caution** On the Workflow Settings page, the start options for Reusable workflows are different from all other dialogs where you can set the start options. In this section they are negated, which means you have to disable the options you don't want to be available.

Workflow Editor

To create and edit declarative workflows, SharePoint Designer 2010 uses the Workflow Editor page. You can reach this page by clicking Edit Workflow on the ribbon bar, using the link in the Workflow Settings page when editing a workflow, or using one of the buttons for creating a new workflow from various pages in SharePoint Designer. As you see in Figure 16–19, the layout of the workflow editor has been completely redesigned compared to previous versions.

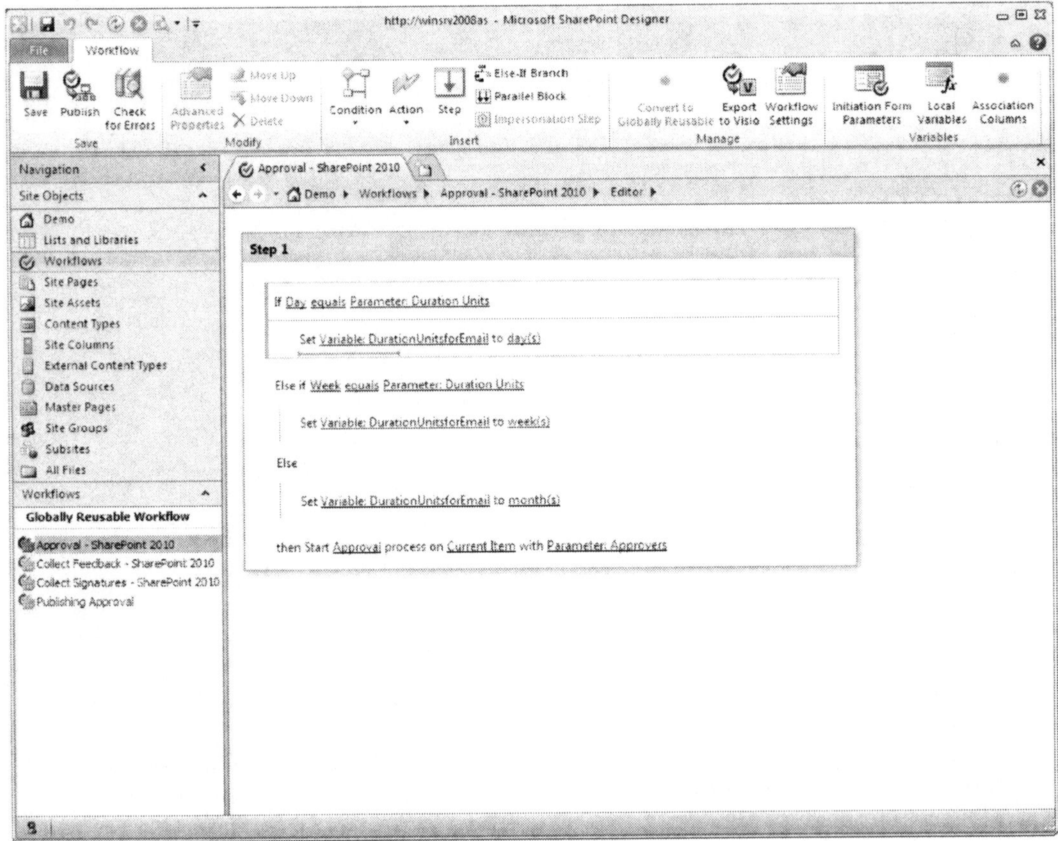

Figure 16–19. Editing a declarative workflow in SharePoint Designer 2010

Workflows are structured using steps that are represented by gray boxes with a heading that can be renamed by clicking the text. You can add actions and conditions to your workflow at any location within a step.

Every action or condition is represented by a sentence that consists of several parameters. These parameters either can be set by the workflow editor to constant values or can be filled from workflow variables or item properties.

We will show how workflow can be designed with SharePoint Designer in more detail in the "Workflows with SharePoint Designer" section.

Visual Studio 2010: Custom Workflows

To leverage the full potential of SharePoint workflows, you can create custom workflows using Visual Studio. Although this allows full control and flexibility over workflows in SharePoint, the approach requires a thorough knowledge of SharePoint development and is solely aimed at professional developers familiar with .NET. Fortunately, Visual Studio 2010 contains project templates for SharePoint workflows and integrates well with SharePoint, which alleviates development complexity.

To get started with developing a custom workflow, create a new project in Visual Studio and select either Sequential Workflow or State Machine Workflow from the SharePoint 2010 templates (as displayed in Figure 16–20). Both templates will result in similar solutions, except for the type of workflow integrated into the project.

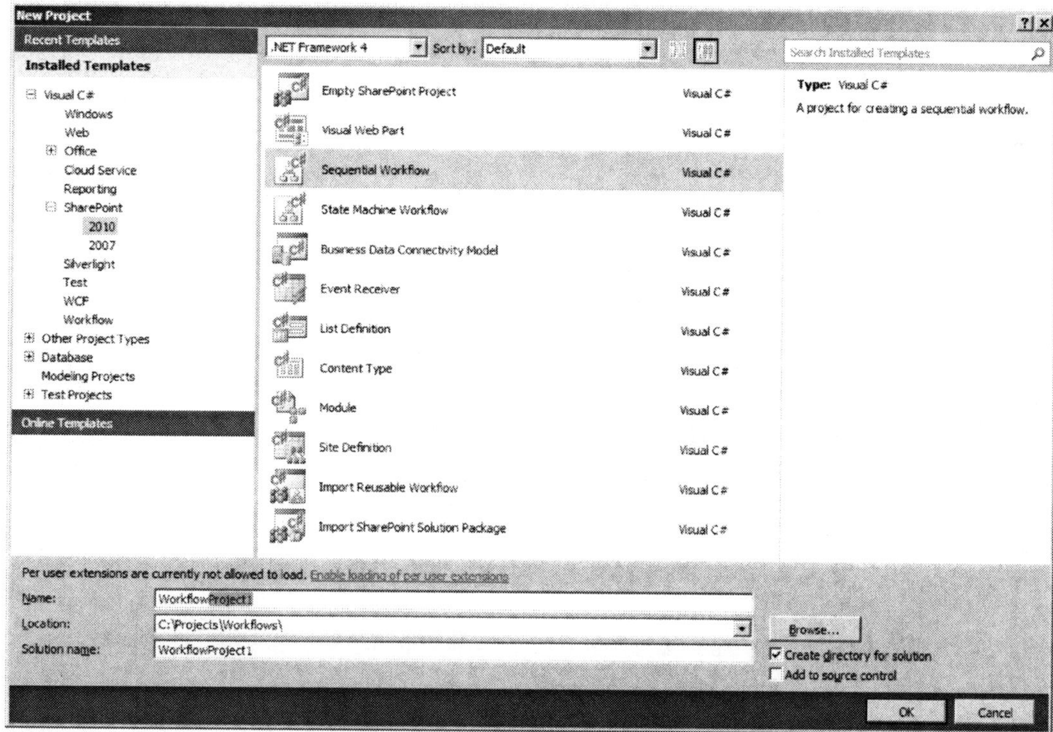

***Figure 16–20.** Creating a workflow project in Visual Studio 2010*

■ **Note** Don't be confused if .NET Framework 4.0 is selected by default when choosing the SharePoint 2010 workflow templates. Although you can select this option, you won't be able to work with 4.0 Workflow facilities. Even if you select 4.0, the resulting project will still be using .NET Framework 3.5.

Once you have started your project creation, wizards are used to gather basic settings for your project. At first you will be asked to enter a local site for debugging (see Figure 16–21). This SharePoint site is used when you debug your workflow (Microsoft often calls this the "F5 experience," since you are able to debug SharePoint solutions directly from within Visual Studio). In this dialog, the option to deploy as a sandboxed solution is disabled, because custom workflows always need to be deployed as a farm solution.

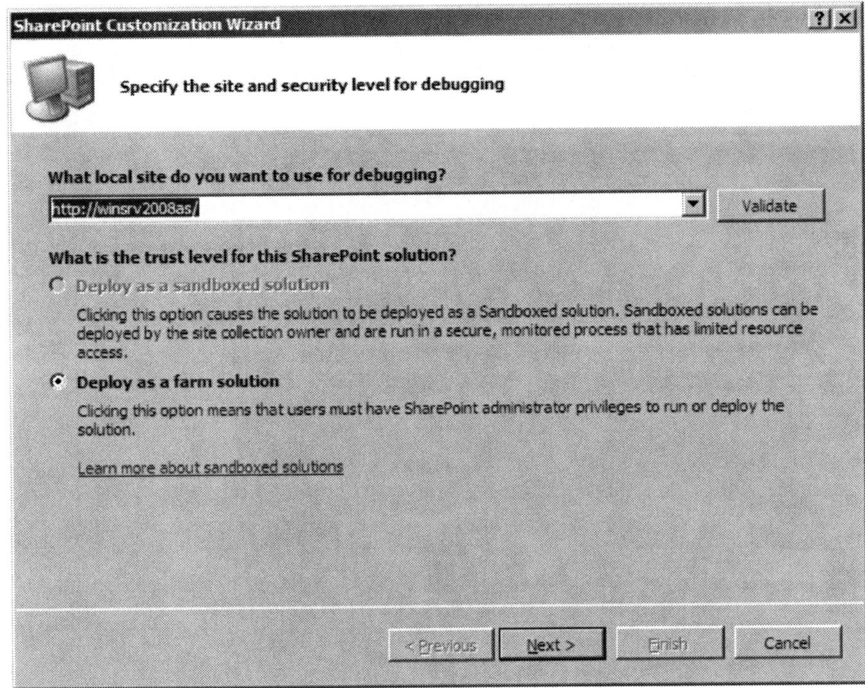

Figure 16–21. *Creating a new workflow project*

In the subsequent wizards, you can specify various settings that are used for debugging. These are the same settings as already described in SharePoint user interface in the "Using Workflows in SharePoint" section. They include a workflow name, the workflow template (list or site workflow), the list to which the workflow is associated, the task list and history list, and, finally, the options surrounding when the workflow should be started.

Once the solution is created, you should see a Visual Studio solution similar to Figure 16–22, depending on your Visual Studio configuration. In the central window is the graphical workflow designer, showing the sequential flow (or the states for a state machine workflow). The toolbox on the left side contains all the available shapes that you can drag on the designer surface to model your workflow. The shapes are categorized into the standard Windows Workflow Foundation shapes and the SharePoint-specific shapes. In the Solution Explorer are all the relevant items for a SharePoint solution including your workflow. The project structure created by the template builds a SharePoint solution including a feature that will be deployed to the local SharePoint when you debug or deploy your solution.

(We will show how to develop custom workflows using Visual Studio in detail in the "Custom Workflows with Visual Studio" section.)

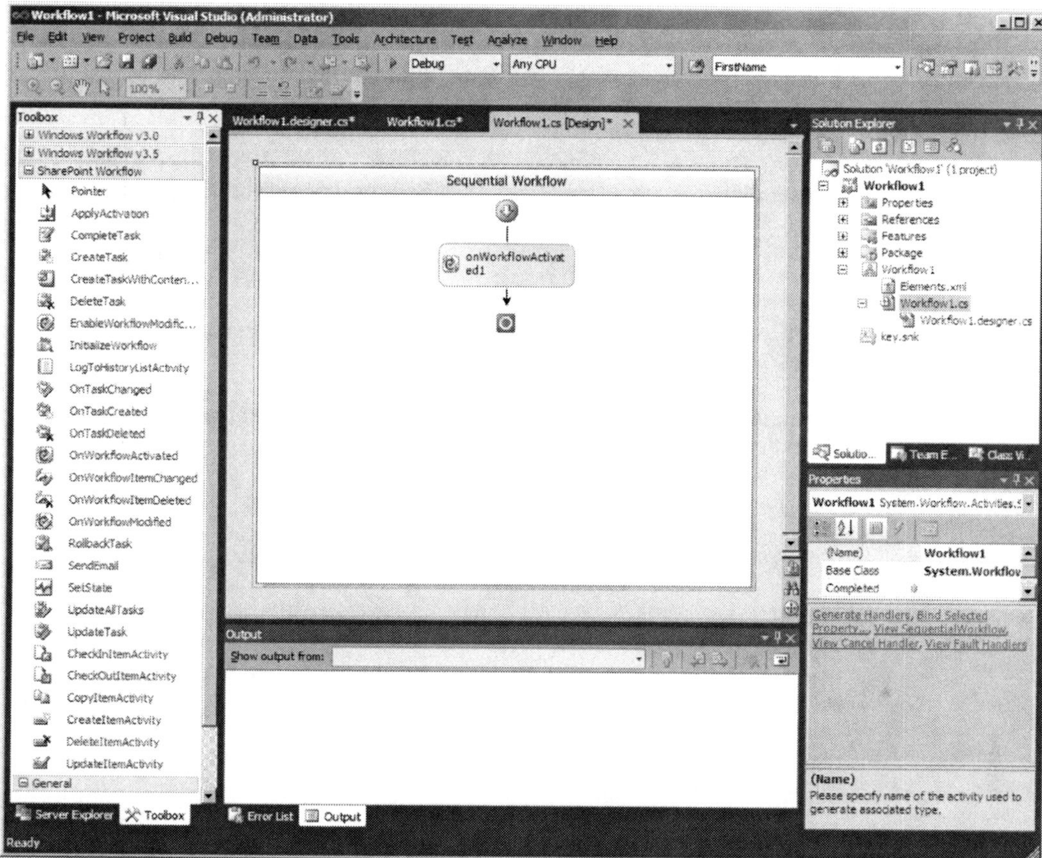

Figure 16–22. Developing workflows in Visual Studio 2010

Tool Comparison

Both tools, SharePoint Designer and Visual Studio, support developing elaborate workflows for the SharePoint environment. Visio 2010, on the other hand, can be used only for designing workflows—to finally create a workflow, you always have to use either SharePoint Designer or Visual Studio. Table 16–2 compares the salient features of these two tools for creating workflows:

Table 16–2. Comparing Workflow Facilities in SharePoint Designer 2010 and Visual Studio 2010

Facility	SharePoint Designer 2010	Visual Studio 2010
Intended audience	Designer/power users	Professional developer
Workflow development	Declarative description	Code based
Supported workflows	Sequential	Sequential and state machine
Reusability	Within the site or site collection, export to WSP	Reusable throughout farm
Reusable workflows	For lists, libraries, and content types	For lists, libraries, content types, and sites
Deployment	Automatically to the site into the workflows list	Using SharePoint feature
Debugging	Not supported	Debugging using Visual Studio
Remote deployment	Supported	Not possible
Workflow type	XOML markup files	Compiled into assembly
Forms	Automatically selected: InfoPath or ASP.NET	Both can be specified in feature
Activities	Built-in activities, custom activities can be developed	Built-in activities, custom activities can be developed
Association	Lists, libraries, content types, and sites	Lists, libraries, content types, and sites
Association and initiation forms	Both supported	Both supported
Modification	Not supported	Modification supported
Import Visio diagrams	Directly supported	Only via Designer to export WSP

Workflows with SharePoint Designer

The previous section covered the fundamentals of SharePoint workflows and a quick overview of the tools that you can use to develop workflows with SharePoint. In this section, we explain how you can use

SharePoint Designer to create declarative workflow solutions. We start by showing how you can create a workflow using only SharePoint Designer, as well as the available actions and conditions.

Later in this chapter, we describe how you can create custom activities with Visual Studio that can be integrated in SharePoint Designer to extend the existing actions and conditions. This approach is especially interesting since these actions can be shared with workflow designers who are not capable of SharePoint workflow development. Therefore, you will also learn a few essentials about the internals of SharePoint Designer workflows and how the actions and conditions are built.

Creating Workflows with SharePoint Designer

SharePoint Designer has been completely redesigned in the 2010 version and offers an impressive interface for designing SharePoint workflows using a declarative approach. Although the interface is very intuitive, some of the concepts of declaring SharePoint Designer workflows need to be explained. To leverage the full potential of declarative workflows, all the available actions and conditions will be described in this chapter to give you a complete understanding of what is possible using the Workflow Designer.

Declaring a Workflow using Actions and Conditions

To start declaring a workflow, open the Workflows page in SharePoint Designer and select one of the available workflow types from the ribbon bar in the Workflows page. In the ensuing dialog, enter a name for the workflow and a description. The workflow is created, and you are able to start developing your workflow in the Workflow Editor page.

What follows is a description of actions and conditions using an example action. The steps for all actions and condition in the example are similar and can easily be comprehended following the basic description.

Looking at the editor window, you will notice a single, horizontal orange bar, which indicates the current cursor position. You can use the keyboard to control the cursor position and insert actions and conditions from the ribbon, or you can click the position where you want to insert an action and enter a part of the name of the action or condition you want to insert. SharePoint Designer will automatically show you a drop-down list of all available actions and conditions for your search, as shown in Figure 16–23.

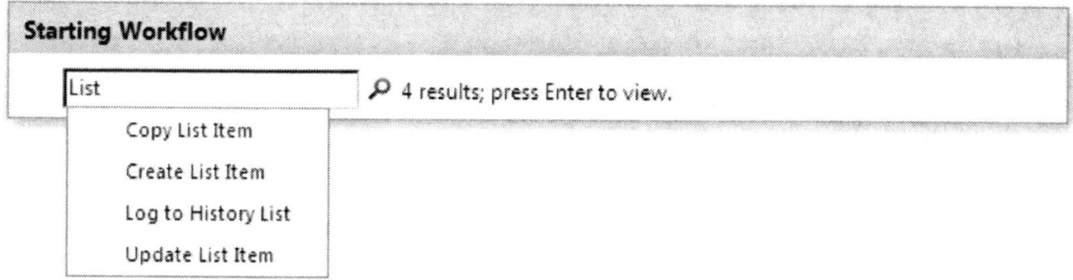

***Figure 16–23.** Selecting an action by entering its name*

After you select an action or condition, an entry will be created that describes the action or condition in one sentence. This sentence contains a number of editable parameters. They are underlined and can be edited by a simple click (Figure 16–24).

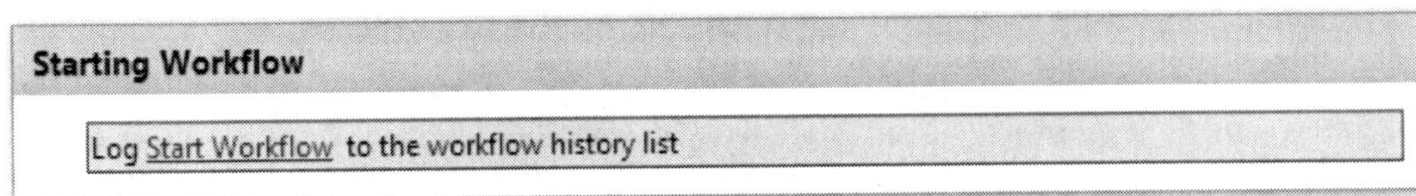

Figure 16–24. A sentence with editable parameters

When you click a parameter, you will see different options for editing. You can directly enter a static value in the textbox, or you can click one of the buttons next to the text box. Depending on the parameter type, you may see the two buttons shown in Figure 16–25.

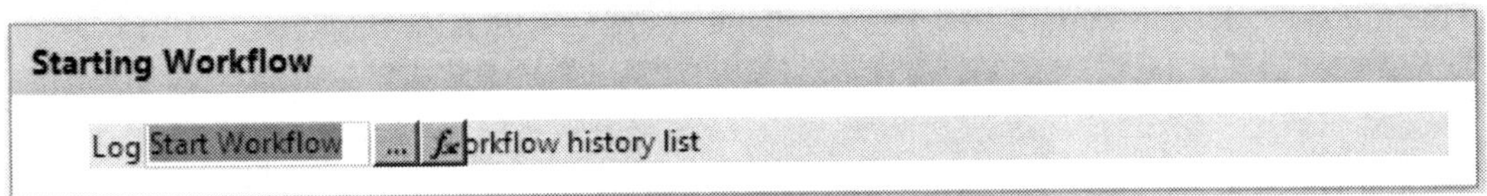

Figure 16–25. Editing an action parameter

The left button with the ellipsis symbol (...) opens the String Builder dialog, which can be used to construct dynamic strings. The button with the function symbol opens the Lookup dialog (Figure 16–26), which enables you to lookup a value from one of the following sources:

- *Current Item*: This is the item on which the workflow was started and to which the workflow instance belongs.
- *Workflow variables and constants*: Select a value from one of the variables that you can define for your workflow. You can manage these variables using Local Variables from the ribbon.
- *Workflow context*: This contains information about the workflow instance, such as the initiator, date, and time of workflow start or the current user.
- *Association: History List*: You can select a value from an item in the associated history list. You can specify a condition composed of a field that you want to compare and a value to select a specific item.
- *Association: Task List*: You can also select a value from an item in the associated task list. As for the history list, a field/value combination can be specified to select an item.
- *Current List*: Select a value from an item in the current list, which is identified by a field together with the value to look for.
- *List within Site*: You will see all available lists within the current site to look up a value. You can specify a condition to select a specific item within the list.

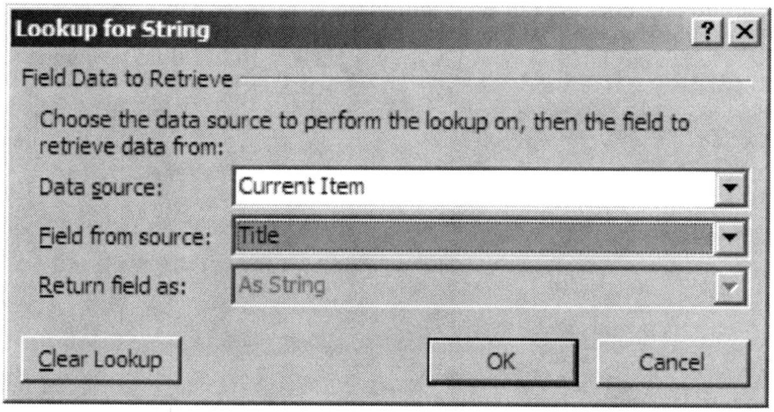

Figure 16–26. Lookup dialog

Figure 16–27 shows the String Builder dialog, used to create dynamic strings. Within the String Builder you can click the Add or Change Lookup button to invoke the Lookup dialog to insert dynamic values (described earlier). This dialog will be available whenever a string parameter is expected.

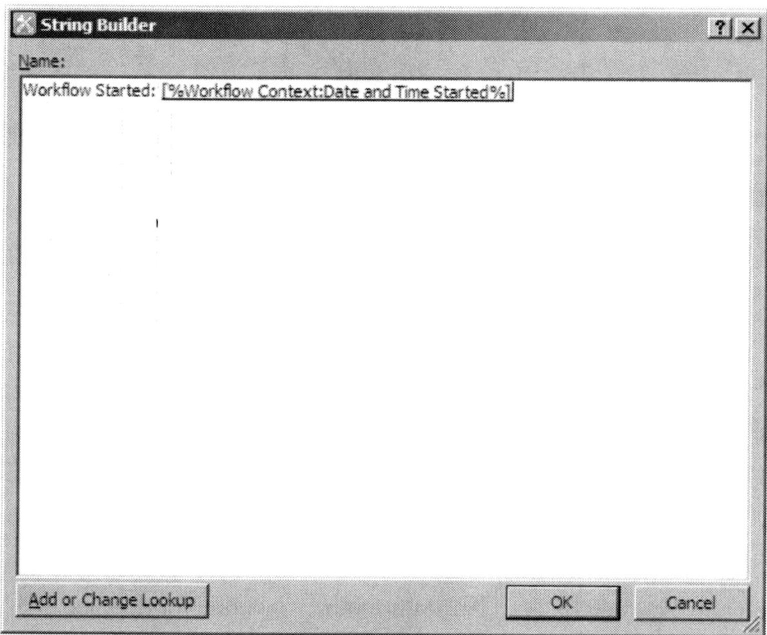

Figure 16–27. String Builder in SharePoint Designer

Instead of editing the properties of an activity by clicking the underlined parameters in the activity sentence, you can also select Advanced Properties from the ribbon to edit all the properties of an activity. For some activities, you will find additional parameters within the Properties windows, as shown in Figure 16–28. In this example, you can see that the action Log to History List shows additional parameters, whereas in the sentence shown earlier, you can only specify the text that should be logged.

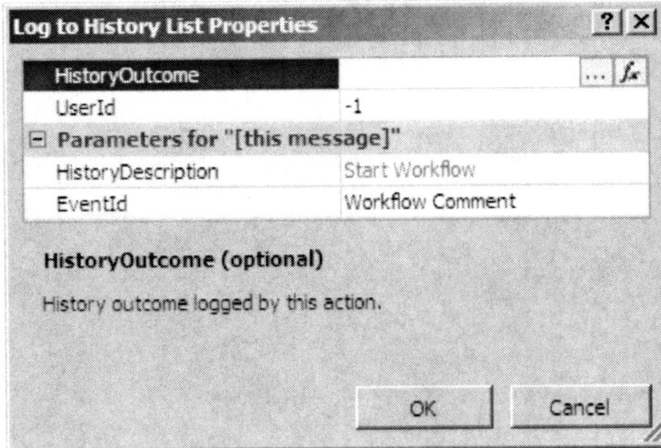

Figure 16–28. *Properties dialog for SharePoint Designer activities*

Actions and Conditions

SharePoint Designer offers a huge selection of actions that can be used to model elaborate declarative workflows. These actions are categorized according to their purpose and the items to which they apply. Table 16–3 lists all available actions and gives a short description for each of them.

Table 16–3. *Workflow Actions in SharePoint Designer 2010*

Category	Action Name	Platform	Description
Core	Add a comment	Foundation	Similar to Log to History List.
Core	Add Time to Date	Foundation	Adds a certain amount of time to a `DateTime` value.
Core	Do Calculation	Foundation	Calculates the result of a mathematical operation on two parameters. Supported operations: plus, minus, multiply by, divide by, and mod.
Core	Log to History List	Foundation	Logs a message to the History List.
Core	Pause for Duration	Foundation	Pauses workflow execution for the specified amount of time.
Core	Pause until Date	Foundation	Pauses workflow execution until the specified `DateTime` value is reached.

Category	Action Name	Platform	Description
Core	Send an Email	Foundation	Sends an e-mail to the specified users. The dialog for sending an e-mail allows specifying the recipients, the subject, and the e-mail body with rich-text capabilities.
Core	Set Time Portion of `DateTime` Field	Foundation	Sets the time value of a `DateTime` parameter.
Core	Set Workflow Status	Foundation	Sets the custom workflow status. Instead of In Progress, Complete, or Error Occurred, a custom value that better describes the workflow's state can be supplied.
Core	Set Workflow Variable	Foundation	Sets a workflow variable to the specified value. Depending on the type of the selected variable, different dialogs are available.
Core	Stop Workflow	Foundation	Stops the workflow and logs the specified error message to the History List.
Document Set	Capture a version of the Document Set	Server	Takes a snapshot of a document set specifying the versioning method.
Document Set	Send Document Set to Repository	Server	Submits a document set to the specified destination using the specified action.
Document Set	Set Content Approval Status for the Document Set	Server	Sets the content approval status for the document set.
Document Set	Start Document Set Approval Process	Server	Starts the approval process for the document set.
List	Add List Item Permissions	Foundation	Assigns permissions on the specified list item to the selected users. This action is only available in the impersonation step.
List	Check In Item	Foundation	Performs check in on an item in a document library. The item can be selected using the Choose List Item dialog.
List	Check Out Item	Foundation	Performs check out on an item in a document library. The item can be selected using the Choose List Item dialog.
List	Copy List Item	Foundation	Copies a list item from one list into another list.
List	Create List Item	Foundation	Creates a new list item in the specified list and allows you to set the field values for the new list item. The ID of the new list item is saved in a workflow variable.
List	Declare Record	Server	Declares the current item as a record for records management.

Category	Action Name	Platform	Description
List	Delete Item	Foundation	Deletes a list item in a specified list. You can specify the list item using a condition in the Choose List Item dialog.
List	Discard Check Out Item	Foundation	Discards a check out on an item in a document library. The list item can be selected using the Choose List Item dialog.
List	Inherit List Item Parent Permissions	Foundation	Inherits permissions from the selected list item. This action is only available in the impersonation step.
List	Remove List Item Permissions	Foundation	Removes permissions for the specified users from the selected list item. This action is only available in the impersonation step.
List	Replace List Item Permissions	Foundation	Replaces permissions for the specified users on the selected list item. This action is only available in the impersonation step.
List	Set Content Approval Status	Foundation	Sets the status of content approval on the current item to the specified value.
List	Set Field in Current Item	Foundation	Sets the specified field in the current list item to the specified value.
List	Undeclare Record	Server	Undeclares the current item as a record for records management.
List	Update List Item	Foundation	Updates a list item in a list with the specified values. You can choose any of the available lists and specify a condition to select the list item, as in the Choose List Item dialog. Subsequently, you can specify a value for each of the fields in the list.
List	Wait for Field Change in Current Item	Foundation	Waits until a condition on a field in the current item is met.
Relational	Lookup Manager of a User	Server	Returns the manager of the specified user from its profile.
Task	Assign a Form to a Group	Foundation	Creates a task with a survey form that will be assigned to a group of people. The values entered by the users will be stored in the task list. The workflow will wait for the task to complete before continuing execution.
Task	Assign a To-do Item	Foundation	Creates a to-do task that will be assigned to the specified users, and the workflow will wait for all tasks to complete before continuing execution.

Category	Action Name	Platform	Description
Task	Collect Data from a User	Foundation	Assigns a task with a custom form to a user. The form fields can be specified, and the values will be stored in the task item. The task ID will be returned to the workflow to allow referencing the task from the workflow. The workflow will wait for the task to complete before continuing execution.
Task	Start Approval Process	Server	Creates an approval task for all specified users on the specified item. The workflow waits for all approval tasks to be finished. Depending on the approval outcome, the workflow status is set accordingly.
Task	Start Custom Task Process	Server	Similar to the approval process, except that you can customize the behavior of the entire process. You can edit all available events and react to individual task events and overall process events.
Task	Start Feedback Process	Server	Similar to the approval process, except that instead of content approval, tasks are assigned to the specified users, and the workflow waits for them to be completed.
Utility	Extract Substring from End of String	Foundation	Copies the last characters of the specified string into a new string variable. The parameter length defines the number of characters to be copied from the end of the string.
Utility	Extract Substring from Index of String	Foundation	Copies a substring of a specified string into a new variable, starting at the specified index until the end of the string.
Utility	Extract Substring from Start of String	Foundation	Copies the first characters of a specified string into a new variable. The parameter length defines the number of characters that should be copied from the start of the string.
Utility	Extract Substring of String from Index with Length	Foundation	Copies a substring of a specified string into a new variable, starting at the specified index. The parameter length defines the number of characters that should be copied starting at the index.
Utility	Find Interval Between Dates	Foundation	Returns the interval between two `DateTime` values. You can select the scale in which the result should be returned to be minutes, hours, or days.

To control the flow of a workflow, several conditions are available that allow you to include decisions into your workflow based on `If-Else` statements. You can concatenate conditions using "and" and "or" statements by adding another condition directly underneath the `If` statement. Furthermore, you can use multiple `Else-If` branches, each containing conditions to be evaluated. Table 16–4 shows the available conditions in SharePoint Designer 2010.

Table 16–4. *Workflow Conditions in SharePoint Designer 2010*

Category	Condition Name	Description
Common	If any value equals value	Compares two values using one of the available operands. Each of the values can be specified using the lookup dialog.
Common	If current item field equals value	Similar to the condition "If any value equals value," except that for the first parameter only a field in the current item can be chosen.
Other	Check list item permission levels	Checks if the specified users have at least the specified permission level on the selected list item.
Other	Check list item permissions	Checks if the specified users have at least the specified permissions on the selected list item.
Other	Created by a specific person	Checks whether the current item was created by the specified person.
Other	Created in a specific date span	Checks whether the current item was created within the time span specified by two `DateTime` values.
Other	Modified by a specific person	Checks whether the current item was modified by the specified person.
Other	Modified in a specific date span	Checks whether the current item was modified within the time span specified by two `DateTime` values.
Other	Person is a valid SharePoint user	Checks whether the user identified by their username is a valid user within SharePoint.
Other	Title field contains keyword	Checks whether the field title in the current item contains the specified string as a substring.

All available actions and conditions are defined within the following files in the SharePoint folder under `TEMPLATE\1033\Workflow`:

- `WSS.ACTIONS`: This file contains all actions and conditions that are available in SharePoint Foundation. The name WSS stands for Windows SharePoint Services, which denoted the SharePoint Foundation functionality in previous SharePoint versions.
- `MOSS.ACTIONS`: This file contains all actions and conditions that are exclusively available to SharePoint Server installations.

Working with Steps and Branches

To structure your workflow, you can use different workflow steps. Each step can contain any number of actions and conditions. A step is displayed as a box with a gray border and has a name that can be changed. You can use steps to structure your workflow and make it comprehensible to others. Steps can be nested within other steps, offering useful flexibility in organizing your workflows. It is even possible to insert steps within `If-Else` branches. Actions and conditions can only be added within a step.

A step is implemented as a `SequenceActivity` in the resulting workflow. This WF activity is a container that executes all child activities in a forward direction until its last activity is finished. Since even the sequential workflow is itself derived from `SequenceActivity`, there is no difference in the execution of your workflow when adding extra steps. They are merely used for logical structuring.

One step is special in its execution behavior: the Impersonation Step. You can use this step like any other step. The difference is small yet very powerful—the activities inside this step will be executed with the permissions of the workflow author. Usually, every workflow is executed using the privileges of the user who started the workflow. This can be a significant limitation for workflow development, when the action to be executed depends on the user's permissions. The user starting the workflow needs access to the current list the workflow will be started on, but what if the workflow needs to write information into another list, on which the user has no permission to write? This is where the impersonation step can be used to overcome this issue. In previous SharePoint versions, this problem drastically limited the use of SharePoint Designer workflows.

Another option to organize your workflow is the use of parallel blocks. Whenever you want multiple actions to be executed simultaneously, you can employ a *parallel block*. Within the parallel block, you can specify actions, conditions, and steps that will be executed in parallel.

Working with Tasks

Tasks in a workflow handle user interaction with the workflow. Whenever you use an action related to a task in your workflow, the workflow execution will be paused until the task is completed by the assigned user. Within SharePoint Foundation, there are three task-related activities available: Assign a Form to a Group, Assign a To-do Item, and Collect Data from a User. For all these task activities, SharePoint Designer will automatically create a task form to display to the users. The information entered by users into the task forms is stored inside the task. The Collect Data from a User activity is especially designed to access this information from the workflow.

When you add this action to your workflow, a wizard is presented that lets you enter a name and description for that task. You can specify custom form fields for the user to fill in, as shown in Figure 16–29. You can define the field name, the data type, and the detailed settings depending on the data type, such as default values and constraints. The fields you enter in this dialog will be added as columns to the task list used by the workflow. When the workflow is published, SharePoint automatically creates a task form for that workflow. This form will be displayed to the user when they edit the task item.

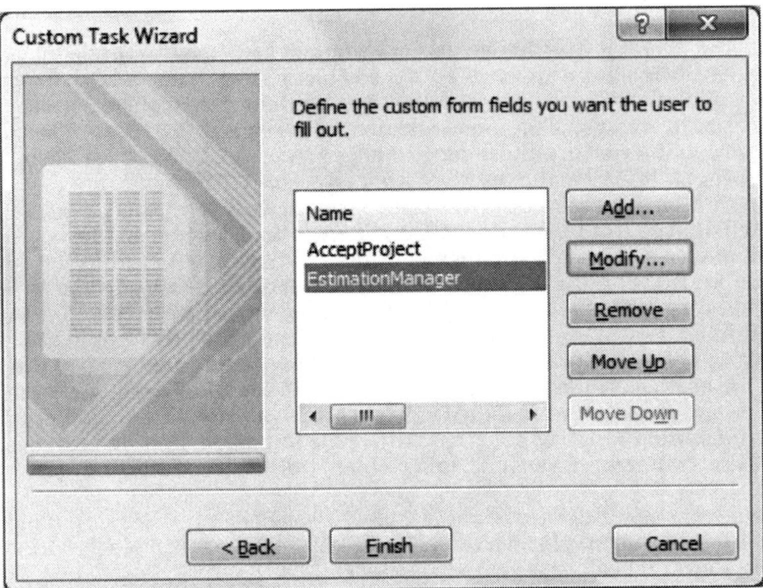

Figure 16–29. Custom Task Wizard

To access the information that was entered by the users, the activity defines an output variable of type TaskId, which stores the list item ID of the task into a workflow variable. Using this ID, you can access the task item in your workflow that was edited by the user and access the fields, which were completed in the task form. To accomplish this, use a lookup within an action, for example Set Workflow Variable, and specify the Task List for your workflow as the data source and the field that was entered through the task form, as shown in Figure 16–30.

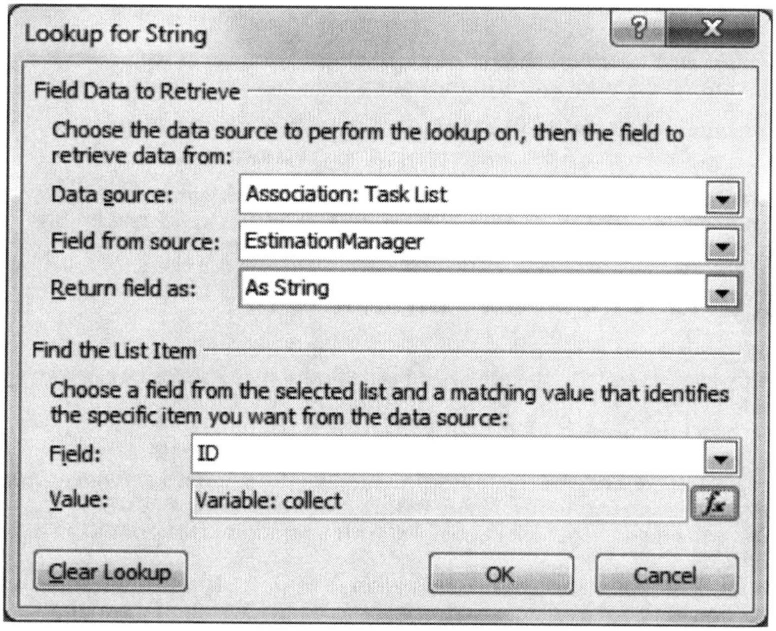

***Figure 16–30.** Lookup results of a custom task*

To identify the correct item in the task list, you need to specify the Find the List Item setting properly. Select ID as the field that is used for comparison, and set the value to the workflow property containing the result of the task action (which is "collect" in the previous example). Now the lookup will select the task item that has the ID of the task that was created by the workflow and returns the selected field value.

You can use this procedure to access any list item or item in a library and select the desired field using the Lookup dialog. All you need is the ID of the list item. Of course, you can also specify any other field value combination to select list items.

■ **Note** When you specify field value combinations that do not return a single list item, the first list item that matches the condition will be returned. Unfortunately, you can only specify one field for comparison, and there is no option for advanced queries on the list.

Source Files of SharePoint Designer Workflows

As mentioned earlier, SharePoint Designer workflows are declarative workflows that are compiled at runtime. These workflows consist of the following files:

- *Workflow markup file .xoml*: Contains the declarative description of the workflow

- *Workflow rules file .rules*: Contains the rules that are used for conditions in the workflow
- *Workflow configuration file .xml*: Contains general workflow configuration as well as the content types that are used for the forms in the workflow.
- *Forms for association, initiation, and tasks*: Either InfoPath or ASPX forms used in the workflow

You can access these files via the All Files section in the SharePoint Designer navigation and then select Workflows. These files can be saved to a local disk using the Export File button in the ribbon bar.

Developing Custom Activities for SharePoint Designer

SharePoint Designer 2010 offers a variety of actions and conditions to develop custom workflows to meet the business requirements. However, even with the advanced workflow activities in SharePoint Server, there will be requirements that cannot be implemented with the standard activities that are shipped with SharePoint. Whenever you encounter limitations in SharePoint Designer workflows, you have two options: either switch to Visual Studio to develop your workflow using code, or develop a custom activity for SharePoint Designer to enhance the facilities provided by the standard activities with your own activities. Both scenarios will require you to use Visual Studio, but by building a custom activity for SharePoint Designer, you will enable other users working with SharePoint Designer to also use this functionality for their workflows.

To construct custom activities for SharePoint Designer, you need to develop a Visual Studio solution that implements a workflow activity and makes it available to the SharePoint environment through configuration files. Breaking it down further, the following steps are required:

1. Create a Visual Studio solution based on the SharePoint 2010 Empty Project template.
2. Add a project using the Workflow Activity Library template to the solution.
3. Implement a class that is derived from `System.Worfklow.ComponentModel.Activity` containing the business logic for your custom action.
4. Describe the workflow behavior for SharePoint Designer within an `.ACTIONS` file.
5. Configure settings in the `web.config` file for your web application.

Throughout the following subsections, these steps will be described in greater detail while developing a small yet useful example: a custom action will be built to select a list item based on a CAML query. The action will require, as input parameters, a SharePoint list—which can be selected from the available lists—and a CAML-based query string. It will return the ID of the first item in the specified list that matches the CAML query. The example shows how you can pass parameters to and from the custom action and how to access the context of a SharePoint Designer workflow. Of course, you will also learn how to develop an activity class containing the business logic of the workflow.

Setting Up the Visual Studio Solution

Before you can implement your custom action using .NET code, you first have to set up your solution. Select the SharePoint 2010 Empty Project template as the basis for a new solution. This project will be used to deploy all the necessary files and configurations to the SharePoint environment. Add another

project to the solution by selecting the Workflow Activity Library template from the Workflows category. This template is not specific to SharePoint workflow development and can also be used to develop reusable activities for WF workflows.
The WF project will contain the code for the custom activity and will be compiled into an assembly. Since the assembly needs to be registered in the GAC, you need to supply a strong name key file to sign the assembly. Add references to the following assemblies to your workflow project:

- `Microsoft.SharePoint.dll`: Required to work with the SharePoint object model
- `Microsoft.SharePoint.WorkflowActions.dll`: Will be used to access the `WorkflowContext` of the SharePoint Designer workflows

To deploy the solution to SharePoint, add a feature to the empty SharePoint project with its scope set to Web Application. This scope is required, because the feature needs to edit the `web.config` for the web application. In addition, the assembly that will be created by the workflow project needs to be added to the `<SafeControl>` section of the `web.config` file. You can do this by editing the properties of the package in the SharePoint project.

An additional file with the extension `.actions` needs to be deployed to the folder `TEMPLATE/1033/Worfklow` below the SharePoint 12 hive. This file is used by SharePoint Designer to gather all the relevant information about the custom action. (There are more details about this file later in this section.) To include the file, add a SharePoint-mapped folder to the SharePoint project, and select the target path for the file. Any subfolders created by Visual Studio can be removed. The `.actions` file will later be put into this mapped folder, which will cause this file to be deployed to the desired path during deployment.

Figure 16–31 illustrates the solution structure, and you can see all the relevant elements required for a custom action.

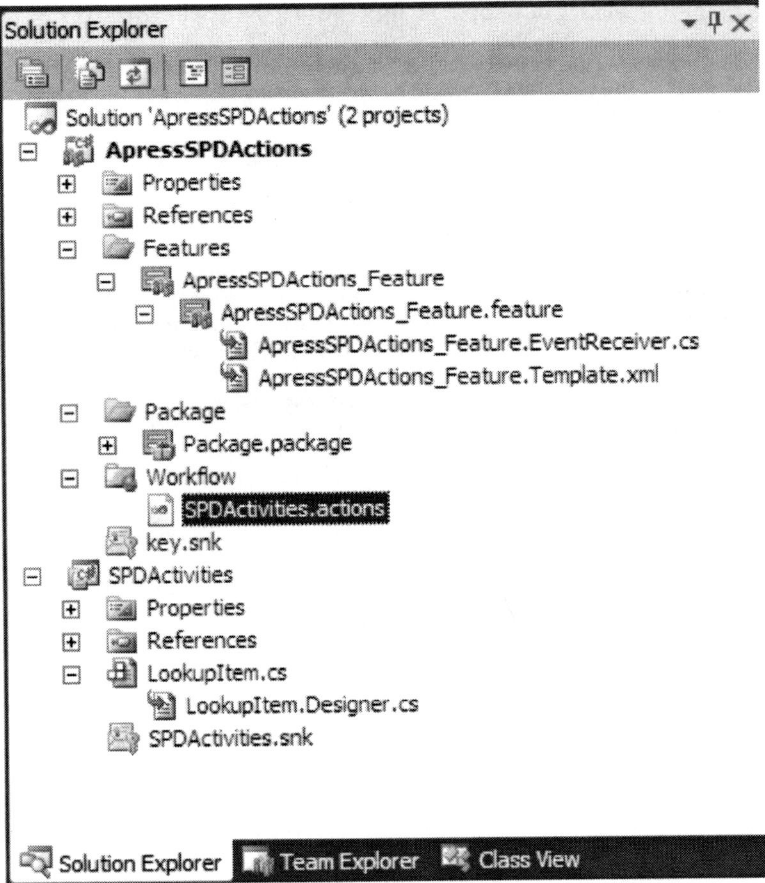

Figure 16–31. *Solution for creating a Custom SharePoint designer action*

To sum up, these are the essential steps for creating a solution:

1. Create a Visual Studio solution based on a SharePoint Empty Project template.
    a. Add a feature to the project with web application scope.
    b. Add the assembly of the workflow project to the safe controls in the package.
    c. Add a SharePoint-mapped folder for the actions file.
2. Add a solution based on the Workflow Activity Library template.
    a. Add a strong name key file.
    b. Add references to the `Microsoft.SharePoint` assembly and the `Microsoft.SharePoint.WorkflowActions`.

Implementing the Activity Class

After the project has been set up, you can begin implementing the custom activity in the Workflow Library project.

In general, the following steps are important for implementing a custom activity class:

1. Create a class that is derived from `System.Workflow.ComponentModel.Activity`.
2. Define class properties.
3. Register class properties as dependency properties.
4. Implement the `Execute` method.

First add a new Activity to your project, and switch to the code view of the activity. Listing 16–1 contains the code for the example activity. (A detailed explanation follows, later.)

The namespaces `Microsoft.SharePoint` and `Microsoft.SharePoint.WorkflowActions` should be included via suitable `using` statements to work with the SharePoint object model and to use the workflow context. The class can be implemented as a subclass of `System.Workflow.ComponentModel.Activity`. The `Activity` class already defines and handles the required events for interacting with the workflow. You only need to define the properties for your workflow activity and override the `Execute` method to define your business logic for this activity.

To access properties from the workflow environment, the `DependencyProperty` object must be used. In the Custom Workflows with Visual Studio section, dependency properties will be described in more detail. The `DependencyProperty` allows loose coupling between workflow activities and the workflow instances. Workflows store their properties in a dictionary, which can be accessed by the activities via dependency properties. The workflow runtime engine makes these properties available to all activities and manages all dependency properties from the activities within a workflow. To register a `DependencyProperty` with the workflow, you first have to define a static variable in your class of type `DependencyProperty`. Then you can call the static `Register` method on `DependencyProperty`, providing a name for the property, the type of the property, and the type of the activity class, and assign the result to your variable.

```
public static DependencyProperty ListIdProperty = DependencyProperty.Register(
                                "ListId", typeof(string), typeof(LookupItem));
```

Once the dependency property is registered, you can add a property to your class with the name that was registered with the dependency property earlier. This property is defined like any other property, except that instead of storing the value to a local variable, the getter and setter method will use the dependency property to access the value. The `GetValue` and `SetValue` methods are inherited from `DependencyObject` and can be accessed using the base keyword. Both methods require the `DependencyProperty` as a parameter and will store a new value or retrieve the current value from the dependency property in the workflow instance.

```
[BrowsableAttribute(true)]
[DesignerSerializationVisibilityAttribute( DesignerSerializationVisibility.Visible)]
[ValidationOption(ValidationOption.Required)]
public string ListId
{
    get
    {
        return (string)base.GetValue(LookupItem.ListIdProperty);
    }
    set
    {
        base.SetValue(LookupItem.ListIdProperty, value);
```

```
    }
}
```

The properties exposed as dependency properties can be made available to SharePoint Designer as parameters for the workflow action.

All the properties in the example are built in the same way, though one property requires special attention: `__Context`. This property holds an object of type `WorkflowContext`, containing useful information about the context in which the workflow is running. This includes the current item on which the workflow was started and information about the workflow instance such as the `WorkflowInstanceId` or the `StartedDateTime`. SharePoint sets several parameters during workflow activation, and some of them are exposed by the SharePoint Designer workflow environment, like `__Context`. These parameters are automatically set to a certain value and are available to every workflow. You simply specify a property with the correct name and bind it correctly to the workflow using the `.actions` file. The parameters shown in Table 16–5 are made available.

Table 16–5. *Properties That Are Available to All Custom Workflow Actions*

Property	Type	Description
`__Context`	`Microsoft.SharePoint.WorkflowActions.WorkflowContext`	Contains information about the workflow instance and useful helper methods
`__ListId`	`System.String`	The GUID (as a String) of the list on which the workflow has been started
`__ListItem`	`System.Int32`	The ID within the list, of the item on which the workflow has been started
`__ActivationProperties`	`Microsoft.SharePoint.Workflow.SPWorkflowActivationProperties`	

With the dependency properties implemented, it is time to write the business logic of the Action. Override the `Execute` method of the `Activity` class. This method is called by the workflow runtime environment when the activity is executed. Within the `Execute` method, you can access the properties of the action and create your own business logic. At the end of the `Execute` method, you need to return the appropriate `ActivityExecutionStatus`. This status can take several values throughout the life cycle of an activity. For the `Execute` method in custom SharePoint Designer actions, the status `Closed` should be used. It indicates that the activity has finished as expected.

Listing 16–1. *Implementing a Custom SharePoint Designer Action*

```
using System;
using System.ComponentModel;
using System.Workflow.ComponentModel;
using System.Workflow.ComponentModel.Compiler;
using Microsoft.SharePoint;
using Microsoft.SharePoint.WorkflowActions;

namespace Apress.SP2010.Workflows.SPDActivities
{
```

```
public partial class LookupItem : Activity
{
    public LookupItem()
    {
        InitializeComponent();
    }

    // Bind Dependency Properties
    public static DependencyProperty __ContextProperty =
           DependencyProperty.Register("__Context",
           typeof(WorkflowContext), typeof(LookupItem));
    public static DependencyProperty ListIdProperty =
           DependencyProperty.Register("ListId", typeof(string),
           typeof(LookupItem));
    private static DependencyProperty SearchQueryProperty =
           DependencyProperty .Register("SearchQuery", typeof(string),
           typeof(LookupItem));
    public static DependencyProperty ResultItemIdProperty =
           DependencyProperty.Register("ResultItemId", typeof(int),
           typeof(LookupItem));

   [BrowsableAttribute(true)]
   [DesignerSerializationVisibilityAttribute(
                                 DesignerSerializationVisibility.Visible)]
   [ValidationOption(ValidationOption.Required)]
   public string ListId
   {
       get
       {
           return (string)base.GetValue(LookupItem.ListIdProperty);
       }
       set
       {
           base.SetValue(LookupItem. ListIdProperty, value);
       }
   }

   [BrowsableAttribute(true)]
   [DesignerSerializationVisibilityAttribute(
                                 DesignerSerializationVisibility.Visible)]
   [ValidationOption(ValidationOption.Required)]
   public string SearchQuery
   {
       get
       {
           return (string)base.GetValue(LookupItem.SearchQueryProperty);
       }
       set
       {
           base.SetValue(LookupItem.SearchQueryProperty, value);
       }
   }
```

```
[BrowsableAttribute(true)]
[DesignerSerializationVisibilityAttribute(
                                DesignerSerializationVisibility.Visible)]
[ValidationOption(ValidationOption.Required)]
public int ResultItemId
{
    get
    {
        return (int)base.GetValue(LookupItem.ResultItemIdProperty);
    }
    set
    {
        base.SetValue(LookupItem.ResultItemIdProperty, value);
    }
}

[ValidationOption(ValidationOption.Required)]
public WorkflowContext __Context
{
    get
    {
        return (WorkflowContext)base.GetValue(
                                    LookupItem.__ContextProperty);
    }
    set
    {
        base.SetValue(LookupItem.__ContextProperty, value);
    }
}

 // Override the Execute method of the Activity
 protected override ActivityExecutionStatus Execute(
                              ActivityExecutionContext executionContext)
 {
     // Retrieve the listGuid using a Helper class in the WorkflowActions
     // namespace
     Guid listGuid = Helper.GetListGuid(this.__Context, this.ListId);
     if ((this.__Context != null))
     {
         SPWeb web = this.__Context.Web;
         if (null != web)
         {
             SPList list = web.Lists[listGuid];
             SPQuery query = new SPQuery();
             query.Query = this.SearchQuery;
             SPListItemCollection items = list.GetItems(query);
             if (items.Count > 0)
             {
                 ResultItemId = items[0].ID;
             }
         }
```

```
            }
            return ActivityExecutionStatus.Closed;
        }
    }
}
```

In the example in Listing 16–1, the Execute method runs a CAML query on the list to be searched. The ListId property is used to get access to the list that is selected in SharePoint Designer from the available lists. The __Context property provides access to the current web object. After the CAML query is processed, the first record of the query response is used to assign the ResultItemId parameter.

Describing a SharePoint Designer Action in the .ACTIONS File

After the class has been implemented, there are further things to do in order to use the new Action in SharePoint Designer. You need to inform SharePoint about the new action and link the parameters in SharePoint Designer to the properties in the Activity class.

Workflow activities are defined in a special XML file, with the file extension of .ACTIONS. We mentioned previously the WSS.ACTIONS and MOSS.ACTIONS files in the SharePoint subfolder 14\TEMPLATE\1033\Workflow, which describe the available actions and conditions for SharePoint Designer in SharePoint Foundation and SharePoint Server. SharePoint Designer parses this folder and reads all the files with the .ACTIONS extension to gather the available actions and conditions for the workflow designer.

Additional actions can be exposed to SharePoint Designer either by adding the relevant information into one of the existing files or by inserting your own .ACTIONS file to the folder. However, it is best practice to add a separate .ACTIONS file to the folder to avoid changes to the standard SharePoint functionality and to keep the system maintainable.

Listing 16–2 shows an example of an .ACTIONS file. The root element is defined as <WorkflowInfo>, which can enclose <Actions> and <Conditions> elements (along with some rather specific elements, which are used in the WSS.ACTIONS file). The two attributes, Sequential and Parallel, of the <Actions> element define the word that will precede the sentence whenever the custom action is placed in a parallel or sequential step. To add a custom action, an <Action> element needs to be inserted inside the <Actions> element.

The <Action> element requires the Name of the action, the full name of the Assembly, and the ClassName of the custom activity. Further, a Category can be specified that defines under which category in the Action ribbon this action will be listed. If a new name is supplied, a new category will be added.

Listing 16–2. *Describing Custom Activities in the .ACTIONS File*

```
<?xml version="1.0" encoding="utf-8" ?>
<WorkflowInfo>
  <Actions Sequential="then" Parallel="and">
    <Action Name="Lookup Item By Title"
      ClassName=" Apress.SP2010.Workflows.SPDActivities.LookupItem"
      Assembly="SPDActivities, Version=1.0.0.0, Culture=neutral,
                PublicKeyToken=07ca925dce31cf11"
      AppliesTo="all"
      Category="List Actions">
      <RuleDesigner Sentence="Find item in %1 with Query %2 (Output to %3)">
        <FieldBind Field="ListId" Text="this list" Id="1"
                   DesignerType="ListNames" />
        <FieldBind Field="SearchQuery" Text="CAML" Id="2"
                   DesignerType="StringBuilder" />
```

```
        <FieldBind Field="ResultItemId"
                   DesignerType="ParameterNames" Text="result" Id="3"/>
      </RuleDesigner>
      <Parameters>
        <Parameter Name="__Context"
                   Type="Microsoft.SharePoint.WorkflowActions.WorkflowContext"
                   Direction="In" DesignerType="Hide" />
        <Parameter Name="ListId"
                   Type="System.String, mscorlib"
                   Direction="In"
                   Description="Canonical form of the list GUID
                                used by this action." />
        <Parameter Name="SearchQuery" Type="System.String, mscorlib"
                   Direction="In"
                   Description="Used to search for an item using CAML." />
        <Parameter Name="ResultItemId"
                   Type="System.Int32, mscorlib"
                   Direction="Out"
                   Description="ID of first item matching the search." />
      </Parameters>
    </Action>
  </Actions>
</WorkflowInfo>
```

The <RuleDesigner> element contains information necessary to render the declarative sentence that is used to describe and configure the action in SharePoint Designer. The mandatory attribute Sentence holds the text that is displayed in the workflow editor within the workflow declaration. This string can contain any number of dynamic variables, which are denoted with %1, %2, and so forth. They behave similarly to the dynamic placeholders you use with String.Format. Figure 16–32 displays the sentence that is created according to the specification in the previously shown .ACTIONS file.

Step 1

Find item in this list with Query CAML (Output to Variable: result6)

Figure 16–32. *Sentence in workflow editor for the example activity*

To substitute the placeholders with dynamic values during workflow runtime, the element <RuleDesigner> can hold any number of <FieldBind> elements as children. Each <FieldBind> element describes one of the variables that were defined in the Sentence of the RuleDesigner. They are associated using the Id attribute of <FieldBind>, which is connected to the corresponding variable in the Sentence. For example, the FieldBind element with Id="1" is bound to the variable %1 in the Sentence.

The <FieldBind> element also requires the attribute Text to be set. This is the text that is displayed as a link in the sentence within workflow designer. More importantly, the Field attribute references a <Parameter> element, which defines input and output parameters to the custom activity.

Another important attribute of the <FieldBind> element is DesignerType. This defines the control that will be presented to the user in the workflow editor of SharePoint Designer. Table 16–6 lists the different designer types that are available and gives a short description of each. If no DesignerType attribute is provided, a text box will be displayed by default.

Table 16–6. Different Designer Types

DesignerType	Description
AddPermission	An advanced control that lets you choose a permission to be assigned to users.
Bool	Drop-down box with `true` and `false` options.
ChooseDoclibItem	Selector for a document library.
ChooseListItem	The default list item selector.
CreateListItem	An advanced control that allows you to select a list and specify the properties to set, when creating a new list item.
Date	Selector for a date/time value.
Dependent	This control is rendered depending on the type of another field. Use the `TypeFrom` attribute to specify the field that will provide the type.
DropDown	A custom drop-down list box control. You can add entries using `<Option>` elements as child elements of `<FieldBind>`.
Email	An advanced control that lets you specify standard e-mail fields, such as To, From, CC, Subject, and Body.
FieldNames	A drop-down list box control with all the field names of the current list or library.
Float	A text box that accepts floating point values.
Hyperlink	A URL browser that builds a link by selecting a local or remote resource.
Integer	A text box that allows positive integer values.
ListNames	A drop-down list box control with all the available lists in the current web.
Operator	Performs an operation on the left and right operands.
ParameterNames	A drop-down list box control with all workflow variables.
Person	A selector for a user or group from the built-in local or domain users and groups.
RemovePermission	An advanced control that lets you select the permission that should be removed.
ReplacePermission	An advanced control that lets you choose the permission that should be replaced.

DesignerType	Description
SinglePerson	A selector for one user or group from the built-in local or domain users and groups.
StatusDropdown	A drop-down list box to select the status of the workflow.
Stringbuilder	A text box to create simple strings.
Survey	Creates a custom workflow task form for user input using a wizard.
Text	The default input text box.
TextBox	The default input text box.
TextArea	The default input text box.
UpdateListItem	An advanced control to select the list item to update and the parameters to set.
WritableFieldNames	A drop-down list box control with all the field names of the current list or library that are editable.

To connect fields that are configured in the workflow editor and are populated with concrete values during workflow execution to the `Activity` class, `<Parameter>` elements are used. They are defined in the `<Parameters>` container following the `<RuleDesigner>` element. Each `<Parameter>` describes a parameter for the rule sentence and references a `DependencyProperty` that is defined in the `Activity` class. The `Name` attribute specifies the name of the dependency property and must exactly match to the name that was used in the `Register` method in the code. The `Type` attribute defines the data type of that parameter and the `Description` can be used to further describe the parameter.

The attribute `Direction` indicates whether a parameter is used as an input or output parameter for the activity class. Specifying `Direction="In"` will cause the runtime to set the value for the corresponding `DependencyProperty`. Conversely, `Direction="Out"` will return the value to the workflow runtime after the activity has completed.

Configuring custom activities for the workflow editor in SharePoint Designer involves the following actions:

1. Create an `.ACTIONS` file in the SharePoint folder …`\14\TEMPLATE\1033\Workflow`.
2. Add an `<Action>` element that specifies the `Class` and `Assembly` for the implementation of the custom activity.
3. Define the `<RuleDesigner>`, and specify the sentence and the dynamic variables.
4. Supply the `<Parameters>` that map the properties from the workflow designer to the assembly code.

■ **Tip** An XML schema definition for some of the elements that are used in the `.ACTIONS` file can be found in the file `WorkflowActions.xsd`, which is located in the SharePoint folder …`\14\TEMPLATE\XML`.

Applying Settings to the Configuration

After the solution has been set up, the custom action has been implemented, and declarations for the workflow editor have been made, there is only one outstanding task: allow the assembly to be used as a custom activity in SharePoint. Because of security constraints, only custom activities with permission to be called as custom activities can be used. To allow your custom activity to be used in SharePoint Designer, you need to add an entry to the web.config file of your web application.

In the web.config file, the element <authorizedTypes> specified by the XPath expression configuration/System.Workflow.ComponentModel.WorkflowCompiler contains a list of <authorizedType> elements. Each defines one type, together with an assembly, that is allowed to be used in workflows. Besides the Assembly, the Namespace and the TypeName must also be supplied. Either the TypeName contains a class name or it can be set to * to authorize all classes within the namespace.

To make the required changes to the configuration, use a feature that is set to the web application scope. Within the SPFeatureReceiver event, these changes can be made during feature activation via the FeatureActivated event. Listing 16–3 shows how these changes can be made to the web.config file for the web application. The SPFeatureReceiver will add this string to the configuration:

```
<authorizedType Assembly="SPDActivities, Version=1.0.0.0, Culture=neutral,
PublicKeyToken=07ca925dce31cf11" Namespace="SPDActivities" TypeName="*" Authorized="True" />
```

Listing 16–3. *Applying Required Settings in web.config Using a FeatureReceiver*

```
[Guid("e72495ca-9fdf-4d9b-8bf4-99df050b577d")]
public class ApressSPDActions_FeatureEventReceiver : SPFeatureReceiver
{
    public override void FeatureActivated(SPFeatureReceiverProperties properties)
    {
        // Get current web application.
        SPWebApplication wappCurrent = (SPWebApplication)properties.Feature.Parent;

        // Create a configuration object and set the parameters as required.
        SPWebConfigModification modAuthorizedType = new SPWebConfigModification();
        modAuthorizedType.Name = "AuthType";
        modAuthorizedType.Owner = "SPDActivities";
        modAuthorizedType.Path = "configuration/System.Workflow.ComponentModel.
                                  WorkflowCompiler/authorizedTypes";
        modAuthorizedType.Type = SPWebConfigModification.
                                 SPWebConfigModificationType.EnsureChildNode;
        modAuthorizedType.Value = "<authorizedType Assembly=\"SPDActivities, " +
        "Version=1.0.0.0, Culture=neutral, PublicKeyToken=07ca925dce31cf11\" " +
        "Namespace=\"SPDActivities\" TypeName=\"*\" Authorized=\"True\" />";

        // Perform the modification to the web.config file.
        wappCurrent.WebConfigModifications.Add(modAuthorizedType);
        wappCurrent.WebService.ApplyWebConfigModifications();
    }
}
```

Custom Workflows with Visual Studio

One of the most advanced tasks in SharePoint workflow development is creating custom workflows using Visual Studio. Whenever your requirements exceed the capabilities of SharePoint Designer or when you want to include your workflow as a part of a complex solution, you will need to deal with custom workflows. With Visual Studio 2010, the support for SharePoint workflow development has improved, and thus tackling custom workflows is easier than ever. For anyone familiar with .NET development, this approach provides the largest amount of freedom in workflow development.

This section begins by describing various primary Workflow Foundation building blocks that you need to grasp to develop SharePoint workflows. These include the fundamental WF classes that are also used in SharePoint. We examine the SharePoint workflow object model and explain in detail how to develop custom workflows using Visual Studio. Further, we will show how to develop custom ASPX forms that are used in workflows and how to use InfoPath forms as workflow forms.

Understanding Workflow Foundation

Earlier in this chapter we introduced some of the basic concepts of WF—activities are the basic building blocks—and described the two basic workflow types: sequential and state machine. This section aims for a more detailed understanding about the object model of WF and about some advanced concepts that are essential for workflow development.

Since this book is not about Workflow Foundation, the coverage of the WF object model is broad and concentrates on the most important objects for working with SharePoint workflows. For WF, the `System` namespace was extended with the `Workflow` namespace. This namespace consists of three namespaces each contained in a separate library with the matching name. Table 16–7 introduces these namespaces.

Table 16–7. *System.Workflow Namespaces*

Namespace	Description
`System.Workflow.ComponentModel`	This namespace contains all the base classes, interfaces, and constructs that are used to create workflow activities and workflows. It contains the `Activity`, t is the base class for all workflow activities. In addition, this namespace contains other basic activities, such as the `CompositeActivity`, which is the base class for all activities that can contain other activities.
`System.Workflow.Activities`	This namespace contains the implementation of extended activities that can be used in a workflow. You will find activities that are derived from `Activity` and `CompositeActivity`, including `CodeActivity` and `DelayActivity`.
`System.Workflow.Runtime`	This namespace contains classes and interfaces that control the workflow runtime engine and workflow instances.

WF Activities and Their Facets

Workflows are constructed from different activities. All those activities share a common base class: `System.Workflow.ComponentModel.Activity`. The `Activity` class is a subclass of `DependencyObject`, which is an abstract base class for all objects that use `DependencyProperties`. Figure 16–33 shows many of the basic activities in the workflow namespace and their relationships.

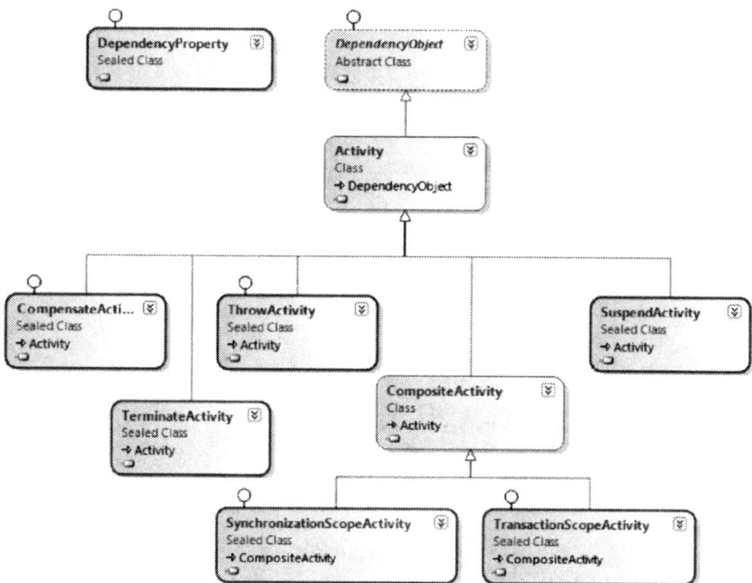

***Figure 16–33.** Basic activities in WF*

An `Activity` defines properties for storing information about the runtime environment, such as the `WorkflowInstanceId`. In addition, an `Activity` defines methods that will be called by the runtime environment and that can be overridden in a derived class to provide custom behavior for an `Activity`. They are as follows:

- `Cancel`: Called to cancel the execution of the current activity instance.
- `Execute`: Contains the execution logic of an activity. It will be called by the runtime to execute the activity. For custom activities, this is the most important method to override.
- `HandleFault`: Called when an error is raised during execution of this activity. The default implementation simply calls the `Cancel` method.

These methods return the `ActivityExecutionStatus` indicating the current state of the activity in the workflow instance. It can take any of the following values—this list illustrates the life cycle of an activity:

- Initialized
- Executing
- Canceling
- Closed
- Compensating
- Faulting

Activities can also be enhanced with additional components that define a specific behavior component. This can be a validator, a serializer, a code generator, or a designer. Such components are attached to an activity using attributes. For example, you can add a custom designer for an activity by implementing a custom class that inherits from System.Workflow.ComponentModel.Design.ActivityDesigner. You can attach this designer to an activity via the following attribute:

```
[System.ComponentModel.Designer(typeof(MyCustomDesigner),
typeof(System.ComponentModel.Design.IDesigner))]
Public partial class MyActivity : Activity
{
}
```

Both namespaces, System.Workflow.ComponentModel and especially System.Workflow.Activities, define a number of different activities offering common workflow behavior. These activities can be used by any workflow, including, of course, by SharePoint workflows. Table 16–8 lists all the activities that are available through the toolbox in the WF 3.0 and WF 3.5 sections, respectively.

Table 16–8. *Available WF Activities in Visual Studio Workflow Designer*

Activity Name	Workflow Type	Description
CallExternalMethod	Both	Calls a method through a local service. You must specify the interface type and the method that should be invoked. Depending on the selected method, you can specify several other properties.
Code	Both	Synchronously executes a method in the code-beside class. Thus, this activity should not depend on external resources. This activity allows you to write custom code.
Compensate	Both	To handle failure and rollback activities that were already completed when an error occurs, you can use the Compensate activity. It can be used only with the CompensatableTransactionScopeActivity and the CompensatableSequenceActivity.
CompensatableSequence	Both	A Sequence activity that allows compensation using the Compensate activity.
ConditionedActivityGroup	Both	This activity allows conditional execution of a collection of child activities. You can specify an Until condition for the group, which specifies the condition under which the execution of the group of activities stops. Each child activity can also specify a When condition to decide whether the activity should be scheduled for execution.
Delay	Both	Pauses workflow execution for the specified amount of time.
EventDriven	Both	A CompositeActivity that allows event-driven execution of its child controls. This activity waits for the specified event to occur, before execution is continued. You must specify an activity of type IEventActivity as the first child activity.

Activity Name	Workflow Type	Description
EventHandlingScope	Both	This CompositeActivity enables event handling during the execution of its child activities, similar to a try statement.
FaultHandler	Both	Similar to a catch statement, this activity handles exceptions of the type specified in the FaultType property.
HandleExternalEvent	Both	This activity handles an external event that is raised by a local service. The activity blocks the execution of the workflow until the event occurs.
IfElse	Both	Similar to an if ... else statement, you specify the conditions to be evaluated, and depending on the result, the execution flow is directed to one or other of the IfElseBranch activities. Each branch can contain multiple activities.
InvokeWebService	Both	You can use this activity to invoke a web service.
InvokeWorkflow	Both	This activity asynchronously calls another workflow.
Listen	Both	This CompositeActivity contains multiple branches, each containing several activities derived from EventDrivenActivity. The activity waits for any of the several events to occur, before continuing execution.
Parallel	Both	This CompositeActivity allows you to execute several sequences of activities independently from each other at the same time. Two or more branches can be added to this activity, each containing a sequence activity. Since the workflow is running within a single thread, this does not allow for true multithreading.
Policy	Both	Using the Rule Set Editor, this activity allows you to add a set of separate business rules to the workflow.
Replicator	Both	This activity creates multiple instances of the activity that is specified as the child activity. As in a foreach statement, you can instantiate a variable number of child activities based on a condition.
Sequence	Both	This CompositeActivity executes its child activities in the specified order.
SetState	State machine	Sets the next state in a state-machine workflow for the transition to the next StateActivity.
State	State machine	This activity represents a state in a state-machine workflow.
StateInitialization	State machine	This SequenceActivity contains child activities that are executed when the workflow state starts running.
StateFinalization	State machine	This SequenceActivity contains child activities that are executed before the workflow transitions to another state.

Activity Name	Workflow Type	Description
Suspend	Both	Suspends the current workflow instance and saves all the state information of the workflow, which will be loaded again when the workflow continues.
SynchronizationScope	Both	This CompositeActivity is granted exclusive access to shared resources in the workflow. Whenever two or more instances try to access the same variable, the runtime uses locking mechanisms to guarantee exclusive access to these resources.
Terminate	Both	This activity terminates the execution of the workflow instance. Terminated instances cannot be resumed.
Throw	Both	Similar to the throw statement in .NET, this activity allows you to throw an exception.
TransactionScope	Both	This CompositeActivity allows you to place activities inside a transaction. When the activity begins, a new transaction is started. When the activity is closed successfully, the transaction is committed. Otherwise, you can roll back the activities.
CompensatableTransactionScope	Both	This CompositeActivity is a compensatable version of the TransactionScopeActivity. You can use the CompensateActivity to perform compensation of an already committed transaction.
WebServiceInput	Both	Receives data from a web service.
WebServiceOutput	Both	Sends data to a web service as a response to a corresponding WebServiceInput activity.
WebServiceFault	Both	Sends an error to the web service as a response to a corresponding WebServiceInput activity.
ReceiveActivity	Both	This SequenceActivity implements a WCF service operation by implementing a WCF service contract.
SendActivity	Both	This activity synchronously calls a WCF service operation and waits for the result or an error before workflow execution continues.

This list of activities should summarize the capabilities and the application of each of the activities. If you need more detailed information on any of these activities, please refer to the MSDN online documentation.

Dependency Properties and Activity Binding

Dependency properties were mentioned earlier regarding SharePoint Designer workflows. We touched on using a DependencyProperty to share properties among different activities. To reiterate, dependency properties allow loose coupling of properties in a workflow, because the other properties do not need to know about the concrete object and can instead get the required properties from the workflow runtime.

These properties are stored in a dictionary that is maintained by the workflow, and the propagation of the value of a DependencyProperty is managed by the workflow.

When an Activity is developed, properties can be exposed to the workflow using a DependencyProperty. But how can they be consumed and used by another Activity? The answer is simply by accessing the property of the activity like any other property. But there is more to it. You can use the ActivityBind class to bind the property of one activity to the property of another activity. Since even the workflow itself is derived from Activity, this concept can be used throughout the workflow. ActivityBind creates a connection between two properties using the Name and Path members. The Name specifies the activity, and the Path represents the member to bind to. The following snippet shows an example of how to bind the property sourceProperty of the activity SourceActivity to MyActivityProperty in myActivity:

```
using System.Workflow.ComponentModel;

ActivityBind activitybind1 = new ActivityBind();
activitybind1.Name = "SourceActivity";
activitybind1.Path = "sourceProperty";
// Call the SetBinding method on the object and pass the static DependencyProperty
// of the class as first parameter.
this.myActivity.SetBinding(MyActivity.MyActivityProperty, activitybind1);
```

This means that at runtime MyActivityProperty gets its value from the SourceActivity.sourceProperty. The SetBinding method that is used to apply the binding is inherited from System.Workflow.ComponentModel.DependencyObject, which is a base class for all activity objects.

Activity binding becomes particularly interesting, since it can be configured using a dialog in Visual Studio to apply bindings. When a DependencyProperty is shown in the properties of an activity, you can select the ellipsis button (...), and the dialog for activity binding is displayed, as shown in Figure 16–34. Simply select the property of your class to bind the property of the existing activity to your property.

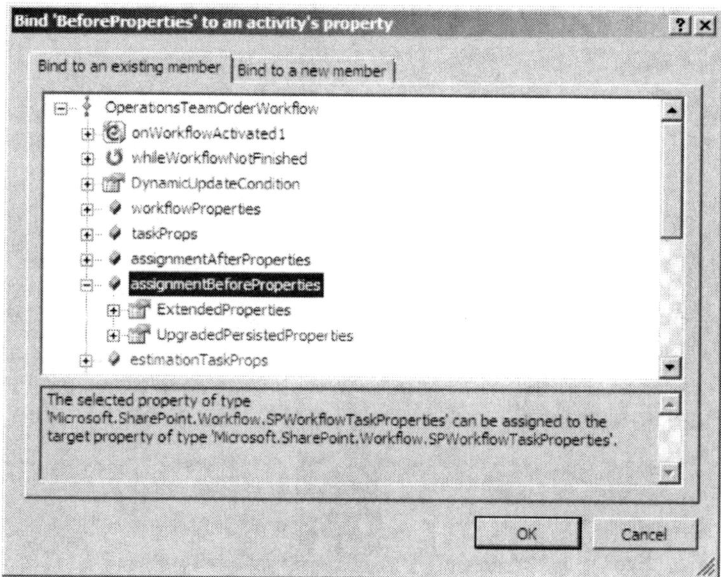

Figure 16–34. Activity binding dialog

Correlation Tokens

One of the important concepts in workflow development is the concept of correlation tokens. Improper use of correlation tokens can result in unpredictable workflow behavior and a great deal of effort to find the origin of such problems.

Because of the loose coupling in the WF infrastructure, a mapping is required between items within a concrete workflow instance and the hosting environment. The workflow runtime environment offers communication capabilities that allow communication between workflow instances and external systems (such as SharePoint). To ensure the communication is addressed to the correct workflow instance and to the correct item within the instance, correlation tokens are used as an identifier.

Consider a correlation token as a meta-variable that defines a common variable across the workflow, such as a specific task that can be used by several activities, for example `CreateTask`, `EditTask`, or `FinishTask`. When multiple activities are working with the same task, they all need the same correlation token. Usually one token is required for the workflow itself and one token for each task that is used inside the workflow.

Correlation tokens can be set in the properties window of an activity, as shown in Figure 16–35. You can either specify an existing token or define a new correlation token.

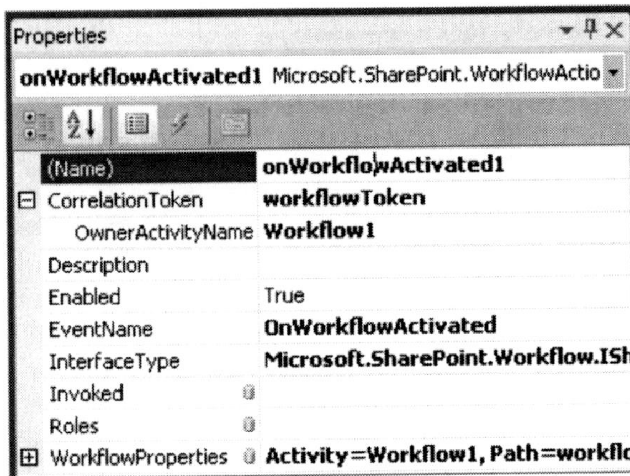

***Figure 16–35.** Setting a correlation token*

The `OwnerActivityName` defines the activity that owns the correlation token. This is especially important within composite activities, such as a sequence within a `while` loop. In this situation, you need to specify the sequence as the `OwnerActivityName` to ensure that for each new sequence a new correlation token will be created on each loop.

SharePoint Workflow Object Model

SharePoint provides its own hosting environment for workflows based on WF. Therefore, SharePoint extends the capabilities of WF and provides its own classes and objects that are specific to the SharePoint workflow life cycle. SharePoint workflow classes employ the following namespaces:

- `Microsoft.SharePoint.Workflow`: Contains the base classes and main entry points for SharePoint workflows.

- `Microsoft.SharePoint.Workflow.Application`: Contains the Three-State workflow classes that are built into SharePoint.
- `Microsoft.SharePoint.WorkflowActions`: Contains the workflow actions or activities that are included with SharePoint. This includes actions for SharePoint Designer as well as activities for custom workflows.
- `Microsoft.SharePoint.WorkflowActions.WithKey`: Contains mirror classes that access list items by using a string identifier.

Since `WorkflowActions` is described in the section about writing custom SharePoint Designer workflows or in the section about custom workflows, they will not be described any further here. The `Application` namespace only contains the class for the implementation of the Three-State workflow and is also not of interest for the SharePoint object model. `WorkflowActions.WithKey` contains mirror classes that already exist in the `WorkflowActions` namespace and have been adapted to work with string identifiers, which are required for working with the new external data sources. In fact, all the base classes that define the SharePoint object model are contained in the `Microsoft.SharePoint.Workflow` namespace. Figure 16–36 shows the most important objects.

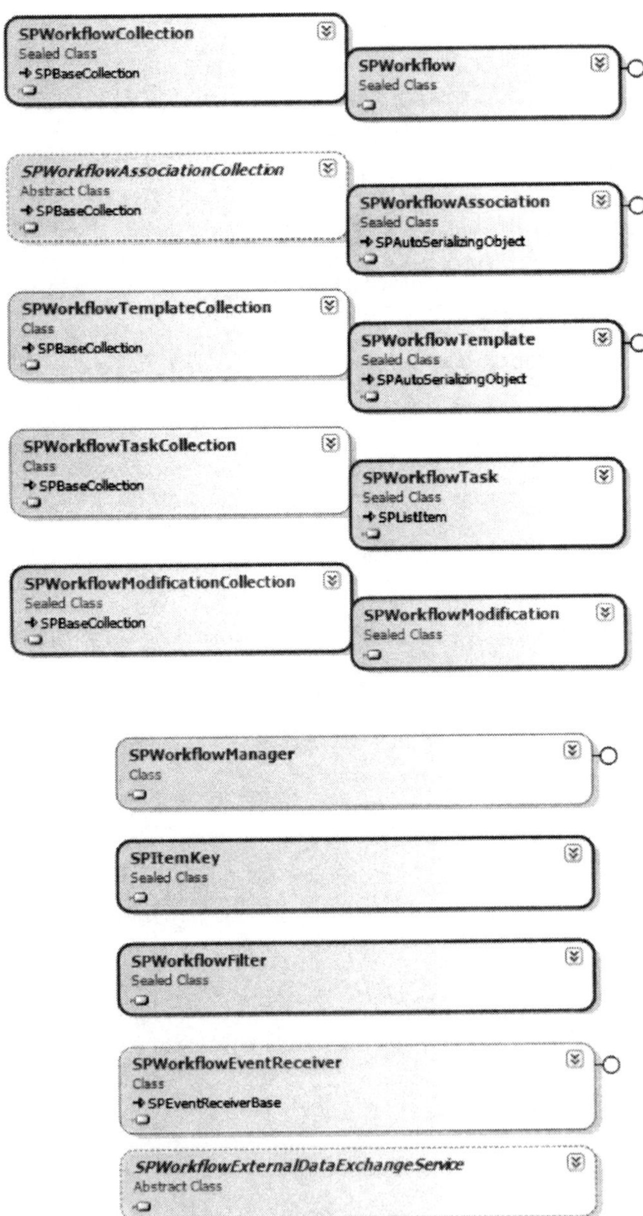

Figure 16–36. *SharePoint workflow object model*

SPWorkflow

The SPWorkflow object is one of the central objects in the SharePoint.Workflow namespace. It represents a workflow instance that is currently running or has already finished running on an item. SPWorkflow has many properties containing detailed information about the workflow instance, including the current state, associated objects such as tasks and lists, and information about users involved in that particular workflow.

Since SPWorkflow represents actual workflow instances, you cannot create new object instances. You always need to provide the workflow instance ID, which will create a SPWorkflow object for this existing instance. You can get SPWorkflow objects as a result of querying an SPListItem for its workflows or by using the SPWorkflowManager to start or cancel workflows.

The following listing retrieves all the workflow instances of an SPListItem and illustrates some of the more significant properties for each workflow:

```
foreach (SPWorkflow wf in listItem.Workflows)
{
    // the ID of the WorkflowAssocation
    GUID associationId = wf.AssociationId;

    // State of the workflow
    SPWorkflowState state = wf.InternalState;

    // Lists for History and Tasks
    SPList historyList = wf. HistoryList;
    SPList taskList = wf.TaskList;

    // All tasks that belong to this instance
    SPWorkflowTaskCollection tasks = wf.Tasks;

    // The name of the SPListItem on which the workflow was created
    String itemName = wf.ItemName;
}
```

SPWorkflowTemplate

The SPWorkflowTemplate represents a workflow template that is deployed to a SharePoint site. It contains several members that return information about the template, such as the AssociationUrl and the InitiationUrl, which return the URLs of the forms that will be used for association and initiation, respectively. Furthermore, you can set various parameters affecting the start behavior of workflows based on this template. You can use the SPWorkflowTemplate and associate it with a SharePoint list or site. The following code selects one specific template from the template collection for a site:

```
// web is the instance of the current SPWeb object
SPWorkflowTemplate template = web.WorkflowTemplates[new GUID("workflowGUID")];
```

SPWorkflowAssociation

The SPWorkflowAssociation class represents the association of a workflow template with a list, content type ,or site. Members of this class contain information about the associated template. You can use the BaseTemplate to get the associated template, the HistoryListId, or the TaskListId for the association. The properties AllowManual, AutoStartChange, and AutoStartCreate control the starting options for the workflow. These properties are exposed for workflow associations via the web interface, described earlier in this chapter. The following snippet selects a collection of SPWorkflowAssociation objects for a list and interrogates several interesting properties:

```
SPWorkflowAssociationCollection associationCollection =
                      parentList.WorkflowAssociations;
foreach (SPWorkflowAssociation association in associationCollection)
{
    // The template on which the association is based
    SPWorkflowTemplate template = association.BaseTemplate;

    // The number of currently running workflow instances that are based on this
    // association
    int runningInstances = association.RunningInstances;

    // The data that was entered during assoication in the association form
    string associationData = association.AssociationData;

    // Whether the workflow is based on declarative description - as a result of
    // SharePoint Designer - or a compiled assembly - the result of Visual Studio.
    bool isDeclarative = association.IsDeclarative;
}
```

To associate a workflow template to a list, content type, or site, you need to create an association object first and then add this object to the list, content type, or site. The creation of a new SPWorkflowAssociation object is handled by the following static methods of the class:

- CreateListAssociation: Creates an association object that can be associated with an SPList object
- CreateListContentTypeAssociation: Creates an association object that can be associated with an SPContentType, of a list
- CreateWebAssocation: Creates an association object that can be associated with an SPWeb object
- CreateWebContentTypeAssociation: Creates an association object that can be associated with a site-level SPContentType, which is available through the ContentTypes collection of an SPWeb

The following snippet shows how you can add a workflow association to an SPList by creating a new SPWorkflowAssociation and adding it to the SPWorkflowAssociationCollection of the SPList:

```
SPWorkflowTemplate template = web.WorkflowTemplates[new GUID("workflowGUID")];
SPList historyList = web.Lists["HistoryList"];
SPList taskList = web.Lists["TaskList"];
SPWorkflowAssociation association = SPWorkflowAssociation.CreateListAssociation(
    template, template.Name, taskList, historyList);
// Set the start option for the association
association.AllowManual = true;
association.AutoStartChange = false;
association.AutoStartCreate = true;

// Add the association to the list of WorkflowAssociation in the SPList
myList.WorkflowAssociations.Add(assocation);
```

SPWorkflowManager

The SPWorkflowManager class is used to control workflow templates and instances. It exposes several members that administer workflow instances across a site collection. You can start or cancel workflows and perform further administrative operations on workflows.

To start a workflow, use the StartWorkflow method—it creates a new workflow instance and starts it. It requires an SPWorkflowAssociation object, a string with event parameters, and either an SPListItem or an Object representing the object on which the workflow should run. Since workflows can be attached to sites, the overloaded method that takes an Object as a parameter has been added to be able to attach workflows to sites as well as to list items.

```
// Create SPSite and SPWeb objects
SPSite site = new SPSite("http://server/site");
SPWeb web = site.RootWeb;

// Get SPList and SPListItem
SPList list = web.Lists[0];
SPListItem listItem = list.Items[0];

// Get the workflow association
SPWorkflowAssociation association = list.WorkflowAssociations[0];

// Get the SPWorkflowManager from the site
SPWorkflowManager manager = site.WorkflowManager;

// Start the workflow on the ListItem
manager.StartWorkflow(listItem, association, association.AssociationData);
```

You can also use the SPWorkflowManager to access several workflow objects for an SPListItem, such as GetWorkflowTasks, GetItemActiveWorkflows, or GetItemWorkflows.

SPWorkflowTask

As mentioned earlier, workflows in SharePoint use tasks for user interaction. Task lists in SharePoint contain all the tasks that need to be completed by users. Those tasks are well integrated into SharePoint. You can use Web Parts to display all the open tasks to the current user or filter the task list to only display all tasks for the current user.

SPWorkflowTask is a special type of SPListItem that is used in task lists, since it is derived from SPListItem. In addition to the members that are inherited from SPListItem, SPWorkflowTask has a property WorkflowId for the GUID of the workflow instance to which the task is assigned. You can use the following snippet to obtain the workflow instance from a task:

```
GUID workflowId = task.WorkflowId;
SPWorkflow workflow = new SPWorkflow(web, workflowId);
```

SPWorkflowModification

The SPWorkflowModification class represents a workflow modification. When workflow modification occurs, the modification form is displayed to the user, and the workflow is modified accordingly. The SPWorkflowModification holds the ContextData, which is a string representation of the data that the user submitted with the modification form. Another useful property is the TypeId. This is the ID of the workflow template on which the modification is based.

You can use the SPWorkflowManager to execute the workflow modification by calling the ModifyWorkflow method, as shown in the following snippet:

```
SPSite site = new SPSite("http://server/site");
SPWeb web = site.RootWeb;
SPList list = web.Lists[0];
SPListItem listItem = list.Items[0];

SPWorkflow workflow = listItem.Workflows[0];
SPWorkflowModification wfModification = workflow.Modifications[0];
String contextString = "<contextData><Value>test</Value></contextData>";
Site.WorkflowManager.ModifyWorkflow(workflow, wfModification, contextString);
```

This code is usually added to the ASPX modification form. The contextString is exposed to the workflow in the ContextData.

SPWorkflowEventReceiver

The SPWorkflowEventReceiver class handles workflow events throughout the lifetime of a workflow.

- *Starting*: Occurs when a workflow is starting
- *Started*: Occurs when a workflow is started
- *Postponed*: Occurs when a workflow is postponed
- *Completed*: Occurs when a workflow is completed

You can register the SPWorkflowEventReceiver with any site, list, or content type.

SPItemKey

In SharePoint 2010, external data sources can be tightly integrated with SharePoint and used like any other SharePoint resource. It is even possible to execute workflows on these data sources, since they appear like a regular SharePoint list. Because list elements of external data source cannot be guaranteed to have an identifier of type Integer, like the Id of a list item in SharePoint, the SPItemKey was introduced. It encapsulates the identification of a list item and therefore contains an Integer value Id for internal lists and a string identifier called Key for external lists. Depending on the concrete list instance, it will offer the correct identification. Some of the activities for SharePoint Designer have been rewritten to support this new type.

Developing Workflows with Visual Studio 2010

Using the Visual Studio 2010 templates for SharePoint 2010 workflow solutions enables a rapid start into custom workflow development. You can choose between a sequential workflow template and a state machine workflow template for your workflow.

The first step in workflow development should always be the design of a proper workflow model, containing all the workflow steps. This model equips you to decide which workflow template to choose. If your workflow becomes very complicated, with many backward connections and conditions to decide the current state of the workflow, you should consider using a state machine workflow.

After designing your workflow, create a Visual Studio project, and lay out your workflow using the workflow activities from the toolbox. Specify the required properties, and bind activity properties to your workflow properties. Once you implement the workflow activities, you can finally deploy your workflow to your SharePoint server. If your workflow contains errors or does not behave as expected, you might also need to debug your workflow.

Modeling the Workflow

Before starting to develop your workflow, you should always construct a detailed model for your workflow and describe what your workflow will do. This involves identifying the stakeholders involved in your business process, the flow of data, and the flow of activities. You can, of course, use Visio 2010 and its SharePoint workflow shapes to model the workflow or any other suitable graphical representation. More important than the tool you use is that you consider everything that is involved in your workflow before you start programming. Otherwise, you might encounter problems during development that necessitate changing the entire process and consequently losing a lot of time.

To demonstrate how to develop a workflow with Visual Studio 2010, the following simple scenario is used. Imagine a technical department for product development. Within this department different types of projects are initiated. To allow employees to request a new project and to view a summary of all the projects in the department, a project list should be introduced. Furthermore, a workflow is needed to handle the estimation and approval of new projects. Figure 16–37 shows a graphical representation of this workflow.

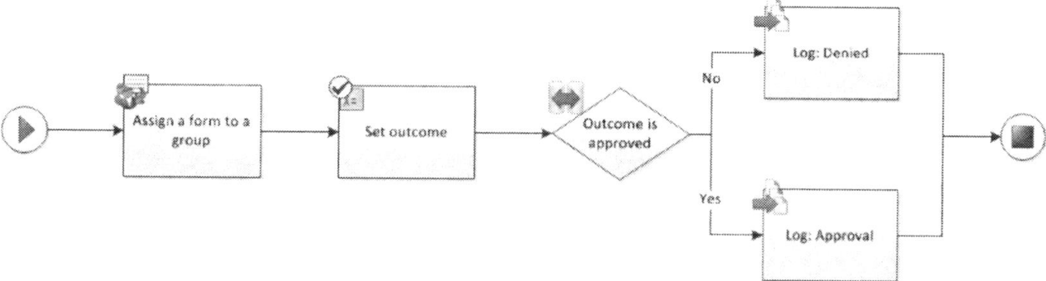

Figure 16–37. *Example workflow for creating new projects in a department*

Users can add new entries to the projects lists using the list edit form. After the project has been saved, the workflow will start automatically, and a task will be assigned to an estimation manager. The estimation manager has to decide whether to accept the new project and estimate the project costs. Depending on the outcome, an entry will be written to the history list.

To achieve this solution, the following items need to be developed:

- A project list with the required fields to store all relevant information. Since this is not within the scope of this example, we will assume that this list already exists.
- A sequential workflow including the following:
  - An association form to select the manager for the department
  - A task form for the estimation

Developing the Workflow

To start developing the workflow, create a new project in Visual Studio 2010 using the SharePoint 2010 Sequential Workflow project template. Specify your workflow name, and select a List workflow in the resultant wizard. Further, specify the debugging options and the settings for starting the workflow in the development environment in the subsequent steps of the wizard.

Once the project is created, you should see an empty project, like the one shown in Figure 16–38. The template automatically creates a feature and a solution package to deploy the workflow. Under the workflow node in the Solution Explorer is an `Elements.xml` manifest file, together with the workflow file. (The feature and manifest, which are required to deploy the workflow, will be described in more detail in the "Developing the Workflow" section.)

When you select the workflow code file, the Visual Studio Workflow Designer opens and shows a basic workflow that consists of one activity, called `onWorkflowActivated`. This activity is required as the first activity in every workflow. It initializes the correlation token for the workflow and binds the `WorkflowProperties` to make them available throughout the workflow.

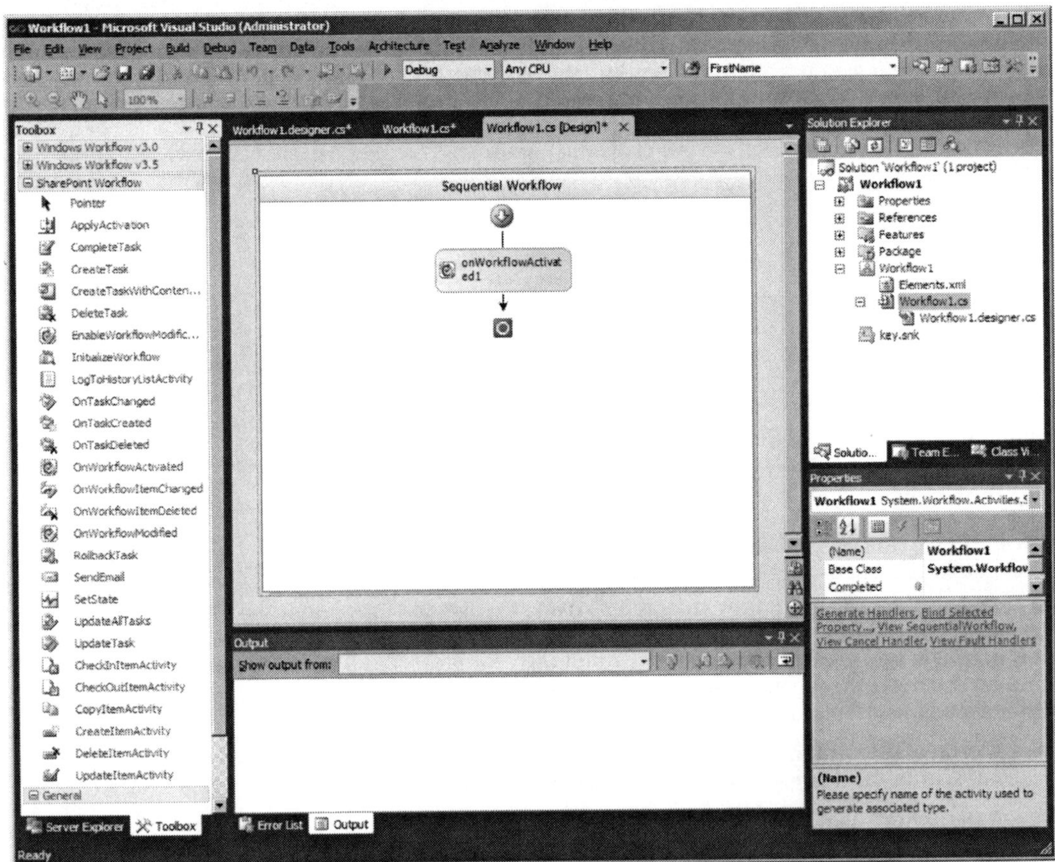

***Figure 16–38.** New Sequential Workflow project*

You can start to develop your workflow by dragging activities from the toolbox—displayed on the left side in Figure 16–38—onto the Workflow Designer surface. Every workflow activity has a set of properties that can be managed in the Properties dialog. Assign values to the properties or use activity binding to bind them to properties within your code. You can access the code that is called through event handlers by double-clicking an activity, or you can edit the entire workflow code by selecting View Code from the context menu on the workflow file in the Solution Explorer.

The toolbox contains all the available activities for creating a SharePoint workflow. In addition to the basic WF activities described earlier, you can also choose the SharePoint-specific workflow activities. The different toolbox entries are separated into different categories according to their origin. Table 16–9 lists the available activities for the SharePoint Workflow category and gives a short description for each.

Table 16–9. *Available SharePoint Workflow Activities in Visual Studio 2010*

Activity Name	Description
`ApplyActivation`	Updates initial workflow properties with information using `SPWorkflowActivationProperties`.
`CompleteTask`	Updates a task and marks it as completed. The task is referenced using the `TaskId` property.
`CreateTask`	Creates a new SharePoint task item in the Task list. Using the property `TaskProperties` allows you to set values for the task. You also need to set the `TaskId` property to a new `Guid` to reference the task in your workflow.
`CreateTaskWithContentType`	Creates a SharePoint task item based on a specific content type. When working with different task forms based on ASPX, you need to use this activity to specify the content type that should be used to display the correct task edit form.
`DeleteTask`	Deletes a SharePoint task item.
`EnableWorkflowModification`	Enables a workflow modification form for the workflow. This allows users to perform workflow modifications.
`InitializeWorkflow`	Initializes a new instance of the workflow.
`LogToHistoryListActivity`	Adds a new entry to the history list that is associated with the workflow. This information can be viewed by users via the workflow information in the workflow settings.
`OnTaskChanged`	This activity responds to the event that is raised when an associated workflow task is modified.
`OnTaskCreated`	This activity responds to the event that is raised when an associated workflow task is created.
`OnTaskDeleted`	This activity responds to the event that is raised when an associated workflow task is deleted.
`OnWorkflowActivated`	This activity is called when a new workflow instance is initiated. This is the first activity in a workflow.

Activity Name	Description
OnWorkflowItemChanged	This activity is called when the item to which the workflow instance is bound is changed.
OnWorkflowItemDeleted	This activity is called when the item to which the workflow instance is bound is deleted.
OnWorkflowModified	This activity is called when a user submits a workflow modification form.
RollbackTask	This activity performs a rollback of changes made to a task since the last changes were committed.
SendEmail	Sends an e-mail to the specified users.
SetState	Sets the status of the workflow. This status is displayed in the status column of a workflow that is attached to a list and in the workflow status page.
UpdateAllTasks	Updates all tasks that are assigned to a workflow instance and are not yet finished.
UpdateTask	Updates a task with the specified properties.
CheckInItemActivity	This activity performs a check-in of the specified document into its document library.
CheckOutItemActivity	This activity performs a check-out of the specified document from its document library.
CopyItemActivity	Copies the specified document from its document library to the specified document library.
CreateItemActivity	Creates a new item in the specified list or document library.
DeleteItemActivity	Deletes an item in the specified list or document library.
UpdateItemActivity	Updates an item in the specified list or document library with the specified properties.

As you lay out the flow of activities on the design surface, whenever important settings for an activity are missing, the designer indicates this with a red exclamation mark in the upper-right corner of the shape or in the Properties window at the affected property. For example, if you place a CreateTask activity after the onWorkflowActivated activity, you are notified that the correlation token needs to be specified.

To implement the example workflow, drag the following activities to the design surface resulting in the sequential workflow, as shown in Figure 16–39 (the names of the activities have already been changed to reflect the flow of activities):

- `CreateTaskWithContentType`: Place this activity right after the `OnWorkflowActivated` shape. This will create a new task that uses a custom ASPX form. When working with only one task type, you could also use the `CreateTask` activity, but since the `CreateTaskWithContentType` is more complex to use, we will show you how to use this activity.
- `WhileActivity`: Place this shape after the activity to create the task. The `while` loop is necessary, to wait until the task has been correctly completed.
- `OnTaskChanged`: Place this shape inside the `WhileActivity`. This activity is executed whenever the task is changed, and the `WhileActivity` holds a condition to wait for the task to be completed and retrieves the information from the task form.
- `CompleteTask`: Places this shape after the `WhileActivity`. It sets the outcome of the task and finishes it.
- `IfElseActivity`: Places this shape below the `CompleteTask` activity and adds a Declarative Rule Condition to the left branch using the Properties window. This rule stipulates that, to enter the left branch in the example workflow, the outcome of the task must equal Approved.
- `LogToHistoryListActivity`: Place one into the `if` branch and another one into the `else` branch to log a custom message to the history log, reflecting the result of the task.

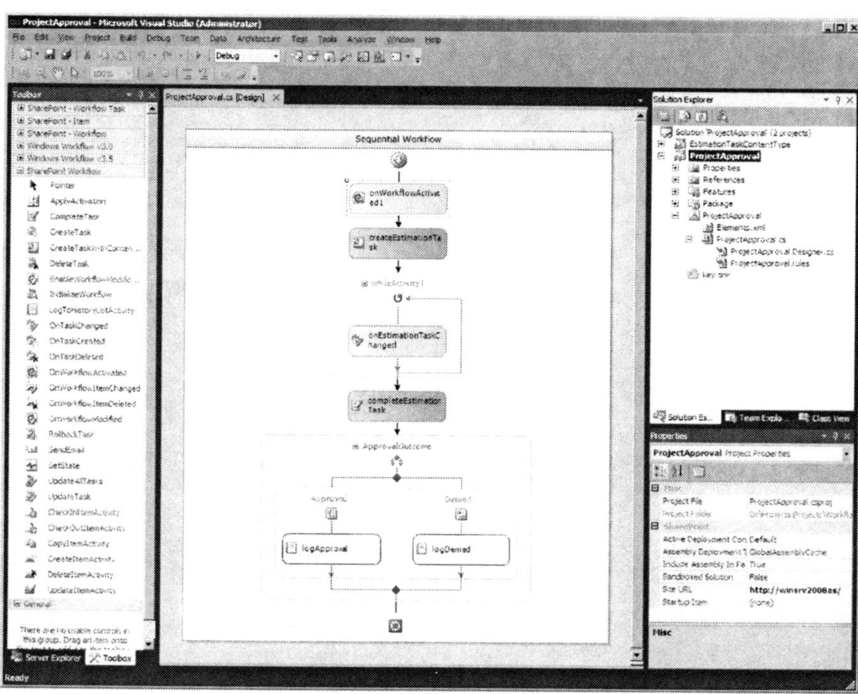

Figure 16–39. Layout of the example workflow

After the workflow flow is completed, you need to set the properties for the previous activities. To accomplish this, either you can define the required properties in the workflow code and bind them using the Properties window or you can select "Bind to a new member" from the binding dialog. In this case, enter a name for the new member, and select the option Create Field to have Visual Studio create and bind the member for you.

Specify the following properties for the activities in the workflow:

- `CreateTaskWithContentType`: Analogous to Figure 16–26, you need to set the following properties:
    - `CorrelationToken`: Specify a token for the task by entering a token that is different from the workflow token.
    - `ContentTypeId`: You need to define a `ContentType` for the task form and assign the ID of the `ContentType` to this property. The definition of the `ContentType` is described in the "Using ASPX Workflow Forms" section.
    - `TaskId`: Bind this property to a new member that holds the `Guid` for this task.
    - `TaskProperties`: Bind this property to a new member of type `SPWorkflowTaskProperties` that holds the properties of this task.
- `WhileActivity`: To define the condition for the `while` loop, you need to specify the following property:
    - `Condition`: Select Code Condition, and choose the method `taskNotFinished`, defined in the workflow code shown in Listing 16–4.
- `OnTaskChanged`: Specify the following properties:
    - `CorrelationToken`: Define the same correlation token as in the `CreateTaskWithContentType` activity.
    - `AfterProperties`: To access the properties of the task after the change, bind this property to a new member of type `SPWorkflowTaskProperties`, as shown in Figure 16–40.

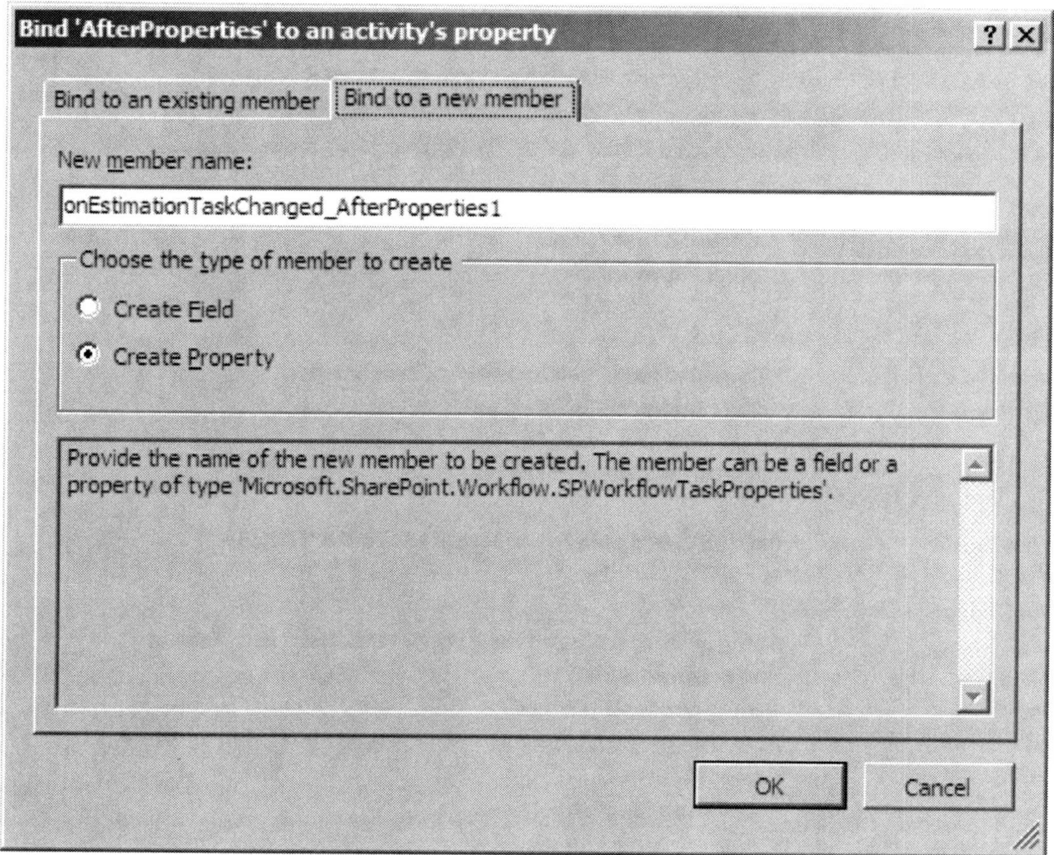

Figure 16–40. Binding the AfterProperties to a new member

    - `BeforeProperties`: To access the properties of the task before the change, bind this property to a new member of type `SPWorkflowTaskProperties`.
    - `TaskId`: Binding the `TaskId` to the existing member that was used in the `CreateTaskWithContentType` activity connects the `OnTaskChanged` activity with the right task.

- `LogToHistoryList`: For both activities, you need to specify the result that should be logged:
    - `HistoryDescription` : Set a description text to log to the history list.
    - `HistoryOutcome`: Set a text for the outcome that should be logged to the history list.

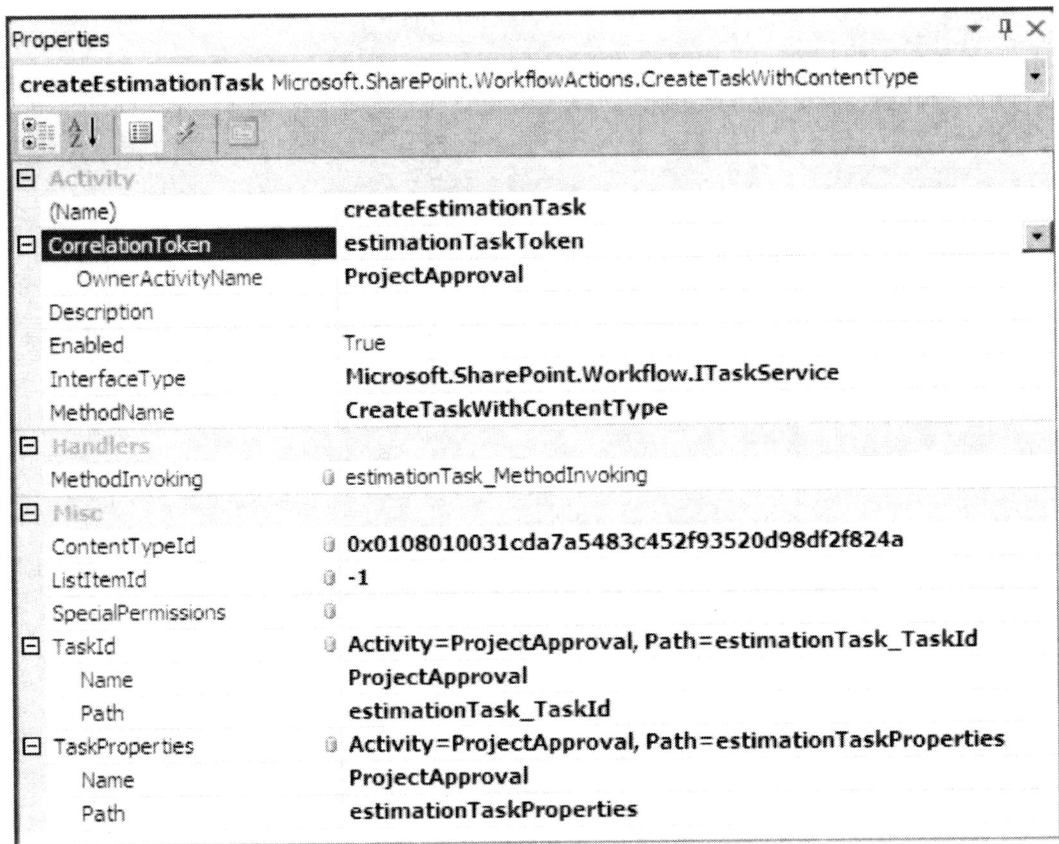

Figure 16–41. *Specifying properties for a CreateTaskWithContentType activity*

After the properties for the activities have been bound, further programming is needed to achieve the desired workflow behavior. Listing 16–4 shows the complete workflow code for the example. As you can see, the `ProjectApproval` class is derived from `SequentialWorkflowActivity`, which manages the execution of its child activities and is used for sequential workflows. The class contains all the members that were defined automatically when the properties of the different activities were bound to new members.

Furthermore, various methods for the activities are created when you double-click the activity shapes in the workflow designer. You can write code to be executed by the activity.

The method `estimationTask_MethodInvoking` is called when a new task is created. At first, a new `Guid` is assigned to the `estimationTask_TaskId`, which has been bound to the `TaskId` of the activity. Additional properties for the task are set, including the name of the user the task is `AssignedTo` and the `Title` of the task. The title is assembled using the `workflowProperties` and gets the title of the item on which the workflow is running.

The method `taskNotFinished` is used as a Code Condition for the `WhileActivity`. It assigns `false` to the `ConditionalEventArgs` that are passed as a parameter to the method, as long as the task has not been finished appropriately. The variable `isTaskComplete` is set to `true` in the method `onTaskChanged1_Invoked` as soon as the task is finished.

Finally, the onTaskChanged1_Invoked method saves two task properties that have been set in the task form into local variables. You can use the afterProperties to access all the properties of the task. Special properties that are not part of the task ContentType are stored by the task form in a HashTable called ExtendedProperties. Use a String key, such as _EstimatedCosts and _Outcome in the example code, to access the corresponding stored values.

Listing 16–4. *Workflow Code*

```
using System;
using System.Workflow.Activities;
using Microsoft.SharePoint.Workflow;

namespace ProjectApproval
{
    public sealed partial class ProjectApproval : SequentialWorkflowActivity
    {
        public ProjectApproval()
        {
            InitializeComponent();
        }

        public Guid workflowId = default(System.Guid);
        public SPWorkflowActivationProperties workflowProperties = new
                                            SPWorkflowActivationProperties();
        public SPWorkflowTaskProperties estimationTaskProperties = new
                                                  SPWorkflowTaskProperties();
        public Guid estimationTask_TaskId = default(System.Guid);
        public SPWorkflowTaskProperties estimationTask_BeforeProperties = new
                                                  SPWorkflowTaskProperties();
        public SPWorkflowTaskProperties estimationTask_AfterProperties = new
                                                  SPWorkflowTaskProperties();
        bool isTaskComplete = false;

        public string costs = default(System.String);
        public string outcome = default(System.String);

        private void onWorkflowActivated1_Invoked(object sender,
                                                 ExternalDataEventArgs e)
        {
            workflowId = workflowProperties.WorkflowId;
        }

        private void estimationTask_MethodInvoking(object sender, EventArgs e)
        {
            estimationTask_TaskId = Guid.NewGuid();
            estimationTaskProperties.AssignedTo = "wapps\\administrator";
            estimationTaskProperties.Title = "Approve_" +
                                            workflowProperties.Item.Title;
        }

        private void taskNotFinished(object sender, ConditionalEventArgs e)
        {
            e.Result = !isTaskComplete;
```

```
        }

        private void onTaskChanged1_Invoked(object sender, ExternalDataEventArgs e)
        {
            isTaskComplete = true;
            costs = estimationTask_AfterProperties.ExtendedProperties
                                              ["_EstimatedCosts"].ToString();
            outcome = estimationTask_AfterProperties.ExtendedProperties
                                                    ["_Outcome"].ToString();
        }
    }
}
```

Deploying Workflows

As with any other SharePoint artifact, a workflow is deployed to SharePoint via a feature. The feature definition for a workflow is relatively straightforward, as you can see in Listing 16–5. Apart from the Title, Description, Id, and Scope attributes, the main aspect of the feature is the manifest file in the ElementManifest element.

***Listing 16–5.** Feature Definition for Example Workflow*

```
<?xml version="1.0" encoding="utf-8"?>
<Feature xmlns="http://schemas.microsoft.com/sharepoint/"
    Title=" ProjectApproval Workflow"
    Description="Feature for ProjectApproval Workflow "
    Id="44f1409b-8578-4657-8810-bcf06aba7dfa"
    Scope="Site">
    <Properties>
        <Property Key="GloballyAvailable" Value="true" />
    </Properties>
    <ElementManifests>
        <ElementManifest Location="ProjectApproval\Elements.xml" />
    </ElementManifests>
</Feature>
```

The manifest file describes a workflow, within a <Workflow> element, as shown in Listing 16–6. The Name, Description, and Id are similar to elements in a feature. CodeBesideClass and CodeBesideAssembly reference the workflow class that implements the workflow, which is ProjectApproval in our example.

To specify custom ASPX pages for association, initiation, modification, or task forms, use the following attributes of the <Workflow> element:

- AssociationUrl: As in the example, supply the path to a custom ASPX page, which can be used to gather additional information during workflow association.
- InstantiationUrl: Enter the path to a custom ASPX form to provide a custom initiation form.
- ModificationUrl: In the same vein, a custom modification form can also be defined by providing the path to a custom ASPX page.

- TaskListContentTypeId: Unlike the previous forms, a custom task form can only be specified using a separate content type. The ID of this content type can be entered here. When only one task form is required, the TaskListContentTypeId can be used in conjunction with the CreateTask activity. For multiple different task forms, the ID must be specified directly with each CreateTaskWithContentType activity.

To stipulate the kind of SharePoint item to which the workflow will be assigned, enter a value (List, Site, or ContentType) for the element <AssociationCategories>.

Listing 16–6. *Workflow Manifest File*

```
<?xml version="1.0" encoding="utf-8" ?>
<Elements xmlns="http://schemas.microsoft.com/sharepoint/">
    <Workflow
        Name="ProjectApprovalWorkflow"
        Description="My SharePoint Workflow"
        Id="5d2fd6e5-996a-43c9-b8c1-5b1a27e9af33"
        CodeBesideClass="ProjectApproval.ProjectApproval"
        CodeBesideAssembly="$assemblyname$"
        AssociationUrl="_layouts/ProjectApprovalForms/
                                        ProjectApprovalAssociationForm.aspx"
        InstantiationUrl="..."
        ModificationUrl="..."
        TaskListContentTypeId="..."
     >
    <Categories/>
    <MetaData>
        <AssociationCategories>List</AssociationCategories>
        <StatusPageUrl>_layouts/WrkStat.aspx</StatusPageUrl>
    </MetaData>
  </Workflow>
</Elements>
```

After you deployed your workflow together with the missing forms, described next, you can test your workflow.

WORKFLOW DEBUGGING

Workflow debugging is significantly easier with Visual Studio 2010 because you can simply select Start Debugging from the development environment. You can work with the debugger as you do with any other project, including setting breakpoints and stepping through the code.

You can also attach to the `w3wp.exe` process and start debugging your SharePoint application directly.

Sometimes you may encounter problems during workflow association or during workflow start. In this situation, examine the SharePoint log files located in `%SharePointRoot%\14\Logs`. Here you will usually find an error message that provides more information about your problem.

Using ASPX Workflow Forms

SharePoint uses either ASPX or InfoPath forms for user interaction in a workflow. However, in SharePoint Foundation, only ASPX forms are available. You can use APSX forms for association, initiation, and modification of a workflow. In addition, you can indicate custom task forms to be used to edit a task and thus collect additional information from users.

Custom Workflow Association Form

Listing 16–6 already showed how a custom association form can be specified for a workflow. You need to construct the custom association form and deploy it to the server. Unfortunately, developing custom workflow forms is a complex task, because the form needs to perform the association. When using the standard association form, described at the beginning of this chapter, you can select several settings, such as the task list and the starting options, and then associate the workflow to the list or site. If SharePoint detects a custom association form, this form is displayed after the standard form to gather additional input. Since all the relevant information must be collected before the association can be performed, this requires the custom form to read the information entered in the standard form and then perform the association itself.

However, the good news is that Visual Studio 2010 includes a template for association and initiation forms that already contains the necessary code to handle the parameters entered in the standard forms and performs the association or initiation. The following example demonstrates how to develop a custom association form. (An initiation form works in the same manner.)

Before you begin, add a SharePoint-mapped folder to the Layouts directory. This controls the deployment of the form to the `_layouts` folder in SharePoint and will be the path to the form that you need to enter in the workflow manifest file. Once done, add a new association form to this folder, selecting the appropriate template.

The template generates an ASPX file that already contains the markup for a SharePoint application page and provides a code-behind file that handles the association. In the markup code, the buttons to trigger the association or to cancel the association are already inserted. You can add controls to the placeholder `PlaceHolderMain` and thus create your own form. Of course, you can change the entire page, but to keep the example simple, only a `TextBox` to enter the username of the estimation manager was added, as shown in Listing 16–7.

Listing 16–7. *Markup Code for Association Form*

```
<asp:Content ID="Main" ContentPlaceHolderID="PlaceHolderMain" runat="server">
    <br />
```

```
    Approver: <asp:TextBox runat="server" ID="EstimationManager"></asp:TextBox>
    <br />
    <br />
    <asp:Button ID="AssociateWorkflow" runat="server"
                OnClick="AssociateWorkflow_Click" Text="Associate Workflow" />
         
    <asp:Button ID="Cancel" runat="server" Text="Cancel" OnClick="Cancel_Click" />
</asp:Content>
```

In the autogenerated code, you can use the methods PopulateFormFields and GetAssociationData to fill your controls with existing values and to pass the values in your controls to the association. The code will create or update an SPWorkflowAssociation object and assign it to the corresponding SharePoint list, site, or content type. This SPWorkflowAssociation object has a member called AssociationData, which is a string that holds additional association data like the data that is entered into the controls on the custom association form. The AssociationData is usually XML to allow for multiple parameters.

Therefore, the GetAssociationData method in the example shown in Listing 16–8 creates an XML string containing an element named EstimationManager, which holds the estimation manager that was entered into the TextBox.

When the PopulateFormFields method is called, a SPWorkflowAssociation object is passed as a parameter, which represents an existing association. In case an association is already present, the AssociationData string will be parsed, and the TextBox for the EstimationManager is populated with the existing value.

You can access the AssociationData in your workflow and process the XML in a similar way.

At the end of the autogenerated code is a section containing all the standard code that should normally be left unchanged.

Listing 16–8. *Code-Behind for Association Form*

```
using System;
using System.Globalization;
using System.Web;
using System.Web.UI;
using Microsoft.SharePoint;
using Microsoft.SharePoint.Utilities;
using Microsoft.SharePoint.WebControls;
using Microsoft.SharePoint.Workflow;
using System.Xml;
using System.IO;
using System.Text;

namespace EstimationTaskContentType.Layouts.ProjectApprovalForms
{
    public partial class ProjectApprovalAssociationForm : LayoutsPageBase
    {
        private const int CreateListTryCount = 100;
        private string historyListDescription = "Custom History List";
        private string taskListDescription = "Custom Task List";
        private string listCreationFailed = "Failed to create list {0} as a
                                    list with same name already exists";
        private string workflowAssociationFailed = "Error occured while
                                    associating Workflow template. {0}";

        protected void Page_Load(object sender, EventArgs e)
```

```
{
    InitializeParams();
}

// This method is called during form load and is used to populate form
// fields with existing values when an existing association is edited.
private void PopulateFormFields(SPWorkflowAssociation existingAssociation)
{
    string data = existingAssociation.AssociationData;
    if (!string.IsNullOrEmpty(data))
    {
        XmlDocument doc = new XmlDocument();
        doc.LoadXml(data);
        XmlNamespaceManager nsmgr = new XmlNamespaceManager(
                                                    doc.NameTable);
        nsmgr.AddNamespace("my",
            "http://schemas.microsoft.com/office/infopath/2003/myXSD");
        XmlNode node = doc.SelectSingleNode(
                            "/my:myFields/my:EstimationManager", nsmgr);
        EstimationManager.Text = node.InnerText;
    }
}

// This method is called when the user clicks the button to associate the
// workflow.
private string GetAssociationData()
{
    StringBuilder sb = new StringBuilder();
    XmlTextWriter writer = new XmlTextWriter(new StringWriter(sb));
    writer.WriteStartElement("my", "myFields",
           "http://schemas.microsoft.com/office/infopath/2003/myXSD");
    writer.WriteElementString("EstimationManager",
            "http://schemas.microsoft.com/office/infopath/2003/myXSD",
             EstimationManager.Text);
    writer.WriteEndElement();
    writer.Flush();
    return sb.ToString();
}

protected void AssociateWorkflow_Click(object sender, EventArgs e)
{
    // Optionally, add code here to perform additional steps before
    // associating your workflow
    try
    {
        CreateTaskList();
        CreateHistoryList();
        HandleAssociateWorkflow();
        // Redirect to the default SharePoint page for workflow settings
        SPUtility.Redirect("WrkSetng.aspx", SPRedirectFlags.
                          RelativeToLayoutsPage, HttpContext.Current,
```

```
                                 Page.ClientQueryString);
            }
            catch (Exception ex)
            {
                SPUtility.TransferToErrorPage(String.Format(
                         CultureInfo.CurrentCulture, workflowAssociationFailed,
                         ex.Message));
            }
        }

        protected void Cancel_Click(object sender, EventArgs e)
        {
            // Redirect to the default SharePoint page for workflow settings
            SPUtility.Redirect("WrkSetng.aspx",
                    SPRedirectFlags.RelativeToLayoutsPage, HttpContext.Current,
                    Page.ClientQueryString);
        }

        #region Workflow Association Code - Typically,
                                   the following code should not be changed
        ...
        #endregion
    }
}
```

After deploying your workflow and custom form to SharePoint, you can test your association form. Instead of an OK button at the bottom of the workflow association form, a Next button is displayed that navigates to your custom association form. When you click Associate Workflow, the association is performed.

Custom Workflow Task Form

Creating a custom ASPX task form requires a separate content type for each task form. Such a content type defines fields to store the values entered into the form and defines the forms that are used to edit and display the task.

To define and deploy this content type, add a project to the solution, based on the Empty SharePoint Project template. Add a SharePoint-mapped Layouts folder and a content type to this project. The Layouts folder will contain the task form, and the Content Type folder will specify the additional fields and the content type itself, as shown in **Figure** 16–42.

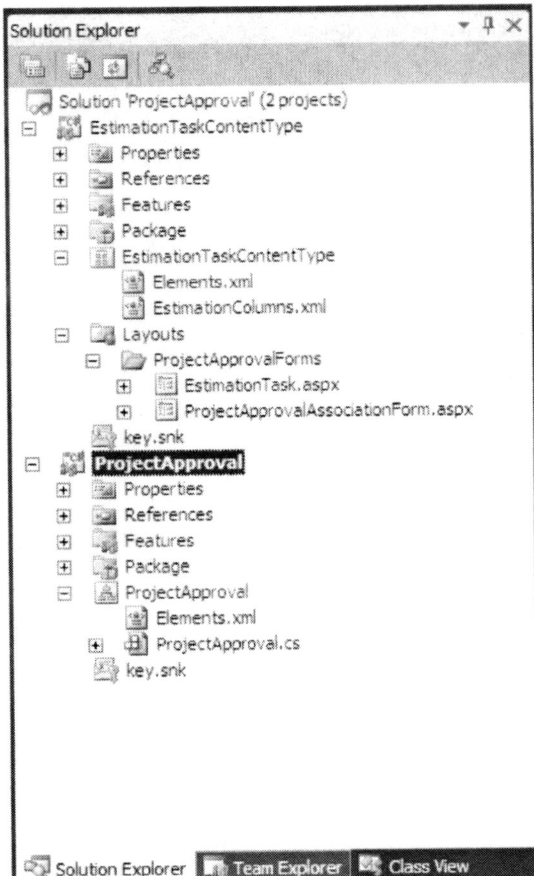

Figure 16–42. *Add a project for the form content type.*

Add a second XML file to the Content Type folder, which is used to define the fields for the content type. (In the example, it is named `EstimationColumns.xml`.) In this file, define your columns, as shown in Listing 16–9. (For more details on this, please refer to Chapter 7.)

For the example, two fields are defined for the estimation task: `EstimatedCosts` and `Outcome`. These columns are used in the content type definition for the workflow task form.

Listing 16–9. *Field Definitions for Custom Task*

```
<?xml version="1.0" encoding="utf-8" ?>
<Elements xmlns="http://schemas.microsoft.com/sharepoint/">
  <Field ID="{6CBABC50-4BC1-4399-BDC0-7C0155F2CC89}"
         Name="EstimatedCosts"
         DisplayName="Estimated Costs"
         StaticName="EstimatedCosts"
         Description="The estimated costs for the project"
```

```
            Type="Number"
        ></Field>
          <Field ID="{074AE023-34DD-4C2A-AA67-F9B88063C2BC}"
            Name="Outcome"
            DisplayName="Outcome"
            StaticName="Outcome"
            Description="The estimated costs for the project"
            Type="Text"
        ></Field>
</Elements>
```

In the content type definition shown in Listing 16–10, define an ID for the content type that inherits from `Workflow Task`, which has the ID 010801 in the following form: 0x010801 + 00 + < GUID>, where you have to generate a new GUID for your content type.

Add references to the fields that were defined in the Custom Columns definition earlier using `<FieldRef>` elements.

Finally, add an `<XmlDocument>` element to the `<XmlDocuments>` and indicate the custom form you want to use for the `Edit`, `Show`, and `New` forms.

Listing 16–10. *Content Type Definition for Custom Task*

```
<?xml version="1.0" encoding="utf-8"?>
<Elements xmlns="http://schemas.microsoft.com/sharepoint/">
  <!-- Parent ContentType: WorkflowTask (0x01080100) -->
  <ContentType ID="0x0108010031cda7a5483c452f93520d98df2f824a"
               Name="EstimationTaskContentType"
               Group="Project Approval"
               Description="Custom Task for ProjectApproval"
               Version="0">
    <FieldRefs>
      <FieldRef ID="{6CBABC50-4BC1-4399-BDC0-7C0155F2CC89}" DisplayName="EstimatedCosts"
Name="EstimatedCosts"/>
            <FieldRef ID="{074AE023-34DD-4C2A-AA67-F9B88063C2BC}" DisplayName="Outcome"
Name="Outcome"/>
    </FieldRefs>
    <XmlDocuments>
      <XmlDocument
NamespaceURI="http://schemas.microsoft.com/sharepoint/v3/contenttype/forms/url">
        <FormUrls xmlns="http://schemas.microsoft.com/sharepoint/v3/contenttype/forms/url">
          <Edit>_layouts/ProjectApprovalForms/EstimationTask.aspx</Edit>
          <Show>_layouts/ProjectApprovalForms/EstimationTask.aspx</Show>
        </FormUrls>
      </XmlDocument>
    </XmlDocuments>
  </ContentType>
</Elements>
```

To create the task form, add a new application page to the layouts folder that was mapped to the project earlier. In the markup code of the form, add the required controls within the `PlaceHolderMain` content placeholder. In the example shown in Listing 16–11, the controls are a `TextBox` for the estimated costs and a `RadioButtonList` for the outcome of the approval.

Listing 16–11. Markup Code for Estimation Task Form

```
<asp:Content ID="Main" ContentPlaceHolderID="PlaceHolderMain" runat="server">
    <div>
        Task Title:
        <asp:Label ID="lblTitle" runat="server"></asp:Label>
        <br /><br />

        Please estimate the project costs:
        <asp:TextBox runat="server" ID="EstimatedCosts"></asp:TextBox>
        <asp:RequiredFieldValidator id="valRequired" runat="server"
             ControlToValidate="EstimatedCosts" ErrorMessage="* Enter Number"
             Display="dynamic" type="Integer">
        </asp:RequiredFieldValidator>

        <asp:radiobuttonlist id="Outcome" runat="server">
            <asp:listitem id="Approve" runat="server" value="Approve" />
            <asp:listitem id="Deny" runat="server" value="Deny" />
        </asp:radiobuttonlist>

        <br /><br />

<asp:Button runat="server" ID="btnSubmit" OnClick="btnSubmit_Click" Text="Submit" />
</div>
</asp:Content>
```

The code-behind for the task form is responsible for passing the information from the form to the workflow. This is done via the AlterTask method of the SPWorkflowTask class. This method requires a reference to the current SPListItem in the task list and a Hashtable containing the new values of the fields that should be set for the task.

SharePoint passes relevant information to the form through request parameters. This way, you can access the Guid of the list and the ID of the item in the list, allowing you to load the correct SPListItem.

The Hashtable can be created using the information from the form to set values in the task item. It is passed to the AlterTask method for processing. If a key matches one the task fields, this field will be populated with the corresponding value in the Hashtable. All the entries in the Hashtable are also available in the workflow through the ExtendedProperties collection of the SPWorkflowTaskProperties object of the task. Only keys that are available through the standard task content type can be accessed directly from the SPWorkflowTaskProperties object.

Listing 16–12 shows how to access the request parameters in the Page_Load method and how to use the AlterTask method in the btnSubmit_Click method.

The final lines of code in Listing 16–12 are responsible for closing the custom task form. Since the form is shown in a modal dialog using the SharePoint dialog framework, you need to close the dialog using JavaScript.

Listing 16–12. Code-Behind for Task Form

```
using System;
using Microsoft.SharePoint;
using Microsoft.SharePoint.WebControls;
using Microsoft.SharePoint.Workflow;
using System.Collections;
using System.Globalization;
```

```
namespace EstimationTaskContentType.Layouts.ProjectApprovalForms
{
    public partial class EstimationTask : LayoutsPageBase
    {
        protected SPList _taskList;
        protected SPListItem _taskListItem;
        protected Guid _workflowGuid;
        protected string _listGuid;
        protected string _listItemId;

        protected void Page_Load(object sender, EventArgs e)
        {
            this._listGuid = Request.Params["List"];
            this._listItemId = Request.Params["ID"];

            using (SPWeb web = SPContext.Current.Site.OpenWeb())
            {
                this._taskList = web.Lists[new Guid(this._listGuid)];
                this._taskListItem =
this._taskList.GetItemById(Convert.ToInt32(this._listItemId));
            }
        }

        protected void btnSubmit_Click(object sender, EventArgs e)
        {
            Hashtable hashTable = new Hashtable();
            hashTable["EstimatedCosts"] = EstimatedCosts.Text;
            hashTable["_EstimatedCosts"] = EstimatedCosts.Text;
            hashTable["Outcome"] = Outcome.SelectedValue;
            hashTable["_Outcome"] = Outcome.SelectedValue;
            hashTable["TaskStatus"] = "complete";
            hashTable["PercentComplete"] = "1";

            SPWorkflowTask.AlterTask(this._taskListItem, hashTable, true);
            this.Page.Response.Clear();
        this.Page.Response.Write(
                string.Format(CultureInfo.InvariantCulture,
                  @"<script type=\"text/javascript\">
                   window.frameElement.commonModalDialogClose(1, '{0}');
                   </script>",
                  null));
            this.Page.Response.End();
        }
    }
}
```

■ **Note** In the assignment of the `Hashtable` values, the two fields from the custom content type are defined twice. The second time, the field name is prefixed with an underscore, but the value is the same as before. The reason for this approach is that SharePoint allows you to access known columns in the `ExtendedProperties` collection only by the `Guid` of the column, if the key matches an existing column. Therefore, this workaround allows you to set the value in your task using the column name in the `Hashtable` and access the field by its name using the leading underscore. You can see that in Listing 16–4, the key with an underscore prefix is used to access the properties.

Integrate InfoPath Forms with Workflows

In SharePoint Server 2010, InfoPath forms can be used as workflow forms instead of ASPX forms. The type of forms you choose does not influence the overall workflow behavior, but working with InfoPath forms is slightly different at some points. In general, InfoPath forms are a little easier, because you don't need to build a separate content type for each task form, and you don't need to program the forms. The forms are rendered by existing application pages that already do some of the work, which needs to be done manually in the case of custom ASPX pages. The following description is based on the previous example for ASPX forms, and thus only the differences are noted.

The first step is to build the InfoPath forms similar to the ASPX forms: an association form with a field for the estimation manager and a task form with one field for the estimated costs and a second field for the outcome of the approval. Both forms need to be published to the local disk using the Publish to a Network Location Wizard. (For details on form publishing, refer to Chapter 15.)

To include these InfoPath forms into the workflow feature, you need to adjust your feature definition file as follows:

- Add the `ReceiverAssembly` and `ReceiverClass` as described in Listing 16–13. This feature receiver will also upload your forms so they can be used in the workflow.
- Add a `<Property>` with the attribute key set to `RegisterForms` with the value `*.xsn`. This will tell the feature receiver to process all `.xsn` files.
- Add an `<ElementFile>` element to the `<ElementManifests>` for each form, and use the `Location` attribute to specify the form relative to the feature definition file.

These settings include your forms into the feature, and the feature receiver will deploy them appropriately.

Listing 16–13. *Feature Definition with InfoPath Forms*

```
<?xml version="1.0" encoding="utf-8" ?>
<Feature xmlns="http://schemas.microsoft.com/sharepoint/"
    ReceiverAssembly="Microsoft.Office.Workflow.Feature, Version=14.0.0.0,
                             Culture=neutral, PublicKeyToken=71e9bce111e9429c"
    ReceiverClass="Microsoft.Office.Workflow.Feature.WorkflowFeatureReceiver"
    Title="ProjectApproval Workflow IP"
```

```
    Description="My SharePoint Workflow Feature"
    Id="cb83bf08-3423-4c45-9396-ac5ff6b5043d" Scope="Site">
    <Properties>
        <Property Key="GloballyAvailable" Value="true" />
        <Property Key="RegisterForms" Value="*.xsn" />
    </Properties>
    <ElementManifests>
        <ElementManifest Location="ProjectApproval\Elements.xml" />
        <ElementFile Location="ProjectApproval\AssociationForm.xsn" />
        <ElementFile Location="ProjectApproval\EstimationTaskForm.xsn" />
    </ElementManifests>
</Feature>
```

In the element manifest file, all that needs to be done is to change the URLs for the forms. The AssociationUrl, InitiationUrl, and ModificationUrl need to be set to special SharePoint application pages that work with InfoPath forms. Listing 16–14 shows how to set these attributes.

To specify the actual InfoPath association form to be used, add an <Association_FormURN> element to the <MetaData>. As the text for this element, enter the URN of the association form. You can get this number from the InfoPath Designer in the Form Template Properties dialog in the field called ID.

Task forms are specified using the <Task[X]_FormURN>, where [X] is the number of the task, starting at zero. Again, the content of the element needs to be set to the URN of the relevant InfoPath form.

***Listing 16–14.** Manifest File with InfoPath Forms*

```
<?xml version="1.0" encoding="utf-8" ?>
<Elements xmlns="http://schemas.microsoft.com/sharepoint/">
    <Workflow
        Name="ProjectApprovalWorkflowIP"
        Description="My SharePoint Workflow with InfoPath"
        Id="0AE6882C-C69E-4455-A2E5-463DA0957B19"
        CodeBesideClass="ProjectApprovalIP.ProjectApprovalIP"
        CodeBesideAssembly="$assemblyname$"
        AssociationUrl="_layouts/CstWrkflIP.aspx"
        ModificationUrl="_layouts/ModWrkflIP.aspx"
        InstantiationUrl="_layouts/IniWrkflIP.aspx"
        StatusUrl="_layouts/WrkStat.aspx">

        <Categories/>
        <MetaData>
            <AssociationCategories>List</AssociationCategories>
            <Association_FormURN>urn:schemas-microsoft-com:office:infopath
                              :AssociationForm:-myXSD-2010-04-09T13-56-22
            </Association_FormURN>
            <Task0_FormURN>urn:schemas-microsoft-com:office:infopath
                          :EstimationTaskForm:-myXSD-2010-04-09T15-40-32
            </Task0_FormURN>
            <StatusPageUrl>_layouts/WrkStat.aspx</StatusPageUrl>
        </MetaData>
    </Workflow>
</Elements>
```

In the workflow code, working with InfoPath forms is similar to working with ASPX forms. You can access the form fields through the ExtendedProperties collection when using task forms. Association and Initiation forms store the InfoPath form as an XML string in the AssociationData property of the SPWorkflowAssociation.

When creating task forms, one additional property needs to be set to define which form is created, since the manifest file supports multiple task forms that are identified by an index, as shown in Listing 16–14. Use the CreateTask activity, and specify the index of the task in the TaskType property of the SPWorkflowTaskProperties object. For example, in Listing 16–15 the TaskType is set to 0, because only one task is specified in the manifest using the <Task0_FormURN> element.

■ **Caution** To access the InfoPath fields in your code, you should use only a flat structure of your form data. If you employ group elements in your schema, SharePoint won't be able to associate the fields to the ExtendedProperties collection.

Listing 16–15. *Creating Task with InfoPath Task Form in a Workflow*

```
private void createTask1_MethodInvoking(object sender, EventArgs e)
{
    estimationTask_TaskId = Guid.NewGuid();
    estimationTaskProperties.TaskType = 0;
    estimationTaskProperties.AssignedTo = "wapps\\administrator";
    estimationTaskProperties.Title = "Approve_" + workflowProperties.Item.Title;
    estimationTaskProperties.ExtendedProperties["Title"] =
                                        workflowProperties.Item.Title;
}
```

To pass parameters from your workflow to the InfoPath task edit form, you can use a special schema file called ItemMetadata.xml. This file is defined as shown in Listing 16–16. It contains only one element, <z:row>, and an attribute for every task property that should be passed to the form. The attributes are named with the prefix ows_ followed by the name of the attribute. For instance, ows_Title in the example will be used to pass the Title attribute to the form using the ExtendedProperties collection, as shown in Listing 16–15.

Listing 16–16. *ItemMetadata.xml*

```
<z:row xmlns:z="#RowsetSchema" ows_Title="" />
```

The ItemMetadata.xml file must be added to the InfoPath form as a secondary data source that is loaded when the form is opened and included as a resource file. You can then select the fields from the secondary data source as default values for the fields in your form.

SharePoint passes the task data to the InfoPath task form during form load. The ItemMetadata schema enables the form to process this data and makes the data accessible to the form.

■ **Caution** Since SharePoint always passes the task information during the form load event, the ItemMetadata.xml file is mandatory for every InfoPath task form. If this is not specified as a secondary data source—even if you don't use task data in the form—an error will be generated.

Summary

This chapter described the immense variety of possibilities for creating elaborate workflows in the SharePoint environment. SharePoint workflows are unique because they operate on SharePoint items, such as lists and sites, and involve human interaction.

Starting with SharePoint workflow basics, this chapter gave an overview of how to work with workflows in SharePoint and which tools can be used in workflow development. With SharePoint 2010, workflow development has greatly improved for codeless workflows that can be described using SharePoint Designer 2010. In addition, Visio 2010 can now be used to design workflows, and the integration of tools has been greatly improved.

Declarative workflows with SharePoint Designer were explained, together with the opportunities to enhance their functionality with custom actions. Custom workflows can be developed using Visual Studio 2010. These workflows are very powerful, exposing a wide scope for customization by skilled developers and overcoming certain limitations of declarative workflows. Forms based on ASP.NET or InfoPath can be integrated into workflows to allow the workflow to interact with users.

CHAPTER 17

Administrative Tasks

This chapter will give you ideas about several core tasks that could be performed using the administrative API. At first glance, the SharePoint API and the object model behind it can be intimidating. The platform is complex, huge, and at times confusing, and there isn't an obvious a set of best practices beyond the simple, entry-level examples that explain the first steps.

Often, developers start with SharePoint by supporting the administration of conventionally designed SharePoint applications. Administrative tasks are also a good place to begin learning the internals of the API from the ground up.

In this chapter you'll learn

- Why you should automate administrative tasks
- How to create the necessary objects
- How to maintain the `web.config` settings programmatically

You'll also find code samples for a collection of common tasks in this chapter.

Introduction

Chapter 1 outlined everything you need to establish a working environment for your applications. While regular SharePoint applications, Web Parts, and features run inside SharePoint, administrative tasks can run standalone. While they execute against an existing server and on the server, they are separate from SharePoint—being perhaps a console task, a web application, or even a WPF solution. For some such tasks there is no alternative to such a standalone approach. Creating a new web site in SharePoint can't be accomplished from a feature, which requires an existing web site. The final choice of the type of application is up to you. A few recommendations may assist with your decision:

- Use a console application if you plan to run tasks automatically—in batch files, for instance. Experienced administrators generally favor a console-based approach. This enhances what you get through `stsadm` and PowerShell.
- Use a WPF or Windows Forms application if you need
  - A very advanced UI containing many distinct options, or heavily graphical output, such as charts
  - To monitor an important parameter and track its state over time
  - High security over who is allowed to access or run the application

- For most other cases, a web application is the best solution. It provides a graphical UI and is easy to deploy. You can reach a broader audience and add more features from time to time just by adding pages. The lack of instant response could be overcome with techniques like Ajax, though; a Windows application would always run more smoothly here.
- A SharePoint feature is the best option if you want to allow site users or site administrators to execute basic administrative tasks. Usually such features simplify regular tasks or aggregate several frequently launched tasks together into one action. There is a danger, though, in exposing the administrative API to people who may be unaware of the consequences: tread carefully!

Why Automate Tasks?

You may be wondering why you should bother programming things you can already program using Central Administration or the Site Settings dialogs. Besides, many scripting tasks are better accomplished with `stsadm` or PowerShell.

There are several good reasons for automating certain tasks using the API. For one, `stsadm` does not provide a UI. As a scripting tool, it's extremely powerful; however, if you perform an operation repeatedly, it's hard to process return values, error prompts, success messages, and so forth, and assemble a useful report from them all. Even Central Administration is suboptimal if you want to create hundreds of sites or, for example, provision a Web Part to 1,500 existing web sites, each with a slightly different setting.

There are several more advantages of using the API as well. Sooner or later you will start writing site templates for your installation. Customized site templates allow users to build enterprise-specific sites with special features for fulfilling certain tasks. Creating, maintaining, and deploying site templates is challenging work. It is not best practice to customize existing templates. Internally, SharePoint holds the definition of the templates in the database. Your customized version of such an STP file is merely a collection of changes. At runtime, the server merges the existing template with your data (i.e., a merge between content from the database and the file system). As you might imagine, this process can take time. In addition, your definitions may grow unexpectedly. Imagine you need to add a few simple definitions to the `onet.xml` file, each requiring hundreds of lines. Five additional definitions and a few requirements later, and you face 3,000 lines of XML.

When developers first consider SharePoint, the XML-based configuration seems to be a boon. With IntelliSense, editing such files seems to be a task that even those who don't speak C# fluently could manage. However, sooner or later, depending on how quickly new requirements are added, your solution becomes unworkable.

The answer to all this is the SharePoint API and the deployment framework. The deployment framework consists of two major parts—solutions and features. Solutions contain the distributed parts, assemblies, XML files, resources, and data. A feature is similar to a solution and frequently distributed as a solution. However, it has several ways it can be managed by the SharePoint UI. Users with administrative privileges can activate and deactivate features. The developer of the feature can run code whenever it's activated or deactivated. The feature runs inside SharePoint and has full access to the API.

There are, though, some administrative tasks that are beyond the scope of a feature. For instance, if you wish to configure a farm or create a new web site, you can't use a feature, because features are designed to run inside an already existing site. In those situations, the administrative tasks require a standalone solution. Despite the availability of the `stsadm` program, or the PowerShell equivalent—and both are adept for such tasks—a more interactive approach would be an advantage. Besides, despite the vast number of features `stsadm` provides, it still lacks support for some of the tasks you may eventually need. Again, this is where again the SharePoint API appears to be the most flexible and powerful option.

Large SharePoint installations typically include multiple servers. Often they are configured to form a farm, while other installations may require separate servers. To distribute templates among your computing center, automation tasks are essential.

Creating Objects

Typical tasks include the creation of web applications and sites, and provisioning of web sites. The internal steps for building a new web application are as follows:

1. Create a unique entry in the configuration database and assign a GUID.
2. Create a web site in IIS and configure it.
3. Create the root folder where the pages and resources will be stored.
4. Create an application pool in IIS and assign it to the web site.
5. Configure authentication and encryption as required by the administrator.
6. Create the first content database for this web application.
7. Assign the search service.
8. Define the public name visible in Central Administration.
9. Create the first site inside the web—the root site that's always required.
10. Configure the web to apply the settings specified by the creator.

There are several optional tasks that might also take place. For example, you can assign alternative URLs to your application. Obviously, executing all these tasks manually could be complicated, error-prone; automating them with a more sophisticated, interactive process provides a significant productivity gain. Now that you have persuaded yourself that it's an advantage to program against the administrative object model, let's start writing code.

Creating a Web Application

The `SPFarm` object is one key entry point into the object model. For administrative tasks, the code to obtain an `SPFarm` object looks like this:

```
SPFarm farm = SPWebServices.AdministrationService.Farm;
```

Given an `SPFarm` object, you can now undertake the necessary tasks. To create and maintain a web, use the `SPWebApplicationBuilder` class. Running its `Create` method, an `SPWebApplication` object is returned, which gives you further access to the freshly created web. The example shown in Listing 17–1 reveals how to construct a new web. It consists of a simple console application with fixed values that performs the creation. Consider using parameters in real life applications.

Listing 17–1. *Console to Create a New SharePoint Web*

```
using System;
using System.Collections.Generic;
using System.Linq;
using System.Text;
using Microsoft.SharePoint.Administration;
```

```
namespace Apress.SP2010.NewWeb
{
    class Program
    {
        static void Main(string[] args)
        {
            string WebName = "Test";     // Change before execute
            int port = 999;              // Change before execute
            SPFarm farm = SPWebService.AdministrationService.Farm;
            SPWebApplicationBuilder builder = new SPWebApplicationBuilder(farm);
            builder.ApplicationPoolUsername = "Administrator";
            builder.ApplicationPoolPassword = new System.Security.SecureString();
            builder.ApplicationPoolPassword.AppendChar('S');
            builder.ApplicationPoolPassword.AppendChar('h');
            builder.ApplicationPoolPassword.AppendChar('a');
            builder.ApplicationPoolPassword.AppendChar('r');
            builder.ApplicationPoolPassword.AppendChar('e');
            builder.ApplicationPoolPassword.AppendChar('P');
            builder.ApplicationPoolPassword.AppendChar('o');
            builder.ApplicationPoolPassword.AppendChar('i');
            builder.ApplicationPoolPassword.AppendChar('n');
            builder.ApplicationPoolPassword.AppendChar('t');
            builder.ApplicationPoolPassword.AppendChar('2');
            builder.ApplicationPoolPassword.AppendChar('0');
            builder.ApplicationPoolPassword.AppendChar('1');
            builder.ApplicationPoolPassword.AppendChar('0');
            builder.ApplicationPoolId = String.Format("AppPool_{0}", WebName);
            builder.DatabaseName = String.Format("SPContentDB_{0}", WebName);
            builder.Port = port;
            builder.Create();
        }
    }
}
```

When you deal with administrative tasks, you will frequently need to assign passwords. This is a critical aspect, as unencrypted passwords in code create a security hole. For this reason, the SharePoint API forces you to use `System.Security.SecureString` when handling passwords. This class ensures that the password values cannot be extracted from the memory while your code is running. However, if an attacker gets the compiled code, storing passwords in the code does not hide it. If you're wondering how someone could get access to your highly secured enterprise network, remember that several people—administrators, developers, and managers—may have access to the servers on which your code is running, or at least to the development machines. Also, your code could spread over time and eventually slip into an unsecured domain. You must ensure that your passwords remain completely secure. So, while the following code may look smart, it's actually quite dangerous from a security standpoint:

```
string password = "SharePoint2010";
foreach (char c in password)
{
    builder.ApplicationPoolPassword.AppendChar(c);
}
```

The variable password is now in memory, and as long as the garbage collector doesn't clean up this section of memory, the string is readable from a sniffer tool. This might sound not obvious, but it's a common method if the sources and assemblies are not reachable.

Another issue is with the various GUIDs SharePoint uses. You must either reference the right GUID or create a new one. In code, you can generate a new GUID easily in one line:

```
Guid guid = Guid.NewGuid();
```

To check what GUIDs already exist, ask the configuration database. (See the section "Retrieving the Configuration Database" near the end of this chapter for more details.)

Having created a new `SPWebApplication` object, the next step is to configure it. Once you have made all your configuration changes to the new `SPWebApplication`, call the `Update` method to persist the settings and update the server farm.

Creating a Site Collection

Large enterprises require an amazing number of site collections. Imagine a company with dozens of divisions split into hundreds of independent departments. Each department can run one or more site collections for its specific purpose. The management of hundreds of site collections is a challenging task for administrators; significantly automating that task saves time and money. Creating site collections programmatically ensures that their internal structures will be well defined and will strictly adhere to the enterprise policies.

For administrative purposes you need to think about automation tasks. Using XML (see Listing 17–2) to define the configuration for an action is a common approach.

Listing 17–2. *XML File for a Site Collection Definition*

```
<?xml version="1.0" encoding="utf-8" ?>
<SiteDefinition>
  <Url>/sites/BlankInternetSite</Url>
  <Title>Generated Site</Title>
  <Description>This site is being genereated by a script.</Description>
  <LCID>1033</LCID>
  <WebTemplate></WebTemplate>
  <OwnerLogin>Administrator</OwnerLogin>
  <OwnerName>Administrator</OwnerName>
  <OwnerEmail>joerg@krause.net</OwnerEmail>
</SiteDefinition>
```

▒ **Tip** If the XML file is part of your project, you can set the value of the file's "Copy to output Directory" property to "Copy always." Visual Studio will copy the file to the output folder alongside the freshly compiled executables.

A console application—see listing 17–3—is used to read this file (assuming it's in the same folder as the executable).

Listing 17–3. *A Console Application That Creates a Site Collection from an XML file*

```
using System;
using System.Collections.Generic;
using System.Linq;
using System.Text;
```

```
using Microsoft.SharePoint;
using Microsoft.SharePoint.Administration;
using System.Xml.Linq;

namespace Apress.SP2010.CreateSiteCollection
{
    class Program
    {
        static void Main(string[] args)
        {
            System.Environment.ExitCode = CreateSiteCollection();
        }

        private static int CreateSiteCollection()
        {
            try
            {
                string srvUrl = "http://sharepointserve";
                using (SPSite site = new SPSite(srvUrl))
                {
                    // Current collection
                    SPSiteCollection coll = site.WebApplication.Sites;
                    XDocument definition = XDocument.Load("SiteDefinition.xml");
                    XElement root = definition.Element("SiteDefinition");
                    SPSite newSite = coll.Add(
                        root.Element("Url").Value,
                        root.Element("Title").Value,
                        root.Element("Description").Value,
                        Convert.ToUInt32(root.Element("LCID").Value),
                        (String.IsNullOrEmpty(root.Element("WebTemplate").Value) ?
                                        null : root.Element("WebTemplate").Value),
                        root.Element("OwnerLogin").Value,
                        root.Element("OwnerName").Value,
                        root.Element("OwnerEmail").Value
                        );
                    return 0;
                }
            }
            catch (Exception ex)
            {
                Console.WriteLine(ex.Message);
                return 1;
            }
        }
    }
}
```

The application does not output anything—the return value is merely used to let it run as part of a batch file. After executing this script, which will take a while, you can open the site. If you didn't provide a template, the user will be prompted to select one (see Figure 17–1). (However, this user will have to have an appropriate permission level to do this.)

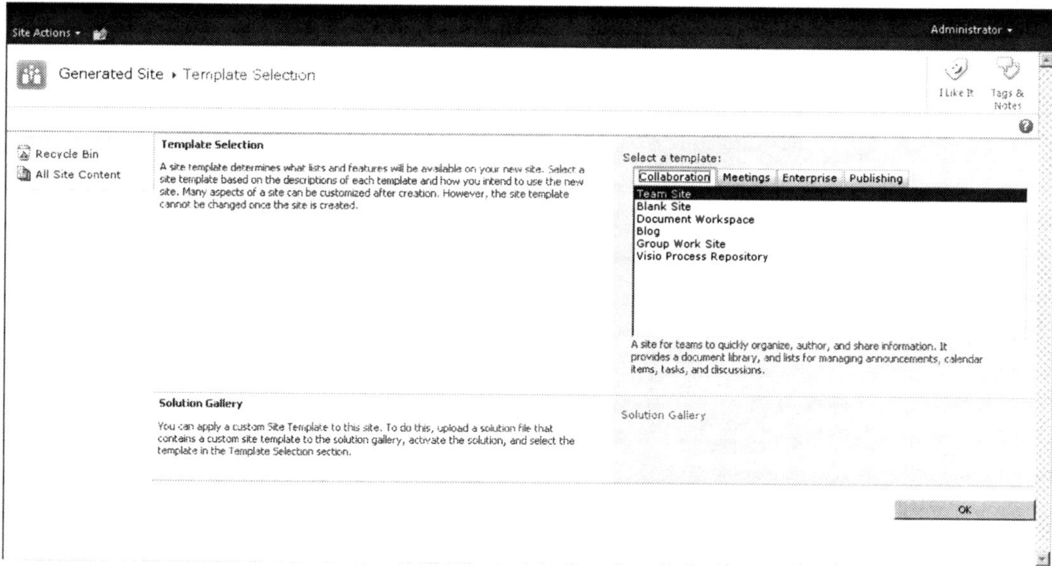

Figure 17–1. *If a site is created without a template, the user will be prompted to choose one.*

To provide a valid template, you must use the internal name, as defined in `%SharePointRoot%/TEMPLATES/SiteTemplates`. The AdventureWorks example template, for instance, has the internal name `BLANKINTERNET`. In XML, the element would look like this:

```
<WebTemplate>BLANKINTERNET</WebTemplate>
```

You can extend this example by investigating the other overloads provided by the `Add` method of the `SPSiteCollection` class.

Creating a Web

When you create a new site collection, it automatically contains one web site: the root web. However, you can create any number of web sites within the site collection to further structure the content. The main reason to create subwebs is to break role inheritance and assign different permissions to users working with particular webs.

From an object model viewpoint, each web site corresponds to an `SPWeb` object. You need to provide an existing site collection, represented by an `SPSite` object, to which your new web site will be added. This solution follows a similar approach to the previous example and uses an XML file to define the parameters.

Listing 17–4. *XML File for a Web Using the Blog Template*

```
<?xml version="1.0" encoding="utf-8" ?>
<SiteDefinition>
  <Url>InternetBlog</Url>
  <Title>Generated Site</Title>
  <Description>This site is being genereated by a script.</Description>
```

```
  <LCID>1033</LCID>
  <WebTemplate>Blog</WebTemplate>
  <UniquePermissions>False</UniquePermissions>
  <ConvertIfThere>False</ConvertIfThere>
</SiteDefinition>
```

The code assumes that you have a site collection already. (If you have executed the examples in the order they appear in the book, you should have one.)

Listing 17-5. A Console Application That Generates a New Web

```
using System;
using System.Collections.Generic;
using System.Linq;
using System.Text;
using System.Xml.Linq;
using Microsoft.SharePoint;
using Microsoft.SharePoint.Administration;

namespace Apress.SP2010.CreateWeb
{
    class Program
    {
        static void Main(string[] args)
        {
            System.Environment.ExitCode = CreateWeb();
        }

        private static int CreateWeb()
        {
            try
            {
                string srvUrl = "http://sharepointserve/sites/BlankInternetSite";
                using (SPSite site = new SPSite(srvUrl))
                {
                    // Current collection
                    XDocument definition = XDocument.Load("WebDefinition.xml");
                    XElement root = definition.Element("SiteDefinition");
                    SPWeb newWeb = site.AllWebs.Add(
                        root.Element("Url").Value,
                        root.Element("Title").Value,
                        root.Element("Description").Value,
                        Convert.ToUInt32(root.Element("LCID").Value),
                        (String.IsNullOrEmpty(root.Element("WebTemplate").Value) ?
                                    null : root.Element("WebTemplate").Value),
                        Boolean.Parse(root.Element("UniquePermissions").Value),
                        Boolean.Parse(root.Element("ConvertIfThere").Value)
                        );
                    return 0;
                }
            }
            catch (Exception ex)
            {
                Console.WriteLine(ex.Message);
```

```
                    return 1;
                }
            }
        }
}
```

The XML file references the Blog template. The Url is relative to your current site collection. In the example, the absolute address of the new blog is

http://sharepointserve/sites/BlankInternetSite/InternetBlog/default.aspx

The settings provided by the XML appear in the web, as shown in Figure 17–2.

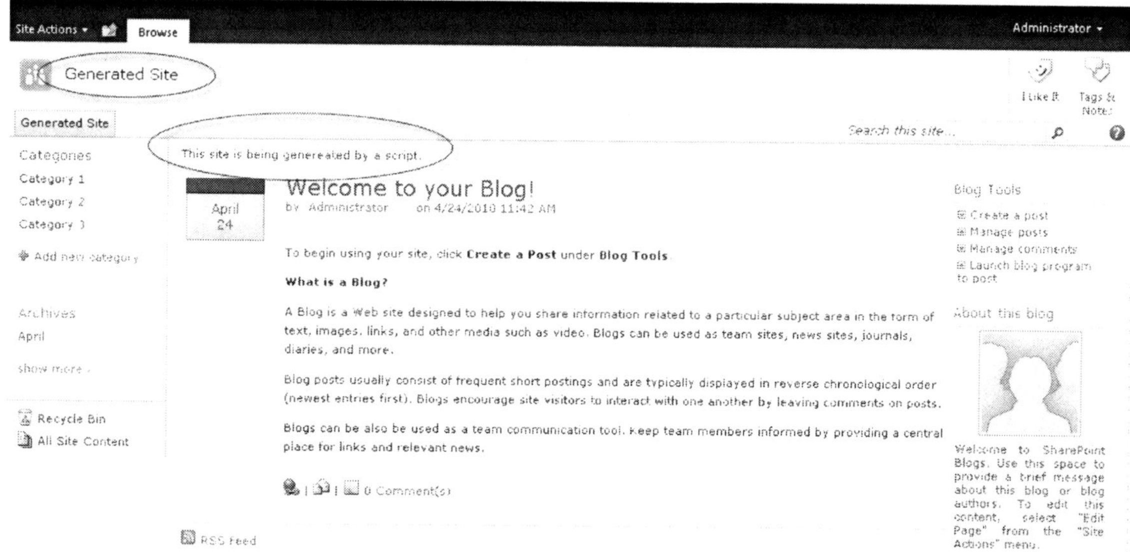

***Figure 17–2.** An automatically created blog*

Working with Site Configurations

Creating and removing objects is a frequent task when administering a SharePoint farm. Another is maintaining the configuration in order to handle all the requests users may make.

Working with Site Properties

Each site includes a property bag, which is widely used internally by SharePoint. However, there is no reason why you cannot also use this property bag to store common settings related to a site. You can regard the bag as an application settings collection, equivalent to what you would normally define in a web.config or app.config file. As in the configuration files, the settings are a collection of key/value pairs.

The properties you use for your own purpose should be clearly distinguishable from those used internally. The best way to achieve this is by adding a unique prefix, such as myprop_. You access the properties through the Properties property of the SPWeb object.

The code shown in Listing 17–6 uses the site collection previously created in this chapter to add a private value to the property bag.

Listing 17–6. Creating a Custom Site Property

```
using System;
using System.Collections.Generic;
using System.Collections.Specialized;
using System.Linq;
using System.Text;
using Microsoft.SharePoint;
using System.Collections;

namespace Apress.SP2010.ReadAddModifyProperties
{
    class Program
    {

        const string PREFIX = "myprop_";

        static void Main(string[] args)
        {
            using (SPSite site =
                   new SPSite("http://sharepointserve/sites/BlankInternetSite/"))
            {
                using (SPWeb web = site.RootWeb)
                {
                    foreach (DictionaryEntry entry in web.Properties)
                    {
                        Console.WriteLine("{0} = {1}", entry.Key, entry.Value);
                    }
                    string key = PREFIX + "AutoCreator";
                    if (!web.Properties.ContainsKey(key))
                    {
                        web.Properties.Add(key,
                            String.Format("Created by {0} at {1}",
                            Environment.UserName,
                            DateTime.Now));
                        web.AllowUnsafeUpdates = true;
                        web.Properties.Update();
                    }
                }
            }
            Console.ReadLine();
        }
    }
}
```

The code displays the existing properties first. To see your new property you must execute the application twice (see Figure 17–3 for the second output). Because this code changes site settings, the `AllowUnsafeUpdates` property must first be set to `true`. An additional reset is not required. With the call of the `Update` method of the `Properties` collection, the new property is persisted to the site. Calling `SPWeb`'s `Update` method has no effect here.

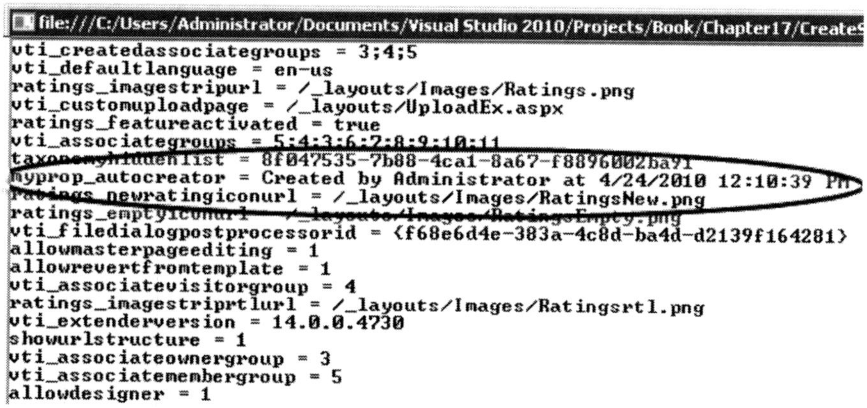

```
file:///C:/Users/Administrator/Documents/Visual Studio 2010/Projects/Book/Chapter17/CreateS
vti_createdassociategroups = 3;4;5
vti_defaultlanguage = en-us
ratings_imagestripurl = /_layouts/Images/Ratings.png
vti_customuploadpage = /_layouts/UploadEx.aspx
ratings_featureactivated = true
vti_associategroups = 5;4;3;6;7;8;9;10;11
taxonomyhiddenlist = 8f047535-7b88-4ca1-8a67-f88960002ba91
myprop_autocreator = Created by Administrator at 4/24/2010 12:10:39 PM
ratings_newratingiconurl = /_layouts/Images/RatingsNew.png
ratings_emptyiconurl = /_layouts/Images/RatingsEmpty.png
vti_filedialogpostprocessorid = {f68e6d4e-383a-4c8d-ba4d-d2139f164281}
allowmasterpageediting = 1
allowrevertfromtemplate = 1
vti_associatevisitorgroup = 4
ratings_imagestriprtlurl = /_layouts/Images/Ratingsrtl.png
vti_extenderversion = 14.0.0.4730
showurlstructure = 1
vti_associateownergroup = 3
vti_associatemembergroup = 5
allowdesigner = 1
```

Figure 17–3. *Adding a custom property*

You can now use your custom properties in your code by accessing the `Properties` collection.

Maintaining Settings in web.config Programmatically

Since SharePoint is built on top of ASP.NET, that means that the distinct configuration method for ASP.NET, the `web.config` file, plays a pivotal role. As a developer you consider this file part of your project, along with the central `web.config` file that configures the server, and optionally those sections dedicated to parts of your application. Maintaining, deploying, and reverting configuration file settings are common tasks. Handling the settings in configuration files and providing deployment strategies for them works well for small implementations. However, once your SharePoint farm starts growing, things become more difficult. Not only does the number of settings increase, but the sheer volume of files also makes it hard to find the specific entry to modify for the desired effect. Configuration files form a hierarchy, and the flexible model allows subsequent files to overwrite settings, replacing those added at higher levels. More confusing, settings at higher levels can define themselves as not overwritable to prevent unpredictable changes. The result is that the final values for settings are sometimes hard to explicitly predict, leading to yet another administrative nightmare.

Using the API is much more powerful and opens up the opportunity to confidently maintain configuration settings throughout a farm. Servers added to the farm receive the current settings automatically, and SharePoint ensures that the settings match. In particular, the `SafeControl` setting, which registers Web Parts as safe to use by end users, can drive you crazy. Whenever a Web Part is deployed, all `web.config` files in the farm must be updated. Moreover, even a simple change in the version number to get the latest update necessitates changes across the farm. If the Web Part is deployed as part of a feature, either the feature must change the settings, or some manual action must be performed to do so. That's certainly not the picture of an easy-to-administer server farm—missing an obscure step can cause your features to stop working.

Setting Up the Configuration

The entry point into the `web.config` configuration is the `SPWebConfigModification` class. This class is related to `SPWebApplication`. This means that each web application has its own list of modifications. The `SPWebConfigModification` class is useful if you have particular entries that you'd like to set. The settings are stored in the content database and applied to existing `web.config` files. If a new server is added or a new `web.config` appears, SharePoint ensures that the registered changes are applied automatically. However, for this to happen, there are some preconditions to be met and several aspects to consider:

- The modification store contains all changes—not just yours, but also all those made by any other application for the current web.
- Every modification has an owner, each with a corresponding `Owner` property. In fact, this is a unique string that identifies the owner, and you're free to use any name for it. We suggest using the assembly or feature name. (You could also use a GUID for the entry name, but this would make reading such entries much harder.)
- Removing changes is easier if you can refer to the owner. If you change a value and remove it later, the original value will be restored. Therefore, you can regard removing as a undo step. This implies that you are not forced to remember the previous settings to restore them later. That's rather useful when a feature sets values, as once it's deactivated, the remove step will restore the previous settings. Reassigning the values explicitly would issue another register cycle, and this could confuse the configuration store. Hence, undo is the better option.
- You should connect modifications to features. If the feature has no other task, you can hide it. Using features guarantees the distribution of the modifications across all servers in the farm without any additional code.

To change the settings of an existing entry is easy using this class. The addressing of such entries is straightforward—it uses XPath to navigate within the XML—provided you have a working knowledge of XPath. To access an entry, you can start with the following code:

```
SPWebConfigModification mod = new SPWebConfigModification();
```

The object created by this expression has several additional options (see Table 17–1).

***Table 17–1.** Properties That Modify the Element-Changing Procedure*

Property	Description
`Name`	Gets or sets the name of the attribute or section node to be modified or created. This is an XPath expression relative to the parent node. The parent is specified by the `Path` property.
`Path`	Gets or sets the XPath expression that is used to locate the node that is being modified or created. The expression can address either a node or an attribute, depending on what you'd like to change or get.
`Owner`	Specifies a unique string to register the modifications against a person, application, process, or whatever is responsible. This is important for ensuring that subsequent changes made by others do not scramble your settings.

Property	Description
Sequence	Accepts values within a range of 0 to 65,536. If the same setting is applied multiple times, a lower sequence number is applied first.
Type	Specifies the type of modification. An enum with the following values:EnsureChildNode: Ensures that the node exists. If it does not, it creates the node. EnsureAttribute: Ensures that the attribute exists. If it does not, it creates it. EnsureSection: Ensures that the section exists. If it does not, it creates the sections. Sections cannot be removed, so use this option with caution.
Value	Specifies the value to be written,
UpgradePersistedProperties	Returns a collection of modified fields as key/value pairs.

Some typical scenarios should clarify things. Imagine you want to set the error handling and show all exceptions, instead of a short, meaningless message. The following entry in `web.config` would do the trick:

```
<configuration>
   <system.web>
      <customErrors mode="Off">
   <system.web>
<configuration>
```

You can access this entry and effect this change in code:

```
private void ExtendErrorSettings()
{
   SPWebApplication web = new SPSite(txtUrl.Text).WebApplication;
   var mod = new SPWebConfigModification();
   mod.Name = "mode";
   mod.Path = "//system.web/customErrors";
   mod.Owner = "WebConfigSettings.aspx";
   mod.Sequence = 0;
   mod.Type = SPWebConfigModification.SPWebConfigModificationType.EnsureAttribute;
   mod.Value = "Off";
   web.WebConfigModifications.Add(mod);
   web.Farm.Services.GetValue<SPWebService>().ApplyWebConfigModifications();
   web.Update();
}
```

The complete sample code contains a web form that enables you to enter the application's address in a `TextBox` named `txtUrl`. The name of the ASPX page is used as the owner's name.

■ **Caution** In the code snippet, the current `Context` is set to `null`. This is required if and only if you run a separate ASP.NET application to launch the code. Internally, SharePoint checks whether an `HttpContext` exists and, if there is one, tries to retrieve the current web from it. If the application runs outside the context of

SharePoint, this fails. It works fine within a console application, however. Here, the HttpContext is null, and the internal code checks this and skips the steps that rely on it.

You might consider adding code to restore the HttpContext object, if it is required in subsequent steps made on the same page.

Removing the setting is as straightforward as creating it:

```
private void RemoveErrorSettings()
{
    SPWebApplication web = new SPSite(txtUrl.Text).WebApplication;
    var coll = from c in web.WebConfigModifications
               where c.Owner.Equals("WebConfigSettings.aspx")
               select c;
    if (coll.Count() > 0)
    {
        for (int i = coll.Count() - 1; i >= 0; i--)
        {
            // Ensure that we remove from end
            SPWebConfigModification mod = coll.ElementAt(i);
            web.WebConfigModifications.Remove(mod);
        }
        // If run outside SharePoint, this line is required
        HttpContext.Current = null;
        web.Farm.Services.GetValue<SPWebService>().ApplyWebConfigModifications();
        web.Update();
    }
}
```

Here, we use a LINQ statement to retrieve the modifications for a particular owner. The collection's elements are removed immediately, so you can't loop using a foreach statement. Instead, the for loop ensures that the elements are deleted by removing the elements in order from last to first.

The modification process is performed by a timer job, and runs quickly but not immediately. If you call the ApplyWebConfigModifications method several times, you could encounter an exception that says, "A web configuration modification is already running." As a best practice you should aggregate all modifications together and call the method only once. Assembling several settings and deploying them as one feature is an acceptable strategy. Creating a number of separate features is harder work and causes more stress for the system.

Accessing the Current Settings

The configuration changes are stored in the Objects table of the configuration database. You can retrieve the stored values via the following SQL statement:

```
SELECT * FROM Objects WHERE Name LIKE 'WebConfigChanges%'
```

You can find the changes easily. However, the values stored in the database are out of sequence. Instead, it seems like they are stored in the database in descending order based on the SPWebConfigModification.Name property. Changing the Name and Value properties leads to a sequence like this:

```
Name = "remove[@sequence='" + sequence + "']"
Value = "<remove verb='*' path='*.asmx' />"
Name = "add[@sequence='" + sequence + "']"
Value = "<add verb='*' path='*.asmx' validate='false'
              type='System.Web.Script.Services.ScriptHandlerFactory, "
              + Constants.AJAXExtensionsAssembly + "' />"
```

The `add[@path='*.asmx']` code will always come before the `remove[@path='*.asmx']` part, even if you put the remove part in the collection first and give it a lower sequence number.

You can use the Sequence property to resolve this issue. If you increment the sequence number for each change, you can use this as the key to finding the node. This will put in order all items that have the same tag, but still doesn't fix the ordering for items with different tag names. (Plus, adding this extra attribute isn't the cleanest code, either.)

Working with Features

Features are a core concept of SharePoint. It is common to create site collections and provide users a collection of features that add particular functionality. If you build many features, you can employ hidden features to deploy support documents, for example. However, hidden features are not visible in the UI, and if it fails you need code or `stsadm` to remove the feature. To handle this issue, building your own administration environment could be a good idea.

This example shows you how to build a simple WPF application to handle features. It's not as attractive as it could be, but it should give you an idea of how to handle features at different scopes (see Figure 17–4).

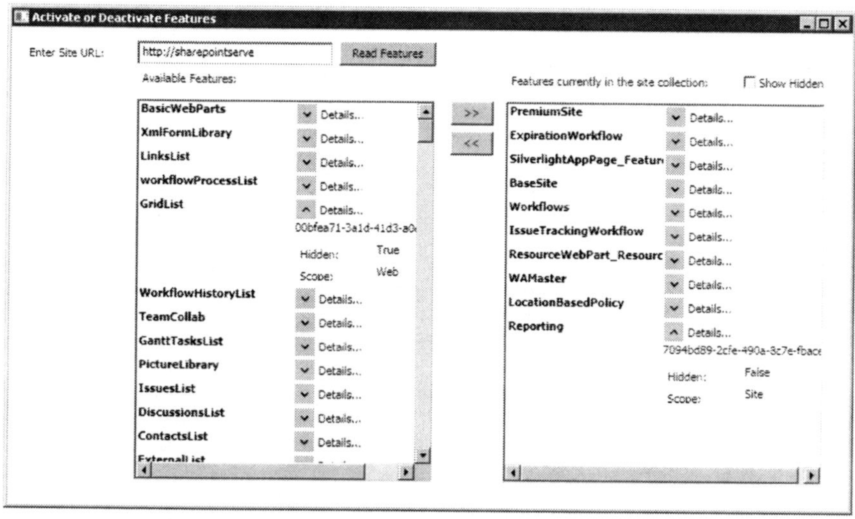

Figure 17–4. A simple WPF application for handling site features

The WPF application (see Listing 17–7) is composed of two parts: the XAML that defines the UI and binding and the code-behind that retrieves the data and handles user actions.

Listing 17-7. XAML Code for the Application's UI

```
<Window x:Class="ActivateFeatures.MainWindow"
        xmlns="http://schemas.microsoft.com/winfx/2006/xaml/presentation"
        xmlns:x="http://schemas.microsoft.com/winfx/2006/xaml"
        Title="Activate or Deactivate Features" Height="487" Width="831">
    <Grid>
        <TextBox Height="23" HorizontalAlignment="Left" Margin="124,12,0,0"
                 Name="txtUrl" VerticalAlignment="Top" Width="191" />
        <Label Content="Enter Site URL:" Height="23" HorizontalAlignment="Left"
               Margin="12,12,0,0" Name="label1"
               VerticalAlignment="Top" Width="106" />
        <Button Content="Read Features" Height="23" HorizontalAlignment="Left"
                Margin="321,11,0,0" Name="btnRead"
                VerticalAlignment="Top" Width="95" Click="btnRead_Click" />
        <ListBox Height="368" ItemsSource="{Binding}" HorizontalAlignment="Left"
                 Margin="124,68,0,0" Name="lstFarm"
                 VerticalAlignment="Top" Width="292">
            <ListBox.ItemTemplate>
                <DataTemplate>
                    <StackPanel Orientation="Horizontal">
                        <TextBlock Text="{Binding DisplayName}" Height="21"
                                   Margin="0,0,0,0" Width="150"
                                   FontWeight="Bold" VerticalAlignment="Top" />
                        <Expander Header="Details..." Margin="0,0,0,0"
                                  BorderThickness="1"
                                  BorderBrush="AliceBlue"
                                  VerticalAlignment="Top">
                            <Grid Width="160">
                                <Grid.ColumnDefinitions>
                                    <ColumnDefinition />
                                    <ColumnDefinition />
                                </Grid.ColumnDefinitions>
                                <Grid.RowDefinitions>
                                    <RowDefinition Height="21" />
                                    <RowDefinition Height="21" />
                                    <RowDefinition Height="21" />
                                </Grid.RowDefinitions>
                                <TextBlock Text="{Binding Id}" Grid.ColumnSpan="2"
                                           Grid.Row="0" Grid.Column="0" />
                                <Label Content="Hidden:" Grid.Row="1"
                                       Grid.Column="0" VerticalAlignment="Top" />
                                <TextBlock Text="{Binding Hidden}" Grid.Row="1"
                                            Grid.Column="1" />
                                <Label Content="Scope:" Grid.Row="2" Grid.Column="0"
                                       VerticalAlignment="Top"/>
                                <TextBlock Text="{Binding Scope}" Grid.Row="2"
                                           Grid.Column="1"/>
                            </Grid>
                        </Expander>
                    </StackPanel>
                </DataTemplate>
            </ListBox.ItemTemplate>
```

```
</ListBox>
<ListBox Height="368" HorizontalAlignment="Left" Margin="485,68,0,0"
         Name="lstSite" VerticalAlignment="Top" Width="312">
    <ListBox.ItemTemplate>
        <DataTemplate>
            <StackPanel Orientation="Horizontal">
                <TextBlock Text="{Binding DisplayName}" Width="150"
                           Margin="0,0,0,0" FontWeight="Bold"
                           VerticalAlignment="Top"/>
                <Expander Header="Details..." BorderThickness="1"
                          BorderBrush="AliceBlue" Margin="0,0,0,0"
                          ExpandDirection="Down" VerticalAlignment="Top">
                    <Grid Width="160">
                        <Grid.ColumnDefinitions>
                            <ColumnDefinition />
                            <ColumnDefinition />
                        </Grid.ColumnDefinitions>
                        <Grid.RowDefinitions>
                            <RowDefinition Height="21" />
                            <RowDefinition Height="21" />
                            <RowDefinition Height="21" />
                        </Grid.RowDefinitions>
                        <TextBlock Text="{Binding Id}" Grid.ColumnSpan="2"
                                   Grid.Row="0" Grid.Column="0" />
                        <Label Content="Hidden:" Grid.Row="1"
                               Grid.Column="0" VerticalAlignment="Top" />
                        <TextBlock Text="{Binding Hidden}" Grid.Row="1"
                                   Grid.Column="1" />
                        <Label Content="Scope:" Grid.Row="2" Grid.Column="0"
                               VerticalAlignment="Top"/>
                        <TextBlock Text="{Binding Scope}" Grid.Row="2"
                                   Grid.Column="1"/>
                    </Grid>
                </Expander>
            </StackPanel>
        </DataTemplate>
    </ListBox.ItemTemplate>
</ListBox>
<Label Content="Available Features:" Height="28" HorizontalAlignment="Left"
       Margin="124,36,0,0" Name="label2"
       VerticalAlignment="Top" Width="106" />
<Label Content="Features currently in the site collection:" Height="28"
       HorizontalAlignment="Left" Margin="485,36,0,0"
       Name="label3" VerticalAlignment="Top" Width="229" />
<Button Content="&gt;&gt;" Height="23" HorizontalAlignment="Left"
        Margin="431,68,0,0" Name="btnAdd"
        VerticalAlignment="Top" Width="42"
        IsEnabled="{Binding ElementName=listBox1, Path=SelectedIndex}"
        Click="btnAdd_Click" />
<Button Content="&lt;&lt;" Height="23" HorizontalAlignment="Left"
        Margin="431,97,0,0" Name="btnRemove" VerticalAlignment="Top"
       Width="42" Click="btnRemove_Click" />
<CheckBox Content="Show Hidden" Height="16" HorizontalAlignment="Left"
          Margin="716,41,0,0" Name="checkBox1" VerticalAlignment="Top"
```

```
                  IsChecked="True" Checked="checkBox1_Checked"
                  Unchecked="checkBox1_Checked" />
    </Grid>
</Window>
```

This UI is shown in Figure 17–4 already filled with sample data. For clarity, the exception handling is omitted. The basic functionality is quite simple (see Listing 17–8). The left-hand list shows the available features. An Expander element is used to display a feature's scope, ID, and whether it's hidden. The right-hand list presents the currently activated features. The check box in the upper-right corner allows the user to hide or show features defined as hidden.

Listing 17–8. *Code for the Application*

```
using System;
using System.Collections.Generic;
using System.Linq;
using System.Text;
using System.Windows;
using System.Windows.Controls;
using System.Windows.Data;
using System.Windows.Documents;
using System.Windows.Input;
using System.Windows.Media;
using System.Windows.Media.Imaging;
using System.Windows.Navigation;
using System.Windows.Shapes;
using Microsoft.SharePoint.Administration;
using Microsoft.SharePoint;

namespace Apress.SP2010.ActivateFeatures
{
    /// <summary>
    /// Interaction logic for MainWindow.xaml
    /// </summary>
    public partial class MainWindow : Window
    {

        SPSite site;
        SPWeb web;

        public MainWindow()
        {
            InitializeComponent();
            txtUrl.Text = "http://sharepointserve";
        }

        private void ReadSource()
        {
            if (!String.IsNullOrEmpty(txtUrl.Text.Trim()))
            {
                try
                {
                    site = new SPSite(txtUrl.Text);
                    web = site.RootWeb;
```

```
            var features = from f in site.Features
                           where f.Definition.Hidden == checkBox1.IsChecked
                           select f.Definition;
            lstSite.ItemsSource = features;
            var farmdefs = from f in SPFarm.Local.FeatureDefinitions
                           where (f.Scope == SPFeatureScope.Web
                               || f.Scope == SPFeatureScope.Site)
                           && !features.Contains(f)
                           select f;
            lstFarm.ItemsSource = farmdefs;
        }
        catch (Exception ex)
        {
            MessageBox.Show(ex.Message, "Error", MessageBoxButton.OK);
        }
    }
}

private void btnRead_Click(object sender, RoutedEventArgs e)
{
    ReadSource();
}

private void btnAdd_Click(object sender, RoutedEventArgs e)
{
    if (lstFarm.SelectedIndex != -1)
    {
        SPFeatureDefinition definition =
                       lstFarm.SelectedItem as SPFeatureDefinition;
        if (definition.Scope == SPFeatureScope.Site)
        {
            site.Features.Add(definition.Id);
        }
        if (definition.Scope == SPFeatureScope.Web)
        {
            web.Features.Add(definition.Id);
        }
        ReadSource();
    }
}

private void btnRemove_Click(object sender, RoutedEventArgs e)
{
    if (lstSite.SelectedIndex != -1)
    {
        SPFeatureDefinition definition =
                       lstSite.SelectedItem as SPFeatureDefinition;
        site.Features.Remove(definition.Id);
        ReadSource();
    }
}

private void checkBox1_Checked(object sender, RoutedEventArgs e)
{
```

```
            ReadSource();
        }

    }
}
```

The two buttons in the middle of the screen add or remove features. An add is performed by adding a feature definition to the site or web's Feature property. A remove is the reverse. The data source used to bind to the lists uses LINQ to select the desired data.

Working with Site Information

Not all tasks are primarily for administrators. Reading information about a site's current structure is a common way to create smarter controls. The SPSiteDataQuery class is a good entry point for information retrieval projects. The class is available for sandboxed solutions. To work with the class, you assign CAML queries as strings to the appropriate properties, as shown in Listing 17–9.

Listing 17–9. *Data Retrieval with a Web Part*

```
public class ContactViewer : WebPart
{
   private GridView grid;

   protected override void CreateChildControls()
   {
      base.CreateChildControls();
      // Add an instance of the GridView control
      this.grid = new GridView();
      this.Controls.Add(this.grid);
   }

   protected override void RenderContents(HtmlTextWriter writer)
   {
      SPWeb web = SPContext.Current.Web;
      SPSiteDataQuery query = new SPSiteDataQuery();

      // Ask for all lists created from the contacts template
      query.Lists = "<Lists ServerTemplate=\"105\" />";

      // Get the Title (Last Name) and FirstName fields
      query.ViewFields = @"<FieldRef Name='Title' />
                           <FieldRef Name='FirstName' Nullable='TRUE'/>";

      // Set the sort order
      query.Query = @"<OrderBy>
                        <FieldRef Name='Title' />
                      </OrderBy>";

      // Query all web sites in this site collection
      query.Webs = @"<Webs Scope='SiteCollection' />";

      DataTable dt = web.GetSiteData(query);
```

```
        DataView dv = new DataView(dt);

        // Set up the field bindings
        BoundField boundField = new BoundField();
        boundField.HeaderText = "Last Name";
        boundField.DataField = "Title";
        this.grid.Columns.Add(boundField);

        boundField = new BoundField();
        boundField.HeaderText = "First Name";
        boundField.DataField = "FirstName";
        this.grid.Columns.Add(boundField);

        this.grid.AutoGenerateColumns = false;
        this.grid.DataSource = dv;
        this.grid.DataBind();

        this.grid.AllowSorting = true;
        this.grid.HeaderStyle.Font.Bold = true;

        this.grid.RenderControl(writer);
    }
}
```

Retrieving the Configuration Database

To check the internal configuration, you can gather values from the configuration database directly. This is useful for checking what IDs or GUIDs are already in use on your farm, to help administration tools checking out references, for instance. The code shown in Listing 17–10 demonstrates this approach.

Listing 17–10. *Retrieving Values from the Configuration Database*

```
using System;
using Microsoft.SharePoint;
using Microsoft.SharePoint.Administration;

namespace Apress.SP2010.ConfigDatabase
{
    class Program
    {
        static void Main(string[] args)
        {
            using (SPSite site = new SPSite("http://sharepointserve"))
            {
                SPContentDatabase cb = site.ContentDatabase;
                Console.WriteLine("Content Database: {0}", cb.DisplayName);
                Console.WriteLine("Connection String: {0}",
                                        cb.DatabaseConnectionString);
                Console.WriteLine("Size: {0} Bytes", cb.DiskSizeRequired);
                foreach (SPSite s in cb.Sites)
                {
                    Console.WriteLine(" Sites: {0}", s.Url);
```

```
                }
            }
            Console.ReadLine();
        }
    }
}
```

Beginning from the root site collection, the `SPContentDatabase` object is retrieved. The object contains several methods and properties. In this example, the name, current size, and database connection string are output, as shown in Figure 17–5. In addition, the `foreach` loop retrieves all the other site collections that store their data in the same content database.

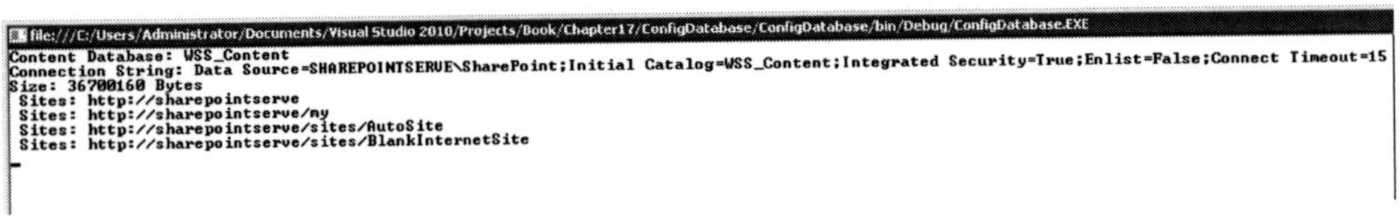

```
file:///C:/Users/Administrator/Documents/Visual Studio 2010/Projects/Book/Chapter17/ConfigDatabase/ConfigDatabase/bin/Debug/ConfigDatabase.EXE
Content Database: WSS_Content
Connection String: Data Source=SHAREPOINTSERUE\SharePoint;Initial Catalog=WSS_Content;Integrated Security=True;Enlist=False;Connect Timeout=15
Size: 36700160 Bytes
 Sites: http://sharepointserve
 Sites: http://sharepointserve/my
 Sites: http://sharepointserve/sites/AutoSite
 Sites: http://sharepointserve/sites/BlankInternetSite
```

Figure 17–5. *Values read from configuration database*

Summary

In this chapter you learned about programming administrative tasks. Several classes are provided by the API to support you're ability to create command-line tools, Web Parts, and applications that help users perform particular administrative actions. Several administrative help maintain the systems, and get information about the health and internal state beyond what the UI and Central Administration allow.

In an ASP.NET environment, the `web.config` file plays a significant role. Manipulating this file gives an administrator full control over an application's behavior. Mistakenly changing configuration elements can cause general failure. Automate such manipulation tasks to avoid human errors and reduce the risk of an outage of a production system.

CHAPTER 18

Enterprise Features

While most of the features you need for programming SharePoint are part of the SharePoint Foundation, eventually you will encounter advanced matters that require SharePoint Server. Programming enterprise features is another vast conglomerate of assemblies, namespaces, and classes. Describing all these features thoroughly would fill an entire book. In this chapter, we will give a brief introduction to some subjects that SharePoint Server adds to the mix.

This chapter includes the following:

- *Search*: Query the index and present search results.
- *My Sites and personalization*: Create and maintain My Sites and personalization settings.
- *Publishing webs*: Publish content and documents and work with Publishing webs.
- *Advanced document features*: Learn to check documents in and out, understand versions, and program against the taxonomy API.
- *Records management*: Understand records management and how to deal with documents under the surveillance of the records store.

This chapter merely provides some ideas and entry points. You may need more information to create real applications. We have provided several links to the MSDN documentation and other sources for your further research.

Enterprise Search

SharePoint as a collaboration platform can access information stored in SharePoint lists and libraries or throughout the enterprise as external content. To search this information, SharePoint offers various options. With SharePoint 2010, the importance of search is elevated, as indicated by the large number of search products available with this release.

Search Products

Starting with SharePoint Foundation 2010 and its basic support for searching, you can choose from a variety of tools to implement enterprise search in SharePoint:

- *SharePoint Foundation 2010*: Basic search functionality is already available in SharePoint Foundation. Although the functionality and performance are limited in this edition, the basic setup is similar to all other search versions. With SharePoint Foundation 2010, search is limited to only one site at a time—you cannot search across multiple sites.
- *Search Server 2010 Express*: This is the free edition of Search Server 2010; it allows crawling and indexing of content.
- *Search Server 2010*: This offers improved scalability and performance for enterprise search in SharePoint. While the Express edition only supports up to a maximum of 10 million indexed items, the Search Server 2010 supports up to 100 million entries.
- *SharePoint Server 2010*: In the SharePoint Server edition, searching is supported with similar features as those in Search Server 2010. In addition, people search and social components as well as taxonomies are available in this edition.
- *FAST Search Server 2010 for SharePoint*: This will meet the most sophisticated needs for enterprise search in SharePoint with a rich set of APIs and connectors.

Preparing Index and Query Services

Before you can search in SharePoint, you need to configure the search service and the crawler that builds the index. You can manage the service applications for search in Central Administration, under Application Management ➤ Service Applications ➤ Manage services on server. Figure 18–1 shows the settings page for SharePoint Server 2010. You can select from the various settings in the left menu to change the behavior for crawling the content and to specify further settings to improve the search results.

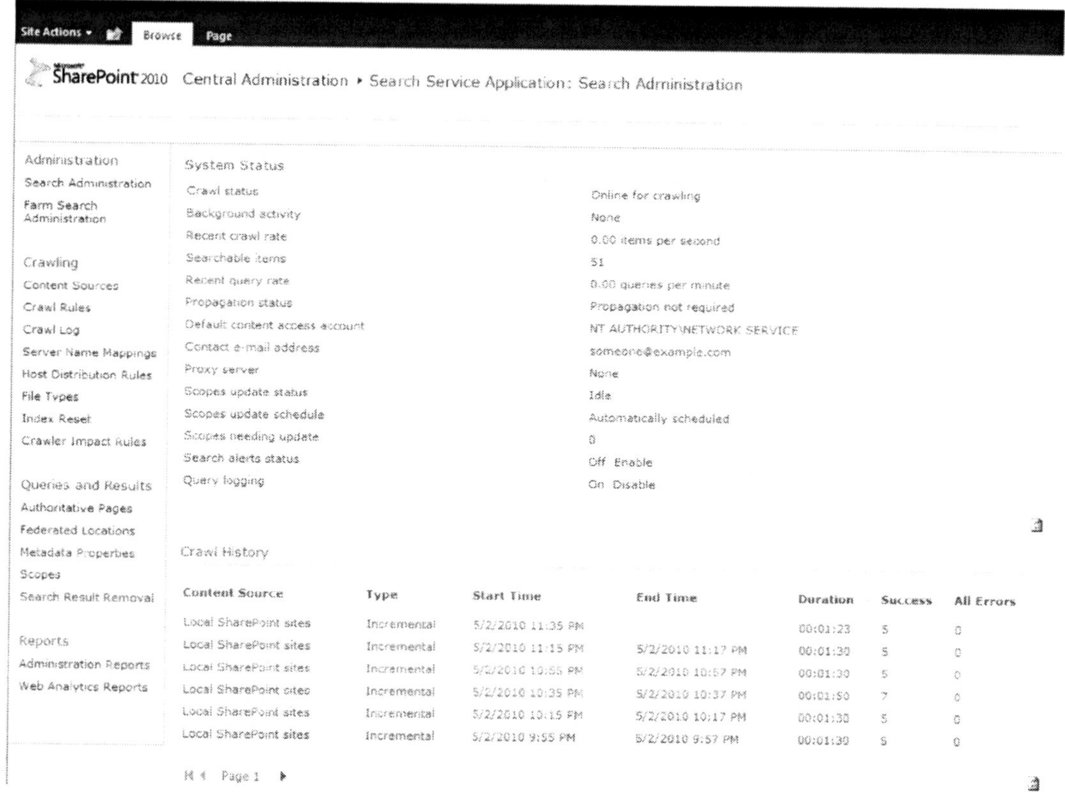

Figure 18–1. *Managing search in Central Administration*

Query Results from the Index

To access the index from code to retrieve the search results in SharePoint Server 2010, you can choose between two object models:

- *Federated search object model*: This object model allows you to gather information from multiple search engines or repositories. You can query against SharePoint Server search, FAST Search Server 2010 for SharePoint, and custom search runtimes. This object model actually calls the query object model to execute the search for SharePoint Server search and FAST search.

- *Query object model*: You can use the query object model to build custom search Web Parts and search applications. You can use this object model to query against SharePoint Server search and FAST Search Server 2010 for SharePoint. The class FullTextSqlQuery allows you to build complex search queries based on SQL syntax. The KeywordQuery class can be used to issue search queries based on simple query syntax. With Fast Search Server 2010, this class can also be used to run queries based on the Fast Query Language (FQL), which supports advanced queries in enterprise environments.

Both object models are implemented in the Microsoft.Office.Server.Search.Query namespace and require references to the following DLLs:

- Microsoft.Office.Server.dll
- Microsoft.Office.Server.Search.dll
- Microsoft.SharePoint.dll

Working with SharePoint Foundation, there is another namespace available that contains a subset of the SharePoint Server functionality. It is called Microsoft.SharePoint.Search.Query, and it comprises the query object model with reduced functionality. It is contained in Microsoft.SharePoint.Search.dll.

As an example of how to use custom search queries, Listing 18–1 demonstrates using the query object model to issue a search query based on a keyword search with the KeywordQuery class. This example is built as an application page with a text input field called txtSearch, a button for submitting the query called btnSearch, and an SPGridView called searchGrid.

The OnClick handler for the button creates a KeywordQuery object and passes the text from the text field to the QueryText property. After calling Execute, the results are available through the ResultTable at the index ResultType.RelevantResults in the returned ResultTableCollection. Using a DataTable, these results are bound to the SearchGrid for display. The relevant table columns are bound using the SetGridColumns method during Page_Load.

***Listing 18–1.** Custom Search with the Query Object Model*

```
using System;
using Microsoft.SharePoint;
using Microsoft.SharePoint.WebControls;
using System.Data;
using Microsoft.Office.Server;
using Microsoft.Office.Server.Search;
using Microsoft.Office.Server.Search.Query;

namespace Apress.SP2010.Layouts.CustomSearch
{
    public partial class ApplicationPage1 : LayoutsPageBase
    {
        protected void Page_Load(object sender, EventArgs e)
        {
            if (!IsPostBack)
            {
                SetGridColumns();
            }
        }

        // The event is called when the search button is pressed
        protected void btnSearch_Click(object sender, EventArgs e)
```

```
        {
            DataTable search = new DataTable();
            using (SPSite site = new SPSite(SPContext.Current.Web.Site.Url))
            {
                KeywordQuery query = new KeywordQuery(site);
                query.ResultsProvider = Microsoft.Office.Server.Search.Query.
                                                SearchProvider.Default;
                query.ResultTypes = ResultType.RelevantResults;
                query.KeywordInclusion = KeywordInclusion.AllKeywords;
                query.QueryText = txtSearch.Text;
                ResultTableCollection results = query.Execute();

                if (results.Count > 0)
                {
                    ResultTable relevant = results[ResultType.RelevantResults];
                    search.Load(relevant);

                    DataView view = new DataView(search);
                    // Fill the SPGridView defined in the page markup
                    searchGrid.DataSource = search;
                    searchGrid.DataBind();
                }
            }
        }

        private void SetGridColumns()
        {

            SPBoundField fieldTitle = new SPBoundField();
            fieldTitle.HeaderText = "Title";
            fieldTitle.DataField = "Title";
            SearchGrid.Columns.Add(fieldTitle);

            SPBoundField fieldPath = new SPBoundField();
            fieldPath.HeaderText = "Path";
            fieldPath.DataField = "Path";
            SearchGrid.Columns.Add(fieldPath);

            SPBoundField fieldAuthor = new SPBoundField();
            fieldAuthor.HeaderText = "Edited";
            fieldAuthor.DataField = "Write";
            SearchGrid.Columns.Add(fieldAuthor);
        }
    }
}
```

Before you can run search queries, you also need to specify the search server that should be used for indexing in Central Administration, under Application Management ➤ Databases ➤ Manage Content Databases ➤ [Your content DB] > Search Server.

This basic example indicates how to search in SharePoint. Particularly when using FAST Search, there are numerous additional features that enable you to implement feature-rich enterprise search in SharePoint.

When working with SharePoint Foundation, you need to use the `Microsoft.SharePoint.Search.Query` namespace (instead of `Microsoft.Office.Server.Search.Query`) in the previous example. SharePoint Foundation provides only a subset of the search functionality available to SharePoint Server or FAST Search Server. Table 18–1 compares some of the search capabilities for different SharePoint products.

Table 18–1. *Comparing Search Capabilities*

Feature	SharePoint Foundation 2010	SharePoint Server 2010	FAST Search Server 2010
Basic search	Yes	Yes	Yes
Document preview	No	No	Yes
Indexing sites	Yes	Yes	Yes
Indexing external content	No	Yes	Yes
People search	No	Yes	Yes
Query federation	No	Yes	Yes
UI-based administration	Limited	Yes	Yes
Visual best bets	No	Limited	Yes

■ **Tip** You can find detailed information about the different search capabilities at `www.microsoft.com/downloads/details.aspx?FamilyID=d7c0091e-5766-496d-a5fe-94bea52c4b15&displaylang=en`.

User Profiles and My Sites

Using data from user profiles and My Sites enables you to enrich your SharePoint 2010 application with user-specific content. You can work with all the data that the user profiles and My Sites contain. The following sections show you how to do the following:

- Use data from a user profile and work with it
- Create a My Site programmatically and work within its context
- Personalize a user's settings

Each section contains examples that give you the basic ideas for creating real applications.

Using User Profiles

The user profile page (see Figure 18–2) in SharePoint Server 2010 is laid out like many social networks such as Facebook or LinkedIn. A profile page contains the following:

- Information about the user
- A note board
- The latest activities
- Organization chart and colleagues
- Tags, membership in groups, and so on

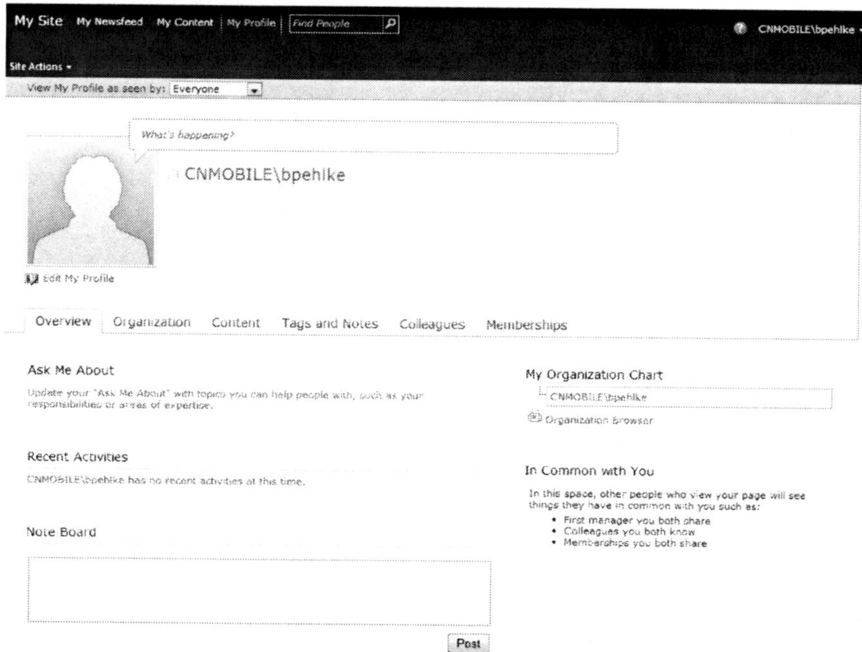

Figure 18–2. A typical user profile page

On the code side, the basic class for working with user profiles is the `UserProfileManager` class in the `Microsoft.Office.Server` namespace.

With the `UserProfileManager` class, you can basically create, get, and remove user profiles. If you want to maintain the user profile metadata such as properties, you should use the `UserProfileConfigManager` class because the `UserProfileManager` class's metadata access is meant to be read-only.

Listing 18–2 shows you how to create a user profile and display the colleagues of the current user in a `ListBox` control. It's supposed to run on a web form and put output in a `ListBox` control named `lbCollegues`.

Listing 18–2. Display Colleagues of the Given User

```
public void GetColleaguesFromUserProfile()
{
   // Get the current site context
   strUrl = "http://localhost";
   SPSite site = new SPSite(strUrl);
   SPServiceContext serviceContext = SPServiceContext.GetContext(site);

   // Initialize the user profile manager
   UserProfileManager upm = new UserProfileManager(serviceContext);

   // Create a user profile
   string sAccount = "domain\\bpehlke";
   if (!upm.UserExists(sAccount))
        upm.CreateUserProfile(sAccount);

   // Get the colleagues from user profile
   UserProfile u = upm.GetUserProfile(sAccount);
   foreach (var colleague in u.Colleagues.GetCommonColleagues())
   {
      lbColleagues.Items.Add(colleague.DisplayName);
   }
}
```

You can extend this example by displaying the latest changes of the current user's profile, for instance, in a custom Web Part that you can put on a Team Site home page. Listing 18–3 shows you how to retrieve these changes for a given user. It's supposed to run on a web form and put output in a `Label` control named `lblOutput`.

Listing 18–3. Display Latest Changes of the Specified User Profile in a Label Control

```
public void GetChangesForUserProfile()
{
   //get current service context
   strUrl = "http://localhost";
   SPSite site = new SPSite(strUrl);
   SPServiceContext serviceContext = SPServiceContext.GetContext(site);

   //initialize user profile manager
   UserProfileManager upm = new UserProfileManager(serviceContext);

   //get the changes for the user profile
   string sAccount = "domain\\bpehlke";
   UserProfile u = upm.GetUserProfile(sAccount);
   foreach (var change in u.GetChanges())
   {
    lblOutput.Text += "<br>" + change.ChangeType + " "
                             + change.ChangedProfile + " "
                             + change.EventTime.ToShortDateString();
   }
}
```

■ **Tip** You can find more information about using user profiles at `http://msdn.microsoft.com/en-us/library/microsoft.office.server.userprofiles.userprofilemanager(office.14).aspx`.

Work Within the Context of My Sites

To create and work with My Sites, you need the user profiles and the `UserProfileManager` class. Listing 18–4 shows you how to create a My Site and work within the context of this site.

***Listing 18–4.** Display Latest Activities of the Current User*

```
public void CreatePersonalSite()
{
   //get current service context
   SPServiceContext serviceContext = SPServiceContext.Current;

   //initialize user profile config manager
   UserProfileManager upm = new UserProfileManager(serviceContext);
   string currentUser = "domain\\bpehlke";
   UserProfile up = upm.GetUserProfile(currentUser);
   up.CreatePersonalSite();
   SPSite mysite = up.PersonalSite;

   using (SPWeb web = mysite.OpenWeb())
   {
     //do something in the My Site context
   }
}
```

This way, it is very easy to work with the My Sites programmatically.

Personalize a User's Settings

A lot of information is stored in the user profile properties, including the following:

- Name, address, and telephone number
- E-mail, department, job title, and so on

With the `UserProfileConfigManager` class, you can maintain properties like these easily. Whereas this class lets you add, edit, and remove properties, the properties itself can be read and set by the user profile object.

Listing 18–5 shows you how to work with the properties and use the data stored in it. It's supposed to run on a web form and put output in a `Label` control named `lblOutput`.

***Listing 18–5.** Using User Profile Properties*

```
public void CreatePersonalSite()
{
   //get current service context
```

```
    SPServiceContext serviceContext = SPServiceContext.Current;

    //initialize user profile manager
    UserProfileManager upm = new UserProfileManager(serviceContext);
    string currentUser = "domain\\bpehlke";
    UserProfile u = upm.GetUserProfile(currentUser);

    //get a list of all user profile properties
    foreach (var prop in u.Properties)
    {
        lblOutput.Text += "<br>" + prop.DisplayName;
    }
    //set the department property
    string department= "IT-Services";
    u[PropertyConstants.Department].Add(department);
    u.Commit();
    //read the new department value
    lblOutput.Text += "<br>" + "New department value: "
                              + u[PropertyConstants.Department].Value.ToString();
}
```

Web Content Management

SharePoint 2010 ships with a rich set of functions for developing professional web content management (WCM) solutions. From configuration, customization, page authoring, and deployment to optimization and web analytics, SharePoint offers a broad range of WCM features.

This section provides an overview of the most important WCM functions and includes the entry points to the API for developers.

■ **Tip** You can find a good entry point for working with the WCM API in MSDN at `http://msdn.microsoft.com/en-us/library/ff512785(office.14).aspx`.

The WCM programming model is also known as the Publishing API. Table 18–2 describes several important namespaces when working with this API.

Table 18–2. Important Namespaces of the Publishing API

Namespace	Description
`Microsoft.SharePoint.Publishing`	Provides the fundamental publishing infrastructure for web content management.
`Microsoft.SharePoint.Publishing.Administration`	Provides content deployment configuration, path, and job functionality.
`Microsoft.SharePoint.Publishing.Cmdlet`	Code to support PowerShell cmdlet object model used for publishing features.
`Microsoft.SharePoint.Publishing.Fields`	Contains the fields, field values, and field behavior, including base types, the content type ID, HTML fields, tags, and validation, as well as image fields and field values, the publishing schedule start dates and end dates, summary link fields, and field values.
`Microsoft.SharePoint.Publishing.Navigation`	Provides classes that represent the node, type, collection, data source, provider, and proxy functionality to support navigation.
`Microsoft.SharePoint.Publishing.WebControls`	Supports the structure, appearance, and behavior of SharePoint Server web controls. These include types such as base fields, selectors, and other containers, along with the display types, fields, panels, state objects, and Web Parts.

Source: `http://msdn.microsoft.com/en-us/library/ff512785(office.14).aspx`

Working with SPPublishingWeb Class

To work with the Publishing API, there is a class called `PublishingWeb`. This class is a wrapper class for the `SPWeb` object. Listing 18–6 shows how to check whether an `SPWeb` instance has the SharePoint Publishing feature activated. For this, the static method `PublishingWeb.IsPublishingWeb` is used, passing in an `SPWeb` instance as a parameter. To obtain a `PublishingWeb` instance, you can use the static method `PublishingWeb.GetPublishingWeb` (see Listing 18–6).

Listing 18–6. *Using the PublishingWeb Class*

```
PublishingWeb publishingWeb = null;
if (PublishingWeb.IsPublishingWeb(web))
{
    publishingWeb = PublishingWeb.GetPublishingWeb(web);
}
else
{
```

```
    throw new System.ArgumentException(
                 "The SPWeb " + web.Title + " is not a PublishingWeb", "web");
}
```

With the PublishingWeb class, you can access the various page layouts (GetAvailablePageLayouts) and also all the publishing pages residing in the site (GetPublishingPages). Listing 18–7 demonstrates how to use those methods to add a new page to the site pages library.

Listing 18–7. *Adding a New Publishing Page to the Site Pages Library*

```
PublishingWeb publishingWeb = PublishingWeb.GetPublishingWeb(web);
string pageName = "MyTestPage.aspx";

PageLayout[] pageLayouts = publishingWeb.GetAvailablePageLayouts();
PageLayout currPageLayout =  pageLayouts[0];

PublishingPageCollection pages = publishingWeb.GetPublishingPages();
PublishingPage newPage = pages.Add(pageName,currPageLayout);

newPage.ListItem[FieldId.PublishingPageContent] = "This is my content";
newPage.ListItem.Update();
newPage.Update();
newPage.CheckIn("This is just a comment");
```

In this code, a PageLayout instance with index 0 is selected from all the available page layouts. By using the PageLayout instance, a new page of type PublishingPage is added to the site pages library. Afterward, the content of a field, identified by FieldId.PublishingPageContent, is set to a HTML text value, followed by an update and check-in.

Content Deployment

The deployment of content from source to destination is a common task in web publishing scenarios. Therefore, SharePoint provides a rich deployment API under the namespace Microsoft.SharePoint.Publishing.Administration. The deployment process always follows these three steps:

1. Export content from the site collection of a source farm.
2. Transport content from the source farm to the destination farm.
3. Import content into a site collection of a destination farm.

■ **Note** Content deployment always proceeds one-way (from source to destination). More complex scenarios, such as deploying from several sources to one destination, are *not* supported.

In a common content deployment scenario, the content of site collection SC1 in farm A will be deployed to site collection SC2 in farm B. To do so, content deployment uses the classes ContentDeploymentPath and ContentDeploymentJob:

- An instance of the class `ContentDeploymentPath` is a connection between the site collection of a source farm and the site collection of a destination farm. It also contains information about authentication on the destination farm.
- The class `ContentDeploymentJob` is associated with an instance of type `ContentDeploymentPath`. It defines the schedule and the sites for the deployment and thus when and what (sites/`SPWebs`) should be deployed.

Listing 18–8 shows how to deploy content between servers; a site collection from URL `http://serverA/sites/SC1` is deployed to a destination site collection at URL `http://serverB/sites/SC2`.

Listing 18–8. *Console Application to Deploy Content Between Servers*

```
using System;
using System.Collections.Generic;
using System.Text;
using Microsoft.SharePoint.Publishing.Administration;

namespace Apress.Sp2010.DeploymentAPI
{
    public class Program
    {
        static void Main( string[] args )
        {
            Example example = new Example();
            example.Invoke();
        }
    }

    public class Example
    {
        public void Invoke()
        {
            // Path settings
            string pathName = "My Deployment Path";
            Uri sourceServerUri = new Uri( "http://serverA" );
            string sourceSiteCollection = "/sites/SC1";

            Uri destinationAdminUri = new Uri( "http://serverB:50000" );
            Uri destinationServerUri = new Uri( "http://serverB" );
            string destinationSiteCollection = "/sites/SC2";

            // Job settings
            string jobName = "My Content Deployment Job";

            ContentDeploymentPath path = null;
            ContentDeploymentJob job = null;

            try
            {
                // Note: the DESTINATION farm must be configured
                // to accept incoming deployment jobs.
                ContentDeploymentConfiguration config =
                            ContentDeploymentConfiguration.GetInstance();
```

```
                config.AcceptIncomingJobs = true;
                config.RequiresSecureConnection = false;
                config.Update();

                // Create a deployment path.
                ContentDeploymentPathCollection allPaths =
                        ContentDeploymentPath.GetAllPaths();
                path = allPaths.Add();

                path.Name = pathName;
                path.SourceServerUri = sourceServerUri;
                path.SourceSiteCollection = sourceSiteCollection;
                path.DestinationAdminServerUri = destinationAdminUri;
                path.DestinationServerUri = destinationServerUri;
                path.DestinationSiteCollection = destinationSiteCollection;
                path.Update();

                // Create a job associated with the path
                job = ContentDeploymentJob.GetAllJobs().Add();
                job.JobType = ContentDeploymentJobType.ServerToServer;
                job.Name = jobName;
                job.Path = path;
                job.Update();
                job.Run();
            }
            catch ( Exception ex )
            {
                Console.Error.WriteLine( ex.StackTrace );
                throw;
            }
            finally
            {
                // Delete the job that was created.
                if ( job != null ) job.Delete();

                // Delete the path that was created.
                if ( path != null ) path.Delete();
            }
        }
    }
}
```

What's New in SharePoint 2010 Web Content Management

On top of the PublishingWeb and ContentDeplyment classes, compared to older versions, SharePoint 2010 offers many great user interface improvements. This section gives a short overview of the most conspicuous points.

Page Authoring Experience

SharePoint 2010 provides a modern AJAX-based in-page web-editing experience. The ribbon UI makes it easy for authors to maintain their content, and the rich-text editor supports multiple browsers without the need to install any third-party controls, such as ActiveX controls. The complete UI implementation of SharePoint is no longer table-based. It uses CSS for element positioning, which reduces the complexity and size of the HTML output. Furthermore, the markup code is fully XHTML compliant and supports the Web Content Accessibility Guidelines (WCAG) 2.0 out of the box. Another interesting feature is that Web Parts can be inserted just like normal content (see Figure 18–3).

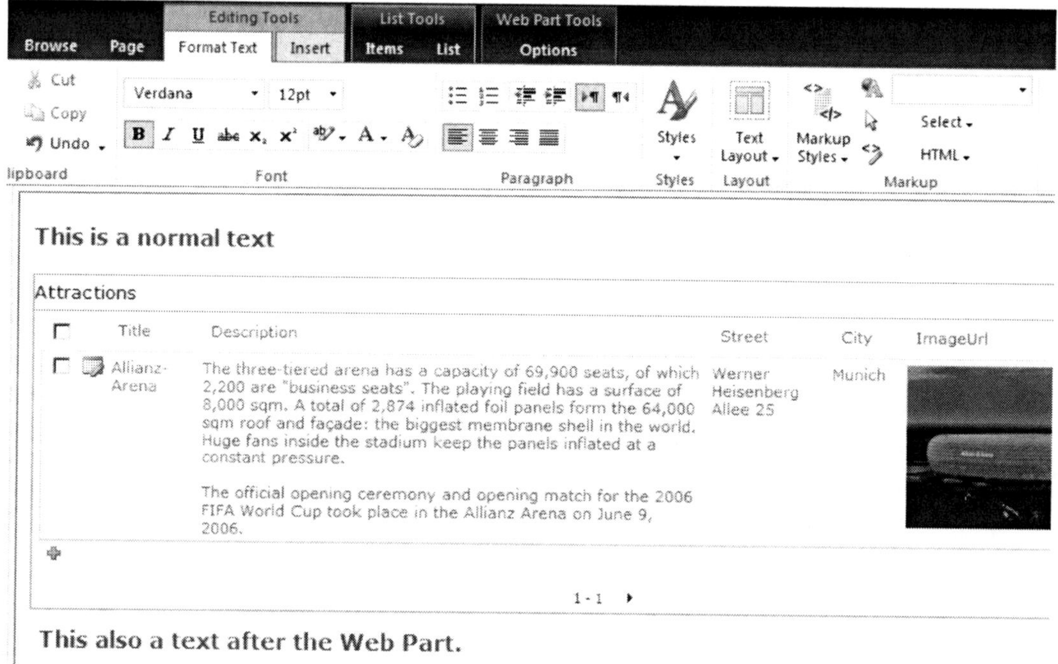

Figure 18–3. Web page containing a Web Part surrounded by HTML text

Rich Media Integration

SharePoint 2010 makes it very easy for users to embed rich media content, such as videos. Featuring contextual options in the ribbon, there is picker functionality to assist in easily loading video content on a SharePoint page, up to and including preview functionality on mouse-over. You can choose whether all videos begin to autoplay when the page is rendered. Video has quickly become a very important component of managed content sites. There is considerably more support in SharePoint Server 2010 for video and rich media, including a skinnable Silverlight player and various storage options.

Content Query Web Part

Another great improvement in the WCM area is the new version of the Content Query Web Part (CQWP). The new CQWP simplifies working with item styles by introducing *slots*. A slot is a marker in the item-style template that is filled with the content at runtime. The Content Query Web Part allows you to set the mappings between the slots and the fields using the property pane—allowing you to create more semantic and reusable item style templates.

Another great feature of the new Content Query Web Part is the *content-to-content* concept. Content-to-content introduces two tokens that can be used in the Content Query Web Part filters. The `PageQueryString` token allows you to include in the query a value from a query string parameter, and the `PageFieldValue` token gives you the option to filter the query results using a value of another field on the same page. This makes it very easy to provide functionality such as related content.

Web Analytics

SharePoint's Web Analytics feature contains several new reports, the ability to schedule alerts and reports, and the What's Popular Web Part. Replacing the usage analysis in the previous version of SharePoint, the new Web Analytics service application provides a good overview of your site, via such measures as most-hit pages, size, and so forth. Note that this isn't a comprehensive analytics package with sophisticated trending analysis of the paths people are taking through your site. Instead, you can set up alerts and use included Web Parts to show your users the most popular pages in the site.

Advanced Document Management and Metadata

While SharePoint has been widely recognized as a content management system in the past, its usage as a document management system (DMS) is not as popular. This was affected by the lack of several standard DMS features in SharePoint 2007, but SharePoint 2010 has addressed those shortcomings.

Document Management

The integration with Microsoft Office client applications enables users to create high-value, easy-to-use knowledge repositories. SharePoint 2010 document management is built on the success of that integration and around several key ideas including the following:

- Managing unstructured silos
- Use of metadata
- The browser as a document management application

Unstructured silos are an answer to the meandering taxonomies and strongly structured hierarchy that rarely reflects reality. The rise of powerful search engine appliances provides users with their web's search experience through Google or Bing, even on local enterprise content management systems.

A core concept is the document set, which allows users to group related documents and share metadata, workflows, home pages, and archiving processes. (We described this earlier in Chapter 4.) The document management features such as document sets can be very rigid, concerning regulatory submissions, policies, and archiving, and they can also be informal to allow teams to simply assemble a few documents together.

However, unstructured silos of documents are not the final answer. Using metadata, users can supply additional information to construct a form of taxonomy without the rigid requirement to store documents in very specific places. SharePoint allows a consistent metadata management through content types and document libraries.

The creation of web sites, pages, and content is a core feature SharePoint users engage in every day. Creating and working with documents is part of a document management solution. SharePoint 2010 supports this through the integration with Office 2007 and Office 2010 as well as the Office web applications. The Content Query Web Part is an integrated module that allows users to retrieve a set of related documents very easily.

■ **Note** Here's the definition of *managed metadata* from Microsoft TechNet: "Managed metadata is a hierarchical collection of centrally managed terms that you can define, and then use as attributes for items in Microsoft SharePoint Server 2010."

Working with Metadata Navigation

Metadata-based navigation can be based on the managed metadata as well as other list properties, such as content type or choice fields.

You can administer this navigation through the Library Settings page entitled "Metadata navigation settings" (see Figure 18–4). Essentially, you can define three things here:

- *Navigation hierarchy*: You can set navigation fields based on content type, choice, or managed metadata.
- *Key filters*: SharePoint can give users not only a tree-view style of navigation but also navigation via typing in fields in order to make navigation easier.
- *Indices*: You can define indices for metadata-based navigation in order to improve performance.

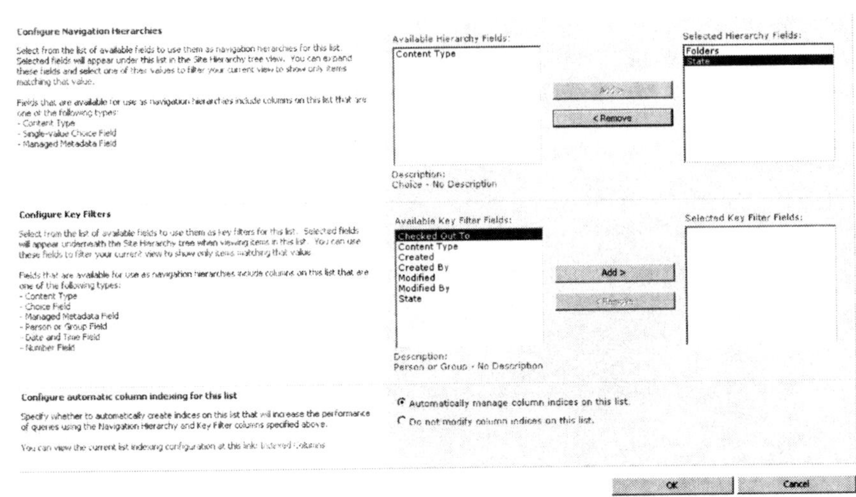

Figure 18–4. Creating a navigation hierarchy using hierarchy fields

Working with Metadata Taxonomies

Taxonomies is a term used in SharePoint to express metadata support. Through Site Settings ➤ Site Actions ➤ Term Store Management, you can set and maintain your metadata taxonomies using the UI (see Figure 18–5).

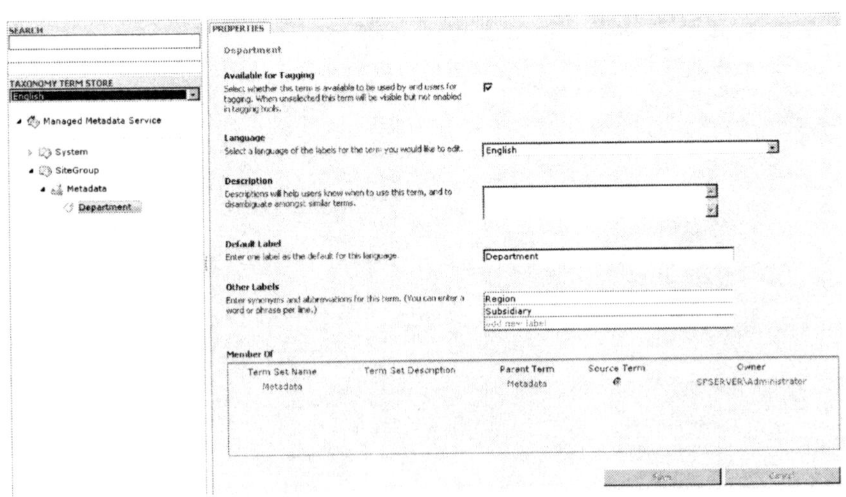

Figure 18–5. Managing metadata through the term store

Before exploring sample code, you need to understand a few terms that are used when working with taxonomies:

- *Term*: A word or phrase that can be associated with an item in SharePoint Server.
- *Term set*: A collection of related terms.
- *Keyword*: A word or phrase that has been added to SharePoint Server items. All managed keywords are part of a single, nonhierarchical term set called the *keyword set*.
- *Label*: A name for a term used on the UI layer.
- *Term store*: A database that stores both managed terms and managed keywords.
- *Group*: In the term stores, all term sets are created within groups. Hence, a group is the parent container for term sets.

To manage or access the term store settings through code, you must reference `Microsoft.SharePoint.Taxonomy.dll`. Listing 18–9 shows how to read the current taxonomy settings.

Listing 18–9. *Retrieve the Current Term Store*

```
using System;
using System.Collections.Generic;
using System.Linq;
using System.Text;
using Microsoft.SharePoint;
using Microsoft.SharePoint.Taxonomy;

namespace Apress.SP2010.DocumentManagement
{
    class Program
    {
        static void Main(string[] args)
        {
            using (SPSite site = new SPSite("http://sharepointserve"))
            {
                using (SPWeb web = site.OpenWeb())
                {
                    TaxonomySession tx = new TaxonomySession(site, true);
                    TermStore store = tx.DefaultSiteCollectionTermStore;
                    Group group = store.Groups["SiteGroup"];
                    TermSet set = group.TermSets["Metadata"];
                    Term t = set.Terms["Department"];
                    foreach (Label label in t.Labels)
                    {
                        Console.WriteLine(label.Value);
                    }
                }
            }
            Console.ReadLine();
        }
    }
}
```

Refer to Figure 18–5 regarding the `Groups`, `TermSets`, and `Terms` names used in the example. The output of this console application consists of three labels: `Department`, `Region`, and `Subsidiary`. It should look like Figure 18–6.

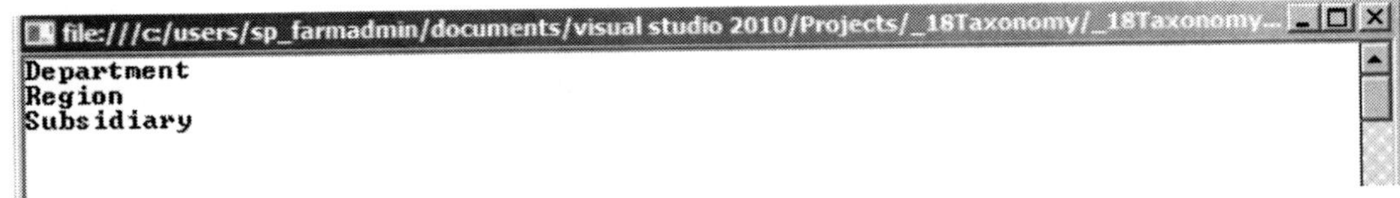

Figure 18–6. Output produced by the example

Several methods such as CreateGroup, CreateTermSet, and CreateTerm let you create taxonomies through code. The corresponding delete methods are available, too. After performing write operations, you need to call CommitAll. The taxonomy API is transactional—once committed, all changes (or no changes, if there's an error) are applied.

Check In and Check Out

While dealing with high-level taxonomies, don't forget that some very basic features of a document management environment are available, too. Usually users can check out and check in documents through the UI. The user currently locking a document is stored automatically (CheckedOutBy field), and the handling from workflows is as straightforward as from the user interface.

Listing 18–10 shows how to check out, change, and check in a document programmatically.

***Listing 18–10.** Check Out, Retrieve the Current State, and Check In*

```
using System;
using System.Collections.Generic;
using System.Linq;
using System.Text;
using Microsoft.SharePoint;

namespace Apress.SP2010.CheckinCheckout
{
    class Program
    {
        static void Main(string[] args)
        {
            using (SPSite site = new SPSite("http://sharepointserve"))
            {
                using (SPWeb web = site.OpenWeb())
                {
                    SPDocumentLibrary docs =
                          (SPDocumentLibrary)web.Lists["DocumentSilo"];
                    foreach (SPFile file in docs.RootFolder.Files)
                    {
                        if (file.CheckOutType == SPFile.SPCheckOutType.None)
                        {
                            file.CheckOut();
                        }
                    }
                    // Added, but not yet checked in.
                    foreach (SPCheckedOutFile file in docs.CheckedOutFiles)
```

```
                    {
                        Console.WriteLine(file.LeafName);
                    }
                    // Checked out regularly.
                    var checkedout = from f in
                                         docs.RootFolder.Files.OfType<SPFile>()
                                     where f.CheckOutType ==
                                         SPFile.SPCheckOutType.Online
                                     select f;
                    foreach (var file in checkedout)
                    {
                        Console.WriteLine(file.Name);
                    }
                    // Check in and add a comment.
                    foreach (SPFile file in docs.RootFolder.Files)
                    {
                        if (file.CheckOutType != SPFile.SPCheckOutType.None)
                        {
                            file.CheckIn("Programmatically Checked In");
                        }
                    }
                }
            }
            Console.ReadLine();
        }
    }
}
```

This code assumes you have document library called DocumentSilo and at least one document stored there. `CheckedOutFiles` returns files that are added by a user but not yet checked in for the first time. `CheckOutType` is the property the `SPFile` type provides to check the current state of a regular check-out.

Versioning

You can activate versioning for each list or library. This allows you to track changes made by users and roll back to a previous version for any reason. The versions are stored as a collection of items; the collection is also accessible through code.

Assuming that versioning is activated for a particular list, you can use the code shown in Listing 18–11 to retrieve version information.

Listing 18–11. *Retrieve the File's History from Version Store*

```
using System;
using System.Collections.Generic;
using System.Linq;
using System.Text;
using Microsoft.SharePoint;

namespace Apress.SP1010.Versioning
{
    class Program
    {
```

```
        static void Main(string[] args)
        {
            using (SPSite site = new SPSite("http://sharepointserve"))
            {
                using (SPWeb web = site.OpenWeb())
                {
                    SPList docs = web.Lists["DocumentSilo"];
                    Console.WriteLine("Versioning is active: ",
                                      docs.EnableVersioning);
                    foreach (SPFile file in docs.RootFolder.Files)
                    {
                        Console.WriteLine("File {0} has next
                                          version {1}. Version History:",
                            file.Url,
                            file.UIVersionLabel);
                        foreach (SPFileVersion v in
                                file.Versions.Cast<SPFileVersion>().Reverse())
                        {
                            Console.WriteLine("  Version {0} checked in
                                              at {1} with this comment: '{2}'",
                                v.VersionLabel,
                                v.Created,
                                v.CheckInComment);
                        }
                    }
                }
            }
            Console.ReadLine();
        }
    }
}
```

This code assumes you have a document library called DocumentSilo that has documents in it and versioning enabled. The outer `foreach` loop inspects all the files, while the inner loop retrieves all the versions for each file. The `Reverse` method reverses the order to process the most recent version first. Access to file details is obtained through the `SPFileVersion` type. This type supports all typical file operations, such as `Recycle` to send the file to the recycle bin or `OpenBinaryStream` to retrieve the file contents. `VersionLabel` is the property that contains the version as displayed in the SharePoint UI. Because versions for files are usually created by a check-in procedure, it makes sense to retrieve the comment by using `CheckInComment`.

Records Management

Companies of every size need to preserve information in a secure and reliable way, not only as a standard practice within the company but also to meet regulatory requirements.

Records management refers to documents and other content that exists in an official, stable state. These are documents that the organization has declared as records and should not be changed. Records are often archived, tracked, and audited. The most common scenario for records management is legal or regulatory compliance, ensuring that the document is retained, unchanged, and purged according to a designated schedule.

Records management in SharePoint Server 2010 enables you to create a repository to retain business documents that are necessary for regulatory compliance and business continuity. SharePoint

Server 2010 provides a site template called Records Center, which is located within the enterprise site templates. This template enables you to create a site collection with features that help manage records within your organization, as shown in Figure 18–7.

■ **Note** When you create your Records Center, we recommend you create a new web application that will enable you to manage your records separately from your "everyday" documents.

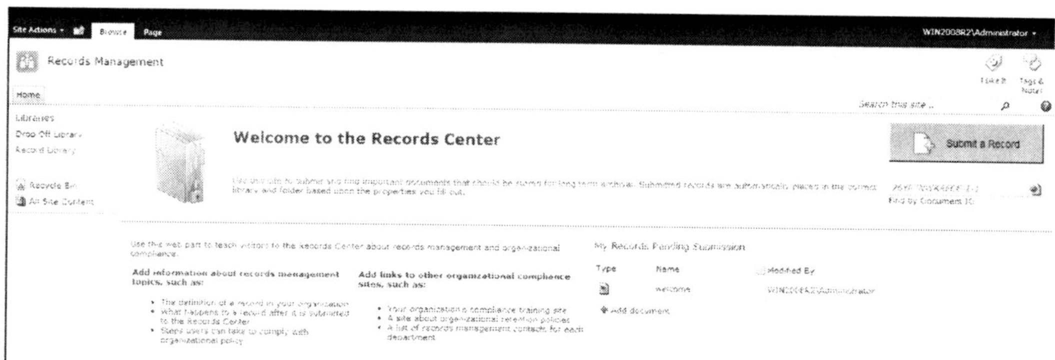

Figure 18–7. The Records Center: records management in SharePoint 2010

Moving Documents to the Records Center Using the API

The SharePoint API and its web services can be used to write your own code to interact with the Records Center. You will find the necessary classes for records management programming in the following six namespaces:

- `Microsoft.Office.RecordsManagement.Holds`
- `Microsoft.Office.RecordsManagement.InformationPolicy`
- `Microsoft.Office.RecordsManagement.PolicyFeatures`
- `Microsoft.Office.RecordsManagement.RecordsRepository`
- `Microsoft.Office.RecordsManagement.Reporting`
- `Microsoft.Office.RecordsManagement.SearchAndProcess`

■ **Note** A complete reference to the necessary classes for records management is on MSDN at `http://msdn.microsoft.com/en-us/library/ff465318%28v=office.14%29.aspx`.

The central function of the object model in the Records Center is to send documents programmatically to the Records Center and to hold and unhold them. These documents can be used, for example, in workflows and event handlers in libraries.

To upload a document to the Records Center using the object model, you can use code similar to Listing 18–12 (the routine can be used in a console application directly or, by modifying the output, in any other type of application).

Listing 18–12. *Move a Document to the Records Center Using the API*

```
static void MoveDocumentToRecordsCenter()
{
   try
   {
      string additionalInformation = string.Empty;
      OfficialFileResult operationResult;

      using (SPSite mySite = new SPSite("http://ServerName"))
      {
          using(SPWeb myWeb = mySite.OpenWeb())
          {
            SPFile myDoc = myWeb.GetFile("DocLib/DocName.docx");
            operationResult =
                 myDoc.SendToOfficialFile(out additionalInformation);

            Console.WriteLine("Operation State: " + operationResult);
          }
      }
   }
   catch (Exception ex)
   {
      Console.WriteLine("Error - " + ex.ToString());
   }
}
```

Two objects, of types `SPSite` and `SPWeb`, respectively, are created to make a reference to the document (`myDoc`, of the `SPFile` type) to be uploaded to the center. The `SendToOfficialFile` method of the `SPFile` class takes care of the upload procedure and returns the results of the action to the variable `operationResult`, indicating its successful completion or whether there was an error (the valid values can be `FileCheckedOut`, `FileRejected`, `InvalidConfiguration`, `MoreInformation`, `NotFound`, `Success`, or `UnknownError`). You can examine the value of the `additionalInformation` parameter to find out what went wrong.

■ **Tip** If the object model cannot be used, SharePoint has a default web service to upload documents to the Records Center; see `http://ServerName:port/_vti_bin/officialfile.asmx`.

Maintain Retention Policies

A retention policy specifies operations on documents at certain points in time. The defined actions require little involvement from users, because policies are automatically and transparently enforced.

Policies enable administrators to control who can access information and how long to retain information and also to evaluate how effectively people are complying with the policy. You can apply policies to manage your content according to business processes and legal or regulatory reasons. Each policy is a collection of sets of instructions for one or more policy features. A policy feature is an assembly that provides certain content management functionality such as expiration or auditing. An extensibility framework enables you to create, customize, and deploy your own policies and policy features. For example, you can implement your own retention policies within a feature and deploy it as a solution. Create a feature with a feature receiver, as shown in Listing 18–13. The scope of the feature should be web application, so your records management policy is scoped to everywhere your content may be located.

Listing 18–13. *Feature Receiver*

```
using Microsoft.Office.RecordsManagement.PolicyFeatures;
using Microsoft.Office.RecordsManagement.InformationPolicy;

public override void FeatureActivated(SPFeatureReceiverProperties properties)
{
   string xmlManifest;
   TextReader policyStream = new
       StreamReader(Assembly.GetExecutingAssembly().GetManifestResourceStream(
                   "Apress.SP2010.RMPolicies.policy.xml"));
       xmlManifest = policyStream.ReadToEnd();
       PolicyResource.ValidateManifest(xmlManifest);
       PolicyResourceCollection.Add(xmlManifest);
}
```

The feature receiver adds a `policy.xml` definition to your web application. Listing 18–14 shows the file's content.

Listing 18–14. *The policy.xml File*

```
<PolicyResource
      xmlns="urn:schemas-microsoft-com:office:server:policy"
      id = "CustomExpiration.CustomExpirationFormula"
      featureId="Microsoft.Office.RecordsManagement.PolicyFeatures.Expiration"
      type = "DateCalculator">
  <Name>Apress Filtered Expiration</Name>
  <Description>Items expires based on a filtered critereon.</Description>
    <AssemblyName>Apress.RMPolicies, Version=1.0.0.0,
       Culture=neutral,PublicKeyToken=44050b881185bf1b</AssemblyName>
   <ClassName>Apress.RMPolicies.FilteredExpiration</ClassName>
</PolicyResource>
```

Each policy is implemented in a class method (such as the example shown in Listing 18–15). The method name is declared in the `ClassName` element of the `policy.xml` file.

Listing 18–15. *Custom Policy Code*

```
public class FilteredExpiration : IExpirationFormula
{
   #region IExpirationFormula Members
   public DateTime? ComputeExpireDate(SPListItem item,
                                       System.Xml.XmlNode parametersData)
```

```
    {
        if (item["DeleteNow"].ToString().Equals("Yes"))
        {
            return DateTime.Now;
        }
        else
        {
            return null;
        }
    }
    #endregion
}
```

Summary

Search is an important part of almost every SharePoint installation. A number of products and features are available to support different requirements. This chapter covered what assemblies you need to reference to program against the features and extend or customize their behavior.

The section "User Profiles and My Sites" explained how to work with user profiles and My Sites. It demonstrates how easy it is to retrieve user-specific data from a user profile in order to use it for different purposes. These purposes can include custom Web Parts and application pages and reports or even extending the social network features in SharePoint 2010.

Web content management consists mainly of the Publishing feature. This allows users to create and publish content. You can even deploy content from farm computers to other farms or servers. SharePoint 2010 provides many new features that support content creation and content management for end users.

Document management is another complex feature that consists of several functions supported by the API. In addition to the libraries and document sets described in Chapter 4, you can work with document versions and lock documents automatically during editing sessions using check-in and check-out actions. Organizing documents in data silos requires adding metadata to aid search engines to quickly find the right document. Programming against the taxonomy API allows you to create hierarchies of metadata and keywords to organize data instead of placing them into a strict hierarchy.

Records management is another crucial subject in the enterprise. Each document has a life cycle, and records management ensures that documents are retained or archived at the right time. The API allows you to construct custom rules for policies that control the document's life cycle.

Index

A

B

C

D

E

F

G

H

I

J

K

L

N

O

P

Q

R

S

T

U

V

W

X, Y

Z

CPSIA information can be obtained at www.ICGtesting.com
Printed in the USA
LVOW131924301211
261759LV00002B/17/P